CREATED EQUAL

D1530098

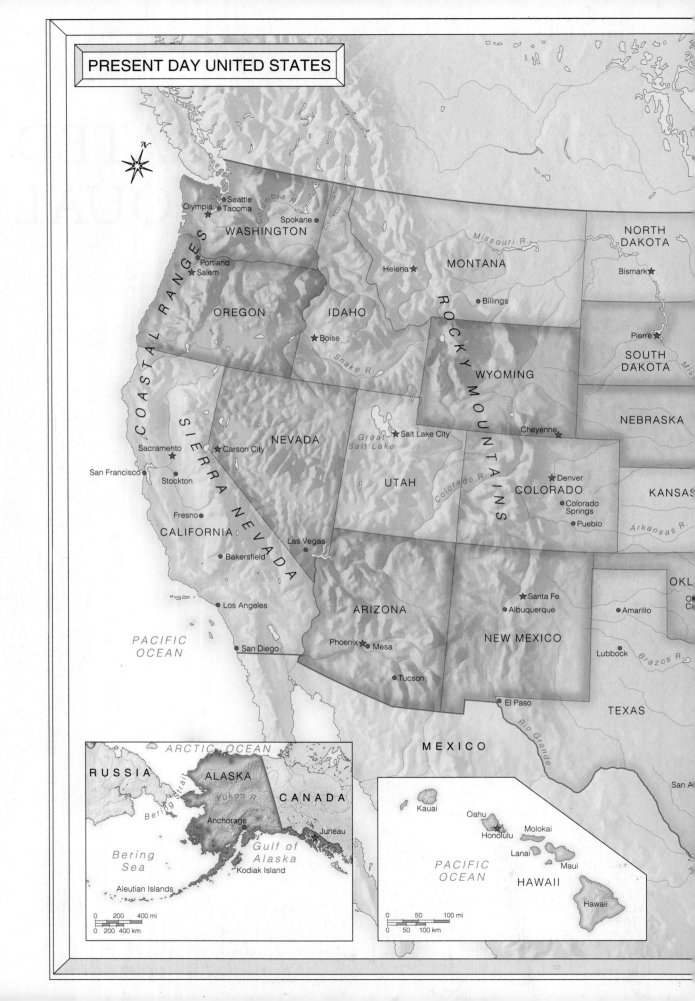

PRESENT DAY UNITED STATES

CREATED EQUAL

A HISTORY OF THE UNITED STATES
COMBINED VOLUME

BRIEF THIRD EDITION

Jacqueline Jones
University of Texas at Austin

Peter H. Wood
Duke University

Thomas Borstelmann
University of Nebraska

Elaine Tyler May
University of Minnesota

Vicki L. Ruiz
University of California, Irvine

Prentice Hall
Boston Columbus Indianapolis New York San Francisco Upper Saddle River
Amsterdam Cape Town Dubai London Madrid Milan Munich Paris Montréal Toronto
Delhi Mexico City São Paulo Sydney Hong Kong Seoul Singapore Taipei Tokyo

Editorial Director: Craig Campanella
Executive Editor: Ed Parsons
Editorial Project Manager: Tracy Clough
Editorial Assistant: Alex Rabinowitz
Supplements Editor: Emsal Hasan
Senior Manufacturing and Operations
  Manager for Arts & Sciences: Nick Sklitsis
Operations Specialist: Christina Amato
Director of Marketing: Brandy Dawson
Senior Marketing Manager: Maureen E. Prado Roberts
Marketing Assistant: Marissa C. O'Brien
Senior Managing Editor: Ann Marie McCarthy
Senior Project Manager: Denise Forlow

Manager, Visual Research: Beth Brenzel
Director of Media and Assessment: Brian Hyland
Media Editor: Sarah Kinney
Media Project Manager: Tina Rudowski
Senior Art Director: Maria Lange
Cover Design: DePinho Design
Cover Image: National Archives and Records Administration
AV Project Manager: Mirella Signoretto
Full-Service Production, Interior Design, and
  Composition: PreMediaGlobal
Printer/Binder: Courier/Kendallville
Cover Printer: Courier/Kendallville
Text Font: Minion Pro Regular 10.5/12.8

Credits and acknowledgments borrowed from other sources and reproduced, with permission, in this textbook appear on appropriate page within text (or on pages C1-C-4).

Copyright © 2011, 2008, 2005 Pearson Education, Inc., publishing as Prentice Hall, One Lake Street, Upper Saddle River, NJ 07458. All rights reserved. Manufactured in the United States of America. This publication is protected by Copyright, and permission should be obtained from the publisher prior to any prohibited reproduction, storage in a retrieval system, or transmission in any form or by any means, electronic, mechanical, photocopying, recording, or likewise. To obtain permission(s) to use material from this work, please submit a written request to Pearson Education, Inc., Permissions Department, One Lake Street, Upper Saddle River, NJ 07458.

Many of the designations by manufacturers and seller to distinguish their products are claimed as trademarks. Where those designations appear in this book, and the publisher was aware of a trademark claim, the designations have been printed in initial caps or all caps.

Library of Congress Cataloging-in-Publication Data

Created equal : a history of the United States / Jacqueline Jones . . . [et al.]. — Brief 3rd ed.
  p. cm.
Includes bibliographical references and index.
1. United States—History.   2. United States—Sopcial conditions.   3. United States—Politics and government.
4. Cultural pluralism—United States—History.   5. Minorities—United States—History.   I. Jones, Jacqueline, 1948-
E178.C68 2010
973—dc22

2010019153

10 9 8 7 6 5 4 3 2 1

Prentice Hall
is an imprint of

www.pearsonhighered.com

Combined Volume
ISBN 10: 0-205-72890-1
ISBN 13: 978-0-205-72890-9

Examination Copy
ISBN 10: 0-205-76404-5
ISBN 13: 978-0-205-76404-4

Volume 1
ISBN 10: 0-205-72888-X
ISBN 13: 978-0-205-72888-6

Volume 1 a la carte
ISBN 10: 0-205-84216-X
ISBN 13: 978-0-205-84216-2

Volume 2
ISBN 10: 0-205-72889-8
ISBN 13: 978-0-205-72889-3

Volume 2 a la carte
ISBN 10: 0-205-84217-8
ISBN 13: 978-0-205-84217-9

BRIEF CONTENTS

CONTENTS

INTERPRETING HISTORY
*"These Gods That We Worship Give Us Everything
We Need"*   20

INTERPRETING HISTORY
*Anne Bradstreet: "The Tenth Muse, Lately Sprung
Up in America"*   48

INTERPRETING HISTORY
Demobilization: "Turned Adrift Like Old Worn-Out Horses"   192

INTERPRETING HISTORY
A Farmer Worries About the Power of "The Few," 1798   232

INTERPRETING HISTORY
Cherokee Women Petition Against Further Land Sales to Whites in 1817   252

INTERPRETING HISTORY
Eulalia Pérez Describes her Work in a California Mission, 1823   *276*

INTERPRETING HISTORY
Senator John C. Calhoun Warns Against Incorporating Mexico into the United States   *304*

INTERPRETING HISTORY
Professor George Howe on the Subordination of Women   *320*

INTERPRETING HISTORY
NSC-68   *565*

INTERPRETING HISTORY
Rachel Carson, Silent Spring   *592*

INTERPRETING HISTORY
Martin Luther King Jr. and the Vietnam War   *607*

> **INTERPRETING HISTORY**
> *The Church Committee and CIA Covert Operations*   625

> **INTERPRETING HISTORY**
> *Religion and Politics in the 1980s*   646

> **INTERPRETING HISTORY**
> *Vermont Civil Union Law*   662

INTERPRETING HISTORY
The Slow Food Movement 692

MAPS

FIGURES AND TABLES

Figures

Tables

PREFACE

"We hold these truths to be self-evident: That all men are created equal; that they are endowed by their Creator with certain unalienable rights; that among these are Life, Liberty, and the pursuit of Happiness. . . . "

Ever since the Continental Congress approved the Declaration of Independence on July 4, 1776, the noble sentiments expressed in the document have inspired people in the United States and around the world. The Founding Fathers conceived of the new nation in what we today would consider narrow terms—as a political community of white men of property. Gradually, as the generations unfolded, diverse racial and ethnic groups, as well as women of all backgrounds, cited the Declaration in their struggle to achieve a more inclusive definition of American citizenship. American history is the story of various groups of men and women, all "created equal" in their common humanity, claiming an American identity for themselves.

In fact, the cloth of American history is distinguished by many major threads—territorial growth and expansion, the rise of the middle class, generations of technological innovation and economic development, and ongoing U.S. engagement with the wider world. *Created Equal* incorporates these traditional narratives into a new and fresh interpretation of American history, one that includes the stories of diverse groups of people and explores expanding notions of American identity. Fresh scholarship, new perspectives, and changing global conditions call for constant refinement and revision, so over the past three years all five of us have devoted ourselves to developing a new edition that will meet current needs. We want the brief third edition of *Created Equal* to be the best yet. We intend it to be both definitive and suggestive, addressing traditional questions and provoking new ones. Ideally, each reader will find parts of his or her own family and community stories reflected here, while also engaging with other less familiar stories that make up the entire American fabric.

What's New to This Edition

This third brief edition of *Created Equal* retains and strengthens the basic structure of the previous edition because dedicated users of the book told us that they appreciated its unique style and many distinctive elements. These elements include a strong chronological narrative that is readable and engaging. The text emphasizes significant political developments throughout American history and uses the stories of individuals, familiar and unfamiliar, to enliven the narrative. Throughout, it intertwines three key themes: our rich social diversity, our changing relation to the varied natural environment, and the vital intersection of foreign and domestic affairs throughout American history. We have added new material related to all of these topics, especially the third theme which relates to ongoing globalization. Also, we continue to underscore two of the book's common-sense assumptions. The first concerns our belief that the social and political realms are deeply interconnected and must be explored together. The second involves our awareness that socioeconomic class and power systems have shaped American society and growth in profound ways that cannot be ignored.

Without straying from this core commitment to a chronological narrative that addresses overarching themes, we have worked to make this edition more user-friendly in several important ways.

- We strengthened transition passages, sharpened conclusions, and increased the number of subheadings to assist readability.

- We added questions within and after each chapter to assist reader comprehension of unfamiliar material.

- A new "Key Terms" section appears at the end of each chapter, defining and reinforcing boldfaced terms throughout the chapter.

- With the goal of coherence in mind, several of the "part introductions" have been redrafted and a number of the chapter openings have been re-written as well.

- This edition contains expanded treatment of such topics as the abolition of the international slave trade (Chapter 10), the Emancipation Proclamation (Chapter 14), Social Darwinism (Chapter 16), and imperialism (Chapter 18).

- Naturally, we have lengthened Chapter 30 to include the bursting of the housing market bubble, the onset of a steep recession, and the federal government's controversial Wall Street "bailout" at the end of the George W. Bush administration, plus the historic election of 2008 and the trouble-filled first year of Barack Obama's presidency.

- Several maps have been updated, and a new map in Chapter 30 shows Iraq and Afghanistan.

- In the "Interpreting History" feature, we have retained the questions after each selection to encourage students to hone their critical thinking skills, and in multiple chapters we have created new entries.

Each "Interpreting History" feature uses primary source material—a document or an object—to drill down on an intriguing topic that relates to the chapter text from a surprising or revealing angle. In Chapter 3, for example, the new "Interpreting History" selection discusses a possible winter journey beyond the Mississippi River by a Frenchman in 1688, and in Chapter 5 the topic is eighteenth-century fascination with mastadon bones from the Ohio River Valley. Chapter 7 introduces a little-known letter from the patriot publicist, Thomas Paine, and in Chapter 11, Eulalia Pérez describes her work in a California mission in the 1820s. The fresh "Interpreting History" selection in Chapter 20 concerns a 1915 Supreme Court ruling on whether an American woman should lose her citizenship if she marries a foreigner, and the new entry in Chapter 30 highlights the difficult early policy decisions surrounding the post 9/11 "War on Terror."

In addition, there is new material in both the text and the graphics. Where a new paragraph seemed necessary, we have added it, often prompted by fresh research in the field or the comments of a helpful reader. Additional pictures have been added, such as the image of a hunter that opens Chapter 1 or the photo in Chapter 9 of actress Kameshia Duncan playing Ona Judge, an enslaved woman who escaped from the household of George and Martha Washington. A revised glossary at the end of each chapter defines terms that are highlighted in the body of the text, providing a handy reference for readers encountering unfamiliar words and phrases.

Significantly, this new brief edition is not only stronger, but *shorter* as well—by more than sixty pages. Working closely with our publishing team, we have managed to implement this win-win change. Some economies have come from sharp editing and careful re-writing—the same things we ask of our own students and colleagues.

Three Central Themes

We have chosen to highlight three significant themes that run throughout American history.

- **Diversity.** The formation of social identity is a central element of the American story, so the theme of diversity runs throughout *Created Equal*. We examine how individual Americans have understood and identified themselves by such factors as gender, religion, region, income, race, and ethnicity. Native Americans, African Americans, Spanish-speaking inhabitants of the Southwest, immigrants from every part of the world, women of all groups—all of these people have played a major role in defining what it means to be an American. Identity is never simple or static; it is always complex and shifting. For example, in the early twentieth century, a Russian immigrant garment worker on New York's Lower East Side might think of herself in any number of ways—as a Jew, an employee, a union member, a single woman, a resident of a thriving city—and these forms of identity might change over time, depending on the woman's circumstances.

- **Globalization.** The deep international recession and the distant wars that remain facts of current American life are reminders of the country's complex ties to the rest of the world. The globalization of the United States' economy and society has been increasing sharply in recent decades. But our culture, shaped by generations of immigrants, has long been engaged with the nations of the world. Since the earliest days of colonial settlement, newcomers and their descendants have traded goods, cultural practices, and ideas with peoples outside their borders. Moreover, America's foreign and domestic relations have always been intertwined. Recall how diplomatic and then military ties to France helped to decide the American War of Independence, or consider the way that economic and political relations with Great Britain, a key consumer of southern cotton, influenced the unfolding of the Civil War. After World War II, American fears of communism and the Soviet Union exerted a profound effect upon the country's politics and society. In our own era, in the wake of the terrorist attacks of September 11, 2001, all Americans were forced to confront the role of the United States in the larger world, with all the opportunities and dangers that role entailed. This wide-angle perspective on the American story is central to *Created Equal*.

- **Environment.** The role of North America's diverse environment has always been significant in American history. But its central importance is only now becoming more clearly understood and more widely debated. From the outset, the physical landscape has been changed by American society in every era. Likewise, each new generation has in turn been shaped by the continent's climate, resources, and landscapes in numerous ways. Before the advent of trains, cars, and planes, North America's rivers, lakes, and harbors played a key role in shaping settlement and connecting communities. The theme of the environment is key to understanding cultural, political, and economic developments. Many Native American groups shared a sense of oneness with the land; for them, the material and spiritual worlds were intimately related. In contrast, many European Americans saw the land as a means of making a living, as a commodity for speculation, or as the source of valuable raw materials—in other words, as a thing to be bought, sold, and used. The vast richness of the American landscape has provoked violent conflict over the years, even as it has formed a key component in American wealth and power. Throughout, we examine meaningful regional differences—not just along the eastern seaboard, but in all of the country's geographical areas.

These three themes serve as the lenses through which we view the traditional narrative framework of American history. Readers of *Created Equal* will understand the major political developments that shaped the country's past, as well as the role of diverse groups in initiating and reacting to those developments. Thus, *Created Equal* builds upon the basic history that forms the foundation of most major textbooks and offers a rich and comprehensive look at the past by including the stories of all Americans.

Chronological Organization

One of the challenges in writing *Created Equal* has been to emphasize the way in which the major themes come together and influence each other, affecting specific generations of Americans. Thus the text is organized into ten parts, most of these covering a generation. Many textbooks organize discussions of immigrants, cities, the West, and foreign diplomacy (to name a few topics) into separate chapters that cover large time periods. In contrast, *Created Equal* integrates material related to a variety of topics within individual chapters. Although the text adheres to a chronological organization, it stresses coherent discussions of specific topics within that framework. This provides students with a richer understanding of events. Chapter 15, for example, which covers the years just after the Civil War, deals with Reconstruction in the South, Indian wars on the High Plains, and the rise of the women's and labor movements, stressing the relationships among all these developments. To cite another example: many texts devote a chapter exclusively to America's post–World War II rise to global power; *Created Equal* integrates material related to that development in a series of six chapters that cover the period of 1945 to 2010. Each of these chapters illustrates the effects of dramatic world developments on American social relations and domestic policy on a decade-by-decade basis. This approach allows readers to appreciate the rich complexity of any particular time period and to understand that major events do not occur in a vacuum, but in a larger social context.

Special Features

The book includes a number of features designed to make American history clear and engaging to the reader, and to encourage students to "do" history on their own. These features include:

- **Parts and timelines.** *Created Equal* consists of ten parts covering three chapters each. An opening section that lays out the basic themes of the period introduces each part. Each chapter includes a useful timeline highlighting major events covered in the chapter.

- **Chapter introductory vignettes and conclusions.** Each chapter begins with a story that introduces the reader to groups and individuals representative of the themes developed in the chapter. Among the chapter introductory vignettes are the stories of a Norwegian immigrant woman in Wisconsin (Chapter 12), a group of runaway slaves accused of treason by Confederate authorities in wartime Florida (Chapter 14), Spanish-speaking inhabitants of northern New Mexico struggling to retain their culture in the face of an onslaught of European American settlers (Chapter 17), and a Sioux Indian boy at a government boarding school (Chapter 18). At the end of each chapter, a concluding section sums up the chapter's themes and points the reader toward the next chapter.

- **Maps, charts, and pullout quotes.** Illustrations—photographs, tables, and figures—enhance the narrative. Large maps offer geographical detail and invite students to see the relationship between geography and history. Quotes in the margin help readers grasp the chapter's major themes.

- **"Interpreting History."** Every chapter includes a boxed feature entitled "Interpreting History." Each full-page box highlights an intriguing primary document or object that relates to the contents of the chapter and its underlying themes. Through these documents, we hear the voices of a variety of Americans, such as a woman poet in seventeenth-century New England, a prominent senator from antebellum South Carolina, industrial titan

Andrew Carnegie, and environmental activist Rachel Carson. We have added a brief introduction before each original text, and we have placed several questions at the end of the feature in order to guide study and prompt further discussion.

- **Glossary.** The third edition includes a revised glossary of terms culled from the text and defined at the end of each chapter. Sample terms (out of several hundred) include *pocket veto, aqueduct, canal locks, sit-down strike, antebellum, carpetbaggers, scalawags, vigilantes,* and *fatigue work*. Each chapter's glossary terms are highlighted in **boldface type** in the chapter text and defined at the end of each chapter.

Exploring the Past to Face the Future

With all its changes and improvements, the third brief edition of *Created Equal* still remains true to the vision that first inspired this book. We continue to offer a basic overview of American history that focuses on the political events and social developments discussed in most textbooks. But from the outset we have pushed to make *Created Equal* distinctive in several ways. It offers a broad geographical scope and environmental awareness from the very beginning of the narrative. This emphasis is becoming increasingly relevant to students as the twenty-first century unfolds. At the same time, the text remains consistently attentive to matters of economic, cultural, and political power. We hope that readers will gain an understanding of the power relations that have shaped our past—which groups have had influence and how they have maintained and wielded that influence.

Along the way, we incorporate numerous groups and individuals who impelled, and experienced, the nation's most significant changes. Their stories, both familiar and unfamiliar, enliven the narrative and help to provide a more direct, subtle, and compelling view of the American past. *Created Equal* tells the evolving saga of a diverse and idealistic people. Our continuing aim is to offer an accurate and thorough account that will help readers become more informed, empowered, and independent in facing the future.

The Authors

Supplements for Qualified College Adopters	Supplements for Students
myhistorylab	**myhistorylab**
MyHistoryLab (www.myhistorylab.com) Save Time. Improve Results. MyHistoryLab is a dynamic website that provides a wealth of resources geared to meet the diverse teaching and learning needs of today's instructors and students. MyHistoryLab's many accessible tools will encourage students to read their text and help them improve their grade in their course.	*MyHistoryLab (www.myhistorylab.com) Save Time. Improve Results.* MyHistoryLab is a dynamic website that provides a wealth of resources geared to meet the diverse teaching and learning needs of today's instructors and students. MyHistoryLab's many accessible tools will encourage you to read your text and help you improve your grade in your course.
Instructor's Resource Manual with Test Bank Available at the Instructor's Resource Center, at **www.pearsonhighered.com/irc**, the Instructor's Resource Manual with Test Bank contains chapter outlines, summaries, key points and vital concepts, and information on audio-visual resources that can be used in developing and preparing lecture presentations. The Test Bank includes multiple choice questions and essay questions and is text specific.	*CourseSmart* **www.coursemart.com** CourseSmart eTextbooks offer the same content as the printed text in a convenient online format—with highlighting, online search, and printing capabilities. You **save 60% over the list price** of the traditional book.
PowerPoint Presentation Available at the Instructor's Resource Center, at **www.pearsonhighered.com/irc**, the PowerPoints contain chapter outlines and full-color images of maps and arts. They are text specific and available for download.	*Books à la Carte* Books à la Carte editions feature the exact same content as the traditional printed text in a convenient, three-hole-punched, loose-leaf version at a discounted price—allowing you to take only what you need to class. You'll **save 35% over the net price** of the traditional book.
MyTest Available at **www.pearsonmytest.com**, MyTest is a powerful assessment generation program that helps instructors easily create and print quizzes and exams. Questions and tests can be authored online, allowing instructors ultimate flexibility and the ability to efficiently manage assessments anytime, anywhere! Instructors can easily access existing questions and edit, create, and store using simple drag-and-drop and Word-like controls.	*Library of American Biography Series* **www.pearsonhighered.com/educator/series/Library-of-American-Biography/10493.page** Pearson's renowned series of biographies spotlighting figures who had a significant impact on American history. Included in the series are Edmund Morgan's *The Puritan Dilemma: The Story of John Winthrop*, B. Davis Edmund's *Tecumseh and the Quest for Indian Leadership*, J. William T. Youngs, *Eleanor Roosevelt: A Personal and Public Life*, and John R. M. Wilson's *Jackie Robinson and the American Dilemma*.
Retrieving the American Past Available through the Pearson Custom Library (**www.pearsoncustom.com**, **keyword search | rtap**), the *Retrieving the American Past* (RTAP) program lets you create a textbook or reader that meets your needs and the needs of your course. RTAP gives you the freedom and flexibility to add chapters from several best-selling Pearson textbooks, in addition to *Created Equal, Brief Edition, 3/e*, and/or 100 topical reading units written by the History Department of Ohio State University, all under one cover. Choose the content you want to teach in depth, in the sequence you want, at the price you want your students to pay.	*Penguin Valuepacks* **www.pearsonhighered.com/penguin** A variety of Penguin-Putnam texts is available at discounted prices when bundled with *Created Equal, Brief Edition, 3/e*. Texts include Benjamin Franklin's *Autobiography and Other Writings*, Nathaniel Hawthorne's *The Scarlet Letter*, Thomas Jefferson's *Notes on the State of Virginia*, and George Orwell's *1984*.
	A Short Guide to Writing About History, 7/e Written by Richard Marius, late of Harvard University, and Melvin E. Page, Eastern Tennessee State University, this engaging and practical text helps students get beyond merely compiling dates and facts. Covering both brief essays and the documented resource paper, the text explores the writing and researching processes, identifies different modes of historical writing, including argument, and concludes with guidelines for improving style. **ISBN-10: 0205673708; ISBN-13: 9780205673704**
	Longman American History Atlas This full-color historical atlas designed especially for college students is a valuable reference tool and visual guide to American history. This atlas includes maps covering the scope of American history from the lives of the Native Americans to the 1990s. Produced by a renowned cartographic firm and a team of respected historians, the Longman American History Atlas will enhance any American history survey course. **ISBN: 0321004868; ISBN-13: 9780321004864**
	Study Card for American History This timeline of major events in American social, political, and cultural history distills course information to the basics, helping you quickly master the fundamentals and prepare for exams. **ISBN: 0321292324; ISBN-13: 9780321292322**

MyHistoryLab (www.myhistorylab.com)

Save TIME. Improve Results. MyHistoryLab is a dynamic website that provides a wealth of resources geared to meet the diverse teaching and learning needs of today's instructors and students. MyHistoryLab's many accessible tools will encourage students to read their text and help them improve their grade in their course.

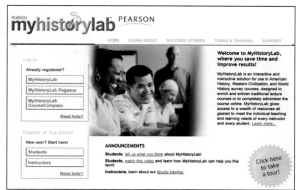

Here are some of the features that will help you and your students save time and improve results:

- Pearson eText—Just like the printed text, students can highlight and add their own notes. Students save time and improve results by having access to their book online.

- Gradebook—Students can follow their own progress and instructors can monitor the work of the entire class. Automated grading of quizzes and assignments helps both instructors and students save time and monitor their results throughout the course.

- History Bookshelf—Students may read, download, or print 100 of the most commonly assigned history works like Paine's *Common Sense* or DuBois's *The Souls of Black Folk.*

- Audio Files—Full audio of the entire book is included to suit the varied learning styles of today's students.

New Read/View/See/Watch/Hear/Study and Review Icons integrated in the text lead to Web-based expansions on topics, allowing instructors and students access to extra information, videos, and simulations. The icons draw attention to the most high-interest material available, although many more resources may be accessed at www.myhistorylab.com.

Read the **Document**

Points students to primary and secondary source documents related to the chapter.

View the **Image**

Identifies primary and secondary source images, including photographs, fine art, and artifacts to provide students with a visual perspective on history.

See the **Map**

Directs students to atlas and interactive maps, that present both broad overviews and detailed examinations of historical developments.

Watch the **Video**

Notes pertinent archival videos and videos by Pearson History authors that probe various topics.

Hear the **Audio**

Marks audio clips from historically significant songs and speeches that enrich students' engagement with history.

Study and **Review**

Alerts students to study resources for each chapter of the textbook available online through www.myhistorylab.com. These resources include practice tests and flashcards.

MEET THE AUTHORS

Jacqueline Jones teaches American history at the University of Texas at Austin, where she is Mastin Gentry White Professor of Southern History and Walter Prescott Webb Chair in History and Ideas. She was born in Christiana, Delaware, a small town of 400 people in the northern part of the state. The local public school was desegregated in 1955 when she was a third grader. That event, combined with the peculiar social etiquette of relations between blacks and whites in the town, sparked her interest in American history. She attended the University of Delaware in nearby Newark and went on to graduate school at the University of Wisconsin, Madison, where she received her Ph.D. in history. Her scholarly interests have evolved over time, focusing on American labor, and women's, African-American, and southern history. In 1999 she received a MacArthur Fellowship. One of her biggest challenges has been to balance her responsibilities as teacher, historian, wife, and mother (of two daughters). In 2008 she published *Saving Savannah: The City and the Civil War;* and she is the author of several other books, including *Soldiers of Light and Love: Northern Teachers and Georgia Blacks* (1980); *Labor of Love, Labor of Sorrow: Black Women, Work, and Family Since Slavery* (1985), which won the Bancroft Prize and was a finalist for a Pulitzer Prize; *The Dispossessed: America's Underclasses Since the Civil War* (1992); and *American Work: Four Centuries of Black and White Labor* (1998). In 2001 she completed a memoir that recounts her childhood in Christiana: *Creek Walking: Growing Up in Delaware in the 1950s.*

Peter H. Wood was born in St. Louis (before the famous arch was built). He recalls seeing Jackie Robinson play baseball against the Cardinals, visiting the courthouse where the *Dred Scott* case originated, and traveling up the Mississippi to Hannibal, birthplace of Mark Twain. Summer work on the northern Great Lakes aroused his interest in Native American cultures, past and present. He studied at Harvard (B.A., 1964; Ph.D., 1972) and at Oxford, where he was a Rhodes Scholar (1964–1966). His pioneering book *Black Majority* (1974), concerning slavery in colonial South Carolina, won the Beveridge Prize of the American Historical Association. From 1975 to 2007 he taught early American history at Duke University, where he also coached the women's lacrosse club for three years. The topics of his articles range from the French explorer LaSalle to President Gerald Ford's pardon of Richard Nixon. In 1989 he coedited *Powhatan's Mantle: Indians in the Colonial Southeast.* His demographic essay in that volume (now in a new edition) provided the first clear picture of population change in the eighteenth-century South. His other books include *Strange New Land: Africans in Colonial America* (2003) and *Near Andersonville: Winslow Homer's Civil War* (2010). Dr. Wood has served on the boards of the Highlander Center, Harvard University, Houston's Rothko Chapel, and the Institute of Early American History and Culture in Williamsburg. He is married to colonial historian Elizabeth Fenn; his varied interests include archaeology, documentary film, and growing gourds. He keeps a baseball bat used by Ted Williams beside his desk.

Thomas ("Tim") Borstelmann, the son of a university psychologist, taught and coached at the elementary and high school levels in Washington state and Colorado before returning to graduate school. From 1991 to 2003, he taught American history at Cornell University while living in Syracuse, New York, before becoming the Elwood N. and Katherine Thompson Distinguished Professor of Modern World History at the University of Nebraska–Lincoln. He lives with his wife, a health care administrator, and two sons in Lincoln. An avid bicyclist, runner, swimmer, and cross-country skier, he earned his B.A. from Stanford University in

1980 and Ph.D. from Duke University in 1990. He became a historian to figure out the Cold War and American race relations, in part because he had grown up in the South. His first book, *Apartheid's Reluctant Uncle: The United States and Southern Africa in the Early Cold War* (1993), won the Stuart L. Bernath Book Prize of the Society for Historians of Foreign Relations. His second book, *The Cold War and the Color Line,* appeared in 2001. His commitment to the classroom earned him a major teaching award at Cornell, the Robert and Helen Appel Fellowship. He found writing *Created Equal* a natural complement to what he does in the classroom, trying to provide both telling details of the American past and the broad picture of how the United States has developed as it has. A specialist in U.S. foreign relations and modern world history, he is equally fascinated with domestic American politics and social change. His new book on the United States and the world in the 1970s will be published in 2011.

Elaine Tyler May grew up in the shadow of Hollywood, performing in neighborhood circuses with her friends. She went to high school before girls could play on sports teams, so she spent her after-school hours as a cheerleader and her summer days as a bodysurfing beach bum. Her passion for American history developed in college when she spent her junior year in Japan. The year was 1968. The Vietnam War was raging, along with turmoil at home. As an American in Asia, often called on to explain her nation's actions, she yearned for a deeper understanding of America's past and its place in the world. She returned home to study history at UCLA, where she earned her B.A., M.A., and Ph.D. She has taught at Princeton and Harvard Universities and since 1978 at the University of Minnesota. Her books examine the relationship between politics, public policy, and private life. Her widely acclaimed *Homeward Bound: American Families in the Cold War Era* was the first study to link the baby boom and suburbia to the politics of the Cold War. The *Chronicle of Higher Education* featured *Barren in the Promised Land: Childless Americans and the Pursuit of Happiness* as a pioneering study of the history of reproduction. *Lingua Franca* named her coedited volume *Here, There, and Everywhere: The Foreign Politics of American Popular Culture* a "Breakthrough Book." Most recently she published *America and the Pill: A History of Promise, Peril and Liberation.* She has served as president of the Organization of American Historians (2010) and the American Studies Association (1996). In 1997 she was the Distinguished Fulbright Professor of American History in Dublin, Ireland. She is married to historian Lary May and has three children, who have inherited their parents' passion for history.

Vicki L. Ruiz is dean of the School of Humanities and professor of history and Chicano/Latino studies at the University of California, Irvine. For her, history remains a grand adventure, one that she began at the kitchen table, listening to the stories of her mother and grandmother, and continued with the help of the local bookmobile. She read constantly as she sat on the dock, catching small fish ("grunts") to be used as bait on her father's fishing boat. As she grew older, she was promoted to working with her mother, selling tickets for the *Blue Sea II.* The first in her family to receive an advanced degree, she graduated from Gulf Coast Community College and Florida State University, then went on to earn a Ph.D. in history at Stanford in 1982, the fourth Mexican American woman to receive a doctorate in history. Her first book, *Cannery Women, Cannery Lives,* received an award from the National Women's Political Caucus, and her second, *From Out of the Shadows: Mexican Women in 20th-Century America,* was named a *Choice* Outstanding Academic Book of 1998 by the American Library Association. She and Ellen Carol DuBois published three editions of *Unequal Sisters: A Multicultural Reader in U.S. Women's History.* In 2008, the fourth edition appeared with Ruiz as sole editor. She and Virginia Sánchez Korrol edited the three-volume *Latinas in the United States: A Historical Encyclopedia,* which received a 2007 Best in Reference Award from the New York Public Library. Ruiz and Sánchez Korrol were recognized by *Latina*

Magazine as Latinas of the Year in Education for 2000, and in 2005 they received a "21 Leaders for the 21st Century" award by women's e-news network. In addition, she and Donna Gabaccia created the anthology *American Dreaming, Global Realities: Re-Thinking U.S. Immigration History.* Active in student mentorship projects, summer institutes for teachers, and public humanities programs, Dr. Ruiz served as an appointee to the National Council of the Humanities. A fellow in the Society of American Historians, she was elected to the national governing bodies of the American Historical Association, the Organization of American Historians, and the American Studies Association. Like Professor May, she is a past president of both the Organization of American Historians and the American Studies Association. She is currently on the national advisory board of the Smithsonian's National Museum of American History. The mother of two grown sons, she is married to Victor Becerra, urban planner and gourmet cook extraordinaire.

ACKNOWLEDGMENTS

As authors, we could not have completed this project without the loving support of our families. We wish to thank Jeffrey Abramson, Lil Fenn, Lynn Borstelmann, Lary May, and Victor Becerra for their interest, forbearance, and encouragement over the course of several editions. Our own children have been a source of inspiration, as have our many students, past and present. We are grateful to scores of colleagues and friends who have helped shape this book, both directly and indirectly, in more ways than they know. Along the way, Matt Basso, Chad Cover, Rob Heinrich, Jeff Manuel, Rob McGreevey, Eben Miller, Andrea Sachs, Mary Strunk, and Melissa Williams provided useful research and administrative assistance; their help was invaluable. Louis Balizet provided careful reading of several chapter drafts.

Our friends at Pearson have continued their generous support and assistance for our efforts. We thank all the creative people associated with Pearson (and there are many) who have had a hand in bringing this book to life, as well as Lindsay Bethoney and all those who deftly guided this brief third edition through the many phases of production.

Finally, we wish to express our deep gratitude to the following individuals who read and commented on the first brief edition. Their thoughtful criticism, advice, and suggestions have all helped improve the book: S. Carol Berg, *College of St. Benedict*; Roger Bromert, *Southwestern Oklahoma State University*; Charlotte Brooks, *State University of New York—Albany*; Eduardo Canedo, *Columbia University*; Nancy Carnevale, *Montclair State University*; John A. Collins, *Freed-Hardeman University*; Cole P. Dawson, *Warner Pacific College*; Barbara C. Fertig, *Armstrong Atlantic State University*; Van Forsyth, *Clark College*; Martin Hershock, *University of Michigan, Dearborn*; Richard Hughes, *Eastern Oregon University*; Kimberly Jensen, *Western Oregon University*; Cynthia M. Kennedy, *Clarion University of Pennsylvania*; Annette Laing, *Georgia Southern University*; Michael Lansing, *Augsburg College*; Carolyn J. Lawes, *Old Dominion University*; Sandy Moats, *University of Wisconsin—Parkside*; Earl F. Mulderink, *Southern Utah University*; C. Samuel Nelson II, *Ridgewater College*; Jason C. Newman, *Cosumnes River College*; David R. Novak, *Purdue University*; Melissa Soto-Schwartz, *Cuyahoga Community College*; Deborah Syrdal, *Humboldt State University*; Michael M. Topp, *University of Texas, El Paso*; Sylvia Tyson, *Texas Lutheran University*; Mark D. Van Ells, *Queenborough Community College, CUNY*; David Voelker, *University of Wisconsin—Green Bay*; Charles Westmoreland, *University of Mississippi*; Julie Winch, *University of Massachusetts, Boston*; David Wolcott, *Miami University*; and Jason Young, *State University of New York, Buffalo*.

This brief edition also owes much to the many conscientious historians who reviewed the full-length edition of the textbook. For their insights and constructive critiques, we are indebted to the following reviewers:

Ken Adderley, *Upper Iowa University*; Gretchen Adams, *Texas Tech University*; Leslie Alexander, *Ohio State University*; Marynita Anderson, *Nassau Community College*; John Andrew, *Franklin and Marshall College*; Abel Bartley, *University of Akron*; Donald Scott Barton, *Central Carolina Technical College*; Mia Bay, *Rutgers University*; Chris Bierwith, *Treasure Valley Community College*; Charles Bolton, *University of Arkansas at Little Rock*; Susan Burch, *Gallaudet University*; Tommy Bynum, *Georgia Perimeter College*; Robert B. Carey, *Empire State College-SUNY*; Todd Carney, *Southern Oregon University*; Kathleen Carter, *Highpoint University*; Jonathan Chu, *University of Massachusetts*; Barak Cook, *University of Missouri*; Amy E. Davis, *University of California–Los Angeles*; Judy DeMark, *Northern Michigan University*; James A. Denton, *University of Colorado*; Joseph A. Devine, *Stephen F. Austin University*; Margaret Dwight, *North Carolina Agricultural and Technical*

University; Nancy Gabin, *Purdue University;* Lori Ginzberg, *Pennsylvania State University;* Gregory Goodwin, *Bakersfield College;* Amy S. Greenberg, *Pennsylvania State University;* Charlotte Haller, *Worcester State College;* Nadine Isitani Hata, *El Camino College;* James Hedtke, *Cabrini College;* Traci Hodgson, *Chemeketa Community College;* Rose Holz, *University of Nebraska–Lincoln;* Fred Hoxie, *University of Illinois;* Tera Hunter, *Carnegie Mellon University;* Creed Hyatt, *Lehigh Carbon Community College;* David Jaffe, *City College of New York;* Jeremy Johnson, *Northwest College;* Yvonne Johnson, *Central Missouri State University;* Kurt Keichtle, *University of Wisconsin;* Anne Klejment, *University of St. Thomas;* Dennis Kortheuer, *California State University–Long Beach;* Rebecca Kosary, *Texas Lutheran University;* Joel Kunze, *Upper Iowa University;* Joseph Laythe, *Edinboro College of Pennsylvania;* Chana Kai Lee, *Indiana University;* Dan Letwin, *Pennsylvania State University;* Gaylen Lewis, *Bakersfield College;* Kenneth Lipartito, *Florida International University;* Kyle Longley, *Arizona State University;* Edith L. Macdonald, *University of Central Florida;* Lorie Maltby, *Henderson Community College;* Sandra Mathews-Lamb, *Nebraska Wesleyan University;* Noeleen McIlvenna, *Wright State University;* Constance M. McGovern, *Frostburg State University;* Henry McKiven, *University of South Alabama;* James H. Merrell, *Vassar College;* Carl Moneyhan, *University of Arkansas–Little Rock;* Earl Mulderink, *Southern Utah State University;* Cynthia Neverdon-Morton, *Coppin State University;* Jason C. Newman, *Consumnes River College;* Steven Noll, *University of Florida;* Jim Norris, *North Dakota State University;* Elsa Nystrom, *Kennesaw State University;* Keith Pacholl, *California State University–Fullerton;* William Pelz, *Elgin Community College;* Melanie Perrault, *University of Central Arkansas;* Delores D. Petersen, *Foothill College;* Robert Pierce, *Foothill College;* Louis Potts, *University of Missouri–Kansas City;* Sarah Purcell, *Central Michigan University;* Niler Pyeatt, *Wayland Baptist University;* Steven Reschly, *Truman State University;* Arthur Robinson, *Santa Rosa Junior College;* Robert E. Rook, *Fort Hays State University;* Thomas J. Rowland, *University of Wisconsin–Oshkosh;* Steven Ruggles, *University of Minnesota;* Leonard J. Sadosky, *Iowa State University;* Rebecca Shoemaker, *Indiana State University;* Howard Shore, *Columbia River High School;* James Sidbury, *University of Texas;* Arwin D. Smallwood, *Bradley University;* Margaret Spratt, *California University of Pennsylvania;* Rachel Standish, *Foothill College;* Jon Stauff, *St. Ambrose University;* David Steigerwald, *Ohio State University–Marion;* Kay Stockbridge, *Central Carolina Technical College;* Daniel Thorp, *Virginia Tech University;* Michael M. Topp, *University of Texas–El Paso;* Clifford Trafzer, *University of California–Riverside;* Deborah Gray White, *Rutgers University;* Scott Wong, *Williams College;* Bill Woodward, *Seattle Pacific University;* Nancy Zens, *Central Oregon Community College;* and David Zonderman, *North Carolina State University.*

CREATED EQUAL

PART ONE

North American Foundations

FOR GENERATIONS, AMERICAN SCHOOL CHILDREN LEARNED ABOUT their country's foundations by returning to the English colonies of the early seventeenth century. They imagined themselves among initial settlers at Jamestown or Plymouth. Then they marched quickly forward to salute the Founding Fathers, the men who met in Philadelphia and drafted our enduring frame of government during the Revolutionary Era. It was a compelling story, but it was narrow, brief, and oversimplified. We can now see that the first chapters of American history are far broader and longer.

Researchers are finally discovering the depth and richness of North America's earliest foundations, stretching back across the continent's long human history. We must explore far back in time to find the varied men and women who were the continent's first founders. Two kinds of foundation builders emerge: the distant ancestors of today's Native Americans and the newcomers from abroad who colonized North America in the sixteenth and seventeenth centuries.

Our earliest human ancestors evolved in Africa and then spread across the landmass of Eurasia. In the Southern Hemisphere, they managed to cross to Australia roughly 40,000 years ago. But evidence suggests that they reached the Americas from Asia much later, probably less than 20,000 years ago. These first arrivals took advantage of the land bridge that joined Siberia to Alaska when Ice Age glaciers caused a dramatic decline in sea levels. Roughly 14,000 years ago, these hunters apparently bypassed melting glaciers to reach the North American interior. They came on foot, but additional newcomers may have skirted the Pacific coast in small boats or even drifted across the South Pacific.

We still understand very little about these earliest Americans and their changing continent. What we do know is that they spread rapidly across North America over the next thousand years, and they continued to hunt mammoths and other large animals until these ancient species became extinct. Did the climate shift gradually, or did the impact of an enormous comet nearly 13,000 years ago cause sudden changes, as some scientists now suggest? We know for certain that later generations adapted to a wide range of environments, learning to fish, hunt for smaller game, and gather berries. It has been 3,000 years since the early signs of American agriculture.

By 500 C.E., complex cultures were beginning to appear in equatorial America. A succession of diverse and rich societies had arisen in the Americas by the time a second set of founders appeared around 1500.

Although Vikings from Scandinavia had preceded Christopher Columbus by five centuries, their small outpost on the coast of Newfoundland lasted only a few years. In contrast, when Columbus reached the West Indies from Spain in October 1492, his voyage launched a human and biological exchange between the Eastern and Western Hemispheres that has never ceased. Spanish and Portuguese ships were soon followed by vessels from England, France, and Holland.

Europeans brought new materials such as iron and new animals such as horses, cattle, and pigs. They also brought deadly diseases previously unknown in the Americas, such as measles and smallpox, which had a catastrophic impact on Native American societies. By 1565 Europeans had established their first lasting outpost in the North American continent, the town of St. Augustine in Spanish Florida. Two decades later the English tried, unsuccessfully, to plant a similar colony at Roanoke Island along the coast of what is now North Carolina.

In the first decades of the seventeenth century, permanent European settlements took hold at Quebec on the St. Lawrence River and at Santa Fe near the Rio Grande. A transatlantic outpost of English society appeared at Jamestown on Chesapeake Bay in 1607. Farther north, behind the sheltering hook of Cape Cod, other English settlers formed additional coastal outposts and renamed the region New England.

Numbers were small at first, but these communities and others endured and expanded, often with crucial help from Native Americans who knew the keys to survival in their own domains. The success of these European footholds prompted competition to control land and resources. Disappointed in early searches for easy mineral wealth, new arrivals took advantage of other opportunities: cutting timber, catching fish, raising tobacco, or trading for furs. The French in particular, with aid from Native Americans, explored the continent's interior. By 1700 they had laid claim to the entire Mississippi River valley and established a colony on the Gulf of Mexico.

Each new colonizing enterprise in the seventeenth century took on a distinctive life of its own—or, rather, numerous lives. First of all, there was the internal life of the community: who would be allowed to take part, how would participants govern themselves, and how would they subsist? In each instance, relations with the region's native inhabitants constituted a second unfolding story. Complicated ties to Europe—economic, religious, social, and political—made a third crucial narrative. Furthermore, relations between colonies and between the distant European powers that backed them had a determining influence, as when England took over the Dutch colony at New Netherland in the third quarter of the seventeenth century, renaming it New York. Finally, there was the compelling drama of the newcomers' relationship to the environment itself. These founding generations labored to understand—or to subdue and exploit without fully understanding—the continent they had started to colonize.

1533	Pizarro overthrows Inca Empire in Peru
1534 to 1543	Expeditions of Cartier (Canada), de Soto (Southeast), and Coronado (Southwest) probe North America
1565	Spanish establish St. Augustine
1577 to 1580	Voyage of Drake challenges Spanish dominance in the Pacific
1585 to 1590	English attempt to establish Roanoke colony fails
1588	Spanish Armada fails in effort to invade England
1599	Spanish colonize New Mexico
1607	England's Virginia Company launches colony at Jamestown
1620	*Mayflower* passengers establish Plymouth Colony
1630	English Puritans found Massachusetts Bay Colony
1637	Pequot War in New England
1660	Restoration of monarchy in England under Charles II
1664	Charles II grants charter to his brother James, Duke of York, sanctioning the takeover of the Dutch New Netherland colony and the creation of New York
1675 to 1676	Metacom's War in New England
1676	Bacon's Rebellion in Virginia
1680	Pueblo Revolt in New Mexico
1681	Quaker William Penn receives charter for Pennsylvania
1682	La Salle explores the Mississippi River and claims Louisiana for France
1689	Dutch leader William of Orange and his wife Mary become joint English sovereigns in the Glorious Revolution, replacing King James II
1691	Witchcraft trials in Salem, Massachusetts
1699	Iberville begins colony in French Louisiana
1711 to 1715	Tuscarora Indians in North Carolina, and then the Yamasee in South Carolina, resist English colonial expansion

1

First Founders

"This is real old C.S.I.," Hugh Berryman told reporters. As a forensic anthropologist, Dr. Berryman knew all about "crime scene investigation." He had come to Seattle in 2005 as part of a team to examine the bones of a deceased human. "It's the type of skeleton that comes along once in a lifetime," commented another member of the team.

In 1996, two outdoorsmen near the Columbia River in Kennewick, Washington, had stumbled on the bones of a middle-aged man. At first, authorities guessed they had the corpse of an early white settler. But tests revealed it to be much older—9,400 years old, in fact. That touched off years of legal wrangling over control of one of the most ancient skeletons ever found in the Americas.

When the team of experts finally won the right to examine Kennewick Man, they found him to be five feet nine inches tall and roughly 40 years old. Evidence of early arthritis and prior injuries suggested a tough life: Years before his death, an enemy attack had embedded a stone point in his right hipbone. "This is like an extraordinary rare book," Berryman observed, "and we are reading it one page at a time."

The discovery of Kennewick Man followed a century of mounting study into when and how human beings first came to inhabit North America. In 1907, on the 300th anniversary of Jamestown, amazingly little was understood about who had lived in North America before the first successful English colonists arrived. Everyone knew that the Italian explorer Christopher Columbus had reached the Caribbean while attempting to sail to the Indies for Spain in 1492. They had learned in school that Columbus, thinking he had reached the Asian islands close to India and China ("the Indies"), mistakenly lumped America's peoples together as "Indians." But most Americans still knew very little about these earliest North Americans.

In the past century, our knowledge of the continent's first inhabitants has changed dramatically. An expanding American history now stretches back in time far before the Jamestown settlement and reaches broadly from coast to coast. Its earliest roots lie with the ancient Indians of the continent over many millennia. In addition, the foreigners who suddenly intruded into portions of the Native American world in the sixteenth century—speaking Spanish, French, and occasionally English—also represent a significant beginning. All these people now number among America's first founders.

Ancient America

Early in the twentieth century near Folsom, New Mexico, archaeologists found a manmade spear point resting between the rib bones of a type of ancient bison that had been extinct for 10,000 years. They named such thin projectile tips Folsom points, after the site. Their discovery proved that humans had lived and hunted on the continent far earlier than scientists had ever imagined. It sparked a revolution in North American archaeology. Soon after the Folsom find, amateurs at nearby Clovis, New Mexico, spotted some large, well-chipped spearheads. In 1932, collectors found more of these so-called Clovis points in the same vicinity, this time beside the tooth of an extinct mammoth. They lay underneath a soil layer containing Folsom points, so they were clearly even older.

Since then, scientists have unearthed Clovis-like points throughout much of North America. According to the latest calculations, humans started creating these weapons roughly 13,900 years ago and ceased about 12,900 years ago. This means that people were hunting widely on the continent nearly 14,000 years ago. Archaeologists continue to push back and refine the estimated date for the appearance of the first people in the Americas. Recently, they have unearthed evidence suggesting the possible presence of pre-Clovis inhabitants.

The Question of Origins

Like all other peoples, the Native American societies retain rich and varied accounts of their own origins. No amount of scientific data can diminish or replace tribal creation stories that serve an important cultural purpose. In these powerful sagas, America's first humans emerge from the earth, are created by other animals, or receive life from the Great Spirit. At the same time, modern researchers continue to compile evidence about the origin and migrations of the diverse peoples who inhabited the Americas for thousands of years before the arrival of Christopher Columbus.

Scientists have determined that the most recent ancestors of modern humans moved from Africa to spread across the Eurasian landmass, the area comprising Europe and Asia, scarcely 70,000 years ago. By 40,000 years ago, some of these Stone Age hunter-gatherers had already reached Australia. Others lived on the steppes of central Asia and the frozen tundra of Siberia. They had perfected the tools they needed to survive in a cold climate: flint spear points for killing mammoths, reindeer, and the woolly rhinoceros; and bone needles to sew warm, waterproof clothes out of animal skin.

Over thousands of years, bands of these northern hunters migrated east across Siberia in search of game. Eventually they arrived at the region where the Bering Strait now separates Russia from Alaska. Between 25,000 and 11,000 years ago, cold conditions expanded arctic ice caps, trapping vast quantities of the earth's water in the form of huge glaciers. As a result, ocean levels sank by 300 feet—enough to expose a bridge of land 600 miles wide between Asia and America.

The Bering Land Bridge formed part of a frigid, windswept region known as Beringia. Small groups of people could have subsisted in this cold landscape by hunting mammoths and musk oxen until Ice Age glaciers receded about 14,000 years ago. As the climate warmed and the ocean rose again, some headed farther east onto higher ground, near the headwaters of the Tanana River in eastern Alaska. These newcomers would have been cut off permanently from Siberia as water once more submerged the land bridge. But the same warming process also eventually opened a pathway through the glaciers blanketing northern America.

This ice-free corridor along the eastern slope of the Rocky Mountains could account for the sudden appearance of Clovis hunters across much of North America nearly 14,000 years ago. Small bands of people, armed with razor-sharp Clovis points, spread rapidly across the

What types of evidence are used to explain the arrival of humans in North America?

Read the **Document**
Iroquois Creation Story at
www.myhistorylab.com

■ When forensic anthropologists examined the ancient skeleton of Kennewick Man in 2005, they noticed an enlarged right arm, strengthened by hurling spears with the throwing device known as an atlatl.

View the **Image**
Clovis Points at
www.myhistorylab.com

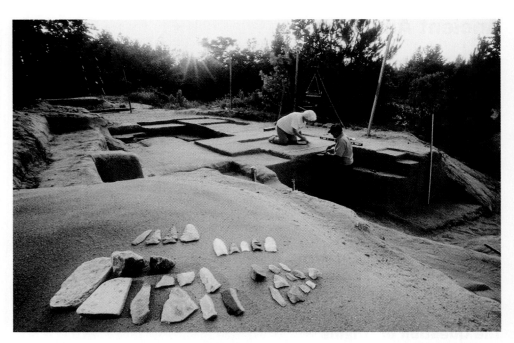

■ Archaeologists digging at Cactus Hill, Virginia, and several other sites have unearthed artifacts that suggest human habitation before the arrival of hunters using Clovis points. The foreground objects are laid out clockwise by apparent age, with the most recent at the top. Clovis-like spearheads appear in the second group. The third and fourth groups, taken from lower layers of soil, are thought to be older items, some reaching back well beyond 14,000 years. With the most primitive tools, it becomes difficult to separate implements made by humans from natural rock fragments.

continent, destroying successive herds of large animals that had never faced human predators before. According to this theory, generations of hunters known as **Paleo-Indians** could have migrated as far as the tip of South America within several thousand years.

In recent decades, three new developments have complicated the picture. At Cactus Hill, Virginia, and other sites, archaeologists have uncovered artifacts suggesting the presence of immediate predecessors to the Clovis people. In addition, a provocative discovery in South America—a campsite at Monte Verde, Chile, dating back more than 14,000 years—suggests to some that small groups may have used a coastal route around the North Pacific rim to reach the Americas by water. Meanwhile, genetic comparisons of different peoples, present and past, are yielding increasingly specific, if controversial, details about ancient migrations and interactions. Advances in understanding DNA—the genetic material that determines our physical make-up and transmits it to our offspring—may someday sharpen or change our awareness regarding the origins of the earliest Paleo-Indians.

Genetic comparisons of different peoples are yielding increasingly specific, if controversial, details about ancient migrations and interactions.

The Archaic World

Some 10,000 years ago, the Paleo-Indian period in North America gradually gave way to the **Archaic** period, which lasted for roughly 7,000 years. Major changes in wildlife played a large part in the transition. As the continent warmed further and the great glaciers receded north, more than 100 of America's largest species disappeared. These included mammoths, mastodons, horses, camels, and the great long-horned bison. Researchers debate whether these large animals were hunted to extinction, wiped out by disease, or destroyed by climate change.

One recent theory suggests that a major meteorite, striking earth some 12,900 years ago (perhaps near the Carolina coast), altered the North American environment drastically. Did an enormous impact from outer space lead to the extinction of numerous large mammals and to the swift, puzzling demise of Clovis Culture?

While scientists ponder evidence for sudden changes caused by a "Clovis Comet," they agree that gradual environmental shifts forced human groups to develop new methods of survival. On the northern plains, Archaic-era bands learned to drive whole herds of bison over cliffs and use the remains for food, clothing, and tools. A weighted spear-throwing device, called an **atlatl**, let hunters bring down medium-sized game. Archaic peoples also devised nets, hooks, and snares for catching birds, fish, and small animals. By 4,000 years ago, they were even using duck decoys in the Great Basin of Utah and Nevada.

Though genetically similar, these far-flung bands of Archaic Indians developed diverse cultures as they adapted to very different landscapes and environments. Nothing illustrates this diversity more clearly than speech. A few early languages branched into numerous language families, then divided further into hundreds of separate tongues. Similar cultural variations emerged in everything from diet and shelter to folklore and spiritual beliefs.

The Rise of Maize Agriculture

One condition remained common to all the various Archaic American groups, despite their emerging regional differences: they all lacked domesticated animals. Archaic Indians, like their Asian forebears, did possess dogs, and settlers in the Andes domesticated the llama over 5,000 years ago. But no mammal remaining in the Americas could readily be made to provide humans with milk, meat, hides, and hauling power.

Although their prospects for domesticating animals were severely limited, early Americans had many more options when it came to the domestication of plants. Humans managed to domesticate plants independently in five different areas around the world, and three of those regions were located in the Americas. First, across parts of South America, inhabitants learned to cultivate root crops of potatoes and manioc (also known as cassava, which yields a nutritious starch). Second, in **Mesoamerica** (modern-day Mexico and Central America), people gradually brought squash, beans, and maize (corn) under cultivation—three foods that complement one another effectively in dietary terms.

Maize agriculture became a crucial ingredient for the growth of complex societies in the Americas, but its development and diffusion took time. Unlike wheat, the Eurasian cereal crop which offered a high yield from the start, maize took thousands of years of cultivation in the Americas to evolve into an extremely productive food source. The differences between Mesoamerica and North America proved substantial when it came to mastering maize agriculture. Southwestern Indians in North America began growing thumb-sized ears of maize only about 3,000 years ago (at a time of increasing rainfall), well after the crop had taken hold in Mesoamerica. More than a thousand years later, maize reached eastern North America, where it adapted slowly to the cooler climate and shorter growing season.

In the East, a different agriculture had already taken hold, centered on other once-wild plants. This was the third zone where the independent domestication of plants occurred in the Americas. As early as 4,000 years ago, eastern Indians at dozens of Archaic sites were cultivating squash and sunflowers. These domesticated plants provided supplemental food sources for eastern communities that continued to subsist primarily by hunting and gathering until the arrival of maize agriculture in the eastern woodlands during the first millennium C.E.

About 3,000 years ago, as maize cultivation began in the Southwest and gardens of squash and sunflowers appeared in the Northeast, the first of several powerful Mesoamerican cultures—the Olmec—emerged in the lowlands along the southwestern edge of the Gulf of

Southwestern Indians in North America began growing thumbsized ears of maize only about 3,000 years ago.

Mexico. Their name meant "those who live in the land of rubber," for they had learned how to turn the milky juice of several plants into an unusual elastic substance. The Olmec grew maize and manioc in abundance, and their surplus of food supported a hierarchical society. They built large burial mounds and pyramids, revered the jaguar in their religion, developed a complex calendar, and played a distinctive game with a large ball of solid rubber. Since they traded widely with people across Mesoamerica, they passed on these cultural traits, which reappeared later in other societies in the region.

Olmec traders, traveling by coastal canoe, may even have encountered and influenced the Poverty Point culture that existed in northeast Louisiana 4,200 to 2,700 years ago. The Poverty Point culture, with a trade network on the lower Mississippi River and its tributaries, stands as a mysterious precursor to the mound-building societies of the Mississippi Valley that emerged much later. Remnants of these more extensive Mississippian cultures still existed when newcomers from Europe arrived to stay, around 1500. In many parts of North America, smaller and less stratified Archaic cultures remained intact well into the era of European colonization. To subsist, they combined hunting for a variety of animals with gathering and processing local plant foods.

A Thousand Years of Change: 500 to 1500

The Olmec grew maize and manioc, and their surplus of food supported a hierarchical society.

The millennium stretching from the fifth century to the explorations of Columbus in the fifteenth century witnessed dramatic and far-reaching changes in the separate world of the Americas. In the warm and temperate regions on both sides of the equator, empires rose and fell as maize agriculture and elaborate irrigation systems provided food surpluses, allowing the creation of cities and the emergence of hierarchical societies.

On the coast of Peru, the expansive Inca empire emerged in the 1400s, building on previous societies. Inca emperors, ruling from the capital at Cuzco, prompted the construction of a vast road system throughout the Peruvian Andes. Stonemasons built large storage facilities at provincial centers to hold food for garrisons of soldiers and to store tribute items such as gold and feathers destined for the capital. Until the empire's fall in the 1530s, officials leading pack trains of llamas ferried goods to and from Cuzco along mountainous roadways.

Similarly, Mesoamerica also saw a series of impressive civilizations—from the Maya to the Aztec—in the millennium spanning 500 to 1500 in the western calendar. Developments in North America in the same millennium were very different but bear enough resemblance to patterns in Mesoamerica to raise difficult questions about early contacts. Did significant migrations northward from Mesoamerica ever take place? And if not, were there substantial trade links at times, allowing certain materials, techniques, ideas, and seeds to reach North American peoples? Or did the continent's distinctive societies, such as the Anasazi in the Southwest and the Cahokia mound builders on the Mississippi River, develop almost entirely independently?

Valleys of the Sun: The Mesoamerican Empires

In Mesoamerica, the Maya and the Aztec established rich empires where worship of the sun was central to their religious beliefs. Mayan culture flourished between 300 and 900. The Maya controlled a domain stretching from the lowlands of the Yucatan peninsula to the highlands of what is now southern Mexico, Guatemala, Honduras, and El Salvador. They derived their elaborate calendar—a 52-year cycle made up of 20-day months—and many other aspects of their culture from the earlier Olmec, but they devised their own distinctive

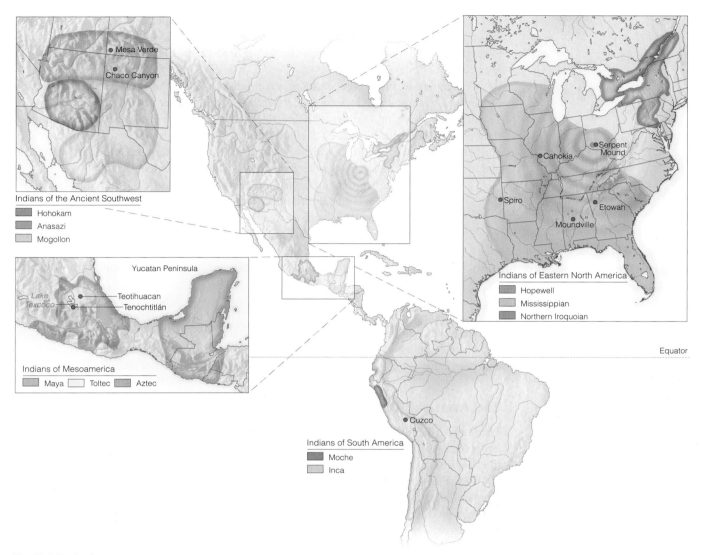

■ MAP 1.1
AMERICA BEFORE COLUMBUS
Distinctive cultures emerged in the Americas during the ten centuries before 1500. But debate continues over the extent of trade and travel networks at any given time.

civilization. The Maya built huge stone temples and held ritual bloodletting ceremonies to appease their gods. Recently, researchers have deciphered the complex pictographs, or glyphs, that appear throughout Mayan art.

The Maya declined rapidly after 750, and dominance in Mesoamerica moved farther west, where great cities had arisen in central Mexico. The people who constructed the metropolis of Teotihuacan in the Mexican highlands remain an enigma. They appear to have traded with the Maya and perhaps with the Olmec before that. They laid out their immense city in a grid, dominated by the 200-foot Pyramid of the Sun. By 500, the city held more than 100,000 inhabitants, making it one of the largest in the world. But Teotihuacan's society declined fast, for unknown reasons, succeeded first by the Toltec and then by the Aztec.

The Aztec (or Mexica) had migrated to the central Valley of Mexico from the north in the twelfth century. Looked down upon at first by the local people, they swiftly rose to power through strategic alliances and military skill. According to legend, the Aztec's war god instructed their priests to locate the place where a great eagle perched on a cactus. They found such a spot, on a swampy island in Lake Texcoco. By the 1400s the Aztec had transformed the island into Tenochtitlán, an imposing urban center, located on the site of modern Mexico City.

The impressive city of Tenochtitlán, surrounded by Lake Texcoco and linked to shore by causeways, became the Aztec capital. Its architecture imitated the ruined temple city of Teotihuacan, which lay 35 miles to the north. The Aztec also adopted many other features of the cultures they had displaced. They used the cyclical 52-year Mesoamerican calendar, and they worshipped the great god Quetzalcoatl, the plumed serpent associated with wind and revered by the Toltec, their predecessors in the Valley of Mexico.

> *Like the Inca of Peru, the Aztec imposed harsh treatment on the peoples they conquered, extracting heavy annual taxes.*

Eager to expand their empire, the Aztec launched fierce wars against neighboring lands. But their primary objective was not to kill enemies or gain more territory. Instead, Aztec warriors demanded tribute and took prisoners from the people they subdued. They then sacrificed numerous captives at pyramid temples to placate the gods. These deities, they believed, would in turn protect them as they conducted further wars of capture, leading to more tribute and sacrifices.

Like the Inca of Peru, the Aztec imposed harsh treatment on the peoples they conquered, extracting heavy annual taxes. This ruthless policy caused outlying provinces to resent Aztec authority and made the centralized empire vulnerable to external attack. When a foreign assault prompted the empire's downfall in the early sixteenth century, the challenge came from a direction Aztec priests and generals could not predict.

The Anasazi: Chaco Canyon and Mesa Verde

The great urban centers of Peru and Mesoamerica had no counterparts farther north. The peoples inhabiting North America in the millennium before Columbus never developed the levels of **social stratification**, urban dynamism, architectural grandeur, astronomical study, or intensive corn agriculture that characterized the Maya, Inca, or Aztec. Yet elements of all these traits appeared in North America, especially in the Southwest and the Mississippi Valley, with the emergence of increasingly settled societies and widening circles of exchange.

In the North American Southwest, three identifiably different cultures were already well established by the year 500. The Mogollon occupied the dry, mountainous regions of eastern Arizona and southern New Mexico. These expert potters lived in sunken pit houses that were cool in summer and warm in winter. The Hohokam, their neighbors to the west in south-central Arizona, constructed extensive canal and floodgate systems to irrigate their fields from the Gila and Salt rivers. Farther north, where Utah and Colorado meet Arizona and New Mexico, lived the people remembered as the Anasazi, or "ancient ones."

By 750, the Anasazi inhabited aboveground houses of masonry or adobe clustered around a circular ceremonial room dug into the earth. They entered this sunken religious chamber, known as a kiva, by descending a ladder through the roof. The climb back up symbolized the initial ascent of humans into the Upper World from below. European explorers later used the Spanish word for town, *pueblo*, to describe the Anasazis' multiroom and multistory dwellings.

Beginning in the 850s, Chaco Canyon in northwest New Mexico emerged as the hub of the Anasazi world. Researchers at this site in the San Juan River basin have identified a north–south traffic in turquoise, highly prized in both Mexico and the Southwest. Wide, straight roads radiating out from Chaco let builders haul hundreds of thousands of logs for use as roof beams in the nine great pueblos that still dot the canyon. The largest, Pueblo Bonito, rises five stories high in places and has 600 rooms arranged in a vast semicircle.

After 1130, a prolonged drought gripped the area, and the turquoise workshops of Chaco Canyon fell silent. Gradually—with populations growing, the climate worsening, and competition for resources stiffening—many Anasazi headed north and moved into sheltered cliff dwellings. The remarkable Cliff Palace at Mesa Verde in southwestern Colorado has 220 rooms and 23 kivas. Reached only by ladders and steep trails, these pueblos offered protection from enemies and shelter from the scorching summer sun. When another prolonged drought (1276–1299) forced the Anasazi to move once again, survivors dispersed south into lands later occupied by the Hopi, Zuni, and Rio Grande peoples.

The Mississippians: Cahokia and Moundville

Earlier, in the Mississippi Valley, the Hopewell people had prospered for half a millennium before 500 C.E. (in the era of the Roman Empire in Europe). The Hopewell lived mainly in Ohio and Illinois. But their network of trade extended over much of the continent. Hopewell burial sites have yielded pipestone and flint from the Missouri River valley, copper and silver from Lake Superior, mica and quartz from Appalachia, seashells and shark teeth from Florida, and artwork made from Rocky Mountain obsidian and grizzly-bear teeth.

Hopewell trading laid the groundwork for larger mound-building societies, known as the Mississippian cultures, that emerged in the Mississippi Valley and the Southeast in roughly the same centuries as the great civilizations of Mesoamerica and the Anasazi in the Southwest. The Mississippian tradition developed gradually after 500. Then after 900, it flourished broadly for six centuries.

Shifts in technology and agriculture facilitated the rise of the Mississippians. Bows and arrows, long used in arctic regions of North America but little known elsewhere, became widespread in the eastern woodlands around 700. At the same time, maize underwent a transformation from a marginal oddity to a central staple crop. Across the East, food supplies expanded as Native American communities planted corn in the rich bottomland soil along the region's many rivers. With greater productivity, commercial and religious elites took advantage of farmers and asserted stronger control over the community's increasing resources.

Mississippian mound-building centers have been found as far apart as Spiro, in eastern Oklahoma, and Etowah, in northern Georgia. The largest complex was at Cahokia in the 25-mile floodplain below where the Illinois and Missouri rivers flow into the Mississippi. On Cahokia Creek, near East St. Louis, Illinois, dozens of rectangular, flat-topped temple mounds still remain after almost a thousand years. The biggest mound—indeed, the largest ancient earthwork in North America—rises 100 feet in four separate levels, covering 16 acres and using nearly 22 million cubic feet of earth. Nearby, residents erected 48 posts in a huge circle, 410 feet in diameter. This creation, now called Woodhenge after England's Stonehenge, functioned as a calendar to mark the progression of the sun throughout each year.

Cahokia's mounds rose quickly in the decades after 1050. A succession of powerful leaders reorganized the vicinity's small, isolated villages into a strong regional chiefdom that controlled towns on both sides of the Mississippi River. These towns provided the chiefdom's centralized elite with food, labor, and goods for trading. Around 1100, the population of Cahokia exceeded 15,000 people. It then waned steadily over the next two centuries as the unstable hierarchy lost its sway over nearby villages. As Cahokia declined, other regional chiefdoms rose along other rivers. The most notable appeared at Moundville in west-central Alabama, 15 miles south of modern Tuscaloosa. The site, with more than 20 flat-topped mounds, became a dominant ceremonial center in the thirteenth century. But by 1400, a century before the appearance of Europeans, Moundville's Mississippian elites had started to lose their power.

View the Image
Reconstructed View of Cahokia at **www.myhistorylab.com**

■ The most striking Mississippian earthwork to survive is the enigmatic Serpent Mound, built in the eleventh century by the Fort Ancient people in southern Ohio. The snake (holding an egg in its mouth) has links to astronomy because its curves are aligned toward key positions of the sun. The serpent may even represent Halley's Comet, which blazed in the heavens in 1066. Completely uncoiled, the earthwork would measure more than a quarter mile in length.

Linking the Continents

Why is the first voyage of Columbus in 1492 still viewed as such an earth-changing event?

Estimates vary widely, but probably around one-sixth of the world's population—as many as 60 to 70 million people—resided in the Americas when Columbus arrived in 1492. Most of them lived in the tropical zone near the equator, but roughly one-tenth of the hemisphere's population (six to seven million) dwelt in North America, spread from coast to coast.

We cannot rule out the appearance in America of ancient ocean travelers on occasion. Around 400, Polynesian mariners sailed their double-hulled canoes from the Marquesas Islands in the South Pacific to the Hawaiian **archipelago**. Conceivably, in the millennium before 1500, one or two boats from Africa, Ireland, Polynesia, China, or Japan sailed—or were blown—to the American mainland. But any survivors of such a journey would have had little genetic or cultural impact, for no sustained back-and-forth contact between the societies occurred. Even the seafaring Norse from Scandinavia, known as Vikings, never established a lasting colony. Their brief settlement at L'Anse aux Meadows in northern Newfoundland a thousand years ago is now well documented, but they remained only a few years at this coastal site. Native American societies, therefore, knew nothing of the people, plants, animals, and microbes of the Eastern Hemisphere.

America's near isolation ended dramatically, beginning in the late fifteenth century, after innovations in deep-sea sailing opened the world's oceans as a new frontier for human exploration. Chinese sailors in the North Pacific or Portuguese mariners in the South Atlantic could well have been the first outsiders to establish ongoing contact with the peoples of the Western Hemisphere. Instead, it was Christopher Columbus, an Italian navigator in the service of Spain, who became the agent of this sweeping change. He encountered the Americas by accident and misinterpreted what he had found. But his chance encounter with a separate realm sparked new patterns of human migration, cultural transfer, and ecological exchange that would reshape the modern world.

Oceanic Travel: The Norse and the Chinese

Scandinavian settlers had colonized Ireland in the 830s and Iceland in the 870s. A century later, these seafarers—led by Erik the Red—reached Greenland in the 980s. When Erik's son Leif learned that Norse mariners blown off course had sighted land farther west, he sailed from Greenland to the North American coast. Here he explored a region near the Gulf of St. Lawrence that he named Vinland.

Around 1000, Leif Eriksson's relatives directed several return voyages to Vinland, where Norse Vikings built an outpost. The tiny colony of 160 people, including women and children, lived and grazed livestock in Vinland for several years until native peoples drove them away. The Greenlanders returned occasionally to cut timber, and they traded with inhabitants of northeastern Canada for generations. But by 1450 Norse settlements in Greenland had died out completely.

Whether sailors in Europe knew much about Norse exploits in the North Atlantic remains a mystery. What Europeans did know, vaguely, was the existence of the distant Chinese Empire. They called the realm Cathay, a term used by Italian merchant Marco Polo, who journeyed from Venice across Asia along the fabled Silk Road in the 1270s. Polo returned to Italy in 1292 to publish his *Travels*, an account of adventures in China during the reign of Kublai Khan.

Marco Polo told of many things unknown to Europeans, including rocks that burned like wood (coal) and spices that preserved meat. Asian spices such as nutmeg, cinnamon, pepper, ginger, and cloves, if they could be obtained, would offer new preservatives. When renewed Islamic power in the Middle East cut off the Silk Road to Cathay, Europeans searched for other ways to reach that far-off region.

The desire to obtain oriental spices at their source fueled European oceanic exploration, leading eventually to the transformation of the Americas. Yet it was China, not Europe, that first mastered ocean sailing on a large scale. Chinese strength in overseas exploration and trade reached its height in the early fifteenth century under Admiral Zheng He (pronounced "Jung Huh"). Between 1405 and 1433, this brilliant officer led seven large fleets to the Indian Ocean, sailing as far as east Africa. His immense treasure ships, 400 feet long and equipped with cannon, carried strange items—even giraffes—home to Asia.

Then, abruptly, China turned away from the sea, passing up its chance to become the first global maritime power and to play a leading role in shaping the destiny of North America. Within a century of Zheng He's accomplishments, the royal court grew dismissive of foreign trade and turned inward. Chinese officials destroyed the log books of earlier voyages and curtailed production of oceangoing vessels. Instead of powerful China on the Pacific, it was tiny Portugal, overlooking the Atlantic, which emerged as the leader in maritime innovation and exploration in the fifteenth century.

Portugal and the Beginnings of Globalization

Geography and religious zeal helped to spur Portugal's unlikely rise to world prominence. Its strategic location exposed the tiny maritime country to the ongoing conflict between Christianity and Islam. The religion founded by Muhammad (born at Mecca in 570) had spread rapidly across North Africa from Arabia. By the eighth century, followers of Islam (known as Muslims, Moslems, or Moors) had crossed the Straits of Gibraltar to establish a kingdom in southern Spain. Centuries later, Spanish and Portuguese Christians rallied to force Islam out of the **Iberian** peninsula—a campaign that concluded in 1492—and to join other militant Europeans in fighting against Islamic power in the Middle East.

When Christian crusades to the holy land failed to defeat the Muslims and reopen over-land trade routes to China, European strategists dreamed of skirting Africa by sea to reach Asia. The Portuguese were well positioned to lead this flanking movement around the areas under Muslim control. And if no such oceanic route to Asia existed, some speculated that

■   **Prince Henry of Portugal rarely went to sea himself. Instead, he established a base at Sagres, overlooking the Atlantic Ocean. From here, beginning in 1418, he sent mariners south along the African coast. They quickly laid claim to the islands of the eastern Atlantic, and by the 1440s they had initiated trade along the west African coast, carrying gold and slaves back to Portugal.**

Portuguese exploration south by sea still might provide links to a strong Christian ally. Fanciful rumors persisted regarding a wealthy black Christian ruler somewhere in Africa known as Prester John.

Intellectual and economic motives also existed for Portuguese ventures beyond the Sahara Desert, along the coast of sub-Saharan Africa. Such journeys, presenting new challenges in shipbuilding and navigation, could boost European knowledge of the unknown and open new markets. The first step involved an investment of leadership and resources, before early efforts could bear fruit and give the exploration process a momentum of it own.

Prince Henry of Portugal (1394–1460) provided these initial ingredients. In 1415 the young prince—later honored as "Henry the Navigator"—had crossed the Straits of Gibraltar to fight Muslims at Ceuta in North Africa. Committed to the campaign against Islam, Henry then waged a religiously inspired crusade-at-sea, building his headquarters at Sagres in southwest Portugal. From there, his sailors launched a far-reaching revolution in human communication and trade, perhaps the most momentous single step in a **globalization** process that continues to the present day.

Henry's innovative ships, known as caravels, pushed south along the African coast. Their narrow hulls were well suited for ocean sailing, and they used triangular lateen sails. This sail design, borrowed by Mediterranean sailors from Arab boats on the Red Sea, helped mariners maneuver against headwinds. Henry's experts at Sagres drew on the work of Jewish cartographers to develop state-of-the-art charts, astronomical tables, and navigational instruments. By the 1440s, his captains had mastered the winds and currents near West Africa. They initiated trade in gold and ivory, and, most ominously, they began buying African slaves and selling them in Europe. But when Henry died in 1460, his mariners had only sailed as far as what is now Sierra Leone.

Looking for the Indies: Da Gama and Columbus

During the 1480s, following a war with Spain, the Portuguese renewed their African designs. In 1482 they erected a trading fort called Elmina Castle on the Gold Coast (modern Ghana) to guard against Spanish competition and to support exploration toward the east. Finally, in 1487, Bartolomeu Dias rounded the southernmost tip of Africa, around the Cape of Good Hope, proving that a link existed between the Atlantic and Indian oceans. The Portuguese could now sail to India and tap into the rich spice trade. Success came a decade later with the voyage (1497–1499) of Vasco da Gama. When his ship returned from India laden with pepper and cinnamon, the Portuguese had at last opened a southeastern sea route to the silk and spice markets of the East.

Meanwhile, the rulers of rival Spain gambled on finding a profitable *westward* route to the Indies. In 1492, King Ferdinand and Queen Isabella finally succeeded in driving Islam from their realm by military means. The monarchs imposed Christian orthodoxy and forced Jews into exile. That same year, they agreed to sponsor an Atlantic voyage by an Italian-born navigator, Christopher Columbus. Leaving Spain with 90 men aboard three small vessels, Columbus headed for the Canary Islands and then sailed due west on September 6. After a voyage of three or four weeks, he expected to encounter the island of Cipangu (Japan), which Marco Polo had mentioned, or to reach the coast of Asia.

Why these huge misunderstandings? The mariner made several crucial mistakes. Like other Europeans, Columbus knew the world was round, not flat. He also accepted the idea of the ancient geographer Ptolemy that by using north–south lines, one could divide the globe into 360 degrees of longitude. But he questioned Ptolemy's estimate that each degree measures 50 nautical miles at the equator. (Each actually measures 60 miles.) Instead, Columbus accepted an alternative figure of 45 miles, making the circumference of his theoretical globe 25 percent smaller than the real distance around the earth. Besides *under*estimating the world's circumference, he compounded his error by *over*estimating two other crucial distances: the breadth of the Eurasian landmass and the extent of Japan's separation from China. The first distance is actually 130 degrees of longitude, and the second is 20. Columbus used authorities who suggested 225 and 30 degrees, respectively. His estimates placed Japan 105 degrees closer to Europe, at the longitude that runs through eastern Lake Superior and western Cuba.

Early on October 12, the distressed sailors finally sighted a small island in the Bahamas, naming it San Salvador after their Christian savior. The inhabitants proved welcoming, and Columbus recorded pleasure over the "gold which they wear hanging from their noses. But I wish to go and see if I can find the island of Cipangu." He did find a large and beautiful island (Cuba, not Cipangu), and he estimated that the Asian mainland of the Great Khan was only "a 10 days' journey" farther west. He claimed a nearby island as La Isla Española, the Spanish island, or Hispaniola (current-day Haiti and the Dominican Republic). He noted stories of hostile islanders farther south called Caribs, or Caniba, who were said

Embarcadero de los Cavallos,

■ Horses, absent from the Americas for nearly 10,000 years, returned aboard Spanish ships. They awed Native Americans at first and played a crucial role in European conquests. "After God," the Spanish wrote, "we owe victory to the horses."

Watch the **Video**
The "Achievement of Columbus" at **www.myhistorylab.com**

The largest Chinese vessels of Zheng He (400 ft.) were nearly five times longer than Columbus's flagship (85 ft.).

PACIFIC OCEAN

NORTH AMERICA

ATLANTIC OCEAN

Columbus (first voyage)

CUBA

Line created by Treaty of Tordesillas (1494)

SOUTH AMERICA

Magellan

Strait of Magellan

Major expeditions

- - - Marco Polo: from Venice (1271) to China along the Silk Road
—— Zheng He: from China to East Africa with a fleet of huge ships (1420s)
—— Prince Henry's ships: from Portugal as far as Sierra Leone (1420–1460)
—— Columbus: first voyage west from Spain via Canary Islands (1492–1493)
—— Da Gama: from Portugal to India via Cape of Good Hope (1497–1499)
—— Magellan's circumnavigation, completed by his crew (1519–1522)

■ **MAP 1.2**
OPENING NEW OCEAN PATHWAYS AROUND THE GLOBE, 1420–1520
In the 1420s, ships from Portugal and China explored opposite coasts of Africa. But China withdrew from oceanic trade, and European mariners competed to explore the world by sea. Within a century, Magellan's ship had circled the globe for Spain. The colonization in North America is a chapter in this larger saga of global exploration.

to devour their enemies. "I repeat," he asserted, "the Caniba are no other than the people of the Grand Khan." (Upon hearing of these fierce Caribs, Europeans soon fashioned the word *cannibal* and named the region the Caribbean.)

    Bolstered by these encounters, the explorers returned hastily across the Atlantic on a more northerly route. They weathered a horrendous winter storm to reach Spain in March 1493. Columbus told the Spanish court that he had touched the Indies off the Asian coast, and he displayed several natives he called "Indians" to prove it. His three later voyages did not shake this belief, which he clung to until his death in 1506. Columbus had not reached the lands he sought, but his exploits would have immediate and extraordinary consequences.

◆●◆ Read the Document

From the Journal of Christopher Columbus at **www.myhistorylab.com**

In the Wake of Columbus: Competition and Exchange

Within months of Columbus's return, the pope in Rome issued a papal bull, or decree. This pronouncement, titled *Inter Caetera*, viewed the whole world as the rightful inheritance of Christianity. It brashly divided the entire earth between two Christian powers, Spain and Portugal, by drawing a line down through the Atlantic Ocean from the North Pole to the South Pole. West of the line, the Spanish alone could continue to seek access to Asia.

East of the line, on the other half of the globe, Portugal would have a monopoly. The two Iberian powers affirmed this division of the earth in the Treaty of Tordesillas (1494).

European navigators and cartographers quickly began to comprehend the geographic reality that Columbus had so thoroughly misunderstood. When Amerigo Vespucci, another Italian in the service of Spain, crossed the South Atlantic in 1499, he described what he saw not as part of Asia but as a *Mundus Novus*, or New World. European geographers wrote his name, *America*, across their maps. Meanwhile, a third Italian navigator—John Cabot (or Caboto)—obtained a license from the English king, Henry VII, to probe the North Atlantic for access to Cathay. In 1497 Cabot sailed west from Bristol across the Atlantic to Newfoundland and perhaps Nova Scotia. Clearly, the ventures of Columbus had sparked widespread excitement and curiosity in European ports, and increasing knowledge fueled greater transatlantic contact.

After thousands of years, the long separation of the hemispheres had been broken. The destinies of the world's most divergent continents swiftly became linked. Those links fostered human migrations of an unprecedented scale. With European ships came transfers of seeds and viruses, bugs and birds, plants and animals that forever reshaped the world. Scholars call this phenomenon the **Columbian Exchange**. The term underscores the two-way nature of the flow. West across the Atlantic went horses, cows, sheep, pigs, chickens, honeybees, and important foods such as sugar cane, coffee, bananas, peaches, lemons, and oranges. But Europeans' westbound ships also carried devastating diseases unknown in the Americas, such as smallpox, measles, malaria, and whooping cough. East in the opposite direction traveled corn, potatoes, pumpkins, chili peppers, tobacco, cacao, pineapples, sunflowers, turkeys—and perhaps syphilis. The planet and all its inhabitants would never be the same again.

View the Image
Early Botanical Illustrations-New World Plants at **www.myhistorylab.com**

Spain Enters the Americas

What factors motivated and shaped Spain's rapid intrusion into sixteenth-century America?

Throughout the sixteenth century, European mariners, inspired by the feats of Columbus and da Gama, risked ocean voyaging in hopes of scoring similar successes. Those who survived brought back novelties for consumers, information for geographers, and profits for ship owners. New wealth prompted further investment in exploration, and expanding knowledge awakened cultural changes for both explorers and the people they met. The dynamic European era known as the Renaissance owed much to overseas exploration. Returning mariners brought reports of surprising places and people. Their experiences challenged the inherited wisdom of traditional authorities and put a new premium on rational thought, scientific calculation, and careful observation of the natural world.

In turn, Europe's Renaissance, or rebirth, stimulated ever wider exploration as breakthroughs in technology and navigation yielded practical results. Sailing south around Africa and then east, Portuguese caravels reached China by 1514 and Japan by 1543. Sailing west, Spanish vessels learned first that the Caribbean did not offer a passage to Asia and then in 1522—through Magellan's global voyage—that the ocean beyond America was enormous. In the West Indies, and then elsewhere in the Western Hemisphere, Native Americans began to pay dearly for the exchange that ships from Spain had initiated.

The Devastation of the Indies

Spanish arrival in the West Indies in 1492 triggered widespread ecological and human disaster within decades. Well-armed and eager for quick wealth, the early colonizers brought havoc to the Taino Indians and Caribs who inhabited the islands. The strange newcomers killed and enslaved native peoples and extracted tribute from the survivors in the form of gold panned from streams. Spanish livestock trampled or consumed native gardens, prompting severe food shortages. Worse, European diseases ravaged countless villages. The West Indian population plummeted as island societies totaling more than one million lost 19 of every 20 people within a generation.

This near-extinction had three consequences. First, when Dominican friars reached Cuba in 1510, these devout missionaries denounced Spanish brutality as sinful. The Indians, they argued, possessed souls that only Christian baptism could save. A Spanish soldier named Bartholomé de Las Casas, who repented and joined the Dominican order, led the outcry for reform. In his scathing exposé titled *The Devastation of the Indies*, he opposed genocide and urged conversion.

Second, in response to the steep drop in population, Spanish colonizers began importing slaves from Africa to replace the decimated Indian workforce. The same Christians who bemoaned Native American enslavement (including Las Casas) justified this initiative and overlooked the contradictions. The first importation of Africans came in 1502, following the Portuguese precedent in the Azores.

Third, decimation in the islands prompted the Spanish to intensify their explorations. They sought new sources of Indian labor close at hand, fresh lands to exploit, and easy passageways to the Pacific. They pushed out from the Caribbean in several directions. In 1513, Vasco Núñez de Balboa pressed across the narrow **isthmus** of Panama to glimpse the Pacific. That same year, Juan Ponce de León sailed northwest from Puerto Rico, hoping the nearby peninsula, which he named Florida, would yield new gold and slaves. But Florida's Indians were already familiar with Spanish raiders; they turned Ponce de León away after he claimed the region for Spain.

The Spanish Conquest of the Aztec

By 1519, the Spanish had determined that the Gulf of Mexico offered no easy passage to Asia. They needed fresh alternatives. In Spain, crown officials sought someone to sail southwest, around the South American continent that Columbus and Vespucci had encountered.

For this perilous task, they dispatched a Portuguese navigator named Ferdinand Magellan, who had sailed in the Indian Ocean. On his epic voyage (1519–1522), Magellan located a difficult passage through the tip of South America—now called the Strait of Magellan—and revealed the vast width of the Pacific, which covers one-third of the earth's surface. Warring factions in the Philippines killed Magellan and 27 of his men, but one of his ships made it back to Spain, becoming the first vessel to circumnavigate the globe.

As news of Magellan's voyage raced through Spain in 1522, word also arrived that a Spanish soldier, or *conquistador*, named Hernán Cortés had toppled the gold-rich empire of the Aztec in central Mexico. Like other ambitious conquistadores, Cortés had followed Columbus to the Caribbean. In 1519, hoping to march overland to the Pacific as Balboa had done, Cortés established a base camp at Vera Cruz on Mexico's east coast. He quickly realized he had reached the edge of a powerful empire.

At Tenochtitlán the Aztec emperor, Moctezuma, reacted with uncertainty to news that bearded strangers aboard "floating islands" had appeared off his coast. If the newcomers' leader was the returning god Quetzalcoatl, the court had to welcome him with the utmost care. The emperor sent basketloads of precious objects encrusted with gold to Cortés's camp. But the elaborate gifts only alerted Cortés and his men to the Aztec's wealth.

■ As the Indian population of the Caribbean plummeted in the face of new diseases and exploitation, the Spanish began importing Africans to the New World as slaves. Many were put to work mining precious metals. Here men are forced to dig for gold nuggets beside a mountain stream, then wash them in a tub and dry them over a fire, before handing them to their Spanish master to weigh in his hand-held scale.

Although the Spanish numbered scarcely 600, they had several key advantages over the Aztec. Their guns and horses, unknown in America, terrified the Indians. When Cortés found coastal peoples staggering under heavy Aztec taxes, he recruited them as willing allies. An Indian woman (christened Doña Marina, or La Malinche) acted as his translator and companion. In an aggressive show of force, Cortés marched directly to the capital and seized Moctezuma as his hostage.

The Spanish still faced daunting obstacles, but sickness worked decisively to their advantage. Smallpox was a disease the Aztec had never encountered before, so they lacked any immunity. The European illness reached the mainland with the invading army, and a crushing epidemic swept the Aztec capital in 1521. The disaster let Cortés conquer Tenochtitlán (which he renamed Mexico City) and claim the entire region as New Spain.

Magellan and Cortés Prompt New Searches

Cortés's conquest of Mexico raised Spain's hopes of additional windfalls in the Americas. In 1531 Spanish raiders under Francisco Pizarro set sail from Panama for Peru, with plans to overthrow the Inca empire. Pizarro had limited resources (180 men and 37 horses), but smallpox assisted him, as it had helped Cortés, and his invaders accomplished their mission. Marching overland to Cuzco in 1533, they killed the emperor, Atahualpa, and sacked the mountain capital for the gold it contained. Meanwhile, Cortés dispatched three ships west

INTERPRETING HISTORY

"These Gods That We Worship Give Us Everything We Need"

Three years after Cortés captured Tenochtitlán in central Mexico, twelve missionaries from the Franciscan Order arrived in the city to preach Christianity to the conquered Aztec. In several meetings with principal elders and priests, they explained their beliefs and laid out their plans through a translator. Similar talks would take place throughout America in later generations.

No transcript of the 1524 conversations exists, but another Franciscan, the famous preserver of Aztec culture Bernardino de Sahagún, gathered recollections of the encounter from both sides and reconstructed the dialogue. He published his version in 1564, creating parallel texts in Spanish and Nahuatl, the Aztec language. "Having understood the reasoning and speech of the twelve," Sahagún reports, the city leaders "became greatly agitated and fell into a great sadness and fear, offering no response." The next morning, they requested a complete repetition of the unsettling message. "Having heard this, one of the principal lords arose, asked the indulgence of the twelve, . . . and made the following long speech."

Our lords, leading personages of much esteem, you are very welcome to our lands and towns. . . . We have heard the words that you have brought us of the One who gives us life and being. And we have heard with admiration the words of the Lord of the World which he has sent here for love of us, and also you have brought us the book of celestial and divine words.

You have told us that we do not know the One who gives us life and being, who is Lord of the heavens and of the earth. You also say that those we worship are not gods. This way of speaking is entirely new to us, and very scandalous. We are frightened by this way of speaking because our forebears who engendered and governed us never said anything like this.

On the contrary, they left us this our custom of worshiping our gods. . . . They taught us how to honor them. And they taught us all the ceremonies and sacrifices that we make. They told us that. . . . we were beholden to them, to be theirs and to serve countless centuries before the sun began to shine and before there was daytime. They said that these gods that we worship give us everything we need for our physical existence: maize, beans, chia seeds, etc. We appeal to them for the rain to make the things of the earth grow.

These our gods are the source of great riches and delights, all of which belong to them. . . . They live in very delightful places where there are always flowers, vegetation, and great freshness, a place. . . . where there is never hunger, poverty, or illness. . . . There has never been a time remembered when they were not worshiped, honored, and esteemed. . . .

It would be a fickle, foolish thing for us to destroy the most ancient laws and customs left by the first inhabitants of this land. . . . We are accustomed to them and we have them impressed on our hearts. . . . How could you leave the poor elderly among us bereft of that in which they have been raised throughout their lives? Watch out that we do not incur the wrath of our gods. Watch out that the common people do not rise up against us if we were to tell them that the gods they have always understood to be such are not gods at all.

It is best, our lords, to act on this matter very slowly, with great deliberation. We are not satisfied or convinced by what you have told us, nor do we understand or give credit to what has been said of our gods. . . . All of us together feel that it is enough to have lost, enough that the power and royal jurisdiction have been taken from us. As for our gods, we will die before giving up serving and worshiping them. This is our determination; do what you will.

Questions

1. *Why would the Aztec priests fear an uprising of the common people under these circumstances? How would you respond to a similar situation?*

2. *As suggested near the end of this chapter, a similar religious confrontation was taking place in Europe in 1524, during the early years of the Protestant Reformation. Contrast and compare these two situations.*

Source: Kenneth Mills and William B. Taylor, *Colonial Spanish America: A Documentary History.* Wilmington, DE: Scholarly Resources, 1998, pp. 21–22.

from Mexico across the Pacific, and one actually reached the Philippines. By the 1560s Spanish cargo ships, known as galleons, were making the lengthy round trip from Acapulco to the Philippines and back across the Pacific.

In 1524, Italian navigator Giovanni da Verrazzano sailed west for the French, hoping to find a swift northern passage from Europe to Asia that was easier than Magellan's arduous southern route. He reached North America near North Carolina's Outer Banks, later cruising north to enter New York harbor before abandoning his search. In 1526, Lucas Vásquez de Ayllón led 500 men and women from the Spanish Caribbean to the Santee River region (near present-day Georgetown, South Carolina) to settle and explore. But Ayllón fell sick and died, and the colony proved short-lived.

In 1528, a rival of Cortés and Ayllón named Pánfilo de Narváez launched another ill-fated expedition from Cuba, landing near Florida's Tampa Bay. Narváez intended to bring wealth and glory to his 400 soldiers, but disease, hunger, and Indian hostilities plagued the party's journey along the Gulf Coast. Only four men—three Spanish and one North African black named Esteban—survived to make an extended trek on foot across the Southwest from Galveston Bay to Mexico City. Their leader, Álvar Núñez Cabeza de Vaca, wrote about the remarkable odyssey after he returned to Spain in 1537. Scholars now recognize Cabeza de Vaca's *Relation* (1542) as an early classic in North American literature.

Three New Views of North America

Even before Cabeza de Vaca published his narrative, Europeans initiated three more expeditions into North America. Each probed a separate region of the continent, hoping to gauge the land's dimensions, assess its peoples, and claim its resources. Together, the three enterprises made 1534 to 1543 the most extraordinary decade in the early European exploration of North America, for Native Americans and newcomers alike.

In the Northeast, Frenchman Jacques Cartier visited the Gulf of St. Lawrence in 1534 and bartered for furs with the Micmac Indians. He returned the next year and penetrated southwest up the St. Lawrence River into Canada. (The name comes from *kanata*, the Huron–Iroquois word for "village.") After a friendly reception at the large Indian town of Hochelaga near modern Montreal, the French returned downriver to camp at Stadacona, the future site of Quebec. Following a hard winter, in which he lost 25 men to scurvy, the explorer and his remaining crew sailed for France.

●●►**Read** the **Document**
Jacques Cartier: First Contact with the Indians at **www.myhistorylab.com**

Cartier came back to Quebec in 1541, seeking precious minerals and signs of a water passage farther west to the Pacific Ocean. He found neither, but a colonizing expedition followed in 1542, led by a nobleman named Roberval. It contained several hundred French settlers, including women for the first time. But again, scurvy and cold took a heavy toll at the Quebec campsite, and the weakened colony withdrew after a single winter. Despite a decade of effort, the French still had not established a beachhead in the New World. Nevertheless, they had demonstrated their resolve to challenge Spain's exclusive claim to American lands.

The Spanish, meanwhile, launched two intrusions of their own—one in the Southeast and one in the Southwest. News of Pizarro's 1533 triumph over the Incas in Peru helped renew the search for wealthy kingdoms to conquer. In 1537, Emperor Charles V of Spain granted one hardened veteran of the Peruvian campaign—Hernando de Soto—the right to explore in and beyond Florida, establishing a personal domain for himself. The conquistador spent most of his fortune assembling a force of more than 600 soldiers that reached Tampa Bay in 1539. The enterprise included several women and priests, along with scores of servants and African slaves, plus 200 horses. De Soto had also brought along a herd of 300 pigs that multiplied rapidly and provided food during the long march through the interior.

Over the next four years, de Soto's party traveled through parts of ten southern states. They hoped to find a city as wealthy as Cuzco in Peru or Tenochtitlán in Mexico. Instead, they encountered only scattered villages. Towns that refused to provide the intruders with

■ Two decades after Verrazzano's explorations, this 1547 chart shows the early claims of France in North America. It depicts the men and women of Roberval's short-lived colonizing expedition as they disembarked in 1542, watched by Native Americans. Perhaps to feature the large St. Lawrence River, the European mapmaker put North at the bottom and South at the top. Hence, the Atlantic coast seems upside-down to our eyes, with Florida appearing in the upper right-hand corner.

porters or guides met with brutal reprisals that included the use of attack dogs. At Mabila near modern-day Selma, Alabama, de Soto's mounted army, brandishing swords and lances, killed several thousand Native Americans who had dared to attack them with bows and arrows. Still, Spanish frustrations grew due to difficult terrain, stiff Indian resistance, and failure to find riches. After exploring beyond the Mississippi River, de Soto died of a fever in 1542. His disheartened followers escaped downstream to the Gulf of Mexico the next year, leaving epidemic sickness in their wake.

At the same time, another encounter was unfolding in the Southwest. In Mexico, speculation about gold in the north had intensified after the appearance of Cabeza de Vaca. His African companion, Esteban, guided a reconnaissance party north in 1539. Esteban was killed by the Zuni Indians, but exaggerated accounts of the region's pueblos prompted rumors about seven golden cities, including two named Cíbola and Quivira. The next year, aspiring conquistador Francisco Vásquez de Coronado set out from northern Mexico to reach these wealthy towns before de Soto could. He left his post as a frontier governor and assembled a huge expedition with more than 300 Spanish adventurers and 1,000 Indian allies. However, his grandiose expectations were quickly dashed. The pueblos of the Zuni, he reported, "are very good houses, three and four and five stories high," but the fabled "Seven Cities are seven little villages."

Spanish newcomers imposed a heavy burden on the Pueblo Indians, demanding food and burning helpless towns. Desperate to get rid of Coronado, the Pueblo recruited a Plains Indian to lead the Spaniards to some far-off "Quivira," hoping men and horses "would starve to death." In the spring of 1541, the Indian guided Coronado's party northeast onto the Great Plains, past endless herds of buffalo. But mighty Quivira proved to be only a Wichita Indian village in what is now central Kansas. The irate Spanish strangled their deceitful guide and made their way back south to New Spain. As they crossed northern Texas, they even came within 300 miles of de Soto's ill-fated party in eastern Arkansas. But neither de Soto nor Coronado—nor Cartier in the north—ever discovered wealthy cities or a sea passage to the Far East.

> *Neither de Soto nor Coronado— nor Cartier in the north—ever discovered wealthy cities or a sea passage to the Far East.*

The Protestant Reformation Plays Out in America

In 1520, while Cortés vied with the Aztec for control in Mexico and Magellan maneuvered around South America, the pope excommunicated a German monk named Martin Luther. Three years earlier, Luther had nailed a list of 95 theses to the church door at Wittenberg, challenging papal authority. Luther's followers questioned lavish church spending and long-standing church practices such as the selling of religious pardons to raise money. They also rejected the church's elaborate hierarchy and criticized its refusal to translate the Latin Bible into modern languages. Luther's reform movement triggered the division of western Christianity into competing faiths. For their written protestations against the papacy, Luther and his fellow insurgents received the enduring name *Protestants*. Their movement became known broadly as the Reformation. Those who opposed it, siding with Rome, launched a Counter-Reformation to defend and revitalize the Roman Catholic Church.

For the first time in history, a controversy in Europe made waves that washed onto American shores. Throughout the remainder of the sixteenth century, European national and religious conflict played out in part overseas, a pattern that repeated itself in future centuries. France and Spain, competing in Europe, wrestled to claim control of Florida. England, an upstart Protestant monarchy with a rising population and an expanding navy, seized control of Ireland and launched its first attempt to plant a colony in North America.

How did Europe's sharp religious split influence the early colonization of North America?

Reformation and Counter-Reformation in Europe

Beginning in 1517, zeal for Luther's religious reforms spread across Europe, sparking armed conflict. In Switzerland, militant priests abolished the practice of confession, condemned the church calendar full of fasts and saints' days, and defied the tradition of a celibate clergy by marrying. The Swiss Reformation found its leader in a French Protestant named John Calvin who arrived in Geneva in 1541 and ruled the city as a church-centered state for more than two decades.

Calvin imposed his own strict interpretation on Lutheranism and drew dedicated followers to his church. Offended by expensive vestments and elaborate rituals, he donned a simple black "Geneva" robe. He argued that faith alone, not "good works," would lead Christians to be saved. Salvation, he preached, was determined by God, not bought by giving **tithes** to the church. Only a select few people, Calvin explained, were destined to be members of God's chosen elect. Moreover, only an informed clergy and the careful study of scripture could reveal signs of a person's status. Soon, Calvinist doctrine helped shape Protestant communities across northern Europe: Huguenots in France, Puritans in England, Presbyterians in Scotland, and the Dutch Reformed Church in the Netherlands.

The Protestant Reformation that Luther had ignited coincided roughly with another important change in Europe: the emergence of the modern nation-state. Kings and queens gradually expanded court bureaucracies and asserted greater control over their subjects and economies. They strengthened their armies, gaining a near monopoly on the use of force, and they took full advantage of the new medium of printing. As religious ferment spread and local allegiances gave way to a broader sense of national identity, strong sovereigns moved to distance themselves from papal authority in Rome.

The emergence of England as a nation-state (under the Tudor dynasty founded by Henry VII in 1485) illustrates this shift in power away from Rome. In 1533, when the pope refused to grant England's next king an annulment of his first marriage, Henry VIII wrested control of the English church from papal hands and had Parliament approve his divorce and remarriage. The new Church of England, or Anglican Church, continued to follow much of the Catholic Church's doctrine. However, its "Protector and only Supreme Head" would now be the English monarch. During her long reign from 1558 to 1603, Henry VIII's daughter Queen Elizabeth I managed to steer the Church of England on a middle course between advocates of Catholicism and extreme Protestants.

Throughout Europe, as zealous believers on both sides of the debate staked out their positions, attempts to heal religious divisions gave way to confrontation. Challenges to the pope in Rome, whether from dissenting parishes or powerful monarchs, met with stiff resistance as Catholic leaders mobilized opposition. Their followers rallied to defend Roman Catholicism through efforts known collectively as the Counter-Reformation.

A militant new Catholic religious order called the Society of Jesus, or the Jesuits, represented one dimension of the Counter-Reformation. Led by a Spanish soldier named Ignatius Loyola and willing to give their lives for their beliefs, these dedicated missionaries and teachers helped to reenergize the Catholic faith and spread it to distant parts of the world. Another institution, the Inquisition, reflects a different side of the Counter-Reformation. In 1542, Catholic authorities established a new religious-judicial proceeding, known as the Inquisition, to help resist the spread of Protestantism. Heretics—persons accused of denying or defying church doctrine—were brought before the Inquisition's strict religious courts; those who refused to renounce their beliefs suffered severe punishment. These heresy trials made clear to Inquisition leaders that the advent of printing was helping to spread the works of Luther and his Protestant allies. In 1557, therefore, the Vatican issued an "Index" of prohibited books.

In Spain, King Philip II, who ruled from 1556 to 1598, led an Inquisition to root out Protestant heresy. The Spanish monarch came close to overpowering Protestant England as well. In 1588 he sent a fleet of warships—the Spanish Armada—to reconquer England for the Catholic Church. A timely storm and hasty mobilization by the island nation foiled the Spanish king's invasion. But Philip II's confrontation with the navy of Elizabeth I epitomized the sharp new division between Catholic and Protestant power in Europe. This deepened antagonism—religious, ideological, and economic—shaped events overseas in the second half of the sixteenth century. The struggle became especially clear in Florida, the vague region claimed by Spain that encompassed Indian lands from Chesapeake Bay to the Gulf of Mexico.

> *In 1542, Catholic authorities established a new religious-judicial proceeding, known as the Inquisition, to help resist the spread of Protestantism.*

Competing Powers Lay Claim to Florida

As Spain used force to obtain the dazzling wealth of New World societies, its European rivals looked on jealously. As early as 1523, French sea raiders had captured Spanish ships returning from Mexico with Cortés's Aztec bounty of gold, silver, and pearls. Ten years later,

In 1562, French Protestants established a short-lived colony at Port Royal Sound on the South Carolina coast. "The commander, on landing with some soldiers, found the country very beautiful, as it was well wooded with oak, cedar, and other trees. As they went through the woods, they saw Indian peacocks, or turkeys, flying past, and deer going by." Traveling upstream beyond Parris Island, they surprised an encampment of Indians, "who, on perceiving the boats, immediately took flight," leaving behind the meat "they were roasting."

French pirates made a similar haul. To protect the flow of riches from America, the Spanish soon initiated a well-armed annual convoy to escort their wealth from Havana to Seville. Each year, Spain's huge West Indies treasure fleet made an enticing target as it followed the Gulf Stream along the Florida coast.

But France had its own designs on Florida, furthered by the special concerns of French Huguenots. Unsure of their future in a religiously divided country, these Protestants took a leading role in the colonization efforts of France. In 1562 French Huguenots established a settlement at Port Royal Sound (Parris Island, South Carolina), close to the route of Spain's annual treasure fleet. The effort lasted only two years and aroused Spanish suspicions of "Lutheran" intruders.

Undaunted, the French backed a larger colonizing effort to Florida in 1564. When French Protestants erected Fort Caroline on the St. John's River at present-day Jacksonville, the Spanish crown took swift action. In 1565, Philip II sent 300 soldiers and 700 colonists under Pedro Menéndez de Avilés to oust the French and secure Florida. Menéndez captured

> *Each year, Spain's huge West Indies treasure fleet made an enticing target as it followed the Gulf Stream along the Florida coast.*

New
Albion

Grand
Canyon

Coronado

Cabeza de Vaca/Esteban

PACIFIC
OCEAN

Drake from England (1579)

Gulf of
Mexico

Mabila

Narváez

De Soto

Pardo

Roanoke
Island

Cofitachequi

Port Royal Sound

St. Augustine

Ayllón from Hispaniola

Ponce de León from Puerto Rico

ATLANTIC
OCEAN

Chesapeake
Bay

Stadacona
(Quebec)

Hochelaga
(Montreal)

Cartier from France

Verrazzano

Several English Voyag

Verrazzano from Fra

North American exploration in the 16th century

—— Ponce de León, 1513	—— Cartier, 1534/1535
—— Verrazzano, 1524	—— De Soto, 1539–1543
—— Ayllón, 1526	—— Coronado, 1540–1542
—— Narváez, 1528	—— Pardo, 1566–1567
—— Cabeza de Vaca and Esteban, 1528–1536	—— Drake, 1577–1580

■ **MAP 1.3**

THE EXTENT OF EUROPEAN EXPLORATION OF NORTH AMERICA BY 1592
By 1592, a century after Columbus's initial voyage, European explorers and colonists had touched the edges of North America, and a few had ventured far inland. But they had not found riches or a passageway to the Pacific, and only the Spanish had managed to establish a lasting foothold along the Florida coast.

Fort Caroline and massacred hundreds of French Huguenots. The heretics, he feared, might attack the treasure fleet, forge alliances with Florida's Indians, or provoke revolt among slaves in the Spanish Caribbean. To prevent further French incursions on Florida's Atlantic coast, Menéndez established a new outpost at nearby St. Augustine. He also sent Juan Pardo north from Port Royal Sound to establish forts in the interior.

With French threats defeated, the Spanish at St. Augustine attempted to plant strategic missions farther north to convert Native Americans to Christianity and secure Spain's land claims. In 1570, eight missionaries from Loyola's Society of Jesus sailed north from Florida to Chesapeake Bay. There, the Jesuits established a mission to convert local Indians and looked for "an entrance into the mountains and on to China." But the friars' rules and beliefs antagonized the Native Americans. By the time Menéndez visited the region in 1572, all the missionaries had been killed. Spain's failure to secure a foothold on Chesapeake Bay soon proved costly, as a new European rival appeared on the scene. Almost overnight, Protestant England emerged as a contending force in the Atlantic world. Now English adventurers began challenging Spanish dominance in the Caribbean and along North America's southeastern coast.

The Background of English Expansion

The voyages of John Cabot and the visits of Bristol fishing vessels to Newfoundland's Grand Banks had stimulated an early English interest in the Atlantic. But for several reasons this curiosity intensified after 1550. Henry VIII had used his power, plus the wealth he had seized from the Catholic Church, to build a sizable navy before he died in 1547. The merchant fleet grew as well, carrying English wool and cloth to Antwerp and other European ports. In addition, the English population, which had declined in the previous 150 years, grew steadily after 1500. Overall numbers more than doubled during the sixteenth century, creating pressure on limited resources, especially land.

Adding to the squeeze, property owners, eager to enclose pastures for sheep grazing, pushed tenants off their land. This "enclosure movement" set countless rural people adrift to seek work in towns and cities. London's population soared from 50,000 in 1500 to 200,000 a century later. When Europe's saturated woolen textile market collapsed suddenly, English cloth exports fell 35 percent in 1551. Merchants searched hastily for new avenues of foreign commerce.

Starting in the 1550s, therefore, England's overseas exploration pushed in all directions. Investors in the new Muscovy Company sent ships north around Scandinavia through the Arctic Ocean, but they failed to find a northeastern route above the Asian landmass to China. Other English vessels sailed south to Morocco and the Gold Coast, challenging the Portuguese monopoly of the African trade. English mariner John Hawkins conducted three voyages to West Africa during the 1560s. Horning in on the growing transatlantic slave traffic, he purchased Africans and then sold them in Caribbean ports to Spanish buyers.

Philip II, having driven the French out of Florida, had had enough of Protestant interlopers. A Spanish fleet forced Hawkins and his young kinsman Francis Drake out of Mexican waters in 1568. But thereafter, English sea rovers, with quiet support from Elizabeth, stepped up their challenges to Spain's empire. Drake proved the most wide-ranging and successful. On a voyage to the Pacific (1577–1580), he plundered Spanish ports in Peru and landed near San Francisco Bay. He claimed California for England as New Albion and then sailed around the globe. In the 1580s, Drake continued, in his words, "to singe the Spaniard's beard." He sacked ports in the West Indies, encouraged slave uprisings against the Spanish, and attacked the settlement at St. Augustine. He also captured numerous treasure ships, sank two dozen enemy vessels in their home port at Cadiz, and helped to defeat Philip II's Spanish Armada in 1588.

England's anti-Catholic propagandists made Drake a national hero. Moreover, they painted Spanish cruelties toward Indians in the New World in the worst possible terms. To bolster their case, they translated the vivid writings of Las Casas into English. But the English were not blameless themselves. In the Elizabethan years, they established their own pattern of violence during their brutal conquest of Ireland. Many who played leading roles in this bloody takeover came to view a colony in America as the next logical step in England's aggressive overseas expansion.

Lost Colony: The Roanoke Experience

Sir Humphrey Gilbert, who had served in Ireland, was one Elizabethan with an eye on America. In 1576 Gilbert promoted the idea of a short northwestern passage to China, and Martin Frobisher, another veteran of the Irish campaign, undertook voyages to locate such a route. Writing an essay on "How Her Majesty May Annoy the King of Spain," Gilbert proposed a colony in Newfoundland. The queen granted him a patent—a license giving him exclusive rights—for such a project. But shipwrecks and desertions doomed the venture to failure. When Gilbert died at sea on the homeward voyage, his half-brother, Walter Raleigh, obtained a similar patent to plant a colony in North America.

■ John White took part in several voyages to Roanoke Island in the 1580s. A skilled artist, the Englishman made valuable firsthand drawings of Native Americans living in what is now coastal North Carolina, including the wife and daughter of a local leader. The woman kept her "haire trussed opp in a knott," had tattoos on her arms, wore "a chaine of great pearles," and often carried "a gourde full of some kinde of pleasant liquor." The girl holds an English doll, for Indian children "are greatly Deligted with puppetts . . . brought oute of England."

●●●▶ Read the Document

Charter to Sir Walter Raleigh at
www.myhistorylab.com

In 1584 Raleigh sent explorers to the Outer Banks, the string of coastal barrier islands below Chesapeake Bay that Verrazzano had glimpsed sixty years earlier. They brought back two Indian informants and positive reports about the land near Roanoke Island. The next month, Richard Hakluyt, England's foremost advocate and chronicler of overseas expansion, handed Elizabeth I an advisory paper entitled "Western Planting." The document called for the establishment of a strategic outpost on the North American coast, where the English could launch attacks against Spanish shipping, hunt for useful commodities, and convert Indians to Protestant Christianity.

Raleigh's three efforts to establish such an outpost failed in rapid succession. In 1585, he first sent Ralph Lane, a hardened veteran of the Irish campaigns, to build a fort at Roanoke Island. But storms at sea scattered his ships, and most of Lane's initial force never arrived. Those who did, including scientist Thomas Harriot and artist John White, fared badly because of scarce food, bad discipline, and hostile relations with the Indians. Francis Drake, arriving in 1586 after harassing the Spanish in the West Indies and Florida, expected to find a thriving enterprise. Instead, he carried the disheartened soldiers back to England. They had paid a price, Hakluyt commented, "for the cruelty and outrages committed by some of them against the native inhabitants of that country." A second expedition diverted to the Caribbean to prey on enemy shipping, after leaving a few men at Roanoke, who did not survive.

In May 1587 John White led a third English venture to America, with 110 people, including women and children. They planned to settle on Chesapeake Bay, but a contentious captain refused to carry them farther north after an initial stop at Roanoke Island. In August the settlers agreed to send White back to England for more supplies; they would leave a message for him if they moved. When he finally returned in 1590—delayed by England's clash with the Spanish Armada—he found the site deserted. The word *Croatoan* carved on a post suggested that survivors had joined the nearby Croatan Indians, but the Lost Colony's fate remains a source of endless speculation. The Spanish, worried by the English foray, drew up plans for a fortification at Chesapeake Bay, but warfare between Spain and England kept both countries preoccupied elsewhere until Philip II and Elizabeth I had died.

CONCLUSION

Over approximately 150 centuries, people of distant Asian ancestry had explored and settled the bountiful Western Hemisphere. In every region of North America, from the arctic North to the semitropical Florida Keys, they had adapted and prospered over countless generations. Then suddenly, in a single century, unprecedented intrusions by sea brought newcomers from foreign lands to the coasts of the Americas. Their numbers only increased with time. In the next century, the contest for European control of the Atlantic seaboard began in earnest.

For Review

✓•⌐Study and Review at www.myhistorylab.com

1. Why did complex societies develop in Mesoamerica and Peru, close to the equator?

2. If you lived in Madrid, Spain, in 1525, how might your understanding of world geography differ from your grandparents' views fifty years earlier?

3. Describe at least three ways in which the Columbian Exchange dramatically altered history in North America and elsewhere by 1600.

4. After reading this chapter, where would you mark the beginning of American history? Defend your choice in comparison to other options for an earlier or later starting point.

Chronology: 14,000 Years Ago to 1590 C.E.

14,000 years ago	Early Paleo-Indians in Florida and Pennsylvania regions, and also in Monte Verde, Chile.
13,900 to 12,900 years ago	Clovis hunters spread across North America.
10,000 to 3,000 years ago	Archaic Indians flourish in diverse settings.
4,200 to 2,700 years ago	Poverty Point culture exists in Louisiana.
300 to 900 C.E.	Mayan culture flourishes in Mesoamerica.
500 to 600	Teotihuacan in central Mexico becomes one of the world's largest cities.
900 to 1100	Anasazi culture centers in Chaco Canyon in Southwest.
1000	Norse explorers establish a Vinland colony in Newfoundland.
1100	Cahokia in Illinois becomes one focus of Mississippian culture.
1400	Aztec build capital at Tenochtitlán (site of modern Mexico City).
1405 to 1433	Chinese fleet of Admiral Zheng. He reaches Indian Ocean and Africa's east coast.
1418 to 1460	Prince Henry of Portugal sends ships to explore Africa's west coast.
1492	First voyage of Columbus.
1494	Treaty of Tordesillas arranges division between overseas claims of Spain and Portugal.
1517	Martin Luther launches Protestant Reformation.
1519	Cortés invades Mexico.
1519 to 1522	Magellan's ship circumnavigates the globe and returns to Spain.
1534 to 1543	Expeditions of Cartier (Canada), de Soto (Southeast), and Coronado (Southwest) probe North America.
1565	Spanish establish St. Augustine.
1585 to 1590	English attempt to establish Roanoke colony fails.

Key Terms

Archaic The second long stage of North American habitation, covering about 7,000 years, from roughly 8,000 BCE to 1000 BCE (or from 10,000 to 3,000 years ago). During this period, inhabitants adapted to diverse local environments, gathering plants and hunting smaller animals than during the previous Paleo-Indian period. p. 6

Archipelago A group of islands, such as the Hawaiian archipelago. p. 12

Atlatl A weighted, handheld device that enabled early Native Americans to throw spears with added power and velocity. p. 7

Columbian Exchange The significant two-way interchange of plants, animals, microbes, and people that occurred once Christopher Columbus established regular contact by sea between the eastern and western hemispheres. For thousands of years before 1492, despite occasional encounters, these two separate and different "worlds" had remained isolated from each other. p. 17

Globalization The process of integration—economic, but also cultural—of different parts of the world into a more unified system of trade and communication. p. 14

Iberian Relating to Europe's Iberian Peninsula, the location of Spain and Portugal. p. 13

Isthmus A narrow strip of land connecting two larger land areas (such as the isthmus of Panama). p. 18

Mesoamerica The transitional region between North and South America, composed of Mexico and Central America. p. 7

Paleo Indians The earliest human inhabitants of North America, who first migrated to the continent from Siberia more than 15,000 years ago. Faced with a warming climate and the disappearance of many large game animals roughly 10,000 years ago (8,000 BCE), they learned to hunt smaller animals and adapted to varied local conditions during the Archaic Period (to c. 1000 BCE). p. 6

Social stratification The schematic arrangement of a population into a ranking of horizontal of social layers (strata), or an identifiable hierarchy of classes within a society. p. 10

Tithe A levy or donation (generally a tenth part) given to provide support, usually for a church. p. 23

2

European Footholds in North America, 1600–1660

In the summer of 1621, an Englishman and an Indian left Plymouth Village on foot to visit a Native American leader named Massasoit and secure his support for the struggling English colony. During their forty-mile journey, Stephen Hopkins and Squanto saw numerous signs of a wave of disease that had swept the New England coast four years earlier, killing thousands of Indians. Unburied skulls and bones still lay aboveground in many places. The two men who encountered these grim scenes had come together from strikingly different backgrounds.

Back in 1609, Hopkins had left England in a fleet heading for Jamestown in Virginia. When a storm wrecked his ship on the uncharted island of Bermuda, he and others rebelled against their official leader. Accused of mutiny and sentenced to hang, Hopkins pleaded his case and narrowly escaped the noose. Hopkins made it back to England and started a family, but in 1620 he decided to return to America. At the English port of Plymouth, Hopkins, his pregnant wife Elizabeth, and several children and servants became paying passengers on a ship called the *Mayflower*. The vessel had been chartered to carry a group of English Protestants to America from their exile in Holland.

During the arduous passage, tensions mounted. Hopkins was among those who muttered "mutinous speeches" and argued that "when they came ashore, they should use their own libertie, for none had power to command them." But after Elizabeth gave birth, Hopkins joined the other forty men aboard in signing the Mayflower Compact.

The agreement bound all the passengers together in a "Civil Body Politic" to be governed by laws best suited "for the general good." They reached New England in early winter, and Hopkins and others laid out the village of Plymouth in the snow. There, the newcomers met Squanto, a local Native American with a command of English who helped them negotiate with neighboring Indians.

Like Hopkins, Squanto had also experienced earlier Atlantic travel. He remembered the first French and English fishing vessels, which had appeared when he was a small boy. In 1614, Squanto was among twenty-seven Indians taken hostage aboard an English ship. He spent time in Spain, England, and Newfoundland before returning home in 1619, only to find his entire village swept away by disease.

The *Mayflower* pilgrims, arriving a year after Squanto's return, would also suffer heavy losses. Of the 102 settlers who had begun the voyage, half of them died in Plymouth Colony by the next spring. But in New England, as elsewhere in America, death seemed to play favorites in the following years. As colonization continued, recurrent epidemics took a particularly heavy toll on Native Americans, who lacked immunity when exposed to foreign diseases for the first time.

In 1622, Squanto fell sick and died of a fever, leaving no relatives behind. In contrast, Stephen and Elizabeth Hopkins lived on to see numerous children and grandchildren thrive.

By the middle of the seventeenth century, English settlements had taken root in both the Chesapeake region and New England. The success of these colonies would exert a lasting influence on the future direction of American society. But their stories unfolded as part of a far wider North American drama that included a diversity of European groups and embraced both the Atlantic and the Pacific shores. Whether confronting newcomers from Spain, France, Holland, or England, scores of Native American communities faced new challenges that altered traditional Indian ways of living and sometimes threatened their very survival.

■ A *Mayflower* replica is now part of the restored Plymouth Colony site in Massachusetts.

Spain's Ocean-Spanning Reach

In 1580, Spain's Philip II laid claim to the throne of Portugal. This consolidation (which endured until 1640) unified Europe's two richest seaborne empires but also created new problems. First, combining with Portugal put huge additional burdens on the overstretched Spanish bureaucracy. Second, the global success of the combined Iberian empires invited challenges from envious rivals in northern Europe. The new international competition came from the French, the Dutch, and the English, aspiring naval powers with imperial ambitions that touched the Pacific as well as the Atlantic.

What motivated Spain to extend the northern borders of its New World empire?

By 1600, for example, a Dutch ship had entered the Pacific, defying Spanish claims for control of that ocean, and had reached Japan, where the new Tokugawa dynasty (1600–1868) was consolidating its control. The pilot, an Englishman named Will Adams, visited Edo—the rising military town that would grow into modern-day Tokyo. He even built a ship for the *shogun* (ruler). Adams's experience in Japan serves as a reminder that by 1600 competition for oceanic control stretched far beyond the Atlantic. Who would dominate Pacific sea-lanes to America?

Vizcaíno in California and Japan

In April 1607, a letter from the king of Spain reached Mexico City. The king commanded his viceroy in charge of affairs in Mexico (New Spain) to create an outpost on California's Monterey Bay. Spanish galleons returning from the Philippines through the North Pacific to the west coast of Mexico desperately needed a haven along the route, after crossing the immense ocean. Monterey Bay was well supplied with water, food, and timber. The sheltering harbor would provide a perfect way station, where ships could take on supplies and make repairs before heading south.

But the viceroy in Mexico City had other ideas. He diverted the necessary funds into a search for the fabled North Pacific isles of Rica de Oro ("Rich in Gold") and Rica de Plata ("Rich in Silver"). In 1611, the viceroy dispatched Sebastián Vizcaíno to hunt for these mysterious islands. The seasoned Pacific navigator found no isles of gold and silver, but he did visit Japan. When Vizcaíno returned across the Pacific in 1613 aboard a vessel built in Japan, he brought 180 Japanese with him to Mexico. This unique delegation was bound for Spain and Italy to open doors between East and West. However, the Tokugawas soon began to persecute the European traders and Christian missionaries who had been allowed in the Japanese islands for a generation, so the frail link between Europe and Japan through Mexico never developed further.

Tokugawa officials, it seems, feared that tolerating foreigners in Japan's ports might foster the spread of Christianity and undermine their supremacy. Moreover, developing Japanese fleets might bring guns to warlords and disrupt hard-won peace. So Japan passed up an opportunity for naval expansion, just as Ming China had done two centuries earlier after the voyages of Zheng He. Instead, the new dynasty adopted a policy of commercial and cultural isolation that lasted for more than 200 years. Otherwise, the history of North America and the world would almost certainly have taken a very different path.

Spain wondered whether to maintain its existing North American colony in Florida and its newest frontier province: New Mexico.

For the Spanish, Vizcaíno's Pacific adventure consumed crucial funds, and the possibility of a Spanish settlement at Monterey quickly disappeared. Concerned that their empire had already become overextended, Spanish officials postponed plans to colonize California's coast. In addition, Spain wondered whether to maintain its existing North American colony in Florida and its newest frontier province: New Mexico.

Oñate Creates a Spanish Foothold in the Southwest

In 1598, Juan de Oñate renewed the northern efforts of Coronado's expedition several generations earlier. Setting out from New Spain, he led 500 men, women, and children north into the upper Rio Grande valley to create the province of New Mexico. Aided by Franciscan friars (organized followers of St. Francis loyal to the pope), Oñate and his colonists expected to convert the Pueblo Indians to Christianity. Expanding outward from the compact apartment-like native towns, or pueblos, the intruders hoped to open a vast new colonial realm "greater than New Spain."

But Oñate drastically underestimated the difficulties. When embittered Indians at Acoma pueblo killed eleven of his soldiers in 1599, he retaliated by bombarding the mesa-top citadel, killing 800 inhabitants and enslaving nearly 600 others. Following the brutal repression of Acoma, neighboring pueblos reluctantly submitted to Spanish demands for labor and food. Colonial reinforcements arriving in 1600 were dismayed by the harsh conditions; Oñate needed new discoveries for the colony to prosper. In 1601, he launched an expedition east into the Great Plains, but the venture proved as futile as Coronado's earlier march had been.

To make matters worse, drought gripped the Rio Grande valley, and many of the recent settlers departed, complaining that the region lacked woods, pastures, water, and suitable land. When Oñate returned from the plains, he found that two-thirds of his tiny colony had given up and returned to Mexico. Foiled on the east and weakened along the Rio Grande, Oñate next pressed west to seek a link to the Pacific. When he reached the Gulf of California in 1605, he envisioned a possible link to the Pacific trade.

In fact, however, Oñate's new "Mexico" remained isolated and impoverished. The desperate colonists, strapped for food and clothing, pressed hard on the native peoples. They demanded tribute in the form of cotton blankets, buffalo hides, and baskets of scarce maize. In winter, ill-equipped Spanish-speaking soldiers stripped warm robes off the backs of shivering women and children; in summer, they scoured each pueblo for corn, torturing residents to find out where food was hidden.

Meanwhile, a few hundred Pueblo Indians—intimidated by the Spanish, desperate for a share of the food they had grown, and fearful of attacks by neighboring Apache—began to accept Christian baptism and seek Spanish protection. By 1608, when the crown threatened to withdraw support from the struggling province, the colony's Franciscan missionaries appealed that their converts had grown too numerous to resettle and too dependent to abandon. Their argument may have been exaggerated, but it caught the attention of authorities.

Spanish exploration by land and sea
- Spanish territory, 1610
- Juan de Oñate, 1598–1601
- Juan de Oñate, 1604–1605
- Sebastián Vizcaíno, 1602–1603
- Sebastián Vizcaíno, 1611–1613

Present state boundaries provided for orientation

■ **MAP 2.1**
THE SPANISH SOUTHWEST IN THE EARLY SEVENTEENTH CENTURY

Besides, England and France were launching new colonies in Virginia and Canada. Since mapmakers still could not accurately calculate longitude (east–west position on the globe), no one was sure whether these bases created by international rivals posed a threat that was dangerously close at hand. Worried Spanish officials finally agreed with the Franciscan friars that New Mexico must carry on. They replaced Oñate with a new governor and asserted royal control over the few dozen settlers who remained in the colony.

New Mexico Survives: New Flocks Among Old Pueblos

The Spanish decision to hold on in New Mexico reshaped life for everyone in the region. At least 60,000 Indians living in nearly sixty separate pueblos found their world transformed and their survival threatened over the next half-century. In 1610 the new governor, ruling over scarcely fifty colonists, created a capital at the village of Santa Fe. Within two decades, roughly 750 colonists inhabited the remote province, including Spanish, Mexican Indians, Africans, and mixed-race children.

■ Acoma, often called Sky City, sits atop a high sandstone mesa west of Albuquerque, New Mexico. The name means "place that always was," and the pueblo has been continuously inhabited for roughly 1,000 years. Acoma's Native American community survived a devastating attack by Spanish colonizers in 1599.

The racial and ethnic diversity of New Mexico repeated the colonial pattern established in New Spain. Similarly, labor practices and religious changes also followed models established after the conquest of the Aztec in Mexico. As in New Spain, certain privileged people in the new colony received **encomiendas**; such grants entitled the holders (known as *encomenderos*) to the labor of a set number of Native American workers. With labor in short supply throughout the Spanish colonies, settlers led occasional raids against nomadic Plains Indians, keeping some captives and shipping others south to toil as slaves in the Mexican silver mines.

Meanwhile, the number of Franciscan missionaries rose rapidly. They forbade traditional Pueblo celebrations, known as **kachina** dances, and destroyed sacred kachina masks. Their combination of intense zeal and harsh punishments prompted many Indians to learn Spanish and become obedient converts. However, it also drove the Indians' own religious practices underground—literally, into the hidden, circular kivas that had long been a focal point for Native American spiritual activities in the region. There, people kept their traditional faith alive in secret and passed sacred rituals along to the next generation.

The Spanish brought more than Christianity to New Mexico. The newcomers also transferred novel crops (wheat, onions, chilies, peas) and planted new fruits (peaches,

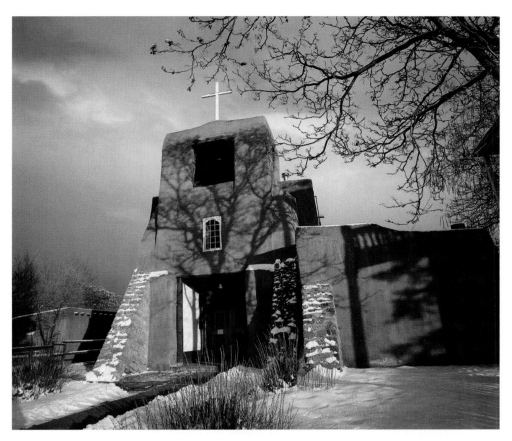

■ The Spanish made Santa Fe the capital of their New Mexico colony in 1610 and built the church of San Miguel there in 1626. Though destroyed in the Pueblo Revolt of 1680, it was rebuilt and has remained in use. "The floor is bare earth," wrote an eighteenth-century observer, "the usual floor throughout these regions."

plums, cherries). Settlers introduced metal hoes and axes, along with donkeys, chickens, and other domesticated animals previously unknown to the native inhabitants. Horses and cattle, led north from New Spain, eventually revolutionized life across the North American West. But the most immediate impact came from Spanish sheep. Each friar soon possessed a flock of several thousand, and Pueblo artisans wove wool into cloth.

But the Pueblo world, like Squanto's world, was eroding under the onslaught of new European diseases. The large Pueblo population, cut in half in the sixty years after Coronado's appearance, still numbered more than 60,000 in 1600. Sickness, along with warfare and famine, cut this number in half again by 1650 and in half once more by 1680.

Conversion and Rebellion in Spanish Florida

By 1600, Spanish Florida also disappointed imperial officials. Dreams of gold-filled kingdoms and a strategic passage from the Southeast to the Orient had never materialized. The Spanish government regarded the outpost at St. Augustine as an undue burden and planned to disband the colony. But Franciscan missionaries won the day, as in New Mexico. They argued that scores of Indian towns appeared ready to receive Christianity. By 1608, the crown had decided to let the colony continue.

■ The Spanish found that glass beads, colorful and easy to transport, made fine gifts and trade items in their contacts with Florida Indians. Chiefs often received special quartz crystal beads and pendants to retain their loyalty.

A handful of missionaries fanned out among the Indians of northern Florida, erecting small churches and mission schools. They recruited Indian students aggressively without regard to age or sex. In 1612, Francisco de Pareja published an illustrated, bilingual confessional in Castilian Spanish and Timucuan, the earliest text in any North American Indian language. The book enabled wary friars to ask villagers, "Have you said suggestive words?" and "Have you desired to do some lewd act with some man or woman or kin?"

Contact with Christian beliefs and books came at a steep price, for each inland village was expected to help feed the colonial garrison at St. Augustine. Native women neglected household crops to grow additional maize and grind it into meal. Annually, Spanish officials requisitioned Indian men from each village to transport the cornmeal overland to the Atlantic coast and return to the mission carrying supplies for the Franciscans. Imported candles, communion wine, and mission bells all had to be hauled inland.

Friars and Indian bearers traveling to the interior also carried sicknesses from St. Augustine. Epidemics of foreign diseases—measles, bubonic plague, malaria, typhus, smallpox, and influenza—took a devastating toll on the Native Americans. As whole villages disappeared, Hispanic entrepreneurs began to expand cattle ranching across northern Florida. Faced with encroaching farms, crushing labor demands, and frightful mortality, local native leaders saw their power reduced and their communities depleted. These conditions sparked a short-lived revolt by Indians at Apalachee in 1647. Nine years later, when the governor at St. Augustine feared a possible attack by English ships, a wider Native American uprising shook Timucua in north-central Florida.

In the end, the English threat to Spanish Florida did not materialize in 1656, but the rumor underscored how much had changed in the preceding half-century. Two generations earlier, in 1600, no European power besides Spain had possessed a solid foothold in any portion of the Americas. But over the next six decades, France, Holland, and England all asserted claims on the American mainland.

◉ See the **Map**

Native American Population Loss, 1500–1700 at **www.myhistorylab.com**

France and Holland: Overseas Competition for Spain

At the turn of the seventeenth century, interlopers from Holland challenged Spanish colonizers in the Philippines and Portuguese traders in Japan. These Dutch efforts illustrated the growing competition between European powers for control of the world's oceans. In London, commercial leaders received a royal charter to create the English East India Company in 1600. Two years later merchants in Amsterdam, hoping to capture Portugal's lucrative Asian trade, established the Dutch East India Company to send ships to eastern oceans. By 1652 they had founded a Dutch colony at Cape Town, near the southern tip of Africa.

The united powers of Spain and Portugal proved even more vulnerable in the Atlantic. To be sure, Spanish convoys continued to transport Mexican gold and silver to Europe annually, along with Asian silks and spices shipped to Mexico via the Pacific trade. Portuguese vessels carried Africans to the New World at a profit. But ships from rival European nations preyed on these seaborne cargoes with increasing success.

Defiantly, European competitors also laid claim to numerous islands in the Caribbean. By 1660, the English had taken control of Barbados, Providence Island, Antigua, and Jamaica; the Dutch had acquired St. Maarten, St. Eustacius, Saba, and Curaçao; and the French had claimed Guadeloupe, Martinique, Grenada, and St. Lucia. For France, however, the most promising Atlantic prospects lay farther north in Canada. There, Spanish power was absent, hopes for a Northwest Passage persisted, and French imperial claims stretched back generations.

How did the expanding beaver trade shape the French and Dutch colonies before 1660?

The Founding of New France

Since the time of Jacques Cartier, fishing boats from the coast of France had crisscrossed Newfoundland's Grand Banks. The trade increased after 1580 as crews built seasonal stations along the American coast for drying codfish. These stations prompted greater contact with Indians; soon Europeans were exchanging metal goods for furs on terms that pleased all. A Native American could trade a worn-out robe made from beaver skins for a highly valued iron kettle. A European artisan could craft a beaver hat that proved fashionable and profitable.

As North Atlantic fishing and trading expanded, the domestic situation in France improved. In 1598, King Henry IV issued the Edict of Nantes, a decree granting political rights and limited toleration to French Protestants, or Huguenots. With religious wars curtailed, the king could contemplate new colonization initiatives in America. An experienced French soldier and sailor named Samuel de Champlain emerged as a key leader in this effort. From 1602 until his death in 1635, Champlain devoted himself to the St. Lawrence River region, where Acadia on the Atlantic coast and Canada along the extensive river valley made up the anticipated realm of New France.

In 1608 Champlain and several dozen other men established an outpost at Quebec, where Cartier and Roberval had wintered generations earlier. In June 1609 Champlain joined a band of Algonquin and Huron Indians in a raid on the Iroquois in what is now upstate New York. When they engaged their Iroquois enemies in battle, Champlain fired his gun—a novelty in the region—killing several war chiefs and sparking a rout. For the powerful **Iroquois League** south of the St. Lawrence (the Five Nation confederation composed of the Seneca, Cayuga, Onondaga, Oneida, and Mohawk Indians), the defeat spawned lasting bitterness. For the French, their victory sealed good relations with the Algonquin and Huron, ensuring the survival of Quebec and spurring unprecedented commerce. Within fifteen years, Native Americans were trading 12,000 to 15,000 beaver pelts annually via the St. Lawrence River valley.

In 1627 the powerful first minister in France, Cardinal Richelieu, pressed for greater French settlement in Canada through a new private company. He banned Huguenots from participating and pushed to make sure that only Roman Catholics were allowed to migrate to Canada. But his expansive policies alarmed rival England, which captured Quebec briefly in 1629. When restored to French control several years later, the tiny outpost contained fewer than 100 people. In an effort to expand the meager settlement and populate the fertile valley upriver from Quebec, French authorities began granting narrow strips of land with river frontage to any Catholic lord who would take up residence there and bring French tenants to his estate.

Competing for the Beaver Trade

Cardinal Richelieu's power in France epitomized the ongoing Counter-Reformation. This outpouring of Catholic zeal reached as far as North America. In 1635 Jesuits founded a college in Quebec, and in 1639 six nuns arrived to begin a school for Indian girls and a hospital. Other religious workers established a station farther west in 1641 in territory recently dominated by the Iroquois; the strategic outpost marked the beginnings of Montreal. From there, the French planned to control the beaver trade as it expanded west. They also hoped to prevent the Iroquois League from diverting furs south to Holland's new colony on the Hudson River.

But the desperate Iroquois nations, facing collapse, took a stand. Increasing contact with Europeans and their contagious diseases had brought catastrophic epidemics to the Iroquois homelands below Lake Ontario. Beginning in 1633, sicknesses that were new to the region swept away some 10,000 people and cut the Five Nations' population in half within a decade, emptying the distinctive longhouses that made up Iroquois villages.

According to Iroquois tradition, mourning survivors must replace deceased individuals swiftly with captives to maintain the community's strength and continuity. Pressed by grieving families, Iroquois warriors initiated a generation of violent campaigns intended to capture and absorb neighboring groups. These so-called mourning wars are also remembered as the Beaver Wars because they included a clear economic motive. Besides captives, the Iroquois aggressors sought furs. If they could seize pelts before the valuable items reached the French, they could trade them to the Dutch for guns and powder. Well armed, they could then engage in further wars for captives and furs.

This spiral of aggression put the Iroquois on a collision course with the Huron and their allies, a small band of Jesuit missionaries willing to risk martyrdom in New France. Eager for Native American converts, the Jesuits focused their attention on the region east of Lake Huron, where 30,000 Huron Indians lived in large villages. The Jesuits erected chapels at four of these towns and constructed a central base at St. Marie near Georgian Bay. Having volunteered for hardship, they witnessed far more of it than they ever imagined.

First came the same foreign epidemics that had wasted the Iroquois; smallpox cut down roughly two-thirds of the Huron population, or 20,000 people, between 1635 and 1640. Then came the Iroquois themselves, bent on capturing Huron women and children to revitalize their longhouses, swept by disease in the 1630s. Armed by Dutch traders eager for furs, 1,000 Iroquois warriors descended on the weakened Huron in March 1649. They burned villages, secured captives, tortured several priests to death, and seized large stocks of pelts. The Iroquois then launched raids on the St. Lawrence River valley, disrupting the fur trade and frightening the several thousand French inhabitants. By 1660, it seemed that New France—thinly settled, weakly defended, and poorly supplied—might face the same extinction that the much older and larger Huron community had suffered.

■ **MAP 2.2**
EUROPEAN AND NATIVE AMERICAN CONTACT IN THE NORTHEAST, 1600–1660
French and English colonization efforts brought devastating diseases to the Five Nations of the Iroquois League. Eager to take captives and profit from the growing trade in furs, the Iroquois ranged north and west to make war on the French and their Huron Indian allies.

A Dutch Colony on the Hudson River

The Dutch traders who supplied firearms to the Iroquois in exchange for furs owed their start to English-born navigator Henry Hudson. In 1609, sailing for the Dutch East India Company, Hudson crossed the Atlantic in search of a western passage to the Orient. He visited Chesapeake Bay and Delaware Bay, then rediscovered modern-day New York harbor, the bay that Verrazzano had entered in 1524. Flying the Dutch flag above his vessel, the *Half Moon*, Hudson sailed north up the broad river that now bears his name. The Dutch moved quickly to gain a foothold in the region. Ships from Amsterdam appeared far up the Hudson, exchanging metal goods for beaver pelts. Soon the Dutch had established a year-round trading post at Fort Orange, near present-day Albany.

In 1621, responsibility for New Netherland—the region claimed between the Delaware and Connecticut rivers—fell to the newly chartered Dutch West India Company (DWIC). Modeled on the Dutch East India Company, the DWIC concentrated on piecing together an empire in the South Atlantic. Dutch ships seized part of sugar-rich Brazil (1632), the island of Curaçao near Venezuela (1634), and Portugal's African outpost at Elmina, on the coast of modern-day Ghana (1637). But the DWIC also laid plans for a North American colony.

To begin, the company transported a group of French-speaking Belgians to New Netherland in 1624. To secure the boundaries of the province, officials deposited farm families far up the Hudson at Fort Orange and along the Connecticut and Delaware rivers. However, Peter Minuit, the colony's director from 1626 to 1631, saw danger in this dispersal.

To consolidate settlement, he purchased Manhattan Island at the mouth of the Hudson from the local Indians in 1626. By 1630, the village of New Amsterdam boasted 270 settlers at the southern tip of Manhattan.

When the company threw open the Indian trade to others besides its own agents, the careless and greedy actions of unregulated traders sparked a series of violent wars with coastal tribes. Also, the Dutch squabbled constantly with neighboring English settlers over fur-trading rights and other matters. The small colony of New Sweden, which materialized on the west side of the Delaware River in 1637, posed yet another problem. The settlers who built Fort Christina (now Wilmington, Delaware) were Swedes and Finns hoping to establish their own trade with the Indians. But in 1655, these several hundred Scandinavians were obliged to surrender to a Dutch fleet.

"All Sorts of Nationalities": Diverse New Amsterdam

The symbol of Dutch power in the region, and the commander of the fleet that seized New Sweden, was Peter Stuyvesant. He ruled New Netherland aggressively for several decades before England seized the colony in 1664. Stuyvesant had served as governor of Dutch Curaçao, losing his right leg in a battle with the Spanish. When he arrived in New Netherland in 1647 as director general for the DWIC, he moved swiftly to assert control.

Stuyvesant limited beer and rum sales, fined settlers for promiscuity and knife fighting, and established a nine-member night watch. When a group of English Quakers, members of the newly formed Society of Friends, arrived at New Amsterdam in 1657, he attempted to expel the radical Protestants and fine any who gave them shelter. However, Dutch residents of Flushing, on Long Island, defied Stuyvesant's ban and signed a public letter of objection stressing religious toleration.

Collection of the New-York Historical Society, (Neg #1049)

■ **New Amsterdam Fort on Manhattan Island**

To address the colony's chronic labor shortage, Stuyvesant endorsed trade in African slaves and used his Caribbean connections to expand this traffic. When the Portuguese forced Holland out of Brazil in 1654 and closed that sugar colony to Dutch slave vessels, some of the ships brought their cargoes to New Amsterdam instead. Like the Dutch-speaking blacks already living in the colony, most of these newcomers were enslaved for life. But the DWIC, the largest importer and owner of slaves in New Netherland, granted "half-freedom" to some whom it could not employ year-round. These people, in return for an annual fee, could travel freely and marry, acquire property, and hire out their labor. By 1664, black residents made up over 10 percent of New Netherland's population and 20 percent of New Amsterdam, the colony's capital.

New Amsterdam, home to fewer than 2,000 people, also had a small Jewish contingent, the first in mainland North America. In 1654, twenty-three Sephardic Jews reached Manhattan, forced out of Brazil by the Portuguese. Stuyvesant, strident in his anti-Semitism, claimed such "blasphemers of the name of Christ" would "infect and trouble this new colony." But the DWIC, which included Jewish stockholders and was eager for newcomers of all kinds, overruled the governor's request to expel the refugees. In the end, colony officials authorized a Jewish ghetto, or segregated neighborhood, where the newcomers could pray together freely in private. At first, however, they were not allowed to construct a synagogue for public worship.

In the early 1660s, the colony continued to grow, "slowly peopled by the scrapings of all sorts of nationalities," as Stuyvesant complained. Huguenots occupied New Paltz near the Hudson; farther north, other newcomers founded Schenectady in 1661. Swedes and Finns continued to prosper along the Delaware, and numerous English had settled on Long Island. Compared with New France, New Netherland seemed far more populous, prosperous, and ethnically diverse. But whereas the French colony to the north endured for another century, the Dutch enterprise soon was absorbed by England. For despite a slow start, the English managed to outdistance all their European rivals and establish thriving North American colonies in the first half of the seventeenth century.

> *Compared with New France, New Netherland seemed far more populous, prosperous, and ethnically diverse.*

English Beginnings on the Atlantic Coast

What factors worked for and against the early English colonization efforts in America?

When Queen Elizabeth I passed away in 1603, several important elements were already in place to help England compete for colonial outposts. Thousands of rural tenants had been pushed off farms; these landless people, who flocked to urban centers in search of work, formed a restless supply of potential colonists. Also, the country had an expanding fleet of English-built ships, sailed by experienced mariners. In addition, England had a group of seasoned and ambitious leaders. A generation of soldiers (many of them younger sons of the property-holding elite known as the gentry) had fought in Europe or participated in the brutal colonization of Ireland.

Because Elizabeth I died without heirs, the king of Scotland, James Stuart, succeeded her as ruler. During the reigns of James I (1603–1625) and his son Charles I (1625–1649), religious and economic forces in England prompted an increasing number of people to consider migrating overseas. With the expansion of the country's Protestant Reformation, religious strife escalated toward civil war, which erupted in 1642. During the tumultuous 1630s, English public officials were glad to transplant Puritans and Catholics alike to foreign shores. In turn, many ardent believers—weary of conflict or losing hope for their cause at home—welcomed the prospect of a safe haven abroad. Economically, the development of joint stock organizations enabled merchants to raise capital and spread the high risk of colonial ventures by selling numerous shares to small investors. At the same time, the fluctuating domestic economy prompted many people to consider seeking their fortunes elsewhere.

The Virginia Company and Jamestown

For Richard Hakluyt, England's leading publicist for overseas expansion, the proper focus seemed clear: "There is under our noses," he wrote in 1599, "the great & ample countrey of Virginia." Great and ample, indeed, especially before the rival Dutch established New Netherland. On paper, the enormous zone that England claimed as Virginia stretched north to south from the top of modern-day Vermont to Cape Fear on Carolina's Outer Banks. From east to west, it spanned North America from the Atlantic to the Pacific, however narrow or wide the continent might prove to be.

In 1606, James I chartered the Virginia Company as a two-pronged operation to exploit the sweeping Virginia claim. Under the charter, a group of London-based merchants took responsibility for colonizing the Chesapeake Bay region. Meanwhile, merchants from the English seaports of Plymouth, Exeter, and Bristol took charge of developing the northern latitudes of the American coast. In 1607, two ships from Plymouth deposited roughly a hundred colonists at the Sagadahoc (Kennebec) River in Maine. The Sagadahoc settlers erected a fort and buildings, but frostbite, scurvy, and dwindling supplies prompted a retreat home in 1608.

A parallel effort by the Londoners proved more enduring—but just barely. In April 1607, three ships from the Thames bearing 105 men sailed into Chesapeake Bay. The newcomers disembarked on what appeared to be a secluded island near a broad river. Within months, these subjects of James I had named the waterway the James River and established a fortified village beside it called Jamestown. In June, hoping for quick rewards, they shipped to London various stones that they thought contained precious gems and gold ore.

When the rocks proved worthless, the colonists' dreams of easy wealth evaporated. So did their fantasies about pushing west to the Pacific. During the outpost's first winter, a fire destroyed the tiny settlement, and death from hunger, exposure, and sickness cut the garrison's population in half. The governor and council appointed by the Virginia Company bickered among themselves, providing poor leadership. Fully one-third of the early arrivals claimed to be gentlemen, from England's leisure class—a proportion six times higher than in England—and most proved unaccustomed to hard manual labor. Moreover, all the colonists were employees of the company, so any profits from their labor went to repay London investors.

Despite the unsuitable make-up of the garrison, conditions improved briefly with the emergence of John Smith as a vigorous leader. Captain Smith dealt brazenly with the local Powhatan Indian confederation, numbering more than 13,000 people. He reached a tenuous accommodation with the paramount chief, Powhatan, who had been steadily expanding his power across the Tidewater region. (Later, Smith claimed to have been assisted and protected by Powhatan's young daughter, Pocahontas.) Still, the Jamestown colony limped along with meager support, living in fear of Spanish attacks.

With hopes of a swift bonanza dashed, the London merchants decided to alter their strategy. They would salvage the venture by attracting fresh capital. Then they would recoup their high initial costs by recruiting new settlers who could produce staple products suited for export—perhaps grapes, sugar, cotton, or tobacco. In 1609, the company began to sell seven-year joint stock options to the English public. Subscribers could invest money or they could sign on for service in Virginia. Company officials promised such adventurers at least a hundred acres of land when their investment matured in 1616. In June 1609, 500 men and 100 women departed for the Chesapeake aboard nine ships.

View the Image

Mural of Jamestown Settlement at
www.myhistorylab.com

"Starving Time" and the Seeds of Representative Government

When the battered fleet arrived at Jamestown, the new arrivals found insufficient supplies. Moreover, the first settlers had failed to discover a profitable staple crop. The colonists depended heavily on the Native Americans for food, and Powhatan's Confederacy proved increasingly unwilling and unable to share its harvest. In a grim "starving time," the ill-equipped newcomers scavenged for berries and bark. Extreme hunger drove a few to cannibalize the dead before dying themselves. By the spring of 1610, seven of every eight people had died; scarcely sixty remained alive.

In June, these survivors abandoned their ghost town altogether. But as they set sail for England, they encountered three long-overdue ships entering Chesapeake Bay with fresh supplies and 300 new settlers. Reluctantly, they agreed to try again. More years of harsh discipline, Indian warfare, and scarce resources followed. A severe seven-year drought, from 1606 through 1612, also conspired against the hapless newcomers.

Relief came from an unexpected quarter: the "bewitching vegetable" known as Orinoco tobacco. The plant, grown in parts of the West Indies and South America, had captured English taste in the previous generation. Sales of this New World product in England sent profits to the Spanish crown and prompted James I to launch a vigorous antismoking campaign in 1604. But John Rolfe, reaching Jamestown in 1610, wondered whether the "noxious weed" might provide the colonists with a viable staple crop. Rolfe, a smoker himself, suspected that sweet-flavored Orinoco tobacco could prosper in Virginia soil. Within a year, Rolfe had somehow managed to obtain seeds, and by 1612 his patch of West Indian tobacco was flourishing. Desperate settlers and impatient London investors were delighted by Rolfe's successful experiment. Soon production of the leaf soared at Jamestown, to the neglect of all other pursuits.

During Virginia's initial tobacco boom, recently starving settlers saw handsome profits within reach. Because land was plentiful, the only limitations to riches were the scarcity of workers and the related high cost of labor. Any farmer who could hire half a dozen field hands could increase his profits fivefold, quickly earning enough to obtain more land and import more servants. The company transported several shiploads of apprentices and servants to the labor-hungry colony. When a Dutch captain delivered twenty enslaved blacks in 1619, settlers eagerly purchased these first Africans to arrive in English Virginia. They also bid on the 100 women who disembarked the same year, shipped

•••–[**Read** the **Document**

John Smith, "The Starving Time" at **www.myhistorylab.com**

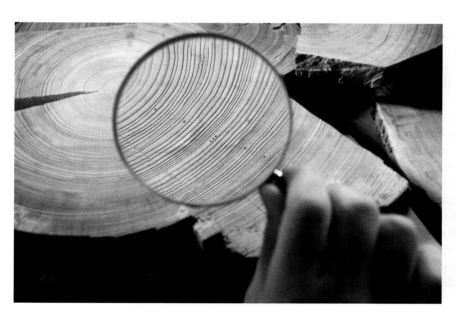

■ Inexperience prompted initial English difficulties at Roanoke and Jamestown, but so did poor weather. Scientists studying the region's bald cypress trees have recently shown (from certain narrow rings) that terrible droughts struck the coastal area in the late 1580s and again from 1606 through 1612. These two sequences of narrow annual rings are visible under the magnifying glass.

from England by the company to be sold as wives and workers. Still, men continued to outnumber women more than three to one for decades to come.

To encourage English migration further, the Virginia Company offered transportation and fifty acres to tenants, promising them ownership of the land after seven years of work. Men who paid their own way received fifty acres and an additional **headright** of fifty acres for each household member or laborer they transported. The Virginia Company went out of its way to assure colonists of access to such established English freedoms as the right to trial by jury and to a representative form of government. The company established civil courts controlled by English common law, and it instructed Virginia's governor to summon an annual assembly of elected **burgesses**—the earliest representative legislature in North America. First convened in 1619, the House of Burgesses wasted no time in affirming its commitment to fundamental English rights. The governor, the house said, could no longer impose taxes without the assembly's consent.

> *The Virginia Company went out of its way to assure colonists of access to established English freedoms.*

Launching the Plymouth Colony

To attract additional capital and people, the Virginia Company also began awarding patents (legal charters) to private groups of adventurers. The newcomers would live independently on a large tract, with only minimal control from the governor and his council. Two such small colonies originated among English Protestants living in exile in Holland because their separatist beliefs did not allow them to profess loyalty to the Church of England. The first group of 180, based in Amsterdam, departed for America late in 1618 on a crowded ship. Winter storms, sickness, and a shortage of fresh water destroyed the venture; scarcely fifty survivors straggled ashore in Virginia.

A second group of English Separatists, residing in the smaller Dutch city of Leiden, fared better. Most had migrated to Holland from northeast England in 1608. This group openly opposed the hierarchy, pomp, and inclusiveness of the Church of England. Instead, they wanted to return to early Christianity, where small groups of worthy (and often persecuted) believers formed their own communities of worship. After a decade in Holland, many of them had wearied of the foreign culture. They were dismayed by the effect of worldly Leiden on their children, and they also sensed, correctly, that warfare would soon break out in Europe. A few families pushed for removal to America, despite the obvious dangers of such a journey.

Possible destinations ranged from South America to Canada. But in the end, the Separatists decided to use a patent granted by the Virginia Company to a group of English capitalists. On the negative side, the migrants had to work for these investors for seven years. They also had to take along paying passengers who did not share their beliefs. On the positive side, they received financial support from backers who paid to rent a ship. Moreover, instead of having their daily affairs controlled from London, they had the power to govern themselves.

Read the Document

Agreement Between the Settlers at New Plymouth (Mayflower Compact) at **www.myhistorylab.com**

In September 1620, after costly delays, thirty-five members of the Leiden congregation and additional Separatists from England departed from Plymouth, along with other passengers. They were crowded aboard the *Mayflower*, a 160-ton vessel bound for Virginia. But a stormy two-month crossing brought them to Cape Cod, in modern-day Massachusetts, no longer considered part of the Virginia Company's jurisdiction. Sickly from their journey and with winter closing in, they decided to disembark at the spot they called Plymouth rather than push south to Chesapeake Bay. Earlier, they had signed a solemn compact aboard the *Mayflower* binding them together in a civil community.

William Bradford, the chronicler and longtime governor of Plymouth Colony, later recalled their plight: "They had now no friends to welcome them nor inns to entertain or refresh their weather-beaten bodies . . . . Besides, what could they see but a hideous and desolate wilderness." Bradford could scarcely exaggerate the challenge. His own wife drowned (an apparent suicide) shortly after the *Mayflower* dropped anchor. And by the time the ship departed in April, an illness had swept away half the colonists. When those remaining planted barley and peas, the English seeds failed to take hold.

Still, settlers had abundant fish and wildlife, along with ample Indian corn, and soon reinforcements arrived from England bringing needed supplies. The newcomers also brought a legal patent for the land of Plymouth Plantation. With Squanto's aid, the settlers secured peaceful relations with Massasoit's villages. When a good harvest assured survival for another winter, they invited Massasoit and his Indians to join in a three-day celebration of thanksgiving so that, according to one account, all might "rejoice together after we had gathered the fruit of our labors."

The Puritan Experiment

After more than a generation of costly colonization attempts, England still had little to show for its efforts when Charles I inherited the throne in 1625. Then two forces prompted rapid change: positive publicity about America and negative developments at home. John Smith, long a key promoter of overseas settlement, drew inspiration from the early efforts at Jamestown and Plymouth. In 1624 he published a best-seller predicting future success for these regions. Ironically, the book's popularity depended in large part on the grim religious, political, and economic conditions in England that suddenly gave such literature a broad appeal.

How were the Puritans strengthened or weakened by seeing themselves as God's chosen people?

Puritan Unrest Leads to the Massachusetts Bay Company

European Christianity had taken a number of different forms since the religious upheaval sparked by Luther a century earlier. The first Protestants had demanded a reformation of the Roman Catholic Church and had questioned papal authority over Christians. Now many non-Catholic English worshippers doubted whether the Church of England (also known as the Anglican Church) had gone far enough toward rejecting the practices of Rome. They lamented what they saw as the church's bureaucratic hierarchy, ornate rituals, and failure to enforce strict observance of the Christian Sabbath each Sunday. They scoffed at the gaudy vestments of Anglican bishops, elaborate church music, and other trappings of worship unjustified by biblical scripture. Instead, they praised the stark simplicity that John Calvin had brought to his church in Geneva.

As English Calvinists grew in number, their objections to the Church of England increased. They protested that the Anglican Church, like the Catholic Church, remained inclusive in membership rather than selective. They argued for limiting participation only to the devout, and they insisted that the Church of England should be independent and self-governing rather than tied to the monarchy. This keen desire for further cleansing and purity, so common to reformers, spurred the ongoing movement known as Puritanism.

Some of the most radical members of the broad Puritan coalition (including Bradford and the Plymouth pilgrims) became known as Separatists because they were committed to an extreme position: complete separation from what they saw as the corrupt Church of England. But many more Puritans (including most of the reformers who migrated to Massachusetts Bay) resisted separation. They hoped to stay technically within the Anglican fold while taking increased control of their own congregations—a practice known as congregationalism.

Unwilling to conform to practices that offended them, these nonseparating Congregationalists remained determined to save the Anglican Church through righteous example, even if it meant migrating abroad for a time to escape persecution and demonstrate the proper ways of a purified Protestant church.

An emphasis on instructive preaching by informed leaders lay at the heart of the Puritan movement. Puritans believed that the sermon should form the center of the Christian worship service. Their churches resembled lecture halls, emphasizing the pulpit more than the altar. In preaching, Puritans stressed a "plain style" that the entire congregation could understand. Moreover, they urged listeners to play an active role in their faith—to master reading and engage in regular study and discussion of scripture. In response to mounting public interest in these practices, Puritan ministers intensified their preaching and published their sermons. In effect, they dared authorities to silence them.

Reprisals came swiftly, led by William Laud, bishop of London. Laud instructed all preachers to focus their remarks on biblical passages and avoid writing or speaking about controversial religious matters. As England's church grew more rigid and its monarchy more controlling, the nation's economy took a turn for the worse. Rents and food costs had risen more rapidly than wages, and workers paid dearly. Jobs became more scarce, and unemployed workers staged local revolts. In 1629, entrepreneurs who viewed New England as a potential opportunity teamed up with disaffected Puritans to obtain a charter for a new entity: the Massachusetts Bay Company. Through a generation of costly trial-and-error experiments, the English had amassed great expertise in colonization. And given the worsening conditions at home, especially among the Puritan faithful, proposals for overseas settlement attracted widespread attention.

•••[**Read** the **Document**
"The Cambridge Agreement" at
www.myhistorylab.com

"We Shall Be as a City upon a Hill"

During the next dozen years, more than 70,000 people left England for the New World. Two-thirds of them sailed to the West Indies. But a large contingent of Puritans embarked for the new Massachusetts Bay colony, adjacent to the Plymouth settlement. A loophole in the king's grant permitted them to take the actual charter with them and to hold their company meetings in America. This maneuver took them out from under the usual control of London investors and let them turn the familiar joint stock structure into the framework for a self-governing colony. By 1629, advance parties had established a post at Salem for people who "upon the account of religion would be willing to begin a foreign plantation."

In England, meanwhile, a Puritan squire named John Winthrop assumed leadership of the Massachusetts Bay Company. "God will bring some heavy Affliction upon this lande," he predicted to his wife, but the Lord "will provide a shelter & a hidinge place for us and others." In exchange, God would expect great things from these chosen people, as from the Old Testament Israelites. "We are entered into covenant with him for this work," Winthrop told his companions aboard the *Arbella* en route to America in 1630.

Winthrop laid out this higher Calvinist standard in a memorable shipboard sermon titled "A Model of Christian Charity." Far from hiding in obscurity, dedicated Puritans must set a visible example for the rest of the world, Winthrop declared. "We shall be as a city upon a hill."

The *Arbella* was one of seventeen ships that brought more than 1,000 people to New England in 1630. The English newcomers chose Winthrop as governor and established Boston as their port. By the time civil war erupted in England in 1642, nearly 20,000 people had made the journey, eager to escape the religious persecution and governmental tyranny of Charles I. Whole congregations migrated with their ministers; other people (more than 20 percent) crossed as servants. But most came as independent families, setting up stable households where women played important parts. They took an immediate role in crucial aspects

■ Port records for 1635 show that groups leaving London varied markedly, depending on their colonial destination. Young children were common aboard ships heading for New England, as were women and girls. Among passengers for New England, eight of every twenty were female. In contrast, females made up only three in twenty of those going to Virginia and one in twenty among people heading for Barbados.

of domestic manufacture and production, and their numerous children provided additional hands where labor was in short supply.

Earlier settlers traded food, lodging, and building materials to fresh arrivals in exchange for textiles, tools, money, and labor. When new groups of church members wanted to establish a village, they applied for land to the General Court, a legislature made up of representatives elected from existing towns. Well before 1640, English settlements dotted the coast and had sprung up inland along the Connecticut River, where smallpox had decimated the Indians in 1633. There, English outposts rose at Wethersfield, Hartford, and Springfield, where English traders hoped to attract furs away from the French and Dutch.

Dissenters: Roger Williams and Anne Hutchinson

Like the biblical Hebrews before them, the Puritans—self-appointed saints—believed that God had chosen them for a special mission in the world. The Almighty, they believed, would watch carefully, punish harshly, and reward mightily. Inevitably some devout people, raised to question authority in England, continued to dissent in New England. Not everyone accepted the idea that Puritans should dominate Indians or that women should defer to men. Roger Williams, a graduate of Cambridge University, and Anne Hutchinson, the talented daughter of an English minister, stand out as two of the earliest and most effective challengers to leadership in the Massachusetts Bay colony.

When Williams arrived in Boston, his Separatist leanings angered Bay Colony authorities, who still hoped to reform the Anglican Church rather than renounce it.

INTERPRETING HISTORY

Anne Bradstreet: "The Tenth Muse, Lately Sprung Up in America"

The Puritans who migrated to America stressed literacy and education as part of their faith. They left extensive court records, sermons, and diaries, but few of these surviving documents come from the pens of women. The poems and reflections of Anne Bradstreet provide a notable exception. "Here you may find," she told her children shortly before her death in 1672, "what was your living mother's mind."

The lifelong poet was born Anne Dudley in Lincolnshire, England, in 1612. She already "found much comfort in reading the Scriptures" by age seven. "But as I grew to be about 14 or 15," she recalled, "I found my heart more carnal, and....the follies of youth took hold of me. About 16, the Lord . . . smote me with the smallpox . . . . and again restored me." That same year, she married Simon Bradstreet, the son of a minister. Two years later, despite a frail constitution, she sailed for Massachusetts Bay with her husband and her father (both future governors of the colony) aboard the Arbella.

Anne Bradstreet was alert to all that seemed strange and different in America. When I "came into this country," she related, "I found a new world and new manners." The young couple set up housekeeping in the town of Cambridge, on the Charles River, but life was difficult at first. Anne suffered from "a lingering sickness like a consumption." Moreover, "It pleased God to keep me a long time without a child, which was a great grief to me and cost me many prayers and tears." Finally, she bore a son in 1633, and seven more children followed.

As the family grew and moved about, "Mistress Bradstreet" wrote poems and meditations, although detractors hinted that she should put down her quill pen and take up a sewing needle. "If what I do prove well, it won't advance," she lamented in rhyme; "They'l say it's stol'n, or else it was by chance." Nevertheless, a book of her poems was published in England in 1650, hailing her as "The Tenth **Muse**, Lately Sprung Up in America."

As a writer, Anne Bradstreet was more interested in spiritual improvement than literary grace. "Many speak well," she observed, "but few can do well." Throughout life, she followed a simple creed: "There is no object that we see; no action that we do; no good that we enjoy; no evil that we feel or fear, but we may make some spiritual advantage" of it. Nothing epitomizes this belief more clearly than "some verses upon the burning of our house, July 10th, 1666." Bradstreet composed the lines on an unburned scrap of paper as she groped to make sense of the calamity. The poem helped her to mourn her loss, take stock of her blessings, and renew her faith. In part, it reads,

In silent night when rest I took,
For sorrow neer I did not look,
I waken'd was with thundring nois
And Piteous shreiks of dreadfull voice....

I, starting up, the light did spye,
And to my God my heart did cry. . . .
Then coming out beheld a space
The flame consume my dwelling place.

And, when I could no longer look,
I blest his Name that gave and took,
That layd my goods now in the dust:
Yea so it was, and so 'twas just. . . .

When by the Ruines oft I past,
My sorrowing eyes aside did cast,
And here and there the places spye
Where oft I sate, and long did lye.

Here stood that Trunk, and there that chest;
There lay that store I counted best:
My pleasant things in ashes lye,
And them behold no more shall I. . . .

Then streight I gin my heart to chide,
And did thy wealth on earth abide?
Didst fix thy hope on mouldring dust,
The arm of flesh didst make thy trust? . . .

Thou hast a house on high erect
Fram'd by that mighty Architect. . . .
The world no longer let me Love,
My hope and Treasure lyes Above.

Questions

1. How might Anne Bradstreet's eventful life before age twenty have shaped her into a poet?
2. Imagine losing your home and belongings in a storm, flood, or fire. Would it deepen or weaken your religious beliefs? How about your need for material possessions?

Source: Anne Bradstreet, "Verses Upon the Burning of Our House, July 18, 1666," 1666.

Cambridge, on the Charles River near Boston, was a small village in the 1660s. The large building in the foreground is Harvard College, founded in 1636, and the smaller brick building beside it is the Indian College, built in 1655. The village was even smaller when Anne Bradstreet resided there briefly after her arrival in Massachusetts Bay. When John Smith gave a map of the region to Charles I, England's king named the Charles River for himself.

The Pull to Settle in America
1. Word-of-mouth information about America
2. Effective work and writing by recruiters
3. Appeal of land and economic opportunities
4. Desire to join earlier migrants to America
5. Safe pursuit of personal religious beliefs
6. Hope of educating and converting Indians

The Push to Leave Home in Europe
1. Escape from direct religious persecution
2. Fear regarding the religious future at home
3. Anxiety about political change in Europe
4. Dismay over economy; need for farmland
5. Relief from joblessness or personal adversity
6. Restlessness and desire for adventure

■ **FIGURE 2.1**
THE TOUGH CHOICE TO START OVER

Williams's other contentions proved equally distressing. The young minister argued that civil authorities, inevitably corrupt, had no right to judge religious matters. He even pushed for an unprecedented separation of church and state—to protect the church. He also contended that the colony's land patent from the king had no validity. The settlers, he said, had to purchase occupancy rights from the Native Americans. Unable to silence him, irate magistrates banished Williams from Massachusetts Bay in the winter of 1635. Moving south, he took up residence among the Narragansett Indians and built a refuge for other dissenters, which he named Providence. In 1643, Williams returned to London, where he persuaded leaders of England's rising Puritan revolution to grant a charter (1644) to his independent colony of Rhode Island.

A more explosive popular challenge centered on Anne Hutchinson, who had grown up in England with a strong will, a solid theological education, and a thirst for spiritual perfection. She married a Lincolnshire textile merchant and took an active part in religious discussions while also bearing fifteen children. When her Puritan minister, John Cotton, departed for New England, Hutchinson claimed that God, in a private revelation, had instructed her to follow. In 1634, the family migrated to Boston, where Hutchinson attended Cotton's church and hosted religious discussions in her home. The popularity of these weekly meetings troubled authorities, as did her argument that the "Holy Spirit illumines the heart of every true believer." Hutchinson downplayed outward conformity—modest dress or regular church attendance—as a route to salvation. Instead, she stressed direct communication with God's inner presence as the key to individual forgiveness.

Most Puritans sought a delicate balance in their lives between respected outer works and inner personal grace. Hutchinson tipped that balance dangerously toward the latter. To the colony's magistrates, especially Winthrop, such teaching pointed toward dangerous anarchy—more troublesome when it came from a woman. These officials labeled Hutchinson and her followers as Antinomians (from *anti*, "against," and *nomos*, "law"). But the vehement faction grew, attracting merchants who chafed under economic restrictions, women who questioned men's domination of the church, and young adults who resented the strict authority of their elders. By 1636, this religious and political coalition had gained enough supporters to turn Winthrop out as governor.

Challenged by this Antinomian Crisis, members of the Puritan establishment fought back. They divided the opposition to win reelection for Winthrop, and they established Harvard College to educate ministers who would not stray from the fold. Also, they staged a flurry of trials for contempt and sedition (inciting resistance to lawful authority), and they made a special example of Hutchinson herself. After a two-day hearing in which she defended herself admirably, Winthrop sentenced Hutchinson to banishment as "a woman not fit for our society." Forced into exile, Hutchinson moved first to Rhode Island and later to New Netherland, living at Pelham Bay near the estate of Joseph Bronk (now called the Bronx). There, she and most of her family were killed by Indians in 1643. A river and a parkway in New York still bear her name.

Expansion and Violence: The Pequot War

Immigration to New England slowed during the 1640s because of religious and political upheaval at home. In England, Puritans and supporters of Parliament formed an army and openly challenged royal authority during the English Civil War. After seizing power, these revolutionaries beheaded Charles I in 1649, abolished the monarchy, and proclaimed England a republican Commonwealth. Settlers in Massachusetts Bay struggled to square such sweeping developments in England with Winthrop's earlier assurance that the eyes of God and humankind would be fixed on New England.

Making matters worse, religious and economic controversies intensified as New England's next generation came of age. Needing new farmland and intellectual breathing room, fresh congregations began to "hive off" from the original settlements like swarms of bees. By 1640, New Hampshire, Rhode Island, and Connecticut each had at least four new towns that would provide the beginnings for independent colonies.

But the northeastern forest was not an empty wilderness, any more than the Chesapeake tidewater, the Florida interior, or the mesas of New Mexico had been. As the Hutchinsons discovered, newcomers who pushed inland were co-opting the land of longtime residents. Pressure on New England's Native Americans erupted in armed conflict in the Pequot War of 1637, at the height of the Antinomian Crisis. The Pequot Indians, English allies recently weakened by smallpox, resided near the mouth of the Connecticut River. But John Winthrop, whose son was leading a settlement effort in the area, fanned fears that the Pequot "would cause all the Indians in the country to join to root out all the English."

Recruiting Narragansett and Mohegan Indians to the English side, the colonists unleashed all-out war against the Pequot. The campaign culminated in a dawn raid on a stockaded Pequot town that sheltered noncombatants. The invaders torched the village (at Mystic, Connecticut) and shot or put to the sword almost all who tried to escape. Some 400 Indian men, women, and children died. The Puritans' Indian allies were shocked by the wholesale carnage. English warfare, they protested, "is too furious, and slaies too many men." Chastened by this intimidating display of terror and weakened by recurrent epidemics, the tribes of southern New England negotiated away much of their land over the next generation, trading furs to the rapidly multiplying colonists and seeking to understand their perplexing ways.

Having gained the upper hand, the Bible-reading English made gestures to convert their Native American neighbors. The Massachusetts General Court encouraged missionary work, forbade the worship of Indian gods, and set aside land for "praying towns" to encourage "the Indians to live in an orderly way amongst us." In Cambridge, the Reverend John Eliot labored to create and print a 1,200-page Indian Bible. Officials at Harvard, committed by their charter to the "education of the English and Indian youth of this Country," erected a well-publicized Indian College.

The Chesapeake Bay Colonies

On Chesapeake Bay, settlers' relations with the Indians remained strained at best during the first half of the seventeenth century. In 1608, in an effort to secure the support of Indian leadership, the English performed an elaborate ceremony granting a scarlet cloak and a copper crown to Chief Powhatan. But two years later, suspicious that he was harboring runaway colonists, the English burned the nearest Indian villages and unthinkingly destroyed much-needed corn. A wife of one Indian leader, taken captive, watched English soldiers throwing her children in the river and shooting them in the head before she herself was stabbed to death.

In what ways did the rapid spread of tobacco help or hurt the Chesapeake colonies?

For both sides, hopes of reconciliation rose briefly in 1614 with the match between Pocahontas, daughter of Powhatan, and John Rolfe, the prominent widower who had introduced tobacco. But the marriage proved brief; Pocahontas died in England three years later, after bearing one child. Leaders intended the wedding alliance as a diplomatic gesture toward peace. But it did little to curtail the settlers' bitterness over their lingering dependence on Indian supplies, or Native Americans' resentment regarding English encroachment and arrogance.

The Demise of the Virginia Company

Powhatan's death in 1618 brought to power his more militant younger brother, Opechancanough, the leader of the Pamunkey tribe. His encounters with the English had been frequent and unfriendly. By 1618, the English tobacco crop was booming, and more newcomers were arriving annually. Over the next three years, forty-two ships brought 3,500 people to the Chesapeake colony. The influx disheartened the Indians, and Opechancanough and his followers in the Powhatan Confederacy sought ways to end the mounting intrusion.

Briefly, disease seemed to work in the Indians' favor. Immigrants who made the long sea voyage with poor provisions often fell ill in the swampy, unhealthy environment of Jamestown. By 1622, the colony's inhabitants were dying almost as rapidly as newcomers arrived. Sickness had carried off 3,000 residents in the course of only three years. Opechancanough sensed a chance to deliver the finishing blow.

Early in 1622, the Powhatan Confederacy coordinated a sudden offensive along the lower James River. On March 22, Opechancanough's forces surprised the English, attacking the outlying settlements and sparing no one. Of the 1,240 colonists, nearly 350 lost their lives. Warned by an Indian, Jamestown survived the uprising, but hope for peaceful relations ended.

The attack of 1622 fueled opposition to the Virginia Company among disgruntled English investors. In 1624, King James I annulled the company's charter, making Virginia a royal colony controlled by the crown. In the colony's first seventeen years, more than 8,500 people, almost all of them young, had embarked for the Chesapeake. By 1624, only fifteen of every 100 remained alive.

The surviving colonists placed a bounty on Opechancanough's head, but attempts to ambush or poison him failed. The Indian leader lived on, nursing his distrust of the English. In 1644, he inaugurated a second uprising that killed some 500 colonists. But the English settlement had grown too large to eradicate. By this time old age forced the "Great General" to be carried on a litter. When the English finally captured him and brought him to Jamestown in 1646, Opechancanough was too old to walk unassisted. Still, he remained defiant until shot in the back by one of the Englishmen guarding him.

After two years of brutal warfare, the Pamunkey and their allies in the Powhatan Confederacy conceded defeat and submitted to English authority. From then on, they would pay a token annual tribute for the privilege to remain on lands that had once belonged to them. With the way cleared for Chesapeake expansion, land-hungry English settlers appeared in ever-increasing numbers in Virginia and the smaller, younger Maryland colony.

Maryland: The Catholic Refuge

●**⧗**⊢Read the Document
The Charter of Maryland (1632) at
www.myhistorylab.com

Maryland owed its beginnings to George Calvert, a respected Catholic member of England's government. He was named the first Baron of Baltimore, in Ireland, in 1625. Calvert, now Lord Baltimore, had a keen interest in colonization, and in 1632 he petitioned Charles I for land in the Chesapeake. The king granted him 10 million acres adjacent to Virginia, to be named Maryland in honor of England's Catholic queen, Henrietta Maria. The Maryland charter gave the proprietor and his heirs unprecedented personal power, especially in the granting of lands to colonists without limitations based on religious belief.

Because Calvert died before the royal charter took effect, his eldest son, the second Lord Baltimore, took charge of the settlement effort. In 1634, the *Ark* and the *Dove* carried more than 200 settlers—both Protestants and Catholics—to the new colony. There, they established a capital at St. Mary's, near the mouth of the Potomac River. With the execution of the king in 1649 and the creation of an anti-Catholic commonwealth in England, the Calvert family provided a haven in Maryland for their coreligionists. However, Catholics never became a majority in the Chesapeake colony.

In 1649, Maryland's assembly passed an Act Concerning Religion, guaranteeing toleration for all settlers who professed a belief in Jesus Christ. This assertion of religious toleration, though limited, proved too broad for many to stomach. In the 1650s, supporters of the English Puritan cause seized power in Maryland, repealed the act, and briefly ended the Calverts' proprietorship. But by 1660, with the restoration of the Stuart monarchy in England, proprietary rule returned to the prosperous farming colony.

Tobacco Becomes a Way of Life

By 1660, Virginia and Maryland totaled roughly 35,000 settlers, scattered along the edges of the bay and its adjoining tidewater rivers. In contrast to New England, the Chesapeake still could not maintain its colonial population without steady infusions of newcomers. A sickly climate kept life expectancy low, and men continued to outnumber women by more than two to one. Early experiments with oranges, pineapples, and grapes led nowhere. Chesapeake lumber sold well at first, but it was John Rolfe's tobacco plant that emerged as the tidewater's unlikely crop of choice.

Virginia's annual tobacco exports grew from a total weight of 2,000 pounds in 1615 to 500,000 in 1626. By 1630, saturated markets and stiff taxes led to slumping tobacco prices, so Virginians diversified their efforts. The beginning of the Massachusetts Bay colony created a demand for food that Chesapeake farmers met with well-timed coastal shipments. In 1634, they reported selling to "their zealous neighbours of New England tenne thousand bushels

MAP 2.3
CULTURES MEET ON THE CHESAPEAKE

The Chesapeake Region, 1600–1660
- Powhatan Confederacy in 1607
- English settlement by 1650
- New Sweden, 1637–1655
- Maryland boundary in 1632
- Current state boundaries

of corne for their releefe, besides good quantities of beeves, goats and hoggs, whereof this country hath great plentie." Such diversification proved brief, however. By 1640, London was receiving almost 1.4 million pounds of Chesapeake tobacco annually.

Though tobacco prices remained low throughout much of the seventeenth century, new-comers to Virginia and Maryland still managed to eke out a profit. They could grow the plants amid stumps in partially cleared fields. They could learn the many necessary procedures—planting, weeding, worming, suckering, topping, cutting, stripping, and curing—as the crop progressed. In short, it took hard work, but little farming experience, to bring cured tobacco to waterfront docks. Since captains charged by volume rather than weight, planters reduced shipping costs by devising a uniform barrel size and developing ways to press more leaves into each cask.

Still, the problems were formidable. Tobacco depleted the soil rapidly, so crop yields dwindled after several years. Then farmers had to leave their plots fallow, allowing them to recover, while clearing new fields for planting. This time-consuming task forced them onto marginal land that was poorly drained and less fertile. It also moved them away from navigable rivers, raising transportation costs. Storms, droughts, and crop diseases posed constant threats, and dependence on a single product in a distant and uncertain overseas market created added dangers.

By mid-century, Chesapeake tobacco planters worried about market saturation and overproduction. But by then, for better or worse, growing the noxious weed had become a way of life. Virginia and Maryland settlers found themselves enmeshed in the high-risk world of tobacco farming. Dependence on the troublesome crop would expand across the upper South for centuries to come.

CONCLUSION

During half a century, the French, Dutch, and English had all moved to challenge Spanish claims in North America. By 1660, all four of these maritime powers of western Europe had taken aggressive steps to establish permanent footholds on the fringes of the enormous continent. In each instance, the European colonizers benefited first from the presence of knowledgeable Native Americans and then from the sharp decline of those same people through warfare and the onslaught of new diseases.

Granted, warfare with foreign invaders and death from unknown diseases had become a part of Native American history in the preceding century. But the sixteenth century was an era of tentative European exploration. In contrast, the first half of the seventeenth century saw Europeans move beyond occasional forays to permanent colonization. Spain, France, Holland, and England each had formidable assets in Europe and on the high seas. By 1660 all had sponsored colonial settlements that had endured for several generations, and each had begun to taste the seductive fruits of empire in North America and elsewhere.

The English, slowest to become involved in overseas colonization, had caught up with their competitors by 1660. Among European countries, England had proven the most aggressive in forming expansive family-based colonies rather than military garrisons or trading outposts. As a result, by 1660 England's fledgling North American colonies had already outstripped all rivals in total population, and they were growing at an increasing pace, thanks in particular to the rapid expansion in New England. This emerging superiority in numbers would prove advantageous in the imperial clashes that lay ahead.

For Review

√●─[Study and **Review** at www.myhistorylab.com

1. What relevance did Spain's access to the Pacific have to its ambitions for colonization in the New World?

2. Why was Dutch New Netherland more culturally diverse than French Canada?

3. Among the forces shaping early migration to America shown in Figure 2.1 on page 49, which proved most important in colonizing Virginia? New England?

4. For Chesapeake colonists who survived past 1620, what large forces (often beyond their control) shaped their settlement over the next four decades?

Chronology: 1598–1660

1598 Spanish colonize New Mexico.

1607 England's Virginia Company launches colony at Jamestown.

1608 Champlain establishes Quebec.

1610 Santa Fe becomes capital of Spanish New Mexico.

1619 Virginia creates an elected assembly.

1620 *Mayflower* passengers establish Plymouth Colony.

1622 Opechancanough leads surprise attack on Jamestown colonists.

1626 Dutch establish New Amsterdam on Manhattan Island.

1630 English Puritans found Massachusetts Bay Colony.

1636 Antinomian Crisis stirred by Anne Hutchinson divides Massachusetts Bay.

1637 Pequot War in New England.

1641 Montreal established in New France.

1644 Roger Williams obtains charter for his Rhode Island colony.

1649 Parliament executes King Charles I and abolishes the monarchy during England's Civil War.

1660 Restoration of monarchy in England under Charles II.

Key Terms

Burgess A representative elected to the popular branch of the colonial legislature in either Virginia or Maryland. p. 44

Encomienda The Spanish encomienda system, imposed in Spain's American empire, requiring Indian communities to supply labor or pay tribute to a local colonial overlord (identified as an encomendero). p. 34

Headright Under the headright system, English colonial governments granted a fixed amount of land, usually 50 acres, to any head of household for every family member or hired hand that person brought into the colony. Sometimes fewer acres were granted for women and children on the grounds that they would clear and plant less land. p. 44

Iroquois League A Native American confederacy, located in central New York, originally composed of the Cayuga, Mohawk, Oneida, Onondaga, and Seneca Indians, and later including the Tuscarora as well. p. 37

Kachina An Indian religious system, inspired by Mexican traditions, and present in the American Southwest for more than 800 years. The kachina cult used masks for group performances associated with rain, curing, fertility, warfare, and the ancestors. Among many Pueblo and Hopi Indians, this tradition was epitomized by kachina (or katsina) dolls. p. 34

Muse In Greek mythology, one of the nine sister goddesses who preside over music, poetry, and the arts. p. 48

3

Controlling the Edges of the Continent, 1660–1715

I n April 1704, Marguerite Messier Le Sueur, joined by her five children, loaded a large canoe on the Montreal waterfront. She worked with her brother and a guide to prepare for an immense inland journey to a new French outpost on the Gulf of Mexico. There she planned to meet her husband, explorer-trader Pierre-Charles Le Sueur. At age twenty-eight, Marguerite had already been married half her life, having wed Pierre-Charles in 1690 when he was thirty-four and she was only fourteen.

Marguerite was deeply involved, through family ties, in the dramatic changes taking place throughout the vast North American hinterland claimed by France. Her cousin, an adventurous Canadian named Pierre Le Moyne d'Iberville, had established the French colony of Louisiana near the mouth of the Mississippi River in 1699, and three years later Iberville and his younger brother Bienville had started the village of Mobile (near present-day Mobile, Alabama) to serve as the first capital. In 1702, Marguerite's husband, long active in Canada's far-flung western trade, had paddled down the Mississippi, taking furs to the new outpost at Mobile. After building a house for his family there, he accompanied Iberville back to France.

In 1704, confident about the future success of the Louisiana venture, Le Sueur sent word to his wife in Montreal to attempt the inland journey of nearly 2,000 miles to Mobile. Pierre-Charles himself departed from France aboard the *Pelican* for the same destination, hoping to reunite with his family. Marguerite and her party set out from Montreal on April 30, 1704, making their way up river and passing through Lake Ontario and Lake Erie. After more than a year, they reached Kaskaskia in southern Illinois and began to descend the Mississippi River. Marguerite's brother and a daughter died before the travelers finally reached their destination. When the survivors arrived at Mobile in August 1705, more bad news awaited them: the voyage of the *Pelican* had met with disaster.

Marguerite's husband had boarded the ship in France, joining missionaries, soldiers, and potential brides recruited to go to Mobile. But at a stopover in Cuba, Pierre-Charles and others caught yellow fever and died before the immigrants reached Mobile. The town—home to just 160 men and a dozen women—hardly had enough food and shelter for the sickly newcomers, and yellow fever spread quickly. The epidemic swept away forty residents in two months and decimated nearby Indian villages.

Still, life at the outpost persisted. Townsmen welcomed the *Pelican*'s eligible young women, ages fourteen to eighteen, and priests celebrated thirteen marriages within the first three weeks. New children were being born to these couples by the late summer of 1705, when Marguerite arrived from Montreal. Moving into the house her late husband had built, she resumed her maiden name, Marguerite Messier, and determined to begin a fresh chapter of her life in the Louisiana colony.

The changes taking place in North America during Marguerite Messier's lifetime occurred within a broad international context. In the second half of the seventeenth century, European maritime powers were caught up in a global race to expand and protect their overseas empires, and the chessboard was constantly changing. For example, by the 1670s Dutch authorities had been forced to withdraw entirely from North America. As the Dutch departed, the Spanish, French, and English intensified their competition, starting towns wherever possible in order to stake their claims.

In the East, England expanded the number and size of its coastal colonies, creating new port towns along the Atlantic seaboard. English newcomers also pressed inland along numerous rivers to found frontier outposts. Many of these towns (such as William Byrd's trading post that became Richmond, Virginia) appeared at the "fall line," the point where waterfalls blocked passage upstream and provided water power to run grist mills.

Pushing up from the South, meanwhile, Spain struggled to retain its foothold in Florida and New Mexico and to lay claim to parts of Arizona and Texas as well. New Spanish towns appeared at Albuquerque, El Paso, and Pensacola. Of the three competing powers only France, pressing west and south from the St. Lawrence Valley, managed to penetrate the interior of the continent extensively. A string of forts from the Great Lakes to the Gulf of Mexico—Detroit, Peoria, Mobile and others—all came into being under the French flag.

■ **French fort at Mobile, 1705.**

One fundamental question recurred in numerous places: Who has the right to govern? After 1660, boundaries remained vague and structures of control were tenuous. Religious dissenters and political rebels who felt excluded or exploited could openly question the legitimacy of those in charge. In congregations, towns, and whole colonies, challenges to authority arose repeatedly; violent disruptions became familiar experiences.

France and the American Interior

The potential wealth of the North American interior had long intrigued government ministers in France. If Canadian fur traders could explore this vast domain and befriend its Indian inhabitants, France might control some of the continent's most fertile farmland and keep its extensive natural assets out of the hands of European rivals. If the French could recruit enough Native Americans as loyal allies, they might even threaten the rich mines of the Spanish empire in Mexico and challenge the growing English colonies lying to the east of the Appalachian Mountains. But for France to realize such wide ambitions, the French king, Louis XIV, would need to make North American colonization a national priority, and the extent of his commitment remained uncertain.

Why did France gain access to North America's interior before other European powers?

The Rise of the Sun King

King Louis XIV stood at the center of France's expanding imperial sphere. Indeed, so much seemed to revolve around him that he became known as the "Sun King." In 1661, at age twenty-two, he assumed personal control of a realm of 20 million people. During most of his long rule—until his death in 1715 at age seventy-seven—Louis dominated European affairs. Always a builder of monuments, he expanded the Louvre in Paris and then dazzled the French nobility and clergy with his opulent new palace at Versailles.

In religion, the Sun King challenged the Catholic pope on one hand and suppressed French Protestants (Huguenots) on the other. In politics, he centralized the monarchy's power as never before. Louis' administration consolidated the laws of France, strengthened the armed forces, built roads, and expanded commerce. His government ministries foreshadowed the power of modern nation-states by regulating industry and imposing tariffs and taxes.

Throughout Louis XIV's reign, his officials followed a set of policies known as **mercantilism**, a system in which a government stressed economic self-sufficiency and a favorable balance of trade. By avoiding foreign debts and drawing in valuable resources from its competitors and its own colonies, a state could pay for wars abroad and costly projects at home. The French mercantilist strategy was to exploit labor efficiently and import raw materials cheaply, while exporting expensive manufactured products, such as glassware, wine, silk, and tapestries, in exchange for gold and silver. Colonists were expected to generate much-needed natural resources and to consume manufactured goods from the mother country.

In Paris, finance minister Jean-Baptiste Colbert emerged as the chief architect of this strategy of aggressive mercantilism. At home he taxed foreign imports, removed domestic trade barriers, and improved internal transportation. Moreover, he reduced worker holidays and outlawed strikes. Colbert improved France's ports and created a code to regulate maritime shipping. He expanded the naval fleet and pressed French sailors into its service. Pushing still harder, he organized overseas trading companies and provided insurance for their expensive ventures. In addition, he sanctioned France's involvement in the African slave trade. Colbert yearned to acquire new territory to increase the empire's self-sufficiency and keep overseas resources out of enemy hands. To that end, he and his successors encouraged French exploration of North America on an unprecedented scale.

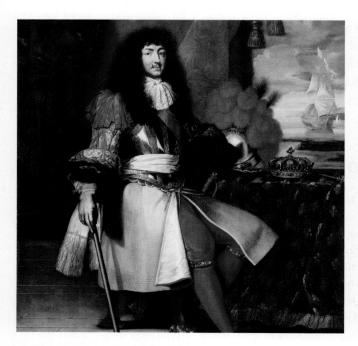

■ **Portrait of Louis XIV, the Sun King.**

The government of Louis XIV assumed direct control over New France from a private company in 1663. Colbert hoped to diversify production away from the fur trade, so he shipped artisans to the colony, plus livestock and tools. To promote domestic life and population growth, the government also transported young single women and announced cash incentives for early marriages and large families. Many of the soldiers sent to protect New France from Iroquois and English threats stayed on to establish farms.

On balance, however, Colbert's plans for a prosperous, well-populated colony failed. The small population of New France—10,000 by 1680—never grew as rapidly as French imperial strategists desired. The harsh winters and short growing seasons hindered the expansion of agriculture. Also, Louis XIV imposed restrictions to make sure that any colonist sent overseas was a pious and loyal Catholic. In 1685, when he revoked the Edict of Nantes (which had granted French Protestants their legal rights), thousands of frightened Huguenots prepared to leave the country. But the king forbade the dissenters from traveling to France's colonies. In contrast to the English, the French did not use their overseas colonies as havens for outcasts, troublemakers, and religious dissidents.

■ **MAP 3.1**
FRANCE IN THE AMERICAN INTERIOR, 1670–1720

Routes of important French explorations

La Salle, 1670	La Salle's party, 1687
Joliet and Marquette, 1673	Iberville, 1699
La Salle, 1679–1682	St. Denis, 1714
La Salle and colonists from France, 1685	La Harpe, 1719
† Spanish Missions 1716–1717	French Fort
	■ Spanish settlements

Present state boundaries provided for orientation

Exploring the Mississippi Valley

In New France, intrepid explorers had probed steadily across the Great Lakes, reaching the western shores of Lake Michigan in 1634. There, Winnebago Indians (today's Ho-Chunk Nation) told of a river called the "Messisipi," and rumors of this river circulated among the French for a generation. Finally, in 1673, trader Louis Jolliet, joined by a Jesuit priest named Jacques Marquette, entered the upper Mississippi and descended the great stream to the mouth of the Arkansas River. If the Mississippi waterway flowed south into the Gulf of Mexico, instead of west to the Pacific as some explorers hoped, perhaps the river could give France a path to the wealth of New Spain and provide French settlers with access to a warm-water port.

Avantures mal-heureuses du Sieur de la Salle.

■ When La Salle's French expedition landed on the Texas coast in 1685, one ship ran aground and broke up; another departed quickly from Matagorda Bay. La Salle's colonists only had the *Belle* (foreground), and it sank in a storm the following year. In 1995, archaeologists found the vessel in shallow water and salvaged the remains.

Officials in Quebec moved to exploit these western prospects, making effective use of an experienced young adventurer: René-Robert Cavelier, Sieur de La Salle. In 1679, inspired by word of Jolliet's exploits, La Salle and his men pushed west through the Great Lakes to erect forts on the Illinois River, a tributary of the Mississippi. These outposts strengthened French trading ties with local Indians and provided a launching point for exploring the Mississippi Valley. In 1682, La Salle led a contingent of French and Indians south from the Illinois to the mouth of the great river, showing that it emptied into the Gulf of Mexico. Before returning to Canada and France, he claimed the entire river basin for France, naming it "Louisiana" to honor his king.

But La Salle, hindered by poor maps and crude navigational instruments, had miscalculated the position of the Mississippi's mouth. Therefore, when he tried to return by sea, sailing from France with four ships and several hundred colonists, he mistakenly disembarked on the Texas coast early in 1685. Slowly, the entire colonization plan unraveled. When one ship sank near shore, the hapless settlers lost valuable supplies and any hope of relocating. Jealous lieutenants eventually killed La Salle before he could find the Mississippi River. Most of the colonists he had brought from France perished in the Texas wilderness.

King William's War in the Northeast

The French colonizers had overreached themselves. They had failed to challenge Spanish power in the Gulf of Mexico or to establish a southern port. The lure of finding a westward route to the Pacific continued. But in the East, French Canadians faced renewed Iroquois attacks along the St. Lawrence River in the 1680s. Moreover, a strengthened Protestant regime emerged in London with the ascent of William III to the English throne in 1689. This transition started more than 100 years of bitter conflict between Protestant England and Catholic France, an ideological and military struggle that often included North America.

The American conflict began in the Northeast with the outbreak of King William's War in 1689, when the Iroquois, well supplied with English arms, launched raids near Montreal. The French struck back, sending parties south to terrorize the English frontier, setting fire to outposts in New York and New England. At Fort Loyal (modern Portland, Maine) raiders butchered 100 English men, women, and children who had surrendered, and they took others captive. Leaving their dead unburied, the survivors fled south toward Salem and Boston in Massachusetts. Many who experienced the attack viewed it as part of a wider design to undo the Reformation and expand the authority of the Catholic Church.

After eight years of bloodshed, King William's War ended in a stalemate in 1697. Hurt by the hostilities, the Iroquois soon promised to remain neutral during any future colonial wars between France and England, a pledge they generally honored for more than half a century. The French, having strengthened their position in Canada, revived the "southern strategy" for a Gulf Coast colony that had so obsessed Colbert and La Salle.

A turn in European events opened the door for renewed French efforts in the American heartland. King Carlos II of Spain fell ill without an immediate heir, and the royal courts of

Europe competed to determine his successor. Louis XIV, eager to acquire Spain's European realm and American dominions for France, proposed that his grandson, Philip of Anjou, receive the Spanish crown. But England supported an opposing candidate, so the War of Spanish Succession (1701–1714) broke out soon after Carlos died.

Founding the Louisiana Colony

Even before new hostilities erupted in Europe in 1701, Louis XIV and his ministers took steps to secure French claims in the Gulf of Mexico, despite Spain's naval dominance in the area. By renewing La Salle's plan for a Louisiana colony, France could strengthen its hand in the impending war over succession to the Spanish throne. A colony on the Gulf of Mexico would provide a southern outlet for the French fur trade and a strategic outpost to counter Spain's new fort at Pensacola in western Florida.

England also saw advantages to establishing a base on the lower Mississippi. Such a post could challenge Spanish and French claims to the Gulf region and increase English trade with the Chickasaw and other southern Indians. In 1698, a London promoter quietly made plans to transport a group of Huguenot refugees to the mouth of the Mississippi. Catching wind of this scheme, the French organized their own secret expedition to the Gulf of Mexico under an aspiring Canadian officer, Pierre Le Moyne d'Iberville.

Coming from a large and well-connected Montreal family, the Le Moynes, Iberville quickly drew several siblings into the gulf colonization plan, including his teenage brother, Bienville. Iberville and his party sailed for the Gulf of Mexico from the French port of Brest in 1699. Their ship entered the mouth of the Mississippi in time to repel the English expedition at a site on the river still known as English Turn. They also managed to build a fort at nearby Biloxi Bay before returning to France.

The two brothers were now well on their way to creating the Gulf Coast colony that La Salle and his followers had failed to establish. A second voyage let Iberville conduct further reconnaissance of the lower Mississippi. On a third trip, in 1702, he established Fort Louis, near Mobile Bay, giving French traders access to the Choctaw Indians. Young Bienville, placed in charge of Fort Louis, labored to sustain the tiny outpost at Mobile. Iberville himself left to pursue other schemes and died an early death in 1706.

Enmeshed in the War of Spanish Succession, France ignored its new Gulf colony. Epidemics reduced Louisiana's newcomers and took a far heavier toll on Indian neighbors. Settlers drawn from Canada, with prior wilderness experience, maintained close ties with local Native Americans and resented the incompetence and haughtiness of colonists sent from France. The latter complained about the poor living conditions and looked down on the uneducated Canadians. However, despite social friction and a chronic lack of supplies from France, the small community at Mobile survived.

Far to the north, additional posts reinforced French territorial claims, fostered the fur trade, and protected neighboring Indians against Iroquois raids. The village of Peoria sprang up on the Illinois River in 1691. Catholic missions appeared nearby at Cahokia (1697) and Kaskaskia (1703). Fort de Chartres took shape in southern Illinois in 1719. Further north, the French established two other strategic posts. In 1689, they laid out a garrison where Lake Huron joins Lake Michigan. In 1701, they created a lasting town on the strait (*le détroit* in French) connecting Lake Erie to Lake Huron. The founder of this village, Antoine de La Mothe Cadillac, foresaw a prosperous future for the new trading post, since Detroit would be accessible "to the most distant tribes which surround these vast sweet water seas."

In 1712 the French crown, its resources depleted by a decade of warfare in Europe, granted control over Louisiana to a powerful Paris merchant, Antoine Crozat. Drawing Cadillac from Detroit to serve as Louisiana's governor general, Crozat hoped to develop

been linked with the Spanish over several generations. The attackers were embittered by colonial slave raids that took Indian captives to work in Mexican silver mines. In retaliation, these raiding parties, riding stolen Spanish horses, killed livestock and seized scarce food. When colonial soldiers proved unable to fend off the hit-and-run attacks, their credibility among local Pueblo Indians weakened.

Third, a smoldering controversy over religion flared during the 1670s. When an epidemic struck in 1671, Spanish missionaries could not stem the sickness with Christian

INTERPRETING HISTORY

Large Enough to Be Called a City

Jean-Jacques Rousseau's Enlightenment ideas about the "noble savage." Today, some scholars suspect Letter XVI

Numbers were equally large upstream, where Lahontan's party received "a very honorable reception" at the towns

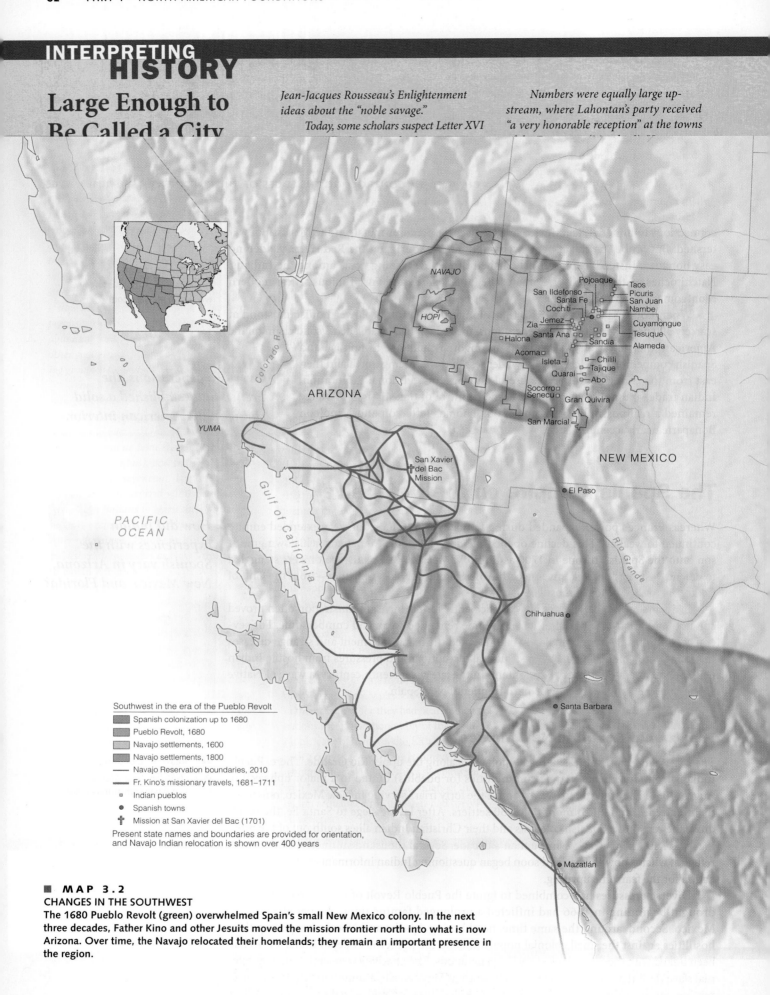

Southwest in the era of the Pueblo Revolt

- Spanish colonization up to 1680
- Pueblo Revolt, 1680
- Navajo settlements, 1600
- Navajo settlements, 1800
- Navajo Reservation boundaries, 2010
- Fr. Kino's missionary travels, 1681–1711
- □ Indian pueblos
- ● Spanish towns
- ✝ Mission at San Xavier del Bac (1701)

Present state names and boundaries are provided for orientation, and Navajo Indian relocation is shown over 400 years

■ MAP 3.2
CHANGES IN THE SOUTHWEST

The 1680 Pueblo Revolt (green) overwhelmed Spain's small New Mexico colony. In the next three decades, Father Kino and other Jesuits moved the mission frontier north into what is now Arizona. Over time, the Navajo relocated their homelands; they remain an important presence in the region.

prayers. In response, traditionalist Indian priests revived age-old Pueblo religious customs. Horrified, the Spanish friars and government officials punished what they saw as backsliding away from Catholicism within the Pueblo population. At Santa Fe in 1675, they hanged three Indian leaders for idolatry and whipped and imprisoned

■ Horses and sheep arrived in the Southwest with the Spanish, and both became central to the Navajo (or Diné) culture in northern Arizona and New Mexico. Navajo women continue to herd sheep and weave their wool into rugs and blankets, as they have done for more than three centuries.

forty-three others—including a militant leader from San Juan pueblo named Popé. Before the captives could be sold into slavery, armed Indians successfully demanded the release of Popé and the other prisoners.

Popé withdrew to Taos, the northernmost pueblo in New Mexico. From there, he negotiated secretly with like-minded factions in other pueblos, unifying resistance to Spanish domination and forging an underground movement. In part, he built support around widespread resentment of the Spanish **encomienda** system (requiring Indian communities to supply labor or pay tribute) and the Catholic Church (which forbade traditional Indian religious ceremonies). Indian women whom Spanish priests or soldiers had abused took Popé's side in this cultural clash. The movement also received covert support from numerous **mestizos** and **mulattos**, mixed-race people whose lack of "pure" Spanish blood cost them any chance for advancement. Popé sent runners to each conspiring pueblo, fixing the date for the rebellion. When the time came, his Pueblo warriors swiftly routed their adversaries. Unified in triumph, the zealous victors smeared excrement on Christian altars and bathed themselves to remove the stigma of baptism.

But initial cohesion gave way to friction. The successful rebels soon quarreled over who should hold power and how best to return to ancient ways. Kivas would replace churches, and the cross would give way to the **kachina**. But what other parts of the imported culture should the Indians abandon? Various Pueblo groups could not agree on which Spanish words, tools, and customs to discard or which foreign crops and animals to retain.

In 1681, the Pueblo fended off a Spanish attempt at reconquest. But they remained divided among themselves and more vulnerable than ever to Apache raids. Within a decade, rival factions had deposed Popé, and another Spanish colonial army, under Governor Diego de Vargas, had entered New Mexico. It took the new governor several years to subdue the province, and the Pueblo managed another full-scale rebellion in 1696. But Vargas anticipated the revolt and crushed the opposition, just as Oñate had done a century earlier. In 1706, several soldiers and their families established the town of Albuquerque. Learning from prior mistakes, Spanish officials did not reimpose the hated *encomienda* system. A new generation of Franciscan missionaries tolerated indigenous Pueblo traditions as long as the Indians also attended Catholic mass.

Navajo and Spanish on the Southwestern Frontier

The repercussions of rebellion and reconquest along the upper Rio Grande echoed through the Southwest. To the north, Pueblo refugees joined the Navajo and brought valuable experience as corn farmers. Corn, already known to the Navajo, now became an increasingly important food and sacred symbol for them.

Moreover, these Pueblo refugees shared knowledge learned from the Spanish about planting peach orchards and raising sheep. Navajo women—the weavers in their society— soon owned large flocks and created wool blankets on their traditional portable looms. The Pueblo also brought more Spanish horses, a key asset that let the Navajo spread their domain west into fine grazing country in what is now northeast Arizona.

Despite limited resources, authorities in Mexico City sent missionaries north to spread Christianity to hostile Indians near the Gulf of California. Year by year, these friar-explorers edged toward what is now southern Arizona, reaching the cactus-studded landscape of the Sonoran Desert by the 1690s.

Eusebio Kino, a tireless Jesuit missionary born in Italy and educated in Germany, spearheaded the early exploration of the Arizona region. In 1701, this padre on horseback established a mission at San Xavier del Bac, below modern Tucson. But Father Kino's missions languished after his death in 1711. Twenty-five years later, a silver strike at "Arizonac," near present-day Nogales on the U.S.-Mexican border, provided a new name for the region, which would eventually become the state called Arizona.

Borderland Conflict in Texas and Florida

The encounters on Spain's other North American frontiers took different forms, in part because European rivals appeared on the scene. Conflict with the French led the Spanish to found missions in Texas, a land they named after the local Tejas Indians. At first, responding to news about La Salle's ill-fated French colony, the Spanish made a brief attempt to establish a Texas mission in 1690, departing again in 1693. They renewed their effort two decades later, after Governor Cadillac sent explorers from Louisiana across eastern Texas to forge ties with Spanish communities south of the Rio Grande. Eager to open trade with the Spanish, these French visitors reached San Juan Bautista, below the modern U.S.-Mexican border, in 1714.

Spanish authorities, taken by surprise, dusted off plans for colonizing Texas. By 1717, they had established half a dozen small missions near the Sabine River, the boundary between modern Texas and Louisiana. The next year, to expand their missionary activities and secure the supply route from San Juan Bautista to these distant outposts in east Texas, the Spanish built a cluster of settlements beside the San Antonio River, at a midpoint in the trail. Within two decades, a string of missions stretched along the river. Indian converts tended herds of cattle and sheep and constructed aqueducts to irrigate new fields of wheat and corn. The earliest mission, San Antonio de Valero (1718), provided a nucleus for the town of San Antonio. Later known as the Alamo, the mission also strengthened Spanish claims to Texas against threats of French intrusion.

During the second half of the seventeenth century, the Indians of Florida, like the Pueblo in New Mexico, debated whether to reject generations of Spanish rule. The Columbian Exchange had altered their lives in dramatic ways. They ate new foods such as figs, oranges, peas, and cabbages. They used Spanish words—*azucár* (sugar), *botija* (jar), *caballo* (horse)—and metal hoes from Europe allowed them to produce more corn. But expanding contact with missionaries created major problems as well. By 1660 devastating epidemics had whittled away at Florida's Native American towns. The Indians still outnumbered the newcomers more than ten to one, but they had to expend enormous energy raising, processing, and hauling food for the Spanish. When colonists grew fearful of French and English attacks after 1670, they forced hundreds of Indians to perform even more grueling labor: constructing the stone fortress of San Marcos at St. Augustine.

Nothing proved more troubling to Florida's Indians than the spread of livestock farming. St. Augustine's elite had established profitable cattle ranches on the depopulated savannas of Timucua, near present-day Gainesville in north-central Florida. These entrepreneurs ignored requirements to keep cows away from unfenced Indian gardens, and they enforced harsh laws to protect their stock. Any Florida Indian who killed cattle faced four months of servitude; people caught raiding Spanish herds had their ears cut off.

Resentment grew in Florida's scattered mission villages. Restless Indian converts wondered whether the English, who had founded their Carolina colony in 1670, might make viable allies. The English seemed eager to trade for deerskins, and they offered the Native Americans a steadier supply of desirable goods than the Spanish could provide. Several Indian communities moved closer to Carolina to test this new alternative for trade. But when France and Spain joined forces against the English after 1700, Florida's Indians found themselves caught up in a struggle far larger than they had bargained for.

> *During the second half of the seventeenth century, the Indians of Florida, like the Pueblo in New Mexico, debated whether to reject generations of Spanish rule.*

Ever since the days of Francis Drake, the English had schemed to oust the Spanish from St. Augustine. In 1702, led by South Carolina Governor James Moore, English raiders and their Indian allies rampaged through the Florida town. Yet the new stone fortress of San Marcos held firm, protecting the inhabitants. Two years later, Moore invaded Apalachee (near modern Tallahassee). His troops crushed the mission towns, killing hundreds and carrying away more than 4,000 Indian captives. Most of them were women and children, whom the English sold as slaves. By 1706, the mission villages in Apalachee and Timucua lay in ruins.

England's American Empire Takes Shape

In 1660, as Louis XIV began his long reign in France and Spanish missionaries labored in obscurity in New Mexico and Florida, England experienced a counterrevolutionary upheaval that dramatically influenced American colonial affairs. Amid violent civil war, rebels supporting Puritans and Parliament defeated the royal army and overthrew the ruling Stuart family. In 1649, they tried and executed King Charles I, and then abolished hereditary monarchy altogether.

What are the contrasting origins of England's Restoration-Era American colonies?

For a brief period, England became a republican commonwealth without a king. But Oliver Cromwell, the movement's dictatorial leader and self-styled Lord Protector, died in 1658. Pressures quickly mounted to undo the radical Puritan Revolution and return to monarchical government. In May 1660, a strong coalition of conservative interests welcomed the late king's son back from exile and restored him to the throne as King Charles II. The renewed Stuart dynasty ruled from 1660 to 1688, a period remembered in English politics and culture as the **Restoration Era**.

The shift in London's political winds could hardly have been more sudden, and Charles II moved quickly in 1660 to underscore the end of England's Puritan experiment. He ordered the execution of those who had beheaded his father. Many who had fought to end monarchy and strengthen Parliament sought refuge in the American colonies when their religious and political beliefs abruptly fell out of favor at home. But other elements of colonial demographics—early marriage, high birth rates, and a low level of mortality in most places—did even more to prompt expansion up and down the Atlantic coast.

Monarchy Restored and Navigation Controlled

Because most English colonists still lived within fifty miles of the Atlantic, an increase in people steadily broadened the opportunities for seaborne trade. Growing ship traffic, in turn, sparked government desires to regulate colonial navigation to benefit the restored monarchy. In 1660, Parliament passed a major new law, based on mercantilism, designed to promote English shipping and trade.

The Navigation Act of 1660 laid out important conditions that shaped England's colonial commerce for generations. First, merchants could not conduct trade to or from the English colonies in foreign-owned ships. Second, key non-English products imported from foreign lands—salt, wine, oil, and naval stores (the tar, pitch, masts, and other materials used to build boats)—had to be carried in English ships or in ships with mostly English crews. Third, the law contained a list of "enumerated articles" produced overseas—tobacco, cotton, sugar, ginger, indigo, and dyewoods—that could no longer be sent directly from a colony to a foreign European port. Instead, merchants had to ship them to England first and then reexport them, a step that directly boosted England's domestic economy. Another Navigation Act (1663) required that goods moving from the European continent to England's overseas colonies must pass through England, arriving and departing on English ships.

A later measure—the Plantation Duty Act of 1673—tried to close loopholes regarding enumerated articles. The new act required captains to pay a "plantation duty" before they sailed between colonial ports with enumerated goods. Otherwise, colonial vessels carrying such goods had to post bond before leaving harbor to ensure that they would sail directly to England. To enforce these rules, the government sent customs officers to the colonies for the first time. Backed by the Navigation Acts, England's fleets grew and colonial trade became a major sector in England's economy.

Even the Great Plague, which swept England in 1665, could not blunt this mercantile growth. And when a catastrophic fire destroyed most of London the next year, planners redesigned the city with the broad streets and impressive buildings that suited the prosperous hub of an expanding empire. The fashionable coffee shops that sprang up as a novelty in late-seventeenth-century London became common meeting places for exchanging news and views about England's increasingly profitable activities overseas.

Multituds flying from London by water in boats & barges.

Flying by land.

Burying the dead with a bell before them.   Searchers.

Carts full of dead to bury.

■ Images of the Great Plague in London (1665).

Dutch New Netherland Becomes New York

At the beginning of his reign, Charles II knew he had to build loyalty and strengthen an economy weakened by civil war. The king, with expensive tastes and a depleted treasury, found that he could reward loyal family members and supporters, at no cost to the crown, by granting them control over pieces of England's North American domain. With this prospect in hand, the king and his ministers sought to bolster foreign trade, strengthen the royal navy, and outstrip England's commercial rivals. They focused first on the Dutch.

As London stepped up its search for new profits, English officials moved to strengthen control over existing colonies and establish (or seize) new ones wherever possible. The Navigation Acts cut sharply into the Dutch carrying trade and spurred a decade of renewed warfare between England and Holland. For the most part, these intermittent Anglo-Dutch Wars ended in stalemate. But at the final Peace of Westminster in 1674, the English emerged with several important gains in Africa and America.

Read the **Document**

Navigation Acts at
www.myhistorylab.com

In West Africa, the English captured and held several key coastal outposts: an island at the mouth of the river Gambia (renamed James Fort for the Duke of York) and Cape Coast Castle on the Gold Coast (near Elmina, the African headquarters of the Dutch West India Company). This encroachment challenged Dutch dominance of commerce with Africa for gold and ivory. It also gave England the footholds it needed to force its way into the Atlantic slave trade. Charles II had already moved to take advantage of the situation. He granted a monopoly to the Royal Adventurers into Africa (1663) and then the Royal African Company (1672) to exploit the grim but highly profitable slave traffic. Within several generations, this ruthless initiative reshaped England's American colonies at enormous human cost.

Across the Atlantic, the English had seized the Dutch colony of New Netherland and its poorly defended port of New Amsterdam. Charles II claimed that the land had belonged to England from the time his grandfather endorsed the Virginia Company in 1606. In 1664, the king used his royal prerogative to regain control of this domain. He issued a charter putting the entire region between the Delaware and Connecticut rivers under the personal control of his brother James, Duke of York. That same year, James sent a fleet to claim his prize. When Governor Peter Stuyvesant surrendered the Dutch colony without a fight, both the province and its capital on Manhattan Island each received the name New York. Fort Orange on the Hudson became Albany because England's traditional name was *Albion*.

The Duke of York controlled an enormous domain (including the Dutch and English settlements on Long Island), and he wielded nearly absolute powers over his new dukedom. James never visited New York, but as proprietor, he chose the colony's governor. That official ruled with an appointed council and enforced "the Duke's Laws" without constraint by any assembly. English newcomers to the colony resented the absence of an elected legislature, and the governor finally authorized an elected body in 1683. But when the new assemblymen approved a Charter of Liberties endorsing government by consent of the governed, the Duke of York disallowed the legislature.

Married women living in New Netherland lost ground in the transition to English rule. Dutch law codes had ensured their full legal status, whereas English common law assigned wives to an inferior status known as **coverture**. They could not own property or keep control over money they earned, and they lacked any independent standing before the law.

As the English asserted political control over New York, the Dutch presence remained evident everywhere. Many English married into Dutch families and worshiped in the Dutch Reformed Church. English-speaking New Yorkers borrowed such Dutch words as *waffle*, *cookie*, *coleslaw*, and *baas* (boss). Anyone who was bilingual, such as Albany merchant Robert Livingston, had a special advantage. Livingston, an immigrant from Scotland, had learned to speak Dutch in Holland in his youth. His marriage linked him to powerful Dutch families in the Hudson Valley, and much of his early wealth came from his ability to translate commercial documents between English and Dutch.

The New Restoration Colonies

Charles II had spurred England's seizure of New Netherland by issuing a charter for control of the contested region to his brother, the Duke of York. To reward supporters, the king continued issuing royal charters for American land, hoping to expand colonization at no cost to the crown. In 1670, for example, he granted a charter to the Hudson's Bay Company. The deal gave the company's proprietors a monopoly on trade, minerals, and land across northern Canada. Farther south, Charles used charters to redistribute control along major portions of the Atlantic coast. His actions prompted an unprecedented scramble for colonial property and profits. Within decades, the English launched important settlement clusters along the Delaware River valley and the Carolina coast. Each depended upon lucrative charters for a small network of friends.

Well-placed people belonged to the Councils for Trade and Plantations in London. Created in 1660, these groups linked England's powerful merchants with crown officials.

Most of these well-placed people belonged to the Councils for Trade and Plantations in London. Created in 1660, these advisory groups linked England's powerful merchants with crown officials. When Charles II issued a charter for Carolina in 1663, five of its eight initial proprietors served on those councils. In 1665, two of these same eight men became the proprietors of New Jersey. In addition, three of the eight played an active role in the Royal African Company, four became founders of the Hudson's Bay Company, and five became initial proprietors of the Bahamas.

Occasionally, Charles reached beyond this small group of friends. In 1679, he made New Hampshire a proprietorship (an ill-fated experiment that lasted to 1708). In 1681, he paid off a debt to Quaker aristocrat William Penn by granting him a charter for Pennsylvania. (The generous arrangement included the "Lower Counties" that became Delaware in 1704.)

Penn's "holy experiment" to create a Quaker refuge benefited from earlier colonization south of New York. Dutch and Swedish settlers had inhabited the lower Delaware Valley for more than a generation. In 1665, the Duke of York carved off a portion of his vast proprietorship, granting the area between the Delaware and the Hudson to two friends: Lord John Berkeley and Sir George Carteret. They named the area New Jersey because Carteret had been born on the Isle of Jersey in the English Channel. Berkeley and Carteret promptly announced liberal "Concessions"—a representative assembly and freedom of worship—to attract rent-paying newcomers from England and the existing colonies. But their plans for profit made little headway.

In 1674, the proprietors divided these fertile lands into two separate provinces. East Jersey—where Newark was established in 1666—attracted Puritan families from New England, Dutch farmers from New York, and failed planters from Barbados. West Jersey was sold to members of the Society of Friends (including William Penn) who inaugurated a Quaker experiment along the Delaware River. Filled with egalitarian beliefs, the Quakers created a one-house **unicameral** legislature, used secret ballots, and gave more power to juries than to judges. Their forward-looking "Concessions and Agreements" of 1677 barred taxation without the consent of the governed. West Jersey's idealistic effort foundered within decades, and by 1702 all New Jersey came under crown control as a single royal colony. But by then, the Quakers had established a foothold in the neighboring colony of Pennsylvania.

●◖• ⌐Read the Document

Penn, Description of Pennsylvania (1681) at **www.myhistorylab.com**

Contrasting Worlds: Pennsylvania and Carolina

Proprietor William Penn laid out his capital for the Pennsylvania colony in 1682, naming it Philadelphia. Within two decades, this market center had more than 2,000 inhabitants. An earnest Quaker, Penn professed pacifism. He made it a point to deal fairly with the Lenni-Lenape (Delaware) Indians. After purchasing their land, he resold it on generous terms to English, Dutch, and Welsh Quakers who agreed to pay him an annual premium, called a **quitrent**. He also emphasized religious tolerance. A growing stream of German Protestants and others facing persecution in Europe began to flow into Pennsylvania after 1700.

Penn drew inspiration from James Harrington, the English political philosopher. Harrington's book *Oceana* (1656) argued that the best way to create an enduring republic was for one person to draft and implement its constitution. After endless tinkering, Penn devised a progressive "Frame of Government" that allowed for trial by jury, limited terms of office, and no use of capital punishment except in cases of treason and murder. But he remained ambivalent about legislative democracy. Settlers resented his scheme for a lower house that could approve acts drafted by the governor but could not initiate laws. In a new Charter of Privileges in 1701, Penn agreed to the creation of a unicameral legislature with full lawmaking powers. Penn's expansive proprietorship belonged to his descendants until colonial rule ended in 1776.

In contrast to William Penn, the proprietors of the new Carolina colony—which split into North and South Carolina a generation later—aspired to establish a stable aristocratic system. Their leader, Anthony Ashley-Cooper, also drew inspiration from Harrington, since *Oceana* stressed that land distribution determined the nature of any commonwealth. Ashley-Cooper (later the first Earl of Shaftesbury) worked in 1669 with his young secretary, John Locke (later an influential political philosopher), to prepare a set of "Fundamental Constitutions." They proposed a stratified society in which hereditary nobles controlled much of the land and wealthy manor lords employed a lowly servant class of "leetmen." Their unrealistic document tried to revive the elaborate feudal hierarchy of medieval times.

The new government framework also endorsed racial slavery, declaring that "Every Freeman of Carolina shall have absolute Power and Authority over his Negro Slaves." This endorsement was not surprising, given the proprietors' involvement with England's new slave-trading monopoly in Africa and their initial recruitment of settlers in 1670 from the Caribbean sugar island of Barbados. When Carolina colonists relocated Charlestown (later Charleston) between the Ashley and Cooper rivers in 1680, the proprietors had already modified aspects of their complicated scheme, setting aside feudalism to encourage greater immigration. Nevertheless, their endorsement of slavery shaped the region's society for hundreds of years.

Bloodshed in the English Colonies: 1670–1690

The appearance of English settlements along the Atlantic coast did little, in most places, to alter the traditional rhythms of life. Year after year, the daily challenges of subsistence dominated American life for Indians and colonists alike. The demanding seasonal tasks of clearing fields, planting seeds, and harvesting crops remained interwoven with the incessant chores of providing clothing, securing shelter, and sustaining community.

Over time, however, changing circumstances in America and Europe introduced new pressures up and down the Atlantic seaboard. On occasion after 1670, familiar routines gave way to episodes of bloodshed that threatened to tear whole colonies apart. Elsewhere in North America, Pueblo rebels were resisting the Spanish in New Mexico, and Iroquois warriors were challenging the French in Illinois country. The English, with their larger numbers, posed an even greater cultural and economic problem for Native American inhabitants.

In 1675 embittered Indians rose up across southern New England in Metacom's War (or King Philip's War). The next year, frontier tensions in Virginia sparked the upheaval known as Bacon's Rebellion. A decade later, events in England prompted further tremors. In London, mounting opposition forced the unpopular James II to surrender the English throne to William of Orange. Parliament emerged from this "Glorious Revolution" with enhanced powers. In America, the end of rule by the Stuart dynasty was punctuated by controversy and violence in one colony after another.

To what degree was colonial violence after 1670 sparked by internal tensions, or by affairs in England?

On occasion after 1670, familiar routines gave way to episodes of bloodshed that threatened to tear whole colonies apart.

Metacom's War in New England

By 1675, the Indians of southern New England, like the Pueblo in New Mexico, had endured several generations of colonization. Yet they disagreed over how much English culture they should adopt. Many used English words for trading, English pots for cooking, and English weapons for hunting. Some had converted to Christianity, living in protected "praying towns." Several young men had enrolled in Harvard's Indian College, where they learned to write English and Latin with an eye toward entering the ministry.

Massasoit, the Wampanoag **sachem** (leader) who had assisted the Pilgrims at Plymouth, made sure that his sons, Wamsutta and Metacom, learned English ways. The two men raised pigs and fired guns, and the colonists called them Alexander and Philip, after the kings of ancient Macedon. But when Wamsutta died in the 1660s, shortly after succeeding his father, Metacom (now called King Philip) suspected foul play by the English. And Metacom had other grievances. Colonial traders made the Indians drunk and then cheated them. English livestock trampled Wampanoag corn, and if Indians shot the cattle, colonial courts imposed punishments. Worst of all, colonists now outnumbered the remaining 20,000 Indians in southern New England by more than two to one.

When a white man shot and wounded a Native American in 1675, it triggered a long-expected conflict. Metacom's warriors ravaged towns along the Connecticut River valley and closer to the coast, using the victories to recruit additional Indian allies. The colonists, unprepared after forty years of peace and unchallenged dominance, were caught off guard. Distrusting even the Christian Indians, Massachusetts officials relocated whole praying towns of Indian converts to windswept Deer Island in Boston Harbor.

By December, the Connecticut and Rhode Island colonies, terrified of being wiped out, united with Plymouth and Massachusetts Bay to create a force of more than 1,000 men. An Indian captive led them to a stronghold of the still-neutral Narragansett in a swamp a dozen miles west of Newport, Rhode Island. The colonists surprised and overwhelmed the fortified village, setting it ablaze during the fierce fighting. Indian survivors fled, leaving behind more than 600 dead. Many of the men, women, and children were "terribly Barbikew'd," minister Cotton Mather later recorded.

This "Great Swamp Fight," reminiscent of an earlier battle in the Pequot War, infuriated the Narragansett survivors, who joined Metacom's growing alliance. But as spring arrived in 1676, the coalition weakened and the tide turned. Sickness broke out among the fighters, who lacked food and gunpowder. The powerful Mohawk of the Iroquois Confederacy opposed Metacom from the west. Numerous Christian Indians joined the colonial forces, despite their painful internment at Boston's Deer Island.

With Metacom facing defeat, defections increased. In August, a former ally betrayed the resistance leader, shot him, and delivered his head to the English. As the struggle ground to a close, the colonists captured Metacom's wife and child, selling them into slavery in the West Indies along with hundreds of other prisoners of war. New England's remaining Indians became second-class inhabitants, confined to reservation-like enclaves, while the colonists soon rebuilt and extended their domain.

Bacon's Rebellion in Virginia

While smoke still billowed over New England, new flames broke out in Virginia. Social unrest had been growing under the stern governorship of Sir William Berkeley. England's wars with the Dutch cut into the tobacco trade, and unfree tobacco workers—more than 6,000 indentured Europeans and nearly 2,000 enslaved Africans—chafed against their harsh treatment. On the frontier, colonists resented the dependent Indians (Occaneechi, Pamunkey, and others) who traded furs in exchange for protection from enemy tribes. Settlers also feared the well-armed Susquehannock living near the Potomac River. "Consider us," Berkeley wrote to the king in 1667, "as a people press'd at our backes with Indians, in our Bowills with our Servants . . . and invaded from without by the Dutch."

By 1676, tensions in Virginia reached the breaking point. Officials had increased taxes to pay for fortifications, servant plots and mutinies abounded, and corruption ran rampant among Berkeley's close associates. The aging governor ruled from Green Spring, his huge estate near the capital, Jamestown. Fearing the hostile views of free men who did not own property, Berkeley had revoked their right to vote. He had not dared to call an election in fourteen years. He also dreaded outspoken preachers, free schools, and printing presses. "How miserable that man is," he wrote, "that Governes a People where six parts of seaven at least are Poore Endebted Discontented and Armed."

Even wealthy newcomers such as Nathaniel Bacon had trouble gaining access to Berkeley's inner circle. When Bacon arrived from England in 1674 at age twenty-seven, he received a council seat because of his connections. But rivals denied the ambitious gentleman a license to engage in the fur trade. Impatient, Bacon condemned Berkeley's ruling Green Spring faction as sponges who "have sukt up the Publique Treasure." When frontier tensions erupted into racial violence, Bacon threw himself into the conflict, challenging Berkeley's leadership and launching aggressive campaigns. His frontier followers, eager for Indian land, killed friendly Occaneechi as well as hostile Susquehannock.

Bacon's army continued to grow, as backcountry leaders joined landless poor and runaway workers—both black and white—to support his anti-Indian cause. When Berkeley called for a rare election to assert his strength, Bacon's supporters dominated the new House of Burgesses. The desperate governor retreated across Chesapeake Bay and hid on Virginia's eastern shore.

Throughout the summer of 1676, rumors swirled that Bacon might join malcontents in Maryland and in the Albemarle region south of Virginia to carve out an independent enclave and seek aid from the Dutch or the French. The new assembly quickly restored the vote to propertyless men and forbade excessive fees. It limited sheriffs to one year in office and passed other measures to halt corruption and expand participation in government. As an

•••—Read the Document
Bacon's Declaration (1676)
at **www.myhistorylab.com**

■ **William Berkeley's Green Spring, the largest mansion in Virginia at the time of Bacon's Rebellion, symbolized the autocratic rule of Governor Berkeley and his "Green Spring Faction." The estate was seized by Nathaniel Bacon's forces in 1676 and later restored by Berkeley's widow.**

incentive for enlistment in the frontier war, the assembly granted Bacon's recruits the right to sell into slavery any Indians they captured.

For their part, slaves and indentured servants took advantage of the breakdown in public controls to leave their masters and join Bacon. Networks of "news wives" (women who used facts and rumors to fan worker discontent) spread stories of oppressive conditions. In June rebel soldiers talked openly of sharing estates among themselves, and in August they took over Green Spring Plantation, where Berkeley kept sixty horses and 400 head of cattle. A month later, Bacon's army burned Jamestown to the ground.

But by October, the tide had turned. Bacon was dead, struck down by dysentery, and reinforcements for Berkeley were on the way from England. With armed vessels patrolling the rivers, Berkeley dared to return from the eastern shore. Soon propertied men who had joined with Bacon were changing sides again and receiving amnesty from the governor.

The revolt had been crushed, but the impact of the tumult proved huge. On the frontier, Bacon's violent campaign against the Indians had killed or enslaved hundreds and fostered bitter hatreds. In the Tidewater, the uprising had raised a frightening prospect for wealthy tobacco planters: a unified and defiant underclass of white and black workers. From then on, Virginia's gentry applied themselves to dividing the races and creating a labor force made up of African slaves. In London, the recently formed Royal African Company stood ready to further such a design.

The "Glorious Revolution" in England

No sooner had peace returned to New England and Virginia than Stuart policies brought a new round of turmoil on both sides of the Atlantic. In England, debate revived over who would succeed Charles II on the throne. The irreligious Charles, an Anglican in name only, had no legitimate children. Therefore, his brother James, a convert to Catholicism, was first in line to inherit the crown.

In 1678, rumors spread regarding a "Popish Plot" by Catholics to kill the king so that James could take power. The House of Commons, fearful of rule by a Catholic king, urged that James be excluded from the line of succession. Instead of James, House members argued, why not consider James's Protestant daughters by his first marriage: either Mary (recently wedded to her Dutch cousin, William of Orange) or Anne? Angered by such interference, Charles II dissolved Parliament in 1681 and ruled on his own for the last four years of his life.

When Charles II died in 1685, the traditional rule of succession prevailed: James II took over the English throne. In France that same year, Louis XIV revoked the Edict of Nantes, which had protected French Protestants. Fear spread among England's Protestant majority that their country's new Catholic ruler, James II, might also sanction persecution of non-Catholics. These concerns mounted when James disbanded Parliament, raised a standing army, and placed a Catholic in command of the navy. Then in 1688, James's queen gave birth to a male heir. Protestant anxieties about a pending Catholic dynasty erupted into open resistance.

United by their fear of Catholicism, rival factions among England's political elite (known for the first time as "Whigs" and "Tories") temporarily papered over their differences. They invited the Protestant William of Orange, James's Dutch son-in-law, to lead an army from Holland and take the English crown.

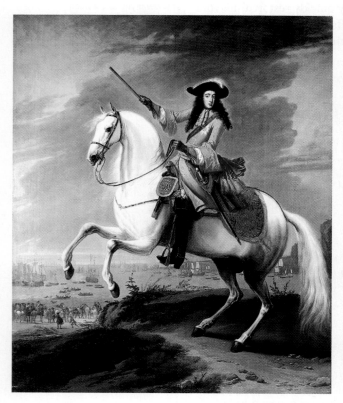

■ Protestants in England and America opposed to King James II welcomed news that William of Orange (above) had arrived from Holland with his army in 1688 to take over the English throne.

In November 1688, he crossed the English Channel with 15,000 men, prompting James to abdicate the throne and escape into exile. William and Mary were proclaimed joint sovereigns in 1689, accepting a Bill of Rights that limited royal power.

Its position now enhanced, Parliament moved to grant toleration to Protestant dissenters, establish limited freedom of the press, and ensure regular parliamentary sessions. It also imposed limits on any permanent, paid military forces, known as standing armies, because they could accrue their own power and jeopardize civil authority. The English had thus preserved Protestantism and curtailed royal absolutism, all without bloodshed. Parliament hailed King William III as "our great Deliverer from Popery and Slavery." The propertied classes, who benefited most from the peaceful transition, hailed it as the "Glorious Revolution."

The "Glorious Revolution" in America

The succession of James II in 1685 did not bode well for England's American colonies. The new king not only professed the Catholic faith but also cherished absolute monarchy and distrusted elected assemblies. In colonial affairs, James favored revenue-generating reforms and direct obedience to the crown. He detested the powerful leaders in Massachusetts since, as Congregationalists, they believed in a decentralized Protestant church. James also resented the fact that they disobeyed the Navigation Acts and asserted their right to self-rule, even after the crown revoked their charter in 1684. Moreover, he rejected the notion that colonists possessed the precious right claimed by the English at home: not to be taxed without giving their consent. The king envisioned an extensive reorganization of the American colonies.

When James assumed the throne, his own colony of New York automatically became a royal province. Convinced of his divine right to set policy, the king nullified the charters of certain colonies in order to bring them under his control. As the cornerstone of his reorganization plan, James linked the New England colonies (plus New York and New Jersey in 1688) into one huge *Dominion of New England*. This consolidation, under an appointed governor general, would make it easier for England to suppress dissent, enforce shipping regulations, and defend the Dominion's frontiers—at least in theory.

In practice, the effort to forge a Dominion of New England proved a disaster. Control of the Dominion went to a military officer, Sir Edmund Andros, who met stiff resistance from the start. The heavy-handed Andros attempted to rule from Boston through a council he appointed, made up of loyal associates, without aid or interference from any elected legislature. He asserted the crown's right to question existing land patents, and he requisitioned a Congregational church for Anglican services. Worse, he offended local leaders by strictly enforcing the Navigation Acts to collect revenue. When participants in democratic town meetings raised objections, he jailed the leaders.

Colonists seethed with resentment toward this revival of Stuart absolutism, which claimed total obedience to the king and his officers as a divine right for the Stuart monarchy. Rumors of French invasions and Catholic plots swirled among staunch Protestants. In April 1689, welcome news that the Protestant William of Orange had invaded England inspired a revolt in Boston. Mobs showed public support for overthrowing the Stuart regime, and local leaders locked Governor Andros in jail.

Colonists seethed with resentment toward this revival of Stuart absolutism, which claimed total obedience to the king and his officers as a divine right for the Stuart monarchy.

The success of William and the demise of the Dominion of New England did not end royal efforts to tighten imperial control over New England. The new Massachusetts charter of 1691 consolidated neighboring Plymouth and Maine into the Massachusetts Bay colony. Moreover, it proclaimed that future governors would be appointed by the monarchy, as in other colonies. The men of Massachusetts, who had elected their own governor since the days of John Winthrop, would no longer have that right.

Emboldened by Boston's actions in 1689, New Yorkers ousted their own Dominion officials and set up a temporary government headed by Jacob Leisler. This German-born militia captain was a staunch Calvinist and hostile to the town's growing English elite. In Leisler's Rebellion, long-standing ethnic and religious rivalries merged with vague class hostilities: Leisler's supporters resented their treatment at the hands of the rich. They freed imprisoned debtors and attacked the houses of leading merchants. After a new governor arrived to take charge in 1691, the elite fought back. They lowered artisan wages and pressured the governor into hanging Leisler, on the grounds that his rebel followers were "growing dayly very high and Insolentt."

Similar tremors shook the Chesapeake region. In Maryland, where the Catholic proprietor ruled over a large and restive Protestant population, the governing Calvert family waited too long to proclaim its loyalty to King William. Fearing a "Popish" plot, assemblyman John Coode and a force of 250 armed Protestants marched on St. Mary's City and seized the government by force. The "happy Change in England" had replaced divine right rule with a more balanced constitutional monarchy, and Maryland settlers were determined to show their support.

Consequences of War and Growth: 1690–1715

How did worldly success and wartime profits contribute to colonial unrest after 1690?

The success of the Glorious Revolution hardly brought peace to England or its empire. On the contrary, warfare marked the reign of William and Mary and also that of Mary's sister, Queen Anne, who ruled from 1702 until her death in 1714. English involvement against France in two protracted wars on the European continent had implications for colonists and Indians living in eastern North America. The War of the League of Augsburg in Europe became known to English colonists in America as King William's War (1689–1697), and the protracted War of Spanish Succession was experienced in America as Queen Anne's War (1702–1713).

Nowhere was the impact of these imperial wars more evident than in the rapidly growing colonies of the Northeast. Indeed, the earlier bloodshed of Metacom's War, starting in 1675, had already aroused consternation and soul-searching. Bible-reading New Englanders viewed the violent decades that followed as a harsh test, or a deserved punishment, sent from the Almighty. They believed that God had watched closely over the initial Puritan "errand into the wilderness." Could it be, ministers now asked from the pulpit, that the Lord had some special controversy with the current generation? As communities grew more prosperous and became caught up in the pursuit of worldly success, were church members forgetting their religious roots and leading less pious lives? Invoking the Old Testament prophet Jeremiah, clerics interpreted personal and collective troubles as God's punishment for the region's spiritual decline.

But such a sweeping explanation of misfortune only raised deeper questions. New Englanders could see clearly that the consequences of rapid change were not spread equally among all towns, congregations, and families. As in most war eras, some people and localities suffered more than others. Certain individuals and groups seemed to benefit economically while others fell behind. Some anxious believers saw the hand of Satan in the day-to-day struggles of village life. Others argued that the worldly success and wartime profits of an expanding elite had undermined the community ideals of earlier generations. While flames engulfed isolated Massachusetts communities such as Deerfield and portions of the Maine frontier, fiery passions were also being aroused in older settlements, such as Salem and Boston.

Salem's Wartime Witch Hunt

One of the most memorable disruptions, the Salem witch hunt, occurred in Essex County, Massachusetts, a two-day ride on horseback from the embattled Maine frontier. In 1692, an outburst of witchcraft accusations engulfed the farm community of Salem Village. The strange episode remains one of the most troubling in early American history.

Among European Christians, a belief in witches with a supernatural power to inflict harm stretched back for centuries. In the 1600s, witchcraft trials abounded in Europe, and in New England zealous believers had executed several dozen supposed witches in isolated cases. Three-fourths of those accused (and even more of those executed) were women. Most were beyond childbearing age, often poor or widowed, with limited power to protect themselves in the community. But Salem's hysteria went far beyond other colonial incidents, with over 200 people accused and twenty put to death.

Early in 1692, more than half a dozen young women in Salem Village, ranging in age from nine to twenty, began to suffer violent convulsive fits. With reduced appetites and temporary loss of hearing, sight, and memory, they also experienced choking sensations that curtailed their speech. Vivid hallucinations followed. By April the adolescents had accused ten people of being witches. Then some of the ten named others in their elaborate confessions, and the hysteria snowballed.

In a world where people considered satanic influence very real, frightened authorities seriously weighed the young women's stories of people appearing to them as devilish specters and apparitions. Overriding tradition, jurists allowed such "spectral evidence" in court, and convictions mounted. The court ordered public hangings on Gallows Hill that continued through September. Only when accusations reached too high in the social hierarchy and when several accusers recanted their stories did the new governor finally intervene. He emptied the jails, forbade further imprisonments, and pardoned the surviving accused until the tremor could subside.

Why this terrible outburst? Some historians argue that strained relations between farm families and more prosperous urban residents nearby may have influenced the craze. Some emphasize the zeal and gullibility of those first assigned to investigate. Still others speculate that the absence of central authority, until Governor Phips arrived in the colony in May, allowed a troubled situation to spin out of control. Finally, commentators stress a perverse psychological dynamic that arises in any witch hunt, ancient or modern. In such cases, accused suspects often can save their own lives by supplying damaging and vivid confessions implicating others rather than by offering heartfelt denials of guilt. One or more of these factors surely came into play.

Yet devastation on the Maine frontier also contributed to what happened in Salem Village. Traumatized survivors from King William's War—the current conflict against the Abenaki and French—had trickled into the Massachusetts community. Significantly, more than half the young women who leveled witchcraft accusations had lost one or both parents in the brutal Indian wars. On February 5, just weeks before the first accusations, attackers had burned the Maine village of York 80 miles north of Salem, killing forty-eight people, and taking 73 captives. Word of the raid no doubt triggered shocking memories among Salem's war refugees, especially the orphans who worked as servants in local households.

Fears deepened in April when one of the accused testified that the Devil had tempted her while she had been living in Maine. Then a servant named Mercy Short, who had been captured and orphaned by Indians, recalled disturbing dreams of the Devil. She told minister Cotton Mather that in her dreams Satan and his minions (who had "an Indian colour") had made "hideous assaults" upon her. Much of what Mather and others recorded as the work of Satan may actually have been posttraumatic stress in a frayed community during wartime.

••●•–Read the **Document**
Ann Putnam, Deposition (1692)
at **www.myhistorylab.com**

••●•–Read the **Document**
Ann Putnam, Confession (1706)
at **www.myhistorylab.com**

The Uneven Costs of War

Throughout the 1690s and beyond, King William's War and then Queen Anne's War made conflict a constant element of colonial life, but the burdens fell unevenly. For many colonial families, incessant warfare brought only death and dislocation. But for others, it offered new opportunities as the colonial economies expanded. Farmers with access to port towns shifted away from subsistence agriculture and grew crops for commercial sale. In doing so, they exposed themselves to greater financial risks, given transportation costs and market fluctuations. But they hoped to reap large profits.

Overseas trade and wartime smuggling offered investors even higher gains and larger risks. The crews of **privateers** (boats licensed to harass enemy shipping in wartime) made money if they captured a foreign vessel as a prize. Profits for outright pirates were greater still. Therefore, some colonial mariners chose to become buccaneers who operated for their own gain while avoiding the arm of the law. Englishman Edward Teach, known as Blackbeard, won notoriety as a privateer-turned-pirate, haunting the Carolina coast until his death in 1718.

Everywhere, poorer families were most likely to sink under the burdens of war. Regressive taxes, requiring the same amount from a poor carpenter as from a rich merchant, obviously hurt impoverished people the most. So did high wartime prices for food and other basic necessities. Furthermore, many of the poor men recruited by the military became casualties of combat or disease, increasing the number of widows living in poverty. As New England towns expanded, the growing distance between rich and poor struck local residents. The moral ties and community obligations—known as the social covenant—that Puritan elders had emphasized two generations earlier were loosening. In their place emerged a focus on secular priorities and a new, individualistic spirit.

■ For protection, the pirate Blackbeard often brought his ship into the shallow waters behind the barrier islands that form North Carolina's Atlantic coast. There, his crew bartered stolen goods at Ocracoke Island and reveled on the beach with local inhabitants.

In Boston, troubled ministers decried the hunger and poverty that they saw deepening in their parishes alongside unprecedented displays of wealth. Between 1685 and 1715, the share of all personal wealth in the town controlled by the richest 5 percent climbed from 26 percent to 40 percent. Angry writers published irate pamphlets encouraging working people to take political action. They charged once-respected elites with studying "how to oppress, cheat, and overreach their neighbours." Predictably, when an English fleet of sixty warships carrying 5,000 men docked at Boston in 1711, powerful merchants who controlled the flow of provisions reaped huge rewards from this windfall.

Storm Clouds in the South

Peace returned to New England's frontier villages and port towns in 1711, as negotiations began for ending Queen Anne's War in America and the related War of Spanish Succession in Europe. British diplomats gained favorable terms from France and Spain when they signed a treaty at Utrecht two years later. (The formal union of England and Scotland in 1707 under the name *Great Britain* had transformed the *English* empire into the *British* empire.) But London officials could not prevent fresh violence in North America, given the expansion of their British colonies. The Wampanoag, Narragansett, and Abenaki Indians had attempted to roll back the advancement of northeastern settlers into Connecticut, Massachusetts, and Maine. Now Native Americans in the Southeast sought to counter the encroachments of newcomers along the Carolina coast.

By the 1660s, settlers drifted into what would become the colony of North Carolina. Some were English radicals fleeing the Restoration. Others, such as John Culpeper, had moved north from the Carolina settlement on the Ashley River, resentful that Shaftesbury and Locke had given Carolina proprietors firm control over the new colony. Still others were runaway servants from Virginia, and later came refugees escaping after Bacon's uprising. In 1677 these newcomers, led by Culpeper, seized control in the Albemarle region. The proprietors suppressed "Culpeper's Rebellion," but in 1689 they agreed to name a separate governor for the portion of Carolina "That Lies north and east of Cape Feare." Another disturbance, "Cary's Rebellion" in 1710, led to official recognition of "North Carolina, independent of Carolina," the next year. (Surveyors marked off the dividing line with Virginia in 1728.)

In 1680, Native Americans still outnumbered newcomers in eastern North Carolina by two to one, but within thirty years that ratio had been reversed. The Naval Stores Act of 1705, passed by Parliament to promote colonial production of tar and pitch for shipbuilding, drew a stream of settlers to the pine forests of eastern North Carolina. By 1710, English communities existed on Albemarle Sound, at what is now Edenton, and on Pamlico Sound, at Bath (where Blackbeard and other pirates were frequent visitors). Farther south, Protestant immigrants from Bern, Switzerland, had staked out the town of New Bern on the site of a Native American village. John Lawson, who had explored the Carolinas before helping to lay out Bath and New Bern, conceded that the Indians had been "better to us than we are to them."

Eventually, the Tuscarora Indians struck back. Frustrated by corrupt traders and land encroachment, they killed Lawson and launched a war in 1711 to drive out the intruders. But they had waited too long. Within two years, the settlers—aided by a South Carolina force of several dozen whites and nearly 500 Yamasee Indians—had crushed the Tuscarora resistance. Most of the Tuscarora survivors migrated north, where they became the sixth nation within the powerful Iroquois Confederacy.

Yamasee warriors from the Savannah River region helped British colonists quell the Tuscarora uprising. But in 1715 they led their own rebellion against advancing settlers and corrupt traders linked to Charleston. They received support from Creek Indians, Spanish settlers in Florida, and French traders at the new Alabama outpost of Fort Toulouse. The still-powerful Cherokee in southern Appalachia opted not to join in the Yamasee War. Otherwise, the Indians might have overwhelmed the South Carolina colony.

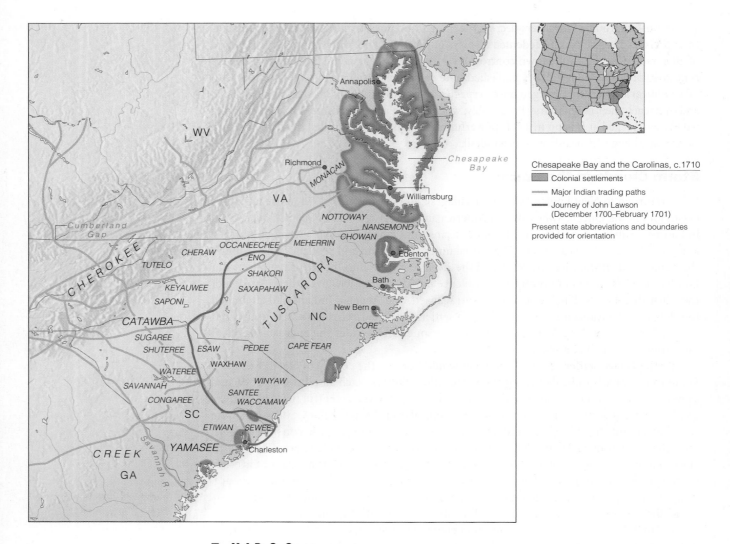

■ MAP 3.3
VIRGINIA AND THE CAROLINAS, c. 1710
After John Lawson made a 1,000-mile journey through the Carolina interior (1700–1701), he became an advocate for colonial growth. The expanding settlements of North Carolina and South Carolina pressed the Tuscarora and Yamasee Indians, who staged wars of resistance after 1710.

CONCLUSION

◉ See the Map

Native Population Loss, 1500–1700 at
www.myhistorylab.com

Inspired by the exploits of La Salle and a generation of voyageurs and missionaries, the French had made inroads into the huge Mississippi Valley. But most European intrusions remained confined to the fringes of the vast continent. The French established themselves in Louisiana, and small numbers of Spanish held onto footholds in New Mexico and Florida, while venturing into parts of Arizona and Texas. The English newcomers, far more numerous, remained clustered along the Atlantic seaboard.

When English colonists penetrated up eastern rivers, warfare with traditional inhabitants ensued. Along the length of eastern North America, from the Kennebec River to the Savannah, hundreds of settlers and Indians died violently during the half-century before 1715. Often the frontier struggles became entwined with wider conflicts between the rival European empires. These wilderness skirmishes seem minute compared with the battles raging in Europe at the same time. Despite the small scale of the conflicts in North America, however, Europe's imperial wars had started to influence developments in the English colonies.

Another element of Europe's expansion overseas—the transatlantic slave trade—had also begun to alter the shape of England's North American colonies. What had seemed only a small cloud on the horizon in the early seventeenth century had grown into an ominous force, with a momentum of its own, by the early eighteenth century. The storm hit hardest along the Southeast coast, where the arrival of thousands of Africans soon shaped a distinctive and repressive world of enslavement and exploitation that endured for generations. No sooner had the English gained control along the Atlantic edge of North America than they orchestrated a "terrible transformation" that placed thousands in bondage and altered the shape of American history.

For Review

√●⎯Study and **Review** at **www.myhistorylab.com**

1. What made the Pueblo Revolt of 1680 the most successful uprising against a colonizing power in the early history of North America?

2. How did the restoration of the monarchy in London in 1660 influence the evolution of England's American colonies over the next two generations?

3. Carolina explorer John Lawson observed that by 1710 the Indians had been "better to us than we are to them." Do you agree?

4. Were developments during the half-century after 1660 as important to the future of North America as the earlier founding of Virginia and the New England colonies? Explain.

Chronology: 1660–1715

1660	Restoration of monarchy in England under Charles II.
1664	Charles II grants a charter to his brother James, Duke of York, sanctioning the takeover of the Dutch New Netherland colony and the creation of New York.
1675 to 1676	Metacom's War in New England.
1676	Bacon's Rebellion in Virginia.
1680	Pueblo Revolt in New Mexico.
1681	Quaker William Penn receives charter for Pennsylvania.

1682	La Salle explores the Mississippi River and claims Louisiana for France.
1689	Dutch leader William of Orange and his wife Mary become joint English sovereigns in the Glorious Revolution, replacing King James II.
1692	Witchcraft trials in Salem, Massachusetts.
1699	Iberville begins colony in French Louisiana.
1711 to 1715	Tuscarora Indians in North Carolina, and then the Yamasee in South Carolina, resist English colonial expansion.

Key Terms

Coverture French term for the dependent and legal status of a woman during marriage. Under English law, the male family head received legal rights, and his wife lost independent status, becoming, in legal terms, a *femme covert*. p. 69

Kachina An Indian religious system, inspired by Mesoamerican traditions, and present in the American Southwest for more than 800 years; the kachina cult used masks for group performances associated with rain, curing, fertility, warfare, and the ancestors. Among many Pueblo and Hopi Indians, this tradition was epitomized by kachina (or katsina) dolls. p. 65

Mercantilism A commercial policy that sought to achieve economic self-suffiency and a favorable balance of trade (often by planting colonies) in order to promote a country's prosperity, strength, and

independence. Rival European imperial powers favored the strategy of mercantilism in the seventeenth and eighteenth centuries. p. 58

Mestizo A person of mixed European and American Indian ancestry. p. 65

Mulattos A person of mixed European and African ancestry; the first-generation offspring of a Caucasian and a Negroid parent. p. 65

Privateers Ships (and their crew members) licensed to harass enemy shipping in wartime. p. 78

Unicameral A legislative body that has only one chamber, or house. p. 70

Sachem Algonquin Indian term for a Native American leader or chief. p. 72

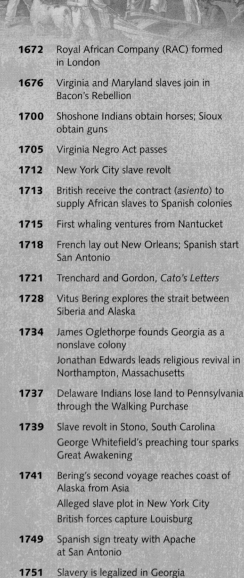

PART TWO

A Century of Colonial Expansion to 1775

ON APRIL 19, 1775, NEW ENGLAND FARMERS BATTLED BRITISH soldiers at Concord Bridge. The confrontation marked the start of the American Revolution. (Each spring in Massachusetts, the date is still set aside as Patriots' Day and celebrated with the running of the Boston Marathon.) But how did colonies that were weak outposts before 1700 become strong enough to challenge the power of the British Empire in the second half of the eighteenth century? The answer is not a simple one. Life changed in dramatic ways during the century before 1775, not only in New England but throughout much of North America.

The rapid spread of Spanish horses across the West allowed Native Americans, such as the Comanche and Sioux, to become mounted buffalo hunters on the Great Plains. The arrival of Russian fur traders disrupted traditional cultures on the Aleutian Islands and the coast of Alaska. At the same time, the gradual success of the new Louisiana colony gave France access to much of the Mississippi River valley. But the potential for a dominant French-speaking empire in America evaporated with the stunning defeat of French forces by the British in the Seven Years' War. As that global conflict ended in 1763, the Spanish also lost ground in North America. After claiming Florida for 200 years, they finally ceded the peninsula to the British, even as they began to extend Spanish missions up the coast of California.

Other changes were even more dramatic. In the eighteenth century, race slavery became an established aspect of colonial society in North America. Hints of coming change appeared even in the generation before 1660. During the next half century, race slavery rapidly took hold as a dominant institution in the coastal Southeast. The English had come late to the transatlantic slave trade, but they became aggressive participants in the lucrative traffic in human beings. English colonizers fashioned harsh slave-based societies in the Caribbean, then in the Chesapeake colonies of Virginia and Maryland, next in North and South Carolina, and finally, after 1750, in the recently established colony of Georgia.

Race slavery transformed the mainland colonies in terrible ways and had far-reaching results. Thousands of Africans arrived in North American ports in the eighteenth century. Strikingly, they were only a small fraction of the much greater transport of Africans to the Caribbean and Central and South America. Nevertheless, by 1750 there were nearly 250,000 African Americans living in North America. Most lived in the South, and most were enslaved, including several hundred in Spanish East Florida and several thousand in French Louisiana. By 1775 the number exceeded half a million. By then, blacks made up more than 20 percent of the population of the British colonies, and the legal and social constraints that shackled their world remained tighter than ever.

Newcomers from Europe, as well as from Africa, altered the make-up of Atlantic colonies that had once been almost entirely English. Many of these newly arrived Europeans, unable to afford the cost of passage, had to pledge their labor for a period of years. But in contrast to the Africans, most European migrants came to America voluntarily and were free from obligations within a few years. The Atlantic crossing could be harrowing, of course, but for thousands the long-term advantages outweighed the short-term drawbacks. Artisans of all kinds were in high demand, and land was cheap. Colonial governments ruled with a light hand in comparison to the monarchies of Europe, and they competed with one another to attract newcomers. This competition for new arrivals bred relative religious and ethnic tolerance.

Pushed by events in Europe and drawn by opportunities in America, non-English families flocked to Britain's North American colonies. This new flow from Europe and the British Isles, combined with the African slave trade, quickly generated a far more diverse colonial society on top of foundations set by earlier English immigrants. Prior generations of colonists had laid out towns, formed governments, and founded the rudimentary institutions of colonial social life. They had established an ambiguous pattern of interaction with Native Americans that involved warfare and displacement as well as trade and intermarriage. Also, they had located harbors, carved out roads, and started to build an economic infrastructure.

As numbers rose and diversity increased, a series of regional economies emerged along the eastern seaboard. Each sustained the local inhabitants while also serving the wider needs of the British Empire. For much of the eighteenth century, the British crown promoted economic growth in the colonies through a workable combination of protectionist controls and benign neglect.

But the British victory over the French brought drastic new problems to eastern North America after 1763. Native Americans lost a valued trading partner and military ally when the French withdrew. Britain faced an enormous war debt and looked to its burgeoning colonies as a source of much-needed revenue. Within little more than a decade, Britain's North American colonists went from resentment and resistance to overt rebellion and an anticolonial war of independence.

4

African Enslavement: The Terrible Transformation

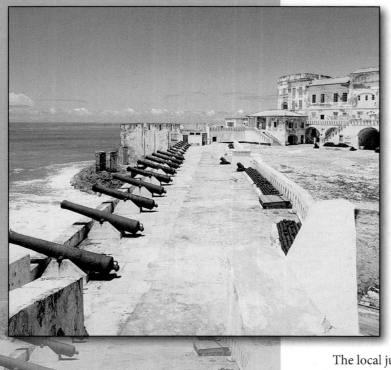

On a wintery day in January 1656, a mulatto servant named Elizabeth Key went before the local court in Northumberland County, Virginia. She was twenty-five years old. The late Colonel John Mottrom, a justice of the peace, had held Elizabeth as a slave, kept in perpetual bondage. She objected strongly, and she wanted to sue the executors of Mottrom's estate for her freedom and back pay. Bess, as she was known, presented a threefold argument. First, as the daughter of a free man, she should inherit her father's legal status according to English law. Second, as a baptized Christian, she should not be enslaved. And third, she could produce a document showing that as a small child she had been "put out" to work until she was fourteen, following local custom. Such contracts for apprenticing a child for a fixed number of years were common in America, where labor was in short supply. But her term of work had expired long ago.

Key was accompanied in court by her white attorney and lover, William Greensted. They had had two children together and would marry six months later, when they finally won a favorable verdict. The young couple produced witnesses who testified that Bess was the daughter of Thomas Key, a white man serving in the Virginia General Assembly, and his "Negro woman." One witness told the jury that Bess's mother had lived openly with Mr. Key and had said that the girl was Key's daughter.

Further testimony established that in 1636, not long before he died, Key had bound little Bess to Humphrey Higginson, a member of the Council of State. Higginson "promised to use her as well as if shee were his own Child"; that is, "more Respectfully than a Comon servant or slave." He even stood as her godfather when Bess was christened.

To be raised in a Christian church was no small matter at a time when Europeans viewed non-Christians captured in wars to be uniquely vulnerable to legal enslavement. For Bess, this circumstance helped her cause greatly, for she proved "able to give a very good account of her fayth." Furthermore, she produced clear evidence that her father had sold her to Higginson for nine years. Mr. Key had demanded that Higginson not dispose of her to any other person, such as to Colonel Mottrom. Rather, he was to give her the usual "freedom portion" of corn and clothes "and lett her shift for her selfe," either in England or Virginia, when her term expired.

The local jury accepted Elizabeth Key's three-part argument and pronounced her free. But the General Court overturned the verdict on appeal, only to be overruled in turn by a committee of the General Assembly. In the end, the committee determined that

"Elizabeth ought to bee free." The assemblymen also argued that her last master owed her a "freedom portion," plus back pay "for the time shee hath served longer than Shee ought to have done." Still, the matter generated debate among settlers. Several decades later, Elizabeth's case would have been decided differently. Moreover, the courts of Virginia might well have enslaved her children for life. And their offspring would have inherited slavery status as well.

A terrible transformation was under way in English co-lonial culture that would warp American society for centuries to come. It spread gradually, like a cancer, revealing a different pace and pattern in each mainland colony. During the 1620s and 1630s, a few black servants were working alongside white servants. But well before the end of the century, the grand-children of those workers had been separated by skin color and physical appearance, according to emerging notions of "race." Free blacks persisted in the English colonies, but in most communities they became anomalies, for the tide was flowing against them. From now on, people of African ances-try were to be legally enslaved for life. Elizabeth Key and her children and grandchildren experienced the painful transition firsthand.

■ Africans arriving in America often had ornamental scarification (known as "country marks") on their bodies, as well as brands inflicted by slave traders and physical scars from the middle passage.

The Descent into Race Slavery

Some major transitions in human affairs evolve slowly, even imperceptibly. Nothing shaped colonial cultures more forcefully than the European colonists' gradual commitment to the legalized enslavement of hundreds of thousands of people and their descendants. It is impor-tant to examine the slippery slope that led to perpetual servitude based on race.

How important was precedent in the English shift to hereditary enslavement of Africans?

The Caribbean Precedent

The roots of race slavery in the Americas extend back to the era of Columbus, when warfare, sickness, and exploitation quickly decimated the native populations of the Caribbean after 1492. Hungry for human labor, the Spanish intruders began to import people from Africa to grow crops and dig for gold in the Caribbean islands. As the native population declined sharply through epidemics, the traffic in black newcomers expanded.

Spanish pressure for labor in the New World intensified further with the discovery of additional mines for precious metals in Mexico and Peru. To meet the growing demand, Spain's king even issued a contract (called the **asiento**) that allowed other European powers—such as Portugal, France, or the Netherlands—to import African slaves to the Spanish colonies. High profits drew eager participation. In the half-century between 1590 and 1640, more than 220,000 people arrived in chains from Africa at the Spanish colonial ports in Central and South America.

Meanwhile, the Portuguese purchased enslaved Africans to work their own expanding sugar plantations. They imported more than 75,000 slaves, mostly from the Congo River re-gion of West Central Africa, to the Atlantic island of São Tomé in the sixteenth century. When Portuguese sugar production spread to coastal Brazil, so did the exploitation of African labor.

By 1625 Brazil imported the majority of slaves crossing the Atlantic each year and exported most of the sugar consumed in Europe.

Long before the 1660s, therefore, Europeans had set a precedent for exploiting African workers in New World colonies. Religious and secular authorities frowned on actively enslaving people, especially if they were fellow Christians, but purchasing so-called infidels (those who followed other religions), could be tolerated, particularly if slavery had already been imposed on them by someone else. These West African victims were non-Christians, and most had already been enslaved by others, captured by fellow Africans in war.

Confident in this rationale, the Spanish and Portuguese adapted their laws to accept the enslavement of Africans. Moreover, the condition would be hereditary, with children inheriting at birth their mother's legal status. The Catholic Church backed the new labor system, though priests occasionally worked to alleviate suffering among Africans in the Americas. The pope did nothing to condemn the growing traffic, nor did the Protestant Reformation have a dampening effect. On the contrary, the rising Protestant sea powers of northern Europe proved willing to assist in the slave trade and take part in the dramatic "sugar revolution," growing sugar on a massive scale for expanding Atlantic markets.

The Dutch, for example, ruled Brazil for a generation in the first half of the seventeenth century, importing slaves to South America and exporting sugar. When the Portuguese regained control of Brazil at midcentury, they pushed out Dutch settlers. These outcasts took their knowledge about managing sugar plantations to the islands of the Caribbean. Some appeared in the new English possessions of Barbados and Jamaica, and soon they were directing African slaves in cutting, pressing, and boiling sugar cane to make molasses. The thick molasses could then be processed further to make rum and refined sugar for export. By the 1650s slavery and sugar production were engulfing England's West Indian possessions, just as these twin features had already become central to the New World colonies controlled by Spain and Portugal. A looming precedent had been set. But as late as 1660, it was not at all clear that African slavery would gain a prominent place, or even a lasting foothold, in any North American colonies.

> *As late as 1660, it was not at all clear that African slavery would gain a prominent place, or even a lasting foothold, in any North American colonies.*

Ominous Beginnings

As far back as the sixteenth century, African men had participated in Spanish explorers' forays into the Southeast, and some had remained, fathering children with Indian women. African slaves had helped to establish the small Spanish outpost at St. Augustine in 1565, but a century later no additional coastal colonies had yet appeared on the mainland anywhere south of Chesapeake Bay.

Granted, Africans were present farther north in the fledgling settlements of the French, Dutch, and English. But their numbers remained small—several thousand at most—and few of these newcomers had come directly from Africa. Most had lived for years in the Caribbean or on the mainland, absorbing colonial languages and beliefs. So they and their children, like Bess Key, were not viewed as complete outsiders by the European colonists. The legal and social standing of these early African Americans remained vague before the 1660s. Everywhere, workers were in demand, and most black newcomers found themselves laboring alongside European servants.

In the Massachusetts Bay colony, early Puritan settlers, seeking viable markets and new sources of labor, exchanged goods for slaves in the Caribbean. In 1644, seafaring New Englanders even attempted direct trade with Africa. But the following year, Massachusetts authorities ordered a New Hampshire resident to surrender a black worker he had purchased in Boston. They argued that the man had been stolen from Africa, not captured in war, and should be returned to his home. In 1652 Rhode Island passed a law limiting all involuntary service—for Europeans or Africans—to no more than ten years.

Along the Hudson River, the Dutch colonists had close ties with the sugar islands of the West Indies, where race slavery was already an accepted system. In New Netherland, therefore, the laws discriminated against black workers and limited their rights. But the statutes also provided loopholes that permitted social and economic advancement to the community's Africans, most of whom spoke Dutch.

Chesapeake Bay lay even closer to the main routes of the Atlantic slave traffic. In 1619 a Dutch warship brought to Virginia more than twenty African men and women acquired as slaves in the Caribbean. Like people deported from England to the Chesapeake, they were sold as servants. Terms of service varied, and some black newcomers earned their freedom quickly and kept it. But others saw their terms extended arbitrarily. In 1640 Virginia's General Court considered punishment for "a negro named John Punch" and two European servants who had escaped to Maryland. When apprehended, the Dutchman and the Scotsman each received four additional years of service, but the African was sentenced to unending servitude "for the time of his natural life." That same year, Virginia passed a law that prevented blacks from bearing arms. A 1643 law taxing productive field hands included African-American women but not white women.

These early efforts to separate Africans from Europeans by law set an ominous precedent in the use of skin color as a distinguishing marker. Still, rules governing the lives of people of color and their offspring remained ambiguous for several decades, and (as the case of Bess Key makes clear) efforts at exploitation could often be undone in court. But new forces would come into play in the mainland American colonies after 1660, consolidating the transition to hereditary enslavement of Africans.

■ This summary of an African slave-trading voyage shows wealthy planters boarding a French ship upon its arrival in the West Indies in order to buy slaves newly arrived from Angola. The crew has used an iron fence dividing the deck to protect against revolt during the voyage. The captain conducts business under an awning in the stern.

Alternative Sources of Labor

The legal status of African newcomers to English North America became distinctly clearer and less hopeful in the decades after 1660. The transatlantic slave trade, already more than a century old, provided certain English colonies with a ready source of African workers at a time when more obvious streams of inexpensive labor—captured Native Americans and impoverished Europeans—were dwindling.

For labor-hungry colonists, Native Americans were close at hand and knew the country well. They took captives when fighting one another, so colonists could buy Indian prisoners or seize them in frontier warfare. Europeans felt they could enslave such people in good conscience, since they were non-Christians who had been taken captive in war. But Native American numbers were declining steadily, owing to epidemics. And those who did become enslaved knew the countryside well enough to escape. Besides, traffic in Indian slaves disrupted the profitable deerskin trade, undermined wilderness diplomacy, and sparked conflict on the frontier.

Efforts to maintain a steady flow of cheap labor from Europe ran into different problems. The Great Plague of 1665 devastated the English population, and the London Fire the following year created a new need for workers of all kinds to rebuild the capital. England's labor surplus, which had been a boon to the first colonies half a century earlier, rapidly disappeared. The use of **indentures** persisted, whereby people too poor to buy their own passage would agree to sell their labor for a fixed period. When these indentured workers reached America, they served a set term for room and board; then their employer needed to find replacements.

Equally important, when indentured servants were mistreated, they had little difficulty in relaying their complaints home to other potential workers. The flow of ships back and forth between Europe and North America grew steadily in the century after 1660, so word of places where indentured servants were regularly abused or swindled quickly reached the other side of the Atlantic. In contrast, the African slave trade lacked any similar "feedback loop." As a result, the brutal treatment of black workers never had a chance, through accurate feedback across the Atlantic, to influence the future flow of captives from Africa.

The Fateful Transition

In general, powerful Chesapeake tobacco planters were encouraged in 1660 by news of the Restoration of Charles II, since England's new king was likely to support their interests and reward their loyalty. These men had noticed the rising profits that sugar growers were making by using slaves in the Caribbean. In Virginia and Maryland, therefore, planters passed a series of laws that sharpened distinctions between servants working for a fixed period and slaves consigned to labor for life.

In shaping new legislation, local leaders even challenged long-standing English legal traditions, such as the right of children to inherit their father's status. In 1662 Virginia's General Assembly considered whether any child fathered "by an Englishman upon a negro woman should be slave or Free." In a crucial reversal of precedent, the legislature said that in such cases children shall be "bond or free *only according to the condition of the mother.*" From now on, the infant of any female slave would be enslaved from birth. Slavery was becoming a hereditary condition.

Could enslaved persons receive their freedom if they accepted Christianity, as sometimes happened in Spanish colonies? A 1664 Maryland law closed off that prospect. The act made clear that the legal status of non-Christian slaves did not change if they experienced religious conversion. Three years later, Virginia's government agreed that "the conferring of baptisme doth not alter the condition of the person as to his bondage." By removing religion as a determining factor, legislators shifted the definition of who could be enslaved from someone who was not Christian to someone who did not look European.

In scarcely a generation, black bondage had become a hereditary institution, and the conditions of life had grown markedly worse for African Americans. Increasingly, they faced corporal punishments: whippings and mutilation. Black slaves—and often free blacks—lost their right to accuse, or even testify against, a white person in court. "And further," stated Virginia's formative slave law of 1680, "if any Negro" raises a hand, even in self-defense, "against any Christian, he shall receive thirty lashes, and if he absent himself . . . from his master's service and resist lawful apprehension, he may be killed."

> *In scarcely a generation, black bondage had become a hereditary institution, and the conditions of life had grown markedly worse for African Americans.*

The Growth of Slave Labor Camps

What factors created a vicious circle that sealed the fate of African workers in Virginia?

Over two generations, beginning in the late seventeenth century, tobacco growers in the Chesapeake and rice producers in the new colony of South Carolina embraced the system of hereditary race slavery that had developed in the Caribbean. For those forced to cut the trees, drain the swamps, and harvest the crops, the shift in production strategy represented—in

■ Rice plantations that emerged in coastal South Carolina around 1700 became labor camps where enslaved blacks were confined for generations, without wages or legal rights. In the 1850s, distant descendants of the region's first African workers were still being forced to plant, harvest, and process the huge rice crops that made their masters rich.

modern terminology—the emergence of slave labor camps. These people received no wages, had no legal rights, and were denied freedom to marry or move about. This deterioration in conditions occurred first, and most dramatically, in Virginia, where several thousand African Americans lived and labored by the 1670s.

Black Involvement in Bacon's Rebellion

Nothing did more to consolidate Virginia's slide toward race slavery than Bacon's Rebellion, the major uprising that shook the Chesapeake region in 1676 (see Chapter 3). The episode pitted aspiring gentry, led by Nathaniel Bacon, against hard-pressed Indian groups on the frontier and an entrenched elite in Jamestown.

Free men, would-be farmers in search of land, made up part of Bacon's following, but diverse unfree workers also proved eager recruits. Such ill-treated people remained legally indentured to large landholders for varying terms, and many of the Africans were undoubtedly bound for life. Together, they raised the colony's annual tobacco crop, and the backbreaking labor prompted frequent unrest. These ragged workers, however long their term of service might be, had the most to gain and the least to lose from Bacon's revolt. According to the Virginia Assembly, "many evill disposed servants . . . taking advantage of the loosenes of the tymes . . . followed the rebells in rebellion." When Bacon died in October 1676, many of his wealthier supporters gave up, renewing their loyalty to the colonial government. But bound workers who had escaped from their masters continued the fight.

A letter reaching London that fall suggested that at the height of the rebellion Bacon had "proclam'd liberty to all Servants and Negroes." Clearly, the widespread unrest had given hope to downtrodden tobacco pickers, about a quarter of whom were black. When military reinforcements arrived in Chesapeake Bay from England in November, the commander, Captain Thomas Grantham, found hundreds of laborers still in active revolt.

Impressed by their strength, Grantham chose to use deceit when he met with 800 heavily armed rebels, both white and black, at their headquarters near the York River. Making vague promises regarding pardons and freedom, he persuaded most of the white men to surrender and return home. Only about "Eighty Negroes and Twenty English" demanded "their hoped for liberty and would not quietly laye downe their armes." But when these last holdouts boarded a sloop, Grantham disarmed the rebels and chained them below decks for return to their masters.

The Rise of a Slaveholding Elite in the Chesapeake Tidewater

With Bacon's death and the arrival of British ships, propertied Virginians had narrowly averted a successful multiracial revolution, fueled from below by workers who resented their distressed condition. But clearly some future revolt might succeed, so the great planters of the Chesapeake Tidewater region moved to tighten their hold on political and economic power. After Bacon's Rebellion, a strategy of divide and conquer seemed in order. They moved to improve conditions for poor whites in ways that would ensure class deference and racial solidarity among Europeans. At the same time, they further reduced the legal status of blacks and solidified their enslavement for life.

For precedent, planters had the model provided by slavery-based colonial societies in the West Indies, including the English sugar island of Barbados. Their uneasiness continued over importing non-Christian strangers who spoke little, if any, English. But such doubts were more than offset by the prospect of laying claim to the children of slaves and to the lives and labor of all generations to come. Increasing life expectancy in the Chesapeake region meant that Africans enslaved for life would yield profitable service for an increasingly long time. Besides, all their healthy offspring who survived childhood could then be forced to clear more land to grow additional crops.

Seizing the moment, a circle of aggressive entrepreneurs established themselves as the leading families of Virginia. These ambitious merchant-planters expected that the English-speaking Africans already present could assist in teaching newcomers to receive orders. They also assumed that slave laborers from diverse African societies could not communicate well enough with one another to cause dangerous disturbances. And of course, having now made skin color a determining feature of social order, they knew that black runaways could be spotted and apprehended readily. As the profitability of the slavery option increased, so did its appeal. By 1700 some 4,500 people were enslaved in Maryland in a total population of 35,000. And the colony's assembly was actively encouraging the importation of slaves. Growing demand meant that merchants and sea captains now devoted more time and larger ships to slave-trading, making African workers more available and affordable.

As the supply of enslaved black newcomers grew larger, planters eager to strengthen their position manipulated the established headright system. Traditionally, under this system, the colonial government granted to any arriving head of household 50 acres for every family member or hired hand he brought into the colony. The incentive was intended to spur migration from Europe, expand the free population, and develop the land through the establishment of family farms. But the wealthy planters who saw African slavery as a profitable labor source also controlled Virginia's legal system. For their own benefit, therefore, they extended the headright system so that a land bonus also went to anyone who purchased an African arrival as a lifelong slave. Thus, before the seventeenth century closed, a Virginia investor buying twenty slaves could also lay claim to headrights worth 1,000 acres of land.

To consolidate their new regime, planters worked through the church and the legislature to separate whites from blacks socially and legally. They undermined the position of free blacks and stigmatized interracial ties. A 1691 Virginia statute decried the "abominable mixture and spurious issue" that resulted from "Negroes, mulattoes and Indians intermarrying" with English or other white people. All such couples were "banished from this dominion forever." It also prohibited masters from freeing any black or mulatto unless they paid to transport that person out of the colony within six months.

> *To consolidate their new regime, planters worked through the church and the legislature to separate whites from blacks socially and legally.*

Virginia's Negro Act of 1705 further underscored the stark new boundaries. It mandated that white servants who were mistreated had the right to sue their masters in county court. Slaves, in contrast, had no such right. Any enslaved person who tried to escape could be tortured and even dismembered in hopes of "terrifying others" from seeking freedom. When masters or overseers killed a slave while inflicting punishment, they were automatically free of any felony charge. If slaves were killed or put to death by law, the owners would be paid public funds for the loss of their "property." In scarcely forty years, prominent whites had used the law to transform the labor system of the Chesapeake, entrapping Africans and their descendants in perpetual slavery.

Read the **Document**
Of the Servants and Slaves in Virginia (1705) at **www.myhistorylab.com**

England Enters the Atlantic Slave Trade

The Atlantic slave trade remains the largest and longest-lasting deportation in human history. In nearly four centuries, more than 10 million people were torn from their homelands against their will and transported to the Caribbean and to Central, South, and North America. Several million more perished in transit. By 1700, more Africans than Europeans had already crossed the Atlantic to the Western Hemisphere. Their numbers grew over the following century as the traffic reached its height. The importation of Africans to North America expanded after 1700, but it remained a small proportion of the overall Atlantic slave trade.

Why did England, once suspicious of the trade, become a leader in transporting enslaved Africans?

England took little part in the trade at first. However, the development of Barbados as a lucrative sugar colony and the expansion of English overseas ambitions changed matters quickly after 1640. With the restoration of the English monarchy in 1660, Charles II immediately granted a monopoly on African trade to a small group of adventurers, and in 1672 he chartered the powerful new Royal African Company (RAC).

The RAC dispatched from England a steady flow of merchant ships along a triangular trade route. The first leg took captains to English outposts along the coast of West Africa, where they exchanged textiles, guns, and iron bars for gold, ivory, and enslaved Africans. After a transatlantic **middle passage** of one to three months, the captains sold slaves and took on sugar in the West Indies before returning to England on the final leg of the triangle. English slave trading expanded when the company's monopoly ended officially in 1698. It ballooned further after 1713 when England obtained the *asiento*, the lucrative contract to deliver Africans to Spain's colonies in America. By the 1730s, British ships controlled the largest share of the Atlantic slave trade. They continued to dominate the traffic for the next seventy years.

The Slave Trade on the African Coast

By the 1680s, Africa's western sub-Saharan coastline contained dozens of trading depots, each controlled by some rival European power. (These imperial posts became known as *factories*, since each was run by a *factor*, or manager.) This string of European outposts began at the mouth of the Senegal River, just above Cape Verde, the continent's westernmost point; it ended below the mouth of the Congo River, in present-day Angola. In between, the coastline curved some 5,000 miles. It embraced diverse geographic environments—from open savannas to thick forests—and scores of distinctive cultures. All along this coastline, villagers caught fish and gathered salt for trade with herders and farmers living farther inland.

Generations of contact with oceangoing ships brought new pressures and opportunities to African coastal communities. Local merchants, who traded gold and ivory to sea captains for imported textiles and alcohol, formed alliances with European trading partners in response to the growing demand for human labor. They consolidated their positions near suitable harbors and navigable rivers. From there, they bartered local servants and war captives to white agents for linen, beads, metalwares, and muskets.

Inland traders, alert to the rising demand for slaves in the port towns, annually brought thousands of captives from the backcountry to the coast. The traders traveled by land and water, binding their prisoners together in small groups to form a **coffle** (from the Arabic word for "caravan"). The overseas goods they received as payment included firearms, gunpowder, and knives, which they used in additional wars to secure more captives.

By the 1660s and 1670s, the pace of deportation across the Atlantic had reached an average rate of nearly 15,000 people each year. It rose steadily to a high of more than 65,000 people per year a century later. As the traffic grew, it became increasingly organized, competitive, and routine. Shrewd African traders played one European vessel against another for the best deals. Hardened European agents learned to curry favor with local officials and to quell unrest among captives, confined in the holding pens known as **barracoons**. Experienced captains timed their ventures to avoid the months when sickness was most rampant in the tropics. Through repeated voyages, improved charts, and accumulated lore, they came to differentiate and exploit half a dozen major slaving regions along Africa's Atlantic coast. On occasion, they even ventured to Mozambique in southeast Africa and the nearby island of Madagascar.

■ FIGURE 4.1
GOODS TRADED IN AFRICA
As European ship captains expanded trade along the African coast, they tailored their cargoes to suit the demands of local markets.

■ **MAP 4.1**
REGIONS OF THE AFRICAN SLAVE TRADE IN 1700

The closest market where Europeans bargained for goods and slaves was Senegambia, where Gorée Island, off the coast of Senegal, and James Fort, located in the mouth of the Gambia River, served as slave-trading centers. The long Windward Coast extending to the southeast beyond Sierra Leone became known for its pepper, grain, and ivory. To the east, from the area of Cape Three Points to the factory at Accra, stretched the Gold Coast. There, the Portuguese had established Elmina to draw trade from the Asante gold fields in the interior. Farther east, the Slave Coast reached along the Bight of Benin to the huge delta of the Niger River. Trading depots at Whydah, Ardra, and Lagos drew captives from secondary ports in between. Beyond the Niger, where the African coast turns south near Cameroon, lay the Bight of Biafra. English captains quickly learned the preferences for trade goods in each district, carrying textiles to the Gold Coast and metals to the Bight of Biafra.

The largest and most southerly region, known as Congo-Angola or West Central Africa, was the only one below the equator. Here, Catholic missionaries and Portuguese traders

■ Slaves were held as prisoners in the interior before being marched to the African Coast in groups known as coffles.

established footholds. Before 1700 more than half of all Atlantic slaves departed from West Central Africa. In the eighteenth century the proportion remained over one-third. Later, north of the Congo River, French and English interests came to dominate the slave traffic out of Loango and Cabinda. During the entire span of the slave trade, the Congo-Angola hinterland furnished roughly 40 percent of all African deportees to the Americas: more than 4.5 million men, women, and children.

The Middle Passage Experience

Read the **Document**

Equiano, the Middle Passage (1788) at www.myhistorylab.com

The grim transatlantic exodus was different for every person. Nevertheless, the long nightmare of deportation contained similar elements for all. The entire journey, from normal village life to enslavement beyond the ocean, could last a year or two. It unfolded in at least five stages, beginning with capture and deportation to the African coast. The initial loss of freedom—the first experience of bound hands, harsh treatment, and forced marches—was made worse by the encounters with strange landscapes and unfamiliar languages. Hunger, fatigue, and anxiety took a steady toll as coffles of young and old were conveyed slowly toward the coast through a network of traders.

The next phase, sale and imprisonment, began when a contingent reached the sea, and African traders transferred "ownership" of the captives. Europeans buyers subjected their new property to demeaning inspections and burned brands into their skin. Then they were put in irons alongside hundreds of other captives and guarded in a secure spot to prevent escape. After several months, canoes transported the captives through the surf to a waiting vessel. (Their hands were bound, so if a canoe capsized, it meant certain drowning.) Once aboard, they might languish in the sweltering hold for weeks while the captain cruised the coast in search of additional human cargo. Crew members sometimes raised nets surrounding the deck to prevent attempts at escape or suicide.

View the **Image**

Diagram of a Slave Ship at www.myhistorylab.com

The ship's captain decided when to begin crossing the Atlantic, the harrowing third phase that constituted the middle passage. The Africans below deck now faced an utterly alien plight, trapped in a strange wooden hull. When the crew unfurled the vessel's huge sails, the captives could only anticipate the worst. The dark crowded hold became increasingly fetid and foul. The rolling of the ship on ocean swells brought seasickness and painful chafing from lying on the bare planks. Alexander Falconbridge, who sailed as a surgeon on several slave ships, recorded that "those who are emaciated frequently have their skin and even their flesh entirely rubbed off, by the motion of the ship, from the . . . shoulders, elbows and hips so as to render the bones quite bare."

Historians have documented more than 27,000 slave voyages from Africa to the Americas, and in each one an array of variables came into play to shape the Atlantic crossing. These included the route, the season, the adequacy of supplies, the crew's navigational skills, and the vessel's condition. The resolve of the prisoners, the vagaries of piracy and ocean warfare, and the ravages of disease also became factors. A change in weather conditions or in the captain's mood could mean the difference between life and death.

■ England's Royal African Company maintained more than a dozen small posts along the Gold Coast. Each outpost funneled slaves to this strong seventy-four-gun fortress known as Cape Coast Castle. Cut into rock beneath the parade ground, the vaulted dungeon inside could "conveniently contain a thousand Blacks . . . against any insurrection."

While the grim details varied, the overall pattern remained the same. The constant rolling of the vessel; the sharp changes in temperature; the crowded, filthy conditions; and the relentless physical pain and mental anguish took a heavy toll. Pregnant mothers gave birth or miscarried; women were subjected to abuse and rape by the crew. Sailors threw the deceased to the sharks and even used corpses as bait, catching sharks which they fed to the captives.

●●●──Read the Document

Falconbridge, the African Slave Trade (1788) at **www.myhistorylab.com**

Saltwater Slaves Arrive in America

For the emaciated survivors of the Atlantic ordeal, two further stages remained in their descent into slavery: the selling process and the time called "seasoning." The selling process on American soil could drag on for weeks or months, as prospective owners examined and prodded the newcomers in dockside holding pens. Those purchased were wrenched away from their shipmates with whom they had formed strong links during their miseries at sea. Slaves often were auctioned in groups, or parcels, to ensure sale of the weak along with the strong. A final journey brought them to the particular plantation where many would work until they died.

●──View the Image

Slave Dealers at **www.myhistorylab.com**

Most Africans did not begin their forced labor immediately. Instead, they entered a final stage, known as seasoning, which lasted several months or longer. The newcomers were distinguished as "saltwater slaves"—in contrast to "country-born slaves" who had grown up in America from birth. Seasoning gave newcomers time to mend physically and begin absorbing a new language. Inevitably, many suffered from what we call posttraumatic stress disorder.

As adults and children recovered from the trauma of the middle passage, they faced a series of additional shocks. They confronted foreign landscapes, strange foods, unfamiliar tasks, and even new names. Worst of all, fresh arrivals encountered a master or overseer determined to turn them into compliant bondservants. Repeatedly, the powerful stranger used arbitrary force to demand the slaves' obedience, destroy their hope, and crush any thoughts of resistance.

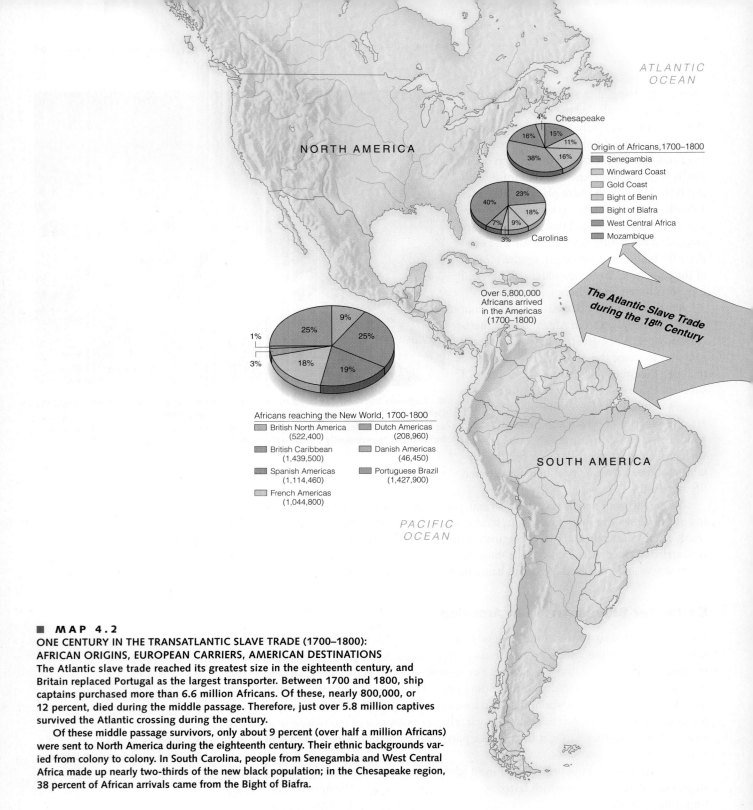

ATLANTIC OCEAN

NORTH AMERICA

4% Chesapeake
15%
16% 11%
38% 16%

Origin of Africans, 1700–1800
- Senegambia
- Windward Coast
- Gold Coast
- Bight of Benin
- Bight of Biafra
- West Central Africa
- Mozambique

23%
40% 18%
7% 9%
3% Carolinas

Over 5,800,000 Africans arrived in the Americas (1700–1800)

The Atlantic Slave Trade during the 18th Century

9%
25% 25%
1%
3% 18% 19%

Africans reaching the New World, 1700–1800
- British North America (522,400)
- British Caribbean (1,439,500)
- Spanish Americas (1,114,460)
- French Americas (1,044,800)
- Dutch Americas (208,960)
- Danish Americas (46,450)
- Portuguese Brazil (1,427,900)

PACIFIC OCEAN

SOUTH AMERICA

■ MAP 4.2

ONE CENTURY IN THE TRANSATLANTIC SLAVE TRADE (1700–1800): AFRICAN ORIGINS, EUROPEAN CARRIERS, AMERICAN DESTINATIONS

The Atlantic slave trade reached its greatest size in the eighteenth century, and Britain replaced Portugal as the largest transporter. Between 1700 and 1800, ship captains purchased more than 6.6 million Africans. Of these, nearly 800,000, or 12 percent, died during the middle passage. Therefore, just over 5.8 million captives survived the Atlantic crossing during the century.

Of these middle passage survivors, only about 9 percent (over half a million Africans) were sent to North America during the eighteenth century. Their ethnic backgrounds varied from colony to colony. In South Carolina, people from Senegambia and West Central Africa made up nearly two-thirds of the new black population; in the Chesapeake region, 38 percent of African arrivals came from the Bight of Biafra.

Survival in a Strange New Land

How did diverse Africans, enslaved in America, find common ground for resistance?

By 1700, race slavery was accepted throughout the mainland colonies. Africans found themselves scattered from New England to Louisiana, but their distribution was far from even. Among roughly 247,000 slaves in the North American colonies in 1750, only 30,000 (or 12 percent) resided in the North, where they made up just 5 percent of the overall population

EUROPE

ATLANTIC
OCEAN

AFRICA

INDIAN
OCEAN

Nations participating and their share
in the slave traffic, 1700-1800

- Britain (3,100,100)
- The Netherlands (349,600)
- Portugal (1,846,900)
- Denmark (52,770)
- France (1,028,950)
- British Colonies/U.S.A. (211,100)

SENEGAMBIA

WINDWARD
COAST

GOLD
COAST

BIGHT OF
BENIN

BIGHT OF
BIAFRA

WEST
CENTRAL
AFRICA

MOZAMBIQUE

Roughly
800,000
Africans
perished
at sea

Approximately
6,600,000
departed
from Africa
(1700–1800)

Africans taken to the Americas, 1700-1800

- Senegambia (389,150)
- Bight of Biafra (1,174,050)
- Windward Coast (521,100)
- West Central Africa (2,440,000)
- Gold Coast (758,550)
- Mozambique (131,000)
- Bight of Benin (1,187,300)

from Pennsylvania to New Hampshire. More than one-third of these northerners (11,000) lived in the colony of New York, where they constituted 14 percent of the colonial inhabitants. All the rest of the people of African descent in North America—some 217,000 men, women, and children by the mid-eighteenth century—lived and worked in the Chesapeake region and the lower South. Fewer than 500 of these black southerners were in Spanish Florida, and fewer than 5,000 resided in French Louisiana.

African Rice Growers in South Carolina

In eighteenth-century North America, by far the greatest number of enslaved workers lived in Virginia or Maryland: 150,000 by 1750. But South Carolina had the highest *proportion* of slaves; there Africans began outnumbering Europeans by 1708. By 1750 South

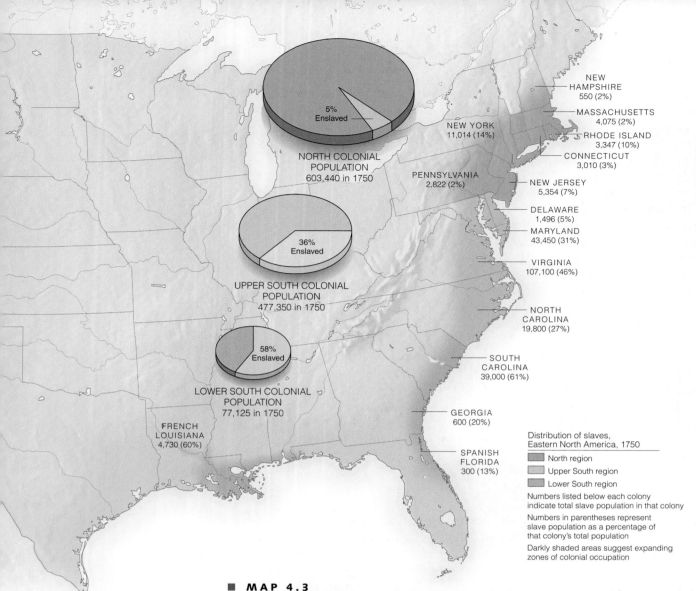

NEW
HAMPSHIRE
550 (2%)

MASSACHUSETTS
4,075 (2%)

RHODE ISLAND
3,347 (10%)

CONNECTICUT
3,010 (3%)

NEW YORK
11,014 (14%)

NEW JERSEY
5,354 (7%)

PENNSYLVANIA
2,822 (2%)

DELAWARE
1,496 (5%)

MARYLAND
43,450 (31%)

VIRGINIA
107,100 (46%)

NORTH
CAROLINA
19,800 (27%)

SOUTH
CAROLINA
39,000 (61%)

GEORGIA
600 (20%)

SPANISH
FLORIDA
300 (13%)

FRENCH
LOUISIANA
4,730 (60%)

**NORTH COLONIAL
POPULATION**
603,440 in 1750

5%
Enslaved

**UPPER SOUTH COLONIAL
POPULATION**
477,350 in 1750

36%
Enslaved

**LOWER SOUTH COLONIAL
POPULATION**
77,125 in 1750

58%
Enslaved

Distribution of slaves,
Eastern North America, 1750

North region

Upper South region

Lower South region

Numbers listed below each colony
indicate total slave population in that colony

Numbers in parentheses represent
slave population as a percentage of
that colony's total population

Darkly shaded areas suggest expanding
zones of colonial occupation

■ **MAP 4.3**

**ENSLAVED PEOPLE LIVING IN NORTH AMERICA IN 1750: DISTRIBUTION BY COLONY, PERCENTAGE
OF TOTAL POPULATION**

By 1750 nearly a quarter of a million people lived as slaves in eastern North America—more than
21 percent of the colonial population. Almost all were Africans or the descendants of Africans, along
with a few thousand Native American and mixed-race slaves. In the North, slaves made up a small
fraction of a large population. By far the greatest number of slaves lived in the Chesapeake area, where
they made up more than a third of the total population. Enslaved people were less numerous but much
more concentrated in the lower South, making up a clear majority of the overall inhabitants. White
settlers had already smuggled several hundred slaves into the fledgling colony of Georgia, even though
the exploitation of slave labor did not become legal there until 1751.

Carolina's black majority (40,000 people) constituted more than 60 percent of the colony's
population. Almost all had arrived through the deepwater port of Charleston. Sullivan's
Island, near the entrance to the harbor, with its so-called **pest house** to quarantine
incoming slaves and reduce the spread of shipborne disease, has been called the Ellis
Island of black America.

What explains the emergence of South Carolina's slave concentration? For one thing,
the colony was closer than Virginia to Africa and to the Caribbean. Moreover, it had been
founded in 1670, just as the English were embracing plantation slavery and the African trade.
Indeed, some of the colony's original proprietors owned stakes in the Royal African Company. Also, some of Carolina's influential early settlers came directly from Barbados, bringing
enslaved Africans and planter ambitions with them.

In the earliest days, South Carolina colonists lacked sufficient labor to clear coastal forests and plant crops. Instead, newcomers let their cattle and pigs run wild. With easy foraging and warm winters, the animals reproduced rapidly. Settlers slaughtered them and shipped quantities of meat to the Caribbean, along with firewood for boiling sugar cane and wooden barrels for transporting sugar. Ship captains also carried enslaved Native Americans to the West Indies and brought back African slaves.

The arriving Africans understood South Carolina's subtropical climate, with its alligators and palmetto trees, better than their European owners did. Many of these enslaved newcomers were already familiar with keeping cattle. Others, obliged to feed themselves, began growing rice in the fertile swamplands just as they had in West Africa. Slave owners quickly realized that this plant, unfamiliar to much of northern Europe, held the answer to their search for a profitable staple crop. Soon, people who had tended their own irrigated rice crops near the Gambia River were clearing cypress swamps along the Ashley and Cooper rivers to grow rice for someone else. They planted and harvested the crop, pounding the grain by hand. They made the fanner baskets used to winnow the rice and wooden barrels needed to export it.

Before long, Carolina entrepreneurs were shipping tons of rice to Europe, where it proved a cheap grain for feeding soldiers, orphans, and peasants. By the middle of the eighteenth century, their fortunes improved even more when indigo, another African crop, joined rice as a profitable export commodity. Outnumbered by their enslaved workers, South Carolina's landowners passed strict Negro Acts that prohibited slaves from carrying guns, meeting in groups, raising livestock, or traveling without a pass. Everywhere, mounted patrols enforced the regulations with brutal severity.

Patterns of Resistance

In South Carolina and elsewhere, enslaved African Americans pressed to relieve their condition in any possible way. Like any other imprisoned population, they spread rumors, refused to work, broke tools, feigned illness, or threatened violence. In response, their owners tried to divide them in order to control them. Masters rewarded workers who were obedient and diligent or who informed on fellow slaves. They imposed harsh punishments—whipping, mutilation, sale, or death—on those suspected of taking food, sowing dissent, or plotting revolt. And they encouraged the formation of black families, not only to gain another generation of laborers at no cost but also to create the emotional ties that they knew would hold individuals in check for fear of reprisals against loved ones.

Owners confined residents in the slave labor camps with curfews and pass systems, denying them literacy and limiting communication with neighbors and relatives. Enslaved families had no viable system for expressing grievances or appealing arbitrary punishments. Faced with such steep odds, many slaves submitted to the deadening routine of the prison camp to survive. But others resorted to diverse strategies to improve their situation or undermine their masters' dominance. Running away, even for a brief period, provided relief from forced work and deprived owners of the labor they depended on. Because arson created serious damage and was difficult to detect, some slaves burned down barns at harvest time. Others succeeded in killing their masters or overseers. Such acts of pent-up rage usually proved suicidal, but they also confirmed slave owners' worst fears.

Above all, the prospect of open rebellion burned in the minds of prisoners and jailers alike. Often, therefore, it is hard to untangle episodes of white paranoia from incidents of actual revolt. Many innocent slaves were falsely accused. But countless others did discuss plans for resistance, and a few freedom fighters avoided detection or betrayal long enough to launch serious uprisings. Word of one upheaval, real or imagined, could spark others.

An early wave of slave unrest erupted in the dozen years after 1710, highlighted by violence in New York City in the spring of 1712. The leaders of the conspiracy were

"Coromantee," or Akan people from Africa's Gold Coast region. Several dozen enslaved Africans and Indians, determined to obtain their freedom and kill all the whites in the town, set fire to a building. As citizens rushed to put out the blaze, the rebels attacked them, killing eight and wounding more. When the militia prevailed, six of the insurgents committed suicide. Authorities executed eighteen, burning some at the stake, hanging others and leaving their bodies on display.

A Wave of Rebellion

A second wave of black resistance swept the mainland colonies after 1730, fueled by the largest influx of Africans to date. In Louisiana, as French landowners staked out riverfront plantations, they also imported African slaves. The several thousand black workers soon outnumbered European settlers, and in 1731 fearful whites broke up two presumed slave plots. One involved a scheme to rebel while Catholic colonists attended a midnight mass on Christmas. Another apparent plot was revealed by the careless boast of a black servant woman. It included several hundred Bambara newcomers from Senegal who aspired to massacre whites, enslave other Africans, and take control of the region. When torture by fire failed to force confessions from key suspects, officials hanged the servant woman. Then the leader and half a dozen other men were "broken on the wheel" (put to death slowly by being tied to wagon wheels and having their bones broken).

The largest slave uprising in colonial North America broke out in 1739 near the Stono River, twenty miles southwest of Charleston. Several factors fueled the Stono Rebellion. By 1739 blacks exceeded whites nearly two to one among South Carolina's 56,000 people. The proportion of recently imported slaves had reached an all-time high. In addition, working conditions had worsened steadily as rice production expanded. Moreover, for several decades the Spanish in Florida had been luring slaves from South Carolina, knowing that the promise of freedom might destabilize Carolina's profitable slave regime. More than a hundred fugitives had escaped to Florida by 1738, when Florida's governor formed them into a free black militia company at St. Augustine. Hoping to win more defections, he allowed thirty-eight African-American households to settle north of the town and build a small fortress—Fort Mose.

■ Archaeologists have recently excavated the site of Fort Mose, near St. Augustine, Florida. Dozens of slaves who escaped from South Carolina received their freedom from the Spanish and established an outpost there in the 1730s.

Meanwhile, the wide commercial rivalries of Spain and Britain led to open warfare in 1739. The slave uprising at Stono erupted just after word reached Charleston that war had broken out between the two Atlantic empires. Other factors may also have influenced the rebels' timing. An epidemic in Charleston had disrupted public activities, and a new Security Act requiring all white men to carry arms to church was to take effect before the end of September.

••••┤**Read** the **Document**
Oglethorpe, Stono Rebellion (1739)
at **www.myhistorylab.com**

Early on Sunday, September 9, 1739, twenty slaves from a work crew near the Stono River broke into a local store. There they seized weapons and executed the owners, then raised a banner and marched south, beating drums and shouting "Liberty!" The insurgents burned selected plantations, killed a score of whites, and gathered more than fifty new recruits. But armed colonists overtook them and blocked their escape to St. Augustine.

Dozens of rebels died in the ensuing battle. In the next two days, militia and hired Indians killed twenty more and captured an additional forty people, whom they immediately shot or hanged.

Yet even fierce reprisals and a harsh new Negro Law could not quell black hopes. In June 1740 several hundred slaves plotted to storm Charleston and take arms from a warehouse. However, a comrade revealed the plan. According to a report, "The next day fifty of them were seized, and these were hanged, ten a day, to intimidate the other negroes." In November, a great fire of suspicious origin consumed much of Charleston.

Fire also played a role in hysteria that broke out in New York City in 1741. In March, a blaze consumed the residence of New York's governor and a local fort. Other fires soon focused suspicions on a white couple, John and Sarah Hughson, who had often entertained blacks at their alehouse. The Hughsons—thought to fence stolen goods for a black crime ring—were accused of inciting working-class unrest. In exchange for her freedom, a sixteen-year-old Irish indentured servant at the Hughsons' tavern testified that she had overheard the planning of an elaborate plot.

In a gruesome spiral of arrests and executions, New York authorities put to death thirty-four people, including four whites, and banished seventy-two blacks. On one hand, the debacle recalled the Salem witch trials, as a fearful community engaged in judicial proceedings and killings on the basis of rumors and accusations. On the other hand, the New York Slave Plot recalled Bacon's Rebellion, for evidence emerged of cooperation between impoverished blacks and whites eager to see a redistribution of property. According to his accusers, a slave named Cuffee had often observed that "a great many people had too much, and others too little." He predicted that soon his master "should have less, and that he (Cuffee) should have more." Instead, he was burned at the stake.

The Transformation Completed

The mechanisms for extorting labor from tens of thousands of people were firmly in place. But to maintain the slave labor system, local governments had to be vigilant and repressive, prompting debates within the white population. Some colonists saw slavery as too morally degrading and physically dangerous to maintain. Powerful supporters of the institution, however, found it too rewarding to give up and suggested modifications instead.

What prevented antislavery ideas from gaining a stronger foothold in the American colonies?

Debating Racial Status in the South and the North

Stakes were highest in the South, where most African Americans lived. As race-based slavery expanded, white colonists treated the continuing presence of free blacks as a contradiction and a threat. As early as 1691, the Virginia assembly passed an act restricting **manumissions** (grants of individual freedom by masters) because "great inconvenience may happen to this country by setting of negroes and mulattoes free." According to the act, such people fanned hopes of freedom among enslaved blacks. Besides, when they grew old and infirm, their care at public expense could constitute "a charge upon the country." By 1723 additional Virginia statutes prevented free people of color from voting, taxed them unfairly, and prevented them from owning or carrying firearms. Lawmakers went on to prohibit all manumissions, except when the governor rewarded "meritorious service," such as informing against other enslaved workers.

Following the Stono uprising, whites in South Carolina conducted their own debate. Leaders imposed a heavy import duty on new African arrivals for several years, hoping to increase the colony's ratio of whites to enslaved blacks. At a time of growing humanitarian concerns in Enlightenment Europe, it took great effort to maintain the rationale for building slavery-based societies in the South. But free people who questioned the institution met stiff resistance from those with vested interests.

While the southern planters labored to intimidate enslaved populations and weaken or contain free black communities, African Americans in the North, both enslaved and free, faced related challenges. Northern slave populations, though far smaller than those in the South, were growing steadily. As the North's involvement in the Atlantic slave trade expanded, its economic and legal commitment to race slavery increased. Rhode Island's slave ranks jumped from 500 in 1720 to more than 3,000 in 1750. Everywhere, new laws made manumission more difficult, and African Americans faced growing discrimination when attempting to hold jobs, buy land, obtain credit, move freely, and take part in civic life. Only in the century after 1760 did northern free black communities gain the numerical and social strength to offer effective opposition to enslavement.

See the **Map**
The Colonies to 1740 at
www.myhistorylab.com

Whereas free blacks lacked the means to oppose slavery, prominent white Christians lacked the will. Even in Massachusetts, where religion remained a dominant force at the turn of the century and the number of slaves had scarcely reached 1,000 people, many leaders already owned black servants, and most ministers defended the practice.

The protests that did appear were ambivalent at best. Judge Samuel Sewell questioned African enslavement in *The Selling of Joseph* (1700). But the tract revealed Sewell's sense of superiority and his skepticism that blacks could play a part in "the Peopling of the Land." African Americans, the judge commented, "can seldom use their freedom well; yet their continual aspiring after their forbidden Liberty, renders them unwilling servants." Reverend Cotton Mather, a slave owner who once berated Sewell as one who "pleaded much for Negroes," was even more ambivalent. In *The Negro Christianized* (1706), the influential Puritan stressed that conversion and Christian instruction, far from earning African slaves their freedom, would make them into "better servants."

Is This Consistent with Christianity or Common Justice?

The conversion and instruction of slaves, rather than the abolition of slavery, became a mission for earnest whites such as Thomas Bray. This well-to-do English philanthropist was committed to spreading the Anglican faith in America among Europeans, Indians, and Africans. In 1701 Bray established the Society for the Propagation of the Gospel in Foreign Parts (SPG). The SPG strengthened the Church of England abroad in the eighteenth century by providing dozens of ministers to serve in the colonies.

But this Anglican foothold came at a steep price. Southern planters made SPG ministers agree that any hopes they offered to slaves regarding heavenly salvation would not include hints of earthly freedom. With few exceptions, the Anglican clergy gave in, strengthening religious support of race slavery. In 1723 a heartfelt petition from a mulatto slave to the Bishop of London, in which the author protested "Cruell Bondegg" in Virginia, went unanswered. That same year, Bray set up a trust of "Associates" to carry on his work. With limited success, they focused on converting blacks in the British plantation colonies.

By the 1730s, only a few whites in Europe or America dared to press publicly for an end to slavery. Christian Priber, who arrived in the South in 1735, was one such activist. The idealistic German hoped to start a utopian community in southern Appalachia. But his radical proposal for a multiracial "Paradise" uniting Indians, Africans, and Europeans posed a huge threat to South Carolina authorities. "He enumerates many whimsical Privileges and natural Rights, as he calls them, which his Citizens are to be entitled to," wrote a scornful detractor, fearful that this egalitarian haven "at the Foot of the Mountains among the Cherokees" was to be "a City of Refuge for all Criminals, Debtors, and Slaves who would fly thither from Justice or their Masters." Priber's brief career as a social agitator challenging the status quo ended in 1743, when he was arrested and brought to jail in Charleston. He died—or was killed—before his case could be heard in court.

At the same time, a New Jersey tailor and bookkeeper named John Woolman posed a less defiant but more enduring threat to race slavery. In 1743, at age twenty-three, this shy Quaker began to question his role in writing out bills of sale when his fellow Quakers purchased slaves. It struck him forcefully that "to live in ease and plenty by the toil of those whom violence and cruelty have put in our power" was clearly not "consistent with Christianity or common justice." Woolman traveled widely to Quaker meetings, north and south, pressing an issue that most Quakers preferred to ignore. When he drafted *Some Considerations on the Keeping of Negroes* (1754), members of the Quaker Yearly Meeting in Philadelphia published his booklet and circulated it widely. Four years later, led by Anthony Benezet, this group outlawed slaveholding among its local members. They set a precedent that many Quakers followed in the next generation, and they challenged other denominations to do the same.

Oglethorpe's Antislavery Experiment

The most sustained early challenge to the slavery system in the American South came in the Georgia colony. In 1732 a group of well-connected London proprietors (known as trustees) obtained a twenty-year charter for the region between English South Carolina and Spanish Florida. Ten of the twenty-one initial trustees were members of Parliament. They included James Oglethorpe, who had recently organized and chaired a "committee on jails" to investigate the condition of debtors in English prisons.

See the **Map**

Oglethorpe, "Establishing Georgia" (1733) at **www.myhistorylab.com**

The trustees foresaw three related purposes—charitable, commercial, and military—for their experimental colony, which they named after King George II. Georgia would provide a haven for England's worthy poor, selected members of the neediest classes who could be transported across the Atlantic and settled on small farms. These grateful newcomers would then produce warm-weather commodities—olives, grapes, silk—to support the empire. Their prosperity would create a growing market for English goods. Finally, their presence would provide a military buffer to protect South Carolina from further warfare with the Yamasee and Creek Indians and from possible invasion by the Spanish in St. Augustine.

With Oglethorpe as their governor, an initial boatload of 114 settlers arrived in 1733 and began building a capital at Savannah. By 1741 the town, located on a bluff 15 miles up the Savannah River, boasted more than 140 houses. By then, more than a 1,000 needy English, plus 800 German, Swiss, and Austrian Protestants, had journeyed to Georgia at the trustees' expense. Another thousand immigrants had paid their own way. Like earlier colonizers, Georgia's first arrivals had trouble adjusting to a strange environment. Alligators, rattlesnakes, and hurricanes tested their resolve. Tension over governance only deepened their discouragement.

The idealistic trustees in London declined to accumulate property and profits for themselves in the colony, but they felt justified in controlling every aspect of Georgia's development. For example, they knew that gin was becoming a source of debt and disruption in Europe and that rum and brandy sold by traders was poisoning colonial relations with southeastern Indians. So in 1735 they outlawed the use of every "kind of Spirits" while still allowing consumption of wine and beer. Georgia's early experiment with prohibition of hard liquor proved difficult to implement, and officials quietly stopped enforcing the law in 1742.

Other efforts at control from above went further. The trustees refused to set up a legislature or to let settlers buy and sell land. Instead, they gave 50 acres of farm land to each family they sent over, plus a house lot in a local village, so all new towns could be well defended. But they parceled out land with little regard for variations in soil fertility. They also stipulated that owners could pass land on to sons only. To prevent the concentrations of wealth that they saw developing in other colonies, the trustees said that no one could own more

INTERPRETING HISTORY

"Releese Us Out of This Cruell Bondegg"

*A*s researchers pay increasing attention to African bondage in the colonial era, new pieces of evidence continue to appear. This halting but powerful appeal, written in Virginia in 1723 by a mulatto Christian slave, was rediscovered in a London archive in the 1990s and transcribed by historian Thomas Ingersoll. It is addressed to Edward Gibson, the newly appointed Bishop of London, whose position gave him religious oversight over all the Anglican parishes in England's American colonies, including Virginia. Gibson had voiced an interest in the Christianization of enslaved Africans, but like many contemporary church leaders, he showed less interest in the liberation of slaves. This heartfelt document, prepared with great labor and at enormous risk, was simply filed away with the bishop's vast correspondence. It never received a response or prompted any inquiry into conditions in Virginia.

August the forth 1723

to the Right Raverrand father in god my Lord arch Bishop of Lonnd. . . .

this coms to sattesfie your honour that there is in this Land of verJennia a Sort of people that is Calld molatters which are Baptised and brouaht up in the way of the Christian faith and followes the ways and Rulles of the Chrch of England and sum of them has white fathars and sum white mothers and there is in this Land a Law or act which keeps and makes them and there seed Slaves forever. . . .

wee your humbell and poore partishinners doo begg Sir your aid and assisttancce in this one thing . . . which is that your honour will by the help of our Sufvering [i.e., sovereign] Lord King George and the Rest of the Rullers will Releese us out of this Cruell Bondegg. . . . and here it is to bee notd that one brother is a Slave to another and one Sister to an othe which is quite out of the way and as for mee my selfe I am my brothers Slave but my name is Secrett

wee are commandded to keep holey the Sabbath day and wee doo hardly know when it comes for our task mastrs are has hard with us as the Egypttions was with the Chilldann of Issarall. . . . wee are kept out of the Church and matrimony is deenied us and to be plain they doo Look no more upon us then if wee ware dogs which I hope when these Strange lines comes to your Lord Ships hands will be Looket in to. . . .

And Sir wee your humble perticners do humblly beg . . . that our childarn may be broatt up in the way of the Christtian faith and our desire is that they may be Larnd the Lords prayer the creed and the ten commandements and that they may appeare Every Lord's day att Church before the Curatt to bee Exammond for our desire is that godllines Shoulld abbound amongs us and wee desire that our Childarn be putt to Scool and Larnd to Reed through the Bybell

My Riting is vary bad. . . . I am but a poore Slave that writt itt and has no other time butt Sunday and hardly that att Sumtimes. . . . wee dare nott Subscribe any mans name to this for feare of our masters for if they knew that wee have Sent home to your honour wee Should goo neare to Swing upon the gallass tree.

than 500 acres. Prohibiting massive estates would allow for thicker settlement and therefore greater manpower to defend the colony militarily.

But the most important prohibition, by far, involved slavery. Oglethorpe began his career as a deputy governor of the Royal African Company, but he died in 1785 opposing the slave trade. His sojourn in Georgia turned him against slavery. In neighboring South Carolina, he saw firsthand how the practice degraded African lives, undermined the morals of Europeans, and laid that colony open to threats of revolt and invasion. So Oglethorpe persuaded the trustees to create a free white colony, convincing them to enact a law in 1735 that prohibited slavery and also excluded free blacks. He believed that this mandate would protect Georgia from the corruptions of enslavement while also making it easier to apprehend black runaways heading to Florida from South Carolina.

In 1739, the Stono Rebellion and the outbreak of war between England and Spain strengthened Oglethorpe's belief that slavery undermined security by creating internal enemies who would support foreign attackers. He saw further evidence in 1740, when he failed in a wartime attempt to capture St. Augustine from Spain. Unable to take the Florida stronghold, the governor seized neighboring Fort Mose, the bastion erected by anti-English slaves who had escaped from Carolina. Later, a Spanish force relying heavily on Indian and African-American fighters retook Fort Mose, showing Oglethorpe the intensity with which ex-slaves would fight the English, their former masters.

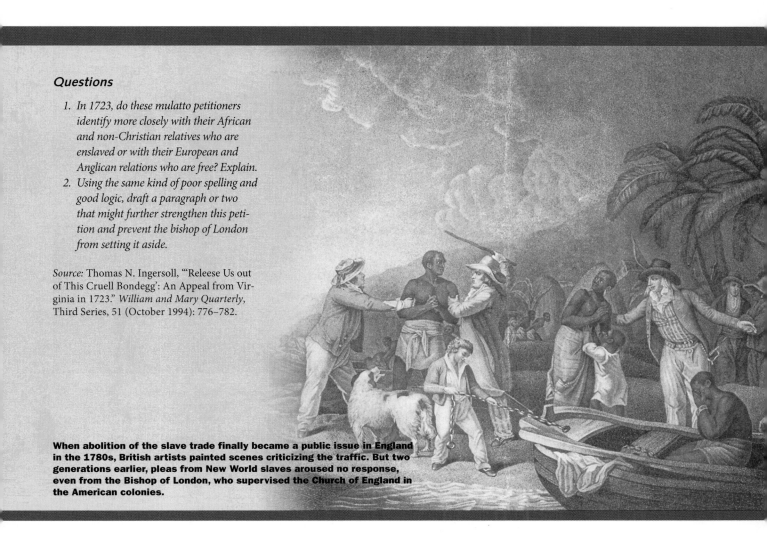

Questions

1. *In 1723, do these mulatto petitioners identify more closely with their African and non-Christian relatives who are enslaved or with their European and Anglican relations who are free? Explain.*
2. *Using the same kind of poor spelling and good logic, draft a paragraph or two that might further strengthen this petition and prevent the bishop of London from setting it aside.*

Source: Thomas N. Ingersoll, "'Releese Us out of This Cruell Bondegg': An Appeal from Virginia in 1723." *William and Mary Quarterly,* Third Series, 51 (October 1994): 776–782.

When abolition of the slave trade finally became a public issue in England in the 1780s, British artists painted scenes criticizing the traffic. But two generations earlier, pleas from New World slaves aroused no response, even from the Bishop of London, who supervised the Church of England in the American colonies.

The next year, fearing a counterattack, Oglethorpe issued a warning to imperial officials. He predicted that if Spanish soldiers captured Georgia, a colony inhabited by "white Protestants and no Negroes," they would then send agents to infiltrate the vulnerable colonies farther north and stir black rebellion.

The End of Equality in Georgia

As Britain's war with Spain continued, few whites could deny the Georgia governor's assertion that slavery elsewhere in British America was a source of internal weakness and strategic danger. Just as Oglethorpe had predicted, Spain pushed from Florida into Georgia with an eye toward destabilizing the colonies farther north. In 1742, Oglethorpe's troops repulsed the invading Spanish force in the crucial Battle at Bloody Marsh on St. Simon's Island.

The victory at Bloody Marsh reduced the immediate threat to Britain's North American colonies, especially neighboring South Carolina, where Oglethorpe and his idealistic policies had numerous powerful opponents. These opponents now joined a group of so-called Malcontents in Savannah to question Georgia's continued prohibition against slavery. By challenging the trustees' antislavery stance, this self-interested coalition prompted the first protracted North American debate about enslavement.

Given Georgia's numerous drawbacks—including a sickly climate, poor soil, restrictive land policies, and lack of representative government—a well-organized faction argued that

■ In 1729 James Oglethorpe (seated, right front) chaired a parliamentary committee exposing the harsh conditions in English jails. When William Hogarth portrayed the committee's visit to Fleet Street Prison, the artist showed Oglethorpe's concern for a dark-skinned prisoner, a hint of the philanthropist's future opposition to slavery in Georgia.

the colony needed slavery in order to prosper. But not everyone agreed. In 1739 Scottish Highlanders living at Darien on the Altamaha River had contacted Oglethorpe to lay out their practical arguments against importing Africans. Their petition expressed shock "that any Race of Mankind, and their Posterity, Should be sentenced to perpetual slavery." Immigrants from Salzburg, Germany, residing at Ebenezer on the Savannah River drafted a similar statement. But Georgia's Malcontents pushed back, demanding the right to import slaves. They drew encouragement and support from powerful merchant-planters in South Carolina, eager to expand their trade in slaves from Africa and to extend their successful rice operations into coastal Georgia.

Oglethorpe warned that the proslavery lobby, hungry to create large estates, seemed bent on "destroying the Agrarian Equality" envisioned in Georgia's initial plan. But over time, the colony's trustees in London grew less unified, committed, and informed. Eventually, the persistent efforts of the proslavery pamphleteers bore fruit. In 1750 the trustees gave in on the matter of land titles. They allowed acreage to be bought and sold freely in any amount. This invited the creation of large plantations, and that pointed toward the drastic step to allowing slavery. The trustees finally caved in on the question of bondage, letting Georgians purchase enslaved workers. The 1750 law permitting slavery after January 1, 1751, made futile gestures to ensure kind treatment and Christian education for slaves. But the dam had broken. Hundreds of slave-owning South Carolinians streamed across the Savannah River to invest in Georgia land. In 1752 the trustees disbanded, their patent expiring, their vision undone. By 1754 Georgia had become a royal colony.

Slave labor camps producing rice and indigo for export soon dotted the lowcountry on both sides of the Savannah River. Georgia's assembly passed a harsh slave code in 1755, based on South Carolina's. Two years later, it legislated a system of patrols to keep the brutal new

To the Honble the Trustees for establishing the Colony of Georgia in America
This View of the Town of Savanah is humbly dedicated by their Honours
Obliged and most Obedient Servant.
Peter Gordon.

■ Savannah, the capital of Oglethorpe's Georgia, was one year old when this view was sketched in 1734. The following year, Georgia's trustees officially outlawed slavery, creating a sharp contrast with the other British colonies in North America, especially neighboring South Carolina on the opposite bank of the Savannah River.

regime in place. Georgia's effort to counter race slavery in North America had failed, a case of too little too late. After holding out for nearly two decades, the colony fell victim to the same divisive institution that had already taken root elsewhere.

◉ View the Image
Slave Quarter, Hermitage Plantation, Savannah, Georgia
at **www.myhistorylab.com**

CONCLUSION

Bit by bit, the slavery system gained a firm foothold in North America during the century after 1660. In southern colonies the system shaped the entire economy and social structure, creating a society based on race slavery. Farther north, where the institution never dominated, it still persisted as a disturbing element of colonial life. Two final observations provide a wider Atlantic context. First, the influx of African slaves into English North America occurred long after the **diaspora**, or dispersion, to Mexico, Brazil, and the Caribbean was well established. The North American portion of the gigantic African traffic did not expand steadily until after the 1670s. A century later, on the eve of the American Revolution, the proportion of blacks in the colonial population (over 20 percent) was higher than it has ever been in the United States since then.

Second, even at its height, the North American trade remained marginal in relation to the wider Atlantic commerce in African labor. For example, whereas roughly 50,000 enslaved men and women reached all the docks of North America between 1721 and 1740, the small West Indian islands of English Barbados and French Guadeloupe *each* received more than 53,000 Africans during the same period. In the next two decades, while Britain's mainland

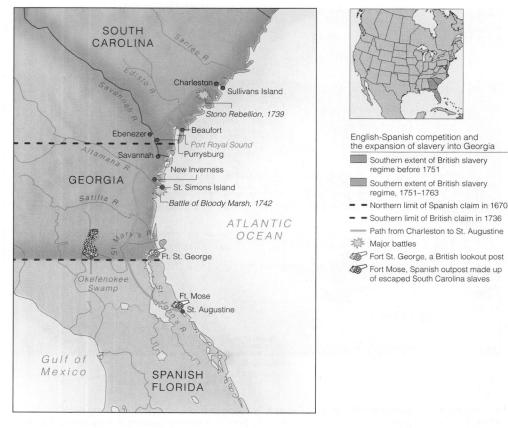

■ MAP 4.4

ENGLISH-SPANISH COMPETITION AND THE EXPANSION OF SLAVERY INTO GEORGIA
The Spanish and the British had competing land claims along the southeast coast after 1670. Creation of the Georgia colony in 1732 intensified the rivalry. The Spanish in Florida offered freedom to any slaves who escaped from South Carolina to St. Augustine, sparking the Stono Revolt in 1739. During the war between Britain and Spain (1739–1743), Georgians defeated the Spanish at Bloody Marsh and secured the disputed "Sea Island" region for the British. Within a decade, slavery became legal in Georgia, and scores of new labor camps appeared between the Savannah and the St. Mary's River, producing rice for export.

colonies purchased just over 100,000 Africans, Caribbean Islands such as English Jamaica (120,000) and French Saint Domingue (159,000) absorbed many more slaves.

During this single forty-year span (1721–1760), Brazil bought 667,000 African workers—more than would reach North America during the entire slave trade. All told, scholars currently estimate that some 650,000 Africans were brought to North America over several centuries. They represented roughly 6 percent of the total Atlantic commerce in enslaved people. Still, the number of mainland slaves expanded from scarcely 7,000 in 1680 to nearly 29,000 in 1700 and to more than 70,000 in 1720. Half a century later in 1770, because of importation and natural increase, 470,000 individuals from New Hampshire to French Louisiana were confined to enslavement.

A century had passed since Elizabeth Key's generation saw the terrible transformation begin. Relative openness had given way to systematic oppression, and slavery's corrosive effects were felt at every level of society. An English visitor to the South in 1759 found provincial planters "vain and imperious," subject "to many errors and prejudices, especially in regard to Indians and Negroes, whom they scarcely consider as of the human species." It took another century before pressures developed that could unseat race slavery, sanctioned by law, as a dominant institution in the land.

For Review

✓•─│Study and **Review** at www.myhistorylab.com

1. What role did the English Restoration of 1660 play in the establishment of African slavery in England's North American colonies?

2. What evidence exists that enslaved Africans, stripped of so much in the Middle Passage, still brought knowledge, skills, and cultural values with them to the New World?

3. If you had been an enslaved person, how would you have responded to harsh, arbitrary treatment? Why?

4. "In retrospect, the best time and place to halt and reverse the 'Terrible Transformation' would have been. . . . " How would you complete this thought?

Chronology: 1672–1751

1672 Royal African Company (RAC) formed in London.

1676 Virginia and Maryland slaves join in Bacon's Rebellion.

1705 Virginia approves Negro Act.

1712 New York City slave revolt.

1713 British receive the contract *(asiento)* to supply African slaves to Spanish colonies.

1734 James Oglethorpe launches Georgia as a nonslave colony.

1739 Slave revolt in Stono, South Carolina.

1741 Alleged slave plot in New York City.

1751 Slavery is legalized in Georgia.

Key Terms

Asiento A contract negotiated by the Spanish crown (between 1595 and 1789) with other European powers such as Portugal, France, England, and the Netherlands to provide a fixed number of slaves annually to Spain's American colonies for a set payment. p. 85

Barracoon An enclosure or barrack used for the confinement of slaves before their forced deportation from the African coast. p. 92

Coffle A procession or train of enslaved prisoners, bound together for travel (from the Arabic word for "caravan"). p. 92

Diaspora The dispersion of a population abroad, whether forced or voluntary. The term is often applied to Jewish settlement outside the eastern Mediterranean region, and to the spread of Africans across the Americas, due to the Atlantic slave trade. p. 107

Indenture A document binding one person to work for another for a given period of time. Indentured servants received food, shelter, and clothing, plus "freedom dues" when their terms of service ended to help them get started independently. p. 88

Manumission A formal emancipation from slavery; the act (by an individual owner or government authority) of granting freedom to an enslaved person or persons. p. 101

Middle passage For European slave ships, the middle passage was the second of three legs in the triangular round-trip voyage from Europe to Africa to America and back to Europe. For enslaved Africans, the middle passage came to mean not only the transatlantic journey itself, but the entire process of removal from an African homeland and ultimate sale to an American master. p. 91

Pest house In colonial times, a shelter to quarantine those possibly infected with contagious diseases (such as newcomers arriving in American ports from Africa or Europe) to prevent the spread of shipborne pestilence. p. 98

5

An American Babel, 1713–1763

In 1749 peace seemed a welcome prospect in the Spanish settlement of San Antonio in south-central Texas. On an August morning, hundreds of people gathered in the town plaza. Captain Turibio de Urrutia, the local military commander, was there along with Father Santa Ana, who presided over the local missions. Across from them stood four Apache Indian chiefs with many of their people. Between the two groups, in the center of the plaza, Spanish and Indian workers began to dig a deep pit with steep sides. Those attending were about to witness one of the most important events in the town's brief history.

Three decades earlier, in 1718, a small Spanish expedition had established the town next to the San Antonio River. The newcomers built houses and excavated irrigation ditches to divert river water onto their fields. But they had occupied contested ground. In 1720 Apache bands, moving south under pressure from the Comanche, attacked several settlers. The Spanish responded with their own raids, capturing Apache women and children and selling them into Mexico as slaves.

Father Santa Ana protested such harsh tactics. The cleric hoped to make peace with the Apache and draw them into the expanding mission system, where they would learn Spanish and accept Christianity. At Santa Ana's urging, Captain Urrutia modified his approach in 1749. After the spring raids, he ordered humane treatment for the 175 prisoners brought back to San Antonio. Rather than sell them as slaves, he merely detained them and sent several captives back to Apache country with a proposal for peace.

When these messengers (two women and a man) returned with word that important Apache chiefs were prepared to negotiate, the townsfolk welcomed the Apache delegation. There was feasting, important for such occasions, and the four chiefs attended a mass conducted by Father Santa Ana. After two days of discussion through translators, the Spanish released some Apache prisoners as a goodwill gesture, and both sides agreed to hold a formal peace ceremony in the plaza.

The next day all gathered to watch the workers digging the deep pit. Then the longtime adversaries buried their differences in an elaborate symbolic ritual. They lowered a live horse into the hole, along with other emblems of warfare: a lance, a hatchet, and a bundle of arrows. Next, the four chiefs linked hands and walked solemnly around the pit, accompanied by the Spanish leaders. At a signal, all the onlookers suddenly grabbed up loose earth and tossed it into the hole. The horse was completely buried—a sacrifice for peace—and the ceremony broke up with shouts and celebration.

Though striking, the encounter between the Spanish and Apache at San Antonio was not unique. During the same era, Europeans and Native Americans met to parley and trade in Detroit, Albany, Philadelphia, Charleston, Savannah, St. Augustine, Mobile, New Orleans, and other colonial towns. Such formal occasions highlight a wider process of contact and interaction throughout the North American colonies in the half-century between 1713 and 1763. Everywhere, colonial expansion brought together Europeans, Africans, and Native Americans in surprising new contacts. Equally important, it forced different peoples *within* each of these three categories, despite contrasting backgrounds, to rub shoulders with one another in unfamiliar ways.

These encounters had all been set in motion by the colonization process. Spanish missionaries lived among Tejas Indians in eastern Texas; French explorers dominated, and then lost, the Mississippi Valley; escaped African slaves fought militiamen from Georgia on the outskirts of St. Augustine. Everywhere, motives differed, accents jarred, and cultures clashed. In Philadelphia, Benjamin Franklin, a newcomer from Boston, protested the way in which Germans "swarm into our settlements, and by herding together establish their language and manner to the exclusion of ours."

For many Christians, the new confusions recalled the story of **Babel**. The people in that biblical city, despite their high ambitions, could not understand one another well enough to work together. Eventually, they scattered abroad across the face of the earth. Bible-reading Americans no doubt recalled that tale, especially during the great religious awakening that shook the English colonies in the 1740s, when the prospect of building something new and transcendent seemed close at hand. The German-born utopian Christian Priber even attempted to establish an egalitarian realm in Appalachia where Europeans, Africans, and Native Americans could live peaceably together. Such dreams were not to be, however. Instead, the existing colonies continued to build up regional economies of their own, under British protection, and elements of a dominant Anglo-American culture began to emerge amid the Atlantic Babel's many voices.

■ Mission San Francisco de la Espada, at San Antonio, had 1,100 cattle, 80 horses, and 16 pairs of oxen when this chapel was being constructed in the 1740s. By the time the United States annexed Texas a century later (1845), the church had fallen into disrepair.

New Cultures on the Western Plains

It makes sense that the Apache chose to bury a horse during their elaborate ceremony at the Spanish presidio (military post) in 1749. By this time the horse, recently introduced to the Indians, was transforming life on the Great Plains. It also makes sense that they buried arrows and hatchets rather than guns. From the time of Spain's arrival in the New World, official Spanish policy had forbidden the sale of firearms to Native Americans.

In contrast, the French, Dutch, and English desired trade at almost any cost. They showed less hesitation about supplying Indians with guns in return for furs, so firearms had become

How and why did life change dramatically for the Comanche and Sioux Indians after 1700?

familiar to many eastern Indians in the seventeenth century. In the eighteenth century, guns began to spread west across the Mississippi River. Combined with the movement of horses from the south, this development had enormous consequences. New patterns of warfare altered Indian cultures, and more powerful hunting techniques affected the regional economies and ecologies of the Native American West.

The Spread of the Horse

Although small horses once roamed the ancient West, they migrated into Asia thousands of years ago and became extinct in America. Horses returned with the early Spanish explorers. Around 1600, when New Mexico's early colonists brought mares north for breeding, horse herds developed in the Rio Grande valley. After the Pueblo Revolt in 1680, Spanish horses taken by the Indians were rapidly traded northward from one culture to another.

By 1690, the Ute had obtained horses and traded them to the Shoshone. Before the mid-eighteenth century, horses had moved west of the Rocky Mountains to the Nez Perce and north to the Blackfoot. The Apache brought horses east to the Caddoan cultures near the Red River and then north to the Pawnee, Arikara, and Hidatsa. Even tribes in the Southeast acquired Spanish horses from the West before they obtained English horses from the Atlantic coast. When a Chickasaw leader drew a regional map on deerskin in 1723, he showed a Native American leading a horse east of the Mississippi River.

The first horses seemed utterly strange to the Indians. "The people did not know what they fed on. They would offer the animals pieces of dried meat," one elder recalled. "He put us on mind of a Stag that had lost his horns," another remembered, "and we did not know what name to give him. But as he was a slave to Man, like the dog, which carried our things, he was named the Big Dog." For generations, Native Americans had used dogs to pull provisions and

■ The horse offered new mobility for hunting, as in this modern painting of Navajo riders. Tribes that had once tracked buffalo on foot at the edge of the Great Plains could now pursue herds across miles of open grassland. This was true for the Cheyenne, who were living in fixed villages in what is now South Dakota in the early eighteenth century. "After they got the first horses," recalled John Stands-in-Timber, "they learned there were more of them in the South and they went there after them." Cheyenne life would never be the same again.

bedding on a **travois**, an A-frame device made with tent poles. A larger animal could haul bigger loads, including longer tent poles that allowed for more spacious tipis.

Whether or not a tribe used tipis as dwellings, it could readily use the horse as a new source of food and as an aid in hunting. As herds expanded and horsemanship improved, warriors rode into battle. On horses, they could conduct lightning raids over long distances. Soon raising, trading, and stealing horses became important activities, and a family's wealth and status depended partly on the number of horses at its command.

The Rise of the Comanche

By the 1770s, mounted Comanche warriors commanded respect and fear across a vast domain. Their territory stretched south nearly 600 miles from western Kansas to central Texas, and it spanned 400 miles from eastern New Mexico to what is now eastern Oklahoma. This area, known as the Comanchería, roughly equaled all the English settlements on the Atlantic coast in size, but its origins were recent and humble. The Comanche's Shoshone-speaking ancestors had been hunter-gatherers on the high plains of Wyoming, living on small game, roots, and berries. The arrival of the horse around 1690 changed everything, allowing family bands to migrate southeast from the Rockies to the western edges of the Great Plains. There, they could hunt buffalo and then ride south annually to trade hides for additional horses at Taos and Santa Fe.

The Comanche were not the first to make their homes in what is now eastern Colorado. For generations, groups of Apache had settled in the region near the upper reaches of the Platte and Arkansas rivers. The Apache settlements—with their irrigated gardens and herds of horses—provided easy targets for Comanche newcomers. Within two decades, the Comanche had hammered their enemies south through one river valley after another. When Apache bands reached San Antonio, they stole livestock from the new Spanish settlement to survive. Threatened by the Comanche moving into central Texas, the hard-pressed Apache chose to seal a pact with the Spanish at San Antonio in 1749.

The Spanish soon began building a mission and presidio among their new Apache allies. But the outpost, 150 miles northwest of San Antonio on the San Saba River, had been established for less than a year when the Comanche attacked it in 1758. They returned the next year, capturing 700 horses. "The heathen of the north are innumerable and rich," exclaimed a Spanish officer at San Saba. "They dress well, breed horses, [and] handle firearms with the greatest skill." The Comanche onslaught continued, and the attacks finally forced the Spanish to withdraw from San Saba in 1767.

In less than two decades, the Comanche had overrun most of Texas. They continued to absorb smaller Native American groups and swell in numbers. By 1780 they had grown into a proud Indian nation of more than 20,000 people. Their domain, the Comanchería, remained a powerful entity in the Southwest for decades.

The Expansion of the Sioux

Comanche strength depended not only on mounted warfare but also on using the horse as a trade commodity to obtain guns. Because Spanish policy prohibited the sale of firearms to Native Americans, the Comanche looked east for weapons. They discovered that by selling horses to their eastern allies, such as the Wichita Indians, they could receive French muskets from Louisiana in return. But the Comanche were not alone; the Sioux also took advantage of the gun frontier as it inched steadily west.

By 1720 the French had established settlements at Peoria, Cahokia, and Kaskaskia in Illinois and at New Orleans, Natchez, and Natchitoches in Louisiana. French traders at these sites provided guns and other metal goods to Indians in exchange for salt, deerskins, beaver pelts, horses, and war captives. Native American groups that took advantage of this

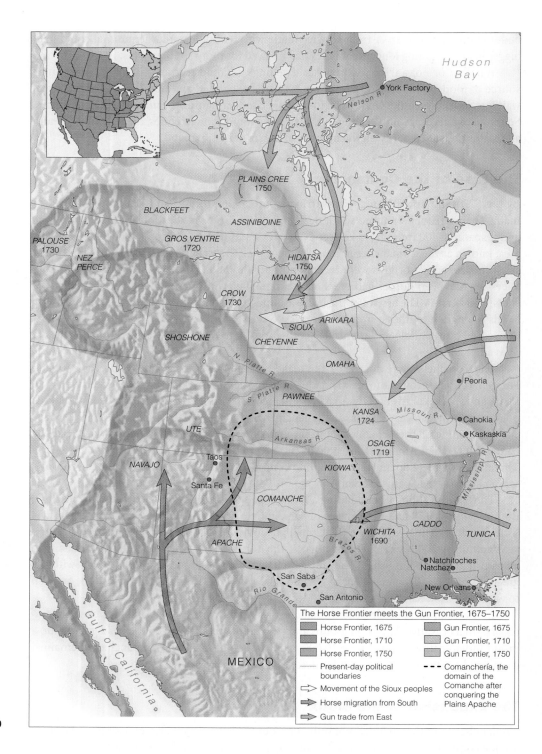

■ MAP 5.1
THE HORSE FRONTIER MEETS
THE GUN FRONTIER, 1675–1750

trade included the Tunica beside the Mississippi, the Caddo and Wichita along the Red and Arkansas rivers, and the Osage, Pawnee, and Omaha tribes near the Missouri.

Farther north, muskets carried west from French posts on the Great Lakes and south from English bases on Hudson Bay proved especially important among the Sioux peoples, who trapped game and gathered wild rice by the lakes of their Minnesota homeland. When the Sioux first encountered a gun from French voyageurs in the mid-seventeenth century, they called it *mazawakan*, meaning "mysterious or sacred iron." Initially, they used the few muskets they could obtain to fight their less well-armed Indian neighbors. By 1700 French traders, moving from the east, had established direct trade with the Sioux, offering a steady supply of guns and powder in exchange for furs.

For a generation, several Sioux bands (the Teton and Yanktonai) walked between two worlds. In the summers, they followed the buffalo onto the prairies, with dogs pulling travois and women carrying heavy burdens. As cold weather approached, they retreated to the edge of the woodlands to gather firewood and seek beaver. In the spring, after trading meat and pelts to the French for guns and ammunition, they returned to the edge of the plains. They glimpsed their first horses not long after 1700. But it was several generations before the western Sioux had acquired enough mounts to drop their old customs and adopt a horse-centered way of life.

By midcentury, the horse frontier on the northern Great Plains had met the gun frontier. Saukamappee, a Cree Indian living with the Blackfoot, remembered vividly the surprise of the initial encounter. When he was a young man, his war party—well-armed and on foot—had gone into battle against the Shoshone. "We had more guns and iron headed arrows than [ever] before," he recalled years later. "But our enemies . . . had Misstutim [Big Dogs, that is, Horses] on which they rode, swift as the Deer."

As the overlap of horse and gun proceeded after 1750, Sioux women assumed the burdensome task of processing slain buffalo. Sioux men, meanwhile, used muskets to acquire more mounts and dominate the buffalo grounds. Their competitors now had guns and horses as well, but within several decades, the Sioux pushed their domain west to the Missouri River. Like the Comanche farther south, they emerged as a dominant power on the Great Plains.

Britain's Mainland Colonies: A New Abundance of People

West of the Mississippi, horses and guns brought dramatic shifts as the eighteenth century progressed. But east of the Appalachian Mountains, a different force prompted striking change: population growth. Several factors came together to push the demographic curve upward at an unprecedented rate after 1700. From our vantage point in the twenty-first century, the colonial seaports and villages appear tiny, and rural settlement seems sparse. But by the mid-eighteenth century, the coastal colonies represented the largest concentration of people that had ever occupied any portion of the continent.

In what ways did Britain's North American colonies become "less English" after 1700?

On both sides of the North Atlantic, population growth characterized eighteenth-century life. But in Europe numbers rose at a gradual pace, while the population along the eastern seaboard of North America surged at an astounding rate. England in 1700 had 5.1 million people, a figure that increased a mere 14 percent to 5.8 million by 1750. In contrast, during the same half-century, the colonial population in British North America more than quadrupled, from 260,000 to nearly 1.2 million.

During these same decades, the Atlantic seaboard colonies also made a permanent and dramatic shift away from a population that was almost entirely of English origin. As the numerous cultures and languages indigenous to western Europe, western Africa, and eastern North America mixed and mingled, they gave rise to an American Babel.

Population Growth on the Home Front

Natural increase—more births than deaths—played an important role in colonial population growth. Marriages occurred early, and the need for labor created an incentive for couples to have large families. Benjamin Franklin, who rose to become the best-known colonist of his generation, was born in Boston in 1706. He grew up in a household of seventeen children. Large families had long been commonplace, to compensate for frequent infant deaths. What made the Franklin children unusual was that all survived childhood and started families of their own.

Although a high birth rate typified most preindustrial cultures, it was the low death rate and long average life span that pushed up American population numbers. With no huge urban centers, colonial epidemics proved less devastating than in Europe. Food was plentiful, and housing improved steadily. Newborns who survived infancy could live a long life. (Franklin himself lived eighty-four years.) Moreover, the 1720s and 1730s proved peaceful compared to earlier decades, so soldiering did not endanger lives among men of military age. For women, death related to pregnancy and childbirth still loomed as a constant threat. (Franklin's own mother was his father's second wife; the first wife died after bearing seven children.) Yet women still outnumbered men among people living into their seventies and eighties.

Although grandparents often endured far into old age, the average age for the total population stayed remarkably young. (See Figure 5.1.) The reasons seem clear. The ratio between men and women was becoming more even over time, the marriage rates for women remained extremely high, and there was no effective means of contraception. Women could resort to sexual abstinence to avoid pregnancy, and mothers could extend the time between births by nursing their infants for a long period (since lactation reduces the chances of conception). Not surprisingly, children abounded.

"Packed Like Herrings": Arrivals from Abroad

Frequent births and improving survival rates were only part of the population story. Immigration—both forced and free—also contributed mightily to the colonies' growth. The unfree arrivals came in two different streams from two separate continents and faced very different prospects. The largest flow of unfree arrivals came from Africa, and these forced migrants faced a bleak new life with few options for improvement. By the 1730s, the expanding transatlantic slave trade brought at least 4,000 Africans to the colonies every year, and the rate increased steadily.

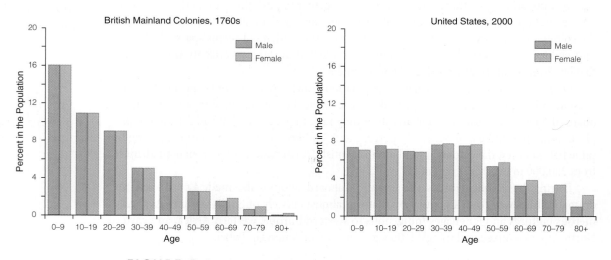

■ **FIGURE 5.1**

COMPARISON OF OVERALL POPULATION STRUCTURE BY AGE COHORT AND SEX: BRITISH MAINLAND COLONIES, 1760S, AND UNITED STATES, 2000
In the mid-eighteenth century, more than half of all people in the British mainland were under age twenty and fewer than two in ten were forty or older. In contrast, among all the living Americans at the start of the twenty-first century (281.4 million people), fewer than three in ten are under twenty, and more than four in ten are age forty or older.

A separate stream of unfree laborers came to the colonies from Europe. Compared with enslaved Africans, these European migrants faced long-term prospects that were far more promising. Every year, hundreds of detainees in British jails were offered transportation to the colonies and a term of service laboring in America as an alternative to prison time or execution. Deported felons joined the larger flow of unfree migrants from Europe: poor people, unable to pay for their own passage, who accepted transportation to America as indentured servants. All were sold to employers to serve as workers, with scant legal rights, until their indenture expired, usually after three to six years.

In the 1720s, Philadelphia shippers devised a variation on indentures known as the redemption contract. Under this **redemption system**, agents in Europe recruited migrants by contracting to loan them money for passage and provisions. On arrival in America, the recruits could then sign a pact with an employer of their own choosing. That person agreed to pay back the shipper, "redeeming" the original loan that had been made to the immigrant. In exchange, the newcomer (called a redemptioner) promised to work for the employer for several years, receiving no more than room and board. After that, the redemptioners were on their own, and their prospects usually improved.

Besides Africans who remained unfree for life and Europeans who gained freedom after a period of service, a smaller stream of newcomers involved free families arriving from Europe who could pay their own way. Poor conditions at home pushed these risk-takers to try their luck in the New World, and glowing descriptions of abundant land at bargain rates caught their attention. American land speculators hoped to rent forest tracts to immigrant farmers who would improve the value of the land by clearing trees and building homes. Britain's imperial administrators also sought to recruit non-English families from the European continent. Their immigrant settlements near the American frontier could bolster colonial defenses against foreign rivals and provide a buffer to ward off Indian attacks.

Even for those newcomers who paid for their own crossing, the Atlantic passage was a life-threatening ordeal. "The people are packed densely, like herrings," Lutheran minister Gottlieb Mittelberger recorded after a voyage to Pennsylvania. "During the journey the ship is full of pitiful signs of distress—smells, fumes, horrors, vomiting, various kinds of sea sickness, fever, dysentery, headaches, heat, constipation, boils, scurvy, cancer, mouth-rot, and similar afflictions." Despite such hardships, newcomers found economic opportunities awaiting them in America. They often wrote home glowing accounts of colonial life, and their letters helped boost the rising population further.

Non-English Newcomers in the British Colonies

Colonies that were thoroughly English at their origin became decidedly more varied after 1700. By far the largest change came from North America's increasing involvement in the Atlantic slave trade. By 1750, 240,000 African Americans made up nearly 20 percent of the population of the British colonies. Native Americans had been drawn into the mix in small numbers as slaves, servants, spouses, and Christian converts. But roughly four out of five colonists were of European descent. Among them, as among the Africans and Indians, many spoke English with a different accent, or as a second language, or not at all.

The New England colonies remained the most homogenous, but even there, 30 percent of the residents had non-English roots by 1760. The new diversity was most visible in New York because of the colony's non-English origins. A 1703 census of New York City shows that the town remained 42 percent Dutch, with English (30 percent) and Africans (18 percent) making up nearly half the population. The remainder included a Jewish community (1 percent) and a growing number of French Protestants (9 percent).

The French New Yorkers had fled to America after Louis XIV ended protection for the Protestant minority of France. When the king revoked the long-standing Edict of Nantes in 1685, he also prohibited Huguenot emigration, but several thousand French Protestants

Read the **Document**
"The Passage of Indentured Servants" (1750) at **www.myhistorylab.com**

John Wollaston, *Mary Spratt Provoost Alexander*, undated. Museum of the City of New York, Gift of William Hamilton Russell (50.215.4)

■ Like many New Yorkers of her generation, shopkeeper Mary Spratt Provoost Alexander (1693–1760) spoke both Dutch and English. Her Dutch mother had married a Scottish immigrant, and Mary was the wife of a local attorney who also came from Scotland.

escaped illegally and sought refuge in America. They established small communities such as New Rochelle in New York. Everywhere, they intermarried with the English and prospered in commerce. By the 1760s, several families with humble Huguenot origins, such as the Faneuils in Boston and the Laurenses and Manigaults in Charleston, had amassed enormous fortunes.

At a time when France and Great Britain were at war, another infusion of French-speaking refugees, the Acadians, fared less well. In 1755 authorities evicted French Catholics from Acadia in British Nova Scotia, fearing they might take up arms for France. Officials burned their homes and deported more than 6,000 to various coastal colonies farther south. These Acadian newcomers, struggling to get by, found themselves resented for their Catholicism and feared as enemies during wartime. Many moved on to French Louisiana where, known as **Cajuns**, they became a lasting cultural force.

Scotland provided a much larger flow of migrants than France, stemming from two different sources. A growing stream of families, at least 30,000 people by 1770, came from Scotland itself. They were pushed by poverty, land scarcity, famines, and a failed political rebellion in 1745. In addition, a larger group known as the Scots-Irish came from Ulster in Northern Ireland. The British had encouraged these Scottish Presbyterians to settle in Ireland in the seventeenth century, displacing rebellious Irish Catholics. In Ulster the Scottish newcomers soon faced restrictions from Parliament and the Anglican Church. By 1770 nearly 60,000 Scots-Irish had opted to leave Ireland for America.

Another stream, German-speaking immigrants, nearly equaled the combined flow of Scots and Scots-Irish settlers. They began to arrive shortly after 1700, as religious persecution, chronic land shortages, and generations of warfare pushed whole communities out of southern Germany and neighboring Switzerland. By 1770 the total had reached 85,000. These refugees generally came as whole families, taking up farmland on the fringes of the colonies. Germans occupied New York's Mohawk Valley and Virginia's Shenandoah Valley, and they fanned out from Germantown across the rich farmland of Pennsylvania. Swiss founded New Bern, North Carolina, in 1710.

Almost all of the white, non-English newcomers, including several thousand migrants from Wales, were Protestant Christians. Many clung to their language and traditions. But most arrivals learned English, and their children intermarried with English settlers. A French visitor described a typical American "whose grandfather was an Englishman, whose wife is Dutch, whose son married a French woman, and whose present four sons have now four wives of different nations."

The Varied Economic Landscape

What role did geography play in shaping the emerging regional colonial economies?

Population growth had consequences, and the changes began at the water's edge. The seaports of Boston, New York, Philadelphia, and Charleston each grew from a village to a commercial hub, absorbing manufactured goods from Britain and shipping colonial produce abroad. All four towns developed an active coastal trade with secondary ports located on nearby rivers. In contrast, Chesapeake Bay had no single dominant port. There, Annapolis,

Alexandria, and Norfolk all expanded, joined by the new town of Baltimore. But given the bay's many rivers, Atlantic ships often visited riverside plantations and villages to conduct separate business.

In Chesapeake Bay and elsewhere, inland commerce was conducted by boat wherever possible. Hartford on the Connecticut River, Albany on the Hudson, Trenton on the Delaware, and Augusta on the Savannah all become riverside trading centers. Trails and former Indian paths connected these river-based communities, easing the way for travelers in the hinterland. By the 1740s, a pathway known as the Great Wagon Road headed southwest from Philadelphia to Winchester in Virginia's Shenandoah Valley and then south through gaps in the Blue Ridge Mountains to the Piedmont region of Carolina.

See the **Map**

Colonial Products at **www.myhistorylab.com**

Widening networks of contact, using boats and wagons, extended inland from the primary ports. And expanding fleets of ships tied each major hub to distant Atlantic ports. As a result, farmsteads and villages that had been largely self-sufficient before 1710 gradually became linked to wider markets. Local production still met most needs. But increasingly, the opportunity existed to obtain a new tool, a piece of cloth, or a printed almanac from far away. The new possibility of purchasing such goods lured farmers to grow crops for market rather than plant only for home consumption.

As local commercial systems gained coherence and strength, a string of regional economies developed along the Atlantic seaboard. Coastal vessels and a few muddy roads linked them tenuously to one another. But geographical and human differences caused each to take on a character of its own. Migration patterns reinforced this diversity, since arrivals from Europe often sought out areas where others already spoke their language or shared their

■ In 1729, Maryland planters founded Baltimore to provide a port on Chesapeake Bay for shipping tobacco. The community had only 50 homes and 200 inhabitants when this early sketch was made in 1752, but the town grew rapidly after that.

form of worship. The influx of German farmers through Philadelphia, for example, gave unique traits to Pennsylvania. (Because the newcomers spoke German, or *Deutsch*, they became known as Pennsylvania Dutch.) Likewise, the rising importation of Africans helped shape the economy and culture of Chesapeake Bay and of coastal South Carolina. Besides the diversity among arriving peoples, American ecological differences played a role as well. Variations in land and climate contributed to the emergence of five distinct economic regions along the Atlantic coast.

Sources of Gain in the Carolinas and Georgia

Two related but distinctive regions took shape along the southeastern coast, linked respectively to the two Carolina colonies. The larger one centered on the lowcountry of coastal South Carolina and Georgia. There, the warm Gulf Stream current provided a long growing season. It also assured mild winters, meaning that cattle and hogs could forage unattended for most of the year. As livestock multiplied, settlers sold meat, barrel staves, and firewood to the sugar islands of the West Indies, purchasing African slave labor in return.

Some of the newcomers had grown rice in Africa before their enslavement. Planting rice for their own use, they soon showed that the crop could thrive in Carolina. Once African know-how made clear the potential for rice cultivation, a system of plantation agriculture, imported from Barbados, took hold quickly after 1700. Rice production spread to Georgia after that colony legalized slavery in 1751. Another African plant, indigo, also took root as a money-making staple crop. For several generations after 1740, indigo from South Carolina provided the blue dye for England's rising textile industry. Beside the barrels of rice and indigo that piled up on Charleston's docks, casks also appeared containing deerskins from the interior. At the height of that trade before 1750, Creek and Cherokee hunters provided more than a million deerskins per year.

In North Carolina, a second regional economy evolved. North of Cape Fear, the sandy barrier islands known as the Outer Banks prevented easy access for oceangoing vessels and hindered efforts to promote staple crop agriculture. So colonists turned to the pine forest to make a living. An extensive band of longleaf pine stretched inland for a hundred miles. With labor, this pine forest yielded naval stores: the tar and pitch used by sailors to protect their ships and rigging. Workers hauled the finished products to Wilmington on the Cape Fear River, the colony's best outlet to the sea. By the 1770s, the port was well known for exporting naval stores, and a dozen sawmills dotted the river.

Farther inland, Scots-Irish and German families moved down the Great Wagon Road after 1740 to carve out farms across the Carolina Piedmont on lands controlled largely by several absentee owners in Britain. By 1763 Ben Franklin estimated that Pennsylvania had lost 10,000 families to North Carolina. Typical of this migration were the Moravians, who established towns at Nazareth and Bethlehem, Pennsylvania, in the 1740s. In 1753 members of this German-speaking religious group bought a tract near modern-day Winston-Salem, North Carolina. They named it Wachovia, meaning "Peaceful Valley." Within several years they had developed prosperous farms, a pottery shop, and a tannery around their initial settlement, called Bethabara. The newcomers bartered seeds and tools with one another and shipped extra produce overland to South Carolina and Virginia.

Chesapeake Bay's Tobacco Economy

North of the Carolinas, farmers in the colonies bordering Chesapeake Bay committed to tobacco production in the seventeenth century. They clung to that staple crop despite a long decline in its market price. After 1710, demand for tobacco revived and prices rose again, in part because snuff (pulverized tobacco inhaled through the nostrils) became popular among Europeans. Tobacco continued to dominate the Chesapeake economy.

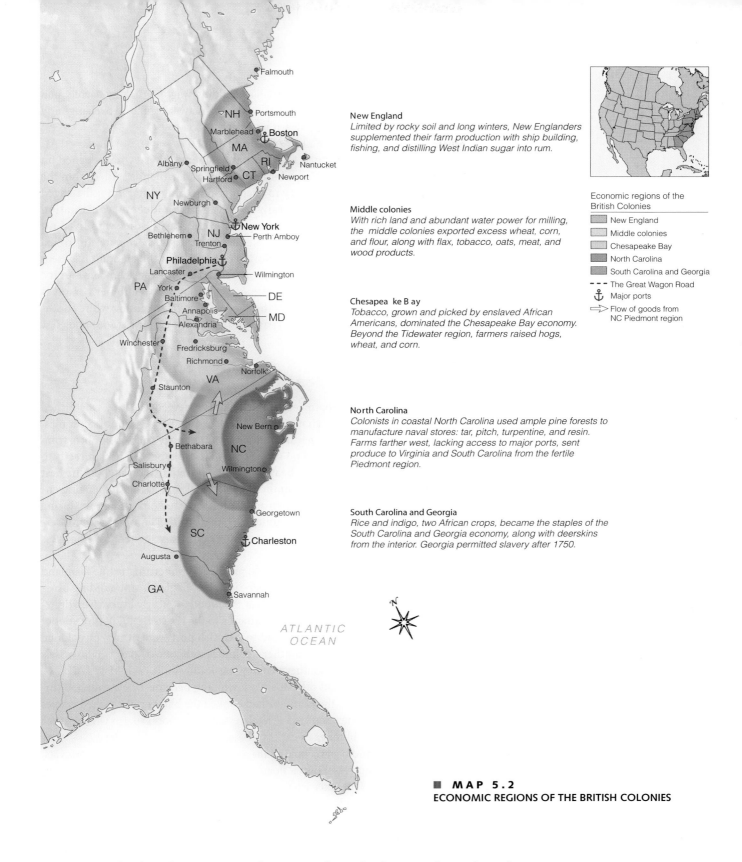

New England
Limited by rocky soil and long winters, New Englanders supplemented their farm production with ship building, fishing, and distilling West Indian sugar into rum.

Middle colonies
With rich land and abundant water power for milling, the middle colonies exported excess wheat, corn, and flour, along with flax, tobacco, oats, meat, and wood products.

Chesapea ke B ay
Tobacco, grown and picked by enslaved African Americans, dominated the Chesapeake Bay economy. Beyond the Tidewater region, farmers raised hogs, wheat, and corn.

North Carolina
Colonists in coastal North Carolina used ample pine forests to manufacture naval stores: tar, pitch, turpentine, and resin. Farms farther west, lacking access to major ports, sent produce to Virginia and South Carolina from the fertile Piedmont region.

South Carolina and Georgia
Rice and indigo, two African crops, became the staples of the South Carolina and Georgia economy, along with deerskins from the interior. Georgia permitted slavery after 1750.

Economic regions of the British Colonies

	New England
	Middle colonies
	Chesapeake Bay
	North Carolina
	South Carolina and Georgia

- - - The Great Wagon Road
⚓ Major ports
⇨ Flow of goods from NC Piedmont region

ATLANTIC OCEAN

■ **MAP 5.2**
ECONOMIC REGIONS OF THE BRITISH COLONIES

However, local conditions in parts of Virginia and Maryland prompted crop diversification as the century progressed. Constant tobacco planting depleted the soil. Moreover, most farms lay far from any navigable river, and rolling huge casks of tobacco many miles to market proved expensive. Wheat and corn thus became important secondary staples. These new crops, along with flax, hemp, and apples for making cider, provided a buffer against poor tobacco harvests and spurred related activities such as building wagons, making barrels, and constructing mills. These trades, in turn, produced widening networks of local exchange and prosperity for white yeoman families, with or without slaves.

Before 1700, all the mainland colonies could be described as *societies with slaves*. After that, the northern colonies continued to allow enslavement, but they never relied on it. In contrast, the southern colonies, except for certain inland farmlands settled from the north, shifted early in the eighteenth century to become something different: full-fledged *slave societies*, tied economically and culturally to slavery. By midcentury, plantation owners remained less wealthy than their counterparts in the West Indies who lived off the profits of slave-grown sugar. But on average, members of the southern elite controlled far more wealth than their counterparts in the North. The profits of the plantation system spread widely, though unevenly, through the rest of the European American community. By the 1770s, whites in the South averaged more than twice as much wealth per person as whites in the North. An estimate for 1774 puts the average net worth among white southerners at £93, a sharp contrast to their counterparts in the middle colonies (£46) and New England (£38).

New England Takes to the Sea

North of Chesapeake Bay, two overlapping economic regions emerged: the long-established New England colonies and the somewhat newer and more prosperous middle colonies. New England faced peculiar disadvantages, beginning with the rocky soil. As imports from London increased, New Englanders found no staple crop that could be sold back directly to Britain to create a balance of trade. All the beaver had been hunted, and much of the best land had been occupied. The region's farm families had adapted well to the challenging environment and short growing seasons. Both men and women worked on handicrafts during the long, hard winters, and networks of community exchange yielded commercial prosperity in many towns. But with a rapidly growing population, successive generations had less land to divide among their children.

By 1770, three out of four ships sailing from New England to a British port were owned by colonial residents.

Increasingly, young men with little prospect of inheriting prime farmland turned to the sea for a living. In timber-rich New England, shipbuilding prospered. Colonists established shipyards at the mouth of nearly every river, drawing skilled carpenters and willing deckhands to the coast. By 1770, three out of four ships sailing from New England to a British port were owned by colonial residents. In contrast, in the southern colonies only one of every eight vessels sailing for Britain from a southern colony was locally built.

On Nantucket Island off Cape Cod, whaling became a new source of income. For generations, the islanders had cooked the blubber of beached whales to extract oil for lamps. In 1715, they outfitted several vessels to harpoon sperm whales at sea and then return with the whale blubber in casks to be rendered into oil. In the 1750s, they installed brick ovens on deck and began cooking the smelly blubber at sea in huge iron vats. This change turned the whaling vessel into a floating factory, and it allowed longer voyages in larger ships. By the 1760s, Nantucket whalers were cruising the Atlantic for four or five months at a time and returning loaded with barrels of oil.

The fishing industry also prospered. All along the coast, villagers dispatched boats to the Grand Banks, the fishing grounds off Newfoundland. When the vessels returned, laden with fish, townspeople graded, dried, and salted the catch. The colonists sent the best cod to Europe in exchange for wine and dry goods. Yankee captains carried the lowest grade to the Caribbean sugar islands, where planters bought "refuse fish" as food for their slaves. In return, skippers brought back kegs of molasses to be distilled into rum. By 1770, 140 American distilleries, most of them in New England, produced five million gallons of rum annually. Much of it went to colonial taverns and Indian trading posts. But some also went to Africa, aboard ships from Britain and New England. American rum, along with various wines and spirits from Europe, made up one-fifth of the total value of goods utilized to purchase African slaves.

As the New England economy stabilized, it became a mixed blessing for women. On the farm, their domestic labors aided the household economy and helped to offset bad harvests. Mothers taught their daughters to spin yarn, weave cloth, sew clothes, plant gardens, raise chickens, tend livestock, and churn butter. The products from these chores could be used at home or sold in a nearby village to buy consumer goods. While the husband held legal authority over the home, a good wife served as a "deputy husband," managing numerous household affairs, or perhaps earning money as a midwife to help make ends meet. She took charge entirely if her husband passed away or went to sea.

But for all their labors, women seemed to lose economic and legal standing to men as New England towns became larger and more orderly. Networks of local officials, consisting entirely of men, drafted statutes and legal codes that reinforced male privileges. Women found it difficult to obtain credit or receive a business license, and the law barred married women from making contracts, limiting their chance for activities outside the home. Gradually, male apothecaries and physicians with a smattering of formal training pushed traditional midwives away from the bedside. Overseers of the poor had the power to remove children from a widowed mother and place them in the **almshouse**.

Economic Expansion in the Middle Colonies

The fifth regional economy, the one that flourished in the middle colonies between New England and Chesapeake Bay, improved upon these two neighboring worlds. The Europeans who resettled Indian lands in Delaware, Pennsylvania, New Jersey, and New York found a favorable climate, rich soil, and numerous millstreams. Unlike New Englanders, they developed a reliable staple by growing an abundance of grain. They exported excess wheat, flour, and bread as effectively as southerners shipped tobacco and rice. But unlike the planters in Virginia and South Carolina, middle-colony farmers did not become locked in the vicious cycle of making large investments in enslaved workers and exporting a single agricultural staple. Instead, they developed a more balanced economy, using mostly free labor. Besides grain products, they also exported quantities of flaxseed, barrel staves, livestock, and pig iron. Large infusions of money from Britain during its long war against France in the 1750s further boosted this prosperous economy.

Whereas the Chesapeake had no dominant seaport, the middle colonies boasted two major ports of entry. European craftsmen, unwilling to compete with unpaid slave artisans in the South, flocked to the middle-colony seaports instead. Both Philadelphia and New York grew faster than rival ports in the mid-eighteenth century, passing Boston in size in the 1750s. By 1763 Philadelphia had more than 20,000 people, New York had nearly as many, and both cities faced a set of urban problems that had already hit Boston.

As the port towns grew, so did economic and social distance between rich and poor. Large homes and expensive imports characterized life among the urban elite. In contrast, the poorest city dwellers lacked property and the means to subsist. By the 1760s, Philadelphia's almshouse and the new Pennsylvania Hospital for the Sick Poor were overflowing. In response, Quaker leaders established a voluntary Committee to Alleviate the Miseries of the Poor, handing out firewood and blankets to the city's needy. They also built a "Bettering House," patterned on Boston's workhouse, that provided poor Philadelphians with food and shelter in exchange for work. To limit urban poverty, New York and Philadelphia authorities moved newcomers to the countryside, where Dutch and German settlers had already established an efficient farming tradition. As immigration rose, the region slowly expanded its economy far up the Hudson Valley, east into Connecticut and Long Island, and south toward Maryland.

((•─**Hear** the **Audio**
"The Connecticut Peddler" at
www.myhistorylab.com

The farm frontier pushed west as well. The acquisitive Thomas Penn had inherited control of Pennsylvania from his more idealistic father, founder William Penn. In 1737, the young proprietor defrauded the Delaware Indians out of 1,200 square miles of potential farmland west of the Delaware River. In the infamous Walking Purchase, Penn claimed a boundary that could be walked in a day and half. Then he hired runners who covered more than 55 miles in 36 hours, giving him title to a huge tract. Land-hungry settlers pressed the reluctant Delaware west toward the Allegheny Mountains and occupied the rich river valleys of eastern Pennsylvania. Land agents and immigrant farmers called the fertile region "the best poor man's country."

Matters of Faith: The Great Awakening

Why did economic and demographic growth go hand in hand with fresh religious intensity after 1730?

Philadelphia epitomized the commercial dynamism of the eighteenth-century British colonies. The city was a hub in the fastest-growing economic region on the Atlantic seaboard. Ben Franklin, arriving there in 1723 at age 17, achieved particular success. Within seven years he owned a printing business. Within 25 years he was wealthy enough to retire, devoting himself to science, politics, and social improvement. He created a lending library, developed an efficient stove, promoted schools and hospitals, supported scientific and philosophical organizations, and won fame experimenting with electricity.

The outburst of scientific inquiry and religious skepticism spreading through the Atlantic world at the time became known as the Enlightenment, and its spirit of rational questioning and reason was greatly aided by the printing press. In America, Franklin and his fellow printers personified the new Age of Enlightenment. By 1760 the British mainland colonies had 29 printing establishments, more presses per capita than in any country in Europe. These presses squeezed out 18 weekly newspapers and countless public notices, fostering political and business communication throughout the colonies. But American printers also published an array of religious material, for the colonial spirit of worldly enterprise existed uneasily beside a longing for spiritual community and social perfection.

In the first half of the eighteenth century, colonists witnessed breakthroughs in religious toleration and controversies within the ministry. They also experienced a revivalist outpouring with roots in Europe and America, later known as the **Great Awakening**. This stirring began in the 1730s, and it gained momentum through the visits from England of a charismatic preacher named George Whitefield (pronounced Whitfield). The aftershocks of the Awakening persisted for a full generation.

Seeds of Religious Toleration

The same population shifts that made Britain's mainland colonies more diverse in the eighteenth century also created a new Babel of religious voices that included many non-Christians. Africans, the largest of all the new contingents, brought their own varied beliefs across the Atlantic. Some slaves from Portuguese Angola had had exposure to Catholicism in their homeland. But most Africans retained much of their traditional cultures and showed skepticism toward Christianity. Efforts to convert Native Americans also had mixed results. A minister living near the Iroquois reported that Indians would beat a drum to disrupt his services and then "go away Laughing."

Another non-Christian contingent, Jewish immigrants, remained few in number, with only several hundred families by 1770. Merchants rather than farmers, they established communities in several Atlantic ports, beginning in Dutch New Amsterdam (1654) and in Newport (1658). Most were Sephardic Jews; that is, their ancestral roots were in Spain and Portugal. They came by way of the Caribbean, reaching Charleston in 1697, Philadelphia after 1706,

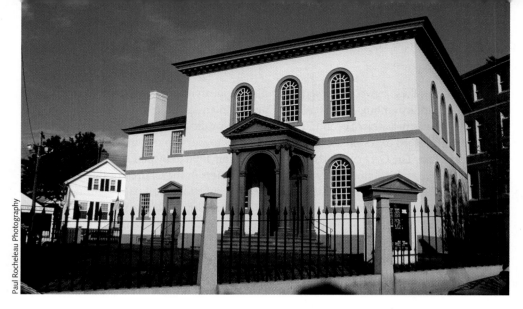

Paul Rocheleau Photography

■ Members of the Jewish community in Newport started Touro Synagogue in 1759, a century after the arrival of their first ancestors in the Rhode Island seaport. Completed in 1763, this gem of colonial architecture is the oldest existing synagogue in the United States.

and Savannah in 1733. A few of their children married into the Protestant culture, but more than 80 percent of Jewish young people found partners within their own small communities.

The majority of eighteenth-century newcomers to the British colonies were Christians. A few, such as the Acadians, were Catholics, but the rest had some Protestant affiliation. In the two centuries since the Reformation, numerous competing Protestant denominations had sprung up across Europe. Now this wide array made itself felt in America, as Presbyterians, Quakers, Lutherans, Baptists, Methodists, and smaller sects all increased in numbers. To attract immigrant families, most colonies abolished laws that favored a single "established" denomination. Nevertheless, New England remained firmly Congregational, while the southern gentry (plus merchant elite everywhere) concentrated increasingly within the Anglican Church.

Rhode Island had emphasized the separation of church and state from the start, and Pennsylvania had likewise favored toleration, both as a matter of principle and as a practical recruitment device to attract new settlers. Since migration from Europe was a demanding ordeal, those who took the risk were often people with strong religious convictions. Such newcomers looked for assurances that they could practice their religion freely, and colonies competed to accommodate them. In many places, religious tests still limited who could hold public office, but tolerance for competing beliefs was expanding.

Many felt that if any institution threatened the growing religious toleration in the colonies, it was, ironically, the British king's own denomination. The monarch headed the Anglican Church, and it had influential American members, including almost every colonial governor. Therefore, repeated talk by the Church of England about installing a resident bishop in America aroused suspicions among colonists who worshiped in other denominations. This was especially true in New England, where Congregationalists had long opposed ideas of religious hierarchy. In 1750, Boston, which had 18 churches, rose up against a plan for an Anglican bishop. In a passionate sermon, Reverend Jonathan Mayhew preached that the town must keep "all imperious bishops, and other clergymen who love to lord it over God's heritage, from getting their feet into the stirrup."

The Onset of the Great Awakening: Pietism and George Whitefield

As relative toleration became a hallmark of the British colonies, no one benefited more than German-speaking Protestant groups. Numerous religious sects, such as the Moravians, Mennonites, Schwenkfelders, and Dunkers, were escaping from persecution as well as poverty at home. Their numbers multiplied after 1730, and hymns in German became a common sound on Sabbath day. In 1743, before any American printer produced an English-language Bible, a press in Pennsylvania put out a complete German edition of Luther's Bible, using type brought from Frankfurt.

Collectively, these newcomers were part of a European reform movement to renew piety and spiritual vitality among Protestant churchgoers in an age of increasing rationalism and worldliness. Pietism, as this "Second Reformation" was called, had roots in eastern Germany and stressed the need to restore emotion and intensity to worship that had become too rational and detached. The German pietists reached out after 1700 to inspire Huguenots in France and Presbyterians in Scotland. They influenced reformers in the Church of England such as John Wesley, the founder of Methodism and a teacher at Oxford University. Through Wesley, pietist ideas touched George Whitefield, a preaching prodigy in Oxford's class of 1736. Over the next decade, "the boy parson" sparked a widespread religious awakening in the American colonies.

Whitefield's mentor, Wesley, had preached briefly in Georgia. So in 1738, at age 23, Whitefield spent several months in the new colony, where he laid plans for an orphanage near Savannah. Arriving back in England, Whitefield quickly achieved celebrity status, drawing large crowds with fiery sermons that criticized the Anglican Church. His popularity preceded him in 1739 when he returned to America for an extended tour, the second of seven transatlantic journeys during his career. Building on religious stirrings already present in the colonies, Whitefield preached to huge and emotional crowds nearly 350 times in 15 months. He made appearances from Savannah to Boston, something no public figure had ever done. "God shews me," he wrote in his journal, "that America must be my place for action."

The timing was perfect. Whitefield's brother was a wine merchant who understood the expanding networks of communication and consumption in the British Atlantic world. So Whitefield realized that in America, as newspapers multiplied and roads improved, he could advertise widely and travel extensively. He had little taste for Protestant debates over church organization and sectarian differences. Instead, he believed that an evangelical minister should simply preach the Bible fervently to a wide array of avid listeners. Everywhere he went, Whitefield served as a catalyst for religious activity.

"The Danger of an Unconverted Ministry"

The heightened commotion in American churches had local origins as well. The same tension felt in European parishes—between worldly, rational pursuits and an emotional quest for grace and salvation—also troubled colonial congregations. Occasional local revivals had taken place in America for decades. The most dramatic one occurred in Northampton, Massachusetts, in 1734–1735, spurred by a talented minister named Jonathan Edwards. As the colonies' most gifted theologian, Edwards anticipated Whitefield's argument that dry, rote "head-knowledge" made a poor substitute for "a true living faith in Jesus Christ." "Our people do not so much need to have their heads stored," Edwards observed, "as to have their hearts touched."

In a fast-growing society, who would prepare suitable church leaders for the next generation? Candidates for the ministry could train at Harvard College (founded 1636), William and Mary (1693), Yale (1707), or one of several small academies. But these institutions could not instruct sufficient numbers. The shortage of educated ministers, combined with

Courtesy, Winterthur Museum (63.639)

■ George Whitefield visited America seven times. In 1739, at age 24, his preaching spurred the Great Awakening.

geographic expansion, meant that one preacher might oversee several parishes. Even if he tended only a single parish, the great distances separating parishioners made it hard for any pastor to travel widely enough to address their needs.

Problems in the pulpit included quality as well quantity. Many college graduates had too much "head-knowledge." Their fluency in Latin and Greek often earned them more disdain than respect from down-to-earth congregations. Most foreign-born ministers, such as Anglicans sent from England and Presbyterians from Scotland, had failed to find good positions at home. Too often, they showed limited appreciation for the local church members who paid their salaries, and they resented those who criticized their ministries.

One such critic was William Tennent, a Scots-Irish immigrant who arrived in Pennsylvania with his family in 1716. Dismayed by the cold, unemotional outlook of Presbyterian ministers, Tennent opened a one-room academy in a log house to train his four sons and other young men for the ministry. But local Presbyterian authorities challenged his credentials and disparaged the teachings of his "Log College." Eventually, the school moved and grew, becoming linked to the new College of New Jersey in 1746, which later evolved into Princeton University. But before this happened, Tennent's preacher sons allied themselves with Whitefield and managed to shake the colonial religious establishment to its roots.

One of Tennent's sons, Gilbert, eventually led a Presbyterian church in Philadelphia created by Whitefield's supporters. In 1740, at the time of Whitefield's triumphal tour, young Gilbert Tennent delivered a blistering sermon entitled "The Danger of an Unconverted Ministry" that became a manifesto for the revival. Cutting to the heart of the matter, he condemned the "sad security" offered by incompetent, uncaring, and greedy ministers. "They are as blind as Moles, and as dead as Stones," he charged, "without any spiritual Taste and Relish." He argued that congregations should turn away from these "Letter-learned . . . Old Pharisee-Teachers" and listen to traveling preachers instead.

The Consequences of the Great Awakening

Whitefield hailed Gilbert Tennant and his brothers as "burning and shining lights" of a new kind. All the ministers and worshipers who joined in the movement began to call themselves "New Lights." Opponents, whom they dismissed as "Old Lights," continued to defend a learned clergy and emphasized head-knowledge on the difficult road to salvation. The Old Lights opposed the disruptions caused by so-called "itinerant ministers" who moved freely from parish to parish without invitation. The New Light ministers, in contrast, appealed to people's emotions and stressed the prospect of a more democratic salvation open to all. They defended their wanderings, which made them more accessible to a broader public and less likely to become set in their ways. "Our Blessed Saviour was an Itinerant Preacher," they reminded their critics; "he Preach'd in no other Way."

Just as New Light preachers moved readily across traditional parish boundaries, they also transcended the lines between different Protestant sects. Their simple evangelical message reached across a wide social spectrum to diverse audiences of every denomination. Moreover, their stress on communal singing, expressive emotion, and the prospects for personal salvation drew special attention from those on the fringes of the culture, such as young people, women, and the poor. Not surprisingly, New Light ministers also made headway in spreading Christianity within various African American and Native American communities.

Members of the religious establishment, once secure as unchallenged leaders in their communities, now confronted a stark choice. Some powerful churchmen acknowledged their New Light critics and reluctantly welcomed the popular renegades into the local pulpits. Such a strategy might blunt the thrust of the revival, and it would surely raise church

Read the **Document**

Edwards, "Sinners in the Hands of an Angry God" at **www.myhistorylab.com**

View the **Image**

Jonathan Edwards at **www.myhistorylab.com**

INTERPRETING HISTORY

"The Creature Must Have Been the Size of a Small House"

By the mid-eighteenth century, scientific observers on both sides of the Atlantic were corresponding earnestly to expand European knowledge of unfamiliar American plants and animals. This 1762 letter to Philadelphia naturalist John Bartram was written by a fellow Quaker in Delaware County, Pennsylvania. A century before Charles Darwin proposed evolution, these two amateur scientists were trying to learn more about huge fossils found at a salt lick near the Ohio River. For millennia, animal herds had been drawn to these springs in modern Boone County, Kentucky, to lick salty sediments deposited by glaciers more than 18,000 years ago.

In 1739, a French officer descending the Ohio had gathered several enormous bones at this site and shipped them to France, labeled "animal de l'Ohio." Local Shawnee Indians often visited "the licks" to hunt buffalo and gather salt. Perhaps Bartram heard of the large fossils through the saga of Mary Draper Ingles, captured from Virginia's frontier and taken to the Ohio Valley during the French and Indian War. Ingles recalled being forced to obtain salt for her Shawnee captors at a spot strewn with gigantic bones. In 1755, this young wife and mother escaped and retraced her steps eastward, covering 800 miles in 42 days. How old were the bones she described, Bartram wondered, and did such creatures still exist?

August 22nd 1762

Respected friend

Pursuant to thy request, I have made as particular an enquiry relating to those bones thou mentions, as I possibly could from two sensible Shawnee Indians, assisted by an interpreter. The place where they lie is about 3 miles from the Ohio in the midst of a large savannah, on the east side of the river. There appear to be the remains of 5 entire skeletons, near together, supposed to have fallen at the same time.

When [asked] to describe several parts, they said a man could but just grasp [one skull] in both his arms. The shoulder blade, when set on end, reached to their shoulders, and they were both tall men. What they called the cup (or socket) of this bone, was equal in size to a large bowl. Asked if they had seen those long bones they called horns [i.e., tusks], they answered they had and showed them to be 10 or 12 feet long. They judged the creature when alive must have been the size of a small house, pointing from the window to a stable.

I asked them [about the location]. They answered, the place was salt and wettish, and by having been much trod and licked, was something lower than the adjacent land. There were many roads through this extent of land, beaten by buffalos and other creatures. I asked if they, or their fathers, had ever seen any such large creatures living, as these bones were supposed to be part of. They answered they had never heard them spoken of, nor ever heard of any creature ever having been seen by the oldest man, or his father.

They had indeed a tradition, such mighty creatures once frequented those Savannahs. There were then men of a size proportionable to them, who used to kill them as an Indian now does a deer. When

---

attendance. Other Old Lights, however, took the opposite approach; they clung to tradition and stability, challenging their new rivals openly. They condemned itinerancy and disputed the interlopers' right to preach. They mocked the faddish popularity of these overemotional zealots and even banned the New Light itinerants from local districts for the good of the parishioners.

In the end, neither tactic stemmed the upheaval, which peaked in the North in the 1740s and in the South during the 1750s and 1760s. But the long-term consequences of the Great Awakening were mixed. Zealous New Light men and women tried to transcend the competing denominations and create a broad community of Protestant believers. But the reformers could never create such unity, and they left behind no new set of doctrines or institutional structures. Nevertheless, they created an important legacy. First, they infused a new spirit of piety and optimism into American Christianity that countered older and darker Calvinist traditions. Second, they established a manner of fiery evangelical preaching that found a permanent place in American life. Finally, and most importantly, they underscored democratic tendencies in the New Testament gospels that many invoked in later years when faced with other apparent infringements of their liberties.

> *Zealous New Light men and women tried to transcend the competing denominations and create a broad community of Protestant believers.*

there were no more of these strong men left alive, God killed these mighty creatures, that they should not hurt the present race of Indians. These the Shawnee said were their traditions. I shall be pleased if what small information I have gained will be agreeable to thee, and shall be glad to oblige thee at any time to the utmost of my power.

I am thy assured friend

James Wright

Shortly after Bartram received this letter, his friend Benjamin Franklin became intrigued by these fossil remains of elephant-like creatures at Big Bone Lick, and scientific interest in the puzzle continued. Thomas Jefferson wondered whether such giant animals still roamed the West, and he advised Meriwether Lewis to pause at the site in 1803 before exploring the Louisiana Purchase. What if these massive mastodons had disappeared long ago? Enlightenment thinkers wondered if the earth was much older than they suspected, and theologians questioned why a knowing God who had created all living things would allow an entire species to become extinct.

Questions

1. *Why did the idea of species extinction cause such intellectual shock waves for Europeans nearly 250 years ago?*
2. *Why is this salt lick near the Ohio River considered "the birthplace of American Vertebrate Paleontology"?*

Source: Edmund Berkeley and Dorothy Smith Berkeley, eds., *The Correspondence of John Bartram, 1773–1777* (Gainesville: University Press of Florida, 1992), 568–569. Text condensed and modernized for clarity.

The American mastodon (Mammut americanum) existed in North America for several million years, but has been extinct for more than 10,000 years. The discovery of fossilized mastodon bones in America in the eighteenth century challenged Enlightenment scientists and theologians. (This skeleton, recovered near Newburgh, New York in 1845, is now in the American Museum of Natural History.)

The French Lose a North American Empire

In 1739, while George Whitefield launched his tour of the English colonies and the Stono slave rebellion erupted in South Carolina, the French dreamed of expanding their American empire. When Pierre and Paul Mallet set out up the Mississippi River from New Orleans that year, the two French Canadians suspected that the Missouri River, the Mississippi's mightiest tributary, stretched to New Mexico. If so, they hoped to claim a new trading route for France. Pausing in Illinois to gather seven French Canadian recruits, the Mallet brothers pushed up the Missouri, hoping it flowed from the southwest.

What key factors undermined the French position in America in the decades after 1740?

But the river flowed from the northwest instead. Disappointed, the party left the river in Nebraska, purchased horses at an Omaha Indian village, and set off across the plains, reaching Santa Fe in July. After a nine-month stay, most of them returned east across the southern plains the next year. When the Mallets completed their enormous circuit and returned to New Orleans, they brought word from the West of Indian and Spanish eagerness to engage in greater trade. From their perspective, the future of France in America looked bright indeed. But the promise disappeared entirely within their lifetimes.

Veue et Perspectiue
de la nouuelle Orleans
1726

Prospects and Problems Facing French Colonists

In 1740 French colonists had grounds for cautious optimism. France already claimed a huge expanse of North America, and its wilderness empire ran strategically through the center of the continent. The potential for mineral resources and rich farmland seemed boundless. Moreover, no Europeans had shown greater skill in forging stable and respectful relations with Native Americans. French forts stretched up the Mississippi River and then east to the lower Great Lakes and the St. Lawrence Valley. These posts facilitated trade with Native Americans and secured ties between Canada and Louisiana. With Indian support, more outposts could be built farther east near the Appalachian Mountains to contain the English settlers and perhaps one day to conquer them.

At least three problems marred this scenario. First, the French population in America paled in comparison to the large number of English settlers. Canada still had fewer than 50,000 colonial inhabitants in 1740, whereas Britain's mainland colonies were rapidly approaching 1 million. Louisiana contained only 3,000 French people, living among nearly 4,000 enslaved Africans and 6,000 Native Americans. Second, French colonists lacked sufficient support from Paris to develop thriving communities and expand their Indian trade. The importation of goods from France was still meager and unpredictable. Finally, an ominous trickle of British hunters and settlers was beginning to cross the Appalachian chain. Carolina traders already had strong ties with the Chickasaw Indians living near the Mississippi River, and Virginia land speculators were eyeing lands in the Ohio Valley.

What seemed a promising situation for the French in 1740 was soon put to the test. Britain and France had long been on a collision course in North America. Colonial subjects of the two European superpowers had already clashed in a series of wars. After several decades of peace, warfare was about to resume. King George's War (1744–1748) and the French and Indian War (1754–1763) preoccupied colonists and Native Americans alike over the next two decades. In 1763 the Treaty of Paris ended the French and Indian War, part of a far broader conflict known in Europe as the Seven Years' War. At that point, less than a quarter century after the Mallet brothers' optimistic journey through the heartlands, the British gained the upper hand. The expansive French empire in North America suddenly vanished.

FLEVVE DE St LOVIS OV MISSISSIPI

■ By 1726 New Orleans, with 100 cabins and nearly 1,000 inhabitants, was receiving shipments of trade goods from France and distributing them up the Mississippi River and its tributaries. Following a Louisiana hurricane in 1722, the levies along the waterfront were expanded, but flooding remains a threat to the low-lying city even today, as the devastation of Hurricane Katrina in 2005 made clear.

British Settlers Confront the Threat from France

These colonial conflicts of the mid-eighteenth century, generally linked to wider warfare in Europe, had a significant impact on everyone living in the British mainland colonies. A few people took advantage of the disturbances to become rich. They provisioned troops, sold scarce wartime goods, sponsored profitable privateering ventures, or conducted forbidden trade with the enemy in the Caribbean. But many more people paid a heavy price because of war: a farm burned, a job lost, a limb amputated, a husband or father shot in battle or cut down by disease. From London's perspective, the Americans made ill-disciplined and reluctant soldiers. From the colonists' viewpoint, the British offered them little respect and less assistance.

Adding insult to injury, a hard-won victory in North America could be canceled out at the peace table in Europe. In 1745, during King George's War, Massachusetts called for an attack on Louisburg, the recently completed French fortress on Cape Breton Island that controlled access to the St. Lawrence River and nearby fishing grounds. After a long siege, New England's forces prevailed. But British diplomats rescinded the colonial victory, handing Louisburg back to France in 1748 in exchange for Madras in India.

Whatever their differences, the American colonists and the British government saw potential in the land west of the Appalachian Mountains, and both were eager to challenge French claims there. In 1747 colonial speculators formed the Ohio Company of Virginia to develop western lands. Two years later the crown granted them 200,000 acres south of the Ohio River, if they would construct a fort in the area. Moving west and north, the Virginians hoped to occupy a valuable spot (modern-day Pittsburgh, Pennsylvania) where the Monongahela and Allegheny rivers come together to form the Ohio River. But the French had designs on the same strategic location.

In 1753 the Virginia governor sent an untested young major in the colonial militia named George Washington—at age 21 already regarded as a promising officer—to warn the French to leave the area. The next spring Virginia workers began erecting a fort at the Fork of the Ohio, but a larger French force drove them off and constructed Fort Duquesne on the coveted site. When Major Washington returned to the area with troops, he probed for enemy forces. In a skirmish on May 28, 1754, near modern Uniontown, Pennsylvania, his men killed ten French soldiers, the initial casualties in what soon became the world's first truly global war. With 450 men and meager supplies, Washington fortified his camp, calling it Fort Necessity, and dug in to prepare for a counterattack.

Throughout the British colonies in the early summer of 1754, fears spread about the dangers of the French offensive and the loyalties of Native American allies. Officials in London requested that all the colonies involved in relations with the Iroquois send delegates to a special congress in Albany, New York, to improve that Indian alliance. Seven colonies sent 23 representatives, who hoped to strengthen friendship with the Iroquois nations and also discuss a design for a union of the colonies. The delegates to the Albany Congress adopted a proposal by Benjamin Franklin for a colonial confederation. The colonies would be unified by an elected Grand Council and a president general appointed by the crown. But no colonial legislature ever ratified Franklin's far-sighted Albany Plan. "Everyone cries, a union is necessary," Franklin wrote, "but when they come to the manner and form of the union, their weak noodles are perfectly distracted."

> *"Everyone cries, a union is necessary, but when they come to the manner and form of the union, their weak noodles are perfectly distracted."*

The main distraction came from Pennsylvania. On July 3, word arrived that the French had defeated Washington's small force at Fort Necessity. But the British were not willing to give up their claims to the Ohio Valley without a fight. The crown responded by dispatching General Edward Braddock and two regiments of Irish troops to America. Early in 1755, his force arrived in Virginia, where preparations were already under way for a campaign to conquer Fort Duquesne. In June Braddock's combined British and colonial army of 2,500 began a laborious march west to face the French.

Read the **Document**
Albany Plan of Union at
www.myhistorylab.com

An American Fight Becomes a Global Conflict

The early stages of the war in America could hardly have been more disastrous for Britain or more encouraging for France. A French and Indian force ambushed Braddock's column in the forest near Fort Duquesne, cutting it to pieces in the most thorough defeat of the century for a British army unit. Elsewhere, Indian raids battered the frontiers, spreading panic in the northern colonies. With the local militia away at war, fears of possible slave uprisings swept through the South. The French commander, the Marquis de Montcalm, struck into New York's Mohawk Valley from Lake Ontario in 1756, then pushed south down Lake Champlain and Lake George in 1757. After a seven-day siege, he took 2,000 prisoners at Fort William Henry. In an episode made famous in *The Last of the Mohicans*, France's Huron Indian allies killed more than 150 men and women after their release from the fort.

View the **Image**
The Seven Years' War at
www.myhistorylab.com

The change in British fortunes came with the new ministry of William Pitt, a vain but talented member of the House of Commons. Pitt was an expansionist committed to the growth of the British Empire at the expense of France. He brought a daring new strategy to the war effort, and he had the determination and bureaucratic skill to carry it out. Stymied in Europe by the military might of the French army, the British would now concentrate their forces instead on France's vulnerable and sparsely populated overseas colonies. Under Pitt, the British broadened the war into a global conflict, taking advantage of their superior naval power to fight on the coasts of Asia and Africa and in North America as well. By 1758, Britain had undertaken a costly military buildup in America, with nearly 50,000 troops.

To win colonial support for his plan, Pitt promised to reimburse the colonies generously for their expenses. In the South, guns, ammunition, and trade goods flowed freely to Britain's Native American allies. In the North, France lost Louisburg again in July 1758. Fort Frontenac on Lake Ontario fell in August. In November, the French destroyed and

MAP 5.3
THE BRITISH CONQUEST OF NEW FRANCE, 1754–1760

British conquest of New France

- French settlements
- British settlements
- Iroquois settlements
- - - Land claimed by the Ohio Company of Virginia
- French victories
- British victories
- French forts
- British forts

1 Washington gives up Ft. Necessity to French, July 3–4, 1754

2 Braddock's army destroyed near Ft. Duquesne, July 9, 1755

3 British yield Ft. William Henry to Montcalm, Aug. 9, 1757

4 British capture French fort at Louisburg, July 26, 1758

5 British take Ft. Frontenac from the French, Aug. 27, 1758

6 Johnson captures Ft. Niagara from the French, July 25, 1759

7 Wolfe defeats Montcalm, Plains of Abraham, Sept. 13, 1759

8 Amherst accepts French surrender of Montreal, Sept. 8, 1760

abandoned Fort Duquesne. The British seized the strategic site at the Fork of the Ohio, erecting a new post (aptly named Fort Pitt) and laying out the village of Pittsburgh beside it. In Canada, autumn brought a poor harvest, followed by the harshest winter in memory. Ice in the St. Lawrence, plus a British naval blockade, cut off overseas support from France. The Marquis de Montcalm huddled in Quebec with his ill-equipped army.

In the spring of 1759, the British pressed their advantage, moving against Canada from several directions. Britain's superintendent of Indian affairs in the region, Sir William Johnson, sensed that many Native Americans were eager to support the winning side. Johnson successfully recruited 1,000 formerly neutral Iroquois to join 2,000 British regulars on the shores of Lake Ontario to lay siege to Fort Niagara. The fort fell in July, a British victory that effectively isolated enemy posts farther west and obliged the French to abandon them. In August, a British force under Jeffery Amherst captured Ticonderoga and Crown Point on Lake Champlain. The stage was set for an assault on Quebec.

■ *Quebec, the Capital of New France.* Thomas Johnson, a New England printer eager to celebrate the fall of Quebec in 1759, copied an old image of the city from a French map. The sketch emphasizes the Catholic churches and seminaries that Louis XIV had promoted in the previous century. But in fact, British cannon fire during the siege of 1759 had devastated much of the town.

Quebec Taken and North America Refashioned

In London, William Pitt knew that capturing Quebec would conquer Canada. Months earlier, he had ordered James Wolfe "to make an attack upon Quebeck, by the River St. Lawrence." Wolfe's **flotilla**, with 8,500 troops, anchored near the walled city in late June. But the French held their citadel despite weeks of heavy shelling. Desperate and sick, Wolfe resorted to a ruthless campaign against the countryside that left 1,400 farms in ruins. Even this strategy failed to draw Montcalm's forces out to fight.

As a last resort, Wolfe adopted a risky plan to climb a steep bluff and attack the vulnerable west side of the city. On the night of September 12, 1759, he dispatched troops to float quietly past French sentries and scale the formidable cliffs. At daybreak, 12 British battalions emerged on a level expanse known as the Plains of Abraham. The future of the continent and its inhabitants hinged on a pitched battle between opposing European armies. Montcalm and Wolfe staked everything in the clash, and both lost their lives in the encounter. By nightfall, the British had won a decisive victory, and four days later the surviving French garrison surrendered the city of Quebec.

Montreal fell to Britain the following year, and fighting subsided in America. But Pitt continued to pour public money into the global war, and one military triumph followed another. The British conquered French posts in India, took French Senegal on the West African coast, and seized the valuable sugar islands of Martinique and Guadeloupe in the French West Indies. When Spain came to France's aid in 1762, British forces captured the Philippines and the Cuban city of Havana. But British taxpayers resented the huge costs of the war. Many also worried that the effort to humiliate France and Spain could spark retaliation. Rising criticism pushed Pitt from office, and peace negotiations began.

In a matter of months, the European powers redrew the imperial map of North America. Their complex swaps constituted the largest single rearrangement of territory in the history of the continent. First, France ceded to Spain the port of New Orleans and all of the Louisiana territory west of the Mississippi River. Then, in the 1763 Treaty of Paris, Spain turned over East Florida to Britain, receiving back Havana and the Philippines in return. France gave Britain its holdings between the Appalachians and the Mississippi River as well as the parts of Canada not already claimed by the Hudson's Bay Company. For this vast acquisition, the British returned the sugar islands of Martinique and Guadeloupe, and they allowed France to retain fishing rights off Newfoundland.

Those negotiating the peace agreed that French Canadians could choose between leaving Canada or becoming British subjects. But the Paris treaty made no mention of the thousands of Native Americans whose homelands were being reassigned. The final results were striking. Britain emerged as the world's leading colonial power, and, after two centuries, the empire of France in North America abruptly disappeared.

CONCLUSION

For half a century, the complex currents of colonial life had recalled the ancient tale of Babel, as told in the Book of Genesis in the Bible. A confusion of voices, interests, and cultures competed and interacted over a wide expanse in North America. In the process, a string of five distinct economic regions emerged along the eastern seaboard. The British colonies that composed these regions varied in ethnic make-up, but they were all expanding rapidly in population.

In 1763, Britain's mainland colonies contained more than 1.6 million people. The figure had quickly come to dwarf all the other population totals on the continent. Amazingly, in the 13 years between 1750 and 1763, the British mainland colonies added more than 400,000 people. This number of new inhabitants—reflecting natural increase, European immigration, and the slave trade combined—exceeded the entire population that had been living in those same British colonies five decades earlier, in 1713.

The growth in numbers during the decades to come would be equally rapid, and the changes for the continent were even more dramatic and long lasting. In the dozen years after 1763, the same colonies that had failed to embrace Franklin's Albany Plan of 1754 proved increasingly willing to cooperate in their opposition to new and troubling British policies. The colonists, for the first time, frequently referred to themselves—rather than to the Indians—as *Americans*. This shared identity contributed to the outbreak of the War of Independence in 1775.

For Review

✓•—Study and **Review** at **www.myhistorylab.com**

1. How does the rapid appearance of horses on the Great Plains relate to the "Columbian Exchange" described in Chapter 1?

2. How did non-English newcomers—both European and African—help shape the regional cultures in Britain's Atlantic Coast colonies in this era?

3. Do you agree with those experts who see the fall of Quebec in 1759 as one of the most important single events in early American history? Why?

4. Describe at least three major changes in this period that had a lasting impact on the future course of American history.

Chronology: 1715–1763

1713 First whaling ventures from Nantucket.

1718 French lay out New Orleans; Spanish start San Antonio.

1734 Jonathan Edwards leads religious revival in Northampton, Massachusetts.

1737 Delaware Indians lose land to Pennsylvania through the Walking Purchase.

1739 George Whitefield's preaching tour sparks Great Awakening.

1741 British forces capture Louisburg.

1749 Spanish sign treaty with Apache at San Antonio.

1753 Moravians establish Bethabara in North Carolina.

1754 War breaks out in America between French and British. Franklin's Albany Plan.

1755 Braddock is defeated near Fort Duquesne.

1758 Comanche attack Spanish at San Saba Mission.

1759 Quebec falls to the British.

1760 George III becomes king of England. French surrender Montreal to British.

1763 Treaty of Paris ends the French and Indian War.

Key Terms

Babel A city described in the Old Testament where constructing a tower was made impossible by the confusion of varied languages. This term from the Book of Genesis is used to describe any scene of clamor and confusion. p. 111

Cajuns The Louisiana word for French-speaking people from Acadia (Nova Scotia) who were forced to move south in 1755 during the French and Indian War. Many of these refugees eventually moved to French Louisiana, where they have had a lasting impact on the culture. p. 118

Flotilla Any sizeable fleet of ships, or, more specifically, a naval term for a unit consisting of two or more squadrons of small warships. p. 134

Great Awakening The title that was applied, in retrospect, to the interdenominational Christian revival that swept Britain's North American colonies between the 1730s and the 1750s, inspired at first by the preaching of Jonathan Edwards and George Whitefield (A religious revival in the early nineteenth century became known as the Second Great Awakening). p. 124

Redemption system An eighteenth-century arrangement in which potential migrants in Europe signed up with an agent who agreed to pay for their Atlantic passage. Reaching America, the newcomer signed a pact to work for several years for an employer. In exchange for much-needed labor, the employer agreed to pay back the shipper, "redeeming" the original loan that had been made to the immigrant "redemptioner." p. 117

By the 1760s, Boston had grown into a busy seaport of 16,000 people. With this expansion, the gap between rich and poor had widened steadily, and the Seven Years' War (the French and Indian War) had only worsened the growing inequality. During the war, wealthy Boston families such as the Hancocks multiplied their fortunes, building stately homes and importing elegant fashions. In 1764 young John Hancock, heir to his uncle's vast shipping business, inherited an immense fortune of £80,000.

However, most Bostonians lived in a very different world. Half the townspeople had property and savings worth less than £40, and half of those possessed £20 or less. George Hewes, five years younger than Hancock, was born into this other Boston in 1742. At age seven, Hewes lost his father, a butcher who also sold soap and candles. But unlike Hancock, George had no rich uncle; he became an apprentice shoemaker at age fourteen.

Despite the town's growth, rich and poor still encountered one another on occasion. If anything, those contacts increased during the tumultuous decade that gave rise to the American Revolution. Politics—both imperial and local—heated up in the 1760s, opening rifts in the ruling elite. Throughout the colonies, British officials and other people who supported the crown's policies became known as Loyalists, or Tories. The wealthy among them saw social and economic dominance as their birthright and scorned their rivals for courting favor with the poor. In contrast, leaders of the emerging opposition (known as Whigs or Patriots) consisted of less conservative—often young and ambitious—members of the educated and professional classes. These people downplayed their rank and privilege to win popular support from those beneath them on the social scale.

In Boston, John Hancock was one such person. In 1763, after Hewes repaired an expensive shoe for Hancock, the merchant invited the young cobbler to a New Year's open house at his impressive mansion. In his old age, Hewes still recalled the occasion vividly. Intimidated by the wealth around him, he remembered being scared "almost to death" when the magnate toasted him and gave him a silver coin.

The two men met again on very different terms after a decade had passed. In December 1773 the shoemaker joined other activists, disguised as Indians, to empty chests of British tea into Boston Harbor. Recalling that night as an old man, Hewes was one of the first to refer to the event as a "tea party." And he swore that in the darkness he had rubbed elbows with Hancock himself and had joined him in smashing a crate of tea. Symbolically, the two men were now working shoulder to shoulder. They came together across

The Limits of Imperial Control, 1763–1775

CHAPTER OUTLINE

New Challenges to Spain's Expanded Empire

New Challenges to Britain's Expanded Empire

"The Unconquerable Rage of the People"

A Conspiracy of Corrupt Ministers?

Launching a Revolution

Conclusion

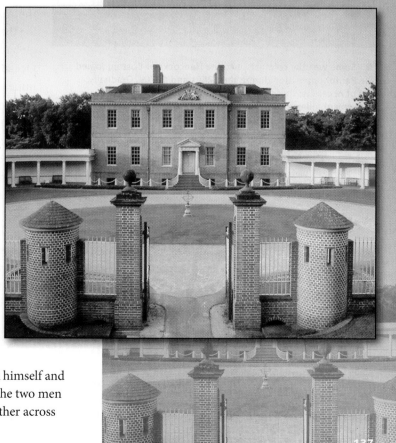

class lines in a coalition that would soon challenge Europe's strongest empire, Britain, and spark the Atlantic world's first successful anticolonial revolution.

America's implausible alliance between a portion of the colonial elite and a wide spectrum of working people developed gradually and imperfectly. During the decade before 1776, class and regional interests still divided British colonists on many occasions. Urban artisans, rural farmers, enslaved African Americans, and numerous wives and widows, for example, did not necessarily share common views and concerns. Indeed, they were frequently at odds. Nevertheless, between 1763 and 1775, colonists from separate regions and backgrounds began to speak of themselves as Americans—a term that had previously applied only to Indians.

At times, this self-conscious new identification with North America went too far, as in the creation of a *Continental* Congress; it was not, of course, a body of the entire North American continent at all. In fact, in the Midwest in 1763, thousands of Native Americans under the leadership of Pontiac were fighting to assert their own independence from European encroachment. On the Great Plains, the Comanche and Sioux contended for new territories. Still farther west, other peoples experienced the initial shocks of colonial contact. Suddenly, inhabitants of the Hawaiian Islands and the Alaskan coast were encountering European intruders for the first time. For rival European empires, competing globally for mastery in the Atlantic, Pacific, and Indian Oceans, North America remained only one prize in a wider imperial contest.

Following the departure of the French, the push of rival powers to establish permanent control over the North American continent continued. But geographic ignorance, limited resources, weak bureaucracies, huge distances, strong-willed colonists, and resilient native inhabitants all posed limits for maintaining and expanding far-flung empires. Russia's foothold in Alaska and Spain's presence in California were new and tenuous at best. Spanish dominance at older outposts in Arizona, New Mexico, and Texas remained partial, and Spain's grip on its newly acquired Louisiana territory was even more nominal. East of the Mississippi River, long-term British control finally seemed certain. But even Britain, secure after its victory over France, would soon be fighting a losing battle to retain much of North America that it confidently claimed to control.

■ Some wealthy colonists, like the Hancocks of Boston, joined the Patriot opposition during the 1760s and 1770s. Gradually, out of necessity, these merchants and planters forged a loose and convenient alliance with colonial artisans and workers who came from a very different world.

New Challenges to Spain's Expanded Empire

How did French, English, and Russian explorers in the Pacific threaten Spain's American empire?

With Spain's acquisition of Louisiana from France in 1763, the Spanish held nominal title to the entire West, from the Mississippi to the Pacific, populated by more than one million Native Americans. But whether Spain could explore and defend this vast domain, stretching north toward Alaska, remained an open question. After all, envious rivals were already prob-ing North America's Pacific coast. French and British exploration voyages challenged Spain's dominance in the Pacific, and Russian colonization in Alaska spurred the Spanish to establish posts along the coast of California. These rivalries, in turn, brought new pressures to bear on the West's diverse Indian peoples, even before the United States emerged as a separate entity with expansionist ambitions of its own.

Pacific Exploration, Hawaiian Contact

Defeat in the Seven Years' War removed the French from North America in 1763. Burdened with heavy war debts, France sought fresh prospects in the unexplored South Pacific. Not to be outdone, British captains pressed their own Pacific explorations. The most skilled and successful was James Cook, who ranged from the Arctic Circle to Antarctica during three momentous voyages beginning in 1768. In January 1778, during Cook's final voyage, his two vessels happened upon the Hawaiian Islands, eight major volcanic islands, plus 114 minor isles, stretching over 300 miles. More than thirteen centuries earlier (A.D. 300–500), seafaring Polynesians had migrated here in ocean-sailing canoes. They had arrived from the Marquesas Islands far to the south, and their descendants, perhaps as many as 300,000 people, lived in agricultural and fishing communities dominated by powerful chiefs.

The Hawaiians treated Cook with hospitality and respect. "No people could trade with more honisty," the captain observed. During the next twelve months, Cook cruised up the west coast of North America. Two centuries after Francis Drake's visit, English mariners still hoped to find a sea passage through North America to shorten voyages from the Atlantic to Asia. But Cook encountered a solid coastline stretching all the way to Alaska. Along the way, he traded with Northwest Coast Indians for sea otter pelts.

Cook's vessels returned south in 1779, and they were again greeted with fanfare on the big island of Hawaii. But admiration turned to resentment as the English outstayed their welcome, and an angry crowd of Hawaiians killed Cook and four of his mariners. After the

■ When Captain Cook anchored at Hawaii's Kealakekua Bay in 1779, he wrote in his journal that the islanders crowded aboard his two vessels and paddled around them in "a multitude of Canoes." Hundreds of others swam about the ships, along with "a number of men upon pieces of Plank." One such surfboarder is visible in the foreground.

captain's death, his two sloops stopped at Macao in China, where the crew sold their furs at a huge profit. They then sailed back to England in 1780 with word of money to be made selling North American sea otter pelts in China. The voyagers also confirmed a disturbing rumor: Russia already had a foothold in this lucrative Pacific traffic.

The Russians Lay Claim to Alaska

Half a century before Cook visited Hawaii, a Danish captain in the Russian naval service trekked across Siberia. Vitus Bering reached the Kamchatka peninsula on the Pacific Ocean in 1728, From there, he built a boat and sailed north through the strait that bears his name. The journey ended European speculation that Asia was linked to North America. On a second expedition in 1741, Bering visited the Alaskan mainland and claimed it for Russia. He died during the return voyage, after a winter shipwreck on a frozen island.

Bering's crew finally returned to Kamchatka with valuable pelts. Over the next generation, Russian merchants sent several expeditions to Alaska each year, bringing back furs that they traded with the powerful Chinese Empire. In Alaskan waters, the Russian trappers lacked the numbers and the skill to collect furs on their own. So they captured native women and children as hostages, then ransomed them back to their men in exchange for a fixed number of furs. Native Alaskans resisted these rough intruders, but many eventually submitted in a desperate effort to survive.

In the quarter-century before 1780, thirty different Russian companies sponsored expeditions to Alaskan waters. The competing newcomers, bringing diseases, firearms, and their brutal hostage-taking system, reduced the population of the Aleutian Islands. As the number of humans and animals on the Aleutian Islands declined, the Russians pushed farther east in search of new hunters and hunting grounds. The Russian voyages from Kamchatka grew longer and more expensive.

To facilitate operations Grigorii Shelikov and a partner formed a new company in 1781 and planned an Alaskan base. In 1784 they founded a permanent colonial settlement on Kodiak Island east of the Aleutians, despite fierce opposition from the island's native residents. By 1799 the firm had absorbed smaller competitors to become the Russian-American Company, with a monopoly from the **czar**.

■ In 1991, 250 years after Vitus Bering's voyage to Alaska, Russians from Kamchatka sailed replicas of Bering's three small vessels across the North Pacific to Alaska. Aleksandr Maslov-Bering, a descendant of the explorer, poses beside the carved bow of one boat.

In 1790, with the Kodiak base secure, Russians forced more than 7,000 island inhabitants to embark on vast fur hunts in their versatile two-seat **kayaks**. That same year, Shelikov hired Alexander Baranov to oversee the Kodiak post and expand operations down the Alaskan coast. In 1799 Baranov established an additional outpost at Sitka in southeast Alaska. Called New Archangel at the time, the post became the capital of Russian America in 1808. From here, Baranov eventually extended the company's reach south toward California, seeking new hunting grounds and a longer growing season.

Spain Colonizes the California Coast

The Seven Years' War had left Spain's king, Carlos III, with vast new land claims in western North America. His bureaucrats in Spanish America struggled to control the huge domain. Across the Southwest, many Native Americans resisted military suppression and slave raids. In addition, clerics offered their own resistance to government designs. The powerful Jesuits opposed administrative reform in the colonies, and in 1767 Carlos III expelled them from the Spanish realm. Unruly colonists posed a threat of their own. French inhabitants of New Orleans led a brief rebellion against Spanish rule in 1768. Finally, officials feared challenges in the Pacific from the British and the Russians. As early as 1759, a Spanish Franciscan had published *Muscovites in California*, warning of Russian settlements.

Mindful of the Russian threat, Spanish leaders in Mexico City moved to establish a token presence along the California coast. In 1769 Gaspar de Portolá and Franciscan friar Junípero Serra led a small vanguard north to establish an initial outpost at San Diego Bay. Portolá then pressed farther up the coast, building a presidio (or military garrison) at Monterey in 1770 to "defend us from attacks by the Russians, who," he believed, "were about to invade us."

After Carlos III removed all Jesuits from Spanish America in 1767, members of the competing Franciscan order expanded their work and took on new responsibilities. Following the lead of Father Serra, other Franciscans soon planted several missions between San Diego and Monterey. These included the San Gabriel mission in 1771, where colonists established the town of Los Angeles ten years later. In 1775 a Spanish captain sailed into San Francisco Bay, and the next year a land expedition laid out the presidio and mission of San Francisco. A town sprang up at nearby San José the following year. As Franciscan fathers labored to convert the coast's diverse Indians, Spanish vessels pushed far up the Pacific shoreline. Captain Ignacio de Arteaga reached the Gulf of Alaska in 1779, fourteen months after Captain Cook had been there.

Since Spanish ships had difficulty supplying the few dozen settlers in California, authorities looked for an overland supply route. In 1774 Juan Bautista de Anza set out in search of a land route to California from the presidio he commanded at Tubac, south of Tucson. Accompanied by a Franciscan named Father Garcés, he forded the Colorado River and then crossed desert and mountains to reach the coast at San Gabriel. The next year, Anza led 240 reinforcements—mostly Spanish women and children—along a similar route, pausing at San Gabriel and heading north to San Francisco Bay.

Further explorations proved less successful. In July 1776 Fathers Domínguez and Escalante left Santa Fe on horseback. The Franciscans headed northwest across Colorado and Utah in search of a more northern route to Monterey on the Pacific coast. But no such trail existed. Instead, their 1,800-mile trek revealed the huge expanse of the Great Basin. Moreover, the path to California that Anza had established proved short-lived. The Yuma Indians, near the Colorado River soon grew to resent Spanish trespassers, and they rebelled in the summer of 1781. Hopes for a rapid expansion of the Spanish colony in California died in the bloody Yuma Revolt.

Despite these problems, Spain managed to retain control over its recently expanded North American empire. The same could not be said for the British in their own newly enlarged empire farther east. They had taken French Canada, and their military might dominated the Atlantic world. But their fortunes in North America were about to change.

The Spanish entry into Alta (upper) California

- 🗲 Fort
- ✝ Mission
- ▪ Presidio
- ● Town
- ▣ Mission and Presidio
- ◉ Town and Presidio
- ── Portolá, 1769
- ── Anza and Garcés, 1774
- ── Anza, 1775–1776
- ── Garcés, 1776
- ── Domínguez and Escalante, 1776
- ── Modern state boundaries shown for orientation

(1769) Years indicate the date of founding

POMO
MIWOK
San Francisco Bay
Ft. Ross (Russian, 1812)
San Francisco (1776)
Santa Clara (1776)
San José (1777)
COSTANOAN
Monterey (1770)
San Antonio (1771)
SALINAN
San Luis Obispo (1772)
CHUMASH
San Gabriel (1771)
San Juan Capistrano (1776)
CAHUILLA
San Diego (1769)
YUMA
PACIFIC OCEAN
CALIFORNIA

Great Salt Lake
UTE
Great Basin
Mohave Desert
Grand Canyon
Colorado R.
HOPI
NAVAJO
ZUNI
Santa Fé
Albuquerque
Yuma (1780)
Indian Uprising, 1781
Gila R.
PAPAGO
APACHE
Tucson
Tubac
NEW MEXICO
Rio Grande

Horcasitas

Loreto (1697)
Gulf of California
BAJA CALIFORNIA

■ **MAP 6.1**
SPANISH EXPLORATION AFTER 1760 AND THE START OF THE CALIFORNIA MISSIONS

New Challenges to Britain's Expanded Empire

Why did the removal of French and Spanish interests pose new problems for Britain's North American empire?

In September 1760, French forces at Montreal submitted to British commander Jeffery Amherst. For Native Americans living east of the Mississippi, the French defeat in Canada had an immediate impact. General Amherst, who despised Indians as "contemptible," intended to alter Native American relations in the interior to reflect the new balance of power. He promptly sent James Grant to South Carolina with instructions "to chastise the Cherokees," who had taken up arms against the growing number of English traders and settlers in western Carolina. Grant invaded Cherokee country in 1761, burning fifteen villages.

With the Cherokee chastened in the South, Amherst turned his attention to the Indians north of the Ohio River. Here his harsh policies brought a sudden retaliation from the Native Americans; their actions took many lives and cost Amherst his command. And if Indians in the Midwest posed fresh challenges to Britain, so did the colonists themselves.

Midwestern Lands and Pontiac's War for Indian Independence

As soon as the British unseated their French competitors in the Ohio River valley, they prohibited traffic with Indians in such goods as knives, tomahawks, muskets, powder, and lead. As French traders withdrew, the British took over their strategic posts at Detroit and at Michilimackinac. English settlers built new forts in the Ohio Valley and erected Fort Pitt over the ruins of Fort Duquesne. Then, early in 1763, word spread among Indians that France would cede Louisiana to Spain and give up Canada and the entire Midwest to Great Britain. This shocking news undercut moderate Native American leaders and strengthened the hand of pro-war factions.

Word that a treaty in far-off Paris might disrupt the entire region drew attention to Neolin, a Delaware Indian prophet urging a return to ancient ways and a sharp separation from the corrupting Europeans. Neolin's popular vision of renewing Native American independence by driving out the British appealed to Pontiac, a militant Ottawa warrior. In April, Pontiac addressed a secret council of more than 400 Ottawa, Potawatomie, and Huron, meeting within ten miles of Fort Detroit. Invoking the Delaware Prophet's vision, he announced that the Master of Life resented the British and wanted them removed: "Send them back to the lands which I have created for them and let them stay there." By May, Pontiac had mobilized a coalition and laid siege to Detroit.

Soon Indians from eighteen nations had joined in Pontiac's widespread uprising. By mid-June 1763, both Detroit and Fort Pitt were under siege, and the British had lost every other Ohio Valley and Great Lakes outpost. As Indian raiding parties ravaged white communities in western Virginia and Pennsylvania, embittered settlers responded with racial killing. In December, white men from Paxton Creek descended on Christian families of Conestoga Indians near Lancaster, Pennsylvania, executing more than thirty peaceful converts. When easterners protested this outrage, the "Paxton Boys" marched on Philadelphia to demand increased protection on the frontier. General Amherst ordered his officers to spread smallpox if possible, and to take no prisoners. The Indians deserved extermination, he ranted, "for the good of mankind."

The violence ended in a stalemate. Without French support, Native American munitions ran short, and Detroit and Fort Pitt endured. Indian militancy waned, and Pontiac was killed by a Peoria Indian in 1765. Still, the uprising proved costly for the British and prompted a shift in policy. To avoid further expensive warfare, officials moved to restore the Indian trade, keep squatters and debt evaders out of Indian country, and prevent colonial speculation in western lands. In October 1763, Major General Thomas Gage replaced Amherst in command of British forces.

In England, the crown went further. Late in 1763, it issued a proclamation forbidding colonial settlers from moving west across the Appalachian summit. Beyond that dividing line, all the land east of the Mississippi River would be reserved for Indians and a few authorized British soldiers and traders. While the Proclamation Line of 1763, drawn along the crest of the Appalachians, had only limited success, it frustrated Virginia's gentry. Such prominent men as George Washington and Thomas Jefferson were investors in land companies that speculated in large western tracts, hoping to obtain property cheaply from Native Americans and sell small parcels to eager settlers at a steady profit. But the British government, fearful of sparking unified Indian opposition and additional warfare, denied the Virginians' wishes and aroused their resentment.

Grenville's Effort at Reform

In 1763 King George III appointed George Grenville to head a new government in London. Grenville's ministry immediately faced a series of intertwined problems. Britain's victory over the French in the Seven Years' War had proved costly, nearly doubling the national debt to a staggering £146 million. As England's postwar depression deepened, returning soldiers swelled the ranks of the unemployed. In addition, rural mobs protested a new tax on domestic cider, imposed to help whittle away at the war debt.

No one promoted opposition to the government more than John Wilkes, a flamboyant member of Parliament (MP). Wilkes published the *North Briton*, an outspoken periodical which attacked the king's peace settlement with France and the king himself. Grenville reacted by arresting the publisher, despite his status as an MP. Angered by government suppression of dissent, protesters made "Wilkes and Liberty!" a popular rallying cry.

Pressured at home, Grenville set out to impose order on Britain's growing American colonies through a series of reforms. The first step was to maintain a military presence of nearly 7,000 troops in North America. The move would protect newly acquired territories while keeping young British men employed overseas rather than jobless at home. Strapped for funds, Grenville hoped to pay for the transatlantic forces with money drawn from the American colonies, reminding them of their subordination to the British Parliament.

A second step involved raising revenue by strengthening customs enforcement in colonial ports. Grenville dispatched forty-four navy ships to America to assist customs officials in nabbing smugglers, and he convinced Parliament to pass the American Duties Act of 1764. This new revenue law, also known as the Sugar Act, increased the duty on sugar and various other products entering the empire from non-British ports. Most importantly, it cut in half the import duty of sixpence per gallon on foreign molasses. Officials hoped that New England rum distillers, who had been secretly importing cheap molasses from the French West Indies without paying customs, would be willing to pay threepence per gallon. If enforced, the act would reduce smuggling and boost revenues.

> *"What has America done,"* *protested critics, "to be stripped of so invaluable a privilege as the trial by jury?"*

To ensure compliance, the Sugar Act established the first of several vice-admiralty courts. The court sat at Halifax, Nova Scotia, so defendants had large travel expenses, and they faced a single appointed judge instead of a favorable hometown jury. "What has America done," protested critics, "to be stripped of so invaluable a privilege as the trial by jury?"

Colonists found Grenville's next statutes equally dismaying. The Currency Act of 1764 prohibited colonial assemblies from issuing paper money or bills of credit to be used as legal tender to pay off debts. The move worsened the money shortage in British America, where a lopsided trade balance was already draining gold and silver from the colonies to England. The next year Parliament passed a Quartering Act that obliged colonists to assist the army by allowing soldiers to use vacant barns and other buildings as temporary quarters. The local governor was to supply the soldiers, at colonial expense, with such basic necessities as firewood, candles, bedding, salt, vinegar, utensils, and beer. Colonial assemblies had willingly voted such support during colonial wars. However, these peacetime requisitions, ordered by a distant Parliament, challenged their authority and smacked of indirect taxation.

■ Lawyers and artisans in the Sons of Liberty encouraged demonstrations against the Stamp Act. But they ran the risk, suggested here, that poor workers, black slaves, and women in the crowds might give their own meanings to the shouts of "Liberty!"

The Stamp Act Imposed

There was nothing indirect about Grenville's most important reform: the Stamp Act. Early in 1765, Parliament approved the new statute "for raising a further revenue" to pay for "defending, protecting, and securing" the British colonies in America. The new act was patterned on a similar law in England, and it required stamps (like those on modern packs of cigarettes) to appear on a variety of articles in America after November 1, 1765. The list included legal contracts, land deeds, liquor licenses, indentures, newspapers, almanacs, and playing cards. Colonial lawyers and printers were to purchase these stamps from designated agents; the official stamp distributor in each colony would receive a handsome fee from all stamp sales. The British treasury anticipated taking in £100,000 per year, to be spent only for government operations in America.

Grenville's stamp bill generated little debate in England. Granted, colonists had no actual representation in the Parliament, but neither did the majority of subjects in England. Most of them did not have the right to vote in Parliamentary elections, yet all were said to be "virtually" represented by MPs, who supposedly had the interests of the entire country at heart. If MPs looked out for nonvoting subjects at home, surely they could provide the same sort of "virtual representation" for British subjects throughout the empire.

Most MPs viewed Grenville's stamp measure as appropriate and well conceived. They saw no legal distinction between external duties used to regulate trade and internal taxes imposed by Parliament within the colonies themselves to raise revenue. Because the stamp tax applied to daily articles used throughout the colonies, its mild burden would be widely distributed. Even better, revenues would grow steadily as colonial economic activity continued to expand.

So as not to cause alarm in the colonies, Parliament set initial stamp prices in America lower than those charged in England, although it could always raise the rates as colonists grew accustomed to the tax. Moreover, the tax was to be gathered quietly by Americans themselves in the course of doing business rather than extracted from citizens by tax collectors. Prominent colonists were eager to accept the lucrative stamp distributorships, and no one predicted an upheaval in ports where the stamps were to be sold. But the Stamp Act soon unleashed a storm of organized resistance.

The Stamp Act Resisted

At first, colonial assemblies had mixed responses to the new tax. But in late May, the youngest member of the Virginia House of Burgesses—a rising attorney named Patrick Henry—galvanized American resistance to the Stamp Act. As the House session was winding down, Henry introduced a series of fiery resolves challenging Parliament's right to impose taxes. The twenty-eight-year-old orator gained narrow passage of five separate resolutions.

Henry's fifth and most provocative resolve asserted that Virginia's assembly had the "sole exclusive right and power to lay taxes" on the colony's inhabitants. The resolution passed by just one vote. In fact, opponents reintroduced it the next day, after Henry left town, and voted it down. But the spark had been struck. Distant newspapers were soon reprinting Henry's "Virginia Resolves," including the resolution that had been voted down plus two that had been drawn up but never introduced for a vote. These provocative draft resolutions said that Virginians were "not bound to yield obedience" to such a tax, and anyone arguing otherwise must "be deemed an enemy" to the colony.

In Massachusetts, the assembly took a different approach. It issued a call for each colony to send delegates to a Stamp Act Congress in New York in October 1765 to "implore relief" from Parliament. Local citizens, inflamed by Virginia's resolutions and squeezed by an economic depression, prepared to take more direct action. In Boston, a small group of artisans and merchants known as the Loyal Nine mobilized to force the designated stamp distributor, Andrew Oliver, to resign before the stamps arrived from England. On August 16, a crowd of

Read the **Document**
Otis, "The Rights of the British Colonies Asserted and Proved" at **www.myhistorylab.com**

View the **Image**
Stamp Act Stamps at **www.myhistorylab.com**

View the **Image**
1765 Stamp Act Protest at **www.myhistorylab.com**

several thousand hanged an effigy of Oliver and tore down his Stamp Office. The protesters ransacked Oliver's elegant house, drinking his wine and smashing his furniture. The next day, Oliver resigned his appointment.

As word of the protest spread, crowds took to the streets in scores of towns. Often the mobs were encouraged by local leaders who opposed the Stamp Act. These prominent citizens had started to organize themselves in secret groups, which they called the Sons of Liberty. The crowds forced the resignation of potential stamp distributors in ports from New Hampshire to the Carolinas. When a shipment of stamps finally arrived in New York City, nearly 5,000 people risked open warfare to confiscate the hated cargo.

Throughout the second half of 1765, the Sons of Liberty promoted street violence against specific targets. But they could not always control the demonstrations, since the debtors, sailors, blacks, and women drawn to such crowds all had separate grievances of their own. For example, on August 26 in Boston, just ten days after the raid on Oliver's house, a second mob launched a broader assault. Without sanction from the Loyal Nine or the Sons of Liberty, the crowd went after the homes of several wealthy office holders, including the house of Lieutenant Governor Thomas Hutchinson. Because he also served as chief justice of the Superior Court, Hutchinson had offended townspeople by issuing numerous warrants for debtors and collecting large fees for administering bankruptcies. Hutchinson recounted how he fled when "the hellish crew fell upon my house with the Rage of devils and . . . with axes split down the doors."

In South Carolina the spirit of insurrection also went well beyond the careful boundaries intended by the Sons of Liberty. They were pleased when Charleston artisans hanged a stamp distributor in effigy, with a sign reading, "Liberty and no Stamp Act." And they gave tacit approval when white workers harassed the wealthy slave trader and potential stamp distributor Henry Laurens with chants of "Liberty, Liberty!" Soon, however, enslaved African Americans also took to the streets, raising their own defiant cry of "Liberty, Liberty!" Fearing an insurrection by South Carolina's black majority, the same people who had sanctioned earlier street demonstrations quickly shifted their focus, believing that ideas of freedom had spread too far. The colonial assembly temporarily banned further importation of Africans. Local leaders expanded slave patrols and placed Charleston briefly under martial law.

▶●●▶ Read the **Document**

Franklin, Testimony Against the Stamp Act at **www.myhistorylab.com**

Elsewhere, too, the colonial elites took steps to contain the turbulence. Many moved—often reluctantly—toward more radical positions, joining the Sons of Liberty and ridiculing the British concept of virtual representation. Colonial assemblies condemned Grenville's intrusive reforms. The Stamp Act Congress passed resolutions vehemently protesting both the Sugar and Stamp acts. But even as they challenged Parliament, these same local leaders stressed their loyalty to the crown and moved to control the violence, some of which was directed at them. Such moderation appealed to cautious merchants in Atlantic seaports, who reluctantly agreed to stop ordering Britain goods. They hoped that exporters in Britain, feeling the economic pinch of a colonial boycott, might use their political strength to force a repeal of the Stamp Act and defuse the tense situation.

When politics in London prompted Grenville's sudden removal from office, hopes rose in America for a possible compromise resolving the Stamp Act crisis. In March 1766, these hopes were nearly fulfilled. The new ministry of Lord Rockingham, responding to merchant pressure as predicted, and also to the compelling rhetoric of William Pitt, persuaded Parliament to repeal the Stamp Act. But colonial victory seemed hollow, for the repeal bill was accompanied by a blunt Declaratory Act. In it, Parliament declared its power "to make Laws . . . to bind the Colonists and People of America . . . in all Cases whatsoever."

Hudson Bay
Company

Nova Scotia

Quebec

● Halifax

Three Rivers

□ Annapolis
Royal

ME
(part of Mass.)

Lake
Nipissing

St. Lawrence R.

Quebec

Montreal

Edward Augustus,
abandoned June 15, 1763

Ft. Michilimackinac,
June 2, 1763

NH

● Portsmouth

Windham ●— Salem

●— Marblehead

Albany ●

Lebanon ●
Hartford ●

NY

MA

● Boston
● Pomfret
● Plymouth

Wethersfield ●

RI

□ Ft. Niagara

Wallingford ●
New Haven ●

CT

● Norwich
●— Newport

Ft. Presque Isle,
June 14–17, 1763

West Haven ●
Milford ●

Lyme ●
Stratford ●

● New London

PA

Woodbridge ●

Fairfield ●
New York ●

Ft. Detroit □

Ft. Venango,
June 13, 1763

Paxton ●

Piscataway ●
Amwell Twp ●

Elizabeth Town ●
Perth Amboy ●

Ft. St. Joseph,
May 25, 1763

Ft. Le Boeuf,
June 18, 1763

Ft. Sandusky,
May 16, 1763

□ Ft. Pitt

Lancaster ●
Conestoga ●

NJ

Brunswick ●

● Philadelphia

Salem ●

Ft. Miami,
May 27, 1763

Frederick Town ●

Baltimore ●

Talbot ●

Elk Ridge Landing ●

Ft. Ouiatenon,
May 31, 1763

Annapolis ●

● Lewes

Dumfries ●

MD

DE

ATLANTIC
OCEAN

□ Ft. Chartres

Indian
reserve
(by proclamation 1763)

Leeds ●
Tappahannock ●

VA

Williamsburg ●

Spanish
Louisiana

Norfolk ●

Mississippi R.

NC

New Bern ●

Cross Creek ●

● Duplin

Wilmington ●
Brunswick ●

● Fort Johnson

Proclamation Line 1763

SC

Boundary after 1764

Charleston ●

West Florida

GA

Boundary in 1763

St. Mary's R.

Savannah ●

Mobile ●

Pensacola ●

□ Ft. Apalachee

□ St. Augustine

New Orleans ●

East
Florida

Gulf of
Mexico

British dominance in eastern North America

- Acquired by Britain from France
- Acquired by Britain from Spain
- Prior British colonies, as of 1763
- Reserved to Indians under British rule
- Spanish Louisiana

Points of violence, 1763–1766

- British forts seized during Pontiac's Rebellion in 1763
- ● Towns demonstrating against the Stamp Act in 1765

Distribution of British troops

- □ British posts 100–250 soldiers
- British posts 250–600 soldiers
- British posts over 600 soldiers

■ **MAP 6.2**

BRITISH NORTH AMERICA, 1763–1766
In 1763 the British worked to govern their new provinces
in Canada and Florida while suppressing an Indian
uprising in the Midwest. With widely dispersed troops,
they also tried to keep colonists out of the Mississippi
Valley and halt opposition to the 1765 Stamp Act.

"The Unconquerable Rage of the People"

How did events in America and Britain in the 1760s confirm the skeptical worldview of "Real Whigs"?

As news of the Stamp Act repeal spread, the Sons of Liberty organized elaborate celebrations in British America. But word of the Declaratory Act had a sobering effect. Clearly, the problems surrounding colonial taxation and representation remained unresolved. The atmosphere of mutual suspicion that had erupted during the Stamp Act crisis divided colonists further in the years ahead. A flurry of pamphlets from colonial presses broadened awareness of the issues and inspired new coalitions in a time of economic recession. As colonial leaders collaborated, they discovered a shared viewpoint that gave added meaning and importance to each new event. This emerging ideology had deep roots stretching back into English history.

Power Corrupts: An English Framework for Revolution

The radical ideas that had appeared during England's Civil War in the 1640s, when English subjects briefly overthrew their monarchy and proclaimed a Puritan Commonwealth, lived on long after the Restoration in 1660. English Whigs who led the Glorious Revolution in 1688 invoked some of these principles when they limited the monarchy's power and strengthened Parliament's authority. Succeeding generations hailed the rights of English subjects and congratulated themselves that Great Britain (as England and Scotland became known in 1707) had achieved a truly balanced government. They drew on the ancient Greek philosopher Aristotle to explain their accomplishment.

Aristotle, his modern readers noted, had observed a cycle in politics. He believed that too much power vested in a king could eventually corrupt the monarchical form of government. Unbounded royal power led to a tyranny, misrule by a despot wielding absolute control. When nobles then asserted themselves against the tyrant (as English barons had done when they forced King John to sign the Magna Carta in 1215), the resulting aristocracy could easily turn corrupt. Abuse of power by such an oligarchy of self-serving nobles could then prompt the common people, known as the commons, to rise up. If the commons gained sway, they might build a democracy, but it too could degenerate, leaving only anarchy. Such a "mobocracy" paved the way for an opportunistic leader to once more seize the scepter of royal power and start the cycle over again.

Confident Whigs claimed that England had halted this vicious cycle by balancing the power of the nation's three estates: the king epitomized the legitimate interests of monarchy, the House of Lords represented the aristocracy, and the House of Commons represented the rest of the population. However, a few of the more radical Whig theorists continued to oppose this consensus view long after 1700. Calling themselves the Real Whigs, these skeptics charged that Britain's mixed government—which claimed an ideal and lasting balance between monarchy, aristocracy, and commons—was actually less perfect and more vulnerable than most people suspected.

A truly balanced government, they argued, is hard to achieve and difficult to maintain, for power inevitably corrupts. Schemers who obtain public office can readily disrupt such a fragile system, so its protection, these critics stressed, demanded constant vigilance. They urged citizens to watch for the two surest signs of decay: the concentration of wealth in a few hands and the political and social corruption that inevitably follows. Where others saw stability in England's exuberant growth, these Real Whigs perceived clear signs of danger in the powerful new Bank of England, the expanding stock market, and the rise in public debt.

No Real Whigs proved more vigilant than John Trenchard and Thomas Gordon. The two men sensed around them the same luxury and greed that had undermined the Roman Republic. They pored over the works of ancient writers such as the Roman statesman Cato, who described and challenged corrupt behavior. In 1721 they published *Cato's Letters: Essays*

Read the Document
Magna Carta at
www.myhistorylab.com

on Liberty, cautioning against "the Natural Encroachments of Power" and warning that "public corruptions and abuses have grown upon us."

Trenchard and Gordon took particular offense at Britain's corrupt patronage system. Too many people gained public positions through political ties rather than through skill or training. The authors of *Cato's Letters* felt each new act of corruption set a dangerous precedent, if unopposed. They reminded readers that tyranny is usually imposed through small, subtle steps, for "if it is suffered once, it is apt to be repeated often; a few repetitions create a habit." Before citizens realize that they are losing their liberties, the permanent "Yoke of Servitude" is in place, supported by military force. All hope of successful protest has disappeared. The encroachment of power over liberty, Trenchard and Gordon concluded, is "much easier to prevent than to cure."

Americans Practice Vigilance and Restraint

Cato's Letters earned a wide American following during the 1760s, for colonists saw disturbing parallels between the warnings of Real Whig authors and current events in America. Now, as throughout history, a government tainted by corruption might deny adequate representation, initiate unjust taxes, or replace jury trials with arbitrary courts. Officials might curtail freedoms of press or religion to consolidate their power. Moreover, weak ministers might advise the king poorly or keep citizens' pleas from reaching his ears. If the populace relaxed its guard, these ministers might even sanction a standing army in peacetime to impose arbitrary rule over their own population.

> *During the 1760s, colonists saw disturbing parallels between the warnings of Real Whig authors and current events in America.*

According to Real Whig doctrine, ordinary people must be alert but circumspect; a measured response to these threats was all-important. One stubborn or mistaken act by officials did not prove a pattern of conspiracy, and it could be counterproductive to raise alarms too often. So prudent citizens should turn first to legal methods of **redress**. If the system was functioning properly, claims of real abuses would bring forth proper corrections. Even if forced to take to the streets as a last resort, crowds should be organized, not uncontrolled. They should threaten property before people and hang effigies, not actual office holders.

For the most part, the Stamp Act demonstrations had followed this logic of restraint and had gained the desired effect. "In every Colony," wrote John Adams, "the Stamp Distributors and Inspectors have been compelled, by the unconquerable Rage of the People, to renounce their offices." But did individual demands for liberty have limits? Could slaves seek liberty from their masters? What about wives from husbands? Could tenants press for redress from rich landlords, or debtors from powerful creditors? Such questions generated widespread, heated debate in the turbulent quarter-century ahead.

Rural Unrest: Tenant Farmers and Regulators

In local controversies, both large and small, the "Rage of the People" frequently boiled up from below. "The People, even to the lowest Ranks, have become more attentive to their Liberties," John Adams observed, "and more determined to defend them." While stamp protesters demonstrated in New York City, aggrieved tenant farmers staged a violent revolt against powerful landholders in the Hudson River valley. They chose an Irish immigrant as their leader, established a council, organized militia companies with elected captains, and broke open jails to free debtors. They even set up their own people's courts to try captured Hudson Valley gentry, before British troops finally suppressed the revolt.

Unrest also shook the Carolinas in the interior region known to colonists as the back-country, or the Piedmont. In South Carolina, the absence of civil government beyond the coastal parishes fostered lawlessness among white settlers until the governor extended circuit courts into the interior in 1769. In North Carolina, migrants seeking fertile land moved

INTERPRETING HISTORY

"Squez'd and Oppressed": A 1768 Petition by 30 Regulators

*I*n the 1760s, corruption prevailed among appointed officials in central North Carolina. Often holding numerous offices at once, these men managed elections, controlled courts, and gathered taxes. Apparently not all the tax money they collected made it to the public treasury. Nevertheless, any farmer who resisted paying might lose the plow horse or the milk cow that sustained the family. It could be "seized and sold" to cover a small tax payment or minor debt, with "no Part being ever Return'd" from the proceeds.

Banding together to better regulate their own affairs, these farmers sought relief through every possible legal means. By 1768 these organized Regulators had exhausted most avenues of peaceful protest. The western counties where they resided were badly underrepresented in the colonial assembly. As a new session prepared to convene, they fired off a final round of petitions, assuring

legislators that they were law-abiding citizens willing to pay their legal share of taxes. In this message of October 4, 1768, 30 Regulators begged for the appointment of honest public officials.

To the Worshipful House of Representatives of North Carolina

Your Poor Petitioners [have] been Continually Squez'd and oppressed by our Publick Officers both with Regard to their fees as also in the Laying on of Taxes as well as in Collecting. . . . Being Grieved thus to have our substance torn from us [by] . . . such Illegal practices, we applied to our public officers to give us some satisfaction . . . which they Repeatedly denied us.

With Regard to the Taxes, . . .we labour under Extreem hardships. . . . Money is very scarce . . . & we exceeding Poor & lie at a great distance from Trade which renders it almost Impossible to gain sustenance by our utmost Endeavours. . . .

To Gentlemen Rowling in affluence, a few shillings per man may seem trifling. Yet to Poor People who must have their Bed and Bedclothes, yea their Wives Petticoats, taken and sold to Defray, how Tremenious [tremendous] . . . must be the

Consequences. . . . Therefore, dear Gentlemen, to your selves, to your Country, and in Pity to your Poor Petitioners, do not let it stand any longer to Drink up the Blood and vitals of the Poor Distressed.

After seeking relief from existing taxes, the petitioners went on to question new burdens, such as the law imposing an additional tax "to Erect a Publick Edifice" for Governor Tryon in New Bern.

Good God, Gentlemen, what will become of us when these Demands come against us? Paper Money we have none & gold or silver we can Purchase none of. The Contingencies of Government Must be Paid, and . . . we are Willing to Pay, [even] if we [must] sell our Beds from under us. And [yet] in this Time of Distress, it is as much as we can support. . . . If, therefore, the Law for that Purpose can be happily Repealed, . . . May the God of Heaven Inspire you with sentiments to that Purpose.

We humble Begg you would . . . Use your Influence with our Worthy, Virtuous Governor to discontinue . . . such Officers as would be found to be ye Bane of Society, and [instead to] Put in the Common Wealth [officials willing] to Encourage the Poor and . . . to stand [up] for them. This

south from Virginia and Pennsylvania in a steady stream. When they arrived in the Piedmont, they found a local elite already appointed to county posts by the governor. The newcomers disliked these grasping office holders who possessed strong family and financial ties to powerful planters and merchants farther east. They seemed to epitomize, at the local level, the sorts of corruption that had long troubled Real Whig pamphleteers.

As backcountry settlers grew in numbers, they protested against their inadequate representation in North Carolina's assembly. They began organizing into local groups to better "regulate" their own affairs, and they soon became known as Regulators. These small farmers, many in debt, protested loudly against regressive taxes that imposed the same burden on all colonists, regardless of their wealth. The Regulators' discontent turned into outrage when coastal planters who dominated the assembly voted public funds to build a stately mansion in New Bern for William Tryon, the colonial governor. By this act, the eastern slaveholding elite hoped to establish North Carolina's permanent capitol building on the coast, and yet Piedmont farmers would bear most of the cost of constructing the mansion.

The decision to erect "Tryon's Palace" at public expense confirmed backcountry suspicions that leading officials were looking out for their own interests at the expense of the public. Both sides dug in their heels. In 1771 Governor Tryon finally called out the militia and marched into the Piedmont. After defeating several thousand angry farmers at the battle of Alamance in May 1771, Tryon hanged six Regulator leaders in Hillsborough would Cause Joy and Gladness to Spring from every Heart. This would cause Labour and Industry to prevail over Murmuring Discontent. This would Raise your poor Petitioners . . . to a flourishing Opulent and Hoping People. Otherwise . . . disatisfaction and Melancholy must Prevail over such as Remain, and Numbers must Defect the Province and seek elsewhere an Asylum from Tyranny and Oppression. . . .

We leave it to you . . . in your great Wisdom . . . to pass such Act or Acts, as shall be Conducive to the welbeing of a whole People over Whose welfare ye are plac'd as Guardians. . . . For the Lords Sake, Gentlemen, Exert your selves this once in our favour.

Questions

1. *How, specifically, do the tone and content of this petition reflect the widespread political outlook, combining vigilance and restraint, described in Cato's Letters?*

2. *Pick some current issue that concerns you deeply and draft a brief, impassioned petition to your legislators. In compelling language, lay out your best arguments for action. Then see if 30 people will sign your petition.*

Source: William S. Powell, James K. Huhta, and Thomas J. Farnham, eds., *The Regulators of North Carolina: A Documentary History, 1759–1776* (Raleigh: State Department of Archives and History, 1971), pp. 187–189.

In 1768 the creation of Tryon's Palace, a mansion for the North Carolina governor at New Bern, prompted backcountry protests. Irate farm families, feeling heavily taxed and poorly represented, joined the Regulator Movement. They filed petitions, withheld taxes, closed courts, and harassed corrupt officials, protesting the "unequal chances the poor and weak have in contentions with the rich and powerful."

Photo courtesy of Tryon Palace Historic Sites & Gardens

and forced the farmers to swear an oath of loyalty. Many refused, migrating farther south to Georgia or west to the Appalachian Mountains. Their leader, a Quaker named Herman Husband, barely escaped with his life. In North Carolina, just as in the Hudson Valley, well-to-do members of the Sons of Liberty dismissed the organized and militant farmers as misguided rabble.

A Conspiracy of Corrupt Ministers?

Numerous sharp divisions—some leading to armed conflict—continued to separate colonists of different classes and regions. But ill-timed steps by successive administrations in London attracted widening attention throughout British America, prompting uneasy new alliances. Colonists familiar with the dire warnings of Real Whig pamphleteers asked themselves a question: in the weak and short-lived ministries that succeeded Grenville's, were the leaders simply ill-informed, or were they actively corrupt? Colonists wondered whether some official conspiracy existed to chip away at American liberties. Even loyal defenders of the crown expressed frustration with new policies that appeared too harsh to calm irate colonists, yet too weak to force them into line.

Did the Boston Massacre highlight justifiable colonial grievances, or was it a provoked attack, exploited by dissidents?

●●●—Read the **Document**

John Dickinson, "Letters . . ." at
www.myhistorylab.com

Parliament's first new imposition after repeal of the Stamp Act was the Revenue Act of 1766. The act further reduced the molasses duty, from threepence per gallon to a single penny, to discourage smuggling and raise revenue. Colonial merchants accepted this measure as an external tax designed to regulate imperial trade. Most paid the new duty, and customs revenues rose. But Real Whig warnings reminded them that compliance with seemingly innocuous legislation could set a dangerous precedent.

The skeptics had a point, for Parliament soon imposed new hard-line measures. Before his sudden death in 1767, Charles Townshend, the Chancellor of the Exchequer (or chief finance minister) put these distasteful statutes in motion. Townshend's new duties sparked angry responses from colonists. The most telling came from John Dickinson, a moderate Philadelphia lawyer. He drafted a series of widely circulated "Letters from a Farmer in Pennsylvania," urging colonists to respond "peaceably—prudently—firmly—jointly." He dismissed any distinction between external and internal taxation, and he also rejected the idea that Americans had virtual representation in Parliament. "We are taxed without our own consent," Dickinson proclaimed to his readers. "We are therefore—SLAVES."

The Townshend Duties Prompt an American Boycott

In search of funds, Parliament passed the Townshend Revenue Act of 1767. It obliged colonists to pay duties on imported glass, paint, lead, paper, and tea. Proceeds were to be spent in the colonies for "the administration of justice, and the support of civil government," a seemingly benevolent gesture. But Dickinson and other colonists pointed out what these two phrases actually meant. "The administration of justice" cloaked expanded searches of American homes and shops in which customs officers used hated "writs of assistance" to ferret out smuggled goods. "The support of civil government" ensured that governors and appointed office holders could draw their pay directly from the new duties instead of depending on an annual salary grant from the local assembly. In short, the new act removed from colonial legislatures one of their strongest bargaining tools in dealing with the crown: the power to pay or withhold yearly salaries for key officials sent from Britain.

Similar acts and instructions followed. Asserting its sovereignty, Parliament disciplined the New York Assembly for defying the Quartering Act of 1765. The crown instructed governors in America, now less dependent for their salaries on colonial lower houses, to disapprove any measures from legislatures asserting their traditional control over how members were chosen, what their numbers should be, and when they would meet. Equally galling, the Customs Act of 1767 established a separate Board of Customs for British North America. Ominously, the commissioners would live in Boston rather than London. To strengthen the board's hand, in 1768 Britain expanded the number of vice-admiralty courts in North America from one to four, adding new courts in Boston, Philadelphia, and Charleston. Furthermore, to look after its troublesome mainland colonies, the British government created a new American Department, overseen by Lord Hillsborough. It also began to move British troops in America from remote frontier outposts to major Atlantic ports, both as a cost-cutting measure and as a show of force.

Americans found these measures threatening, especially when considered as a whole. In February 1768, the Massachusetts legislature, led by forty-six-year-old Samuel Adams, petitioned the king for redress. The legislators circulated a call to other colonial assemblies for similar protests. Condemning the Townshend Revenue Act as unconstitutional, they argued that it imposed taxation without representation. By removing control of the governors' salaries from colonial legislatures, they said, Parliament set the dangerous precedent of making royal officials "independent of the people." Lord Hillsborough demanded an immediate retraction of this provocative "Circular Letter" and ordered the dissolution of any assembly that took up the matter.

In June, events in Boston took a more radical turn. Defying Hillsborough, the Massachusetts assembly voted against rescinding its circular letter. On June 5, a dockside crowd faced down a "press-gang" from a British warship and protected local sailors from being forced (or "pressed") into naval service. Five days later, customs officials seized John Hancock's sloop, *Liberty*, and demanded that he pay import duties for a cargo of Madeira wine. This move sparked a huge demonstration as citizens dragged a small customs boat through the streets and then burned it on Boston Common. Impatient Sam Adams was heard to say, "Let us take up arms immediately and be free."

Emotions ran high. But most leaders sensed that any escalation of the violence would be premature and perhaps suicidal. They reined in demonstrations and instead initiated a boycott of British goods. Nonimportation plans called upon colonists to refrain from imported luxuries and opt instead for virtuous self-sufficiency. The prospect of nonviolent resistance held broad appeal. As the nonimportation movement expanded, women of all ranks, self-proclaimed Daughters of Liberty, turned to making and selling homespun garments. Local associations sprang up, pledging to forgo imported tea and London fashions. A dozen colonial assemblies voted to halt importation of selected goods. In New York, the value of imports from Britain shrank from £491,000 to just £76,000 in a single year.

The damage to English shipping proved substantial. Britain was losing far more revenue in colonial trade than it was gaining through the expanded customs duties. Soon influential British exporters were pressing their government for relief. When Baron Frederick North, who succeeded Townshend, established a new ministry in January 1770, he received the king's consent to work toward a better arrangement with the colonies. Lord North quickly persuaded Parliament to repeal all the Townshend Duties except the one on tea. The move defused the colonial boycott, but it offered too little too late. Like the earlier Declaratory Act, this measure reaffirmed Parliament's disputed right to tax the colonists at will. Moreover, the repeal came on March 5, 1770, the exact day that violence escalated in Boston.

Hear the Audio
"The Liberty Song" at
www.myhistorylab.com

> *Impatient Sam Adams was heard to say, "Let us take up arms immediately and be free."*

View the Image
Signing an Anti-Tea Agreement at
www.myhistorylab.com

The Boston Massacre

After the *Liberty* riot in June 1768, tensions had mounted in Boston, especially with the arrival in October of two regiments of British soldiers, well armed and dressed in their traditional red coats. According to Real Whig beliefs, any appearance by a standing army in peacetime constituted danger. Artisans in a sluggish economy welcomed the increased business that the men in uniform generated, but numerous unemployed workers resented the soldiers' "moonlighting," trying to earn extra pay by applying for local jobs. With 4,000 armed men encamped in a seaport of scarcely 16,000, confrontation seemed inevitable. Affairs "cannot long remain in the state they are now in," wrote one observer late in 1769; "they are hastening to a crisis. What will be the event, God knows."

In March 1770, protesters took to the streets after a run-in between local workers and job-seeking soldiers. Rumors spread about a larger confrontation, and on March 5, around 9 p.m., a crowd gathered outside the customs house. When a harassed sentry struck a boy with his rifle butt, angry witnesses pelted the guard with snowballs. As fellow soldiers pushed through the mob to assist him, firebells summoned more townspeople to the scene. The British fixed their bayonets, loaded their rifles, and aimed at the crowd.

■ In Paul Revere's image of the 1770 Boston Massacre, soldiers defend the hated customs house by moonlight, while a sniper fires from a window clearly labeled "Butcher's Hall." Revere's partisan engraving spread an anti-British view of the bloody event.

Read the Document

Boston Gazette, Description of the Boston Massacre at
www.myhistorylab.com

Into this tense standoff marched several dozen sailors, waving banners and brandishing clubs. Their leader was Crispus Attucks, an imposing ex-slave who stood 6 feet 2 inches. The son of a black man and an Indian woman, he had run away from his master and then taken up a life at sea. Damning the soldiers and daring them to fire, Attucks pressed his band of colonial sailors to the front, waving a long stick in the moonlight. In the mayhem, a British gun went off, prompting a volley of fire from the other soldiers. The crowd recoiled in disbelief at the sight of dead and wounded Americans lying in the street. According to a printed report, Attucks and four others had been "killed on the Spot." The anti-British cause had its first martyrs.

By grim coincidence, the bloody episode in New England occurred only hours after Lord North addressed the House of Commons to urge removal of most Townshend Duties. His effort at reconciliation immediately became lost in a wave of hostile publicity. Paul Revere, a Boston silversmith, captured the incident in an inflammatory engraving. The Sons of Liberty quickly named the event of March 5 the Boston Massacre. "On that night," John Adams remarked, "the foundation of American independence was laid."

Creating Committees of Correspondence

The overzealous conduct of customs officers gave colonists further cause for distrust. In 1769, after crown agents confiscated John Hancock's vessel, the *Liberty*, and converted it into a customs vessel, citizens in Newport, Rhode Island, destroyed the sloop. In the Delaware River region, residents jailed a customs collector in 1770, and the next year local protesters stormed a customs schooner and beat up the crew. In June 1772, the *Gaspée*, another customs boat said to harass local shipping, ran aground near Pawtuxet, Rhode Island. In a midnight attack, more than a hundred raiders descended on the stranded schooner and set fire to the vessel.

The destruction of the *Gaspée* renewed sharp antagonisms. The irate Earl of Hillsborough, secretary of state for the American colonies, sent a royal commission from London to investigate and to transport suspects to England for trial. But many of the attackers, such as John Brown of Providence, came from important Rhode Island families. Even a £500 reward could not induce local inhabitants to name participants. Besides, many viewed the order to deport accused citizens to England as a denial of their fundamental right to trial by a jury of their peers.

When the colonists took action, Virginia's House of Burgesses again led the way, as it had in the Stamp Act crisis. In March 1773, Patrick Henry, Thomas Jefferson, and Richard Henry Lee pushed through a resolution establishing a standing committee to look into the *Gaspée* affair and to keep up "Correspondence and Communication with our sister colonies" regarding the protection of rights. Following Virginia's example, ten other colonial legislatures promptly established their own Committees of Correspondence. In Massachusetts, people formed similar committees, linking individual towns. Within months a new act of Parliament, designed to rescue the powerful East India Company from bankruptcy, gave these emerging communication networks their first test.

Could the British, through a more creative response to the Boston Tea Party, have averted the ensuing escalation toward violence?

Launching a Revolution

In 1767, before Parliament imposed the Townshend Duties, Americans annually imported nearly 870,000 pounds of tea from England. But the boycott movement cut that amount to less than 110,000 pounds by 1770; colonists turned to smuggling Dutch blends and brewing homemade root teas. When nonimportation schemes lapsed in the early 1770s, purchase of English tea resumed, though a duty remained in effect. Encouraged by this apparent acceptance of parliamentary taxation, Lord North addressed the problem facing the British East India Company, which owed a huge debt to the Bank of England and had 18 million pounds of unsold tea rotting in London warehouses. Many MPs held stock in the East India Company, so Parliament passed a law to assist the ailing establishment.

The Tempest over Tea

The Tea Act of 1773 let the struggling East India Company bypass the expensive requirement that merchants ship Asian tea through England on its way to colonial ports. Now they could send the product directly to the colonies or to foreign ports, without paying to unload, store, auction, and reload the heavy chests. Any warehouse tea destined for the colonies would have its English duty refunded. These steps would reduce retail prices and expand the tea market. They would also quietly confirm the right of Parliament to collect a tea tax of threepence per pound.

The company promptly chose prominent colonial merchants to receive and distribute more than 600,000 pounds of tea. These consignees would earn a hefty 6 percent commission. But wary colonists in port towns, sensing a repetition of 1765, renewed the tactics that had succeeded against the Stamp Act. Sons of Liberty vowed to prevent tea-laden ships from docking, and crowds pressured local distributors to renounce participation in the scheme. "If they

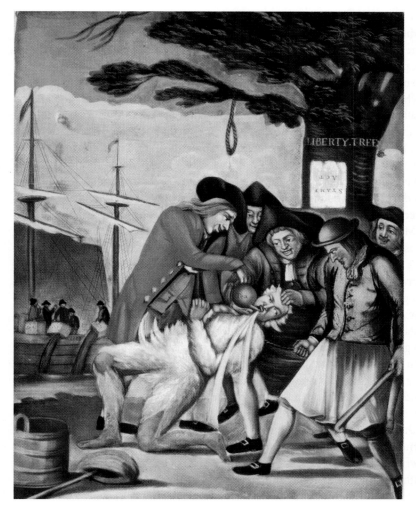

■ A 1774 London cartoon expressed anger that Boston's Sons of Liberty, defying British authority, could overturn the Stamp Act, tar and feather revenue agents, dump East India Company tea, and use their "Liberty Tree" to hang officials in effigy.

succeed in the sale of that tea," proclaimed New York's Sons of Liberty, "then we may bid adieu to American liberty."

In Boston, where tea worth nearly £10,000 arrived aboard three ships in November, tension ran especially high. The credibility of Governor Thomas Hutchinson, who had taken a hard line toward imperial dissent, had suffered in June when Benjamin Franklin published private correspondence suggesting the governor's willingness to trim colonial rights. When Hutchinson's sons were named tea consignees, the appointments reinforced townspeople's suspicions. The governor could have signed papers letting the three vessels depart. But instead he decided to unload and distribute the tea, by force if necessary.

On December 16, the largest mass meeting of the decade took place at Boston's Old South Church. A crowd of 5,000, including many from other towns, waited in a cold rain to hear whether Hutchinson would relent. When word came that the governor had refused, the cry went up, "Boston Harbor a teapot tonight!" A band of 150 men, disguised as Mohawk Indians and carrying hatchets, marched to the docks and boarded the ships.

As several thousand supporters looked on, this disciplined crew spent three hours methodically breaking open chests of tea and dumping the contents overboard. The well-organized operation united participants representing all levels of society—from merchants such as John Hancock to artisans such as George Hewes—and news of the event spurred similar acts of defiance in other ports. Sixty years later, as one of the oldest veterans of the Revolution, Hewes still recalled with special pride his role in "the destruction of the tea."

The Intolerable Acts

"The crisis is come," wrote General Thomas Gage, commander of British forces in America, responding to the costly Tea Party in Boston Harbor; "the provinces must be either British colonies, or independent and separate states." Underestimating the strength of American resolve, Parliament agreed with King George III that only stern measures would reestablish "the obedience which a colony owes to its mother country." Between March and June 1774, it passed four so-called Coercive Acts to isolate and punish Massachusetts.

The first of the Coercive Acts, the Boston Port Act, used British naval strength to cut off the offending town's sea commerce—except for shipments of food and firewood—until the colonists paid for the ruined tea. By the Administration of Justice Act, revenue officials or soldiers charged with murder in Massachusetts (as in the Boston Massacre) could have their trials moved to another colony or to Great Britain. The Quartering Act gave officers more power to requisition living quarters and supplies for their troops in the colonies. Most important, the Massachusetts Government Act removed democratic elements from the longstanding Massachusetts Charter of 1691. From now on, the assembly could no longer elect the colony's Upper House, or Council. Instead, the governor would appoint council members, and any locality would need his written permission to hold a town meeting.

Lord North's government went even further. It replaced Hutchinson with Gage, installing the general as the governor of Massachusetts and granting him special powers and three additional regiments. It also secured passage of the Quebec Act, new legislation to address nagging problems of governance in Canada after a decade of English rule. The act accommodated the Catholic faith and French legal traditions of Quebec's inhabitants. Moreover, it greatly expanded the size of the colony to draw scattered French settlers and traders under colonial government. Suddenly, Quebec took in the entire Great Lakes region and all the lands north of the Ohio River and east of the upper Mississippi River.

Expanding the province of Quebec to the Ohio River might extend British government to French wilderness outposts and help to regulate the Indian trade. But the move also challenged the western land claims of other American colonies. The Quebec Act appeared to favor French Catholics and Ohio Valley Indians—both recent enemies of the crown—over loyal English colonists. Resentment ran especially high in New England, where Protestants had long associated Catholicism with despotism. The Quebec Act, which denied the former French province a representative assembly and jury trials in civil cases, set an ominous precedent for neighboring colonies.

The Coercive Acts and the Quebec Act—lumped together by colonial propagandists as the Intolerable Acts—brought on open rebellion against crown rule. Competing pamphlets debated the proper limits of dissent. In *A Summary View of the Rights of British America*, Thomas Jefferson went beyond criticisms of Parliament to question the king's right to dispense land, control trade, and impose troops in America. Within months, Massachusetts called for a congress of all the colonies and established its own Provincial Congress at Concord, a village 17 miles west of Boston. Out of reach of British naval power, this **de facto** Massachusetts government reorganized the militia into units loyal to its own Committee of Public Safety. These farmer-soldiers became known as Minutemen for their quick response to Gage's repeated efforts to capture patriot gunpowder supplies.

From Words to Action

While Massachusetts chafed under new restrictions, shifting coalitions in each colony, ranging from conservative to radical, vied for local political control. Extralegal committees, existing outside the authorized structure of colonial government, took power in hundreds of hamlets. In Edenton, North Carolina, fifty-one women signed a pact to abstain from using imported products for the "publick good." London cartoonists mocked the action as the "Edenton Ladies' Tea Party," but women in other colonies made similar agreements to boycott British tea and textiles. During the summer, all colonies except Georgia selected representatives to the First Continental Congress.

In September 1774, fifty-six delegates convened at Carpenters Hall in Philadelphia. Most had never met before, and they disagreed sharply over how to respond to the Intolerable Acts. Joseph Galloway, a wealthy lawyer and land speculator from Pennsylvania, urged a compromise with Britain modeled on the Albany Congress of 1754. His plan called for the creation of a separate American parliament, a grand council with delegates elected by the colonial legislatures. The less conservative delegates opposed this idea for a colonial federation, under a president-general appointed by the king. Led by Patrick Henry of Virginia, they managed to table the Galloway Plan by a narrow vote.

When Paul Revere arrived from Boston on October 6, bearing a set of militant resolves passed in his own Suffolk County, further rifts appeared. Moderates from the South expressed sympathy for Massachusetts but still resisted calls for a nonexportation scheme that would withhold southern tobacco, rice, and indigo from Great Britain. By the time the Congress adjourned in late October, it had issued a Declaration of Rights and passed a range of measures that seemed to balance competing views. On one hand, the Congress endorsed the fiery Suffolk Resolves, which condemned Parliament's Coercive Acts as unconstitutional and spoke of preparation for war. On the other, it humbly petitioned the king for relief from the crisis and professed continued loyalty. But in practical terms, Galloway and the more conservative members had suffered defeat. Most importantly, the delegates signed an agreement to prohibit British imports and halt all exports to Britain except rice. They called for local committees to enforce this so-called Association, and they set a date—May 10, 1775—for a Second Congress.

Before delegates could meet again in Philadelphia, the controversy that had smoldered for more than a decade on both sides of the Atlantic erupted into open combat. Predictably, the explosion took place in Massachusetts, where General Gage had received secret orders to arrest the leaders of the Massachusetts Provincial Congress and regain the upper hand before the strained situation grew worse. He was to use force, even if it meant the outbreak of warfare.

On April 18, Gage ordered 700 elite troops from Boston to row across the Charles River at night, march ten miles to Lexington, and seize John Hancock and Sam Adams. Next, the

•••┌Read the **Document**

"Give Me Liberty or Give Me Death" at **www.myhistorylab.com**

Hudson Bay
Company

HALIFAX, Regional Vice-Admiralty
Court for everything above 43 degrees,
15 minutes

44°30'

43°15'

41°

40°30'

Nova Scotia

Quebec

Three Rivers

Montreal

ME
(part of Mass.)

BOSTON, Regional Vice-Admiralty
Court for everything between 44 degrees,
and 40 degrees 30 minutes

Lake
Nipissing

Quebec

NH

NY

Concord

Lexington

MA

Woodstock

Marshfield

Ft. Michilimackinac

RI
CT

Ft. Niagara

New Haven
Fairfield
New York

36°15'

PA

NJ

Ft. Detroit

MD

Baltimore

DE

Alexandria

PHILADELPHIA, Regional Vice-Admiralty
Court for everything between 41 degrees,
and 36 degrees 15 minutes

Fredericksburg

VA

King William

ATLANTIC
OCEAN

Kaskaskia

Williamsburg

Indian
Reserve

Chowan
Edenton

Spanish
Louisiana

Alamance

Hillsborough

NC

New Bern
Onslow

Wilmington

SC

CHARLESTON, Regional Vice-Admiralty
Court for everything below 36 degrees,
15 minutes

GA

British dominance in eastern North America

British-ruled providence of Quebec, 1774

Boundary set by Quebec Act of 1774

British-ruled providence of East Florida

British-ruled providence of West Florida

Reserved to Indians under British Rule

Spanish Louisiana

Major battles

West Florida

St. Mary's R.

Mobile

Pensacola

St. Augustine

Distribution of British troops

□ British posts 100–300 soldiers

■ British posts 300–500 soldiers

◼ British post 4,800 soldiers

East
Florida

N

Gulf of
Mexico

The spread of news concerning the battles
of Lexington and Concord, April 19, 1775

▲ Within 1–7 days

▲ Within 8–14 days

▲ More than 14 days

■ **MAP 6.3**

BRITISH NORTH AMERICA, APRIL 1775

**Rising colonial unrest brought strong countermeasures. The British government organized regional
vice-admiralty courts to punish smugglers; it greatly expanded Quebec in 1774; and it reallocated
troops to the Boston area. When warfare erupted there in April 1775, the news spread throughout the
colonies within weeks.**

soldiers were to proceed seven miles to Concord to capture a stockpile of military supplies.
Alerted by signal lanterns, express riders Paul Revere and William Dawes eluded British
patrols and spurred their horses toward Lexington along separate routes to warn Hancock
and Adams. Bells and alarm guns spread the word that the British were coming. By the time

■ **The shots fired at dawn by British troops, dispersing local militia from Lexington's town green, were the opening volley of the American Revolution. Amos Doolittle, a Connecticut soldier who responded to the alarm, later depicted the events of April 19, 1775. The date is still honored in New England as Patriots' Day.**

the British soldiers reached Lexington, shortly before sunrise, some seventy militiamen had assembled on the town green. When the villagers refused to lay down their arms, the redcoats dispersed them in a brief skirmish that left eight militiamen dead.

The British column trudged west to Concord and searched the town for munitions. Four hundred Minutemen who had streamed in from neighboring communities advanced on the town in double file, with orders not to shoot unless the British fired first. At the small bridge over the Concord River, British regulars opened fire. "The shot heard 'round the world" killed two men. The Americans loosed a volley in return, killing three. By noon, exhausted British forces were retreating toward Boston in disarray. The redcoats made easy targets for the more than a thousand Americans who shot at them from behind stone walls. A relief party prevented annihilation, but the British suffered severe losses: 73 killed and 200 wounded or missing. The Americans, with only 49 dead, had turned the tables on General Gage, transforming an aggressive raid into a punishing defeat.

●◆●⎯[**Read** the **Document**
Warren, "Account of the Battle of Lexington" at **www.myhistorylab.com**

CONCLUSION

For Britain, festering administrative problems in America had suddenly become a military emergency. A decade of assertive but inconsistent British policies had transformed the colonists' sense of good will toward London into angry feelings of persecution and betrayal. The years of incessant argument and misunderstanding reminded many, on both sides of the Atlantic, of watching a stable household unravel into mutual parent-child recrimination. They saw a once-healthy family becoming increasingly dysfunctional and troubled. The colonies, like assertive children, grew steadily in strength, while British officials, chafed like aging parents receiving diminished respect. Predictably, authorities in London found the once-dependent colonists to be ungrateful, intemperate, and occasionally paranoid. With equal assurance, the American subjects saw Parliament, government ministers, and eventually the king himself as uninformed, selfish, and even deceitful.

Britain's overseas empire, which had expanded steadily for two centuries, now seemed on the verge of splitting apart. As the limits of imperial control in North America became more evident, colonists worked to overcome the regional and ethnic differences that had long been a fact of eighteenth-century life. Political independence no longer seemed implausible. With effort, class hostilities and urban-rural divisions could also be overcome. Redirecting old local resentments toward the British crown could increase a sense of unity among people with different personal backgrounds and resources.

Nor would British colonists be alone if they mounted a rebellion. On one hand, they could make the unlikely choice of liberating half a million slaves, empowering colonial women, and embracing the anti-British cause of Pontiac and numerous Native Americans. Such revolutionary moves would increase their strength dramatically in one direction. On the other hand, they could also take a more cautious and less democratic route. If men of substance could gain control of the forces that were being unleashed, they might curb potential idealism among slaves, women, tenant farmers, and the urban poor, giving precedence instead to policies that would win vital support from the continent of Europe in an American fight for independence. France, recently evicted from North America, and Spain, anxious about British designs in the Pacific, might both be willing allies, despite their commitment to monarchy. Such an alliance, if it ever came about, could push the limits of British imperial control to the breaking point.

For Review

✓•—Study and Review at www.myhistorylab.com

1. Was the creation of Spanish missions in California a milestone, or a footnote, in early American history? Explain.

2. How does the Regulator upheaval in North Carolina relate, if at all, to wider patterns of American resistance?

3. "By demanding 'obedience' in 1774, King George III treated his American colonies as unruly children, not as grown family members." Explain.

4. List (and prioritize) four main factors that explain how British colonists made the rapid shift from loyal subjects to irate rebels.

Chronology: 1763–1775

1763 Treaty of Paris ends the French and Indian War.
Proclamation Line limits westward expansion of British colonies.
Pontiac's Rebellion.

1764 Sugar Act; Currency Act.

1765 Quartering Act; Stamp Act.
Virginia Resolves; Stamp Act demonstrations.
Tenant riots in Hudson Valley.

1766 Stamp Act repealed Declaratory Act.
Bougainville explores the South Pacific for France.

1767 Townshend Acts.

1768 James Cook makes first of three voyages to explore the Pacific.
Massachusetts Circular Letter.

1770 Boston Massacre.

1771 Battle of Alamance ends the Regulator Movement in North Carolina.

1772 Burning of the *Gaspée*.

1773 Boston Tea Party.

1774 Intolerable Acts.
First Continental Congress meets.
Suffolk Resolves.

1775 Battles of Lexington and Concord.

Key Terms

Czar The title for a male ruler, or king, of Russia during the centuries before the Russian Revolution of 1917. p. 140

De facto Latin phrase meaning "in reality," sometimes applied to a government that is exercising real power, though it has not been legally constituted. p. 157

Kayak A highly maneuverable, decked-in canoe used by Native Alaskans for travel and hunting. The light frame is covered with skins, and the paddle has a blade at each end. Popular modern versions of this traditional boat are made with canvas or fiberglass. p. 140

Redress A remedy for a wrong; a correction or reparation. As a verb, to redress means to correct, to set right, or to remove the cause of a grievance. p. 149

PART THREE

The Unfinished Revolution, 1775–1803

IN 1775 GREAT BRITAIN STILL POSSESSED ALL OF NORTH AMERICA EAST of the Mississippi River, from Hudson Bay to the Gulf of Mexico. If the British could suppress the troublesome rebellion along the Atlantic seaboard, their prospects for expansion in America looked promising. Farther west, Spain had recently acquired the vast Louisiana Territory from France. The Spanish retained their dominance in the Southwest, and they were finally beginning to expand their claim to California by building a series of new missions and presidios.

Within a year, a revolution had erupted against the British Empire in America, as 13 Atlantic colonies declared their independence. Rejecting monarchy, these new states formed a loose confederation and fought to remove imperial control. The rebellious Americans, with support from Britain's European rivals, eventually gained victory in a protracted war. Moreover, they followed this improbable success by overcoming economic duress and internal struggles to establish the innovative framework for a viable constitutional government.

By 1803, therefore, the broad picture had changed markedly. In the Pacific Ocean, Europeans had encountered the Hawaiian Islands for the first time, Russian fur traders had consolidated their hold in Alaska, and Spanish vessels along the Pacific coast faced increasing competition from the ships of rival nations. The British still held Canada and Florida, but the United States of America had emerged as an independent republic and had started to acquire new territories. Its most spectacular acquisition was the Louisiana Territory, which President Thomas Jefferson purchased in 1803, after Spain had returned the region to the control of France.

Few could have foreseen such an unlikely series of events in the brief span since young Jefferson had drafted the Declaration of Independence in 1776. His generation had reluctantly become the effective leaders of a revolutionary movement, contending ably with those who pushed for greater democratization, those who desired the stability of military rule, and even those who longed for the protection of the British monarchy.

These unlikely leaders were by no means united in all their views and actions. They argued fervently over constitutional issues, domestic policies, and foreign alignments. Most managed to reap personal gains from the new society, and they saw to it that rewards reached far beyond their own households. Urban artisans, frontier farmers, and immigrant newcomers benefited as well.

While the revolutionary era fulfilled optimistic expectations for numerous citizens, it failed to meet the hopes and aspirations of other Americans. Many American merchants and planters, indebted to British interests before 1776, gained by the separation from Great Britain as creditors and investors in the new society. Many frontier farmers and army veterans, on the other hand, faced burdensome debts after the Revolutionary War.

Women worried that the numerous written constitutions of the period were unresponsive to their interests. In 1776 New Jersey gave the vote to "all free inhabitants" who were also property holders. This included some single women, and in 1790 the state's election law referred specifically to "he or she" among voters. But this novel provision was undone a generation later, in 1807, when New Jersey men objected to the idea of any women having the right to vote. Female access to education and the courts improved somewhat in the last quarter of the eighteenth century, but for most American women the advances were more symbolic than real.

For African Americans the disappointments were greater still. British offers of freedom prompted thousands of enslaved Southerners to take up the Loyalist cause at great personal risk. Other free blacks and slaves, primarily in the North, shouldered arms for the Patriots, drawn by the rhetoric of liberty and the prospect of advancement. Even though they had chosen the winning side, they reaped few benefits. Although the number of free blacks increased after the Revolutionary War, the African slave trade to the United States resumed and gained official protection. Slavery itself gained renewed significance with the transition to cotton production in the South and a federal constitution that sanctioned the power of slaveholders. Even in the North, where gradual emancipation became the norm by the end of the century, free blacks found their welcome into white churches and schools to be so half-hearted that many began organizing their own separate institutions.

Eastern Indians, like African Americans, had good reason to distrust the Revolution and its leaders. The majority, including most Iroquois and Cherokee warriors, sided with the British and paid a steep price in defeat. Throughout the Mississippi Valley, Native Americans who still remembered the benefits of French trade and British military support faced relentless pressure as American speculators, soldiers, and settlers dissected their homelands. After 1803, government officials promised that the newly acquired lands beyond the Mississippi would become an Indian Territory, providing a refuge for displaced eastern tribes. If so, what was to become of the Native American nations that already inhabited the western plains?

Like most political upheavals, the American Revolution left many questions unanswered and much business unfinished. Even the new federal government itself, in operation for little more than a decade by 1803, remained a work in progress. The specific roles and relative power of the government's three separate branches spurred endless debate, as did the proper place of the military and the most suitable direction for foreign policy. The Constitution ratified in 1789 seemed promising, but it remained an uncertain and largely untested framework.

1792 Washington is reelected president
Mary Wollstonecraft, *Vindication of the Rights of Woman*

1793 Washington issues Neutrality Proclamation
Eli Whitney invents the cotton gin

1794 U.S. troops defeat forces of Ohio Confederacy
Whiskey Rebellion

1795 Jay's Treaty
Treaty of San Lorenzo

1796 Washington's farewell address
John Adams is elected president

1797 XYZ Affair

1798 Quasi War with France (to 1800)
Alien and Sedition Acts
Kentucky and Virginia Resolutions (1798–1799)

1799 Seneca Leader Handsome Lake proclaims *gai'wiio*, or "Good Message"

1800 Thomas Jefferson is elected president
Gabriel plot is exposed in Richmond, Virginia

1801 Judiciary Act of 1801
War against Barbary pirates
Spain secretly cedes Louisiana Territory to France

1803 Louisiana Purchase
Marbury v. Madison

7

Revolutionaries at War, 1775–1783

The shots fired at Concord Bridge in April 1775 resounded through all the villages of New England. In Peterborough, New Hampshire, a town of 549 people, a company of recruits shouldered their rifles and marched toward Boston. Before the long Revolutionary War ended in 1783, most of Peterborough's adult men had performed some sort of Patriot military service.

In Peterborough, as in countless other American towns, reasons for enlisting differed, and length of service varied greatly. At a moment of regional crisis, such as when General Burgoyne's British army threatened to isolate New England by thrusting down the Hudson Valley in 1777, most able-bodied men in Peterborough, young and old alike, entered the militia for several months. But overall, the town's most prosperous merchants and farmers served least, while fewer than two dozen men, driven by poverty, ambition, or patriotic zeal, did most of the fighting.

No one in the community saw more action than William "Long Bill" Scott, a 33-year-old husband and father when the war began. "I was a Shoemaker, & got my Living by my Labor." In April 1775, when Scott enlisted in the local militia company headed by his cousin, he refused to serve as a private. Convinced that his own "Ambition was too great for so low a Rank," he talked his relative into granting him a lieutenant's commission.

At Bunker Hill in June, Lieutenant Scott suffered severe wounds. Taken captive, he hid his convictions from the British, claiming that he had only risked his life for personal advancement: "If my Captain was killed," he explained, "I should rise in Rank." Regarding the "Dispute between Great Britain and the Colonies," Scott told his captors, "I know nothing of it; neither am I capable of judging whether it is right or wrong."

Perhaps, but in contrast to many whose initial zeal seemed stronger, Long Bill Scott stayed the course. When the British evacuated Boston, they deported him to Nova Scotia. But he escaped and fought at New York the following year, only to be captured again. In his next dramatic escape, he tied his sword around his neck, pinned his watch to his hat, and swam across the Hudson River at night. Scott returned to Peterborough in 1777 to recruit a company of his own, serving for several more years before old wounds made marching difficult. He finished the war as a volunteer on a navy frigate.

In all, a dozen Scott relatives from Peterborough gave 40 years in wartime service to the army, the navy, and the state and local militias. In addition to Long Bill, his father and many of his cousins saw action, as did several of his sons, one of whom died of camp fever after six years of service. Long Bill himself sustained nine wounds and was captured twice, but his rewards proved slim. His military pay depreciated sharply, and when he sold his farm to cover debts, the notes he received in payment lost 98 percent of their worth within three years. He lost the down payment on another farm, and when his wife died he was unable to care for his children. Destitute, he returned to army service in the mid-1790s. He died at Fort Stanwix in New York in 1796, at age 54.

Despite his early disclaimers, Long Bill Scott's commitment to the Patriot cause proved unwavering. But for most, the War of American Independence was not a clear, two-sided struggle, with all the colonists banding together to oppose the English monarchy.

■ In April 1775, riders spread word across New England that violence had erupted near Boston. William Ranney's history painting, *First News of the Battle of Lexington* (1847), shows a small town preparing to send reinforcements. The ominous storm clouds suggest impending war.

North Carolina Museum of Art, Raleigh, Purchased with funds from the State of North Carolina (52.9.25)

Instead, within each small community and within the Atlantic theater as a whole, alliances often proved the old adage that "My enemy's enemy is my friend." Powerful merchants like John Hancock and Henry Laurens threw in their lot with the people in part because they had grown disillusioned with Parliament's political and commercial controls. Many enslaved blacks, eager for liberty from their masters, escaped to join the British. On the international scale, the monarchies of France and Spain swallowed their dislike for America's republican rhetoric and joined in a war that allowed them an opportunity to attack their long-standing rival, Britain. On the other hand, many Cherokee and Iroquois Indians, disillusioned by contact with land-hungry settlers, cast their lot with the British forces from overseas.

Not all Indian warriors or enslaved Africans sided with the British, and by no means all New England farmers or Virginia planters embraced the Patriot cause. In a landscape marked by uncertainty, large numbers of people at all levels of society opted for cautious neutrality as long as they could, while others shifted their allegiance as the winds changed. The final outcome of the conflict, therefore, remained a source of constant doubt. Looking back, Americans often view the results of the Revolutionary War as inevitable, perhaps even foreordained. In fact, the end result—and thus independence itself—hung in the balance for years.

"Things Are Now Come to That Crisis"

New England's Minutemen had rallied swiftly at Lexington. In the ensuing months, Congress took the initial steps to form a Continental Army. It also launched efforts to force the British out of Boston and to pull Canada into the rebellion. If these predominantly Protestant rebels hoped to draw the French Catholics of Quebec into their revolt, would free whites also be eager to include the blacks of Boston, Williamsburg, and Charleston in the struggle for liberty? Or would it be the British who recruited African Americans and furnished them with arms? The answers to such questions became clear in the 15 months between the skirmish at Lexington and the decision of Congress to declare political independence from Britain in July 1776.

How were the Americans able to drive British forces out of Boston in March 1776, less than a year after the Battle of Lexington?

The Second Continental Congress Takes Control

●•◆•┤Read the Document

Royal Proclamation of Rebellion
at **www.myhistorylab.com**

■   In June 1775, Congress selected a wealthy Virginia planter to command its army. The choice of George Washington reassured southern slave owners and disappointed blacks and whites in the North who saw slavery as a contradiction in the struggle for freedom.

Enthusiasm ran high in Philadelphia in May 1775 as the Second Continental Congress assembled, and the delegates moved quickly to put the colonies on a wartime footing. They instructed New York to build fortifications, and they paid for a dozen companies of riflemen to be sent north to aid the Minutemen surrounding Boston. They created an Army Department under the command of a New York aristocrat, General Philip Schuyler, and approved an issue of $2 million in currency to fund the military buildup.

In late May, word arrived from Lake Champlain in New York of a victory for soldiers under Benedict Arnold of Connecticut and for the Green Mountain Boys (farmers from the area that became Vermont, led by Ethan Allen). They had captured Fort Ticonderoga, along with its cannons, just the sort of heavy arms needed by the new Army Department. This initiative not only secured the Hudson Valley against a British attack from the north; it also allowed Schuyler to propose a strike against Montreal and Quebec via Lake Champlain. Congress approved the assault, to be led by General Richard Montgomery. It also approved a daring scheme submitted by Arnold. He planned to lead separate forces up the Kennebec River. They would assist Montgomery in seizing Quebec and winning Canada before the region could become a staging ground for British armies.

No single action by Congress had greater implications than the one taken on June 15, 1775. That day, members voted unanimously to appoint George Washington, a 43-year-old delegate from Virginia, "to command all the continental forces." Colonel Washington already headed a committee drawing up regulations to run the new army, and he had notable military experience. But his strongest asset may have been his southern roots. Northern delegates sensed the need to foster colonial unity by placing a non–New Englander in charge of the army outside Boston. In military and political terms, the selection of Washington proved auspicious. The tall, imposing master of Mount Vernon emerged as a durable and respected leader in both war and peace. But putting a plantation owner in command reduced the prospect of freedom for slaves. It also signaled the beginning of an unlikely alliance between wealthy regional leaders of the North and South, contributing to the particular shape of the Federal Constitution a dozen years later.

"Liberty to Slaves"

The selection of Washington sent a strong message to half a million African Americans, spurring many of them to risk siding with the British. For their part, the British sensed an opportunity to undermine rebellious planters. In June 1775, the British commander in America, Thomas Gage, wrote to London: "Things are now come to that crisis, that we must avail ourselves of every resource, even to raise the Negros, in our cause."

In the South, rumors of liberation swept through the large African-American community during 1775. Slaveholding rebel authorities countered with harsh measures to quell black unrest. In South Carolina that spring, attention focused on a prominent free black man named Thomas Jeremiah, a skilled pilot in the port of Charleston. In April, Jeremiah supposedly told an enslaved dockworker of a great war coming and urged slaves to seize the opportunity. Weeks later, nervous Patriot planters made the well-known free black into a scapegoat, accusing him of involvement in a plot to smuggle guns ashore from British ships to support a slave uprising. In August 1775, despite a lack of hard evidence against him, Jeremiah was publicly hanged and then burned sending a fearsome message.

That September, a Georgia delegate to Congress made a startling comment. He said that if British troops were to land on the southern coast with a supply of food and guns, offering freedom to slaves who would join them, 20,000 blacks would respond. In November, the beleaguered royal governor of Virginia, Lord Dunmore, attempted just such a scheme. Dunmore issued a proclamation granting freedom to any slave, owned by a rebel, who agreed to take up arms on behalf of the king. Hundreds responded to Dunmore's proclamation. They formed the Ethiopian Regiment and wore sashes proclaiming "Liberty to Slaves."

The Struggle to Control Boston

In the North, British forces had been confined in Boston ever since the Battle of Lexington. They would remain isolated on the town's main peninsula for nearly a year, supported by the Royal Navy. In early July 1775, Washington arrived at nearby Cambridge to take up his command and oversee the siege of Boston. He quickly set out to improve order among his men, tightening discipline, calming regional jealousies, and removing incompetent officers. In addition, he wrote scores of letters to civilian political leaders and the president of Congress to muster support for his feeble army.

Washington made clear that nearly everything was in short supply, from tents and uniforms to muskets and cannons. He dispatched 25-year-old Henry Knox, a former bookseller and future general, to retrieve the cannons captured at Ticonderoga. The Patriots' siege could not succeed without heavy fieldpieces to bombard the city from the heights at Dorchester and Charlestown that lay across the water from Boston.

Even before Washington's arrival, the British and the Americans had vied for control of these strategic heights. Indeed, General Gage drew up plans to secure Charlestown peninsula by seizing its highest point, Bunker Hill. But the Patriots learned of the scheme. On the night of June 16, 1775, they moved to fortify the area. The next afternoon, 1,500 Patriots confronted the full force of the British army in the Battle of Bunker Hill.

Gage might easily have sealed off Charlestown peninsula with his naval power. Instead, he used 2,500 British infantry to launch three frontal attacks from the shoreline. The first two uphill charges fell back, but a third assault finally dislodged the Americans. Although the Battle of Bunker Hill was technically a British victory, success came at a terrible price. The encounter left 42 percent of British troops (1,054 men) wounded or dead—the worst casualty figures of the war. Gage lost his command, replaced by General William Howe, and the Royal Army no longer appeared invincible.

With Washington and his army encamped outside Boston, Henry Knox worked to retrieve the British **ordnance** captured at Ticonderoga. Using oxen, sledges, and local volunteers, he hauled 43 heavy cannons east, across trails covered with snow and ice, from the Hudson Valley to the coast. His men delivered the guns in late winter, and in March 1776 the Americans, in a surprise move, placed them on Dorchester Heights, where they could bombard the enemy huddled in Boston. Threatened, and unable to counterattack, General Howe evacuated his army, retreating by ship to Halifax, Nova Scotia. There, he made plans to attack the rebels again at New York, where Loyalist support was stronger.

Declaring Independence

In the context of the entire year 1776, why was Washington's successful crossing of the Delaware River on December 25 so significant?

As Washington laid siege to Boston, other Americans converged on British forces in Canada. General Montgomery's troops seized Montreal in November 1775. They then descended the St. Lawrence River to join Benedict Arnold's men, who had struggled north toward Quebec under brutal winter conditions. Their combined force attacked the walled city during a fierce snowstorm on the night of December 30. But their assault failed, and Montgomery perished in the fighting. When British reinforcements reached Quebec in May, the Americans retreated toward Lake Champlain. They left behind most of their baggage and hundreds of sick companions, dying from smallpox. Hundreds more died during the withdrawal or spread the deadly pox as they returned to New England towns. Everywhere, strained loyalty to the British was turning to explosive anger.

"Time to Part"

Read the **Document**

"Common Sense" by Thomas Paine at **www.myhistorylab.com**

In January 1776, a brilliant pamphlet, *Common Sense*, captured the shifting mood and helped propel Americans toward independence. The author, a former corsetmaker named Thomas Paine, had endured personal and economic failures in England before sailing to Philadelphia in 1774. At 37, the gifted writer found a fresh start in America and began to compose bold newspaper essays.

Common Sense sold an amazing 120,000 copies in three months. Paine promised to lay out "simple facts, plain arguments, and common sense" on the precarious American situation. He lambasted "the so much boasted constitution of England," attacking hereditary monarchy and the divine right of kings. "One honest man," Paine proclaimed, is worth more "than all the crowned ruffians that ever lived." He urged the creation of an independent constitutional republic that could become "an asylum for all mankind." "Reconciliation is now a fallacious dream," he argued: "'TIS TIME TO PART."

Paine's avid readers agreed. In the spring of 1776, one colony after another instructed its representatives to the Second Continental Congress to vote for independence. But many among the well-to-do held strong social and economic ties to London. They feared the loss of British imperial protection and the startling upsurge of democratic political activity among the lower orders. At first, Congress vacillated. Finally, with no sign of accommodation from England, most members agreed with Robert Livingston of New York that "they should yield to the torrent if they hoped to direct its course." In early June, young Livingston, age 30, joined the committee assigned to prepare a formal statement declaring independence from Great Britain. The Committee of Five also included Benjamin Franklin, John Adams, Roger Sherman, and the second youngest member of the Continental Congress, Thomas Jefferson.

The 33-year-old Jefferson willingly took responsibility for crafting the document. He framed a stirring preamble, drawing on British philosopher John Locke's contract theory of government. Locke (1632–1702) believed that the sovereign power ultimately resided not in government but in the people themselves, who chose to submit voluntarily to civil law to protect property and preserve basic rights.

According to Locke, rulers possessed conditional, not absolute, authority over the people. Citizens therefore held the right to end their support and overthrow any government that did not fulfill its side of the contract. For any people facing "a long train of abuses," Jefferson wrote, "it is their right, it is their duty, to throw off such government and to provide new guards for their future security." He went on to catalogue the "repeated injuries and usurpations" committed by King George III. On July 2, when Congress voted on a statement affirming that "these United Colonies are, and of right, ought to be, Free and Independent States," 12 colonies approved, with the New York delegation abstaining. Having made the fundamental decision, the delegates then considered how to "declare the causes" behind their momentous choice to separate from Great Britain.

Over the next two days, Congress members edited the draft declaration submitted by the Committee of Five. They kept Jefferson's idealistic assertion that "all men are created equal." But they removed any reference to slavery, except for the charge that the king had "excited domestic insurrections amongst us," a veiled reference to the Thomas Jeremiah debacle in Charleston and to Lord Dunmore's proclamation. With other changes in place, they finally voted to approve the revised Declaration of Independence on July 4, 1776.

John Hancock, the president of the Congress, signed the document with a flourish, and printers hastily turned it into a published broadside. The other signatures (contrary to folklore) came two weeks later, after New York had finally offered its approval. Then 56 delegates gathered to sign their names to "The unanimous declaration of the 13 United States of America." They did so at great risk, for signing the document exposed them to charges of treason, punishable by death.

● View the Image

Signing of the Declaration of Independence at **www.myhistorylab.com**

The British Attack New York

While the Second Continental Congress debated independence, the British maneuvered to suppress the rebellion. Strangling the revolt with a naval blockade appeared impossible, given the length of the American coastline. But two other strategies emerged—one southern and one northern—that shaped British planning throughout the conflict.

The southern design rested on the assumption that loyalty to the crown remained strongest in the South. If the British could land forces below Chesapeake Bay, support from white loyalists and enslaved blacks might enable them to gain the upper hand and push north to reimpose colonial rule elsewhere. In June 1776, troops under General Henry Clinton arrived off the South Carolina coast with such a mission in mind. On June 28, British ships bombarded Sullivan's Island, at the mouth of Charleston harbor. But the Americans' log fortress withstood the cannon fire, and the attackers withdrew. The British did not renew their southern design for several years, concentrating instead on a separate northern strategy.

According to Britain's northern plan, troops would divide the rebellious colonies in two at the Hudson River valley, seizing New York City and advancing upriver while other forces pushed south from Canada. Then, having sealed off New England, they could finally crush the radicals in Massachusetts who had spearheaded the revolt while restoring the loyalties of inhabitants farther south. Lord George Germain, the aggressive new British cabinet minister in charge of American affairs, favored this plan. An overwhelming strike, he asserted, could "finish the rebellion in one campaign."

Early in 1776, Germain set out to generate a land and sea offensive of unprecedented scale, renting thousands of mercenaries from the German states. Eventually, 30,000 German troops traveled to America, so many of them from the state of Hesse-Cassel that onlookers called all of them Hessians. Canada, having already repulsed an American invasion, could provide a loyal staging ground in the north. "I have always thought Hudson's River the most proper part of the whole continent for opening vigorous operations," observed "Gentleman Johnny" Burgoyne, the dapper British general who arrived at Quebec with reinforcements in May 1776.

But plans for a strike south from Canada had to wait. Britain made its first thrust toward the mouth of the Hudson River by sea. In June, a convoy under General William Howe sailed from Halifax to Staten Island, New York, with 9,000 soldiers. By August, the general had received 20,000 reinforcements from across the Atlantic. His brother, Admiral Richard Howe, hovered nearby with 13,000 sailors aboard seventy naval vessels. On orders from Congress, General Washington moved south to defend New York City, a difficult task

■ John Trumbull spent years gathering portraits for his famous painting *The Declaration of Independence.* This engraving identifies individuals in the painting with their signatures. The artist placed the Drafting Committee in the center (31–35). He omitted signers for whom he had no likeness, and he included several nonsigners, such as John Dickinson.

made harder by ardent Loyalist sentiment. Short on men and equipment, the general weakened his position further by dividing his troops between Manhattan and Brooklyn Heights on nearby Long Island.

A month after Congress members signed the Declaration of Independence, Washington nearly lost his entire force—and the cause itself. General Howe moved his troops by water from Staten Island to the Brooklyn area and then outflanked and scattered the poorly trained Americans in the Battle of Long Island on August 27. Remarkably, the British leader called off a direct attack that would have overrun the American batteries on Brooklyn Heights. Under cover of night, rebel troops slipped back across the East River to New York City in small boats.

"Victory or Death": A Desperate Gamble Pays Off

View the Image

New York Burning (1776) at www.myhistorylab.com

Washington's narrow escape from Long Island in August 1776 was the first of numerous retreats. His army left New York City on September 15. The rebels withdrew from upper Manhattan and Westchester in October and from Fort Washington and Fort Lee on the Hudson—with heavy losses—in November. The Americans "fled like scared rabbits," one Englishman wrote. With winter at hand, the Continental forces retreated southwest toward Philadelphia.

As the ragged American army withdrew across New Jersey late in 1776, General William Howe repeatedly failed to press his advantage. The British commander and his brother had received a commission from Lord North, who headed the government in London, permitting them to negotiate a peace settlement with the Americans whenever possible. They hoped that a strong show of force, without a vicious offensive that might alienate civilians, could bring the enemy to terms. Howe's troops offered pardons to rebels and encouraged desertions from Washington's army. In early December, the dwindling American force hurried through Princeton and slipped across the Delaware River into Pennsylvania. Confident of victory, the British failed to pursue them, instead making camp at Trenton. Washington realized that unless circumstances changed quickly, "the game will be pretty well up."

Distressed by civilian talk of surrender, Tom Paine again took up his pen. On December 19, he launched a new series of essays ("The American Crisis") that began, "These are the times that try men's souls." Paine mocked "the summer soldier and the sunshine patriot" who shrank from extreme trials. "Let it be told to the future world, that in the depth of winter, when nothing but hope and virtue could survive," vigilant citizens, "alarmed at one common danger, came forth to meet and to repulse it."

Action soon followed words. On Christmas Day 1776, Washington issued a new code phrase for sentinels: "Victory or Death." He ordered Paine's words read aloud to the troops. Then, after dark, his men recrossed the windswept Delaware River in a driving snowstorm and advanced on Trenton. Holiday festivities and foul weather had left the enemy unprepared. The Americans inflicted a startling defeat, killing several dozen and capturing more than 900 Hessian soldiers. As Washington advanced again on December 30, Howe sent fresh troops forward under Charles Cornwallis to confront the rebels, pinning them down near Trenton. But when the British paused before attacking, the Americans left their campfires burning and slipped out of reach. They then circled behind Cornwallis to defeat his reinforcements at Princeton on January 3. It was not the last time that Washington bested Cornwallis.

■ This picture showing the noise and movement of the American victory at the Battle of Princeton was created by deaf painter William Mercer, whose father, Brigadier General Hugh Mercer, died in the battle.

INTERPRETING HISTORY

"By What Means Do You Expect to Conquer America?" Tom Paine, *American Crisis II* (Philadelphia, January 1777)

*W*eeks after Thomas Paine lifted American spirits with his first "American Crisis" essay, he was back in print with another installment. "American Crisis II" appeared in Philadelphia in January 1777, only eleven months after his publication of Common Sense. In it, the skilled propagandist rolled out a new phrase, "The United States of America." Paine's confident tone reflected the Patriots' improved situation after Washington's victories at Trenton and Princeton.

The short pamphlet took the form of a defiant public letter to Admiral Richard Howe. Besides stressing "the wickedness" of the British cause, the author reminded the commander of "the impossibility of conquering us." "Your experiment in the Jerseys," Paine chided, "is like robbing an orchard in the night before the fruit be ripe, and running away in the morning. . . . The mighty subduers of the continent are retreated into a nutshell." Though brash, Paine also proved astute. In this abridged excerpt, he warns Lord Howe why the British might not prevail in a drawn-out war.

To Lord Howe

Soon after your return to New York, you published a very illiberal and unmanly handbill against the Congress, "with their extravagant and inadmissible claim of independence." Why, God

When Thomas Paine drafted a public letter to Admiral Howe in 1777, he mocked the British war effort and reminded readers that time, geography, and principle were all working in favor of the American cause.

bless me! What have you to do with our independence? We ask no leave of yours to set it up; we ask no money of yours to support it; we can do better without your fleets and armies than with them.

By what means, may I ask, do you expect to conquer America? If you could not effect it in the summer, when our army was less than yours, nor in the winter, when we had none, how are you to do it? In point of generalship you have been outwitted, and in point of fortitude outdone; your advantages turn out to your loss, and we can always prevent a total defeat. You see that we have two to one the advantage of you, because we conquer by a drawn game, and you lose by it.

In all the wars which you have formerly been concerned in you had only armies to contend with; in this case you have both an army and a country to combat with. In former wars, the countries followed the fate of their capitals; Canada fell with Quebec. . . . Here it is

otherwise; if you get possession of a city here, you are obliged to shut yourselves up in it, and can make no other use of it, than to spend your country's money in. This is all the advantage you have drawn from New York; and you would draw less from Philadelphia, because it requires more force to keep it, and is much further from the sea.

Were you to garrison the places you might march over, your army would be like a stream of water running to nothing. By the time you extended from New York to Virginia, you would be reduced to a string of drops not capable of hanging together; while we, by retreating from State to State, like a river turning back upon itself, would acquire strength in the same proportion as you lost it, and in the end be capable of overwhelming you. What we contend for is worthy the affliction we may go through. What are salt, sugar and finery, to the inestimable blessings of "Liberty and Safety!" Or what are the inconveniences of a few months to the tributary bondage of ages?

'Tis the unhappy temper of the English to be pleased with any war, right or wrong, be it but successful; but they soon grow discontented with ill fortune, and it is an even chance that they are as clamorous for peace next summer, as the king and his ministers were for war last winter. What lately appeared to us misfortunes, were only blessings in disguise; the more surface you spread over, the thinner you will be, and the easier wiped away. "We have put, sir, our hands to the plough, and cursed be he that looketh back."

Questions

1. Why does Paine tell the British that if the war ends in a draw, the Americans win "and you lose by it"?
2. Was Paine correct to warn that "the possession of a city here" would not aid the British cause? If so, why?

Source: Eric Foner, ed., *Thomas Paine: Collected Writings* (New York: Library of America, 1995), pp. 100–115.

The Struggle to Win French Support

The success at Trenton and Princeton restored a glimmer of hope for the tattered Continental Army and its supporters. As American forces took up winter quarters at Morristown, Howe withdrew his army from much of New Jersey to await the spring campaigns. As a result, anxious civilians who had sworn their loyalty to the crown felt deserted. Public sentiment in the region again swung toward the rebels. More importantly, news of the victories spurred support overseas for the American cause. French officials, eager to see their European rival bogged down in a colonial war, dispatched secret shipments of munitions to aid the revolutionaries.

One young aristocrat, the idealistic Marquis de Lafayette, was already on his way from France to volunteer his services to General Washington. But drawing forth an official French commitment to the American cause would take a larger show of success. That triumph finally came at the end of the next campaign season, with the Americans' stunning victory at Saratoga, deep in the Hudson Valley, 185 miles above New York City.

If the rebellious Americans opposed monarchy, why did the French crown decide to back their cause?

Breakdown in British Planning

Among the Americans, two years of grim conflict had dampened the initial zeal that had prompted citizens to enlist. Washington felt armed resistance could not continue for long unless more men made longer commitments to fight. He insisted that soldiers needed tighter discipline and better pay. In response, Congress expanded his disciplinary powers and offered a bonus to those who enlisted for a three-year term.

In a slumping economy, numerous recruits answered the call, including immigrants and unemployed artisans who lacked training, supplies, and experience. Many rural recruits also lacked immunity to smallpox, since they had never been exposed to the disease. When smallpox broke out among the soldiers at Morristown, Washington ordered a mass inoculation, a decision that left his recuperating army vulnerable for weeks.

Despite American vulnerability, the British were slow to move. Lord North's ministry had fallen victim to its own contradictions. By seeking a decisive blow *and* a negotiated settlement in 1776, the British had achieved neither objective. They had also underestimated the persistence of Washington's army. During the 1777 campaigns, they learned further lessons about the difficulty of their task and the need for coordinated plans.

By seeking a decisive blow and a negotiated settlement in 1776, the British had achieved neither objective.

General Burgoyne, returning to London for the winter, won government support for a major new offensive. He planned to lead a large force south from Canada, using the Hudson Valley to drive a wedge through the rebellious colonies. In support, a combined British and Indian force would strike east from Lake Ontario, capturing Fort Stanwix and descending eastward along the Mohawk River to meet Burgoyne at Albany. William Howe would push north from New York City to complete the design.

But General Howe had formed a different plan. Assuming Burgoyne would not need his help in the Hudson Valley, he intended to move south against Philadelphia. The two generals never integrated their separate operations, and the results were disastrous. In one six-month span, the British bungled their best chance for victory and handed their enemies an opening that permanently shifted the course of the war.

Saratoga Tips the Balance

The isolated operations of Burgoyne and Howe got off to slow starts in late June 1777. Howe took two months to move his troops by sea from New York harbor to the headwaters of Chesapeake Bay. This delay gave the Americans time to march south, but an

The Revolutionary War in the North

— British
— Patriots
✸ British victories
✸ Patriot victories

1. Arnold leads winter journey to Quebec, 1775
2. Montgomery fails to conquer Canada, 1775–1776
3. Knox hauls cannon from Ft. Ticonderoga, 1776
4. William Howe withdraws from Boston to Halifax, 1776
5. Howe brothers capture New York with huge force, 1776
6. Washington retreats, then re-crosses the Delaware, 1776–1777
7. William Howe sails from New York, moves on Philadelphia, 1777
8. Washington meets Howe at Brandywine and Germantown, 1777
9. Burgoyne tries to seize Hudson Valley from Canada , 1777
10. Arnold defeats British near Ft. Stanwix, 1777
11. Gates forces Burgoyne's surrender at Saratoga, 1777
12. Clinton retreats from Philadelphia to New York, 1778
13. Marching from Valley Forge, Washington wins at Monmouth, 1778
14. Brant/Butler attack Wyoming Valley, 1778; Cherry Valley, 1779
15. Sullivan attacks Iroquois villages, 1779

■ **MAP 7.1**
THE REVOLUTIONARY WAR IN THE NORTH

engagement at Brandywine Creek on September 11, 1777, failed to check the British advance on Philadelphia. The British finally entered the city in late September only to find that the rebel Congress had retreated to York, Pennsylvania.

Just north of Philadelphia, Washington attacked the large Hessian garrison at Germantown on October 4. The surprise succeeded, but morning fog created so much confusion that the inexperienced Patriot troops allowed victory to slip away. Despite defeats at Brandywine and Germantown, the Americans had gained combat experience and had made Howe pay heavily for his hollow capture of Philadelphia. As Washington's battered army took up winter quarters at nearby Valley Forge, he looked expectantly northward, hoping "all New England" would "turn out and crush Burgoyne."

Moving south from Canada in late June, "Gentleman Johnny" saw little likelihood of being crushed. The British officers believed their huge army to be invincible. The worried Americans fell back from Crown Point and Ticonderoga on Lake Champlain. But as British supply lines lengthened, the crown's army grew less certain of victory. Burgoyne's soldiers expended valuable time cutting a roadway through the wilderness. Also, the reinforcements anticipated from the West had been turned back by Benedict Arnold's men at Fort Stanwix. Even worse, American militia near Bennington badly mauled a British unit of 600 sent to forage for corn and cattle. With cold weather approaching and supplies dwindling, Burgoyne pushed south toward Albany, unaware that Howe would not be sending help up the Hudson to meet him.

As Burgoyne's situation worsened, the American position improved. An arrogant British proclamation demanding submission from local residents only stiffened their resolve and drew out more rebel recruits. While Burgoyne's army crossed to the Hudson River's west bank at Saratoga, General Horatio Gates's American forces dug in on Bemis Heights, ten miles downstream.

On September 19, 1777, Patriot units under two aggressive officers, Benedict Arnold and Daniel Morgan, confronted the enemy at Freeman's Farm, not far from Saratoga. In the grueling battle, British forces suffered 556 dead or wounded, nearly twice the American losses. Gates's refusal to commit reinforcements prevented the Patriots from achieving total victory. Nevertheless, the American ranks swelled with new recruits who sensed a chance to inflict losses on Burgoyne's forces. On October 7, the beleaguered British tried once more to smash southward, only to suffer defeat in a second battle at Freeman's Farm. Morgan and Arnold once again played key roles, though Arnold suffered a crippling leg wound. When Burgoyne's entire army of 5,800 surrendered at nearby Saratoga ten days later, Gates took full credit for the stunning triumph.

Forging an Alliance with France

Ever since declaring independence, Congress had maneuvered to win international recognition and aid for the new nation. Benjamin Franklin was sent to Paris as part of a commission seeking European support. Since the French government doubted the rebellion's chances for success, it moved cautiously at first, confining itself to covert assistance. Word of the American victory at Saratoga suddenly gave Franklin greater leverage. When he hinted that he might bargain directly with London for peace, the French foreign minister, Comte de Vergennes, moved immediately to recognize American independence.

In negotiating a vital alliance, France agreed to renounce forever any claim to English land in North America, and Franklin promised that the Americans would help defend French holdings in the Caribbean. Both parties pledged to defend the liberty of the new republic, and each agreed not to conclude a separate peace with Great Britain or to cease fighting until U.S. independence had been ensured by formal treaty. In May 1778 the Continental Congress approved this alliance. The next month, France entered the war, adding its enormous wealth

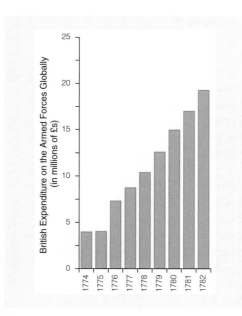

■ **FIGURE 7.1**
BRITISH GOVERNMENT EXPENSES ON ARMED FORCES THROUGHOUT THE WORLD (IN MILLIONS OF POUNDS), 1774–1782
Britain's war budget soared after France entered the conflict in 1778, but major resources flowed toward India and the Caribbean, limiting the share available for North America.

and power to the American cause. A year later, Spain—unwilling to ally itself directly with the upstart republic but eager to protect its vast American assets from Great Britain—entered the war on the side of France.

For the British, what had been a colonial brushfire swiftly flared into a global conflict reminiscent of the Seven Years' War. Hostilities with France meant possible invasions at home and inevitable attacks on outposts of Britain's empire. French ships seized Senegal in West Africa, took Grenada in the West Indies, and burned trading posts on Hudson Bay in Canada. London's annual war expenditures climbed from £4 million in 1775 to £20 million in 1782.

As war costs mounted in Britain, domestic opposition to the American conflict intensified. Some members of Parliament pushed for a swift settlement. In 1778 a peace commission led by Lord Carlisle offered concessions to the Continental Congress, hoping to tear the French alliance apart. But the Carlisle Commission failed to win a reconciliation. Other Britons went further in opposing the war. Their diverse reasons included fear of French power, desire for American trade, disgust over war profiteering, ties to friends in America, and idealistic belief in the revolution's principles. Many drank toasts to General Washington and openly supported the American cause.

Faced with growing economic and political pressure, the king and his ministers briefly considered withdrawing all troops from the rebellious colonies and focusing on the French threat. Instead, when General Howe resigned as commander in chief in America, they instructed his successor, Sir Henry Clinton, to retreat from Philadelphia to New York and devote his main resources to attacking the French in the Caribbean. Within Britain, discontent over an uncertain war strategy continued to escalate, as the government failed to either pacify the Americans or crush their rebellion.

Legitimate States, a Respectable Military

If Americans were so fearful of centralized authority, how did they coordinate a successful political and military revolt against the powerful British Empire?

Even with the new French alliance, the rebellious American states faced serious challenges on both the civilian and military fronts. They had thrown out their colonial governors and embarked on a dangerous war, but two fundamental questions still confronted them. First, how would the once-dependent colonies now be governed? And second, how could they shape a military force strong enough to defend themselves but not so powerful and unchecked as to seize control from their new civil governments?

The Articles of Confederation

The Continental Congress had taken prompt initiative. Without clear authority, it had declared independence, raised an army, issued currency, borrowed money from abroad, and negotiated an alliance with France. Then it moved to bring greater stability and legitimacy to its work. In November 1777, one month after the victory at Saratoga, it approved the Articles of Confederation and presented this formal plan for a lasting and unifying government to the states for ratification. Citizens were already debating how much authority each new state government would have in relation to the larger federation. Who would have the power to levy taxes, for example, and who would control the distribution of land?

The Articles declared "The United States of America" to be a "firm league of friendship" between the 13 former colonies. Each independent state in this weak alliance retained all rights and powers not "expressly delegated" to the Confederation Congress. Indeed, ties between the sovereign states seemed so loose that France considered sending 13 separate ambassadors to America.

According to the Articles, Congress could not collect taxes or regulate trade; it could only requisition funds from the states. Shares would vary depending on each state's free population. Moreover, the Confederation had no separate executive branch; executive functions fell to various committees of the Confederation Congress. In addition, to the dismay of land speculators, the Congress would not control the western domains that several large states had claimed. Maryland, a small state without western claims, protested this arrangement and refused to ratify. To win the required approval from all 13 states, drafters changed the plan and granted the Confederation control of western lands. After four years, the Articles finally won ratification in 1781.

Given the importance of the states, the task of designing new state governments became a top priority, even for members of the Continental Congress. In May 1776, for example, two of Jefferson's friends in the Virginia delegation in Philadelphia returned home to help implement this state-level process. They left their younger colleague behind, but they carried his written draft for a possible state constitution. Those already at work in Virginia accepted Jefferson's proposed preamble, and on June 29, 1776, Virginia led the way, adopting the first republican state constitution.

Virginia had already pioneered in another respect. Two weeks earlier, Virginia representatives approved a Declaration of Rights drawn up by George Mason. He affirmed the revolutionary concepts that all power derives from the people and that magistrates are their servants. He went on to endorse trial by jury, praise religious freedom, and condemn hereditary privilege. Over the next eight years, many states adopted a similar bill of rights to enumerate the fundamental limits of government power.

Creating State Constitutions

Each of the thirteen states had removed a functioning colonial government, and each needed to reestablish the rule of law under some new system. Britain itself possessed no written constitution, but the colonies had been ruled under published charters, and Americans believed in the value of such clear and open arrangements. Thus they readily envisioned an explicit controlling document, or constitution, for each new state. Besides, the novel idea that government flowed from the people—as an agreement based on the consent of the governed—called for some all-encompassing, written legal contract.

A new written constitution, whether for a state or a union of states, represented something more fundamental and enduring than a regular law. It needed to be above day-to-day legal statutes and political whims. Somehow the people, through chosen representatives, had to prepare a special document that citizens would affirm, or ratify, only one time. After the new government structure was in place, the constitution itself would be difficult, though not impossible, to change.

In 1779 Massachusetts legislators, under pressure from the public, fixed upon a method for providing the elevated status and popular endorsement for such a new document. Local voters in town meetings chose representatives for a specific constitution-drafting convention. These delegates, building on a model suggested by John Adams, crafted a suitable document, and their proposed constitution was then submitted to all the state's free men (regardless of race or property) for ratification. This widened constituency was intended to give special weight to the endorsement process.

Approval of the Massachusetts document was hotly debated. Many objected to the limits on popular power that were part of Adams's novel design. A reluctant revolutionary, Adams argued that "interests" (like-minded groups), rather than people, should receive equal representation. In addition, he proposed sharing legislative responsibilities between a house, a senate, and a chief executive. Property requirements for these offices were steep,

Read the **Document**

John Adams, Thoughts on Government
at **www.myhistorylab.com**

so wealthy interests would have power far beyond their numbers. The Massachusetts state constitution, ratified by a narrow margin, implemented these ideas. They signaled a turn away from the strongest popular radicalism of 1776 and foreshadowed the more conservative balance of interests that James Madison championed in the federal Constitution drafted in 1787.

This extended experiment in constitution writing was unprecedented. Never before in history, John Adams observed, had several million people had numerous opportunities "to form and establish the wisest and happiest government that human wisdom could contrive." Initial state efforts yielded varied results as citizens debated novel approaches to self-government. By 1780 the desire of established elites to rein in democratic power was evident. Yet in comparison to the overseas monarchy Americans had rejected, even the most conservative new state constitutions seemed risky and bold. Several common threads ran through all these documents.

First, fearing executive might, drafters curtailed the power of state governors to dismiss assemblies, raise armies, declare war, fill offices, or grant privileges. Colonial governors had been appointed from above, by proprietors or the crown, and they could serve terms of any length. In contrast, state governors would now be elected annually (usually by the assembly) and would be subject to impeachment and term limits. In Pennsylvania, the most radical of the new constitutions did away with a single governor altogether, placing executive power in the hands of a twelve-member council elected by the people.

Second, drafters expanded the strength of legislatures and increased their responsiveness to the popular will. They made elections more frequent, and they enlarged the size of assemblies to allow greater local involvement. They also reduced property requirements for holding office and changed limits on the right to vote to allow wider participation.

Third, constitution-makers feared that corruption emerged when people held more than one office at a time. Having experienced these glaring conflicts of interest under imperial rule, they stressed the separation of executive, legislative, and judicial posts. Preventing members of the executive branch from also holding a legislative seat removed any prospect for a cabinet-style government along the lines of the British model.

Tensions in the Military Ranks

Any new republican order required a fighting force to defend itself. But the new state militias and Washington's national army, which was controlled and paid by the Continental Congress, prompted debate from the start. Discussions erupted as to what constituted equitable pay, appropriate discipline, suitable tactics, and a proper distribution of limited supplies. Citizens argued over whether wealth, popularity, vision, military experience, political savvy, European training, or influential ties should play a role in determining who received, or retained, the cherished right to command.

One heated topic involved the election of officers. Wealthy gentry assumed that they would command the state militias, while citizen soldiers demanded the right to choose their own leaders. Another topic concerned opting out of military service. Should a prosperous individual have the right to buy an exemption or to send a paid substitute? In 1776, as Washington's army had retreated into Pennsylvania, militia in Philadelphia had chastised "Gentlemen who formerly Paraded in our Company and now in the time of greatest danger have turn'd their backs." They asked whether state authorities meant "to force the poorer kind into the field and suffer the Rich & the Great to remain at home?"

Three years later, some of these same Philadelphia militia staged a bitter demonstration that became known as the Fort Wilson Riot. In October 1779, spurred by soaring food prices, impoverished militiamen marched past the stately home of James Wilson, where wealthy Patriots had gathered. "The time is now arrived," the demonstrators' handbill proclaimed, "to prove whether the suffering friends of this country, are to be enslaved, ruined and starved, by a few overbearing Merchants, . . . Monopolizers and Speculators." Shots were exchanged, and six died in the melee at "Fort Wilson." (Wilson himself went on to become a leader of the 1787 Constitutional Convention.)

Subtle class divisions also beset the Continental Army, where jealousies over rank plagued the status-conscious officer corps. Congressional power to grant military commissions, often on regional and political grounds, only intensified disputes. Also, Americans representing Congress abroad were empowered to promise high military posts to attract European officers. Some of these recruits served the American cause well, such as Johann de Kalb and Friedrich von Steuben (both born in Germany) and Thaddeus Kosciusko and Casimir Pulaski from Poland. In France, at age 19, the Marquis de Lafayette secured a commission to be a major general in America, and he assisted Washington impressively throughout the war.

In contrast, other foreign officers displayed arrogance and spread dissension. Irish-born Thomas Conway, for example, courted congressional opponents of Washington and encouraged the desires of General Horatio Gates to assume top command. Whether or not a concerted "Conway Cabal" ever existed, Washington managed to defuse tensions from Valley Forge during the hard winter of 1777–1778. His numerous letters helped to consolidate his position with Congress and to patch frayed relations with Gates.

Another rival for command of the army, English-born Charles Lee, met disfavor several months later, when Washington ordered him to attack the rear guard of Clinton's army as it withdrew from Philadelphia to New York. Lee mismanaged the encounter at Monmouth, New Jersey, on June 28, 1778, and only Washington's swift action stopped a premature retreat. The Battle of Monmouth ended in a draw, but American troops claimed victory and took pride in their swift recovery and hard fighting.

Shaping a Diverse Army

The army's improved effectiveness came in large part from the efforts of Friedrich von Steuben, a European officer recruited by Benjamin Franklin after charges of homosexuality disrupted his German military career. He had arrived at Valley Forge in February 1778, offering to serve without pay. There he found soldiers with poor food, scant clothing, and limited training. Many Americans still wanted to see a more democratic citizen army, with elected officers and limited hierarchy. But Washington hoped to mold long-term soldiers into a more "Europeanized" force, and Steuben suited his needs. The German worked energetically to drill soldiers who, in turn, trained others.

New discipline helped boost morale. Still, terms of service and wage levels remained sources of contention. So did the disparities in treatment and pay between officers and enlisted men. There were other grievances: inept congressional committees overseeing the war effort, incompetent officers filling political appointments, and a frustrating shortage of new recruits. Arguments also persisted over whether women or African Americans could serve in the army.

Women organized in diverse ways to assist the war effort, making uniforms and running farms and businesses for absent husbands. A few American women, such as Deborah Sampson of Massachusetts, disguised themselves as men and fought. Far more accompanied the troops of both armies, earning scant pay to do cooking and washing. They also carried water to the weary and wounded on the battlefield. As many as 20,000 women may have accompanied the American army during the war. Mary Hays, wife of a Pennsylvania soldier, endured the winter at Valley Forge and later hauled pitchers of water on the battlefield at Monmouth. When her husband was wounded, she is said to have set down her jug and joined his gun crew, earning folk legend status as the cannon-firing "Molly Pitcher."

After petitioning to fight, free blacks were allowed to join the revolutionary army. Rhode Island even formed an African-American regiment. But repeated proposals to arm southern

View the Image
George Washington at Valley Forge at **www.myhistorylab.com**

Read the Document
Letter from a Revolutionary War Soldier at **www.myhistorylab.com**

■ More than a century after the grim winter at Valley Forge, artist Edwin Abbey composed this mural of Steuben drilling Washington's soldiers in February 1778.

slaves met with defeat. South Carolina and Virginia even moved in the opposite direction, offering to give away slaves captured from Loyalist planters as a bonus to white recruits. Not surprisingly, thousands of enslaved people, especially in the South, risked their lives to escape to British lines.

The War at Sea

Even as the Americans' army grew into a respectable force, their lack of naval strength proved a constant disadvantage. As early as October 13, 1775, the Continental Congress had agreed to arm two vessels to prey on British supply ships. The vote marked the birth of the American navy. Despite objections, Congress promptly appointed a committee to acquire sailing craft, and most of the 13 states built up their own small navies, adding to the confusion. The lack of central coordination proved deadly. When Massachusetts sent its ships along the Maine coast to challenge a Loyalist buildup at Castine in 1779, British vessels cornered the fleet at Penobscot Bay and crushed the enterprise.

Despite its strength, the British navy faced increasing challenges as more European powers joined the fray: France in 1778, Spain in 1779, and Holland in 1780. The English feared possible invasion, and French corsairs harassed Britain's coastline, joined by American captains. One such captain, a Scottish immigrant named John Paul Jones, arrived in European waters from America in early 1778. In April, Jones raided the port of Whitehaven in his native Scotland, and the propaganda triumph of an American success in British waters proved huge. The brazen young captain won an even greater victory the next year when his crew managed to board Britain's sleek new H.M.S. *Serapis* and capture the frigate before their own vessel sank.

In all, the Continental Navy equipped more than 50 vessels and captured nearly 200 British craft as prizes. But these numbers pale in comparison to the activities of American privateers. More than a thousand private shipowners obtained licenses from Congress to seize enemy ships and divide the proceeds among themselves and their crew. With international commerce curtailed, shipowners and sailors were eager to try their luck. Their small, quick boats swarmed the Atlantic like troublesome gnats, frustrating England's mighty navy. By war's end the British had surrendered 2,000 ships, 12,000 men, and goods valued at £18 million. And privateering drew merchant investors into the Patriot war effort, helping to bind the coastal elite more firmly to the American cause.

The Long Road to Yorktown

By July 1778, Clinton's British forces had returned to New York City, and their situation had not improved. Frustrated in New England and the middle tier of states, Clinton revived the southern strategy discussed at the beginning of the war. The South supposedly contained numerous Loyalists, and its lengthy growing season would mean more fodder for military horses. Besides, the long southern coastline had little protection, and Washington's distant army would have trouble defending the region. Moreover, nearly 500,000 slaves posed a threat to Patriot planters and represented potential support for British invaders. Finally, the same whites who dreaded slave rebellion also feared war with Native Americans, so the possible use of Indian allies also entered Britain's strategic calculation.

What conditions and events in America and Europe led to final American success in the War for Independence?

Indian Warfare and Frontier Outposts

Most Native Americans in eastern North America remained loyal to the British. Exceptions existed, such as the Oneida, Tuscarora, and Catawba, but many Indians had long-standing grievances about white encroachments. In Appalachia, colonial land investors and frontier squatters had defied the king's Proclamation Line for more than a decade. When dissident Cherokee, led by a young war chief named Dragging Canoe, attacked intruders on the Watauga River in July 1776, whites struck back. In all, 6,000 troops pushed into the mountains, laying waste to Cherokee villages.

Daniel Boone had already led migrants through Cumberland Gap in western Virginia to establish a fort on the Kentucky River at Boonesborough in 1775. By 1777, these pioneer families faced constant warfare against Indian adversaries fighting for their homelands. The Native Americans were also being urged on by Henry Hamilton, the British commandant at far-off Detroit. In one six-month span, Hamilton, who became known as the Scalp Buyer, received 77 prisoners and 129 scalps from this frontier warfare. Along the upper Ohio, violence escalated in 1777, when Americans killed Shawnee leader Cornstalk and his son during a truce. The next year, they murdered the neutral Delaware leader, White Eyes. Four years later, at the village of Gnadenhutten (south of modern-day Canton, Ohio), militia from Pennsylvania massacred 100 peaceful Delaware men, women, and children who had been converted to Christianity by missionaries of the Moravian Church.

By then, conflict involving Native Americans had also flared farther north. Joseph Brant, a mixed-race Mohawk leader educated in New England and loyal to the British, pushed south from Fort Niagara on Lake Ontario, attacking poorly guarded frontier settlements. First in the Wyoming Valley of northeastern Pennsylvania and later in New York's Cherry Valley, the raiders killed hundreds of non-Indian settlers. In the summer of 1779, American General John Sullivan led a campaign to annihilate Indian towns in reprisal.

Sullivan's revenge-minded troops, numbering more than 4,000, destroyed forty villages of the four tribes in the Iroquois Confederacy most linked to the British cause: the Mohawk, Onondaga, Cayuga, and Seneca. They avoided towns of the two Iroquois groups sympathetic to the Americans—the Oneida and Tuscarora—but elsewhere they chopped down orchards, torched crops, and sent Indian refugees streaming to Fort Niagara. Hunger and retaliatory raids haunted the region until the end of the war.

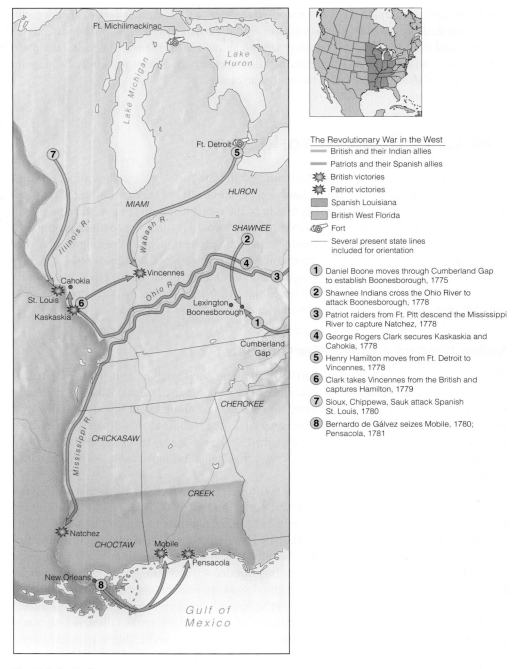

The Revolutionary War in the West
- British and their Indian allies
- Patriots and their Spanish allies
- British victories
- Patriot victories
- Spanish Louisiana
- British West Florida
- Fort
- Several present state lines included for orientation

1. Daniel Boone moves through Cumberland Gap to establish Boonesborough, 1775
2. Shawnee Indians cross the Ohio River to attack Boonesborough, 1778
3. Patriot raiders from Ft. Pitt descend the Mississippi River to capture Natchez, 1778
4. George Rogers Clark secures Kaskaskia and Cahokia, 1778
5. Henry Hamilton moves from Ft. Detroit to Vincennes, 1778
6. Clark takes Vincennes from the British and captures Hamilton, 1779
7. Sioux, Chippewa, Sauk attack Spanish St. Louis, 1780
8. Bernardo de Gálvez seizes Mobile, 1780; Pensacola, 1781

■ **MAP 7.2**
THE REVOLUTIONARY WAR IN THE WEST

While the British were passing arms and supplies to the divided Iroquois Confederacy through Fort Niagara, they were also using several western posts to arm other Indian allies and seek an advantage in the interior. Soldiers at Fort Michilimackinac recruited Sioux, Chippewa, and Sauk warriors for an unsuccessful attack on Spanish-held St. Louis in 1780. At Fort Detroit, Hamilton continued to equip war parties of Ottawa, Fox, and Miami Indians to attack American newcomers migrating into the Ohio Valley.

In 1778, with support from his home state of Virginia, a young Patriot surveyor named George Rogers Clark organized a foray west to counter these raids and lend support to Spanish

■ The British used Fort Niagara (on the southwest edge of Lake Ontario, at the mouth of the Niagara River) to launch attacks on American settlements and to shelter Indian allies. During the harsh winter of 1779–1780, 5,000 Iroquois refugees, made homeless by the scorched-earth campaign of General John Sullivan, camped near the fort in five feet of snow.

and French allies in the upper Mississippi Valley. He secured settlements on the Mississippi River, and in February 1779 he led a grueling winter march to surprise the fort at Vincennes, on the Wabash River in southern Indiana. Clark's men managed to capture Henry Hamilton, but they failed to seize Detroit.

The Unpredictable War in the South

The rebel war effort beyond the Appalachian Mountains expanded south in 1778, when Patriot raiders captured Natchez on the lower Mississippi and seized property in British West Florida. But it was the energetic governor of Spanish Louisiana, Bernardo de Gálvez, whose actions proved decisive. Living in New Orleans, Gálvez maintained a careful neutrality between the Americans and their British rivals through 1778. But when Spain allied with France and declared war on Britain the next year, the governor acted quickly to keep the British from gaining ground on the Gulf Coast.

Moving from west to east, Governor Gálvez drove the British from the Mississippi River in 1779, seized their fort at Mobile in 1780, and conquered Pensacola, the capital of British West Florida, in 1781. The fall of Mobile and Pensacola cut British supply lines to the southeastern interior, hurting Creek and Cherokee warriors. Without additional guns, knives, and powder, the Indians could offer little assistance in Britain's ambitious plan to win back the South. It was support the British could ill afford to lose.

Still, the crown's forces regained control of most of Georgia from the rebels in 1778. The next year, they blocked American and French efforts to retake Savannah. Early in 1780, British generals Clinton and Cornwallis ferried troops by sea from New York to South Carolina, and by May they had isolated Charleston and forced the surrender of 5,500 American troops— the largest loss of American men and weapons during the entire war. A confident Clinton returned to New York, leaving Cornwallis in command in South Carolina as fierce fighting erupted across the state. Banastre Tarleton's British cavalry, along with Loyalist supporters, went head to head against the guerrilla bands led by Thomas Sumter, Andrew Pickens, and Francis Marion.

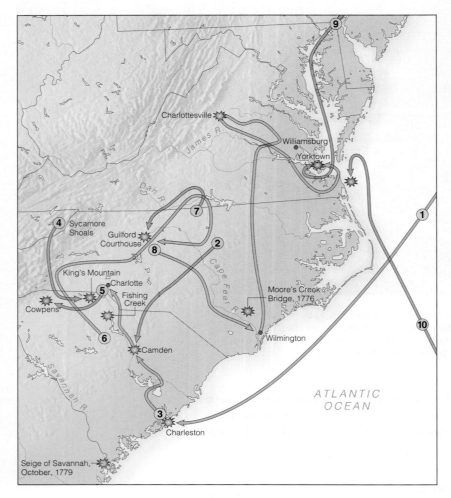

The Revolutionary War in the South

━━━ British and their Loyalist allies
━━━ Patriots and their French allies
✦ British victories
✦ Patriot victories

① Clinton and Cornwallis force surrender of Charleston, May 1780
② Gates moves the American army to Camden, August 1780
③ Cornwallis bests Gates at Camden and moves North, August 1780
④ Americans defeat Ferguson at Kings Mountain, October 1780
⑤ Morgan meets British at Cowpens, defeats Tarleton, January 1781
⑥ Cornwallis pursues Greene's army across the Dan River, February 1781
⑦ Greene confronts Cornwallis at Guilford Courthouse, March 1781
⑧ After a retreat to Wilmington, Cornwallis moves to Virginia, April 1781
⑨ Washington moves south, pins Cornwallis at Yorktown, August 1781
⑩ De Grasse from West Indies, defeats the British fleet, September 1781

■ **MAP 7.3**
THE REVOLUTIONARY WAR IN THE SOUTH

In June 1780, Congress appointed Horatio Gates to take command of southern operations, and he hurried to the Carolinas with fresh troops. On August 16, Gates's army confronted Cornwallis at Camden, South Carolina, 120 miles north of Charleston. The Americans, short on rest, food, and leadership, suffered a stinging defeat. Two days after the Camden disaster, as Gates fled north, Tarleton's cavalry landed another blow. They surprised Sumter's band of 800 partisans at Fishing Creek near the Catawba River and took 300 prisoners. Suffering almost no losses themselves, the cavalry inflicted 150 casualties and freed several hundred Loyalists and British regulars.

That September, as Washington absorbed word of the defeats at Camden and Fishing Creek, he received another rude shock. Benedict Arnold—in command of West Point, the key outpost controlling the Hudson River—had plotted to defect and yield the post to the British. An admired leader, Arnold was also self-centered. When Congress failed to promote him, he became alienated from the Patriot cause. The capture of General Arnold's British contact, Major John André, alerted Washington to the scheme. He hanged the major as an enemy spy, but Arnold escaped and received command of British troops.

Five years of war left Washington and Congress facing severe problems: soaring inflation, scarce resources, sinking citizen morale, and mounting disobedience among enlisted men. Early in 1780, soldiers from Massachusetts, New York, and Connecticut had mutinied in separate incidents. Members of the Pennsylvania and New Jersey Lines soon staged similar strikes over disputed terms of enlistment. The British had reason for optimism as Cornwallis pressed into North Carolina in the fall of 1780. But the next 12 months saw a dramatic reversal in their fortunes.

That reversal began in October with a surprising Patriot victory in the southern back-country, where Cornwallis had sent Major Patrick Ferguson with a troop of South Carolina Loyalists to guard the army's flank and harry rebel supporters. More than 800 frontiersmen rallied at Sycamore Shoals in the Watauga Valley and raced south to challenge the British at King's Mountain, just below North Carolina's southern border. On October 6, these sharp-shooters surrounded and decimated the Loyalist troops. Ferguson died in the one-sided affair, and his force lost more than 1,000 men—killed, wounded, or captured.

The Final Campaign

A shrewd change in American leadership followed the victory at King's Mountain. Congress, on Washington's advice, replaced Gates in the southern command with General Nathanael Greene, an experienced Rhode Islander who had served as the army's quartermaster general. Greene arrived in Charlotte, North Carolina, in December 1780, taking charge of a tattered army of 1,600. Shocked by the violence of partisan warfare and conscious of the need to win public support, he urged restraint on such experienced guerrilla fighters as Sumter and Marion while weaving them into his overall plans to conduct an elusive "fugitive war." Greene decided to divide his small army and send half his men into South Carolina under the seasoned Daniel Morgan to harass the British flank. "It makes the most of my inferior force," he explained, "for it compels my adversary to divide his, and holds him in doubt as to his own line of conduct."

Cornwallis took the bait and dispatched Tarleton, who caught up with Morgan at Hannah's Cowpens, west of King's Mountain, on January 17, 1781. The outnumbered rebel militia lacked experience and discipline, but Morgan turned this weakness to an advantage at the Battle of Cowpens. He stationed the militia units in front of his Continental forces with orders to fire two rounds and fall back. The British force of 1,100, sensing an enemy retreat, advanced too far too fast, and Morgan's men promptly overwhelmed them. Tarleton managed to escape, but he left behind 100 dead, 800 prisoners, and most of his horses and ammunition. Morgan's victorious Patriot force suffered only 148 casualties. He rightly called the Battle of Cowpens "a devil of a whipping."

Though frustrated, Cornwallis clung to the belief that "a successful battle may give us America." He discarded all excess baggage and pursued the rebel army 200 miles across North Carolina. Greene, continuing his elusive "fugitive war," directed a speedy retreat over swollen rivers to the Virginia border. Then he doubled back to confront the weary British in the Battle of Guilford Courthouse on March 15. Although the American forces eventually withdrew from the field, Cornwallis sustained such heavy losses that he was forced to alter his plans.

The British retreated to the coast at Wilmington, North Carolina, and then marched north in early summer 1781 to Yorktown, Virginia. There, Cornwallis hoped to obtain reinforcements by sea, rally Loyalists in the Chesapeake region, and divide the rebelling colonies. The design's success hinged on naval superiority and timely support from General Clinton in New York. But Cornwallis could be assured of neither.

In August the French fleet in the Caribbean set out for Chesapeake Bay. Admiral François De Grasse planned to spend eight weeks in North American waters. The move gave Washington (still in the north) brief access to impressive naval power, and he seized his chance. He sent word south to Lafayette in Virginia to keep Cornwallis contained at Yorktown. Then, to hold Clinton's forces in New York, he ordered his men to make a show as if preparing for a lengthy siege. But instead of besieging New York City, American soldiers and their French allies slipped away, secretly marching south to lay a trap for the British army.

■ The joint American-French victory at the siege of Yorktown, Virginia, in October 1781 ended British hopes for preventing American independence. As Cornwallis's troops marched out to lay down their arms, a band played "The World Turned Upside Down." "Finally," Lafayette wrote proudly, "everything came together at once, and we had a sensational turn of events. . . . The play is over."

Admiral De Grasse reached Chesapeake Bay with two dozen ships at the end of August. On September 5, he repulsed a British fleet off the mouth of the bay, dashing Cornwallis's hopes for relief by sea and allowing Washington to tighten the noose. When 9,000 Americans and 7,800 French converged on Yorktown in late September, they outnumbered their 8,000 opponents by more than two to one, and the siege proved brief. Plagued by sickness and shortages of food and munitions, the British surrendered on October 19, 1781. For Washington and his army, Yorktown was a stunning victory. Intermittent warfare continued for another year. But the Americans finally had powerful leverage to bargain for peace and force Britain to recognize their independence.

Winning the Peace

◉ See the Map

The American Revolution
at **www.myhistorylab.com**

After Yorktown, the final phase of the war played out in European courts. There, the diplomatic maneuvering proved complicated and risky, with Benjamin Franklin, John Adams, and John Jay as the key American players. Often at odds, the three men nevertheless managed to achieve a final triumph that proved as unlikely and momentous as Washington's victory in Virginia. They did it, wrote the immodest Adams, "in spite of the malice of enemies, the finesse of Allies, and the mistakes of Congress."

For the British, the road to the peace table had been long and unpleasant. Early feelers about a negotiated settlement—from the Howes in 1776 and the Carlisle Commission in 1778—had not mentioned independence. But conditions changed drastically after Yorktown. Domestic unrest in Britain had already boiled into riots, and the expanded war was going poorly in India and the West Indies. "O God, it is all over!" Lord North muttered when he received the news of Cornwallis's defeat in Virginia.

Within months, Sir Guy Carleton replaced Clinton in command of the remaining British forces in America, the hawkish Lord Germain stepped down from the Cabinet, and North resigned after 12 years as prime minister. Even the king spoke of abdicating. But instead, he approved a new ministry more suited to the rising antiwar sentiment in Parliament. The Earl of Shelburne became prime minister in July 1782. Even before he assumed office, he had authorized peace discussions with his old acquaintance, Benjamin Franklin.

Franklin was in a difficult position. The crucial alliance he had negotiated with France stated that the Americans would not sign a separate peace with Britain. Moreover,

Congress, grateful for vital French military and financial support, had instructed the American negotiators to defer to the wishes of Vergennes. The Americans did not realize that the French foreign minister had already entertained thoughts of a truce that would leave London in control of all the territory it currently held in America, including New York City and parts of the lower South. Vergennes opposed the Americans' republican principles, and he refused to treat the American diplomats as equal partners.

Still, the American peace commissioners fared surprisingly well in the treacherous waters of European diplomacy, starting with Franklin's first informal talks with the British. He laid out four "necessary" points, leading with the recognition of American independence. To this he added the removal of British troops, the right to fish in Newfoundland waters, and the revision of the Canadian border, which the Quebec Act of 1774 had pushed south to the Ohio River. Franklin then noted some "desirable" items for later bargaining. The British, he suggested, should consider paying an indemnity for war damages, an act that would officially acknowledge their own blame for the war. Perhaps they should cede Canada to the United States as well.

For its part, Britain sought compensation for roughly 70,000 American Loyalists who had been driven from their homes, plus the right to collect old debts that colonists had owed to British merchants before 1776. Hoping to disrupt the American-French alliance and to reestablish trade with their former colonies, the British negotiated preliminary peace terms with the Americans in November 1782. In return for independence, troop withdrawal, and fishing rights, the Americans agreed vaguely that their Congress would "recommend" that individual states approve compensation for confiscated Loyalist property.

■ The final American victory in the War of Independence came at the peace table, when negotiators John Jay, John Adams, and Benjamin Franklin won favorable terms in the 1783 Treaty of Paris. Benjamin West's unfinished painting also includes the absent Henry Laurens (rear) and Franklin's grandson (right), the delegation's secretary.

On the Canadian boundary question, the Americans scored another success, but one that came at the expense of Indian nations. By giving up their bid for all of Canada, the negotiators persuaded Britain to relinquish the Ohio Valley and accept a northern boundary for the United States defined by the Great Lakes and the St. Lawrence River. In the west, the United States would reach to the Mississippi River, and Americans would gain free navigation on that waterway, despite Spanish opposition. In the South, the thirty-first parallel, above East and West Florida, would provide the American boundary.

The diplomats endorsed the final peace terms at Versailles, France, in September 1783. Amid all the other treaty terms, the British yielded East and West Florida to Spain. In the process, however, they made no mention of the Indians who had served as allies in the American conflict. Abandoned, the Native Americans had to confront their new situation alone. To end up "betrayed to our Enemies & divided between the Spaniards and the Americans is Cruel & Ungenerous," protested the Creek leader, Alexander McGillivray. His people had been "most Shamefully deserted."

CONCLUSION

The War for Independence that began at Lexington had lasted eight years. Like any lengthy armed struggle, it took a heavy toll on combatants and noncombatants alike. Personal survival was far from certain, as encounters with sickness and the enemy carried off enlisted men. American forces lost an estimated 25,000 soldiers, a huge number in proportion to the small overall population.

For those who avoided death, lesser dangers abounded. Uprooting from home became commonplace, losses of property were extensive, and indebtedness proved widespread. Despite constant uncertainties at the individual level, a makeshift revolutionary army, learning as it marched, had forced the British to concede American independence.

As in all wars, some of the most decisive action occurred far from the battlefield. In London, weakness in the chain of command, a lumbering bureaucracy, and divided public sentiment undermined the British war effort. Elsewhere in Europe, skillful American diplomats forged vital alliances needed to secure victory and won favorable peace terms. An unprecedented flurry of constitution writing had launched more than a dozen newly independent states, and the Articles of Confederation, approved after long delay, had knit them together into a formal league with a common Congress. The new and difficult art of republican self-government remained a work in progress, with some of the most difficult and contentious choices still to come. The fragile unity built on fighting a common enemy would be strained to the limit as new debates erupted over the meaning and direction of the unfinished revolution.

For Review

✓•⃞Study and Review at www.myhistorylab.com

1. Was undermining or ending racial slavery a realistic strategic possibility for one or both sides in 1775–1776? Explain.

2. To what extent did poor military planning by the British lead to the costly defeat of General Burgoyne's campaign at Saratoga in 1777?

3. How did the initial state constitutions, drafted soon after 1776, reflect the recent political experiences of wary former British colonists?

4. In what specific ways did French support make possible the American victory in the War of Independence?

Chronology: 1776–1783

1776 Thomas Paine, *Common Sense*. Declaration of Independence. Washington crosses the Delaware and wins victory at Trenton. New Jersey gives women the right to vote.

1777 Burgoyne surrenders at Saratoga. Washington defuses "Conway Cabal."

1778 U.S. forges an alliance with France.

1779 Sullivan's campaign against the Iroquois. "Fort Wilson" Riot, Philadelphia.

1780 Charleston falls to the British. British Major John André hanged as spy.

1781 Morgan defeats Tarleton at Cowpens, S.C. Cornwallis wins costly victory over Greene's American forces at Guilford Courthouse, N.C. Cornwallis surrenders at Yorktown. Articles of Confederation are ratified.

1782 Christian Delaware Indians massacred at village of Gnadenhutten in Ohio.

1783 Treaty of Paris ends the war.

Key Term

Ordnance Cannons, artillery, and by extension general military supplies including weapons, ammunition, combat vehicles, and tools. p. 167

During the revolutionary war years, between 1775 and 1782, a huge smallpox epidemic ricocheted relentlessly across broad sections of North America. At times the epidemic entwined itself with the war, traveling on supply ships and moving with marching troops. In the Northeast, it struck during the siege of Boston and the attack on Quebec. In the South, the disease cut down hundreds of Virginia slaves at the start of the war and claimed additional victims during the British siege of Charleston in 1780.

Like the war itself, smallpox erupted first in Massachusetts. But the devastating contagion spread far more widely than the military destruction, proving truly continental in scope. It gained a foothold in New Orleans, Mexico City, and the trading posts that dotted the Canadian interior. In 1781 the disease ravaged Indian villages on the Northwest Coast, devastated missions on the Baja Peninsula, and erupted at California's San Gabriel Mission, where Spanish-speaking newcomers were building a new village that would grow into modern-day Los Angeles. On the Atlantic coast, smallpox menaced Virginia as French and American troops surrounded the British at Yorktown. As the War of Independence ended, the transcontinental epidemic also drew to a close. Over eight years, the fearsome virus took more than 130,000 North American lives, many times the 25,000 Americans lost in service during the Revolution.

As the dual scourges of epidemic and war subsided, fresh problems confronted North America's inhabitants. Great Britain's mainland colonies had won their independence, but questions remained as to which European powers would exert the most influence on the huge continent. British power ruled Canada; Spanish authority claimed much of the West; and French officials still dreamed of regaining control over the Mississippi Valley. In the North Pacific, Russians intruded on the Alaskan coast, and soon the prospect of trade with China lured sea captains from the United States to seek furs along the Northwest Coast.

In the woodlands between the Appalachian Mountains and the Mississippi River, Indians whom Pontiac had sought to unify a generation earlier once again endured sudden transfers of their ancestral land between distant powers. Now the rapid incursion of American settlers intensified the dilemma. Farther east, inhabitants of the Atlantic seaboard faced an array of thorny problems. Most importantly, half a million people remained legally enslaved, and they were potential allies for any European power seeking to disrupt the fragile new **federation**.

8

New Beginnings: The 1780s

CHAPTER OUTLINE

Beating Swords into Plowshares

Competing for Control of the Mississippi Valley

Debtor and Creditor, Taxpayer and Bondholder

Drafting a New Constitution

Ratification and the Bill of Rights

Conclusion

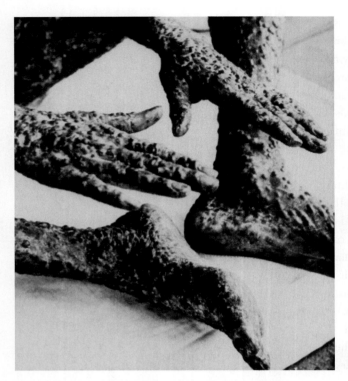

■ Smallpox "spread like lightning through all the missions," causing "havoc which only those who have seen it can believe. The towns and missions were . . . deserted, and bodies were seen in the road." Time and again, "the poor little children, abandoned beside the dead, died without help," wrote Father Luis Sales from Baja California in 1781. This modern photo shows that smallpox persisted until its global eradication in the 1970s.

In addition, members of the Confederation's Continental Congress in Philadelphia had a restless army to pay, a weak government to reform, and enormous war debts to confront. Acceptance of the Articles of Confederation in 1781 had not come easily, and all assumed that the basic structure of governance would demand further revision and adjustment. However, few could foresee that within eight years it would be set aside for a more centralized federal design.

Beating Swords into Plowshares

Thanks to military victory and skillful diplomacy, the initial survival of the new United States seemed assured. The former colonies had banded together under the Articles of Confederation, finally ratified in 1781, which placed specific governmental powers in the hands of an elected national legislature, or Continental Congress. But deeper questions persisted regarding the republican experiment, now that peace was at hand. How would citizens transform their "swords into plowshares," as urged by the Biblical prophet, Isaiah? Should power rest primarily with the victorious army, the wealthy merchants, or the artisans and farmers central to the revolutionary movement? Should authority be consolidated in the hands of a well-educated, new national elite, or should it be widely dispersed, with local communities and states empowered to manage their own affairs? Equally important, what cultural patterns would take hold within the fledgling society in these postwar years?

Why did the prospect of a Newburgh Conspiracy and the creation of the Society of the Cincinnati upset many Americans?

Will the Army Seize Control?

After their triumph at Yorktown, Washington's men had moved north to press British forces to evacuate New York City. More than 10,000 American troops and 500 officers encamped at Newburgh, on the Hudson River. Exhausted soldiers were eager to receive long-overdue pay and return home. Clearly, they could negotiate best for promised wages while they were still together and armed. Officers were especially reluctant to disband without certain assurances of money. In 1780 they had extracted from the Congress a promise of half pay for life. In December 1782, with no sign of compensation in sight, disgruntled officers sent a delegation to Philadelphia to press their claims.

Within Congress, the men around financier Robert Morris, including James Wilson and Alexander Hamilton, wanted to bolster and centralize the Confederation's finances. To that end, they sought a new duty of 5 percent on imported goods to raise money from the states. Revenue from this "continental impost" could make the Confederation solvent and allow it to assume responsibility for paying off war debts. In turn, this commitment would tie the interests of wealthy citizens to the Confederation government's success. Morris even threatened to resign his post if the "nationalists" did not get their way. Rumblings from the officer corps would help these politicians push through the impost measure, crucial to their long-term goals. So they quietly encouraged the military dissidents in Newburgh.

The spread of smallpox, 1775–1782

▬▬ Known transmission route

▬▬ Probable transmission route

Modern state and provincial boundaries
are provided for reference

■ **MAP 8.1**
THE SPREAD OF SMALLPOX ACROSS NORTH AMERICA, 1775–1782
A great smallpox epidemic swept North America during the Revolutionary era. In 1781 it
moved up the Baja Peninsula with settlers heading for San Gabriel, the Spanish mission
that became Los Angeles, California.

In March 1783, inflammatory petitions circulated among officers at Newburgh, hinting
at a military takeover to impose stability after a turbulent revolution. These anonymous
"addresses" urged officers to sit tight, neither fighting nor laying down their arms, until
Congress guaranteed their payment. Without Washington's approval, the officers arranged a
meeting to discuss their plight.

INTERPRETING HISTORY

Demobilization: "Turned Adrift Like Old Worn-Out Horses"

Joseph Plumb Martin was born in western Massachusetts in 1760. He enlisted in the Continental Army before his sixteenth birthday and was encamped at West Point, New York, when peace finally arrived. Later, in a compelling narrative of his wartime experiences, he recalled the demobilization process from the perspective of a common soldier.

William Ranney painted *Revolutionary War Veterans Returning Home* in 1848, when the United States was at war with Mexico. The image offered a positive reminder of earlier American military success. But the artist suggested that some soldiers leaving the Continental Army in 1783 had clearly fared better than others.

William Ranney, *Veterans of 1776 Returning from the War,* c. 1848. Dallas Museum of Art, Museum League Fund, Special Contributors and General Acquisitions Fund

[On April 19, 1783,] we had general orders read which satisfied the most skeptical, that the war was over and the prize won [after] eight tedious years. But the soldiers said but little about it; their chief thoughts were closely fixed upon their situation. . . . Starved, ragged and meager, not a cent to help themselves with, and no means or method in view to remedy or alleviate their condition. This was appalling in the extreme. . . .

At length, the eleventh day of June 1783, arrived. "The old man," our captain, came into the room, with his hands full of papers. . . . He then handed us our discharges, or rather furloughs, . . . permission to return home, but to return to the army again if required. This was policy in government; to discharge us absolutely in our present pitiful, forlorn condition, it was feared, might cause some difficulties. . . .

Some of the soldiers went off for home the same day that their fetters were knocked off; others stayed and got their final settlement certificates, which they sold to procure decent clothing and money. . . . I was among those. . . . I now bid a final farewell to the service. I had obtained my settlement certificates and sold some of them and purchased some decent clothing, and then set off from West Point. . . .

When those who engaged to serve during the war enlisted, they were promised

a hundred acres of land, each. . . . When the country had drained the last drop of service it could screw out of the poor soldiers, they were turned adrift like old worn-out horses, and nothing said about land to pasture them upon. . . . Congress did, indeed, appropriate lands, . . . but no care was taken that the soldiers should get them. [Instead,] a pack of speculators . . . were driving about the country like so many evil spirits, endeavoring to pluck the last feather from the soldiers. The soldiers were ignorant of the ways and means to obtain their bounty lands. . . . It was, soldiers, look to yourselves; we want no more of you.

We were, also, promised six dollars and two thirds a month. . . . And what was six dollars and sixty-seven cents of this "Continental currency," as it was called, worth? It was scarcely enough to procure a man a dinner. . . . I received one month's pay in specie while on the march to Virginia, in the year 1781, and except that, I never received any pay worth the name while I belonged to the army. . . . It is provoking to think of it. The country was rigorous in exacting my compliance to *my* engagements . . . but

equally careless in performing her contracts with me, and why so? One reason was that she had all the power in her own hands and I had none. Such things ought not to be.

After the war, Martin settled on the Maine frontier, and a speculator bought his right to 100 acres of bounty land in Ohio. In 1818, as a disabled laborer with a large family, he successfully petitioned Congress for a small pension to support the household. He died poor in 1850.

Questions

1. *Why did the government worry about discharging soldiers such as Martin in 1783, and why did many of them sell their final settlement certificates?*

2. *Do elements in Martin's complaints relate to the situation of modern American combat veterans?*

Source: James Kirby Martin, ed., *Ordinary Courage: The Revolutionary War Adventures of Joseph Plumb Martin,* 2nd ed. (New York: Brandywine Press, 1999), pp. 159–164.

If the plotters at Newburgh hoped to draw Washington into the scheme, they were sorely disappointed. He did attend the officers' meeting on March 15, but he used his commanding presence to discredit the ill-advised plan. His eyes weakened by endless wartime correspondence, he drew a pair of spectacles from his pocket, a surprising gesture that underscored his years of dedication and sacrifice. He then read a letter from Congress containing assurances of support, and he urged his officers not to take any actions that would undermine the honor they had earned.

Within Congress, the frightening prospect of a coup dissolved resistance to certain demands from the officers. Chastised by Washington, the officers disavowed the "infamous propositions" and accepted a congressional offer of full pay for the next five years. In April 1783, as Congress accepted a version of the 5 percent impost, momentous news arrived from Europe. Word spread that preliminary articles of peace had been signed in Paris. By June most soldiers were headed home.

The Society of the Cincinnati

Washington's strong stance against the suspected Newburgh conspiracy reminded his admirers of the familiar story of Cincinnatus, a general in Rome's early Republic. The Roman Senate called Cincinnatus from his farm to command an army against invaders. After defeating the enemy, he put down his sword and took up his plow again rather than seize power as a military ruler. His selfless act earned Cincinnatus the lasting respect of the Roman people. Similarly, at a crucial moment for the American republic, Washington urged fellow officers to respect the fragile principle of civilian control over the military. Your action, Thomas Jefferson told Washington, "has probably prevented this revolution from being closed as most others have been by a subversion of that liberty it was intended to establish."

Still, Jefferson and others had grounds to fear that some military officers might meddle in politics while hiding behind the noble name of Cincinnatus. In May 1783, General Henry Knox announced formation of the Society of the Cincinnati. The new organization invoked the name of the famous Roman, in a plural form, to put its members in the best light. But it was open only to officers in the Continental Army, their descendents, and invited honorary members, so some onlookers sensed that the "Cincinnati Club" had a sinister purpose. After all, members contributed to a charitable fund that resembled a political war chest, and they maintained contact with each other through newsletters concerning "the general union of the states." Critics feared a separate, self-perpetuating aristocracy of the very kind Americans had fought to erase.

Washington was automatically a member of the society, but Jefferson and other friends urged the general not to accept a leadership position. Struck by this "formidable" opposition, Washington suggested changes in the society, including doing away with the hereditary and honorary memberships. However, he never played a central role in the organization, and Washington's well-publicized alterations were never implemented. The Cincinnati exerted influence as a pressure group before receding from politics in future generations.

Renaming the Landscape

The controversy over the Society of the Cincinnati represented part of a larger debate about the direction of postwar life. Many Americans—despite continuing disagreements—set out to build a national culture and a shared identity. Like the Puritans before them, they aspired to provide new models for the Atlantic world.

They began with names. Everywhere, people christened new towns, counties, streets, and schools and renamed old ones. They replaced numerous British names, such as those of hated prewar governors, so Virginia's Dunmore County received the Indian name *Shanando*

●●─[Read the **Document**

George Washington, The Newburgh Address at **www.myhistorylab.com**

(later spelled *Shenandoah*). Because most people found references to royalty distasteful, King Street in Boston quickly became State Street. Still, royal figures who had aided the revolution received their due. Newcomers on the Ohio River named their town Louisville, honoring America's wartime alliance with King Louis XVI of France.

Political leaders popularized Christopher Columbus as well. For generations, the English had downplayed the explorer's importance as they contested Spanish claims in the Western Hemisphere. Now, American writers coined the ringing term *Columbia* for their land to stress its separation from Britain. In South Carolina, citizens named their new capital Columbia in 1786. Five years later, the proposed national capital was christened the District of Columbia. In New York City, when King's College reopened in 1784 under local governance, it was called Columbia College (later Columbia University).

Of all the new names, those honoring individual war heroes became the most popular. Citizens hailed foreign supporters of the revolution—such as Lafayette, Pulaski, and Steuben—by using their names on streets and towns. They saluted American officers the same way. Washington's name was used most often, but those of Montgomery, Wayne, Greene, Lincoln, Mercer, Marion, and others popped up as well. North Carolina named one of its trans-Appalachian forts on the Cumberland River Nashborough, after General Francis Nash, who had died at the battle of Germantown. Citizens changed the fort's name to Nashville in 1784. Two years later, inhabitants of a site on the Tennessee River named their new town Knoxville in honor of General Knox, who had become the Confederation's secretary of war the previous year.

An Independent Culture

New names were just part of the story. Many felt that the American language needed to be made more independent and accessible. Noah Webster, a schoolteacher who had fought against Burgoyne, believed that "as an independent nation, our honor requires us to have a system of our own, in language as well as government." In his *American Spelling Book* (1783), Webster championed a simple, uniform written language that rejected English conventions. Words such as *colour* and *labour* lost their silent *u*, *theatre* became *theater*, and *plough* was shortened to *plow*. The New Englander followed this success with an influential grammar book and a popular reader. Webster went on to produce *An American Dictionary of the English Language* (1828) that incorporated 5,000 new words, many of them reflecting Indian origins (*tomahawk*) and American nature (*rattlesnake*).

> *Noah Webster believed that "as an independent nation, our honor requires us to have a system of our own, in language as well as government."*

Webster also joined other reformers in lobbying state legislatures for copyright laws to protect the literary works that poured from the pens of ambitious writers. Philip Freneau, a classmate of James Madison at Princeton, drafted a poem titled "The British Prison Ship" (1781), about his war experiences. Authors living near Hartford, known as the Connecticut Wits, wrote similarly nationalistic poetry. Timothy Dwight, future president of Yale College, created "The Conquest of Canaan" (1785), and Joel Barlow composed an epic titled "The Vision of Columbus" (1787), heralding a bright future.

Increasingly, the land itself captured the imagination of Americans. In 1784 a Connecticut silversmith engraved the first map of the new United States. Jedidiah Morse, who published *Geography Made Easy* and *The American Geography* in the 1780s became known as the "Father of American Geography." In Philadelphia, Quaker naturalist William Bartram drafted a pioneering nature book about his travels throughout the Southeast, and the versatile painter and patriot Charles Willson Peale launched a museum to promote interest in art and the natural world. At his Virginia estate called Monticello, Thomas Jefferson pursued his own fascination with the American landscape. He promoted exploration, tested new crops, and excavated ancient Indian mounds. In *Notes on the State of Virginia* (1785), Jefferson detailed his region's geography, society, and natural history.

In 1782 Hector St. John de Crèvecoeur, a Frenchman who made his home in America, published *Letters from an American Farmer*, posing the question "What is an American?" According to Crèvecoeur, free people flourished in America because "a new mode of living" nurtured community growth. Societies for bettering jails, assisting debtors, and building libraries had existed before independence, but after the war Crèvecoeur watched a burst in the creation of voluntary associations. Reformers launched more than thirty new benevolent organizations between 1783 and 1789, offering aid to the poor, the sick, and the disabled.

In 1785 prominent New Yorkers John Jay and Alexander Hamilton joined like-minded citizens to form a Society for the Promotion of the Manumission of Slaves. In Connecticut, citizens banded together in an early **temperance** organization to stop the abuse of liquor. Similar efforts to reform and improve the new nation sprang up everywhere. Amid such postwar cultural optimism, the former colonists of the British Empire began to speak of shaping an expansive empire of their own.

Natural History Museum, London

■ Exploring near the Altamaha River in Georgia, John Bartram and his botanist son William found "several curious shrubs, one bearing beautiful good fruit." They named it the Franklin tree after their scientist friend in Philadelphia, Benjamin Franklin. William drew a watercolor of the rare plant and saved seeds to protect the species.

Competing for Control of the Mississippi Valley

"It has ever been my hobby-horse," John Adams wrote in 1786, "to see rising in America an empire of liberty, and a prospect of two or three hundred millions of freemen, without one noble or one king among them. You say it is impossible. . . . I would still say, let us try the experiment." Westward expansion became a persistent American theme. But during the postwar decade, interest and activity centered mostly on the land just beyond the Appalachian Mountains, territory reserved for Indians until Britain ceded the region at the end of the Revolution.

In the South in the 1780s, pioneer families searching for land pushed west through Cumberland Gap and spread out across parts of the lower Mississippi River valley, an area that eventually became known as the Old Southwest. These homesteaders promptly faced resistance from Native American inhabitants and their Spanish supporters. At the same time, north of the Ohio River, other American migrants were flocking to newly claimed woodlands later remembered as the Old Northwest. They, too, met stiff opposition from Native Americans and their British allies in neighboring Canada. By the time the Constitutional Convention met in Philadelphia in the summer of 1787, the Continental Congress of the existing Confederation government was busy revising an elaborate plan to draw this territory into the Union.

Why did control of the Mississippi Valley matter so much to Americans after the Revolution?

Disputed Territory: The Old Southwest

For a generation, Spain had been rebuilding its position north of the Gulf of Mexico and east of Texas in the Old Southwest. The Spanish had acquired Louisiana from France in 1763 and had conquered West Florida. In a 1783 treaty, Britain gave back East Florida to the Spanish and agreed that Spain would retain West Florida as well. The Spanish occupied St. Augustine, Pensacola, New Orleans, and Natchez, as well as St. Louis farther north.

Because Spain controlled both banks of the lower Mississippi, the Spanish determined who could use the huge river for trade. Since 1763 they had let British subjects navigate

■ **MAP 8.2**

SOUTHERN LAND DEBATES AFTER 1783
Following the Revolution, competing forces collided in the trans-Appalachian South. The United States claimed land reaching the Mississippi River down to 31 degrees latitude, and the Spanish claimed territory north to the Tennessee River. Although major Indian tribes continued to possess much of the region, coastal states also claimed sweeping jurisdiction. In Georgia, for instance, settlement remained confined near the Savannah River, but the state sold speculators large tracts as far west as the Yazoo River.

freely on the Mississippi, so trans-Appalachian fur traders had become accustomed to using this thoroughfare. Louisiana merchants paid for goods in Spanish silver, and settlers upriver needed the hard currency. During the Revolutionary War, Americans had retained access to the river, and the Spanish in New Orleans depended on produce from the north. Still, Spanish authorities feared American expansion into the Mississippi Valley. They debated whether to resist migrants pushing from the east, or to welcome newcomers and profit from their trade.

In 1783 Spain was shocked when Britain, through its separate treaty with the United States, granted the Americans a generous southern boundary: the thirty-first parallel. The treaty terms also included the right of Americans to navigate on the Mississippi. The Spanish believed that they alone should decide whose boats had access to the river. Moreover, Spain had good reason to claim that its West Florida province stretched north *above* 31 degrees at least to the mouth of the Yazoo River and perhaps as far as the Tennessee River.

For its part, the new Confederation had the force of numbers working to its advantage. The threat of Indian attacks had dammed up westward expansion since 1775. After the war, Americans migrated by the thousands to three existing centers of Anglo settlement in the Old Southwest. By 1785, 10,000 recent migrants clustered along several rivers above Knoxville. Nearly three times that many newcomers had already staked claims to the rich land between Lexington and Louisville. In addition, another 4,000 were clearing farms along the Cumberland River around Nashville. Aggressive Americans talked about pushing even farther west. They imagined establishing a foothold on the Mississippi at Chickasaw Bluffs (modern Memphis) or perhaps seizing Natchez or New Orleans.

Southern Claims and Indian Resistance

In the southern states, powerful land speculators pressed their legislatures to support expansion. Georgia, unlike many other states, had not relinquished its western lands to the Confederation. The state's 35-million-acre Yazoo claim stretched west from the Chattahoochee River (Georgia's present boundary with Alabama) to the Mississippi River and from the lower border of modern-day Tennessee to the thirty-first parallel. "I look forward to a time, not very far distant," wrote Judge George Walton, when Georgia "will be settled and connected . . . from the shores of the Atlantic to the banks of the Mississippi." By 1789 Walton had been elected governor of the state, and the land business boomed. During his tenure, Walton signed warrants for huge tracts up to 50,000 acres, sometimes selling unusable or even nonexistent acreage.

Unlike Georgians, pioneers from Virginia and the Carolinas faced a rugged mountain barrier. But they still trekked west through Cumberland Gap. In the decade after the war, backwoodsman Daniel Boone worked as a surveyor for these migrants in the transAppalachian region of Virginia that became Kentucky in 1792. During that same decade, North Carolina issued more land patents than it had created during the entire colonial era, most of them deeds for homesteads west of the mountains. Some of North Carolina's western landholders tried to create their own separate jurisdiction: the mountain state of Franklin. Without recognition from the Confederation government, their venture soon failed. Instead, all of North Carolina's western territory—from the Appalachians to the Mississippi—became the state of Tennessee in 1796.

> *Native American southerners, living in all these lands, suddenly found themselves caught between the competing claims of Spain and the United States.*

Native American southerners, living in all these lands, suddenly found themselves caught between the competing claims of Spain and the United States. The Cherokee, Creek, Choctaw, and Chickasaw—some 40,000 people—all debated which individuals and strategies to follow. Some responded to their new situation by selecting leaders with ties to European Americans. Among the Creek, for example, Alexander McGillivray rose to prominence. The son of a wealthy Scottish trader and a Creek woman, he had been raised on his father's Georgia plantation before becoming the Creek leader in 1782. He was well equipped to bargain with Spanish and American officials.

The renegade Cherokee warrior Dragging Canoe, who had split with tribal elders before the Revolution broke out, offered a different approach. Hundreds of militant Indians, discouraged by the compromises of their leaders, had joined his band of guerrilla fighters known as the Chicamauga living along the Tennessee River. From this well-protected location—near where Alabama, Georgia, and Tennessee now meet—the Chicamauga recruited allies and led forays to stop American encroachment. But Dragging Canoe died in 1792 before he could build a strong alliance with Indians north of the Ohio River.

"We Are Now Masters": The Old Northwest

Native Americans in the North also struggled to maintain their way of life and resist the newcomers. But white Americans lost no time in claiming Indian domains ceded by Britain in the 1783 Treaty of Paris. "We are now Masters of this Island," General Philip Schuyler boasted to the Iroquois, "and can dispose of the Lands as we think proper." Britain refused to vacate western forts on the pretext that Americans still owed prewar debts to London merchants. Even so, the British could provide little material support to the region's Indians.

American delegations moved quickly to draft treaties with the Iroquois and the Ohio Valley tribes. Delegates bluntly asserted the right of the new United States government to Indian lands, treating the Native Americans as dependents rather than equals. The negotiators even took hostages to force the Indians to accept their terms. Ordinary Americans sealed these claims with a surge of migration into western Pennsylvania and beyond. "The Americans . . . put us out of our lands," Indian leaders complained to the Spanish in 1784, "extending themselves like a plague of locusts in the territories of the Ohio River which we inhabit."

Americans initially remained divided among themselves over who would control the region. Connecticut retained a "western reserve" of 4 million acres south of Lake Erie that it used to satisfy claims from the state's war veterans. Similarly, Virginia held onto land rights for an even larger "military district" to repay soldiers and war victims. But one by one, the states of Massachusetts, New York, Connecticut, and Virginia ceded large territorial claims to the Confederation government.

These western acquisitions transformed the Confederation into something more than a league of states. With lands of its own to organize, the Confederation government took on attributes of a sovereign ruling body. As cessions increased, Congress put Thomas Jefferson in charge of a committee to draft "a plan for the temporary Government of the Western territory." Before he departed for Europe to replace Benjamin Franklin as the American minister to France, Jefferson drew up a design for western land distribution.

⊙─See the **Map**

Western Land Claims Ceded by the States at **www.myhistorylab.com**

■ A sketch by Congressman Thomas Jefferson shows his proposal to divide the new interior territories into fourteen states (with Number 7 to be named Saratoga after the crucial Revolutionary War victory). By suggesting numerous compact states, Jefferson hoped to maximize the congressional voting power of western farmers. Others, eager to limit western power in Congress, pushed successfully for fewer, larger states.

University of Michigan, William L. Clements Library, Map Division

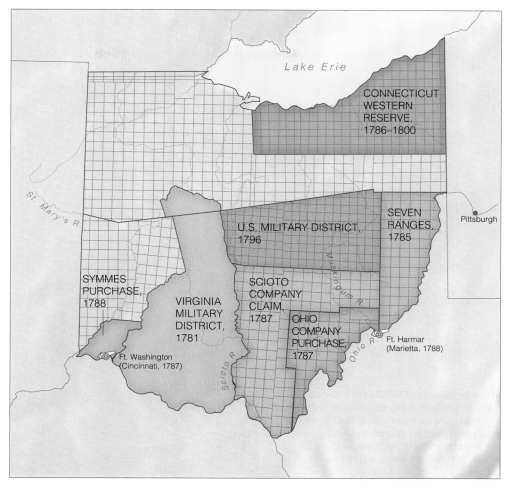

■ **MAP 8.3**
SETTLERS' OHIO, AFTER 1785
In 1785 the American government began to impose a novel grid system on the territory northwest of the Ohio River. Later, surveyors laid out similar straight geometric boundaries for states and counties across the natural landscape of the American West.

After Jefferson sailed for France, his report became the basis for the Land Ordinance of 1785. Jefferson knew that in the South, where surveyors often staked out piecemeal claims on a first-come, first-served basis, the best property had gone to wealthy investors. Moreover, odd-shaped lots had prompted endless boundary litigation. To avoid these complications, the 1785 ordinance called for surveyors to lay out a grid of square townships, beginning at the point where the Ohio River flowed out of Pennsylvania. A township would contain 36 numbered sections, each 1 mile square (640 acres). The ordinance reserved the income from one valuable section near the heart of every township to support public education.

Orderly surveying and public education were just parts of Jefferson's plan. Hoping to populate the region with self-sufficient yeomen farmers, he proposed that the government give away land in small parcels. He envisioned self-government for these enterprising pioneers, not colonial status. For Jefferson, the more weight these independent farmers obtained in the American government the better, so he urged the rapid entry of numerous new territories into the Union on an equal footing with the 13 original states. He suggested

■ Marie-Thérèse Lasselle (1735–1819) witnessed a generation of transitions in the Great Lakes region. She and her husband ran a trading post at Kekionga on the Maumee River (now Fort Wayne, Indiana). Long after the Revolutionary War drove them to Detroit, she created this self-portrait, using watercolor on embroidered silk.

Courtesy, Monroe County Historical Commission, Monroe, MI

creating up to 14 small, rectangular districts in the west. At least nine would be north of the Ohio River, and each could become a separate state with voting rights in Congress.

According to Jefferson's report, the first settlers arriving in a district were to form a temporary government. When the local population reached 20,000, residents could call a convention, frame a constitution, and send a delegate to Congress. When the district's population equaled the number of free inhabitants living in the smallest of the 13 original states, that district could enter the Union if certain conditions were met. Each new state must agree to support a republican form of government, remain part of the Confederation, and accept a share of the federal debt. It must also agree to exclude slavery after 1800. Congress accepted Jefferson's report, but then it modified the plan greatly. In its Land Ordinance of 1785, Congress removed his call for numerous districts, dismissed the notion of free land, and dropped the idea of ending slavery.

The Northwest Ordinance of 1787

The huge task of surveying the wilderness north of the Ohio River into neat geometric squares would take years to complete. Almost immediately—and long before the initial ordinance could take hold—political shifts produced an entirely new law from

Congress: the Northwest Ordinance of 1787. This law determining how territories north of the Ohio River would be governed contained a number of additional changes. For example, it reversed direction on the slave question once again, introducing an immediate prohibition of slavery north of the Ohio River. However, it made arrangements to deport fugitive slaves back to their owners in slaveholding states.

In various ways, the new ordinance proved less democratic than earlier versions. Congress cut the possible number of new districts in the Old Northwest, specifying there could be only three to five new states. This move limited the potential political weight of the vast territory. In addition, the ordinance increased property requirements for citizens who wanted to vote or hold office. It also slowed the process by which new states could gain admission to the Union. Eventually, Congress granted statehood to five new entities, but the process took more than half a century.

●●●─[Read the **Document**
Northwest Ordinance (1787)
at **www.myhistorylab.com**

Most members of Congress feared democratic governance in the Old Northwest and the prospect of giving a strong voice to people with different regional interests. To retain control over the domain, they provided for the appointment of territorial officials—a governor, a secretary, and three judges—instead of allowing elected governments. Even when territorial legislatures formed, the governor would have veto power over their actions. James Monroe, head of the committee that moved the bill through Congress, wrote candidly to Jefferson, "It is in effect to be a colonial gover[nme]nt similar to wh[at] prevailed in these States previous to the revolution."

These changes benefited eastern speculators—some of whom were members of Congress—who hoped to control these lands for profit. In 1786 former army officers in New England, joined by five surveyors, organized the Ohio Company to buy up western land. They dispatched Massachusetts minister Manasseh Cutler to lobby Congress to sell a huge tract at bargain rates. Cutler joined forces with congressional insiders associated with another venture, the Scioto Company. Together, they engineered a deal providing 1.5 million acres to the Ohio Company and another 5 million acres for Scioto investors.

Whatever suspicious bargains surrounded congressional passage of the Northwest Ordinance of 1787, the new law still granted basic rights to western residents. These guarantees—following state bills of rights—included religious freedom, trial by jury, and access to common-law judicial proceedings. Most important, the western territories were assured of full entry into the Union as equal states rather than receiving dependent status as permanent colonies. This system established an orderly method for bringing new regions into the Union, starting when Vermont became the fourteenth state in 1791.

Debtor and Creditor, Taxpayer and Bondholder

The end of the Revolutionary War brought widespread economic depression. The money spent by foreign armies for goods and services dried up, and the split with Britain disrupted established patterns of commerce. When peace returned, merchants scrambled to find profitable markets and new trade routes. At the same time, those who had preserved their holdings or made money during the war paid to buy goods from abroad that had been scarce during the fighting. These foreign purchases drained hard currency away from the states and increased the Confederation's debt.

Citizens everywhere felt the brunt of the postwar slump as prices dropped and the money supply shrank. As credit tightened, merchants called in their loans and unpaid bills.

Why did large bondholders care so deeply about what forces were in control of the state and national governments?

Families in debt, especially poor artisans and subsistence farmers, suddenly faced the threat of foreclosure and loss of their property. They fought back in local elections, in state legislatures, and even in the streets. Violence broke out in state after state, from New Hampshire to Georgia, as hard-pressed people, many of them veterans, decried fiscal policies that favored wealthy bondholders. Heavy taxes were being used to pay annual interest on bonds held by members of the moneyed classes. When armed conflict erupted in Massachusetts, fear of wider rebellion helped prompt a drastic effort to restructure and strengthen the national government through a special, closed-door convention in Philadelphia.

New Sources of Wealth

In 1783, the British government managed to fire one parting shot at the former colonies. To nurture Britain's maritime trade and punish New England shippers, it restricted Americans from trading with the British West Indies. The move barred American ships from a key portion of Britain's imperial commerce, forcing merchants to seek out new avenues of trade. In 1784 an American vessel entered the Baltic Sea and established trade relations with Russia. Meanwhile, the Massachusetts ports of Nantucket and New Bedford stepped up their search for whales to provide oil for American lamps. Captains had no trouble finding sailors in need of work, and ships sailed wherever they sensed possible profits.

Early in 1783, a Savannah merchant named Joseph Clay commented that a "vast number" of slaves had fled the South in wartime. As rice plantations renewed production, African workers were "exceeding scarce and in demand." Sensing a profit, foreign slave traders shipped 15,000 Africans to Georgia and South Carolina by 1785. New England captains soon joined in, sailing ships to Africa in hopes of renewing a trade that had been interrupted during the war. Antislavery sentiment had increased with the idealism of the Revolution, and several states, including Virginia, had outlawed slave imports. But these developments did not prevent American vessels from transporting Africans across the Atlantic. "The Negro business is a great object with us," Clay reported in 1784. "It is to the Trade of this Country, as the Soul to the body."

Financier Robert Morris took a global perspective, realizing that profits could be made by opening new trade routes to the Orient. The project would take an enormous investment—ten times the amount needed to send a ship to Europe—but the potential rewards were irresistible. Morris's first vessel, the *Empress of China*, left New York harbor for Canton by way of the Indian Ocean early in 1784. It carried almost 30 tons of ginseng root—procured from western Virginia—highly prized by the Chinese. The ship's cargo also included $20,000 in hard currency (a huge drain on New York's economy) and 2,600 furs.

In six months, the American vessel reached Canton, China's outlet for foreign commerce. "The Chinese had never heard of us," one sailor noted, "but we introduced ourselves as a new Nation" and gave them "a description of our Country." Chinese merchants welcomed trade with "the new people" and called their strange country "the flowery flag kingdom" because the stars on the American flag resembled blossoms. In May 1785 the *Empress of China* returned to New York loaded with tea, chinaware, and silk. Morris and his partners raked in a hefty 20 percent return on their investment.

Other traders took notice. In 1787 the Browns, wealthy merchants in Providence, diverted a slave ship from the African trade to the China tea trade. That same year, six Boston investors sent several vessels around Cape Horn to trade for furs on the American Northwest Coast, pioneering new Pacific routes for American ships. Among the Nootka Indians, Captain Robert Gray exchanged cloth and iron goods for sea otter pelts. Then he sailed the *Columbia* across the Pacific, pausing at Hawaii for supplies. Reaching Canton in 1789, Gray

George Davidson, Attacked at Juan de Fuca Straits, c. 1792.

ATACKTED at JUAN, DE, FUCA, STRAITS.

■ This painting on glass shows Northwest Coast Indians menacing the American ship *Columbia* from their large war canoes. Cannon smoke above the deck suggests warning shots have been fired. Captain Robert Gray was conducting trade for sea otter pelts to transport across the Pacific Ocean to China, where the soft fur was highly valued.

traded profitably and proceeded home through the Indian Ocean, making the *Columbia* the first American ship to circumnavigate the globe.

Because Gray's voyage affirmed the rewards of trade along the Northwest Coast, a diplomatic controversy flared the following year at Nootka Sound, on the west side of Vancouver Island. Although Spain protested British and American trading activities in the area, Gray was back on the Northwest Coast by 1792. He entered a powerful stream—where Washington and Oregon now meet—and named it the Columbia River, after his ship. When he planted the American flag at the mouth of this major waterway, his action foreshadowed later territorial claims by the United States in the Oregon region.

While American merchants probed for new markets abroad, they also moved to strengthen their economic and political position at home. Some wealthy investors bought up a variety of loan certificates, paper notes, and wartime securities issued by state governments and the Continental Congress, paying only a small fraction of the original value. Certificates issued to soldiers at the end of the war became part of this speculative market when the original recipients sold their notes to prosperous speculators for needed cash. In Maryland, for example, the claims on $900,000 owed by the state became concentrated in the hands of only 318 people by 1790. Moreover, 16 of these people controlled more than half of the total value, and these wealthy investors took an increasing interest in political events. They realized that whoever controlled the reins of power at the state and national levels would determine how the various notes of credit might be redeemed. Speculators who had purchased numerous notes for a fraction of their face worth stood to reap enormous profits from any government that would pay interest on, and then buy back, all these paper arrangements at their original high value.

"Tumults in New England"

The few people who had acquired most of the paper securities wanted their holdings redeemed for hard money. But the majority of citizens, faced with rising debts amid an economic downturn, resented the heavy taxes needed to pay interest on the debt to these wealthy speculators. Favoring much easier credit, they urged their states to issue new paper money. But local elites wanted to limit paper money in ways that favored their new position as powerful creditors and holders of wartime certificates. Their opponents argued that issuing paper money could take the pressure off cash-strapped farmers and help retire enormous war debts. In seven states, these advocates of economic relief carried the day. State government presses put additional notes in circulation.

Local battles over debt, credit, and currency issues hit hardest in the Northeast. In Massachusetts, a legislature sympathetic to creditors consolidated the state's huge war debts in a way that placed extreme tax burdens on ordinary citizens. Also, Britain's ban on American commerce in the British West Indies undermined New England's economy. The fish, grain, and lumber from that region could no longer be sold to the Caribbean colonies in exchange for much-needed hard currency.

Britain's ban on American commerce in the British West Indies undermined New England's economy.

These changes had an immediate impact. In New Hampshire courts, debt cases rose sixfold from 1782 to 1785. The heavy costs of traveling to court and paying high legal fees pushed thousands of rural families into bankruptcy. Embittered farmers saw their livestock and household property seized and auctioned off at low prices. Hard times often spark drastic responses, and New England's pot soon boiled over. Early in 1787, Washington's secretary in Virginia noted that the "tumults, insurrections, and *Rebellion* in New England have of late much engrossed the minds of the people here."

Newspaper accounts told of disturbing events in Rhode Island. Rural politicians seeking relief for indebted farmers swept into power during the April 1786 election, routing rich Providence merchants from their longtime domination of the assembly. The newcomers quickly implemented their paper money platform. The Rhode Island region had a withered economy, and the state government carried a burdensome war debt. To address these matters, assemblymen approved a huge outlay of paper money. To ensure the plan's success, legislators declared that all creditors had to accept the money as legal tender.

Not surprisingly, creditors and speculators resented Rhode Island's currency law. They fumed at the new legislature's unwillingness to assume a share of the national debt and pay interest to wealthy bondholders, as other states had done. So rich merchants in Providence fought back, closing their stores rather than accept the new bills. Some even left the state to avoid being forced to accept debt payments in paper money. When judges who favored the merchants' cause finally declared the new statute unconstitutional, creditors everywhere sighed with relief. Their newspapers condemned the "Rogue Island" currency law as a dire example of the dangers of democracy.

Shays' Rebellion: The Massachusetts Regulation

In Massachusetts and New Hampshire, unlike Rhode Island, powerful merchants retained control over the state assemblies, and they resisted public pressure to generate more paper money. Instead, these creditors pushed to enforce debt collection by the courts. As in other states, wealthy speculators had bought up, at bargain rates, most of the public securities and certificates issued during the war. They anticipated huge profits if a government they controlled could redeem these notes, in gold and silver, at their full face value.

In New Hampshire, by 1785, securities valued at nearly £100,000 belonged to just 4.5 percent of the state's adult male population: 1,120 men among approximately 25,000. A mere 3 percent of this group—34 men—controlled more than a third of this vast speculative

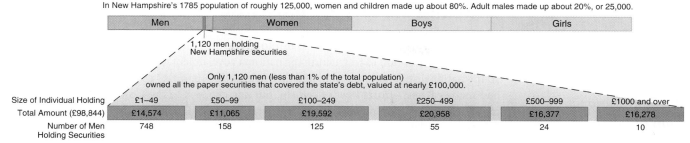

In New Hampshire's 1785 population of roughly 125,000, women and children made up about 80%. Adult males made up about 20%, or 25,000.

Men	Women	Boys	Girls

1,120 men holding
New Hampshire securities

Only 1,120 men (less than 1% of the total population)
owned all the paper securities that covered the state's debt, valued at nearly £100,000.

Size of Individual Holding	£1–49	£50–99	£100–249	£250–499	£500–999	£1000 and over
Total Amount (£98,844)	£14,574	£11,065	£19,592	£20,958	£16,377	£16,278
Number of Men Holding Securities	748	158	125	55	24	10

Who held New Hampshire's Security Notes, 1785

■ **FIGURE 8.1**
CONCENTRATION OF SECURITY NOTES IN THE HANDS OF A FEW: THE EXAMPLE
OF NEW HAMPSHIRE IN 1785

investment. Most of these men had close ties to the prevailing government, situated in Exeter, near the coast. When farmers organized conventions to voice their economic grievances, merchants infiltrated and disrupted their meetings. In September 1786, 200 citizens, many of them armed war veterans, marched on Exeter to demand money reforms before conditions "drive us to a state of desperation." Officials organized cavalry units to confront the furious citizens, arresting their leaders from the crowd "as a butcher would seize sheep in a flock." As soon as the state's governor, General John Sullivan, had suppressed the dissenters, he issued a proclamation forbidding further conventions. He then wrote to the Massachusetts governor, James Bowdoin, offering to help crush similar unrest in the neighboring state.

Early in 1786, the Commonwealth of Massachusetts had imposed a heavy direct tax on its citizenry. Western farmers lacked sufficient cash and already faced a wave of foreclosures for debt. They protested the tax law at town meetings and county conventions. When their complaints fell on deaf ears, they took action, "regulating" events as the North Carolina Regulators had done two decades earlier. The Massachusetts Regulation became known as Shays' Rebellion when a former army officer named Daniel Shays emerged as one of its popular leaders. At first, these New England Regulators focused on closing the courts. In August 1786, 1,500 farmers marched against the Court of Common Pleas in Hampshire County and shut it down. The next month, another band closed the court in Worcester.

The confrontation escalated as winter set in. By January more than 1,000 Shaysites, knowing that their allies in New Hampshire had been defeated, moved to seize the federal arsenal in Springfield. But Governor Bowdoin had mobilized an army, financed largely by wealthy merchants in Boston. This private militia overpowered the westerners and forced all who did not flee to sign an oath of allegiance. Disarmed but not silenced, the dissidents succeeded in extracting some relief from the legislature. They also managed to defeat Bowdoin in the next election and replace him with a more popular governor, John Hancock.

The unrest in New England played into the hands of those advocating a stronger national government. (Rumors even circulated that nationalists had provoked the violence to rally support for their cause.) In May 1787, Henry Knox expressed fear to Governor John Sullivan that "we are verging fast to anarchy." He urged Sullivan to send delegates from New Hampshire to a crucial meeting that was about to begin in Philadelphia.

•••—Read the Document
Miltary Reports on Shays' Rebellion
at **www.myhistorylab.com**

The unrest in New England played into the hands of those advocating a stronger national government.

Drafting a New Constitution

How did nationalist leaders use their political skills to bring about the Constitutional Convention in Philadelphia?

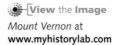

View the Image
Alexander Hamilton—Portrait
at **www.myhistorylab.com**

Even before Yorktown, Alexander Hamilton, Washington's youthful aide-de-camp, had proposed a convention to restructure the national government. Now he worked with another young nationalist, James Madison, and their energetic supporters to bring it about. Congress had made earnest efforts toward reform, but any changes to the Confederation's governing articles required approval from all 13 states. Thus, vital amendments—which would let Congress regulate commerce, raise revenue, and establish a judiciary, for example—proved nearly impossible. For some powerful leaders, especially merchants and creditors, a major political revision seemed in order.

"Many Gentlemen both within & without Congress," wrote Madison, desire a "Convention for amending the Confederation." Still, it would take impressive leadership—Madison provided much of it—to seize the initiative and then generate enough momentum to change the rules of national government. Extensive compromise, both between elite factions and toward resistant popular forces, would be necessary at every stage. After all, it would take an enormous push to engineer such a convention, to guide it to restructure the government along nationalist lines, and finally to persuade voting Americans to ratify the proposed changes and accept their legitimacy. To begin such a task, would-be reformers needed to convince the Confederation Congress to allow their revision plans to move forward. For that, they needed to recruit the enormous prestige of George Washington.

Philadelphia: A Gathering of Like-Minded Men

View the Image
Mount Vernon at
www.myhistorylab.com

The path began at Mount Vernon in 1785 when Washington hosted commissioners appointed by Maryland and Virginia to resolve state boundary disputes regarding the Potomac River. During the gathering, these men (including James Madison) scheduled a broader meeting on Chesapeake trade for the next year at Annapolis, Maryland. They invited all the states to send representatives. Only 12 delegates from five states showed up at Annapolis in September 1786, but news of the unrest in New England prompted talk of a more extended meeting.

Alexander Hamilton, as a representative from New York, persuaded the other delegates to call for a convention in Philadelphia the following May to discuss commerce and other matters. Madison won endorsement for the proposal from the Virginia legislature and then from Congress. Reform-minded congressmen, such as James Monroe, saw an opportunity to amend and improve the existing Confederation structure. But when the states sent delegates to Philadelphia the following spring, many of the appointees thought that amendments might not go far enough. They were open to the more sweeping changes that Madison and other nationalists had in mind. So the gathering called to consider commercial matters and propose improvements to the Articles of Confederation soon became a private meeting to design and propose an entirely new structure for governing the United States.

Madison reached Philadelphia in early May 1787. He immediately began drafting plans for drastic change and lobbying delegates, some of whom came early to attend a secret gathering of the Society of the Cincinnati. On May 25, when representatives from seven states had arrived, they launched the convention and unanimously chose Washington as the presiding officer. Participants agreed that they would operate behind closed doors and each state delegation would have one vote. There would be no public discussion or official record of their proceedings. Soon, delegates from 12 states had joined the gathering. Only Rhode Island did not send representatives.

The 55 delegates had much in common. All were white, male, and well educated, and many already knew one another. These members of the national elite included 34 lawyers,

30 public creditors, and 27 members of the Society of the Cincinnati. More than a quarter of the participants owned slaves, and nearly a dozen had done personal business with financier Robert Morris of the Pennsylvania delegation. Not surprisingly, all seemed to agree that the contagion of liberty had spread too far. One called the current situation "an excess of democracy."

Specifically, these men feared recent legislation passed by state assemblies to assist hard-pressed citizens: laws that delayed tax collection, postponed debt payments, and issued paper money. Most delegates hoped to replace the existing Confederation structure with a national government capable of controlling finances and creating creditor-friendly fiscal policy. To be effective, they believed, a strengthened central government must have greater control over the states. Only Robert Yates and John Lansing of New York and Luther Martin of Maryland staunchly resisted expanding central power.

Many delegates, especially those from heavily populated states, thought the national legislature should be based on proportional representation according to population rather than each state receiving equal weight regardless of its numbers. Also, most wanted to see the single-house (unicameral) Congress of the Confederation replaced by an upper and lower house that would reflect the views and values of different social classes. John Adams had helped create such a two-house (bicameral) system in the Massachusetts constitution, thereby limiting pure democracy and giving more political power to propertied interests.

Besides calling for checks within the legislative branch itself, Adams had also laid out strong arguments for separating, and checking, the powers of each competing branch of government. For a sound and lasting government, Adams had argued, there should be **separation of powers**; the legislative branch should be balanced by separate executive and judicial branches that are equally independent. Most delegates agreed with this novel system of **checks and balances**, intended to add stability and remove corruption.

Compromise and Consensus

The Philadelphia gathering, which lasted through the entire summer, would later be known as the Constitutional Convention of 1787. Even as a consensus emerged within the small meeting, countless personal, practical, and philosophical differences persisted. Hamilton delivered a six-hour speech in which he staked out an extremely conservative position. He underscored "the imprudence of democracy" and stressed a natural separation between "the few and the many"—the "wealthy well born" and the "turbulent and changing" people. Hamilton's conservative oration called for the chief executive and the senators to be chosen indirectly, by elected representatives rather than by the people themselves, and he recommended that these high officials should serve for life. Such ideas undoubtedly appealed to many of his listeners, but all of the delegates knew that a majority of citizens would never accept such proposals. Pierce Butler of South Carolina invoked Solon in ancient Greece, "who gave the Athenians not the best government he could devise but the best they would receive."

This attentiveness of convention members to what the public would accept is illustrated by their approach to **suffrage** (the right to vote). Property ownership was no longer a universal voting requirement, and state constitutions varied on whether religion, race, or gender could determine eligibility. James Wilson of Pennsylvania, second only to Madison in working to build a practical nationalist majority in the convention, pointed out that "it would be very hard and disagreeable" for any person, once franchised, to give up the right to vote. Accordingly, the delegates proposed that in each state all those allowed to vote for any "branch of the state legislature" would also be permitted to cast ballots for members of the House of Representatives. But they shied away from accepting

● ● ● Read the Document

The Debates in the Federal Convention of 1787 reported by James Madison at **www.myhistorylab.com**

direct election for the Senate or the president, and they deferred suffrage matters to the states.

Time and again during the 16-week convention, these like-minded men showed their willingness to bargain and compromise. Lofty principles and rigid schemes often gave way to balancing and improvisation. The unlikely creation of the **electoral college** for selecting a president is one example. Delegates who differed over the length for the chief executive's term of office and right to run for reelection also disagreed on the best method of presidential selection. Some suggested that ordinary voters should elect the president; others proposed that the state governors, or the national legislature, or even electors chosen by the lower house should choose the chief executive.

Finally, the aptly named Committee on Postponed Matters cobbled together an acceptable system: a gathering (or "college") of chosen electors from each state would cast votes for the presidency. This electoral college plan had little precedent, but it managed to balance competing interests. Under the scheme, state legislatures would set the manner for selecting electors. The least populous states would get a minimum of three electoral votes, and states with more people would choose more electors in proportion to their numbers, giving them added weight in the decision. The people could also participate in the voting process, though only if their state legislatures called for it. If no candidate won a majority in the electoral college, the House of Representatives had the right to determine the president, with each state having one vote. The system was far from elegant or democratic, but it placated varied interests, and it won prompt approval.

Questions of Representation

As deliberations stretched across the long, hot summer of 1787, two central issues threatened to unravel the convention: political representation and slavery. Questions of representation pervaded almost every discussion, pitting the states with the largest populations, such as Virginia, Pennsylvania, and Massachusetts, against the less populated states. Madison's well-organized Virginians offered a comprehensive blueprint outlining a new national government that would have three separate branches. This design, called the "Virginia Plan," recommended a bicameral national legislature with proportional representation in each body. The House of Representatives would be chosen by popular election, the Senate by the lower house.

> *As deliberations stretched across the long, hot summer of 1787, two central issues threatened to unravel the convention: political representation and slavery.*

Madison's system clearly favored populous states. Not surprisingly, a coalition of small-state delegates led by William Paterson of New Jersey submitted an alternative "New Jersey Plan." This less sweeping revision built on the current Articles of Confederation. It called for a continuation of the current unicameral legislature, in which each state received an equal vote. A committee chaired by Benjamin Franklin finally broke the impasse between the two plans. The idea of an upper house, or Senate, would be retained, and each state, whatever its size, would hold two senate seats. Seats in the House of Representatives would be determined proportionally, according to the relative population of each state. Moreover, this lower house would have the power to initiate all bills dealing with finance and money matters.

To implement proportional representation in a fast-growing society, the delegates devised a radical innovation: a national census every ten years. This regular headcount in turn raised a thorny question. Should slaves—people enumerated in the census yet denied the rights of citizens—be counted in determining a state's proportional representation in the national government? Slaveholding states wanted their human property to count because that would give those states more representation. The convention resolved this dilemma in mid-July with a "three-fifths" formula that made every five enslaved people equivalent to three free people in apportionment matters.

In an ironic twist, the same week the Constitutional Convention delegates approved the notorious **three-fifths clause**, the existing government of the United States leaned in the opposite direction. Meeting in New York, members of the Confederation's Congress passed the Northwest Ordinance, which outlawed slavery in the new territory above the Ohio River. Because there was much contact between the two meetings, some scholars speculate that powerful Southerners agreed to give away the prospect of slavery north of the Ohio River in exchange for more support of slavery within the new plan taking shape in Philadelphia.

Slavery: The Deepest Dilemma

During the debate over the three-fifths clause, Madison commented that the greatest division in the United States "did not lie between the large & small States: it lay between the Northern & Southern," owing to "the effects of their having or not having slaves." This highly charged issue simmered beneath the surface for most of the summer. In late August, with most other matters resolved, delegates could no longer postpone questions surrounding slavery. Yet again, a committee deliberated, and a bargain was struck. This time, hundreds of thousands of human lives were at stake.

Planter delegates from Georgia and South Carolina refused to support any document that regulated the slave trade or curtailed slavery itself. They asserted that such a charter could never win acceptance at home. In part they were bluffing: Constraints on slavery had wide popular appeal in the expanding backcountry of the Deep South. There, independent farmers outnumbered planters, ministers questioned slavery, and pioneers wanted national support in confronting powerful Indians. Few delegates challenged the proslavery posturing, possibly because strong antislavery opinions could have prolonged or even deadlocked the convention. Weary participants were eager to complete their work and fearful of unraveling their hard-won consensus.

Rather than force the matter, even those who disapproved of slavery rushed to compromise, heaping a huge burden on future generations. Southern delegates dropped their protests against giving Congress the power to regulate international shipping. In exchange, the framers approved a clause protecting the importation of slaves for at least 20 years. They also added a provision governing fugitive slaves that required the return of "any person held to service or labor." Through a calculated bargain, delegates had endorsed slavery and drawn the South into the Union on terms that suited that region's leaders. The word *slave* never appeared in the finished document.

In early September, the convention members put the finishing touches on their proposal and wondered whether Americans would accept it. Winning state-by-state approval would involve an uphill battle, especially given the absence of a bill of rights. George Mason, who had drawn up Virginia's Declaration of Rights 11 years

■ In a crucial decision, members of the Constitutional Convention chose to protect the slave trade and preserve slavery. One African American who had already taken matters in her own hands was Mumbet, a slave in Massachusetts and widow of a Revolutionary War soldier. In 1781 she sued for her freedom on the grounds that "all were born free and equal." Her court victory proved a landmark in New England. Proudly, she took the name **Elizabeth Freeman.**

earlier, reminded members that such a set of guarantees "would give great quiet to the people." But in the convention's closing days, many delegates resisted the notion, and all were eager to adjourn. They overwhelmingly voted down Mason's suggestion.

Without a bill of rights, Mason and Edmund Randolph of Virginia refused to endorse the final document, along with Elbridge Gerry of Massachusetts. Other delegates who dissented had already departed. Of the 74 delegates chosen at the convention's outset, 55 actually attended the proceedings, and only 39 agreed to sign the finished plan. It was approved "by the unanimous consent of the States present" on September 17, 1787.

Ratification and the Bill of Rights

Why was a bill of rights expected by citizens, omitted by the drafters of the Constitution, and later added?

Committed nationalists now faced their most difficult task: winning public acceptance for an alternative structure that defied existing law. After all, the proposed constitution ignored the fact that the Articles of Confederation—the document governing the United States at the time—could be amended only with the approval of all 13 states. Instead, the text drafted in Philadelphia stated that ratification (acceptance through voting) by conventions in any nine states would make the new document take effect in those places. Moreover, the proposed ratification process left no room for partial approval or suggested revisions. Each state, if it wanted to enter the debate at all, had to accept or reject the proposed frame of government as offered.

The Campaign for Ratification

The Confederation Congress had acquiesced in allowing the 1787 convention to occur in the first place. Most congressional representatives had expected the meeting to produce proposals for amending the current government, not discarding it. But now that the Philadelphia conclave had ended, the Congress sitting in New York City balked at endorsing the revolutionary document. To avoid a lengthy and troublesome debate, proponents of the new constitution urged Congress simply to receive the frame of government as a possible proposal and then transmit it to the states without an endorsement. Congress did so on September 28, 1787, and the document's advocates portrayed the unanimous vote as an expression of approval.

Supporters had no time to lose because Pennsylvania's assembly was set to adjourn on the next day. An early victory in that large and central state would be crucial in building momentum, so they rushed the congressional letter of transmittal from New York to Philadelphia. There, the assembly faction dominated by Robert Morris won a hasty vote to schedule a state ratifying convention. Over the next three months, Pennsylvania towns and counties elected delegates, a convention met, and the state voted to approve the new plan. Delaware had approved it unanimously on December 7, and New Jersey and Georgia followed suit. By the end of January, Connecticut had also ratified. Other states called elections and scheduled conventions. Only Rhode Island, which had not sent delegates to the drafting convention, refused to convene a meeting to debate ratification.

By seizing the initiative early, the proponents of the new framework shaped the terms of debate. The drafters, anything but a cross-section of society, worked to portray themselves as such. They noted that their document began with the ringing phrase "We the people of the United States," a last-minute addition by Gouverneur Morris of New York. And Madison told the public that the text sprang from "*your* convention."

Most important, in a reversal of logic and contemporary usage, the nationalists who supported the new constitution took for themselves the respected name of **Federalists**. They gave their opponents the negative-sounding term **Anti-Federalists**. The Federalists then used

■ In 1788 newspapers tracked ratification of the new "federal superstructure" state by state. Massachusetts ratified the proposed U.S. Constitution in March—apparently aided by the Hand of God! New Hampshire provided the "ninth and sufficient pillar" in June, followed by Virginia four days later.

their ties to influential leaders to wage a media war for public support. They dashed off letters and published essays praising the proposed constitution.

The strongest advocacy came from Alexander Hamilton and James Madison. The two men composed 80 essays for the New York press under the pen name *Publius*. John Jay added five more, and in the spring of 1788 the collection appeared as a book titled *The Federalist*. In the most famous piece, "Number 10," Madison challenged the widely accepted idea that a republic must be small and compact to survive. Turning the proposition around, he argued that minority opinions would fare better in a large nation, where diverse competing interests would prevent a unified majority from exerting control.

•••[**Read** the **Document**
Madison Defends the Constitution at **www.myhistorylab.com**

Dividing and Conquering the Anti-Federalists

Opponents of the new plan found themselves on the defensive from the start. Many of them had supported some government change, and most conceded the presence of economic difficulties. But Federalist predictions of impending chaos seemed exaggerated. "I deny that we are in immediate danger of anarchy," one Anti-Federalist writer protested.

Richard Henry Lee, president of the Confederation Congress, condemned the Federalists as a noisy "coalition of monarchy men, military men, aristocrats and drones." Other prominent figures joined him in opposition: George Clinton in New York; Luther Martin in Maryland; and Patrick Henry, George Mason, and Benjamin Harrison in Virginia. Such notables became the spokespeople for a far wider array of skeptics.

•••[**Read** the **Document**
Henry, Against the Ratification of the Constitution at **www.myhistorylab.com**

Collection of the New-York Historical Society, (#1176)

■ **Celebrations in July 1788 hailed the new Constitution of the United States. "Columbus" on horseback led New York City's parade, followed by artisan groups. The silk banner of the pewterers proclaimed that under the Federal Plan, "All Arts Shall Flourish in Columbia's Land, And All Her Sons Join as One Social Band."**

Many opponents of the proposed constitution protested the plan's perceived threat to local political power. Despite Madison's reassurances in *Federalist* Number 10, they believed that local and state governments represented voters more fairly and responded to their needs more quickly than a distant national authority could. For some critics this belief expressed a radical democratic principle; for others it represented their provincial bias. In short, Anti-Federalists were too diverse to speak with a single voice. They included subsistence farmers living far from urban markets and war veterans who saw their influence in republican government diminished by the proposed system. Many indebted people also opposed ratification, fearing that a strong national government would favor the interests of bondholders and foreign creditors ahead of the economic well-being of ordinary citizens.

If Anti-Federalists were numerous in the remote countryside, Federalists predominated in coastal commercial centers. Using a variety of tactics, they pressed their advantages in the fight to control state ratifying conventions. They lured prominent Anti-Federalist delegates with hints of high office, and they ridiculed vocal opponents as Shaysite extremists. In state after state, they forged coalitions linking commercial farmers living near towns and rivers with aspiring artisans and city-based entrepreneurs. Through intensive politicking, they garnered approval in Massachusetts in February 1788, but only by a thin margin (187 votes to 168 in the ratifying convention). This commitment from "the Bay State" helped to sway Maryland in April, South Carolina in May, and New Hampshire in June. The Federalists could now claim the nine states needed to implement their plan, and in July they staged parades to hail the new Constitution of the United States.

The approved Constitution promptly became the law of the land. But in Massachusetts, the Federalists had triumphed only by promising to add an explicit bill of rights that gave written protection for valued civil liberties. They had to make similar assurances to secure slim majorities in Virginia (89 to 79) and New York (30 to 27). North Carolinians had voted down the proposed frame of government at their first ratifying convention because it lacked a bill of rights. A second North Carolina convention, called in 1789, withheld approval until a bill of rights had actually been introduced into the first Federal Congress as proposed amendments to the Constitution. In 1790, Rhode Island narrowly voted approval for the new framework (34 to 32) rather than risk being left in economic and political isolation.

Adding a Bill of Rights

In a society consisting of almost 3 million people, the franchise remained a limited privilege, open primarily to white men with property. All told, only about 160,000 voters throughout the country took part in choosing representatives to the state ratifying conventions. And only about 100,000 of these people—less than 7 percent of the entire adult population—cast votes for delegates who supported the Constitution. Federalists knew, therefore, that they would have to fulfill their pledge to incorporate a bill of rights. Madison, goaded by Jefferson, promised Virginians that he would push for the inclusion of specific rights as amendments to the Constitution. He had several motives. First, he hoped to ensure his own election to the nation's new House of Representatives. Second, he wanted to head off talk of another convention "for a reconsideration of the whole structure of government."

In compiling a list of protections, or bill of rights, Madison drew from scores of proposals for explicit amendments put forward by the state ratifying conventions. He selected those, mostly dealing with individual rights, that could pass a Federalist-dominated Congress and would not dilute any of the proposed new government's powers. He set aside suggestions for limiting the government's right to impose taxes, raise a standing army, or control the time and place of elections. True to his word, he pushed 12 less controversial statements through the Congress as constitutional amendments, despite congressional apathy and opposition. Within two years, three-fourths of the states ratified ten of these weighty pronouncements. Hence, the first ten amendments—the **Bill of Rights**—quickly became a permanent part of the U.S. Constitution.

Many of the protections provided by the Bill of Rights harked back to lessons learned in earlier struggles with Parliament. The ten amendments guarded the right of the people to bear arms, limited government power to quarter troops in homes, and banned unreasonable searches or seizures. They also ensured the right to trial by jury, outlawed excessive bail and fines, and prohibited "cruel and unusual punishments." The First Amendment secured freedom of speech and of the press, protected people's right to assemble and petition, and prohibited Congress from meddling in the exercise of religion. By securing these freedoms, Madison engineered a final set of compromises that ensured the acceptance and longevity of the Constitution he had done so much to frame.

CONCLUSION

The War for Independence exhausted the new nation. Managing the difficult task of demobilization and reconstruction consumed American energy and resources in the 1780s. So did the new western domain, where Americans had to balance prospects for national expansion against the military threats posed by European empires and Native American groups that claimed the region. Also, economic differences set aside during the war quickly reemerged; questions of wealth and property loomed large.

Therefore, when confederation leaders imposed unprecedented taxes to pay off the war bonds gathered up by wealthy speculators, irate farmers and veterans protested that Congress was gouging "the Many" to enrich "the Few." These numerous dissenters pressured state governments to provide debt relief and issue paper money. But wealthy creditors reacted forcefully: these like-minded men maneuvered to create a new and stronger central government that could support their interests and override state-level economic measures favoring the common people. Sidestepping the existing government, they drafted a new constitution at a closed convention in Philadelphia in 1787, and they campaigned successfully for its ratification by 1789.

The reins of power had nearly slipped from the hands of established American leaders during the tumultuous 1770s. They had restored their secure grip on political affairs by the end of the 1780s in the face of bitter and varied opposition. But the fierce debate over ratification of the Constitution raised fresh uncertainties about the long-term survival of the union. Much hinged on selection of the initial president. Inevitably, George Washington emerged as the overwhelming favorite to become the first chief executive of the new republic.

For Review

✓•⌐Study and Review at www.myhistorylab.com

1. For the numerous debtors during the postwar economic depression of the 1780s, what factors worked for, and against, their interests?

2. To what extent is the genius of the American Constitution found in its unique, innovative structure of checks and balances?

3. If the Constitution's notorious "three-fifths clause" had been a "five-fifths clause" instead, who would have benefited?

4. Did leading nationalists exaggerate the difficulties of the 1780s to suit their agenda, or did they save the new union in a dire situation? Explain.

Chronology: 1783–1789

1783   Treaty of Paris.
Newburgh Conspiracy is thwarted.
Society of the Cincinnati is formed.

1785   Land Ordinance of 1785.

1786   Shays' Rebellion in Massachusetts.

1787   Constitutional Convention meets in Philadelphia.
Constitution of the United States is drafted and signed.
Northwest Ordinance creates Northwest Territory.

1788   Publication of *The Federalist*.
Ratification of the Constitution.
Madison agrees to draft Bill of Rights.

1789   George Washington is elected the first president of the United States.

Key Terms

Anti-Federalists A diverse and unsuccessful coalition that opposed ratification of the Constitution and feared the increased power of the proposed central government. The Anti-Federalists were named by their opponents, the Federalists. p. 210

Bill of Rights A set of amendments assuring basic rights, proposed by James Madison to help ensure acceptance of the newly drafted Constitution, and based on suggestions from the states. Ten of the twelve items passed by Congress were ratified by the states in 1791.

Taken together, these first ten amendments to the Constitution became known as the Bill of Rights. p. 213

Checks and balances The rules controlling interactions among the executive, legislative, and judicial branches of government, making up a novel system designed to prevent any single branch from overreaching its powers, as set forth in the Constitution in 1787. p. 207

Electoral college An intricate system in which each state appoints electors, equal in number to its representation in Congress, to elect the president and vice president. The electoral college is a provision of the Constitution (Article II, Section 1) because the framers were unwilling to approve the direct election of president and vice president. This group, or "college," of electors still makes the selection, voting according to prior party commitments rather than individual choice. p. 208

Federalists A coalition of nationalist leaders who favored creating a stronger central government to replace the Articles of Confederation. They labeled their opponents as Anti-Federalists in the late 1780s. The strongest essays endorsing their proposed new Constitution were entitled *The Federalist*. p. 210

Federation An alliance or compact between political units that agree to surrender certain powers to a central authority while still retaining other powers. p. 189

Separation of powers The novel idea that the powers of the three branches of government—legislative, executive, and judicial—should be kept separate from one another, so that each can check and balance the powers of the other two. p. 207

Suffrage The right to vote. p. 207

Temperance A social movement embracing either total opposition to alcohol consumption or support for its moderate use. p. 195

Three-fifths clause A controversial clause of Article I, section 2, of the U.S. Constitution said that each slave would count as "three-fifths of all other Persons" when representatives and direct taxes were being apportioned to states according to population. Slaves had no rights of citizenship, but the clause gave southern slave states additional power in Congress. Section 2 of the Fourteenth Amendment did away with the clause in 1868. p. 209

9

Revolutionary Legacies, 1789–1803

Revolutionary ideals of freedom and equality were contagious. In the wake of the American Revolution, a young enslaved woman named Ona Judge acted on those ideals and escaped from bondage; she fled the household of her master and mistress, President George Washington and his wife, Martha Custis Washington.

In 1789, when the Washingtons moved from Virginia to New York, and later to Philadelphia (the nation's first capital), they took seven enslaved household workers, including mulatto teenager Ona Judge, the first lady's personal attendant. By the mid-1790s, Ona Judge had made secret plans to escape from Philadelphia. Later, she said that she feared returning to the Washington's Mount Vernon estate, explaining: "I knew that if I went back to Virginia, I should never get my liberty." With help from other blacks in Philadelphia, the young woman found her way to Portsmouth, New Hampshire. There, she hoped, she would begin a new life of freedom.

The president's official duties and his personal interests clashed as he sought to locate the runaway. In 1793, Washington had signed into law the Fugitive Slave Act. This law provided that any owner of a fugitive must receive authorization from a local judge in order to retrieve his or her "property." However, the chief executive ignored this provision of the law and instead directly approached Josiah Whipple, the U.S. customs collector at Portsmouth. Washington claimed that his slave had been abducted by a mysterious Frenchman and directed Whipple to locate and return her.

Whipple managed to find Judge, but after talking to her, he doubted the president's claim that the young girl was the victim of a kidnapping. In a letter to Washington, Whipple noted that "she had not been decoyed away as had been apprehended, but that a thirst for compleat freedom . . . had been her only motive for absconding." He reported that Judge was willing to make a bargain with her master. Because she missed her family at home, she agreed to return to Virginia if Washington would promise to free her. The indignant president refused to negotiate, but at the same time, he did not want to risk causing a public uproar by ordering Whipple to forcibly return her. And so Ona Judge settled into life in New Hampshire. She married John Staines, an African-American sailor, in 1797, and started a family.

The story of Ona Judge reveals that revolutionary ideals reverberated throughout the new nation. After the war, many different groups sought to claim the freedom denied them by law or custom. In New England and the Upper South, increasing numbers of free people of color struggled to assert their rights. Throughout the states, some women had maintained a high degree of political engagement; New Jersey even granted propertied women the right to vote, if only for a brief period. Artisans also sought to wield new political clout. Western migrants, free blacks, women voters, artisan-politicians—they all revealed both the social tensions mounting in the new republic and the promise it offered to these same groups.

During the decade after the Revolution, the population of the new nation grew in size and diversity. The first census of the United States, conducted in 1790, tallied 3,929,214 people. Of this number, 757,208 were black. Throughout the states, people of various ethnicities clustered together in pockets. German-born people accounted for one-third of all Pennsylvanians, and almost one-fifth of New York residents were Dutch. Numbers of Northerners and Southerners were about equal. However, ethnic and regional differences proved less significant in shaping the emerging two-party system than the persistent split between urban-based merchants and rural interests such as southern planters. The Revolution also unleashed enormous creative energy as some people, freed of restrictions imposed by Great Britain, pursued new economic opportunities. In contrast, many artisans and small farmers continued to stagger under a burden of debt and new federal taxes. These groups considered the Revolution a betrayal of their vision for America.

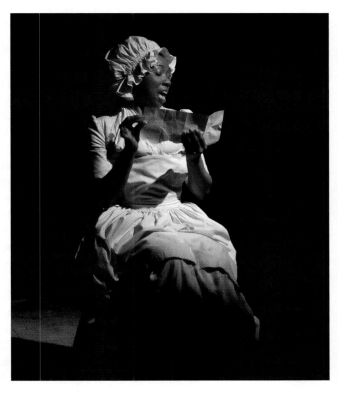

■ **Actress Kameshia Duncan plays the runaway slave Ona Judge in the 2007 Florida Stage production of the play "A House with No Walls" by Thomas Gibbons.**

The impulse for association so evident in the union of states helped to shape postwar society. In the Northwest, Ohio Indians created a confederacy among several groups in order to increase their collective power, much as the colonies had done before the war. And throughout the United States, ordinary people put into practice the grand theories of the Revolution by coming together to effect change. Exhorting their brothers and sisters to join in religious fellowship, revivalists formed new spiritual communities. Reform groups wrote constitutions for themselves in an effort to commit their principles to paper. Temperance advocates joined together and called on men and women to cast off the tyranny of drink.

Most dramatically, opponents of slavery kept alive the rhetoric and the ideals of the Revolution. In 1800, Gabriel, an enslaved blacksmith in Richmond, Virginia, plotted a rebellion to seize the city. His actions gave voice to the egalitarian principles articulated in Philadelphia in 1776 and again in Saint-Domingue in 1791, when slaves staged a bloody revolt against their French masters. (In 1804 they renamed the country Haiti.) Gabriel's rebels used the words of the nation's founders to justify their actions, rallying around the cry "Death or Liberty." One even compared himself to George Washington in his struggle to "obtain the liberty of [his] countrymen." Gabriel's vengeful plans to kill all whites except abolitionists failed when informants betrayed him to Richmond authorities. The foiled slave rebellion in Virginia expressed enslaved people's desire to share in the freedom of the new nation. More generally, in the 1790s, almost all Americans, regardless of creed or color, wrestled with the legacy of the Revolution.

Competing Political Visions in the New Nation

What were the disagreements between the Federalists and the Democratic-Republicans in domestic policy? In foreign policy?

In the first two decades of the new nation, domestic politics remained entwined in relations with the great European powers. For all their bold talk of freedom and liberty, the heirs of the Revolution continued to formulate public policies based upon the models offered by Great Britain and France. Specifically, some Americans found much to admire in British traditions of social order and stability, traditions shaped by a strong central authority in the form of a monarchy. Other Americans derived inspiration from the French Revolution, which began in 1789. They believed that, for all its bloody excesses, the revolution represented an ideal of true democracy, an ideal at odds with entrenched privilege in the form of monarchies and aristocracies. The British model appealed to Federalists, supporters of a strong central government. In contrast, the French model appealed to Anti-Federalists, soon to be called **Democratic-Republicans**, supporters of the rights of the states and of the active participation of ordinary citizens in politics. These divergent views shaped both foreign and domestic policy in the 1790s.

Within this contentious atmosphere, George Washington assumed the presidency in 1789, backed by the unanimous endorsement of the electoral college. Neither the ratification of the Constitution nor Washington's election silenced the continuing debate over civil liberties and the nature of the national government. Responding to the concerns of the Anti-Federalists, Congress quickly passed ten amendments to the Constitution, collectively called the Bill of Rights. Ratified by the necessary number of states in 1791, the amendments were intended to protect white men from the power of government, whether local, state, or national. The Judiciary Act of 1789 established a national, federal court system that included a five-member Supreme Court and the office of attorney general, charged with enforcing the nation's laws.

Like other public figures of the time, Washington believed that ideological differences between political leaders should never become institutionalized in the form of separate parties. These leaders believed politicians should debate issues freely among themselves, without being bound by partisan loyalty to one view or political candidate over another. However, by the late 1790s, the intense rivalry between Alexander Hamilton, Washington's secretary of the treasury, and Thomas Jefferson, his secretary of state, had produced a **two-party system** that proved remarkably durable. Representing two competing political visions, Hamilton and his supporters (known as Federalists) and Jefferson and his supporters (called Democratic-Republicans) disagreed on foreign diplomacy and domestic economic policies. Hamilton advocated a strong central government that would promote commerce and manufacturing. In contrast, Jefferson favored states' rights bolstered by small, independent farmers who would serve as the nation's moral and political center.

In 1792 Washington ran for and won a second term. Four years later, Washington declined to run for a third term. His successor was his vice president, John Adams, an unabashed Federalist who rankled Jefferson and other more egalitarian-minded citizens. Between 1789 and 1800, the clash between the Federalists and the Democratic-Republicans reverberated in the halls of Congress, on the high seas, and in Indian country.

Federalism and Democratic-Republicanism in Action

An outspoken Federalist, Hamilton took bold steps to advance the commercial interests of the new nation. In 1789, as Washington's secretary of the treasury, he persuaded Congress to enact the first U.S. **tariff**, or tax, on imported goods. He argued this move would encourage home manufactures and raise money for the treasury.

Hamilton also sought to strengthen the federal government through **monetary policy**. At his prodding, in 1790 Congress agreed to fund the national debt—that is, to assume responsibility for repaying the government's creditors including paying interest on the debt (a total of $54 million). Congress also assumed responsibility for debts that the individual states had incurred during the Revolution. To pay for all this, federal officials stepped up debt collection and imposed new taxes on individuals. In 1791 Congress also issued a 20-year charter to the first Bank of the United States. Hamilton believed this institution, modeled after the Bank of England, would help stimulate the economy by circulating surplus funds held by the government.

Read the **Document**
Alexander Hamilton, "Bank"
at **www.myhistorylab.com**

An advocate of agricultural interests and the power of individual states, Jefferson disagreed with Hamilton on all these issues. Jefferson bitterly opposed the Bank of the United States, arguing that only the states could issue charters for financial institutions. He favored a lower tariff, arguing that high-priced imports hurt farmers and other small consumers. The leader of the Democratic-Republicans believed that the government should not interfere in the lives of its citizens by imposing new taxes on individual households or on imported goods. According to Jefferson, governments, like individuals, should exercise restraint in their spending and should avoid accumulating debt. Hamilton and Jefferson's opposing views of government shaped the American political party system for generations to come.

The different views epitomized by Hamilton and Jefferson found expression in American reactions to Europe's political turmoil surrounding the French Revolution. Since France had recently been a crucial wartime ally, most Americans at first supported the dramatic events unfolding there in 1789. By imposing constitutional constraints on their king, Louis XVI, the French seemed engaged in a heroic struggle much like that of the Patriots of 1776, who had challenged the enormous power of the British monarch. But when French radicals launched what became known as the Reign of Terror, American public opinion grew more critical.

In January 1793, leaders in Paris beheaded the French king and went on to execute aristocrats and presumed opponents of the revolution. In response, Federalist politicians argued that the bloody excesses in France should push American citizens toward a moderate and stable central government for the United States, more like that of Great Britain. Months later, when France and England went to war over territorial claims in Europe and the West Indies, American public opinion was divided. Fearing dangerous entanglements, President Washington issued a Proclamation of Neutrality at the outbreak of the war, but few Americans could resist taking sides.

Tensions between France and the United States took a turn for the worse when France's first envoy to the United States, Citizen Edmund Genêt, ignored the Neutrality Proclamation and tried to enlist American support for French designs on Spanish Florida and British Canada. Nor did Britain endear itself to its former American subjects during these years. Pursuing French military forces in 1793, the British navy seized 300 American merchant ships plying the West Indian seas, forcing American sailors into service. In a practice known as **impressment**, British sea captains boarded American ships and captured sailors at gunpoint. Meanwhile, along the United States' northwest border, British officials were supplying the Indians of the Ohio Confederacy with guns, alcohol, and encouragement in their fight against the Americans. Feeling squeezed by foreign powers in such ways, many Americans hoped that economic growth could assist the fledgling United States in resisting pressures from European rivals.

Planting the Seeds of Industry

As debates swirled regarding American involvement in international affairs, questions arose over how to deal with the emerging industrial economy at home. During the late eighteenth century, most manufacturing still took place in individual households. Master artisans

Ralph Earl, *Elijah Boardman*, Metropolitan Museum of Art. Bequest of Susan W. Tyler, 1979. (1979.395)

■ **Elijah Boardman of New Milford, Connecticut, poses at his desk in 1789.** The portrait highlights Boardman's success as a merchant. His business prospered because wealthy Americans wanted to dress fashionably, as he did, with his ruffled sleeves, silk stockings, and fancy shoe buckles. By the late eighteenth century, New England merchants were at the center of a thriving worldwide exchange of goods between Europe, the U.S. and China. Their profits helped to finance the country's industrial revolution.

employed journeymen (skilled workers) and apprentices as well as their own wives and children. Throughout New England and the Mid-Atlantic, family businesses made everything from soap and candles to cloth and shoes.

In the 1790s, however, signs of a novel manufacturing economy emerged, especially in the region stretching from New England to New York, New Jersey, and Pennsylvania. This area had all the ingredients for an American Industrial Revolution: water power from rushing rivers, a faltering agricultural economy that western producers would soon eclipse, capital from successful merchants, and a dense population offering both workers and consumers.

Key individuals helped spark the early changes, including Samuel Slater, a 21-year-old English inventor who arrived in the United States in 1791. With financial support from Moses Brown, a wealthy merchant of Providence, Rhode Island, Slater constructed the first American machine for spinning cotton thread and launched his Steam Cotton Manufacturing Company in nearby Pawtucket. The nine boys and girls (ages seven to twelve) hired by Slater to operate the machinery were among America's first factory workers.

In 1793 another innovator, Massachusetts-born Eli Whitney, invented the cotton gin. This machine gave a tremendous boost to both the southern plantation economy and the fledgling northern industrial system. By quickly removing the seeds and other impurities from raw cotton, Whitney's cotton gin fostered the emergence of a new cotton economy. Southern planters expanded their holdings in land and slaves, rushing to meet the rising demand for cotton from mill owners in both England and New England.

By the mid-1790s, Hamilton and his supporters were praising the nation's economic growth and regional specialization. Traditional products of the Atlantic seaboard—tar and turpentine in North Carolina, tobacco in the Chesapeake region, wheat in the Mid-Atlantic states—flourished once again, as early canal and turnpike construction encouraged new markets. In New England, shipbuilding prospered, free from earlier British restrictions, and the fishing and whaling fleets expanded. The forests of Maine and New Hampshire produced wood for hulls, masts, planks, and barrels. In the Deep South, enslaved workers raised cotton, first in South Carolina and Georgia, later in the fertile lands of Alabama and Mississippi. Between 1792 and 1800, annual cotton production jumped from 3 million to 35 million pounds. The figure would soar to 93 million pounds by 1815.

Echoes of the American Revolution: The Whiskey Rebellion

●◗●▪ Read the Document

Whiskey Rebellion Address at **www.myhistorylab.com**

Despite Hamilton's optimism about the economy, Washington's administration faced violent resistance to its policies from certain quarters. In 1794, farmers and grain distillers in southwestern Pennsylvania refused to pay their federal taxes. This **Whiskey Rebellion** was the culmination of a lengthy rural protest against Hamilton's "hard money" policy. By favoring hard currency (coinage) over the more plentiful paper money, the government constricted financial credit. With less money to lend, creditors charged high interest rates for loans. Courts forced debtors such as small farmers to repay loans, even when money was extremely scarce. Those who could not pay their taxes or repay their loans faced foreclosure on their property.

Eager to strengthen the federal government and reduce the national debt, Hamilton devised a federal excise tax on whiskey. The plan was aimed at distillers rather than consumers, and it imposed a higher rate on small producers. Therefore, the tax fell especially hard on backcountry farmers, who distilled their bulky grain harvest into whiskey for efficient shipment to eastern markets. Using the tactics of the Stamp Tax rioters a generation earlier, western Pennsylvania farmers attacked officials and tarred and feathered a man charged with collecting the whiskey tax. They closed courts, blocked roads, and organized mass protests.

Hamilton, believing that a show of force would strengthen the federal government, urged the president to make western Pennsylvania a test case for enforcing the tax. In September, the government federalized 13,000 men from state militias to subdue the rebellion. To underscore the supremacy of the national government over the states, Washington personally led the troops into western Pennsylvania. However, when the soldiers arrived, they found that organized resistance had collapsed.

Washington claimed that the Whiskey Rebellion had been incited by ignorant men who twisted the facts with their "suspicions, jealousies, and accusations of the whole government." Yet he failed to gauge the extent of country dwellers' economic distress. By defying federal authority so openly, the farmers expressed the general grievances of westerners who felt underrepresented in state legislatures and the halls of Congress. They also revealed the deep current of resentment against Federalist policies that was running through rural America.

Courtesy, American Canal and Transportation Center

■ This logo advertises the Hampshire machine. A precursor of the canal lock, the machine consisted of a pulley that carried a canal barge in a cart up an inclined plane. Invented in 1795, it was used on the Connecticut River in western Massachusetts. However, it proved too cumbersome in the long run. Most canals used locks, sections closed off with gates so that the water level could be raised or lowered.

Securing Peace Abroad, Suppressing Dissent at Home

At the same time Washington was dealing with unruly farmers, he also had to address international concerns. In 1794 the president sent Chief Justice John Jay to England to negotiate a key treaty. The negotiations were intended to resolve several problems: British forts in the Northwest Territory, British seizure of American ships and sailors in the West Indies, barriers to Americans trading freely with European belligerents in wartime, and American debts owed to British creditors.

Jay obtained a treaty but failed to extract meaningful compromises from the British government. England grudgingly agreed to evacuate its northern forts and to stop seizing American ships. Jay, however, acquiesced to English demands that individual Americans pay the debts they had owed to English creditors since before the Revolution. The Americans believed that their victory in the war exempted them from long-standing financial obligations to their English creditors. The Democratic-Republicans took alarm at Jay's concessions. In their view, the new agreement humiliated all Americans and threatened southern planters in particular.

Western agricultural interests also sought trade protections from Washington's administration. With the Pinckney Treaty of 1795 (the Treaty of San Lorenzo), they did better than their southern counterparts. Under this agreement, Spain allowed the United States to navigate the Mississippi River freely and to land goods at New Orleans free of taxes for three years.

With their eye on the next presidential election, the Democratic-Republicans began a vigorous campaign in favor of their own candidate, Virginia's Thomas Jefferson. They contrasted Jefferson, the friend of the small farmer, with the Federalists' choice, Vice President John Adams of Massachusetts, an advocate of strong central government run

●●●─ Read the Document
The Jay Treaty (1794) at www.myhistorylab.com

●●●─ Read the Document
The Treaty of San Lorenzo at www.myhistorylab.com

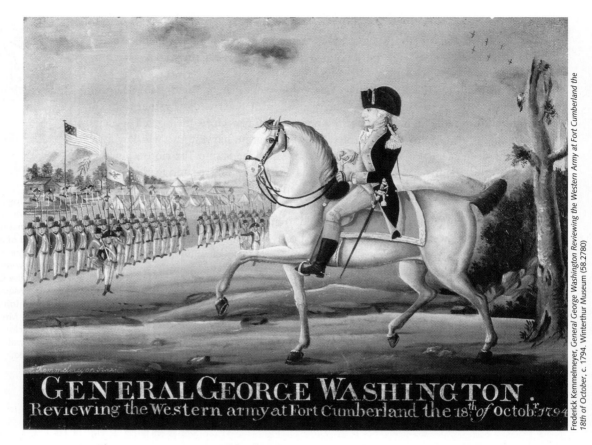

Frederick Kemmelmeyer, General George Washington Reviewing the Western Army at Fort Cumberland the 18th of October, c. 1794. Winterthur Museum (58.2780)

■ This 1794 painting seemingly evokes the American Revolution, when General Washington reviewed American troops. However, in this scene, President Washington is surveying some of the 13,000 state militiamen he commanded in an effort to suppress the Whiskey Rebellion in western Pennsylvania. Farmers objected to the new government tax on whiskey. With cries of "Liberty and No Excise," the protesters harassed federal tax collectors, reminiscent of anti–Stamp Act demonstrations three decades before. The Whiskey Rebellion melted away quickly. Critics objected to Washington's willingness to use such a huge force against protesting American citizens.

by the educated and wellborn. Jefferson's party expressed particular dismay over Washington's haste to crush the rebellious Pennsylvania farmers in 1794 and over Jay's Treaty. Backed by the New England states, Adams won the election, though narrowly. Because Jefferson received the second largest number of electoral votes—68 to Adams's 71—the Virginian became the new vice president according to the terms of the Constitution then in effect (Article II, section I).

In his farewell address, printed in newspapers but not delivered in person, Washington warned against the "insidious wiles of foreign influence" and against entangling alliances with foreign powers that could compromise America's independence and economic well-being. Nevertheless, upon assuming the presidency in 1797, Adams found that European powers still had a hold on American domestic and foreign relations. France began to seize American merchant vessels (300 of them by mid-1797) in retaliation for what it saw as favoritism toward England in Jay's Treaty. In October of that year, President Adams sent John Marshall and Elbridge Gerry to join the U.S. ambassador to France,

TABLE 9-1

The Election of 1796

Candidate	Political Party	Electoral Vote
John Adams	Federalist	71
Thomas Jefferson	Democratic-Republican	68
Thomas Pinckney	Federalist	59
Aaron Burr	Democratic-Republican	30

Charles Pinckney, to negotiate a new treaty with France. However, French intermediaries (referred to only as X, Y, and Z in the Americans' dispatches) demanded that the three U.S. commissioners arrange for a loan of $12 million to France and pay a $250,000 bribe. Only then would the envoys be allowed to speak to the foreign minister, Charles Talleyrand. The sentiments of the American public, outraged at the idea of paying a bribe and willing to defend their new nation against all aggressors, were captured in the cry "Millions for defense, but not one cent for tribute." Adams called the commissioners home, ending the "XYZ Affair."

Federalists throughout the country called for war against France, and the Adams administration sought to shore up the country's military forces by creating the Navy Department and the Marine Corps. Hoping to rid U.S. coastal waters of French ships that were preying on American vessels, in May 1798 Congress authorized American captains to seize such armed "pirates" sent from the Republic of France. Over the next two years, the undeclared so-called Quasi War pitted the American navy against its French counterpart until the two nations signed a treaty, called the Convention of 1800, in Paris.

Conflicts also continued to simmer on the domestic front. The Federalist-dominated Congress passed the **Alien and Sedition Acts** in 1798 to suppress the rising chorus of criticism from rural people, Democratic-Republican leaders, and newspaper editors. Such dissent, Congress charged, amounted to sedition—an act of insurrection against the government. These new laws made it more difficult for immigrants to become resident aliens, gave the president the power to deport or imprison aliens, and branded as traitors any people (U.S. citizens included) who "unlawfully combine or conspire together, with intent to oppose any measure or measures of the government of the United States."

Even though the Alien and Sedition Acts were unconstitutional—they violated the First Amendment's guarantee of freedom of speech—the Federalist-dominated Supreme Court upheld them. Consequently, Democratic-Republicans were by definition guilty of treason, for they advocated policies and supported candidates opposed by the Federalists, the party in power.

●●●─┤Read the Document
The Alien and Sedition Acts at **www.myhistorylab.com**

Ten newspaper editors were convicted, and many others charged and jailed, under the Sedition Act. Some Democratic-Republican lawmakers also spent time in jail because their speech offended their partisan rivals. Congressman Matthew Lyon of Vermont (founder of a newspaper called *Scourge of Aristocracy*) went to prison for suggesting that President Adams showed "unbounded thirst for ridiculous pomp, foolish adulation, and selfish avarice."

In 1798 and 1799, the state legislatures of Kentucky and Virginia issued a series of resolutions condemning the Alien and Sedition Acts. Outraged at what they saw as the Federalists' blatant power grab, the two legislatures proposed that individual states had the right to declare such measures "void and of no force." Thomas Jefferson (for Kentucky) and James Madison (for Virginia) wrote the actual resolutions. As authors of the **Kentucky and Virginia Resolutions**, the two Founding Fathers unwittingly laid the theoretical framework for Southerners to attempt to nullify federal laws in the future.

●●●─┤Read the Document
The Virginia and Kentucky Resolutions at **www.myhistorylab.com**

People of Color: New Freedoms, New Struggles

Despite the rhetoric of equality, North American elites demonstrated a preoccupation with the idea of race as a means of categorizing people. Spanish officials in colonial New Mexico conducted a 1790 census that divided the population into groups based on ethnicity, with specific terms to designate varieties of mixed-race parentage. In the United States, a 1790

In what ways did the legacy of the Revolution shape the lives of African Americans in the North and South?

■ **After the Revolution and well into the early nineteenth century, African Americans, both enslaved and free, served as sailors in disproportionate numbers. This picture suggests the dangers faced by all men who labored on whaling ships. By the 1790s, American whalers were searching for sperm whales as far away as the South Pacific. These whales were the source of several prized substances, including sperm oil (a fuel), spermaceti (used to make candles), and ambergris (an ingredient in expensive perfumes). During the heyday of the sperm whale industry, American fleets were killing 10,000 whales annually.**

Naturalization law limited naturalized U.S. citizenship to "free white persons," mocking the oft-heard claim that all people were equal under the law.

In the United States, the crosscurrents of the revolutionary legacy showed themselves most obviously in the status of African Americans. Most remained enslaved, and their numbers were increasing annually, due to the continuation of the Atlantic slave trade. African Americans like Ona Judge showed extraordinary resourcefulness in escaping slavery and claiming freedom. But even free African Americans faced an uphill struggle in their efforts to achieve political rights and economic well-being. Free people of color created educational and religious institutions that affirmed their sense of community and shared heritage. But persistent white prejudice, sanctioned by law, limited their employment options and condemned many black men and women to poverty. Lacking full citizenship rights, they saw the Revolution as an unfulfilled promise rather than a glorious achievement.

> *In the United States, the crosscurrents of the revolutionary legacy showed themselves most obviously in the status of African Americans.*

Blacks in the North

Between 1790 and 1804, all the northern states abolished slavery. Some, such as New York and New Jersey, did so gradually, stipulating that the children of slaves must serve a period of time (as long as 28 years in certain states) before they could gain their freedom. In 1800 over 36,500 blacks in the North were still enslaved, and some 47,000 were free.

Pennsylvania did not liberate its last slave until 1847. Yet throughout the North, blacks—whether enslaved or free—were only a small percentage of the total population, ranging from less than 1 percent in Vermont to almost 8 percent in New Jersey. Most black men worked as farm hands or manual laborers, most black women as domestic servants or laundresses. Nevertheless, some whites saw black men as rivals for their jobs and as a threat to the well-being of the white population.

At both the state and national levels, most free blacks lacked basic citizenship rights. In 1792, two years after Congress limited naturalized U.S. citizenship to "free white persons," it restricted the militia to white men. State legislatures in New England and the Mid-Atlantic region imposed various other restrictions on free people of color. These measures limited blacks' right to vote, serve on juries, and move from place to place. Rectifying an "oversight" in their state constitutions, New Jersey and Connecticut later took special pains to disfranchise African-American men. Massachusetts offered free blacks the most rights, including the right to vote (for men) and the right of blacks and whites to intermarry.

As slaves, blacks had served in a variety of skilled capacities in the North. Yet as free people, they faced mounting pressures in trying to live independently. Certain jobs, such as those with the federal postal service, remained closed to them by law. And municipal authorities refused to grant them licenses to ply their trades, such as wagon driving. Lacking the means to buy tools and equipment and the ability to attract white customers, many black artisans had to take menial jobs. Increasingly, free black men worked as laborers, sailors, and domestic servants, and black women worked mostly as domestic servants and laundresses.

Still, free blacks in the North set about creating their own households and institutions. They moved out of the garrets and back rooms in houses owned by whites and set up housekeeping on their own. In Boston in 1790, one in three African Americans lived outside white households; 30 years later, eight in ten did so. In response to efforts of white Methodists to segregate church seating, Philadelphia black leaders formed the Free African Society in 1787. The first independent black church in the North, St. Thomas Protestant Episcopal Church, was founded in Philadelphia in the early 1790s. Black people also continued to celebrate their own festivals, typically featuring parades in which men, women, and children came

■ An anonymous artist captured this scene, probably in the slave quarters of a South Carolina plantation, in 1800. It is unknown what kind of entertainment or celebration the musicians and dancers are engaged in. The two men on the right are playing musical instruments of West African origin: a banjo and a quaqua, or skin-covered gourd used as a drum. On large lowcountry plantations especially, Africans and their descendants preserved traditional musical forms and social rituals.

■ MAP 9.1

THE NORTHWEST TERRITORY
After the Revolution, the Northwest Territory became a battleground. Indians—both long-term residents and newcomers—as well as European American squatters and speculators vied for control of the land. The Northwest Ordinance of 1787 provided for territorial governments before an area could apply for statehood. The present-day states of Ohio, Indiana, Michigan, Illinois, and Wisconsin were carved out of Northwest Territory. All had gained statehood by 1848, but only after almost 60 years of bloodshed between Indians and U.S. troops in the region.

together to strut their finery, play drums and other African musical instruments, and proclaim their identity as a free people. The festivals gave blacks an opportunity to escape the confines of the workplace, even if only for a short time, and eat, drink, and dance with other people of color.

Manumissions in the South

Some southern slaves achieved freedom through legal means initiated by their owners. George Washington was not the only wealthy Southerner to move to free his own slaves in his will. In 1782 the Virginia state legislature lifted a 59-year-old ban on manumission, a process by which owners released selected people from bondage. Over the next ten years, approximately 10,000 Virginia slaves gained their freedom through manumission. Some planters believed that the Revolution was the will of God, and they came to believe that slavery violated their religious principles. Some, taking to heart the rhetoric of the Revolution, objected to the glaring contradiction between the ideal of liberty and the reality of bondage. In 1802 a Maryland woman freed her slaves because, she said, the institution went against "the inalienable Rights of Mankind."

In the Upper South, especially, private manumissions dramatically increased the free black population. There, the emergence of a more diversified economy, including craft shops and grist mills, had lowered slave prices and encouraged abolitionist sentiment among some lawmakers, clergy, and slave owners.

> *Some planters objected to the glaring contradiction between the ideal of liberty and the reality of bondage.*

Virginia planters George Washington and Robert Carter were unusual in terms of the numbers of slaves they manumitted (several hundred) and their efforts to ease the transition to freedom for people who possessed neither land nor financial resources. Washington arranged apprenticeships for younger freed blacks and pensions for aged ones. In 1792 Carter granted his older slaves small plots of land. In general, however, newly emancipated men and women had difficulty finding employment as free workers. Nor was their freedom guaranteed: the 1782 Virginia manumission law provided that black debtors could be returned to slavery.

Despite the growth in the free black population, the number of slaves actually increased in the Upper South, from over 520,000 in 1790 to almost 650,000 in 1810. In the South, slavery proved to be an extraordinarily durable institution. At the same time, the institution of bondage spread west with the nation.

Continuity and Change in the West

Blacks may have derived inspiration from the struggle against Great Britain, but as the nation expanded west, so did the institution of slavery and notions of white supremacy. Western communities tended to duplicate their eastern counterparts. The opening of federal lands proved a boon for speculators, who extended credit to homesteaders and profited from the sale of small land parcels. Charged high prices for their purchases and forced to buy expensive supplies transported across the Appalachians, some newcomers rapidly sank into debt. Nor did black Americans fare well, whether slave or free. Before 1800, many white families seeking a fresh start in the trans-Appalachian South took slaves with them into the new states of Kentucky and Tennessee. Even in the Northwest Territory (above the Ohio River), where slavery was prohibited by law, African American arrivals faced the same prejudices that shaped social relations in the East. Rather than extend the bounds of liberty, western settlement solidified ideas about white supremacy.

What were sources of conflict for people who lived in the Northwest Territory and the southern borderlands?

From the Canadian border to Georgia, the trans-Appalachian West had become a cultural battlefield. European Americans warred against Indians, but Indian leaders also disagreed bitterly with one another about how to respond. Should they defend their hunting grounds to the death or seek refuge elsewhere? For most, the answer was neither total resistance nor complete capitulation to an alien culture. Yet one generalization holds true for all inhabitants: the abundance of land and natural resources, combined with the clash of cultures and the prevalence of armed men of different backgrounds, made life particularly dangerous in the borderlands.

Indian Wars in the Great Lakes Region

Native Americans residing in the Northwest Territory in the 1790s included peoples who had long occupied the Great Lakes region and the Upper Midwest, such as the Miami, Potawatomi, Menominee, Kickapoo, Illinois, Fox, Winnebago, Sauk, and Shawnee. Also present were refugees from the East: Ottawa, Ojibway, Wyandot, Algonquin, Delaware, and Iroquois displaced by the Revolutionary War. As they resettled in villages, they managed to retain some elements of their cultural identity, but in the seven years immediately after the Revolution, thousands died in Indian-white clashes in the region.

What caused this violence? By encouraging European Americans to stake their claim to the area, the Northwest Ordinance inflamed passions on both sides: whites' determination to occupy and own the land, and Indians' equal determination to resist this incursion. In 1790, under orders from President Washington, Brigadier General Josiah Harmar led a force of about 1,500 men into the Maumee River Valley in the northwest corner of modern-day Ohio.

Orchestrating two ambushes in September, Miami chief Little Turtle and his men killed 183 of Harmar's troops, driving the general back in disgrace. The next year, Washington chose another officer, General Arthur St. Clair, to resume the fight. But when St. Clair's men met Little Turtle's warriors in November 1791 near the upper Wabash River, the Americans suffered an even greater defeat, losing over 600 men.

Washington tried once more to find a commander equal to Little Turtle. This time he chose General Anthony Wayne, a Revolutionary War hero dubbed "Mad Anthony" for his bold recklessness. Wayne mobilized a force of 3,000 men and constructed a string of new forts as well. At the battle of Fallen Timbers in August 1794, near present-day Toledo, hundreds of Indians perished before Wayne's forces. The withdrawal of British support helped to doom the Ohio Confederacy. On August 3, 1795, 1,100 Indian leaders met at Fort Greenville (in western Ohio) and ceded to the United States a vast tract of Indian land: all of present-day Ohio and most of Indiana. Little Turtle helped negotiate the agreement.

Patterns of Indian Acculturation

White newcomers swiftly made clear their belief that men should farm and herd sheep and cattle, while women should milk cows, raise chickens, tend the garden, spin thread, and weave cloth. However, Indian groups differed in their responses to the various attempts to persuade—or force—them to "acculturate" by adopting novel customs. At first, all learned from each other, as newly arrived settlers and indigenous peoples traded foodways, folk remedies, and styles of dress, adopting foreign habits while still retaining some old ways. Little Turtle himself chose among European-American cultural traits; he drank tea and coffee, kept cows, and shunned leather breeches in favor of white men's clothing. The fact that his wife made butter suggested that she was skilled in the ways of European-American homemakers.

Adopting some habits of European Americans—for example, liquor consumption—amounted to self-destruction. Alcohol was a prized trade item. Moreover, European Americans and Indians often used it to lubricate political negotiations and cultural rituals. Yet conflicts over liquor, and tensions vented under the influence of liquor, became increasingly common—and deadly. Some Indian leaders, such as Joseph Brant and Little Turtle, came to view the drinking of alcohol as a full-blown crisis among their people. Both believed that Indians must reject the white man's bottle if they were to survive.

The migration of whites into Indian hunting grounds rapidly depleted their game supply and devastated their crop fields.

But liquor was only one piece of a larger cultural puzzle, as the experience of the Cherokee, Chickasaw, Choctaw, Creek, and Seminole Indians in the southeastern United States revealed. The migration of whites into their hunting grounds rapidly depleted their game supply and devastated their crop fields. Unable to hunt efficiently for food, many in these groups took up new forms of agriculture after the Revolution, and they became known to whites as the Five Civilized Tribes. Women, who had traditionally tended crops using hoes, gave way in the fields to men, often using plows provided by the federal government. Protestant missionaries encouraged Indian women to learn to spin thread and weave cloth. For more than a generation, the willingness of these southern tribes to accommodate themselves to European-American law and divisions of labor allowed them to stay in their homeland and retain key elements of their cultural identity.

In southwest and far west borderland areas, Spanish officials met with mixed success in their attempts to convert Indians to Christianity and encourage them to engage in sedentary farming. For example, between 1772 and 1804, Spanish priests established 19 missions among the Chumash, hunter-gatherers living in permanent villages along the California coast. When large numbers of the Indians moved to these settlements, they forfeited their traditional kin and trade networks, and their distinctive culture began to fade. Birth rates plummeted due to disruptions in family life (more women than men lived in the missions), and mortality rates increased dramatically as contact with the Spanish introduced new diseases.

In contrast, along the Texas Gulf Coast, the Spanish made little headway in their efforts to bring the Karankawa Indians into the missions. Members of this nomadic tribe arrived at the mission gates only when their own food reserves were low; in essence, the Karankawa simply included the missions in their seasonal migrations between the Gulf Coast and the coastal plain.

Land Speculation and Slavery

The West was not necessarily a place of boundless economic opportunity for all people who settled there. Eager investors and creditors thwarted many homesteaders' quest for cheap land. Schemes such as the Ohio Company of Associates foreshadowed the significance of land speculation in shaping patterns of settlement and property ownership further west in later generations. With backing from wealthy investors, the Ohio Company quickly bought up tracts of land and then sold parcels to family farmers at inflated rates. A similar venture was initiated in Georgia in 1795, when speculators bribed state legislators for the right to resell huge tracts to the west of the state, land that the state did not even own. The state legislature passed the so-called Yazoo Act (named for a Georgia river) because of these bribes. The act resulted in the defrauding of thousands of buyers, whose land titles were worthless.

By protecting slavery and opening new territory to European-American settlement, the new nation condemned southern blacks to a kind of legal bondage that stood in stark contrast to revolutionary principles. Many settlers relied on slave labor. By the late eighteenth century, Kentucky slaves numbered 40,000—more than 18 percent of the state's total population. On wilderness homesteads, where farmers owned just one or two slaves, African Americans faced a kind of isolation unknown on large plantations in the Southeast.

Patterns of land use directly affected the spread of slavery into the West. Despite eastern planters' use of European soil conservation techniques (crop rotation, use of manure as fertilizer), many of them had to contend with depleted soil in the Upper South. Generations of tobacco growers had worn out the land, depriving it of nutrients. As a result, many growers were forced to abandon tobacco. Some of them moved west into Indian lands in the Mississippi Territory to cultivate cotton. The scarcity of labor motivated slave owners to push workers to the limits of their endurance. Slaves cleared potential farmland of underbrush, rooted out tree stumps, and prepared the ground for cultivation. Once cotton could be planted, these same slaves worked in gangs under the sharp eye of a white overseer or black driver. Men, women, and children labored as human machines, forced to plant, hoe, and harvest as much cotton as quickly as possible.

Many free people of color also found a less than hospitable welcome in the West. In 1802 delegates to the first Ohio territorial convention moved to restrict blacks' economic and political opportunities, even though fewer than 400 were living in Ohio at the time. Although slavery was outlawed in Ohio and other territories, blacks still lacked the right to vote. Soon after Ohio became a state in 1803, the legislature took steps to prevent the in-migration of free blacks altogether. In 1803 the territorial legislature of Indiana passed a "black law" prohibiting blacks or Indians from testifying in court against white people. Black families in the Northwest Territory were also vulnerable to kidnapping: some white men seized free blacks and sold them as slaves to plantation owners in the South.

■ In 1791, an artist made this sketch of the wife of a Spanish soldier stationed at the presidio, or military garrison, in Monterey, California. Many elite Spaniards in the Americas went to great lengths to dress like their European counterparts. This woman is wearing the elegant dress, elaborate jewelry, and dainty shoes that befit her status. One eighteenth-century resident of New Mexico wrote that, despite the hot climate, European Americans "will go up to their ears in debt simply to satisfy their pride in putting on a grand appearance." However, most Nuevomexicanos adopted some elements of Indian-style clothing, such as practical leather moccasins and garments made of buckskin and coarse woolens.

Whites in the western territories preserved and adopted slavery to extract financial profit from new areas of settlement.

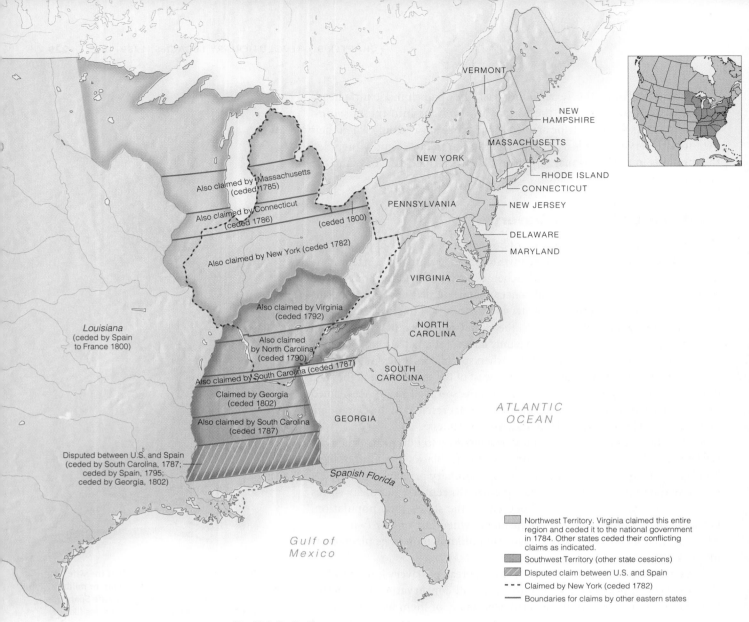

■ MAP 9.2
WESTERN LAND CLAIMS OF THE STATES
Several of the original thirteen colonies, including Massachusetts, Connecticut, New York, Virginia, South Carolina, North Carolina, and Georgia, claimed land west of the Appalachian mountains. By 1802 these states had ceded their western lands to the federal government. The Land Ordinance of 1785 provided that this expanse be auctioned off in parcels no less than 640 acres each, with a minimum price of one dollar per acre—too expensive for many family homesteaders, thus opening the way for investors to purchase and profit. Hoping to raise money through land sales, the federal government did not object to speculation.

What kinds of traditional hierarchies were challenged by different groups of Americans in the wake of the Revolution? How successful were those challenges?

Shifting Social Identities in the Post-Revolutionary Era

The nation's founders had argued for an egalitarian society, one in which people prospered according to their talents and ambition. Of course, their definition of egalitarianism encompassed only white men. Still, it was a revolutionary idea and led to challenges of social hierarchies after the Revolution. These hierarchies included the patriarchal (male-headed) family, established Protestant denominations, power systems based on social standing, and

■ Men and women participate in a Shaker worship service in New Lebanon, New York. The formal name of the church was the United Society of Believers in Christ's Second Appearance. The group's more familiar name derived from their peculiar worship style, which involved trembling and shaking. Members of the group reconfigured traditional family relations. They forbade marriage and sexual intercourse, depending on new converts to expand their ranks. Like several other Protestant denominations, they encouraged congregants to call each other brothers and sisters.

ideas about race and gender. Ordinary men and women penned letters to local newspapers, glorifying common laborers and questioning the claim to power of elite citizens.

In the early nineteenth century, voluntary reform organizations multiplied across the nation. As their numbers proliferated, both the possibilities and limitations of reform became clear. Some groups—for example, white working men—sought to advance their own self-interest without showing much concern for the plight of African-American laborers. In other cases, people banded together to target the behavior of a specific group: drunkards, slave owners, the irreligious, or prostitutes. These moral reform groups welcomed diversity among members, as long as new converts supported the cause.

Artisan-Politicians and Menial Laborers

In the decades after the Revolution, residents of port cities along the eastern seaboard grew accustomed to public parades marking special occasions: a visit from George Washington, the ratification of the Constitution, the Fourth of July. Most of these parades consisted of groups of artisans marching together, carrying the banners of their respective occupations. As one example, the bricklayers' flag declared, "Both Buildings and Rulers Are the Works of Our Hands."

Proud of their role in the Sons of Liberty and other revolutionary organizations, bricklayers—along with tanners, carpenters, glassblowers, weavers, and other groups of artisans—proclaimed themselves the proud citizens of the new nation. American worker organizations built on a distinct revolutionary heritage that stressed the equality of all (white) freeborn men. Master artisans in several cities—including Boston, Albany,

INTERPRETING HISTORY

A Farmer Worries About the Power of "The Few," 1798

After the Revolution, many ordinary Americans debated the challenges faced by the new nation. For example, C. William Manning, a tavern keeper and farmer in Massachusetts, in 1798 wrote an essay titled "The Key of Liberty." Manning warns about the power of "the few"—the wealthy and influential—over the power of "the many"—ordinary people who must work hard for a living.

"In the sweat of thy face shalt thou get thy bread, until thou return to the ground," * is the irreversible sentence of Heaven on man for his rebellion. To be sentenced to hard labor during life is very unpleasant to human nature. There is a great aversion to it perceivable in all men; yet it is absolutely necessary that a large majority of the world should labor, or we could not subsist. For labor is the sole parent of all property; the land yields nothing without it, and there is no . . . necessary of life but what costs labor and is generally esteemed valuable according to the labor it costs. Therefore, no person can possess property without laboring unless he gets it by force or craft, fraud or fortune, out of the earnings of others.

But from the great variety of capacities, strength, and abilities of men, there always was and always will be a very unequal distribution of property in the world. Many are so rich that they can live without labor—also the merchant, physician, lawyer, and divine, the philosopher and schoolmaster, the judicial and executive officers, and many others who could honestly get a living without bodily labors. As all these professions require a considerable expense of time and property to qualify themselves therefore, . . . so all these professions naturally unite in their schemes to make their callings as honorable and lucrative as possible.

Also, as ease and rest from labor are reasoned among the greatest pleasures of life, pursued by all with the greatest avidity, and when attained at once create a sense of superiority; and as pride and ostentation are natural to the human heart, these orders of men generally associate together and look down with too much contempt on those that labor.

As the interests and incomes of the few lie chiefly in money at interest, rents, salaries, and fees, that are fixed on the nominal value of money, they are interested in having money scarce and the price of labor and produce as low as possible. . . .

Providence, Portsmouth, Charleston, Savannah, and New York—created organizations called the General Society of Mechanics and Tradesmen that brought together skilled workers from a variety of fields. The proliferation of newspapers let these artisans participate in a new, more open public forum. Such participation in turn helped them to gain greater influence within local politics. In some towns, as many as 85 percent of adult men owned property of some kind and thus were eligible to vote. Indeed, artisans' organizations soon became quasi-political groups, extending their reach in ways that pre-Revolutionary trades-based associations had not.

But not all workers were so secure. The diggers who constructed the early canals of the 1790s included men from all walks of life: part-time farmers, indentured servants, slaves, and white transients. Moving around in search of work, they led an unsettled existence that contrasted greatly with the more predictable life of urban artisans. Canal diggers represented a transition workforce of sorts, bridging the worlds of traditional, outdoor work with the more disciplined, regimented pace of the factory.

The plight of menial laborers (in the countryside and the cities) suggests the ironies that accompanied the decline of indentured servitude and the rise of the "free laborer." To be sure, master artisans attained a degree of economic independence. But for men and women who lacked skills, money, and wealthy patrons, freedom often meant financial insecurity and, in some cases, reliance on public or private charity. Those who did find work usually had the kinds of jobs that came with the booming economy of the late eighteenth century: moving goods from one place to another, building new structures, and providing personal services for the merchants who profited from all this commercial activity.

But the greatest danger the many are under in these money matters is from the judicial and executive officers, especially so as their incomes for a living are almost wholly gotten from the follies and distress of the many—they being governed by the same selfish principles as other men are. They are the most interested in the distresses of the many of any in the nation; the scarcer money is and the greater the distresses of the many are, the better for them. . . .

This is the reason why they ought to be kept entirely from the legislative body; . . . For in all these conceived differences of interests, it is the business and duty of the legislative body to determine what is justice, or what is right and wrong; and it is the duty of every individual in the nation to regulate his conduct according to their decisions. . . .

The reason why a free government has always failed is from the unreasonable demands and desires of the few. They cannot bear to be on a level with their fellow creatures, or submit to the determinations of a legislature where (as they call it) the swinish multitude is fairly represented, but sicken at the idea, and are ever hankering and striving after monarchy or aristocracy, where the people have nothing to do in matters of government but to support the few in luxury and idleness.

For these and many other reasons, a large majority of those that live without labor are ever opposed to the principles and operation of a free government; and though the whole of them do not amount to one-eighth part of the people, yet, by their combinations, arts, and schemes, have always made out to destroy it sooner or later.

Genesis 3:19

Questions

1. *According to Manning, why have attempts at "free government" failed in the past?*
2. *How do you think Manning would view the institution of slavery?*
3. *What is the significance of the fact that Manning never published his views? What does this fact tell us about the nature of political debates during this time?*
4. *Do you think Manning is referring to Federalists when he condemns "the few"? Why or why not?*

Source: C. William Manning, "The Key of Liberty" (1798), in *Major Problems in American History, Vol. 1: To 1877*, Elizabeth Cobbs Hoffman and Jon Gjerde (Houghton Mifflin, 2002), 170–171.

"Republican Mothers" and Other Well-Off Women

The post-Revolutionary period was a time of flux for various groups of women as well as for male workers. Some well-educated women in the United States read English writer Mary Wollstonecraft's *Vindication of the Rights of Woman* published in England and America in 1792. In that manifesto, Wollstonecraft argued that young men and women should receive the same kind of education. She objected to a special female curriculum that exclusively emphasized skills such as needlepoint and musical accomplishments; this "false system of education," she charged, left women "in a state of perpetual childhood."

In 1801 an anonymous "American Lady" published an essay titled "A Second Vindication of the Rights of Woman." In it, she claimed that "a good kitchen woman [that is, a household drudge], very seldom makes a desirable wife, to a man of any refinement." The anonymous "American Lady" and others who shared her opinion celebrated a new kind of woman—the **Republican mother**—who provided cultured companionship for her husband and reared her children to be virtuous, responsible members of society. This image of womanhood promoted the idea that well-off women should dedicate themselves to tending the home fires rather than aspiring to a more public role in business or politics.

Prior to the Revolution, women tended to bear many children, since additional hands were needed to labor in the fields. But as the sons of farmers became store managers and bookkeepers, they had less need for the unpaid labor of their own children. The decline in white women's fertility rates after the Revolution suggests that the economy had shifted. And some women could now buy products their grandmothers had made at home. In particular, a small but influential group of well-to-do women in the cities were shedding their roles as producers of candles, soap, and textiles. Instead, they became consumers of these staples and of luxury goods, and they managed household servants. "Republican mothers" participated in the public life of the new nation as the guardians of the home and the socializers of children.

But the idea of the "Republican mother" also suggested a more radical notion. If such a woman wanted to earn the respect accorded all intelligent human beings, she must strive for an education equal to that of men's. In the 1790s, a number of academies for "young ladies" opened in New England. These schools offered courses in such "womanly pursuits" as needlework, etiquette, and music. But many also offered a classical curriculum consisting of mathematics, foreign languages, and geography. This system of study encouraged young women to think for themselves. In this respect, female academies challenged the view that women were intellectually inferior to and necessarily dependent on men.

A Loss of Political Influence: The Fate of Non-Elite Women

The Revolution had given elite white women a rationale for speaking out in the realm of politics. Yet the war had a very different impact on other groups of women. Many Native American women, feeling the pressure of non-Indian cultures, found their traditional roles

■ James Peale completed this painting of his family in 1795. Peale came from a distinguished family of artists. The picture represents the ideal of post-Revolutionary citizenship and family life. Husband and wife are both featured prominently, although their roles differ. The husband represents the household in the public, political sphere. The wife, a devoted mother, is responsible for preparing the children to be virtuous citizens of the new republic. Growing up in a well-to-do home, these playful children are exempt from the hard labor associated with childhood in the colonial period and, in the 1790s, still characteristic of childhood among enslaved, rural, and poor families.

had been weakened by the end of the eighteenth century. For example, among the Cherokee, the introduction of a European-American division of labor lessened women's customary political influence as leaders and diplomats. Most European Americans believed that only men should serve in positions of authority, and so Cherokee women felt pressed to refrain from taking part in political negotiations and to subordinate themselves to men.

In the West, Indian women bore the brunt of ongoing conflicts between their own people and European-American settlers. In New Mexico, female Indian captives from Plains tribes (such as the Apache, Comanche, and Kiowa) became *indios servientes* in Hispanic households. In the East, Native American women dispossessed of their land pieced together a meager existence. For example, in Natick, Massachusetts, women turned to weaving and peddling baskets and brooms while their men scrounged for wage labor.

For some Americans, the postwar years brought unprecedented opportunities to buy, sell, and trade. However, commercial development, combined with race and gender discrimination, offered only modest possibilities for many impoverished women and women of color. Like other free blacks, Chloe Spear of Boston "worked early and late" at a number of jobs, such as laundering and ironing clothes. Eventually, she managed to purchase her own home. In Rhode Island, Elleanor Eldrige started her work career at age ten in 1795. Thereafter, she labored as a domestic servant, spinner, weaver, dairymaid, and nurse. She finally went into business, first as a soapboiler and then as a wallpaperer and house painter. However, like many free blacks, Eldrige remained vulnerable to the machinations of white men who tried to defraud her of her hard-won earnings.

> *Commercial development, combined with race and gender discrimination, offered only modest possibilities for many impoverished women and women of color.*

Some white women also felt the effects of fluctuations in the market economy. In Philadelphia in the mid-1790s, two former servants—Polly Nugent (married to a blacksmith who had just lost his job) and Grace Biddle (newly widowed)—had to plead for assistance from their former mistress, Elizabeth Drinker. The city's "Bettering House" for indigent people housed men and women, blacks and whites. In the period after the Revolution, many women had neither the resources nor the opportunities to improve their lot.

The Election of 1800: Revolution or Reversal?

The social turbulence of these years also played out in the political arena. The campaign of 1800 pitted Thomas Jefferson and his vice-presidential running mate, Aaron Burr, against the incumbent, John Adams, and his vice-presidential nominee, Charles Pinckney. Certain elements of the campaign were predictable. The Democratic-Republicans blasted Alexander Hamilton's economic policies and the Adams administration's military buildup. Jefferson's party also condemned the Alien and Sedition Acts, used to silence Adams's political opponents. For their part, the Federalists portrayed Jefferson as a godless supporter of the French Revolution. They also charged that he had fathered children by one of his slaves, Sally Hemings. (Two centuries later, the preponderance of evidence, including the Hemings family's oral traditions and DNA evidence, suggests that this assertion was true.)

In what ways did the election of the Democratic Republican Thomas Jefferson signal a new direction for the new nation?

Jefferson prevailed in the 1800 election, but his victory did not come easily. The electoral college allowed delegates to vote separately for president and vice president, and as a result Jefferson tied with Burr. Each man received 73 votes. Then the decision went to the House of Representatives, which was dominated by Federalists. After a series of tied votes, Jefferson finally gained a majority. His selection in February 1801 marked the orderly transfer of power

TABLE 9-2		
The Election of 1800		
Candidate	Political Party	Electoral Vote
Thomas Jefferson	Democratic-Republican	73
Aaron Burr	Democratic-Republican	73
John Adams	Federalist	65
Charles C. Pinckney	Federalist	64

from the Federalists to the Democratic-Republicans, a peaceful revolution in American politics.

As chief executive, Jefferson did little to change the direction of the country. Aware of his razor-thin victory, he retained many Federalist appointees. And his eagerness to expand the boundaries of the United States—which culminated in the Louisiana Purchase of 1803—solidified the Hamiltonian principles that favored commerce and trade over agrarian values.

The Enigmatic Thomas Jefferson

Who was Thomas Jefferson? In 1800 Jefferson, the presidential candidate, wrote, "I have sworn upon the altar of God eternal hostility against every form of tyranny over the mind of man." Yet Jefferson's own views on ordinary people were less heroic. Specifically, his deep skepticism about African American equality and the viability of Indian cultures helped to justify violent assaults on both groups in the early nineteenth century.

Many Americans today know Jefferson as the author of the Declaration of Independence. But he also sought to defend slavery as a central institution in the new republic, and he regarded blacks as lacking in imagination and intelligence. Jefferson wrote much about the noble calling of the yeoman farmer. Yet he assigned the task of tilling the soil on his own estate (Monticello, near Charlottesville, Virginia) to his enslaved workers.

The president's views on Indians also did nothing to reverse the course of aggression in the West. He believed that land ownership created the stable institutions necessary for civilized behavior. Yet the system of private property, and the violent methods that whites used to enforce it, spelled the destruction of traditional Indian ways of life.

View the **Image**
Jefferson and Liberty at
www.myhistorylab.com

It is tempting to excuse Jefferson's prejudiced beliefs by saying he merely reflected his time. But in fact, a significant number of Jefferson's contemporaries were voicing their misgivings about slavery. While Jefferson acknowledged their arguments, he did not share their beliefs. A citizen of a trans-Atlantic "republic of ideas," he corresponded with political thinkers—from John Adams to the Marquis de Lafayette—who understood the inherent tension between freedom for whites and slavery for blacks. Obviously, Jefferson knew that some of the northern states had written constitutions that incorporated the sentiments of the Declaration of Independence in ways that justified the abolition of slavery. Moreover, a notable number of Jefferson's wealthy Virginia compatriots (including George Washington) had chosen to free their slaves, either by their own hand or through provisions of their wills, to practice in their own households what they preached to British tyrants.

The United States provided the political theory and rhetoric to inspire abolitionists around the globe, but within the new nation, the debate over the institution of slavery continued to rage.

Jefferson lived in an age when revolutionary enthusiasm was sweeping the western world. Challenges to slavery had rocked Europe; France outlawed the practice in 1794, although Napoleon later reinstated it. Abolition had also transformed the Western Hemisphere with the successful rebellion of the Saint-Domingue slaves in 1791. The United States provided the political theory and rhetoric to inspire abolitionists around the globe, but within the new nation, the debate over the institution of slavery continued to rage. The southern states, in particular, took decisive steps to solidify the institution within their own boundaries.

Protecting and Expanding the National Interest

As president, Jefferson reconsidered his original vision of the United States: a compact country in which citizens freely pursued modest agrarian interests without interference from the national government or distractions from overseas conflicts. Indeed, during his years in office, the federal government moved toward increasing its power.

Just before Jefferson assumed the presidency, the Federalist-dominated Congress had strengthened the national court system by passing the Judiciary Act of 1801. The act created 16 circuit (regional) courts, with a judge for each, and bolstered support staff for the judicial branch in general. President Adams appointed these judges (so-called midnight judges because they were appointed right before Jefferson took office). Before stepping down, Adams had also appointed Secretary of State John Marshall as chief justice of the Supreme Court.

Adams's last-minute acts had long-term consequences. Marshall remained on the bench for 34 years. He presided over the court when it rendered its landmark *Marbury v. Madison* decision in 1803, which established the judiciary's right to declare acts of both the executive and legislative branches unconstitutional. Chief Justice Marshall wrote: "It is emphatically the province and duty of the judicial department to say what the law is."

In the realm of international affairs, Jefferson asserted his own authority. Challenges from foreign powers prompted the Democratic-Republican president to take bold steps to protect U.S. economic and political interests abroad and along the country's borders. In 1801 Jefferson's administration launched a war against Barbary pirates in North Africa when Tripoli (modern-day Libya) demanded ransom money for kidnapped American sailors. (Together, the North African kingdoms of Tunis, Tripoli, Algeria, and Morocco were known as the Barbary States.) The war against Tripoli, which spanned four years, revealed the extent of U.S. trade interests even at this early point in the nation's history. The United States signed a peace treaty with Tripoli in 1805 and paid $60,000 for the release of the American captives.

At the beginning of the nineteenth century, the European powers continued their operations in the territory west of the United States. In 1801 Napoleon persuaded the King of Spain to secretly cede the trans-Mississippi region called Louisiana to France. Retaining control of New Orleans, Spain denied Americans the right to use that city as a depository for goods awaiting shipment. In 1803 Jefferson sent his fellow Virginian, and prominent Anti-Federalist, James Monroe to Paris. Together with American ambassador Robert Livingston, Monroe set out to secure American trading rights to New Orleans. To the Americans' surprise, Napoleon agreed to sell the whole area to the United States. At the time, Louisiana included most of the territory between the Mississippi River and the Rocky Mountains—a total of 828,000 square miles. The United States agreed to pay $15 million for the Louisiana Purchase.

The European powers continued their operations in the territory west of the United States.

The Louisiana Purchase reversed the roles of Jefferson and his Federalist rivals. The president advocated territorial expansion, but his opponents remained suspicious of the move. Devoted to a strict interpretation of the Constitution, Jefferson traditionally favored limiting federal authority. Yet he sought to justify the purchase by pointing out that it would finally rid the area of European influence. He proposed shifting Indians from the Mississippi Territory (part of present-day Alabama and Mississippi) to the West so that American newcomers could have the eastern part of the country to themselves. For their part, the Federalists feared that Louisiana would benefit mainly agrarian interests and eventually dilute New England's long-standing political influence and power. They suspected Jefferson of attempting to expand the influence of his own political party.

CONCLUSION

In his first inaugural address, Jefferson suggested that both parties, despite their differences, shared similar views about the role of government and the importance of economic opportunity for ordinary people. Seeking unity after a partisan campaign, he reminded political leaders, "We are all Republicans, we are all Federalists." Indeed, most public officials at the time held a common suspicion of groups that professed religious beliefs that lay outside the mainstream of Protestantism or liberal Deism (a general belief in God without ties to a particular religious denomination). They considered slavery less a moral issue than a political matter that individual states must address. They united behind the idea that Indians, blacks, and women should have no formal voice in governing the nation.

Nevertheless, the post-Revolutionary era saw the rise of two opposing camps—those favoring local control and those supporting federal authority. Many people defined political interests in "either-or" terms: either the French system of political equality or the British monarchy; either the individual states or the federal government; either the farm or the factory. Such thinking promoted a narrow view of the United States, already a society of great economic and ethnic diversity.

Despite this ideological split, the new nation gave white men opportunities practically unknown in the rest of the world. Regardless of their background, many white men could aspire to own property, to enjoy impressive legal rights, and to participate in the political process. The federal government supported economic growth by facilitating territorial expansion, technological innovation, and the protection of private property. As much for the prosperity it promoted as for the noble ideas it nourished, the Revolution continued to inspire liberation movements within the United States and throughout the world.

For Review

✓●–⌐Study and Review at www.myhistorylab.com

1. What were the limitations of the "either-or" clash of ideas between the Federalists and the Democratic-Republicans? How might an enslaved Southerner, or a member of one of the Five Civilized tribes, have perceived this political debate?

2. Choose three different groups and describe the ways the legacy of the Revolution affected their postwar experiences. Consider, for example, these issues: legal status, religious beliefs, labor, community life, and culture.

3. How did relations with European countries shape political debates in the United States between 1789 and 1803? In what ways had the new nation not fully achieved its independence?

4. In political terms, at least, the United States emerged from the Revolution as a unified nation. In what ways did regional distinctions challenge the notion—or ideal—of unity among all Americans?

Chronology: 1789–1803

1789 Judiciary Act of 1789 establishes national court system.

1790 Congress restricts citizenship to "free white persons." Northern states take steps to abolish slavery.

1791 Bill of Rights is ratified.
Slaves revolt in Saint-Domingue (Haiti). Samuel Slater constructs first spinning machine on U.S. soil.
Bank of the United States is chartered.

1792 Washington is reelected president. Mary Wollstonecraft publishes *A Vindication of the Rights of Woman*.

1793 Washington issues Neutrality Proclamation.
Eli Whitney invents the cotton gin.

1794 U.S. troops defeat forces of Ohio Confederacy.
Whiskey Rebellion takes place in Pennsylvania.

1796 John Adams is elected president.

1797 XYZ Affair stirs anti-French sentiment.

1798 Quasi War waged with France (to 1800).
Alien and Sedition Acts passed.

1800 Thomas Jefferson is elected president.

1801 War waged against Barbary pirates.

1803 Jefferson buys Louisiana Purchase. *Marbury v. Madison* decided.

Key Terms

Alien and Sedition Acts Laws enacted by the Federalist-dominated Congress in 1798 to limit the speech of their critics and to make it more difficult for immigrants to become citizens. p. 223

Democratic-Republicans The political party that emerged after the Revolution to oppose the Federalists' support for a strong central government; favored states' rights and the agrarian way of life. Thomas Jefferson, a leader of the Democratic-Republicans, was elected president in 1800. p. 218

Impressment A policy that authorizes the seizure of persons or private property in the service of a government. p. 219

Kentucky and Virginia Resolutions Resolutions issued by two state legislatures in 1798 in response to the Alien and Sedition Acts passed by Congress; proclaimed that individual states had the right to declare such measures "void and of no force." p. 223

Marbury v. Madison An 1803 Supreme Court decision establishing the right of the judiciary to declare acts of both the executive and legislative branches unconstitutional. p. 237

Monetary policy Government policies designed to affect the national economy through bank lending policies, interest rates, and control of the amount of money in circulation. p. 219

Republican mother A wife and mother whose primary role is caring for and socializing future citizens (her children); an ideal favored by some elites after the American Revolution. p. 233

Tariff A government tax on imported goods. p. 218

Two-party system A system of government characterized by two major political parties that compete against each other in "winner take all" elections. p. 218

Whiskey Rebellion Protest in 1794 by western Pennsylvania farmers and grain distillers who objected to a high federal tax on the whiskey they produced. p. 220

PART FOUR

Expanding the Boundaries of Freedom and Slavery, 1804–1848

IN THE FIRST HALF OF THE NINETEENTH CENTURY, FEW IF ANY NATIONS could rival the United States's remarkable record of growth. At its founding, the country consisted of 4 million people living in 13 states that hugged the eastern seaboard of North America. By the mid-nineteenth century, the nation's population had grown to 23.2 million people as a result of reproduction, foreign immigration, and the conquest of indigenous and Spanish-speaking peoples. Because of a mix of diplomatic pressure and military aggression, dramatic geographic expansion accompanied the burgeoning population growth. By 1850 the country sprawled the breadth of the continent to the Pacific Ocean.

Territorial expansion, economic growth, and increasing ethnic diversity profoundly shaped American politics in the first half of the nineteenth century. Innovations in transportation (the steamboat), communication (the telegraph), and the production of crops and textiles (reapers and mechanical looms) allowed Americans to move materials, people, and information more quickly and to produce food and goods more efficiently. Meanwhile, the immigration of large numbers of western Europeans, the rapid expansion of the free black population, and the conquest of Spanish-speaking peoples in the Southwest in 1848 challenged the United States's view of itself as an exclusively Anglo-Protestant nation.

Some citizens declared that the United States had a God-given duty and God-given right to expand its borders in opposition to the British and Russians in the Northwest and in opposition to Spain and later Mexico in the South and Southwest. Thus, territorial expansion brought the United States into conflict with other countries and groups that claimed the land. America's victory in the War of 1812 secured the nation's Great Lakes border and at the same time proved that American soldiers and sailors were the equal of England's seasoned fighting forces. In 1823, fearful that

European powers would take advantage of independence movements in Latin America, the United States issued the Monroe Doctrine, stating that the era of colonization of the Americas was over.

Nevertheless, Indian tribes continued to resist the incursion of European Americans who believed that land was a commodity to be wrested from native peoples and then bought and sold. In the southern part of the country, the Five Civilized Tribes and other Native American groups occupied territory coveted by both gold seekers and cotton growers. Many American voters demanded that their political leaders work to expand the nation's boundaries through a variety of means: treaty, negotiation, or military force.

Andrew Jackson, who assumed the presidency in 1828, seemed a fitting symbol and a representative politician of the age. Determined to expand the power of the executive branch of government, Jackson claimed to represent the interests of ordinary people in his political battles against the Second Bank of the United States and the Supreme Court and in his forceful removal of Indian tribes from the Southeast to Indian Territory (present-day Oklahoma). Like other politicians of the time, Jackson conceived of citizenship as a system of rights and privileges for white men only.

Still, European Americans trumpeted the arrival of a new era of egalitarianism. Western settlers laid claim to political power, and suffrage restrictions based on property ownership crumbled in the wake of egalitarian legislation and rhetoric. Americans were restless, moving out west and back east again, around the countryside, and in and out of cities. Believing that people could and should work together to reform society, many created reform associations, embraced new religious beliefs, and joined political parties. New forms of association yielded new kinds of communities in an era characterized by great geographical mobility.

At the same time, two distinct power systems coalesced to ensure that certain groups would monopolize the political and economic life of the country. In the South, cotton planters launched an aggressive defense of the institution of slavery. In the North, an emerging socioeconomic class system deepened the differences between the political influence and material well-being of factory owners and machine operators.

For the country, therefore, growth brought great promise and great peril. Abolitionists, associations of working people, nativists (people hostile to immigrants), women's rights advocates, and a variety of other groups proclaimed their agendas for social change. Most significantly, by 1848 it was becoming more difficult for national legislators to resolve the question of whether to allow slavery in the territories. As passions rose, few could imagine a political compromise that would satisfy abolitionists and proslavery advocates alike. As midcentury approached, more and more Americans seemed prepared to express their convictions—or their prejudices and resentment—through violent means.

1827	Workingmen's Party founded in Philadelphia
1828	*Cherokee Phoenix* begins publication
1829	Gold discovered on Cherokee lands in Georgia
1831	Nat Turner leads slave rebellion in Virginia
	William Lloyd Garrison publishes *The Liberator*
1832	Nullification crisis
	Worcester v. Georgia
	Jackson vetoes Second Bank of the United States
	Black Hawk War
1833	Great Britain abolishes slavery
	National Road completed
1834	Cyrus McCormick patents reaper
	First strike at Lowell mills
	Whig Party organized
1835	Alexis de Tocqueville, *Democracy in America*
	Texas revolts against Mexico
1836	Congress passes gag rule on antislavery petitions
	Republic of Texas founded
1837	Panic of 1837
	John Deere invents steel plow
1838	Pennsylvania revokes black male suffrage
	Cherokee removal begins; Trail of Tears
1840	Liberty Party founded
1841	John Tyler assumes presidency after death of William Henry Harrison
	Supreme Court rules in favor of *Amistad* Africans
1844	Mormon leader Joseph Smith killed by mob in Nauvoo, Illinois
1845	Irish potato famine
	Frederick Douglass, *Narrative of the Life of Frederick Douglass*
	Texas becomes twenty-eighth state
1846	Great Britain cedes southern part of Oregon Country to United States
	Mexican-American War begins
1847	United States wins battles of Buena Vista, Vera Cruz, Mexico City
	Capture of San Patricio soldiers, Battle of Churubusco
1848	Treaty of Guadalupe Hidalgo ends Mexican-American War
	Women's Rights convention in Seneca Falls, New York
	Popular revolutions sweep Europe

10

Defending and Expanding the New Nation, 1804–1818

In early November 1804, a group of soldiers worked feverishly to construct a rough military garrison on the north bank of the Missouri River, near several Mandan Indian villages just west of modern Washburn, North Dakota. The soldiers knew they had to work quickly. Within a month, winter would descend on the northern Great Plains, and the temperature would plummet. In fact, not long after Fort Mandan was completed, the temperature registered at 45 degrees below zero Fahrenheit.

The garrison provided shelter for the members of the **Lewis and Clark Expedition**, a party of exploration led by Meriwether Lewis and William Clark. Both captains in the U.S. Army, Lewis and Clark had been commissioned by President Thomas Jefferson to explore the upper reaches of the newly acquired Louisiana Territory, which had doubled the size of the country. With the ultimate goal of reaching the Pacific Coast in what today is Oregon, their party spent the winter at Fort Mandan and joined the buffalo hunts and nightly dances sponsored by their hosts, the Mandan Indians. Between November 1804 and March 1805, Lewis and Clark also found time to record their observations on all manner of things natural and cultural. In their journals and their letters to President Jefferson, they described the language of the Hidatsa Indians and the beadwork of the Arikara, the medicinal properties of native plants, and the contours of the Missouri River. In a shipment prepared for the president, they included deer horns, pumice stones, and the pelt of a white weasel. Among an assortment of live animals, only a magpie and a prairie dog survived the journey to Washington, D.C.

Lewis and Clark's trek took 28 months to complete and covered 8,000 miles. Their expedition's purpose was partly scientific, but Jefferson had also commissioned them to chart a northwestern waterway passage to the Pacific coast. The president hoped to divert the profitable fur trade of the far Northwest away from British Canada and into the hands of Americans by locating a river connecting this larger Northwest directly to eastern U.S. markets. Jefferson also instructed Lewis and Clark to initiate negotiations with various Indian groups, to pave the way for miners and ranchers to move into the area.

Lewis and Clark's party consisted of a diverse group of people, including British and Irish enlisted men, and Lewis's African-American slave, York. At Fort Mandan, the group picked up Toussaint Charbonneau, a French Canadian, and his 15-year-old wife, Sacajawea, a Shoshone Indian. The explorers came to rely on Sacajawea's skills as an interpreter. And because women never traveled with Indian war parties,

Sacajawea's presence reassured suspicious Native Americans that the goal of the expedition was peaceful.

During the first two decades of the nineteenth century, the United States faced a number of challenges from within and outside its borders, challenges that had longlasting political and economic effects. Indians in general were a persistent threat to the new nation. Indeed, in the Great Lakes region, various tribes maintained political and military alliances with the British in Canada. Nevertheless, in this period the United States successfully met its most severe test to date: a war with Great Britain that raged from 1812 to 1815. The effects of this "Second American Revolution" were far-reaching. The conflict eliminated the British from the Old Northwest once and for all. The war also spurred industrialization and stimulated commerce. In the South, the cotton plantation system began to shape the political and economic life of the entire region, in the process expanding human bondage.

👁️ **See** the **Map**

Louisiana Purchase and Exploration of the Trans-Mississippi West at **www.myhistorylab.com**

▶️ **Watch** the **Video**

Lewis and Clark: what were they trying to accomplish? at **www.myhistorylab.com**

■ **Captain Meriwether Lewis posed in Indian dress for this watercolor completed in 1807 by French artist C.B.J. Fevret de Saint-Memin.**

British Aggression on Land and the High Seas

In the election of 1804, Democratic-Republican Thomas Jefferson and his vice-presidential running mate, George Clinton, easily bested their Federalist opponents, Charles C. Pinckney and Rufus King. Developments overseas preoccupied Jefferson during his second term in office. England and France continued to challenge each other as the reigning powers of Europe. In 1805 the British navy, under the command of Lord Nelson, defeated the French and Spanish fleets in the Battle of Trafalgar off the coast of Spain. That same year, France reveled in its own triumph on land when Napoleon conquered the Austrian and Russian armies at the Battle of Austerlitz. Supreme on the seas, England in 1806 passed the Orders in Council, which specified that any country that wanted to ship goods to France must first send them to a British port and pay taxes on them. Many Americans believed that England's policies amounted to acts of military and economic aggression against the United States.

What were the domestic and international consequences of Britain's persistent challenges to U.S. territorial sovereignty and trade relations with other nations?

The Embargo of 1807

Not content to control trade across the Atlantic as decreed by the 1806 Orders in Council, the British also seized sailors from American ships, claiming that these men were British seamen who had been lured away from their own vessels by American captains promising

The Lewis and Clark expedition to the Pacific

— Pittsburgh to Camp Wood, 1803

— Camp Wood to Pacific and return, 1804–1805

••• Continental Divide

⚔ Fort   🏠 Camp

Lewis and Clark returned east from the Pacific to St. Louis by slightly different routes in 1806

Present state names and boundaries provided for orientation

■ **MAP 10.1**

LEWIS AND CLARK, 1803–1806

This map, showing the route of the Lewis and Clark expedition, suggests the importance of interior waterways in facilitating travel and exploration in the West. Spain feared, rightly, that the Americans would use western rivers to establish trade links with the Indians and thereby challenge Spain's northern border with the United States.

■ Lewis and Clark were not the only explorers; they were also pioneering naturalists committed to gathering, recording, and studying plans and animal life in the West. William Clark drew this sketch of a eulachon, also called a candlefish, as part of his journal entry for February 25, 1806. Pacific Indians dried the oily fish and used it as a torch.

them higher wages. In some cases these claims were probably true. However, U.S. political leaders charged that an estimated 6,000 U.S. citizens had been seized by the British navy between 1808 and 1811, including an unknown number of African Americans, many of whom were working as mariners. With limited economic opportunities on shore, black sailors accepted the danger and long absences from home. However, neither black nor white sailors had bargained for enforced service in His Majesty's Royal Navy.

Seizure, or impressment, reminded Americans of their pre–Revolutionary War days, when British "press gangs" prowled the docks of American port cities and seized colonial merchant sailors. In 1807 the tensions over impressment erupted into violence. Just 10 miles off the shore of Virginia, the American ship *Chesapeake* came under attack from a British vessel. British naval officers claimed that the Americans were harboring four British deserters. In the ensuing exchange of cannon fire, three Americans were killed and 18 wounded. Jefferson demanded that England leave American sailors and ships alone, but he was rebuffed.

President Jefferson decided to place an embargo on all exports to the European powers in an effort to force those nations to respect the rights of Americans on the high seas. The **Embargo Act of 1807** passed by Congress halted the shipment of goods from the United States to Europe. Because Europe—including England—relied heavily on American grain and timber, Jefferson hoped that the move would force England to respect American independence. The president saw this measure as preferable to either war or capitulation to England. But the move aroused intense opposition in Federalist-dominated New England, where the regional economy depended heavily on foreign trade. As the effects of the embargo took hold, the New England grain growers saw the markets for their products dry up, and the timber industry suffered when local shipbuilding ground to a standstill. Southern tobacco and cotton planters faced similar hardship because of the embargo. By 1808 some of them had joined with Northerners to circumvent the embargo by moving their goods through Canada and then to Europe.

Yet Jefferson held his course, prodding Congress to enforce the unpopular act. His efforts provoked a backlash as New England politicians threatened to take their states out of the union. Despite all the uproar, the embargo did benefit Americans by promoting industrialization at home. At the same time, the embargo seemed only to intensify, not lessen, tensions between England and the United States.

On the Brink of War

The consequences of the Embargo of 1807 were some of the many challenges American political leaders faced during the first decade of the nineteenth century. Both the Federalists and the Democratic-Republicans suffered a blow to their leadership in 1804. That year, the Federalist party lost one of its original leaders with the death of Alexander Hamilton at the hand of his rival, Aaron Burr. Both successful New York attorneys, the two men had risen together through the political ranks in the 1780s and 1790s. Burr served as Jefferson's running mate in the election of 1800; four years later he ran for governor of New York. Incensed by a report that Hamilton had claimed he was "a dangerous man, and one who ought not to be trusted with the reins of government," as well as "still more despicable rumors," Burr challenged his antagonist to a pistol duel at Weehawken, New Jersey, in July 1804. Hamilton, mortally wounded in the affair, died the next day, and Burr's political career fell into ruins.

Jefferson, declining to run for a third presidential term in 1808, left the stage as well. Soon after the inauguration of the new president, James Madison, Congress repealed Jefferson's embargo and replaced it with the Non-Intercourse Act, which eased the complete ban on exports to Europe. This measure permitted American exporters to ship their goods to all European countries except for France and England, still at war with one another. New Englanders opposed even this limited embargo.

Meanwhile, the Federalists' influence in Congress was waning. The partisan division within Congress—the Federalists, with their emphasis on a strong national government, against the localist Democratic-Republicans—gradually eased. By 1810 a different split had emerged—between young, hotheaded representatives from the West and their

TABLE 10-1

The Election of 1804

Candidate	Political Party	Electoral Vote
Thomas Jefferson	Democratic-Republican	162
Charles C. Pinckney	Federalist	14

TABLE 10-2

The Election of 1808

Candidate	Political Party	Electoral Vote
James Madison	Democratic-Republican	122
Charles C. Pinckney	Federalist	47
George Clinton	Democratic-Republican	6

This lithograph of the Prophet (Tenskwatawa) was based on an 1824 painting of the Shawnee mystic and holy man. Early in life, he suffered an accident with bows and arrows, losing his right eye. He and his older brother Tecumseh called on all Indians to resist the encroachment of their lands by whites and to renounce the way of life followed by whites, including the use of liquor. After the Indians' defeat at the Battle of Tippecanoe in 1811, the Prophet retreated to Canada. He returned to the United States in 1826. By that time he no longer wielded influence as a leader of the Shawnee.

more conservative seniors from the eastern seaboard. The western group, or "**war hawks**," called on the nation to revive its former glory. Americans must uphold U.S. honor, they declared, by opposing European, especially British, claims to military dominance. The war hawks also yearned to vanquish the Indians who impeded settlement of the area west of the Mississippi.

Looking eastward, the war hawks saw an England determined to defile the honor of their young nation. Looking westward, these same men saw an equally threatening menace: the rise of an ominous Indian resistance movement that blended military strength with native spirituality. The movement was led by Shawnee brothers Tecumseh and Tenskwatawa (also known as the Prophet), who founded Prophet's Town in Indiana in 1808. They envisioned a sovereign Indian state and the preservation of Native American culture. Tenskwatawa spoke of a time and place where Indians would reject alcohol and scorn "the food of whites" as well as the "wealth and ornaments" of commercial trade. Tecumseh set out to deliver the message to as many Indian groups as possible, traveling the broad swath of territory from Florida to Canada.

Meanwhile, in 1809, the territorial governor of Indiana, William Henry Harrison, plied a group of Indian leaders with liquor, then got them to agree to sell 3 million acres to the U.S. government for just $7,600. Upon hearing of the deal, Tecumseh decried a new form of American aggression: "treaties" between U.S. officials and Indians who lacked the authority to sell their people's homeland. "All red men," Tecumseh proclaimed, must "unite in claiming a common and equal right in the land, as it was at first, and should be yet; for it never was divided, but belongs to all, for the use of each."

In November 1811, Harrison led 1,000 U.S. soldiers in an advance on Prophet's Town. But before they could reach the settlement, several hundred Shawnees under the command of Tenskwatawa attacked their camp on the Tippecanoe River. The Indians suffered a sound defeat before the superior U.S. weapons, and Harrison burned Prophet's Town to the ground. Clearly, military technology, not just determination, would shape the western conflict.

■ **MAP 10.2**
THE PUBLIC DOMAIN IN 1810
This map indicates the expanse of western lands owned by the U.S. government in 1810, after the Louisiana Purchase. American war veterans received land warrants in return for military service in the Revolutionary War and the War of 1812. A warrant entitled the bearer to settle a specific number of acres of unoccupied lands. Warrants could be transferred, sold, and traded like stocks and bonds. After the War of 1812, the government issued 29,186 land warrants for a total of 4.8 million acres.

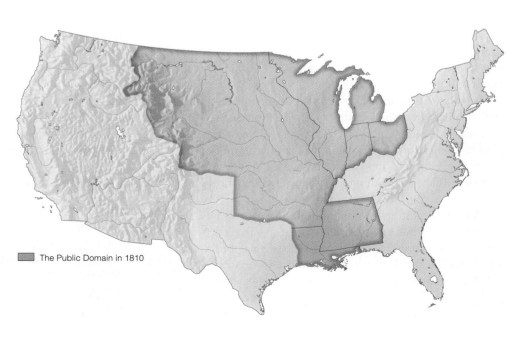

The Public Domain in 1810

Yet in the ensuing war, the Americans faced not just Indian foes, but also one of the mightiest military forces in the world—the British army and navy.

The War of 1812

The defeat of the Shawnees at Tippecanoe encouraged western war hawks' resolve to break the back of Indian resistance. But to achieve this goal, the United States would have to invade Canada and eliminate the British arms suppliers who had been trading with the Indians. Claiming the mantle of patriotism, western and southern members of the House of Representatives agitated for a war that would eliminate both the British threat on the high seas and the Canada-based Indian-British alliance. These Americans wanted a war that would win for them a true independence once and for all. "On to Canada! On to Canada!" became the rallying cry of the war hawks.

In a secret message sent to Congress on June 1, 1812, President Madison listed Americans' many grievances against England: the British navy's seizure of American citizens, the blockades of American goods, and continued conflict "on one of our extensive frontiers," the result of "savages" who had the backing of British traders and military officials. Madison left it up to Congress whether Americans would continue to endure these indignities or would act "in defense of their natural rights." Seventeen days later, the House voted 79 to 49 and the Senate voted 19 to 13 to declare war on England and, by extension, the western Indians.

The **War of 1812** united Americans behind a banner of national expansion. But at the same time, it exposed dangerous divisions between regions of the country and between political viewpoints. Many New Englanders saw the conflict as a plot by Virginia Democratic-Republicans primarily to aid France in opposition to England and to add agrarian (that is, slave) states to the Union. In an ironic twist, the New England Federalists—usually staunch defenders of the national government—argued that states should control their own commerce and militias.

What were the political and economic interests of the United States, the Indian tribes, and Great Britain and why did those divergent interests clash during the War of 1812?

⊙ See the **Map**
The War of 1812
at **www.myhistorylab.com**

TABLE 10-3		
The Election of 1812		
Candidate	Political Party	Electoral Vote
James Madison	Democratic-Republican	128
De Witt Clinton	Federalist	89

Pushing North

Although the Americans were better armed and organized than the western Indians, they were at a disadvantage when they took on the soldiers and sailors of the British Empire. The United States had not invested in its military and thus was ill-prepared for all-out war. The American navy consisted merely of a fleet of tiny gunboats constructed during the cost-conscious Jefferson administration. The charter for the Bank of the United States had expired in 1811, depriving the country of a vital source of financial credit. Suffering from a drop in tax revenues as a result of the embargo on foreign trade, the nation lacked the funds to train and equip the regular army and the state militias. Nevertheless, in the fall of 1812, the Americans launched an ambitious three-pronged attack against Canada, striking from Niagara, Detroit, and Lake Champlain. All three attempts failed miserably.

In the West in late 1812, Tecumseh (who had accepted a commission as a brigadier general in the British army) and British General Isaac Brock captured Detroit. Yet the Americans scored some notable successes in 1813. That September, Commodore Oliver H. Perry defeated a British fleet at Put-in-Bay on Lake Erie. Exhilarated, he declared, "We have met the enemy and they are ours."

Courtesy, Dartmouth College Library

BIG DICK AT THE 'MERMAID'S RETREAT.' SEE CHAPTER II.

■ **In 1815 approximately 6,000 American prisoners of war were confined to Britain's dark Dartmoor Prison in Devonshire, England. Many of them were African Americans, who represented one-fifth of all U.S. sailors who fought in the war. Among that group was Richard Craftus. An imposing man, Craftus earned the title "King Dick" by serving as the leader of the central barracks at Dartmoor, where blacks were held. He strolled through the cellblock, carrying a large club and settling disputes between prisoners.**

■ MAP 10.3

THE NORTHERN FRONT, WAR OF 1812

Much of the fighting of the War of 1812 centered in the Great Lakes region. It was there, the war hawks charged, that the British were inciting Indians to attack American settlements. Conducted in 1812 and 1813, the campaign against Canada was supposed to eliminate the British threat and, some Americans hoped, win Canadian territory for the United States.

Perry's hard-won victory forced the British back into Canada, over Tecumseh's objections. General William Henry Harrison followed in hot pursuit. British Colonel Henry Proctor marched his troops to eastern Ontario, leaving Tecumseh to try holding the Americans at bay. At the Battle of the Thames that October, Harrison defeated the Indians. Many perished, Tecumseh among them.

Later that autumn, an American campaign against Montreal failed. The Americans trudged back into New York state, the British close behind them. Flush with their victory in Montreal, the British captured Fort Niagara and set Buffalo and other nearby towns aflame.

By mid-1814, the English and their allies had also crushed Napoleon in Europe. This success freed up 15,000 British troops, who promptly sailed for North America. Still, in July 1814 the Americans, under the leadership of Major General Jacob Brown and Brigadier General Winfield Scott, managed to defeat the British at the Battle of Chippewa, across the Niagara River from Buffalo. But by the end of that year, the Americans had withdrawn to their own territory and relinquished their goal of invading and conquering Canada. The arrival of fresh British troops forced the Americans to defend their own soil.

Fighting on Many Fronts

For the United States, the most humiliating episode of the war came with the British attack on the nation's capital. On August 24, 1814, the British army, backed by the Royal Navy, sailed into Chesapeake Bay. At the Battle of Bladensburg, Maryland, they scattered the American troops they encountered. The Redcoats then advanced to Washington, where they torched the Capitol building and the White House, causing extensive damage to both structures.

Residents of the capital city had received word that the British were advancing. On Sunday, August 21, public officials frantically packed up their books and papers. Private citizens gathered up their furniture and other belongings and left town. By Tuesday, the city stood nearly empty. As a ragtag American force succumbed to the British, a Baltimore newspaper reported, President Madison "retired from the mortifying scene, and left the city on horseback."

Yet the Americans rallied, pursued the British, and bested them in the Battle of Baltimore. This victory inspired an observer, Francis Scott Key, to write "The Star Spangled Banner" as he watched "the bombs bursting in air" over Baltimore's Fort McHenry. The Americans scored another crucial victory in September, when U.S. naval commander Thomas McDonough crushed the British fleet on Lake Champlain near Plattsburgh, New York.

In the Southeast, Tecumseh's message of Indian unity had resonated with particular force among Native Americans once the war broke out. Some Cherokee and Choctaw cast their lot with the United States. However, a minority of Creek were emboldened by Tenskwatawa's call to war against the whites. By 1813 a group of warriors called Red Sticks (for their scarlet-painted weapons) stood ready to do battle with U.S. forces. Yet they faced opposition from some of their own people, the White Sticks, who counseled peace. The Red Sticks finally decided to attack Fort Mims, north of Mobile.

In response, Andrew Jackson, leader of the Tennessee militia, received a commission as major general. His mission was to retaliate against the Indians. Jackson had speculated in Indian lands in Mississippi Territory, and he called Native Americans "blood thirsty barbarians." Even

■ This engraving, published in 1814, depicts the bombardment of fort McHenry by British warships in September of that year. When he witnessed the battle, Francis Scott Key, a Washington lawyer, was aboard a prisoner exchange boat in Baltimore Harbor. He was seeking release of a friend captured by the British. After penning the poem "The Star Spangled Banner," Key set the words to music, using the tune of a popular English drinking song. Congress declared the song the national anthem in 1931.

in a country where anti-Indian sentiment ran high, his views were extreme. He often boasted about collecting the scalps of all his Indian victims, and he relished his new assignment.

Jackson's 3,500 troops laid waste to Creek territory. Regiments of Cherokee, Choctaw, and Chickasaw Indians, as well as White Sticks, helped them. During a monumental battle in March 1814, more than three-quarters of the 1,000 defending Red Sticks and a number of Indian women and children died at Horseshoe Bend (in modern-day Alabama). In the Treaty of Horseshoe Bend that followed, the Americans forced the Creek Nation to give up 23 million acres. The remnants of the Red Sticks fled to the swamps of Florida, where they joined additional Creeks, other Florida Indians, and numerous fugitive slaves in an emerging group known as the Seminoles.

Jackson next marched to New Orleans to confront the British. Knowing he would be facing some of Europe's finest soldiers, he assembled 7,000 men, U.S. soldiers and militiamen from the states of Louisiana, Kentucky, and Tennessee. Two Kentucky regiments consisted of free Negro volunteers, about 400 men in total. The Battle of New Orleans, fought on January 8, 1815, began with a ferocious assault by British soldiers. But within just half an hour, 2,000 of them lay dead or wounded. The Americans lost only 70. Jackson's back-country sharpshooters had vanquished the army of Europe's greatest military power.

Later, many Americans associated Andrew Jackson with the war's decisive battle and most glorious victory. But in fact, American and British negotiators had actually signed a peace agreement ending the war two weeks before the British defeat in New Orleans. The Battle of New Orleans might have been a glorious victory for the Americans, but it was hardly the decisive battle of the war.

An Uncertain Victory

Before the Battle of New Orleans, in the fall of 1814, President Madison had decided to end the war. He dispatched John Quincy Adams, son of former president John Adams, to the Belgian city of Ghent to start negotiations. Representative Henry Clay and three other American envoys accompanied Adams. At first, English representatives at the meeting made two demands. The Americans, they said, must agree to the creation of an Indian territory in the upper Great Lakes region. They must also cede much of the state of Maine to England. The Americans refused, and the negotiations dragged on.

In the meantime, the New England states had grown increasingly impatient with what they called "Mr. Madison's war." As with the embargo, they saw the effort as a mistake and a threat to their regional commercial interests. In December 1814, Massachusetts, Connecticut, Rhode Island, New Hampshire, and Vermont sent delegates to a gathering in Hartford, Connecticut, to consider a course of action. The delegates demanded that the federal government give their states financial aid to compensate for the revenue they had lost as a result of disrupted trade. Some delegates even hinted that their states wanted to secede from the union. Although most delegates shied away from immediate action, the majority of them apparently wanted to leave open the possibility of secession.

> *American nationalism came at the expense of vast Indian homelands and thousands of lives on both sides.*

Back in Ghent, the British had reversed their initial position by late December. They had lost recent battles in upper New York and in Baltimore and, as always, were still worried about new threats from France. They dropped their demands for territory and for an Indian buffer state in the upper Midwest. They also agreed to an armistice that, in essence, represented a draw: both combatants would retain the same territory they had possessed when the war began. The British made no concessions to the Americans' demands that they stop impressing American sailors and supplying the western Indians with arms or that they revoke the Orders in Council. Still, most U.S. citizens considered the war a great victory for the United States. After Congress ratified the **Treaty of Ghent**, which ended hostilities between the two nations in 1815, the Americans and the British never again met each other across a battlefield as enemies.

●●●–[**Read** the **Document**

The Treaty of Ghent (1815)
at **www.myhistorylab.com**

The "Era of Good Feelings"?

In 1816, the Democratic-Republicans nominated James Monroe for president, to run against Federalist candidate Rufus King. Although Monroe only narrowly won his party's endorsement, he soundly defeated King in the general election. Monroe benefited from several developments that had mortally wounded the Federalist party: the War of 1812 victory, presided over by a Democratic-Republican chief executive; the New England Federalists' flirtation with secession (and treason) during the war years; and the strong nationalist tendencies of both the Jefferson and Madison administrations, which had stolen the Federalists' thunder.

Did political and social realities justify the use of the term "the Era of 'Good Feelings'" to describe the period after the War of 1812?

Addressing Congress in December 1817, President Monroe expressed optimism about the state of the nation. The country's boundaries were secure, and the Indians had little choice but to retreat farther and farther west. The president predicted that, shortly, "Indian hostilities, if they do not altogether cease, will henceforth lose their terror." Equally inspiring, the Americans had once again defied the British Empire and won. Two treaties with Britain—the Rush-Bagot of 1817 and the pending Convention of 1818—set the U.S.-Canadian border at the forty-ninth parallel and provided that the two countries would jointly occupy Oregon Territory for ten years.

TABLE 10-4		
The Election of 1816		
Candidate	**Political Party**	**Electoral Vote**
James Monroe	Democratic-Republican	183
Rufus King	Federalist	34

Monroe called on Congress to acknowledge "the vast extent of territory within the United States [and] the great amount and value of its productions" and to facilitate the construction of roads and canals. It was this "happy situation of the United States," in Monroe's words, that ushered in what some historians call the **Era of Good Feelings**, a period relatively free of partisan political strife. Although voters continued to disagree over some issues of the day—such as the national bank, sectionalism, and internal improvements—they did not necessarily express those disagreements in the form of bitter partisan wrangling. Still, the term "good feelings" may fully apply only to a narrow group of enfranchised citizens, men who shared common beliefs about territorial expansion and economic development.

●●●—Read the Document
Western Country Ohio (1816)
at **www.myhistorylab.com**

Praise and Respect for Veterans After the War

American veterans of the War of 1812 won the praise of a grateful nation. Even the British expressed a grudging respect for Americans' fighting abilities. One British naval officer admitted, "I don't like Americans; I never did, and never shall." He had "no wish to eat with them, drink with them, or consort with them in any way." But, he added, he would rather not fight with "an enemy so brave, determined, and alert, as they have always proved." To reward veterans for their service, Congress offered them 160-acre plots of land in the territory between the Illinois and Mississippi rivers. These grants did much to encourage families to emigrate west and establish homesteads.

Some military heroes of the war parlayed their success into impressive political careers. Andrew Jackson won election to the presidency in 1828 and 1832, as did William Henry Harrison in 1840. Countless others earned recognition within their own communities, and European American veterans were not the only ones to gain status and influence as a result of the conflict. For example, a Cherokee leader named the Ridge earned the gratitude of American officials for his contributions to the war effort. He had accepted the government's attempts to press the Cherokee to adopt European American ways; he had settled in a log cabin rather than in a traditional Cherokee dwelling when he married a Cherokee woman named Susanna Wickett in the early 1790s. During the war against the Red Sticks, the Ridge served under Andrew Jackson and earned the title of major. For the rest of his life, the Cherokee leader was known as Major Ridge. His wife devoted herself to tending an orchard, keeping a garden, and sewing clothes, tasks traditionally performed by European American but not Native American women. Eventually, the family prospered, bought African-American slaves, and became Christians as well.

INTERPRETING HISTORY

Cherokee Women Petition Against Further Land Sales to Whites in 1817

In traditional Cherokee society, men took responsibility for foreign affairs while women focused on domestic matters, leading to a roughly equal division of labor. However, European-American diplomats, military officials, and traders dealt primarily with Indian men. As a result, beginning in the eighteenth century, Cherokee women's traditional influence was eroding within their own communities. In this new world, Indian warriors wielded significant power.

Nevertheless, Cherokee women insisted on presenting their views during the crisis of 1817–1819, when men of the group were deciding whether to cede land to U.S. authorities and move west. The following petition was supported by Nancy Ward, a Cherokee War Woman. This honorific title was bestowed on women who accompanied and attended to the needs of war parties. Ward had supported the colonists' cause during the American Revolution.

Amovey [Tennessee] in Council 2nd May 1817

The Cherokee Ladys now being present at the meeting of the Chiefs and warriors in council have thought it their duties as mothers to address their beloved Chiefs and warriors now assembled.

Our beloved children and head men of the Cherokee nation we address you warriors in council we have raised all of you on the land which we now have, which God gave to us to inhabit and raise provisions we know that our country has once been extensive but by repeated sales has become circumscribed to a small tract, and [we] never have thought it our duty to interfere in the disposition of it till now, if a father or mother was to sell all their lands which they had to depend on which their children had to raise their living on which would indeed be bad and to be removed to another country we do not wish to go to an unknown country [to] which we have understood some of our children wish to go over the Mississippi but this act of our children would be like destroying your mothers. Your mothers your sisters ask and beg of you not to part with any more of our lands, we say ours. [Y]ou are our descendants and take pity on our request, but keep it for our growing children for it was the good will of our creator to place us here and you know our father the great president [James Monroe], will not allow his white children to take our country away for if it was not they would not ask you to put your hands to paper for it would be impossible to remove us all for as soon as one child is raised, we have others in our arms for such is our situation and will consider our circumstance.

Therefore children don't part with any more of our lands but continue on it and enlarge your farms and cultivate and raise corn and cotton and we your mothers and sisters will make clothing for you which our father the president has recommended to us all we don't charge anybody for selling any lands, but we have heard such intentions of our children but your talks become true at last and it was our desire to forewarn you all not to part with our lands.

Nancy Ward to her children[:] warriors to take pity and listen to the talks of your sisters, although I am very old yet cannot but pity the situation in which you will hear of their minds. I have great many grand children which I wish they do well on our land.

In addition to Nancy Ward, 12 Cherokee women signed the petition. Their

In 1987, Wilma Mankiller became the first woman to be elected Principal Chief of the Cherokee Nation of Oklahoma.

names suggest the varying degrees of assimilation to white ways on the part of Cherokees in general. Petitioners included Cun, o, ah and Widow Woman Holder, as well as Jenny McIntosh and Mrs. Nancy Fields.

It is unclear what effect, if any, this petition had on Cherokee male leaders. The Cherokee nation did halt land cessions to whites between 1819 and 1835.

Questions

1. How and why did motherhood confer authority on Cherokee women?
2. What is the significance and meaning of the land in Cherokee culture?
3. Does this petition provide evidence for the view that early nineteenth-century Cherokee men and women were adopting elements of European American culture? If so, what elements, and in what ways?

Source: Cherokee Women to Cherokee Council, May 2, 1817, series 1, Andrew Jackson Presidential Papers.

■ Southeastern Indians varied widely in their willingness to adopt European American ways. Some argued that the best way to preserve their community and remain on the land of their forebears was to accommodate themselves to white practices of trade, textile production, and farming. This 1805 painting shows Benjamin Hawkins, a government Indian agent, at a Creek settlement near Macon, Georgia. Hawkins expresses evident satisfaction with the Indians' neat cabins, well-tended fields, flocks of sheep, and bountiful harvest of vegetables.

The Ridge's battlefield experiences earned him the respect of other Cherokee who embraced the "civilization" program that missionaries and government officials promoted. At the same time, the Ridge vehemently resisted U.S. officials' attempts to persuade the Cherokee to give up their lands to whites and move west. He believed that his people should adopt some elements of white culture but should also hold fast to their native lands in opposition to white settlers and politicians.

A Thriving Economy

The end of the War of 1812 saw an upsurge in internal migration. New Englanders, especially, pushed west in search of new opportunities. Between 1800 and 1820, the population of Ohio grew from 45,000 to 581,000. New means of transportation—and new means to fund them—facilitated the movement of goods and people. In 1807 an entrepreneur named Robert Fulton piloted the *Clermont*, his new kind of boat powered by steam, up the Hudson River from New York City. Steamboats traveled upriver, against the current, ten times faster than keelboats, which had to be pushed, pulled, or hauled by men or mules. Within a few years, therefore, such vessels were plying the Mississippi River and its major tributaries.

Improvements in land transportation stimulated economic growth. The profits that the Philadelphia and Lancaster Turnpike raked in by charging travelers tolls inspired other local private corporations to invest in roads. By 1810 several thousand such corporations were building roads up and down the East Coast. Funding came from a variety of sources, both public and private. Philadelphia textile mill owners financed transportation links with the city's hinterland (rural areas to the west) to carry their goods to the largest number of customers. Individual cities also invested in routes westward. The state of Virginia authorized a board of

Improvements in land transportation stimulated economic growth.

public works to expend funds for roads and other internal improvements. Western politicians flexed their political muscle in 1806 by securing congressional authorization for the building of the Cumberland (later National) Road, which snaked through the Allegheny Mountains and ended at the Ohio River.

The acceleration of commerce in the West, combined with the disruption in trade from Europe that had come with the Embargo of 1807 and the War of 1812, stimulated manufacturing throughout the United States. Philadelphia's growth proved particularly dazzling. During the war, the city's craft producers did not have to worry about foreign competition. Local merchant-financiers, who otherwise might have been pouring their money into trade ventures, began to invest in manufacturing. As early as 1808, the city's new factories had compensated for the glass, chemicals, shot, soap, lead, and earthenware that no longer flooded in from England. Philadelphia soon took the lead in production of all kinds, whether carried out in factories, artisans' shops, or private homes. Metalworking, ale brewing, and leather production counted among the array of thriving industries that made Philadelphia the nation's top industrial city in 1815. Still, in 1820 about two-thirds of all Philadelphia workers labored in small shops employing fewer than six people.

Transformations in the Workplace

Even the earliest stages of the Industrial Revolution transformed the way people lived and worked. Some crafts—for example, the production of leather, barrels, soap, candles, and newspapers—expanded from small shops with skilled artisans into larger establishments with unskilled wage earners. In these cases, production was reorganized; now wage earners under the supervision of a boss replaced apprentices and journeymen who had formerly worked alongside a master artisan. These workers performed a single task many times a day instead of using their specialized skills to see a production process through to completion.

New England rapidly became the center of mechanized textile production in the United States. By the late eighteenth century, Boston shippers were making handsome profits by supplying Alta California (the area north of San Diego, encompassing present-day California, Nevada, and parts of Arizona and Utah) with cloth, shoes and tools, selling western otter pelts in China; and returning home laden with Chinese porcelains and silks. These profits helped to finance New England's mechanized textile industry. By 1813 seventy-six cotton mills housing over 51,000 spindles were operating within the vicinity of Providence, Rhode Island.

Faced with a shortage of adult men (many were moving west), New England mill owners sought other local sources of labor. The Rhode Island system of production had relied on child spinners working in small mills. This system gave way to the Lowell model, based in Waltham and Lowell, Massachusetts, which brought young women from the surrounding countryside to work in gigantic mills. Many of the women were eager to earn cash wages and to escape the routine of farm life. Still, New England mill owners realized that they had to reassure Yankee parents that their daughters would find the factories safe, attractive places to work. Mill owners offered the young women housing in dormitory-like boardinghouses staffed by older women, called matrons, who looked after them.

The Market Revolution

As new means of transportation facilitated the movement of ideas, goods, and people, natural barriers separating farms from towns and the West from the East began to crumble. Factory workers quickly and efficiently processed raw materials—leather into shoes, cotton into clothing. Wage earning gradually replaced family labor and indentured servitude as the dominant labor system in the North. Together, all of these rapid economic transformations in the early nineteenth century fueled what some scholars have called the **market revolution**. Driven by improvements in transportation, increasing commercialization, and the rise of factories, powerful economic changes affected ordinary Americans and their everyday routines at home and on the job.

The gradual changes of the Market Revolution were driven by investment. Wealthy New England merchants led the way, but a wide variety of private individuals and public institutions proved willing to invest their money and energy in new economic opportunities. Profits from foreign trade helped to build the textile factories that dotted the northeastern landscape. States and even towns used the money of taxpayers and private investors to build turnpikes and later to finance canals and railroads. Entrepreneurs pioneered the putting out system, a form of production (of hats and other forms of clothing, for example) that enlisted the efforts of single women in the cities, as well as farm families during the winter season. These workers received raw materials from a merchant-capitalist and engaged in piecework in return for wages. Combined public-private investment in new forms of business organization and technology spurred American economic growth.

These changes spilled over into American social and religious life, encouraging some people to adopt an optimistic worldview about the possibilities inherent in American life—possibilities that included moving from one place to another, making money by selling new products, altering the natural landscape to make way for canals or factories, and aspiring to buy goods rather than produce goods at home. Foreign visitors often commented on the "restlessness" of Americans, their "acquisitiveness," and their impatience with tradition.

Not all Americans adopted this new way of looking at the world, but almost all groups felt its effects. Slave owners pushed black men, women, and children to work even harder in the fields of the South so that more cotton and rice could be exported to northern and European markets. Western Indians suffered the effects of European American conquest, as whites chopped down forests and cleared the land for farms, violently displacing native populations in the process. In New England textile mills, women and children operated the machines that produced cloth. These operatives served as the vanguard of the Industrial Revolution in America.

By the second decade of the nineteenth century, America had clearly defined itself as a nation that embraced many different kinds of change in transportation and technology. Yet traditional forms of inequality and hierarchy endured, serving as distinguishing features of the Market Revolution.

The Rise of the Cotton Plantation Economy

The growth and spread of the cotton economy redefined the institution of slavery, the southern political system, and, ultimately, all of American history. With the invention of the cotton gin and the acquisition of the Louisiana Territory, cotton production boomed, and the enslaved population expanded. About 700,000 slaves resided in the United States in 1790; just two decades later, that figure had jumped to 1.1 million.

The **Abolition Act of 1808** outlawed the importation of foreign slaves. Northern abolitionists had first called for an end to the international slave trade during the U.S. Constitutional debates of the late 1780s. Anti-slavery activists from New York, for example, argued that such traffic in human beings was repugnant to the "ideas of mankind which form the basis of the government of the United States." Yet even after the Act had passed, some southern plantation owners found ways to smuggle slaves into the country illegally. The expansion of the United States into the vast Louisiana territory and the astounding profitability of cotton heightened the demand for labor. Slave traders in New Orleans responded by building a

How did staple-crop production shape the labor, culture, and family lives of slaves?

highly successful contraband market in foreign slaves and evading detection by the U.S. Marshals Service. Still, the Abolition Act forced an important shift as planters increasingly relied on natural reproduction among slaves and on the domestic slave trade—the forced migration of slaves from the upper South to the lower South.

The institution of slavery was marked by increasingly sharp regional variations, reflecting the impact of cotton cultivation on local economies. At the same time, the contours of an African-American culture emerged. This culture had certain characteristics regardless of place, such as strong ties that bound nuclear and extended family members, rich oral and musical traditions heavily influenced by West African customs, and individual and collective resistance to slavery. White people as a group understood little of this culture; they viewed black people primarily as workers who would never become citizens. As U.S. military strength and nationalistic pride grew, southern planters imposed a harsher, more regimented system of slavery on the black population. The tension between the rhetoric of freedom and equality and the reality of slavery continued to shape southern—and American—life for the next four decades.

Regional Economies of the South

Throughout the South, shifts in production methods transformed the demographic and economic make-up of specific regions. For example, by the early nineteenth century, the Chesapeake tobacco economy had declined as a result of worn-out lands and falling prices. In its place arose a more diversified economy based on crafts, the cultivation of corn and wheat, and the milling of flour. Owners put enslaved men to work making barrels and horseshoes while forcing their wives, sisters, and daughters to labor as spinners, weavers, dairymaids, personal servants, and livestock tenders.

The lower South states of Georgia and South Carolina also saw their economies change during this period. The indigo export business never recovered from the Revolution, since colonial cultivators of the plant had relied heavily on British subsidies to shore up their profits. European customers now had to turn to Louisiana and Central America for indigo. In contrast, the lowcountry (coastal) South Carolina rice economy recovered and flourished after the war. In a particularly rich rice district, All Saints Parish, one out of two slaves lived on a plantation with more than a hundred slaves in 1790; 30 years later, four out of five lived on such large establishments. In these areas, the plantation owners themselves often lived elsewhere, and black people constituted almost the entire population.

Adding to the wealth of South Carolina and Georgia was the rapid development of cotton cultivation, especially in the interior, away from the coast. There, prosperous cotton planters began to rival their lowcountry rice-growing counterparts in social status and political influence, and these slaveholders pushed steadily for further western expansion. Cotton planters rushed into the newly-purchased Louisiana Territory after 1803. They accelerated an economic process that had begun in the late eighteenth century: the replacement of a frontier exchange economy with plantation agriculture. (Sugar dominated the New Orleans region; cotton, the rest of the lower Mississippi Valley.) By 1800 slaves in lower Louisiana were producing 4.5 million pounds of sugar annually.

The reaches of the lower Mississippi took on an increasingly multicultural flavor. A strong Spanish influence persisted as a vestige of colonial days. French-speaking planter-refugees and their slaves from revolutionary Saint-Domingue came to New Orleans while the city was still in French hands (1800 to 1803). Between 1787 and 1803, nearly 3,000 slaves arrived from Africa, Spanish West Florida, and the Chesapeake to be sold in New Orleans, followed by even larger numbers of slaves from the North after 1803. Slave owners who settled in Natchez, on the banks of the Mississippi River, grew cotton—and grew rich.

◉▸View the Image

Plantation and Southern Commerce
at **www.myhistorylab.com**

Black Family Life and Labor

By 1820, the enslaved population reached 1.5 million and continued to increase rapidly over the next four decades. Since importation of Africans ended officially in 1808, this number suggests a tremendous rate of natural increase. Some planters continued to buy slaves brought into the country illegally after 1808, but most of the increase stemmed from births. The preferences of both slave owners and slaves account for this development. Southern planters encouraged black women to bear many children. At the same time, enslaved African Americans valued the family as a social unit; family ties provided support and solace for a people deprived of fundamental human rights. Even under harsh conditions, black people fell in love, married (albeit informally, without the sanction of law), had children, and reared families. Despite the lack of protection from local, state, and national authorities, the slave family proved a remarkably resilient institution.

The stability of individual slave families depended on several factors, including the size and age of the plantation and the fortunes and life cycle of the slave owner's family. Very large or long-established plantations had more two-parent slave families than did the small or newer holdings, which tended to have more unrelated people. Slave families were broken up when whites died and their "property" was bequeathed to heirs. Slaves might also be sold or presented to other family members as gifts. Many slave families suffered disruption in response to the growing demand for slaves in the fresh cotton lands of Alabama and Mississippi. The forced migration from upper South to lower South necessarily severed kin ties, but slaves often reconstituted those ties in the form of symbolic kin relationships. Families adopted new, single members of the slave community, and the children called these newcomers "Aunt" or "Uncle."

> *Despite the lack of protection from local, state, and national authorities, the slave family proved a remarkably resilient institution.*

■ British artist John Antrobs titled his 1860 painting "Plantation Burial." Held at night, after the workday, slave funerals provided an opportunity for the community—including slaves from nearby plantations—to come together in mourning. Planters remained suspicious of such gatherings, which were marked by African musical and religious forms. Whites feared that slaves would conspire under the cover of darkness.

Since plantations functioned as slave labor camps, owners generally showed little or no inclination to take family relationships into account when they parceled out work assignments to men, women, and children. Rather, those assignments, and the conditions under which slaves performed them, reflected the size and crops of a particular plantation. During the period 1790 to 1860, an estimated 75 percent of slaves worked primarily as field hands. On large plantations the division of labor could be quite specialized. Men served as skilled carpenters, blacksmiths, and barrelmakers, and women worked as cooks, laundresses, nursemaids, and personal maids.

Rice slaves continued to work under the task system. Each day, after they completed a specific assigned task, they spent their time as they chose, within limits. Even in the cotton-growing regions, where blacks labored under the regimented gang system, slaves tried to work for themselves in the little free time they had on Saturday afternoons and Sunday. In Louisiana, one white observer noted that the slave man returning to his living quarters after a long, hot day in the fields "does not lose his time. He goes to work at a bit of the land which he has planted with provisions for his own use, while his companion, if he has one, busies herself in preparing some for him, herself, and their children." Family members who grew or accumulated a modest surplus—of corn, eggs, vegetables—in some cases could sell their wares in a nearby market or to slaves on another plantation.

Some slaves took goods from their master's storeroom and barn and sold or traded them to other slaves or to poor whites. These transactions often took place under the cover of darkness. Planters complained of slaves who stole their cattle, hogs, chickens, sacks full of cotton, farm equipment, and stores of ham and flour. Thus slaves' various forms of labor fell into at least three categories: work performed at the behest of and directly under the supervision of whites, labor performed by and for family members within the slaves' living quarters, and the sale (or sometimes clandestine exchange) of goods with masters, other slaves, and poor whites.

100 DOLLS. REWARD.

RAN AWAY

From me, on Saturday, the 19th inst.,

Negro Boy Robert Porter,

aged 19; heavy, stoutly made; dark chesnut complexion; rather sullen countenance, with a down look; face large; head low on the shoulders. I believe he entered the City of Washington on Sunday evening, 20th inst. He has changed his dress probably, except his boots, which were new and heavy.

I will give $50 if taken and secured in the District of Columbia, or $100 if taken north of the District, and secured in each case and delivered before the reward shall be good.

Dr. J. W. THOMAS.

Pomunky P. O., Charles Co., Md.

■ From colonial times through the abolition of slavery in 1865, runaways were a persistent problem for slaveholders. This advertisement was published in the Centerville, Maryland, *Times and Eastern-Shore Public Advertiser.* Typically, the owner describes the runaways in terms of their height, skin color, and their distinguishing characteristics.

Resistance to Slavery

Slaves resisted the harsh demands made by their masters; that resistance took many forms, including cultural expression. In 1817, the New Orleans City Council decreed that enslaved men and women could sing and dance at a stipulated place—Congo Square—every Sunday afternoon. Thereafter, a variety of groups came together to make music. These groups included recent émigrés from Saint-Domingue and slaves newly imported from Africa; slaves from neighboring plantations, in town for the day; and free people of color (Creoles), who often blended Spanish and French classical music traditions. In towns and on plantations throughout the South, black people drew from West African musical styles, using drums as well as banjo-like instruments, gourd rattles, and mandolins. Over the generations several uniquely American musical styles flowed from Congo Square and other southern gathering places: the blues, gospel, ragtime, jazz, swing, and rock 'n' roll.

In their artistic expression, dress, hairstyles, and language, black people sought to preserve their cultural uniqueness and create an existence that slaveholders could not touch. In the South Carolina lowcountry, slaves spoke Gullah. Originally a pidgin—a blend of words and grammatical structures from West African languages and English—Gullah later developed into a more formal Creole language. Slaves throughout the United States also mixed West African religious beliefs with Christianity. In slave quarters, spiritual leaders not only preached a Christianity of equality but also told fortunes and warned away "haunts" (spirits of the dead).

Black resistance to slavery took many forms. Slaves might work carelessly in an effort to resist a master's or mistress's demands. During the course of their workday, some broke hoes and other farm implements. A cook might burn the biscuits, thus spoiling a special dinner party for her mistress. Striking out more directly, the African-influenced "conjurer"—often a woman who had a knowledge of plants and herbs—could wreak havoc on a white family by concocting poisons or encouraging disruptive behavior among other enslaved workers.

Slaves also stole goods from their masters and at times stole themselves by running away. (This practice was more common among young, unmarried men than among those who had family obligations.) Despite the extraordinary peril involved, some slaves revolted. In St. Charles and St. John the Baptist parishes in Louisiana, an 1811 revolt of 400 slaves cost two whites their lives and left several plantations in flames. The original participants, led by a free man of color, Charles Deslondes, acquired new members as they marched toward New Orleans. U.S. troops cut their advance short, killing 66 of them. In the Southeast in 1817 and 1818, 400 to 600 black fugitives converged on the swamps of central Florida, uniting with Indian refugees from the Red Stick War. Together, they raided Georgia plantations until Andrew Jackson and his soldiers halted them in April 1818.

To justify their own behavior, masters and mistresses created a number of myths about the black people they exploited. Whites had a vested interest in believing that their slaves felt gratitude toward them. Skilled in the so-called deference ritual, some slaves hid their true feelings and acted submissively in the presence of white people. Owners and overseers alike interpreted this behavior as a sign of black contentment.

Although some planters boasted of their fatherly solicitude for their slaves, most slave owners harbored deep fears about the men and women they held in bondage. These fears explain the barbaric punishments that some owners inflicted on men, women, and children. Even in "respectable" southern families, slave owners branded, mutilated, and beat enslaved workers for resisting discipline or to deliver a warning to other potentially defiant workers. In the slave South, American cries of freedom, equality, opportunity, and the blessings of citizenship rang hollow.

CONCLUSION

During the first two decades of the nineteenth century, striking historical developments stirred the spirit of American nationalism. The Louisiana Purchase magnified the natural wealth of the young nation, and the federal government encouraged citizens to exploit that wealth through trade and settlement. The Embargo of 1807 and the War of 1812 freed the country from the British menace in the Northwest Territory and on the high seas. The war also bolstered the American economy by stimulating technological innovation and the growth of manufacturing. Territorial expansion combined with economic development created new jobs for a burgeoning population.

Southern cotton planters and northern factory owners derived their newfound prosperity from very different sources: staple crop agriculture on one hand and the emerging industrial system on the other. At the same time, these two groups had much in common. As they expanded their operations, whether sprawling plantations or gigantic mill complexes, they displaced smaller landowners and raised land prices. Members of both elite groups proved restless entrepreneurs, eager to move around to find the freshest lands and the cheapest labor. Their personal wealth and their political power set them apart from the people under them—the slaves and wage earners—who produced that wealth. And both the southern "lords of the lash" and the northern "lords of the loom" depended on large numbers of slaves to grow cotton. Producing and processing cotton yielded tangible benefits for a few and created a new, harsher world of work for many.

For Review

✓•─ Study and **Review** at www.myhistorylab.com

1. Who were the war hawks, and why did they emerge as such a potent political force in Congress? Why were most from the West?

2. In the United States, what were the political, social, and economic consequences of the War of 1812?

3. Explain the market revolution and its effects on American society. Which groups benefited?

4. Which elements of African-American culture revealed the slaves' struggle to live life on their own terms, rather than on the terms dictated by white masters and mistresses? Within the plantation, in what ways was the power of slaveholders limited or restricted?

Chronology: 1804–1818

1804 Lewis and Clark Expedition (1804–1806).

1805 British navy defeats French and Spanish fleets at Battle of Trafalgar.

1806 Congress authorizes funds for construction of National Road.

1807 Jefferson places embargo on all U.S. exports to Europe.
U.S.S. *Chesapeake* attacked by British vessel.
Robert Fulton pilots first steamboat up the Hudson River.

1808 Congressional ban on slave trade takes effect.
Non-Intercourse Act prevents exports to France and England.
Tecumseh and Tenskwatawa found Prophet's Town in Indiana.

1811 Battle of Tippecanoe. Revolt of 400 slaves in Louisiana.

1812 War of 1812 begins.

1813 Red Sticks battle U.S. troops at Battle of Horseshoe Bend.

1814 British forces attack Washington, D.C.

1815 Treaty of Ghent ends War of 1812.
Battle of New Orleans.

1816 Tariff of 1816.

1818 Andrew Jackson battles Seminole in Florida.

Key Terms

Abolition Act of 1808 Also called the Slave Trade Act, prohibited the importation of foreign slaves into the U.S. p. 255

Embargo Act of 1807 A law passed by Congress, at the urging of President Thomas Jefferson, to halt the shipment of U.S. goods to Europe in response to British military and naval aggression. p. 245

Era of Good Feelings A term used by historians to describe the presidency of James Monroe (1816–1820), when partisan tensions eased among voters and their political leaders. p. 251

Lewis and Clark Expedition A "corps of discovery" commissioned by President Thomas Jefferson in 1804 to explore the newly acquired Louisiana Territory. Led by Meriwether Lewis and William Clark and lasting 28 months, the party reported on an array of subjects, including the cultural practices of western Indians and the natural features of the land, but failed to find a water route that would connect the Pacific Northwest to eastern markets. p. 242

Market Revolution The combined effects of transportation innovation, technological change, and economic growth, especially during the first half of the nineteenth century. p. 255

Treaty of Ghent Peace treaty signed by the United States and Great Britain in 1815, ending the War of 1812. p. 250

War hawks Politicians who favor specific forms of military action as a tool of U.S. foreign policy. p. 246

War of 1812 A military and naval conflict that pitted U.S. forces against the British and their Indian allies. The end of the war eliminated the post-Revolutionary British threat to U.S. sovereignty. p. 247

Campaigning for political office in Tennessee in the 1820s was not an activity for the faint of heart. Candidates competed against each other in squirrel hunts, the loser footing the bill for the barbecue that followed. A round of speech-making often was capped by several rounds of whiskey enjoyed by candidates and supporters alike. Into this boisterous arena stepped a man unrivaled as a campaigner. David Crockett ran successfully for several offices, including local justice of the peace in 1818, state legislator in 1821 and 1823, and U.S. congressman in 1827, 1829, and 1833. The plainspoken Crockett knew how to play to a crowd and rattle a rival. He bragged about his skill as a bear hunter and ridiculed the fancy dress of his opponents. He condemned closed-door political caucuses (small groups of party insiders who hand-picked candidates) and praised grassroots democracy. Crockett claimed he could out-shoot, out-drink, and out-debate anyone who opposed him. If his opponent lied about him, why, then, he would lie about himself: "Yes fellow citizens, I can run faster, walk longer, leap higher, speak better, and tell more and bigger lies than my competitor, and all his friends, any day of his life." Crockett's blend of political theater and folksy backwoods banter earned him the allegiance of voters like him—men who, though having little formal education, understood the challenges of carving a homestead out of the dense thickets of western Tennessee.

During the 1820s, European American settlers in the trans-Appalachian West transformed the style and substance of American politics. In 1790, 100,000 Americans (not including Indians) lived west of the Appalachians; half a century later that number had increased to 7 million, or about four out of ten Americans. Beginning with Kentucky in 1792, western states began to relax or abolish property requirements for adult male voters. Even the English that Americans spoke changed. New words introduced into the political vocabulary reflected the rough-hewn, woodsman quality of western electioneering: candidates hit the campaign trail, giving "stump" speeches along the way. They supported their party's platform with its "planks" (positions on the issues). As legislators, they voted for "pork-barrel" projects that would benefit their constituents at home. Emphasizing his modest origins, David Crockett became widely known as Davy Crockett. (It is hard to imagine anyone calling the Sage of Monticello Tommy Jefferson.)

Western settlers attacked what they considered centralized, eastern-based institutions of wealth and privilege. They scorned a six-person Supreme Court that could overturn the laws of Congress and the individual states. They charged that the privately owned

11

Society and Politics in the "Age of the Common Man," 1819–1832

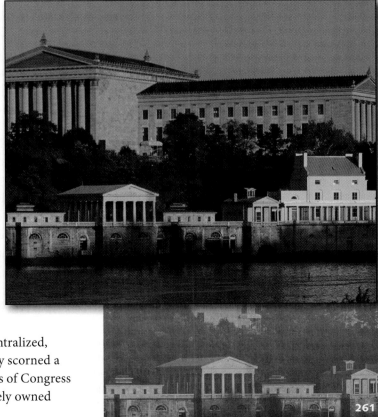

Read the **Document**

Davy Crockett, Advice to Politicians (1833) at **www.myhistorylab.com**

■ **John Gadsby Chapman painted this portrait of Davy Crockett.**

Second Bank of the United States enriched its own board of directors at the expense of indebted farmers. Western voters rejoiced with the 1828 election of Andrew Jackson to the presidency; here, they claimed, was a man who would battle eastern financiers and at the same time support white settlers' claims to Indian lands in the West. Jackson held out the promise that ordinary people would have a political voice and access to expanding economic opportunities.

During his two terms in office (1828–1836), Andrew Jackson of Tennessee so dominated the American political landscape that historians have called him the symbol of an age and the representative man of his time. Born in humble circumstances, orphaned at age 14, Jackson achieved public acclaim as a lawyer, military officer, and finally president. He promoted a strong central government, and the authority of the chief executive in particular, and he had fought against foreign military forces (the British in the War of 1812) and Native Americans. He clashed with southern states' rights advocates.

Democracy had its limits during this period. While voter participation in presidential elections soared, from 25 percent of eligible voters in 1824 to 50 percent in 1828, even most free people could not vote, including Native Americans, women, and free people of color. Further complicating this age was the rise of distinct social classes. Acquiring great economic and political significance, the class system seemed to mock the idea of equality. The outlines of this system appeared in the 1820s in the Northeast, where business and factory managers received salaries, not hourly wages, and their wives were full-time homemakers and mothers. New forms of popular literature, such as the *Ladies Magazine*, published in Boston, glorified the middle-class family, especially the pious wife and mother who held moral sway over it.

The "age of the common man" was thus rife with irony. Jackson himself embodied many apparent contradictions. An Indian-fighter, he adopted a young Indian boy as his ward. A foe of privilege, he was a slave owner. A self-professed champion of farmers and artisans, he expressed contempt for their representatives in Congress. He also took steps to expand the power of the executive branch. The 1820s revealed these larger contradictions as national leaders pursued a more democratic form of politics on one hand and supported a system based on class and so-called racial differences on the other. The resulting tensions shaped American society and politics in the third decade of the nineteenth century.

The Politics Behind Western Expansion

How did western expansion affect the nation's politics and economy in the 1820s?

As the United States gained new territory through negotiation and conquest, and people moved west, the nation felt the impact. President Monroe warned Europeans not to intervene any longer in the Western hemisphere. Americans settling west of the Appalachian mountains found a spokesman in Andrew Jackson. Once in the West, settlers faced the same kinds

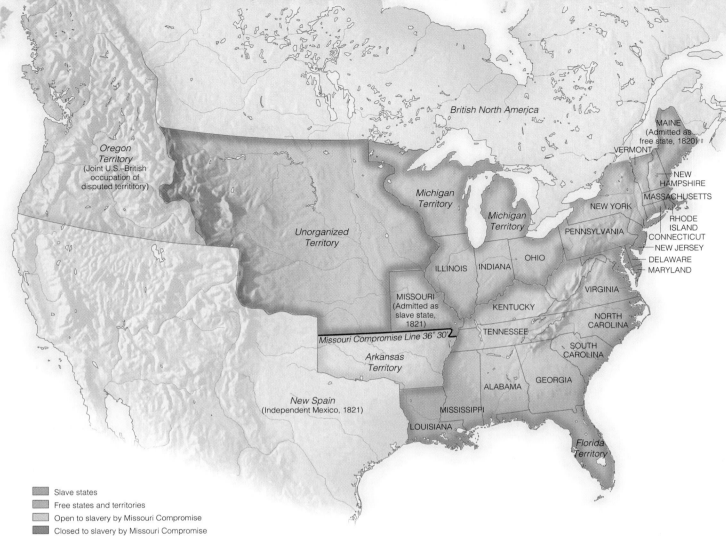

Slave states
Free states and territories
Open to slavery by Missouri Compromise
Closed to slavery by Missouri Compromise

■ MAP 11.1
THE MISSOURI COMPROMISE
Missouri applied for statehood in 1819, threatening the balance between 11 free and 11 slave states. According to a compromise hammered out in Congress, Missouri was admitted as a slave state, and Maine, formerly part of Massachusetts, was admitted as a free state. Slavery was banned above the 36°30′ parallel.

of conflicts that increasingly preoccupied Easterners, especially those between masters and slaves and debtors and creditors. Congressional debates over whether Missouri should be admitted to the Union as a slave or free state sent shock waves throughout the country. Of the political conflict over the fate of slavery in the territories, the elderly Thomas Jefferson wrote, "This momentous question, like a firebell in the night, awakened and filled me with terror. I considered it at once as the death knell of the Union."

•:•–Read the Document
Expanding American and Internal Improvements at **www.myhistorylab.com**

The Missouri Compromise

In 1819 the United States consisted of 22 states. Slavery was legal in half of them. Late that year, the territory of Missouri applied for statehood. This move set off panic in both the North and South because a twenty-third state was bound to upset the delicate balance of senators between slave and free states. The debate over the future of Missouri occupied Congress from December 1819 to March 1820.

In the Senate, Rufus King of New York claimed that Congress had the ultimate authority to set laws governing slavery. However, his colleague William Pinckney of Maryland retorted that new states possessed the same rights as the original 13; that is, they could choose

■ MAP 11.2

PRINCIPAL CANALS BUILT BY 1860

Many canals were expensive ventures and, in some cases, engineering nightmares. The Erie Canal had a competitive advantage because it snaked through the Mohawk Valley, the only major level pass through the mountain chain that stretched from Canada to Georgia. In contrast, the Pennsylvania Main Line Canal, which ran from Harrisburg to Pittsburgh, used a combination of inclined planes and steam engines in ten separate locations to haul boats up and down the Allegheny Mountains.

whether to allow slavery. Maine's application for admission to the Union suggested a way out of the impasse. Speaker of the House of Representatives Henry Clay of Kentucky successfully proposed a plan. Missouri would join the Union as a slave state at the same time that Maine, originally part of Massachusetts, would become the twenty-fourth state and be designated a free one. In the future, slavery would be prohibited from all Louisiana Purchase lands north of latitude 36°30′, an area that included all territory north of present-day Missouri and Kansas. The House and Senate finally approved the compromise, which maintained the balance between the number of slave and free states.

The day Congress sealed the compromise, Secretary of State John Quincy Adams of Massachusetts walked home from the Capitol with Senator John C. Calhoun of South Carolina. The two men engaged in a muted but intense debate over slavery. Calhoun claimed that the institution "was the best guarantee to equality among the whites." Slavery, he asserted, demonstrated that all white men were equal to one another and superior to all blacks. Unnerved by Calhoun's comments, Adams concluded that the debate over Missouri had "betrayed the secret of [Southerners'] souls." By reserving backbreaking toil for blacks, wealthy planters fancied themselves aristocratic lords of the manor. Adams confided in his diary that night, "They look down upon the simplicity of a Yankee's manners, because he has no habits of overbearing like theirs and cannot treat negroes like dogs." Adams feared that North-South conflicts might someday imperil the nation itself.

Ways West

Missouri was just one of the territories west of the Mississippi River where the population had increased during this period. Through land grants and government financing of new methods of transportation, Congress encouraged European American migrants to push their way west and south. The Land Act of 1820 enabled westerners to buy a minimum 80 acres at a price of $1.25 an acre in cash—even in those days, a bargain homestead. Built with the help of government legal and financial aid, new roads and canals, steamboats, and, after the early 1830s, railroads facilitated migration. Between 1820 and 1860, the number of steamboats plying the Mississippi River jumped from 60 to more than 1,000. Canals linked western producers to eastern consumers of grains and cattle and connected western consumers to eastern producers of manufactured goods. Shipping costs and times between Buffalo and New York shrank. Cities such as Rochester and Syracuse, New York, and Cincinnati, Ohio, flourished because of their geographic position along key waterways.

((•—Hear the Audio
The Erie Canal at
www.myhistorylab.com

Among the most significant of these waterways was the **Erie Canal**. Completed in 1825, this engineering marvel used 83 canal locks to link the Great Lakes directly to the East Coast by way of the Hudson River. Public acclaim was thunderous. Upstate New York's economy thrived. And New York City, at the mouth of the Hudson, emerged as the most important port and financial center in the country.

Americans took a variety of routes west. In the 1820s, desperate planters moved out of the exhausted lands of the upper South (the states of Virginia and Maryland), the Carolinas, and Georgia, westward into Alabama, Arkansas, Louisiana, and Mississippi. This migration across the Appalachian Mountains furthered the nationalist idea of the "expansion of liberty

HAULING THE WHOLE WEEKS PICKING

■ The rich bottomlands of the Mississippi Delta proved ideal for growing cotton. After the forced removal of the Five Civilized Tribes from the Old Southwest, slave owners established expansive plantations in the delta. This scene, painted in 1842 by artist William Henry Brown, shows a group of slaves bringing in "the whole weeks picking" of cotton on the Vick plantation near Vicksburg, Mississippi.

■ **MAP 11.3**

MEXICO'S FAR NORTHERN FRONTIER IN 1822

This map shows Mexico's far northern frontier in 1822. When Moses Austin died suddenly in 1821, the task of supervising the settlement of in-migrants from the United States fell to his son Stephen. The Mexican government authorized the younger Austin to act as empresario of the settlement. He was responsible for the legal and economic regulations governing the settlements clustered at the lower reaches of the Colorado and Brazos rivers.

and freedom," a view held by many white men regardless of political affiliation. Yet it also spread slavery. The sight of slave coffles—groups of men, women, and children bound together in chains, hobbling down a city street or a country road—became increasingly common in this western region. In 1821 Virginia, North Carolina, South Carolina, and Georgia had produced two-thirds of the nation's cotton crop; the rest came from recently settled areas. Just a dozen years later the proportions shifted: Tennessee, Louisiana, Alabama, Mississippi, and Florida together produced two-thirds of all cotton, and the remaining one-third came from older areas.

European Americans also migrated across the border into Mexican territory. In 1821 Spain approved the application of a U.S. citizen, Moses Austin, to settle 300 American families on 200,000 fertile acres along the Colorado and Brazos river bottoms in southeastern Texas. Austin died soon after, but his son Stephen carried on his legacy. Within two years, the younger Austin had received permission (now from the government of newly independent Mexico) to bring in another 100 families. These settlers, together with squatters, numbered about 1,500 people. Although the Mexican constitution prohibited slavery, some of the newcomers brought their slaves with them, and some free people of color came on their own. All these migrants from the United States called themselves **Texians** to distinguish themselves from the **Tejanos**, or Spanish-speaking residents of the region. These newly arrived Texians agreed to adopt the Roman Catholic faith and become citizens of Mexico. During the rest of the decade, 900 additional families sponsored by Austin arrived in Texas. They were followed by 3,000 more squatters. Mexican officials feared that they would lose authority over the mass of American newcomers within their borders.

The Panic of 1819 and the Plight of Western Debtors

In 1819 a financial panic swept across the nation, followed by an economic depression that hit western states and territories particularly hard. The Second Bank of the United States played a major role in triggering this economic downturn, which came to be called the Panic of 1819. Granted a 20-year charter by Congress in 1816, the Second Bank resembled its predecessor, seeking to regulate the national economy through loans to state and local banks. In 1819 the bank clamped down on small, local **wildcat banks**, which had extended credit to many people who could not repay their loans. Many homesteaders were not self-sufficient farmers but producers of staple crops or proprietors of small enterprises. They relied on credit from banks and local private lenders. As a result, the bank's crackdown on wildcat banks had a devastating impact on western households. Debtors unable to meet their obligations had their mortgages foreclosed, their homes seized, and their crops and equipment confiscated. Ruined by the Panic of 1819, many western farmers developed an abiding hatred of the Bank of the United States and a deep resentment of eastern financiers.

Davy Crockett's own family history suggests the plight of families dependent on bank credit to create homesteads out of western territory. The son of a propertyless squatter, Crockett had an intense fear of debt. Although he campaigned as a hunter and a farmer, he had built several enterprises on land he leased or owned on Shoal Creek in south-central Tennessee: a water-powered grist mill, a gunpowder factory (worked by slaves), an iron ore mine, and a liquor distillery. For each venture, he had to borrow money from local creditors. Spending much of his time away from home, Crockett relied on his wife, Elizabeth, and his children to manage these businesses. (He had three children by his first wife, Polly, who died in 1815, and eventually would have a total of nine by Elizabeth.)

The depression of 1819 cut off Crockett's sources of credit, and in 1822 a flash flood swept away his grist mill and powder factory. Without milled grain, the distillery could no longer operate. Creditors immediately set upon the family, demanding payment of their debts. The Crocketts were fortunate enough to own land they could sell, using the proceeds to repay their debts and then moving farther west in Tennessee.

Others were not so lucky. Small farmers who lost their land through foreclosure in the Panic of 1819 could not produce crops for the eastern market, contributing to the rise in the price of food. Deprived of credit, small shopkeepers also felt the effects of the depression. With rising unemployment, consumers could not afford to buy cloth, and as the demand for cotton fell, southern plantation owners, too, felt the contraction. Within a few years Andrew Jackson would capitalize on the fears and resentments of working men, farmers, planters, and tradesmen, as he championed the "common man" in opposition to what debtors called the "eastern monied interests." In doing so he would transform the two-party system.

The Monroe Doctrine

Despite the troubled economy, James Monroe won reelection easily in 1820. On the international front, his second term opened on a tense note. Foreign nations had started claiming land or promoting their own interests near U.S. borders. The United States remained especially wary of the Spanish presence on its southern and western borders. In 1818 President Monroe had authorized General Andrew Jackson to broaden his assault on the Seminole Indians—a group composed of Native Americans and runaway slaves—in Florida. For the past two years, U.S. troops had pursued fugitive slaves into Spanish-held Florida.

TABLE 11-1

The Election of 1820

Candidate	Political Party	Electoral Vote
James Monroe	Democratic-Republican	231
John Quincy Adams	Democratic-Republican	1

Now Jackson and his men seized the Spanish fort at Pensacola and claimed all of western Florida for the United States. The United States demanded that Spain either suppress the Seminole population or sell all of east Florida to the United States. With the Transcontinental Treaty of 1819, Spain gave up its right to both Florida and Oregon (although Britain and Russia still claimed land in Oregon). In 1822 General Jackson became the first governor of Florida Territory.

Farther north, in 1821 the emperor of Russia, Czar Alexander I, forbade non-Russians from entering the territory north of the fifty-first parallel and the open sea 100 miles off the coast of what is now Canada and Alaska. The Russians had established trading posts up and down that coast, some almost as far south as San Francisco Bay. Meanwhile, rumors circulated that European monarchs were planning new invasions of Latin America.

Fearful of an alliance among Russia, Prussia, Austria, Spain, and France, President Monroe and Secretary of State John Quincy Adams formulated a policy that became a landmark in American diplomatic history. Adams rejected a British proposal that Great Britain and the United States join forces to oppose a further Spanish encroachment in Latin America. He convinced Monroe that the United States must stand alone against the European powers—Spain in the south and Russia in the northwest—if it hoped to protect its own interests in the Western Hemisphere. In his annual message to Congress in December 1823, the president declared that the era of Europe's colonization of the Americas had ceased. Henceforth, he said, foreign nations would not be allowed to intervene in the Western Hemisphere.

●●●—Read the Document

The Monroe Doctrine (1823)
at **www.myhistorylab.com**

The United States conceived the **Monroe Doctrine** as a self-defense measure aimed specifically at Russia, Spain, and Britain. With the Russo-American Treaty of 1824, Russia agreed to pull back its claims to the area north of 54°40′, the southern tip of the present-day Alaska panhandle. However, the United States did not have the naval power to back up the Monroe Doctrine with force. The doctrine was at first more a statement of principle than a blueprint for action, intended to discourage European powers from political or military meddling in the Western Hemisphere. The doctrine would have greater international significance in the late nineteenth century, when the United States developed the military might to enforce it.

Andrew Jackson's Rise to Power

The election of 1824 provided a striking contrast to the bland affair four years earlier in which Monroe had been elected. In 1824 the field of presidential nominees was crowded, suggesting a party system in disarray. Although all the candidates called themselves "Democratic-Republicans," the label meant little more than the fact that most politicians sought to distance themselves from the outmoded "Federalist" label, which hearkened back to the post-Revolutionary period rather than pointing forward to the nation's new challenges. Nominees included Secretary of State John Quincy Adams, Representative Henry Clay of Kentucky, and Andrew Jackson, now a senator from Tennessee. Jackson received the highest number of electoral votes (99), but no candidate achieved a majority. As a result, the election went to the House of Representatives.

Clay withdrew from the race. He had promised Jackson his support but then endorsed Adams, whom the House subsequently elected. When Adams named Clay secretary of state, Jackson's supporters cried foul. The election, they charged, amounted to nothing more than a corrupt deal between two political insiders.

Haunted by these charges, Adams served his four-year term under a cloud of public distrust. A member of a respected New England family and the son of former president John Adams, the new chief executive had served with distinction in Monroe's cabinet. Still, Adams proved ill suited to the rough-and-tumble world of what came to be called the New Democracy. Adams advocated a greater federal role in internal improvements and public education, a variation on Henry Clay's "American System," a set of policies which promoted a national bank, public funding of canals and turnpikes, and a high tariff to protect domestic manufactures.

Adams's party, now calling itself the **National Republicans**, faced a formidable challenge in the election of 1828. Having seethed for four long years, Andrew Jackson's supporters (the Democratic-Republicans) now urged "the people" to reclaim the White House. The campaign was a nasty one. Jackson's opponents attacked his personal morality and that of his wife and his mother. Jackson's supporters countered with the charge that Adams himself was corrupt and that he and his cronies must be swept from office.

Jackson won a stunning victory, with his supporters hailing the well-to-do slaveholder as the president of the "common" (meaning white) man. In office, Jackson tightened his party's grip on power by introducing a national political spoils system. Through this process, successful candidates rewarded their supporters with jobs and tossed their rivals out of appointed offices. The spoils system let the Democratic-Republicans—now called the Democrats—build a nationwide political machine. Not surprisingly, it also provided fertile ground for corruption and fueled the debate over the use and limits of federal authority.

TABLE 11-2

The Election of 1824

Candidate	Political Party	Popular Vote (%)	Electoral Vote
John Quincy Adams	Democratic-Republican	30.5	84
Andrew Jackson	Democratic-Republican	43.1	99
William H. Crawford	Democratic-Republican	13.1	41
Henry Clay	Democratic-Republican	13.2	37

Read the **Document**

Andrew Jackson, First Annual Message to Congress (1829)
at **www.myhistorylab.com**

TABLE 11-3

The Election of 1828

Candidate	Political Party	Popular Vote (%)	Electoral Vote
Andrew Jackson	Democratic	56.0	178
John Quincy Adams	National Republican	44.0	83

■ Some commentators disapproved of what they considered the excessively lively inauguration gala for President Jackson in 1829. One described the affair this way: "On their arrival at the White House, the motley crowd clamored for refreshments and soon drained the barrels of punch, which had been prepared, in drinking to the health of the new Chief Magistrate. A great deal of glassware was broken, and the East Room was filled with a noisy mob."

Federal Authority and Its Opponents

How did Jackson expand the power of the presidency? Who supported and who opposed Jackson's policies regarding federal authority?

When Americans defeated the British in the War of 1812, they ensured the physical security of the new nation. However, the war's end left a crucial question unanswered: what role would federal authority play in a republic of states? During Andrew Jackson's tenure, Congress, the chief executive, and the Supreme Court all jockeyed for influence over one another and over the states. Jackson claimed a broad popular mandate to increase the power of the presidency, and used it to end the charter of the Second Bank of the United States.

At the same time, militant southern sectionalists regarded the growth of federal executive and judicial power with alarm. If the president could impose a high tariff on the states and if the Supreme Court could deny the states the authority to govern Indians within their own borders, might not high-handed federal officials someday also threaten the South's system of slavery?

Judicial Federalism and the Limits of Law

In a series of notable cases, the Supreme Court, under the leadership of Chief Justice John Marshall, sought to limit states' power to control people and resources within their own boundaries. In *McCulloch v. Maryland* (1819), the Court supported Congress's decision to grant the Second Bank of the United States a 20-year charter. The state of Maryland had imposed a high tax on notes issued by the bank. Declaring that "the power to tax involves the power to destroy," the Supreme Court ruled the state's action unconstitutional. The court justices held that, although the original Constitution did not mention a national bank, Congress retained the authority to create such an institution. This fact implied that Congress also had the power to preserve it. This decision relied on what came to be called a "loose construction" of the Constitution to justify "implied powers" of the government, powers not explicitly stated in the Constitution.

In 1832 a case involving the rights of the Cherokee nation brought the Court head to head with President Jackson's own brand of federal muscle-flexing. With the expansion of cotton cultivation into upland Georgia in the early nineteenth century, white residents of that state increasingly resented the presence of their Cherokee neighbors. At the same time, some Cherokee worked and worshipped in ways similar to European Americans: they cultivated farmland, converted to Christianity, and established a formal legal code. On July 4, 1827, Cherokee leaders met in convention to devise a republican constitution. In the grand tradition of the Patriots of 1776, the group proclaimed the Cherokee a sovereign nation, responsible for its own affairs and free of the dictates of individual (U.S.) states.

By the late 1820s, however, many white people, including the president, were calling for the removal of the Cherokee from the Southeast. The 1829 discovery of gold in the Georgia hills brought 10,000 white miners to Cherokee territory in a gold rush that the Indians called the "Great Intrusion." President Jackson saw the very existence of the Cherokee nation as an affront to his authority and a hindrance to Georgia's economic well-being. He resented the fact that the Cherokee considered themselves a sovereign nation, independent of the U.S. president. Jackson, in fact, favored removing all Indians from the Southeast to make way for whites. He declared that Georgia should be rid of "a few thousand savages" so that "towns and prosperous farms" could develop there. In 1830, with the president's backing, Congress passed the Indian Removal Act. The act provided for "an exchange of lands with the Indians residing in any of the states or territories, and for their removal west of the river Mississippi."

Outraged by this naked land grab, the Cherokee nation refused to sign the removal treaties specified by Congress as part of the Indian Removal Act. In a petition to Congress in 1830, members of the group declared, "We wish to remain on the land of our fathers. We

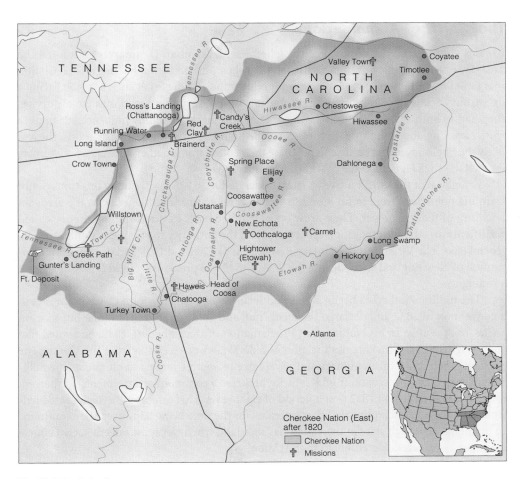

■ **MAP 11.4**
THE CHEROKEE NATION AFTER 1820
This map shows the Cherokee nation on the eve of removal to Indian Territory (present-day Oklahoma).
The discovery of gold in the region sparked a constitutional battle over control of Cherokee land.
In 1832 the Supreme Court ruled that the federal government had ultimate authority over Indian nations.
The state of Georgia ignored the ruling and sought to enforce its own laws in Cherokee territory.

have a perfect and original right to claim this, without interruption or molestation." In an effort to protect their land titles, the Cherokee first tried to take their case to Georgia courts, but Georgia refused to allow them to press their claim. The Georgia legislature maintained that it had authority over all the Indians living within the state's borders, and that the Cherokee nation lacked jurisdiction over its own people. The Cherokee nation appealed to the Supreme Court.

The Cherokee hoped that the Supreme Court would support their position that they were an independent entity, not bound by the laws of Georgia. In a set of cases—*Cherokee Nation v. Georgia* (1831) and *Worcester v. Georgia* (1832)—the Court agreed that Georgia's authority did not extend to the Cherokee nation. The Court proclaimed that Indian self-governing bodies were "domestic dependent nations" under the authority of the U.S. government, not the individual states. Under this ruling, Georgia lacked the authority to force Indians from their land. More generally, the states must defer to the federal government in issues related to the welfare and governance of the Indians. The governor of Georgia rejected these Supreme Court rulings, as did Jackson. Of the *Worcester* decision, Jackson declared, "John Marshall has made his decision. Now let him enforce it." In 1832 the president instead sent troops to Georgia to begin forcing the Indians out of their homeland.

•●•⌐Read the Document
Memorial of the Cherokee Nation (1830) at **www.myhistorylab.com**

The "Tariff of Abominations"

Besides engineering the removal of the Cherokee, Jacksonian Democrats continued the post–War of 1812 policy of high tariffs. In 1828 they pushed through Congress legislation that raised fees on imported manufactured products and raw materials such as wool. Facing a disastrous decline in cotton prices after the Panic of 1819, Southerners protested: to survive, they had to both sell their cotton on the open world market and buy high-priced supplies from New England or Europe. In their view, the higher the tariff on English goods, the less likely the English were to continue to purchase their cotton from southern planters. Southerners dubbed the 1828 legislation the "Tariff of Abominations."

A renewal of the tariff four years later moderated the 1828 rates. But by this time, South Carolina politicians were in no mood to sit back and accept what they saw as the arrogant wielding of federal power. They drew on past precedents in developing a theory called **nullification**—the idea that individual states had the authority to reject, or nullify, specific federal laws. The Virginia and Kentucky Resolutions of 1798 and 1799 and the Hartford Convention of New England states during the War of 1812 had previously raised this issue of state sovereignty.

The nullification crisis began when politicians led by Senator John C. Calhoun met in a convention in 1832 and declared the tariff "null and void" in South Carolina. But Jackson struck back swiftly. In his Nullification Proclamation of December 10, 1832, he argued that states' rights did not include nullification of federal laws or secession from the Union. The president then sent a token military and naval force to South Carolina to intimidate the nullifiers. Henry Clay, now senator from Kentucky, brokered a compromise agreement: a 10 percent reduction in the Tariff of 1832 over a period of eight years. This compromise finally eased tensions, and the South Carolina nullifiers retreated for the time being. However, they continued to maintain "that each state of the Union has the right, whenever it may deem such a course necessary . . . to secede peaceably from the Union."

● ●—Read the Document

Proclamation Regarding Nullification at www.myhistorylab.com

The "Monster Bank"

A similar struggle unfolded over the power of the federal government regarding a central bank. The repository of federal funds ($10 million), the Bank of the United States in the 1830s had 30 branches and controlled the money supply by dictating how state banks should repay their loans: in paper notes or in currency. As a central (though privately held) institution, the bank also aided economic growth and development by extending loans to commercial enterprises.

In 1832 Jackson vetoed a bill that would have renewed the charter of the Second Bank of the United States, which was due to expire in 1836. Somewhat contradictorily, Jackson claimed to represent the interests of small borrowers such as farmers, but he also advocated hard money (currency in the form of gold or silver, not paper or credit extended by banks). Traditionally, small lenders objected to hard-money policies, which kept the supply of currency low and interest rates for borrowers high. Jackson also objected to the bank's work as a large commercial institution. For example, he blamed the bank for precipitating the Panic and Depression of 1819 by withholding credit from small banks, causing them to recall their loans and, in some cases, fail.

Jackson condemned the bank as a "monster" intent on devouring hardworking people and enriching a few eastern financiers. By vetoing the bank bill, Jackson angered members of Congress and his own cabinet. They had urged

TABLE 11-4			
The Election of 1832			
Candidate	Political Party	Popular Vote (%)	Electoral Vote
Andrew Jackson	Democratic	55.0	219
Henry Clay	National Republican	42.4	49
John Floyd	Independent	—	11
William Wirt	Anti-Masonic	2.6	7

him to recharter the bank because they believed the credit system was necessary for economic progress and expansion. Convinced that Jackson had overextended his reach, his opponents seized on the issue as a sign of the chief executive's political vulnerability. However, Congress upheld Jackson's veto of the Second Bank (the bank closed when its charter expired in 1836). Nominated for president by the National Republicans in 1832, Henry Clay drew support from merchants who had benefited from Bank of the United States loans and from the sizable contingent of Jackson-haters. But Jackson won in a landslide, carrying not only his stronghold, the West, but also the South and substantial parts of New York, Pennsylvania, and New England.

While in office, Jackson used his veto power a total of 12 times. All his predecessors *combined* had used it just ten times. When his opponents finally formed a political party in 1834, they called themselves **Whigs**, after the English antimonarchist party. In choosing this name, their intention was to ridicule "King Andrew." The Whigs opposed the man who had built up the power of the presidency in defiance of Congress and the Supreme Court.

Americans in the "Age of the Common Man"

In the early 1830s, a wealthy Frenchman named Alexis de Tocqueville visited the United States and wrote about the contradictions he saw. In his book *Democracy in America* (published in 1835), Tocqueville noted that the United States lacked the rigid hierarchy of class privilege that characterized European nations. With universal white manhood suffrage, white men could vote and run for office regardless of their class or religion. However, Tocqueville also noted some sore spots in American democratic values and practices. He commented on the plight of groups deprived of the right to vote, whose lack of freedom stood out starkly in the otherwise egalitarian society of the United States. He sympathized with the southeastern Indians uprooted from their homelands. He raised the possibility that conflicts between blacks and whites might eventually lead to bloodshed. He even contrasted the situation of young unmarried white women, who seemed so free-spirited, with that of wives, who appeared cautious and dull. He concluded, "In America a woman loses her independence forever in the bonds of matrimony." Tocqueville saw America for what it was: a blend of freedom and slavery, of independence and dependence.

How did the work of Indians, free and enslaved African Americans, and women change during the "Age of the Common Man"?

Wards, Workers, and Warriors: Native Americans

Population growth in the United States—and on the borderlands between the United States and Mexican territory—put pressure on Indian societies. Yet different cultural groups responded in different ways to this pressure. Some, like the Cherokee, conformed to European American ways and became sedentary farmers. Others were forced to work for whites. Still others either waged war on white settlements and military forces or retreated farther and farther from European American settlements in the hope of avoiding clashes with the intruders.

Nevertheless, prominent whites continued to denigrate the humanity of all Indians. In the 1820s, Henry Clay claimed that Indians were "essentially inferior to the Anglo-Saxon race . . . and their disappearance from the human family will be no great loss to the world." In 1828 the House of Representatives Committee on Indian Affairs surveyed the Indians of the South and concluded that "an Indian cannot work" and that all Indians were lazy and notable for their "thirst for spirituous liquours." According to the committee, when European settlers depleted reserves of wildlife, Indians as a group would cease to exist.

■ This photo of the Fairmont Waterworks in Philadelphia shows the effects of Greek architecture on American public buildings in the early nineteenth century. Designed by Frederick C. Graff, the waterworks were completed in 1822. Numerous banks, colleges, commercial buildings, and large private homes built during this period were designed in the Greek Revival style. The United States saw itself as the embodiment of democracy, a form of government associated with Athens and other early Greek city-states.

◉ See the Map

Native American Land Cessions to 1829 at www.myhistorylab.com

Members of the Cherokee nation bitterly denounced these assertions. "The Cherokees do not live upon the chase [for game]," they pointed out. Neither did the Creek, Choctaw, Chickasaw, and Seminole—the other members of the Five Civilized Tribes, so called for their varying degrees of conformity to white people's ways.

In parts of California, Spanish missionaries conquered Indian groups, converted them to Christianity, and then forced them to work in the missions. In missions up and down the California coast, Indians worked as weavers, tanners, shoemakers, bricklayers, carpenters, blacksmiths, and other artisans. Some herded cattle and raised horses. Indian women cooked for the mission, cleaned, and spun wool. They wove cloth and sewed garments.

But even Indians living in or near missions resisted the cultural change imposed by the intruders. Catholic missionaries complained that Indian women such as those of the Chumash refused to learn Spanish. The refusal among some Indians to completely assimilate signaled persistent, deep-seated conflicts between native groups and incoming settlers. In 1824 a revolt among hundreds of newly converted Indians at the mission *La Purisima Concepción* north of Santa Barbara revealed a rising militancy among native peoples.

After the War of 1812, the U.S. government had rewarded some military veterans with land grants in the Old Northwest. Federal agents tried to clear the way for these new settlers by ousting Indians from the area. Overwhelmed by the number of whites, some Indian groups such as the Peoria and Kaskaskia gave up their lands to the interlopers. Others took a stand against the white intrusion. In 1826 and 1827, the Winnebago attacked white families and boat pilots living near Prairie du Chien, Wisconsin. Two years later, the Sauk chief Black Hawk (known to Indians as Ma-ka-tai-me-she-kia-kiak) assembled a coalition of Fox, Winnebago, Kickapoo, and Potawatomi. Emboldened by the prospect of aid from British Canada, they clashed with federal troops and raided farmers' homesteads and miners' camps.

In August 1832 a force of 1,300 U.S. soldiers and volunteers struck back, killing 300 Indian men, women, and children encamped on the Bad Axe River in western Wisconsin. The massacre, the decisive point of what came to be called the Black Hawk War, marked the end of armed Indian resistance north of the Ohio River and east of the Mississippi.

Slaves and Free People of Color

In the 1820s, the small proportion of free blacks within the southern population declined further. Southern whites perceived free blacks, like Indians, as an unwelcome and dangerous presence, especially given the possibility that they would conspire with enslaved people

■ Artist Charles Bird King painted this portrait of Sequoyah while the Indian leader was in Washington, D.C., in 1828. Government officials honored him for developing a written form of the Cherokee language. He is wearing a medal presented to him by the Cherokee nation in 1825. He later settled permanently in Sallisaw, in what is today Sequoyah County, Oklahoma.

to spark a rebellion. For these reasons some states began to outlaw private manumissions (the practice of individual owners freeing their slaves) and to force free blacks to leave the state altogether. In the 1820s the small proportion of free blacks within the southern population declined further.

One free black who inspired such fears was Denmark Vesey. Born on the Danish-controlled Caribbean island of St. Thomas in 1767, Vesey was a literate carpenter as well as a religious leader. In 1799 he won $1,500 in a Charleston, South Carolina, lottery and used some of the money to buy his freedom. In the summer of 1822, a Charleston court claimed to have unearthed evidence of a "diabolical plot" hatched by Vesey together with plantation slaves from the surrounding area.

Yet the historical record strongly suggests that no plot ever existed. Black "witnesses" who feared for their own lives provided inconsistent and contradictory testimony to a panel of judges. Authorities never located any material evidence of a planned uprising, such as stockpiles of weapons. Under fire from other Charleston elites for rushing to judgment, the judges redoubled their efforts to embellish vague rumors of black discontent into a tale of a well-orchestrated uprising and to implicate growing numbers of black people. As a result of the testimony of several slaves, 35 black men were hanged and another 18 exiled outside the United States. Of those executed, Vesey and 23 other men said nothing to support even the vaguest charges of the court.

In the North, some blacks were granted the right to vote after emancipation in the late eighteenth century; however, many of those voting rights were lost in the early nineteenth century. New Jersey (in 1807), Connecticut (1818), New York (1821), and Pennsylvania (1838) all revoked the legislation that had let black men cast ballots. Free northern blacks continued to suffer under a number of legal restrictions. Most were not citizens and therefore perceived themselves as oppressed like the slaves in the South.

> *Some states began to outlaw private manumissions and to force free blacks to leave the state altogether.*

A new group of black leaders in the urban North began to link their fate to that of their enslaved brothers and sisters in the South. In Boston, North Carolina–born David Walker published his fiery *Walker's Appeal to the Coloured Citizens of the World* in 1829. Walker called for all blacks to integrate fully into American society, shunning racial segregation whether initiated by whites or by blacks themselves. Reminding his listeners of the horrors of the slave trade, he declared that black people were ready to die for freedom: "I give it as a fact, let twelve black men get well armed for battle, and they will kill and put to flight fifty whites."

●●●—| Read the Document

An Account of the Late Intended Insurrection Among a Portion of Blacks of this City at **www.myhistorylab.com**

Northern black leaders disagreed among themselves on the issues of integration and black separatism—for example, whether blacks should create their own schools or press for inclusion in the public educational system. A few leaders favored leaving the country altogether, believing that black people would never find peace and freedom in the United States. Founded by whites in New Jersey in 1817, the American Colonization Society (ACS) paid for a small number of black Americans to settle Monrovia, later named Liberia, on the west coast of Africa. The ACS drew support from a variety of groups, including whites in the upper South who wanted to free their slaves but believed that black and white people could not live in the same country, and some slaves and free people of color convinced that colonization would give them a fresh start. A small number of American-born blacks settled in Liberia. However, most black activists rejected colonization. They had been born on American soil, and their forebears had been buried there. Maria Stewart, a black abolitionist and public speaker in Boston declared, "Before I go [to Africa] the bayonet shall pierce me through."

> *Northern black leaders disagreed among themselves on the issues of integration and black separatism.*

Northern whites sought to control black people and their movements. Outspoken black men and women such as Walker and Stewart alarmed northern whites who feared that if blacks could claim decent jobs, white people would lose their own jobs. African Americans

INTERPRETING HISTORY

Eulalia Pérez Describes her Work in a California Mission, 1823

Born to Spanish parents in Baja, California, Eulalia Pérez was a widow with five daughters when she became the chief housekeeper for the San Gabriel Mission in the early 1820s. She secured her position by winning a cooking competition between herself and two other Spanish women. Here she gives an account of her many duties in the mission.

I made several kinds of soup, a variety of meat dishes and whatever else happened to pop into my head that I knew how to prepare. . . .

Because of all this, employment was provided for me at the mission. At first they assigned me two Indians so that I could show them how to cook. . . .

The missionaries were very satisfied; this made them think more highly of me. I spent about a year teaching those two Indians. I did not have to do the work, only direct them, because they already had learned a few of the fundamentals.

After this, the missionaries conferred among themselves and agreed to hand over the mission keys to me. This was in 1821, if I remember correctly. . . .

The duties of the housekeeper were many. In the first place, every day she handed out the rations for the mess hut. To do this she had to count the unmarried women, bachelors, day-laborers, vaqueros [cowboys]. . . . Besides that, she had to hand out daily rations to the heads of households. In short, she was responsible for the distribution of supplies to the Indian population and to the missionaries' kitchen. She was in charge of the key to the clothing storehouse where materials were given out for dresses for the unmarried and married women and children. Then she also had to take care of cutting and making clothes for the men.

Furthermore, she was in charge of cutting and making the vaqueros' outfits, from head to foot—that is, for the vaqueros who rode in saddles. Those who rode bareback received nothing more than their cotton blanket and loincloth, while those who rode in saddles were dressed the same way as the Spanish-speaking inhabitants; that is, they were given shirt, vest, jacket, trousers, hat, cowboy boots, shoes and spurs; and a saddle, bridle and lariat for the horse. Besides, each vaquero was given a big silk or cotton handkerchief, and a sash of Chinese silk or Canton crepe, or whatever there happened to be in the storehouse.

They put under my charge everything having to do with clothing. I cut and fitted, and my five daughters sewed up the pieces. When they could not handle everything, the father was told, and then women from the town of Los Angeles were employed, and the father paid them.

Besides this, I had to attend to the soap-house, . . . to the wine-presses, and to the olive-crushers that produced oil, which I worked in myself. . . .

I handled the distribution of leather, calf-skin, chamois, sheepskin, Morocco leather, fine scarlet cloth, nails, thread, silk, etc.—everything having to do with the making of

who worked outdoors as wagon drivers, peddlers, and street sweepers were taunted and in some cases attacked by whites who demanded deference from blacks in public. In October 1824, a mob of white men invaded a black neighborhood in Providence, Rhode Island. They terrorized its residents, destroyed buildings, and left the place "almost entirely in ruins." The catalyst for the riot had come the previous day, when a group of blacks had refused to yield the inside of the sidewalk—a cleaner place to walk—to white passersby.

In the South, whites in 1831 took steps to reinforce the institution of slavery, using both violent and legal means. That year Nat Turner, an enslaved preacher and mystic, led a slave revolt in Southampton, Virginia. In the 1820s, the young Turner had looked skyward and had seen visions of "white spirits and black spirits engaged in battle . . . and blood flowed in streams." Turner believed that he had received divine instructions to lead other slaves to freedom, to "arise and prepare myself, and slay my enemies with their own weapons." In August he and a group of followers that eventually numbered 80 moved through the countryside, killing whites wherever they could find them. Ultimately, nearly 60 whites died at the hands of Turner's rebels. Turner himself managed to evade capture for more than two months. After he was captured, he was tried, convicted, and executed.

In the wake of the Turner revolt, a wave of white hysteria swept the South. In Virginia near where the killings had occurred, whites assaulted blacks with unbridled fury. The saddles, shoes and what was needed for the belt- and shoe-making shops.

Every week I delivered supplies for the troops and Spanish-speaking servants. These consisted of beans, corn, garbanzos, lentils, candles, soap and lard. To carry out this distribution, they placed at my disposal an Indian servant named Lucio, who was trusted completely by the missionaries.

When it was necessary, some of my daughters did what I could not find the time to do.

Questions

1. *What were some of the things produced at the mission?*
2. *Why did the position of housekeeper confer such high status?*
3. *What other kinds of workers in the mission does Pérez mention?*
4. *How does this account reveal some of the larger purposes of Spanish missions? In what ways were these missions colonial as well as religious enterprises?*

Source: Eileen Boris and Nelson Lichtenstein, eds., *Major Problems in the History of American Workers*, 2nd ed. (New York: Houghton Mifflin, 2002), 93–95.

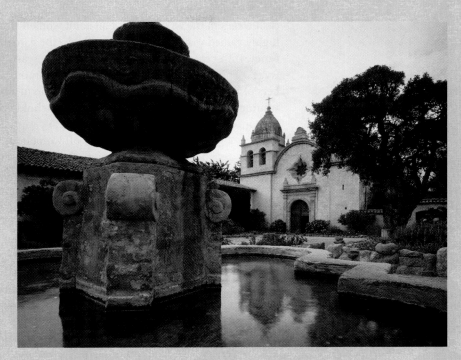

Mission San Carlos Borromeo in Carmel, California. Beyond the fountain is the mission's central courtyard. On the left is the rancheria, where Indians lived. In this and other missions along the California coast, Indians maintained separate residences in traditional-style dwellings. Even Indians who worked and prayed at the missions attempted to preserve their own customs related to clothing, food, and kin and family relations.

Virginia legislature seized the occasion to defeat various antislavery proposals. Thereafter, all the slave states moved to strengthen the institution of slavery. For all practical purposes, public debate over slavery ceased throughout the American South.

Read the **Document**
The Confession of Nat Turner (1831)
at **www.myhistorylab.com**

Legal and Economic Dependence: The Status of Women

Regardless of where they lived, enslaved women and Indian women had almost no rights under either U.S. or Spanish law. However, legal systems in the United States and the Spanish borderlands differed in their treatment of women. In the United States, most of the constraints that white married women had experienced in the colonial period still applied in the 1820s. A husband controlled the property that his wife brought to the marriage, and he had legal authority over their children. Indeed, the wife was considered her husband's possession. She had no right to make a contract, keep money she earned, vote, run for office, or serve on a jury. In contrast, in the Spanish Southwest, married women could own land and conduct business on their own. At the same time, however, husbands, fathers, and local priests continued to exert much influence over the lives of these women.

European-American women's economic subordination served as a rationale for their political inferiority. The "common man" concept rested on the assumption that men had the largest stake in society because only they owned property. That stake made them responsible citizens.

Yet women contributed to the economy in myriad ways. Although few women earned cash wages in the 1820s, almost all adult women worked. In the colonial period, society had highly valued women's labor in the fields, the garden, and the kitchen. However, in the early nineteenth century, work was becoming increasingly identified as labor that earned cash wages. This attitude proved particularly common in the Northeast, where increasing numbers of workers labored under the supervision of a boss. As this belief took root, men began valuing women's contributions to the household economy less and less. If women did not earn money, many men asked, did they really work at all?

> *Although few women earned cash wages in the 1820s, almost all adult women worked.*

In these years, well-off women in the northeastern and mid-Atlantic states began to think of themselves as consumers and not producers of goods. They relied more and more on store-bought cloth and household supplies. Some could also afford to hire servants to perform housework for them. Privileged women gradually stopped thinking of their responsibilities as making goods or processing and preparing food. Rather, their main tasks were to manage servants and create a comfortable home for their husbands and children.

In contrast, women in other parts of the country continued to engage in the same forms of household industry that had characterized the colonial period. In Spanish settlements, women played a central role in household production. They made all of their family's clothes by carding, spinning, and weaving the wool from sheep. They tanned cowhides and ground blue corn to make tortillas, or *atole*. They produced their own candles and soap, and they plastered the walls of the home. In the Spanish mission of San Gabriel, California, the widow Eulalia Pérez cooked, sewed, ministered to the ill, and instructed children in reading and writing. At Mission San Diego, Apolonaria Lorenzana worked as a healer and cared for the church sacristy and priestly vestments.

Indian women also engaged in a variety of essential tasks. Sioux and Mandan women, though of a social rank inferior to men, performed a great deal of manual labor in their own villages. They dressed buffalo skins that the men later sold to traders. They collected water and wood, cooked, dried meat and fruit, and cultivated maize (corn), pumpkins, and squash with hoes made from the shoulder blades of elk. These women worked collectively within a network of households rather than individually within nuclear families.

Some women worked for cash wages during this era. New England women and children, for example, were the vanguard of factory wage-earners in the early manufacturing system. In Massachusetts in 1820, women and children constituted almost a third of all manufacturing workers. In the largest textile factories, they made up fully 80 percent of the workforce.

The business of textile manufacturing took the tasks of spinning thread and weaving cloth out of the home and relocated those tasks in factories. The famous "Lowell mill girls" are an apt example. Young, unmarried white women from New Hampshire, Vermont, and Massachusetts, these workers moved to the new company town of Lowell, Massachusetts, to take jobs as textile machine operatives. In New England, thousands of young men had migrated west, tipping the sex ratio in favor of women and creating a reserve of female laborers. But to attract young women to factory work, mill owners had to reassure them (and their parents) that they would be safe and well cared for away from home. To that end, they established boarding houses where employees could live together under the supervision of a matron—an older woman who served as their mother-away-from-home. Many young women valued the friendships they made with their coworkers and the money they made in the mills. Some of these women sent their wages back home so that their fathers could pay off the mortgage or their brothers could attend school.

Most ordinary women received little in the way of formal education. Yet elite young women had expanded educational opportunities, beginning in the early nineteenth century.

Emma Willard founded a female academy in Troy, New York, in 1821, and Catharine Beecher established the Hartford (Connecticut) Female Seminary two years later. For the most part, such schools catered to the daughters of wealthy families, young women who would never have to work in a factory to survive. Hailed as a means to prepare young women to serve as wives and mothers, the schools taught geography, foreign languages, mathematics, science, and philosophy, as well as the "female" pursuits of embroidery and music.

Out of this curriculum designed especially for women emerged women's rights activists, women who keenly felt both the potential of their own intelligence and the degrading nature of their social situation. Elizabeth Cady, an 1832 graduate of the Troy Female Seminary, later went on to marry Henry B. Stanton and bear seven children. But by the 1840s, she strode onto the national stage as a tireless advocate of women's political and economic rights.

Ties That Bound a Growing Population

As the nation expanded westward, population growth and migration patterns disrupted old bonds of community. When people left their place of birth, they often severed ties with their family and original community. New forms of social cohesion arose to replace these traditional ties. New religions sought to make sense of the changing political and economic landscape. High literacy rates among the population created a new community of readers—a dispersed audience for periodicals as well as for a new, uniquely American literature. Finally, opinion makers used the printed word to spread new ideas and values across regional boundaries. These ideas, such as glorification of male ambition, helped knit together far-flung segments of the population, men and women who began to speak of an "American character."

In what ways did Americans maintain a sense of community in the face of unprecedented migration and population growth?

New Visions of Religious Faith

New forms of religious faith arose in response to turbulent times. During the Indian Wars in the Old Northwest, a Winnebago prophet named White Cloud helped Black Hawk create a **coalition** of Winnebago, Potawatomi, Kickapoo, Sauk, and Fox Indians. A mystic and medicine man, White Cloud preached against white people and exhorted his followers to defend their way of life, an Indian way that knew no tribal boundaries. White Cloud, the religious leader, and Black Hawk, the military leader, surrendered together to federal troops on August 27, 1832, their alliance signifying the spiritual component in the Indians' militant resistance to whites. Through the rest of the nineteenth century, a number of Indian groups found inspiration, and in some cases common ground, in the teachings of Indian religious leaders.

New religious enthusiasms took hold in other parts of the country as well. In the late 1820s and early 1830s, the **Second Great Awakening** swept western New York. The fervor of religious revivals so heated the region that people began to call it "the Burned-Over District." Huge crowds of people of various Protestant denominations attended week-long prayer meetings, sat together on the "anxious bench" for sinners, and listened, transfixed, as new converts told of their path to righteousness.

What explains this wave of religious enthusiasm? A major factor was a clergyman named Charles Grandison Finney, who managed to tap into the wellspring of hope and anxiety of the time. A former lawyer, Finney preached that people were moral free agents, fully capable of deciding between right and wrong and doing good in the world. Finney's message had great appeal during this period of rapid social, economic, and technological change. In New England and New York, for example, canals were bringing new kinds of goods to rural areas and longtime residents were departing for the Midwest. Traditional social relationships seemed threatened.

Watch the Video
Evangelical Religion and Politics, Then and Now at
www.myhistorylab.com

Throughout the country, religious institutions also grappled with questions about slavery. As the fear of possible black uprisings spread, white clergy in the South began to turn away from their former willingness to convert anyone. Instead, they began seeking respectability in the eyes of the well-to-do, slave-owning class. Incorporating masculine imagery into their sermons, they strove to reinforce the power of husband over wife, parent over child, and master over slave, relations that defined the typical plantation household.

Elsewhere, some church leaders sought to purge Christianity of what they saw as its too-worldly nature and to revive the early, simple church that Jesus and his disciples had established. On April 6, 1830, a young farmer named Joseph Smith founded the Church of Jesus Christ of Latter-Day Saints (also called the Mormons) in Fayette, New York. Smith said that, in a vision, an angel named Moroni presented him with the text of a holy book originally written by a Native American historian more than 1,400 years earlier. The text was called the *Book of Mormon*. Together with the Old and New Testaments, it formed the basis of a new faith. Over the next few years, the Mormon Church grew rapidly, claiming 8,000 members by the mid-1830s. However, the young church also aroused intense hostility among mainstream Protestant denominations that regarded the new group's theology and textual inspiration with suspicion. It was almost impossible for religious institutions to escape the worldly realm of politics and social fragmentation.

Literate and Literary America

Around the same time, a young widow named Sarah Hale broke new ground for women. In 1821 she became the first woman to edit an American periodical when she accepted responsibility for editing the Boston-based *Ladies Magazine*, later renamed *Godey's Lady's Book*. Once a hatmaker but now a published poet and novelist, Hale portrayed women as especially devout and thus powerful: men might claim as their domain "the government and the glory of the world," she wrote in 1832, "but nevertheless, what man shall become depends upon the secret, silent influence of women." That influence, Hale and other men and women like her believed, derived from women's roles as nurturers and caretakers. Thousands of similar magazines—most short-lived—appeared between 1825 and 1850.

Just as sentimental fiction and poetry attracted a large readership among women, a number of male writers staked their claim to emerging American literature. Washington Irving, James Fenimore Cooper, and William Cullen Bryant all explored regional histories and landscapes in their works. In *Rip Van Winkle* (1819) and the *Legend of Sleepy Hollow* (1820), Irving wrote about the legends of upstate New York. Cooper explored the western New York middle ground contested by the British, Americans, French, and Indians in the late eighteenth century in such works as *The Spy* (1821) and *The Last of the Mohicans* (1826). Bryant, inspired by the sight of the Illinois plains in 1832, penned "The Prairies," a praise-song to the vast plains as beautiful and "quick with life."

Along with this new American literary tradition, small towns across the nation began publishing newspapers to educate, inform, and entertain readers. News stories about national elections and legislation, about foreign monarchs and conflicts, reached log cabins in the West as well as elegant townhouses in Boston and Philadelphia. Wrote Washington Irving in 1820, "Over no nation does the press hold a more absolute control than over the people of America, for the universal education of the poorest classes makes every individual a reader." Widely distributed newspapers, books, and magazines promoted a set of values that writers claimed described an enduring American character. The ideal American supposedly was ambitious—ready to seize opportunity

The ideal American supposedly was ambitious—ready to seize opportunity wherever it could be found—and at the same time devoted to home and family.

Henry F. Darby, *The Reverend John Atwood and His Family*, 1845. Gift of Maxim Karolik for the M. and M. Karolik Collection of American Paintings, 1815–1865, 62.269. Museum of Fine Arts, Boston. Reproduced with permission. Copyright 2003 Museum of Fine Arts, Boston. All Rights Reserved

■ **The Rev. John Atwood and family reading the Bible, 1845.**

wherever it could be found—and at the same time devoted to home and family. In fact, these values strongly resembled those adopted by the British middle classes at the same time. Indeed, the United States spawned its own brand of middle-class sensibility called Victorianism, after the English queen who reigned from 1837 to 1901.

Five core values defined early American Victorianism. First, the Victorians believed in the significance of the individual. People should be judged on the basis of their character, not on the circumstances of their birth. This belief, however, generally applied only to white men. Second, individuals should have the freedom to advance as far as their talents and ambition took them; no person should claim advantages over others by virtue of a noble title or aristocratic lineage. Third, work was intrinsically noble, whether performed by a canal digger wielding a pick-axe or a merchant using a quill pen. All people, regardless of their trade, deserved to reap the fruits of their labor. Fourth, everyone should exercise self-control and restraint in activities such as drinking and engaging in sexual relations. Finally, men and women occupied separate but complementary spheres. American society could be orderly and stable only if men could find a haven from the heartless world of work in their own homes. There, wives tended the hearth and infused the household with their love, self-sacrifice, and religious devotion.

CONCLUSION

Western settlement infused American politics with raw energy in the 1820s. Andrew Jackson was the first in a long line of presidents who boasted of their humble origins and furthered their careers by denouncing what they called the privileges enjoyed by wealthy Easterners. The challenges faced by western settlers in establishing homesteads and paying their debts emerged as national, not purely local, issues. Through the sheer force of his personality, Andrew Jackson exemplified these dramatic changes in the political landscape. Almost single-handedly, he extended the limits of executive power and remade the American party system in the process.

At the same time, the contradictions in Jacksonian politics became ever more glaring. As the nation expanded its borders and diversified its economy, distinctions between social classes sharpened. The country also staked its claim to foreign territory, using violence to advance democratic values. Meanwhile, the North and South eyed each other with increasing distrust. And the contrast between those who moved from place to place voluntarily and those who were forced to move became even more striking.

For Review

✓●─Study and Review at www.myhistorylab.com

1. How did Jackson shape the role of the presidency and the federal government? What was the significance of the nullification crisis? The clash over the national bank?

2. What factors account for the rise of new political parties during this period?

3. Discuss the constitutional principles at stake in debates over the rights of the Cherokee.

4. Who benefited from the "Age of the Common Man"? Who was left out?

Chronology: 1819–1832

1819 Spain cedes Florida to United States.
Tallmadge Amendment.
Panic of 1819 triggers economic depression.

1820 Missouri Compromise maintains North–South balance of power.
Washington Irving, "The Legend of Sleepy Hollow."

1821 Mexico gains independence from Spain.
Sequoyah completes Cherokee syllabary.

1822 Charleston officials convict and hang blacks in Vesey "plot."

1823 Monroe Doctrine declares Western Hemisphere off limits to Europe.
Catharine Beecher establishes Hartford Female Seminary.
Lowell textile mills open.

1824 Erie Canal opens.

1826 American Society for the Promotion of Temperance founded.

1827 Workingmen's party founded in Philadelphia.

1828 *Cherokee Phoenix* begins publication.

1829 Gold discovered on Cherokee lands in Georgia.

1831 Nat Turner leads slave rebellion in Virginia.
William Lloyd Garrison publishes *The Liberator*.

1832 Nullification crisis. *Worcester v. Georgia*.
Jackson vetoes Second Bank of the United States.
Black Hawk War.

Key Terms

Coalition An alliance of parties, factions, or nations. p. 279

Erie Canal Waterway linking the New York cities of Troy and Albany, on the Hudson River, with Buffalo, on the eastern tip of Lake Erie; in the 1820s, the opening of the Erie Canal revolutionized trading between the Midwest and East Coast and established New York City as the most important financial center in the United States. p. 265

Monroe Doctrine Policy announced by President James Monroe in 1823 that the era of European colonization of the Americas had ceased; warned foreign powers, especially Russia, Spain, and Britain, that the United States would not allow them to intervene in the Western Hemisphere. p. 268

National Republicans A political party, led by John Adams in the 1820s, that favored a greater federal role in funding internal improvements and public education; forerunner of the Whigs, formed in opposition to President Andrew Jackson. p. 269

Nullification The doctrine that a state has the right to ignore or nullify certain federal laws with which it disagrees. p. 272

Second Great Awakening A series of Protestant religious revivals that began in the 1790s and continued through the 1820s. Prominent revivalists such as Charles Grandison Finney sought to link the life of the spirit with political action and reform efforts. p. 279

Tejanos Spanish-speaking residents of the Mexican (and later, U.S.) state of Texas. p. 266

Texians The name used by U.S.-born citizens who lived in the Mexican state of Texas. p. 266

Whigs A national political party formed in 1834 in opposition to the presidency of Andrew Jackson and his policy of expanding the power of the president. The Whigs favored congressional funding for internal improvements and other forms of federal support for economic development. p. 273

Wildcat banks Small banks that make loans unsupervised by the state or other financial institutions. p. 267

12

Peoples in Motion, 1832–1848

I n the spring of 1847, Jannicke Saehle left her home in Bergen, a city on the western coast of Norway, and boarded a ship bound for New York City. From New York, the young woman traveled by steamship up the Hudson River to Albany. There she boarded a train to Milwaukee, Wisconsin. Although arduous, the journey had its pleasures. Piloted by a charming captain, the steamship resembled, in Saehle's words, "a complete house four stories high, and very elegantly furnished, with beautiful rugs everywhere." On the train, the passengers enjoyed each other's company as well as "the noteworthy sights that we rushed past." By the summer, Saehle was living with and working as a domestic servant for a Norwegian family, the Torjersens, in Koshkonong in southeastern Wisconsin. Founded in 1840, Koshkonong was a rapidly growing settlement of Norwegian immigrants farming the fertile prairie.

Jannicke Saehle was eager to make a new life for herself in the United States. For just a few months of service in the Torjersen household, she received the harvest of three acres of wheat for three years. In the fall, she found a job washing and ironing at a tavern in Madison. For the first five weeks, she earned a dollar a week. Then she received a raise of 25 cents a week, with the promise of another raise, and relief from washing, at the end of the winter. Although she could not speak English, she was pleased to "enjoy the best treatment" from the tavern owners and patrons.

In September 1847, Jannicke Saehle wrote of her good fortune in America in a letter to her family back in Norway. She described "the superabundance of food" in the Torjersen home. On his 40-acre farm, Torjersen kept swine and produced "tremendous amounts" of wheat, potatoes, beans, cabbage, cucumbers, onions, and many other kinds of vegetables. At the Madison tavern, she had "food and drink in abundance" and dined on the same fare served to the guests: for breakfast, "chicken, mutton [lamb], beef or pork, warm or cold wheat bread, butter, white cheese, eggs, or small pancakes, the best coffee, tea, cream and sugar." For supper she feasted on "warm biscuits, and several kinds of cold wheat bread, cold meats, bacon, cakes, preserved apples, plums, and berries, which are eaten with cream, and tea and coffee." Saehle felt heartbroken to see excess food thrown to the chickens and pigs, for, she wrote, "I think of my dear ones in Bergen, who like so many others must at this time lack the necessaries of life."

Jannicke Saehle was one of the more than 13,000 immigrants from Norway, Sweden, and Denmark who arrived in the United States during the 1840s. This migration continued to increase over the course of the nineteenth century. In the 1880s, more than 655,000 Scandinavians, fleeing poverty and military conflict, came to

America. Many traveled to Wisconsin and Minnesota, where they farmed small homesteads and found the cold winter climate similar to that of their homeland.

In the 1830s and 1840s, patterns of settlement and employment among immigrant groups varied widely in the United States. For example, most Irish immigrants lacked the resources to move much farther west than the eastern seaboard ports where they landed. In contrast, many Germans arrived with enough money to buy farmland in the Midwest or take up a trade in eastern cities. Many immigrants relied for jobs and housing on compatriots who had already arrived. Communities of immigrants built their own religious institutions and mutual aid societies.

In the 1830s and 1840s, the United States was home to many peoples in motion. Groups of Indians in the Southeast and Midwest and slaves in the upper South were forced at gunpoint to move from one region of the country to another. From western Europe came poor and persecuted groups drawn to the United States by the demand for labor and the promise of religious and political freedom. Some Americans eagerly pulled up stakes and moved to nearby cities or towns in search of better jobs. Migrants with enough resources made the long journey across the Sonoran Desert in the Southwest to California or to the Oregon Territory in the Northwest.

■ Norwegian immigrants to the United States, 1880s.

Population movements and economic change generated new forms of community and group identity. In their native lands, many newcomers to the United States had lived and labored as peasants under the control of aristocratic landlords. Now in America these immigrants worked as wage earners or as small farmers. Urban workers founded the National Trades Union, an organization that tried to help laboring people wield political influence. Some women and men challenged basic institutions such as the nuclear family, slavery, and white supremacy. Some reformers established new communities based on alternative notions of marriage and child-rearing.

In politics, the so-called Second Party system had emerged by 1836, as Jacksonian Democrats squared off against the Whigs on familiar issues including tariffs and new systems of transportation. Some Americans turned to violence to advance or defend their causes. Urban mobs vented their wrath against African Americans, abolitionists, and Irish immigrants and other Roman Catholics. The government itself sponsored violence, which peaked in the late 1830s with the forced removal of southeastern Indians to the West, and again in the late 1840s, when the United States wrested a vast expanse of land from Mexico. Indeed, within the larger society, physical force seemed to be an acceptable means of resolving disputes; politicians of all persuasions followed Andrew Jackson's lead and staked their claim to national leadership on the basis of their records as soldiers, military officers, and Indian-killers.

Mass Migrations

When foreign visitors called Americans a "restless" people, they were referring to patterns of both immigration to and migration within the country. Between 1830 and 1850, 2.3 million immigrants entered the United States, up from a total of 152,000 during the two previous decades. Most newcomers came from Ireland, Germany, England, Scotland, and

What caused some groups to migrate voluntarily? Why were others forced to move against their will?

Scandinavia. In the United States itself, individuals and families moved around the country with almost dizzying frequency in search of better jobs. They migrated from rural to urban areas, from one city to another, out West and then back to the East. In the late 1840s, almost half of all urban residents moved within a 12-month period. For the country as a whole, an estimated one family in five moved every year, and on average every family moved once every five years. Many westward migrants had enough money to move overland and buy a homestead once they arrived in Wisconsin or Oregon. However, much of the population turnover in urban areas stemmed from landless people's relentless quest for higher wages and cheaper places to rent.

Some people moved because other people forced them to—under the crack of a whip and in manacles. Slave traders in the upper South transported thousands of enslaved men, women, and children to the lower South for sale "on the block." U.S. soldiers forced Indians to walk from their homelands in the southeast to Indian Territory (now the state of Oklahoma). In the less settled West, however, older identities of race and ethnicity sometimes gave way to new identities forged from mixed cultures.

Europeans marveled at Americans' apparent willingness to search out new opportunities. But to some Americans, moving meant the death of dreams and the loss of hope for a better life.

Newcomers from Western Europe

During this period, hardships in Western Europe led to increased immigration to the United States, especially from Ireland and the German states.

During this period, hardships in Western Europe led to increased immigration to the United States, especially from Ireland and the German states. For the long-suffering people of Ireland, life had become more precarious than ever by the early nineteenth century. Over the generations, small farm plots had been subdivided among heirs to the point that most holdings consisted of fewer than 15 acres each. At the same time, the population of Ireland had grown exponentially—to more than 4 million people in 1800. England treated Ireland like a colony that existed purely for the economic gain of the mother country (or, in the eyes of the Irish, an occupying power). A series of English laws and policies mandated that farmers export most of the island's grain and cattle, leaving the impoverished people to subsist mainly on a diet of potatoes. Then, beginning in 1845, a blight devastated the potato crop. In the next five years, 1 million people died and another million fled to the United States. The great Irish migration had begun.

Large numbers of poor Irish had settled in the United States even before the potato famine of the mid-1840s. In the 1820s, about 50,000 such immigrants arrived; the following decade saw a spike in numbers to more than 200,000. Then as the 1840s and 1850s unfolded, 1.7 million Irish men, women, and children emigrated to the United States. This exodus continued over the next century as more than 4.5 million Irish arrived.

By the 1870s, the Irish constituted fully 20 percent of the population of New York City, 14 percent of Philadelphia, and 22 percent of Boston (the "hub of Gaelic America"). Most Irish immigrants remained along the eastern seaboard, since they lacked the resources to move farther inland. The newcomers quickly formed mutual aid associations and other community organizations. In cities across America, the Sisters of Mercy, a Roman Catholic order founded in Dublin, established homes to provide lodging for single women and day nurseries for the children of working mothers.

The Irish newcomers soon realized that their struggle against poverty, discrimination, and religious persecution would not end in the United States. The arrival of large numbers of Irish immigrants in the 1830s threatened the jobs of native-born Protestants, who reacted with resentment and violence. Employers posted signs outside their doors reading "No Irish Need Apply." Despised for their Roman Catholicism and their supposed clannishness, the Irish competed with African Americans for the low-paying jobs at the bottom of the economic

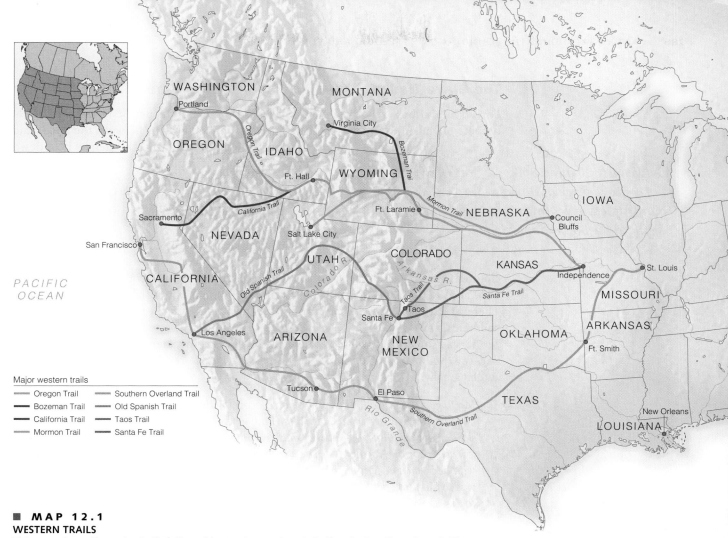

■ **MAP 12.1**

WESTERN TRAILS

This map shows the major trails followed by western emigrants in the nineteenth century. Settlers endured long and dangerous journeys. For example, beginning at Independence, Missouri, and stretching to Portland, Oregon, the Overland Trail was 2,000 miles long. Covering the entire trail could take four to six months. Wagon trains had to traverse rocky terrain, scale mountains, and ford rivers. Along the way, outposts such as Fort Laramie and Fort Hall gave travelers a chance to refresh their supplies, rest their livestock, and repair their wagons. Though resentful of such incursions, Indians rarely attacked large wagon trains.

ladder. In 1834 a mob destroyed the Ursuline convent in Charlestown, near Boston, after terrifying the women and children residents and ransacking the building.

Nevertheless, by the 1850s the Irish had gained a measure of influence. They filled many high positions in the U.S. Catholic Church and became active in the Democratic party. They believed that their white skin entitled them to distance themselves from blacks and lay claim to full American citizenship.

The hardship endured by the Irish in the early nineteenth century mirrored the political and economic distress of many other people living in Europe at the time. In the revolutions of 1848 in France, the German states, the Austrian Empire, and parts of Italy, people struck out against monarchy and called for constitutional government. The Germans immigrated in especially dramatic numbers, with more than half a million arriving in the United States between 1831 and 1850. Those numbers exploded in the next few decades, as a failed uprising against the authoritarian Prussian state in 1848 led many German intellectuals, farmers, and workers to flee the region. Across western Europe, rising unemployment and dramatic population increases made food scarce in both rural and urban areas, further stimulating immigration across the Atlantic.

The Slave Trade

Forced migration of enslaved workers increased during this period as the slave trade became big business. Many wealthy traders made regular trips between the upper and lower South. Traders transported men, women, and children by boat down the eastern seaboard or down the Mississippi River or chained and forced them to walk as much as 20 miles a day for seven or eight weeks at a time. Eventually, slaves stood on the block in the markets of New Orleans, Natchez, Charleston, and Savannah, where white men inspected them for health, strength, and compliance.

Between 1800 and 1860, the average price of slaves quadrupled, revealing a growing demand for bound labor.

Between 1800 and 1860, the average price of slaves quadrupled, revealing a growing demand for bound labor. As many as one out of every ten slave children in the upper South was sold to the lower South (many to cotton planters) between 1820 and 1860. Slave households in Virginia bore the brunt of these forced separations. There, an estimated three-quarters of the people sold never saw their spouse, parents, or children again.

It was sometimes worse if they did. Moses Grandy, standing on a sidewalk one day, saw his wife in chains, in a coffle passing by. He recalled the scene in his 1844 autobiography:

> Mr. Rogerson was with them on his horse, armed with pistols. I said to him. "For God's sake, have you bought my wife?" He said he had; when I asked him what she had done, he said she had done nothing, but that her master wanted money. He drew out a pistol and said that if I went near the wagon where she was, he would shoot me. I asked for leave to shake hands with her which he refused, but said I might stand at a distance and talk with her. My heart was so full that I could say very little. . . . I have never seen or heard from her from that day to this. I loved her as I love my life.

See the **Map**
Slavery in the South at
www.myhistorylab.com

Voluntary migrations of African Americans formed the counterpoint of the slave trade as runaways and free people of color made their way out of the old slave states. An estimated 50,000 enslaved workers tried to escape each year, but few made it to the North and freedom. Some southern free people of color headed to northern cities. By 1850 more than half of all Boston blacks had been born outside Massachusetts. Of those migrants, about one-third had been born in the South, most in Virginia, Maryland, and the District of Columbia. Slave runaways who lived in fear of their safety and their lives eluded census takers, but by mid-century as many as 600 fugitives lived in Boston.

Regardless of their place of origin, many migrants took up residence with other blacks, who helped ease the newcomers' transition to city life. These boarding arrangements strengthened ties between the enslaved and the free communities. For example, when authorities arrested the runaway George Latimer in Boston in 1842, free blacks in that city took immediate action. They posted signs condemning the police as "human kidnappers." Some tried to wrench him physically from his captors. Still others sponsored protest meetings in the local African Baptist Church and made common cause with white lawyers sympathetic to abolition. Finally a group of blacks and whites raised enough money to buy Latimer from his owner and free him.

Meanwhile, throughout the urban North, whites began eyeing blacks' jobs. Irish immigrants in particular desperately sought work. Skilled black workers found it increasingly difficult to ply their trades as cooks, hotel and boat stewards, porters, brickmakers, and barbers. In 1838, 656 black artisans in Philadelphia reported that they had to abandon their work because white customers would no longer patronize them. White factory owners in Philadelphia preferred white laborers. In that same city, a bustling site of machine shops and textile factories, almost no blacks did industrial labor of any kind.

■ MAP 12.2

INDIAN REMOVAL

This map shows the routes of forced migration of the Five Civilized Tribes in the 1830s. By the 1870s, several groups of Plains Indians, including the Cheyenne, Arapaho, Comanche, and Kiowa, had joined them in Indian Territory (present-day Oklahoma).

Trails of Tears

Like enslaved blacks, many Indians were forced to migrate. Throughout the 1830s, the U.S. government pursued the policy of removing Indians from the Southeast by treaty or by force. The 1832 Treaty of Payne's Landing, negotiated by the Seminole Indians and James Gadsden, a representative of Secretary of War Lewis Cass, aimed to force the Seminole out of Florida and into Indian Territory (present-day Oklahoma). The federal government promised to give individual Indians cash, plus blankets for the men and dresses for the women, in exchange for their lands. Government authorities also hoped to recapture the large number of runaway slaves who had sought refuge in Seminole villages, deep in the swamps of central Florida.

Three years later, many of the Indians had departed for the West. But a small number withdrew deeper into the Everglades and held their ground. They were led by a young man named Osceola, who with his followers waged a **guerrilla war** (based on ambush tactics) against better-armed U.S. troops. Osceola's resistance, called the Second Seminole War, dragged on for seven years. Eventually, the government forced 3,000 Seminole to move West, but not until it had spent $20 million, and 1,500 U.S. soldiers had lost their lives.

The Choctaw of the southern Alabama–Mississippi region, the Chickasaw directly to the north of them, the Creek in central Georgia and Alabama, and the Cherokee of north Georgia suffered the same fate in the 1830s. The Creek remained bitterly divided among themselves on the issue of removal, as did the Cherokee. Major Ridge, his son John Ridge, and Elias Boudinot, leaders of the so-called Treaty Party of the Cherokee nation, urged their people to give up their homeland and rebuild their nation in the West. John Ross and others like him opposed the Ridges and Boudinot. The Cherokee must remain in Georgia at all costs, Ross insisted. He claimed that he spoke for a majority of Cherokee. To silence him, the U.S. government threw him in prison. Then it concluded negotiations with the Treaty Party, which agreed to sell Cherokee land to the federal government for $5 million. Elias Boudinot said, "We can die, but the great Cherokee Nation will be saved." Within a few years, the Ridges and Boudinot died at the hands of anti–Treaty Party Cherokee assassins.

In 1838 General Winfield Scott, with 7,000 troops under his command, began rounding up the citizens of the Cherokee nation. U.S. troops held men, women, and children in concentration camps before forcing them to march west. During the period from 1838 to 1839, nearly 16,000 Indians were forced by federal authorities to make a journey from their homeland in the Southeast to western territory. The Indians called this journey the Trail on Which We Cried, also known as the **Trail of Tears**. Four thousand of them died of malnutrition and disease in the course of the 116-day forced march. Federal troops confiscated or destroyed the material basis of Cherokee culture: sawmills, cotton gins, barns, homes, spinning wheels, meetinghouses, flocks, herds, and the printing press used to publish the *Cherokee Phoenix*. They often forcibly separated families. A soldier who participated in the operation saw children "separated from their parents and driven into the stockade with the sky for a blanket and the earth for a pillow."

U.S. officials claimed that troops had carried out the removal with "great judgment and humanity." However, an internal government report completed in 1841 revealed that the United States had reneged on even its most basic treaty promises: "Bribery, perjury, and forgery, short weights, issues of spoiled meat and grain, and every conceivable subterfuge was employed by designing white men." Many government agents seized goods such as blankets and food intended for Indians and sold these goods for profit. Military authorities suppressed the report, and the public never saw it.

Migrants in the West

For many native-born migrants seeking a new life west of the Mississippi, the road proved neither smooth nor easy. For example, as the Mormon community moved west from New York, they met with religious persecution. The founder of the church, Joseph Smith, aroused the anger of his neighbors in Nauvoo, Illinois. They took alarm at the Nauvoo Legion, a military company formed to defend the Mormon community. They also heard rumors (for the most part true) that Smith and other Mormon leaders engaged in plural marriage or polygamy, allowing men to marry more than one wife.

In 1844 the Nauvoo Legion destroyed the printing press owned by a group of rebellious church members who objected to what they considered Smith's authoritarian tactics. Civil authorities charged Smith and his brother Hyrum with the destruction of private property and arrested and jailed the two men in the nearby town of Carthage. In June 1844, an angry mob of non-Mormons broke into the jail and lynched the brothers.

By 1847 Brigham Young, who had inherited the mantle of leadership from Smith, determined that the Mormons could not remain in Illinois. Migrants, some of them pushing hand-carts loaded with personal belongings, set out for the West. By 1852, 10,000 Mormons had settled in Salt Lake City in what is present-day Utah. With their large numbers and church-inspired discipline, the community prospered. They created an effective irrigation system and turned the desert into a thriving agricultural community.

■ This picture of the Whitman mission at Waiilatpu, Oregon, in 1845 shows the missionaries' house on the left, a mill in the background, a blacksmith shop in the right center, and a gathering place for worshippers on the far right. By this time the Whitmans had turned their attention from converting Indians to preaching to European American emigrants recently arrived from the East.

But the Mormons had not settled an uninhabited wilderness. Around Salt Lake, Canadian trappers, Paiute Indians, and Spanish speakers from New Mexico crossed paths, some to hunt, others to gather roots and berries, herd sheep, or trade captives. A Christmas dinner celebrated near Great Salt Lake around this time revealed the multicultural mix of western life. The guests included Osborne Russell (a European American trader), a Frenchman married to a Flathead woman, and various other intermarried Cree, Snake, and Nez Percé Indians. The group feasted on the meat of elk and deer, a flour pudding, cakes, and strong coffee. After the meal, the women cleared the table. The men smoked pipes and then went outside and conducted target practice with their guns.

European Americans also migrated to the Northwest during this period. Protestant missionaries initially settled Oregon beginning in 1834. But in contrast to the Mormons, these northwestern colonists found themselves in the midst of hostile Native Americans. One young doctor and his wife from western New York, Marcus and Narcissa Whitman, established a mission near present-day Walla Walla, Washington. More than a thousand more emigrants from the East followed the Whitmans to Oregon during the "Great Migration" of 1843.

The U.S. government aided this westward movement when it commissioned its Topographical Corps of Engineers to survey the Oregon Trail. That task fell to an expedition headed by John Charles Frémont in 1843–1844. The expedition's final report had immense practical value for the emigrants, for it mapped the way west and provided crucial information about pasture, sources of water, and climate.

Some settlers established successful homesteads in Oregon, but the settlements founded by missionaries were fragile affairs. Discouraged and overwhelmed by homesickness, Narcissa Whitman eagerly awaited copies of the latest *Mothers' Magazine* sent to her by female relatives in the East. After 1843 the influx of newcomers brought her some consolation but also brought outbreaks of measles, to which the Native Americans had no immunity. An ensuing epidemic among the Cayuse claimed many lives. In 1847, blaming the missionaries for the deaths of their people, several Indians attacked the Whitman mission, killing 12 whites, including Narcissa and Marcus Whitman.

New Places, New Identities

Like the West, the Midwest and the borderlands between U.S. and Spanish territories were meeting places for many different cultures. Leaving established communities behind, some migrants challenged rigid definitions of who was black, Indian, Hispanic, or European American. Moving from one place to another enabled—or forced—people to adopt new individual and group identities.

People who fell into one racial category in the East sometimes acquired new identities in the West. Some people classified as "black" in the South became "white" outside the region. For example, the commonwealth of Virginia classified the light-skinned George and Eliza Gilliam as black. Beginning their married life near Petersburg, they were well aware of Virginia's tightening restrictions on free people of color and their uncertain future in Virginia, where local officials knew who they were and who their parents were. In 1831, the couple decided to make a new life for themselves in western Pennsylvania. Eliza died in 1838, and George remarried nine years later. He prospered over the course of his lifetime. He worked as a doctor and druggist and invested in and sold real estate. George and his second wife, Frances, eventually moved to Illinois, and the couple finally settled in Missouri. Several of the Gilliam children attended college in Ohio. In 1870, the census listed the value of his estate at $95,000 (the equivalent of $2 million dollars today). Public records in Pennsylvania, Illinois, and Missouri listed family members as white. Outside the slave South, the Gilliams managed to reinvent themselves and embrace opportunities sought by many other Americans in this era of migration.

> *Leaving established communities behind, some migrants challenged rigid definitions of who was black, Indian, Hispanic, or European American.*

Throughout the West, migrants forged new identities as a matter of course. For example, many people straddled more than one culture in the western borderlands. In 1828 Mexican military officer Jose Maria Sanchez described the *Tejano* settlers (Spanish-speaking natives of Mexico) he met in the province of Tejas (Texas): "Accustomed to the continued trade with the North Americans, they have adopted their customs and habits, and one may say truly that they are not Mexican except by birth, for they even speak Spanish with a marked incorrectness." In other provinces of northern Mexico, European American Protestant traders and travelers mingled with Catholic native Spanish speakers.

In parts of the West, traditional social identities yielded to new ones, based less on a single language or ethnicity than on a blend of cultures and new ways of making a living from the land. The 1830s and 1840s marked the height of the Rocky Mountain fur trade. The trade could generate huge profits for the eastern merchants who controlled it. Individual trappers fared more modestly, ranging freely across national boundaries and cultures, going wherever the bison, bear, and beaver took them. These men demonstrated a legendary ability to navigate among Spanish, French, European American, and Native American communities. Westerners coined new terms to describe the people representative of new kinds of cultural identity within trading communities. Some white men became "white Indians," and the children they had with Indian women were called "métis" (mixed bloods). William Sherley "Old Bill" Williams, a convert to the religion of the Osage Indians of the southeastern Plains, was not unusual in the ways he crossed cultural boundaries. He married an Osage woman, and when she died, he wed a New Mexican widow. His third wife was a Ute woman. Williams's life story suggests the ways that Indian and Hispanic women could serve as cultural mediators between native peoples and European American traders.

A Multitude of Voices in the National Political Arena

The increasing diversity of the American population, combined with specialized regional economies, also heightened tensions within and between different groups and sections of the country. The Second Party system, which replaced the Federalist–Anti-Federalist rivalry of the early nineteenth century, was characterized by intense competition between the Jacksonian Democrats and anti-Jackson Whigs. But this new system could not accommodate the old or new conflicts based on race, religion, ethnicity, regional loyalties, and political beliefs. Social and cultural disputes between nativists and immigrants, and between abolitionists and defenders of slavery, spilled out of the courthouse and the legislative hall and into the streets. Public demonstrations ran the gamut from noisy parades to bloody clashes. During these displays, resentments between ethnic and religious groups, arguments over political issues, and opposition to reformers often blended together.

Why did debates over the rights (or lack thereof) of workers, slaves, and immigrants lead to the rise of new political organizations?

Whigs, Workers, and the Panic of 1837

One polarizing elected official, Andrew Jackson—ill with tuberculosis—did not run for a third term in 1836. The Democrats nominated Jackson's vice president and friend Martin Van Buren of New York for president. The Jackson-haters, led by Senator Henry Clay and other congressmen, formed a political party called the Whigs. They drew their support from several groups: advocates of Clay's American System (policies that supported a national bank, public funding of canals and turnpikes, and protective tariffs), states' rights Southerners opposed to Jackson's heavy-handed use of national power, and merchants and factory owners in favor of the Second Bank of the United States. **Evangelical Protestants** from the middle classes also joined the anti-Jackson forces; they objected to his rhetoric stressing class differences because they believed that individual religious conviction, not a group's material status, should shape politics and society. Still somewhat disorganized, these allied groups fielded three candidates: Hugh White of Tennessee, Senator Daniel Webster of Massachusetts, and General William Henry Harrison of Indiana. Benefiting from the Whigs' disarray, Van Buren narrowly won the popular vote but swept the electoral college.

During this period, political candidates of all persuasions in northeastern cities began to court the allegiance of workers aligned with a new trade union movement. People worried about making a living tended to favor the Democratic party, which spoke against class privilege and the wealthy. In the late 1820s and early 1830s, a variety of trade organizations had formed to advance the interests of skilled workers (the "producing classes," they called themselves). These unions pressed for a ten-hour workday, the abolition of debtors' prisons and paper money (so that workers would receive their wages in hard currency rather than bank notes), and higher wages.

The founding of the **National Trades Union** (NTU) in 1834 made workers more politically visible. The union represented workers as diverse as jewelers, butchers, bookbinders, and factory workers. In Philadelphia in the early 1830s, for example, the local NTU organization, called the General Trades Union, consisted of 50 trade societies and sponsored a number of successful strikes. Both Whigs and Democrats professed allegiance to the union,

Read the **Document**

Clay, "Defense of the American System" at **www.myhistorylab.com**

TABLE 12-1

The Election of 1836

Candidate	Political Party	Popular Vote (%)	Electoral Vote
Martin Van Buren	Democratic	50.9	170
William Henry Harrison	Whig	36.6	73
Hugh L. White	Whig	9.7	26
Daniel Webster	Whig	2.7	14
W.P. Magnum	Independent	—	11

but neither party went out of its way to represent the interests of workers over other groups, such as farmers and bookkeepers.

A major depression, the **Panic of 1837**, created even larger troubles for the trade union movement. Brought on by overspeculation—in canals, turnpikes, railroads, and slaves—the panic deepened when large grain crops failed in the West. British creditors worsened matters when they recalled loans they had made to American customers. The depression lasted until the early 1840s and devastated the NTU and its constituent organizations. Up to one-third of all Americans lost their jobs when businesses failed. Those fortunate enough to keep their jobs were in no position to press for higher wages. Not until the Civil War era did members of the laboring classes recapture political momentum at the national level.

Suppression of Antislavery Sentiment

Enslaved black workers were also at the center of contention in these years. In 1831 a Boston journalist named William Lloyd Garrison launched *The Liberator*, a newspaper dedicated to "immediate emancipation" of all slaves. Two years later, a group of 60 blacks and whites formed the American Anti-Slavery Society. That same year, Great Britain had abolished slavery in the British West Indies. This move encouraged like-minded Americans eager to cooperate with their British counterparts to abolish slavery everywhere. In the United States, the abolitionist movement enlisted the energies of a dedicated group of people who believed not only that slavery was immoral but also that the federal government must take immediate steps to destroy this "peculiar institution."

●●●—|Read the Document

Garrison, First Issue of "The Liberator" at **www.myhistorylab.com**

Both northern communities of free people of color and white women and men provided moral and financial support to the society. All the supporters showed a great deal of courage within a larger American society indifferent to the issue of slavery. Well-to-do black leaders, including Henry Highland Garnet, Charles Lenox Remond, and his sister Sarah Parker Remond, spoke out on behalf of southern blacks in chains. Fugitive slaves, including Frederick Douglass, Solomon Northup, and William and Ellen Craft, electrified northern abolitionist audiences with their firsthand accounts of the brutality of slavery and of their own daring escapes from bondage.

A few white women also became active in the abolitionist cause. Sarah and Angelina Grimké, for example, left the household of their slave-owning father in Charleston, South Carolina, and moved to Philadelphia. The Grimké sisters spoke before groups composed of men and women, blacks and whites in the North, an act offensive to many other whites. They were struck by what they perceived to be the similar legal constraints of slaves and white women. White men considered both groups to be unworthy of citizenship rights, childlike in their demeanor, well-suited for domestic service, and inherently unintelligent and overly emotional.

Abolitionist activities provoked outrage not only from southern slave owners but also from anti-abolitionists and their allies in Congress—in other words, most northern whites. In Washington, D.C., the House of Representatives imposed a gag rule on antislavery petitions, forbidding them to be read aloud or entered into the public record. Supporters of slavery also resorted to violence. In 1834 a mob of whites attacked a school for young women of color operated by a white teacher, Prudence Crandall, near New Haven, Connecticut. A local paper charged that the school was fostering "levelling [egalitarian]

Samuel J. Miller, "Frederick Douglass," 1847/52. Cased half-plate daguerreotype, plate: 14 × 10.6 cm; plate in closed case: 15.2 × 12 × 1.4 cm; plate in open case: 15.2 × 24 × 2 cm. Major Acquisitions Centennial Endowment, 1996.433. Reproduction, The Art Institute of Chicago. Photography © The Art Institute of Chicago.

■ Born a slave in Maryland in 1818, Frederick Douglass became a leading abolitionist speaker, editor, and activist. Not content to condemn southern slaveholders exclusively, he also criticized northern employers for not hiring blacks. Trained as a ship caulker, Douglass faced job discrimination in the shipyards of New Bedford, Massachusetts, where he and his wife, Anna, settled soon after he escaped slavery and they moved north (in 1838).

Library Company of Philadelphia (1835—7/P.8658)

■ The artist titled this print *New Method of Assorting the Mail, as Practiced by Southern Slave-Holders*. In July 1835, a proslavery mob broke into the U.S. post office in Charleston, South Carolina, and burned abolitionist literature. The sign on the side of the building offers a "Reward for Tappan." The brothers Arthur and Lewis Tappan were wealthy New York City merchants who funded abolitionist activities. Southern slaveholders hoped to stem the North-South flow of abolitionist literature, which took the form of sermons, pamphlets, periodicals, and resolutions.

principles, and intermarriage between whites and blacks." The next year in Boston a different mob attacked the *Liberator* founder, William Lloyd Garrison, tying a rope around him and parading him through the streets of that city while onlookers jeered. In 1837 in Alton, Illinois, a group of whites murdered outspoken abolitionist Rev. Elijah P. Lovejoy. Hounded out of Missouri because of his antislavery pronouncements, Lovejoy had moved directly across the river to Alton, in free-state Illinois, where he published the *Alton Observer* and organized the Illinois Anti-Slavery Society. Antiblack riots broke out in New York City, Philadelphia, and Cincinnati in 1834, and again in Philadelphia in 1842. Indeed white workers attacked blacks so often in the 1830s and 1840s that bricks and stones became known as "Irish confetti" because of the way immigrants used them as weapons.

Still, these dramatic episodes had little noticeable impact on the two major political parties. In 1840, the Democrats renominated Van Buren, although many people blamed him for the depression. Eager to find a candidate as popular as Andrew Jackson, the Whigs selected William Henry Harrison; his supporters called him "Old Tippecanoe" in recognition of his defeat of Indians at the battle of the same name in 1811. As Harrison's running mate the Whigs chose John Tyler, who had been both governor of and a senator from Virginia. To counter their reputation as well-heeled aristocrats, which in fact they were, the Whigs promoted Harrison as a simple, humble man living in a log cabin and drinking hard cider. They rallied around the slogan "Tippecanoe and Tyler Too."

By this time, the Whigs had gained strong support among wealthy southern planters, who worried that Van Buren would not protect their interests in slavery. Harrison won the election, but he contracted pneumonia at his inauguration and died within one month of

TABLE 12-2

The Election of 1840

Candidate	Political Party	Popular Vote (%)	Electoral Vote
William Henry Harrison	Whig	53.1	234
Martin Van Buren	Democratic	46.9	60
James G. Birney	Liberty	<1	—

taking office. Ridiculed as "His Accidency," Tyler assumed the presidency and soon lost his core constituency, Whigs who favored a strong central government, by vetoing bills for both a national bank and higher tariffs. The new president represented members of the Whig party who were ardent supporters of states' rights. As a result, he proved a poor standard-bearer for the numerous nationalist-minded Whigs.

Tyler learned a hard lesson: that members of his own party were a loose coalition of groups with varying views on a range of issues rather than a unified party bound to a single idea or principle.

Abolitionists could claim few victories, either real or symbolic, during these years. However, they did take heart from the *Amistad* case. In 1839 Spanish slave traders attempted to transport 53 illegally purchased Africans to Havana, Cuba, on a ship named *Amistad*. En route to Havana, the Africans, under the leadership of a young man named Cinqué, rebelled, killed the captain, and took over the ship. Soon after, U.S. authorities captured the ship off the coast of Long Island. President Van Buren wanted to send the blacks to Cuba. However, a federal district court judge in Hartford, Connecticut, ruled that because the African slave trade had been illegal since 1808, the Africans had been wrongfully enslaved. The U.S. government appealed the case to the Supreme Court.

To raise funds for the *Amistad* case, Philadelphia black leader Robert Purvis paid to have Cinqué's portrait painted; then antislavery activists sold copies for $1 each. In 1841 former president John Quincy Adams argued the Africans' case before the high court. The court ruled in their favor. Of the original 53 men, women, and children, 35 had survived the ordeal, and they returned to Africa. Slavery advocates and abolitionists alike pondered the question: Could the law be used to dismantle slavery?

Nativists as a Political Force

Immigration, like slavery, aroused strong feelings. Among the active players on the political scene in the early nineteenth century were the **nativists**, who opposed immigration and immigrants. The immigrants who came to the United States were a varied group in terms of their jobs, religion, and culture. Some farmed homesteads in Michigan, and others worked in northeastern factories. But to nativists, these distinctions made little difference: all immigrants were foreigners and thus unwelcome. Some nativists were also **temperance** advocates calling for the prohibition of alcohol; they objected to the Irish drinking in taverns and the Germans drinking in their *Biergarten*. Protestants worried that large numbers of Catholic immigrants would be loyal to the pope in Rome, the head of the Catholic Church, and thus undermine American democracy. Members of the working classes, black and white, feared the loss of their jobs to desperate newcomers who would accept low, "starvation" wages. But nativists objected just as much when immigrants kept to themselves—in their Catholic schools or in their German *Turnverein* (gymnastics clubs). They also complained when immigrants participated in U.S. politics as individual voters and members of influential voting blocs.

Samuel F. B. Morse, the artist and inventor, was among the most vocal nativists. In the early 1840s, he ceased painting portraits and turned his creative energies to developing a form of long-distance electric communication. Congress financed construction of the first telegraph line, which ran from Washington to Baltimore. In May 1844, Morse sent a message in code, "What hath God wrought!" and the modern telegraph was born. The precursor of all later communication innovations, the telegraph revolutionized the spread of information and tied the country together.

■ Abolitionists hailed the eventual freeing of the *Amistad* captives as one of their few successes in the fight against slavery before the Civil War. This picture shows the Spanish slave ship, commandeered by the captives under the leadership of Cinque, anchored off Culloden Point, Long Island, in 1839. Initially charged with the murder of the ship's captain, the Africans were held in New Haven, Connecticut, until a U.S. Supreme Court ruling led to their release and return to Africa in 1842.

Morse was convinced that Catholic immigrants in particular (mostly the Irish) were a grave threat to American democracy. In his book *Imminent Dangers to the Free Institutions of the United States* (1835), Morse charged that Catholics favored "monarchical power" over republican governments. Catholicism was like a cancer, he wrote: "We find it spreading itself into every nook and corner of the land; churches, chapels, colleges, nunneries and convents are springing up as if by magic every where." In his fears, Morse expressed nostalgia for a simpler past, even as his technical ingenuity paved the way for the modern world.

●●●—[Read the Document
Morse, Foreign Immigration
at **www.myhistorylab.com**

Library Company of Philadelphia (59541.D)

■ Taken on May 9, 1844, this daguerreotype is one of the first American photographs to record an urban civil disturbance. A crowd gathers outside Philadelphia's Girard Bank, at the corner of Third and Dock streets. At the time, soldiers called in to quell the riot were occupying the bank. Called the Bible Riots, the clash between Protestant and Catholic workers revealed tensions arising from nativism, temperance activism, and the use of the Protestant version of the Bible in the public schools.

In 1844 an openly nativist political organization, the American Republican party, elected six of its candidates to Congress and dozens of others to local political offices. In 1849 nativists founded the Order of the Star-Spangled Banner. Also called the Know-Nothing party, the group got its name by cautioning its members to profess ignorance when asked about its existence.

In some cases, anti-Catholic prejudices in particular helped to justify territorial expansion. Many U.S. Protestants believed the government was justified in seizing the land of Spanish-speaking Catholics in the West. They claimed religious and cultural superiority over Hispanics. As Protestant explorers, traders, and travelers reported on their experiences in the Southwest, their condemnation of Mexican Roman Catholics set the stage for the U.S. conquest of northern Mexico in the late 1840s.

Reform Impulses

What were the major reform movements of the 1830s and 1840s? What were the various strategies used by reformers to effect social change?

In August 1841, writer Lydia Maria Child recorded a striking scene in New York City: a march sponsored by the Washington Society, a temperance group, was snaking its way through the streets. The procession stretched for two miles and consisted of representatives from "all classes and trades." The marchers carried banners depicting streams and rivers (the pure water favored over liquor) and poignant scenes of the grateful wives and children of reformed drunkards. Stirred by the martial sounds of trumpets and drums, Child wrote that the music was "the voice of resistance to evil." She added, "Glory to resistance! for through its agency men become angels."

Inspired by faith in the perfectibility of human beings and heartened by the rapid pace of technological progress, many Americans set about trying to "make angels out of men," in Child's words. In the process, various reform associations targeted personal habits such as dress and diet, conventional beliefs about sexuality and the status of women, and institutions such as schools, churches, and slavery. Their efforts often brought women out of the home and into public life. Yet not all Americans shared the reformers' zeal, and even those who did rarely agreed about the appropriate means to transform society.

Public Education

In the eyes of some Americans, a growing nation needed new forms of tax-supported schooling. As families moved from one area of the country to another, public education advocates pointed out, children should be able to pick up in one school where they had left off in another. Members of a growing middle class wanted to provide their children with schooling beyond basic literacy instruction (reading and writing skills) and had the resources to do so.

Watch the Video

Who was Horace Mann and why are so many schools named after him? at **www.myhistorylab.com**

Horace Mann, a Massachusetts state legislator and lawyer, was one of the most prominent educational reformers. In 1837 Mann became secretary of the first state board of education. He stressed the notion of a **common school system** available to all boys and girls regardless of class or ethnicity. In an increasingly diverse nation, schooling promoted the acquisition of basic knowledge and skills. But it also provided instruction in what Mann and others called American values: hard work, punctuality, and sobriety.

By the 1840s, public school systems attended by white children had cropped up across the North and the Midwest. Local school boards eagerly tapped into the energies of women as teachers. School officials claimed that women were naturally nurturing and could serve as "mothers away from home" for small children. Furthermore, schools could pay women only a fraction of what men earned. Between the 1830s and 1840s, the number of female school-teachers in Massachusetts jumped more than 150 percent. In 1846 writer and educator

Catharine Beecher created a Board of National Popular Education, which sent unmarried female New England teachers to the Midwest.

Despite the lofty goals of Mann and other reformers, public schooling did not offer a "common" experience for all American children. Almost exclusively, northern white children benefited from public school systems. Slightly more than one-third of all white children attended school in 1830; 20 years later, the ratio had increased to more than one-half. In northern cities, these proportions were considerably higher; there reformers were able to provide elementary-school instruction for relatively large numbers of white children, both immigrant and native-born.

Despite the lofty goals of Mann and other reformers, public schooling did not offer a "common" experience for all American children.

By contrast, few black children had the opportunity to attend public schools. In the South, slave children were forbidden by law to learn to read and write. Recalled one former slave many years later, "dey [owners] didn't teach 'em nothin' but wuk [work]." By the 1830s, schools for even the children of free people of color had to meet in secret. In the North, many black households needed the labor of children to survive, resulting in black school-attendance rates well below those of whites. Throughout the Northeast and Midwest, black children remained at the mercy of local officials, who decided whether they could attend the schools their parents' tax dollars helped to support.

All over the country, education remained an intensely grassroots affair, belying the reformers' call for uniform systems. Local communities raised money for the teacher's salary, built the schoolhouse, and provided wood to heat the building. Southern states did not develop uniform public education systems until the late nineteenth century. Lacking local, popular support for tax-supported schooling, poor white children remained illiterate, while wealthy parents hired tutors for their own children or sent them to private academies.

An increase in the literate population resulted in an increased demand for higher education. Between 1830 and 1850, the number of colleges more than doubled (46 to 119). Founded in 1837, Mount Holyoke, a college for women in Massachusetts, and Oberlin in Ohio, which accepted black men as well as white and black women, were unusual for their liberal admission policies. Lyceums—informal lectures offered by speakers who traveled from place to place—attracted hordes of adults regardless of their formal education. By the mid-1830s, approximately 3,000 local lecture associations, mostly in New England and the Midwest, were sponsoring such series. In addition, local agricultural fairs offered informal practical instruction to rural people.

Formal training for professionals such as physicians and lawyers also changed during this period. By the 1830s, almost all states required that doctors be licensed. The only way to attain such a license was to attend medical school, and these schools excluded women. In regions of the country where medical schools appeared, the self-taught midwife gradually yielded to the formally educated male physician. In contrast, in rural communities of black and white Southerners, Native Americans, and Hispanics, women continued to practice time-honored ways of midwifery and healing.

Alternative Visions of Social Life

As in education, the crosscurrents of reform showed up clearly in debates about sexuality, the family, and the proper role of women. For example, reformer Sylvester Graham argued that even husbands and wives must monitor their sexual activity. Sexual excess between husband and wife, he claimed, caused ills ranging from headaches, chills, and impaired vision, to loss of memory, epilepsy, insanity, and "disorders of the liver and kidneys." Graham also promoted a diet of special crackers made of wheat flour (now called Graham crackers) and fruit (in place of alcohol and meat) in addition to a regimen of plain living reinforced with cold showers.

The crosscurrents of reform showed up clearly in debates about sexuality, the family, and the proper role of women.

■ Artist Albertus Browere titled this 1844 painting *Mrs. McCormick's General Store.* These barefoot boys are getting into trouble. Reformers advocated universal, compulsory schooling as one way to rid street corners of young mischief makers. Had these youngsters lived in the country, they probably would have been working in the fields.

◉ See the **Map**

Utopian Communities before the Civil War at **www.myhistorylab.com**

Other reformers disagreed with Graham's notion that people must repress their sexuality to lead a good and healthy life. Defying conventional standards of morality, sponsors of a number of experimental communities discouraged marriage-based monogamy (a legal commitment between a man and a woman to engage in sexual relations only with each other) and made child-rearing the responsibility of the entire community rather than just the child's parents. These communities were communitarian—seeking to break down exclusive relations between husband and wife, parent and child, employer and employee—in an effort to advance the well-being of the whole group, not just individuals within it. These communities were also **utopian**, seeking to forge new kinds of social relationships that would, in the eyes of the reformers, serve as a model for the larger society.

Many of these communities explicitly challenged mainstream views related to property ownership and the system of wage labor as well as rules governing relations between the sexes. The Scottish industrialist and socialist Robert Owen founded New Harmony in Indiana in 1825, basing his experiment on principles of "cooperative labor." In 1826 Owen released his "Declaration of Mental Independence," which condemned private property, organized religion, and marriage. By this time, 900 persons had joined the New Harmony order.

Several other prominent communitarian experiments that challenged conventional marital relations were vehemently criticized, and participants were sometimes physically attacked by their neighbors. Salt Lake City Mormons, who practiced plural marriage, continued to meet intense hostility from outsiders. Another group, the Oneida Community, founded in upstate New York near Utica in 1848 by John Humphrey Noyes, went even further than the Mormons in advocating an alternative to monogamy. At its peak, Oneida consisted of 300 members who endorsed the founder's notion of "complex marriage," meaning communal sexual unions and community-regulated parent-child relations. Charges of adultery eventually forced Noyes to flee the country and seek refuge in Canada.

Networks of Reformers

Many moral reforms overlapped with and reinforced each other. For example, women's rights advocates often supported temperance. Husbands who drank, they pointed out, were more likely to abuse their wives and children. Sarah and Angelina Grimké gained prominence as both abolitionists and advocates for women's rights. They also followed Sylvester Graham's program, and for a short time they sported "bloomers" (loose fitting pants, popularized by dress reformer Amelia Bloomer) in place of cumbersome dresses.

Dorothea Dix spearheaded a major reform effort that gained the support of a variety of politicians and activists. As a young woman, Dix had worked as a teacher and writer. In 1836 she visited England, where she met several prominent British reformers. Five years later she volunteered to teach a Sunday school class for women at an East Cambridge jail not far from Boston. Her first day there, in March 1841, changed her life—and the face of American antebellum reform—forever.

Dix found among the inmates not only women accused of prostitution and vagrancy, but also women who were clearly mentally ill. All of them were miserable, shivering in the cold. Dix was horrified that insane persons were imprisoned with criminals. She set out on a campaign to investigate the conditions under which the mentally ill were confined. Over the next 18 months, she investigated every prison, almshouse, and asylum in Massachusetts. She kept careful notes, which later formed the basis of her petitions, or "memorials," demanding better treatment for all insane persons. At one place she found people "confined in *cages, closets, cellars, stalls, pens! Chained, naked, beaten with rods,* and *lashed* into obedience." Dix presented her findings to the Massachusetts state legislature. Heartened by the public outcry she had inspired, she widened her investigation to include the states of Rhode Island and New York. In the late 1840s, she traveled to another dozen states in the South, Mid-Atlantic, and Midwest.

Some women argued that the United States must change its laws and customs to allow women the full legal rights and economic opportunities enjoyed by native-born white men. The organized women's rights movement drew its greatest inspiration from the abolitionist cause. Elizabeth Cady Stanton, for example, and other American women attended the 1840 World Anti-Slavery Convention in London. Male leaders of the British and Foreign Anti-Slavery Society relegated the women delegates to a balcony and excluded them from the formal deliberations. Eight years later, Cady Stanton worked with Lucretia Mott, a Quaker minister, Susan B. Anthony, a women's rights activist, and other similarly inclined men and women to organize a women's rights convention at Seneca Falls, New York.

Women's rights advocates made some progress independent of the abolitionist movement. For instance, in 1839 Mississippi passed the nation's first Married Women's Property Law. The ruling was intended to protect the fortunes of the married daughters of wealthy planters. In 1848 both New York and Pennsylvania passed legislation giving married women control over any real property (land) or personal property they brought to marriage.

Massachusetts resident Margaret Fuller explored many reform impulses of the day during her brief life (1810–1850). Educated in the classics by her father at home in Cambridge, in the 1830s she embraced a new intellectual sensibility called Transcendentalism. Fuller cultivated friendships with two other famous Transcendentalists living in the Boston area: Ralph Waldo Emerson and Henry David Thoreau. Transcendentalists believed in the primacy of the spirit and the essential harmony between people and the natural world. They took their inspiration from European Romantics, who celebrated the beauty of nature in art, music, and literature. In 1845 Fuller published *Woman in the Nineteenth Century,* one of the first feminist essays written by an American. "I would have Woman lay aside all thought, such as she habitually cherishes, of being led and taught by men," wrote Fuller. She then embraced the role of investigative journalist, writing about the plight of slaves, Indians, and imprisoned women for the New York *Tribune.*

The United States Extends Its Reach

Why was seizing the land that would become the state of Texas so important to so many Americans?

Efforts to reform society at home went hand-in-hand with a determination to expand the nation's borders, especially in the Southwest. In the mid-1840s, the editor of the *New York Morning News* declared that the United States had a "manifest destiny" to "overspread the continent" and claim the "desert wastes." Those inhabiting the "desert wastes"—Mexican settlers and a variety of Indian groups—apparently would have little say in the matter. The term **manifest destiny** soon became a catchall phrase, justifying American efforts not only to conquer new territory but also to seek out new markets for its goods across the oceans.

The Lone Star Republic

In the early 1830s, the Mexican government became alarmed by the growing number of American emigrants to Texas. Worried that the settlers would refuse to pledge allegiance to Mexico, that country closed the Texas border to further in-migration. By 1835 only one out of every eight residents of Texas was a *Tejano* (that is, a native Spanish speaker); the rest, numbering 30,000, hailed from the United States. The U.S.-born Texians, together with some prominent *Tejanos*, had become increasingly well armed and militant. They organized volunteer patrols to attack Indian settlements. These forces became the precursor of the Texas Rangers, a statewide organization of law enforcement officers.

> *In the early 1830s, the Mexican government became alarmed by the growing number of American emigrants to Texas.*

In 1836 the Texians decided to press for independence from Mexico. Only by becoming a separate nation, they believed, could they trade freely with the United States, establish their own schools, and collect and spend their own taxes. The pro-independence Texians included Davy Crockett, who had moved there in late 1835. A few months later, Crockett and other armed Texians retreated to a Spanish mission in San Antonio called the Alamo. In March 1836, a military force led by Antonio Lopez de Santa Anna, president of the Republic of Mexico and a general in the army, battled them for thirteen days. All 187 Texians died at the hands of Santa Anna and his men; the Mexican leader lost 600 of his own troops. Historians disagree on whether all of the Alamo defenders died fighting or if some were executed by Mexican soldiers.

In April a force of Texians and their *Tejano* allies, including military leader Juan Seguin, surprised Santa Anna and his men at the San Jacinto River and killed another 600 of them. The victors captured Santa Anna and declared themselves a new nation. Sam Houston, former U.S. congressman from Tennessee and commander-in-chief of the Texian army, became president of the Republic of Texas (also called the Lone Star Republic) in 1837. Some *Tejanos* who objected to Mexican high-handedness joined in supporting the new republic, including Jose Antonio Navarro, Francisco Ruiz, and Lorenzo de Zavala, who became its vice president.

In the northern territories of Mexico, many Spanish speakers had long felt abandoned by the Mexican government, which had made no provisions for their self-government and, as in the case of Texas, inhibited trade relations with the United States. Although other Mexican provinces protested the way they were treated by the government, Texas was the only Mexican state to launch a successful rebellion against Mexico.

Texas's independence raised the fears of U.S. abolitionists and imperiled blacks living in the new republic. In contrast to Mexico, which had abolished slavery in 1829, Texas approved a constitution that not only legalized slavery but also prohibited free blacks from living in the country. Greenbury Logan, a black man who owned a farm near Austin, petitioned to stay. He wrote, "Every privilege dear to a free man is taken away." But **vigilantes** forced him to leave. They also forced out many *Tejanos*. Among them was Juan Seguin, who had helped defeat Santa Anna at the Battle of San Jacinto and was now the mayor of San Antonio. Not until 1981 did another *Tejano*, Henry Cisneros, hold the office of mayor of the city of San Antonio.

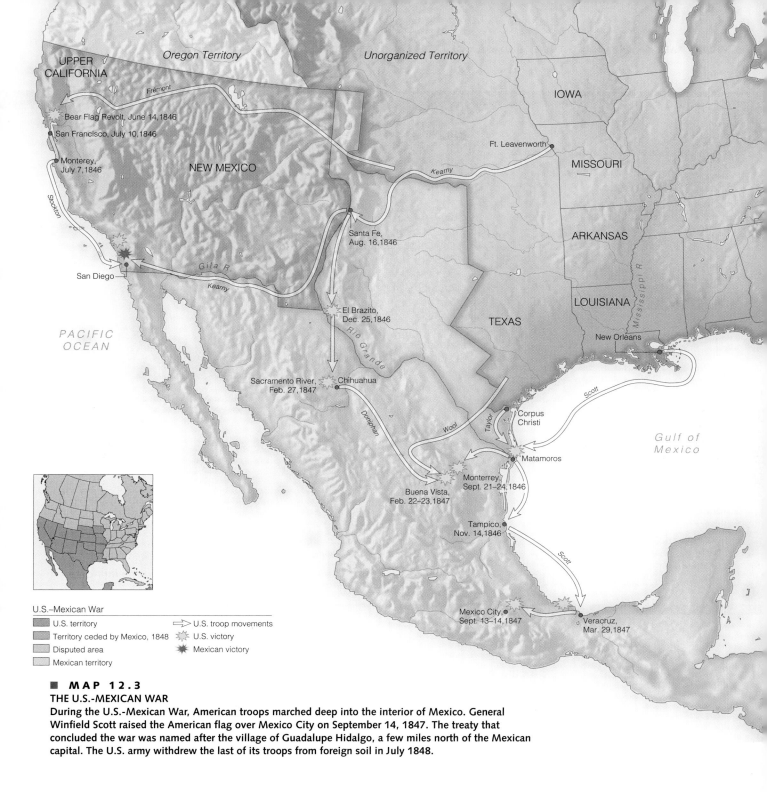

■ **MAP 12.3**
THE U.S.-MEXICAN WAR
During the U.S.-Mexican War, American troops marched deep into the interior of Mexico. General Winfield Scott raised the American flag over Mexico City on September 14, 1847. The treaty that concluded the war was named after the village of Guadalupe Hidalgo, a few miles north of the Mexican capital. The U.S. army withdrew the last of its troops from foreign soil in July 1848.

The Election of 1844

As an independent republic, Texas became a hotly contested political issue in the United States. During the election of 1844, politicians began to debate whether the United States should annex Texas. Van Buren was outspoken in his opposition to the idea. As a result, the frankly expansionist Democrats spurned

TABLE 12-3

The Election of 1844

Candidate	Political Party	Popular Vote (%)	Electoral Vote
James K. Polk	Democratic	49.6	170
Henry Clay	Whig	48.1	105
James G. Birney	Liberty	2.3	—

303

INTERPRETING HISTORY

Senator John C. Calhoun Warns Against Incorporating Mexico into the United States

In January 1848, Senator John C. Calhoun delivered a speech, addressing his remarks to President Polk and to his fellow lawmakers. He urged them to resist calls to incorporate all of a conquered Mexico into the United States. Calhoun favored the spread of slavery into new territories. However, here he expresses the fear that residents of Mexico were incapable of becoming suitable U.S. citizens for "racial" reasons.

It is without example or precedent, either to hold Mexico as a province, or to incorporate her into our Union. No example of such a line of policy can be found. We have conquered many of the neighboring tribes of Indians, but we never thought of holding them in subjection—never of incorporating them into our Union. They have either been left as an independent people amongst us, or been driven into the forests.

I know further, sir, that we have never dreamt of incorporating into our Union any but the Caucasian race—the free white race. To incorporate Mexico, would be the first instance of the kind of incorporating an Indian race; for more than half of the Mexicans are Indians, and the other half is composed chiefly of mixed tribes. I protest such a union as that! . . .

Sir, it is a remarkable fact, that in the whole history of man, as far as my knowledge extends, there is no instance whatever of any civilized colored races being found equal to the establishment of free popular government, although by far the largest portion of the human family is composed of these races. . . . Are we to associate with ourselves as equals, companions, and fellow-citizens, the Indians and mixed race of Mexico? Sir, I should consider such a thing as fatal to our institutions.

Calhoun then moves on to another theme. He disputes the notion that Mexico can begin as a territory and then work

Portrait of John C. Calhoun by Charles Bird King, c. 1818-1825.

its way up to statehood, following the standards Congress set for other western territories.

You can establish a Territorial Government for every State in Mexico, and there are some twenty of them. You can appoint governors, judges, and magistrates. You can give the people a subordinate government, allowing them to legislate for themselves, whilst you

---

the former president as a candidate and nominated James K. Polk of Tennessee. They called for the "reannexation" of Texas and the "reoccupation" of Oregon. Their rallying cry became "Fifty-Four Forty or Fight," a reference to their desire to own the area (expressed in terms of its longitude and latitude coordinates) claimed by the British in present-day Canada south of Alaska and west of the Continental Divide. Kentucky congressman Henry Clay received the Whig nomination after he announced he was against the **annexation** of Texas. But under pressure from Southerners, he later changed his mind, to the disgust of party leaders.

Neither the Democrats nor the Whigs had shown an interest in addressing the issue of slavery directly in the last presidential election. Yet in 1844, the controversy over the annexation of Texas made it impossible for the two parties to ignore the growing controversy over bound labor. Under the banner of the young Liberty party, some abolitionists charged that territorial expansion would mean the continued growth and prosperity of the slave system; they pointed to the public pronouncements of southern planters, who were outspoken in their desire to expand their slaveholdings into the fertile lands of eastern Texas.

For their part, Democrats and Whigs believed, correctly, that most voters would ignore slavery when they cast their ballots. Thus members of both parties tried to silence both sides of the slavery debate. They turned a deaf ear to the proslavery advocates on one hand and squelched northern abolitionist opinion by ignoring petitions to Congress on the other. In the

•••• Read the Document
James K. Polk's First Inaugural Address
at **www.myhistorylab.com**

defray the cost. So far as the law goes, the thing is done. There is no analogy between this and our Territorial Governments. Our Territories are only an offset of our own people, or foreigners from the same regions from which we came. They are small in number. They are incapable of forming a government. It would be inconvenient for them to sustain a government, if it were formed; and they are very much obliged to the United States for undertaking the trouble, knowing that, on the attainment of their majority—when they come to manhood—at twenty-one—they will be introduced to an equality with all other members of the Union. It is entirely different with Mexico. You have no need of armies to keep your Territories in subjection. But when you incorporate Mexico, you must have powerful armies to keep them in subjection. You may call it annexation, but it is a forced annexation, which is a contradiction in terms, according to my conception. You will be involved, in one word, in all the evils which I attribute to holding Mexico as a province. In fact, it will be but a Provincial Government, under the name of a Territorial Government. How long will that last? How long will it be before Mexico will be capable of incorporation

into our Union? Why, if we judge from the examples before us, it will be a very long time. Ireland has been held in subjection by England for seven or eight hundred years, and yet still remains hostile, although her people are of kindred race with the conquerors. A few French Canadians on this continent yet maintain the attitude of hostile people; and never will the time come, in my opinion, Mr. President, that these Mexicans will be reconciled to your authority. . . . Of all nations of the earth they are the most pertinacious—have the highest sense of nationality—hold out the longest, and often even with the least prospect of effecting their object. On this subject also I have conversed with officers of the army, and they all entertain the same opinion, that these people are now hostile, and will continue so. . . .

We make a great mistake, sir, when we suppose that all people are capable of self-government. We are anxious to force free government on all; and I see that it has been urged in a very respectable quarter, that it is the mission of this country to spread civil and religious liberty over all the world, and especially this continent. It is a great mistake. None but people advanced to a very high state of moral and intellectual improvement

are capable, in a civilized state, of maintaining free government; and amongst those who are so purified, very few, indeed, have had the good fortune of forming a constitution capable of endurance.

Calhoun also warns that "these twenty-odd Mexican States" would eventually have power in Congress. He asks his listeners whether they would want their own states "governed by" these peoples.

Questions

1. *Why does Calhoun assume that, if the United States incorporates Mexico into its territory, the federal government "must have powerful armies to keep them [Mexicans] in subjection"?*
2. *On what basis does Calhoun reject the idea of Mexican territories becoming future states?*
3. *How might Calhoun's more extreme expansionist colleagues—those in favor of seizing all of Mexico—have countered his arguments against such action?*

Source: Clyde A. Milner, ed., Major Problems in the History of the American West: Documents and Essays (1989), pp. 219–221.

end, Polk won the election. The expansionists had elected one of their most ardent champions to the highest office in the land.

Still, Polk was not interested in going to war with Great Britain over the vast territory of Oregon. In 1846 the two countries reached a compromise. Britain would accept the 49th parallel as the border between Canada and the United States and retain the disputed islands off the coast of Vancouver. The United States settled for one-half of its original claim to Oregon. Thereafter, it was free to turn its full attention to extending its southern and western borders.

War with Mexico

Texian leaders wanted to become part of the United States. In 1845, as one of his last acts as president, Tyler invited Texas to become the twenty-eighth state. He also understood that annexing Texas was a way to goad Mexico into open hostilities; Mexico had warned the United States that such a move would mean war. A joint resolution of both houses of Congress confirmed Texas statehood in December 1845.

The boundaries between Mexico and the new state of Texas remained in dispute. Mexico recognized the Nueces River as the boundary for Texas. In contrast, Texians and

U.S. politicians envisioned the boundary a hundred miles to the south at the Rio Grande. Complicating matters further, the new president, James K. Polk, had sent an envoy, John Slidell, to purchase California and a disputed section of Texas from Mexico. Mexico refused the deal. Nevertheless, around this time, Polk wrote in his diary that if he could not acquire all of New Mexico and California through diplomatic negotiation, he was determined to obtain them by force. The stage was set for war.

Armed conflict broke out in January 1846. U.S. troops, under the command of General Zachary Taylor (a veteran of wars against Tecumseh, the Seminole, and Black Hawk), clashed with a Mexican force near the mouth of the Rio Grande near Matamoros. Taylor had deliberately moved his troops across the Nueces River into disputed territory; his intention was to provoke an armed response from Mexico. A skirmish ensued, 11 Americans were killed, and Taylor pulled back. Polk used this military action as justification for a declaration of war against Mexico. The president declared, "American blood has been shed on American soil."

Not all Americans supported the war. Transcendentalists such as Henry David Thoreau objected to what they saw as a naked land grab. Refusing to pay taxes for what he considered a war to expand slavery, Thoreau went to jail. Nativists also objected to the war, fearing that the United States would have to assimilate thousands of Indians and Spanish-speaking Roman Catholics. Some members of Congress, including a newly elected U.S. Representative from Illinois named Abraham Lincoln, also condemned Polk's "act of aggression."

> *The Wilmot Proviso declared that "neither slavery nor involuntary servitude shall ever exist" in territories the United States acquired from Mexico.*

Predictably, opponents of slavery were among Polk's most outspoken critics. Soon after the outbreak of war, Representative David Wilmot of Pennsylvania attached an amendment to a bill appropriating money for the war. Called the Wilmot Proviso, the measure declared that "neither slavery nor involuntary servitude shall ever exist" in territories the United States acquired from Mexico. Though a member of the Democratic party, Wilmot spoke primarily as a white Northerner; he wanted to preserve the West for "the sons of toil of my own race and color." Wilmot's views show how racial prejudice and antislavery sentiment coexisted in the minds of many white Northerners. The House approved the proviso, but the Senate did not. Southern Democrats claimed that Congress had no right to deprive slaveholders of their private property anywhere in the nation.

●●◦—|Read the Document
Thomas Corwin, "Against the Mexican War" at **www.myhistorylab.com**

Meanwhile, Polk launched a three-pronged campaign against Mexico. He sent Taylor into northern Mexico and ordered General Stephen Watts Kearny into New Mexico and then into California. Following the third directive of the campaign, General in Chief of the U.S. Army Winfield Scott coordinated an **amphibious landing** of 10,000 soldiers at Vera Cruz, on the Gulf of Mexico coast. Mexican forces tried to defend their homeland using guerrilla tactics. But U.S. soldiers overcame them in part by terrorizing civilians. Scott acknowledged that the men under his command had "committed atrocities to make Heaven weep and every American of Christian morals blush for his country. . . . Murder, robbery and rape of mothers and daughters in the presence of tied-up males of the families."

◉—|See the Map
Mexican-American War, 1846–1848
at **www.myhistorylab.com**

In September 1847, Mexico City surrendered, and the war ended. Mexico had been in no shape to resist superior U.S. firepower. The United States paid for Scott's victory with 13,000 lives and $100 million. The Mexicans lost 20,000 lives. In the Treaty of Guadalupe Hidalgo (approved by the Senate in 1848) Mexico agreed to give up its claims to Texas. The United States gained all of Texas and half of the territory of Mexico: the area west of Texas, comprising present-day New Mexico, Arizona, Utah, Nevada, and California. Male residents of areas formerly held by Mexico were given one year to decide whether to stay in the United States and become citizens or return to Mexico. They were also entitled to retain their titles to the land, a provision that proved difficult to enforce in the face of European American land hunger.

■ This painting shows the U.S. Navy going up the Tuxpan River in Mexico during the U.S.-Mexican War. Located on the Gulf Coast halfway between Vera Cruz and Tampico, Tuxpan was the last significant Mexican port to be seized by U.S. forces by the spring of 1847. Commodore M.C. Perry assembled a formidable force of marines and infantry to take over the town on April 19, 1847.

The U.S. government paid Mexico $18.25 million. Of that amount, $15 million was designated as payment for land lost; the rest was **restitution** to U.S. citizens who might bring claims against Mexico for damaged or destroyed property during the war. Americans had conflicting views of the treaty. Abolitionists saw it as a blood-drenched gift from American taxpayers to slaveholders. Others argued that Polk had squandered a rare opportunity to seize all of Mexico.

CONCLUSION

In the 1830s and 1840s, mass population movements affected almost every aspect of American life. Immigrants from western Europe helped to swell the nation's labor force in midwestern farming communities and eastern cities. The arrival of the Roman Catholic Irish provoked a backlash among native-born Protestants and spawned a nativist political movement. Reformers in the United States and Europe went back and forth across the Atlantic, exchanging ideas related to women's rights, abolition, and utopian communities. As European Americans pushed the boundaries of the country west and south, they clashed with Indians and with foreign powers that claimed those lands as their own. Thus migration and immigration had profound consequences for American politics, ideas, society, and economics.

Most striking was the restlessness among land-hungry slave owners and antislavery forces alike. The war with Mexico in general and the clash over the Wilmot Proviso in particular opened a new chapter in the debate over slavery. In considering the proviso, congressmen gave up their party loyalties as Democrats or Whigs and began to think of themselves as Northerners and Southerners. When Wilmot proclaimed that he wanted to preserve the West for his "own color," he revealed that even antislavery Northerners did not necessarily embrace black people as equals. When Southerners indicated that even the vast expanse of Texas would not satisfy their desire for land, they revealed that the conflict over slavery was far from over. In fact, that conflict was about to enter a new and ominous stage.

For Review

✓• Study and Review at www.myhistorylab.com

1. Why did so many Northerners oppose both slavery and racial equality? (Consider the conflict over the western territories.) What were the various forms of migration that influenced the debate over slavery?

2. Why did some women see their role as social reformers as an extension of their roles as wives and mothers in the home?

3. Did all opponents of the Mexican War agree with one another? Why or why not?

4. How was slavery intertwined with manifest destiny and the Mexican War?

Chronology: 1832–1848

1833 Great Britain abolishes slavery.

1835 Texas revolts against Mexico.

1836 Congress passes gag rule on antislavery petitions.
Republic of Texas founded.

1837 Panic of 1837.

1838 Cherokee removal begins; Trail of Tears.

1840 Liberty party founded.

1841 John Tyler assumes presidency after death of William Henry Harrison.
Supreme Court rules in favor of *Amistad* Africans.

1844 Mormon leader Joseph Smith killed by mob in Nauvoo, Illinois.

1845 Irish potato famine. Frederick Douglass, *Narrative of the Life of Frederick Douglass*.
Texas becomes twenty-eighth state.

1846 Great Britain cedes southern part of Oregon Country to United States.
Mexican-American War begins.

1847 United States wins battles of Buena Vista, Vera Cruz, Mexico City.

1848 Treaty of Guadalupe Hidalgo ends Mexican-American War.
Women's rights convention in Seneca Falls, New York.
Popular revolutions sweep Europe.

Key Terms

Amphibious landing A military assault that begins on the water and ends on land. p. 306

Annexation Addition of territory that had belonged to one nation into another nation. p. 304

Common school system Tax-supported public education to provide elementary schooling free to young children. p. 298

Evangelical Protestants Christians who emphasize the importance of personal faith, as well as seeking new converts. p. 293

Guerrilla war A conflict fought not on the basis of conventional warfare, but rather by mobilizing small groups of fighters who attack and harass superior forces. p. 289

Manifest destiny The idea, first promoted in the 1840s, that the United States had a God-given right to expand its territory; used to justify territorial growth, expansion of economic markets, and conquest. p. 302

National Trades Union Organization formed in 1834 to help workers gain greater political influence. p. 293

Nativists American citizens born in the United States who oppose further immigration, especially from anywhere outside northwestern Europe. p. 296

Panic of 1837 Economic crisis and depression caused by a combination of overspeculation—in bridges, canals, and turnpikes—and a large failure of grain crops in the West. p. 294

Restitution Giving back to the rightful owner something that has been lost or taken away. p. 307

Temperance A social movement embracing either total opposition to alcohol consumption or support for its moderate use. p. 296

Trail of Tears The name Cherokee Indians gave to their forced removal from the Southeast to the West in 1838 and 1839 as part of the federal government's Indian removal policy. During the journey, U.S. troops destroyed the material basis of Cherokee culture and separated many families; over 4,000 Indians died. p. 290

Utopian Relating to communities organized to strive for ideal social and political conditions. p. 300

Vigilantes People who seek to take the law into their own hands and punish or intimidate alleged criminals or persons who resist a certain social order (for example, white supremacy). p. 302

PART **FIVE**

Disunion and Reunion

THE CIVIL WAR WAS THE COUNTRY'S GREATEST POLITICAL AND MORAL crisis. By 1860 the two-party system could no longer contain the dispute between proslavery and antislavery forces. That dispute centered on the fate of slavery in new western territories. Tensions accompanied large-scale migration to the west, and the 1849 Gold Rush pushed California—and the issue of slavery there—to the forefront of the nation's attention. Several dramatic developments—the secession of southern states from the Union, the formation of the Confederate States of America, and a Confederate attack on a federal fort in Charleston Harbor—precipitated all-out war. In the spring of 1861, few people could have anticipated that the conflict would drag on for four long years and claim nearly 700,000 lives.

The Second Party system, based on divisions between Whigs and Democrats, unraveled in the 1850s. Both parties represented coalitions of groups that expressed cultural, not sectional, sensibilities. Yet a series of events led to a realignment of parties into northern and southern camps. Many Northerners chafed under the Fugitive Slave Act of 1850, which required that all citizens assist law enforcement agents in retrieving runaway slaves for their owners. The founding of the Republican party in 1854 gave a political voice to Northerners hoping to preserve the western territories for family farmers who would not have to compete for land and labor with large slaveholders. In 1857 the Supreme Court ruled that black people had no rights that any court was bound to respect. Violent conflicts between proslavery and antislavery forces in Kansas and a failed raid by abolitionists on Harpers Ferry, Virginia, in 1859 revealed that legislators' resolutions and maneuverings were insufficient to stave off bloodshed.

In pursuing a militant nationalism, Confederates hoped to compensate for their relative weakness in terms of population and industrial capacity compared with the North. They believed that they could use a large, docile black labor force to grow food and serve as a support system for the army. They anticipated that European nations, dependent on southern cotton, would extend them diplomatic recognition and that white civilians would rally to the defense of their homeland no matter what the price in money or blood. Confederates also believed that western Indians would gladly assist them in their cause against a hated U.S. army and that brilliant southern generals could indefinitely outstrategize a huge, lumbering invading army. On all these counts they miscalculated, but their miscalculations were revealed only gradually.

During the war, white Southerners had to contend with two major unanticipated consequences of the conflict. First, war mobilization efforts across the South required the centralization of government and economic policymaking. Principled states' rights supporters opposed these efforts. Second, slaves and free blacks alike proved traitorous to the Confederate cause. In myriad ways—running away from their owners and spying for the enemy, slowing their work pace in the fields, and fighting for the Union army—black people served as combatants in the war. They fought for their families and their freedom and for a country that would grant them full citizenship rights. In the North, only in late 1862 did President Abraham Lincoln announce that the United States aimed to destroy slavery, but violent antidraft, antiblack riots in several cities showed that the northern white population was deeply divided over **emancipation**.

Soon after the end of the war and Lincoln's death, in April 1865, congressional Republicans began to challenge President Andrew Johnson's plan for reconstructing the South; they considered it too lenient toward the former Confederate states. In 1867 these political leaders had enough votes to enact their own plan, calling for the enfranchisement of black men in the South, the reorganization of southern state governments under leadership loyal to the Union, and the enactment of a labor contract system between southern landowners and black laborers.

Members of the Republican party backed a strong Union, a federal system in which the central government would ensure that individual men could pursue their own self-interest in the marketplace of goods and ideas. Yet the Civil War era exposed the limits of the Republican vision. The Plains Indians sought not citizenship but freedom from federal interference. Women and working people challenged various components of the Republican ideal, with its emphasis on unbridled individualism and federal subsidies of business. African Americans aspired to own property, vote, and send their children to school, just as other nineteenth-century Americans did. They wanted to farm their own land and care for their own families free from white control. Yet congressional Republicans did not enact large-scale land redistribution programs; most thought that once the rebels were subdued and slavery abolished, their duty was done.

Civil strife persisted into the postwar period. Union generals turned from quelling the southern rebellion to putting down armed resistance among the Plains Indians. Former rebels formed vigilante groups to attack black voters and their allies in the South. By the early 1870s, most Northerners had lost interest in the welfare of the former slaves and acquiesced as former Confederates reclaimed state governments. The last occupying forces withdrew from the South in 1877. In welding the country together as a single economic and political unit, the Republicans had triumphed. However, white Southerners retained control over their local social and political affairs. The revolution to secure African-American civil rights was stalled for nearly 100 years.

1865 Freedmen's Bureau is formed
Confederacy is defeated
Lincoln is assassinated; Andrew Johnson becomes president
Thirteenth Amendment is ratified

1866 Civil Rights Act of 1866
National Labor Union is founded
Equal Rights Association is founded
Ku Klux Klan is organized
Congress approves Fourteenth Amendment

1867 National Grange is founded
United States purchases Alaska from Russia
Reconstruction Act of 1867

1868 Johnson is impeached and acquitted
U.S.-China Burlingame Treaty
Colored Labor Union is founded
Fourteenth Amendment is ratified

1869 Congress approves Fifteenth Amendment
Transcontinental Railroad is completed
National Woman Suffrage Association and American Woman Suffrage Association are formed
Knights of Labor is founded

1870 Fifteenth Amendment is ratified

1871 Ku Klux Klan Act

1872 Apex Mining Act of 1872
Congress creates Yellowstone National Park
Susan B. Anthony attempts to vote
Crédit Moblier scandal

1873 Timber Culture Act
Panic of 1873

1874 Freedman's Savings Bank fails

1875 Civil Rights Act
Resumption Act
Whiskey Ring is exposed

1876 Battle of Little Big Horn
Contested presidential election between Rutherford B. Hayes and Samuel J. Tilden

1877 Compromise of 1877
California Workingmen's party is formed
Great Railroad Strike

13

The Crisis over Slavery, 1848–1860

On January 24, 1848, Henry William Bigler took a break from building a sawmill for John Sutter in California's Sacramento Valley and penned in his pocket diary, "This day some kind of mettle was found . . . that looks like goald."

GOLD! News of the discovery at Sutter's mill spread like wildfire. Immigrants from all over the world and migrants from all over the United States began to pour into the foothills of the Sierra Nevada Mountains in 1849. Dubbed "the Forty-Niners," they journeyed westward across the mountains, from the tenements of New York City and the great plantations of Mississippi; north from Mexico; and over the oceans, from western Europe, China, and South America. Equipping themselves with simple mining tools, the Forty-Niners began to dig for buried treasure, determined to stake a claim and make a fortune.

During the Gold Rush years of 1848 to 1859, various cultural groups were thrown in close proximity to each other. People from Belgium, France, Germany, Scotland, Chile, and Long Island learned to appreciate flour and corn tortillas (*tortillas de harina* and *tortillas de maiz*) and beef cooked in chile, staples of the Mexican diet. The disproportionate number of men permitted small numbers of women to challenge European-American gender conventions. A gold miner might take a break from washing his clothes, straighten his aching back, and watch a Mexican woman and her daughter, well mounted on their horses, rounding up a herd of near-wild cattle. An-Choi, a Chinese immigrant woman, earned a tidy sum by opening a brothel that catered to gold miners. Biddy Mason, an enslaved woman, successfully sued for her freedom and became the first African-American homesteader in Los Angeles.

California came to be part of the United States as a result of the U.S.-Mexican War. In the 1848 Treaty of Guadalupe Hidalgo, Mexico agreed to hand over territory stretching from Texas northwest to California. As a result, the United States obtained a vast expanse of land—almost 530,000 square miles— called the Mexican Cession. In addition to the land, the nation added to its population large numbers of men, women, and children already living in the area—13,000 Spanish speakers and 100,000 Indians (all former Mexican citizens) in California alone. After 1848 many new settlers streamed into California, and the migrants pressed for statehood. The Gold Rush exacerbated tensions over slavery, pushing the nation down the road toward the Civil War.

California became a state in 1850, but only after a bitter Congressional debate over the extension of slavery. The resulting **Compromise of 1850** included several provisions bearing on the issue of slavery: California would be admitted as a free state; slave-trading would be outlawed in the District of Columbia; carved out of the Mexican Cession, the Utah and New Mexico territories could decide for themselves whether or not to legalize slavery. Finally, a harsh new fugitive slave law provided for the capture and return of slaves who found their way to free states in the North or West, including California. Though called a compromise, in fact these provisions inflamed the passions on both sides of the slavery debate—abolitionists in the North and slave owners in the South.

■ **Chinese and European American miners pan for gold in the Auburn Ravine in California in 1852.**

Despite California's status as a free state, the principle of free labor was often violated. In 1850 the state enacted a law that provided for the indenture or apprenticeship of Indian children to white men for indeterminate periods of time. The law also allowed for the hiring out, to the highest bidder, of adult Indians deemed guilty of vagrancy. California also enacted discriminatory legislation against African Americans. The state's Fugitive Slave Law of 1852 decreed that, regardless of his or her current status, a black person who entered the state as a slave and thereafter attempted to remain on free soil was a fugitive slave. That year, three African-American gold miners, Robert Perkins, Carter Perkins, and Sandy Perkins, all former slaves who had been freed by their owner, were arrested under the law and ordered re-enslaved in their native Mississippi.

Other California labor systems revealed that the principle of free labor was not carried out in practice. Chinese immigrants to California entered the country organized in companies, or district associations, indebted to merchants for their transportation and bound to work for an employer until the debt was repaid. Fearing competition from cheap labor, alarmed European Americans labeled these Asian workers "coolies" (i.e., enslaved laborers). By 1852 the Chinese in California (almost all of them men) had been pushed out of mining as a result of the discriminatory Foreign Miners Tax, a measure leveled with special force against both Chinese and Mexican miners. Although the Treaty of Guadalupe Hidalgo guaranteed U.S. citizenship rights to Mexicans, those rights were not enforced under the law. Many Mexicans found themselves vulnerable to violence and land **dispossession** perpetrated by the growing European-American majority.

Continued European-American migration into the Midwest, the Great Plains, and the Southwest intensified conflicts over land with Native Americans and Latinos. Rapid population growth, the coming together of many different cultures, and dramatic economic changes all fueled the conflict over slavery. All over the nation, Americans gradually united around a radical proposition: there could be no compromise on the issue of whether human beings could be held as property.

Regional Economies and Conflicts

It is tempting to view the decade of the 1850s with an eye toward the impending firestorm of 1861. However, in the early 1850s, few Americans could have anticipated the Civil War. At midcentury, the United States was going through a period of rapid transition. New developments such as railroads, the factory system, and more efficient farm equipment led to significant changes in regional economies and began to give form to an emerging national economy.

To what extent, and in what ways, were U.S. regional economies interdependent by 1860? Were certain regions, or groups of people, outside the emerging national economy?

Migration into the Midwest accelerated. Slavery shaped life in the South, though most white Southerners were not plantation owners. Annexation of land in the Southwest and West and the conquest of Indians on the Plains produced wrenching social upheavals for Native Americans in those regions. Meanwhile, Americans continued to wrestle with the role of slavery in this rapidly changing society, while a free labor ideology grew stronger in the North.

Native American Economies Transformed

On the Plains, Indians confronted dramatic transformations in their way of life. Forced to relocate from the Southeast to Indian Territory (present-day Oklahoma), the Five Southern ("Civilized") Tribes, the Cherokee, Choctaw, Creek, Chickasaw, and Seminole, grappled with the task of rebuilding their political institutions. By the 1850s, the Cherokee had established a new capital at Talequah, along with public schools. They published a Cherokee newspaper (the *Advocate*) and created a flourishing print culture in their own language.

In the 1850s, U.S. officials negotiated treaties with various Plains Indian groups to enable European Americans to move west without fear of attack. Most settlers were bent on heading straight for California or the Northwest, traversing the Plains, which they called the Great American Desert in the mistaken belief that the absence of trees there demonstrated the infertility of the soil. The Fort Laramie Treaty of 1851 and the Treaty of Fort Atkinson three years later provided that the government could build roads and establish forts along western trails and that, in return, Indians would be compensated with supplies and food for their loss of hunting rights in the region. A young Cheyenne woman, Iron Teeth, recalled "the government presents" to her people in these terms: "We were given beef, but we did not care for this kind of meat. Great piles of bacon were stacked upon the prairies and distributed to us, but we used it only to make fires or to grease robes for tanning." She and her family sought out other items from government trading posts: "brass kettles, coffee-pots, curve-bladed butcher knives, boxes of black and white thread."

As whites moved west in large numbers to (in the words of a popular song) "scrape the mountains clean and drain the rivers dry," they disregarded U.S. treaties and tribal boundaries and overran the fragile settlements of Indians. Taking leave of the Fort Laramie conclave of 1851, Cut Nose of the Arapaho declared, "I will go home satisfied. I will sleep sound, and not have to watch my horses in the night, or be afraid for my women and children. We have to live on these streams and in the hills, and I would be glad if the whites would pick out a place for themselves and not come into our grounds." But within a generation, the Plains Indians were besieged by the technology, weaponry, and the sheer numbers of newcomers heading West.

Land Conflicts in the Southwest

To the Southwest, the United States had gained control over a vast expanse of land, provoking legal and political conflicts over the rights and labor of the people who lived there, both natives and newcomers. Under the terms of the Treaty of Guadalupe Hidalgo, Mexico ceded not only California but also the province of New Mexico, territory that included the present-day states of New Mexico, Arizona, Utah, Nevada, and western Colorado. In 1853 the United States bought an additional tract of land from Mexico, 55,000 acres located in the area south of the Gila River (in present-day New Mexico and Arizona). Overseen by the U.S. secretary of war, a Mississippi planter named Jefferson Davis, the agreement was called the **Gadsden Purchase** (after James Gadsden, a railroad promoter and one of the American negotiators).

In Texas newly arrived European Americans battled native *Tejanos* (people of Mexican origin or descent) for political and economic supremacy. White migrants from the southern United States brought their slaves with them to the region, claiming that the institution of slavery was crucial for commercial development. German immigrants came to central

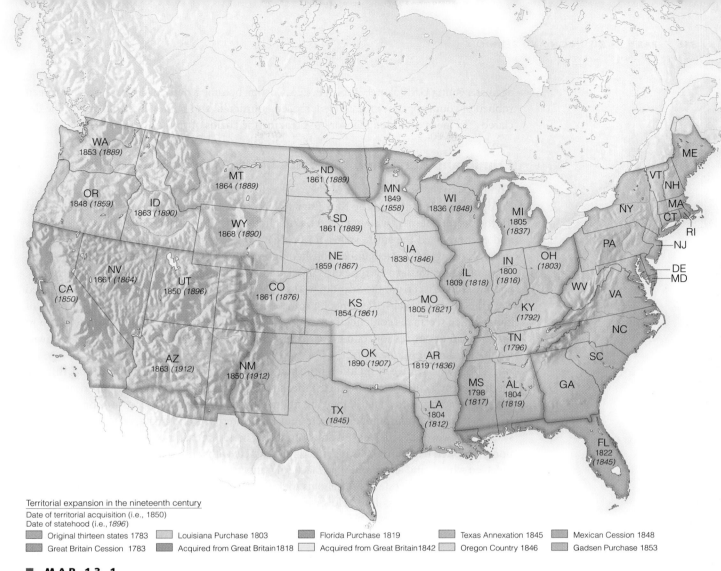

Territorial expansion in the nineteenth century
Date of territorial acquisition (i.e., 1850)
Date of statehood (i.e., *1896*)

Original thirteen states 1783	Louisiana Purchase 1803	Florida Purchase 1819	Texas Annexation 1845	Mexican Cession 1848
Great Britain Cession 1783	Acquired from Great Britain 1818	Acquired from Great Britain 1842	Oregon Country 1846	Gadsen Purchase 1853

■ **MAP 13.1**

TERRITORIAL EXPANSION IN THE NINETEENTH CENTURY
As a result of the Mexican War (1846–1848), the United States won the territory west of Texas by conquest. In 1853, James Gadsden, U.S. ambassador to Mexico, received congressional approval to pay Mexico $15 million for 55,000 square miles in present-day southern Arizona and New Mexico. That year marked the end of U.S. continental expansion.

and east Texas, founding towns with German names such as Fredericksburg, Weimar, and Schulenburg. During the 1850s, commercial farming continued to replace subsistence home-steading as the cattle industry spread and the railroads penetrated the region. Although European Americans monopolized the courts and regional political institutions, *Tejanos* retained cultural influence throughout Texas, dominating the cuisine and styles of music and architecture.

Some Spanish-speaking residents in the Southwest reacted forcefully when U.S. courts disregarded the land titles held by *Californios* and *Tejanos*. In the early 1850s, California authorities battled Mexican social bandits such as Joaquin Murrieta, who, with his men, raided European-American settlements. Murrieta and others argued that they were justified in stealing from privileged European Americans who, they claimed, disregarded the lives and property of Mexicans. In 1859 in the Rio Grande Valley of Texas, tensions between the *Tejano* majority and groups of European-American law enforcement officers known as the Texas Rangers erupted into full-scale warfare. Juan Cortina, who had fought on the side of Mexico during the Mexican War, orchestrated attacks on European Americans and their property in the vicinity of Brownsville. U.S. retaliation led to Cortina's War, pitting the Mexican leader against a young U.S. colonel, Robert E. Lee. Cortina became a hero to *Tejanos*. "You have been robbed of your property, incarcerated, chased, murdered, and hunted like wild beasts," he declared. "To me is entrusted the work of breaking the chains of your slavery."

Ethnic and Economic Diversity in the Midwest

Compared to the Southwest, the Midwest revealed a distinctive social make-up shaped by the European immigrants and the New Englanders who settled there. The Yankee Strip (named for the northeasterners who migrated there) ran through northern Ohio, Indiana, and Illinois and encompassed the entire states of Michigan, Wisconsin, and Minnesota. Here migrants from New England settled and established public schools and Congregational churches. Immigrants from western Europe also made a home in this region—the Germans, Belgians, and Swiss in Wisconsin, the Scandinavians in Minnesota. At times cultural conflict wracked even the smallest rural settlements. In some Wisconsin villages, equally matched numbers of Yankees and Germans contended for control over the local public schools, with the group in power posting notices for school board elections in its own language, hoping that its rivals would not show up at the polls.

The lower Midwest, including the southern portions of Ohio, Indiana, and Illinois, retained strong cultural ties to the southern states, from which many settlers had migrated. Though residing in free states, they maintained broad support for the institution of slavery. In some cases, they outnumbered their Yankee counterparts and managed to shape the legal system in a way that reflected a distinct antiblack bias. For example, Indiana's state constitution prohibited blacks from voting, making contracts with whites, and testifying in trials that involved whites, and also prohibited black migrants from entering the state.

Most rural midwestern households followed the seasonal rhythms characteristic of traditional systems of agriculture. However, by the mid-nineteenth century, family farming had become dependent on expensive machinery and hostage to the national and international grain markets. John Deere's steel plow (invented in 1837) and Cyrus McCormick's horse-drawn mechanical reaper (patented in 1854) boosted levels of grain production. Improved agricultural efficiency meant that the Midwest, both upper and lower, was fast becoming the breadbasket of the nation.

Regional Economies of the South

Like the Midwest, the South at midcentury had its own diversity. The South Atlantic states encompassed a number of regional economies. Bolstered by the high price of cotton on the world market, slave plantations prospered in the Black Belt, a wide swath of fertile soil stretching west from South Carolina. In many areas of the South, planters concentrated their money and energy on cotton, diverting slaves from nonagricultural labor to toil in the fields. During the 1850s, enslaved Virginia sawmill laborers, South Carolina skilled artisans, and Georgia textile mill operatives all found themselves reduced to the status of cotton hands. In some cases, white laborers took their places in mills and workshops. In other parts of the South, slaves combined field work with nonagricultural work.

Increasingly, northern critics described the South as a land of economic extremes, with wealthy planters enjoying their white-columned mansions while degraded blacks slaved obediently in the fields. The reality was more complicated. Even among whites, there were huge variations in material conditions and daily experiences. A large amount of wealth in land and slaves was concentrated among a small percentage of the white population, and many nonslaveholding whites were **tenant farmers**, leasing their land, mules, and implements from wealthy planters. In some areas, as many as one of five farms was operated by tenant farmers.

At the same time, about half the total southern white population consisted of **yeoman** farmers, families that owned an average of 50 acres and produced most of what they consumed themselves, with the occasional help of a hired hand (a leased slave or a wage-earning white person). In upcountry Georgia and South Carolina, yeoman farmers maintained local economies that were little affected by the cotton culture of the great planters in the Black Belt. These families grew what they needed: corn for themselves and their livestock and small amounts of cotton that the women spun, wove, and then sewed into clothing. Men and women alike labored in neighborhood networks of exchange, trading farm produce such as milk and eggs for services such as shoemaking and blacksmithing.

The institution of slavery discouraged immigrants from moving to the rural South in large numbers. German artisans realized that slave labor would undercut their own wages, and Scandinavian farmers understood that they could not compete with large planters in terms of landowning or slave owning. However, the ethnic diversity of southern port cities offered a striking contrast to the countryside, where native-born Protestants predominated. In 1860, 54 percent of all skilled workers and 69 percent of unskilled workers in Mobile, Alabama, were immigrants.

Throughout the slave states, black people continued to challenge the underpinnings of white supremacy. On the back roads of the plantation counties, late at night, poor workers of both races colluded to deprive the planter elite of their ill-gotten gain. Slaves swapped hams pilfered from smokehouses and bags of cotton lifted from storehouses for cash and goods offered by landless whites.

Southern blacks were a diverse group. In the cities, planters allowed highly skilled slaves to hire themselves out and keep part of the money they earned for themselves. In their pride of craft and in their relative freedom to come and go as they pleased, these people inhabited a world that was neither completely slave nor completely free. Located primarily in the upper South and in the largest towns, communities composed of free people of color supported churches and clandestine schools, mocking the white notion that all black people possessed a childlike temperament that rendered them incapable of caring for themselves.

A Free Labor Ideology in the North

In reaction to the southern slave system, the rural areas of the Northeast and Mid-Atlantic spawned a potent **free labor ideology**, which held that workers should reap what they sow, unfettered by legal systems of slavery and indentured servitude. Free labor advocates glorified the family farmer, the sturdy landowner of modest means, the husband and father who labored according to the dictates of the season and owed his soul—and his vote and the land he tilled—to no master. Nevertheless, the reality that sustained this ideal was eroding in the North during the 1850s.

More and more Northerners were earning wages by working for bosses, rather than tilling their own land. Faced with competition from Midwestern farmers and burdened by unfavorable growing conditions imposed by rocky soil and a long winter, New Englanders were migrating to nearby towns and mill villages and to the West. By 1860 the region's textile and shoemaking industries were largely mechanized. From New Hampshire to Rhode Island, growing numbers of water-powered factories perched along the **fall line**, where rivers spilled swiftly out of the foothills and into the coastal plain. The all-white factory workforce included men and women, adults and children, Irish Catholics and native-born Protestants, failed farmers and young men and women eager to

■ Maine textile workers, with their shuttles, pose for a formal portrait around 1860. Although women factory workers developed a collective identity distinct from that of middle-class wives, most young, native-born women eventually married and withdrew from the paid labor force. Many male factory workers were skeptical that women could or should play an effective role in labor organizations such as unions. Nevertheless, women workers in a number of industries, including textiles and shoes, formed labor organizations in the antebellum period.

leave the uncertain, hardscrabble life of the countryside for the promise of the mill towns and the seaport cities.

Although Northerners in general contrasted themselves to the "backward slave South," their region of the country retained elements of unfree labor systems. New Jersey did not officially emancipate the last of its slaves until 1846, and throughout the North, vestiges of slavery lingered through the mid-nineteenth century. As a group of disproportionately poor people, blacks in New England, the Mid-Atlantic, and the Midwest were vulnerable to labor exploitation, including indentured servitude and a system of "apprenticeship" whereby black children were taken from their parents and forced to work for whites.

Many nonslave workers did not receive pay for their labors. As is the case today, wives and mothers throughout the country performed almost all of their work in the home without monetary compensation, although the measure of a white man was calculated more and more in cash terms. On farms and in textile mills such as those of Pawtucket, Rhode Island, children played a key role in the livelihood of individual households but received little or nothing in cash wages. Some members of the white working classes began to condemn "**wage slavery**," a system that deprived them of what they considered a fair reward for their labors and left them at the mercy of merchant capitalists and factory bosses. These workers charged that they were paid so little by employers that their plight was similar to that of black slaves in the South.

While different regions developed specialized economies, these regions relied on each other for the production of staple crops and manufactured goods. The result was a national economy. Southern slaves produced the cotton processed in New England textile mills. Midwestern farmers grew the grain that fed eastern consumers. California Forty-Niners discovered the gold that expanded the national currency supply. Yet these patterns of economic interdependence were insufficient to resolve the persistent political question: which groups of people were entitled to American citizenship, with all the rights and privileges that the term implied?

Individualism Versus Group Identity

In what ways did the American ideal of individualism clash with the group stereotypes and prejudices enshrined in 1850s law and customs?

In every region of the country, discriminatory ideas and practices increasingly exerted force. People were defined ever more strongly on the basis of their nationality, language, religion, and skin color. They were more and more limited in their legal status and the jobs they could obtain. Degrading images of legally vulnerable groups—blacks, Chinese, Hispanos—became a part of popular culture, in the songs people sang and the pictures they saw in books and magazines. Through these means, native-born Americans of British stock sought to distance themselves from people of color and from immigrants.

Paradoxically, some writers began to highlight the idea of American individualism during this time. Such authors extolled what they considered the universal qualities embedded in American nationhood. They believed that the United States consisted not of distinctive and competing groups, but of a collection of individuals, all bent on pursuing their own self-interest, variously defined. They believed that the "representative" American was ambitious and acquisitive, eager to make more money and buy new things.

Yet not everyone could afford to embrace this optimistic form of individualism. Many who were marginalized found emotional support, and in some cases even political power, in a strong group identity. For example, on the Plains, the Sioux Indians resisted the idea that U.S. officials could carve up territory and sell land to individual farmers at the expense of a people that pursued the buffalo across artificial political boundaries. During negotiations at Fort Laramie in 1851, Black Hawk, a leader of the Oglala Sioux, condemned the whites with his understatement, "You have split my land and I don't like it." In contrast to the Plains

George Caleb Bingham, *Raftsmen Playing Cards*, 1847. Saint Louis Art Museum, Ezra H. Linley Fund

■ Just as American writers explored questions of national identity, American artists portrayed everyday scenes related to the vitality of American enterprise and democracy. This painting, *Raftsmen Playing Cards* (1847), was one from George Caleb Bingham's series of pictures of Missouri rivermen. A contemporary observer speculated that the youth on the right is "a mean and cunning scamp, probably the black sheep of a good family, and a sort of vagabond idler." Large rivers such as the Missouri and Mississippi remained powerful symbols of freedom in the American imagination.

Indians, who wanted no role in American politics, African Americans and white women strove for full citizenship rights. These groups looked forward to the day when each person was accorded the same rights and was free to pursue his or her own talents and ambitions.

Putting into Practice Ideas of Social Inferiority

Everywhere, European-American men sought to achieve or preserve the most stable, well-paying, and appealing jobs for themselves. By promoting ideas related to the supposed inferiority of African Americans, Hispanos, and immigrants, European-American men could justify barring these groups from the rights of citizenship and landownership as well as from nonmenial kinds of employment. In California, U.S. officials justified the exclusion of blacks, Indians, Chinese, and the poorest Mexicans from citizenship rights by claiming that members of these groups were nonwhite or, in the words of one state judge writing in 1854, "not of white blood." (Of course, the concept of "white blood" has no scientific basis because the different blood types—A, B, AB, and O—are found among all peoples.)

The precarious social status of various groups was revealed in patterns of their work. In California, white men pursued opportunities on farms and in factories while increasing numbers of Chinese men labored as laundrymen and domestic servants. Indians toiled as field hands under white supervision. In rural Texas, Anglos established plantations and ranches while more and more Mexicans worked as *vaqueros* (cowboys), shepherds, sidewalk vendors, and freighters. In Massachusetts mill towns, white men and women served as the forefront of an industrial labor force while many African Americans of both sexes

INTERPRETING HISTORY

Professor George Howe on the Subordination of Women

*A*ntebellum southern elites prized what they called "natural" hierarchical social relations: the authority of fathers and husbands over daughters and wives, parents over children, rich over poor, and whites over blacks. According to slaveholders, clergy, and scholars, these relationships provided social stability and ensured that the weak and dependent would receive care from the rich and powerful. In July 1850, George Howe, professor of Biblical literature at the Theological Seminary at Columbia, South Carolina, addressed the graduating class of a private women's academy. Howe suggested that the roles of women (elite white women) were enduring and never-changing.

The Endowments, Position and Education of Woman. An Address Delivered Before the Hemans and Sigourney Societies of the Female High School at Limestone Springs

The duties of life to all human beings are arduous, its objects are noble—each stage of its progress is preparatory to some other stage, and the whole a preparation to an interminable existence, upon which, in one sense, we are hereafter to enter, and in another, have already entered. Others may slightly regard the employments, trials and joys of the school girl. I am disposed to put on them a higher value. Our wives, sisters, and our mothers were in the same position yesterday. You will occupy a like [position] with them tomorrow. Whatever of virtue, of patient endurance, of poignant suffering, of useful labor, of noble impulse, of generous endeavor, of influence exerted on society for its good, has been exhibited in their example, in a few short years we shall see exhibited also in yours.

To woman, . . . there must be ascribed . . . acuteness in her powers of perception, . . . instincts . . . and emotions. When these are powerfully excited there is a wonderful vigor and determination of will, and a ready discovery of expedients to accomplish her wishes. She has readier sympathies, her fountain of tears is nearer the surface, but her emotions may not be so constant and permanent as those of man. She has greater readiness and tact, purer and more noble and unselfish desires and impulses, and a higher degree of veneration for the virtuous and exalted, and when she has found the way of truth, a heart more constant and more susceptible to all those influences which come from above. To the gentleness and quiet of her nature, to its affection and sympathy, that religion which pronounces its benediction on the peace-makers and the merciful, which recommends to them the ornament of a meek and quiet spirit, which, in the sight of the Lord, is of a great price, addresses itself with more force and greater attraction than it addresses man. Born to lean upon others, rather than to stand independently by herself, and to confide in an arm stronger than hers, her mind turns more readily to the higher power which brought her into being. . . .

Providence, then, and her own endowments mark out the proper province of woman. In some cases she may strive for the mastery, but to rule with the hand of power was never designed for her.

and all ages were confined to work in kitchens and outdoors as sweepers, cart drivers, and hawkers of goods.

Despite the divergent regional economies that shaped them, emerging ideologies of racial inferiority were strikingly similar. European Americans stereotyped all Chinese, Mexicans, and African Americans as promiscuous, crafty, "degraded," and intellectually inferior to whites. Such prejudices, in places as diverse as Boston, San Antonio, and San Francisco, prevented many people of color from reaching the limits of their own talents in mid-nineteenth-century America.

"A Teeming Nation"—America in Literature

●•◆•[**Read** the **Document**
"Moby Dick" by Herman Melville
at **www.myhistorylab.com**

Ideas about ethnic and racial difference coexisted with notions of American individualism, which stressed forms of universal equality. The variety of voices that gave expression to the national ideals of personal striving and ambition suggested the growth, energy, and vitality of the United States in the 1850s. In the Northeast, writers such as Ralph Waldo Emerson, Henry David Thoreau, Herman Melville, and Walt Whitman promoted a robust sensibility attuned to the challenges posed by the rigors of both the external world of natural beauty and the inner world of the spirit.

When she thus unsexes herself she is despised and detested by man and woman alike. England's Queen Victoria at the present moment, if not more feared, is far more beloved in the quiet of her domestic life, than Elizabeth was, the most feared of her female Sovereigns.

Howe ends his address by drawing an implicit comparison between the South and the North. Like many Southerners, he associated the North with labor radicalism, abolitionism, and challenges to the "natural" position of women.

When women go about haranguing promiscuous assemblies of men, lecturing in public, either on infidelity or religion, on slavery, on war or peace—when they meet together in conventions and pass resolutions on grave questions of State—when they set themselves up to manufacture a public opinion for their own advantage and exaltation—when they meet together in organized bodies and pass resolutions about the "rights of woman," and claim for her a voice and a vote in the appointment of civil rulers, and in the government, whether of Church or State, she is stepping forth from her rightful sphere and becomes disgusting and unlovely, just in proportion as she assumes to be a man.

Louisa McCord was a member of an elite slaveholding family in South Carolina. She was an ardent supporter of slavery. Though an accomplished essayist herself, she believed that white women should remain subordinate to their fathers and husbands. In 1856 she wrote, "The positions of women and children are in truth as essentially states of bondage as any other, the differences being in degree, not kind." She added that the "true definition of slavery" thus "applies equally to the position of women in the most civilized and enlightened countries."

Questions

1. Does Professor Howe believe that women are naturally inferior to men? Why or why not?
2. Why would Howe argue against citizenship rights for women, including the right to vote and serve on juries?
3. What were the tensions implicit in white women's status, considering that they were neither full citizens like their husbands nor slaves like the workers who toiled on their behalf?

Source: George Howe, *The Endowments, Position and Education of Woman. An Address Delivered Before the Hemans and Sigourney Societies of the Female High School at Limestone Springs*, July 23, 1850 (Columbia, SC: I. C. Morgan, 1850), pp. 5, 9, 10–11.

Some forms of literature offered an explicit critique of American materialism. According to Emerson, people were too concerned about possessions; as he put it, things were "in the saddle," riding everyone. During the 1850s, Thoreau's work became more explicitly focused on nature, as in his book *Walden* (1854). An appreciation of the wonders of nature—wonders that could be felt and tasted, as well as seen—amounted to a powerful force of democratization; anyone and everyone could participate. In turn, Thoreau actively supported the abolition of slavery; his love of nature formed the foundation of his belief in the universal dignity of all people in general and the cause of freedom for black people in particular.

In contrast, other writers celebrated busy-ness, whether in the field or workshop. In the introduction to his book of poetry titled *Leaves of Grass* (1855), Walt Whitman captured the restlessness of a people on the move: "Here is not merely a nation but a teeming nation of nations. Here is action . . . magnificently moving in vast masses." To Whitman, the expansiveness of the American landscape mirrored the American soul, "the largeness and generosity of the spirit of the citizen." His sensuous "Song of Myself" constituted an anthem for all Americans poised, gloriously diverse in their individuality, to exploit the infinite possibilities of both body and spirit.

Read the Document
"Walden" by Henry David Thoreau at **www.myhistorylab.com**

Challenges to Individualism

Many men and women remained skeptical of—and, in some cases, totally estranged from—the wondrous possibilities inherent in Whitman's phrase "Me, Me going in for my chances." In northern cities, individualism promoted the kind of creative genius necessary for technological innovation and dynamic economic change, but it had little meaning for Native Americans in the West, most of whom were desperately seeking a collective response to new threats in the form of cattle ranchers and the U.S. cavalry. On the Great Plains, groups such as the Mandan and Pawnee performed ceremonies and rituals that celebrated kinship and village life above the individual.

African Americans in the North forged a strong sense of group identity. Though they rejected notions of white people's "racial" superiority, blacks had little choice but to think of themselves as a group separate and distinct from whites. In northern cities, blacks took in boarders and joined mutual-aid societies in order to affirm the collective interests of the larger black community. In contrast, well-to-do whites were increasingly emphasizing the sanctity of the nuclear family, composed solely of parents and children. Charismatic black Boston preacher Maria Stewart denounced the twin evils of racial and gender prejudice for condemning all black women to a life of menial labor: "How long shall the fair daughters of Africa be compelled to bury their minds and talents beneath a load of iron pots and kettles?"

Some groups of women embraced a collective identity of womanhood, although the definition of that identity took several forms. In the North, writers such as Catharine Beecher articulated a vision of female self-sacrifice fueled by family obligations and emotional relationships. Beecher declared that self-sacrifice formed the "grand law of the system" by which women should live their lives. Informed by religious devotion and sustained by labors of love in the home, this female world offered an alternative to the masculine individualism necessary to profit-seeking, whether on the family farm or in the bank or textile mill. Middle-class women believed they could take pride in rearing virtuous citizens and caring for overworked husbands. Sarah Willis Parton (Fanny Fern) cautioned her readers in a series of sketches published in 1853 (*Fern Leaves from Fanny's Portfolio*) that marriage is "the hardest way on earth of getting a living. You never know when your work is done."

Other groups of women cherished different kinds of aspirations. Organizers of the country's first conference devoted to the status of women, the Seneca Falls Convention held in upstate New York in 1848, derived inspiration from the abolitionist movement and protested the efforts of white men to exclude women from formal participation in it. In their demands for women's rights, Elizabeth Cady Stanton and Lucretia Mott linked the plight of the slave with the plight of free women, arguing that white men exploited and denigrated members of both groups. Though some delegates believed that women's rights should only be pursued in religious and social contexts, Stanton insisted that their activism extend into the political realm. Over the objections

■ Isabella Baumfree was born into slavery in New York State in 1797. Thirty years later she escaped from bondage and became a preacher. In 1843 she changed her name to Sojourner Truth. A powerful orator, she spoke on behalf of abolition and urged white women's-rights activists to embrace the cause of enslaved women. Truth sold small cards, called *cartes de visite*, to support herself. On this card, a portrait taken in 1864, she notes that she must sell her image ("the Shadow") to make a living.

of Lucretia Mott and others, Stanton boldly called upon her fellow delegates to fight for the right of women to vote. In the midst of this debate Stanton, received crucial support from African-American leaders such as Frederick Douglass and Sojourner Truth. Douglass, who published the antislavery newspaper the *North Star* in nearby Rochester, spoke forcefully in favor of female suffrage at Seneca Falls. Denying women the vote, he argued, had for too long resulted in the "maiming and repudiation of one-half of the moral and intellectual power of the government of the world." Delegates to Seneca Falls eventually approved a document called the "Declaration of Sentiments," modeled after the Declaration of Independence: "We hold these truths to be self-evident: that all men and women are created equal." This group of women claimed for themselves a revolutionary heritage and all the rights and privileges of citizenship: to own property in their own names, to vote, to attend schools of higher learning, and to participate "in the various trades, professions, and commerce." Seneca Falls and the declaration it inspired gave rise to the women's rights movement in the United States, a movement that eventually won the vote for women some 70 years later.

Many women, including enslaved workers throughout the South and hard-pressed needleworkers toiling in cramped New York City tenements, could not devote themselves full time to the care of hearth and home, nor could they aspire to a career of public agitation. In her autobiographical novel *Our Nig; or, Sketches from the Life of a Free Black, in a Two-Story White House, North* (1859), Harriet Wilson wrote bitterly of the fate of women such as her mother, a woman "early deprived of parental guardianship, far removed from relatives . . . left to guide her tiny boat over life's surges alone and inexperienced." Like the book's main character, Alfrado, Wilson herself had suffered at the hands of tyrannical white women employers, but at the end of the story Alfrado achieves a measure of dignity and independence for herself by setting up a small business. She thus offered an explicit challenge to both the arrogance of propertied white men and the homebound sentimentality of wealthy white women.

The Paradox of Southern Political Power

At the center of debates about hierarchies and equality, the institution of slavery needed to expand to survive. Decades of intensive cultivation were exhausting the cotton fields in the South. The planter elite was counting on the admission of new territories as slave states to preserve their threatened power in Congress. To slave owners, northern-sponsored efforts to block their expansion amounted to a death sentence for all that the white South held dear. In defense of the slave system, the white South had to mount a strong offense, or die.

In the early 1850s, proslavery forces maintained firm control over all branches of the federal government. This derived in large part from the "three-fifths clause" of the Constitution, which gave disproportionate representation to the slave states, where each slave was counted as three-fifths of a person. Nevertheless, southern planters felt increasingly defensive as the country expanded westward. They warned against "the abolition excitement," which would necessarily upset the delicate balance between slave and free states. Gradually, this tension between southern strength and southern fears led to the fraying and then unraveling of the Jacksonian American party system, which had relied on a truce maintained between Whigs and Democrats on the issue of slavery. A new party, the Republicans, fused the democratic idealism and economic self-interest of native-born Northerners in such a powerful way that white Southerners believed that the institution of slavery was in danger of succumbing to the Yankee onslaught. And so a clash of ideas gradually slipped out of the confines of the polling place and into the realm of armed conflict.

Why could white Southerners dominate all three branches of the national government and still perceive themselves on the defensive, under siege?

The Party System in Disarray

In 1848, eight years after the appearance of the antislavery Liberty party, cracks in the second two-party system of Whigs versus Democrats opened wider with the founding of the Free-Soil party. Free-Soilers challenged the prevailing notion that the Whigs and Democrats could continue to smooth over the question of slavery in the territories with a variety of patch-work policies and piecemeal compromises. The Free-Soil platform promoted a forthright no-slavery-in-the-territories policy and favored the Wilmot Proviso (introduced in Congress in 1846), which would have banned slavery from all land acquired as a result of the Mexican War. In the presidential election of 1848, the Free-Soil party nominated former President Martin Van Buren, Democrat of New York. At the same time, Free-Soilers extended their appeal to the Whig party by supporting federal aid for internal improvements, free western homesteads for settlers, and protective tariffs for northern manufacturers.

Nevertheless, the two major parties persisted in avoidance politics. The Democrats nominated General Lewis Cass, the "father of **popular sovereignty**," a doctrine allowing citizens of new states to decide for themselves whether to permit slavery within their borders. The Whigs put forth General Zachary Taylor, although the Louisiana slaveholder and Mexican War veteran had never held elected office. Taylor managed to parlay his military record into a close win in the fall of 1848. But Taylor died after a year and a half as president and was replaced by his vice president, Millard Fillmore.

In 1849 white Southerners confronted a disturbing reality. Although slave owners controlled the presidency and the Supreme Court and outnumbered the North in the House of Representatives, California's application for statehood in 1849 raised the specter of an unbalanced federal system consisting of 16 free states and 15 slave states. The abolitionist threat appeared in other guises as well: the territories of Utah and New Mexico apparently preparing to ban slavery once they became states, abolitionists clamoring for the immediate emancipation of all slaves, and black men and women, including former slave Harriet Tubman, working with abolitionists in the upper South and the North to facilitate the escape of slaves through a network of safe stops called the **Underground Railroad**. The "railroad" consisted of Northerners, white and black, who sheltered fugitives from southern slavery in their flight to the North or, in some instances, to Canada.

TABLE 13-1

The Election of 1848

Candidate	Political Party	Popular Vote (%)	Electoral Vote
Zachary Taylor	Whig	47.4	163
Lewis Cass	Democratic	42.5	127
Martin Van Buren	Free-Soil	10.1	—

The Compromise of 1850

Against this backdrop of sectional controversy, Congress debated the terms under which California would enter the Union in 1850. A young Democratic senator from Illinois, Stephen Douglas, helped cobble together the Compromise of 1850, under which California would enter the Union as a free state that year. New Mexico and Utah would eventually submit the slavery question to voters and thus put the idea of popular sovereignty to a practical test. The federal government would abolish the slave trade in Washington, D.C. (a move that did not affect the status of slaves already living there), and shore up the Fugitive Slave law of 1793 with a new, harsher measure.

The **Fugitive Slave Law of 1850** essentially did away with the notion of the North as free territory, for it required local and federal law enforcement agents to retrieve runaways no

TABLE 13-2

The Election of 1852

Candidate	Political Party	Popular Vote (%)	Electoral Vote
Franklin Pierce	Democratic	50.9	254
Winfield Scott	Whig	44.1	42
John P. Hale	Free-Soil	5.0	—

matter where they sought refuge in the United States. Blacks were denied a trial or the right to testify on their own behalf. Fugitive slave commissioners earned $10 for each runaway they returned to a claimant. By compelling ordinary citizens to aid in the capture of alleged fugitives, the law brought the issue of slavery to the doorstep of northern whites.

Despite these dramatic events, the presidential campaign of 1852 was a lackluster affair. The Democrats nominated an unknown lawyer, Franklin Pierce. Although he hailed from New Hampshire, Pierce supported slavery. The Whigs turned their back on the undistinguished President Fillmore and chose as their nominee General Winfield Scott, who had gained fame during the Mexican War. Yet the Whigs split into regional factions during the election, Northerners resenting Scott's support of the Fugitive Slave Law and Southerners doubting his devotion to slavery. This split foreshadowed the end of national political parties and the emergence of regional parties, an ominous development indeed.

Expansionism and Political Upheaval

The interests of southern planters affected not only domestic politics, but debates and policies related to foreign affairs as well. Even as Congress was heatedly discussing the Compromise of 1850, Southerners were contemplating ways to extend their reach across and even beyond the continental United States. They wanted to find new, fresh, fertile lands for cotton cultivation, and they hoped to incorporate those lands into the United States. Such expansion would also help to bolster the political power of slave owners in Congress by someday adding new slave states to the Union.

In 1848, President Polk had made a gesture to buy Cuba from Spain, an offer that was rebuffed but one that did not discourage two privately financed expeditions of proslavery Americans from making forays into Cuba in an effort to seize the island by force on behalf of the United States. In 1854 the American ambassadors to Great Britain, France, and Spain met in Ostend, Belgium, and issued a statement declaring that, if Spain would not sell Cuba, the United States would be justified in taking control of the island. According to the Americans, the Monroe Doctrine gave license to the United States to rid the Western Hemisphere of European colonial powers. Noting that two of the three ambassadors hailed from slave states, abolitionists charged that the Ostend Manifesto was just one more ploy to extend the power of slaveholders throughout the Northern Hemisphere.

In 1855, a young proslavery American adventurer, Tennessee-born William Walker, gathered a band of 58 mercenaries and managed to capture Granada, Nicaragua. Declaring himself president of Nicaragua, Walker encouraged the institution of slavery and won U.S. recognition for his regime in 1856. Walker was driven out of the country a year later, but his arrogance and bold move helped set the stage for the Nicaraguan anti-American movement that would resurface in the twentieth century.

The Gadsden Purchase of 1853 marked the end of westward land acquisition on the continent, but in a commercial sense, expansion continued past the edge of the continental United States. Americans saw the Pacific Ocean as a trade route and East Asia as a trading partner. Commodore Matthew Perry commanded a fleet of U.S. Navy ships that steamed into Tokyo Harbor in 1853. The treaty Perry helped arrange with Japan in 1854 protected American whaling ships, sailors, and merchants in that part of the world and opened the door to an increase in trade later in the century.

By the mid-1850s, the uniting of the continent into what would eventually become the 48 contiguous states was a source of sectional tension as well as national pride. Fewer and fewer Northerners supported what they considered proslavery charades, so-called legislative compromises. And the territory of Nebraska, poised on the brink of statehood, forced national lawmakers to confront again the political problem of the expansion of slavery. Once more Senator Douglas from Illinois stepped in to fill the breach. Douglas believed that mutual accommodation between North and South demanded a constant process of negotiation and

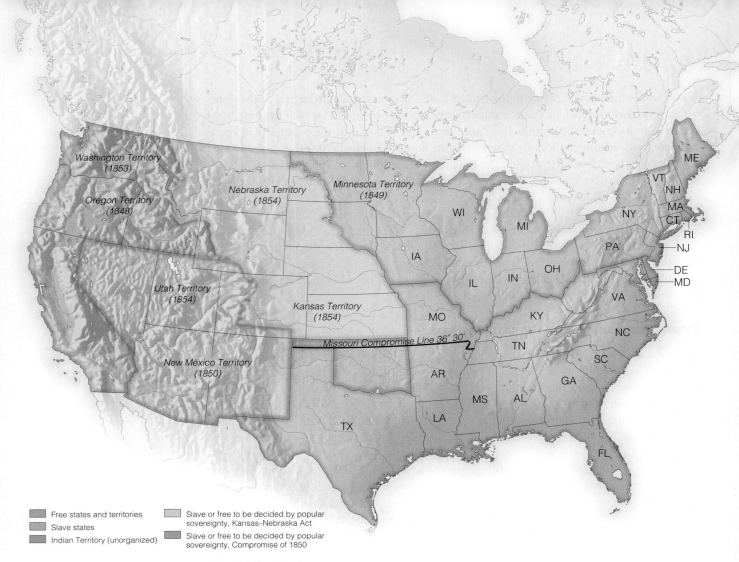

Free states and territories

Slave states

Indian Territory (unorganized)

Slave or free to be decided by popular sovereignty, Kansas–Nebraska Act

Slave or free to be decided by popular sovereignty, Compromise of 1850

■ **MAP 13.2**
THE KANSAS-NEBRASKA ACT, 1854
Stephen A. Douglas, senator from Illinois, proposed the Kansas-Nebraska Act of 1854. Douglas hoped to ensure that any transcontinental railroad route would run through Illinois and benefit his constituents. To secure southern support for the measure, proponents of the bill repealed part of the Missouri Compromise of 1820. As a result of the act, settlers displaced many Plains Indians from their lands. In the mid-1850s, the territory of Kansas became engulfed in an internal civil war that pitted supporters of slavery against abolitionists.

flexibility on both sides. Thus he argued that the gigantic territory be split into two new states, Kansas and Nebraska, whose respective voters would decide the issue of slavery for themselves. His proposal necessitated that part of the Missouri Compromise of 1820, the part that forbade slavery above the 36°30′ line, would have to be repealed.

The Kansas-Nebraska Act became law in 1854, enraging northern Free-Soilers by dismantling the 1820 agreement. They became convinced that what they called the Slave Power Conspiracy would stop at nothing until slavery overran the entire nation. The measure also had a profound effect on the Plains Indians, for it deprived them of fully one-half the land they had been granted by treaty. Specifically, the act wrought havoc on the lives of Ponca, Pawnee, Arapaho, and Cheyenne on the southern and central plains. European-American settlers poured into the region, provoking Indian attacks. In September 1855, 600 American troops staged a retaliatory raid against an Indian village, Blue Water, in Nebraska, killing 85 Sioux and leading to an escalation in violence between Indians and settlers in the area.

In their impatience with the two major parties, Free-Soilers were not alone in the early 1850s. The nativist American party, or Know-Nothings, condemned the growing political influence of immigrants, especially Roman Catholics. With its ranks filled with former Whigs,

◉ See the Map

The Compromise of 1850 and the Kansas-Nebraska Act at www.myhistorylab.com

the party tapped into a deep wellspring of resentment against immigrants on the part of urban, native-born workers as well as Protestant farmers anxious about retaining their influence in public affairs. The party wanted to limit the political participation of all foreign-born men by denying them the right to vote, whether or not they became U.S. citizens.

The Republican Alliance

The rapid rise of the Know-Nothings further indicated that voters had grown disillusioned with the two-party system. Confirmation of that fact appeared on March 20, 1854, in the small town of Ripon, Wisconsin, when a group of disaffected Whigs created the **Republican party**. One core idea informed the party: that slavery must not be allowed to spread into the western territories. From this base, the Republicans built an organization so powerful that it would capture the presidency within six years.

The genius of the Republican party resided in its ability to create and maintain an alliance between groups with vastly different goals. Now forced by the Fugitive Slave Act of 1850 to serve slaveholders (by returning runaway slaves to them) and fearful of the potential of slave-holding Southerners to capture their party, some northern Democrats cast their lot with the Republicans. From the ranks of antislavery men—the long-suffering adherents of the Liberty and Free-Soil parties—came another wing of the Republicans. These party members openly proclaimed their belief in the power of the federal government to halt the relentless march of slavery and ensure that, throughout the land, free soil would be tilled by free labor, free men and women.

Yet antislavery Republicans were by no means unified on major issues apart from the extension of slavery. Many Northerners were willing to tolerate slavery as long as it could be confined to the southern states; they cared little or nothing for the rights of black people, slave or free. In fact, in the Midwest, Republicans saw no contradiction in calling for the end of slavery in one breath and for the end of black migration to the area in the next. They feared that as job competitors, blacks would force whites to work for less money than they were accustomed to, or would push whites out of jobs altogether.

From the ranks of the newly formed Illinois state Republican party emerged a formidable leader. Born in 1809 in Kentucky, Abraham Lincoln came from a modest background and followed a checkered path into Illinois Whig politics: from youthful plowhand and log-splitter, to local postmaster and county surveyor, and finally self-taught lawyer and member of the state legislature (1834–1842). Although his 6-foot 4-inch frame and humble background drew ridicule from wealthy people—a Philadelphia lawyer described him as "a tall rawly boned, ungainly back woodsman, with coarse, ill-fitting clothing"—Lincoln made good use of his oratorical gifts and political ambition in promoting the principles of free soil.

The presidential election of 1856 revealed the full dimension of the national political crisis. The Democrats nominated James Buchanan, a "dough-face" (i.e., proslavery Northerner) from Pennsylvania, with John Breckinridge of Tennessee as his running mate. In their platform, they took pains to extol the virtue of sectional compromise on the slavery issue, by this time a very unpopular position. Meanwhile, the enfeebled Whigs could do little but stand by helplessly and declare as their "fundamental article of political faith, an absolute necessity for avoiding geographical parties," another plank decidedly out of favor with a growing number of voters. The Know-Nothings cast their lot with former President Millard Fillmore, offering voters little more than an anti-immigrant platform.

Drawing on support from members of the Free-Soil and Whig parties, the Republicans nominated John C. Frémont of California for

TABLE 13-3

The Election of 1856

Candidate	Political Party	Popular Vote (%)	Electoral Vote
James Buchanan	Democratic	45.3	174
John C. Frémont	Republican	33.1	114
Millard Fillmore	American	21.6	8

president. Their platform stated in no uncertain terms the party's opposition to the extension of slavery, as well as Republican support for a transcontinental railroad and other federally sponsored internal improvements such as roads and harbors. The document also included the bold, noble rhetoric—in favor of "the blessings of liberty" and against "tyrannical and unconstitutional laws"—that would be the hallmark of the Republican party in the decade to come. Buchanan won the election, but Frémont's carrying 11 of the 16 northern states boded well for the Republican party and ill for the slaveholders' union. In Illinois, Frémont had benefited from the tireless campaigning of Abraham Lincoln, who electrified ever-growing crowds of people with the declaration that "the Union must be preserved in the purity of its principles as well as in the integrity of its territorial parts." The founding of the Republican party, with its unabashed pro-Union, antislavery stand, signaled that the days of political compromise on the issue of human bondage were rapidly coming to an end.

The Deepening Conflict over Slavery

During the 1850s, what specific events and developments pushed the nation toward armed conflict?

Only a small subset of Americans—adult white men—participated directly in the formation of new political parties that set the terms for congressional debates over territorial expansion and slavery. Nevertheless, during the 1850s, increasing numbers of ordinary people were drawn into the escalating conflict over the South's "peculiar institution" as some Northerners mounted concerted challenges, violent as well as peaceful, to the Fugitive Slave Law. The western territory of Kansas became a bloody battleground as abolitionists and proslavery forces fought for control of the new state government. Sites of struggle over the slavery issue also included the streets of Boston, the Supreme Court of the United States, political rallies in Illinois, and a federal arsenal in Harpers Ferry, Virginia. No longer would the opposing sides confine their disagreements to congressional debates over the admission of new states. Nor would words be the only weapons. The country was rushing headlong into nationwide armed conflict.

Watch the Video
Slavery at **www.myhistorylab.com**

The Rising Tide of Violence

The Fugitive Slave Law of 1850 caused fear and alarm among many Northerners. In response to the measure, some African Americans, hiding in northern cities, fled to Canada, often with the aid of conductors on the Underground Railroad. Abolitionists, white and black, made dramatic rescue attempts on behalf of men and women sought by their self-proclaimed southern owners. In Boston in 1851, a waiter named Shadrach Minkins was seized at work and charged with running away from a Virginia slaveholder. During a court hearing to determine the merits of the case, a group of blacks stormed in, disarmed the startled authorities, and, in the words of a sympathetic observer, "with a dexterity worthy of the Roman gladiators, snatched the trembling prey of the slavehunters, and conveyed him in triumph to the streets of Boston." Shadrach Minkins found safety in Montreal, Canada, and a Boston jury refused to convict his lawyers, who had been accused of masterminding his escape. The spectacular public rescue of Minkins, and other such attempts, both successful

Read the Document
Reminiscences of the Underground Railroad (1880) at **www.myhistorylab.com**

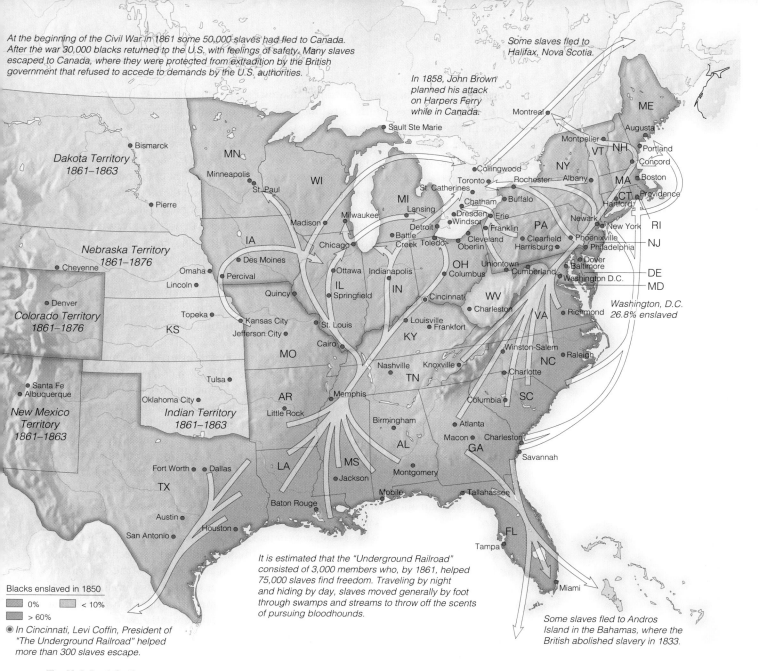

At the beginning of the Civil War in 1861 some 50,000 slaves had fled to Canada. After the war 30,000 blacks returned to the U.S. with feelings of safety. Many slaves escaped to Canada, where they were protected from extradition by the British government that refused to accede to demands by the U.S. authorities.

Some slaves fled to Halifax, Nova Scotia.

In 1858, John Brown planned his attack on Harpers Ferry while in Canada.

Washington, D.C. 26.8% enslaved

Blacks enslaved in 1850
- 0%
- < 10%
- > 60%

In Cincinnati, Levi Coffin, President of "The Underground Railroad" helped more than 300 slaves escape.

It is estimated that the "Underground Railroad" consisted of 3,000 members who, by 1861, helped 75,000 slaves find freedom. Traveling by night and hiding by day, slaves moved generally by foot through swamps and streams to throw off the scents of pursuing bloodhounds.

Some slaves fled to Andros Island in the Bahamas, where the British abolished slavery in 1833.

■ MAP 13.3
THE UNDERGROUND RAILROAD
The Underground Railroad consisted of a network of people who helped fugitives in their escape from slavery en route to the North or Canada. An escaped slave named Harriet Tubman made an estimated 19 separate trips to the South to help an estimated 300 slaves escape to freedom. Harriet Tubman made an estimated thirteen separate trips to the South to help an estimated seventy slaves escape to freedom.

and unsuccessful, throughout the North, brought the issue of slavery into the realm of public performance in northern towns and cities.

Gradually, the war of words over slavery cascaded out of small-circulation abolitionist periodicals and into the consciousness of a nation. In particular, author Harriet Beecher Stowe managed to wed politics and sentiment in a most compelling way. Her novel *Uncle Tom's Cabin* (1852) sold more than 300,000 copies within ten months and a million copies over the next seven years. The book, originally serialized in a magazine, *The National Era*, introduced large numbers of Northerners to the sufferings of an enslaved couple, Eliza and George. Slavery's greatest crime, in Stowe's eyes, was the forced severance of family ties between husbands and wives, parents and children.

Watch the Video
Underground Railroad at
www.myhistorylab.com

Watch the Video
Harriet Beecher Stowe and the Making of Uncle Tom's Cabin at
www.myhistorylab.com

Southern slaveholders were outraged at Stowe's attempt to portray their way of life as an unmitigated evil. A South Carolina slave-holding woman, Louisa McCord, wrote "We proclaim it [slavery], on the contrary, a Godlike dispensation, a providential caring for the weak, and a refuge for the portionless." Another Southerner, George Fitzhugh, took this argument to its logical conclusion. In his book *Cannibals All! Or, Slaves Without Masters* (1857), Fitzhugh claimed that civil society demanded the enslavement of the masses, whether white or black: "Some were born with saddles on their backs, and others booted and spurred to ride them—and the riding does them good." Fitzhugh also argued that slaves, whom he claimed were cared for by benevolent planters, were better off than northern factory workers, whom he asserted were exploited and neglected by indifferent employers.

Meanwhile, the territory of Kansas was becoming engulfed in a regional civil war. Proslavery settlers, aided and abetted by their compatriots (called Border Ruffians) from Missouri, installed their own territorial government at Shawnee Mission in 1855. Opposing these proslavery settlers were the Free-Soilers, some of whom had organized into abolitionist groups, such as the New England Emigrant Aid Company, and armed themselves with rifles.

This dangerous situation soon gave way to terrorism and insurrection on both sides. In 1855, in retaliation for a proslavery raid on the "Free-Soil" town of Lawrence, Kansas, an Ohio abolitionist named John Brown, together with his four sons and two other men, hacked to death five proslavery men at Pottowatamie Creek. The massacre only strengthened the resolve of proslavery advocates, who in the next year drew up a constitution for Kansas, which effectively nullified the principle of popular sovereignty over the issue of slavery. Called the **Lecompton Constitution**, the document decreed that voters might approve or reject slavery, but even if they chose to reject it, any slaves already in the state would remain slaves under the force of law. By throwing his support behind the Lecompton Constitution, President Buchanan alienated northern members of his own party, and the Democrats descended into North-South factionalism.

The spilling of blood over slavery was not confined to the Kansas frontier. In 1856 Senator Charles Sumner of Massachusetts, an outspoken abolitionist, delivered a speech on the floor of the United States Senate condemning "The Crime Against Kansas" (the Lecompton Constitution) and the men who perpetrated it, men he characterized as "hirelings picked from the drunken spew and vomit of an uneasy civilization," men who (like his own colleague Senator Butler of South Carolina) loved slavery the way that degenerates loved their prostitutes. Shortly after this speech, Congressman Preston S. Brooks of South Carolina, a relative of Senator Butler, leapt to the defense of the white South and attacked Sumner on the floor of the Senate, beating him into unconsciousness with a cane. Abolitionists contemplated the necessity of defending themselves and their interests, from the courtrooms of New England and the small towns of the West to the halls of Congress itself.

The *Dred Scott* Decision

●●●◀|Read the Document

The Supreme Court, Dred Scott v. Sandford at **www.myhistorylab.com**

Across the street from the Capitol, proceedings in the Supreme Court were more civil but no less explosive. In 1857 a former slave named Dred Scott sued in federal court, claiming that he was a citizen of Missouri and a free man. Scott maintained that he had become free once his master had taken him onto free soil (the state of Illinois and the territory of Wisconsin). In the case of **Dred Scott v. Sandford** (1857), the court ruled that even residence on free soil did not render a slave a free person, for, regardless of their status, black people had "no rights which the white man was bound to respect." With this single decision, Chief Justice Roger B. Taney and the Court threw off the hard-won balance between slave and free states. In effect, the Court declared unconstitutional the Compromise of 1820, which had banned slavery in the region north of Missouri's southern boundary, because, the justices held, slave owners could not be deprived of their property without due process. This decision threatened the precarious freedom of the South's quarter million free people of color and extended the reach of slavery into the northern states.

◀●▶|Watch the Video

Dred Scott and the Crises that Led to the Civil War at **www.myhistorylab.com**

Most white people residing outside the South never read the Court's ruling, but if they had, they probably would have agreed with the justices' claim that, since the earliest days of the Republic, blacks "had been regarded as beings of an inferior order, and altogether unfit to associate with the white race, either in social or political relations." At the same time, northern opinion makers warned that the decision made Northerners complicit in the slave system. Of the "slave power," the *Cincinnati Daily Commercial* thundered, "It has marched over and annihilated the boundaries of the states. We are now one great homogeneous slaveholding community." Even nonabolitionists had good reason to fear the long-term implications of the ruling, for it suggested that the institution of slavery was about to spill out of the confines of the southern states and into the rest of the country. Free white men and women feared competing with slaves in the workplace, whether in the West or East. These concerns increased with the onset of a depression in 1857 in the northeastern and midwestern states, as the mining of California gold produced inflation in the East.

The Lincoln-Douglas Debates

Against this backdrop of economic turmoil and political conflict, the congressional elections of 1858 assumed great significance. In particular, the Senate contest in Illinois pitted incumbent Stephen A. Douglas against challenger Abraham Lincoln. In a series of seven public debates, the two men debated the political conflict over slavery as it had been shaped during the tumultuous decade after the Mexican War. Though no friend of the abolitionists, Douglas was quickly falling from favor within the Democratic party; the Supreme Court had nullified his proposal for popular sovereignty in the territories, and he had parted ways from his southern brethren when he denounced Kansas's Lecompton Constitution.

•••⌐**Read** the **Document**

The Lincoln-Douglas Debates of 1858 at **www.myhistorylab.com**

Lincoln ridiculed the doctrine of popular sovereignty, which he maintained was as thin as the "soup that was made by boiling the shadow of a pigeon that had starved to death." He had no desire to root out slavery in the South, but, "I have said, and I repeat, my wish is that the further spread of [slavery] may be arrested, and that it may be placed where the public mind shall rest in the belief that it is in the course of ultimate extinction." According to a reporter present, this last remark provoked great applause. And this was no minor confrontation between two candidates; it is estimated that in six of the seven debates, the two men spoke before crowds exceeding 10,000 people each. Lincoln lost the election (in which blacks were not allowed to vote as a matter of Illinois law), but, more significantly, he won the loyalty of Republicans all over the North and put the white South on notice that the days of compromise were almost over. Meanwhile, with the admission as free states of Minnesota in 1858 and Oregon in 1859, Congress began to reflect a distinct antislavery bias.

Harpers Ferry and the Presidential Election of 1860

On a Sunday night in October 1859, John Brown and nineteen other men (including at least five African Americans) launched a daring attack on the federal arsenal in Harpers Ferry, Virginia. They had received guns and moral support from some of the North's leading abolitionists, and their plan was to raid the arsenal and distribute firearms to slaves in the surrounding area, thereby inciting a general rebellion that, they hoped, would engulf the rest of the South. The Virginia militia and a U.S. Marines force, commanded by Lieutenant Colonel Robert E. Lee, captured Brown and his surviving followers, but not before the insurrectionist had killed seven people and injured ten others. Brown was convicted of treason against the United States for his raid on the federal arsenal, murder, and inciting an insurrection. On December 2, 1859, before being led to the gallows, Brown handed a scrap of paper to one of his guards: "I John Brown am now quite *certain* that the crimes of this *guilty land: will* never be purged *away: but with Blood.*" Brown failed as the instigator of a slave rebellion, but he succeeded as a prophet.

■ The election of 1858 pitted Stephen A. Douglas, Democratic senator from Illinois, against his Republican challenger, a lawyer named Abraham Lincoln. The debates between the two candidates revealed the increasing divisiveness of the slavery question. Douglas maintained that compromise on the issue was still possible; he argued that the European American men residing in territories should decide the question for themselves. Although Lincoln lost this election, he articulated a view that was rapidly gaining support throughout the North: the idea that slavery must not be allowed to spread outside the South.

The raid on Harpers Ferry cast a shadow over the party conventions held in the summer of 1860. By then it was apparent that the national party system had all but disintegrated. Southerners in effect seceded from the Democratic party by walking out of their Charleston convention rather than supporting Stephen Douglas as candidate for president. Within a few weeks, representatives of both the northern and the southern wings of the party reconvened in separate conventions in Baltimore. Northerners gave the nod to Douglas and Southerners chose as their standard-bearer John C. Breckinridge, a proponent of extending slavery into the territories and annexing Cuba. Representing the discredited strategy

TABLE 13-4

The Election of 1860

Candidate	Political Party	Popular Vote (%)	Electoral Vote
Abraham Lincoln	Republican	39.8	180
Stephen A. Douglas	Democratic	29.5	12
John C. Breckinridge	Democratic	18.1	72
John Bell	Constitutional Union	12.6	39

of compromise was the candidate of the Constitutional Union party, John Bell of Tennessee.

In Chicago, the Republicans lined up behind Abraham Lincoln and agreed on a platform that had something for everybody, including measures to boost economic growth (as promoted by Henry Clay's American System earlier in the century): a proposed protective tariff, a transcontinental railroad, internal improvements, and free homesteads for western farmers. The Republicans renounced the Know-Nothings. Lincoln himself took the lead in admonishing Republicans who sought to curtail the voting rights of European immigrants, such as the Germans and Scandinavians.

Yet Republicans gave little hope to other groups demanding the rights and protection that flowed from American citizenship. Spanish-speaking residents of California, Chinese immigrants, free people of color throughout the North, Indian tribes from North Carolina to the northwestern states, the wives and daughters of men all over the country—these groups were not included in the Republicans' grand design for a country based on the principles of free labor.

Abraham Lincoln was elected president in 1860, although he received support from only 40 percent of the men who cast ballots. Lincoln won the electoral college, and he also received a plurality of the popular vote. However, ten southern states had refused to list him on the ballot; in that region of the country, he received almost no votes. Stephen Douglas won almost 30 percent of the popular vote; together, Douglas and Breckenridge outpolled Lincoln (2.2 million votes to 1.85 million). Nevertheless, the new president had swept New England, New York, Pennsylvania, and the upper Midwest. The regional interests of North and South took precedence over national political parties. By the end of 1860, South Carolina had seceded from the Union, and the nation headed toward war.

■ Augustus Washington, son of a former slave, took this picture of John Brown in 1846, 13 years before the raid on Harpers Ferry, Virginia. A pioneer daguerreotypist, Washington operated a successful studio in Hartford, Connecticut. After the passage of the Fugitive Slave Law in 1850, Washington emigrated with his family to Liberia, an African settlement for American freeborn blacks and former slaves, founded as a republic in 1847.

CONCLUSION

During the 1850s, Americans on both sides of the slavery issue voiced their opinions, and their frustrations, in ever more dramatic ways. People all over the country came to feel that the institution of slavery had relevance to their lives. In the slave states, black workers remained yoked to a system that denied their humanity and mocked the integrity of their families. In the nonslave states, free people of color understood that northern racial prejudice was but a variation of the slaveholders' theme of domination. New England farm families looking to move west were convinced that western homesteads would not improve their economic security if these homesteads were surrounded by plantations cultivated by large numbers of enslaved workers. Republicans promoted a future full of hope, a future that would fulfill the long-thwarted promise of the young country as a republic of equal rights for all male citizens.

In contrast, southern whites of various classes agreed on a rallying cry that stressed independence from Yankee interlopers and freedom from federal interference. Yet this unifying rhetoric carried different meanings for different groups of Southerners. The owners of large plantations were desperate to preserve their enslaved labor forces, and also hungry for fresh lands and renewed political power; these men scrambled to maintain their own privileges in the face of growing northern influence in Congress. Non-slaveholding farmers sought to produce all household necessities themselves and remain independent of the worldwide cotton market economy so crucial to the wealth of slave masters and mistresses. Yet almost all southern whites, rich and poor, stood allied, determined to take up arms to protect their households and their distinctive "southern way of life."

On the eve of the Civil War, complex forces roiled an ethnically diverse society. Ultimately the North and South marched into combat, each side united enough to mobilize huge armies. However, wartime strains would expose fault lines in the free-labor coalition as well as in the slaveholders' republic.

For Review

✓•—[Study and Review at www.myhistorylab.com

1. How did free labor ideology further the notion of individualism?

2. Is it more accurate to describe the United States of the 1850s in terms of a national, unified economy or in terms of a collection of regional economies? Explain.

3. Why did the white South feel increasingly defensive about slavery in the 1850s?

4. What factors led to the demise of the two-party system that had been dominated by Whigs and Jacksonian Democrats? How would you evaluate the efforts of politicians who sought to "compromise" on the issue of slavery?

Chronology: 1848–1860

1848 Gold is discovered in California.
Women's Rights Convention, Seneca Falls, New York.
Zachary Taylor elected president.

1849 "Forty-Niners" migrate to California.

1850 Compromise of 1850; Fugitive Slave Act.

1851 Fort Laramie Treaty.

1852 American (Nativist) party is founded.
Harriet Beecher Stowe, *Uncle Tom's Cabin*.

1853 Gadsden Purchase.
Matthew Perry's fleet enters Tokyo Harbor.

1854 Kansas–Nebraska Act.
Republican party is founded.

1855 William Walker captures Granada, Nicaragua.
Walt Whitman, *Leaves of Grass*.

1856 Lecompton (Kansas) Constitution.
James Buchanan elected president.

1857 *Dred Scott* Supreme Court Case.

1858 Lincoln–Douglas debates.

1859 Harpers Ferry raid.

1860 Abraham Lincoln elected president.

Key Terms

Compromise of 1850 Congressional legislation that provided that California would enter the Union as a free state that year, and that New Mexico and Utah would eventually submit the slavery question to their voters. As part of this compromise, the federal government abolished the slave trade in Washington, D.C. p. 312

Dispossession Act of taking land or other property from a group of people. p. 313

Dred Scott v. Sandford The 1857 case in which the Supreme Court held that residence on free soil did not render a slave a free person, for black people, enslaved and free, had (in the words of the court) "no rights which the white man was bound to respect". p. 330

Emancipation National or state-sponsored program to free slaves. p. 311

Fall line The geographical division between the Piedmont and the Atlantic coastal plain where the land slopes sharply to the sea. p. 317

Free Labor Ideology The ideas, represented most forcefully by the antebellum Republican party, that workers should profit from their own labor and that slavery is wrong. p. 317

Fugitive Slave Law of 1850 Congressional legislation that required local and federal law enforcement agents to retrieve runaways no matter where they sought refuge in the United States. p. 324

Lecompton Constitution A Kansas state constitution drawn up by proslavery advocates in 1857; sought to nullify the doctrine of popular sovereignty in the state, decreeing that even if voters rejected slavery, any slaves already in the state would remain enslaved under the force of law. p. 330

Gadsden Purchase A total of 29,670 square miles of land (located in present-day southern Arizona and southwestern New Mexico) purchased by the United States from Mexico in 1853. p. 314

Popular sovereignty The idea that residents of a state should be able to make decisions on crucial issues, such as whether or not to legalize slavery. p. 324

Republican party Founded in 1854, this political party began as a coalition of Northerners who opposed the extension of slavery into the western territories. p. 327

Tenant farmer A farmer who raises livestock and crops on land leased from wealthier owners. p. 316

Underground Railroad A secret network of abolitionists developed during the antebellum period to help slaves escape and find refuge, many in the North or in Canada. p. 324

Wage slavery The idea that wage earners are exploited by employers as harshly as slaves are exploited by their owners. p. 318

Yeoman A farmer who owns a modest amount of land (but no slaves). p. 316

14

"To Fight to Gain a Country": The Civil War

Pensacola, Florida, was the site of a dramatic court-martial trial in April 1862, when five men were found guilty of treasonous acts against the Confederate States of America. "Possessed of information well calculated to aid the enemy," and thus capable of "giving intelligence" to the enemy, the defendants had endangered the security of Confederate troops stationed in the area, according to the chief prosecutor. Later, the presiding officer claimed that coastal communities were engulfed in a "general stampede" as planters tried to move slaves and livestock out of the way of the encroaching Union army. At stake in this trial was the very fate of the would-be new nation.

All of the defendants—George, Robert, Stephen, Peter, and William—were runaway slaves. The specific charges lodged against them read, "That the said slaves are intelligent beings possessing the faculties of Conveying information which would prove useful to the enemy and detrimental to the Confederate States." The charges suggest that the Confederates were forced to repudiate elements of their own proslavery beliefs, which held that black people were childlike and servile, incapable of acting on their own, and grateful for the guidance and protection of southern whites.

Prosecuting officers believed that "strong measures" were needed to prevent the nefarious activities of "spys [*sic*] whether white or black." These officials therefore were unprepared for the firestorm of criticism that followed the announcement of the verdict.

The owner of the slaves, General Jackson Morton, expressed outrage that two of his men were marked for summary execution. In a formal complaint to Confederate authorities, Morton denounced the hearing as "vulgar and improper." By the time the controversy faded, an impressive array of Confederate military officers (from sentinels to a lieutenant, a captain, a colonel, a major general, and a general) had had to justify their actions in convening the trial. In the words of one official, "The sacrosanctity of slave property in this war has operated most injuriously to the Confederacy."

Though at a distinct disadvantage compared to the North in terms of troops, supplies, and industrial might, the white South managed to fight on for four long, bloody years. Early on, politicians hailed slaves as a tremendous asset, an immense, easily managed labor force that would grow food and dig trenches. Instead, African-American men and women became freedom fighters, a source of subversion in the heart of the Confederacy. In October 1862, in response to the crisis of wartime slave management, the Confederate Congress passed a measure that exempted from military service one white man for every 20 slaves on a plantation. Many slave owners used this law to shield themselves or their sons from combat duty. In turn, the Twenty-Negro Law inflamed resentment among non-slaveholding small farmers, who charged that this rich man's war was actually a poor man's fight.

As defenders of slavery, the Confederates cast themselves as rebels in an age when the principle of individual rights was gaining ground. The citizens of France, Germany, and Italy were agitating on behalf of modern, democratic nation-states, and systems of serfdom and slavery throughout Europe and the Western Hemisphere were under siege. By early 1865, desperate southern leaders were themselves considering offering slaves their liberty in return for military service.

The Republican conduct of the war revealed the party's nationalistic guiding principles. Yet several groups besides white Southerners objected to a strong federal government, one that would weld the country together geographically as well as economically. The Lincoln administration met bitter resistance from Indian tribes as diverse as the Santee Sioux of Minnesota, the Cheyenne of Colorado, and the Navajo and Apache of the Southwest. In northeastern cities, Irish immigrants battled federal draft agents and attacked black women, men, and children, their supposed competitors in the workplace. The Civil War, then, was less a "brothers' war" between the white farmers of the North and South exclusively and more a conflict that pitted diverse groups against each other over the issues of slavery, territorial expansion, federal power, and local control. Yet by the end of the war in April 1865, the Republican vision of a Union forged in blood had prevailed, at the cost of nearly 700,000 lives.

■ Sgt. F.L. Baldwin, a Union soldier, poses with an American flag as a backdrop.

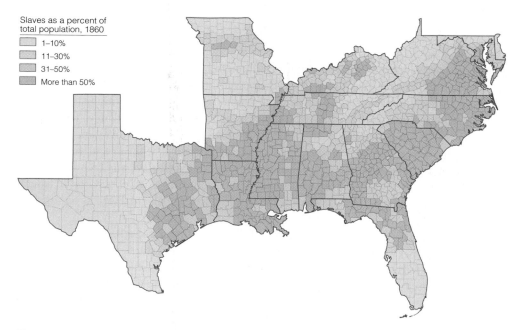

Slaves as a percent of total population, 1860

- 1–10%
- 11–30%
- 31–50%
- More than 50%

■ **MAP 14.1**
SLAVERY IN THE UNITED STATES, 1860
In the South, the areas of the greatest concentration of slaves were also the areas of greatest support for the Confederacy. During the war, the Appalachian mountain region and the upper Piedmont—the area between the mountains and the broad coastal plain—were home to people loyal to the Union and to people who became increasingly disaffected with Confederate policies as the war dragged on.

Mobilization for War, 1861–1862

How did the North and South prepare for war, and how did those preparations reflect each side's strategy for fighting—and winning—the war?

•••—Read the **Document**
Confederate Constitution (1861)
at **www.myhistorylab.com**

On December 20, 1860, less than eight weeks after Abraham Lincoln was elected president of the United States, South Carolina seceded from the Union, determined, in the words of its own Declaration of Independence, to "resume her separate and equal place among nations." By February 1, 1861, Mississippi, Florida, Alabama, Georgia, Louisiana, and Texas (all states dependent on slave-based staple-crop agriculture) had also withdrawn from the United States of America. Three days later, representatives of the seven states met in Montgomery, Alabama, and formed the **Confederate States of America**. They also adopted a new constitution for their new nation. Though modeled after that of the United States, this document invoked the power of "sovereign and independent states" instead of "we, the people." Delegates to the Montgomery convention elected as their president Jefferson Davis, a wealthy Mississippi planter with an impressive record of public service. Davis was a graduate of West Point, a veteran of the Mexican War, and a former United States congressman, senator, and secretary of war.

The Secession Impulse

In some respects, the Civil War seems difficult to explain, for the two sides shared a great deal. Most of the people in the North and South were English-speaking Protestants with deep roots in the culture of the British Isles. Together they celebrated a revolutionary heritage, paying homage to George Washington and the other Founding Fathers.

Why, then, was the white South, especially the slave South, so fearful of Abraham Lincoln? Although Lincoln enjoyed a broad electoral college victory, he won only 40 percent of the popular vote. Lincoln had made it clear that, as president, he would possess neither the authority nor the desire to disturb slavery as it existed in the South. However, he summed up his philosophy before the secession crisis this way: "As I would not be a *slave*, so I would not be a *master*. This expresses my idea of democracy. Whatever differs from this . . . is not democracy."

Not surprisingly, then, southern elites felt threatened by Lincoln in particular and the Republicans in general, pointing to the new president's oft-repeated promise to halt the march of slavery into the western territories. Although he was in no position to achieve this goal by executive order, Lincoln did have the power to expand the Republican base in the South by dispensing patronage jobs to a small group of homegrown abolitionists. He could also make appointments to the Supreme Court as openings became available. The Republican party was not a majority party; it was a sectional party of the North and the upper Midwest. But this sectional party had managed to seize control of the executive branch of government, tipping the antebellum balance of power between slave and free states decisively in favor of the North. Slave owners feared that John Brown's 1859 raid on the federal arsenal at Harpers Ferry, Virginia, was just the first in a series of planned attacks on the slave South (see Chapter 13).

Two last-ditch efforts at compromise failed to avert a constitutional crisis. In December 1860, as South Carolina was seceding and other states were preparing to join it, neither northern Republicans nor lower South Democrats showed any interest in a series of proposed constitutional amendments that would have severely curtailed the federal government's ability to restrict the interstate slave trade or the spread of slavery. Called the Crittenden Compromise (after its sponsor, Senator John J. Crittenden, a Whig from Kentucky), this package of proposed amendments was defeated in the Senate on January 16, 1861. A peace conference, organized by the Virginia legislature and assembled in February, revised the Crittenden Compromise, but key players were missing: the seven Confederate states and five northern states. Congress rejected the conference's recommendations at the end of February. By this time, many Americans, radicals and moderates, Northerners and

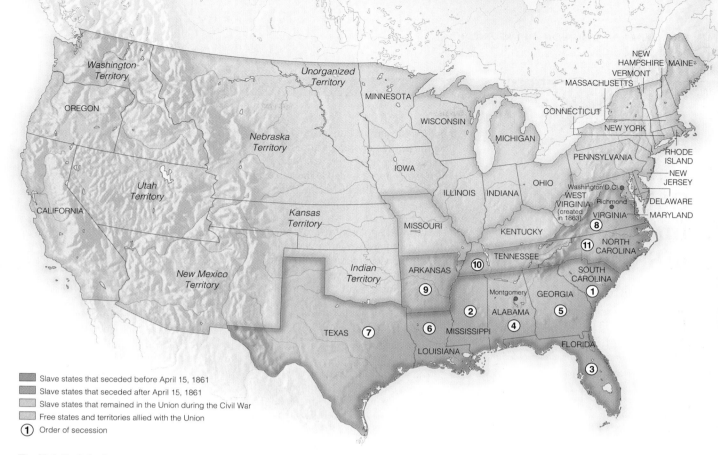

Slave states that seceded before April 15, 1861
Slave states that seceded after April 15, 1861
Slave states that remained in the Union during the Civil War
Free states and territories allied with the Union
① Order of secession

■ MAP 14.2

THE SECESSION OF SOUTHERN STATES, 1860–1861

The southern states seceded from the Union in stages, beginning with South Carolina in December 1860. Founded on February 4, 1861, the Confederate States of America initially consisted of only that state and six Deep South states. The four upper South states of Virginia, Arkansas, Tennessee, and North Carolina did not leave the Union until mid-April, when Lincoln called for 75,000 troops to put down the civil rebellion. The slave states of Delaware, Maryland, Kentucky, and Missouri remained in the Union, but each of those states was bitterly divided between Unionists and Confederate sympathizers.

Southerners, were in no mood to compromise on the issue of slavery, especially its extension into the West.

In his inaugural address of March 4, Lincoln appealed to the South to refrain from any drastic action, invoking the historic bonds of nationhood, the "mystic chords of memory, stretching from every battle-field, and patriot grave, to every living heart and hearthstone." For the most part, Lincoln's plea for unity fell on deaf ears. However, among the Southerners who initially resisted the secessionists' call to arms was the West Point graduate and Mexican War veteran Robert E. Lee of Virginia. Later, after Virginia seceded, Lee cast his lot with the Confederacy: "I cannot raise my hand against my birthplace, my home, my children," he declared. By his home, Lee meant the Commonwealth of Virginia, not the collection of disaffected states.

Indeed, in early April, the Confederacy was a rhetorical powerhouse, full of blustering firebrands. But it was also a poor excuse for an independent nation, with only one-third of the U.S. population and almost no industrial capacity. Over the next few weeks, as the seven Confederate states attempted to coax the upper South to join their revolution, Lincoln emerged as an unwitting ally in their effort.

Located in Charleston Harbor, Fort Sumter was one of two Union forts in southern territory, and in the spring of 1861 it was badly in need of supplies. On April 12, Lincoln took the moral high ground by sending provisions but not troops to the fort. The Confederates found

> *In his inaugural address of March 4, Lincoln appealed to the South to refrain from any drastic action.*

INTERPRETING HISTORY

A Virginia Slaveholder Objects to the Impressment of Slaves

During the Civil War, some southern slave owners bitterly resisted Confederate slave impressment policies. On December 4, 1861, John B. Spiece, an Albemarle County, Virginia, slaveholder and lawyer, wrote to the Confederate attorney general and protested government policy.

Dr Sir, Although a stranger to you, yet in consequence of the excitement and distress in this section of the country, in reference to a certain matter; I am constrained to address you, not merely on my own account; but on behalf of a large number of most respectable citizens. . . .

A practice has prevailed for some considerable time in *this* section of the country of impressing into service of the confederate army, the horses wagons and *slaves* belonging to the people.

The "Press masters" will go to their houses, and drag off their property to Just Such an extent as they choose; until it has not only created great excitement and distress; but bids fair to produce wide spread ruin. And I am told that these "Press masters" are paid by the Government the enormous price of *two dollars and fifty cents for each team which they impress*;—hence their anxiety and untiring exertions to increase the number;—thus making thirty or forty dollars pr day—

While I do not controvert the right of the Government to impress into its service *wagons and teams*; yet I do controvert the right to impress *Slaves*—It does seem to me that no one can be impress'd into military service of any kind, unless he is subject to military duty: because this whole business is relating to the Army, and is purely a military matter.—

The people in this section of the country are much attached to their slaves, and treat them in a humane manner—consequently they are exceedingly pained at having them dragged off at this inclement season of the year, and exposed to the severe weather in the mountains of north western Virginia. . . . Some have already died, and others have returned home afflicted with Typhoid fever, which has spread through the family to a most fatal and alarming extent.—

I am a practicing lawyer myself, but these "Press masters" will hear nothing from any one residing amongst the people.—

Therefore Sir, in consequence of the distress produced by the causes before mentioned, I am constrained to write to you; requesting you if you please, to give your opinion upon the questions involved.

To wit—If a man's wagon and team should be impress'd into Service, can his slave be impress'd to drive the said team—

Secondly—If a man has neither wagon or team can his slave be impress'd to drive some other team (*some* of the "Press masters" yield this *last* point, whilst others do not, and contend that they can impress just as many slaves as they choose from any plantation, taking all the negro men if they think proper.)—

Some few of the people have not been able to sow their grain this fall:—and there is deep dissatisfaction amongst the people—therefore I deem it proper and expedient that the authorities should know it—

Spiece goes on to cite the laws of the Commonwealth of Virginia, as amended in 1860, "by which it seems there is no power to impress Slaves." In the absence of Confederate congressional legislation to that effect, he argues, government authorities lack the legal right to take slaves from their owners. Spiece concludes his letter by suggesting that in taking slaves far from their homes, Confederate authorities were endangering the security of the would-be-new nation.

There is also a serious evil in impressing slaves for the service in North western Virginia:—whilst there they get to talking with *Union men* in disguise, and by that means learn the original

---

the move provocative nonetheless and began firing on the fort. After a 33-hour Confederate bombardment, the heavily damaged fort surrendered without a fight. In response, many white Southerners, such as Mary Boykin Chesnut, the wife of a high Confederate official, cheered and embraced the "pomp and circumstance of glorious war."

Three days after the capture of Fort Sumter, Lincoln (anticipating a conflict no longer than 90 days) called for 75,000 northern volunteers to quell a civil uprising "too powerful to be suppressed by the ordinary course of judicial proceedings." By the end of the month, he had ordered a blockade of southern seaports. Condemning these moves as acts of "northern aggression," the upper South, including Virginia (deprived of its western part, which now formed a new state called West Virginia), Tennessee, Arkansas, and North Carolina all seceded from the Union by May 20. Grateful for the newfound loyalty of Virginia

These slaves are unloading ships at City Point, Virginia. Field hands impressed to work in Confederate factories, on wharves, and in mines experienced a new way of life off the plantation and out of the sight of their owners.

cause of the difficulty between North & South: then return home and inform other negroes:—not long since one of my neighbors negro men went to his master, and desired to let him go again to the north western army— adding "I wish you to let me go further than I went before["]—I have the honor to be most respectfully your Obt Servt.

It is unknown whether Confederate officials responded to Spiece's letter.

Questions

1. *How does John Spiece demonstrate his talents as a lawyer in this letter?*
2. *How does Spiece suggest that slave impressment might actually undermine the security of the Confederacy?*
3. *In what ways does Spiece's reaction to slave impressment suggest changes in, or challenges to, southern planters' ideology of paternalism?*

Source: Ira Berlin, Barbara J. Fields, Thavolia Glymph, Joseph P. Reidy, and Leslie S. Rowland, eds., *Freedom: A Documentary History of Emancipation, 1861–1867*, Series 1, Vol. 1, *The Destruction of Slavery* (1985), pp. 782–83.

and eager to appropriate the Tredegar Iron Works in Richmond, the Confederacy moved its capital from the down-at-the-heels Montgomery to the elegant Richmond on May 11.

Certain segments of the southern population early demonstrated that they would withhold their support from the Confederacy. Yeoman farmers in the upcountry, Louisiana sugar planters dependent on world markets for their profits, and people in the hill country of east Tennessee all voted for Unionist delegates to their respective state conventions that chose secession. Enslaved black workers, of course, could hardly be counted on to defend those who kept them in bondage. The Border States of Missouri, Kentucky, Maryland, and Delaware remained within the Union, although among their residents were many outspoken people who openly sympathized with the South.

Preparing to Fight

Poised to battle each other, the South and the North faced similar challenges. Both sides had to inspire—or force—large numbers of men to fight. Both had to produce massive amounts of cannon, ammunition, and food. And both had to devise military strategies that would, they hoped, ensure victory. In early 1861, white Southerners were boasting of the stockpiles of cotton that, if needed, would serve as leverage for military support, diplomatic recognition, and financial assistance from the great European powers. Plantations brimming with hogs and corn, it was hoped, would sustain both masters and slaves, in contrast to the North, where cotton mills would lie idle and workers would soon descend to poverty and starvation.

From the beginning of the war, Confederates aimed for a strategy calculated to draw on their strengths. They would fight a purely defensive war with small units of troops deployed around the South's 6,000-mile border. Seasoned officers such as Robert E. Lee and Thomas J. Jackson would lead the charge to crush Union armies that ventured into Confederate territory. Finally, the South could command more than 3 million black people (a third of its total population of 9 million), all of whom, it was assumed, would do the bidding of planters and military men. Whereas the North would have to conquer the South to preserve the Union, the Confederacy would only have to survive to win its independence.

At first, the North was inclined to think little past the numbers: in 1860, it possessed 90 percent of the manufacturing capacity and three-quarters of the 30,000 railroad miles in the United States. Its population, 22 million, dwarfed that of the South. The North retained control of the (admittedly less than formidable) U.S. Navy and all other resources of the federal government, including a bureaucratic infrastructure to facilitate troop deployment and communication. Its diversified economy yielded grain as well as textiles; it could not only mobilize a large army but count on feeding it as well.

Early on, the North had a plan, but one that could hardly be dignified by the term *strategy*. It would defend its own territory from southern attack and target Confederate leaders, under the assumption that latent Union sentiment in the South would arise to smash the rebellion before it went too far. Union gunboats positioned along the East Coast and up and down the Mississippi River would seal off the Confederacy from foreign supply lines. The North would also launch a political offensive calculated to undermine Confederate sympathizers by bolstering Unionist sentiment everywhere. Lincoln, for example, continued to appeal to slaveholders loyal to the Union, whether those slaveholders lived in the Border States or deep in the heart of the Confederacy.

Confederates claimed that they were heirs of the noble ideas of the American Revolution. They argued that the tariff on imported goods was a form of taxation imposed on the South without its consent. White Southerners denounced what they called northern "tyranny" and "oppression." Northerners also invoked a Revolutionary heritage to justify their cause. However, they downplayed the issue of unjust taxation and instead stressed the glories of the Union—in Lincoln's words, "the last, best hope of mankind" in an age of kings and emperors.

Barriers to Southern Mobilization

On July 21, 1861, at Manassas Junction (Bull Run), about 30 miles southwest of Washington, D.C., Union and Confederate forces encountered each other on the field of battle for the first time. This was the fight that earned Thomas "Stonewall" Jackson his nickname and burnished his reputation, for Union troops skirmished briefly with the enemy and then turned and fled back to the capital, disgraced. In the coming weeks, Northerners gave up the idea that the effort to suppress the rebels would be an easy one, and Lincoln began to reorganize the country's officer corps and fortify its armies.

■ Farmer's cabin, Block House, New Braunfels, Texas.

To win this initial victory, the Confederates had relied on the massing of several huge forces: those of Generals Joseph Johnston and P. G. T. Beauregard, as well as Stonewall Jackson. Consequently, southern military strategists decided they must continue to defend southern territory while going on the offensive against the Yankees (the "offensive-defensive" strategy was used for the duration of the conflict). In other matters, however, the South learned life-and-death lessons more slowly. Only gradually did the central paradox of the Confederate nation become abundantly clear: that a country founded on an agrarian ideal of "states' rights" needed to industrialize its economy and centralize its government operations to defeat the Union.

The first weeks of the war revealed that the South would pursue its antebellum aims of conquering western territory for slavery. An early victory of Texas forces over Union troops in New Mexico led to the formation of what slaveholders in that region called the Confederate Territory of Arizona. Over the next year, the Confederates launched successful assaults on the cities of Albuquerque and Santa Fe, in present-day New Mexico. However, southern troops amounted to little more than a band of plunderers; in Rio Abajo, for example, farmers and ranchers switched their allegiance to the Union after the rebels raided their homesteads.

Deprived of money raised from customs duties (the U.S. Navy blockade brought a halt to established patterns of overseas trade), the Confederacy relied on floating bonds ($400 million worth), raising taxes, and a 10 percent tax on farm produce. The Confederate Treasury printed money at a furious rate ($1 billion over the course of the conflict), but its value declined precipitously; near the end of the war one Confederate dollar was worth only 1.6 cents.

Raising a volunteer army and impressing slave labor (forcing slaves to labor for the military) met with stiff resistance from various quarters of southern society. For yeoman farm families, long defensive of the independence of their own households, Confederate mobilization efforts came as a rude shock. Antebellum Southerners believed that white fathers should protect and retain control over their dependents at all times. Planters expressed a well-founded fear that slaves impressed for a wide range of tasks, whether saltmaking or chopping trees or tending brick kilns, were difficult to control now that plantation discipline had been loosened. When the Confederate call for volunteers failed to produce the number of soldiers (and menial laborers) needed to fight the Union, the Richmond government in March 1862 implemented a military conscription law (all men between ages 18 and 35—later it became 45—were called up for three years of service). The law exempted certain kinds of workers, such as railroad employees, schoolteachers, miners, and druggists, and allowed the buying of **substitutes** by draftees who could afford the $300 price for them. This last type of exemption allowed wealthy men to pay someone to fight in their place.

These provisions provoked anger not only among ordinary citizens but also among principled states' rights advocates such as governors Joseph Brown of Georgia and Zebulon Vance of North Carolina. Brown exempted large numbers of men from the draft, claiming that the Confederacy posed a greater threat to states' rights than did the Union. On January 1, 1862, 209,852 southern men were present for duty. Yet the northern force was more than twice as large, with 527,204.

Indians and Immigrants in the Service of the Confederacy

Just as the Confederates failed in their attempt to use fully the labor of enslaved workers, so they failed to reap much gain from the vaunted military prowess of Indians, especially those in Indian Territory (present-day Oklahoma). In 1861 southern military officials appealed to the Cherokee and the other Five Tribes for support, promising them arms and protection from Union forces in return. Only gradually and reluctantly did Cherokee leader John Ross commit his men to the Confederacy: "We are in the situation of a man standing alone upon a low naked spot of ground, with the water rising all around him." More devoted to the Confederate cause was Cherokee leader Stand Watie, who, backed by many Cherokee slaveholders, proceeded to mobilize what he called the "United Nations of Indians" as a fighting force on behalf of the Confederacy. Among those responding to the call to arms were Choctaw and Chickasaw men, who formed Company E of the 21st Mississippi Regiment, "the Indian Brigade."

Although Indian Territory was considered of great strategic value to the Confederacy, southern military officials at times expressed frustration with the traditional battle tactics of Indian warriors. They were unused to military encounters that pitted long, straight rows of men on foot against each other. At the Battle of Elkhorn Tavern (Pea Ridge) in March 1862, Indian troops abandoned the battlefield in the face of cannon fire, leading their commander, Albert Pike, to demand that in the future they be "allowed to fight in their own fashion" rather than "face artillery and steady infantry on open ground." By the summer of 1862, the Confederacy had lost its advantage in Indian Territory; the Cherokee and Creek were divided in their loyalties, with some joining Union forces. By this time, the Comanche and Kiowa, resentful of the Confederacy's broken promises

■ **Stand Watie**

(guns and money diverted from them), had joined Union troops and were threatening to invade Texas.

Like Native Americans, immigrants and ethnic minorities in the South were divided in their loyalties. A Jewish lawyer and slaveholder, Judah Benjamin, served as a cabinet member and trusted adviser to Jefferson Davis. Prominent southern military officers included some from Ireland, Prussia, and France. German and Irish workmen from southern cities helped fill the ranks of the Confederate army, as did an estimated 2,500 Hispanos. But ethnic loyalties could also disrupt services deemed necessary to Confederate manufacturing and transportation. The Confederate railroad director in Selma, Alabama, contended with a labor force of immigrants (most probably from Germany and Ireland), men who "do not feel identified in any great degree with the South" and who demanded high wages. They were constantly threatening to run away to Union lines, where they believed they could make more money and enjoy the luxuries denied them in war-torn Alabama.

The Course of War, 1862–1864

When the time came to marshal resources in the service of the national state, Northerners were at a distinct advantage over the states' rights men who dominated the Confederacy. Not only did the Union have more resources, but the Republicans' support for the centralization and consolidation of power also facilitated the war-mobilization process. In Congress, the Republicans took advantage of their new majority status and expanded federal programs in the realm of the economy, education, and land use. However, like Davis, Lincoln encountered vehement opposition to his wartime policies. Meanwhile, on the battlefield, Union losses were mounting. The United States confronted an uncertain fate.

What obstacles did the South face in defending its territory against northern invaders?

The Republicans' War

Worried about disloyalty in the vicinity of the nation's capital, on April 27, 1861, Lincoln gave General Winfield Scott the power to suspend the writ of habeas corpus (a legal doctrine designed to protect the rights of people arrested) in Baltimore. By the end of the year, this policy, which allowed the incarceration of people not yet charged with a crime, was being applied in almost all of the loyal United States. Chief among those targeted were people suspected of interfering with war mobilization of men and supplies. Democrats stepped up their opposition to the president, denouncing him as a tyrant and a dictator. Meanwhile, from the other side of the political spectrum, abolitionists expressed their frustration with the administration's conciliatory policy toward the South in general and toward Unionist slaveholders in particular. Lincoln insisted that his objective was "to save the Union, and . . . neither to save or destroy slavery."

Wartime manufacturing and commerce proved to be a boon to entrepreneurs. In Cleveland a young commission-house operator named John D. Rockefeller was earning enough money to hire a substitute to serve in the army for him. In the middle of the war, he shifted his business from trading grain, fish, water, lime, plaster, and salt to refining the crude oil (used in kerosene lamps) recently discovered in western Pennsylvania. War profiteers seized their opportunities in both the North and the South. In 1862 the *Southern Cultivator*, a magazine published in Augusta, Georgia, ran an article titled "Enemies at Home," denouncing the "vile crew of speculators" who were selling everything from corn to cloth at exorbitant prices.

■ Ulysses S. Grant

■ William Tecumseh Sherman

The Republicans' willingness to centralize wartime operations led in 1861 to the formation of the U.S. Sanitary Commission, which recruited physicians, trained nurses, raised money, solicited donations, and conducted inspections of Union camps on the front. During the war, as many as 20,000 white and black women served as nurses, cooks, and laundresses in Union military hospitals. Black women worked primarily in the latter two categories. A long-time advocate of reform on behalf of the mentally ill during the antebellum period, Dorothea Dix, served as superintendent of nurses.

The Republicans believed that the federal government should actively promote economic growth and educational opportunity, and they enacted measures previously thwarted by Democratic presidents and Congresses. In July 1862, the **Homestead Act** granted 160 acres of western land to each settler who lived on and made improvements to the land for five years. Congress also passed the **Morrill Act**, which created a system of land grant colleges. (Many of these colleges eventually became major public universities, including Colorado State University, Kansas State University, and Utah State University.) Also approved in 1862, the **Pacific Railroad Act** appropriated to the Union Pacific and the Central Pacific railroads a 400-foot right-of-way along the Platte River route of the Oregon Trail and lent them $16,000 to $48,000 (depending on the terrain) per mile.

During the first year and a half of war, Union military strategy reflected a prewar Republican indifference to the rights and welfare of both northern and southern blacks.

■ Robert E. Lee

■ Thomas "Stonewall" Jackson

In September 1861, Lincoln revoked a directive released by General John Frémont that would have authorized the seizure of property and the emancipation of slaves owned by Confederates in the state of Missouri. The president feared that such a policy would alienate slaveholders who were considering switching their allegiance to the Union. Later that fall, the capture of Port Royal, South Carolina, allowed Union soldiers to treat blacks as "contraband of war," denying slaveholders their human property but failing to recognize blacks as free people with rights.

Union military strategy reflected a prewar Republican indifference to the rights and welfare of both northern and southern blacks.

As Union forces pushed deeper into Confederate territory, U.S. officers devised their own methods for dealing with the institution of slavery. By early 1862, the North had set its sights on the Mississippi River valley, hoping to bisect the Confederacy and cut off supplies and men bound from Texas, Arkansas, and Louisiana to the eastern seaboard. In February, General Ulysses S. Grant captured Fort Henry and Fort Donelson on the Tennessee and Cumberland rivers, the Union's first major victory of the war; in April, New Orleans fell to Admiral David Farragut. In New Orleans, General Benjamin Butler attempted to retain the loyalty of Unionist slaveholders by returning runaway slaves to them. This policy was not always greeted with enthusiasm within Union ranks. A Massachusetts soldier, restless under the command of an officer sympathetic to "slave catching brutes," vowed, "I never will be instrumental in returning a slave to his master in any way shape or manner."

■ The bodies of soldiers lie where they fell on September 17, 1862, the single day that claimed the largest number of lives in the Civil War. Like many other battles of the war, Antietam was shaped by the physical features of the battlefield itself, with soldiers on both sides seeking cover in small groves of trees and behind rocks, road ruts, and fences made of stone and wood.

The Ravages of War

◉ See the **Map**
The Civil War Part I: 1861–62
at **www.myhistorylab.com**

In the summer of 1862, the South suffered a hemorrhaging of its slave population as the movement of Union troops up and down the eastern seaboard opened the floodgates to runaways. Yet over the course of the summer the Confederacy persevered on the battlefield, aided by the failure of Union armies to press their advantage. In June, General George McClellan was turned back on the outskirts of Richmond, which convinced Lincoln not only of the incompetence of his chief general but also of the value of a less forgiving approach toward the South. But General John Pope, brought in from the western campaign to command the 50,000-man Army of the Potomac, did little better.

In other parts of the country, the Yankee war against the Confederates spilled over into savage campaigns against Indian tribes. An uprising among the Santee Sioux in Minnesota killed 500 whites before the state militia quashed the rebellion at Wood Lake in the fall of 1862. General James H. Carleton routed the Texas Confederates who had been occupying New Mexico and Arizona, and then provided what he called a "wholesome lesson" to the Mescalero Apache and Navajo who had been menacing Spanish American *placitas* (communities) in the area. Carleton's Union soldiers forced the Mescaleros to accept reservation status at Bosque Redondo in the Pecos River valley. Meanwhile, Colonel Kit Carson conducted a campaign of terrorism against the Navajo, burning *hogans* and seizing crops and livestock, claiming that "wild Indians could be tamed." Many of the survivors undertook the "Long Walk" to Bosque Redondo, a forced march reminiscent of the Cherokee Trail of Tears a generation before.

The bloodiest day of the war occurred on September 17, 1862, on the banks of Antietam Creek in northern Virginia. The Battle of Antietam claimed 20,000 lives and resulted in a Union victory, although a costly one. To journalists and soldiers alike, battles could offer stirring sights of long rows of uniformed men arrayed against each other, their arms at the ready, regimental flags unfurled in the wind. Yet for the women of Shepardstown, Maryland, left to clean up after the Antietam slaughter, there was no talk of the glory of war, only a frantic, round-the-clock effort to feed the Confederates and bind their wounds. Surveying the battlefield wreckage, one observer, Maria Blunt, lamented the carnage: the dead but also men "without arms, with one leg, with bandaged sides and backs; men in ambulances, wagons, carts, wheelbarrows, men carried on stretchers or supported on the shoulder of some self-denying comrade." All over the South, white women established temporary hospitals in barns, private homes, and churches and mourned each human sacrifice to the cause: "A mother—a wife—a sister had loved him."

The extraordinarily high casualty rate in the war stemmed from several factors. Confederates and Federals alike fought with new kinds of weapons (rifles and sharpshooters accurate at up to 1,000 yards) while troops massed in old-style (that is, close) formation. Soft minie balls punctured and lodged in limbs, leading to high rates of amputation that in turn fostered deadly infections. One Alabama soldier observed in 1862, "I believe the Doctors kills more than they cour [cure]." In fact, twice as many Civil War soldiers died of infection and disease—diarrhea, dysentery, typhoid, pneumonia, and malaria—as were killed in combat.

The Emancipation Proclamation

Appalled by the loss of life but heartened by the immediate outcome of Antietam, Lincoln took a bold step. In September he announced that on January 1, 1863, he would proclaim all slaves in Confederate territory free. Lincoln used the Emancipation Proclamation to bolster northern morale by infusing the conflict with moral purpose and at the same time to further the Union's interests on the battleground by encouraging southern blacks to join the U.S. army. The measure left slavery intact in the loyal Border States and in all territory conquered by the Union. Consequently, nearly 1 million black people were excluded from its provisions. Skeptical of the ability of blacks and whites to live together, Lincoln remained committed to the colonization of freed blacks outside the United States (in Central America or the West Indies).

In the congressional elections of 1862, the Democrats had picked up strength in New York, Pennsylvania, and Ohio and carried Illinois. The lower Midwest in general harbored large numbers of Democrats who opposed the war (especially now that it was an "abolition war") and called for peace with the South; these so-called Copperheads disrupted Union enlistments and encouraged military desertions. The Emancipation Proclamation electrified abolitionists, but the war effort and the growing casualties were taking their toll among the laboring classes. Especially aggrieved were the working people who paid higher taxes (relative to those paid by the wealthy) to keep the war machine running, and the dockworkers and others who lost their livelihoods when trade with foreign countries ceased. Their resentment boiled over in the summer of 1863.

Persistent Obstacles to the Confederacy's Grand Strategy

From the beginning of the war, the North's effort to blockade 3,500 miles of southern coastline met with fierce resistance on the high seas. The South made up in resourcefulness what it lacked in a navy, relying for supplies on swift steamers manned by privateers (British arms smuggled onto remote southern beaches could bring up to 700 percent in profits). Seemingly invincible Confederate ships such as the ironclad *Merrimack* and the well-fortified British-built ships *Alabama* and *Florida* prowled the southeastern seaboard, sinking Union vessels and protecting the blockade runners. Nevertheless, by December 1861, Union forces had established beachheads in Confederate territory up and down the East Coast.

■ Kate Cumming of Mobile, Alabama, earned the gratitude of the Confederacy for her work as a hospital matron during the war. Before and during the Civil War, many people believed that respectable women should not work in hospitals. Physicians claimed that women were likely to faint at the sight of blood and that they were not strong enough to turn patients over in their beds. Yet, as the war progressed, more and more northern and southern women defied these stereotypes and served in hospitals as nurses, administrators, and comforters of the ill and dying. Noted Cumming soon after she first entered a hospital, "The foul air from this mass of human beings at first made me giddy and sick, but I soon got over it." Still, in southern hopsitals, soldiers and enslaved workers handled much of the direct patient care.

●●●—Read the Document
Barton, Memoirs about Medical Life at the Battlefield (1865)
at **www.myhistorylab.com**

●●●—Read the Document
"Lee at Fredericksburg" (1886)
by J. Horace Lacy at
www.myhistorylab.com

In November 1861, Union naval forces intercepted a British packet ship, the *Trent*, and seized two Confederate diplomats, James Mason and John Slidell, who were en route to London and Paris, where they planned to plead the South's case in a bid to gain diplomatic recognition. To avoid a rift with England, Lincoln and Secretary of State William H. Seward released the two men. In the process, Mason and Slidell lost whatever influence they might have had with European governments, and Lincoln enjoyed the praise of the British public for his moderation in handling the *Trent* affair.

More generally, Confederate hopes for diplomatic recognition foundered on the shoals of European politics and economics, in England and in the Western Hemisphere. English textile mills drew on their own immense prewar stockpiles of raw cotton and sought out new sources of fiber in Egypt and elsewhere. Also, English workers flexed their political muscle in a successful effort to forestall recognition of the slaveholders' nation. Early in the war the Confederates, who counted 2,500 Hispanos among their ranks, recognized the strategic importance of Mexico, both as a trade route for supplies and as a means of access to ports. In approaching Mexican President Benito Juarez for aid in late 1861, however, Confederate envoy John T. Pickett discovered that, although Mexicans still smarted from their defeat on their own land 13 years before, the Juarez administration remained an ally of the United States.

By the summer of 1862, Britain and France were inclined to mediate peace in favor of Confederate independence, for the two powers assumed that the South's impressive victories in Virginia and Tennessee signaled a quick end to the war. Nevertheless, the Confederacy's autumn setbacks of Antietam and Perryville (in Kentucky), combined with ennobling rhetoric of the soon-to-be-announced Emancipation Proclamation, proved that the Union was still very much alive. The diplomatic recognition the white South so desperately craved remained elusive.

The Other War: African-American Struggles for Liberation

In what ways did black people, northern and southern, enslaved and free, shape the course of the fighting?

From the onset of military hostilities, African Americans, regardless of whether they lived in the North or the South, perceived the Civil War as a fight for freedom. Although they allied themselves with Union forces, they also recognized the limitations of Union policy in ending slavery. Therefore, blacks throughout the northern and southern states were forced to take action to free themselves as individuals, families, and communities. Twenty-year-old Charlie Reason recalled his daring escape from a Maryland slave master and his decision to join the famous 54th Massachusetts Infantry composed of black soldiers: "I came to fight *not* for my country, I never had any, but to gain one." Soon after the 54th's assault on Fort Wagner (outside Charleston Harbor) in July 1863, Reason died of an infection contracted when one of his legs had to be amputated. In countless ways, black people throughout the South fought to gain a country on their own terms.

Enemies Within the Confederacy

Slaveholding whites were shocked when they could not always count on the loyalty of "petted" domestics. Soon after the war began, South Carolina's Mary Boykin Chesnut had expressed unease about the enigmatic behavior of one of her trusted house slaves, Laurence, asking herself of all her slaves, "Are they stolidly stupid or wiser than we are, silent and strong, biding their time?" A few months later, Chesnut's cousin was murdered while sleeping, bludgeoned by a candlestick; the cousin's slaves William and Rhody were

■ All over the South, black people watched and waited for opportunities to claim their own freedom. The movement of Union troops into an area often prompted slaves to flee from the plantation. Individuals and extended families sought safely behind Union lines or in nearby towns or cities, or began the quest for long-lost loved ones.

charged with the crime. Of her own mulatto servant, one of Chesnut's women friends remarked, "For the life of me, I cannot make up my mind. Does she mean to take care of me—or to murder me?" Now rising to the surface, such fears put whites on alert, guarding against enemies in their midst.

Yet no single white man or woman could halt the tide of freedom. Given the chance to steal away at night or walk away boldly in broad daylight, black men, women, and children left their masters and mistresses, seeking safety and paid labor behind Union lines. Throughout the South, black people waited and watched for an opportunity to flee from plantations, their actions depending on the movement of northern troops and the disarray of the plantations they lived on. In July 1862, the Union's Second Confiscation Act provided that the slaves of rebel masters "shall be deemed captives of war and shall be forever free," prompting Union generals to begin employing runaway male slaves as manual laborers. Consequently, military authorities often turned away women, children, older adults, and the disabled, leaving them vulnerable to spiteful masters and mistresses. For black men pressed into Union military and menial labor service, and for their families still languishing on plantations, "freedom" came at a high price indeed.

The Ongoing Fight Against Prejudice in the North and South

In the North, the Emancipation Proclamation spurred the enlistment of black men in the Union army and navy. Eventually, about 33,000 northern blacks enlisted, following the lead of their brothers-in-arms from the South. For black northern soldiers, military service opened up a wider world. Some learned to read and write in camp, and almost all felt the satisfaction of contributing to a war that they defined in stark terms of freedom versus slavery. They wore their uniforms proudly.

Union wartime policies revealed, however, that African Americans would continue to fight prejudice on many fronts. Some northern whites approved recruiting blacks, reasoning that for each black man killed in battle, one white man would be spared. Until late in the war, black soldiers were systematically denied opportunities to advance through the ranks and were paid less than whites. Although they showed loyalty to the cause in disproportionate numbers compared with white men, most blacks found themselves barred from taking up arms at all, relegated to fatigue work deemed dangerous and degrading to whites. They intended to labor for the Union, but, in the words of a black soldier from New York, "Instead of the musket it is the spade and the Whelbarrow and the Axe cuting in one of the horable swamps in Louisiana stinking and misery." For each white Union soldier killed or mortally wounded, two died of disease; the ratio for blacks was one to ten.

Many northern military strategists and ordinary enlisted men showed indifference at best, contempt at worst, for the desire of black fugitives to locate lost loved ones and begin to labor on their own behalf. In the course of the war, Union experiments with free black labor—on the South Carolina Sea Islands under the direction of northern missionaries, and in Louisiana, under the direction of generals Nathaniel Banks and Benjamin Butler—emphasized converting the former slaves into staple crop wage workers under the supervision of Yankees. Some of these whites, in their eagerness to establish "order" in former Confederate territory, saw blacks only as exploitable labor—if not cannon fodder, then hands to dig ditches and grow cotton.

Former slave Susie King Taylor recalled the heady, dangerous days of 1862, when she fled from Savannah and found refuge behind Union lines off the coast of Georgia. Despite the soldiers' little pay and poor treatment in the First South Carolina Volunteers (later known as the 33rd United States Colored Cavalry), Taylor gained a great deal of satisfaction from conducting a school for black children on St. Simon's Island and performing a whole host of tasks for the fighting men, from cleaning rifles to washing clothes and tending the ill. She understood that her own contributions to the war effort showed "what sacrifices we can make for our liberty and rights."

The Emancipation Proclamation did not materially change the day-to-day experiences of any slaves within southern territory, though many derived hope from the Union's new-found commitment to the abolition of bondage. That commitment changed the nature of the war from 1863 onward.

Battle Fronts and Home Fronts in 1863

How did developments on the battlefield affect politics in both the North and South?

In 1863 the North abandoned the strategy of conciliation in favor of an effort to destroy the large southern armies and deprive the Confederacy of its slave labor force. By this time, the war was causing a tremendous hardship among ordinary white folk in the South. Meanwhile, Lincoln found himself caught between African-American freedom fighters who resented the poor treatment they received from many white commanders, and white Northerners who took their opposition to the war in general and the military draft in particular into the streets. Deprivation at home and the mounting casualty rates on the battlefields were reshaping the fabric of American society, North and South.

Disaffection in the Confederacy

The Civil War assaulted Southerners' senses and their land. Before the war, slave owners and their allies often contrasted the supposed tranquility of their rural society with the rude, boisterous noisiness of the North. According to this view, the South was a peaceful place of contented slaves toiling in the fields, whereas the North was the site of workers striking, women clamoring for the vote, and eccentric reformers delivering streetcorner harangues.

The war exploded on the southern landscape with ferocious force, and the rumble of huge armies on the march shook southern society to its foundations. For the first time many Southerners smelled the acrid odor of gunpowder and the stench of rotting bodies. They heard the booms of near and distant cannon and the mournful sounds of church bells tolling for the dead. They saw giant encampments of soldiers cover what used to be cotton fields. Seemingly overnight, both armies constructed gorge-spanning train trestles and huge riverside docks and warehouses, all in preparation for conflict. As soldiers withdrew from the battlefield, they left behind a scarred and blood-spattered land, cornfields mowed down, fires smoldering in their wake.

These sights and sounds were especially distressing to Southerners who objected to the war as a matter of principle or because of its disastrous effects on their households. Scattered throughout the South were communities resistant to the policies of what many ordinary whites considered the Richmond elite—the leaders of the Confederacy. In western North Carolina, a group calling themselves Heroes of America declared their loyalty to the Union. In northern Alabama, the "Free State of Jones [County]" raised troops for the Yankee army. Throughout the rural South, army deserters were welcomed home by their impoverished wives and children; it is estimated that during much of the war, as many as one-third of all Confederate soldiers were absent without leave at any particular time.

During much of the war, as many as one-third of all Confederate soldiers were absent without leave at any particular time.

Groups of poor women resisted the dictates of the Davis administration, wealthy men and women who flaunted an extravagant wartime lifestyle of lavish dinners and parties. Women from Virginia to Alabama protested a Confederate 10 percent "tax-in-kind" on produce grown by farmers and the food shortages that reached crisis proportions. In April 1863, several hundred Richmond women, many of them wives of Tredegar Iron Works employees, armed themselves with knives, hatchets, and pistols and ransacked stores in search of food: "Bread! Bread! Our children are starving while the rich roll in wealth."

Whereas some white women resisted the Confederacy, others leaped to the fore to provide essential goods and services to the beleaguered new nation. Virginia's Belle Boyd kept track of Union troop movements and served as a spy for Confederate armies. Poor women took jobs as textile factory workers, and their better-educated sisters found employment as clerks for the Confederate bureaucracy. Slaveholding women busied themselves running plantations, rolling bandages, and knitting socks for soldiers. Still, many women thought their labors were in vain. Of the Confederacy's stalled progress, Georgia's Gertrude Thomas noted, "Valuable lives lost and nothing accomplished."

The Tide Turns Against the South

In the fall of 1862, Lincoln replaced General McClellan with General Ambrose E. Burnside and then General Joseph ("Fighting Joe") Hooker. In early May 1863, Lee and Jackson encountered Hooker at Chancellorsville, Virginia. The battle left Hooker reeling, but it also claimed the life of Jackson, mistakenly shot by his own men on May 2 in the early evening twilight. The South had lost one of its most ardent champions.

Lee decided to press his advantage by invading Pennsylvania and, it was hoped, encouraging northern Peace Democrats and impressing the foreign powers. The ensuing clash at Gettysburg was a turning point in the war. Drawn by reports of a cache of much-needed shoes, Confederate armies converged on the town, in the south-central part of the state and across the border from Maryland. Union forces pursued. In a three-day battle that began on July 1, the 92,000 men under the command of General George G. Meade were arrayed against the 76,000 troops of Robert E. Lee.

Gettysburg later came to represent the bloody consequences of a war fought by men with modern weapons under commanders with a premodern military sensibility. On the last day of the battle, the men under Confederate Major General George Pickett moved slowly into formation, passing hastily dug graves and the fragments of bodies blown to bits the day before. At 3 p.m., a mile-wide formation of 15,000 men gave the rebel yell and charged three-quarters of a mile across an open field to do battle with Union troops well fortified behind stone walls. Within half an hour, Pickett had lost two-thirds of his soldiers and all 13 of his colonels. The battle's three-day toll was equally staggering: 23,000 Union and 28,000 Confederate soldiers wounded or killed. Fully one-third of Lee's army was dead or wounded.

What made the soldiers of both sides fight on under these conditions? Some remained devoted to a cause. Others cared less about the Confederacy or the Union and more about proving their manhood and upholding their family's honor. Still others sought to memorialize comrades slain in battle or to conform to standards of discipline drilled into them. Some prayed merely to survive.

The Union victory at Gettysburg on July 3 brought rejoicing in the North. The next day, General Ulysses S. Grant captured Vicksburg on the Mississippi River, a move that earned him the rank of lieutenant general (conferred by Congress). Within a year, he assumed the position of supreme commander of the Union armies.

Civil Unrest in the North

●●●─|Read the **Document**

Brewster, Three Letters from the Front (1862) at **www.myhistorylab.com**

Not all segments of northern society joined in the celebration. Even principled supporters of the Union war effort were growing weary of high taxes and inflated consumer prices, not to mention the sacrifices of thousands of husbands, sons, and brothers. In May, federal soldiers had arrested the defiant and outspoken Copperhead Clement Vallandigham at his home in Dayton, Ohio. Subsequently convicted of treason (he had declared the conflict "a war for the freedom of blacks and the enslavement of whites"), Vallandigham was banished to the South.

Following a military draft imposed on July 1, 1863, the northern white working classes erupted. Enraged at the wealthy who could buy substitutes, resentful of the Lincoln administration's high-handed tactics, and determined not to fight on behalf of their African-American competitors in the workplace, laborers in New York City, Hartford, Troy, Newark, and Boston (many of them Irish) went on a rampage. The New York City riot of July 11–15 was especially savage as white men directed their wrath against black men, women, and children. Members of the mob burned the Colored Orphan Asylum to the ground and then mutilated their victims, before the federal government deployed 20,000 troops to New York to quell the violence and discourage other men from resisting the draft elsewhere. On August 19, the draft resumed.

The Desperate South

Meanwhile, the South had to contend not only with dissent and disaffection at home but also with the stunning battle and territorial losses it suffered at Gettysburg and Vicksburg. On August 21, Jefferson Davis proclaimed a day of "fasting, humiliation and prayer." Even as Davis was invoking the name of the Almighty, 450 rebels under the command of William Clarke Quantrill were destroying the town of Lawrence, Kansas (long a hotbed of abolitionist sentiment), and killing 150 of its inhabitants. With the exception of Quantrill and John Singleton Mosby (whose squads of men roamed northern Virginia attacking Union posts and troops in 1863), Confederate military leaders shunned guerrilla warfare, preferring to meet the enemy on a field of honor. The desperate Quantrill raid on Lawrence demonstrated that the Confederate cause was, if not lost, then losing in the late summer of 1863.

Before the year was out, Davis faced other setbacks as well. Grant's successes at Missionary Ridge and Lookout Mountain, in Tennessee, caused both France and England to draw back from offering overt support to the Confederacy in the form of sales of navy warships or diplomatic recognition. The Confederate president had long counted on securing the support of the great European powers; now those hopes were dashed.

Dedicating the national cemetery at Gettysburg on November 19, 1863, Lincoln delivered a short address that affirmed the nation's "new birth of freedom" and its commitment that "the government of the people, by the people, for the people, shall not perish from the earth." Lincoln's speech is one of the great rhetorical masterpieces of American politics. In it he elevated the Civil War from a military conflict exclusively to a great moral struggle against slavery. In the South, more and more whites were flagging in their conviction that the system of bondage was worth the ultimate sacrifice in terms of their own lives and the welfare of their families.

●••─[Read the **Document**
Abraham Lincoln, The Gettysburg Address (1863) at **www.myhistorylab.com**

The Prolonged Defeat of the Confederacy, 1864–1865

By 1864 northern generals, with Lincoln's blessing, had decided to fight a "hard war" against their tenacious enemy. Union troops were authorized to live off the land (denying southern civilians the necessities of life in the process), to seize livestock and other supplies indiscriminately, and to burn everything that the Confederates might find useful. The purposes of this strategy were twofold: to irreparably harm what was left of Confederate morale, and to facilitate the movement of northern troops through hostile territory. If northern troops could sever the area west of Georgia from the Confederacy and take Richmond and destroy its surrounding armies, the Union would be safe at last.

During the last months of the war, what factors contributed to the defeat of the Confederacy?

((•●─[Hear the **Audio**
"When This Cruel War is over" at **www.myhistorylab.com**

"Hard War" Toward African Americans and Indians

The policy of "hard war" should not be confused with total war, characterized by state-approved terrorism against civilians. However, Confederate policies toward black soldiers and Union policies toward Indian insurgents in the West did show elements of total war against particular segments of the population. In April 1864, Confederate General Nathan Bedford Forrest destroyed Fort Pillow, a Union garrison on the Mississippi River. After surrendering, black soldiers were systematically murdered. Wounded survivors were bayoneted or burned to death. Among southern generals, conventions of war (providing for the detention and exchange of prisoners of war) did not apply to African-American soldiers.

Nor were Indians accorded the minimal respect shown to most white combatants. In the early fall of 1864, a group of Cheyenne and Arapaho were camped along Sand Creek in the southeastern corner of Colorado. Black Kettle, a chief of the Cheyenne, had received promises from Union Colonel John M. Chivington and others stationed at Camp Weld in Denver that the two sides would remain at peace with each other. Therefore, on the morning of November 29, 1864, when Black Kettle saw Chivington leading a Colorado volunteer militia toward his settlement, he waved a white flag and stood his ground.

■ In September 1864, the Indian chiefs Black Kettle and White Antelope, with other Cheyenne and Arapaho leaders, met with Colonel John M. Chivington at Camp Weld, Colorado. The purpose of the meeting was to secure a truce between the Indians and European Americans in the area. Two months later, Chivington attacked an encampment of these Indians on the banks of Sand Creek, about 100 miles southeast of Denver.

Chivington did not come in peace. That day he and his men massacred 125 to 160 Indians, mostly women, children, and old people, returning later to mutilate the bodies. In response, the Sioux, Arapaho, and Cheyenne launched their own campaigns against white migrants traveling the South and North Platte trails. Chivington declared that it was "right and honorable" to kill Indians, even children, using any means.

"Father Abraham"

The election of 1864 proceeded without major incident, although Lincoln faced some opposition within his own party. Together with his new running mate, a former slave owner from Tennessee named Andrew Johnson, Lincoln benefited from a string of pre-election military victories won for him by Admiral David G. Farragut at Mobile, Alabama, and by General Philip Sheridan in Virginia's Shenandoah Valley. As a result, he defeated the Democratic nominee, his own former general, George McClellan, who managed to garner 45 percent of the popular vote. One of the keys to Lincoln's success was the "peace platform" that the Democrats had drafted at their convention the summer before. Support among Union soldiers for "Little Mac" dropped precipitously as a result, and Lincoln won three-quarters of the army's vote.

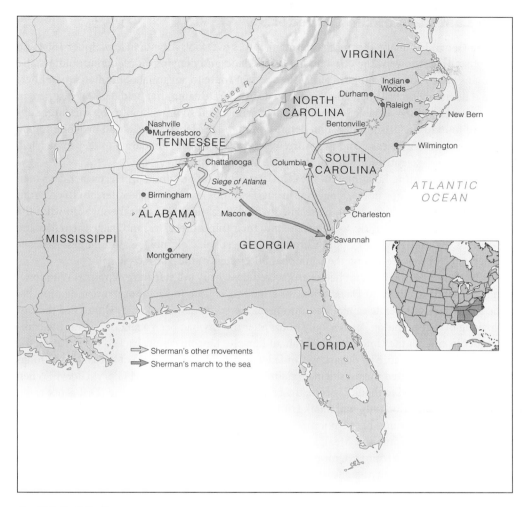

■ **MAP 14.3**
SHERMAN'S MARCH TO THE SEA, 1864–1865
General William T. Sherman's famous march to the sea marked the final phase of the Union effort to
divide and conquer the Confederacy. Sherman's men burned Atlanta to the ground in September 1864.
In late December, they made their triumphant entry into the city of Savannah. Sherman followed a policy
of "hard war" in these final months of the war; he ordered his troops to seize from civilians any food
and livestock they could use and to destroy everything else, whether rail lines, houses, or barns. White
Southerners expressed outrage over these tactics. Still, Sherman never systematically attacked civilians, a
characteristic of the Union's "total war" against Native American peoples in the West.

Despite his limited military experience, Lincoln possessed a strategic sense superior
to that of many of his generals. He played down his own military experience, making light
of his minor part in the Black Hawk War of
1832. In that conflict, he reminisced, he had
engaged in "charges upon wild onions . . . [and]
bloody struggles with the Musquetoes." However, he cared deeply about ordinary soldiers
and talked with them whenever he had the
opportunity. In return, Union troops gave
"Father Abraham" their loyalty on the battlefield and, especially during the election of 1864,
at the ballot box.

TABLE 14-1

The Election of 1864

Candidate	Political Party	Popular Vote (%)	Electoral Vote
Abraham Lincoln	Republican	55.0	212*
George B. McClellan	Democratic	45.0	21

*Eleven secessionist states did not participate.

The Last Days of the Confederacy

Union General William Tecumseh Sherman's forces overtook Atlanta in September 1864 and swept southeast toward the coast, living off the land and denying Confederate soldiers and civilians alike food and supplies along the way. En route to Savannah, Sherman's men liberated Andersonville Prison, a 26-square-acre Confederate camp that held 33,000 prisoners in the summer of 1864. Unable to feed their own armies and so unwilling to commit large supplies of food to the prison, the Confederate commander, Henry Wirz, stood by while 13,000 died of starvation, disease, and exposure. Wirz was the only Confederate officer to be tried, convicted, and executed for war crimes by the U.S. government.

After presenting Lincoln with the "Christmas gift" of Savannah in December, Sherman took his 60,000 troops north, slogging through swamps and rain-soaked terrain to confront the original secessionists. Later, he recalled with satisfaction, "My aim then was to whip the rebels, to humble their pride, to follow them to their inmost recesses, and make them fear and dread us." By mid-February, South Carolina's state capital, Columbia, was in flames. African-American troops were among the triumphant occupiers of the charred city.

By early April 1865, Grant had overpowered Lee's army in Petersburg, Virginia. Withdrawing, Lee sent a telegram to Davis, who was attending church in Richmond, warning him that the fall of the Confederate capital was imminent. Davis and almost all other whites fled the city. Arriving in Richmond on April 3, only hours after the city had been abandoned, was the commander in chief of the Union army, Abraham Lincoln. Lincoln calmly walked the streets of the smoldering city (set afire by departing Confederates), flanked by a group of ten sailors. Throngs of black people greeted the president, exclaiming, "Glory to God! Glory! Glory! Glory!" When a black man kneeled to thank Lincoln, the president said, "Don't kneel to me. That is not right. You must kneel to God only, and thank Him for the liberty you will enjoy hereafter."

On April 9, Lee and his demoralized and depleted army of 35,000 men found themselves outnumbered by Grant and Meade, and Lee surrendered his sword at Appomattox Courthouse in northern Virginia. Union officials ensured rebel soldiers protection from future prosecution for treason, and allowed the cavalry to keep their horses for use in spring planting. When the ragtag members of the so-called Stonewall Brigade—men who had entered the war with Stonewall Jackson four years before—came forward to lay down their arms, the Union army gave them a salute of honor, acknowledging their bravery.

One of the last casualties of the war was Abraham Lincoln. Watching a comedy with his wife, Mary, at Ford's Theater in Washington on the night of April 14, Lincoln was assassinated by John Wilkes Booth, a Confederate loyalist fearful that the president was bent on advancing "nigger citizenship." Lincoln lingered through the night but died the next morning. Booth was caught and shot within a matter of days. Of the departed president, Secretary of War Edwin M. Stanton is reported to have said, "Now he belongs to the ages."

CONCLUSION

Rather than asking why the South lost the Civil War, we might wonder why it took the North four years to win it. Despite all the political dissent and social conflict in the white South, despite the crumbling of the institution of slavery and the lack of support from the European powers, the Confederacy was able to mobilize huge armies under the command of brilliant tacticians such as Lee and Jackson. The war was fought on the battlefield by regiments of soldiers, not on the sea by navies or in the countryside by guerrillas. Therefore, as long as Confederate generals could deploy troops and outwit their foes during brief but monumental clashes, the Confederacy could survive to fight another day.

The South had entered the war armed with a states' rights ideology that held that all whites in the region were unified in support of slavery and that blacks were passive and childlike in their dependence on whites. The course of the war exposed the fallacy of this ideology. Even at the outset of the war, white Southerners differed in their support for the Confederacy, and as the conflict dragged on, many poor whites believed they were sacrificing more for the cause than were their social betters. Blacks proved aggressive in fighting for their freedom, wreaking havoc on plantation discipline and on southern military strategy. And too, many Confederates were forced to accept the fact that in order to fight the war successfully, principled states' rights supporters must yield to those politicians advocating a more centralized effort in behalf of mobilizing for war and fighting the enemy.

In terms of soldiers' lives lost—620,000—the Civil War was by far the costliest in the nation's history. Adding the deaths of slaves who toiled for the Confederate armies, the number of people who died as a result of the Civil War reaches 700,000. (The death toll among American military personnel in the Revolution was 26,000; in World War I, 116,000; in World War II, 400,000; in Vietnam, 58,000.) At the end of the war, the Union was preserved and slavery was destroyed. Yet, in their quest for true freedom, African Americans soon learned that military hostilities were but one phase of a wider war, a war to define the nature of American citizenship and its promise of liberty and equality. Thus April 1865 marked not so much a final judgment as a transition to new battlefields.

Watch the Video
The Meaning of the Civil War for Americans at **www.myhistorylab.com**

For Review

✓●─Study and Review at www.myhistorylab.com

1. Despite the claims of white leaders, the South was not unified in fighting the Civil War. Identify three different social groups within the South and discuss why they either initially withheld their support for the Confederacy or why their initial support for the cause gradually eroded over the course of the fighting.

2. What were the North's advantages over the South in terms of centralizing military, political, and economic operations during the war? Given those advantages, why did the Confederacy nevertheless believe it could win the war?

3. What were the effects and limitations of the Emancipation Proclamation in shaping the course of the war? In shaping southern and black communities during the war?

4. What accounts for the long duration of the Civil War and the very high mortality rates among military personnel during the conflict? Why did neither Jefferson Davis nor Abraham Lincoln seek a negotiated settlement to avoid further bloodshed?

Chronology: 1860–1865

1860 South Carolina secedes from Union.

1861 Confederate States of America is formed.
Civil War begins.

1862 Minnesota (Santee) Sioux uprising.
Congress passes Homestead, Morrill, and Pacific Railroad acts.
Union victory at the Battle of Antietam.

1863 Emancipation Proclamation.
Richmond Bread Riots.
Union victory at Battle of Gettysburg with heavy losses on both sides.
Northern antidraft riots.
Lincoln delivers Gettysburg Address.

1864 Fort Pillow massacre of African-American (Union) soldiers in western Tennessee.
Sand Creek (Colorado) massacre of Cheyenne and Arapaho.
Lincoln re-elected president.
Sherman's March to the Sea.

1865 Confederacy is defeated.
Lincoln assassinated.

Key Terms

Confederate States of America The would-be new nation formed in February 1861 by seven southern states—South Carolina, Mississippi, Florida, Alabama, Georgia, Louisiana, and Texas—in a bid for independence from the United States of America. By late spring 1861, the Confederacy also included Virginia, Arkansas, Tennessee, and North Carolina. p. 338

Homestead Act Legislation passed in 1862 that granted 160 acres of land free to each settler who lived on and made improvements to government land for five years. p. 346

Morrill Act Legislation passed by Republican Congress in 1862 to create a system of agricultural (land-grant) public colleges. p. 346

Pacific Railroad Act Legislation that granted to the Union Pacific and the Central Pacific railroads cash subsidies and a 400-foot right of way along the Platte River route of the Oregon Trail. p. 346

Substitute During war, a man paid to serve in combat in another man's place. p. 344

T he day of jubilee had come at last! In late December 1864, African-American men, women, and children rejoiced when the troops of Union General William Tecumseh Sherman liberated Savannah, Georgia. The city's black community immediately formed its own school system under the sponsorship of a new group, the Savannah Education Association (SEA). The association owed its creation to the desire of freedpeople of all ages to learn to read and write. A committee of black clergy began by hiring 15 black teachers and acquiring buildings (including the Old Bryan Slave Mart) for use as schools. By January 10, 1865, Savannah blacks had raised nearly $800 to pay teachers' salaries, enabling several hundred black children to attend classes free of charge.

Following hard on the heels of the Union army, a group of northern white missionaries arrived in Savannah to seek black converts for two Protestant denominations, the Presbyterians and the Congregationalists. On the first day of school, in January 1865, these northern newcomers watched a grand procession of children wend its way through the streets of Savannah. The missionaries expressed amazement that the SEA was an entirely black-run organization. These whites had believed the former slaves incapable of creating such an impressive educational system.

In March 1865, the federal government, under the auspices of the newly formed Bureau of Refugees, Freedmen, and Abandoned Lands (Freedmen's Bureau), agreed to work with missionaries in opening schools for black children throughout the former Confederate states. In Savannah, missionaries and government officials soon became alarmed that black leaders were willing to accept financial aid from them but not willing to relinquish control of SEA schools to the whites in return. The Northerners were also distressed by the militancy of certain local black leaders. One of these leaders was Aaron A. Bradley, who, armed with a pistol and bowie knife, was urging other black men to vote as a bloc in all elections.

In an effort to wrest control of the SEA from Savannah blacks, northern missionaries and agents of the Freedmen's Bureau decided to withhold funds from the association. By March 1866, these efforts had paid off: the city's black community, swollen by a refugee population, was no longer able to support its own schools. Northern whites took over SEA operations, and the association ceased to exist.

During the months and years immediately after the war, a major conflict raged between supporters of African-American rights and supporters of southern white privilege. Republican congressmen hoped to *reconstruct* the South

15

Consolidating a Triumphant Union, 1865–1877

Courtesy of the Georgia Historical Society, William Wilson Collection

■ **In Savannah, African American Sunday school pupils pose for photographer William Wilson in 1890. After the Civil War, many southern black communities created, or enlarged and solidified, their own institutions, including schools and churches.**

by enabling African Americans to own land and to become full citizens. Southern freedpeople sought to free themselves from white employers, landlords, and clergy and to establish control over their own workplaces, families, and churches. In contrast, President Andrew Johnson appeared bent on *restoring* the antebellum power relations that made southern black people field laborers dependent on white landowners. For their part, many southern whites were determined to prevent black men and women from becoming truly free. Most former rebels remained embittered about the outcome of the war and vengeful toward the freedpeople.

After the war, the U.S. government sought to weld the whole nation into one political and economic unit. Western economic development presented new challenges for men who had fought for the Union. In order to open the West to European-American miners and homesteaders, the U.S. army clashed repeatedly with Native Americans. On the Plains and in the Northwest, Indians resisted white efforts to force them to abandon their nomadic way of life and take up sedentary farming. William Tecumseh Sherman, Philip H. Sheridan, and George Custer were among the U.S. military officers who had commanded troops in the Civil War and now attempted to subdue the Plains Indians and further white settlement. Sherman declared, "We must act with vindictive earnestness against the Sioux, even to their extermination, men, women and children." The former head of the Freedmen's Bureau, General Oliver O. Howard, oversaw the expulsion of Chief Joseph and his people, the Nez Percé, from their homeland in southeast Washington's Walla Walla Valley in 1877.

The Civil War hardened the positions of the two major political parties. The Republicans remained in favor of a strong national government, one that promoted economic growth. The Democrats tended to support states' efforts to manage their own affairs, which included regulating relations between employers and employees, whites and blacks. The railroad industry represented a robust, Republican-sponsored partnership between private enterprise and the federal government. Between 1862 and 1872, the government gave the industry subsidies that included millions of dollars in cash and more than 100 million acres of land. During the postwar period, now called the **Reconstruction era**, federal government officials attempted to complete the political process that the military defeat of the South had only begun: the consolidation of the Union, North and South, East and West. This process encompassed the nation as a whole.

The Struggle over the South

The Civil War had a devastating impact on the South in physical, social, and economic terms. Estimates of fatalities among southern soldiers amounted to 260,000 men, as many as 33 percent of the total who marched off to war. The region had lost an estimated $2 billion in investments in slaves; modest homesteads and grand plantations alike lay in ruins; and gardens, orchards, and cotton fields were barren. More than 3 million former slaves eagerly embraced freedom, but the vast majority lacked the land, cash, and credit necessary to build family homesteads for themselves. Hoping to achieve social and economic self-determination, African-American men and women traveled great distances, usually on foot, in efforts to locate loved ones and reunite families that had been separated during slavery. At the same time, landowning whites considered black people primarily as a source of agricultural labor; these whites resisted the idea that the freedpeople should be granted citizenship rights.

How did various groups of Northerners and Southerners differ in their vision of the postwar South?

In the North, Republican lawmakers disagreed among themselves how best to punish the defeated but defiant rebels. President Abraham Lincoln had indicated early that after the war the government should bring the South back into the Union quickly and painlessly. His successor wanted to see members of the southern planter elite humiliated, but resisted the notion that freedpeople should become independent of white landowners. In Congress, moderate and radical Republicans argued about how far the government should go in ensuring the former slaves' freedom.

Wartime Preludes to Postwar Policies

Wartime experiments with African-American free labor in Union-occupied areas foreshadowed bitter postwar debates. As early as November 1861, Union forces had occupied the Sea Islands off Port Royal Sound in South Carolina. In response, wealthy cotton planters fled to the mainland. Over the next few months, three groups of northern civilians landed on the Sea Islands with the intention of guiding blacks in the transition from slave to free labor. Teachers arrived intent on creating schools, and missionaries hoped to start churches. A third group, representing Boston investors, had also settled on the Sea Islands to assess economic opportunities; by early 1862, they decided to institute a system of wage labor that would reestablish a staple crop economy and funnel cotton directly into northern textile mills. The freed slaves, however, preferred to grow crops for their families to eat rather than cotton to sell, relying on a system of barter and trade among networks of extended families. Their goal was to break free of white landlords, suppliers, and cotton merchants.

Meanwhile, in southern Louisiana, the Union capture of New Orleans in the spring of 1862 enabled northern military officials to implement their own free (that is, non-slave) labor system. General Nathaniel Banks proclaimed that U.S. troops should forcibly relocate blacks to plantations "where they belong"; there they would continue to work for their former owners in the sugar and cotton fields, but now for wages supposedly negotiated annually. The Union army would compel blacks to work if they resisted doing so. In defiance of these orders, however, some blacks went on strike for higher wages, and others refused to work at all. Moreover, not all Union military men relished the prospect of forcing blacks to work on the plantations where they had been enslaved. Thus, federal policies returning blacks to plantations remained contested even within the ranks of the army itself.

The Lincoln administration had no hard-and-fast reconstruction policy to guide congressional lawmakers looking toward the postwar period. In December 1863, the president outlined his Ten Percent Plan. This plan would allow former Confederate states to form new state governments once 10 percent of the men who had voted in the 1860 presidential election had pledged allegiance to the Union and renounced slavery. Congress instead passed the Wade-Davis Bill, which would have required a majority of southern voters in any state to take a loyalty oath affirming their allegiance to the United States. By refusing to sign the bill before Congress adjourned, Lincoln vetoed the measure (through a **pocket veto**). However, the president approved the creation of the **Freedmen's Bureau** in March 1865. The bureau was responsible for coordinating relief efforts on behalf of blacks and poor whites loyal to the Union, for sponsoring schools, and for implementing a labor contract system on southern plantations. At the time of his assassination, Lincoln seemed to be leaning toward giving the right to vote to southern black men.

Presidential Reconstruction, 1865–1867

When Andrew Johnson, the seventeenth president of the United States, assumed office in April 1865 after Lincoln's death, he brought his own agenda for the defeated South. Throughout his political career, Johnson had seen himself as a champion of poor white farmers in opposition to the wealthy planter class. A man of modest background, he had been elected U.S. senator from Tennessee in 1857. He alone among southern senators remained in Congress and loyal to the Union after 1861. Lincoln first appointed Johnson military governor of Tennessee when that state was captured by the Union in 1862 and then tapped him as his running mate for the election of 1864.

Soon after he assumed the presidency, Johnson disappointed congressional Republicans who hoped that he would serve as a champion of the freedpeople. He welcomed back into the Union those states reorganized under Lincoln's Ten Percent Plan. He advocated denying the vote to wealthy Confederates, though he would allow individuals to come to the White House to beg the president for special pardons. Johnson also outlined a fairly lenient plan for readmitting the other rebel states into the Union. Poor whites would have the right to vote, but they must convene special state conventions that would renounce secession and accept the Thirteenth Amendment abolishing slavery. Further, they must repudiate all Confederate debts. The president opposed granting the vote to the former slaves; he believed that they should continue to toil as field workers for white landowners.

Johnson failed to anticipate the speed and vigor with which former Confederate leaders would move to reassert their political authority. In addition, he did not gauge accurately the resentment of congressional Republicans, who thought his policies toward the defeated South were too forgiving. The southern states that took advantage of Johnson's reunification policies passed so-called **Black Codes**. These state laws were an ill-disguised attempt to institute a system of near-slavery. They aimed to penalize "vagrant" blacks, defined as those who did

■ Freedmen's Bureau agents distributed rations to former slaves and southern whites who had remained loyal to the Union. Agents also sponsored schools, legalized marriages formed under slavery, arbitrated domestic disputes, and oversaw labor contracts between workers and landowners. This photo shows the bureau office in Petersburg, Virginia.

not work in the fields for whites, and to deny blacks the right to vote, serve on juries, or in some cases even own land. The Black Code of Mississippi restricted the rights of a freed-person to "keep or carry fire-arms," ammunition, and knives and to "quit the service of his or her employer before the expiration of his or her term of service without good cause." The vagueness of this last provision threatened any blacks who happened not to be working under the supervision of whites at any given moment. People arrested under the Black Codes faced imprisonment or forced labor.

At the end of the war, congressional Republicans were divided into two camps. Radicals wanted to use strong federal measures to advance black people's civil rights and economic independence. In contrast, moderates were more concerned with the free market and private property rights; they took a hands-off approach regarding former slaves. But members of both groups reacted with outrage to the Black Codes. Moreover, when the legislators returned to the Capitol in December 1865, they were in for a shock: among their new colleagues were four former Confederate generals, five colonels, and other high-ranking members of the Confederate elite, including former Vice President Alexander Stephens, now under indictment for treason. All of these rebels were duly elected senators and representatives from southern states. In a special session called for December 4, a joint committee of

•◦•—Read the **Document**

The Mississippi Black Code at **www.myhistorylab.com**

INTERPRETING HISTORY

A Georgia Planter Appeals to a Freedmen's Bureau Officer

In April 1866, M. C. Fulton, a white planter living near Thomson, Georgia, wrote to Brigadier General Davis Tillson, the head of the Freedmen's Bureau in Georgia, appealing for help in getting his black women workers back to work in the fields in time for spring cotton planting.

Dear Sir—Allow me to call your attention to the fact that most of the Freedwomen who have husbands are not at work—never having made any contract at all—their husbands are at work, while they are as nearly as idle as it is possible for them to be, pretending to spin—knit or something that really amounts to nothing for their husbands have to buy them clothing. . . .

Now these women have always been used to working out & it would be far better for them to go to work for reasonable wages & their rations—both in regard to health & in furtherance of their family wellbeing—. . . . It is impossible for one man to do this [work] & maintain his wife in idleness without stealing more or less of their support, whereas if their wives (where they are able) were at work for rations & fair wages—which they can all get; the family could live in some comfort and more happily—besides their labor is a very important percent of the labor of the South. . . .

Now & then there is a woman who is not able to work in the field—or has 3 or 4 children at work & can afford to live on her childrens labor—with that of her husband—Even in such a case it would be better she should be at work—Generally however most of them should be in the field—Could not this matter be referred to your agents[?] They are generally clever men and would do right. I would suggest that you give this matter your favorable consideration & if you can do so to use your influence to make these idle women go to work. You would do them & the country a service besides gaining favor & the good opinion of the people generally.

I beg you will not consider this matter lightly for it is a very great evil & one that the Bureau ought to correct—if they wish the Freedmen & women to do well. . . . I am very respectfully your ob[edien]t servant

M. C. Fulton

Fulton added a postscript:

These idle women are bad examples to those at work & they are often mischief makers—having no employment their brain becomes more or less the Devil's workshop as is always the case with idle people—black or white. . . .

Such people are generally a nuisance—& ought to be reformed if possible or forced to work for a support. . . . Poor white women have to work—so should all poor people—or else stealing must be legalized—or tolerated for it is the twin sister of idleness. . . .

Questions

1. *How does Fulton define "idleness"? Why does he believe that women who stay home and care for their families are not really working?*
2. *Is Fulton making a race-based or a class-based argument in his appeal to Davis? Explain.*
3. *Does Fulton have good reason for assuming—or hoping-- that Davis will be responsive to this letter?*

M. C. Fulton to Brig. Gen. Davis Tillson, 17 April 1866, Unregistered Letters.

After the Civil War, many rural southern blacks, such as those shown here, continued to toil in cotton fields owned by whites.

15 lawmakers (six senators and nine members of the House) voted to bar these men from Congress.

By January 1865, both houses of Congress had approved the Thirteenth Amendment to the Constitution, abolishing slavery. The necessary three-fourths of the states ratified the measure by the end of the year. However, President Johnson was becoming more openly defiant of his congressional foes who favored aggressive federal protection of black civil rights. He vetoed two crucial pieces of legislation: an extension and expansion of the Freedmen's Bureau and the Civil Rights Bill of 1866. This latter measure was an unprecedented piece of legislation. It called on the federal government—for the first time in history—to protect individual rights against the willful indifference of the states (as manifested, for example, in the Black Codes). Congress managed to override both vetoes by the summer of 1866.

In June of that year, Congress passed the Fourteenth Amendment. This amendment guaranteed the former slaves citizenship rights, punished states that denied citizens the right to vote, declared the former rebels ineligible for federal and state office, and voided Confederate debts. This amendment was the first to use gender-specific language, guarding against denying the vote "to any of the male inhabitants" of any state.

Even before the war ended, certain groups of Northerners had moved south, and the flow increased in 1865. Black and white teachers volunteered to teach the former slaves to read and write. Some Northerners journeyed south to invest in land and become planters in the staple crop economy. White southern critics called all these migrants **carpetbaggers**. This derisive term suggested that the Northerners hastily packed their belongings in rough bags made of carpet scraps and then rushed south to take advantage of the region's devastation and confusion. To many freedpeople, whether they worked for a carpetbagger or a Southerner, laboring in the cotton fields was but a continuation of slavery.

Some former southern (white) Whigs, who had been reluctant secessionists, now found common ground with northern Republicans who supported government subsidies for railroads, banking institutions, and public improvements. This group consisted of some members of the humbled planter class as well as men of more modest means. Southern Democrats, who sneered at any alliances with the North, scornfully labeled these whites **scalawags** (the term referred to a scrawny, useless type of horse on the Scottish island of Scalloway).

Soon after the war's end, southern white vigilantes launched a campaign of violence and intimidation against freedpeople who dared to resist the demands of white planters and other employers. Calling itself the Ku Klux Klan, a group of Tennessee war veterans soon became a white supremacist terrorist organization and spread to other states. In May 1866, violence initiated by white terrorists against blacks in Memphis, Tennessee, left 46 freedpeople and two whites dead, and in July, a riot in New Orleans claimed the lives of 34 blacks and three of their white allies. These bloody encounters demonstrated the lengths to which ex-Confederates would go to reassert their authority and defy the federal government.

Back in Washington, Johnson vetoed the Fourteenth Amendment, traveling around the country and urging the states not to ratify it. He argued that policies related to black suffrage should be decided by the states. The time had come for reconciliation between the North and South, maintained the president. (The amendment would not be adopted until 1868.)

Congressional Republicans fought back. In the election of November 1866, they won a two-thirds majority in both houses of Congress. These numbers allowed them to claim a mandate from their constituents and to override any future vetoes by the president. Moderates and radicals together prepared to bypass Johnson to shape their own Reconstruction policies.

H.P. Moore/Collection of the New-York Historical Society, Neg. #37497

■ Residents of Edisto Island, off the coast of South Carolina, pose with a U.S. government mule cart immediately after the Civil War. U.S. troops captured the island in November 1861. The following March, the government began to distribute to blacks the lands abandoned by their former masters. In October 1865, President Andrew Johnson halted the program. A group of angry and disappointed blacks appealed to the president, claiming, "This is our home, we have made these lands what they are." After meeting with the group, General Oliver O. Howard noted, "I am convinced that something must be done to give these people and others the prospect of homesteads."

The Postbellum South's Labor Problem

While policymakers maneuvered in Washington, black people throughout the postbellum South aspired to labor for themselves and gain independence from white overseers and landowners.

While policymakers maneuvered in Washington, black people throughout the postbellum (postwar) South aspired to labor for themselves and gain independence from white overseers and landowners. Yet white landowners persisted in regarding blacks as field hands who must be coerced into working. With the creation of the Freedmen's Bureau in 1865, Congress intended to form an agency that would mediate between these two groups. Bureau agents encouraged workers and employers to sign annual labor contracts designed to eliminate the last vestiges of the slave system. All over the South, freed men, women, and children would contract with an employer on January 1 of each year. They would agree to work for either a monthly wage, an annual share of the crop, or some combination of the two.

According to the Freedmen's Bureau, the benefits of the annual labor contract system were clear. Employers would have an incentive to treat their workers fairly—to offer a decent wage and refrain from physical punishment. Disgruntled workers could leave at the end of the year to work for a more reasonable landowner. In the postbellum South, however, labor relations were shaped not by federal decree but by a process of negotiation that pitted white landowners against blacks who possessed little but their own labor.

For instance, blacks along the Georgia and South Carolina coast were determined to cultivate the land on which their forebears had lived and died. They urged General Sherman to confiscate the land owned by rebels in the area. In response, in early 1865, Sherman issued Field Order Number 15, mandating that the Sea Islands and the coastal region south of Charleston be divided into parcels of 40 acres for individual freed families. He also decreed that the army might lend mules to these families to help them begin planting. Given the provisions of this order, many freed families came to expect that the federal government would grant them "forty acres and a mule."

As a result of Sherman's order, 20,000 former slaves proceeded to cultivate the property once owned by Confederates. Within a few months of the war's end, however, the War Department bowed to pressure from the white landowners and revoked the order. The War Department also provided military protection for whites to return and occupy their former lands. In response, a group of black men calling themselves Commissioners from Edisto Island (one of the Sea Islands) met in committee to protest to the Freedmen's Bureau what they considered a betrayal. Writing from the area in January 1866, one Freedmen's Bureau official noted that the new policy must be upheld but regretted that it had brought the freedpeople into "collision" with "U.S. forces."

During its brief life (1865 to 1868), the Freedmen's Bureau compiled a mixed record. The individual agents represented a broad range of backgrounds, temperaments, and political ideas. Some were former abolitionists who considered northern-style free labor to be "the noblest principle on earth." These men tried to ensure safe and fair working arrangements for black men, women, and children. In contrast, some agents had little patience with the freedpeople's drive for self-sufficiency. Some bureau offices became havens for blacks seeking redress against abusive or fraudulent labor practices, but other offices had little impact on the postwar political and economic landscape. For agents without means of transportation (a reliable horse), plantations scattered throughout the vast rural South remained outside their control. Because white landowners crafted the wording and specific provisions of labor contracts, the bureau agents who enforced such agreements often served the interests of employers rather than laborers.

The outlines of sharecropping, a system that defined southern cotton production until well into the twentieth century, were visible just a few years after the Civil War. Poor families, black and white, contracted annually with landlords, who advanced them supplies, such as crop seed, mules, plows, food, and clothing. Fathers directed the labor of their children in the fields. At the end of the year, many families remained indebted to their employer and, thus, entitled to nothing and obliged to work another year in the hope of

●●●─[Read the **Document**
Southern Skepticism of the Freedmen's Bureau (1866) at **www.myhistorylab.com**

●●●─[Read the **Document**
A Sharecropper's Contract at **www.myhistorylab.com**

repaying the debt. If a sharecropper's demeanor or work habits displeased the landlord, the family faced eviction.

Single women with small children were especially vulnerable to the whims of landlords in the postbellum period. Near Greensboro, North Carolina, for example, planter Presley George Sr. settled accounts with his field worker Polly at the end of 1865. For her year's expenses, Polly was charged a total $69 for corn, cloth, thread, and board for a child who did not work. By George's calculations, Polly had earned exactly $69 for the labor she and her three children (two sons and a daughter) performed in the course of the year, leaving her no cash of her own. Under these harsh conditions, freedpeople looked to each other for support and strength.

Building Free Communities

Independence in the workplace was not the only concern of freedpeople. Soon after the war's end, southern blacks set about organizing themselves as an effective political force and as free communities devoted to the social and educational welfare of their own people. Differences among blacks based on income, jobs, culture, and skin color at times inhibited institution-building. Some black communities found themselves divided by class, with blacks who had been free before the war (including many literate and skilled light-skinned men) assuming leadership over illiterate field hands. In New Orleans, a combination of factors contributed to class divisions among people of African heritage. During the antebellum period, light-skinned free people of color, many of whom spoke French, were much more likely to possess property and a formal education than were enslaved people, who were dark-skinned English speakers. After the Civil War, the more privileged group pressed for public accommodations laws, which would open the city's theaters, opera, and expensive restaurants to all blacks for the first time. However, black churches and social organizations remained segregated according to class.

((•─Hear the **Audio**

"Free At Last" at
www.myhistorylab.com

For the most part, postbellum black communities united around the principle that freedom from slavery should also mean full citizenship rights: the ability to vote, own land, and educate their children. These rights must be enforced by federal firepower: "a military occupation will be absolutely necessary," declared the blacks of Norfolk, "to protect the white Union men of the South, as well as ourselves." Freedpeople in some states allied themselves with white yeomen who had long resented the political power of the great planters and now saw an opportunity to use state governments as agents of democratization and economic reform.

Networks of freedpeople formed self-help organizations. Like the sponsors of the Savannah Education Association, blacks throughout the South formed committees to raise funds and hire teachers for neighborhood schools. Small Georgia towns, such as Cuthbert, Albany, Cave Spring, and Thomasville, with populations no greater than a few hundred, raised up to $70 per month and contributed as much as $350 each for the construction of school buildings. Funds came from the proceeds of fairs, bazaars, and bake sales; subscriptions raised by local school boards; and tuition fees. In the cash-starved postbellum South, these amounts represented a great personal and group sacrifice for the cause of education.

All over the South, black families charted their own course. They elected to take in orphans and elderly kin, pool resources with neighbors, and arrange for mothers to stay home with their children. These choices challenged the power of former slaveholders and the influence of Freedmen's Bureau agents and northern missionaries and teachers. At the same time, in seeking to attend to their families and to provide for themselves, southern blacks resembled members of other mid-nineteenth-century laboring classes who valued family ties over the demands of employers and landlords.

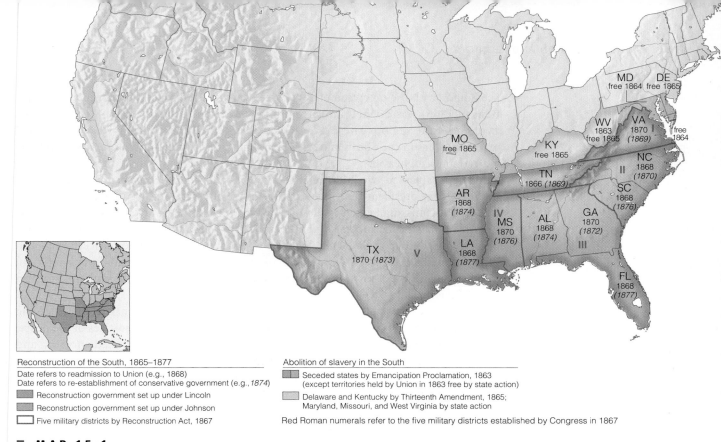

Reconstruction of the South, 1865–1877

Date refers to readmission to Union (e.g., 1868)
Date refers to re-establishment of conservative government (e.g., *1874*)

- Reconstruction government set up under Lincoln
- Reconstruction government set up under Johnson
- Five military districts by Reconstruction Act, 1867

Abolition of slavery in the South

- Seceded states by Emancipation Proclamation, 1863 (except territories held by Union in 1863 free by state action)
- Delaware and Kentucky by Thirteenth Amendment, 1865; Maryland, Missouri, and West Virginia by state action

Red Roman numerals refer to the five military districts established by Congress in 1867

■ **MAP 15.1**
RADICAL RECONSTRUCTION
Four of the former Confederate states, Louisiana, Arkansas, Tennessee, and Virginia, were reorganized under President Lincoln's Ten Percent Plan in 1864. Neither this plan nor the proposals of Lincoln's successor, Andrew Johnson, provided for the enfranchisement of the former slaves. In 1867 Congress established five military districts in the South and demanded that newly reconstituted state governments implement universal manhood suffrage. By 1870 all of the former Confederate states had rejoined the Union, and by 1877 all of those states had installed conservative (i.e., Democratic) governments.

Tangible signs of the new emerging black communities infuriated most southern whites. A schoolhouse run by blacks proved threatening in a society where most white children had little opportunity to receive an education. Black communities were also quick to form their own churches, rather than continue to occupy an inferior place in white churches. Other sights proved equally unsettling: on a main street in Charleston, an armed black soldier marching proudly or a black woman wearing a fashionable hat and veil, the kind favored by white women of the planter class. These developments help to account for the speed with which whites organized themselves in the Klan and various other vigilante groups, aiming to preserve "the supremacy of the white race in this Republic."

Congressional Reconstruction: The Radicals' Plan

The rise of armed white supremacist groups in the South helped spur congressional Republicans to action. On March 2, 1867, Congress seized the initiative. A coalition led by two radicals, Senator Charles Sumner of Massachusetts and Congressman Thaddeus Stevens of Pennsylvania, prodded Congress to pass the Reconstruction Act of 1867. The purpose of this measure was to purge the South of disloyalty once and for all. The act stripped thousands of former Confederates of voting rights. The former Confederate states would not be readmitted to the Union until they had ratified the Fourteenth Amendment and written new constitutions that guaranteed black men the right to vote.

See the **Map**
Reconstruction at
www.myhistorylab.com

The South (with the exception of Tennessee, which had ratified the Fourteenth Amendment in 1866) was divided into five military districts. Federal troops were stationed throughout the region. These troops were charged with protecting Union personnel and supporters in the South and with restoring order in the midst of regional political and economic upheaval.

Congress passed two additional acts specifically intended to secure congressional power over the president. The intent of the Tenure of Office Act was to prevent the president from dismissing Secretary of War Edwin Stanton, a supporter of the radicals. The other measure, the Command of the Army Act, required the president to seek approval for all military orders from General Ulysses S. Grant, the army's senior officer. Grant also was a supporter of the Republicans. Both of these acts probably violated the separation of powers doctrine as put forth in the Constitution. Together, they would soon precipitate a national crisis.

During the Reconstruction period, approximately 2,000 black men of the emerging southern Republican party served as local elected officials, sheriffs, justices of the peace, tax collectors, and city councilors. Many of these leaders were of mixed ancestry, and many had been free before the war. They came in disproportionate numbers from the ranks of literate men, such as clergy, teachers, and skilled artisans. In Alabama, Florida, Louisiana, Mississippi, and South Carolina, black men constituted a majority of the voting

■ This drawing by famous political cartoonist Thomas Nast depicts the first black members of Congress. Left to right, front row: Senator Hiram Revels of Mississippi (the first African American to serve in the U.S. Senate), Representatives Benjamin S. Turner of Alabama, Josiah T. Walls of Florida, Joseph H. Rainey of South Carolina, Robert B. Elliott of South Carolina. Back row: Representatives Robert G. DeLarge of South Carolina, Jefferson Long of Georgia.

public. Throughout the South, 600 black men won election to state legislatures. However, nowhere did blacks control a state government, although they did predominate in South Carolina's lower House. Sixteen black Southerners were elected to the U.S. Congress during Reconstruction. Most of those elected to Congress in the years immediately after the war were freeborn. However, among the nine men elected for the first time after 1872, six were former slaves. All of these politicians exemplified the desire among southern blacks to become active, engaged citizens.

Newly reconstructed southern state legislatures provided for public school systems, fairer taxation methods, bargaining rights of plantation laborers, racially integrated public transportation and accommodations, and public works projects, especially railroads. Nevertheless, the legislative coalitions forged between Northerners and Southerners, blacks and whites, were uneasy and, in many cases, less than productive. Southern Democrats (and later, historians sympathetic to them) claimed that Reconstruction governments were uniquely corrupt, with some carpetbaggers, scalawags, and freedpeople vying for **kickbacks** from railroad and construction magnates. In fact, whenever state legislatures sought to promote business interests, they opened the door to the bribery of public officials. In this respect, northern as well as southern politicians were vulnerable to charges of corruption. In the long run, southern Democrats cared less about charges of legislative corruption and more about the growing political power of local black Republican party organizations.

In Washington in early 1868, President Johnson forced a final showdown with Congress. He replaced several high military officials with more conservative men. He also fired Secretary of War Stanton, in apparent violation of the Tenure of Office Act. Shortly thereafter, in February, a newly composed House Reconstruction Committee impeached Johnson for ignoring the act, and the Senate began his trial on March 30. The president and Congress were locked in an extraordinary battle for political power.

The final vote was 35 senators against Johnson, one vote short of the necessary two-thirds of all senators' votes needed for conviction. Nineteen senators voted to acquit Johnson of the charges. Nevertheless, to win acquittal, he had had to promise moderates that he would not stand in the way of congressional plans for Reconstruction. Johnson essentially withdrew from policymaking in the spring of 1868. That November, with Republicans urging Northerners to "vote as you shot" (that is, to cast ballots against the former Confederates), Ulysses S. Grant was elected president.

Political reunion was an uneven process, but one that gradually eroded the newly won rights of former slaves in many southern states. By the end of 1868, Arkansas, North Carolina, South Carolina, Louisiana, Tennessee, Alabama, and Florida had met congressional conditions for readmission to the Union, and two years later, Mississippi, Virginia, Georgia, and Texas followed. The Fifteenth Amendment, passed by Congress in 1869 and ratified by the necessary number of states a year later, granted all black men the right to vote. However, in some states, such as Louisiana, reunification gave Democrats license to engage in wholesale election fraud and violence toward freed men and women. In 1870–1871, a congressional inquiry into the Klan exposed pervasive and grisly assaults on Republican schoolteachers, preachers, and prospective voters, black and white. The Klan also targeted men and women who refused to work like slaves in the fields. In April 1871, Congress passed the Ku Klux Klan Act, which punished conspiracies intended to deny rights to citizens. But Klan violence and intimidation had already taken their toll on Republican voting strength.

TABLE 15-1

The Election of 1868

Candidate	Political Party	Popular Vote (%)	Electoral Vote
Ulysses S. Grant	Republican	52.7	214
Horatio Seymour	Democratic	47.3	80

Claiming Territory for the Union

What human and environmental forces impeded the Republican goal of western expansion?

While blacks and whites, Northerners and Southerners clashed over power in the South, poet Walt Whitman celebrated the "manly and courageous instincts" that propelled a brave, adventurous people west. Whitman hailed the march across the prairies and over the mountains as a cavalcade of progress. He and other Americans believed that the postbellum migration fulfilled a mission of national regeneration begun by the Civil War. Kansas's population grew by 240 percent in the 1860s, Nebraska's by 355 percent.

To unite the entire country together as a single economic and political unit was the Republican ideal. The railroads in particular served as vehicles of national integration. When the Central Pacific and Union Pacific Railroads met at Promontory Point, Utah, in 1869, the hammering of the spike that joined the two roads produced a telegraphic signal received simultaneously on both coasts, setting off a national celebration.

Meanwhile, regular units of United States cavalry, including two regiments of blacks, were launching attacks on Indians on the Plains, in the Northwest, and in the Southwest. Between 1865 and 1890, U.S. military forces conducted a dozen separate campaigns against western Indian peoples and met Indian warriors in battle or attacked Indian settlements in more than 1,000 engagements. In contrast to African Americans, who adamantly demanded their rights as American citizens, defiant western Indians battled a government to which they owed no allegiance.

Federal Military Campaigns Against Western Indians

In 1871 the U.S. government renounced the practice of seeking treaties with various Indian groups. This change in policy opened the way for a more aggressive effort to subdue native populations. It also hastened the expansion of the reservation system, an effort begun in the antebellum period to confine specific Indian groups to specific territories.

On the Plains, clashes between Indians and U.S. soldiers persisted after the Civil War. In 1867 at Medicine Lodge Creek in southern Kansas, the United States signed a treaty with an alliance of Comanche, Kiowa, Cheyenne, Arapaho, and Plains Apache. This treaty could not long withstand the provocation posed by the railroad, as Indians continued to attack the surveyors, supply caravans, and military escorts that preceded the railroad work crews. The year before, the Seventh U.S. Cavalry, under the command of Lieutenant Colonel George Custer, had been formed to ward off Indian attacks on the Union Pacific, snaking its way across the central Plains westward from Kansas and Nebraska. In November 1868, Custer destroyed a Cheyenne settlement on the Washita River, in present-day Oklahoma. Custer's men murdered women and children, burned tipis, and destroyed 800 horses.

⊕ **View** the **Image**
Geronimo and Natiche Surrender (1886) at **www.myhistorylab.com**

The Apache managed to elude General George Crook until 1875. Crook employed some of these Apache to track down the war chief Geronimo of the Chiricahua. Like many other Indian leaders, Geronimo offered both religious and military guidance to his people. He believed that a spirit would protect him from the white man's bullets and from the arrows of Indians in league with government troops. Yet Geronimo was tricked into an initial surrender in 1877, and was held in irons for several months before gaining his release and challenging authorities for another nine years.

In 1874 Custer took his cavalry into the Black Hills of the Dakotas. Supposedly, the 1868 Treaty of Fort Laramie had rendered this land off-limits to whites. Custer's mission was to offer protection for the surveyors of the Northern Pacific Railroad and to force Indians onto reservations as stipulated in the 1868 treaty. However, the officer lost no time trumpeting the fact that Indian lands were filled with gold. This report prompted a rush to the Black Hills, lands sacred to the Sioux. Within two years, 15,000 gold miners had illegally descended on Indian lands to seek their fortunes. The federal government proposed to buy the land, but leaders of the Sioux, including Red Cloud, Spotted Tail, and Sitting Bull, spurned the offer.

During the morning of June 25, 1876, Custer and his force of 264 soldiers attacked a Sun Dance gathering of 2,500 Sioux and Cheyenne on the banks of the Little Big Horn River in Montana. Custer foolishly launched his attack without adequate backup, and he and his men were easily overwhelmed and killed by Indian warriors, led by the Oglala Sioux Crazy Horse and others. Reacting to this defeat, U.S. military officials reduced the Lakota and Cheyenne to wardship status, ending their autonomy.

Indians throughout the West maintained their distinctive ways of life during these turbulent times. Horse holdings, so crucial for hunting, trading, and fighting, varied from group to group, with the Crow wealthy in relation to their Central Plains neighbors the Oglala and the Arikara. Plains peoples engaged in a lively trading system. They exchanged horses and their trappings (bridles and blankets) for eastern goods such as kettles, guns, and ammunition. Despite their differences in economy, these groups held similar religious beliefs about an all-powerful life force that governed the natural world. People, plants, and animals were all part of the same order.

The Postwar Western Labor Problem

In 1865 the owners of the Central Pacific Railroad seemed poised for one of the great engineering feats of the nineteenth century. In the race eastward from California, they would construct trestles spanning vast chasms and roadbeds traversing mountains and deserts.

■ With this 1870 photograph, the Kansas Pacific Railroad advertised the opportunity for western travelers to shoot buffalo from the comfort and safety of their railroad car. The company's official taxidermist shows off his handiwork. Railroad expansion facilitated the exploitation of natural resources while promoting tourism.

■ Chinese construction workers labor on the Central Pacific Railroad, c. 1868. Many Chinese immigrants toiled as indentured laborers, indebted to Chinese merchant creditors who paid for their passage to California. Isolated in all-male work camps, crews of railroad workers retained their traditional dress, language, and diet. After the completion of the transcontinental railroad in 1869, some immigrants returned to China, and others dispersed to small towns and cities throughout the West.

Government officials in Washington were eager to subsidize the railroad. What the owners lacked was a dependable labor force. The Irish workers who began the line in California struck for higher wages in compensation for brutal, dangerous work. These immigrants dropped their shovels and hammers at the first word of a gold strike nearby—or far away. As a result, in 1866 the Central Pacific had decided to tap into a vast labor source by importing thousands of Chinese men from their native Guangdong province.

The Chinese labored to extend the railroad tracks eastward from Sacramento, California, up to ten miles a day in the desert, only a few feet a day in the rugged Sierra Nevada Mountains. In nerve-wracking feats of skill, they lowered themselves in woven baskets to implant nitroglycerine explosives in canyon walls. Chinese laborers toiled through snowstorms and blistering heat to blast tunnels and cut passes through granite mountains. With the final linking of the railroad in Utah in 1869, many Chinese sought work elsewhere in the West.

Signed in 1868, the Burlingame Treaty, named for Anson Burlingame, an American envoy to China, had supposedly guaranteed government protection for Chinese immigrants as visitors, traders, or permanent residents. Most immigrants were men. (Six out of ten California Chinese women were listed in the 1870 census as prostitutes, most the victims of their compatriots.) Yet the treaty did not inhibit U.S. employers, landlords, and government officials from discriminating against the Chinese.

By 1870, 40,000 Chinese lived in California and represented fully one-quarter of the state's wage earners. They found work in the cigar, woolen-goods, and boot and shoe factories of San Francisco; in the gold mining towns, now as laundry operators rather than as miners as they had before the Civil War; and in the fields as agricultural laborers. White workers began to cry unfair competition against this Asian group that was becoming increasingly integrated into the region's economy.

As a group, Chinese men differed from California Indians, who remained trapped in the traditional agricultural economy of unskilled labor. Whites appropriated Indian land and forced many men, women, and children to work as wage earners for large landowners.

Deprived of their familiar hunting and gathering lands, and wracked by disease and starvation, California Indians had suffered a drastic decline in their numbers by 1870, from 100,000 to 30,000 in 20 years.

Land Use in an Expanding Nation

The Union's triumph in 1865 prompted new conflicts and deepened long-standing ones over the use of the land in a rich, sprawling country. In the South, staple crop planters began to share political power with an emerging elite, men who owned railroads and textile mills. Despairing of ever achieving antebellum levels of labor efficiency, some landowners turned to mining the earth and the forests for saleable commodities. These products, obtained through extraction, included phosphate (used in producing fertilizer), timber, coal, and turpentine. Labor in extractive industries complemented labor in the plantation economy. Sharecroppers alternated between tilling cotton fields in the spring and harvesting the crop in the fall, while seeking employment in sawmills and coal mines in the winter and summer.

As European Americans settled in the West and Southwest, they displaced natives who had been living there for generations. For example, the U.S. court system determined who could legally claim property. Western courts also decided whether natural resources such as water, land, timber, and fish and game constituted property that could be owned by private interests. In the Southwest, European-American settlers, including army soldiers who had come to fight Indians and then stayed, continued to place Hispanic land titles at risk. Citing prewar precedents, American courts favored the claims of recent squatters over those of long-standing residents. In 1869, with the death of her husband (who had served as a general in the Union army), Maria Amparo Ruiz de Burton saw the large ranch they had worked together near San Diego slip out of her control. The first Spanish-speaking woman to be published in English in the United States, de Burton was a member of the Hispanic elite. Nevertheless, she had little political power. California judges backed the squatters who occupied the ranch.

As they controlled more land and assumed public office, some European Americans in the Southwest exploited their political connections and economic power. In the 1870s, the so-called Santa Fe Ring wrested more than 80 percent of the original Spanish grants of land from Hispanic landholders in New Mexico. An alliance of European-American lawyers, businesspeople, and politicians, the Santa Fe Ring defrauded families and kin groups of their land titles and speculated in property to make a profit. Whereas many ordinary Hispanic settlers saw land—with its crops, pasture, fuel, building materials, and game—as a source of livelihood, groups such as the Santa Fe Ring saw land primarily as a commodity to be bought and sold.

Seemingly overnight, boom towns sprang up wherever minerals or timber beckoned: southern Arizona and the Rocky Mountains west of Denver, Virginia City in western Nevada, the Idaho-Montana region, and the Black Hills of South Dakota. In all these places, increasing numbers of workers operated sophisticated kinds of machinery, such as rock crushers. When the vein was exhausted or the forests depleted, the towns went bust.

Railroads facilitated not only the mining of minerals but also the growth of the cattle-ranching industry. Rail connections between the Midwest and East made it profitable for Texas ranchers to pay cowboys to drive their herds of long-horned steers to Abilene, Ellsworth, Wichita, or Dodge City, Kansas, for shipment to stockyards in Chicago or St. Louis. Cattle drives were huge; an estimated 10 million animals were herded north from Texas alone between 1865 and 1890. They offered employment to all kinds of men with sufficient skills and endurance. Among the cowhands were African-American horsebreakers and gunmen and Mexicans skilled in the use of the *reata* (lasso). Blacks made up about 25 percent and Hispanics about 15 percent of all cowboy outfits.

TABLE 15-2

Estimates of Railroad Crossties Used and Acres of Forest Cleared, 1870–1910

Year	Miles of Track	Ties Renewed Annually (millions)	Ties Used on New Construction (millions)	Total Ties Annually (millions)	Acres of Forest Cleared (thousands)
1870	60,000	21	18	39	195
1880	107,000	37	21	58	290
1890	200,000	70	19	89	445
1900	259,000			91	455
1910	357,000			124	620

Source: Michael Williams, Americans and Their Forests (1989), 352. Cambridge University Press.

In knitting regional economies together, federal land policies were crucial to the Republican vision of a developing nation. The Mineral Act of 1866 granted title to millions of acres of mineral-rich land to mining companies, a gift from the federal government to private interests. The Timber Culture Act of 1873 allotted 160 acres to individuals in selected western states if they agreed to plant one-fourth of the acreage with trees. Four years later, the Desert Land Act provided cheap land if buyers irrigated at least part of their parcels.

The exploitation of western resources raised many legal questions: Must ranchers pay for the prairies their cattle grazed on and the trails they followed to market? How could one "own" a stampeding buffalo herd or a flowing river? What was the point of holding title to a piece of property if only the timber, oil, water, or minerals (but not the soil) were of value? The Apex Mining Act of 1872 sought to address some of these issues. This law legalized traditional mining practices in the West by validating titles approved by local courts. According to the law, a person who could locate the apex of a vein (its point closest to the surface) could lay claim to the entire vein beneath the surface. The measure contributed to the wholesale destruction of certain parts of the western landscape as mining companies blasted their way through mountains and left piles of rocks in their wake. It also spurred thousands of lawsuits as claimants argued over what constituted an apex or a vein.

It was during this period that a young Scottish-born naturalist named John Muir began to explore the magnificent canyons and mountains of California. He contrasted nature's majesty with the artificial landscape created by and for humans. In the wilderness, there is nothing "truly dead or dull, or any trace of what in manufactories is called rubbish or waste," he wrote; "everything is perfectly clean and pure and full of divine lessons."

Muir was gratified by the creation of the National Park system during the postwar period. Painters and geologists were among the first Easterners to appreciate the spectacular vistas of the western landscape. In 1864 Congress set aside a small area within California's Yosemite Valley for public recreation and enjoyment. Soon after the war, railroad promoters forged an alliance with government officials in an effort to block commercial development of particularly beautiful pockets of land. Northern Pacific railroad financier Jay Cooke lobbied hard for the government to create a 2-million-acre park in what is today the northwest corner of Wyoming. As a result, in March 1872, Congress established Yellowstone National Park. Tourism would continue to serve as a key component of the western economy.

Muir and others portrayed the Yosemite and Yellowstone valleys as wildernesses, empty of human activity. In fact, both areas had long provided hunting and foraging grounds for native peoples. Yellowstone had been occupied by the people now called the Shoshone since the fifteenth century. This group, together with the Bannock, Crow, and Blackfoot, tried to retain access to Yellowstone's meadows, rivers, and forests after it became a national park. However, U.S. policymakers and military officials persisted in their efforts to mark off territory for specific commercial purposes, while Indians were confined to reservations.

Buying Territory for the Union

Before the war, Republicans had opposed any federal expansionist schemes that they feared might benefit slaveholders. However, after 1865 and the outlawing of slavery, some Republican lawmakers and administration officials advocated the acquisition of additional territory. Secretary of State William Seward led the way in 1867 by purchasing Alaska from Russia. For $7.2 million (about 2 cents an acre), the United States gained 591,004 square miles of land. Within the territory were diverse indigenous groups—Eskimo, Aleut, Tlingit, Tsimshian, Athabaskan, and Haida—and a small number of native Russians. Though derided at the time as "Seward's icebox," Alaska yielded enough fish, timber, minerals, oil, and water power in the years to come to prove that the original purchase price was a tremendous bargain.

The impulse that prompted administration support for the Alaska purchase also spawned other plans for territorial acquisitions. In 1870 some Republicans joined with Democrats in calling for the annexation of the Dominican Republic. These congressmen argued that the tiny Caribbean country would make a fine naval base, provide investment opportunities for American businesspeople, and offer a refuge for southern freedpeople.

However, influential Senator Charles Sumner warned against a takeover without considering the will of the Dominican people, who were currently involved in their own civil war. Some congressmen, in a prelude to foreign policy debates of the 1890s, suggested that the dark-skinned Dominican people were incapable of appreciating the blessings of American citizenship. In 1871 an annexation treaty failed to win Senate approval.

In facilitating western expansion, Republicans upheld the ideal that prosperity would come to all people who worked hard. Indians were not part of the Republican vision of western prosperity. But other groups also questioned the Republican vision as it affected their own interests.

The Republican Vision and Its Limits

What were some of the inconsistencies in, and unanticipated consequences of, Republican notions of equality and federal power?

After the Civil War, victorious Republicans envisioned a nation united in the pursuit of prosperity. All citizens would be free to follow their individual economic self-interest and to enjoy the fruits of honest toil. In contrast, some increasingly vocal and well-organized groups saw the expansion of legal rights, and giving black men the right to vote in particular, as only initial, tentative steps on the path to an all-inclusive citizenship. Women, industrial workers, farmers, and African Americans made up overlapping constituencies pressing for equal political rights and economic opportunity. Together they challenged the mainstream Republican view that defeat of the rebels and destruction of slavery were sufficient to guarantee prosperity for everyone.

Partnerships between government and business also produced unanticipated consequences for Republicans committed to what they believed was the collective good. Some politicians and business leaders saw these partnerships as opportunities for private gain. Consequently, private greed and public corruption accompanied postwar economic growth. Thus, Republican leaders faced challenges from two very different sources: people agitating for civil rights and people hoping to reap personal gain from political activities.

Postbellum Origins of the Women's Suffrage Movement

Watch the Video

The Women's Rights Movement in Ninteenth-Century America at **www.myhistorylab.com**

After the Civil War, the nation's middle class, which had its origins in the antebellum period, continued to grow. Dedicated to self-improvement and filled with a sense of moral authority, many middle-class Americans (especially Protestants) felt a deep cultural connection to their counterparts in England. Indeed, the United States produced its own "Victorians," so called for the self-conscious middle class that emerged in the England of Queen Victoria during her reign from 1837 to 1901.

At the heart of the Victorian sensibility was the ideal of domesticity: a harmonious family living in a well-appointed home, guided by a pious mother and supported by a father successful in business. Famous Protestant clergyman Henry Ward Beecher and his wife were outspoken proponents of this domestic ideal. According to Eunice Beecher, women had no "higher, nobler, more divine mission than in the conscientious endeavor to create a *true home*."

Yet the traumatic events of the Civil War only intensified the desire among a growing group of American women to participate fully in the nation's political life. They wanted to extend their moral influence outside the narrow and exclusive sphere of the home. Many women believed that they deserved the vote and that the time was right to demand it.

In 1866 veteran reformers Elizabeth Cady Stanton, Susan B. Anthony, and Lucy Stone founded the Equal Rights Association to link the rights of white women and African Americans. Nevertheless, in 1867, Kansas voters defeated a referendum proposing suffrage for both blacks and white women. This disappointment convinced some former abolitionists that the two causes should be separated—that women should wait patiently until the rights of African-American men were firmly secured. Frederick Douglass declined an invitation to a women's suffrage convention in Washington, D.C., in 1868. He explained, "I am now devoting myself to a cause [if] not more sacred, certainly more urgent, because it is one of life and death to the long enslaved people of this country, and that is: negro suffrage." But African-American activist and former slave Sojourner Truth warned, "There is a great stir about colored men getting their rights, but not a word about the colored women; and if colored men get their rights, and not colored women get theirs, there will be a bad time about it."

In 1869 two factions of women parted ways and formed separate organizations devoted to women's rights. The more radical wing, including Cady Stanton and Anthony, bitterly denounced the Fifteenth Amendment because it gave the vote to black men only. They helped to found the National Woman Suffrage Association (NWSA), which argued for a renewed commitment to the original Declaration of Sentiments passed in Seneca Falls, New York, two decades earlier. They favored married women's property rights, liberalization of divorce laws, opening colleges and trade schools to women, and a new federal amendment to allow women to vote. Lucy Stone and her husband, Henry Blackwell, founded the rival American Woman Suffrage Association (AWSA). This group downplayed the larger struggle for women's rights and focused on the suffrage question exclusively. Its members supported the Fifteenth Amendment and retained ties to the Republican party. The AWSA focused on state-by-state campaigns for women's suffrage.

In 1871 the NWSA welcomed the daring, flamboyant Victoria Woodhull as a vocal supporter, only to renounce her a few years later. Woodhull's political agenda ranged from free love and dietary reform to legalized prostitution, working men's rights, and women's suffrage. (In the nineteenth century, free love advocates denounced what they called a sexual double standard, one that glorified female chastity while tolerating male promiscuity.) In 1872 one of Woodhull's critics successfully challenged her. Woodhull spent a month in jail as a result of the zealous prosecution by vice reformer Anthony Comstock, a clergyman who objected to her public discussions and writings on sexuality. Comstock assumed the role of an outspoken crusader against vice. A federal law passed in 1873, and named after him, equated information related to birth control with pornography, banning this and other "obscene material" from the mails.

Read the Document

Trial of Susan B. Anthony at **www.myhistorylab.com**

Susan B. Anthony used the 1872 presidential election as a test case for women's suffrage. She attempted to vote and was arrested, tried, and convicted as a result. By this time, most women suffragists, and most members of the NWSA for that matter, had become convinced that they should focus on the vote exclusively; they therefore accepted the AWSA's policy on this issue. In the coming years, they would avoid other, related causes with which they might have allied themselves, including black civil rights and labor reform.

Workers' Organizations

Many Americans benefited from economic changes of the postwar era. Railroading, mining, and heavy industry helped fuel the national economy and in the process boosted the growth of the urban managerial class. In the Midwest, many landowning farmers prospered when they responded to an expanding demand for grain and other staple crops. In Wisconsin, wheat farmers cleared forests, drained swamps, diverted rivers, and profited from the booming world market in grain. Yet the economic developments that allowed factory managers and owners of large wheat farms to make a comfortable living for themselves did not necessarily benefit agricultural and manufacturing wage-workers.

■ A Norwegian immigrant extended family in the town of Norway Grove, Wisconsin, poses in front of their imposing home and up-to-date carriage in this photograph taken in the mid-1870s. Linking their fortunes to the world wheat market, these newcomers to the United States prospered. Wrote one woman to her brother back home in Norway, "We all have cattle, driving oxen, and wagons. We also have children in abundance."

Indeed, during this period growing numbers of working people, in the countryside and in the cities, became caught up in a cycle of indebtedness. In the upcountry South (above the fall line, or Piedmont), formerly self-sufficient family farmers sought loans from banks to repair their war-damaged homesteads. To qualify for these loans, the farmer had to plant cotton as a staple crop, to the neglect of corn and other foodstuffs. Many sharecroppers, black and white, received payment in the form of credit only; for these families, the end-of-the-year reckoning yielded little more than rapidly accumulating debts. Midwestern farmers increasingly relied on bank loans to purchase expensive threshing and harvesting machinery.

Several organizations founded within five years of the war's end offered laborers an alternative vision to the Republicans' brand of individualism and nationalism. In 1867 Oliver H. Kelly, a former Minnesota farmer now working in a Washington office, organized the National Grange of the Patrons of Husbandry, popularly known as the **Grange**. This movement sought to address a new, complex marketplace increasingly dominated by railroads, banks, and grain elevator operators. The Grange encouraged farmers to form cooperatives that would market their crops and to challenge discriminatory railroad rates that favored big business.

Founded in Baltimore in 1866, the National Labor Union (NLU) consisted of a collection of craft unions and claimed as many as 600,000 members at its peak in the early 1870s. The group welcomed farmers as well as factory workers and promoted legislation for an eight-hour workday and the arbitration of industrial disputes.

In 1873 a nationwide depression threw thousands out of work and worsened the plight of debtors. Businesspeople in agriculture, mining, the railroad industry, and manufacturing had overexpanded their operations. The free-wheeling loan practices of major banks had contributed to this situation. The inability of these businesspeople to repay their loans led to the failure of major banks. With the contraction of credit, thousands of small businesses went bankrupt. The NLU did not survive the crisis.

However, by this time, a new organization had appeared to champion the cause of the laboring classes in opposition to lords of finance. Founded in 1869 by Uriah Stephens and other Philadelphia tailors, the Knights of Labor eventually aimed to unite industrial and rural workers, the self-employed and the wage earner, blacks and whites, and men and women. The Knights were committed to private property and to the independence of the farmer, the entrepreneur, and the industrial worker. The group banned from its ranks "nonproducers," such as liquor sellers, bankers, professional gamblers, stockbrokers, and lawyers.

This period of depression also laid the foundation for the Greenback Labor party, organized in 1878. Within three years after the end of the Civil War, the Treasury had withdrawn from circulation $100 million in wartime paper currency ("greenbacks"). With less money in circulation, debtors found it more difficult to repay their loans. The government also ceased coining silver dollars in 1873, despite the discovery of rich silver lodes in the West. To add insult to injury, the Resumption Act (1875) called for the government to continue to withdraw paper greenbacks. Thus, hard money became dearer, and debtors became more desperate. In 1878 the new Greenback Labor party managed to win 1 million votes and elect fourteen candidates to Congress. The party laid the foundation for the Populist party that emerged in the 1890s.

Several factors made coalition building among these American workers difficult. One was the nation's increasingly multicultural workforce. Unions, such as the typographers, were notorious for excluding women and African Americans, a fact publicized by both Frederick Douglass and Susan B. Anthony, to no avail. In 1869 shoe factory workers (members of the Knights of St. Crispin) went on strike in North Adams, Massachusetts. They were soon shocked to see 75 Chinese strikebreakers arrive by train from California. Their employer praised the new arrivals for their "rare industry." The shoemakers' strike collapsed quickly after the appearance of what the workers called this "Mongolian battery."

Employers would continue to manipulate and divide the laboring classes through the use of ethnic, religious, and racial prejudices.

Political Corruption and the Decline of Republican Idealism

Out of the new partnership between politics and business emerged an extensive system of bribes and kickbacks. Greedy politicians of both parties challenged the Republicans' high-minded idealism.

In the early 1870s, the *New York Times* exposed the schemes of William M. "Boss" Tweed. Tweed headed Tammany Hall, a New York City political organization that courted labor unions and contributed liberally to Catholic schools and charities. Tammany Hall politicians routinely used bribery and extortion to fix elections and bilk taxpayers of millions of dollars. One plasterer employed on a city project received $138,000 in "payment" for two days' work. After the *Times* exposé, Tweed was prosecuted and convicted. His downfall attested to the growing influence of newspaper reporters.

Another piece of investigative journalism rocked the political world in 1872. In 1867 major stockholders of the Union Pacific Railroad had formed a new corporation, called the Crédit Mobilier, to build railroads. Heads of powerful congressional committees received shares of stock in the new company. These gifts of stock were bribes to secure the legislators' support for public land grants favorable to the new corporation. The *New York Sun* exposed a number of the chief beneficiaries in the fall of 1872, findings confirmed by congressional investigation. Among the disgraced politicians was Grant's vice president, Schuyler Colfax.

The 1872 presidential election pitted incumbent Grant against the Democratic challenger, *New York Tribune* editor Horace Greeley. Many Republicans, disillusioned with congressional corruption and eager to press forward with civil service reform, endorsed the Democratic candidate. Greeley and his Republican allies decried the patronage (or "spoils") system by which politicians rewarded their supporters with government jobs. Nevertheless, Grant won the election.

By 1872, after four bloody years of war and seven squandered years of postwar opportunity, the federal government seemed prepared to hand the South back to unrepentant rebels. The North showed what one House Republican called "a general apathy among the people concerning the war and the negro." The **Civil Rights Act of 1875** guaranteed blacks equal access to public accommodations and transportation. Yet this act

PLATE 17

■ In 1871 Thomas Nast drew a series of cartoons exposing the corruption of New York City Democratic boss William M. Tweed and his political organization, Tammany Hall. In this drawing, published in *Harper's Weekly* in 1871, Nast depicts Tweed and his cronies engaging in a "wholesale" looting of the New York City treasury with the assistance of compliant police officers. Those same officers stand ready to crack down on the impoverished father who robs a bakery to feed his family. By portraying Tweed as an enemy of the poor, Nash ignored the fact that the political boss gained a large following among immigrant voters.

TABLE 15-3

The Election of 1872

Candidate	Political Party	Popular Vote (%)	Electoral Vote
Ulysses S. Grant	Republican	55.6	286
Horace Greeley	Democratic, Liberal Republican	43.9	66

Read the Document

Samuel Tilden's Speech to the Manhattan Club Conceding the Election of 1876 at
www.myhistorylab.com

TABLE 15-4

The Election of 1876

Candidate	Political Party	Popular Vote (%)	Electoral Vote
Rutherford B. Hayes	Republican	48.0	185
Samuel J. Tilden	Democratic	51.0	184

Watch the Video

The Promise and Failure of Reconstruction at
www.myhistorylab.com

represented the final, half-hearted gesture of radical Republicanism. The Supreme Court declared the measure unconstitutional in 1883 on the grounds that the government could protect only political and not social rights. White Southerners reasserted their control over the region's political economy.

The presidential election of 1876 intensified public cynicism about deal making in high places. A dispute over election returns led to what came to be known as the Compromise of 1877. In the popular vote, Democrat Samuel J. Tilden outpolled Republican Rutherford B. Hayes, a former Ohio governor. However, when the electoral votes were counted, the Democrat had only 184, one short of the necessary number. Nineteen of the twenty votes in dispute came from Louisiana, South Carolina, and Florida, and these three states submitted two new sets of returns, one from each of the two main parties. A specially appointed congressional electoral commission, the Committee of Fifteen, was charged with resolving the dispute. It divided along partisan lines. The eight Republicans outvoted the seven Democrats to accept the Republican set of returns from Florida.

To break the logjam, the Democrats agreed that Hayes could assume office in return for the withdrawal of all remaining federal troops from the South. The Republicans tacitly agreed that their work there was finished and that blacks in the region should fend for themselves. Hayes declined to enforce the Civil Rights Act of 1875. White Southerners were free to uphold the principle of states' rights that had been traditionally invoked to deny blacks their rights in the region. Thus the Civil War failed to solve one of the most pressing issues of the day—the relation between federal and state power in protecting the rights of individuals.

CONCLUSION

During the dozen or so years after the Civil War, both northern Republicans and southern Democrats registered a series of spectacular wins and crushing losses. Though humiliated by the Union victory, southern white supremacists eventually won for themselves the freedom to control their own local and state governments. As landlords, sheriffs, and merchants, these men defied the postwar federal amendments to the Constitution and deprived African Americans of basic citizenship rights. By the end of Reconstruction, northern Republicans had conceded local power to their former enemies. Even an aggressive nationalism, it turned out, could accept traditional southern hierarchies: white over nonwhite, rich over poor.

Yet the Civil War was not only a fight between whites. During the conflict, black people had served as combatants in the struggle for freedom. They saw the war in different terms than did northern white Republicans and southern white Democrats. After the war, blacks pursued full citizenship rights while attempting to maintain institutional and cultural autonomy from white people regardless of political affiliation. In their quest, freed men and women met with mixed success. Black men gained the (formal) right to vote. Yet white Republicans, both in Congress and in southern state legislatures, proved to be disappointing allies to blacks who found themselves, increasingly, at the mercy of white vigilantes and other terrorist groups. During the Reconstruction period, blacks consolidated their families, established their own churches, and sought to work on their own terms in the fields. Yet lacking money and credit, they found it difficult to buy land and in the process achieve true independence from white landowners, bankers, and politicians.

At the end of Reconstruction, Republicans remained in firm control of national economic policy. The white South had secured its right to conduct its own political affairs, but the Republican vision of economic growth and development had become the law of the land. This vision was a guiding principle of historic national and, increasingly, international significance. Economic innovation in particular proved to be a force of great unifying power, stronger even than all the federal military forces deployed during and after the Civil War.

For Review

✓●─Study and Review at **www.myhistorylab.com**

1. In what ways did the outcome of the Civil War challenge the power of states' authority over their own economy and people? Was the war a clear victory for federal authority? Why or why not?

2. Did all workers share the same interests after the war? Choose three groups of workers and describe the challenges they faced during Reconstruction.

3. What did freedom mean to southern black people after the war? What were the limits on their freedom?

4. Was the effort to subdue the Plains Indians after 1865 an extension of the Civil War? Why or why not?

Chronology: 1865–1877

1865   Freedmen's Bureau is formed.
Lincoln is assassinated; Andrew Johnson becomes president.
Thirteenth Amendment abolishing slavery is ratified.

1866   Civil Rights Act of 1866.
Ku Klux Klan is organized.

1867   U.S. purchases Alaska from Russia.
Reconstruction Act of 1867.
Ratification of Fourteenth Amendment protecting civil rights.

1868   Johnson is impeached and acquitted.
Fourteenth Amendment is ratified.

1869   Transcontinental Railroad is completed.
National Woman Suffrage Association and American Woman Suffrage Association are formed.
Knights of Labor is founded.

1870   Fifteenth Amendment enfranchising black men is ratified.

1871   Ku Klux Klan Act.

1873   Panic of 1873.

1874   Congress passes Civil Rights Act.

1876   Battle of Little Big Horn.
Contested presidential election between Rutherford B. Hayes and Samuel J. Tilden.

1877   Compromise of 1877.

Key Terms

Black Code Southern state laws passed after the Civil War to limit the rights and actions of newly liberated African Americans. p. 364

Carpetbaggers A negative term applied by Southerners to Northerners who moved to the South after the Civil War to pursue political or economic opportunities. p. 367

Civil Rights Act of 1875 Congressional legislation that guaranteed black people access to public accommodations and transportation; the Supreme Court declared the measure unconstitutional in 1883. p. 383

Freedmen's Bureau Federal agency created by Congress in March 1865 and disbanded in 1869. Its purposes were to provide relief for Southerners who had remained loyal to the Union during the Civil War, to support black elementary schools, and to oversee annual labor contracts between landowners and field hands. p. 364

Grange An organization founded by Oliver H. Kelly in 1867 to represent the interests of farmers by pressing for agricultural cooperatives, an end to railroad freight discrimination against small farmers, and other initiatives. Its full name was National Grange of Patrons of Husbandry. p. 382

Kickbacks Money paid illegally in return for favors (for example, to a politician by a person or business that has received government contracts). p. 373

Pocket veto An indirect veto of a legislative bill made when an executive (such as a president or governor) simply leaves the bill unsigned, so that it dies after the adjournment of the legislature. p. 364

Reconstruction era The 12 years after the Civil War when the U.S. government took steps to integrate the 11 states of the Confederacy back into the Union. p. 363

Scalawag A negative term applied by southern Democrats after the Civil War to any white Southerner who allied with the Republican party. p. 367

PART **SIX**

The Emergence of Modern America, 1877–1900

THE UNITED STATES BECAME A MODERN NATION DURING THE LAST quarter of the nineteenth century. Vast reserves of coal, timber, and water helped fuel a growing industrial economy. Railroad lines crisscrossed the nation and knit together regional economies. Large numbers of immigrants, many from eastern Europe, arrived in the United States, drawn by America's rising standard of living, high demand for labor, and religious and political freedom.

To raise the money needed to purchase expensive equipment and machinery, coal and oil producers and railroad owners formed modern corporations, businesses that were owned by stockholders rather than individuals. The largest businesses sought to dominate the marketplace by eliminating their competitors. Managers could cut production and operating costs by slashing the wages of workers or by installing labor-saving machinery. Either way, workers paid the price.

The generation that came of age after the Civil War witnessed a series of violent confrontations between workers and employers. Standards of industrial work discipline required laborers to toil for long hours at dangerous, disagreeable jobs. Some workers formed new kinds of labor unions to combat the power of big business. Some organizations, such as the Knights of Labor, were national in scope and inclusive in their membership; others represented the interests of specific groups of workers. Employers, local and state law enforcement officials, and judges used a variety of means to suppress strikes and other forms of collective action among workers. Nevertheless, local communities often supported the strikers, who were their friends and neighbors.

During the late nineteenth century, the national economy began to shift to the production of consumer goods. New products gave Americans new ways to spend their money. Manufacturers of everything from shoes to bathtubs advertised their goods to a mass market. In cities, department stores offered a dazzling array of goods.

Even as the country was becoming more ethnically diverse, advertisers promoted a single standard of physical beauty and material well-being.

At the same time, some scholars and politicians seized on a revolutionary new theory of natural history to argue for the superiority of white, middle-class Americans. Social Darwinism served as the intellectual justification for unfettered economic growth and for the subjugation of darker-skinned peoples, at home and abroad.

Many Americans rejected the trends toward economic standardization and cultural homogeneity. Native Americans in the West continued to resist the railroad and its profound threat to their way of life. By 1890 the U.S. military had forcibly subdued most of these Indians, relegating many to reservations. Together with industrial workers throughout the nation, Hispanic villagers in the Southwest and African-American sharecroppers in the South disputed the notion that progress could be defined exclusively in terms of economic growth and development.

Middle-class reformers sought to mediate between what they perceived to be two dangerous groups: arrogant industrialists and discontented workers. These reformers feared that rapid urban and industrial growth would cause rifts in the social fabric. Middle-class women pioneered in the founding of social settlements and other urban institutions to ease the transition of immigrants into modern American society.

The lines between national standards and local cultural interests often blurred. For example, for a short time Sioux chief Sitting Bull (Tatanka Iyotake) appeared with William ("Buffalo Bill") Cody's "Wild West" show, which played to enthusiastic audiences in the United States and Europe. Yet this Indian leader also led the Plains Indians as they attempted to resist U.S. military authorities. To cite another example: Some groups of Americans who sought to preserve their own cultural traditions nonetheless aspired to a middle-class way of life and its material comforts. Elite Hispanic families in the Southwest remained devoted to their Roman Catholic faith and at the same time followed up-to-date clothing fashions marketed by East Coast department stores.

The promise and the conflicts inherent in the emerging modern social order met head on in the 1890s. A new political party called the Populists mounted a brief but potent challenge to entrenched economic and political power. The Populists failed in their attempt to capture the presidency in 1896, but they offered a vision of a new kind of political party, one that would bring black and white farmers and industrial workers together in opposition to landlords, employers, and bankers.

In 1898, in an effort to protect its interests in the Western Hemisphere and to extend those interests into the Pacific, the United States went to war with Spain. This imperialist venture suggested the links among several impulses, including missionary outreach, commercial expansion, and white supremacist racial ideologies. By 1900 the United States was fast becoming a world leader in terms of manufacturing, technological innovation, and the rapid growth of its prosperous middle class.

1890 Sherman Anti-Trust Act
Wyoming admitted to the Union, first state to enfranchise women
National American Woman Suffrage Association is formed
Wounded Knee Massacre

1891 Populist party formed
Eleven Italian immigrants are lynched in New Orleans

1892 Ellis Island opens as screening site for immigrants
Miners strike in Coeur d'Alene, Idaho
Steelworkers strike at Carnegie's Homestead plant near Pittsburgh

1893 Columbian Exposition opens in Chicago
Pro-American interests stage a successful coup against Queen Liliuokalani of Hawaii
Worst nationwide depression to date

1894 Coxey's Army marches on Washington, D.C.
Pullman workers strike

1896 Supreme Court decides *Plessy v. Ferguson*, upholds segregation
W. E. B. Du Bois is first black person to receive a Ph.D. from Harvard

1898 United States annexes Hawaii
Maine blows up in Havana Harbor
United States defeats Spain in Spanish-American-Cuban-Filipino War
Spain cedes Guam and Puerto Rico to United States, turns over Philippines in return for $20 million

1899 Gen. Emilio Aguinaldo leads Filipino revolt against 70,000 U.S. occupying forces

1900 U.S. troops sent to China to crush Boxer Rebellion

16

Standardizing the Nation: Innovations in Technology, Business, and Culture, 1877–1890

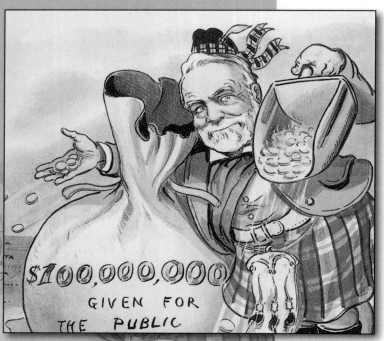

Andrew Carnegie eventually became the richest man in the world, but he began life in modest circumstances. In 1835 Will and Margaret Carnegie were living in the village of Dunfermline, Scotland, where Will was a skilled weaver. The couple had two sons—Andrew, born in 1835, and Tom, born eight years later. When steam-powered textile looms threw Will Carnegie and other handweavers out of work, the family emigrated to the United States and settled in Pittsburgh, Pennsylvania. Eager to work hard, Andrew took a series of jobs to help support the family: bobbin boy in a textile mill, tender of a steam boiler in a factory, clerk and then messenger in a telegraph office. By the time he was 18 years old, he was personal assistant to Thomas Scott, superintendent of the Western Division of the Pennsylvania Railroad. Three years later, after the death of his father, Andrew assumed the role of family breadwinner; he also took over the job of Thomas Scott, who became president of the railroad.

Working for the railroad, Andrew Carnegie learned a great deal about running a gigantic business efficiently and profitably. He also invested in oil and railroads. In 1872 he visited England and gained firsthand information about the production of steel, a lighter, stronger material than iron. Three years later he opened his own steel plant in Pittsburgh, then proceeded to buy rival steel mills.

In his business life, Andrew Carnegie was a man of strong principles. In 1868 he had promised himself that he would not hoard the money he made; instead he would promote the "education and improvement of the poorer classes." Earning $25 million a year by the early 1890s, he nonetheless believed that "The amassing of wealth is one of the worst species of idolatry." During the course of his career, Carnegie gave away 90 percent of his fortune, founding the Carnegie Endowment for International Peace, as well as many public libraries around the country.

It was significant that Carnegie spent his formative years in business learning about railroads. These lessons paved the way for his own success in the steel industry. By 1877 the emergence of a national rail system signaled the rise of big business. The railroad industry produced America's first business bureaucracies, employing gigantic workforces to maintain, schedule, operate, and staff trains that traversed 93,000 miles of track. By 1890 the Pennsylvania Railroad had become the nation's largest employer, with 110,000 workers on its payroll. About one out of seven people worked in the rail industry. The personnel in charge of coordinating these vast operations were among the country's first professional, salaried managers.

The railroad industry was both a great centralizer and a great standardizer. Trains ran on schedules that were set by a central office, and those schedules relied on definitions of actual time that were standard throughout the nation. Moreover, trains broke down regional boundaries by transporting goods to all areas of the country. For the first time, trains carried brand-name goods and commodities to a national market. A California wheat farmer could purchase replacement parts for his McCormick reaper manufactured in Chicago. An Iowa farm family ordered a new cookstove through a mail-order catalogue. Levi-Strauss, a small clothier in San Francisco, shipped its famous denim pants to cowboys in Texas. Pillsbury Flour of Minnesota distributed its products to bakeries throughout the Midwest. Armour Meatpacking of Chicago sent its sausages to the East Coast. With the introduction of the new refrigerated railroad car, trains also began carrying larger loads of fruits and vegetables over longer distances. The new traffic in produce stimulated commercial agriculture in the South and on the West Coast.

Few Americans amassed the fabulous fortunes of rich industrialists like Carnegie, yet most people aspired to a better life, even in modest terms. Proprietors, managers, and office workers filled the ranks of the comfortable middle class, men and women freed of the danger and drudgery of manual labor. Between 1880 and 1900, clerical workers tripled in number, and business managers increased from 68,000 to more than 318,000. Enjoying steady work and cash salaries, middle-class employees began to move their families out of the city. Urban areas were becoming increasingly befouled by smokestacks and congested with new factories and workshops.

Providers of goods and services celebrated a "standard" American viewed as white, native born, middle class, heterosexual, and Protestant. This image assumed special significance in the marketing of consumer products and in the appeal of new forms of leisure activities. Mass advertising techniques heightened distinctions that European Americans drew between themselves and people they considered inferior, exotic, or foreign.

Yet the energy and vitality associated with American popular culture served as a magnet for people all over the world. Beginning in the 1880s, eastern European immigrants streamed to the United States. They were also eager to partake of the country's plentiful jobs, material

■ When Andrew Carnegie retired in 1901, he sold the Carnegie Steel Company to American banker and financier J.P. Morgan for $480 million. Carnegie's personal fortune was about $500 million.

■ The "Great Labor Uprising" of July 1877 was the first national strike in U.S. history. As railroad lines proliferated, owners slashed wages in a bid to remain competitive. Railroad workers in some cities destroyed trains, tracks, and other equipment. Spreading eventually to 14 states, the conflict claimed the lives of more than 100 people and resulted in the loss of millions of dollars worth of private property.

prosperity, and democratic openness. Well into the twentieth century, the nation still showed the ethnic and cultural diversity that was shaped by patterns of immigration during the late nineteenth century.

The New Shape of Business

What were the challenges faced by large business owners and managers who sought to mass produce and mass market their goods?

In 1882 prospectors discovered gold in the creeks of Idaho's Coeur d'Alene region (in Indian territory, about 90 miles east of Spokane, Washington). Multiethnic boomtowns mushroomed in the region. The Northern Pacific Railway promoted settlement, and the primitive techniques that had been used in surface mining soon yielded to far more efficient hydraulic methods of extraction (a process in which powerful water hoses wash the soil away to expose gold deposits).

The mining industry in the region soon emerged as a big business. In 1885 an unemployed carpenter named Noah S. Kellogg set in motion a dramatic chain of events. Kellogg discovered a lode containing not only gold but also zinc and lead. In short order, he sold his mines to a Portland businessman, who paid a whopping $650,000 for them. A group of eastern and California investors, and finally several large corporations, soon controlled major interests in the mines. By the mid-twentieth century, mining companies had dug more than a billion dollars' worth of metal out of Noah Kellogg's original stake.

Crucial to the process of innovation were engineers, who mastered the technical aspects of construction and design. Many American engineers were trained in Germany, but others attended such schools as the Massachusetts Institute of Technology (MIT) or Cornell University, in New York state, both of which introduced electrical engineering into their curricula in 1882. American engineers, such as those who worked in Mexico under the auspices of mining companies and the railroads, served as the vanguard of American capitalism throughout the world.

No matter what industry they were in, advocates of standardized industrial processes and mass marketing hoped to break down regional barriers and create an integrated national economy. Whether they specialized in railroads or shoes, wheat or steel, business owners and managers who possessed the necessary resources and resourcefulness pursued similar goals: to mine, grow, manufacture, or process large quantities of goods and then market them as widely, cheaply, and quickly as possible. Business put a premium on technological innovation, on the efficient use of workers, and on the reduction of uncertainties that accompanied a competitive marketplace. These guiding principles, formulated during the late 1870s and 1880s, laid the foundations of economic progress in late nineteenth-century America.

New Systems and Machines—and Their Price

The free enterprise system thrived on innovation. Indeed, during the 1880s, new machines, new technical processes, new engineering feats, and new forms of factory organization fueled the growth and efficiency of U.S. businesses. Many devices that became staples of American life appeared during this period. Alexander Graham Bell invented the telephone in 1876. Thomas A. Edison developed the phonograph in 1877 and the electric light in 1879. Cash registers, stock tickers, and typewriters soon became indispensable tools for American businesses. Beginning in the 1880s, railroad cars installed steam heat and electric lights, boosting the comfort of passengers.

During these years, more and more businesses perfected the so-called American system of manufacturing, which dated back half a century and relied on the mass production of interchangeable parts. Factory workers made large numbers of a particular part, each part

●•●•Read the Document
Edison, "The Success of the Electric Light" at www.myhistorylab.com

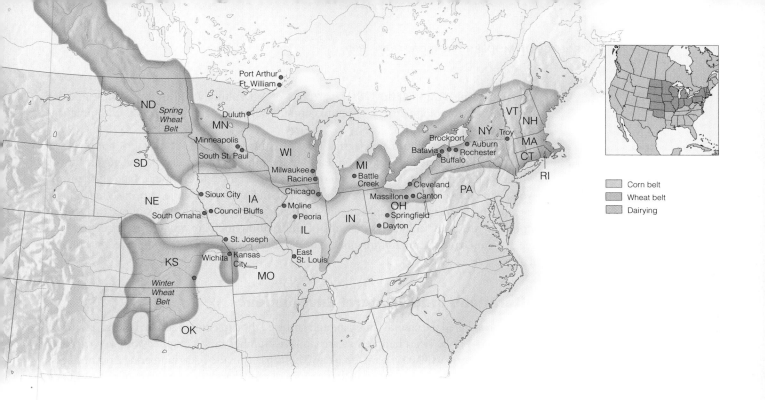

■ **MAP 16.1**

AGRICULTURAL REGIONS OF THE MIDWEST AND NORTHEAST
By 1890 several Midwestern cities served as shipping centers, getting wheat and corn to the growing metropolitan areas of the Northeast and Mid-Atlantic. Farmers complained that the railroads gave discounts to large shippers, such as Standard Oil, and discriminated against small producers.

exactly the same size and shape. This system enabled manufacturers to assemble products more cheaply and efficiently, to repair products easily with new parts, and to redesign products quickly. The engineers who designed the modern bicycle (which has wheels of equal size) used the American system to make their product affordable to almost anyone who wanted one. The bicycle craze of the late nineteenth century resulted from the novelty and cheapness of this new form of transportation and recreation, one enjoyed by males and females of all ages. Production techniques used to make bicycles were later adapted to the manufacture of automobiles.

New technical processes also facilitated the manufacture and marketing of foods and other consumer goods. Distributors developed pressure-sealed cans, which enabled them to market agricultural products in far-flung parts of the country. Innovative techniques for sheet metal stamping and electric resistance welding transformed a variety of industries. By 1880, 90 percent of American steel was made by the Bessemer process, which injected air into molten iron to yield steel.

The agriculture business benefited from engineering innovations as well, which often reached across national boundaries. As just one example, the first modern irrigation systems in the Southwest were constructed by Native Americans and *mestizos* (people of both indigenous and Spanish ancestry). And in the 1870s, Japan began importing American farm implements and inviting U.S. engineers to construct dams and canals for new steam- and water-powered gristmills and sawmills. Technology was a universal language, one that many peoples around the globe sought to master.

Long active in territorial exploration and land surveying, the federal government continued to assume a leading role in applied science. In 1879 the U.S. Geological Survey (USGS) was formed, charged with compiling and centralizing data describing the natural landscape, an effort that had originated in 1804 with the Lewis and Clark expedition. In the 1880s, the federal government also began to systematize and disseminate information useful to farmers through the U.S. Department of Agriculture. In 1881, for example, the department's Entomology Bureau began to combine current research on insects with practical techniques for pest control.

See the Map

Resources and Conflict in the West at **www.myhistorylab.com**

Like factory machines, new agricultural machinery benefited consumers, but the need for hired hands gradually evaporated. Early in the nineteenth century, producing an acre of wheat took 56 hours of labor; in 1880 that number dropped to 20 hours. One agricultural worker in Ohio observed, "Of one thing we are convinced, that while improved machinery is gathering our large crops, making our boots and shoes, doing the work of our carpenters, stone sawyers, and builders, thousands of able, willing men are going from place to place seeking employment, and finding none. The question naturally arises, is improved machinery a blessing or a curse?"

Alterations in the Natural Environment

Innovation altered the natural landscape and hastened the depletion of certain natural resources. By the mid-1870s, Texas had new steam-powered lumber mills equipped with saw rigs that could produce up to 30,000 board feet a day. This capacity made Texas lumbering a big business, especially when it was combined with infusions of capital and the expansion of railroad lines into the piney woods region, along the eastern edge of the state. Texas lumber mills were poised to benefit from the exhaustion of the great forests of the eastern and Great Lakes states.

In the Chesapeake Bay, dredge boats were becoming more efficient in harvesting oysters, and shellfish reserves began to decline. In the mid-1880s, oyster harvesters took a record 15 million bushels from the bay; the shellfish simply could not replenish themselves. New means of commercial fishing also reduced supplies of salmon in the Northwest.

■ Following the wholesale slaughter of buffalo on the Great Plains, settlers earned money by gathering the skeletons. "The bones are shipped East by the carloads," reported the *Dodge City Times*, "where they are ground and used for fertilizing and manufactured into numerous useful articles." This mound of buffalo bones at the **Michigan Carlson Works in Detroit, c. 1880, suggests the extent of the devastation.**

In 1884 in California, a federal court issued a permanent injunction against hydraulic mining, because it contributed to soil erosion and water pollution. Hydraulic mining had washed an estimated 12 billion tons of earth into San Francisco Bay, raising the floor of the bay several feet. At the same time, mercury flowing into nearby streams from gold mines in the San Jose hills was poisoning fish in the bay, creating pollution that would be felt well into the twentieth century. Similar cases of industrial pollution despoiled other parts of the country. In the absence of any laws to restrain them, Chicago meatpackers befouled the Chicago River with the byproducts of sausage, glue, and fertilizer.

> *Population growth spurred the growth of industries that exploited nature.*

By stimulating manufacturing and extractive enterprises alike, the railroads powered these great environmental transformations, for better or worse. Since buffalo herds impeded rail travel, railroads promoted the shooting of buffalo from trains, a "sport" that almost eradicated the species. By the mid-1880s, the great herds had disappeared, victims of ecological change (the incursion of horses into grazing areas), disease (brucellosis spread by domestic livestock), and commercial enterprise. Sioux leader Black Elk decried the slaughter and the heaps of bones left to rot in the sun.

Innovations in Financing and Organizing Business

As agents of economic development and cultural change, the railroads knew no peer. As private enterprises, however, they faced the same challenges that all big businesses ultimately must address. The proliferation of independent lines and the high fixed costs associated with the industry made profits slim and competition intense. As a result, railroad companies began to come together in informal pools to share equipment and set prices industrywide. In the 1880s, these pools gave way to consolidation, a process by which several companies merged into one large company. Moreover, like other large businesses, including oil and steel, the railroads sought to slash wages in order to decrease their cost of doing business. This decision had profound consequences for workers, who in some cases reacted violently.

In these years, U.S. businesses grew larger and more quickly than their western European counterparts. This difference stemmed in large part from America's astonishing population growth and its rich natural resources. Equally significant, the United States possessed a social and legal culture favorable to big business. The absence of an entrenched, conservative elite, along with the spread of state and national laws that protected private property, stimulated the entrepreneurial spirit. The U.S. government refrained from owning industries, although it heavily subsidized the railroad industry. It taxed business lightly and did not tax individual incomes at all until 1913. Finally, American bankers such as J. P. Morgan aggressively promoted growth through their lending practices and bond sales.

Several large enterprises began to conquer not just local but also national markets. Examples include Bell Telephone (founded in Boston), the Kroger grocery business (Cincinnati), Marshall Field department store (Chicago), and Boston Fruit Company. In the South, Midwest, and West, investors rushed to finance gigantic mining operations and agribusinesses, such as the 1.5 million acres devoted to rice cultivation in southeastern Louisiana and bonanza wheat farms (as large as 38,000 acres) in the Red River valley of North Dakota.

Owners of these enterprises devised new forms of business organization that helped their companies grow and survive in a dynamic economy. By combining, or integrating, their operations, manufacturers created large businesses called **trusts** to cut costs and monopolize an entire industry in the process. Unable to withstand the ruthless competition that favored larger enterprises, smaller companies folded. The two icons of American big business in the 1880s—Andrew Carnegie in steel and John D. Rockefeller in petroleum—proved master innovators in both the managerial and technical aspects of business.

Within a year of opening the Edgar Thomson Steelworks, Carnegie was producing steel at half the prevailing market price. He excelled at vertical integration, in which a single firm controls all aspects of production and distribution. Carnegie employed laborers in the

Bonanza farms were huge agricultural enterprises, ranging in size from 15,000 to 50,000 acres. This photo shows a bonanza wheat farm in Oregon, c. 1890. Many of these farms relied not only on sophisticated machinery but also on transient labor forces (up to 1,000 workers at a time) to help plow, plant, harvest, and thresh the crop. Some of the largest landowners abandoned farming when they had an opportunity to sell their vast holdings for a profit.

Lake Superior region to mine the raw material, and he owned the ships and railroads that brought the ore to the mills in Pittsburgh and then transported the manufactured steel to customers.

Another form of business consolidation was horizontal integration, in which a number of companies producing the same product merge to reduce competition and control prices. In 1882 John D. Rockefeller, a former bookkeeper, horizontally integrated the petroleum industry by forming Standard Oil Trust. Stockholders in small companies turned over their shares to Standard Oil, which then coordinated operations and eliminated competition from other smaller firms. Standard Oil also practiced vertical integration. Soon Rockefeller had positioned himself to buy out his rivals—or ruin them. Trusts placed a premium on efficient production, but they also worked to the disadvantage of consumers, who were hostage to high prices within industries that lacked competition.

Immigrants: New Labor Supplies for a New Economy

To operate efficiently, expanding industries needed expanding supplies of workers to grow crops, extract raw materials, and produce manufactured goods. Many of these workers came from abroad. The year 1880 marked the leading edge of a new wave of immigration to the United States. Over the next ten years, 5.2 million newcomers entered the country, almost twice the previous decade's level of 2.8 million.

In the mid-nineteenth century, most immigrants hailed from western Europe and the British Isles—from Germany, Scandinavia, England, and Ireland. Between 1880 and 1890, Germans, Scandinavians, and the English kept coming, but they were joined by numerous Italians, Russians, and Poles. In fact, these last three groups predominated among newcomers for the next 35 years, their arrival rates peaking between 1890 and 1910. At the same time, immigrants from Asia, especially from China, were making their way to the Kingdom of Hawaii, which was annexed by the United States in 1898. Between 1852 and 1887, 26,000 Chinese arrived on the islands. Almost 40 percent of all immigrants to the United States during this period were known as "birds of passage," men who were recruited by American employers and who, after earning some money, migrated back to their native land.

The year 1880 marked the leading edge of a new wave of immigration to the United States. Over the next ten years, 5.2 million newcomers entered the country, almost twice the previous decade's level of 2.8 million.

In some cases, domestic politics affected patterns of foreign immigration to the continental United States. For example, on the West Coast, the Chinese faced intense hostility from native-born white men who feared that "coolies" (Chinese immigrants) would depress their wages and take their jobs. Passed in 1882, the **Chinese Exclusion Act** aimed to stem the flow of Chinese immigration to the United States.

Many of the new European immigrants sought to escape oppressive economic and political conditions in Europe, even as they hoped to make a new life for themselves and their families in the United States. Russian Jews fled discrimination and violent **anti-semitism** in the form of pogroms, organized massacres conducted by their Christian neighbors and Russian authorities. Southern Italians, mostly landless farmers, suffered from a combination of declining agricultural prices and high birth rates. Impoverished Poles chafed under cultural restrictions imposed by Germany and Russia. Hungarians, Greeks, Portuguese, and Armenians, among other groups, also participated in this great migration; members of these groups too were seeking political freedom and economic opportunity.

Immigrants replenished America's sense of itself as a haven for the downtrodden, a place where opportunity beckoned to hard-working and ambitious people. "The New Colossus," written by American poet Emma Lazarus in 1883, pays tribute to the "huddled masses yearning to breathe free"—people from all over the world who sought refuge in the United States. The words of her poem are inscribed on the Statue of Liberty at the entrance to New York harbor.

The story of Rosa Cassettari, a young woman who emigrated from northern Italy to the United States in 1884, suggests the challenges that faced many newcomers during this period. Rosa's husband, Santino, had preceded her to America. He had settled in an iron mining camp in Missouri. Leaving her son with relatives, Rosa received the assurances of friends and relatives: "You will get smart in America. And in America you will not be so poor."

Life in the Missouri iron camp proved harsh—nothing like what Rosa had expected. Her husband, who was much older than she, neglected her; he preferred the company of prostitutes in the town. The iron was almost depleted, and some workers and their wives had moved on to a new mine in Michigan. Rosa's days centered on caring for her new baby and cooking for 13 of the miners.

Despite these realities, within a couple of years, Rosa grew used to America and considered herself an American. She returned briefly to her hometown in Italy but expressed impatience with the rigid social etiquette that separated the rich from the poor. She also yearned for the hearty meals that had become her staple in the iron camp. Back in Missouri, she mustered enough courage to leave Santino, traveling to Chicago and making a new life for herself in the Italian *colonia* (community) there. She eventually married another Italian man (the two had fallen in love in Missouri) and found work as a cleaning woman at Chicago Commons, a social settlement house.

Specific groups of immigrants often gravitated toward particular kinds of jobs. For example, many Poles found work in the vast steel plants of Pittsburgh, and Russian Jews went into the garment industry and street-peddling trade in New York City. California fruit orchards and vegetable farms employed numerous Japanese immigrants. Cuban immigrants rolled cigars in Florida. In Hawaii, the Chinese and Japanese labored in the sugar fields; after they had accumulated a little money, they became rice farmers and shopkeepers. In Boston and New York City, second-generation Irish took advantage of their prominent place in the Democratic party to become public school teachers, firefighters, and police officers.

The experience of Kinji Ushijima (later known as George Shima) graphically illustrates the power of immigrant niches. Shima arrived in California in 1887 and, like many other Japanese immigrants, found work as a potato picker in the San Joaquin Valley. Soon, Shima

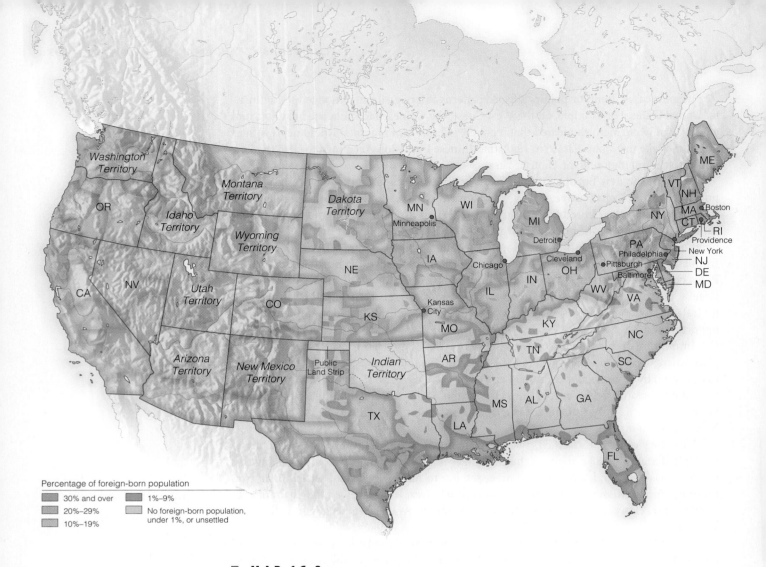

Percentage of foreign-born population

- 30% and over
- 20%–29%
- 10%–19%
- 1%–9%
- No foreign-born population, under 1%, or unsettled

■ **MAP 16.2**

POPULATION OF FOREIGN BORN, BY REGION, 1880
After the Civil War, large numbers of immigrants settled in northeastern cities. In addition, the upper Midwest and parts of the western mining frontier drew many newcomers from western Europe. The area along the country's southwestern border was home to immigrants from Mexico. Cuban cigar makers established thriving communities in southern Florida.

moved up to become a labor contractor, securing Japanese laborers for the valley's white farmers. With the money he made, he bought 15 acres of land and began his own potato farm. Eventually he built a large potato business by expanding his holdings, reclaiming swampland, and investing in a fleet of boats to ship his crops up the coast to San Francisco. Taking advantage of a Japanese niche, Shima prospered through a combination of good luck and hard work.

Efficient Machines, Efficient People

Unlike George Shima, most immigrant workers did not become business owners. By the late nineteenth century, the typical industrial employee labored within an immense, multistory brick structure and operated a machine powered by water or steam. Smoky, smelly kerosene lamps gave way to early forms of electric lighting, first arc and then incandescent light bulbs. Long-standing industries, such as textiles and shoes, were now fully mechanized.

The new products flooding the economy—locomotives and bicycles, cash registers and typewriters—streamed from factories designed to ensure maximum efficiency from both machines *and* the people who tended them.

In the 1880s, a few factory managers hired efficiency experts. The experts' goal was to cut labor costs in the same way that industry barons had shaved the costs of extracting raw materials or distributing final products. With huge quantities of goods flowing from factories, even modest savings in wages could mean significant profits in the long run. Frederick Winslow Taylor, chief engineer for the Midvale Steel Plant outside Philadelphia, pioneered in the techniques of efficient "scientific management."

By the late nineteenth century, the typical industrial employee labored within an immense, multistory brick structure and operated a machine powered by water or steam.

Southern textile mill owners in the Piedmont region of South Carolina and Georgia devised their own strategies for shaping a compliant workforce. They employed only white men, women, and children as machine operators, but threatened to hire blacks if the whites protested low wages and poor working conditions. Poor whites lived in company housing, their children attended company schools, and they received cash wages. In contrast, blacks remained in the countryside, impoverished and without the right to vote. In the cities of the North as well as the textile villages of the South, factory workers remained exclusively white until well into the twentieth century.

The Birth of a National Urban Culture

In the 1880s, visitors to the territory of Utah marveled at the capital, Salt Lake City, where Mormon pioneers had made the desert bloom. Situated at the foot of the magnificent snow-covered Wasatch Range, this oasis in the Great Salt Basin boasted a built landscape almost as impressive as the natural beauty that surrounded it. In the heart of Salt Lake City lay Temple Square. This broad plaza contained the Mormon Tabernacle, a huge domed structure. Next to it stood the Mormon Temple, a soaring six-spired granite cathedral still under construction. The city had the advantage of rail service (Promontory Point, where the transcontinental railroad was joined, was not far away). Mines in nearby Bingham Canyon yielded rich lodes of silver and large local smelters refined copper ores. Irrigation systems made the city self-sufficient in the production of foodstuffs. A settlement inspired by religious faith, Salt Lake City was at the same time thoroughly modern.

What technological and managerial innovations shaped the nation's largest cities in the late nineteenth century?

Not just Salt Lake City, but other cities around the country began to assume monumental proportions. In New York, the 1880s marked the completion of Central Park and the Brooklyn Bridge and the arrival of the Statue of Liberty from France. Chicago, rebuilding after a disastrous fire in 1871, became a sprawling rail hub dotted with yards for western cattle, northern timber, and the trains that hauled them. In 1885 Chicago also became the location for a major architectural breakthrough by engineer William LeBaron Jenney. He designed the ten-story Home Insurance Building, the world's first metal frame skyscraper. The steel skeleton weighed only one third as much as the thick stone walls needed to support a similar masonry building, and the design left room for numerous windows. Urban architecture would never be the same again.

Cities represented American notions of progress and prosperity; they were places where innovation, consumer culture, and new forms of entertainment grew and flourished. From 1875 to 1900, American cities developed increasingly sophisticated systems of communications and transportation. Streetlights, transportation networks, and sewer lines provided basic services to swelling populations of immigrants and rural in-migrants. Cities also represented a new cultural diversity in American life. At times uneasily, they accommodated immigrants from around the world. San Francisco's Chinatown formed a "city within a city" as hostile

■ Admirers hailed New York City's Brooklyn Bridge as the eighth wonder of the world when it was completed in 1883. With a central span of 1,595 feet, it became the largest suspension bridge in the world. Built over 14 years, the bridge linked Brooklyn to Manhattan across the East River, using steel suspension cables that are nearly 16 inches thick. Its total cost was about $18 million.

European Americans sought to circumscribe its residents. These growing cities required larger local governments to manage the services necessary for daily life. Politics, prejudice, and technology came together to shape the urban landscape.

Economic Sources of Urban Growth

Northeastern and mid-Atlantic cities emerged as centers of concentrated manufacturing activity. Yet, with the aid of eastern capital, western cities also flourished. New York's Wall Street and Boston's State Street, home to the nation's largest investment bankers, financed the Main Streets of the Midwest and West. Some urban areas prospered through milling, mining, or other enterprises, such as lumber and flour milling in Minneapolis and ore smelting in Denver. Others focused on manufacturing to serve a growing western population. Chicago was rivaled only by New York in terms of its industrial economy and the vast territory that it supplied with raw materials, processed food, and manufactured goods. Salt Lake City produced goods for the so-called Mormon Corridor of settlements that stretched west from the city to southern California. By the 1880s, San Francisco had a commercial reach that encompassed much of the West as well as Hawaii and Alaska.

No trend supported urban growth more than the arrival of newcomers from abroad. To stoke its furnaces, mill its lumber, and slaughter its cattle, Chicago relied on immigrants from Ireland, Slovakia, Germany, Poland, and Bohemia. The three cities with the highest percentage of foreign-born residents in 1880 were San Francisco (45 percent), Chicago (42 percent), and New York (40 percent). Yet all large cities also attracted migrants from America's own countryside, as native-born men and women fled the hardships of life on the farm. Moreover, the use of increasingly efficient agricultural machines meant that rural workers had fewer job opportunities. Most of the immigrants from rural areas to the cities were young women; they included Yankee girls from the hardscrabble homesteads of New England, daughters of Swedish immigrants in Minnesota, and native-born farm tenants in Indiana.

Rural folk sought the steady work and wages afforded by jobs in the city, but they were also drawn to the excitement that had become the hallmark of the urban scene. In the early nineteenth century, Thomas Jefferson had located the heart of America in its sturdy yeoman farmers. By the late nineteenth century, that heart had shifted to the city.

Building the Cities

The American city was emerging as a technological marvel. Through a combination of money and engineering skill, cities managed to provide an adequate water supply for private and commercial purposes, move large numbers of people and goods efficiently, get rid of waste materials, and illuminate thoroughfares at night. Professionals, such as landscape contractors, construction architects, and civil engineers, designed the parks, bridges, public libraries, and museums that made cities so attractive.

Cities grew upward and outward as a result of developments in mass production and technology. Elevators extended living and office spaces upward. The invention of the electric streetcar in 1888 permitted cities to spread out. Soon, residential suburbs cropped up many miles from urban commercial cores. Wealthy and middle-class urban residents followed the streetcar lines out of the city, hoping to find a green refuge from the grime and noise of downtown while maintaining a manageable commute to work.

As cities expanded, the challenges associated with providing services also grew more complex and expensive. A polluted water supply, for example, meant epidemics of diphtheria and cholera, so city taxpayers demanded waterworks that delivered drinkable water through intricate systems of dams, pumps, reservoirs, and pipes. Chicago had long pumped its sewage into Lake Michigan, the source of its drinking water. In the 1880s, the city financed the building of a canal and the reversal of the flow of the Chicago River. These changes sent the city's sewage away from Lake Michigan and westward into the Mississippi River instead. Begun in 1889, the 28-mile Chicago Sanitary and Ship Canal was completed seven years later. One awed observer marveled at the "powerful machinery for digging and hoisting, steam shovels, excavators, inclines, conveyors, derricks, cantilevers, cableways, channelers, steam drills, pumps, etc." The cost: $54 million.

Local Government Gets Bigger

These new systems of services, combined with the mushrooming immigrant neighborhoods, changed both the quality and the quantity of urban problems. Zoning issues—who could build what, where, and when—became flashpoints for conflict as the interests of homeowners, developers, storekeepers, and municipal engineers collided. Urban political leaders struggled to improve the city's public works while meeting the needs of multiple ethnic groups. Governing a city was an expensive, full-time enterprise and one that had the potential to be very lucrative to businesspeople and politicians alike.

Although New York's "Boss" Tweed had been convicted on charges of corruption in the early 1870s, the infamous Tammany Hall gang carried on his legacy. The Democratic officials associated with this social and political organization perfected a system of kickbacks linked to municipal construction projects. Under this system, contractors paid politicians for city construction contracts. For example, a New York City courthouse that was supposed to cost a quarter of a million dollars ended up costing taxpayers 52 times that amount, or twice as

> *In the 1880s, secretive networks of corruption linking law enforcement personnel, city officials, and construction contractors flourished in many cities.*

much as the United States paid Russia for Alaska! In the 1880s, secretive networks of corruption linking law enforcement personnel, city officials, and construction contractors flourished in many cities. These webs, or "machines," characterized urban life for decades to come.

Urban machines existed to secure jobs for their loyal supporters and line the pockets of those at the highest levels of power. Deal-making blurred the lines between private enterprise and public service as everyone from mayors to local ward organizers benefited from the modernization of the American city. In the process, urban bosses ensured that the streets were paved, tenement buildings erected, sewer lines laid, and trolley tracks extended. But taxpayers footed the bill, which included outrageous amounts of money used for bribes and kickbacks.

Local officials went out of their way to support the provision of illegal services, such as prostitution and gambling, demanded by their constituents. Corrupt politicians, judges, and police extorted "hush money" from brothels, gambling parlors, and unlicensed taverns. Urban bosses also had a vested interest in sponsoring new money-making venues for professional sports and supporting other forms of commercialized leisure activity. Baseball parks, boxing rings, and race tracks yielded huge sums in the form of kickbacks from contractors. Once built, stadiums and boxing rings generated profits indefinitely as fans filled the stands.

Despite the outcry of reformers, who condemned corrupt urban bosses, these local politicians gained favor among their constituents when they provided needed goods and services, especially among the poor. The boss who provoked the wrath of "good government" men and women also won the loyalty of immigrants whom he helped by providing jobs, food, clothing, loans, and proper burials for loved ones. For the boss, charity was good politics.

Thrills, Chills, and Toothpaste: The Emergence of Consumer Culture

What were the social and economic consequences of the new consumer culture?

On a hot summer day in 1890, a young mother named Emily Scanlon, with her three-year-old daughter in tow, paid the five cent admission fee to a popular ride called the Toboggan Slide at the Brandywine Springs Amusement Park near Wilmington, Delaware. The two of them ascended a stairwell to the top of the three-story-high structure and then stepped into a car that ran on a wooden trough. When the attendant released the brakes, the car descended, pulled by gravity. It moved slowly at first, then picked up speed around a curve. Suddenly, Emily Scanlon stood up in the car (perhaps to retrieve her hat, which had blown off), and she and her daughter were thrown from the car. Mrs. Scanlon died instantly of a broken neck, but the youngster survived. Significantly, the tragedy did not provoke a shutdown of the ride or the installation of safety measures. Instead, park managers simply posted a sign that read, "Passengers must keep their seats." Patrons continued to enjoy the thrills of the toboggan.

Brandywine Springs boasted an ornate gateway that proclaimed "Let All Who Enter Here Leave Care Behind." In cities around the country, amusement parks brought men and women, girls and boys together to enjoy merry-go-rounds, prizefights, and circus sideshows. By 1880 railroads and steamships were transporting crowds out of Manhattan to Coney Island, where working-class people mingled with the self-proclaimed "respectable" middle classes.

Late in the century, Americans of all kinds began to sample a new realm of sensual experience—one of physical daring, material luxury, and visual fantasy—either as participants or as observers. Central to this emerging consumer culture was mass advertising, a form of appeal that sought to instill in consumers the desire for things that were new and visually attractive. Colorful spectacles of all kinds—whether in the form of a department store window or a well-publicized athletic event—became an integral part of American life.

Shows and Sports as Spectacles

Public officials, college administrators, and ambitious entrepreneurs alike discovered that Americans craved new and stimulating forms of entertainment and were willing to pay for them. Athletic events began to draw large crowds, revealing their potential as big business. Traveling circus and road shows promoted new products and services by charming their audiences with exotic performances. Though modest by today's standards, such spectacles found a ready market in the United States and other countries.

In the quarter-century after Reconstruction, three major sports began to attract large national audiences. Organized baseball had existed since 1846, when the Knickerbocker Base Ball Club of New York met the New York Nine in Hoboken, New Jersey. (The score was 23 to 1, in favor of the Nine.) The National Baseball League, consisting of eight professional teams, was founded in 1876, the American League in 1900. In the 1880s, several new regulations—those governing the overhand pitch, foul balls, and swingless strikes—helped to standardize the game.

Also in the 1880s, Walter Camp, a former Yale University football player, introduced rules—for instance, the system of downs and the center snap to the quarterback—that made that sport quicker and more competitive. Camp was also behind the selection of the first "All America" team (1889) to stimulate fan interest. By this time towns, high schools, and colleges were fielding football teams.

Likewise, boxing emerged as a national, regulated sport. John L. Sullivan, an American, won renown as the world's bare-knuckled champion in 1882, even as more and more fighters had started wearing gloves. Sullivan then joined a traveling theatrical group and demonstrated gloved boxing to enthusiastic crowds all over the country. In 1889, Sullivan defeated an opponent in a 75-round match, the last heavyweight, bare-knuckled championship.

Performances based on skills of all kinds gained national audiences, as the career of William "Buffalo Bill" Cody reveals. Born in Iowa in 1846, Cody parlayed his early years as a Pony Express postal rider, cavalry scout, Indian fighter, and buffalo hunter into a form of mass entertainment. In his "Buffalo Bill Combination" show, cowboy and Indian actors performed skits depicting dramatic events in western history (from a European-American point of view, at least).

In 1882 Cody produced "Buffalo Bill's Wild West," a traveling road show that featured sharpshooter Annie Oakley, cowboy musicians, and Sioux warriors performing authentic Native American dances. Sioux leader Sitting Bull (Tatanka Iyotake), long an admirer of Annie Oakley (he called her "Little Sure Shot"), joined the show in 1885. Like other Indians who worked for Cody, Sitting Bull took advantage of the opportunity to escape the confines of the

■ "Buffalo Bill" Cody and Sitting Bull pose for a promotional photo for the 1885 season of the "Wild West." Cody refrained from calling the production a "show," maintaining that it demonstrated frontier skills and recreated historical encounters (such as Custer's Last Stand and stagecoach robberies). The "Wild West" toured Canada and Europe and inspired many imitators.

reservation (in his case, Standing Rock in North Dakota). As a member of the "Wild West" troupe, he also enjoyed decent food and accommodations. At a time when whites were denigrating Indian culture, Sitting Bull affirmed that culture by demonstrating his shooting and riding skills. However, white audiences jeered him—they saw him as less an entertainer and more an enemy warrior—and he left after just a year. By the 1890s, Cody was playing to audiences in Europe as well as the United States, dramatizing a West that was fast disappearing.

Mass Merchandising as Spectacle

In the cities of the late nineteenth century, the act of shopping for goods, especially luxury goods, became an adventure in itself. A new piece of the cityscape, the department store, welcomed customers into a world of luxury and abundance, a place of color, light, and glamour. These "palaces of consumption" showcased a variety of technological innovations. In Marshall Field's "Grand Emporium" (Chicago), Wanamaker's (Philadelphia), and Lord & Taylor (New York), shoppers glided from story to story on escalators and in elevators. Warmed by central heating, they browsed display cases, racks, and tables laden with enticing goods and illuminated by arc lighting. Their money streamed into cash registers or to a central clerk through cash conveyors.

Thus, department stores not only offered a dazzling array of goods but also made shopping an exciting experience. Middle-class women in particular had the leisure time and the cash to indulge in day-long shopping excursions. In 1880 a New Yorker could arrive at Macy's by taking the Sixth Avenue elevated train and spend the morning exploring any number of specialized departments: ribbons, women's and children's muslin underwear, toys, candy, books, men's furnishings, china and glassware, and so on. Fatigued at noon, she might visit the lunchroom to partake of a modest meal and then devote the rest of her day to examining the colored dress silks, a new department established the year before.

The department store was an exclusively urban phenomenon, but mass merchandising reached far beyond cities. The material riches of American society became accessible to rural people through the mail-order catalogue. This marketing device was pioneered in 1872 by the Chicago company Montgomery Ward, the official supply house for the Farmers' Grange. On homesteads throughout the Midwest, family members gathered to pore over the thousands of items displayed in "The Great Wish Book." The company's motto? "Satisfaction guaranteed or your money back." Farm wives delighted in the latest Parisian fashions, their husbands pondered the intricacies of McCormick threshing machinery, and the children studied the newest line of toys and fishing rods. Late in the decade, a competitor appeared on the scene in the form of the Sears, Roebuck Catalogue.

■ Refugio Amador and her five daughters, Emilia, Maria, Clotilde, Julieta, and Corina, were members of an elite Hispanic family in Las Cruces, New Mexico. Her husband, Martin Amador, was a prominent politician, merchant, hotel owner, and freighter. A subcontractor for the U.S. government, he supplied military troops in the area. The family shopped by mail-order catalogue from Bloomingdale's Department Store in New York City.

The mass production needed to satisfy eager customers depended on mass advertising, an enterprise still in its infancy in the 1880s. Yet some of the principles that would shape the future of this business were in place even at this early date. For instance, soon after the Civil War, the makers of Sozodont dentifrice (toothpaste) plastered the name of their product all over weekly religious magazines and more mainstream publications, such as *Harper's* and *Scribner's*. They labeled the natural landscape as well. Indeed, the word *Sozodont* on Maiden's Rock in Red Wing, Minnesota, was so large that steamboat passengers on the Mississippi River three miles away could plainly read it.

◉ Watch the Video

"Rural Free Delivery Mail" at
www.myhistorylab.com

Defending the New Industrial Order

By the late 1870s, as consumer culture expanded, intense conflict over fundamental issues all but evaporated from national politics. Although ethnic and cultural loyalties continued to inflame local and state elections, Republicans and Democrats at the national level disagreed about little except the tariff. Adhering to tradition, Republicans favored a higher tariff that would benefit domestic businesses by making imported goods more expensive. In contrast, Democrats argued that a higher tariff, and resulting higher prices for goods produced in the United States, would harm consumers. Members of the Republican party called themselves the Grand Army of the Republic; they "waved the **bloody shirt**"—that is, reminded voters that many of their Democratic opponents, especially those in the South, had supported secession a generation before. Still, the two major parties openly shared a similar goal: to win as many jobs as possible for their respective supporters. Politics served as a vehicle for patronage and favors rather than as a conduit for ideas and alternative visions of the nation's future.

Many politicians also shared a belief in the idea of *laissez-faire* (a French phrase meaning to leave alone, referring to the absence of government interference in the economy). Laissez-faire was actually a flexible concept, invoked to justify government indifference in some areas but government intervention in others. Indeed, politicians tended to favor laissez-faire in social matters more than in the economy. Thus, support for manufacturers and railroads in the form of tariff protection and land grants, for example, was justified. At the same time, however, Congress, the president, and the Supreme Court were reluctant to enact bold measures to redress the growing gap between rich and poor. In fact, certain clergy, business-people, and university professors sought to explain and defend the inequality between the captains of industry and the masses of ill-paid laborers. They argued that the system of industrial capitalism was desirable because it was "natural."

One view of this period was provided by Mark Twain (Samuel Clemens) and Charles Dudley Warner in *The Gilded Age* (1873). Their book satirized the trend toward corruption in public affairs and the wild financial speculation that produced both poverty and great wealth. The growth of large businesses that received economic and political support from government officials served to enrich employers, investors, and politicians at the expense of workers and farmers. The term *Gilded Age* became synonymous with the excess and extravagance on the part of politicians and businessmen alike during the last quarter of the nineteenth century.

What arguments were offered by defenders of the new industrial order, including politicians, business owners, and influential writers and thinkers?

The Contradictory Politics of Laissez-Faire

In 1880 the undistinguished President Rutherford B. Hayes chose not to run for office again. That summer the Republicans nominated James A. Garfield of Ohio, a former mule driver who had become a Civil War general. To counter the "bloody-shirt" effect, Democrats put forth their own former Union general: Winfield S. Hancock, who had been wounded at Gettysburg. Garfield won the popular vote by a narrow margin but overwhelmed Hancock in the electoral college.

Garfield's arrival in the White House set off a race for patronage jobs among loyal Republicans. Indeed, overwhelmed by office-seekers, the new president remarked, "My God! What is there in this place that a man should ever want to get into it?" Then on July 2, 1881, Charles J. Guiteau, who had unsuccessfully sought the position of U.S. consul in Paris, shot Garfield in a Washington, D.C., train station. Garfield languished for a few months, finally dying on September 19.

TABLE 16-1			
The Election of 1880			
Candidate	**Political Party**	**Popular Vote (%)**	**Electoral Vote**
James A. Garfield	Republican	48.5	214
Winfield S. Hancock	Democratic	48.1	155
James B. Weaver	Greenback-Labor	3.4	—

Vice President Chester A. Arthur, a former New York politician, assumed the reins of government. Arthur's administration supported certain forms of government intervention in society, or "social engineering." Arthur and others believed that laissez-faire policies had their limits; strong measures were needed to counter what they and other conservatives considered immoral personal behavior. In 1882 Congress passed the **Edmunds Act**. Targeting Mormons, the act outlawed polygamy (the practice of having more than one wife at a time), took the right to vote away from the law's offenders, and sent a five-member commission to Utah to oversee local elections.

That same year, Congress responded to pressure from West Coast European-American politicians, the San Francisco Workingmen's Party in particular, and approved the Chinese Exclusion Act. The act became the first piece of legislation to bar a particular national group from entering the United States. Most Chinese immigrants took jobs that native-born whites shunned. Moreover, unemployment among California white manufacturing workers in the 1870s was caused not by Chinese competitors, but by the flood of cheap eastern-made goods carried into the state by the transcontinental railroad. As eastern goods entered California, manufacturers in the West laid off workers and closed factories. The Chinese thus became scapegoats for groups hit hard by larger economic changes.

In 1883 the Supreme Court set back the cause of blacks' civil rights by declaring the Civil Rights Act of 1875 unconstitutional. The five cases involved in the Court's decision focused on exclusions of blacks from hotels, railroad cars, and theaters. The Court held that state governments could not discriminate on the basis of race but that private individuals could do so. This decision put an official stamp of approval on racist practices of employers, hotels, restaurants, and other providers of jobs and services.

Arthur surprised his critics by embracing the cause of **civil service reform**. This movement sought to inject professional standards into public service and rid the country of the worst excesses of the corrupt "spoils system," where political victors put loyal supporters into public jobs regardless of their qualifications. In response to Garfield's assassination by Guiteau, the disappointed patronage-seeker, Congress passed the **Pendleton Act** (1883). This measure established a merit system for federal job applicants and created the Civil Service Commission, which administered competitive examinations to candidates in certain classifications.

In 1884 Arthur fell ill (he would die shortly), and the Republicans nominated James G. Blaine of Maine as their candidate for the presidency. Blaine, who had benefited from corrupt deals in the past, offended the sensibilities of a group of reform-minded Republicans, who called themselves Mugwumps. (The term reportedly had its roots in an Indian word that meant "holier than thou.") As a result, Blaine was bested in the national election by the former mayor of Buffalo, Grover Cleveland, who became the first Democratic president in 28 years.

TABLE 16-2			
The Election of 1884			
Candidate	Political Party	Popular Vote (%)	Electoral Vote
Grover Cleveland	Democratic	48.5	219
James G. Blaine	Republican	48.2	182

Throughout the 1880s, Congress and the chief executive applied the laissez-faire principle selectively—for example, to the status of Indians. Like other critics of federal Indian policy, writer Helen Hunt Jackson in her 1881 book *A Century of Dishonor* called for applying the "protection of the law to the Indian's rights of property." Moved to act, Congress passed the Dawes General Allotment (Severalty) Act in 1887. The new act was intended to improve the economic condition of Indians by eliminating common ownership of tribal lands in favor of a system of private property. The law distributed plots of land to individual Indians who renounced traditional customs. The law also encouraged these landowners to become sedentary farmers and to adopt "other habits of civilized life." In the end, however, the act amounted to little more than a land-grab on the part of whites; between 1887 and 1900, Indian-held lands decreased from 138 million acres to 78 million acres.

By the 1880s, local citizens, through the Grange and their elected public officials, were calling for the states to restrict the monopolistic practices of the railroads, which routinely gave shipping discounts to large corporations. Nevertheless, in *Wabash v. Illinois* (1886), the Supreme Court invalidated a state law regulating railroads, ruling that only Congress, and not the states, could control interstate transportation. The next year Congress passed the Interstate Commerce Act of 1887. This legislation mandated that the railroads charge all shippers the same rates and refrain from giving rebates to their largest customers. The act also established the Interstate Commerce Commission to oversee and stabilize the railroad industry. Congress thus acknowledged that the public interest demanded some form of business regulation, although enforcement of the act was less than vigorous.

Cleveland invoked laissez-faire principles in 1887 when he vetoed legislation that would have provided seeds for hard-pressed farmers in Texas. As the president put it, "Though the people support the government, the government should not support the people." Cleveland also favored lower tariff rates, but most Americans favored government protection of domestic manufacturing in the form of higher tariffs. The Republicans exploited Cleveland's unpopular views on this issue in the 1888 campaign, nominating Benjamin Harrison, grandson of President William Henry ("Tippecanoe") Harrison. The younger Harrison defeated his rival in the electoral college but not in the popular vote.

The principle of government laissez-faire was of little use in addressing a central paradox of the late nineteenth century: the free enterprise system was being undermined by the very forms of business organization it had spawned and nourished. Trusts and combinations were inherently hostile to competition. In 1890 Congress passed a piece of landmark legislation, the **Sherman Anti-Trust Act**, designed to outlaw trusts and large business combinations of all kinds.

> *Read the Document*
> *Interstate Commerce Act* at **www.myhistorylab.com**

TABLE 16-3

The Election of 1888

Candidate	Political Party	Popular Vote (%)	Electoral Vote
Benjamin Harrison	Republican	47.9	233
Grover Cleveland	Democratic	48.6	168
Clinton B. Fisk	Prohibition	2.2	—
Anson J. Streeter	Union Labor	1.3	—

Social Darwinism and the "Natural" State of Society

In the late nineteenth century, human-made devices and engineering feats helped create a new social order, one marked by a few very wealthy industrialists, a growing middle class, and an increasingly diverse workforce of ill-paid field and factory hands. Brazenly borrowing from the theories of Charles Darwin, a British naturalist who had pioneered the study of evolution, some prominent clergy, businesspeople, journalists, and university professors sought to defend this new order as God-ordained or "natural." These observers drew parallels between Darwin's theory of "survival of the fittest" and the workings of modern society. (In his book *The Origin of Species*, Darwin had discussed the study of animals, not people or societies.) In the United States, Social Darwinists warned that "unnatural" forms of intervention—specifically, labor unions or social welfare legislation—were misguided, dangerous, and ultimately doomed to failure. In essence, Social Darwinists distorted a compelling scientific theory, misusing it to justify exploitation of the poor and laboring classes.

The ideology of **Social Darwinism** evolved in response to class conflict and other forms of social turbulence in the 1870s and 1880s. Famed Brooklyn minister Henry Ward Beecher cited what he called "the great laws of political economy" to preach the virtues of poverty ("it was fit that man should eat the bread of affliction") and the evils of labor unions. Beecher and like-minded thinkers agreed that the government had the right and the obligation to

> *Read the Document*
> *Herbert Spencer, Social Darwinism (1857)* at **www.myhistorylab.com**

INTERPRETING HISTORY

Andrew Carnegie and the "Gospel of Wealth"

In an article titled "Wealth," published in the North American Review in 1889, steel manufacturer Andrew Carnegie defended the amassing of large fortunes on the part of a few. He hailed this trend as a sign of progress.

The conditions of human life have not only been changed, but revolutionized, within the past few hundred years. In the former days there was little difference between the dwelling, dress, food, and environment of the chief and those of his retainers. The Indians are to-day where civilized man then was. When visiting the Sioux, I was led to the wigwam of the chief. It was just like the others in external appearance, and even within the difference was trifling between it and those of the poorest of his braves. The contrast between the palace of the millionaire and the cottage of the laborer with us to-day measures the change which has come with civilization.

This change, however, is not to be deplored, but welcomed as highly beneficial. It is well, nay, essential for the progress of the race, that the houses of some should be homes for all that is highest and best in literature and the arts, and for all the refinements of civilization, rather than that none should be so. Much better this great irregularity than universal squalor. . . . Whether the change be for good or ill, it is upon us, beyond our power to alter, and therefore

This *Judge* cartoon depicts Andrew Carnegie dispersing his fortune. Many of his donations were used for the establishment of public libraries, a worthy cause according to Carnegie's "gospel of wealth."

to be accepted and made the best of. It is a waste of time to criticize the inevitable.

Carnegie believed that wealthy people had the responsibility to give away their money before they died, although he had distinct ideas about to whom—or to what—such money should be given. He elaborated on what came to be called the "gospel of wealth":

There remains, then, only one mode of using great fortunes; but in this we have the true antidote for the temporary unequal distribution of wealth, the reconciliation of the rich and the poor—a reign of harmony—another ideal, differing indeed, from that of the Communist

in requiring only the further evolution of existing conditions, not the total overthrow of our civilization. . . . Under its sway we shall have an ideal state, in which the surplus wealth of the few will become, in the best sense, the property of the many, because it is administered for the common good, and this wealth, passing through the hands of the few, can be made a much more potent force for the elevation of our race than if it had been distributed in small sums to the people themselves. Even the poorest can be made to see this, and to agree that the great sums gathered by some of their fellow-citizens and spent for public purposes, from which the masses reap the principal benefit, are more valuable to them than if scattered through the course of many years in trifling amounts.

In 1901 Carnegie sold his steel company to banker J. P. Morgan for $480 million. By the time of his death, Carnegie had given away an estimated $350 million to a variety of causes and institutions.

Questions

1. How does Carnegie link extremes of wealth and poverty with progress?
2. Why did Carnegie focus his philanthropic energies on building public libraries?
3. Why would Carnegie have rejected as impractical and unreasonable the argument that he should have paid his workers higher wages rather than distributing his profits to charity?

Source: Andrew Carnegie, "Wealth," *North American Review* (1889).

come to the rescue of private companies threatened by angry workers or consumers. These observers also made a distinction between public subsidies to railroads and tariff protection for domestic manufacturers on one hand and public intervention on behalf of workers on the other.

Yale sociologist William Graham Sumner declared that society was like a living organism. For the species to remain healthy, individuals must prosper or decline according to their inherent characteristics. "Society, therefore, does not need any care or supervision," Sumner wrote in his 1883 treatise *What the Social Classes Owe to Each Other*. These views rationalized not only the hierarchies of the workplace but also the triumph of "Anglo Saxons" on the North American continent and beyond. Editors of the *New York Times* interpreted Darwin's ideas as suggesting that "the red man will be driven out, and the white man will take possession. This is not justice, but it is destiny." In his book *Our Country* (1885), the Reverend Josiah Strong also drew on the ideas of Social Darwinism to claim that just as the fittest plants and animals endure in the natural kingdom, so "civilized" whites would eventually displace "barbarous," dark-skinned peoples, whether on the High Plains of South Dakota or on the savannas of Africa.

Not all Americans studied or debated the theories of Charles Darwin, of course. Nevertheless, middle-class opinion-makers, many of them Victorian Protestants, believed that their own religious and cultural values remained superior to those of other groups of people, at home and abroad. The United States was becoming increasingly diverse in both economic and ethnic terms. At the same time, white, prosperous, native-born Protestants contended that they set the standards for the rest of the nation. These standards revolved around the middle-class domestic ideal, with its rigidly proscribed gender roles, devotion to personal achievement (for men at least), and commitment to moral suasion (that is, regulating a person's behavior by appealing to his or her conscience). Agents of the Victorian middle class included schoolteachers, clergy, magazine editors, business leaders, and other well-educated people able and willing to influence the beliefs and behavior of others.

CONCLUSION

Some historians suggest that the great captains of industry were the chief representatives of widely held values in late-nineteenth-century America. Men such as Carnegie and Rockefeller had the vision and personal ambition necessary to build large corporate enterprises. They became fabulously wealthy by providing the United States with the ingredients necessary to an economic revolution: steel, oil, and other materials. Their ideology of unbridled individualism encouraged many people to aspire to entrepreneurial independence: the tailor's hope that he would someday own his own store, the waiter's dream of opening his own restaurant. The explosion of economic activity during this period—a second American industrial revolution—widened the middle class and lent credence to the notion of widespread upward mobility, modest though it was in most cases.

Nevertheless, a case can be made that engineers were the true representatives of the age. As designers of railroad routes, gravity-defying skyscrapers, and new systems of shop-floor management, they oversaw the technical aspects of economic growth and development. Engineers melded science with mass production to yield a form of capitalism that thrived on consumers' deepest desires and anxieties. In the process, a new, complex national culture emerged.

This culture valued innovation, newness, fashion, change, and sensory stimulation. Advertisers sought to convince consumers that they should buy products that were up to date. Customers all over the country desired to experience thrilling and novel theatrical spectacles and athletic contests. "Desires" replaced more traditional "needs" when Americans of all ages contemplated buying clothes and household furnishings. Yet this culture also embraced impulses that were conservative, promoting the idea that white, Protestant, native-born Americans set the standard against which other Americans were judged, and often found wanting. Still, many native-born Americans and immigrants to the United States found this vital consumer culture enormously appealing.

At the same time, the effort to homogenize and standardize American cultural impulses was not without complications. Throughout the nation, various groups rejected standardization in favor of local tradition or new forms of collective action. Thus, politicians and the Social Darwinists were forced to defend their outlook on life. Some of their critics advanced the idea that society was not a living organism at all. Rather, it was like a machine, a creation of people who had the ability—and the duty—to repair or adjust it. Around the country, in fact, the standardizers met with stiff resistance.

For Review

√●─Study and Review at www.myhistorylab.com

1. In assembling large industrial workforces, what were the priorities of business managers? How did the drive for "efficiency" shape certain workplaces?

2. What were the effects of mechanical and technological innovations on midwestern agricultural laborers and steel workers? For these laborers, what was the price of "progress"?

3. What did circuses, baseball games, department stores, and amusement parks have in common in the late 1800s?

4. Contrast life on a western farm or a southern plantation to life in Chicago, New York, or San Francisco in 1890. Why did so many rural people, especially young people, move to the city?

Chronology: 1877–1889

1877 All federal troops withdrawn from the South, ending Reconstruction.
"Great Uprising" of railroad employees and other workers.

1878 Thomas Edison patents the phonograph.
San Francisco Workingmen's party stages anti-Chinese protests.

1879 First telephone line connects two American cities (Boston and Lowell, Massachusetts).

1880 New York City streets lit by electricity.
James A. Garfield elected president.

1881 Charles Guiteau assassinates President Garfield.

1882 Standard Oil Trust is created.
Chinese Exclusion Act.

1883 Pendleton Act (civil service reform).

1884 Grover Cleveland elected president.

1887 Interstate Commerce Act creates Interstate Commerce Commission.
Dawes Act.

1889 First All-American football team, consisting of players from Yale, Harvard, and Princeton.

Key Terms

Anti-semitism Prejudice against Jews. p. 395

"Bloody shirt" A partisan rallying cry used to stir up or revive sectional or party animosity after the American Civil War; for example, post–Civil War Republicans "waved the bloody shirt," associating some Democrats with a treasonous acceptance of secession during the war, while opponents had spilled their blood for the Union. p. 403

Chinese Exclusion Act Congressional legislation passed in 1882 to bar most Chinese workers from entering the United States. p. 395

Civil service reform Measures designed to eliminate the spoils system in government hiring, in favor of maintaining professional standards in public service. p. 404

Edmunds Act Congressional legislation passed in 1882 and aimed at Utah Mormons; it outlawed polygamy, stripped polygamists of the right to vote, and provided for a five-member commission to oversee Utah's elections. p. 404

Laissez-Faire a belief in little or no government interference in the economy. p. 403

Pendleton Act Congressional legislation passed in 1883; established a merit system for federal job applicants and created the Civil Service Commission, which administered competitive examinations to candidates in certain job classifications. p. 404

Sherman Anti-Trust Act Congressional legislation passed in 1890 outlawing trusts and large business combinations. p. 405

Social Darwinism A late-nineteenth-century variation on the theories of British naturalist Charles Darwin, promoting the idea that only the "fittest" individuals will, or deserve to, survive (i.e., the idea that society operates on principles of evolutionary biology). p. 405

Trust A combination of firms or corporations created for the purpose of reducing competition and controlling prices throughout an industry. p. 393

In the spring of 1889, men in San Miguel County, northern New Mexico Territory, armed themselves and donned masks. Mounting their horses, they rode out to attack those whom they considered their enemies. As members of a secret organization called *las Gorras Blancas* (the Whitecaps), they banded together in the dead of the night and destroyed the fences of local cattle ranchers, chopping the wooden posts to pieces and scattering the barbed wire. In some of their raids, the rebels shot and wounded ranchers. Over the next year and a half, *las Gorras Blancas* broadened their targets. They burned bridges, haystacks, and piles of lumber; cut telegraph wires; and took axes to electric light poles and to railroad ties belonging to the Atchison, Topeka, and Santa Fe Railroad. The membership of the group overlapped with that of the Knights of Labor, a national labor union that boasted 20 local assemblies in San Miguel County, east of Santa Fe. On the night of March 11, 1890, *las Gorras Blancas* nailed pieces of paper to the buildings of East Las Vegas, the largest town in the county. These pages, copies of the insurgents' "platform," declared, "Our purpose is to protect the rights and interests of the people in general; especially those of the helpless classes."

Who were these mysterious nightriders? They consisted of Hispanos—Spanish-speaking natives of the area. Their movement began when Juan Jose Herrera, together with his two brothers, Pablo and Nicanor, organized their neighbors in an effort to block European-American ranchers from fencing their land. Labeled *las masas de los hombres pobres* (the masses, the poor people) by a local newspaper, *las Gorras Blancas* were desperately, and violently, struggling to preserve a traditional way of life that was rapidly disappearing. Fenced lands prevented the area's Hispanic settlers from grazing their stock herds in the customary, open-range manner. The fence-cutters believed they were upholding American principles of justice and fair play.

Many Hispanos lived in adobe (baked-clay) dwellings in small river-valley villages surrounded by breathtaking mesas, ponderosa pine forests, and high dry plains. In addition to raising chickens and grazing sheep, families grew chiles, pinto beans, squash, and wheat. Together, villagers relied on the common lands that had come down to them from their ancestors— land originally bestowed through grants from Spain and then Mexico. After the Civil War, European-American interlopers—sheep and cattle ranchers, lawyers, speculators, commercial lumberers, and the railroads—began to encroach on these common lands. Through local courts, the newcomers installed a system of private property that granted exclusive ownership

17

Challenges to Government and Corporate Power, 1877–1890

■ **By 1889 Santa Fe had seen several centuries of cultural conflict.**

to single individuals. It was these groups, with their fences and their laws governing land title registration, that *las Gorras Blancas* targeted.

Las Gorras Blancas had only mixed success. They managed to discourage new European Americans from settling in the area, and they prevented the railroads from buying more rail ties in northern New Mexico. Yet the nightriders could not stem the tide of land loss throughout the Southwest. The Court of Private Land Claims, established in 1891 by the U.S. government, resolved land disputes between Hispanic and European-American claimants. Of the more than 35 million acres of land in dispute in the early 1890s, Hispanic claimants received title to little more than 2 million acres—barely one-twentieth of the land they had held in common.

Las Gorras Blancas represented a unique response to local conditions. But it was also part of a growing, nationwide movement against the standards imposed by industrialization and capitalism. Around the country, a wide variety of individuals and organizations emerged in the late 1870s and the 1880s to challenge employers, landlords, and military and government officials. Members of these latter groups responded with a challenge of their own: business, they proclaimed, must be allowed to develop fully and freely without "unnatural" intervention in the form of regulatory legislation or grassroots rebellions such as that of *las Gorras Blancas*.

It is difficult to generalize about those who contested the emerging order. Even their own names could be misleading. In the early 1890s, another group called "white caps," this one in Mississippi, consisted of whites who terrorized black landowners and mill workers. And although the Knights of Labor was a national union, it shaped its program in accordance with local issues. In San Miguel County, for instance, the issue was land—who controlled it and under what conditions. In Washington, D.C., the Knights' concern was the welfare of workers in the building trades. The Richmond, Virginia, Knights pioneered interracial organizing, living up to the group's motto, "An injury to one is an injury to all." In contrast, the San Francisco Knights spearheaded the move to bar Chinese laborers from the United States and to limit job opportunities for those who remained. Indeed, groups that challenged the authority of government and large business interests often disagreed among themselves about goals and strategies for change.

> *Around the country, a wide variety of individuals and organizations emerged in the late 1870s and the 1880s to challenge employers, landlords, and military and government officials.*

Resistance to Legal and Military Authority

> **?**
> *What were the various protest strategies used by different groups of people who faced discrimination, and at times violence, from employers, government officials, vigilantes, and the U.S. military?*

America's march toward national economic centralization and integration was not steady. On the battlefield and in the courts, European Americans pressed their advantage, but these efforts met with stiff resistance from a variety of aggrieved groups. Members of these groups rightly believed they had much to lose from so-called progress. European Americans repeatedly used the notion of "racial" difference as a justification for depriving darker-skinned peoples of their claims to land, jobs, and education. For example, California lawmakers approved legislation that discriminated against the Chinese as workers and as parents of school-aged children. In an effort to seek redress, some Chinese took their claims to court.

In a similar vein, prejudice against African Americans assumed the form of discriminatory legislation and random violence. Blacks chafed under restrictions intended to bar them from good jobs and from associating with white people on an equal basis. Varieties of black resistance to white authority included migration out of the South to the West, creation of community institutions, and violent retaliation.

For their part, during the late 1880s, the Plains Indians responded to encroaching railroads, settlers, and military regiments by embracing a movement of spiritual regeneration. On the Plains, whites, and especially U.S. military officers, perceived this movement as more dangerous than an armed uprising, and they reacted accordingly.

Chinese Lawsuits in California

Throughout California, unemployed whites agitated for the violent expulsion of Chinese from jobs. (Most of these immigrants received two-thirds the wages of their white counterparts for the same work.) Opposition to the Chinese hardened in the 1880s. In San Francisco, the Knights of Labor and the Workingmen's Party of California helped to engineer the passage of the Chinese Exclusion Act, approved by Congress in 1882. This measure denied any additional Chinese laborers entry into the country while allowing some Chinese merchants and students to immigrate. In railroad towns and mining camps, vigilantes looted and burned Chinese communities, in some cases murdering or expelling their inhabitants. In 1885 in Rock Springs, Wyoming, white workers massacred 28 Chinese and drove hundreds out of town in the wake of an announcement by Union Pacific officials that the railroad would begin hiring the lower-paid immigrants. Cheered on by others, a mob burned the Chinese section of town to the ground.

Whites held that the Chinese, with their distinctive customs, would never fit into American life. Nevertheless, early on the Chinese demonstrated an understanding and appreciation of American political and legal processes. Beginning in Gold Rush days, Chinese immigrants had taken their grievances to court. In 1862 in San Francisco, Ling Sing protested the $2.50 personal tax levied on Chinese miners. The California Supreme Court

•••–Read the Document
Farwell, The Chinese at Home and Abroad at **www.myhistorylab.com**

■ In the West, Chinese mining companies used water-management techniques based on traditional Chinese machinery such as the waterwheel. This photo shows a Chinese river-mining operation in Siskiyou, California, c. 1890. Chinese workers also constructed flumes, dams, canals, tunnels, and pumps to drain areas efficiently.

● ● ● ┌Read the **Document**

Yick Wo v. Hopkins at
www.myhistorylab.com

agreed (in *Ling Sing v. Washburn*) that the group could not be singled out for special taxes. In the 1870s, Chinese merchants used the provisions of the Civil Rights Act to challenge state and local laws that forbade them from holding certain jobs, living in white neighborhoods, and testifying in court.

In San Francisco in 1885, laundry operator Yick Wo was convicted under an 1880 municipal law prohibiting the construction of wooden laundries without a license. A native of China, Yick Wo had arrived in the United States in 1861. By the time of his arrest, he had operated a legal laundry for 22 years. When he applied for a license, the board of supervisors turned him down, just as the board had denied licenses to all Chinese laundry operators who applied. In 1885 his lawyers petitioned the California Supreme Court, which upheld Yick Wo's arrest. The lawyers continued their appeal to the U.S. Supreme Court, maintaining that the board of supervisors intended to bar Chinese from independent laundry work altogether. In *Yick Wo v. Hopkins* (1886), the Supreme Court reversed the state court's decision. The higher court held that the San Francisco laundry-licensing board had engaged in the discriminatory *application* of a law that on the surface was nondiscriminatory.

Still, many cases challenging discriminatory laws never made it to the nation's highest court. And state and local courts in general often refused to acknowledge that Chinese immigrants had any civil rights at all. (Chinese immigrants were not granted citizenship until World War II, although their children born in this country qualified as citizens.) In 1885 the California Supreme Court heard the case *Tape v. Hurley*, brought by Joseph and Mary Tape on behalf of their daughter Mamie. Joseph Tape was a Chinese immigrant with some standing in the San Francisco Chinese community. Mary Tape had been raised in a Shanghai orphanage and had come to the United States with missionaries when she was 11 years old. She grew up to speak English fluently and dressed as a European American. Their daughter Mamie was quite westernized as well.

Even so, Mamie Tape was barred from the city's public school system. The school board claimed that Mamie's presence in the classroom would be "very mentally and morally detrimental" to her classmates. The Tapes sued the city and won, but the school board retaliated by creating a separate school for children of Asian descent within Chinatown. Mary Tape wrote an angry letter to the board: "Dear Sirs, Will you please to tell me! Is it a disgrace to be Born a Chinese? Didn't God make us all!!! What right! have you to bar my children out of the school?" In the end, the Tapes decided to enroll their two children in the segregated school. Yet their legal protest kept alive the ideal of equality under the law.

Blacks in the "New South"

Similar problems plagued African Americans in what Atlanta journalist Henry Grady hailed as the "New South." The former Confederate states, he claimed, were now forward looking, prepared to embrace industrialization and promote the reconciliation of blacks and whites. According to the journalist, it was time for the South to march forward and join with a larger, modernizing America.

Grady's speech about the "New South" provided a label that stuck. Yet he doubtless spoke too soon and in terms too grandiose. True, he could point with pride to some dramatic industrial developments in the South. Soon after James Bonsack invented a cigarette-rolling machine in 1880, James Buchanan Duke pioneered the production of machine-made cigarettes. In 1884, Duke's Durham, North Carolina, company was selling 400,000 of them each day. The southern textile labor force more than doubled between 1880 and 1890. And by the mid-1880s, with the backing of the Tennessee Coal, Iron, and Railway Company, the city of Birmingham, Alabama, specialized in pig iron production.

Factory and professional work in towns and cities offered new opportunities in the South as industry developed. However, these jobs were dominated by white men. Low-paid heavy labor, primarily in rural areas, continued to be the primary source of work for black men.

■ Some Chinese made a prosperous life for themselves in the United States. This photo shows Ah Sue, her husband, Ah Quin, and their twelve children. Ah Sue found refuge in the San Francisco Chinese Mission Home in 1879. Two years later she and Ah Quin celebrated their Christian wedding in the Mission Home. Ah Quin rose from the position of cook to become a successful railroad contractor and merchant in San Diego.

The hardest and lowest-paid jobs, such as digging ore out of a hill in northern Alabama or constructing a railroad through the swamps of Florida, often went to convicts whom private employers had leased from the state. Most of these "convict lease" workers were black men who had been arrested on minor charges and then bound out when they could not pay their fines or court costs. In Mississippi a black man could be picked up for "some trifling misdemeanor," in the words of one observer, fined $500, and compelled to work off the fine (at a rate of 5 cents a day) for a local planter. With an almost unlimited supply of such workers, employers had little incentive to ease the brutal living and working conditions endured by these convicts.

Patterns of migration within and outside the South reveal blacks' efforts to resist discrimination. Some blacks fled the countryside and settled in southern cities, where good jobs were still limited but personal freedom was greater. Gradually, a new black elite arose. These physicians, lawyers, insurance agents, and undertakers reached out to an exclusively black clientele. They also nourished a sense of community. Black men and women continued to sustain their own institutions, such as schools, lodges, benevolent societies, burial organizations, and churches.

Despite Henry Grady's pronouncements, clearly the South had not abandoned its historical legacy of white supremacist ideologies. In fact, in the late 1880s, white Democrats feared the assertiveness of the new black elite. According to whites, this generation of men and women born as free persons and not as slaves must be "put in their place," quite literally. As a result, new state and local laws mandated separate water fountains for blacks and whites, restricted blacks to separate railroad cars and other forms of public transportation, and excluded them altogether from city parks and other public spaces. Long-standing customs barring black people from white-owned theaters, restaurants, and hotels now carried the weight of law. There were two separate school systems, one white and well funded, one black and starved of cash. Legal discrimination against blacks came to be called **Jim Crow**, a set of laws akin to twentieth-century South Africa's system of apartheid mandating the strict segregation (in public) of groups labeled according to their heritage or the color of their skin.

Black leaders throughout the country tried to keep a national spotlight on the legal and violent manifestations of the Jim Crow system. A rising tide of lynching engulfed the South, cresting in the 1890s, but white officials did little or nothing to halt it. Black men, women, and children were all vulnerable to the fury of the white lynch mob—on the most flimsy pretext. Blacks throughout the segregated South rightly feared that they would be targeted if they spoke out against lynching. Yet northern blacks did not hesitate to highlight the hypocrisy of the federal government, which turned a blind eye toward this practice. Frances Ellen Watkins Harper, an educator and writer living in Philadelphia, issued the following challenge to an audience of white club women: "A government which has the power to tax a man in peace, draft him in war, should have the power to defend his life in the hour of peril." Harper condemned "the government which can protect and defend its citizens from wrong and outrage and does not."

"Jim Crow" in the West

Racial segregation was not limited to the South. The U.S. military enforced its own set of Jim Crow regulations. In 1869 Congress created the 24th and 25th Infantries (Colored), composed of African-American soldiers. White officers were appointed to lead these segregated units. Consequently, black men who aspired to positions of military leadership found their way blocked. Some white officers, such as George Custer, refused to command black troops at all.

Military officials assigned black soldiers to the West, where they became known as buffalo soldiers. (The origins of the term are unclear. It may refer to the buffalo robes worn by many of the soldiers or to Plains Indians' respect for the black men's skills on horseback.) Many of these men were proud to wear a U.S. soldier's uniform, an emblem of their newly won citizenship rights. They helped to construct new roads and forts, protect wagon trains of settlers, and patrol the border between the United States and Mexico. They were an integral part of campaigns to subdue the Cheyenne, Comanche, Sioux, Ute, Kiowa, and Apache. They were among the soldiers deployed to quash strikes among workers (silver miners in Idaho, for example) and to fight forest fires in the Northwest.

■ Among the "buffalo soldiers" who served with the U.S. military were these Seminole scouts. The Seminole traced their history to the eighteenth century, when Creek Indians and runaway slaves of African descent established communities together in Florida. After the Seminole Wars (1818–1858), many Seminole were relocated to Indian Territory (present-day Oklahoma). Some fled to Mexico before the Civil War. In 1870 they were recruited by U.S. Army officers to serve as scouts. Their unit was disbanded 11 years later. Discriminatory policies of the military caused some to return to Mexico.

Often the buffalo soldiers encountered hostility from local townspeople, who resented their patronage of local establishments. In 1881 black Tenth Cavalry troops stationed at Fort Concho near San Angelo, Texas, reacted angrily when a local white man killed a black soldier in a saloon. Another soldier had died at the hands of a local white within the previous two weeks. In the absence of justice for the murderers, the soldiers blanketed San Angelo with handbills. Signed "U.S. soldiers," the message read, "If we do not receive justice and fair play . . . someone will suffer, if not the guilty, the innocent. It has gone far enough." When some of the soldiers attacked one of the men they believed guilty, the Texas Rangers entered the town to restore order. The army transferred the black companies out of the area and disciplined the leaders of the protest.

Once they were mustered out of the army, some black soldiers decided to settle permanently in the West. There they joined thousands of black migrants who were fleeing the Jim Crow South. In the late 1870s, 20,000 blacks from Tennessee, Mississippi, and Louisiana, called "Exodusters," migrated into western Kansas. The migrants cited the South's convict lease system, poor schools, and pervasive violence and intimidation as reasons for their flight. Some of these migrants established all-black towns in Kansas, Colorado, Nebraska, and New Mexico. Though generally small and poor, such towns provided places for blacks to live in safety and on their own terms.

The Ghost Dance on the High Plains

Their lands and way of life threatened by whites, western Indians sought desperately to revitalize their culture and protect themselves. In 1889 an Indian named Wovoka offered the Plains Indians a mystical vision of the future, a vision that promised a return to the beloved past. A leader of the Paiute in Nevada, Wovoka preached what came to be called the Ghost Dance, part religion and part resistance movement. In 1889 a solar eclipse occurred while Wovoka was wracked by fever, and he claimed that the conjunction of the two events enabled him to glimpse the afterworld. The Indians could usher in a new day of peace, Wovoka proclaimed, and this new day would be a time free of disease and armed conflict. The buffalo would return, he promised, and the Indian men and women who had died would come back to replenish depleted villages.

Many of the Indians who performed the Ghost Dance fell into a trance-like state, bringing inspiration to impoverished and disheartened reservation communities. However, as the ritual spread across the Plains, U.S. military officials grew anxious. In November 1890, E. B. Reynolds, a Special U.S. Indian Agent, described to his superiors in Washington the strange, seemingly dangerous behavior that had gripped the Indians on Pine Ridge Reservation in South Dakota: "The religious excitement aggravated by almost starvation is bearing fruits in this state of insubordination; Indians say they had better die fighting than to die a slow death of starvation, and as the new religion promises their return to earth, at the coming of the millennium, they have no fear of death."

As tensions between whites and Indians mounted, Sitting Bull emerged as a spiritual and political leader. After leading his followers into Canada, Sitting Bull returned to the United States in 1881 and later performed briefly with Buffalo Bill Cody in the Wild West show. He surrendered at Fort Buford, Dakota Territory, where he was held prisoner for two years. His brief stint as a performer in Buffalo Bill Cody's "Wild West" show left him disgusted with the ways of white people.

Sitting Bull offered a pointed critique of the sedentary, materialistic way of life promoted by whites:

White men like to dig in the ground for their food. My people prefer to hunt buffalo as their fathers did. White men like to stay in one place. My people want to move their tepees here and there to different hunting grounds. The life of white men is slavery. They are prisoners in towns or farms. The life my people want is a life of freedom. I have seen nothing that a white man has, houses or railways or clothing or food, that is as good as the right to move in open country, and live in our own fashion.

Sitting Bull rejected white notions of "progress" in favor of his people's traditions.

Watch the Video
Sioux Ghost Dance at
www.myhistorylab.com

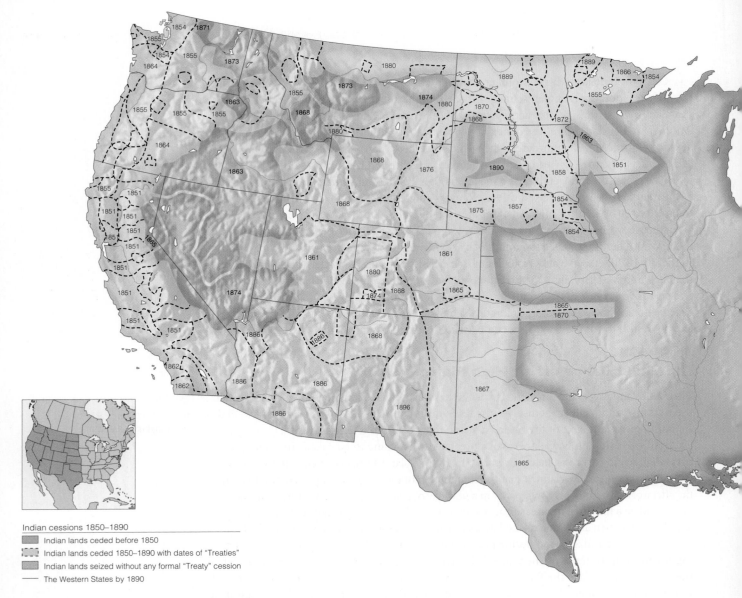

Indian cessions 1850–1890

▨ Indian lands ceded before 1850

┊┊┊ Indian lands ceded 1850–1890 with dates of "Treaties"

▨ Indian lands seized without any formal "Treaty" cession

── The Western States by 1890

■ **M A P   1 7 . 1**

INDIAN LANDS LOST, 1850–1890

Between 1850 and 1890, many "treaties" signed by Indian groups and the U.S. government provided that Indians turn over land in exchange for cash payments. Yet U.S. military forces seized a large portion of western Indian lands by force, without signing any treaty agreements at all. By 1890 many Indians lived on reservations, apart from European American society.

•••[Read the **Document**

Accounts of the Wounded Knee Massacre at **www.myhistorylab.com**

In mid-December 1890, military officials ordered Indian police to arrest Sitting Bull at his cabin on the Standing Rock Reservation in South Dakota. Alarmed by what they perceived as rising Indian militancy, white settlers in Nebraska and South Dakota pressured the government to rid the area of the "savages . . . armed to the teeth," men who were "traitors, anarchists, and assassins." While arresting Sitting Bull, his Indian captors killed him.

A week later, on December 28 and 29, soldiers of the Seventh Cavalry under Colonel James Forsyth attacked Indians at Wounded Knee Creek, South Dakota. Estimates of the number of Indians killed range from 150 to 250. More than 60 women and children were among those slain as they fled the oncoming troops. The massacre at Wounded Knee proved the last major violent encounter between Plains Indians and U.S. cavalry forces. By this time, many Indians throughout the Midwest lived on reservations and engaged in farming. Government agents, eager to create independent farmers, instructed Indian men in the use of the plow. But plowing became a collective effort, as bands would work together until their task was done. Thus some Indian groups attempted to maintain customs of collective endeavor in opposition to the European Americans' glorification of ambition and individualism.

Nevertheless, Chinese immigrants, southern African Americans, and Plains Indians were not the only groups to feel aggrieved at the hands of private and public interests. In some cases, native-born white American men and women also protested against what they perceived to be unfair policies and practices on the part of business and the federal government.

Revolt in the Workplace

During the late nineteenth century, workers launched different kinds of challenges against the system of industrial capitalism, which, many charged, enriched a few industrialists and bankers at the expense of the vast majority of laboring people. Workers joined together in unions, and in many cases they fought the violence of private company security forces with violence of their own. Some men and women destroyed the machinery that threatened to replace them in the workplace. By the early 1890s, critics of the new industrial and agribusiness order—a system driven by technological innovation—had come together in the form of a new political group, the People's party, or **Populists**. This organization aimed to bring together urban and rural, male and female, agricultural and industrial workers to protest the hardships suffered by laborers of all kinds and to demand that the federal government take strong action in rectifying social ills.

What technological and structural changes in the workplace prompted farmers and workers to organize between 1877 and 1890?

Nevertheless, in workplace conflicts, the lines were not always strictly drawn between employees and employers. For example, the late-nineteenth-century laboring classes never achieved the level of unity called for by the Populists. White workers often expressed intense hostility toward their African American and Chinese counterparts. Within small towns, shopkeepers and landlords at times showed solidarity with striking workers; in these cases, community ties were stronger than class differences. Also, despite their critique of big business, workers often embraced the emerging consumer culture. In fact, many of them fought for shorter work days and higher wages so that they could enjoy their share of the material blessings of American life—in department stores, movie theaters, and amusement parks. In the end, Populism was primarily a rural movement composed of small farmers, sharecroppers, and wage hands.

Trouble on the Farm

In the late summer of 1878, the combined effects of the recent national economic depression and the loss of jobs to labor-saving technology catalyzed a rash of machine breaking throughout rural Ohio. In the Midwest, displaced farmhands burned the reapers, mowers, and threshers of their former employers. Some wealthy farmers responded by abandoning their machinery and rehiring their farmhands. Technology, one noted, "ought to be dispensed with in times like these." By contrast, critics charged the machine-breakers with "short-sighted madness." The protests revealed that even family farming had become a business. Now farmers needed to secure bank loans, invest in new machinery, and worry about the price of crops in the world market. These changes had profoundly altered labor relations between farm workers and farmers and between farmers and their creditors.

On the Northern Plains, farmers endured extremes of weather and the anxiety of uncertain harvests. In the mid-1880s, the plight of Plains farmers worsened when a series of natural disasters highlighted their vulnerability to the elements. Drought and declining wheat prices drove half the population of western Kansas and Nebraska back east to Iowa and Illinois between 1888 and 1892. Meanwhile, the bitterly cold winter of 1886–1887 decimated cattle herds throughout the region.

These problems contributed to a radical turn in farmers' politics. In the 1880s, a national movement emerged and tapped into a wellspring of anger and discontent in farming regions

■ A Nebraska farm family poses proudly with their new windmill, c. 1890. Such devices powered water pumps that reached deep into the earth. Though expensive, windmills were necessities for drought-stricken farmers on the Plains, especially during the harsh years of the mid-1880s to the mid-1890s.

throughout the nation. The Southern Alliance in Louisiana, Texas, and Arkansas pressed for an expanded currency, taxation reform, and government ownership of transportation and communication lines. Its members tended to ally with the Democratic party. The Northern Alliance from the Plains states also focused on the expansion of the currency supply— specifically, the coinage of silver—but advocated the formation of a third political party to advance its interests. Both of these large regional groups found adherents in the mountain West. There, miners and farmers joined together to protest the monopolistic powers of the railroads, privately owned water companies, and silver mining interests. These monopolies drove up consumer prices and depressed workers' wages.

Most Alliance men and women farmed modest parcels of land. As small producers, they felt powerless to influence the businesspeople and politicians who affected their livelihoods and their life possibilities. Members of the Alliance also presented themselves as the last line of defense for the noble yeoman in the face of the corrupting influences of modern corporate capitalism. In rural Alabama, where the Farmers' Alliance had links with local schools and churches, the group's newspapers railed against the "filthy city," a "wicked place" of vice, crime, and dissipation. Farm folk thus distanced themselves from the "New South Creed," which promoted materialism and industrialization.

Although the Farmers' Alliance identified itself primarily with agricultural interests, it made some notable forays into coalition-building as well. In 1899, the northern and southern groups attempted to combine with the Colored Farmers' Alliance. Together, these groups claimed more than 4 million members. They also sought to join with the Knights of Labor and thus bring all members of the "producing classes" together. By representing the financial interests of all farmers and highlighting the vulnerabilities of debtors, the organization foreshadowed the wider national appeal of the Populist party in the 1890s.

Militancy in the Factories and Mines

The new economy wrought profound hardship on members of the urban laboring classes as well as on small farmers. Many industrial workers faced layoffs and wage cuts during the depressions of the 1870s and 1880s. The great railroad strikes of 1877 (see Chapter 16) fore-shadowed an era of bitter industrial conflict. Because no laws regulated private industry, employers could impose ten- to fifteen-hour workdays, six days a week. Industrial accidents were all too common, and some industries lacked safety precautions. Steelworkers labored in excessive heat, and miners and textile mill employees alike contracted respiratory diseases. With windows closed and machines speeded up, new forms of technology created new risks for workers. The Chicago meatpackers, who wielded gigantic cleavers in subfreezing lockers, and the California wheat harvesters, who operated complex mechanical binders and threshers, were among those confronting danger on the job.

In 1884, the Massachusetts Bureau of Statistics of Labor issued a report outlining the occupational hazards for working women in the city of Boston. In button-making establishments, female workers often got their fingers caught under punch and die machines. Employers provided a surgeon to dress an employee's wounds the first three times she was injured; thereafter, she had to pay for her own medical care. Women operated heavy power machinery in the garment industry and exposed themselves to dangerous chemicals and processing materials in paper-box making, fish packing, and candy manufacturing.

Some women workers, especially those who monopolized certain kinds of jobs, organized and struck for higher wages. Three thousand Atlanta washerwomen launched such an effort in 1881 but failed to get their demands met. Most women found it difficult to win the respect not only of employers but also of male unionists. Leonora Barry, an organizer for the Knights of Labor, sought to change that. Barry visited mills and factories around the country. At each stop, she highlighted women's unique difficulties and condemned the "selfishness of their brothers in toil" who resented women's intrusion into the workplace. Barry was reacting to men such as Edward O'Donnell, a prominent labor official who claimed that wage-earning women threatened the role of men as family breadwinners.

■ Mining was one of the most hazardous occupations in the United States. Below-surface miners worked with explosives and sophisticated kinds of machinery. As a result, the chances of explosions, cave-ins, rockslides, and fires increased. These conditions help to account for the labor militancy of miners throughout the country. This photo shows a mining operation at Marysville, near Helena, Montana, c. 1885.

See the **Map**

Organizing American Labor in the Late 19th Century at **www.myhistorylab.com**

For both men and women workers, the influx of 5.25 million new immigrants in the 1880s stiffened job competition at worksites throughout the country. To make matters worse, vast outlays of capital needed to mechanize and organize manufacturing plants placed pressure on employers to economize. Many of them did so by cutting wages. Like the family farmer who could no longer claim the status of the independent yeoman, industrial workers depended on employers and consumers for their physical well-being and very survival.

Not until 1935 would American workers have the right to organize and bargain collectively with their employers. Until then, laborers who saw strength in numbers and expressed an interest in a union could be summarily fired, blacklisted (their names circulated to other employers), and harassed by private security forces. The Pinkerton National Detective Agency, founded in 1850 by a Scottish immigrant named Allan Pinkerton, initially found eager clients among the railroads. The Pinkertons, as they were called, served as industrial spies and policemen during some of the most bitter and violent strikes of the late nineteenth century.

The Knights of Labor, a secret fraternal order founded in 1869, came under the leadership of Terence V. Powderly a decade later. With this Irish American at the helm (he was called Grand Master Workman), the labor union made impressive gains in the 1880s. In appealing to many different kinds of workers around the country, the Knights blended a critique of the late-nineteenth-century wage system with a belief in the dignity of labor and a call for collective action. According to the Knights, business monopolies and corrupt politicians everywhere shared a common interest in exploiting the labor of ordinary men and women. The Knights advocated a return to the time when workers controlled their own labor and received a just price for the products they made. "We declare an inevitable and irresistible conflict between the wage system of labor and republican system of government," the Knights proclaimed. By "republican system" the Knights meant a society governed by workers and small farmers.

Read the **Document**

Bellamy, from Looking Backward at **www.myhistorylab.com**

In condemning the concentration of wealth in the hands of a few, the Knights drew on the ideas of popular social critics of the day. In New York City, Henry George, an economist and land reformer, achieved national prominence with his book *Progress and Poverty* (1879), in which he advocated a single tax on property as a means of distributing wealth more equally. In his popular novel titled *Looking Backward* (1888), journalist-turned-novelist Edward Bellamy envisioned a "cooperative commonwealth" in the year 2000, a socialist paradise in which poverty and greed had disappeared and men and women of all classes enjoyed material comfort and harmonious relations with their neighbors.

Between 1885 and 1886, the Knights undertook the difficult task of organizing black workers. Many blacks remained suspicious of white-led unions, and for good reason. Historically, the white labor movement had conceived itself as a way to exclude black men and women from stable, well-paying jobs. Throughout the South, segregation was the norm within biracial unionism. Whites, whether New Orleans dockworkers, Birmingham District coal miners, or lumber workers in East Texas and Louisiana, insisted on separate locals from blacks. Yet African Americans did not necessarily acquiesce to this arrangement.

In 1886 workers around the country began to mobilize on behalf of the eight-hour day. "Eight hours to constitute a day's work" was their slogan. The issue had broad appeal, but the growing diversity of the labor force made unity difficult. In 1880, between 78 and 87 percent of all workers in San Francisco, St. Louis, Cleveland, New York, Detroit, Milwaukee, and Chicago were either immigrants or the children of immigrants. In many places, the laboring classes remained vulnerable to divisive social and cultural animosities. The diversity of ethnic groups, coupled with the fact that many newcomers from Europe adopted racist ideas to become "Americans," drove wedges between workers.

The Haymarket Bombing

The year 1886 marked the end of an era dominated by the Knights of Labor as the organization experienced the difficulties of overcoming its members' diverse crafts, racial loyalties,

INTERPRETING HISTORY

"Albert Parsons's Plea for Anarchy"

On August 10, 1886, the New York Herald published an essay by convicted Haymarket defendant Albert R. Parsons. In it, Parsons defends his views on anarchism. His theories on the inevitable clash between workers and capitalists echo the arguments of Karl Marx, the German political theorist. Marx predicted that the capitalist system would inevitably self-destruct and that the working classes would rise to rule the world.

Albert Parsons

So much is written and said nowadays about socialism or anarchism, that a few words on the subject from one who holds to these doctrines may be of interest to the readers of your great newspaper.

Anarchy is the perfection of personal liberty or self-government. It is the free play of nature's law. . . . It is the negation of force or the domination of man by man. In the place of the law maker it puts the law discoverer and for the driver, or dictator, or ruler, it gives free play to the natural leader. It leaves man free to be happy or miserable, to be rich or poor, to be mean or good. The natural law is self-operating, self-enacting, and cannot be repealed, amended or evaded without incurring a self-imposed penalty. . . .

The capitalist system originated in the forcible seizure of natural opportunities and rights by a few, and converting these things into special privileges, which have since become vested rights formally entrenched behind the bulwarks of statute law and government.

And what of the laborer who for twelve or more hours weaves, spins, bores, turns, builds, shovels, breaks stones, carries loads, and so on? Does his twelve hours weaving, spinning, boring, turning, building, shoveling, etc. represent the active expression or energy of his life? On the contrary, life begins for him exactly where this activity, this labor of his ceases—viz: at his meals, in his tenement house, in his bed. His twelve hours work represents for him as a weaver, builder, spinner, etc., only so much earnings as will furnish him his meals, clothes, and rent. . . . The wage slaves are "free" to compete with each other for the opportunity to serve capital and capitalists to compete with each other in monopolizing the laborer's products.

Parsons argues that it is only a matter of time before the capitalist system "will collapse, will fall of its own weight, and fall because of its own weakness." He asserts that the fall of capitalism will usher in a new era of socialism, a system in which all property is held in common and workers can govern themselves. He concludes:

To quarrel with socialism is silly and vain. To do so is to quarrel with history; to denounce the logic of events; to smother the aspirations of liberty. Mental freedom, political freedom, industrial freedom—do not these follow in the line of progress? Are they not the association of the inevitable?

Ten days after this essay was published, Albert Parsons and the other Haymarket defendants were found guilty and sentenced to be hanged. Four of them, including Parsons, were executed on November 11, 1887. The true identity of the bomb-thrower remains a mystery to this day.

Questions

1. What is the significance of Parsons's claim that the triumph of socialism is "inevitable" and "natural"?
2. What was Parsons's anarchist critique of capitalism?
3. Bring Parsons and Andrew Carnegie into conversation with each other about the "inevitable" future of the U.S. .
4. Why did many Americans identify anarchists with violence?

Source: New York Herald, August 30, 1886.

and political allegiances. Industrialists dug in their heels and, with the aid of hired detectives, took union leaders to court on charges of sabotage, assault, conspiracy, and murder.

On May 1, 1886, 350,000 workers in 11,562 business establishments went out on a one-day strike as part of the eight-hour workday movement. In Chicago, home to militant labor anarchists (men and women who opposed government authority of any kind), 40,000 workers participated in the strike. Among the Chicago leaders was Albert Parsons. A descendant of New England Puritans and a printer by trade, Parsons had lived in Waco, Texas, where he met his future wife, Lucia Gonzalez, an Afro-Latina (probably born a slave). In 1873 the Parsonses moved to Chicago to avoid Texas laws against "race mixing," which prohibited interracial marriage. There Albert joined the International Typographical Union, and Lucia took up dressmaking. They were counted among the most famous and feared radicals in the city.

On May 4, 1886, things took a bloody turn. Strikers called a rally in Chicago's Haymarket Square to protest the murder of two McCormick Reaper strikers the day before. During the rally, a bomb went off, killing a police officer and wounding seven others, who later died. Although the identity of the culprit was never discovered, eight **anarchists** (persons who denounce authority in all its forms), including Albert Parsons, were arrested, tried, and sentenced to death for conspiring to provoke violence in what came to be called the Haymarket bombing. Though Parsons and several of the others had not been present when the bomb exploded, he and three other detainees were hanged in November 1887.

The Haymarket hangings demoralized the labor movement nationwide. Now associated in the minds of the middle class with wild-eyed bomb throwers, the Knights saw their ranks plummet from 700,000 in 1886 to 100,000 by 1890. With the demise of the Knights of Labor, the American Federation of Labor (AFL) emerged to become the most powerful national labor movement. Samuel Gompers, an English immigrant cigarmaker, had founded the new group in 1886 partly in response to the Knights' attempts to usurp the Cigar Makers' International Union with a socialist-dominated local. The AFL garnered the allegiance of skilled trade workers (most of them white men) and promoted basic goals such as better wages and working conditions.

Yet the radical labor tradition persisted. Meeting in Paris in 1889, a congress of world socialist parties voted to set aside May 1, 1890, as a day of worldwide celebrations in support of labor and demonstrations in favor of the eight-hour workday. (May 1 became an international labor day, celebrated annually.) In the United States, the United Mine Workers (founded in 1890) and the American Railway Union (1893) followed the radical labor-organizing principles of the Knights of Labor long after the AFL attained its ascendancy.

Read the Document

Engel, Address by a Haymarket Anarchist at **www.myhistorylab.com**

Crosscurrents of Reform

How did social reformers differ from labor radicals in their assumptions about the need for, and the means of, social change?

In the 1880s, a young Danish-born journalist named Jacob Riis prowled New York's East Side slum district in search of stories for the New York *Tribune* and the Associated Press bureau. In this part of the city, more than 37,000 tenement buildings housed more than 1 million people in inhuman living conditions. In 1890 Riis published a collection of his own photographs, along with explanatory notes, under the title *How the Other Half Lives*. His book galvanized the public in support of slum clearance and housing codes. *How the Other Half Lives* is a powerful indictment of greedy landlords, indifferent city officials, and rapacious sweatshop owners.

During the last decades of the nineteenth century, reformers adopted a range of causes. Some, like Riis, focused on the plight of the urban poor. Others challenged the Indian reservation system, which, they charged, left Indians poor and dependent on the federal government. Settlement house workers aimed to improve the lives of immigrant families. Middle-class women sought to protect and empower women by aiding abused or vulnerable wives and mothers, promoting temperance in alcohol use, and supporting women's suffrage. Many reformers participated in a transatlantic community of ideas, learning about reform strategies and institutions from their European counterparts.

Although reformers professed to favor the full integration of various ethnic groups into American life, at times they could hardly help but look down on the people they aimed to help. (*How the Other Half Lives*, for all its sympathetic portrayals of the poor, reinforces negative ethnic stereotypes of many immigrants.) Some of the people whom reformers hoped to help rejected part of their benefactors' package of values—Protestantism, for example—while accepting forms of concrete aid, such as shelter from abusive husbands. Thus the history of late nineteenth-century reform reveals the value and goals of not just middle-class Americans but of a wide variety of other social groups as well.

"Street Arabs at Night," c. 1890. Museum of the City of New York, The Jacob A. Riis Collection, #123

■ Jacob Riis titled this photograph "Street Arabs in Sleeping Quarters [Areaway, Mulberry St.]". Riis's photos, collected in his book *How the Other Half Lives,* exposed the poverty and wretched living conditions endured by many immigrants in New York's Lower East Side. In certain cases, Riis carefully positioned his subjects before photographing them. It is doubtful that these little boys were sleeping while the photographer noisily set up his equipment a few feet away.

The Goal of Indian Assimilation

In the mid-nineteenth century, many European Americans, including government officials, believed that the reservation system was a much-needed reform to protect western Indians. Whites reasoned that reservation Indians would remain separate from the rest of American society, to the benefit of everyone. Indians could preserve their own culture, and they would remain safe from the attacks of both homesteaders and U.S. Army troops. By segregating this group, European Americans were free to settle on rich farmlands, mine for gold and silver, and take advantage of timber resources in the West.

By the 1870s, the harsh reality of the reservation system had prompted a group composed of both Native Americans and European Americans to call for reform. The reformers pointed out that many western Indians had previously roamed the Plains in search of buffalo and other sources of food, clothing, and shelter. Confining whole tribes to reservations meant that they lost not only their traditional means of feeding and housing themselves but their entire way of life. Reservation lands were often unsuitable for farming, leaving the residents to depend on supplies of food, blankets, and clothing provided by the federal government. Kept apart from the rest of American society, denied the rights of citizenship such as education and the vote, many Indians fell victim to self-destructive behavior, including alcoholism and suicide.

Convinced that the reservation system was a failure, in 1879 reformers began to call for the assimilation of Native Americans into American life. This cause was promoted by some Indians as well as Protestant missionaries. In 1879 Ponca chief Standing Bear toured the East Coast, speaking before large, receptive audiences in Boston, New York, Philadelphia, and Washington.

((•—|Hear the Audio
Omaha Funeral Song at
www.myhistorylab.com

■   Susan LaFlesche was the first Indian woman to become a physician in the United States. Together with her sisters Marguerite and Lucy, Susan attended Hampton Institute in Virginia, a vocational school for African Americans and Indians. This photo, c. 1885, shows Hampton students performing in a pageant at the school. Susan, center, and the woman on the right represented "Indians of the Past." The other students represented "Indians of the Present." Hampton's mission was to prepare its students for farming and the skilled trades.

Standing Bear's appeal helped to galvanize eastern reformers. The campaign for Indian assimilation bore a marked resemblance to the antislavery crusade before the Civil War. Both movements focused on the wrongs perpetrated by the U.S. government (slavery and the Indian reservation system). Both argued that the group in question deserved full citizenship rights. And both promoted the ideal of group self-sufficiency: blacks and Indians tilling the soil, embracing mainstream Christianity, and learning trades.

Beginning in 1883, advocates of Indian assimilation sponsored annual conferences at Lake Mohonk, New York, to plot strategy for the coming year. These conferences brought together scholars, clergy, reformers, and politicians, all of whom considered their cause as part of the tradition of Protestant missionary outreach work. The reformers believed that the values of white middle-class Protestants provided the best guide for Indians seeking to rid themselves of the hated reservation system. Advocates of assimilation also received support from people who simply wanted the Plains Indians removed from their land to make way for European-American settlers.

Out of these conflicting impulses—one on behalf of the Indians' welfare, the other in support of the destruction of Indians' claims to large tracts of land—came two major initiatives that would shape federal Indian policy in the years to come. The first was the Indian boarding school movement, begun in 1879 with the founding of a school near Carlisle, Pennsylvania. The purpose of the movement was to convert Indian children to Christianity, and to force them to abandon their native culture and learn literacy skills. The second was the Dawes Severalty Act of 1887, allowing reservation land to be divided into separate farms for individual

Native American families. However, ambitious land speculators and corrupt government officials sought to enrich themselves from the provisions of the act, which allowed the sell-off of Indian lands to white buyers.

Transatlantic Networks of Reform

During this period, American reformers derived ideas and inspiration from their European counterparts. This transatlantic exchange of ideas was greatly facilitated by improvements in sea transportation. During the 1870s and 1880s, ocean travel became cheaper and safer as well as more efficient and comfortable. In 1890, a tourist embarking from New York could cross the Atlantic in just ten days for about $30 (the price of a bicycle) on a well-appointed steamship.

Contacts between European and American scholars, students, artists, clergy, writers, and reformers enriched the intellectual life of the United States and bolstered the reform impulse. American women's rights supporters conferred with their counterparts in London. American college students attended classes at German universities. Out of these contacts emerged the **Social Gospel**, a moral reform movement that stressed the responsibility of Christians to address the ills of modern urban life.

> *During this period, American reformers derived ideas and inspiration from their European counterparts.*

An idealistic graduate of Rockford (Illinois) Female Seminary, Jane Addams journeyed to Europe for the first time in 1883. The sight of large numbers of poor people in London's East End made a lasting impression on her. In 1888 she went again to England and visited Toynbee Hall, a social settlement founded to alleviate the problems of the laboring classes. Back in Chicago, she and her friend and former classmate Ellen Gates Starr decided to open a settlement house of their own in 1889. Called Hull House, it was located in the Nineteenth Ward, home to 5,000 Greek, Russian, Italian, and German immigrants.

Social settlement houses—so-called because their goal was to help immigrants with the transition of settling in the United States—provided a variety of services for immigrants, including English language classes, neighborhood health clinics, after-school programs for children, and instruction in personal hygiene and infant care. In 1891 six settlements were in operation. By 1900 the number stood at 200.

Women Reformers: "Beginning to Burst the Bonds"

Like the Indian assimilation movement, women's reform work in general during this period had a strong missionary strain. In San Francisco, the Occidental Branch of the Women's Foreign Missionary Society enlisted the aid of well-to-do women in sponsoring a rescue home for Chinese prostitutes. Without the protection of traditional kin ties, these immigrants remained vulnerable to sexual and physical abuse. The rescue home enabled the young women to escape the men who exploited them and, in some cases, to reenter society, now as married women, factory wage-earners, or small merchants.

In Salt Lake City, a group of women challenged the Mormon practice of plural marriage. In 1886 their Industrial Christian Home Association received a subsidy from Congress to provide shelter for "women who renounce polygamy and their children of a tender age." That same year some Denver women founded the Colorado Cottage Home, a rescue home for pregnant girls and women.

The Women's Christian Temperance Union (WCTU) is an apt example of the missionary impulse behind late-nineteenth-century reform. Though best known for its antialcohol crusade, the WCTU also sponsored homes for unwed mothers and day and night nurseries for the children of working women. It also stressed the need for women's "purity," claiming that women and children were the chief victims of men's alcohol consumption. But the group went further to denounce women's victimization at the hands of men in general.

■ Frances Willard (1839–1898) grew up on a farm in Wisconsin Territory. She served as the first dean of women at Northwestern University in Illinois. In the mid-1870s, she decided to devote her life to the cause of temperance. From 1879 until her death, she was president of the Woman's Christian Temperance Union. Willard developed what she called a "Do-Everything policy." Under her leadership, the WCTU addressed a range of issues, including women's suffrage and workers' rights.

By the 1870s, the issue of women's suffrage had captured the attention of men and women throughout the country. The issue had special resonance in the West for several reasons. When European-American women overcame the hardships associated with the challenge of settling the trans-Mississippi West, they considered themselves worthy of having an equal voice in the polling booth. Reflecting on her hard life as a settler in Circle Valley, Utah, Mrs. L. L. Dalton wrote in 1876 that she was "proud and thankful" to see women "beginning to burst the bonds of iron handed custom" and asserting their "co-heirship" with fathers, brothers, and husbands. Abigail Scott Duniway, who sympathized with the plight of over-worked and often lonely farm wives, published a women's rights journal, *New Northwest*, in Portland, Oregon, from 1871 to 1887.

Western politics pitted cattle ranchers against farmers, and religious and cultural groups against each other. These conflicts prompted the men of various groups to seek allies wherever they could find them—within their own households if necessary. The territorial legislature of Wyoming granted women the right to vote in 1869. Utah Territory followed suit in 1870, and Washington Territory in 1883. The states of Wyoming (in 1890), Colorado (in 1893), and Utah and Idaho (both in 1896) approved suffrage for women.

CONCLUSION

In the 1870s and 1880s, the Americans who challenged the power of government and big business represented a wide spectrum of ideologies, tactics, and goals. Some resisted violently. Others formed new institutions such as settlement houses, reform associations, or political parties. Some people hoping to effect social change used the language of evangelical Protestantism, echoing the reform activities of persons who called for the abolition of slavery before the Civil War. Others collected data and interviewed specific groups of workers, women, or immigrants in an effort, first, to expose the conditions under which these groups lived and labored and, second, to propose specific legislation to remedy those conditions. Plains Indians embraced religious mysticism in a failed attempt to halt the incursion of European Americans into their ancient hunting grounds. Thus, powerful groups encountered much resistance from people opposed to their narrow idea of progress—the idea that bigger factories, more efficient farm machinery, and a nationwide network of railroad lines would bring prosperity to all Americans.

As Americans began to think more broadly about their own society, they began to think more broadly about their place in the world. Some men and women hoped to apply the principles of moral and civic reform to other countries west of the United States. The 1880s thus laid the foundations not only for a transatlantic republic of cultural exchange, but also for a trans-Pacific empire of missionary work and trade. In the process, a new ideology of expansionism emerged, one that blended elements of economic gain, national security, and Christian missionary outreach to peoples in far-off lands.

For Review

✓•─[Study and **Review** at **www.myhistorylab.com**

1. Discuss the role of law as both a facilitator of, and barrier to, economic and political equality among all Americans during this period.

2. What were the arguments and counterarguments of the supporters and opponents of the Indian reservation system? Did all Indians share a particular point of view on this issue? Why or why not?

3. Why were so many labor unions, political organizations, and reform associations segregated by race?

4. Why did increasing numbers of middle-class Americans find transatlantic travel, and visits to Europe, so appealing? In what ways did patterns of foreign travel affect domestic life in the United States?

Chronology: 1877–1890

1877 "Great Uprising" of railroad employees and other workers.

1878 San Francisco Workingmen's party stages anti-Chinese protests.

1882 Chinese Exclusion Act.

1886 Accused Haymarket bombers tried and convicted.

1888 Edward Bellamy, *Looking Backward.*
National Farmers' Alliance is founded.

1890 Wyoming admitted to the Union, first state to enfranchise women.
National American Woman Suffrage Association is formed.
Wounded Knee Massacre.

Key Terms

Anarchists Persons who reject all forms of government as inherently oppressive and undesirable. p. 422

Jim Crow The name given to the set of legal institutions that ensured the segregation of nonwhite people in the South. p. 414

Populists Agrarian reformers who formed the Populist, or People's party, a major (third) political party that emerged mostly in the Midwest and South in the late 1880s to address the needs of workers and farmers in opposition to government monetary policies and big business. The party faltered after its presidential candidate, William Jennings Bryan, lost in the 1896 election. p. 417

Social Gospel A reform movement around the end of the twentieth century that stressed the responsibility of religious organizations to remedy a wide range of social ills related to urban life. p. 425

18

Political and Cultural Conflict in a Decade of Depression and War: The 1890s

I n the early 1890s, Luther Standing Bear, a young man of Lakota Sioux origin, found himself suspended between two worlds. Born in 1868 in South Dakota, he had learned to hunt buffalo in the traditional manner of the western Sioux. In 1879 he bowed to the wishes of his father, Standing Bear, who insisted that he learn the ways of "Long Knives," or whites. The youth was among the first pupils to attend the new federal Indian boarding school in Carlisle, Pennsylvania. Once at the school, he discovered that he was to become an "imitation of a white man"—and quickly.

Called Ota Kte, or Plenty Kill, at home, now he was required to pick a new first name from among those listed on a classroom blackboard. He chose Luther. His teachers took away his blanket and moccasins and gave him a coat, pants, and vest to wear. They forbade him to speak his native language, and they cut his long hair. Like most other youths at Carlisle, Standing Bear learned to read and write English and to practice a craft (in his case, tin-smithing). His teachers encouraged him to embrace Christianity.

In 1884, as part of his government-sponsored training, Luther Standing Bear traveled to Philadelphia to work at the Wanamaker department store. After spending a year stocking shelves and performing other tasks at the famous store, Standing Bear returned to South Dakota. There he taught Sioux children in a school near the place of his birth, now the Rosebud Indian Reservation.

In December 1890, U.S. military officials attacked and killed 150 to 200 Indians at Wounded Knee, South Dakota, near Luther Standing Bear's home. The young man moved with his family to the nearby Pine Ridge Reservation, where he began work as a shopkeeper and postal clerk. In the late 1890s, Luther Standing Bear served as an interpreter for Buffalo Bill's "Wild West" show during its tour in London. By 1912 he had become an American citizen and settled in southern California, where he began his acting career in the new motion picture industry. He appeared in some of the first movie westerns and became an Indian activist, speaking out against the "government prison" known as the reservation.

In the 1890s, Luther Standing Bear's journey took place amid economic depression, civil strife, and war. Throughout the decade, workers and employers showed that the United States was not immune to the bloody class conflict that had long plagued Europe. Some scholars lamented the closing of the western frontier, prompting fears that America's unique dynamic of growth and social improvement had come to an end. Native-born whites began to seize upon new categories of racial

■ This group of Chiricahua Apache students arrived at the Carlisle Indian boarding school in 1890. Government-sponsored Indian education included dressing them in European American clothing and cutting their hair.

difference to draw distinctions between various groups in the United States and around the world. Faced with declining consumer demand at home, politicians and businesspeople joined forces to expand American markets and American influence abroad. America's expansionist ventures would reveal a blend of economic interests and missionary outreach, particularly in Cuba and the Philippines.

Native-born whites began to seize upon new categories of racial difference.

Whereas some Americans tried to define rigid racial and nationalistic boundaries, others sought avenues of connections. A new political party, the Populist, or People's, party, aimed to bring together men and women of all backgrounds and regions. By advocating grassroots democracy as well as government action to regulate the economy, the party paved the way for the Progressive reforms of the early twentieth century.

Relying on a variety of means, from new legal and educational systems to commercial expansion and the deployment of military might, American elites attempted to consolidate their political power and cultural influence. In the process, the United States confronted not only the domestic challenges of sustaining a modern industrial society but also the world-wide challenges that pitted the enduring ideal of democracy against the emerging reality of **imperialism**, the notion that stronger powers had the right and even the obligation to assume control over the politics and natural resources of weaker peoples.

Frontiers at Home, Lost and Found

In 1893 historian Frederick Jackson Turner proposed a new way of thinking about American history. According to Turner, the process of settling the West had shaped all of American history. He argued that during the colonial period, the rigors of taming the land had transformed English colonists into more resourceful, more democratic people—in other words, into Americans. With each successive wave of western settlement, American society renewed itself. In his view, the West served as a safety valve, a place of opportunity that beckoned people out of crowded eastern cities. However, Turner noted, an 1890

How did fears about a closing western frontier affect American political, social, and cultural life in the 1890s?

■ Frederick Jackson Turner's 1893 announcement that the western frontier had disappeared was premature. Here, homesteaders in Washington State cut down trees to carve a farm out of the forest, c. 1900. Felling gigantic hardwoods in the Northwest was a formidable challenge to family farmers.

Census Report had concluded that the frontier—the unsettled area of the western part of the country—had recently disappeared. "And now," Turner concluded, "four centuries from the discovery of America, at the end of a hundred years of life under the Constitution, the frontier has gone, and with its going has closed the first period in American history."

Turner's thesis promoted the idea of American "exceptionalism": the idea that its individualism and democratic values made the United States unique among the nations of the world. Yet, in his celebration of the sturdy frontiersman, Turner ignored the bloody legacy of western settlement and its devastating effects on native and Spanish-speaking peoples.

Nevertheless, at the end of the nineteenth century, Turner and others were asking questions. Did America need to conquer new lands and "tame" certain peoples to preserve its distinctive character? Now that the frontier had disappeared, what was to prevent the United States from becoming more like Europe? These concerns led to efforts to assimilate and Americanize certain groups of people and to tighten systems of legal discrimination against others. In addition, some Americans turned their attention to "interior" frontiers of psychology, art, and spirituality. These issues also inspired some Americans to advocate extending the nation's military might and political authority beyond U.S. territorial boundaries. In the view of imperialists, if the American frontier at home was closing, the American frontier abroad should expand.

Claiming and Managing the Land

As less and less land was available for cultivation, grazing, and mining, the politics of rural development entered a new phase. In the early 1890s, the last great parcel of Indian land was opened to European-American farmers. Congress established the Territory of Oklahoma in 1890. Three years later, the Cherokee Outlet in the north-central part of the territory, combined with Tonkawa and Pawnee reservations, was thrown open to settlers and oil developers. On September 16, 1893, 100,000 people claimed 6.5 million newly opened acres in a single day. The "sooners," people who rushed to claim the land, gave the state of Oklahoma its nickname. The "Sooner State" was admitted to the Union in 1907.

Congress took other steps to manage western lands during the 1890s. The Court of Private Land Claims (1891) oversaw land disputes in New Mexico, Colorado, and Arizona. This court favored recent European-American claimants over the Hispanic settlers who had received title to the lands from either Spain or Mexico generations earlier.

Land courts were only one example of an expanded federal role in the settlement of the West and management of the land. During the 1890s, the federal government continued to provide information and services for farmers through the U.S. Department of Agriculture. Policymakers argued over the proper balance between conserving natural resources for use by farmers, loggers, and oilmen and preserving the beauty of unspoiled panoramas for the enjoyment of all. In 1890 Congress established a national park in California's spectacular Yosemite Valley, where the Yosemite Indians had lived for hundreds of years. The 1891 Forest Reserve Act set aside forest reserves in the public domain (the vast tracts of land still owned by the federal government). Logging companies were allowed to exploit these areas for their timber.

With his appointment as chief of the Division of Forestry in 1898, Gifford Pinchot sought to bring the issue of natural resource conservation to national attention. He believed that a managed forest could provide lumber and then renew itself. By contrast, John Muir and others argued that uninhabited regions should be preserved in their natural state, unmarred by dams, mines, or logging operations. In 1892 Muir founded the Sierra Club, a group devoted to preserving wilderness. In 1899 both Muir and the Northern Pacific Railroad lobbied successfully for two new national parks, Mount Rainier in Washington and Glacier in Montana, highlighting the ongoing significance of railroad tourism. "Rusticating," or hiking and enjoying the beauty of nature, became a popular pastime for many Americans in the 1890s.

The Tyranny of Racial Categories

The supposed closing of the western frontier, and with it the disappearance of the "safety valve" for restless Easterners, highlighted urban America's increasing class and cultural diversity. In an effort to categorize social groups, many national opinionmakers—scholars, journalists, and politicians—claimed that people should be distinguished from one another by their inborn, "natural" characteristics, ranging from skin color to facial bone structure and intelligence. Supposedly, these differences defined specific racial categories, such as Caucasoid, Mongoloid, and Negroid. In fact, so-called racial differences between groups were cultural differences. Late-nineteenth-century scientific racists ranked "superior" and "inferior" races on an elaborate hierarchy encompassing all groups, native and foreign born.

Several factors account for this renewed obsession with the idea of race in the 1890s. European and American efforts to colonize and explore the far reaches of the globe brought whites face to face with darker-skinned peoples, whom scholars in the new discipline of anthropology studied and classified. The "New Immigration" from eastern Europe raised concerns about conferring citizenship on non-Anglos, such as Russian Jews, Poles, and Italians. Persistent violence along the U.S.-Mexican border, combined with the resistance of Indians and African Americans to the authority of white people, alarmed local and federal officials. Theories of "racial difference" were used to justify attempts to subordinate these groups, by violence if necessary.

In the South, the doctrine of white supremacy had disastrous consequences for African Americans. Beginning with Mississippi in 1890, over the next 20 years, white Democrats in all the southern states met in state constitutional conventions and imposed restrictions on the voting rights of African-American men, including literacy requirements and poll taxes (fees that people had to pay to vote).

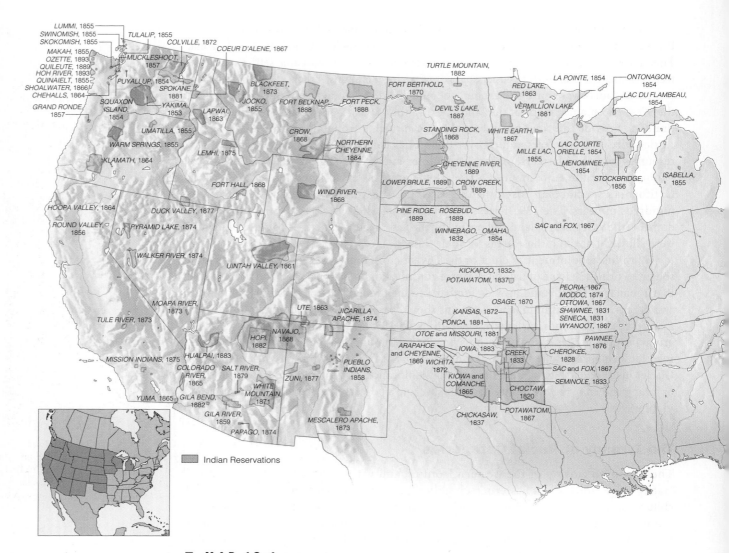

■ **MAP 18.1**
INDIAN RESERVATIONS, 1900
The Dawes Act, passed by Congress in 1887, intended to abandon the reservation system and integrate Indians into mainstream American society. Nevertheless, many reservations remained intact. As a group, Indians lived apart from European Americans. By the early twentieth century, the Indian as a "vanishing race" had become a familiar theme in novels and films. Yet Indian activists continued to press the cause of their people: to preserve native cultures and, at the same time, protest persistent poverty.

In 1896 the Supreme Court put its stamp of approval on segregated schools, trains, and streetcars in its *Plessy v. Ferguson* opinion. By a 7-1 majority, the Supreme Court ruled that such Jim Crow laws did "not necessarily imply the inferiority of either race." Justice John Marshall Harlan dissented from the majority view, pointing out the obvious: "The white race deems itself to be the dominant race," a view that conflicted with the "colorblind" U.S. Constitution.

Between 1882 and 1901, more than 100 people, most of them black men, were lynched every year in the United States; the year 1892 set a record of 230 deaths. In the South, lynch mobs targeted black men and women who refused to subordinate themselves to whites. Many black men victimized by lynch mobs were falsely accused of raping white women. Black Memphis newspaper editor Ida B. Wells charged that accusations of rape were merely a pretext for the murder of black men. The southern white man, wrote Wells, "had never gotten over his resentment that the Negro was no longer his plaything, his servant, and his source of income." Death threats forced the editor to move north.

Yet even in the South, racial definitions were never as clear-cut or self-evident as racists, scientific or otherwise, claimed. For example, Italians and Jews occupied a middle ground between black and white, as class issues intermingled with racial categories. In 1891 in New Orleans, the lynching of a group of 11 Italian prisoners accused of conspiring to murder the city's chief of police met with no public outcry. Instead, a local newspaper condemned the "lawless passions" and "the cutthroat practices" that it claimed were characteristic of all Italian immigrants. However, the Italian government protested loudly against the incident. Armed conflict between the two nations was averted only when the United States agreed to compensate the victims' families.

At the same time, Jewish shopkeepers and merchants in the South gained a conditional entry into the ranks of "whites." In Natchez, Mississippi, the small but prosperous Jewish community owned 45 businesses, about a third of all in the town. However, living in an overwhelmingly Protestant region of the country, many southern Jews found themselves barred from local social organizations.

New Roles for Schools

Between 1890 and 1899, nearly 3.7 million immigrants entered the United States, fewer than 1.4 million of them English speakers from the United Kingdom and Ireland; nearly 2.3 million were non-English speakers from Germany, Italy, Austria-Hungary, and Russia. During this period, public displays of patriotism became increasingly characteristic of American life. The recitation of the Pledge of Allegiance was introduced into public classrooms and courtrooms in the 1890s.

■ A middle-class Powhatan Indian family in Virginia poses for the camera, c. 1900. Since the seventeenth century, the Powhatan had intermarried with the Nanticoke of Delaware as well as African Americans of the mid-Atlantic region. Communities such as these defied the efforts of scientists and others to rigidly categorize people according to race.

Many Americans saw formal education as a great equalizer of social groups, and many younger immigrants and the children of immigrants eagerly embraced American schooling as a means of upward mobility. However, schools did not always fulfill their promise as agents of equal opportunity for all. Increasingly, schools separated and grouped children according to their culture, religion, and class as well as skin color.

Many of the schools established by reformers and missionaries focused not on classical education but on teaching practical trades to students. At the Carlisle Indian school, boys learned to make harnesses, tin pots and pans, wagons, and carriages, among other products, many of which were sold to local residents to raise money for the school. Girls took in laundry and ironed, also part of the school's money-making effort. The goal of such activities was to enable the pupils to become self-supporting upon graduation.

The school as a vehicle for vocational instruction also found support among northern philanthropists concerned about education for southern black children and young people. A generation after the Civil War, the persistent poverty of many rural southern blacks convinced northern reformers that this group of Americans should be educated for a distinct form of second-class citizenship. Philanthropists, such as Julius Rosenwald of Chicago, upheld the notion of segregated public education. They created new institutions, or modified existing ones, to stress the trades and "domestic arts" at the expense of such subjects as philosophy, mathematics, and foreign languages.

•••◦┤Read the **Document**

*Booker T. Washington,
Atlanta Exposition Address*
at **www.myhistorylab.com**

◉┤Watch the **Video**

*The Conflict Between Booker T.
Washington and W.E.B. DuBois*
at **www.myhistorylab.com**

This emphasis on vocational training provoked varied reactions from African-American leaders. Born a slave in 1858, Booker T. Washington had labored in a West Virginia coal mine before attending Hampton Normal (teacher-training) and Agricultural Institute in Virginia. In 1881 he assumed the leadership of Tuskegee Institute, an Alabama school for blacks founded on the Hampton model. Speaking at the Cotton States Exposition, a fair held in Atlanta in 1895, Washington urged southern blacks to "Cast down your buckets where you are"—in other words, to remain in the South and to concentrate on acquiring manual skills that would bring a measure of self-sufficiency to black families and communities. In the same address, Washington proposed that blacks refrain from agitating for civil rights, such as the vote. In return, whites should refrain from attacking innocent men, women, and children. Ignoring this last part of the speech, whites hailed Washington's "Atlanta Compromise" proposal as one that endorsed segregation and second-class citizenship for blacks.

Challenging Washington's message, northern scholar-activist W. E. B. Du Bois ridiculed the notion that blacks should be content to become maids, carpenters, and sharecroppers. Similarly, in 1896 John Hope, a young professor at Roger Williams University in Nashville, Tennessee, and future president of Morehouse College and later Atlanta University, renounced Washington's apparent accommodationist stance: "If we are not striving for equality, in heaven's name for what are we living?" he demanded. "Rise, Brothers! Come let us possess this land. Never say, 'Leave well enough alone.'"

Some immigrant groups, responding specifically to the Protestant agenda of most public school systems, preferred to sponsor their own schools. In many urban areas, Roman Catholic nuns founded and staffed parochial (parish) schools that appealed to certain immigrant communities. By 1900 Catholics constituted the largest single denomination in the country, with 9 million members from diverse backgrounds.

> *By 1900 Catholics constituted the largest single denomination in the country, with 9 million members from diverse backgrounds.*

New forms of schooling reinforced class and cultural distinctions. No longer dependent on the income their children might earn in the workplace, late-nineteenth-century urban middle-class families could allow their sons and daughters to prolong their schooling. High school came to be considered a logical extension of public schooling. Between 1890 and 1900, the number of students graduating from high school doubled, from 43,731 to 94,883.

The spread of private institutions of higher education reflected the wealth of a new industrial owner class and new forms of socialization for young people of privilege. In 1891 Central Pacific Railroad builder Leland Stanford founded Stanford University in California in honor of his recently deceased son. The previous year, Standard Oil's John D. Rockefeller established the University of Chicago.

College life was becoming associated with a particular stage of personal development, a stage marked not only by academic endeavors, but also by uniquely American group activities, such as playing with or cheering for the school football team. The game of basketball was invented in 1891, and soon after, many colleges formed teams that played the new sport. But not everyone viewed these developments as positive. An 1893 editorial in the *Nation* decried "the inordinate attention given to athletics in college" and suggested that "debt, drink, and debauchery" were the natural consequence.

Connections Between Consciousness and Behavior

In the 1890s, some scholars and writers proposed that, although America's geographic frontier was closed, the "interior" frontier (of the human will and imagination) might still attract the curious. In Vienna, professor-physician Sigmund Freud pioneered the study of the human unconscious, the mysterious realm of thought and feeling that lies hidden beneath the mundane activities of everyday life. Freud's *The Interpretation of Dreams* (1900) suggested that dreams reveal the dreamer's unconscious desires and that these desires shape routine behavior. In the United States, the new discipline of psychology owed much to the work of Harvard University professor William James. In his *Principles of Psychology* (1890), James described the human brain as an organism constantly adjusting itself to its environment; people's surroundings profoundly influence their behavior, he argued.

Novelist Stephen Crane combined an unflinching look at reality—a blood-soaked Civil War battlefield or the slums of New York City—with a sensitive probing of human psychology. In *The Red Badge of Courage* (1894), Crane explores the fears and self-delusions of a Union soldier, basing his account on firsthand descriptions of the fighting a generation before. By stripping the story of all ideology—northern soldiers are hardly distinguishable from southern soldiers, and political issues are never mentioned—Crane suggests that the real war was that of the combatants battling their own private demons.

> *In the United States, the new discipline of psychology owed much to the work of Harvard University professor William James.*

Kate Chopin's novel *The Awakening* (1899) prompted outrage among critics. They objected to the sympathetic portrayal of the wealthy married heroine, Edna Pontellier, who anguishes over her inability to reconcile her artistic, free-spirited temperament with her roles of wife and mother. At the end of the story, set in New Orleans, she chooses to commit suicide rather than submit to a life of convention. The novel focuses on Edna's reaction to the expectations other people have of her and on her gradual awakening to the idea that she must live life—or die—on her own terms.

Religious leaders also explored the uncharted territory of the mind. In the late nineteenth century, the Church of Christ, Scientist, founded by Mary Baker Eddy in 1879, prospered and grew. Eddy held that physical illness was a sign of sin and that such illness could be healed by Christian faith and prayer. In 1892 she reorganized her Christian Science faith around a mother church in Boston. Through branch churches, the American-born sect spread to more than 60 countries throughout the world.

The Search for Domestic Political Alliances

In the 1890s, groups of Americans seemed to be estranged from each other as they rarely had been before. A few were enjoying the fruits of astonishing wealth, building for themselves magnificent, multimillion-dollar "summer cottages" reminiscent of glittering European palaces. In 1899 University of Chicago sociologist Thorstein Veblen coined the term **conspicuous consumption** to describe the expensive tastes of the ostentatious rich. Meanwhile, working men and women toiled long hours under dangerous conditions—when they had jobs. In 1895 the average worker was unemployed for three months of the year. Categories of race pitted various groups, native born and immigrant, against one another. Self-styled sophisticated city folk derided the **hayseeds** on the farm.

> *What were the coalitions and institutions that were created and strengthened in an effort to unite diverse groups in common purpose?*

Still, the prosperous middle class hoped that certain unifying forces would connect different classes and ethnic groups. Businessmen, lawyers, and other professionals placed their faith in public schools, such cultural institutions as public museums and libraries, and the desire for a more comfortable life to instill "American" values in newcomers and the poor. The 1890s also witnessed some remarkable alliances between groups of people who had never before found common ground. The Populist party had a profound impact on the nation's political landscape in the 1890s. And women, through their local and national organizations, helped to blend domestic concerns with politics, offering a new model of civic involvement.

> *The prosperous middle class hoped that certain unifying forces would connect different classes and ethnic groups.*

Class Conflict

Congress passed the Pension Act of 1890 to provide pensions for all disabled men who had served in the Union army during the Civil War. To pay for the pensions, Congress imposed a high tariff (named the McKinley Tariff after Representative William McKinley of Ohio) on a wide variety of imported goods. The northeastern states, dependent on domestic manufacturing, traditionally supported a high tariff. Western states supported the McKinley Tariff in return for the Sherman Silver Purchase Act of 1890, under which the federal government promised to buy a total of 4.5 million ounces of silver each month and to issue banknotes for that amount redeemable in gold or silver. As a result, Westerners benefited from the infusion of federal cash used to purchase silver mined in the West.

But the pairing of a high tariff with the purchase of silver produced explosive political and economic results. The tax on imported manufactured goods hurt consumers, and when wages did not keep pace with prices, workers revolted. In 1892 steel magnate Andrew Carnegie and his company chairman Henry Clay Frick initiated a drastic wage cut at the Carnegie Steel Company's Homestead plant, near Pittsburgh. Workers struck in June. They armed themselves with rifles and dynamite and engaged in a pitched battle with some 300 detectives from the Pinkerton agency, men hired by Frick to break the strike. (Homestead town officials had refused Frick's request to subdue the strikers.) Ten people died, and 60 were wounded. In response to the violence, the governor of Pennsylvania mobilized the state's National Guard. The troops escorted strikebreakers to work. The company cut its workforce by 25 percent and reduced the wages of the strikebreakers. The steelworkers' union lay in ruins. Gloated Frick, "Our victory is now complete and most gratifying."

Around the same time, gold, copper, and silver miners in the West faced daunting barriers to labor organization from within and outside their ranks. Protestants harbored suspicions of Roman Catholics. Ancient hatreds prevented the Irish from cooperating with the English. European Americans disdained Mexicans and the Chinese. However, the workers in Idaho's Coeur d'Alene mines managed to overcome these animosities and strike for union recognition. In March 1892, mine owners in the region formed a "protective association" and slashed wages. When workers walked off the job, the owners imported strikebreakers from other areas of the West. The strikers retaliated by blowing up a mine with dynamite. Fifteen hundred state and federal troops arrived on the scene, and the resulting clash left seven miners dead. The troops confined 300 striking miners in bullpens, where they remained for several weeks before their trials. In this case, too, the strikers met with defeat. However, out of this conflict came a new organization, founded in Butte, Montana, in 1893: the Western Federation of Miners.

Widespread discontent over the tariff and simmering resentment on the part of debtors clamoring for unlimited coinage of silver helped unseat President Harrison in the election of 1892. The victorious Democratic candidate, Grover Cleveland, took office once more in 1893 (the only defeated president to be reelected). A new and noteworthy player in the election of 1892 was the People's (Populist) party, whose first national convention took place in Omaha, Nebraska, that summer. The party had emerged from the Farmers' Alliances that had so effectively organized black and white midwestern and southern farmers in the 1880s. In the 1890s, the plight of western farmers reflected the state of American agriculture in general. The price of wheat had been a dollar a bushel in 1870, but it was only 35 cents 20 years later. Dakota farmers lost 15 cents on every bushel of wheat they sent to market.

The Populist party platform endorsed at the Omaha convention supported "free and

TABLE 18-1

The Election of 1892

Candidate	Political Party	Popular Vote (%)	Electoral Vote
Grover Cleveland	Democratic	46.1	277
Benjamin Harrison	Republican	43.0	145
James B. Weaver	Populist	8.5	22
John Bidwell	Prohibition	2.2	—

■ MAP 18.2
MANUFACTURING IN THE UNITED STATES, 1900
During the late nineteenth century, most manufacturing took place in the northeastern United States.
Exceptions included flour milling in Minneapolis, the growing textile industry in the southern Piedmont,
and the emergence of steel production in Birmingham, Alabama, thanks to rich local deposits.

unlimited coinage of silver and gold at the present legal ratio of sixteen to one"; a graduated
income tax; government ownership of railroad, telegraph, and telephone companies; and an
end to land speculation. The delegates condemned government subsidies to private corporations and called for the direct election of U.S. senators. The Populists' 1892 platform also included resolutions sympathizing "with the efforts of organized workmen to shorten the hours
of labor" to an eight-hour workday (many workers were forced to toil 12 to 14 hours daily)
and expressing solidarity with the (now considerably weakened) Knights of Labor in their
struggles against "tyrannical" employers.

The Populists gained strength when a national economic depression hit in 1893. This
dramatic downturn stemmed from several causes. As debtors clamored for "free silver," foreign investors in the United States became nervous, and European bankers began to call in
their loans. A bubble of overbuilding and land speculation burst.

The effects of the depression were widespread. Within six months, 8,000 businesses
failed. As many as 20 percent of all workers lost their jobs. In 1894 Jacob S. Coxey, an Ohio
quarry owner, dubbed himself a "general" and mobilized 5,000 men to march to Washington,
D.C. There, "Coxey's Army" protested the failure of the federal government to provide relief,
now that the country was in the midst of the worst depression ever.

Also in 1894, Eugene V. Debs, head of the American Railway Union (ARU), inspired
the union's 150,000 members to protest conditions at the Pullman Palace Car Company.

Employees in the company town of Pullman, near Chicago, felt squeezed when Pullman cut their wages by one-third but left intact the rents on their company-owned houses. The resulting strike crippled railroads from Chicago to California. President Cleveland declared that he could not stand by while the strikers interfered with the delivery of the U.S. mail. The president sent troops to quell the uprising, crushing the strike. For the first time, a federal court issued an injunction to force workers to go back to their jobs. Debs and other ARU leaders defied the order and went to jail.

To workers all over the country, the response to the Pullman strike signaled a troublesome alliance between government and big business, two powerful forces that the poor and the unemployed could not hope to counter. Judicial decisions confirmed the belief of many farmers and workers that all branches of the federal government were conspiring to favor the rich at the expense of the poor. In 1895 the Supreme Court rendered two opinions that favored big business and the wealthiest Americans. In *United States v. E. C. Knight*, the court ruled that the Sherman Anti-Trust Act of 1890 applied only to interstate commerce and not to manufacturers. The court had decided in favor of the subject of the suit, the sugar trust that controlled 98 percent of the industry. In *Pollock v. Farmers' Loan and Trust Company*, the court struck down a modest federal income tax (2 percent on incomes over $4,000 per year). These decisions helped set the stage for the showdown between the Populists and the two major parties in 1896.

Rise and Demise of the Populists

In 1896 the Republicans nominated Congressman William McKinley of Ohio, whose name had graced the widely unpopular tariff bill of 1890. The Democrats turned their back on Cleveland, regarded as a pariah by members of his own party for his ties to big business and his high-handed tactics against the Pullman strikers. Without an obvious presidential candidate at their convention in Chicago in July, the Democrats seemed at loose ends. Then, out of the audience, a young man rose to address the 15,000 delegates. William Jennings Bryan, a 36 year-old Populist from Nebraska, electrified the assembly with his passionate denunciation of arrogant industrialists and indifferent politicians. The country must abandon the gold standard once and for all, he thundered: "You shall not press down upon the brow of labor this crown of thorns, you shall not crucify mankind upon a cross of gold." One awestruck listener, an alternate member of the Nebraska delegation, later said of Bryan's "Cross of Gold" speech, "There are no words in our language to picture the effect it produced upon the vast multitude which heard it." The next day, the Democrats chose Bryan as their candidate for president.

By nominating William Jennings Bryan, the Democrats took on the Populist cause of free silver.

By nominating this eloquent upstart, the Democrats took on the Populist cause of free silver. Conservative Democrats bolted the party or sat out the election. Meeting in their own convention later in the summer, the Populists also chose Bryan as their candidate for president.

In the general election, McKinley received much support from his friend and political supporter Marcus (Mark) Hanna. A wealthy iron magnate and chair of the Republican National Committee, Hanna coordinated an effort to raise large sums of money for the Republicans ($16 million in total, compared with the Democrats' $1 million). Hanna charged that Bryan as president would mean disaster for businessmen, bankers, and other creditors, who would now be at the mercy of working people, small farmers, and other debtors. McKinley triumphed in November and, as a national force, the People's party rapidly disintegrated after the election of 1896.

TABLE 18-2

The Election of 1896

Candidate	Political Party	Popular Vote (%)	Electoral Vote
William McKinley	Republican	51.1	271
William J. Bryan	Democratic/Populist	45.5	176

Yet as a political movement encompassing disparate elements, the Populists left a mixed legacy. In some areas of the country, the party yielded some remarkable, if short-lived, inter-racial coalitions. In North Carolina, Republican-Populist fusion captured the state legislature in 1894 and the governorship in 1896. Throughout the South, however, the black population was growing—from 4.5 million on the eve of the Civil War to a total of 10 million people in 1890. Frightened by this development, white southern Democrats campaigned to disfranchise black men, beginning in the 1890s. Landless blacks and whites would find no common political ground again until the 1930s.

Barriers to a U.S. Workers' Political Movement

In the 1890s, workers in Europe were forging new political parties to represent their inter-ests and, in some cases, to press a bold socialist agenda, in the forum of national politics. Although late-nineteenth-century America showed dramatic evidence of bitter class conflict, it produced no viable workers' party or socialist movement. Why? The answer is not simple. Together, farmers and members of the industrial laboring classes aspired to self-sufficiency, a life free of debt that released their wives and children from unremitting toil and provided some measure of material comfort. Nevertheless, both groups found it difficult to ally with each other. The large influx of immigrants meant that competition for even low-paying jobs remained fierce among wage-earning men and women.

Employers manipulated racial, ethnic, and religious prejudices among workers to keep them estranged. White Protestant workers seized on ethnic and religious distinctions to win for themselves advantages in the workplace. Their unions excluded certain minority and ethnic groups altogether. Even somewhat egali-tarian unions fell prey to prejudice. In addition, skilled workers, taking pride in their craft and its traditions, distanced themselves from those who tended machines.

Many American workers, regardless of ethnicity, religion, or in-dustry, continued to believe that they could eventually own their own businesses. They resisted casting their lot permanently with unions or other working-class organizations. High rates of geographic mobility also prevented workers from committing themselves to a particular union in a particular place. And the power of antistrike forces proved daunting. Private security agencies, such as the Pinkertons, as well as state-deployed National Guard troops, backed up the authority of em-ployers, judges, mayors, and governors.

Challenges to Traditional Gender Roles

In the 1890s, the women's suffrage, club, missionary, and social set-tlement movements emerged as significant political forces. In 1890 the two major national women's suffrage associations, the National Woman Suffrage Association and the American Woman Suffrage Association, merged to form the National-American Woman Suf-frage Association (NAWSA). Elizabeth Cady Stanton served as the new group's first president for two years. But the suffrage move-ment exhibited contradictory impulses. On one hand, it brought together supporters from around the country and also yielded striking examples of international cooperation. On the other hand, white native-born Protestant American suffragists distanced themselves from the poor, immigrants, African Americans, and the laboring classes within their own country.

■ In 1896 Charles H. Epps, the city sergeant of Richmond, Virginia, ran for reelection. He distributed these cards to prospective voters. The cards suggest the masculine nature of politics at this time. This one doubled as a scorecard for the city's professional baseball team and carried advertisements for a local whiskey manufacturer and liquor and tobacco store.

California Views Historical Photo Collection, Monterey, CA

■ **The diversity of the American workforce and the American economy inhibited the development of a national workers' political party. By the 1890s, some industries were fully mechanized. Others relied on traditional forms of manual labor. In California, Asian workers faced persistent discrimination from labor unions. These immigrants are picking oranges near Santa Ana, c. 1895.**

◉▷ See the **Map**

Women's Suffrage before the 19th Century at **www.myhistorylab.com**

> *Although often associated with immigrants in the largest cities, settlement houses reached diverse populations.*

Identifying themselves primarily as wives and mothers, some women entered the political realm through local women's clubs. They believed that personal intellectual development and group political activity would benefit both their own families and society in general. In the 1880s, the typical club focused on self-improvement through reading history and literature. By the 1890s, many clubs had embraced political activism. They lobbied local politicians for improvements in education and social welfare and raised money for hospitals and playgrounds. The General Federation of Women's Clubs (GFWC), founded in 1892, united 100,000 women in 500 affiliate clubs throughout the nation.

Yet the GFWC specifically excluded African-American clubs. Black women formed their own national federation, the National Association of Colored Women (NACW), in 1896. Through club work, they spoke out against lynch mobs and segregationists and worked to improve their local communities. In some areas of the country, black and white women did make common cause—to further the goals of temperance, for example—although white women embraced these alliances uneasily.

In the West, Protestant-sponsored "mission homes" ministered to women in need. The San Francisco Presbyterian Chinese Mission Home offered a safe haven for Chinese women fleeing abuse and exploitation. Eastern women supported not only the San Francisco mission but also shelters for unwed mothers and abused girls in other cities, in the name of virtuous womanhood.

Social settlements were unique institutions, founded and staffed by well-educated women, many of whom had attended elite women's colleges. The daily operations of the settlement house reflected the priorities of its founders, who often brought activists, public health officials, journalists, and laboring men and women together around the dinner table to discuss problems of the poor. Settlement house workers hoped to instill in poor women the values of domesticity and pride in American citizenship. By 1900 more than 200 social settlement houses were helping to acculturate immigrants by offering classes in a variety of subjects, including English, health, and personal hygiene.

Although often associated with immigrants in the largest cities, settlement houses reached diverse populations. In the late 1890s, a coalition of the Kentucky Federation of Women's Clubs and other organizations sponsored several teachers who organized a summer settlement called Camp Cedar Grove in the eastern part of the state. This venture provided the foundation for the Hindman Settlement School. The school, still in existence, initially aimed to acculturate mountain people to middle-class ways in dress, eating habits, and manners and to preserve traditional mountain music and crafts.

Sensitive to the prejudices of their clients and their neighbors, most early settlements failed to reach out to African Americans. This policy stimulated the development of black-led settlements, such as the Phyllis Wheatley Settlement in Minneapolis and the Neighborhood Union in Atlanta. Founded by Lugenia Burns Hope in 1908, the Neighborhood Union aimed "to bring about a better understanding between the races."

Some women challenged traditional gender relations that relegated women to dependence on men. Emma Goldman, a Russian immigrant and self-proclaimed anarchist, paired the sexual liberation of women with the rights of workers to live a decent life. A radical by any measure, Goldman was, nevertheless, not alone in rejecting the idea that marriage should always be permanent. Between 1890 and 1900, the divorce rate increased from one out of every 17 new marriages to one out of 12. More and more couples, middle class and working class, native born and immigrant, were seeking means to dissolve marriages that had failed.

Charlotte Perkins Gilman was among the most prolific and well-known critics of the conventional division of labor in the home. She proclaimed that women, no longer content to remain dependent on men, must take their rightful place within the economy, working as equals with their brothers and husbands. Gilman proposed that housework be divided into its specialized tasks to be performed by professionals. This system would free women from the unpaid, mind-numbing task of combined "cook-nurse-laundress-chambermaid-housekeeper-waitress-governor." In her critique of gender conventions, Gilman anticipated the feminist movement of the 1960s.

Men also pondered the effects of industrializing society on their own roles. As assistant secretary of the U.S. Navy in the late 1890s, Theodore Roosevelt worried that, in this age of machines, young men lacked the opportunities for "the strenuous life" their grandfathers had enjoyed. He argued that unapologetic masculine bravado provided the key to American strength and rejuvenation on both a national and personal level. In his multivolume history *The Winning of the West* (1889–1896), Roosevelt extolled America's relentless march to the Pacific: "The rude, fierce settler who drives the savage from the land lays all civilized mankind under a debt to him." Imperialism at home and abroad, he declared, was a "race-important work," one that should claim the energies of men as politicians and soldiers. These views helped to propel the United States into the realms of imperialism and international conflict.

American Imperialism

In the 1890s, the United States began to extend its political reach and economic dominance to other parts of the world. Americans looked beyond their borders and saw exotic peoples who represented a variety of opportunities—as consumers of American goods, producers of goods Americans wanted to buy, and objects of American benevolence. This view represented an extension of the reform impulse at home.

How did different groups define, and in some cases further, American interests abroad?

The country's mighty industrial manufacturing sector demanded new markets and a wider consumer base. The depression of 1893, in particular, raised fears that manufacturers would have to contend with surpluses of goods that Americans could not afford to buy. American businesspeople and State Department officials established a partnership that combined private economic self-interest with national military considerations. Some molders of public opinion used the new languages of race and masculine virility to justify an "Anglo-Saxon" mission of conquest of "childlike" peoples. Meanwhile, European countries were carving up Africa and making economic inroads into China. Many Americans believed their own country should join the "race" for riches and "march" to glory as part of the international competition to exploit the natural resources and trade potential of weaker countries.

Cultural Encounters with the Exotic

In early October 1897, 30,000 spectators paid their 25-cent fee to enter New York's Excursion Wharf and observe the novel cargo of the recently arrived steamship *Hope*. Arctic explorer Robert Peary had returned from Greenland, bringing with him six Greenland Eskimo and a 37.5-ton meteorite dislodged from the Cape York region. The American public hailed the intrepid explorer Peary as a hero. The American Museum of Natural History put the Eskimo on display, and New Yorkers regarded their odd clothing, language, and eating habits with intense curiosity.

During the late nineteenth century, Americans were fascinated by artifacts and images dealing with far-away places, especially Africa, the Middle East, and Asia. This impulse, revealed in high art as well as popular culture, stereotyped darker-skinned, non-Christian peoples as primitive, sensual, and inscrutable. Chicago's Columbian Exposition of 1893 featured exhibits depicting harems, spice merchants, and turbaned warriors and performances of "hootchy kootchy dancers," scantily clothed young women writhing to the music of exotic instruments.

Throughout the late nineteenth century, photographers took pictures of Middle Eastern nomads and African villagers. American artists traveled abroad to render romantic scenes of deserts, ancient ruins, and mysterious peoples in oils and in watercolors. These cultural tendencies could be used to sell products and entertainment. The glassmaker-jeweler Tiffany and Co. evoked Islamic art in its tea services and silver patterns. Tobacco companies marketed mass-produced cigarettes with "Oriental" brand names: "Fatima," "Omar," and "Camel." Thus, a fascination with the exotic encompassed a wide range of impulses in American life and letters, bringing together explorers, scientists, artists, and advertising agents.

Initial Imperialist Ventures

The opening of Asia to American trade, combined with the military challenges posed by the major European imperial powers, stimulated the growth of the U.S. Navy in the 1880s. In his book *The Influence of Sea-Power in History, 1660–1763* (1890), Captain Alfred Thayer Mahan contended that if the United States aspired to be a world power, it must control the seas.

Seeking way stations for its ships, the United States negotiated control over both Pearl Harbor in Hawaii and the harbor at Pago Pago in Samoa in 1887. Three years later, Secretary of State James G. Blaine hosted the first Pan-American Conference in Washington, D.C., a gathering of representatives from 19 independent Latin American republics.

In 1895 the United States signaled to Great Britain that it was prepared to go to war to bar Europeans from colonizing or intervening in the Americas, a policy outlined in the Monroe Doctrine more than 70 years before. Britain had persisted in its long-standing claims to the jungle boundary between its colony of British Guiana and the country of Venezuela on the north coast of South America. President Cleveland made clear his intention to enforce the Monroe Doctrine. Britain, sensitive to other threats posed by European imperial powers to the far-flung British empire, backed down. Thereafter, Britain began to concentrate on strengthening its diplomatic ties with the United States.

Meanwhile, in the Pacific, the Hawaiian Islands seemed to pose both a threat and an opportunity for American interests. Located 2,000 miles from the California coast, Hawaii had a population of 150,000 in 1890. In 1875 sugar planters and merchants, many of whom were related to missionaries, had negotiated a treaty with the United States that let them ship the crop to the United States

■ The Greenland Eskimo Minik is shown here soon after his arrival in New York City in 1897 at age 7. Minik was devastated by the death of his widowed father, Qisuk; the two were among six Eskimo brought to New York by Arctic explorer Robert E. Peary. Later in his life, Minik spoke of his father to a newspaper reporter, saying, "He was dearer to me than anything else in the world, especially when we were brought to New York, strangers in a strange land."

duty-free. Production of Hawaiian sugar increased from less than 10,000 tons in 1870 to 300,000 tons by 1900.

By this time, Chinese, Koreans, Filipinos, Puerto Ricans, Japanese, and Portuguese had made their way to the Hawaiian Islands. These groups formed the bulk of the plantation labor force, for disease had decimated the native population. In the fields and in their barracks, immigrant contract workers followed a disciplined regimen under the supervision of mounted, whip-wielding overseers called *lunas*. Indeed, these laborers' workday bore a marked resemblance to that of sharecroppers on the largest cotton plantations of the U.S. South.

The McKinley Tariff of 1890 raised duties on imports of the islands' sugar. This tariff served to overturn the 1875 pro-planter treaty, causing planters (mostly Americans) to panic about their livelihood. They received no support from the islands' native leader, Queen Liliuokalani, who believed foreigners should be barred from running the country. In 1893 the planters, backed by American marines, launched a successful revolt that deposed the queen. They then called for the United States to annex the islands as a territory. Upon investigation, President Cleveland discovered that native Hawaiians opposed annexation, and so refused to agree to the move. His refusal incurred the wrath of American imperialists, who claimed that the "Hawaiian pear" had been "ripe for the plucking."

The Spanish-American-Cuban-Filipino War of 1898

Those seeking to expand American influence also looked just south of Florida. In the Caribbean, Cuban nationalists staged an uprising against the island's Spanish colonial authorities in 1895. Native *insurrectos* under the leadership of José Martí burned crops of sugar cane and attacked passenger trains. American companies with large investments in the Cuban sugar industry (a total of about $50 million) were outraged at the destruction of their property; they had no sympathy for the *insurrectos*. Yet the arrival of Spanish military

⊙ See the **Map**

Activities of the US in the Caribbean, 1898–1930s at **www.myhistorylab.com**

■ The battleship *Maine* exploded and sank in Havana Harbor on February 15, 1898.

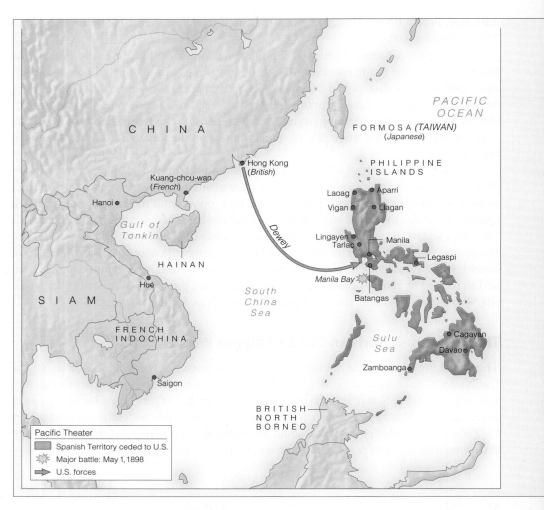

■ MAP 18.3
THE SPANISH-AMERICAN-CUBAN-FILIPINO WAR OF 1898

officials, who herded the rebels into barbed-wire concentration camps, inflamed public opinion in the United States. By 1897, both businesspeople and humanitarians urged President McKinley to intervene in Cuba.

Two major American newspaper publishers, William R. Hearst and Joseph Pulitzer, highlighted Spanish atrocities against Cubans. On February 9, 1898, Hearst published a letter written by the Spanish minister in Washington, D.C., Dupuy de Lôme, in which de Lôme denounced President McKinley as a spineless politician. Six days later, the American battleship *Maine*, which had been sent to Havana harbor to evacuate Americans should the need arise, exploded and sank. Two hundred sixty officers and men were killed. Subsequent investigations concluded that the heat from one of the coal bins had ignited an adjacent powder magazine. But the Hearst papers implied that the Spanish were responsible for the blast. Attempting to expand their readership, the Hearst and Pulitzer newspapers engaged in **yellow journalism**: sensational news reporting that blurred the line between fact and fiction, spontaneous reality and staged theater.

McKinley responded to American businesspeople who feared for their interests in Cuba and to other Americans who decried Spain's brutality toward the *insurrectos*. On April 11, 1898, McKinley called on Congress to declare war against Spain. To war supporters, much

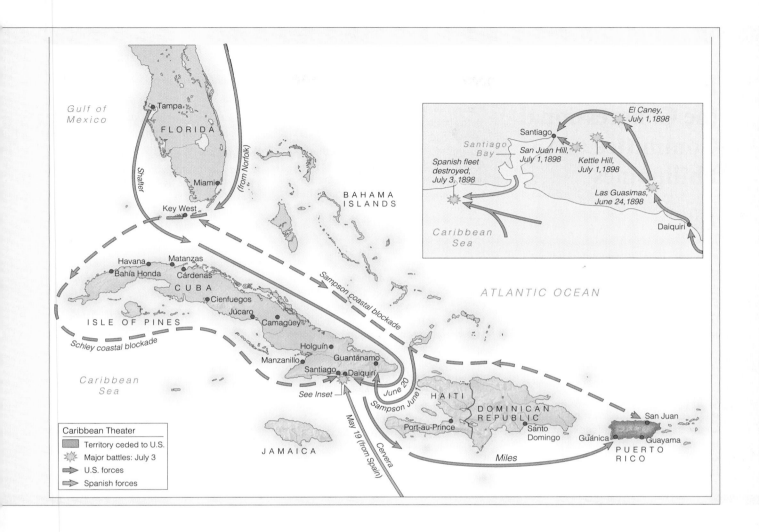

was at stake: the large American sugar investment, trade with the island, and American power and influence in the Western Hemisphere. Congress responded to McKinley's message by adopting the Teller Amendment, which declared that the United States would guarantee Cuba its independence once the Spanish were driven from the island. America went to war on April 29.

McKinley hoped to hobble the Spanish navy by making a preemptive attack on the fleet in the Spanish colony of the Philippines. Commodore George Dewey, stationed with the American Asiatic Squadron in Hong Kong, was dispatched with his ships to Manila Bay, where on May 1, 1898, his force of four battleships sank all ten rickety Spanish vessels, killing 400, with only a few minor American casualties. Dewey waited in the harbor until American reinforcements arrived in August. Then, with the help of Filipino nationalists led by Emilio Aguinaldo, U.S. forces overran Manila on August 13.

Meanwhile, congressional Republicans had found the necessary votes to annex Hawaii. They claimed that the United States needed the Pacific islands to secure a refueling way station for Dewey's troops. McKinley signed the congressional resolution on July 7, 1898. Hawaiian residents were granted citizenship rights, and the islands became an official U.S. territory in 1900.

Earlier in the summer of 1898, halfway around the globe, 17,000 American troops had traveled to Tampa, Florida, in preparation for their incursion into Cuba. Among them

INTERPRETING HISTORY

Proceedings of the Congressional Committee on the Philippines

In January 1900, Congress established the Committee on the Philippines. Senator Henry Cabot Lodge of Massachusetts was appointed chair. The committee's task was to review the American conduct of the war. The testimony of two U.S. officers, which follows, foreshadows the difficulties faced by the United States in fighting a guerrilla war in Vietnam six decades later.

Brigadier General Robert P. Hughes testified in response to questions posed by committee members:

Q: In burning towns, what would you do? Would the entire town be destroyed by fire or would only offending portions of the town be burned?

GEN. HUGHES: I do not know that we ever had a case of burning what you would call a town in this country; but probably a *barrio* or a *sitio;* probably a half dozen houses, native shacks, where the *insurrectos* [rebels] would go in and be concealed, and if they caught a detachment passing they would kill some of them.

Q: What did I understand you to say would be the consequence of that?

GEN. HUGHES: They usually burned the village.

Q: All of the houses in the village?

GEN. HUGHES: Yes, every one of them.

Q: What would become of the inhabitants?

GEN. HUGHES: That was their lookout. . . . The destruction was as a punishment.

Q: The punishment in that case would fall, not upon the men, who would go elsewhere, but mainly upon the women and little children.

GEN. HUGHES: The women and children are part of the family, and where you wish to inflict a punishment you can punish the man probably worse in that way than in any other.

Q: But is that within the ordinary rules of civilized warfare? Of course you could exterminate the family, which would be still worse punishment.

GEN. HUGHES: These people are not civilized.

Sergeant Charles S. Riley also testified in response to the committee's questions:

Q: During your service there [in the Philippine Islands] did you witness what is generally known as the water cure?

A: I did.

Q: When and where?

A: On November 27, 1900, in the town of Igbaras, Iloilo Province, Panay Island.

Riley described to the committee a Filipino man, 40–45 years of age, stripped to the waist, with his hands tied behind him.

Q: Do you remember who had charge of him?

A: Captain Glenn stood there beside him and one or two men were tying him. . . . He was then taken and placed under the tank, and the faucet was opened and a stream of water was forced down or allowed to run down his throat; his throat was held so he could not prevent swallowing the water, so that he had to allow the water to run into his stomach. . . . When he was

Watch the **Video**
Roosevelt's Rough Riders at
www.myhistorylab.com

See the **Map**
World Colonial Empires, 1900
at **www.myhistorylab.com**

were the Rough Riders, volunteers organized by Lieutenant Colonel Theodore Roosevelt, who had resigned his post as assistant secretary of the navy to serve as an officer. The troops landed near Santiago, Cuba, in late June. On July 1, Roosevelt and his men engaged an unprepared Spanish force of about 2,000 men at El Caney and San Juan Hill. The Rough Riders charged up nearby Kettle Hill (they were on foot, not on horses) and into American legend. They received crucial backup support from two African-American regiments that day. By late July, American warships had destroyed the Spanish fleet in Santiago Bay. According to Secretary of State John Hay, it had been "a splendid little war," just 113 days long. Battles claimed 385 American lives (although many times that number died from disease).

On August 12, 1898, Spain signed an armistice and later in the year ceded its claim to remnants of its empire, including Cuba and Puerto Rico in the Caribbean and the island of Guam in the Pacific. The United States forced Cuba to incorporate into its constitution (written in 1901) the so-called Platt Amendment, which guaranteed continuing U.S. influence over the country, including the stationing of American troops at a naval station on Guantanamo Bay. Meeting with Spanish negotiators in Paris, the United States agreed to pay $20 million for the Philippines.

filled with water it was forced out of him by pressing a foot on his stomach or else with their hands. . . .

Q: What had been his crime?

A: Information had been obtained from a native source as to his being an insurgent officer. After the treatment he admitted that he held the rank of captain in the insurgent army—an active captain. . . .

Q: His offense was treachery to the American cause?

A: Yes, sir.

Questions

1. *In what ways did the Filipino insurrection challenge the conventions of what congressional committee members called "civilized warfare"?*

2. *How did General Hughes justify the destruction of whole villages as part of the U.S. effort to suppress the insurrectionists?*

3. *What are the arguments for and against the practice of torture as a means of extracting information from enemy combatants?*

Source: Proceedings of the Congressional Committee on the Philippines, in Harvey Graff, ed., *American Imperialism and the Philippine Insurrection* (Boston, 1969), pp. 64–79.

This photograph of a United States soldier during the War of 1898 is titled "The Church Saint sat on by a *Washington Johnnie*" [soldier]. During the war, photographers produced vivid images that conveyed the dramatic effects of the U.S. invasion on the society and culture of the Philippines. Led by Emilio Aguinaldo, insurrectionists fought for Philippine independence, beginning in January 1899. Two years later, American forces captured Aguinaldo and established a colonial government in the country.

But Filipino rebels were not about to bow to a new colonial power. Over the next two years, the United States committed 100,000 troops to subdue the rebels, using tactics that foreshadowed the U.S. war in Vietnam 70 years later. Hunting down guerrillas hiding in the jungle, American soldiers torched villages and crops. They forced water down the throats of suspected rebel leaders—a form of torture known as the "water cure" then and "waterboarding" today—in an effort to extract information. Four thousand Americans and 20,000 Filipinos died in combat. As many as 600,000 Filipino civilians succumbed to disease and starvation.

Ownership of the Philippine Islands gave the United States a foothold in Asia. In 1894–1895, Japan had waged a successful war against China, and European traders rushed in to China to monopolize local markets and establish their own spheres of influence. Secretary of State John Hay issued a communication called the Open Door note in the summer of 1899; in it, he urged the imperial powers to respect the trading interests of all nations. In 1900 the Boxer Uprising in China prompted cooperation among the western powers. The Boxers, radical Chinese nationalists, killed 200 foreign missionaries and other whites in an effort to purge China of outsiders. Together, the Germans, Japanese, British, French, and Americans sent 18,000 troops to quell the revolt. The United States and European nations continued to compete for the China market well into the twentieth century.

Critics of Imperialism

Theodore Roosevelt seemed to personify the late-nineteenth-century idea of American manifest destiny: the notion that the core of the nation's history was a militant mission to expand its territorial reach. However, not all Americans agreed with Roosevelt. New York financier Mark Hanna called him a "madman" and "that damned cowboy." Writer Mark Twain believed him "clearly insane" and "insanest upon war and its supreme glories." Twain and other prominent people founded the Anti-Imperialist League in 1898 in an attempt to stem the rising tide of militarism.

It is difficult to generalize about the politics of anti-imperialists during this period. Some critics of imperialism advocated a hands-off policy toward other nations in the belief that all peoples were entitled to self-determination. In contrast, other anti-imperialists such as Social Darwinists used arguments about racial hierarchies to justify their opposition to expansion.

In the summer of 1900, the Democrats and Republicans prepared for the upcoming presidential election. Receiving the Democratic nomination once again, William Jennings Bryan was eager to press the outdated cause of free silver. He also condemned the American presence in the Philippines, although this issue, too, was rapidly losing the attention of the electorate. At the Republican convention, Roosevelt's supporters managed to win for him the slot as McKinley's running mate. That fall, the former Rough Rider waged an exuberant campaign. Accompanied by a retinue of gun-toting cowboys, he wrapped the Republicans in the American flag. When McKinley swept to reelection in the fall, few Americans could have anticipated how central Roosevelt's vision would become to the country over the next two decades.

CONCLUSION

As Americans greeted the twentieth century, they might have marveled at the dramatic changes that had occurred in their country over the last 100 years. In 1800 the United States was home to 5.3 million people who lived in 16 states. One hundred years later, the country included 45 states and boasted a population of 76 million people. Many workplaces, fields as well as factories, were dominated by machines and the people who tended them. The economy was shifting toward the mass production of consumer goods.

In 1900 the United States exerted control over the land and peoples of Alaska, the Hawaiian and Samoan Islands, the Philippines, Guam, Puerto Rico, and Cuba. These holdings, notable for their strategic significance, illustrated the growing willingness of the United States to extend its influence and economic reach—by armed force if necessary—to the far corners of the earth. The new drive for worldwide economic and political power ran counter to America's revolutionary heritage, with its values of democracy and self-determination.

For Review

✓●—⌐Study and Review at www.myhistorylab.com

1. Why is it difficult for historians to define the terms "race," "imperialism," and "frontier"?

2. What were the regional and class dimensions in conflicts over U.S. monetary policy?

3. How successful were the Populists in welding together a coalition among farmers and factory workers and blacks and whites throughout the country? What are some of

the problems faced by third parties in American politics more generally?

4. Describe three different kinds of encounters between the United States and foreign countries in the 1890s. What were the commercial implications of Americans' fascination with "the exotic"?

Chronology: 1890–1900

1890 National American Woman Suffrage Association is formed.
Wounded Knee Massacre.

1891 Populist party formed.

1892 Ellis Island opens as screening site for immigrants.
Miners strike in Coeur d'Alene, Idaho.
Steelworkers strike at Carnegie's Homestead plant near Pittsburgh.

1893 Columbian Exposition opens in Chicago.
Pro-American interests stage a successful coup against Queen Liliuokalani of Hawaii.
Worst nationwide economic depression to date.

1894 Coxey's Army marches on Washington, D.C.
Pullman workers strike.

1896 Supreme Court decides *Plessy v. Ferguson*, upholds segregation.
W. E. B. Du Bois is first black person to receive a Ph.D. from Harvard.

1898 United States annexes Hawaii.
Maine blows up in Havana Harbor.
United States defeats Spain in Spanish-American-Cuban-Filipino War.
Spain cedes Guam and Puerto Rico to United States, turns over Philippines in return for $20 million.

1899 Emilio Aguinaldo leads Filipino revolt against 70,000 U.S. occupying forces.

1900 U.S. troops sent to China to crush Boxer Rebellion.

Key Terms

Conspicuous consumption A term coined by the American social theorist Thorstein Veblen to describe the behavior of wealthy persons who flaunt their status through their purchase of fine clothes, large houses, fancy cars, and other highly visible material goods. p. 435

Hayseeds A derogatory term applied to rural people deemed uneducated and naive (in contrast to self-proclaimed sophisticated city dwellers). p. 435

Imperialism The policy of extending a nation's authority by territorial acquistion (through negotiation or conquest) or by

the establishment of political or economic control over other nations. p. 429

Plessy v. Ferguson The 1896 case in which the Supreme Court decided that states could segregate public accommodations by race. p. 432

Yellow journalism Newspaper articles, images, and editorials that exploit, distort, or exaggerate the news in order to inflame public opinion. p. 444

PART **SEVEN**

Reform at Home, Revolution Abroad, 1900–1929

MANY AMERICANS GREETED THE FIRST YEARS OF THE TWENTIETH century with optimism. Developments at home and abroad seemed to promise a new era of prosperity and progress. The mass manufacturing of automobiles proved a boon to the economy and transformed patterns of travel, leisure, and consumption. The beginning of commercial air flights heralded a revolution in communication and transportation. Moving pictures and new musical forms such as jazz delighted millions.

Focused on the new challenges of urbanization and industrialization, Progressive reformers sought to use science to solve a wide range of problems related to public health and welfare. Some advocated overhauling the system of public education; others pressed for legislation banning the sale and distribution of alcohol. Some lobbied for worker health and safety legislation, and still others sought to exercise social control through eugenics and state-mandated sterilization.

A variety of groups challenged white men's exclusive claim to civil rights. African Americans took the national stage to argue for equality under the law and for freedom from state-sanctioned violence in the form of lynching and servitude for debt. Beginning with the Great Migration of World War I, southern blacks abandoned the cotton fields to seek jobs in northern cities.

The changing roles of women bolstered the women's suffrage movement. Growing numbers of women were becoming labor organizers, reformers, and college professors. Rising divorce rates and the emergence of birth control as a political as well as a medical issue signaled challenges to the traditional patriarchal family. At the same time, conflicts among reformers emerged. For example, white middle-class suffragists hoped to maintain their "respectability" in an effort to win the support of reluctant male leaders; in the process, these women distanced themselves from members of the working class and even the African-American women active in the suffrage movement. Suffragists' efforts paid off in 1920, with the ratification of the Nineteenth Amendment to the Constitution.

With its lively consumer culture and rising standard of living, the United States continued to attract newcomers from abroad. Immigrants from Mexico and eastern Europe sought refuge from poverty, oppression, and civil strife at home. In 1914, 1.2 million immigrants came to America, the largest number in a single year before or since that date. Between 1900 and 1930, more than 1 million Mexicans migrated north, most settling in existing Mexican-American communities in the Southwest or creating new communities there or in the Midwest.

World War I shattered the belief among many Progressives that conflicts could be solved in a rational, peaceful way. The end of the war had permanently entangled U.S. interests in European affairs. Moreover, revolutions in Mexico (1910) and Russia (1917) affected the United States directly, the former by spurring immigration across the country's southwest border, the latter by challenging the nation's system of industrial capitalism. Nevertheless, many Americans remained convinced that the country could and should isolate itself from world affairs.

Natural forces also remained beyond the control of reformers and government officials. The San Francisco earthquake of 1906, the great Mississippi flood of 1927, and the Florida hurricane of 1928 exacted devastating tolls in terms of human life and property damage. The local communities that were directly affected struggled for years to recover from these disasters.

But for many Americans, the 1920s were a period of peace and prosperity. New household appliances and conveniences lightened the burdens of housework. Radios and movies proved to be popular forms of entertainment. Traditional social mores gave way to expressions of sexual freedom. Progressive impulses waned as business values rose to take their place.

The decade after the end of World War I revealed both the persistence of old conflicts and the emergence of new conflicts within American society. Conservatives branded labor union organizers and socialists as unpatriotic and subversive. Asian immigrants on the West Coast and blacks in the rural South and urban North faced continued legal discrimination in the workplace and in the courts. Protestant fundamentalists challenged the move toward secularism and rationalism, claiming that religious faith, not science, set the standard for morality in modern life. Responding to those who feared that foreign immigration represented a threat to American society, Congress imposed immigration restrictions in 1924. Put into effect in 1920, the Eighteenth Amendment to the Constitution prohibited the sale and distribution of alcoholic beverages. The three Republican presidents who served during the 1920s—Harding, Coolidge, and Hoover—retreated from the activist stance favored by their predecessors, including Theodore Roosevelt and Woodrow Wilson.

The stock market crash of 1929 revealed fundamental weaknesses in the American economy. A tide of bank failures engulfed individual American families even as it threatened businesses abroad. As the depression deepened, Americans looked to the federal government to address the crisis.

19

Visions of the Modern Nation: The Progressive Era, 1900–1912

Upton Sinclair, a writer and political activist with a vision of a more equitable society, joined the expanding Socialist party in 1902. Four years later, at the age of 28, Sinclair published *The Jungle*, an exposé of the brutal exploitation of immigrant workers in the meat packing industry. The novel tells the story of Jurgis Rudkus, a Lithuanian immigrant who works in one of Chicago's meat packing plants. The book describes the squalid working conditions Jurgis endured in the plant, where filth, rats, and even workers' body parts ended up in the packages of ground meat. Sinclair hoped to win sympathy for the plight of immigrant workers with his vivid descriptions of the appalling conditions, and to turn the nation toward socialism.

The Jungle had a powerful impact, but the effect was not what Sinclair had hoped. Rather than spark interest in socialism, or even improved wages and working conditions, the novel aroused consumer indignation and led to the passage of the Pure Food and Drug Act (1906) and the Meat Inspection Act, which prohibited adulterated or fraudulently labeled food and drugs from interstate commerce. Sinclair later wrote with regret, "I aimed at the public's heart and by accident hit the stomach."

Sinclair's novel and its ultimate impact illustrate the many strains of reform in the early 1900s. As a socialist, Sinclair had a vision of a nation where unionized workers labored in dignity with good wages and working conditions in industries kept in check by government ownership. Most of his readers, however, had a different vision: of an affluent nation where consumers could count on the quality of the products they purchased. Even the leaders of industry had a vision: of a government that would provide a seal of approval to reassure citizens who would purchase their products, so they could reap the rewards of the free enterprise system. The Pure Food and Drug Act and Meat Inspection Act satisfied consumers and industry leaders, but left Sinclair's primary concern—working conditions in the plants—largely unchanged.

Upton Sinclair was one of the many reformers whose responses to the rapid changes taking place in the nation were fueled by a faith in progress and a belief in the possibility for social improvement. During the first years of the twentieth century, the nation began to emerge as something profoundly different from what it had been in the past. The dramatic changes taking place, from industry and technology down to the most intimate levels of life, sparked equally dramatic efforts to control, tame, and regulate them. Because of the flurry of reform activity during this period, historians call it the Progressive Era. People from all parties participated in the wide range of reform efforts known as **Progressivism**.

Progressive Era reformers did not always agree, and sometimes their visions were in conflict. Some Americans pushed vigorously for greater equality; others worked just as hard to maintain prevailing hierarchies. Reform-minded politicians like Theodore Roosevelt led the nation into an era of strong national government with a global reach. Millions of immigrants came to the United States with hopes for a better future; many joined efforts to bring the democratic ideals of their adopted country into reality. Activists for gender and racial equality, labor leaders, and local reformers had a vision of the nation that rested on equal rights, decent wages and working conditions, and vibrant cities.

A wide range of reform activities sprang up to foster, tame, control, or resist the changes taking place. Social and cultural radicals pushed for a freer society liberated from sexual constraints, government controls, and industrial tyranny. Some reformers looked to science as a tool for social improvement. Innovative artists fused their creative energy to new technologies and media to generate and reflect the vibrant urban culture in film, music, literature, and the visual arts.

In all their variety and at all levels, reform movements reshaped the relationship between citizens and government. Despite their differences, those who promoted these reform efforts called themselves Progressives. The tensions among all these visions of the nation shaped the politics of the era.

Expanding National Power

Along with flourishing radical and reform movements at the grassroots, the Progressive Era gave rise to a reformist impulse at the national level. The person who most fully embodied the national Progressive movement was Theodore Roosevelt, president from 1901 to 1908. Roosevelt used his power to regulate big business, intervene in labor disputes, control the uses of the natural environment, and extend the reach of the nation across the world. His hand-picked successor in the White House, William Howard Taft, followed mostly similar policies.

In what ways did Theodore Roosevelt promote Progressive reform?

Theodore Roosevelt: The "Rough Rider" as President

Roosevelt rose to prominence in the Republican party in the 1880s and held several important political posts, including assistant secretary of the Navy (1897–1898) and governor of New York (1899–1900). In 1900 Roosevelt became vice president; in September 1901, President McKinley was assassinated, and at age 42 Roosevelt became the youngest person ever to occupy the Oval Office.

Roosevelt was a strong proponent of American military and commercial presence in the world. He expanded the power of the federal government both at home and abroad and used the "bully pulpit" of the presidency to exert moral leadership. Using the Sherman Anti-Trust Act of 1890, which gave the federal government the power to break up monopolies, Roosevelt earned the title of "trust-buster." But it was not his intention to weaken big business. In fact, he believed that a strong country needed large, powerful industries, and he hoped to regulate them to keep big business strong.

Roosevelt's efforts to strengthen the state and foster American nationalism extended to his attitudes toward immigrants. He believed that discrimination against loyal newcomers harmed democracy: "It is a base outrage to oppose a man because of his religion or birthplace." He was proud of appointing a cabinet in which "Catholic and Protestant and Jew sat side by side."

TABLE 19-1			
The Election of 1900			
Candidate	Political Party	Popular Vote (%)	Electoral Vote
William McKinley	Republican	51.7	292
William Jennings Bryan	Democratic-Populist	45.5	155

■ Lumberjacks topple a giant spruce tree in a forest in Washington state around 1900. President Theodore Roosevelt believed that the federal government should manage timberlands and other natural resources to prevent depletion while allowing their use. Roosevelt preserved some Pacific Northwest forests in national parks and refuges but allowed others to be cultivated for timber.

But Roosevelt did not believe in cultural pluralism, that is, the idea that the United States could include citizens who retained their ethnic heritage. Rather, Roosevelt promoted the idea of a melting pot that would blend all diverse cultures into a unique American "race." Although Roosevelt was a firm believer in Anglo-Saxon superiority, he was also the first president to invite an African-American leader, Booker T. Washington, to the White House.

Protecting and Preserving the Natural World

Industrial smoke had long been a problem in both European and American cities, and Progressive Era reformers established organizations to fight air pollution. At the same time, mining and other industries were depleting natural resources while destroying the natural beauty of the land. More than any previous president, Roosevelt used the federal government to manage the natural world. Although his actions did not please everyone, Roosevelt's environmental efforts were among his most enduring legacies.

Roosevelt advocated both preservation and conservation. His preservation policies doubled the number of national parks, created 16 national monuments, and established 51 wildlife refuges. At the same time, he shared the view of **conservationists** that timberlands, areas for livestock grazing, water, and minerals needed federal government management. Roosevelt transferred 125 million acres of public land into the forest reserves to prevent the depletion of timber and he set aside land for dam sites, oil and coal reserves, and grazing. John Muir and the Sierra Club campaigned to protect the beautiful Hetch Hetchy Valley in Yosemite National Park, but Congress passed the Raker Act in 1913, allowing the city of San Francisco to build a dam and flood the valley. Residents of the Owens Valley in eastern California also protested the building of an aqueduct to divert water to the Los Angeles area. Dams, reservoirs, and aqueducts brought water and electricity to arid regions, allowing such cities as Las Vegas and Los Angeles to flourish in environments that would otherwise be unable to support large populations.

Expanding National Power Abroad

The turn of the twentieth century marked the high point of European and American imperial expansion, bringing 75 percent of the world's land under the control of Europeans or their descendants. Roosevelt hoped to strengthen the federal government at home, develop the nation's military and commercial might, and extend American power abroad. To further these ends, he sent troops to China as part of the international expedition to crush the nationalist Boxer Uprising in 1900. He also proposed the construction of a canal across the Isthmus of Panama, which Congress approved in 1902. But Panama was still a province of Colombia, and Roosevelt was unhappy with the Colombian government's negotiating position regarding an American canal project. So he aided Panamanian nationalists who seceded from Colombia in 1903. In return, the U.S. president got his canal deal with a newly independent Panama.

In 1904 Roosevelt further increased the authority of the United States to intervene in the affairs of nations in the Western Hemisphere through what came to be known as the Roosevelt Corollary to the Monroe Doctrine

TABLE 19-2

The Election of 1904

Candidate	Political Party	Popular Vote (%)	Electoral Vote
Theodore Roosevelt	Republican	57.9	336
Alton B. Parker	Democratic	37.6	155
Eugene V. Debs	Socialist	3.0	—

of 1823. Fearing political uprisings that might threaten American commercial interests, Roosevelt asserted that "chronic wrongdoing" might require the intervention by "some civilized nation" in the affairs of another. "In the Western Hemisphere," he concluded, this "may force the United States . . . to the exercise of an international police power." The Roosevelt Corollary justified later interventions in the Dominican Republic, Cuba, Nicaragua, Mexico, and Haiti. While the Monroe Doctrine had told Europeans to stay out of the hemisphere, the Roosevelt Corollary declared that the United States would intervene where it wanted to.

The bloody U.S. war against Filipino nationalists that began in 1899 lasted four years before the Americans crushed the revolt and established firm colonial rule in the Philippines. William Howard Taft became the colony's first governor-general in 1901. Taft developed a public works program that included roads, bridges, and schools. He also transferred government functions to Filipinos who cooperated with American colonial powers. Although the United States promised to grant Philippine independence, that promise was deferred until 1946.

William Howard Taft: The One-Term Progressive

Roosevelt declined to run for reelection in 1908. The Republicans selected Roosevelt's hand-picked successor, William Howard Taft. Taft was a loyal ally who worked closely with Roosevelt on foreign and domestic policies. Roosevelt assumed that Taft, after his victory in the general election, would fulfill Roosevelt's reform agenda.

Taft's respect for the separation of powers spelled out in the U.S. Constitution made him dubious about some of Roosevelt's extensions of the powers of the presidency. Nevertheless, Taft initiated far more antitrust suits than Roosevelt had during his presidency. Despite similar political inclinations, Roosevelt's support for his protégé cooled. Although Roosevelt counted major business leaders among his own advisors, he was displeased when Taft appointed corporate lawyers rather than activist reformers to his cabinet. Taft departed from Roosevelt's foreign policy as well. In contrast to Roosevelt, who emphasized military might, Taft claimed that **"Dollar Diplomacy"**—"substituting ballots for bullets"—was the best way for the United States to exert influence in the world.

When Taft signed the higher Payne-Aldrich Tariff in 1909, he disappointed progressive Republicans and aligned himself with the conservative old guard of the party, who were critical of Roosevelt. The breach between Taft and the Progressives widened when Taft's secretary of the interior, Richard A. Ballinger, opened up for commercial development 1 million acres of land that Roosevelt had placed under federal protection. In a further affront to conservationists, Gifford Pinchot, still head of the National Forest Service, discovered that Ballinger had sold Alaskan coal deposits to corporate moguls J. P. Morgan and David Guggenheim. When Taft defended Ballinger, Pinchot leaked the news to the press and called for a congressional investigation. Taft subsequently fired Pinchot, but Roosevelt publicly supported Pinchot and signaled his break from Taft.

Roosevelt returned from hunting in Africa to enter the political spotlight again. He toured the country in 1910, describing his plan for a **"New Nationalism,"** a far-reaching expansion of the federal government to stabilize the economy and institute social reforms. When the Republican party's old guard managed to renominate Taft at the Republican National Convention,

■ An earthquake devastated San Francisco on April 18, 1906. Here a Chinese immigrant watches as the city goes up in flames. Chinatown was destroyed, along with much of the downtown.

TABLE 19-3

The Election of 1908

Candidate	Political Party	Popular Vote (%)	Electoral Vote
William H. Taft	Republican	51.6	321
William Jennings Bryan	Democratic-Populist	43.1	162
Eugene V. Debs	Socialist	2.8	—

•●•⌐Read the **Document**
Dollar Diplomacy—William Howard Taft (1912) at **www.myhistorylab.com**

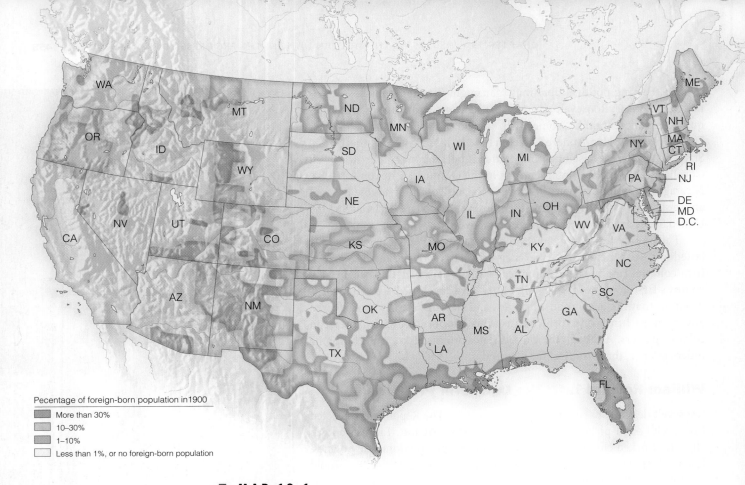

Pecentage of foreign-born population in1900

- ▓ More than 30%
- ▒ 10–30%
- ░ 1–10%
- ☐ Less than 1%, or no foreign-born population

■ **MAP 19.1**

FOREIGN-BORN POPULATION, 1900

Although the most famous points of entry for immigrants during the turn-of-the-century decades were New York's Ellis Island for people from Europe, and Angel Island in San Francisco Bay for people from Asia, most immigrants eventually settled in the upper Midwest and the southwestern region bordering Mexico.

TABLE 19-4			
The Election of 1912			
Candidate	**Political Party**	**Popular Vote (%)**	**Electoral Vote**
Woodrow Wilson	Democratic	41.9	435
Theodore Roosevelt	Progressive	27.4	88
William H. Taft	Republican	23.2	8
Eugene V. Debs	Socialist	6.0	—

Roosevelt and his supporters withdrew from the Republican party and formed the Progressive party. Roosevelt boasted, "I am as strong as a bull moose," inspiring his followers to call themselves the **Bull Moosers**. Their reformist platform called for extensive controls on corporations, minimum wage laws, child labor laws, a graduated income tax, and women's suffrage.

In contrast to Roosevelt's "New Nationalism," Democratic candidate Woodrow Wilson was reluctant to vest so much power in the government. He called his own approach the "New Freedom," believing that the government should dismantle the trusts and then revert to limited powers. The Republican vote split between Taft and Roosevelt, and the victory went to Wilson. Wilson took office amid an overwhelming popular mandate for reform.

Immigration: Visions of a Better Life

Where did immigrants settle, and what did conditions did they encounter?

Between 1900 and 1910, nearly 9 million immigrants entered the United States, the largest number for any single decade in the nation's history until the 1990s. They came particularly from southern and eastern Europe, as well as Mexico and Asia. The United States was one of several potential destinations for these courageous and hopeful sojourners. It was particularly appealing because of its often exaggerated, but nonetheless real, opportunities for jobs and economic advancement, its official commitment to freedom of religion and political thought, and its reputation as a nation that welcomed newcomers from abroad.

On arrival, many found that the "promised land" was not the paradise they expected. They faced crowded living conditions in urban tenements, jobs in sweatshops and factories with long hours, low wages, and miserable working conditions, and a hostile reception. Many Americans—including some whose own parents or grandparents had come to the United States as immigrants—looked down on the newcomers as "racially inferior" and morally suspect, feared competition for jobs, and worried that the masses of poor foreigners in their midst would become a burden on taxpayers and public institutions. The Statue of Liberty may have held up the torch of welcome, but many citizens, from union halls to legislative chambers, wanted the newcomers to leave.

Many did leave. One-third of immigrants to the United States returned to their home countries. Known as "**birds of passage**," some came for only a few years and returned to their native lands, including nearly 90 percent of migrants from the Balkans. Other groups, especially those who faced severe hardships in the lands of their birth, were more likely to make the United States their permanent home. Only 11 percent of the Irish and 5 percent of the Jews returned between 1908 and 1923.

The Heartland: Land of Newcomers

At the dawn of the twentieth century, it was not the coastal cities, with their visible immigrant ghettos, but the settlements in the upper Midwest, along with the lower Southwest, where the greatest concentration of foreign-born residents lived. In the growing towns and cities of the Midwest, newcomers from central Europe and Italy joined the earlier settlers from Germany and Scandinavia to form farming and mining communities on the rich soil and abundant mineral deposits of the region.

In the 1890s, the upper Midwest was sparsely settled. As a result of the Dawes Act of 1887, which divided tribal lands into individual parcels, much of the land originally held by Indians had been divided and sold. Most of the Indians who were native to that region were removed to reservations. The iron-rich areas near Lake Superior, previously the hunting, fishing, and gathering areas of the Native Americans, were now inhabited by lumberjacks who cut the forests. Mining companies discovered the iron deposits and began recruiting workers, first from northern Europe and then, after 1900, from southern and eastern Europe. By 1910 the iron range was home to 35 European immigrant groups. Gradually, these cohesive working-class communities, like others elsewhere, developed their own brand of ethnic Americanism, complete with elaborate Fourth of July celebrations and other festivities that expressed both their distinctive ethnic identities and their allegiance to their adopted country.

The Southwest: Mexican Borderlands

In 1904 a train carrying Irish orphans from a Roman Catholic **foundling home** in New York chugged westward to deliver its small passengers to waiting Catholic families in Clifton and Morenci in the Arizona territory. Church officials at the New York orphanage had screened the families carefully to be certain that the couples hoping to adopt these children were devout churchgoing Catholics,

Watch the **Video**
Ellis Island Immigrants, 1903 at
www.myhistorylab.com

■ **An immigrant family manages the daily routines of life in a tenement flat in 1910. Crowded conditions, poor ventilation, and inadequate plumbing made it impossible for impoverished residents such as these to maintain a clean and healthy environment.**

industrious workers, and respectable members of the community. The local parish priest approved these couples, and on the appointed day, they waited eagerly as the orphans, dressed in their best clothes, departed from the train. But when the Anglo-Protestant residents of the town discovered that Mexican Catholic foster parents claimed these fair-skinned children, they were outraged.

That night, the Anglo women gathered to mobilize their husbands into a vigilante posse. In the middle of the night, during a driving rainstorm, the men went to the homes of the Mexican couples and kidnapped the children at gunpoint. The next day, the children were distributed to the vigilantes' wives and other Anglo foster parents. Although the Catholic foundling home that had placed the children with the Mexican couples fought a lengthy legal battle to regain custody of the children, the Anglos managed to keep the orphans. The Arizona Supreme Court validated the kidnapping in the name of the "best interests of the children," and the U.S. Supreme Court let the ruling stand.

The struggle over the orphans reflected tensions and divisions in the region along lines of class as well as race. Longtime residents of this borderland region of Arizona included many Mexicans, mainly farmers, ranchers, and miners. In the early twentieth century, Mexico's deteriorating economy and prolonged revolution after 1911 prompted large numbers of Mexicans to migrate to California and the Southwest, looking for work. The year before the arrival of the orphans, Mexican mine workers had struck for better wages and working conditions against the Anglo owners of the Arizona Copper Company. The owners put down the strike, and the conflict left bitter feelings on both sides. The vigilante kidnapping of the orphans was, in part, retaliation against the Mexican workers who had organized the strike the previous year.

Asian Immigration and the Impact of Exclusion

Asians continued to face the most severe restrictions on immigration. The Chinese Exclusion Act of 1882, which prohibited most Chinese from immigrating to the United States, was renewed and extended in 1902. As a result, the mostly bachelor Chinese community in the United States declined by nearly half between 1890 and 1920. Many died or returned to China, reducing the numbers from more than 107,000 to about 61,000. The sex ratio remained severely unbalanced, with about 14 men for every woman.

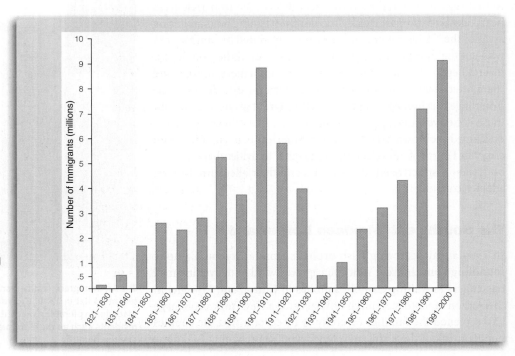

■ **FIGURE 19.1**
NUMBER OF IMMIGRANTS ENTERING THE UNITED STATES, 1821–2000
The number of immigrants entering the United States spiked in the first decade of the twentieth century and then dropped drastically as a result of the immigration restriction laws passed by Congress in the 1920s. Immigration increased again as laws changed after World War II, allowing new immigrant groups to enter.

Asian immigration exclusion

■ Immigration restricted by
Chinese Exclusion Acts (1882–1943)

■ Asiatic barred zone (1917–1952)

■ Japanese and Koreans restricted by
"Gentlemen's Agreement" (1907)
and barred in 1924

■ **MAP 19.2**

AREAS EXCLUDED FROM IMMIGRATION TO THE UNITED STATES, 1882–1952
In 1882 the United States barred Chinese immigrants from entering the country; Japanese and Koreans
were barred in 1924. In 1917 the exclusion was extended to people from India, Indonesia, and the
Arabian Peninsula. Those laws remained in effect until 1943 and 1952, respectively.

During the exclusion era, certain categories of Chinese immigrants were allowed entry.
Wives of Chinese men already in the United States could enter, as could teachers, students, and
merchants. More than 20,000 Chinese arrived during the first decade of the new century.
One such emigrant was Sieh King King, an 18-year-old student. In 1902, at a political meeting,
she addressed a packed hall in San Francisco's Chinatown. The *San Francisco Chronicle*
reported that she "boldly condemned the slave girl system, raged at the horrors of foot-binding
[a traditional Chinese practice in which girls' feet were tightly bound to keep them small]
and, with all the vehemence of aroused youth, declared that men and women were equal and
should enjoy the privileges of equals." Sieh King King expressed ideas that were emerging
among urban radicals in the United States but also reflected political movements in their
home countries.

Individual Chinese could immigrate if they had family members in the United States. As
a result, American-born Chinese frequently traveled back and forth, claiming on their return
that they left a child in China and requesting permission for their offspring to emigrate. In
this way they created spaceholders for imaginary kin, allowing other Chinese to enter the
country. The American authorities knew of this system of "paper sons" and "paper fathers"
and tried to stop the practice with elaborate and lengthy investigations that could last a year
or more while hopeful Chinese immigrants waited as virtual prisoners in wretched conditions
on Angel Island, the immigrant gateway in San Francisco Bay.

In the 1880s, there were only about 3,000 Japanese immigrants in mainland United
States. Japanese immigrants could still enter the country, and nearly 300,000 did so between
1890 and 1920, when opportunities for higher-paying jobs in Hawaii and California offered

an alternative to the economic crisis they faced in Japan. As in many countries around the world, marriages in Japan generally were arranged by families, and some men returned to Japan to meet and marry their brides. But cost and distance often prevented those meetings. Some women came to the United States as "picture brides" after an exchange of photographs. Although some women were disappointed with their often much older husbands, most accepted their fate as they would have accepted an arranged marriage in Japan. Others were delighted with the opportunity for adventure and life in the new land. As one picture bride explained, many of the people from her village had already gone to the United States, and she wanted to go, too: "I didn't care what the man looked like."

Although the Japanese comprised less than 1 percent of California's population, they faced intense nativist hostility. The Japanese in California protested against the discrimination they faced, and in one case they successfully turned a local case of school segregation into an international incident. In response to the segregation of Japanese children in San Francisco, the Japanese government expressed its extreme displeasure. Hoping to avoid a confrontation with Japan—a significant military power that had just won a war with Russia—President Theodore Roosevelt interceded and convinced the San Francisco school board to rescind its segregation order. This incident led to the "Gentlemen's Agreement" of 1907, in which the Japanese government agreed to limit the number of immigrants to the United States. The numbers of immigrants from Japan dwindled, and Japanese immigrants instead began to settle in Brazil.

Newcomers from Southern and Eastern Europe

Eastern European Jews were among the most numerous of the "new" immigrants in the early twentieth century. In 1880 there were about 250,000 Jews in America; by 1920, there were 4 million, the vast majority from eastern Europe. A number of factors motivated Jews to leave their small towns, or *shtetls*. Economic turmoil and restrictions on Jewish land ownership, trade, and business left many Jews impoverished. Antisemitic policies in Russia and eastern Europe confined many Jews to live in restricted areas. Even more devastating was antisemitic violence in the form of riots, or *pogroms*, in which Jewish towns were attacked and many Jews were beaten and killed. Many young Jewish boys emigrated to avoid being conscripted into the czar's army.

One such immigrant was young Morris Bass. At age 12, he left his family and ventured alone across the Atlantic. A butcher in New York's crowded Jewish ghetto quickly offered him a job and a place to sleep on a straw mat behind the shop. Like many others, Morris prospered modestly. After a few years, he was able to strike out on his own as a pushcart peddler. Eventually, he sent home enough money to bring his parents and siblings to America. Some Jewish immigrants struggled to retain the faith and practices of Jewish orthodoxy that had defined their lives in the *shtetl*. But Morris was among those who wanted to assimilate into American life. He retained Jewish cultural practices but abandoned many

California Views Historical Photo Collection, Monterey, CA

■ This young woman was a "picture bride" whose photograph secured her betrothal to her distant future husband. In this way, many men who emigrated from Asia arranged to marry women they had never met. The young fiancee then left her home to join a strange man in a strange land, hoping for the best.

religious rituals, such as refraining from work on Saturdays (the Jewish Sabbath) and wearing distinctive clothes.

Italian immigration also peaked between 1900 and 1914. While 90 percent of the Jews who migrated from Russia came to the United States, Italians ventured to many countries around the world creating a large global Italian diaspora. Turmoil in their home country, resulting from the political and economic consequences of unification of the Italian peninsula, prompted approximately 13 million Italians to emigrate between 1870 and 1920. Out of that number, approximately 3 million came to the United States. The majority of Italians who came to the United States arrived with their families and settled permanently, establishing strong communities and mutual aid societies. Most Italians were committed Roman Catholics, and they preserved their rituals, festivals, and faith in the new country.

Work, Science, and Leisure

As the nineteenth century gave way to the twentieth, working women and men could increasingly expect to be employed in industry rather than farms, in large organizations rather than small shops, and in enterprises that relied more on efficiency than craftsmanship. Towering skyscrapers began to dot the urban landscape, symbolic of the triumph of commerce and corporate power. Science and technology reigned, changing the nature of work as well as the fruits of production. Professional organizations of educators, social workers, physicians, and scientists emerged, while experts with academic credentials became leaders of many public institutions. It seemed as though science could solve virtually any problem. Although social problems like poverty persisted, advances in medical science contributed to improved public health.

■ At Ellis Island this immigrant family received identification tags, indicating that they had been examined and declared healthy. Those who were ill, or youngsters without relatives to meet them, were sent to quarantine houses. Some were refused entry and sent back to their home countries.

INTERPRETING HISTORY

Defining Whiteness

Naturalization laws pertaining to immigrants in the early twentieth century were based on racial categories. Asian immigrants, classified racially as "Mongolians," were not allowed to apply for U.S. citizenship. Naturalization was available only "to aliens being free white persons and to aliens of African nativity and to persons of African descent." Because racial theories were imprecise and fluid, and racial identities were not linked to nationality, immigrants occasionally challenged their racial classification to claim that they were "white." John Svan, who was Finnish, petitioned in federal court to contest the labeling of Finns as Mongolians, claiming he was white and, therefore, allowed to apply for U.S. citizenship. The petition demonstrates the acceptance of racial definitions based on phenotype—particularly skin color—as well as the imprecise nature of those definitions. In the case of "John Svan vs. the United States Government," the court granted Svan's petition, legally changing his racial identity from Mongolian to white and reclassifying Finns as white people. Here is the court's 1908 memorandum, which allowed Svan to become a citizen:

John Svan was born in Finland and calls himself a Finn. . . . According to ethnologists, the Finns in very remote times were of Mongol origin; but the various groupings of the human race into families is arbitrary and, as respects any particular people, is not permanent but is subject to change and modification through the influences of climate, employment, intermarriage and other causes. There are indications that central and western Europe was at one time overrun by the Finns; some of their stock remained, but their racial characteristics were entirely lost in their remote descendants, who now are in no danger of being classed as Mongols.

The Osmanlis, said to be of Mongol extraction, are now among the purest and best types of the Caucasian race. Changes are constantly going on and those occurring in the lapse of a few hundred years with any people may be very great.

The chief physical characteristics of the Mongolians are as follows: They are short of stature, with little hair on their body or face; they have yellow-brown skins, black eyes, black hair, short, flat noses, and oblique eyes. In actual experience we sometimes, though rarely, see natives of Finland whose eyes are slightly oblique. We sometimes see them with sparse beards and sometimes with flat noses; but Finns with a yellow or brown or yellow-brown skin or with black eyes or black hair would be an unusual sight. They are almost universally of light skin, blue or gray eyes, and light hair. No people of foreign births applying in this section of the country for the full rights of citizenship are lighter-skinned than those born in Finland. In stature they are quite up to the average.

This more urban society developed new forms of leisure and entertainment. The film industry emerged in Hollywood, a suburb of Los Angeles. Amusement parks and nightclubs provided new venues for greater intimacy between unmarried men and women. And American art and literature began to emphasize the vitality and diversity in the nation's cities.

The Uses and Abuses of Science

Breakthroughs in science and medicine led to improvements in public health. Reformers exposed the dangers of potions and remedies sold by street vendors, as standards for medications improved. But crowding and lack of sanitation still fostered the spread of disease, especially among the poor. Lack of access to clean water was one of the major causes of disease, along with crowding, lack of medical care, and other chronic problems of poverty. Improved public sanitation alleviated the problem considerably in the early years of the twentieth century, reducing the incidence of typhoid fever by 70 percent. Among those who contributed to better conditions were community nurses. In 1900 the New York Charity Organization Society hired Jessie Sleet Scales, the first African-American public health nurse, to address problems related to tuberculosis. Scales and other public health professionals implemented sanitation standards and provided care for poor communities, helping to control the spread of disease. Public sanitation remained a problem, however, especially in crowded cities.

Confessedly, Finland has often been overrun with Teutons and by other branches of the human family, who, with their descendants, have remained within her borders and are now called Finns. They are in the main indistinguishable in their physical characteristics from those of purer Finnish blood. Intermarriages have been frequent over a very long period of time. If the Finns were originally Mongols, modifying influences have continued until they are now among the whitest people in Europe. It would, therefore, require a most exhaustive tracing of family history to determine whether any particular individual born in Finland had or had not a remote Mongol ancestry. This, of course, cannot be done and was not intended. The question is not whether a person had or had not such ancestry, but whether he is now a "white person" within the meaning of that term as usually understood. This is the practical construction which has uniformly been placed upon the law. . . . Under such law Finns have always been admitted to citizenship, and there is no occasion now to change the construction.

The applicant is without doubt a white person within the true intent and meaning of such law.

The objections, therefore, in my opinion should be overruled and it will be so ordered.

Questions

1. According to the court, what might cause changes in the "groupings of the human race into families" over time?
2. How does the court's opinion reflect prevailing attitudes toward race during the Progressive Era?
3. How did the court explain the transformation of Finns from the classification as "Mongols" to becoming "among the whitest people in Europe"?

These Finnish men living in Minnesota were among those whose racial classification was changed from "Mongolian" to "White" as the result of one Finnish immigrant's petition. Along with the Jews, Italians, Irish, and other immigrant groups now considered "white," Finns were classified as nonwhite until the laws and customs changed. Racial categories were fluid and imprecise, but whiteness conferred status and privileges.

Reflecting an impulse to blame social problems on allegedly flawed individuals or groups was the eugenics movement, which advocated scientific breeding to improve the nation's racial stock. Drawing on theories of white racial superiority and unscientific notions of genetic inheritance, eugenicists believed that character traits were inherited, including tendencies toward criminality, sexual immorality, and lack of discipline leading to poverty. Eugenicists claimed that social problems resulted from the high birthrate of immigrants and others they considered to be racially inferior to educated middle-class Anglo-Saxon Americans with their low birthrate.

President Theodore Roosevelt was an outspoken advocate of eugenics reform. Alarmed by the dramatic decline in the birthrate of native-born Americans and the tendency of some college-educated women to remain single and childless, he feared that the immigrants, with their much higher birthrate, would overrun the nation. Roosevelt called upon Anglo-Saxon women to prevent what he called **race suicide**, much as male citizens had an obligation to defend the country if called to military duty.

Some eugenics crusaders proposed compulsory sterilization of those they deemed unfit for parenthood. Indiana enacted a eugenic sterilization law in 1907 and other states soon followed. These laws gave legal sanction to the surgical sterilization of thousands of men and even greater numbers of women whom government and medical officials deemed "feebleminded." The criteria were vague at best; often sexual impropriety or out-of-wedlock pregnancy landed young women—generally poor and often foreign-born—in institutions for the feebleminded, where the operations took place. The Supreme Court upheld compulsory sterilization laws in the 1920s. Increasingly, women of color were targeted, and the practice continued well into the 1980s.

Scientific Management and Mass Production

Read the Document
Taylor, Scientific Management at
www.myhistorylab.com

In 1911 Frederick Winslow Taylor wrote *The Principles of Scientific Management*, a guide to increased efficiency in the nation's industries. While working in the Midvale Steel Works near Philadelphia, Taylor developed a system to improve mass production in factories to make more goods more quickly. Taylor's principles included analysis of each job to determine the precise motions and tools needed to maximize each worker's productivity, detailed instructions for workers, and wage scales with incentives to motivate workers to achieve high production goals. Over the next decades, industrial managers all over the country drew on Taylor's studies. Business leaders rushed to embrace Taylor's principles, and Taylor himself became a pioneering management consultant.

Watch the Video
*The Rise and Fall of the Automobile
Economy* at **www.myhistorylab.com**

Henry Ford was among the most successful industrialists to employ Taylor's techniques. Born in 1863 on a farm near Dearborn, Michigan, the mechanically inclined Ford became an apprentice in a Detroit machine shop in 1879. Although he did not invent the automobile—the first motor cars were manufactured in Germany—he developed design and production methods that brought the cost of an automobile within the reach of the average worker. Experimenting with the new internal combustion engine in the 1890s, he built his first automobile in 1896. In 1903 Ford established the Ford Motor Company and began a profitable business. He introduced the popular and relatively inexpensive, mass-produced Model T automobile in 1908, which sold for $850. In 1913 Ford introduced the **assembly line**, a production system in which each worker performed one task repeatedly as each automobile in the process of construction moved along a conveyor. Assembly-line manufacturing increased production while cutting costs. In 1914 Ford increased his workers' wages to $5 per day at a time when industrial laborers averaged only $11 per week. By 1916 the price of the Model T dropped to $360. In this sense Ford was a pioneer not only in production but also in consumption. His innovations helped to usher in the **mass consumption society**.

New Amusements

Read the Document
Coney Island, 1904 at
www.myhistorylab.com

As Americans increasingly moved from rural to urban areas, and from farms to factories, new institutions of leisure emerged in the growing cities. Consumer culture was the flip side of business culture in the early twentieth century. One of the great ironies of American history in the twentieth century is that its popular culture—which more than anything else identifies the United States to the rest of the world—was largely a creation of immigrants and people of color. During the very years when these groups faced intense discrimination, they developed the cultural products that came to define America.

The motion picture industry is a case in point. In 1888 Thomas Edison invented the kinetoscope, the early motion picture camera. The pragmatic Edison thought that his new device might be used in education and industry and did not see much commercial potential for the gadget. Not until the early twentieth century did the moving picture begin to reach a wide audience. Moviemakers left the East Coast and moved to the West, taking advantage of the even climate, cheap land, and nonunion labor. Within a few years, the moviemakers, mostly Jewish immigrants, established the film industry. Hollywood emerged as a major center of American popular culture, sending its products across the nation and abroad.

The first motion picture audiences were in the working-class neighborhoods of the growing cities. In New York alone, by 1910, there were 1,000 small storefront theaters and fun houses known as penny arcades where there had been none 20 years earlier. The number of saloons also increased from 7,000 to 9,000, while the Coney Island amusement park drew thousands to its shimmering lights and thrilling rides. During these same years, the sounds of African-American music began attracting audiences among immigrants and native-born whites, as youths from all ethnic groups flocked to dance halls. Glamorous nightclubs, known as cabarets, also began to appear, offering dining, dancing, music, and entertainment to the wealthy.

"Sex O'Clock in America"

The sexual mores and behavior of Americans seemed to be changing so dramatically that one observer announced that "sex o'clock" had struck. Indeed, the codes of the past were challenged at every turn. Among the middle class, unchaperoned dating began to replace the previous system of a man "coming to call" at the home of a woman he hoped to court.

Immigrants often brought traditional courtship patterns to the new world and extended them into the next generation. One Italian man described his thwarted efforts to woo his fiancée in private. When he visited her home, "She sat on one side of the table, and I at the other. They afraid I touch." Finally, less than a month before their wedding, he got permission to take her to the theater. But the family was unwilling to let them go alone. "We came to the aisles of the theater. My mother-in-law go first, my fiancée next, my little sister, my father in law. I was the last one. I had two in between. . . . I was next to the old man." He tried to steal a kiss a few days before the wedding, but his fiancée rebuffed him: "No, not yet."

In spite of efforts by their elders, native-born as well as immigrant youth challenged the sexual codes of the past. Increasing sexual intimacy between unmarried men and women reflected heightened expectations for sexual satisfaction—for women as well as men. These

■ *The Café Francis,* by George Luks, c. 1909. Luks was one of many artists who celebrated urban street life, popular culture, and diverse working-class subjects. This art exuded the vitality of urban life and conveyed a gritty reality without moral condemnation. Their raw and sensual depictions of city entertainments stirred controversy among art critics at the time. Contemptuous critics referred to them as the "Ashcan School," a label they embraced.

years also witnessed a rise in the proportion of brides who were pregnant at marriage, from a low of 10 percent in the mid-nineteenth century to 23 percent by 1910. Artists challenged sexual mores as well. Theodore Dreiser's 1900 novel *Sister Carrie* narrates the story of an independent young woman who uses her sexuality to advance her ambition. Because of the novel's scandalous content, Dreiser's publisher did not promote the book, although it was revived and republished in later years.

Marriage increasingly held the promise not only of love, intimacy, and mutual obligation, as it had in the nineteenth century, but of sexual fulfillment and shared leisure pursuits. However, some women did not marry but instead formed lifelong attachments to other women. Rarely identified as lesbian but often described as **Boston marriages**, these unions signified long-term emotional bonds between women who lived together. Meanwhile, lesbians, as well as gay men, gained greater visibility in the cities. They frequented bars and clubs in such places as Greenwich Village and Harlem, hoping to avoid the attention of police, who were likely to arrest them for indecent conduct.

> *Marriage increasingly held the promise not only of love, intimacy, and mutual obligation, but of sexual fulfillment and shared leisure pursuits.*

Reformers and Radicals

Who were the reformers and radicals, and what strategies did they use to promote their vision of society?

Progressivism included two distinct impulses. On the one hand, many Anglo-Saxon Protestants tried to impose order on a rapidly changing nation. They hoped to stem the tide of immigration, bolster rapidly eroding sexual codes, and quell the movements for social change. On the other hand, women's rights activists, workers, and African Americans struggled to achieve the rights and privileges available to white men of property and standing. The tensions between these two very different approaches to reform shaped the politics of the era.

Muckraking, Moral Reform, and Vice Crusades

Read the Document
Mother Jones, "The March of the Mill Children" at **www.myhistorylab.com**

Read the Document
Steffens, from The Shame of the Cities at **www.myhistorylab.com**

In the early twentieth century, a group of investigative journalists, the **muckrakers**, began to expose the ills of industrial life. Their best-known works illuminated corruption in business and politics. Ida Tarbell wrote a powerful exposé of the ruthless business practices of John D. Rockefeller, who transformed the Standard Oil Company into a monopoly. Lincoln Steffens unearthed scandals in city and state politics.

Child labor was another concern of reformers. Children worked in fields and factories across the country, picking cotton in Texas, mining coal in West Virginia, working in the textile mills of North Carolina, and sewing buttons in urban sweatshops. Children of immigrants and rural migrants often assisted parents on farms or in shops, their labor an accepted part of the household economy. But the jobs available to children in urban industries often were dangerous and unhealthy, characterized by long hours, low pay, and miserable working conditions. Reformers attempted to improve children's working conditions and to establish age limits so that children could attend school and spend time in healthful recreation rather than in grim sweatshops and factories. Ultimately, child labor activists succeeded in passing legislation at the state level that restricted child labor, although these efforts were more successful in northern states than in the South.

Protective legislation for women was also controversial. Reformers campaigned for laws that would establish minimum wages, maximum hours, regulations against night work, and restrictions on heavy lifting. When they were unable to secure such safety measures for all workers, they argued that women needed special protections because of their physical frailty and their role as future mothers. Women's rights activists disagreed over these measures. Some argued that they were necessary to protect women from exploitation and dangerous working conditions. Others claimed that women should be treated the same as men, arguing that protective legislation implied that women needed special care and were not suited for particular kinds of work. The Supreme Court affirmed the ten-hour working day for women—and the principle of protective legislation—in its landmark 1908 decision *Muller v. Oregon.*

Watch the Video

What was the progressive education movement? at **www.myhistorylab.com**

One noted reformer was Helen Keller, whose work on behalf of the blind called attention to the needs of the disabled. Keller lost her sight and hearing from an illness at the age of 19 months and learned to communicate through Braille and sign language, which she mastered through touch, with the help of her extraordinary teacher, Anne Sullivan. Keller went on to study at schools for the deaf and graduated with honors from Radcliffe College in 1904. A passionate socialist and advocate of women's rights along with other radical causes, Keller wrote several books and lectured widely all over the world, with the assistance of interpreters.

Most Progressive reformers were prosperous American-born Anglo-Saxon Protestants. Along with their efforts to improve living and working conditions and alleviate the suffering of the poor, they also hoped to eradicate vice from their society. Vice crusaders in most of the nation's large cities tried to eliminate prostitution and to patrol dance halls, movie theaters, and saloons. Vice crusading culminated in the passage of the Mann Act in 1910, which made it illegal to transport women across state lines for "immoral purposes."

Women's Suffrage

The movement for women's rights, including the effort to gain the vote, was more than half a century old by 1900. But the movement gained momentum at the dawn of the twentieth century. A new generation of women's rights leaders came together in the suffrage movement. The militancy of the suffrage movement in England inspired American activists to develop new tactics and international alliances. These activists achieved legislative success when several western states granted women the right to vote: Washington in 1910, California in 1911, and three more states in 1912. Eventually the movement united around the goal of enacting a federal amendment.

The suffrage movement, for all its radicalism, was largely a movement of white middle-class women. White suffrage leaders feared that any alliance with women of color would alienate Southern voters whom they needed for ratification of the Nineteenth Amendment. They also hoped to win over to their cause racist and nativist critics in the North who feared that granting the vote to women would enfranchise "undesirable" voters, specifically immigrant

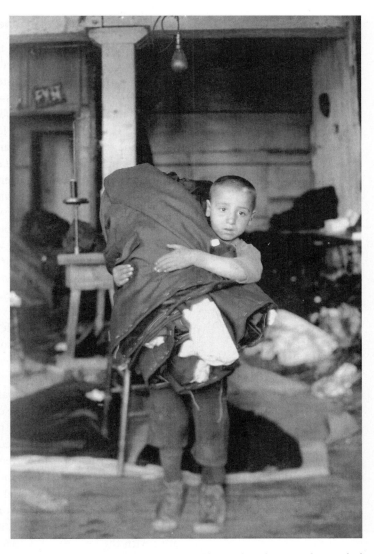

■ In the early twentieth century, many children such as this young boy worked long hours doing hard labor. Photographer Lewis Hine, who took this picture, worked for the National Child Labor Committee. His photographs documented the exploitation of child workers and helped to generate support for child labor laws. Hine also photographed immigrants, industrial work, and urban street life. He was one of many Progressive era artists committed to enriching, expressing, interpreting, and transforming the urban industrial landscape.

and minority women. The suffrage movement also gained the support of conservatives who believed that women would vote for conservative causes such as prohibition and immigration restriction.

Many minority women, such as Hispana activist Adelina Otero Warren, supported the suffrage movement even though white leaders kept their distance and refused to embrace the antiracist campaigns of their nonwhite sisters. The African-American antilynching activist Ida B. Wells (also known by her married name as Ida B. Wells-Barnett) supported women's suffrage but was unable to convince the white women's rights leaders to denounce lynching. Ultimately, the passage of the Nineteenth Amendment resulted from a combination of factors, including radical activism, strong support of a wide range of reformers, and an alliance with conservative, racist, and anti-immigrant forces.

Radical Politics and the Labor Movement

Progressive reformers believed that American capitalist democracy was a fundamentally sound system that simply needed to be fixed to achieve its full promise. Radicals of the era, by contrast, believed that the system itself was flawed and needed to be fundamentally transformed. Emma Goldman, a Russian Jewish immigrant, was one of many radical activists who gained both fame and notoriety for her outspoken support of radical causes.

Clara Lemlich was another Jewish immigrant who arrived in America filled with a passion for the rights of workers. "I am a working girl," she declared in her native Yiddish, "one of those striking against intolerable conditions." Still in her teens, the petite young woman took the podium on the night of November 22, 1909, before thousands of striking workers in New York and roused them with stirring words. The next morning, 15,000 garment workers went on strike, demanding a 52-hour workweek, overtime pay, and union recognition. Soon the number of strikers swelled to more than 20,000. Observers at the time were astonished to see lively, fashionably dressed young women filling the picket lines. Ninety percent of the striking workers were Jewish and Italian immigrants.

The strike ended when the striking workers overwhelmingly rejected an offer of better wages and working conditions that did not include recognition of their union. Calling the strikers "socialists," their more moderate allies broke from the union and left the young female workers vulnerable to the power of the company owners. The coalition of support fell apart, and most of the strikers eventually went back to work.

Less than two years later, a fire broke out in the top floors of the Triangle Shirtwaist Company, one of the centers of the 1919 strike. Scraps of material piled everywhere created a fire trap, quickly spreading the flames into a raging inferno. Eight hundred workers, most of them young Jewish and Italian women, were trapped in the conflagration because company officials had locked interior doors to prevent the women from taking breaks outside.

The flames tore through the building in less than half an hour, leaving 146 young women dead. The factory owners were charged with manslaughter, but their attorney argued that the building was in full compliance with safety laws, so they were acquitted of all wrongdoing. But compliance with the laws did not ensure safety for the workers. No laws at the time required adequate fire escapes or fire drills. Just a few months before the fire, the building had been inspected and declared "fireproof." The brutal working conditions that led to the Triangle Shirtwaist fire prevailed all over the country and mobilized workers in a wide range of industries.

■ Victims of the Triangle Shirtwaist Company fire.

Socialism was never as strong in the United States as it was in Europe, but it did gain strength at the turn of the century. Socialists promoted labor unions and the rights of women and formed their own political party. Socialist leader Eugene V. Debs, who had gained national fame for his role in the 1894 railroad strike, became the spokesperson and leader of the Socialist party. Between 1900 and 1920, he was the party's candidate for president, gaining nearly a million votes, or 6 percent of the electorate, in the 1912 election. Although the socialists never gathered a large enough following to win national elections, they elected hundreds of candidates to local office.

The Industrial Workers of the World (IWW), also known as the **Wobblies**, offered another possibility for labor radicalism. It was organized in 1905 by socialists and labor militants. The IWW included women, blacks, immigrants, and unskilled and migratory laborers, workers generally shunned by the American Federation of Labor (AFL). The Wobblies organized workers in the mines of the Rocky Mountain states, in the lumber camps of the Pacific Northwest and the South, and in the eastern textile and steel mills. IWW membership reached about 3 million people, although no more than 150,000 were members at any one time.

View the Image
Logo for the Industrial Workers of the World at **www.myhistorylab.com**

Resistance to Racism

The Progressive Era was anything but progressive for nonwhite Americans. Although there were notable exceptions, such as Jane Addams, many white Protestant reformers were either indifferent to racial minorities or actively hostile to them. Moreover, most blacks lived in the rural South, not in northern cities where Progressives were most active. Lynching continued into the twentieth century, with nearly 100 lynchings per year between 1900 and 1910. African Americans were the primary targets of lynch mobs, although other minorities were also vulnerable. Between 1850 and 1930, 597 Mexicans died at the hands of vigilante mobs, half of them in Texas. Black leaders spoke out against lynching and other forms of racial injustice. Ida B. Wells-Barnett, who had launched an international crusade against lynching in the 1890s, worked to establish local and national networks of black women's clubs. Although she was unable to persuade white suffrage leaders to support the cause of racial justice, she worked closely with Jane Addams to prevent the establishment of segregated schools in Chicago.

A number of other black leaders came to prominence in the first decade of the twentieth century. In 1905 scholar and civil rights leader W. E. B. Du Bois joined with other black leaders to form the Niagara Movement, which called for an end to segregation and discrimination in unions, the courts, and public accommodations, as well as for equal economic and educational opportunity. In 1909 prominent African Americans joined with white progressive allies to establish the National Association for the Advancement of Colored People (NAACP). The new organization adopted the platform of the Niagara Movement, and Du Bois became the editor of its journal, *The Crisis*.

CONCLUSION

When Woodrow Wilson entered the White House in 1913, the nation looked and behaved differently than it had at the turn of the century. Millions of immigrants from Europe, Asia, and Mexico had arrived in the United States and settled in towns and cities across the nation. Growing urban areas with new amusements and increasingly diverse populations emerged as centers of a national mass culture. New developments in science and technology brought the automobile and the motion picture to American consumers. At the same time, industrial production contributed to environmental damage, pollution, and dangerous working conditions.

Progressive reformers and labor activists mounted efforts to curb the ill effects of urban industrial society. Faith in science and expertise gave rise to pervasive optimism that social problems could be solved. Muckrakers exposed corruption, women's rights activists pushed for the vote, and African-American leaders organized for civil rights and against lynching. In the West and Southwest, Mexicans and Asians challenged discriminatory laws and labor practices. At the same time, moralists and vice crusaders sought to tame what they considered dangerous challenges to the social order.

These years also witnessed a major expansion of national power. Presidents Roosevelt and Taft strengthened the role of the federal government through new efforts to regulate big business and by extending America's military and economic presence abroad. By 1912 most Americans supported a strong reform agenda. But within a few years, the nation became embroiled in a major world war that would challenge the inherent optimism of Progressivism, signaling the end of an era.

For Review

✓●─⌐Study and Review at www.myhistorylab.com

1. Who were the Progressives, and why is this time period known as the Progressive Era?

2. How did Theodore Roosevelt and William Taft use their presidential power? On which issues did they agree and disagree?

3. How did immigrants respond to their adopted country, and how did their American-born neighbors respond to them?

4. How did new leisure institutions and artistic creativity alter urban life?

Chronology: 1901–1912

1901 McKinley is assassinated; Vice President Theodore Roosevelt becomes president.

1902 New Lands Act spurs dam building and irrigation in the Southwest.

1903 First motorized flight by Orville and Wilbur Wright.
Henry Ford founds Ford Motor Company.

1904 Roosevelt Corollary to Monroe Doctrine.

1905 Industrial Workers of the World founded.

1906 San Francisco earthquake.
Upton Sinclair, *The Jungle*.
Pure Food and Drug Act.

1907 "Gentlemen's Agreement" with Japan.
Indiana becomes first state to pass compulsory sterilization law.

1908 *Muller v. Oregon* limits maximum hours for working women.

1909 New York City garment workers' "Uprising of the 20,000."
National Association for the Advancement of Colored People (NAACP) founded.

1910 Mexican Revolution begins.

1911 Triangle Shirtwaist Company fire, New York City.

1912 Theodore Roosevelt helps form Progressive party.
Woodrow Wilson elected president.

Key Terms

Assembly line A form of industrial production popularized by the Ford Motor Company in which workers perform one task repeatedly as the products they are jointly assembling move along a conveyor. p. 464

"Birds of passage" A term applied to immigrants who came to the United States for a brief period of time, and then returned to their home countries. p. 457

Bull Mooser Supporter of Theodore Roosevelt in the 1912 presidential election when he broke from the Republican party and ran as a third-party candidate on the ticket of the Progressive (or Bull Moose) party. p. 456

Boston marriages Unions of two women based on long-term emotional bonds in which the women live together as if married to each other. p. 466

Conservationist Advocate of conserving and protecting the natural world through the use of renewable natural resources. p. 454

"Dollar Diplomacy" President William Howard Taft coined the term to refer to a policy that encouraged economic investment in foreign countries. p. 455

Foundling home A residence for orphaned children. p. 457

Mass consumption society The term refers to a shift in the early twentieth century from a society focused on frugality and production to one that embraced and celebrated consumer goods and leisure pursuits. p. 464

Muckrakers The name given to a group of investigative journalists in the early twentieth century whose exposés often challenged corporate and government power. p. 466

New Nationalism Theodore Roosevelt's plan for a far-reaching expansion of the federal government to stabilize the economy and institute social reforms. p. 455

Progressivism A notion of political reform central to the "Progressive Era" (the first two decades of the twentieth century), when urban reformers with a faith in progress sought to address local and national social problems through political and civic means. p. 452

Race suicide A fear articulated by Theodore Roosevelt and others that the low birthrate of Anglo-Saxon Americans, along with the high birthrate of immigrants from southern and eastern Europe and elsewhere, would result in a population in which "inferior" peoples would outnumber the "American racial stock." p. 463

Wobblies Members of the Industrial Workers of the World (IWW), a radical labor union formed in 1905. p. 469

War and Revolution, 1912–1920

"This is the crisis of the world," wrote prominent African-American scholar and activist W. E. B. Du Bois in his July 1918 editorial in *The Crisis*, as desperate armies struggled on the battlefields of Europe and the outcome of World War I hung in the balance. Du Bois served as editor of this influential NAACP journal, whose circulation soared from 1,000 in its first year of publication in 1910 to over 100,000 by 1918. Arguing that the threat of imperial German power "spells death to the aspirations of Negroes and all darker races for equality, freedom and democracy," Du Bois concluded, "Let us, while this war lasts, forget our special grievances and close our ranks with our own white fellow citizens and the allied nations that are fighting for democracy." World War I, as Du Bois understood, would touch every continent abroad and would reshape American life and politics at home.

At first, from 1910 to 1914, optimism about solving the nation's social problems rose as Progressive reformers attempted to ameliorate some of the worst aspects of modern industrial life. International developments then turned American attentions abroad. Traumatic revolutions swept through Mexico, China, and Russia, and the conflagration of the Great War—World War I, as it became known later—consumed all of Europe from 1914 to 1918 and eventually drew in the United States. What President Woodrow Wilson called the war "to make the world safe for democracy" encouraged people of color, both in the vast European-ruled colonies of Asia and Africa and in the segregated United States, to claim a place of greater equality. But at home the war also created pressures for conformity and intolerance for dissent. The United States emerged from the war with great prestige and power, but the Versailles Treaty of 1919 failed to create a lasting structure for world peace.

A World and a Nation in Upheaval

American politics in the 1910s and the U.S. involvement in World War I must be understood within the context of change and uncertainty in the international system. While world affairs were still dominated by the wealthy nations of western Europe and North America, the first wave of the great revolutions of the twentieth century was beginning to wash away much of the old order. Tensions also sharpened within the United States over traditional hierarchies of color, gender, and class. The struggle between Progressive reform and conservative reaction pervaded public life in the United States and much of the rest of the world.

The Apex of European Conquest

On the eve of World War I, three quarters of the world's population lived under the rule of Europeans or their descendants. Exploration of the most remote parts of the globe filled in the last blank spaces on world maps, including the North (1909) and South (1911) poles. The granting of statehood to Arizona and New Mexico in 1912 completed the 48 main-land states.

Technological innovations in transportation and communication tied the world more closely together. Just as the Suez Canal (1870) and the trans-Siberian railroad (1904) linked Europe more directly to Asia, the Panama Canal (1914) cut in half the travel time by water between the East and West coasts of the United States. Cables laid on the floor of the Atlantic Ocean in 1914 inaugurated telephone service between Europe and the United States.

The competition that arose from the expansion of European power sowed the seeds of World War I. Germany, France, Britain, Italy, and Russia raced each other for new colonies and greater influence across Africa and Asia. The central rivalry emerged between a newly unified Germany (1871) and traditionally dominant Britain. Anticipating trouble, each of the major European powers sought allies to bolster its position. Britain, France, and Russia formed an alliance that became known as the **Entente** or sometimes the Allies. Germany, Austria-Hungary, and Italy established their own alliance, known as the Central Powers.

The United States emerged as a global power in this same period around the turn of the century. Fifteen years after it seized an overseas empire in 1898, the country's economic growth was stunning. In 1913, U.S. consumption of energy from coal and oil equaled that of Britain, Germany, France, Russia, and Austria-Hungary combined. The United States also brought a different history to the world stage. It had been born in 1776 in the first successful revolution by colonies against a European empire. Americans had long understood them-selves as a people who opposed empires and supported self-government. The events of 1898 contradicted this legacy, and Americans remained ambivalent about their country's imperial venture. The U.S. Congress in 1916 promised eventual independence to the Philippines and granted U.S. citizenship to residents of Puerto Rico in 1917.

Confronting Revolutions in Asia, Europe, and the Americas

As nationalist movements in China, Russia, and Mexico overturned weak central govern-ments controlled by foreign investors, American economic and security interests seemed to be at stake on three continents. In Asia, the Chinese deeply resented exclusive foreign enclaves that dominated their nation's coastal region and exempted for-eigners from the constraints of Chinese laws. In 1911, nationalist revolutionaries inspired by Sun Yat-sen, a Hawaiian-educated Christian democratic reformer, overthrew the corrupt Qing dynasty that had proven unable to resist western incursions.

The American desire for an open door into China's trade—a door that no other powerful nation could close at will—conflicted with the rising impe-rial power of the region: Japan. The Tokyo government, which had annexed Korea in 1910, responded to the outbreak of World War I by seizing the valuable German-held Shantung Peninsula in northeastern China. In its Twenty-One Demands to China, issued in January 1915, Japan made clear its plans to dominate the development of the Chinese economy. The American relationship with both China and Japan was undercut at home by continued dis-crimination and violence against immigrants from Asia.

Revolutionary struggles with implications for America also threatened the monarchs who ruled eastern Europe. For Russians, defeat at the hands of Japan in 1905 helped pre-cipitate a thwarted revolution followed by two years of political turmoil. The czar survived to rule another decade, and thousands of political reformers—unionists, anarchists, and

What were the greatest challenges to the existing international and domestic order in the 1910s?

Watch the **Video**
The Outbreak of WWI at
www.myhistorylab.com

■ The son of a Haitian immigrant, W.E.B. Du Bois (1868–1963) was the first African American to earn a Ph.D. at Harvard University. Du Bois became a distinguished historian and sociologist, as well as one of the nation's most influential voices on racial issues.

The United States had been born in the first successful revolution by colonies against a European empire.

Tijuana

Columbus, NM

El Paso

Pancho Villa pursued, 1916–1917

Parral

socialists—joined a growing wave of immigration from Russia and elsewhere to the United States. The wave crested in 1914 at 1.2 million people, most of them from east or south of the Alps. That same year, the assassination of the heir to the Austro-Hungarian throne by a Serbian nationalist in Sarajevo provided the spark that ignited the Great War.

Before World War I, the most important region of the world for the United States was Latin America, especially Central America, Mexico, and the Caribbean islands. This area guarded the nation's strategic southern flank, and American citizens and corporations invested more money in Latin America than in any other region of the world. American anxieties about stability to the south centered on Mexico. "Land for the landless and Mexico for the Mexicans" became the slogan of revolutionaries there between 1910 and 1920. U.S. stakes in the Mexican revolution were high. American investors owned 43 percent of all Mexico's wealth (other foreigners owned another 25 percent), and more than half of the country's trade flowed north to the United States. Moreover, by 1921 Mexico was the world's second largest exporter of oil. Washington feared the spread of radical political ideas northward as almost a million Mexicans crossed their northern border during the revolutionary decade, tripling the number of Americans with recent roots south of the Rio Grande.

Many came through El Paso, the "Ellis Island" for immigrants from the south. Fleeing poverty and violence, they found both discrimination and employment. Most immigrants sought unskilled positions, but members of Mexico's professional class—teachers, architects, and lawyers—also came north, for political asylum. The new arrivals joined Mexican Americans who had lived in the region since it was part of Mexico. They had not crossed the border; in 1848 the border had crossed them.

> *Mexican Americans had lived in the region since it was part of Mexico. They had not crossed the border; in 1848 the border had crossed them.*

Wilson sought unsuccessfully to reestablish in Mexico a political order respectful of the rights of foreign property owners. Wilson twice sent U.S. troops into Mexico, at Veracruz in April 1914 to block a German arms shipment and then in pursuit of Francisco ("Pancho") Villa and his army after their 1916 assault on Columbus, New Mexico. The American forces under General John J. Pershing withdrew in early 1917 as the president prepared to enter the much larger war in Europe. Land redistribution and national control of the country's abundant mineral wealth, particularly oil, were written into Mexico's new constitution passed a few days later, and the revolutionary upheaval ended by 1920.

Social Conflicts at Home

Just as social upheaval threatened monarchies and international investors abroad, less privileged Americans contested traditional lines of hierarchy and control in the United States. The Wilson administration's "New Freedom" slogan did not apply to African Americans, who faced continuing discrimination in employment and housing. The president filled his cabinet with white Southerners who segregated the few federal agencies that had employed blacks. When Wilson took office, African Americans continued to be murdered publicly by vigilante mobs across the South at a rate of more than one person per week. But the president ignored requests from the recently formed NAACP for an antilynching law.

UNITED STATES

ATLANTIC OCEAN

Houston ●

● New Orleans

San Antonio

*Gulf of
Mexico*

● Miami

BAHAMA
ISLANDS
(*British*)

Mexico City

Guantanamo
U.S. Naval Base, 1898

DOMINICAN
REPUBLIC
*Occupied, 1916–1924
Protectorate, 1905–1941*

U.S. VIRGIN
ISLANDS
*Acquired from
Denmark, 1917*

CUBA
*Occupied, 1898–1902,
1906–1909, 1912, 1917, 1922,
Protectorate, 1898–1934*

PUERTO RICO
Annexed, 1898

Veracruz
Occupied, 1914

JAMAICA
(*British*)

HAITI
*Occupied, 1915–1934
Protectorate, 1915–1936*

*Caribbean
Sea*

XICO

BRITISH
HONDURAS

HONDURAS
*Occupied, 1912–1919,
1924–1925*

NICARAGUA
*Occupied, 1912–1925,
1926–1933*

VENEZUELA

GUATEMALA

Canal Zone
*Seized from Colombia, 1903,
then leased from Panama, 1903*

EL SALVADOR

COSTA RICA

COLOMBIA

U.S. interests in the Caribbean, 1898–1939

▨ U.S. and possessions
▨ Occupied by or protectorate of U.S.
⇨ U.S. assaults

PANAMA
Protectorate, 1903–1939

■ MAP 20.1
U.S. INTERESTS AND INTERVENTIONS IN THE CARIBBEAN REGION, 1898–1939
By its size, wealth, and military power, the United States dominated the Caribbean region to its south.
American capitalists invested heavily in Mexico, Central America, and the Caribbean islands, and U.S.
troops often intervened to protect those investments. Puerto Rico (by acquisition from Spain) and the Panama
Canal Zone (by lease from Panama) became particularly important territories ruled by the United States.

Women of all colors lived under particular burdens of discrimination. Their uniquely
intimate relationships—as daughters, wives, mothers—with those who did not treat them
as equals complicated their efforts at reform. So did their dilemma about women's roles in
society: some sought full legal equality with men, and others wanted special protections for
women on the grounds that they were fundamentally different.

American women's long struggle to vote came to a head in this decade. By 1912 a growing number of European nations and nine American states, all in the West, had granted the
franchise to citizens of both sexes. The moderate National American Women Suffrage Association under the leadership of Carrie Chapman Catt worked within the political system,
building an alliance with President Wilson after he endorsed women's suffrage in 1916 and
supporting the U.S. entry into World War I the next year. Alice Paul and other militants
formed the National Women's Party and opposed the war effort as inherently undemocratic

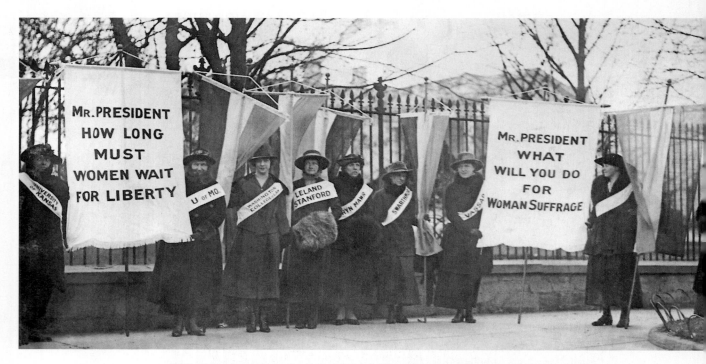

■ In February 1917, as the United States broke relations with Germany and began to prepare to enter World War I, supporters of women's suffrage continued to picket on the sidewalk outside the White House. College women joined the effort to ensure that winning liberty at home would go hand in hand with fighting for democracy abroad.

because half the adult population could not vote. In 1918, suffragist organizers helped elect a more sympathetic Congress that passed the Nineteenth Amendment, ending sex discrimination in voting two years later.

Most adult Americans—workers—continued to find themselves in frequent conflict with their bosses and employers. Industrial capitalism's efficiency produced great material wealth, but 60 percent of it belonged to 2 percent of the population, whereas two-thirds of Americans owned only 2 percent of the wealth. The anticapitalist aspirations of the Socialist party and the Industrial Workers of the World frightened both industrialists and the more conservative labor leaders of the American Federation of Labor, especially when the western-based IWW led two major strikes in the East, one a success in Lawrence, Massachusetts, in 1912 and the other a failure in Paterson, New Jersey, in 1913. The campaign against a wage cut at the vast Lawrence textile factory was especially impressive in uniting 20,000 workers of 40 different national backgrounds.

Some business owners sought to undercut union campaigns by providing better working conditions and even company-run "unions." These carrots of concession were accompanied by the stick of force. Bolstered by sympathetic federal courts and state governors, companies usually refused to negotiate with workers who went on strike. This pattern reached a violent climax on Easter night in 1914 outside Ludlow, Colorado, in a mining camp owned by John D. Rockefeller Jr.'s Colorado Fuel and Iron Company. State militia and company guards broke a strike there with torches and machine guns, burning the miners' tent colony and killing two women and 11 children.

Such brutality by owners against workers appalled most Americans. The Wilson administration slowly began supporting the right of laborers to organize for collective bargaining with their employers. Wilson's strong backing from Samuel Gompers and the AFL in the 1912 election initiated the modern alliance between labor and the Democratic party.

■ Children of the striking coal miners gather in their tent colony outside Ludlow on the high plains of south-central Colorado, at the base of the mountains of the Front Range. Winter snows and cold temperatures made for a difficult life, as did the grueling and dangerous work of mining coal that was common across the state. Miners' children died with their mothers and fathers in the Ludlow massacre on April 20, 1914.

American Neutrality and Domestic Reform

Most Americans had roots of some kind in Europe and had long defined themselves in relation to life on "the continent." But they also considered themselves part of the New World that was separate from the Old World of kings, castles, and rigid social classes. When Europe stepped off the precipice in August 1914 into a war larger than any previously fought or imagined, few Americans wanted any part of it. Make "no entangling alliances," George Washington had urged his fellow citizens. Europeans must stay out of our hemisphere, the Monroe Doctrine had declared. Faithful to this tradition, Americans focused on domestic political reforms and on an economy revived by European demands for war-related goods, which created new jobs that lured many black Southerners north. But international ties proved too important to the well-being of Americans for the country to remain indefinitely on the sidelines of World War I.

What were Americans' priorities from 1914 to 1917?

"The One Great Nation at Peace"

Following traditional U.S. policy, Wilson urged Americans to remain neutral "in fact as well as in name" to promote an eventual "peace without victory." Neutrality was profitable. Wilson stoutly defended the rights of neutrals to trade with belligerents, the same principle that had led the United States into the War of 1812 against England. After the recession of 1913–1914, war-related demand from abroad for American farm and factory products jump-started the economy. In the course of World War I, American bankers extended $10 billion in loans to the Allies (primarily Britain and France), and the United States changed from a debtor nation to the world's largest creditor.

The nature of the fighting in Europe further bolstered the American determination to avoid being drawn into the conflict. Industrialized warfare brought fiendish new ways to kill human beings, including machine guns and poison gas. Gone were the days of bold maneuvers and dashing cavalry charges; now was the time of trench warfare, with its unrelenting misery, terror, and helplessness. Eight and a half million young men lost their lives and another 21 million were wounded, devastating an entire generation of European society. Eight million civilians also died as a result of the fighting, and an international outbreak of influenza in 1918 killed another 20 million around the world.

In the United States, neutrality also made political sense. Immigrants from every part of Europe lived and voted in the United States, so Americans had blood ties to all the belligerents. Commercial and political elites tended to identify with Britain and France, as did many other Americans. But among two of the largest groups of Americans, those with roots in Germany and Ireland, many took a different view. Few Irish Americans equated England with the cause of democracy after centuries of British rule in Ireland. Native-born white Americans were already concerned with preserving unity in their increasingly varied and urban society. Allowing in the hatreds from Europe's battlefields would only exacerbate the ethnic and class tensions that worried social reformers and many politicians, including President Wilson.

Reform Priorities at Home

Americans traditionally considered powerful government a primary threat to individual liberty, but the rise of mammoth corporations at the start of the twentieth century altered that calculation. Competition was disappearing, particularly in critical sectors of the economy such as oil production and railroads. Laissez-faire policies, by which federal agencies encouraged economic expansion, were no longer adequate. Only government, argued Progressive reformers, could balance the new might of the largest companies. This meant modest regulation of some aspects of the marketplace. Wilson's first term also encouraged such democratic reforms as the ratification of the Seventeenth Amendment for the direct popular election of U.S. senators (1913), previously chosen by state legislatures.

Three areas topped the Wilson administration's reform agenda: taxes, the money system, and monopolies. The Underwood-Simmons Tariff of 1913 cut duties—taxes—on imported goods by almost one-half, helping American consumers and promoting freer trade. The Sixteenth Amendment (1913) allowed a federal income tax, which the 1916 Revenue Act put into effect. This was a progressive tax, one that took a larger percentage of the income of the rich than of the poor. The legislation also levied higher taxes on corporate profits and created the first federal estate tax on inheritances.

Congress moved to regulate money in another new way as well. The absence of a centrally managed money system had long contributed to the exaggerated boom-and-bust cycles in the American economy. The Federal Reserve Act of 1913 created a system of 12 Federal Reserve Banks to control the amount of currency in circulation, increasing it in deflationary times and decreasing it when inflation threatened. The system aimed to abolish depressions and prevent bank closures. It did not fully succeed, as the years after 1929 showed, but the Federal Reserve System did stabilize the American banking industry and helped position the dollar to become the central global currency.

⊙ Watch the Video
American Entry into WWI at
www.myhistorylab.com

No issue so dominated American politics between 1913 and 1915 as the tension between huge new corporations and the nation's antimonopoly tradition. The size and market share of companies such as U.S. Steel, American Tobacco, and Du Pont (chemicals) inhibited competition. Congress created the Federal Trade Commission (1914) to investigate business practices that unfairly prevented competition. The Clayton Antitrust Act of 1914 supplemented the 1890 Sherman Antitrust Act by outlawing specific unfair business practices such as local price cutting and granting rebates to undermine competitors.

Another kind of legislation focused on preserving natural landscapes. An increasingly urban, industrial society looked to its most beautiful rural places for solace. Local and state governments set aside parklands throughout

TABLE 20-1			
The Election of 1916			
Candidate	Political Party	Popular Vote (%)	Electoral Vote
Woodrow Wilson	Democratic	49.4	277
Charles E. Hughes	Republican	46.2	254
A. L. Benson	Socialist	3.2	—

■   The body of a soldier lies caught in barbed wire in the "no-man's-land" between opposing trenches on the western front. Technological advances in weaponry helped make the fighting in World War I vastly more destructive than previous wars. The sheer scale of the slaughter stunned combatants and observers, both in Europe and America, and helped turn many in the postwar generation to deep skepticism regarding the use of military force.

the Progressive Era. Wilson followed in Roosevelt's conservationist footsteps by creating the National Park Service in 1916 to provide unified management of such new national treasures as Glacier National Park in Montana (1910), Rocky Mountain National Park in Colorado (1915), Lassen Volcanic National Park in California (1916), and Acadia National Park in Maine (1919).

The Great Migration

The Progressive Era of roughly 1900–1920 was anything but progressive from the viewpoint of many African Americans. White mob violence reached its apex in these years, with hundreds of lynchings and dozens of race riots. Most blacks lived in the South, where segregation and discrimination trapped the majority in poverty. Many therefore seized the unprecedented opportunity offered by the outbreak of the Great War. War-related orders created huge needs for workers in northern factories, and the war also closed the spigot of European immigration, drying up the standard source of new labor. Along with other cities, Chicago and Detroit became centers of the **Great Migration** of more than half a million African Americans out of Dixie during the war years.

Black Southerners still found plenty of discrimination in the urban North. But the large black communities of Philadelphia, Cleveland, and New York offered far greater independence than the rural South they left behind. African Americans could vote, earn higher

■ A migrant family from the South arriving in Chicago, c. 1916. Southerners of all colors, like Europeans, were drawn by the lure of better jobs to the industrial cities of the American Northeast and Midwest. With immigration from Europe slowed to a trickle by the onset of World War I, industry's demand for southern immigrants increased sharply.

◉─⟮See the **Map**

African American Population, 1910 and 1950 at **www.myhistorylab.com**

wages, send their children to better schools, and even sit where they wanted on streetcars. One woman newly arrived in Chicago was stunned the first time she boarded a trolley and saw black people sitting next to whites. "I just held my breath, for I thought any minute they would start something. Then I saw nobody notices it, and I just thought this is a real place for Negroes."

When war in Europe shut off most Atlantic immigration after 1914, it opened the door to newcomers who did not have to cross the submarine-infested ocean. Blacks who boarded trains for the North were joined by a similar number of white Southerners leaving rural poverty to look for jobs. A small stream of French Canadians found work in New England factories. A much larger stream of Mexicans and Mexican Americans flowed to jobs across the American Southwest and Midwest. World War I and the Mexican Revolution increased their numbers sharply, with the growing cities of Los Angeles, San Antonio, and El Paso remaining particular magnets for new immigrants. The number of Mexican Americans in Los Angeles soared from 6,000 in 1910 to nearly 100,000 in 1930.

Limits to American Neutrality

Meanwhile, the fighting in Europe did not diminish, and a steady undertow of interests and inclinations pulled against American neutrality. Most Americans who paid attention to events abroad favored the Allies over the Central Powers. The diversity of Americans' ethnic roots across Europe, Africa, Asia, and Latin America could not mask fundamental cultural and linguistic connections to England, the one-time "mother country." President Wilson deeply admired British political values and institutions, and most influential newspaper editors supported the British cause. Even Americans critical of the British Empire did not want to see the European continent under the autocratic rule of German Kaiser Wilhelm II.

Concrete economic interests also tied the United States to the Allied side. During three years of neutrality (1914–1917), American bankers lent 85 times as much to the Entente nations as to the Central Powers ($2.3 billion versus $27 million), and agricultural and industrial workers earned decent wages in filling Allied war orders.

Certain powerful Americans, concentrated on the East Coast, tried from the start to prepare the country for entering the war. They emphasized that the U.S. military was much smaller than the forces of European states because of Americans' traditional aversion to large standing armies. Republicans such as Theodore Roosevelt and former Secretary of State Elihu Root led the war preparedness movement.

Progressives split over the war. More radical reformers opposed joining it as a matter of principle. "Let the capitalists do their own fighting and furnish their own corpses," Socialist Eugene Debs wrote in 1914, "and there will never be another war on the face of the earth." They feared, presciently, that going to war would take the wind out of the sails of domestic reform.

Most Progressives followed President Wilson's leadership, opposing U.S. involvement in Europe at first but gradually shifting to support it. The president squeaked by conservative Republican nominee Charles Evans Hughes in the 1916 election, winning a second term in the White House. "He kept us out of war," his supporters declared, but Wilson himself was less optimistic. He knew where German submarine warfare might lead: "Any little German lieutenant can put us into the war at any time by some calculated outrage."

Read the Document
Debs, Critique of WWI at
www.myhistorylab.com

The United States Goes to War

Like Lyndon Johnson in 1964 regarding Vietnam, Wilson won reelection as a liberal reformer and a man of peace, only to go to war within six months. On April 2, 1917, Wilson asked Congress for a declaration of war against Germany "to make the world safe for democracy." Congress agreed by a large majority, and four days later the United States entered the Great War. The government limited anti-war criticism in an effort to ensure unity. Mobilization went slowly; it took almost a year before American soldiers in large numbers saw combat in the trenches of northern France. But American foodstuffs and munitions arrived more quickly, as did American naval ships protecting cargo vessels bound for England. The U.S. entry into the war ultimately provided the narrow margin of victory against the Central Powers.

How did fighting in World War I change the United States?

The Logic of Belligerency

Wilson's insistence on the traditional rights of neutral nations to trade with belligerents clashed with German and British efforts to prevent trade destined for their enemy. The German use of the new submarines, or U-boats (from the German *Unterseeboote*), against superior British surface forces pulled Americans into the war. Submarines were extremely vulnerable when not submerged. Before firing on a merchant or passenger ship that might be armed or carrying contraband (war materials), they refused to surface and warn civilian passengers—as required under international law—to evacuate on lifeboats. With Britain arming merchant ships and stowing munitions in the holds of passenger ships, U-boats were the key element in the German campaign to weaken the enemy. The British navy, in turn, seized American goods bound for Germany. But Britain's blockade of the German coastline and neutral ports nearby did not endanger civilians in the same way. "One deals with life; the other with property," Secretary of State Robert Lansing explained.

The deaths of civilians without warning on the high seas shocked and angered the American public, especially the sinking of the magnificent British ocean liner *Lusitania* in May 1915, which killed 128 U.S. citizens and a thousand others. Hoping to keep the United States out of the war, the German government twice put its unrestricted submarine warfare on hold.

Read the Document
Wilson's War Message to Congress at
www.myhistorylab.com

By January 1917 the British blockade had reduced German food rations per person to less than half the prewar level. Facing imminent starvation, Berlin decided to take one last chance with unrestricted submarine warfare. The German government calculated that it could force a British and French surrender before enough American assistance arrived.

Preparing for war with the Americans, German Ambassador Arthur Zimmermann secretly offered German aid to the revolutionary Mexican government "to reconquer the lost territory in Texas, New Mexico, and Arizona" if it joined the Central Powers. Mexico declined, but the Zimmermann telegram leaked to the press on March 1 and outraged Americans. One last hindrance to joining the Allies disappeared with the revolution that same month in Russia, which replaced the monarchy with a social democratic government.

Still guarding American autonomy and wary of close identification with the French, British, and Russian empires, Wilson took the nation into war as an "Associated" power rather than a full-blown member of the Entente. The president believed that the United States, unique among the belligerents, sought only to defend principles rather than to acquire territory. "We have no quarrel with the German people" but only with the "Prussian autocracy" whose U-boats were engaged in "a warfare against mankind," Wilson declared in calling Americans to a great crusade in Europe.

Mobilizing the Home Front

Going to war entailed a complete reorientation of the American economy. For the U.S. Army and Navy to succeed abroad, mass production of war materials had to be centrally planned, and only the federal government could fulfill this role. The Wilson administration created several new agencies to manage the war effort at home. The Selective Service Act established local boards to draft young men into the military. The U.S. Railroad Administration took control of the nation's primary transportation system to solve railroad tie-ups caused by heavy demands for war materials. The War Industries Board supervised all war-related production, allowing large manufacturers to coordinate their schedules without fear of antitrust action. The War Labor Board resolved disputes between workers and employers. The Committee on Public Information had the task of inspiring and maintaining public support for Wilson's war policies.

The close cooperation between industry and government, combined with strong demand for American goods from the Allied governments, caused corporate earnings to soar. "We are all making more money out of this war than the average human being ought to," one steel company official admitted privately. And some of the war gains were spread around, for a collaborative effort entailed keeping workers productive and content. Taking a position unprecedented in the U.S. government, the War Labor Board promoted an eight-hour workday and the right of workers to form unions.

Ensuring Unity

Read the Document

Buffington, "Friendly Words to the Foreign Born" at **www.myhistorylab.com**

The deaths of U.S. soldiers and sailors made support for the war an emotional issue, and a pattern of repressing dissent took hold that outlasted the war itself. Several states banned teaching the German language. Sauerkraut became "liberty cabbage," frankfurters became hot dogs, and many German Americans anglicized their names. Temperance reformers cited German beer drinking in their successful campaign for a constitutional prohibition of alcohol production. Congress approved the controversial Eighteenth Amendment in December 1917 as a way to save grain for the war effort, and the states ratified it in 1919. Anti-German sentiment led to sometimes deadly violence against Americans of German descent by the summer of 1918. Congress passed sharply restrictive immigration legislation in 1917 as anti-German feelings fed broader prewar fears of new immigrants. The Espionage Act (1917) and Sedition Act (1918) banned written and oral organizing against the war.

■ European demand for war-related goods brought the U.S. economy out of the deep recession of 1913–1914 and created hundreds of thousands of new jobs. U.S. entry into the war in April 1917 took several million men into the armed forces, opening better-paying opportunities in manufacturing to many women. Four workers at the Westinghouse Electric Company pause from their labors in 1918.

Most African Americans agreed with W. E. B. Du Bois's call to "close our ranks shoulder to shoulder" with white fellow citizens in support of the war effort, although antiblack violence escalated. The arrival of half a million black Southerners in northern cities increased competition for jobs and housing, causing resentment among many whites. Employers contributed to tensions by recruiting African Americans as strikebreakers and pitting them against white workers. Whites rioted in East St. Louis on July 1, 1917, causing at least 47 fatalities, most of them black. Black soldiers from the North at times rebelled against the Jim Crow restrictions they found on southern military bases.

The War in Europe

When the United States entered the war in Europe in 1917, crisis gripped the Allies. In the east, much of the war effort collapsed in the confusion of Russia's revolution against the czar. In the west, 49 divisions of the French army mutinied, refusing orders to make further suicidal advances. In the south, at Caporetto, Austro-Hungarian forces inflicted a disastrous defeat on the Italian army. It was not clear whether the Americans had joined soon enough to stave off defeat.

No battle-ready American army waited at ports for immediate shipment to the trenches of northern France. U.S. commanders instead had to conscript and train nearly 5 million young men for an American Expeditionary Force (AEF) under General Pershing, and 16,000 young women volunteered for service overseas as nurses and Red Cross workers.

INTERPRETING HISTORY

African-American Women in the Great War

Just as black American men served in the American Expeditionary Forces in France in 1917–1918, black American women served in auxiliary organizations such as the Red Cross and the Young Men's and Women's Christian Associations (YMCA and YWCA), which worked to boost the soldiers' morale. They staffed canteens set up to provide social and educational support for American troops as an alternative to entertainments such as prostitution and gambling. Addie W. Hunton and Kathryn M. Johnson felt a particular calling to encourage African-American soldiers, who suffered from discrimination and segregation even as they fought for democracy. As devout Christians, the two women believed they must model a life of service and compassion, even in the face of persecution. An account of their time in Europe published soon after they returned to the United States suggests some of the complications of a segregated society sending people abroad.

American women supported the war effort in many ways, including working in munitions factories, buying war bonds, single-parenting while husbands were away in the military, and volunteering as nurses for the armed forces in France. Here, African American women entertain black soldiers with music in a service club in Newark, New Jersey, 1918.

Two Colored Women with the American Expeditionary Forces

The relationship between the colored soldiers, the colored welfare workers, and the French people was most cordial and friendly and grew in sympathy and understanding, as their associations brought about a closer acquaintance. It was rather an unusual as well as a most welcome experience to be able to go into places of public accommodation without having any hesitations or misgivings; to be at liberty to take a seat in a common carrier, without fear of inviting some humiliating experience; to go into a home and receive a greeting that carried with it a hospitality and kindliness of spirit that could not be questioned.

These things were at once noticeable upon the arrival of a stranger within the gates of this sister democracy, and the first ten days in France, though filled with duties and harassed with visits from

German bombing planes, were nevertheless a delight, in that they furnished to some of us the first full breath of freedom that had ever come into our limited experience.

The first post of duty assigned to us was Brest. Upon arriving there we received our first experience with American prejudices, which had not only been carried across the seas, but had become a part of such an intricate propaganda, that the relationship between the colored soldier and the French people is more or less a story colored by a continued and subtle effort to inject this same prejudice into the heart of the hitherto unprejudiced Frenchman.

[An order posted by a white officer of a black battalion read:] "Enlisted men of this organization will not talk to or be in company with any white women, regardless of whether the women solicit their company or not."

[Another order read:] "There are two Y.M.C.A.'s, one near the camp, for white troops, and one in town, for the colored troops. All men will be instructed to patronize their own Y."

The account also describes segregation imposed during the return voyage to the United States:

Quite a bit of unpleasantness was experienced on the boats coming home. . . . On [one] boat there were nineteen

colored welfare workers; all the women were placed on a floor below the white women, and the entire colored party was placed in an obscure, poorly ventilated section of the dining-room, entirely separated from the other workers by a long table of Dutch civilians. The writer immediately protested; the reply was made that the southern white workers on board the ship would be insulted if the colored workers ate in the same section of the dining-room with them, and, at any rate, the colored people did not expect any such treatment as had been given them by the French.

Questions

1. *How did serving in France affect the ways African-American men and women viewed their own country?*
2. *What might the impact of blacks' service in France have been on American society when they returned home after the war?*

Source: Addie W. Hunton and Kathryn M. Johnson, *Two Colored Women with American Expeditionary Forces* (New York: Brooklyn Eagle Press, 1920), pp. 28–30, 182–183, 186.

■ **MAP 20.2**
WORLD WAR I IN EUROPE AND THE WESTERN FRONT, 1918
By the time U.S. troops arrived in force on the western front in northern France, the new Bolshevik
(Communist) government of Russia had made peace with the Germans and withdrawn from the war.
Germany now faced enemies only on one front—the western front—and moved all its troops there.
In this dire situation for the French and British, American soldiers helped fill the gap in 1918.

Although the veteran French and British lines had to stand largely on their own against the
final German spring offensive, American soldiers later engaged in fierce combat at Belleau
Wood, Château-Thierry, and St. Mihiel, ultimately losing 114,000 men. As the only army
growing stronger in 1918, the AEF contributed crucially to the fall offensive that convinced
Germany to surrender on November 11.

Events in Russia provoked the greatest long-term concerns. In October 1917, Vladimir
Lenin and his fellow **Bolsheviks** seized control of the government, building a dictatorship of the Communist party in the name of the working class. The Bolsheviks opposed
the Great War as a struggle among rival capitalists. In the czar's archives, they found and
published the secret prewar treaties of the Entente for dividing up their prospective conquests after the war, both in Europe and in the colonies overseas. While Wilson spoke of a

From Art of the October Revolution, Leningrad, Aurora Art Publishers, 1979

■ **"Comrade Lenin Sweeps the Globe Clean."** This Bolshevik (Communist) drawing shows Vladimir I. Lenin (1870–1924), the leader of the Russian revolution and founder of the world's first Communist government, ridding the world of capitalists and monarchs. But Lenin also sought western trade and investment, especially from the United States, as a stimulus to reconstructing the devastated postwar economy of the new Union of Soviet Socialist Republics (USSR).

What kind of new world order did Wilson want, and to what extent did he achieve it?

war for democracy, the Bolsheviks asked Russians, "Are you willing to fight for this, that the English capitalists should rob Mesopotamia and Palestine?"

The answer, as Wilson feared, was no. In January 1918, the president gave the famous "Fourteen Points" speech to the U.S. Congress, outlining his aims of a postwar world built not on expansion and revenge but on national self-determination, open diplomacy, and freedom of commerce and travel, to be guaranteed by a new League of Nations. He hoped to dissuade the Bolsheviks from making a separate peace with Germany that would allow Germany to move all its troops to the western front. But Lenin, facing civil war at home, conceded huge swaths of the old czarist empire in eastern Europe to the Germans to gain peace with the Brest-Litovsk Treaty of March 3, 1918.

The competing visions of Wilson and Lenin for world order contained the roots of the Cold War that would dominate American life after 1945. They agreed that the old diplomacy of imperialist states competing for pieces of property around the globe would no longer work and that only the creation of democratic states would prevent further wars. But they understood democracy very differently. For Wilson, it meant self-governing nations with capitalist economies and republican political practices (at least in Europe and North America, and eventually elsewhere). For Lenin, it meant workers in every land overthrowing the owners of capital and setting up Soviet governments. Whereas Wilson viewed the world as a collection of nations, Lenin saw it as a battleground between two classes.

The Struggle to Win the Peace

World War I killed more than 16 million people and wrought immeasurable physical, social, and psychological damage. Was it worth it? Citizens of the belligerent nations emerged from 1918 convinced that only a future free of war could legitimate such suffering. Some put their hopes in the radical solution unfolding in Russia. Some in the Entente states believed that severe measures against Germany would ensure peace. Most looked to Woodrow Wilson in the winter and spring of 1919, with his vision of a more peaceful, democratic postwar order. The president sailed for Europe in January to lead the conference that would shape the peace. Vast crowds greeted him enthusiastically as he toured England, Italy, and France.

Peacemaking and the Versailles Treaty

War and revolution destroyed the four great empires of Russia, Germany, Austria-Hungary, and the Ottomans (based in modern Turkey). Meeting in Paris from January to June 1919, the "Big Three" of Wilson, French President Georges Clemenceau, and British Prime Minister David Lloyd George took on two major tasks to shape the postwar order. First, the three leaders redrew the map of eastern and central Europe and the Middle East to create nation-states out of the vanished empires. Second, they had to decide what to do about a defeated Germany. The possible spread of revolution gave the negotiations a particular urgency. Anticolonial revolts broke out in India and China, and pro-Soviet workers' councils seized power briefly in Hungary and southern Germany. "We are running a race with Bolshevism," Wilson warned, "and the world is on fire."

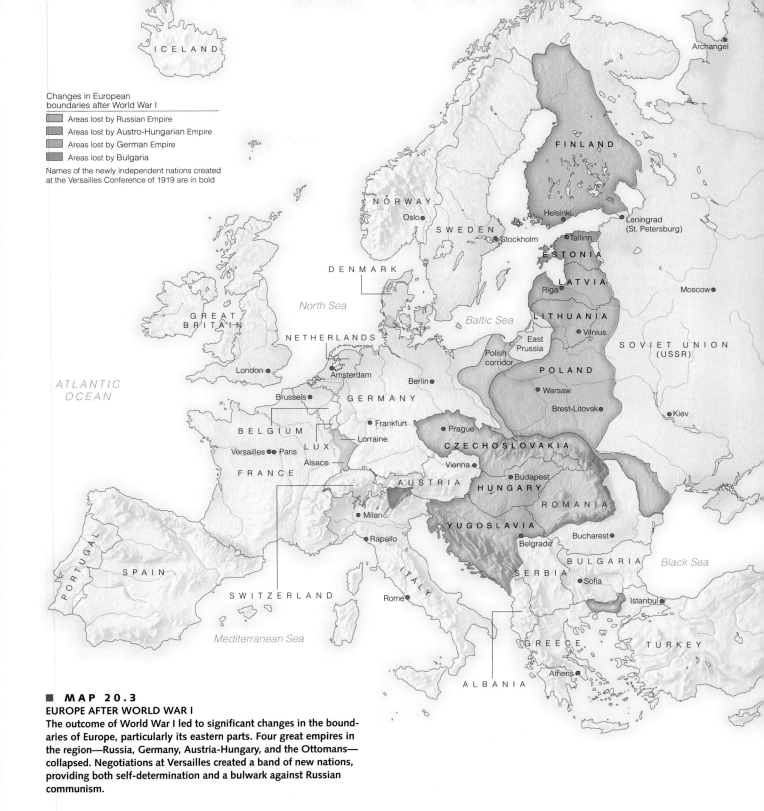

Changes in European
boundaries after World War I

▨ Areas lost by Russian Empire
▨ Areas lost by Austro-Hungarian Empire
▨ Areas lost by German Empire
▨ Areas lost by Bulgaria

Names of the newly independent nations created
at the Versailles Conference of 1919 are in bold

■ **MAP 20.3**
EUROPE AFTER WORLD WAR I
The outcome of World War I led to significant changes in the boundaries of Europe, particularly its eastern parts. Four great empires in
the region—Russia, Germany, Austria-Hungary, and the Ottomans—
collapsed. Negotiations at Versailles created a band of new nations,
providing both self-determination and a bulwark against Russian
communism.

   To put out the fire, the Big Three created a string of new nations running from Finland in
the north to Yugoslavia in the south. Eastern Europeans were to be self-governing within the
new political boundaries. How far would "self-determination" go? Secretary of State Lansing
worried that the president's language of democracy was "loaded with dynamite." The world's
nonwhite majority wondered whether it applied to them. The Big Three created the mandate
system to provide for eventual self-determination for colonies after a period of tutelage under

an established power, and they rejected Japan's proposal to include racial equality as a principle of the new League of Nations.

The German question predominated at the Paris conference. To create a long-term peaceful order in Europe, Wilson wanted lenient terms for Germany. But the French and British had lost much more in the war than the Americans, and they believed Germany must pay for that. To satisfy France and England, Germany had to admit guilt for causing the war and pay $33 billion in reparations, while losing much of its eastern territory to the Polish and Czechoslovakian states. For Wilson the League of Nations was the key: this new and unprecedented global organization would keep the peace by ensuring collective security for all nations.

⦿⦿⊢Read the **Document**

Henry Cabot Lodge's Objections to Treaty of Versailles at **www.myhistorylab.com**

Back home, most Republicans objected on principle to one key aspect of the Versailles Treaty (named for the estate of King Louis XIV, where it was signed): Article 10 of the League of Nations charter, guaranteeing ahead of time a collective response to defend any member's territory from attack. Treaty opponents were determined to preserve complete American autonomy, including freedom of action in Latin America. Henry Cabot Lodge Jr. of Massachusetts, the powerful Republican chair of the Senate Foreign Relations Committee, organized the two Senate votes rejecting American membership in the league. Hoping to stave off defeat for his idealistic plan, Wilson undertook an ill-advised national speaking tour to promote the league. His strenuous effort failed to win American participation in the league, and it ultimately broke his fragile health. Wilson suffered a stroke on October 2, 1919, that left him incapacitated for the rest of his presidency.

Waging Counterrevolution Abroad

Soon after Russia withdrew from the war, Britain, France, and the United States intervened in the civil war there between the Bolsheviks (the "Reds") and the various counterrevolutionary forces (the "Whites"). The initial military rationale in the summer of 1918 was to reopen the eastern front against Germany. The United States landed 7,000 troops in Vladivostock, on Russia's far Pacific coast. In conjunction with the British, 5,000 U.S. soldiers went ashore at Archangel in northern Russia. They quickly became involved in fighting the Red Army. The Wilson administration meanwhile funneled money and military intelligence to leaders of the White forces.

The Bolsheviks rejected certain values cherished by most Americans: the sanctity of private property and contracts, political liberty, and religious freedom. They liberalized divorce laws and legalized abortion, challenging conservative American attitudes about the relationships between women and men. And they established the Comintern in 1919 to promote similar revolutions around the world. Allied intervention in the Russian civil war failed to overthrow Lenin's government, and American troops pulled out in 1920.

The Red and Black Scares at Home

In the United States, industrial unrest provoked fears of a Soviet-style revolution. Four million American workers, one out of every five, went out on strike in 1919—the highest proportion of the workforce ever. They sought improved wages and working conditions as well as recognition of the right to collective bargaining. In Seattle a walkout by shipyard workers mushroomed into a general strike that shut down most of the city for a week. In Pittsburgh the AFL led a bitter strike against U.S. Steel in pursuit of union recognition. The United Mine Workers led walkouts by hundreds of thousands of coal miners, which evolved into open warfare between miners and coal companies in West Virginia over the next two years. In Boston three-quarters of the police force went on strike to protest wages lower than those of common laborers. Between April and June, anarchists mailed or delivered bombs to 36 prominent public figures, including Attorney General A. Mitchell Palmer. All were defused except two.

Whereas many Americans sympathized with struggles for unionization, others viewed them as dangerous to private property and social order. They associated strikes with radical immigrants and anarchists and considered them "un-American." The **Red Scare** of 1919 associated reform and social justice of any kind with subversion. Attorney General Palmer directed the deportation to Russia of 249 foreign-born radicals aboard the *Buford* in December 1919, including anarchist and feminist Emma Goldman. "Palmer raids" led to the arrest of thousands more within a month.

Violence against workers extended to African Americans after World War I. An upsurge in lynching included at least ten black veterans still in uniform and was not limited to the South. White mobs burned entire black communities to the ground, including Tulsa's Greenwood neighborhood in 1921 and the all-black town of Rosewood, Florida, in 1923. The Red Scare merged with the "Black Scare" in Phillips County, Arkansas, where black sharecroppers, many of them veterans, formed a union in 1919 to pursue equitable crop settlements from landlords. Fearing insurrection, local white leaders used 2,500 federal troops and white vigilantes to massacre more than 200 sharecroppers. But any inclination toward deference in the face of brutality was gone, and African Americans fought back fiercely against white marauders in deadly riots in Washington and Chicago in the summer of 1919.

Where was the president during this turmoil? Incapacitated by his stroke, he lay resting in his bed in Washington, the administration managed largely by his wife, Edith, and his secretary, Joseph Tumulty. In any case, Wilson's segregationist policies suggested that he would have been unlikely to provide effective leadership in bridging the nation's racial divides.

■ The Seattle General Strike Committee took on the responsibility of keeping essential services running in the city. Here its members issue groceries to union families, January 1919. The cooperation necessary among organized workers to keep a strike going offered a different model of community interaction than did the individualism often touted by wealthier Americans.

CONCLUSION

How much success could a varied generation of Progressive reformers claim by 1920? Women had won the vote with the Nineteenth Amendment. Daily life for Americans of darker hue continued to entail picking one's way through a maze of discrimination. Most union campaigns stalled by 1920, beaten back by the physical force and cleverness of corporate employers and their government sympathizers. And when the Red Scare dissipated, Americans did not return to the reform spirit of Progressivism. Voter turnout in 1920 dipped below 50 percent for the first time in a century. Those who did vote that year gave the Republican party a sweeping victory and put Ohio Senator Warren G. Harding in the White House. His speeches may have been, as one rival said, "an army of pompous phrases moving over the landscape in search of an idea," but most of the nation sought calm after the upheavals of the previous decade.

American contributions to democracy abroad were similarly ambivalent. Whereas eastern Europeans named streets in their newly independent nations for President Wilson, few Latin Americans believed that U.S. invasions of Caribbean and Central American countries promoted self-government. Russians admired much about American society and the U.S. economy while resenting American troops in their land. Above all hung the problem of Germany, still the most potentially powerful single nation in Europe. The Versailles Treaty imposed harsh terms and embittered a generation of German people. "If I were a German, I think I should not sign it," Wilson admitted privately. The Weimar Republic that replaced the abdicated German Kaiser lasted through the 1920s. But the storms of the Great Depression after 1929 swamped Germany's republican experiment and gave rise to Adolf Hitler.

For Review

✓● Study and Review at www.myhistorylab.com

1. Why did the United States stay out of World War I for three years?

2. Which were the most important Progressive reforms of the 1910s and why?

3. How accurate was Wilson's description of World War I as a war "to make the world safe for democracy"?

4. How did the Wilson administration respond to the 1917 Bolshevik (Communist) Revolution in Russia?

Chronology: 1912–1920

1912   Woodrow Wilson elected president.

1913   Federal Reserve Act.

1914   U.S. troops block German arms shipment to Mexico.
World War I breaks out in Europe.

1915   U.S. marines occupy Haiti.
Germans sink *Lusitania*.
Film *Birth of a Nation* released.

1916   Jeannette Rankin elected first female member of Congress.
U.S. marines occupy Dominican Republic.
Woodrow Wilson reelected president.

1917   United States enters World War I.
Russian Revolution.
Residents of Puerto Rico granted U.S. citizenship.

1918   Spanish influenza epidemic kills 20 million worldwide.
Sedition Act.
Wilson's "Fourteen Points" speech to Congress.

1919   Versailles Treaty ends World War I.
U.S. Senate rejects League of Nations.
Eighteenth Amendment (Prohibition) ratified.

1920   Nineteenth Amendment (women's suffrage) ratified.

Key Terms

Bolsheviks The Communist revolutionaries who overthrew the Russian czar in 1917 and established the Union of Soviet Socialist Republics (USSR). p. 485

Entente The alliance of Britain, France, and Russia, later joined by Italy and the United States, during World War I. p. 473

Great Migration The movement of African Americans out of the South to northern cities, particularly during World War I. p. 479

Red Scare Post–World War I repression of socialists, communists, and other left-wing radicals ("Reds"). p. 489

In the superior court of Los Angeles in 1920, Lorimer Linganfield, a respectable barber, filed for divorce. Although his wife, Marsha, held him in "high regard and esteem as her husband," there were "evidences of indiscretion" in her conduct. She wore a new bathing suit, "designed especially for the purpose of exhibiting to the public the shape and form of her body." To his further humiliation, she had "a desire to sing and dance at cafes and restaurants for the entertainment of the public." When Lorimer complained about her "appetite for beer and whisky" and extravagant tastes for luxury, she replied that he was "not the only pebble on the beach, she had a millionaire 'guy' who would buy her all the clothes, automobiles, diamonds and booze that she wanted." The ultimate insult was her refusal to have any sexual intercourse, claiming that she did not want any "dirty little brats around her." The judge was sympathetic, and Lorimer Linganfield won his suit.

The Linganfields' difficulties represent a larger struggle as Americans shifted from the nineteenth century producer economy, with its clearly defined gender roles and sexual mores, to the **consumer economy** of the twentieth century and to new amusements, changing sexual behavior, and flamboyant "new women." Marsha Linganfield was a "**flapper**," one of the young women of the 1910s and 1920s who broke from time-honored conventions. With short, "bobbed" hair, knee-length dresses, and boyish styles unencumbered by layers of petticoats, flappers flirted, petted, and danced "wild" dances like the Charleston, an African-American dance brought north from South Carolina juke joints. Flappers blurred the line between "good girls" and "bad girls" that had previously defined proper female behavior.

New forms of popular entertainment that developed in the 1920s, especially Hollywood movies and jazz music, became defining features of the nation itself. Popular culture offered Jews and blacks a space for innovation. At a time when white, Anglo-Saxon, Protestant (WASP) men had control of nearly all government and business institutions, Jewish moviemakers and African-American musicians were creating the culture that would soon represent the nation.

The great heroes of the 1920s were celebrities admired for their individual achievements in sports and adventure. In 1927, the same year that Babe Ruth hit a record 60 home runs, Charles Lindbergh flew his small monoplane, *The Spirit of St. Louis*, nonstop from New York to Paris in 33 and one-half hours, a feat that electrified the world and made him an instant hero. Professional sports came of age in the 1920s. In 1926, 19-year-old Olympic gold

21

All That Jazz: The 1920s

medalist Gertrude Ederle became the first woman to swim the English Channel. She broke the world's record with her time of 14 hours and 31 minutes, two hours faster than those of the six men who had preceded her. The nation idolized this new generation of heroes, who dominated headlines and drew cheering crowds wherever they went.

The glamorous life, however, was out of reach for many. Often characterized as the "roaring twenties" of giddy prosperity and reckless good times, these were also years of widespread poverty, especially in rural areas and urban ghettos. But at the end of the decade, almost half of all households did own a car or a radio; almost a third owned a washing machine or a vacuum cleaner and real wages rose steadily.

■ Florine Stettheimer's *Portrait of My Sister Ettie* (1923) conveys the glamour and sensuality of "flappers" like Marsha Linganfield.

> *The great heroes of the 1920s were celebrities admired for their individual achievements in sports and adventure.*

Conservative politics at the national level prevailed throughout the decade. An anti-radical immigrant Red Scare followed World War I, and Prohibition made alcohol consumption illegal until 1933. High-profile court cases revealed public ambivalence about the use of new scientific knowledge. Business values of material acquisition spread as the expansion of consumer credit weakened traditions of saving and frugality. For those with money to invest, Wall Street beckoned. The stock market rose to perilous heights, only to collapse at the end of the decade.

The Decline of Progressive Reform and the Business of Politics

What major developments signaled the end of the Progressive Era?

Reformers who had championed the causes of the marginalized and disadvantaged lost influence in the business-dominated 1920s. After achieving the vote, the women's rights movement splintered as younger women sought new freedoms not through politics but through a social and sexual revolution. Widespread hostility toward immigrants and various ethnic groups was at the root of the outlawing of liquor, new laws restricting immigration, and the rise of the Ku Klux Klan. But progressive political impulses did not entirely disappear, especially among African Americans, who continued to mobilize and organize for civil rights.

In 1924 President Calvin Coolidge declared, "The business of America is business." Despite its many critics, with the support of national political leaders, business reigned. After a recession following World War I, the U.S. economy grew steadily under Republican leadership. The Gross National Product (GNP) increased 5.5 percent annually, from $149 billion in 1922 to $227 billion in 1929. Official unemployment remained below 5 percent throughout the decade, and real wages rose 15 percent. These trends fueled the popularity of the conservative, business-friendly presidents of the 1920s. Economic interests also drove foreign policy during the decade. After World War I, with much of Europe in shambles, the United States made loans to foreign countries, becoming the world's leading creditor nation. International markets opened up for American-made products, leading to a tremendous expansion in foreign trade.

Women's Rights After the Struggle for Suffrage

One indication of the waning of progressive reform was the fragmentation of women's rights activism in the 1920s. The radical wing of the suffrage movement, the National Woman's Party (NWP), in 1923 launched a campaign for the **Equal Rights Amendment** (ERA), which declared simply: "Equality of rights under the law shall not be denied or abridged by the United States or by any state on account of sex."

The debate over the ERA in the 1920s reflected the fundamental divide that would permeate women's rights activism throughout the rest of the twentieth century. On one side were those who believed that women were fundamentally the same as men and deserved equal rights; on the other side were those who argued that women were different and deserved special privileges and protections. Many women's rights activists opposed the ERA because it would undercut efforts to gain special legislative protections for women based on their presumed physical weakness and their potential for childbearing, such as maximum hours, regulations against night work, and limitations on the weights they could lift. These women disapproved of the NWP and formed their own nonpartisan organization, the League of Women Voters, which promoted social and political reform.

Marital breakdown still carried a heavy negative stigma, especially for women. Nevertheless, the divorce rate doubled between 1900 and 1920 and continued to rise throughout the 1920s, in part the result of women's increasing independence. As job opportunities for women increased, more women felt able to abandon unhappy marriages.

■ Speakeasy hostess Mary Louise Guinan appears unrepentant as she is arrested for selling alcohol during the Prohibition era. Law enforcement was futile because speakeasies that were raided and closed simply reopened in new locations.

Prohibition: The Experiment That Failed

The Eighteenth Amendment, prohibiting the manufacture and sale of alcohol, went into effect in January 1920. Several diverse interests came together to ban liquor. Temperance crusaders in the Anti-Saloon League and the Women's Christian Temperance Union had long argued that women and children suffered when men spent their paychecks at the saloon and returned home drunk and violent. World War I prompted others to support a ban on the manufacture of liquor to save grain for the war effort. Anti-immigrant "drys" had political motives for promoting prohibition. They hoped to undercut immigrant and ethnic politicians who used local saloons to forge their constituencies and **political machines**. The "wets" included alienated intellectuals, Jazz Age rebels, and many city dwellers whose social lives revolved around neighborhood pubs, especially in Irish and German communities.

Enforcement was impossible. Federal agents had responsibility for enforcing the law, but their numbers were inadequate. To be effective, federal agents had to work closely with local law enforcement officials. In some urban areas, local officials refused to cooperate with

Watch the Video
Drinking and the Temperence Movement in Nineteenth-Century America at **www.myhistorylab.com**

((•⊢Hear the **Audio**

"Prohibition is a failure" at
www.myhistorylab.com

•◆•⊢Read the **Document**

*Eighteenth Amendment—Prohibition
of intoxicating Liquor (January 16,
1919)* at **www.myhistorylab.com**

federal agents. Americans who wanted to drink liquor found many ways to acquire it. Illegal **"speakeasies"** abounded where customers could buy drinks delivered by rumrunners who smuggled in liquor from Canada, Mexico, and the West Indies. Many people concocted their own "bathtub gin" or "moonshine whiskey," homemade brews using readily available ingredients and household equipment.

Prohibition was intended to cure society's ills. Instead, it provided vast opportunities for crime and profit. Organized crime received a major boost when violence erupted in the scramble to profit from illegal liquor. Chicago witnessed 550 gangland killings in the 1920s, with few arrests or convictions. By 1929 Chicago mob king Al Capone controlled a massive network of speakeasies that raked in $60 million annually.

Prohibition failed to live up to its promise. Although alcohol consumption declined by two-thirds within a year of the passage of the amendment, by 1929 the consumption of alcohol had climbed back up to 70 percent of its pre-Prohibition level.

Reactionary Impulses

The Red Scare after World War I (see Chapter 20) inaugurated a decade of hostility to political radicals and foreigners. Shoemaker Nicola Sacco and fish peddler Bartolomeo Vanzetti were both: Italian **aliens** and self-proclaimed anarchists. In May 1920, the paymaster and guard of a South Braintree, Massachusetts, shoe company was robbed and murdered, and Sacco and Vanzetti were arrested and charged with the crime. Sacco testified that he was in Boston at the time, applying for a passport, and his alibi was corroborated. Both men proclaimed their innocence and insisted that they were on trial for their political beliefs rather than the crime itself. Their Italian accents and advocacy of anarchism in the courtroom did not help their case with many Americans suspicious of foreign radicals, including the judge presiding at their trial. Despite a weak case against them, Sacco and Vanzetti were convicted of first-degree murder and sentenced to death.

■ Nicola Sacco and Bartolomeo Vanzetti, Italian aliens and self-proclaimed anarchists, were accused of murder in May 1920. The men and their supporters claimed they were on trial not for the crime but for their political beliefs and their immigrant status. After all appeals failed, the two were executed in 1927.

Lawyers for the two anarchists appealed the case several times to no avail. The convictions sparked outrage among Italian Americans, political radicals, labor activists, and liberal intellectuals who believed the two men were falsely convicted. The case soon generated mass demonstrations, appeals for clemency, and petitions from around the world. The governor of Massachusetts appointed a commission to review the case, but the commission concluded that there were no grounds for a new trial. Finally, on August 23, 1927, Sacco and Vanzetti were executed by electric chair.

Sacco and Vanzetti's case underscored the anti-immigrant sentiment that prevailed in the 1920s. In 1924 Congress passed the Johnson-Reid Act, imposing a limit of 165,000 immigrants from countries outside the Western Hemisphere and using a quota system for each country based on the year 1890, a time when British, German, and Scandinavian immigrants dominated the foreign-born population. The Johnson-Reid Act limited entry every year to 2 percent of the total number of immigrants from each country who were present in 1890. This measure effectively barred Jews, Slavs, Greeks, Italians, and Poles because their numbers were so small in 1890. The 1924 law also reaffirmed the exclusion of Chinese immigrants and added Japanese and other Asians to the list, effectively closing the door to all migrants from Asia.

Agricultural interests in California and Texas lobbied to keep the door open to Mexicans because of the low-wage labor they provided. In the aftermath of the Mexican Revolution, many Mexicans hoped to find stability and jobs in the United States. Between 1910 and 1930, more than 1 million Mexicans, nearly one-tenth of Mexico's population, migrated to the United States, where they found work on farms, on railroads, and in mines.

One of the most reactionary developments of the 1920s was the revival of the Ku Klux Klan (KKK), which became the most powerful white supremacy group in the nation, remaining active throughout the twentieth century. The Klan used vigilante violence as well as political mobilizations not only to attack African Americans, their primary targets in the South following the Civil War, but also immigrants, Mexicans, Jews, Catholics, communists, feminists, and other radicals, as well as divorced or allegedly promiscuous women. Klan membership included laborers, businesspeople, physicians, judges, social workers, and women who believed their homogenous small-town Protestant culture was threatened by the evils of modern life, brought on by the presence and influence of morally suspect outsiders. The Klan wielded considerable power in the 1920s in certain states, particularly Texas, Oklahoma, Oregon, and Indiana.

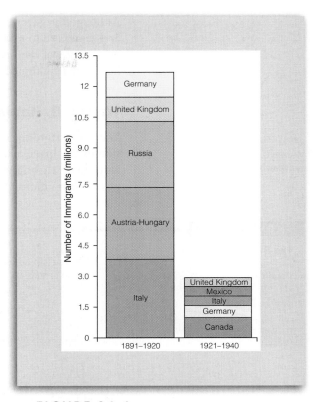

■ **FIGURE 21.1**
NUMBER OF IMMIGRANTS AND COUNTRIES OF ORIGIN, 1891–1920 AND 1921–1940
Before the immigration restriction laws passed in the 1920s, many immigrants came from Russia and southern and eastern Europe. After immigration restriction, most came from western Europe and Canada.

Marcus Garvey and the Persistence of Civil Rights Activism

In the midst of a decade of reactionary policies toward outsiders and political activists, African Americans continued their struggle for civil rights. Jamaican-born black nationalist Marcus Garvey moved to Harlem in 1916 and opened a branch of his Universal Negro Improvement Association (UNIA). Garvey urged black people to establish their own nation-state in Africa: "Africa was peopled with a race of cultured black men, who were masters in art, science, and literature. . . . Africa shall be for the black peoples of the world." By the 1920s, the UNIA had nearly 1 million followers. In keeping with his belief in black-owned businesses, Garvey established the Black Star Line shipping company. But the business ran into problems. In 1922 Garvey was arrested and charged with mail fraud.

Although the government lacked any concrete evidence against him, Garvey was convicted and sentenced to five years in prison, where he kept up his political activities. After his release he was deported to Jamaica as an undesirable alien. Nevertheless, the momentum he sparked continued.

Warren G. Harding: The Politics of Scandal

Watch the Video
Warren G. Harding at
www.myhistorylab.com

Warren G. Harding, a Republican U.S. senator from Ohio, won the 1920 presidential election by the biggest landslide since 1820. He established the conservative agenda that would last throughout the decade. Harding supported immigration restriction and opposed labor unions. After World War I, Harding distanced himself from Woodrow Wilson's peace settlement but promoted international treaties. In 1921 and 1922, Secretary of State Charles Evans Hughes achieved the first major disarmament accord, the Five-Power Treaty, signed by Japan, Britain, France, Italy, and the United States. The five nations agreed to scrap more than 2 million tons of warships in the first such pact of its kind. Hughes extended the power of the United States abroad through economic ties, encouraging banks to provide loans to war-ravaged Europe.

TABLE 21-1

The Election of 1920

Candidate	Political Party	Popular Vote (%)	Electoral Vote
Warren G. Harding	Republican	60.4	404
James M. Cox	Democratic	34.2	127
Eugene V. Debs	Socialist	3.4	—

But Harding's presidency was marred by scandal. He had built his political base by handing out favors and deals to his friends, and he continued to do so as president. His buddies used their offices for personal gain, while Harding caroused with them, drinking, despite Prohibition, and engaging in notorious extramarital affairs. The press initially ignored these abuses, but by 1923, the many scandals finally broke. Harding's cronies were exposed for selling government appointments and providing judicial pardons and police protection for bootleggers.

The most serious scandal of Harding's presidency involved the large government oil reserves at Teapot Dome, Wyoming, and Elk Hills, California. At the urging of Secretary of the Interior Albert Fall, Harding transferred control over the reserves from the U.S. Navy to the Department of the Interior. After accepting a bribe of nearly $400,000 from two oil tycoons, Harry F. Sinclair and Edward L. Doheny, Fall secretly issued leases to them without opening up the competition to other oil companies. Fall went to jail for a year as a result. When he learned of the scandals in his close circle, Harding grew deeply worried. The stress may have been among the causes of the heart attack that killed him in 1923.

Calvin Coolidge: The Hands-Off President

Read the Document
Inaugural Address, Calvin Coolidge (March 1925) at
www.myhistorylab.com

Harding's vice president, Calvin Coolidge, took over the presidency. Sober and serious, this aloof New Englander was not vulnerable to scandal as Harding had been. Coolidge believed that the government should meddle as little as possible in national affairs. He took long naps every day and exerted little presidential leadership. Known mostly for his hostility to labor unions and his laissez-faire attitude toward business, he was a popular president during the complacent mid-1920s.

Not everyone was pleased with Coolidge's probusiness politics, and opposition mobilized for the 1924 election. Progressive Republicans formed a new Progressive party and nominated Robert M. La Follette of Wisconsin for president. The Progressive platform promoted conservation, higher taxes on the wealthy, replacing the electoral college with direct election of the president, and the abolition of child labor. Democrats deadlocked between Catholic candidate Alfred E. Smith, an urban politician from New York, and Protestant

William G. McAdoo, who drew support in the South and West. On the 103rd ballot, delegates finally chose a compromise candidate, John W. Davis, a corporation lawyer. The Republicans nominated Coolidge, who claimed responsibility for the nation's prosperity and won easily, receiving more votes than the other two candidates combined.

TABLE 21-2

The Election of 1924

Candidate	Political Party	Popular Vote (%)	Electoral Vote
Calvin Coolidge	Republican	54.0	382
John W. Davis	Democratic	28.8	136
Robert M. La Follette	Progressive	16.6	13

Herbert Hoover: The Self-Made President

The 1928 election was a major turning point for the presence of ethnic minorities in politics. The Democrats broke tradition by selecting an Irish Roman Catholic, New York governor Alfred E. Smith, as their candidate. It was the first time a major party had nominated a Catholic for president. Coolidge decided not to run for reelection in 1928, and the Republican party selected Secretary of Commerce Herbert Hoover as its nominee. Prohibition—the Eighteenth Amendment banning the manufacture and sale of alcohol—figured prominently in the 1928 presidential campaign. Although the Democratic platform gave lukewarm support to the continuation of Prohibition, Smith made no secret of his support for repealing the Eighteenth Amendment. By contrast, Republican Herbert Hoover praised Prohibition as "a great social and economic experiment." The other major issue of the campaign was religion. Anti-Catholic sentiment was strong throughout the country, especially in the South, where Democrats either sat out the

TABLE 21-3

The Election of 1928

Candidate	Political Party	Popular Vote (%)	Electoral Vote
Herbert Hoover	Republican	58.2	444
Alfred E. Smith	Democratic	40.9	87
Norman Thomas	Socialist	0.7	—

election or voted Republican. Smith's opponents attacked his Catholicism, charging that he was more loyal to the Vatican than to the United States.

Herbert Hoover epitomized the values of the self-made man. He was orphaned as a child and raised by relatives of modest means. After graduating from Stanford University, Hoover went into mining and rose to become a wealthy corporate leader. By age 40, he was already a millionaire. Hoover began his career in government during World War I, when he earned widespread admiration for handling the distribution of food relief to European war refugees. He then served ably as secretary of commerce in the Harding and Coolidge administrations. Shortly after the election, President Hoover predicted, "We in America today are nearer to the final triumph over poverty than ever before in the history of any land." But less than a year into his presidency, his optimism, along with the nation's economy, came crashing down.

Hollywood and Harlem: National Cultures in Black and White

In 1920, for the first time, the majority of Americans lived in towns and cities with populations greater than 2,500. Although this shift often is considered a watershed in the transformation from rural to urban America, it is worth noting that because the census defined any town with more than 2,500 inhabitants as urban, the majority of Americans still lived in small and ethnically homogeneous towns. Many small-town Americans viewed big-city life with suspicion. They feared the decline of traditional Protestant American values of hard work, thrift, and discipline. Yet many were drawn to the new urban life.

What developments in the arts and technology helped forge a national popular culture in the 1920s?

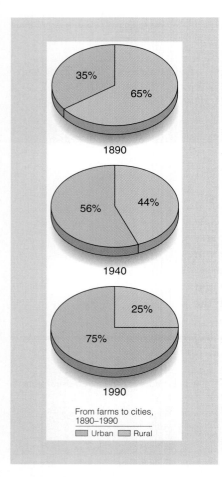

■ **FIGURE 21.2**
**URBAN AND RURAL POPULATION,
1890–1990**
In the nineteenth century, the American population was primarily rural. During the twentieth century, the population became predominantly urban.

Watch the Video
The Harlem Rennaisance at
www.myhistorylab.com

Hollywood on the West Coast and Harlem on the East Coast became centers of cultural innovation. Eventually, the artistic productions of both centers attracted audiences of all racial, class, and regional backgrounds. Increasingly, as Americans moved from place to place, they encountered similar entertainments, music, arts, and consumer products. Movies, automobiles, radios, and advertising all fostered this emerging national culture.

Hollywood Comes of Age

As movie theaters spread into towns and cities across the country, Hollywood's messages began to reach a mass audience and forge a nationwide popular culture. Movie stars provided models for how to adopt new styles of manhood and womanhood. Douglas Fairbanks showed middle-class men how to break free from the humdrum of white-collar work into the world of leisure. His attire of sports clothes changed the way men dressed in their off-work hours. Female stars, such as Clara Bow, epitomized the flapper and taught female viewers how to be "naughty but nice."

Ironically, as the nation closed its doors to immigrants, foreigners on screen captivated the imagination of a native-born population drawn to the allure of the outsider. Movie stars like Greta Garbo from Sweden, Dolores del Rio, Lupe Velez, and Ramon Navarro from Mexico, and Rudolph Valentino from Italy drew audiences with their foreignness. And yet, because movies were silent until the late 1920s, their accented voices were not heard. Sound arrived in the late twenties, bringing their ethnic voices and dialects into the movies. For native-born Americans watching films in small towns and cities, sound movies brought the diverse voices of the cities into their communities. For immigrants, sound movies carried their familiar accents and allowed for identification with the stars on the screen.

The Harlem Renaissance

While Hollywood in the 1920s developed on the West Coast, a flourishing center of African-American culture emerged on the East Coast. The black arts movement known as the Harlem Renaissance drew on European as well as African and African-American artistic traditions and gathered white as well as black intellectuals and artists. The young black poet Arna Bontemps was among the many artists drawn to Harlem. In 1924 he described Harlem as "a foretaste of paradise. A blue haze descended at night and with it strings of fairy lights on the broad avenues. From the window of a small room in an apartment on Fifth and 129th Street, I looked over the rooftops of Negrodom and tried to believe my eyes. What a city! What a world!"

Harlem Renaissance writers claimed their identity as Americans while articulating the culture, aesthetics, and experiences of African Americans. The poet Langston Hughes challenged white America to accept African Americans in his 1925 poem "I, Too, Sing America:"

> I, too, sing America
> I am the darker brother
> They send me to eat in the kitchen
> When company comes,
> But I laugh
> And eat well
> And grow strong
> Tomorrow,
> I'll be at the table
> When company comes

■ Rudolph Valentino dances the tango in this famous scene from the 1920 film *The Four Horsemen of the Apocalypse*. Films in the 1920s featured exotic locales with foreign stars such as the Italian-born Valentino. In keeping with the public's taste for grandeur, lavish movie palaces emerged in cities across the country.

> Nobody'll dare
> Say to me,
> "Eat in the kitchen,"
> Then.
> Besides,
> They'll see how beautiful I am
> And be ashamed—
> I, too, am America.

The music of black America was so prominent that it provided the decade with its most lasting moniker, the Jazz Age. Emanating from New Orleans, Chicago, and St. Louis, jazz was central to the black arts movement and the emerging national culture. With the help of the recording industry and radio, jazz and the blues began to reach a wide audience, primarily among blacks but increasingly among whites as well. Blues lyrics expressed themes of working-class protest and resistance to racism. Women who sang the blues, including Bessie Smith, Ma Rainey, and Ethel Waters, asserted their sexuality, their passion for men or for women, their resistance to male domination, their sorrows, and their strength.

Radios and Autos: Transforming Leisure

Radio played a major role in linking people across regions through shared information, advertising, and entertainment. Annual radio production increased from 190,000 in 1923 to almost 5 million in 1929. Radios brought jazz and other forms of popular music to the

■ **Poet Langston Hughes as a student at Lincoln University, Pennsylvania, in 1927. A major literary figure of the Harlem Renaissance, Hughes expressed the hopes, dreams, and sorrows of black Americans.**

airwaves, transforming the way music was enjoyed in American homes. Americans became more inclined to listen to music on their Victrolas and radios than to make music themselves. By the mid-1920s, sales of records surpassed those of sheet music; production and sales of pianos also dropped precipitously.

The number of radio stations soared from 30 in 1922 to 556 the following year, and national broadcasts began to supersede local ones. Airwaves became so cluttered that by the mid-1920s, the federal government created the Federal Radio Commission to regulate and organize access. Meanwhile, American Telephone and Telegraph (AT&T) and the National Broadcasting Company (NBC) combined to form the first national network system, which gave programs and advertisers access to audiences across the country.

Automobiles extended the mobility of Americans. The automobile offered the possibility of commuting to work without relying on public transportation, encouraging the expansion of suburban communities. The number of passenger cars in the nation more than tripled during the twenties. The Federal Highways Act of 1916 had produced a network of roads all over the country, providing construction jobs and a slew of new roadside businesses, from restaurants to garages. Automobiles also stimulated the tourist industry; Florida, California, and Arizona became vacation destinations in this period.

Automobile production also revolutionized the consumer industry. The pragmatic Henry Ford built inexpensive, functional automobiles that he expected his workers to be able to purchase and keep. But Ford faced serious competition from General Motors' Alfred P. Sloan, Jr., who developed the concept of **planned obsolescence** and emphasized auto styling to encourage customers to trade in their old cars for newer and more expensive models.

The automobile was part of a consumer society increasingly focused on leisure, pleasure, and intimacy. Courtship patterns changed, and sexual activity increased as young couples abandoned the front porch for the back seat. Women gained new freedom and autonomy when they, too, took the wheel. Moralists worried that the automobile would provide youth with too much independence and privacy. One juvenile court judge announced that "the automobile has become a house of prostitution on wheels."

Science on Trial

What did science contribute to American life in the 1920s, and where did scientific ideas fall short?

Although advances in technology and medicine improved the quality of life for many Americans in the early twentieth century, scientific efforts to alter the natural world did not always lead to expected social benefits. One case in point was the engineering project to build levees along the Mississippi River to prevent flooding. Scientific ideas were also tested in the nation's courtrooms. Two major cases, the Scopes trial and the Supreme Court's decision in *Buck v. Bell*, subjected scientific ideas to judicial and cultural scrutiny. The questions raised in these cases continued to generate controversy and debate throughout the rest of the century.

■ **MAP 21.1**
THE MISSISSIPPI RIVER FLOOD OF 1927
The Mississippi River flood in 1927 sent water across a huge area of the South, extending as far west as Texas, covering most of Louisiana, Arkansas, and Mississippi, and reaching north into Kansas, Illinois, and Indiana.

The Great Flood of 1927

For half a century the engineers of the Mississippi River Commission had adhered to a policy of building levees, assuming that strong barricades against the river's banks would prevent flooding. Presumably, the levees would allow the rich soil of the floodplains along the river to be settled and farmed rather than leaving the basins empty to provide places for the river to expand and contract with seasonal rains. But the levee policy proved to be a disastrous example of human efforts to master the natural contours of the land. In March 1927, the rains came, and the river rose. Public authorities and river experts assured those who watched and worried that the levees would hold. They were wrong. Torrential rains caused the river to rage across the levees and the land beyond, submerging 26,000 square miles of prime farmland across seven states. More than 900,000 people were forced from their homes. The flood caused more than $100 million in crop losses and $23 million in livestock deaths. Journalists at the time called it "America's greatest peacetime disaster."

With the help of the Department of Commerce and the National Guard, the Red Cross set up 154 relief camps for flood victims. The camps were racially segregated. Refugees in the white camps were free to come and go and had more comfortable and generous accommodations and rations than those in the black camps. Armed guards patrolled the camps for black refugees and restricted people attempting to enter or leave. Black laborers had to register and give the names of their employers to receive any shelter or assistance.

Federal authorities, including Secretary of Commerce Herbert Hoover, refused to intervene in local camp management. As a result, southern whites were able to force black sharecroppers back to work on their plantations. Despite the prisonlike conditions, many African-American refugees managed to escape and made their way north.

The Triumph of Eugenics: *Buck v. Bell*

Many Americans, including large numbers of policymakers, believed in white racial superiority. Supposedly scientific theories of race bolstered claims that distinct, biologically based characteristics divided humans into superior and inferior races. These theories had no scientific merit and were later thoroughly discredited. But in the 1920s, these dubious theories of racial superiority supported measures such as immigration restriction and eugenic sterilization laws. Eugenics was a pseudo-science based on notions of racial superiority. Eugenicists claimed that the Anglo-Saxon Protestant "race" was superior to all others, including Jews, Southern Europeans, and Catholics, as well as non-whites. Racial superiority, according to eugenic reformers, might be compromised not only by mixing with inferior groups but also by the propagation of individuals whose mental or moral condition rendered them inferior, and whose offspring would diminish the quality of the Anglo-Saxon "stock."

Several states enacted eugenic laws that allowed the state to sterilize "inferior" individuals without their knowledge or consent. These laws authorized government and medical officials to determine whether or not an individual was inferior, or "feebleminded," and to order that the person be sterilized. Opponents of eugenic sterilization, mostly Catholic activists, challenged these laws in several states. Hoping to put an end to such challenges, eugenic advocates decided to test the constitutionality of Virginia's compulsory sterilization law. Their plan was to bring the case all the way to the U.S. Supreme Court, which they expected to uphold the law.

Proponents of the law selected the case of Carrie Buck, in part because she was white. Eugenic advocates did not want race to be at the center of the case, especially because eugenic sterilization laws did not target particular races; they simply targeted the "feebleminded." Feeblemindedness was a loosely defined criterion often used to label poor, immigrant, or minority women who were sexually active. At the age of 17, Carrie Buck, the daughter of an unmarried woman, was raped and became pregnant; as a result, she was sent to a state institution for the feebleminded. Buck was labeled as feebleminded because she had borne a child out of wedlock and was therefore deemed morally unfit for parenthood.

Carrie Buck was sterilized in 1927. The following year, Buck's sister Doris was taken to the Virginia Colony for Epileptics and the Feebleminded and sterilized at age 16. She was told that she had had an appendectomy. Later, Doris Buck married and tried to get pregnant. None of the physicians she consulted told her why she could not conceive. She finally learned the truth in 1979. "I broke down and cried. My husband and I wanted children desperately. We were crazy about them. I never knew what they'd done to me."

No evidence established that Carrie Buck, her mother, or her daughter was below normal intelligence. Buck's daughter died as a child, but her teachers described the girl as bright. In writing the majority opinion for the Supreme Court that upheld the law, Justice Oliver Wendell Holmes wrote, "Three generations of imbeciles are enough." Within the next few years, 30 states had compulsory sterilization laws, and the number of operations rose dramatically. In the 1930s, the Nazis in Germany modeled their sterilization policies on the California law. Finally, in the 1980s, a rare alliance of traditional Catholics and feminist activists succeeded in repealing compulsory sterilization laws.

The Rise and Fall of Man

Primate   **Neanderthal Man**   **Socrates**   **W. J. Bryan**

 This satiric political cartoon, published during the Scopes trial, depicts the theory of evolution as the development of humans from their origins as apes to the "survival of the fittest," portrayed as William Jennings Bryan. Bryan argued the case against evolution in the famous courtroom drama.

Science, Religion, and the Scopes Trial

Populist leader and longtime reformer William Jennings Bryan was among those troubled by eugenics. In his last public crusade, Bryan opposed another scientific theory in a Dayton, Tennessee, courtroom in July 1925. Tennessee had recently outlawed the teaching of Charles Darwin's theory of evolution in the schools. A 24-year-old science teacher from the local high school, John Thomas Scopes, agreed to test the law. Using a state-approved textbook, Scopes taught a lesson on evolutionary theory. He was arrested and quickly indicted by a grand jury. Bryan agreed to represent the prosecution; famed Chicago criminal lawyer Clarence Darrow defended Scopes.

Bryan did not oppose science, but he objected to its misapplication. Darrow did not oppose religion. But he argued that religious fundamentalists—"creationists" who believed in the literal interpretation of the Bible—should not determine how science was taught in the schools. Reporters at the time, and since, cast the trial as a struggle between religion and science, with rural and small-town Americans on the side of creationism and secular urbanites supporting evolution. But the divide was not so clear-cut. Almost all advocates on both sides of the Scopes trial were Christians who disagreed over how to interpret the Bible. They were also believers in science; those opposed to the teaching of evolution considered it to be an unscientific theory.

Almost all advocates on both sides of the Scopes trial were Christians who disagreed over how to interpret the Bible.

The Scopes trial also contained elements of popular entertainment. Dubbed "the Monkey trial" because Darwin's theory of evolution demonstrated that humans evolved from an earlier primate form from which monkeys and chimpanzees also descended, the trial was one of the first national media events. The judge invited reporters from around the country, including broadcast journalists. The Scopes trial was the first jury trial broadcast on live radio. More than 900 spectators packed the courtroom, and hundreds more gathered in the streets, where a carnival atmosphere prevailed, complete with souvenir stands, food vendors, itinerant preachers, and hucksters, including numerous chimpanzees accompanied by their trainers.

The jury reached a guilty verdict in just nine minutes. Bryan technically won the case, but most reporters deemed the spectacle a victory for Darrow and the teaching of evolution. That assessment was premature. The Tennessee Supreme Court overturned the verdict on a technicality, robbing Darrow of his chance to take the case to the U.S. Supreme Court. Before the trial, most science textbooks included discussion of evolution; after the trial, material on evolution began to disappear. Laws against the teaching of evolution remained on the books until the U.S. Supreme Court overturned an Arkansas law in 1968.

The Scopes trial did not resolve the debate between creationists and evolutionists, a controversy that continued throughout the century. As late as 2000, the school officials in Kansas ruled that creationism and evolution were both unproven theories and that both could be taught in the schools.

Consumer Dreams and Nightmares

What were the positive and negative effects of the 1920s consumer culture?

Unlike faith and politics, the material prosperity of many in the Jazz Age seemed a unifying force. During the 1920s, spending on recreation nearly doubled. Faith in continuing prosperity promoted the extension of consumer credit to unprecedented heights. Previously, the only major item routinely purchased on credit was a house. But in the twenties, **installment buying** became the rage for a wide range of consumer goods, from autos and radios to household appliances. Consumer debt rose from $2.6 billion in 1919 to $7.1 billion in 1929. As one official in a midwestern loan company remarked, "People don't think anything nowadays of borrowing sums they'd never have thought of borrowing in the old days. They will assume an obligation for $2,000 today as calmly as they would have borrowed $300 or $400 in 1890." This habit of buying on credit boosted the standard of living for many but also left families in a precarious situation and vulnerable to the vagaries of the broader economy. The stock market crash and subsequent depression made that vulnerability vividly clear.

JUST GOING ALONG
FOR THE RIDE

Many a General spare tire is never put to service during the single ownership of a car—they just go along for the ride. It is this year round freedom from tire worry that has spoiled General Tire users for any other tire. But more important is the factor of safety at today's high speeds. Generals are blowout proof and skid-safe and the exclusive low pressure feature makes comfort a luxurious reality. All of these advantages cost so little when you total up General's almost unheard of big mileage. The General Tire & Rubber Co., Akron, O.

The New
GENERAL
DUAL BALLOON
— *goes a long way to make friends*

■ **In the 1920s, advertisers used sexualized images to sell all sorts of products. This advertisement for automobile tires provides very little information about the product but evokes images of fun and romance to capture consumers' attention.**

Marketing the Good Life

Advertising fueled much of the new spending. As one contemporary reporter noted, "Advertising is to business what fertilizer is to a farm." According to advertisers, consumer goods promised health, beauty, success, and the means to eliminate personal and embarrassing flaws, such as bad breath or dandruff. Cigarette companies used advertising to promote smoking as a symbol of independence for women and as a means to achieve beauty. Clever advertising campaigns promised women that if they would "reach for a Lucky Strike" instead of a sweet, they would remain slim, healthy, and sexually appealing.

Advertising also fostered a vision of big business as a benevolent force, promoting individual happiness. In his 1925 best-seller *The Man That Nobody Knows*, advertising executive Bruce Barton portrayed Jesus as a businessman who gathered a group of twelve followers who believed in his enterprise and, through effective public relations and advertising, sold his product to the world. The consumer culture had its temples: movie palaces, department stores, and the 1920s innovation, the shopping center. Kansas City's elegant Country Club Plaza was the first shopping center in the nation.

A much less successful venture was the Florida land boom. Exaggerated promotions fed fantasies of a consumer paradise, sparking a frenzy of investment in Florida real estate. Developers rushed to construct roads and find new land on which to build, fueling a spree of speculative property purchasing. The boom peaked in 1925 and quickly collapsed. In 1926 a hurricane hit Miami, killing 130 people and causing millions of dollars of property damage. Human folly and nature's fury contributed to the Florida land boom and bust.

Writers and Critics

Some social critics claimed that consumerism fostered not only economic disasters such as the Florida land boom but also a stifling conformity. Sinclair Lewis was one of several novelists of the twenties whose books expressed biting criticism of the frantic pursuit of material gain and status. George Babbitt, the protagonist of Lewis's novel *Babbitt* (1922), struggles to become accepted and successful in his small town by conforming to the empty materialism and standardized opinions accepted and prized by his neighbors.

F. Scott Fitzgerald wrote not about small-town conformity, as Lewis did, but about the modern urban life that was its antithesis. Fitzgerald glamorized, criticized, and in many ways embodied the giddy nightlife and status seeking of the Jazz Age. Born in St. Paul, Minnesota, into a family of modest means, he grew up admiring and emulating the wealthy. He married glamorous flapper Zelda Sayre, daughter of a prominent Alabama judge, and together they embraced the dizzy, indulgent, free-spirited life of the decade. But Fitzgerald's novels, including *This Side of Paradise* (1920), *The Beautiful and the Damned* (1922), and *The Great Gatsby* (1925), criticized the era's obsessions with success, glamour, consumerism, advertising, and status. The Fitzgeralds, along with other writers who were critical of American superficiality and conformity, moved to Paris. Eventually, the life Fitzgerald both lived and criticized caught up with him. By the end of the decade, he—like the nation—was broken by his excesses. In 1931 he came home to Baltimore an alcoholic; Zelda was diagnosed with schizophrenia and spent the rest of her life in mental institutions.

Poverty amid Plenty

Most Americans in the 1920s were neither investing in Florida real estate nor frequenting expatriate American writer Gertrude Stein's Paris salon. Even so, they were not immune to the desires and dreams that the consumer society sparked. The middle class and the more

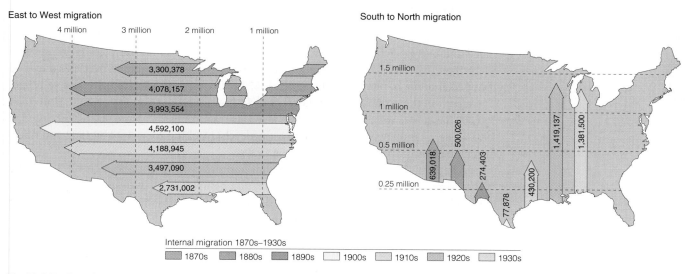

■ **MAP 21.2**
AMERICANS ON THE MOVE, 1870s–1930s
Between the 1870s and the 1930s, millions of Americans moved around the country, mostly from East to West, but also from South to North.

prosperous members of the working class enjoyed many of the comforts, amusements, and appliances that the booming economy made available. The poor, by contrast, struggled just to make ends meet. Throughout the twenties, the nation's poorest people continued to be the most mobile, moving in search of jobs, security, and a place they could settle and call home. Henry Crews, son of a white Georgia sharecropper, longed for "that single house where you were born, where you lived out your childhood . . . your anchor in the world." But he never had such a home. Like many other hardworking sharecroppers and factory workers, his family moved frequently in search of a better life, a dream that often proved elusive.

Sharecropping required hard work and careful planning to carve out a meager life, but many did so with pride. Ed Brown, a young black sharecropper, had no formal education but considered himself "pretty schemy." He worked on six different plantations, moving about in search of better circumstances or to escape from debt or threats of violence. Although he and his wife, Willie Mae, were never able to buy a place of their own, they did improve their circumstances over time. When they finally got out of debt and secured a bit of cash, they used it to adorn their meager cabin. In 1929 they bought an old Model T Ford. But finding it too costly to maintain, they swapped it for a cow and a butter churn and dasher, which provided more practical benefits. Meanwhile, Ed took odd jobs to earn extra money, while Willie Mae took care of the children, picked cotton, took in laundry, and, as Ed noted with appreciation, kept "things . . . lookin very pretty."

Industrial workers struggled throughout the decade, especially in a political climate hostile to unions. With the crushing of labor radicalism in the Red Scare after World War I, union organizing and strikes declined. But workers continued to protest low wages and poor working conditions. In March 1929, young women textile workers in Elizabethton, a small town nestled in the Blue Ridge Mountains of eastern Tennessee, closed down the American Glanzstoff plant in protest against low wages, petty rules, and arrogant employers. Soon, the protest spread to textile mills across the region. At Glanzstoff, the strikers returned to work when the company promised better pay and agreed not to discriminate against union members. But the employers broke their promises, so the women struck again. The governor sent in the National Guard, armed with machine guns. More than 1,000 people were arrested in confrontations with the troops.

The Stock Market Crash

The symbolic end of the 1920s arrived on "Black Tuesday," October 29, 1929, when the inflated and overextended stock market came crashing down. In one day, stocks fell in value $14 billion. By the end of the year, stock prices were down 50 percent; by 1932, they had dropped another 30 percent. In three years, $74 billion of the nation's wealth had vanished. The effect on the economy was catastrophic. Industrial production fell by half. More than 100,000 businesses went bankrupt. Banks failed at an alarming rate: more than 2,000 closed in 1931 alone. Unemployment rose to staggering levels, reaching 25 percent by 1932 and rarely dropping below 17 percent throughout the 1930s.

In keeping with the social policies that had prevailed throughout the 1920s, relief efforts were slim. No federal relief or welfare, no unemployment insurance, no Social Security, no job programs existed to help those who had lost their jobs, their savings, and their homes. Although many wealthy people lost their fortunes, which had been built on speculative investments, the poor suffered the most. People who lost their homes and farms moved into makeshift shelters in shantytowns, which they nicknamed **Hoovervilles** to mock the ineffectual efforts of President Herbert Hoover to respond to their plight.

The causes of the stock market crash and the decade-long depression that followed were complex and varied. Stock prices had risen dramatically, especially at the end of the 1920s. Speculators had been purchasing stocks on 10 percent margins, meaning they put down only 10 percent of the cost and borrowed the rest from brokers and banks.

INTERPRETING HISTORY

F. Scott Fitzgerald, *The Great Gatsby*

F. Scott Fitzgerald's 1925 novel The Great Gatsby expressed the longings of many Americans of the 1920s to partake of the glamorous life of the wealthy and live out their vision of the American dream. The story revolves around the desires of the newly wealthy Jay Gatsby to be accepted into the ranks of New York's elite. He is infatuated with Daisy Buchanan, who lives across the Sound from him in Long Island,

Writer F. Scott Fitzgerald and his flapper wife, Zelda, personified the glamorous literati of the Jazz Age. In his writing, Fitzgerald both romanticized and criticized the decadent consumerism of the aspiring and upwardly mobile middle class. In this page from a scrapbook, their photos are adorned with autographs of other famous literary figures.

a green light from her dock beckoning to him. In this passage from the final paragraphs of the book, the narrator, Nick Carraway, comments on the elusiveness of Gatsby's dream—the American dream. The poignant ending of the novel foreshadows the collapse of the overextended leisure and consumer culture of the 1920s that led to the Great Depression of the 1930s.

I spent my Saturday nights in New York because those gleaming, dazzling parties of his were with me so vividly that I could still hear the music and the laughter, faint and incessant, from his garden, and the cars going up and down his drive. One night I did hear a material car there, and saw its lights stop at his front steps. But I didn't investigate. Probably it was some final guest who had been away at the ends of the earth and didn't know that the party was over.

On the last night, with my trunk packed and my car sold to the grocer, I went over and looked at that huge incoherent failure of a house once more. On the white steps an obscene word, scrawled by some boy with a piece of brick, stood out clearly in the moonlight, and I erased it, drawing my shoe raspingly along the stone. Then I wandered down to the beach and sprawled out on the sand.

Most of the big shore places were closed now and there were hardly any lights except the shadowy, moving glow of a ferryboat across the Sound. And as the moon rose higher the inessential houses began to melt away until gradually I became aware of the old island here that flowered once for Dutch sailors' eyes—a fresh, green breast of the new world. Its vanished trees, the trees that had made way for Gatsby's house, had once pandered in whispers to the last

and greatest of all human dreams; for a transitory enchanted moment man must have held his breath in the presence of this continent, compelled into an aesthetic contemplation he neither understood nor desired, face to face for the last time in history with something commensurate to his capacity for wonder.

And as I sat there brooding on the old, unknown world, I thought of Gatsby's wonder when he first picked out the green light at the end of Daisy's dock. He had come a long way to this blue lawn, and his dream must have seemed so close that he could hardly fail to grasp it. He did not know that it was already behind him, somewhere back in that vast obscurity beyond the city, where the dark fields of the republic rolled on under the night.

Gatsby believed in the green light, the orgastic future that year by year recedes before us. It eluded us then, but that's no matter—tomorrow we will run faster, stretch out our arms farther. . . . And one fine morning—

So we beat on, boats against the current, borne back ceaselessly into the past.

Questions

1. *Why would Fitzgerald use the Dutch sailors of the colonial period as a point of reference in this passage?*
2. *Critics have often pointed to Fitzgerald's ambivalence about modern urban life as expressed in The Great Gatsby. Do you see any ambivalence in this passage?*
3. *In this passage, is Fitzgerald optimistic or pessimistic about the American dream?*

Source: © 1925 by Scribner and Sons; renewed by Frances Scott Fitzgerald Lanahan.

The popularity of installment buying in the consumer goods market had devastating effects when applied in this manner to the stock market. Investors expected to get rich quickly by selling their stocks at a higher price and paying back the loans from their huge profits. This system worked for a few years, encouraging investors with limited funds to make risky investments in the hope of gaining large fortunes. When the price of stocks spiraled out of control, far beyond their actual value, creditors demanded repayment of their loans, and investors were unable to pay their debts. The collapse was the worst of the twentieth century. Nothing of comparable magnitude occurred until 2008, when a similar combination of inflated stock and housing prices and irresponsible, unregulated business practices led to an economic catastrophe.

The collapse of the stock market alone would not necessarily have caused such a severe and prolonged depression. Poor decision making by financial and political leaders exacerbated underlying weaknesses in the economy. The Federal Reserve curtailed the amount of money in circulation and raised interest rates, making it more difficult for people to get loans and pay off their debts. These policies had profound worldwide implications and contributed to an international crisis. Banks in Germany and Austria, for example, depended on loans from the United States, and many went bankrupt, causing a ripple effect across Europe. The Hawley-Smoot Tariff of 1930 also contributed to the downward spiral. The new high tariff was intended to protect American commodities from competition from cheaper foreign goods. Foreign governments retaliated by raising their own tariffs to keep out American goods. These monetary and trade policies backfired, and the economic crisis spread throughout the western industrial world. Only the Soviet Union was spared the effects of the global economic crisis. As a communist state-run economy, it was largely immune from the collapse of worldwide capitalism.

Within the United States, the unequal distribution of wealth exacerbated the effects of the economic downturn. The nation may have looked prosperous, but most of the wealth was concentrated in the hands of a small number of people. If average Americans had been able to buy more cars, household appliances, and other products, those industries might have survived, and the economy might have recovered more quickly. Political leaders, and the business-oriented public policies they had promoted throughout the decade, left the country ill prepared to address the crisis and meet the needs of families deprived of their means of livelihood.

CONCLUSION

The stock market collapse, and the prolonged depression that followed, revealed the flaws in the economic system that spurred the apparent prosperity of the 1920s. Beneath the visible affluence was the hidden poverty that prevailed throughout the decade. National leaders promoted business interests and paid little attention to social welfare, the environment, or the need to regulate the economy. By the end of the 1920s, it was clear that Prohibition was a dismal failure and that the federal government was ill equipped to enforce it.

Although political reform withered, cultural vitality flowered. Hollywood emerged as a major industry, and the Jazz Age reflected the widespread appeal of African-American music. A black arts movement flourished, centered in Harlem, and writers—disenchanted with the status quo—gathered in Greenwich Village or moved to France. Across the country, a youth culture challenged the gender and sexual mores of the past. Consumer culture expanded as increasing numbers of families purchased cars, radios, and new fashions. Few who were involved in the private preoccupations of the decade could have foreseen the disaster ahead, when the stock market crashed and the Depression set in.

For Review

✓●─⌐Study and Review at www.myhistorylab.com

1. How did the U.S. presidents of the 1920s use the power of the presidency?

2. How did outsiders to the American mainstream create the most American forms of popular culture: jazz and Hollywood movies?

3. What was the Scopes trial about and why was it important?

4. What were some of the causes of the 1929 stock market crash?

Chronology: 1920–1929

1920 Harding elected president. Nineteenth Amendment (women's suffrage) ratified.

1921 Sheppard-Towner Act provides nurses for maternal and infant care.

1922 Five-Power Naval Treaty.

1923 Equal Rights Amendment proposed.

1924 Coolidge elected president.
Johnson-Reid Act limits immigration.
Portable radio introduced.

1925 Scopes trial, Dayton, Tennessee.
F. Scott Fitzgerald, *The Great Gatsby*.

1926 Gertrude Ederle is first woman to swim across English Channel.

1927 Charles Lindbergh flies nonstop from New York to Paris.
Al Jolson stars in *The Jazz Singer*, first talking movie.
Sacco and Vanzetti executed.
Buck v. Bell upholds compulsory sterilization laws.

1928 Hoover elected president.
Tamiami Trail across Florida Everglades completed.

1929 Stock market crash.

Key Terms

Alien Foreign-born resident of the United States who has not been naturalized as a U.S. citizen. p. 494

Consumer economy An economic system in which most people work for wages, which they use to purchase manufactured goods and foodstuffs. p. 491

Equal Rights Amendment (ERA) A proposed amendment to the United States Constitution that would have guaranteed equal rights for women. p. 493

Flapper Young woman in the 1910s and 1920s who rebelled against the gender conventions of the era with respect to fashion and behavior. p. 491

Hoovervilles Shantytowns, named for President Hoover and occupied largely by people who lost their homes and farms during the Great Depression. p. 506

Installment buying A system in which a consumer could make a down payment to purchase a product and then pay the remaining installments over time. p. 504

Planned obsolescence A concept whereby producers intend for their products to eventually become obsolete or outdated and require replacement, thus perpetuating a cycle of production and consumption. p. 500

Political machine A group that effectively exercises control over a political party, usually at the local level and organized around precincts and patronage. p. 493

"Speakeasies" Establishments where alcohol was illegally sold during the Prohibition era. p. 494

PART EIGHT

From Depression and War to World Power, 1929–1953

THE GREAT DEPRESSION AND WORLD WAR II TESTED AMERICANS' faith in their federal government to a degree unmatched in the nation's history. Economic collapse in the 1930s and the threat of Nazi and Japanese aggression from 1941 to 1945 presented challenges beyond the reach of ordinary citizens, local communities, and businesses acting alone. The federal government began to take more responsibility for economic and social well-being at home and for the spread of American values around the world.

The Great Depression resulted in a fundamental reordering of American politics. President Franklin Delano Roosevelt (FDR), who took office in 1933, believed that the federal government must assume an active role in banking, agriculture, and social welfare. He sponsored a large number of federal initiatives, known collectively as the New Deal. The New Deal aimed to put people back to work, restore faith in American businesses, boost purchasing power among consumers, and cushion the effects of economic downturns on industrial workers.

The effects of the New Deal were uneven. Many workers, including domestic servants, agricultural laborers, and part-time and seasonal employees, did not qualify for Social Security and other benefits. In the South, government policies that discouraged landowners from planting crops led to the displacement of many black and white sharecropping families. On the other hand, employees of many large companies won higher wages and improved job security as a result of militant labor protests. African-American civil rights activists, local communist organizations such as urban Unemployed Councils, and southern sharecroppers' and tenants' unions gave voice to the groups hit hardest by the Depression.

The New Deal did not end the Depression. On the morning of December 7, 1941, the Japanese conducted a surprise air attack on the U.S. Pacific naval fleet stationed in Pearl Harbor, Hawaii. Americans reacted with shock and outrage to what the president called this "day of infamy." The U.S. entry into World War II put large numbers of Americans back to work, many of them in the expanding defense industries.

The conflict brought Americans together in shared hardship, sacrifice, and national purpose. At the same time, the war placed strains on the social fabric. All over the country, family members separated from one another to search for work. In the Midwest, blacks and whites competed for scarce wartime resources, such as housing. On the West Coast, more than 100,000 Japanese immigrants and U.S. citizens of Japanese descent were forced into internment camps.

Elected to an unprecedented fourth term in 1944, Roosevelt proved to be a commanding leader during wartime as well as economic depression. In the last stages of the war, the president met several times with his British and Soviet counterparts, Winston Churchill and Josef Stalin, to plan for the postwar reconstruction of Europe and Asia. Roosevelt's death in April 1945 catapulted Vice President Harry S. Truman into the presidency. Germany surrendered to the Allies the next month. In August 1945, the new president authorized the dropping of atomic bombs on the Japanese cities of Hiroshima and Nagasaki, effectively ending the war in the Pacific. Together, the two bombs killed 120,000 Japanese civilians and wounded at least 130,000 more. The Atomic Age ushered in a new chapter in the history of human warfare.

Together with its allies, the United States emerged victorious from the war, but unlike its allies, America escaped physical destruction. Yet in many respects the postwar world was radically different from the world of the 1930s. The Soviet Union, an ally in the war against Germany and Japan, emerged as America's greatest enemy. The development of weapons of mass destruction introduced a new and profound threat to the natural environment, as well as to humans. To secure its supremacy in world affairs, the United States helped to form the North Atlantic Treaty Organization (NATO). For the first time, Americans were part of a multinational peacetime alliance, one that required them to defend a member of the alliance even if they themselves were not attacked.

World War II also profoundly altered life in the United States. The perceived communist threat led some Americans to suspect domestic groups of internal subversion: African Americans agitating for their civil rights, labor leaders attempting to organize southern factories, and leftists who expressed support for communism in general and the Soviet Union in particular. Supported by government contracts, the defense industry became an integral part of the nation's economy.

Recovering quickly from the disruptions of war, returning soldiers and their wives hoped to settle down to a normal family life. These couples produced the baby boom, a generation that shaped American culture and society in significant ways. In the new and growing suburbs, many (predominantly white) Americans achieved their dream of home ownership, and businesses found plenty of room to expand in new industrial parks. Yet, not all Americans shared in this newfound prosperity and security, and not all were willing to forgo their rights to free speech and free assembly in the struggle against communism.

1943	Smith-Connally Act
	Zoot-suit riots in Los Angeles. Attacks on blacks in Detroit
1944	Normandy invasion on D-Day (June 6)
	Servicemen's Readjustment Act (GI Bill)
1945	Harry S. Truman becomes president upon death of Roosevelt
	First test of atomic bomb, Alamogordo, New Mexico
	Atomic bombs dropped on Hiroshima and Nagasaki
	V-E Day (May 7); V-J Day (Sept. 2)
	United Nations created
1946	*Morgan v. West Virginia* outlaws segregation in interstate transportation
	Winston Churchill gives "Iron Curtain" speech, Fulton, Missouri
1947	Jackie Robinson joins Brooklyn Dodgers
	Taft-Hartley Act
	Truman Doctrine of containing communism announced
1948	New Mexico and Arizona grant Indians right to vote
	Modern state of Israel founded
	Armed Services desegregated
	Organization of American States (OAS) founded
1949	Billy Graham launches his first evangelical crusade in Los Angeles
	Establishment of People's Republic of China
	USSR acquires nuclear weapons
1950	North Korean troops invade South Korea
	Internal Security Act of 1950
	Senator Joseph McCarthy accuses State Department of harboring communists
1951	Ethel and Julius Rosenberg convicted of treason
1952	McCarran-Walter Act
	Puerto Rico becomes self-governing commonwealth
1953	Korean War ends
	Soviet leader Josef Stalin dies

22

Hardship and Hope: The Great Depression of the 1930s

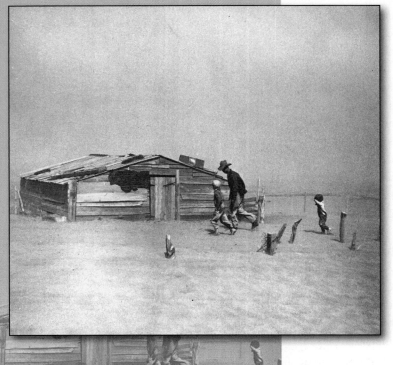

Will Rogers was a Cherokee, a comedian, a plainspoken critic of the nation's rich and powerful, a movie star, a journalist, and an adviser to President Franklin Delano Roosevelt (FDR). Rogers articulated a new vision of American national identity that took shape in the 1930s. In contrast to earlier notions of the United States as an Anglo-Saxon country into which newcomers might assimilate, this new Americanism included ethnic minorities, particularly those of European immigrant background. The Great Depression tarnished the status of the business elite and opened up the political process to party realignments and new leaders. The popular culture expressed and reflected this new Americanism; Will Rogers was its most prominent voice.

In the 1930s, the Great Depression gave rise to a cultural and political upheaval that helped propel Rogers to stardom and political influence. President Franklin Roosevelt coveted his support, and Rogers obliged by promoting the New Deal, the president's program for economic recovery. However, Rogers also pushed the president to the left by advocating such measures as taxing the rich and redistributing wealth. In 1932 Oklahoma nominated Rogers for president as the state's favorite son; three years later, California Democratic leaders urged him to run for the Senate. But in 1935, before any of these possibilities could come to fruition, Rogers died in a plane crash.

The response to Rogers's death illustrates his stature as a national leader and spokesperson for a new multicultural Americanism. Congress adjourned in his memory, President Roosevelt sent a well-publicized letter to Rogers's family, the governor of California proclaimed a day of mourning, flags flew at half staff, bells rang in Rogers's honor in more than 100 cities, and nearly 100,000 people filed by his coffin at Forest Lawn Cemetery. Radio stations across the country broadcast his memorial service from the Hollywood Bowl, presided over by a Protestant minister and a Catholic priest, while a Yiddish performer sang a Hebrew mourning chant. Across town, Mexican-American citizen groups placed a wreath on Olvera Street that read "Nosotros Lamentamos la Muerte de Will Rogers" ("We Mourn the Death of Will Rogers"). An African-American fraternal group in Los Angeles called the Friends of Ethiopia joined black performers from Rogers's films in a parade to honor the Cherokee movie star who had publicly opposed Italy's 1935 invasion of Ethiopia.

In his hometown of Claremore, Oklahoma, Cherokee Indians performed a death dance in memory of their fallen kinsman.

This massive national grieving reveals not only Rogers's popularity, but also the culture of 1930s America. The economic crisis unleashed changes in society that opened the door for a politically radical Cherokee Indian to become one of the most popular figures of the Great Depression. Millions of Americans experienced poverty—many for the first time. The shared experience of loss and suffering permeated the country.

Roosevelt drew a new political coalition into the Democratic party that elected him to the presidency four times. The Great Depression gave him the opportunity to forge a strong national government and to promote a more representative democracy. His inclusiveness brought citizens of recent immigrant background into the political mainstream but stopped short of the color line. Nevertheless, African-American voters abandoned the Republican party to vote for FDR.

The New Deal, a package of remedies put together by Franklin Roosevelt to address the problems of the Depression, provided relief to many Americans in need but did not eradicate poverty or end the Depression. Yet, as American families from every region of the country drew around their radios to hear the president's **fireside chats**, as they made heroes of Will Rogers and other outsider celebrities, and as they held onto their faith in the nation's promise in spite of its worst economic crisis, they helped forge a more inclusive nation.

■ Will Rogers, left, is shown here with William Harrison Hays, one of many powerful political leaders with whom Rogers socialized.

> *The economic crisis opened the door for a politically radical Cherokee Indian to become one of the most popular figures of the Great Depression.*

The Great Depression

The Great Depression defined the 1930s in the United States. It shaped American culture, the political life of the nation, the public policies that resulted, and the cultural expressions that reflected the spirit of the people during a time of national crisis. Its effects permeated the lives of Americans from the mansions of the wealthy to the shanties of the poor and from the boardrooms to the bedrooms. The Depression drove thousands of farmers from the drought-stricken southern Great Plains to California. But the story is not simply one of despair and hardship. It is also one of strong communities, resourcefulness, and hope.

The Great Depression was a global economic catastrophe. Of the major world powers, only the Soviet Union—a communist society with state-directed labor, agriculture, and industry—was immune to the collapse of the capitalist system after 1929. The Soviet economy grew throughout the 1930s, and its relative health led many people in troubled capitalist systems to look to communism as an alternative. Socialism also gained many converts across Europe. The world's powerful nations all moved toward greater government intervention in their economies. England, France, and the United States used deficit spending to help stimulate the economy and instituted relief programs. Italy, Germany, and Japan also increased government intervention in the economy, but they used different strategies to address the crisis, particularly military spending. These varied responses to the Depression contributed to the conflicts and alliances that would eventually culminate in World War II.

What caused the Great Depression, and how did it affect ordinary Americans?

Causes of the Crisis

> *The story of the Depression is not simply one of despair and hardship. It is also one of strong communities, resourcefulness, and hope.*

The Great Depression of the 1930s was the worst economic depression in the twentieth century. But it was neither the first nor the last. A complex set of factors led to the collapse. Economists at the time, and since, have debated its cause, with no widely-shared explanation. **Capitalism**, the economic system that forms the basis of the American economy, has cycles of ups and downs. In the United States, prior to the 1930s, the government stepped in to regulate the economy primarily to protect economic competition. Progressive Era reforms prevented corporations from establishing monopolies, so that competition could flourish. In the free market economy, consumers would determine which companies would succeed, based on the quality of their products and services. Because the government did not determine the levels of industrial or agricultural productivity, and did not set the prices, the economy was subject to changing circumstances that led to times of prosperity and times of recession or, in the case of severe economic downturns, depression.

⊙ See the **Map**
The Great Depression at
www.myhistorylab.com

Before the 1930s, the United States provided no **welfare-state** benefits, such as medical care, relief from poverty, income for the unemployed, or old-age insurance. Without policies that would serve as a safety net for workers who lost their jobs, many wage earners and their families fell into poverty during economic downturns. In the Great Depression of the 1930s, the economic crisis was so severe that one-quarter of the nation's workers,

■ Margaret Bourke-White in this 1937 photograph, "At the time of the Louisville Flood," depicts the painful irony of poverty in the midst of affluence. Here, hungry Americans line up at a breadline in front of a billboard proclaiming American prosperity.

nearly 14 million people, lost their jobs, leaving them and their families—40 million people in all—without any income or security. Many of these people had never known poverty before. Among the newly poor were thousands of middle-class Americans who now faced the loss of their homes and savings. For working-class and poor Americans, the impact of the Depression was devastating because they had little economic security to begin with.

For many Americans, the Depression really began in the 1920s. Food production and distribution stumbled along weakly throughout the 1920s, contributing to widespread rural poverty. During the 1920s, 1,200 big corporations absorbed more than 6,000 independent businesses. By 1929, 200 corporations controlled nearly half of all industry, which limited competition and made it difficult for new, smaller businesses to flourish.

Although the economy looked healthy on the surface, prosperity rested on an unsound foundation. Many people obtained consumer goods on credit, so when people lost their jobs, they could not pay their debts. Throughout the 1920s, the gap between the rich and poor increased. Nearly 80 percent of the nation's families had no savings at all. Americans with high annual incomes of $10,000 or more—2.3 percent of the people—held two-thirds of all savings. The concentration of wealth among the richest Americans during the 1920s contributed to the persistence of the crisis in the 1930s.

Surviving Hard Times

In human terms, the Depression of the 1930s dealt a devastating blow to large numbers of Americans: crushing poverty, hunger, humiliation, and loss of dignity and self-worth. Many felt a profound shame that they could no longer earn a living and support their families. The few jobs available often went to the young, strong, well-fed, and well-groomed. Thousands of citizens poured out their hearts in letters to the president, hoping that the government could provide some assistance. In 1934 an Oklahoma woman lamented, "The unemployed have been so long without food-clothes-shoes-medical care-dental care etc.—we look prety bad—so when we ask for a job we dont' get it. And we look and feel a little worse each day—when we ask for food they call us bums—it isent our fault . . . no we are not bums."

Families provided the first line of defense against disaster, especially in the early days of the crisis. Many families adapted to hard times by abandoning time-honored gender roles. As men lost jobs, women went to work. Working women did not take jobs from men; rather, they held jobs defined as "traditional women's work" as secretaries, nurses, and waitresses. These jobs offered lower wages than most jobs held by men. A white woman working for wages earned, on average, 61 percent of a white man's wages; a black woman earned a mere 23 percent. Still, they provided at least a modicum of much-needed income.

Many parents struggled to provide for their families under difficult conditions, sometimes risking their health and safety to do so. Erminia Pablita Ruiz Mercer remembered when her father was injured while working in the beet fields in 1933. "He didn't want to live if he couldn't support his family," so he risked experimental back surgery and died on the operating table. Young Erminia then dropped out of school to work as "a doughnut girl" to support her mother and sisters.

Enduring Discrimination

For many poor families, hard times were nothing new. As one African American noted, "The Negro was born in depression. It only became official when it hit the white man." Throughout the 1930s, black Americans suffered the impact of economic hard times disproportionately. By 1932 black unemployment reached 50 percent. With local white authorities in charge of relief, impoverished southern blacks had few places to turn for assistance. African Americans also faced increasing violence; the number of lynchings increased from eight in 1932 to twenty in 1935.

Many poor people joined the growing ranks of **hobos**, riding the rails from town to town, looking for work. But poverty did not erase racial hierarchies or sexual codes, especially for nine young African Americans in 1931 who came to be known as the "Scottsboro Boys." The youths were riding the rails when they were arrested in Paint Rock, Alabama. Two white women on the train with them accused them of rape. Narrowly avoiding a lynching, they were taken to jail in Scottsboro. An all-white jury convicted them of rape, and they were sentenced to death. But in November 1932, the U.S. Supreme Court ordered a new trial on the grounds that the defendants did not get a fair trial. But the new trial also resulted in convictions.

The case became a major rallying point for civil rights activists, liberals, and radicals throughout the 1930s. Support for the young men came from all over the world. In 1935 the U.S. Supreme Court reversed the second set of convictions on the grounds that excluding blacks from the jury denied the defendants due process. Yet, in the next two years, five of the defendants were again tried and found guilty. Although none of the Scottsboro Boys was executed, they all spent long years in prison.

Mexican-American families could barely survive on the low wages paid to Mexican laborers. According to a 1933 study, working children's earnings constituted more than one-third of their families' total income. The work was often grueling. Julia Luna Mount recalled her first day at a Los Angeles cannery: "I didn't have money for gloves so I peeled chilies all day long by hand. After work, my hands were red, swollen, and I was on fire! On the streetcar going home, I could hardly hold on my hands hurt so much." Young Julia was lucky—her father saw her suffering and did not make her return to the cannery. But Carmen Bernal Escobar's father could not afford to be soft-hearted about work: "My father was a busboy and to keep the family going . . . in order to bring in a little more money . . . my mother, my grandmother, my mother's brother, my sister and I all worked together" at the cannery.

Those with cannery work, hard as it was, were among the fortunate. Many more Mexicans were deported. Between 1931 and 1934, more than 500,000 Mexicans and Mexican Americans—approximately one-third of the Mexican population in the United States—were sent to Mexico. Most were children born in the United States. Throughout the century, the United States opened or closed its doors to Mexican immigrants depending on the need for their labor. They were deported during the Depression when unemployment was high, then recruited again during the labor shortage of World War II.

The Dust Bowl

Severe drought exacerbated the difficulties of farmers across Oklahoma, Texas, Kansas, Colorado, and New Mexico, an area that came to be known as the **Dust Bowl**. Farmers had used the land mainly for grazing until high grain prices during World War I enticed them to plow under millions of acres of natural grasslands to plant wheat. Plowing removed root systems from the soil, and years of little rainfall caused the land to dry up. By the middle of the decade, high winds picked up the loose topsoil, creating dust storms across the open plains. The ecological disaster drove 60 percent of the population out of the region.

Migrant farm families fleeing the Dust Bowl came to symbolize the suffering wrought by the Depression. The photographs of Dorothea Lange, the songs of Woody Guthrie, and the writings of John Steinbeck all immortalized their plight. Steinbeck's Pulitzer prize–winning novel *The Grapes of Wrath* (1939) and its film version have remained classics of American popular art. Writing in *The Nation* in 1936, Steinbeck described the Dust Bowl migrants streaming into California:

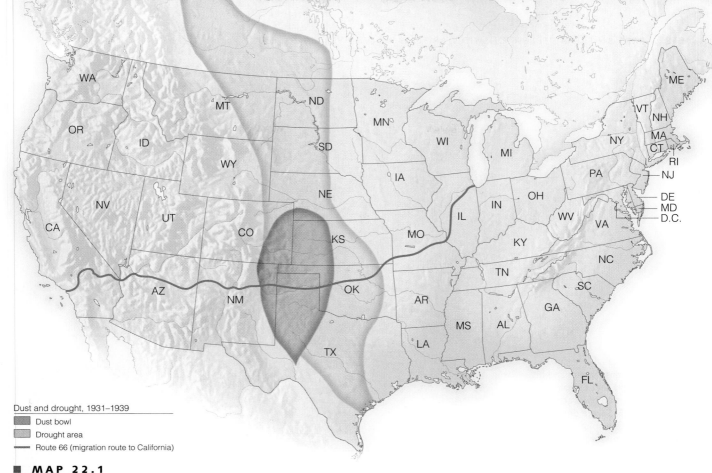

■ **MAP 22.1**

DUST AND DROUGHT, 1931–1939

Drought cut a giant swath across the middle of America during the years of the Great Depression. The hardest hit region was the Dust Bowl area of Oklahoma, Texas, New Mexico, Colorado, and Kansas. Many people fled the afflicted areas, abandoning farms, piling their belongings on their cars, and driving along Route 66 to California.

Dust and drought, 1931–1939
- Dust bowl
- Drought area
- Route 66 (migration route to California)

> *Poverty-stricken after the destruction of their farms, their last reserves used up in making the trip, they have arrived so beaten and destitute that they have been willing at first to work under any conditions and for any wages offered. . . . They are not drawn from a peon class, but have either owned small farms or been farm hands in the early American sense, in which the "hand" is a member of the employing family. They have one fixed idea, and that is to acquire land and settle on it. . . . They are not easily intimidated. They are courageous, intelligent, and resourceful. Having gone through the horrors of the drought and with immense effort having escaped from it, they cannot be herded, attacked, starved, or frightened.*

Thousands of **Okies** piled belongings on their cars and made their way to California in hopes of starting over. There they joined Mexican migrant farm workers, African-American laborers, and others down on their luck, hoping for work.

Presidential Responses to the Depression

Until the economic collapse, President Herbert Hoover's political achievements had earned wide admiration. He seemed the perfect embodiment of the spirit of the prosperous 1920s. But his ideas about politics and economics were ill suited to the crisis of the 1930s. Dissatisfaction with Hoover's response to the Depression gave Franklin Delano Roosevelt a landslide victory in the 1932 presidential election. Promising to take action to ease the nation's suffering, the optimistic Roosevelt seemed to embody hope for an end to the crisis.

How did Presidents Hoover and Roosevelt respond to the Great Depression?

517

■ An Oklahoma farmer and his sons try to find shelter from the storm of dust that blew across the plains in 1935. Severe drought after years of excessive plowing created dry loose topsoil that was picked up by high winds. More than half of the residents of the Dust Bowl moved out of the area as a result of the devastation.

Herbert Hoover: Failed Efforts

Had prosperity continued, Hoover might have left a legacy of presidential leadership to match his earlier achievements as a Progressive administrator of food relief in Europe. Declaring that "excessive fortunes are a menace to true liberty," he favored steeply graduated inheritance and income taxes on the wealthy, with no tax burden on the poor. He believed that society had a responsibility to care for those in need and that the prosperous should bear much of the burden. After the stock market crash, Hoover increased spending for public works—programs in which the government created jobs for people who needed employment—to the unprecedented sum of $700 million. He established the Reconstruction Finance Corporation to make government credit available to banks and other financial institutions. Seeking to restore confidence in the economy, he strove for a balanced budget by raising taxes and cutting spending—a strategy that underestimated the depth of the Depression and made the situation worse.

As the Depression set in and brought widespread misery, Hoover fully expected that charitable organizations would step in and provide aid to the poor. He believed that government relief to the needy had demoralizing effects on people. Even when it was clear that the crisis was beyond the help of charitable groups, Hoover remained strongly opposed to direct relief for the poor. Private giving did increase to record levels; unfortunately, it was not sufficient.

Hoover's popularity reached its lowest ebb in 1932. A group of World War I veterans in Portland, Oregon, organized a march on Washington, D.C., called the Bonus March. The veterans were due to receive a bonus of $1,000 each in 1945. The group had asked to have their bonuses early, in 1932, to help ease their suffering during the Depression. Hoover refused. More than 20,000 veterans traveled to Washington to petition Congress. The determined veterans set up a tent city and settled in with their families. When Hoover refused to meet with the protesters, the veterans began to leave. But some did not depart quickly enough, and a police officer began shooting at the unarmed demonstrators, killing one person.

Army Chief of Staff Douglas MacArthur stepped in and escalated the violence. His troops used tear gas and bayonets to prod the veterans and their families to vacate the area, then set fire to the tent city. The attack injured more than 100 people and killed one baby. The image of federal troops assaulting a group of peaceful veterans stunned the public. Although MacArthur had ordered the brutality, the public blamed Hoover. As most people saw it, Hoover had heartlessly spurned the veterans' legitimate request. By the time of the 1932 election, Hoover had lost most of his public support.

View the Image

Bonus Expeditonary Force March on Washington at **www.myhistorylab.com**

Franklin Delano Roosevelt: The Pragmatist

In contrast to Hoover, Franklin Delano Roosevelt was born into a family of wealth and privilege. Pampered as a child, he was educated at elite schools and colleges. In 1905, he married a distant cousin, Eleanor Roosevelt, the niece of President Theodore Roosevelt. Like Franklin, Eleanor came from a sheltered, upper-class background. But her early life, unlike his, was filled with sadness. Both her parents died when she was a young child, and at age ten her grandmother left her in the care of a harsh governess. The young woman began to flourish when she went abroad to study. The rigorous education developed her strengths and confidence.

Franklin Roosevelt was elected to the New York State Senate in 1911, and in 1913 he became Assistant Secretary of the Navy. His political plans derailed suddenly in 1921 when he was stricken with polio and lost the use of his legs. The painful and incapacitating illness threw the normally ebullient young man into despair. The formerly athletic Roosevelt depended on braces, crutches, and a wheelchair to move around. But his extraordinary reserves of self-confidence and optimism helped to sustain him in the face of his paralysis.

TABLE 22-1

The Election of 1932

Candidate	Political Party	Popular Vote (%)	Electoral Vote
Franklin D. Roosevelt	Democratic	57.4	472
Herbert Hoover	Republican	39.7	59
Norman Thomas	Socialist	2.2	—

■ In this 1941 photograph, FDR is pictured with his dog Fala and Ruthie Bie, a friend's grandaughter, in Hyde Park, New York. This is one of only two known photographs of Roosevelt in his wheelchair. Careful to project an image of strength, vitality, and optimism, FDR avoided photos that would call attention to his physical disability. Yet many Americans found inspiration and hope knowing that their president, like the nation, could triumph over adversity.

INTERPRETING HISTORY

Songs of the Great Depression

Popular songs expressed the spirit, sorrows, and longings of Depression Era Americans. According to folk-music historian Alan Lomax, the 12-year-old daughter of a striking Kentucky mineworker wrote "Which Side Are You On?" in 1937. The song became a popular anthem for labor militancy.

Woody Guthrie (1912–1967) wrote more than a thousand songs about the struggles of common people and the dispossessed. As a teenager, Guthrie left home to hitchhike, ride the rails, live in hobo camps, and follow migrant workers around the country. His song "Union Maid" expresses the hopes and spirit of union workers, and "So Long, It's Been Good to Know Yuh" captures the sorrows of Dust Bowl migrants.

Woody Guthrie, singer and songwriter, immortalized the spirit of ordinary Americans during the struggles of the Great Depression. His songs became anthems of the era and remain classics of American folk music.

Which Side Are You On? By Florence Reece (sung to the tune of an old English song, "Jack Munro")

Come all of you good workers
Good news to you I'll tell
Of how the good old union
Has come in here to dwell.

Chorus
Which side are you on,
Tell me, which side are
    you on?

My daddy was a miner,
He's now in the air an' sun,
Stick with him, brother miners,
Until this battle's won.

They say in Harlan County
There are no neutrals there
You'll either be a union man,
Or a thug for J. H. Blair.

O gentlemen, can you stand it,
O tell me if you can,
Will you be a lousy scab,
Or will you be a man?

FDR's bout with polio did nothing to dampen his political ambitions. He became governor of New York in 1928, following in the footsteps of his Republican cousin, Theodore Roosevelt. In his 1932 Democratic presidential campaign, FDR made few specific proposals, but promised the American people a "New Deal."

"Nothing to Fear but Fear Itself"

◄•••┤Read the Document

Franklin D. Roosevelt, First Inaugural Address (1933) at
www.myhistorylab.com

In his inaugural address, Roosevelt endeavored to ease the nation's anxieties with reassuring words: "Let me assert my firm belief that the only thing we have to fear is fear itself—nameless, unreasoning, unjustified terror which paralyzes needed efforts to convert retreat into advance." Roosevelt launched his advance immediately. Panic had prompted many Americans to pull out their bank savings, causing many banks to fail. To stop the run on banks, FDR announced a "bank holiday," temporarily closing all the nation's banks. He could have nationalized the banking system, a move toward socialism that would likely have received widespread support. But Roosevelt favored government regulation, not government ownership. He proposed the Emergency Banking Bill, providing government support for private banks. Congress passed the bill instantly, to the applause of the bankers who helped draft it.

Don't scab for the bosses,
Don't listen to their lies,
Us poor folks haven't got a chance,
Unless we organize.

Source: Florence Reece/Stormking
Music, 1947.

**Union Maid By Woody Guthrie
(first verse and chorus)**

There once was a union maid
Who never was afraid
Of goons and ginks and company
    finks
And the deputy sheriffs who made
    the raids;
She went to the union hall
When a meeting it was called
And when the company boys came
    'round
She always stood her ground.

Chorus
Oh, you can't scare me.
I'm sticking to the union,
    (3 times)
Oh, you can't scare me.
I'm sticking to the union,
    (2 times)
Till the day I die.

Source: Woody Guthrie, TRO © Copyright
1961. Ludlow Music, Inc., New York, NY.

**"So Long, It's Been Good to Know Yuh
(Dusty Old Dust)" By Woody Guthrie
(selected verses and chorus)**

I've sung this song, but I'll sing
    it again,
Of the place that I lived on the wild,
    windy plains,
In the month called April, the
    county called Gray
And here's what all of the people
    there say:

Chorus
So long, it's been good to know ye;
    (3 times)
This dusty old dust is a-getting my
    home,
And I've got to be driftin' along.

A dust storm hit, and it hit like
    thunder;
It dusted us over, and it covered us
    under;
Blocked out the traffic and blocked
    out the sun.
Straight for home all the people
    did run.

The sweethearts sat in the dark and
    they sparked,
They hugged and kissed in that
    dusty old dark,
They sighed and cried, hugged and
    kissed

Instead of marriage, they talked
    like this:
Honey, so long, it's been good to
    know ye . . .

Now, the telephone rang, and it
    jumped off the wall;
That was the preacher a-making his
    call.
He said, "Kind friend, this may be
    the end;
You've got your last chance of
    salvation of sin."

The churches was jammed, and the
    churches was packed,
And that dusty old dust storm
    blowed so black;
The preacher could not read a word
    of his text,
And he folded his specs and he took
    up collection, said:
So long, it's been good to know ye. . . .

Source: Woody Guthrie, TRO © Copyright
1963. Folkways Music Publishers, Inc.,
New York, NY.

Questions

1. *What makes the songs emblematic
    of the era in which they were written?*
2. *How are issues of class addressed in
    these folk tunes?*

In the first of his "fireside chats" to millions of radio listeners, whom he addressed as "my friends," Roosevelt assured citizens that the reopened banks were sound. He used the medium of radio skillfully to explain his policies and to communicate comforting and reassuring messages that reached people in the intimate setting of their homes. The next day, bank deposits exceeded withdrawals as a result of the confidence he inspired.

●●●─[Read the Document
*Franklin Roosevelt, fireside
chat (September 6, 1936)*
at **www.myhistorylab.com**

The New Deal

The New Deal drew on Progressive Era reform impulses to extend the reach of the federal government to solve social problems. It provided assistance to many Americans suffering the effects of the Depression and established the welfare state that would last half a century. Based on pragmatism, experimentation, and shrewd political calculation, FDR's plan began with a flurry of activity in the first 100 days of his administration and developed into a more progressive agenda by 1935, often called the **Second New Deal**. New Deal programs countered capitalism's cyclical nature and offered a safety net for industrial workers.

*What was the New Deal,
and how did it develop
over time?*

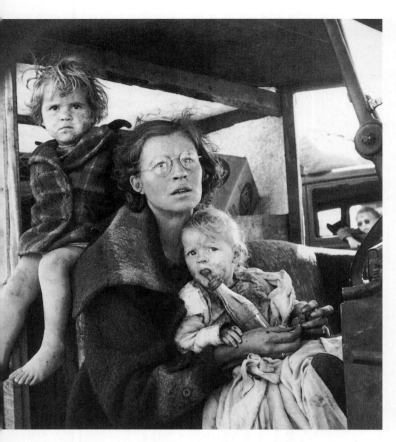

■ Dorothea Lange took photographs for the Farm Security Administration (FSA), documenting the lives of Depression-era migrants. This 1939 photo, "Mother and Children on the Road, Tulelake, Siskiyou County, California," is one of Lange's many portraits of impoverished families.

They legitimized labor unions and established a system of regulation and cooperation between industry and labor. They won Roosevelt a resounding reelection in 1936. Many New Deal programs failed, but those that succeeded created the foundation of the modern American state. The broad-based reform effort, however, did not end the Depression nor eradicate poverty.

The First Hundred Days

Roosevelt acted quickly and pragmatically. As one of his first acts, he encouraged Congress to repeal Prohibition. In 1933 the states quickly ratified the Twenty-First Amendment, repealing the Eighteenth. Repeal of Prohibition helped the economy by providing additional tax revenues from liquor sales, since they were once again legal, and a market for farmers' corn and wheat, which were used to produce liquor. Congress created the Securities and Exchange Commission (SEC) to oversee the stock market and the Federal Deposit Insurance Corporation (FDIC) to reform the banking system and provide insurance for deposits.

One of FDR's most pressing challenges was to prop up prices for producers while keeping them low enough for consumers. Poverty in the midst of plenty was one of the Depression's cruelest ironies. Farmers could not afford to transport their goods to market and food rotted while millions of people went hungry. Through the Agricultural Adjustment Act, the government sought to prop up farm prices by limiting supply. It paid farmers to destroy livestock and take acreage out of production.

Most Americans in need desperately wanted to work. They considered government relief a sign of failure and shame. Many citizens searched for ways to preserve their pride. One woman wrote to Eleanor Roosevelt asking to borrow money to avoid charity:

> *Please Mrs. Roosevelt, I do not want charity, only a chance from someone who will trust me. . . . I am sending you two of my dearest possessions to keep as security, a ring my husband gave me before we were married, and a ring my mother used to wear. . . . If you will consider buying the baby clothes, please keep them (rings) until I send you the money you spent. It is very hard to face bearing a baby we cannot afford to have, and the fact that it is due to arrive soon, and still there is no money for the hospital or clothing, does not make it any easier. I have decided to stay home, keeping my 7 year old daughter from school to help with the smaller children. . . . The 7 year old one is a good willing little worker and somehow we must manage—but without charity.*

In March 1933, Congress passed the Federal Emergency Relief Administration (FERA), which provided $500 million in grants to the states for aid to the needy. The program was headed by Harry Hopkins, an energetic and brash young reformer, who disbursed $2 million during his first two hours on the job. He then persuaded Roosevelt to launch a temporary job program, the Civil Works Administration (CWA). The CWA provided government-sponsored jobs for more than 4 million workers. But the program came under fire from conservatives, and FDR ended it a few months later.

■ **MAP 22.2**
AREAS SERVED BY THE TENNESSEE VALLEY AUTHORITY
The Tennessee Valley Authority (TVA) brought electricity to a large area in western Appalachia, one of the poorest regions in the country. The government-owned project strengthened the economy and improved living conditions in the area. But the many dams, along with other TVA projects, disrupted natural ecosystems and had negative environmental consequences that were unforseen at the time.

The New Deal included two major conservation and environmental programs. In 1933 Roosevelt combined his interest in conservation with his goal of providing work for unemployed young men. The Civilian Conservation Corps (CCC) operated under the control of the Army. CCC workers lived in camps, wore uniforms, and conformed to military discipline. They planted millions of trees, built more than 30,000 wilderness shelters, stocked rivers and lakes with nearly 1 billion fish, and preserved historic sites. Their work revived depleted forests and provided flood control. By 1935 the CCC had employed more than 500,000 young men and kept them, in FDR's words, "off the city street corners."

Another measure that linked natural resources to the recovery effort was the Tennessee Valley Authority (TVA), an experiment in government-owned utilities that brought power to rural areas along the Tennessee River in seven states in western Appalachia—among the poorest areas in the nation. This far-reaching government-owned project offered a radical alternative to American capitalism. Under the TVA, the government built five dams, improved 20 others, and constructed power plants; it produced and sold electricity to farmers and facilitated the development of industry in the region. The TVA also provided flood control and became one of the largest and cheapest suppliers of power in the nation.

In addition to the dams built as part of the TVA, gigantic new dams provided electricity and irrigation in the arid West: Hoover Dam on the Colorado River outside Las Vegas, and

👁 **See the Map**
The Tennessee Valley Authority at
www.myhistorylab.com

•••• **Read the Document**
Tennessee Valley Authority Act at
www.myhistorylab.com

the huge Grand Coulee Dam across the Columbia River in Washington State that provided electricity to much of the Northwest and irrigation for over half a million acres of land in the Columbia basin. The Golden Gate Bridge, another Depression-era project, spanned the entrance to San Francisco Bay. In 1930, construction began on the Empire State Building in New York City, the tallest building in the world up to that time.

The 1933 National Industrial Recovery Act (NIRA) became the centerpiece of the first New Deal. The NIRA established the National Recovery Administration (NRA) to oversee regulation of the economy. In his second "fireside chat," Roosevelt called the NRA "a partnership in planning" between business and government. The NRA enabled businesses in each sector of the economy to form trade associations and set their own standards for production, prices, and wages. Section 7(a) of the NIRA also guaranteed collective bargaining rights to workers, sparking new hope for union organizers.

FDR's first 100 days also included the creation of the Home Owners' Loan Corporation, providing refinancing of home mortgages at low rates. Because the plan helped stem the tide of foreclosures and also guaranteed the repayment of loans, it pleased homeowners, banks, and real-estate interests. It helped FDR gain the support of a large segment of the middle class.

One of the boldest New Dealers was John Collier, whom Roosevelt appointed as Commissioner of Indian Affairs. Collier opposed the policy of land allotment that the Dawes Act of 1887 had enacted. Under allotment, Native-American land holdings had dwindled from 130 million acres to 49 million acres—much of it desert. Collier rejected the assumption that Indians' survival depended on their assimilation into white culture. He altered the government boarding schools' curriculum to include bicultural and bilingual education and eliminated military dress and discipline.

Collier's ideas came to fruition in the 1934 Indian Reorganization Act, which recognized the autonomy of Indian tribes, did away with the allotment program, and appropriated

■ On October 28, 1935, John Collier, Commissioner of Indian Affairs, stands with a group of Flathead Indian chiefs as Secretary of the Interior Harold L. Ickes signs the first constitution providing for Indian self-rule. Franklin Roosevelt appointed Collier to bring the New Deal to Native Americans.

funds to help Indians add to their land holdings. It also provided for job and professional training programs as well as a system of agricultural and industrial credit. In keeping with Collier's goal of Indian self-government, each tribe decided whether to accept the terms of the Indian Reorganization Act. In the end, 181 tribes voted to accept the law, while 77 opted out of it.

Protest and Pressure from the Left and the Right

Despite these accomplishments, challenges to Roosevelt's New Deal took many forms. In spite of FDR's efforts to help businesses survive and remain profitable during the Depression, many business leaders continued to oppose the New Deal, charging that FDR was a dictator and that his program amounted to socialism. At the same time, FDR faced criticism from the left. Many people believed that Roosevelt's policies did not go far enough to ease the suffering caused by the economic crisis. Some thought that New Deal policies aimed at bolstering capitalism were ill-advised, and that capitalism itself was the problem. Disenchantment with capitalism drew many Americans to the cause of socialism and swelled the ranks of the small Communist party.

> *Many people believed that Roosevelt's policies did not go far enough to ease the suffering caused by the economic crisis.*

By 1934 and 1935, much of the pressure on Roosevelt came from workers, whose hopes that the NIRA would guarantee collective bargaining rights were dashed by the intransigence of employers. In 1934 nearly 1.5 million workers participated in 1,800 strikes. Although most African Americans supported FDR and the Democratic party during the Depression, between 3,000 and 4,000 members of the black community of Birmingham, Alabama, joined the Communist party and related organizations during the 1930s. One successful effort at biracial organizing occurred in the Arkansas delta in 1934. The Southern Tenant Farmers' Union (STFU) brought together black and white tenants and sharecroppers to fight for better working conditions.

In addition to the communists, socialists, labor unions, and grassroots organizations that sprang up all over the country, a number of individuals proposed alternatives to Roosevelt's program and gained large followings. The most influential of these were Dr. Francis Townsend, Father Charles E. Coughlin, and Senator Huey P. Long. In 1934 Townsend, a retired physician and health commissioner from Long Beach, California, introduced an idea for a pension plan that sparked a nationwide grassroots movement. Townsend proposed a 2 percent national sales tax that would fund a pension of $200 a month for Americans over age 60. The **Townsend Plan** became hugely popular, especially among elderly Americans. In 1936 a national survey indicated that half of all Americans favored the plan. Though the plan was never implemented, the groundswell of support that it generated probably hastened the development and passage of the old-age insurance system contained in the 1935 Social Security Act.

Coughlin also inspired a huge following. A Catholic priest, he served as pastor of a small church outside Detroit, Michigan. He began to broadcast his sermons on the radio, using his magnetic personality to address political as well as religious issues. Soon he became a media phenomenon, broadcasting through 26 radio stations to an audience estimated at 40 million. The "Radio Priest" called for a redistribution of wealth and attacked Wall Street, international bankers, and the evils of capitalism. But his message turned from social justice populism to right-wing bigotry. His virulent anti-Semitism and admiration for the fascist regimes of Adolf Hitler in Germany and Benito Mussolini in Italy drove away many of his followers. By 1940 Coughlin had ceased broadcasting and abandoned all political activities, under orders of the Catholic Church.

Huey P. Long was among the most powerful, and colorful, politicians of the era. He rose from modest origins to become a lawyer and a public service commissioner. In 1928 Long won the governorship of Louisiana.

> *Huey P. Long was among the most powerful, and colorful, politicians of the era.*

His progressive leadership inspired tremendous loyalty, especially among poor workers and farmers. He did more for the underprivileged people of Louisiana than any other governor. He expanded the state's infrastructure; developed social services; built roads, hospitals, and schools; and changed the tax code to place a greater burden on corporations and the wealthy. Unlike many other southern politicians, his public statements were free of racial slurs. But his ambition had no bounds, and he used any means to accumulate power.

In 1932 Long resigned the governorship and won election to the U.S. Senate. Soon, he gained a huge national following. Initially he supported FDR, but by 1933 he had broken with the president and forged his own political movement based on his Share-Our-Wealth Plan. Giving voice to many Americans' resentment toward "wealthy plutocrats," Long advocated a radical redistribution of the nation's wealth. He called for new taxes on the wealthy and proposed to guarantee a minimum annual income of $2,500 for all those in need. As he put it, "How many men ever went to a barbecue and would let one man take off the table what was intended for nine-tenths of the people to eat? The only way you'll ever be able to feed the balance of the people is to make that man come back and bring back some of the grub he ain't got no business with." By 1935 he was planning to challenge FDR in the next presidential election. But he never had the chance. In September 1935, the son-in-law of one of his vanquished political opponents assassinated him.

Eleanor Roosevelt also pushed FDR to the left, particularly on the issue of civil rights. Although FDR was reluctant to support an antilynching bill in Congress for fear of alienating southern white voters, the First Lady campaigned vigorously against lynching. When the Daughters of the American Revolution (DAR) denied African-American opera star Marian Anderson the right to perform at Constitution Hall in Washington, D.C., Eleanor promptly resigned from the DAR in protest and arranged for Anderson to perform at the Lincoln Memorial on Easter Sunday 1939, where a huge audience stood in the cold to hear her sing.

The Second New Deal

FDR was careful not to alienate southern Democrats by cultivating African-American voters. However, he did reach out to industrial workers. In the spring of 1935, Congress passed the National Labor Relations Act, also known as the Wagner Act, which guaranteed collective bargaining and gave a huge boost to labor unions.

Also in 1935, Congress passed the Social Security Act, perhaps the most important and far-reaching of all New Deal programs. The act established a system of old-age pensions, unemployment insurance, and welfare benefits for dependent children and the disabled. The framework of the Social Security Administration shaped the welfare system for the remainder of the century. But the welfare state established by the Social Security Act left out many of the most needy. It also established a two-track system of welfare. One track provided workers with unemployment insurance and support in their old age (the Social Security program). But Social Security did not cover domestics, seasonal or part-time workers, agricultural laborers, or housewives. The other track made matching funds available to states to provide relief for the needy, mostly dependent women and children with no means of support. Unlike Social Security, which was provided to all retired workers regardless of their circumstances, relief programs, which came to be known as "welfare," were administered according to need.

The architects of this welfare system included many women who had been active reformers, such as Eleanor Roosevelt. These advocates hoped to protect women and children from the destitution that almost certainly resulted if a male breadwinner lost his job, deserted his family, or died. The system presumed that a man ordinarily earned a **family wage** that let him support his wife and children and that women were

TABLE 22-2

Key New Deal Legislation, 1933–1938

Year	Act or Agency	Key Provisions
1933	Emergency Banking Act	Reopened banks under government supervision
	Civilian Conservation Corps (CCC)	Employed young men in reforestation, flood control, road construction, and soil erosion control projects
	Federal Emergency Relief Act (FERA)	Provided federal funds for state and local relief efforts
	Agricultural Adjustment Act (AAA)	Granted farmers direct payments for reducing crop production; funds for payment provided by a processing tax, later declared unconstitutional
	Farm Mortgage Act	Provided funds to refinance farm mortgages
	Tennessee Valley Authority (TVA)	Constructed dams and power projects and developed the economy of a seven-state area in the Tennessee River Valley
	Home Owners' Loan Corporation	Provided funds for refinancing home mortgages of nonfarm homeowners
	National Industrial Recovery Act (NIRA)	Established a series of fair competition codes; created National Recovery Administration (NRA) to write, coordinate, and implement these codes; NIRA's Section 7(a) guaranteed labor's right to organize (act later declared unconstitutional)
	Public Works Administration (PWA)	Sought to increase employment and business activity by funding road construction, building construction, and other projects
	Federal Deposit Insurance Corporation (FDIC)	Insured individual bank deposits
	Civil Works Administration (CWA)	Provided federal jobs for the unemployed
1934	Securities and Exchange Act	Created Securities and Exchange Commission (SEC) to regulate trading practices in stocks and bonds according to federal laws
	Indian Reorganization Act	Restored ownership of tribal lands to Native Americans; provided funds for job training and a system of agricultural and industrial credit
	Federal Housing Administration (FHA)	Insured loans provided by banks for the building and repair of houses
1935	Works Progress Administration (WPA)	Employed more than 8 million people to repair roads, build bridges, and work on other projects
	National Youth Administration (NYA)	WPA program that provided job training for unemployed youths and part-time jobs for students in need
	Federal One	WPA program that provided financial assistance for writers, artists, musicians, and actors
	National Labor Relations Act (Wagner Act)	Recognized the right of employees to join labor unions and to bargain collectively, reinstating the provisions of NIRA's Section 7(a); created the National Labor Relations Board (NLRB) to enforce laws against unfair labor practices
	Social Security Act	Created a system of social insurance that included unemployment compensation and old-age survivors' insurance; paid for by a joint tax on employers and employees
1938	Fair Labor Standards Act	Established a minimum wage of 25 cents an hour and a standard work week of 44 hours for businesses engaged in interstate commerce

necessarily economically dependent on men. Thus, a deeply entrenched gender system prevailed through the 1930s. As a result, some—though not all—male breadwinners received benefits like Social Security. Impoverished women and children, on the other hand, received public charity. These payments were usually meager, not enough to lift a woman and her children out of poverty.

Because there were no nationally established guidelines on how to distribute welfare funds, states could determine who received assistance. As a result, the Social Security Act did little to assist African Americans, especially in the South, where black women were deliberately excluded by local authorities who preferred to maintain a pool of cheap African-American labor rather than to provide relief for black families.

◉—View the Image

WPA Project at Tonawanda Reservation at **www.myhistorylab.com**

In 1935 Congress allocated the huge sum of nearly $5 billion for the Emergency Relief Appropriation. Roosevelt used a significant portion of the money to expand his public works program. By executive order, he established the Works Progress Administration (WPA), which provided millions of jobs for the unemployed. The project mandated that WPA jobs would make a contribution to public life and would not compete with private business. The jobs included building streets, highways, bridges, and public buildings; restoring forests; clearing slums; and extending electricity to rural areas. The WPA National Youth Administration gave work to nearly 1 million students.

The most effective WPA program was Federal One, which provided financial support for writers, musicians, artists, and actors. The Federal Theater Project, under the direction of Hallie Flanagan, former head of Vassar College's Experimental Theater, shaped the project into an arena for experimental community-based theater. The Federal Theater Project included 16 black theater units. Federal One supported thousands of artists and brought the arts to a wide public audience through government-funded murals on public buildings, community-theater productions, local orchestras, and the like.

◉—Watch the Video

Responding to the Great Depression: Whose New Deal? at **www.myhistorylab.com**

The New Deal did not reach everyone. New Deal programs were geared toward full-time industrial workers, most of whom were white men. Domestic workers, Mexican migrant laborers, black and white sharecroppers, Chinese and Japanese truck farmers—all were among those ineligible for Social Security, minimum wages and maximum hours, unemployment insurance, and other New Deal benefits. But the New Deal established the national welfare state and provided assistance and security to millions of working people along with disabled, dependent, and elderly Americans. Such sweeping programs also solidified Roosevelt's popularity among the poor, workers, and much of the middle class.

FDR's Second Term

In the 1936 campaign, FDR claimed that the election was a battle between "the millions who never had a chance" and "organized money." He boasted that the "forces of selfishness and of lust for power" had united against him: "They are unanimous in their *hate* for *me—and I welcome their hatred.*" His strategy paid off. Roosevelt won the election by a landslide of more than 60 percent of the popular vote. His strongest support came from the lower ends of the socioeconomic scale. The election also swept Democrats into Congress, giving them a decisive majority in both the House and the Senate.

With such a powerful mandate, Roosevelt was well positioned to promote a new legislative program. As his first major effort, he took on the Supreme Court. Dominated by conservative justices, the Court had invalidated some major legislation of Roosevelt's first term, including the AAA and the NIRA. Roosevelt feared that the justices would unravel the New Deal by striking down its progressive elements. To shift the balance of power on the Court, he proposed a measure that would let the president appoint one new justice for every one on the Court who had at least ten years of service and who did not retire within six months after turning 70.

Emboldened by his landslide victory, FDR believed that he could persuade Congress and the nation to go along with any plan he put forward, but he was mistaken. Many viewed his "court packing" plan as a threat to the fundamental separation of powers and feared that it would set a dangerous precedent. Powerful Republicans in Congress forged an alliance with conservative Democrats, mostly from the South, to defeat the plan. This informal alliance dominated Congress for the following two decades. The Court blunder cost Roosevelt considerable political capital and

TABLE 22-3			
The Election of 1936			
Candidate	Political Party	Popular Vote (%)	Electoral Vote
Franklin D. Roosevelt	Democratic	60.8	523
Alfred M. Landon	Republican	36.5	8
William Levine	Union	1.9	—

■ In this mural on San Francisco's Coit Tower, "Industries of California," Works Projects Administration (WPA) artist Ralph Stackpole depicts the city's diverse workforce. Across the country, government-funded artists created works of public art that portrayed life in local communities.

empowered his opponents. In the end, his plan proved unnecessary anyway. The Court did not undercut the New Deal. Within the next few years, retirements allowed Roosevelt to appoint several new justices who tipped the balance in his favor.

A New Political Culture

FDR continued to face strong opposition from conservatives on the right and from radicals, communists, and socialists on the left. But his political fortunes benefited from the emergence of a new and more inclusive national culture. This new Americanism emanated from the working class and found expression in the labor movement, popular culture, and the political coalition that came together in the Democratic party. These nationalizing forces cut across lines of class and region and occasionally challenged hierarchies of gender and race.

How did the Depression and the New Deal change the way Americans of different backgrounds thought of themselves and their fellow citizens?

The Labor Movement

The labor insurgency that erupted during the 1930s demonstrated the need for a new national labor movement. The American Federation of Labor (AFL), restricted to skilled workers, left out most of the nation's less skilled industrial laborers. John L. Lewis of the United Mine Workers (UMW) and Sidney Hillman of the Amalgamated Clothing Workers of America were among several union leaders from a number of industries—including mining, steel, rubber, and automobile—who left the AFL to form a new broad-based labor organization, the Congress of Industrial Organizations (CIO). Hillman and others argued that higher wages were good for the economy because workers would then be able to purchase consumer products, benefiting industry as well as workers. Lewis and Hillman played key roles in the CIO's growth into a national force, but the impetus came from the workers themselves.

■ Some strikes became violent, as did this one in 1934 when police battled striking teamsters armed with pipes on the streets of Minneapolis.

The CIO's first major action came in 1936 in Akron, Ohio, where workers in the rubber industry organized a **sit-down strike**, a new strategy whereby laborers stopped work and simply sat down, shutting down production and occupying plants so that strikebreakers could not enter and take their jobs. Sit-down strikes became a prominent labor tactic during 1936 when 48 strikes broke out across the nation. The numbers shot up the following year to about 500 strikes that lasted more than one day.

The most powerful demonstration of workers' discontent came in the automobile industry, where speed-ups of the assembly line drove workers to rebellion. In 1936 a spontaneous strike erupted against General Motors in Atlanta; it soon spread to Kansas City, Missouri; Cleveland, Ohio; and the main plants at Flint, Michigan. Two weeks into the strike, workers clashed with police. Frank Murphy, Michigan's pro-labor governor, refused to use National Guard troops against the strikers, and Roosevelt declined to send in federal troops.

Women as well as men participated actively in the Flint strike. Twenty-three-year-old Genora Johnson Dollinger, wife of a striker and mother of two young sons, organized 500 women into the Women's Emergency Brigade, made up primarily of strikers' wives, sisters, and girlfriends. Wearing red berets and armbands, they ran soup kitchens and first-aid stations. They also entered the fray when necessary, as when they broke plant windows so that the company could not use tear gas effectively against the strikers inside.

The sit-down strike at Flint lasted 44 days and forced General Motors to recognize the United Auto Workers (UAW), which was a CIO union. The strike scored a clear victory for the workers and boosted the CIO's stature as a national union of industrial workers. Membership in the UAW quadrupled in the next year. Bowing to the formidable power of the national union in the wake of the UAW success, U.S. Steel conceded to the CIO even without a strike, ending its policy of hiring nonunion workers and signing an agreement with the Steel Workers' Organizing Committee. The CIO brought together workers from all over the country. Most of its member unions were open to racial and ethnic minorities and women.

The New Deal Coalition

FDR's support of labor unions brought workers solidly into the Democratic fold. They joined a coalition that included voters who had never before belonged to the same party, particularly northern blacks and southern whites. Although African Americans in the South were disenfranchised, blacks in the North had voted Republican for 60 years, loyal to the party of Lincoln. In a dramatic shift, black voters in northern cities overwhelmingly backed FDR in 1936 and remained in the Democratic party for the rest of the century.

Other racial and ethnic minorities also joined the New Deal coalition. In 1939 Latinos organized their first national civil rights assembly, El Congreso de Pueblos de Habla Española (the Spanish-Speaking People's Congress), which opened with a congratulatory telegram from Eleanor Roosevelt. Immigrants from Europe and their children also became loyal Democratic voters.

In spite of this diverse coalition, many Americans remained bitterly opposed to FDR. On the left, socialists and communists criticized the New Deal for patching up capitalism rather than transforming the economic system. On the right, conservative business leaders despised Roosevelt for the constraints he placed on business and the intrusion of the government into the economy. Critics from the political right considered the New Deal akin to communism. In 1938 Congress created the House Un-American Activities Committee (HUAC), chaired by Martin Dies of Texas. Formed ostensibly to investigate American fascists and Nazis in the United States, the committee instead pursued liberal and leftist groups throughout World War II and the Cold War.

A New Americanism

The New Deal coalition reflected not only Roosevelt's popularity but also a new and more inclusive American identity. An expanding mass culture fostered this sensibility, spread

■ Amelia Earhart was the first woman to fly solo across the Atlantic. The legendary aviator gave preliminary flying lessons to her friend Eleanor Roosevelt. FDR convinced his wife not to take up flying, but the First Lady always regretted her decision.

largely through the national media. It is no accident that Franklin Roosevelt found his way into the homes and hearts of Americans through his "fireside chats" over the radio; his mastery of that technology made him the first media-savvy president. During the 1930s, 70 percent of all households owned a radio—more than owned a telephone. The motion-picture industry also expanded into small towns across the country. Talking films brought vernacular speech and a variety of accents to diverse audiences who gathered in neighborhood theaters.

Movie plots portrayed the triumph of common people over the rich and powerful and celebrated love across class and ethnic lines. Although racial stereotypes persisted in motion pictures throughout the decade, notable exceptions, such as Will Rogers's films, featured strong minority characters. Popular movies also challenged traditional gender and class hierarchies. Female stars, such as Katharine Hepburn, Rosalind Russell, Bette Davis, and Mae West, portrayed feisty, independent women.

New sports celebrities also embodied the nation's diversity. Baseball star Joe DiMaggio, son of an Italian immigrant fisherman, became a national hero. African-American boxer Joe Louis, the "Brown Bomber" who was born into a sharecropper family in Alabama, became heavyweight champion of the world at age 23. In 1938, when Louis fought German boxer Max Schmeling at Yankee Stadium, the fight attracted 70,000 fans and grossed more than $1 million. When the black fighter knocked out Schmeling in the first round, he seemed to strike a blow for America against Hitler's Nazi Germany.

A number of women also became heroes in the 1930s for their daring exploits, personal courage, and physical prowess. Athletes like tennis champion Helen Wills and Olympic track star and brilliant golfer "Babe" (Mildred) Didrikson (later Zaharias) greatly expanded the popularity of women's sports. Renowned aviator Amelia Earhart, the first woman to fly solo across the Atlantic, devoted her life to advancing both feminism and commercial aviation. When her plane disappeared during an attempted round-the-world flight in 1937, many of her admirers were so convinced of her invincibility that they refused to believe she had died. Even today, people still speculate about her fate.

CONCLUSION

The New Deal set in place a welfare state that established the principle of government responsibility for the well-being of vulnerable citizens. Before the New Deal, people suffered the fluctuations of the market economy with no recourse beyond the assistance of kin, communities, and charities. Older Americans who could no longer work had no government-guaranteed pensions and often faced poverty in old age. Bank failures could wipe away life savings. Unemployment could mean starvation for a worker's family. The New Deal provided Social Security for the elderly, unemployment compensation for workers who had lost their jobs, minimum standards for hours and wages, and economic aid to women and children who had no means of support. It established national economic regulations and regulatory agencies as well as the right of workers to unionize and engage in collective bargaining. These government protections offered many Americans an unprecedented level of economic security.

Most New Deal policies protected factory workers in large companies. The safety net did not extend to many of the neediest Americans, including Mexican-American migrant workers, African-American and white sharecroppers, seasonal agricultural laborers, and domestic workers. FDR was reluctant to press for antilynching legislation for fear of alienating southern congressmen who still retained enormous power. Although FDR's conservative opponents accused him of socialist leanings, the New Deal actually rescued and shored up capitalism.

The New Deal was the Roosevelt administration's response to a global economic crisis. With the exception of the communist Soviet Union, which had already abandoned capitalism, all industrialized nations responded to the Depression by increasing the role of the state in the economy. Italy, Germany, and Japan moved to fascism and the nearly total state direction of the economy, while Britain and France established welfare states that would become more fully developed after World War II. The U.S. system of social welfare was not as extensive and inclusive as those that emerged in some western European democracies. But it was part of a larger trend toward government intervention in the economy and greater protections for citizens.

For Review

1. What were the most profound effects of the Great Depression on national institutions and American citizens?

2. In what ways did Eleanor Roosevelt use her position as first lady?

✓•⊣Study and Review at www.myhistorylab.com

3. What pressures did Roosevelt encounter from the left and the right of the political spectrum?

4. In what ways did labor unions develop and change during the New Deal, and how did Americans of different backgrounds mobilize as workers?

Chronology: 1930–1939

1930 Beginning of Hoover Dam construction.
1,352 U.S. banks fail.

1931 Nine young African Americans (the "Scottsboro Boys") arrested on charges of rape.

1932 Black unemployment rate reaches 50 percent.
Bonus Army marches on Washington, D.C.

1933 Initial New Deal ("Hundred Days") legislation: AAA, FERA, CCC, TVA, NIRA.
Twenty-first Amendment ratified.

1934 Indian Reorganization Act.
Securities and Exchange Commission (SEC) created.

1935 National Labor Relations (Wagner) Act.
Social Security Act.
Committee of Industrial Organizations (CIO) organized.

1936 Hoover Dam on Colorado River completed, creating Lake Mead.

1937 170,000 workers participate in sit-down strikes.
FDR's court-packing plan fails.

1938 Boxer Joe Louis defeats Max Schmeling.
Fair Labor Standards Act.
Congress creates Special Committee on Un-American Activities.

1939 First meeting of El Congreso de Pueblos de Habla Española.

Key Terms

Capitalism The now almost worldwide economic system of private ownership of property and profit-seeking corporations. p. 514

Dust Bowl The plains regions of Oklahoma, Texas, Colorado, and New Mexico and Kansas? affected by severe drought in the 1930s. p. 516

Family wage A level of income sufficient for an individual worker, usually a man, to support a spouse and family through a single salary. p. 526

Fireside chats The broadcasts by President Franklin Delano Roosevelt during which he spoke directly to American families, often gathered around a radio in their living room. p. 513

Hobos Migrant worker or poor and homeless vagrant who traveled on trains from location to location, usually in search of employment. p. 516

Okie Migrant from Oklahoma who left the state during the Dust Bowl period in search of work. p. 517

Second New Deal The agenda of policies and programs initiated by President Franklin Delano Roosevelt beginning in 1935 that was intended to strengthen the lot of American workers while simultaneously preserving the capitalist system. p. 521

Sit-down strike A strategy employed by workers agitating for better wages and working conditions in which they stop working and simply sit down, thus ceasing production and preventing strikebreakers from entering a facility to assume their jobs. p. 530

Townsend Plan A proposal by Dr. Francis Townsend in 1934 for a 2 percent national sales tax that would fund a guaranteed pension of $200 per month for Americans older than age 60. p. 525

Welfare state A nation in which the government provides a "safety net" of entitlements and benefits for citizens unable to economically provide for themselves. p. 514

23

Global Conflict: World War II, 1937–1945

In 1938, Franz Steiner was a young man with a newly minted law degree. A talented artist and musician, he was well-educated and spoke several languages. But then everything changed when he was rounded up by the Nazis and taken from his home in Vienna, Austria, to the Dachau concentration camp. There he was imprisoned to provide slave labor for the Germans.

In 1938, Dachau was not yet a death camp, but imprisoned Jews who were weak or ill perished nonetheless. Under the brutal conditions—sleeping on cold, straw-covered floors and lacking adequate shoes, clothes, or food—many died. Some could get out if they could prove that they would leave the country immediately. Franz was lucky: he was relatively healthy, and he had a sponsor in the United States, a family friend who agreed to take him in. But the quota of Jews allowed to enter the United States was already filled for the year. In spite of the horror unfolding in Europe, American officials granted few exceptions to the immigration restrictions put into place in the 1920s.

With the doors to the United States closed, Franz secured a ticket on a French ship bound for Shanghai, China, an open city that required no entry visa. After three months in Dachau, Franz was released. His parents assured him that the Nazis would leave them alone, since they were too old and frail to work. Reluctantly, Franz departed, leaving his parents in Austria.

In Shanghai, Franz settled with thousands of other Jews who had fled the Nazis and now lived alongside the local Chinese. Like many European Jewish families, Franz's relatives were rapidly scattering all over the world. Still optimistic that his parents would survive in Vienna, he noted, "Parents write regularly." But he worried about his younger brother, 20-year-old Hans, who had escaped from Austria on a boat with friends.

After a year in Shanghai, Franz was finally allowed to enter the United States. By April 1941, he had settled in San Francisco, changed his name to Frank, and taken a job. But he remained worried about his parents and his brother. He wrote in his diary, "My parents asked for an affidavit" to get out of Austria. "Hans is in Yugoslavia, hope he will survive it."

But Hans did not survive it. The Germans finally caught up with Hans and his friends and shot them all, dumping them in a makeshift grave. Frank did not learn of his brother's fate until after the war. Meanwhile, Frank continued to correspond with his parents in Vienna. The last letter he sent to his parents was returned to him unopened, stamped by the Nazis with the fiction that they had "emigrated" to

Auschwitz. Frank never heard from them again. Along with millions of others, they died in a death camp as part of Hitler's "Final Solution" to rid Europe of Jews.

Frank married an American woman and became a citizen. Half a century later, he donated the last letter he wrote to his parents—still unopened—to the Yad Vashem Holocaust Memorial Museum in Israel.

Frank Steiner's story is one small piece of the global saga of disruption, dislocation, loss, suffering, death, and survival during World War II. The war affected countries and peoples all over the globe. The huge scale of destruction was unlike that of any previous war. At least 55 million people died, including 25 million in the Soviet Union, 10 million in China, and 6 million in Poland. In the **Holocaust**, Nazi Germany's campaign of genocide, 6 million European Jews perished along with thousands of Romani (Gypsies), Poles, mentally and physically disabled people, homosexuals, and others deemed "racially inferior." The war also had a tremendous impact on countries under colonial rule. Germany's bombardment of England and occupation of France, Holland, and Belgium weakened these countries' hold over their vast colonies. Japan's defeat of the American, British, Dutch, and French forces in Southeast Asia from 1940 to 1942 shocked the Western powers and ended white rule in the region, setting in motion a wave of decolonization in Asia and Africa after the war.

■ Franz Steiner just after his release from Dachau. After starving the prisoners, Nazis fed them boiled potatoes to fatten them up before they were released, so their emaciated bodies would not be visible to the outside world. Later in the war, the Nazis no longer many any effort to keep up appearances.

The United States was the only major combatant that did not suffer massive destruction on its home territory. It had two powerful advantages: an ocean barrier on its east and west coasts, plus tremendous natural resources that could provide the materials needed for modern warfare, such as steel and oil. In order to minimize American casualties, President Franklin Delano Roosevelt (FDR) pursued a strategy to make the United States the "arsenal of democracy," providing armaments and supplies to the other Allied powers so that their armies would do most of the fighting. Although the Soviet Union carried the largest burden of fighting the war and suffered the highest losses, millions of Americans also fought, and many died in the conflict. Military service had a leveling effect on social relations, as soldiers came together from all classes and ethnic groups. The vast majority of the troops—more than 85 percent—were white men from a wide variety of backgrounds. Soldiers of color generally fought in segregated units, but their battlefield successes and sacrifices gave them a sense of belonging to the nation and fueled postwar movements for equality and civil rights.

No bombs dropped on the American mainland, yet the war reached into every aspect of national and personal life. Although wartime brought prosperity, the rationing of essential goods and the scarcity of consumer products brought nearly all Americans into the war effort. As soldiers and war industry workers moved around the country, local and regional sensibilities gave way to a stronger national identity. The U.S. military and defense establishment expanded to the formidable scale it would maintain during and after the war, making the United States the most powerful nation in the world.

> *The United States was the only major combatant that did not suffer massive destruction on its home territory.*

The United States Enters the War

Why were most Americans initially opposed to entering the war, and what changed their minds?

During the 1930s, the rise of **fascism** and militarism in Italy, Germany, and Japan created a terrible dilemma for Americans. Disillusioned by World War I and preoccupied with the hardships of the Great Depression, they disagreed strongly about how to respond to overt aggression in Africa, Europe, and Asia. The ensuing "Great Debate" became a turning point in the nation's relationship with the outside world. Mobilizing for the enormous crusade of World War II gave rise to a unity of purpose that lasted throughout the war and into the postwar era.

Fascist Aggression in Europe and Asia

In the 1930s, Depression-era Americans grappled with domestic problems and avoided entanglements abroad. But they found it difficult to ignore events in Europe and Asia. In Italy, Spain, and Germany, where a weak economy and high unemployment created political unrest, fascist leaders rose to power with strong popular support. These new leaders promised economic recovery through strengthening militaries and national expansion. They also encouraged intense nationalist sentiments, urging people to identify strongly with the state. Fascist governments were antidemocratic, antiparliamentary, and frequently antisemitic. These governments generally ruled by police surveillance, coercion, and terror.

Germany emerged as the most powerful fascist state in Europe. After Germany's defeat in World War I and the severe economic depression that Germany experienced in the 1920s, Adolf Hitler's National Socialist (Nazi) party won broad support in the weakened country. On January 30, 1933, Hitler became chancellor of Germany. Extolling fanatical nationalism and the racial superiority of "Aryan" Germans, Hitler blamed Jews for Germany's problems. He began a campaign of terror against Jews, homosexuals, suspected communists, and anyone else he saw as promoting "un-German" ideas. Hitler vowed to unite all German-speaking peoples into a new empire, the "Third Reich."

The fascist governments forged alliances to increase their power and launched campaigns of aggression and expansion. In 1935 Italy invaded Ethiopia, the sole independent African nation. The following year, Nazi troops occupied the Rhineland, in the western region of Germany, in violation of the Versailles agreement. Hitler and Mussolini signed the **Axis Pact**, and Japan forged an alliance with Germany. Soon after that, civil war erupted in Spain. Hitler and Mussolini extended aid to the fascist General Francisco Franco, who was trying to overthrow Spain's republican government.

Although Spanish republicans appealed to antifascist governments for help in the fight against Franco, only the Soviet Union came to their assistance. The United States maintained an official policy of neutrality, but many on the left, including large numbers of writers and intellectuals, championed the beleaguered Spanish government and denounced the fascists. Some joined Soviet-organized international forces to fight against Franco.

In the spring and summer of 1938, Hitler annexed Austria to the Third Reich and then demanded that the Sudetenland be turned over to Germany. After World War I, this German-speaking area had become part of the newly formed Czechoslovakia. In September the leaders of France and Britain met with Hitler in Munich and agreed to let him have the Sudetenland in return for his promise that he would seek no more territory. Soviet leader Josef Stalin feared that the anticommunist leaders of France and Britain were trying to turn Hitler's aggression toward the Soviet Union. To prevent that possibility, Stalin signed a nonaggression pact with Hitler. Eventually, Hitler broke all his promises. Throughout the war and after, the Munich meeting became the symbol of "appeasement," a warning that compromise with the enemy leads only to disaster.

In 1939, with the help of the Soviet Union and in violation of the Munich agreement, Germany invaded Poland, which fell quickly. At that point Britain and France declared war on Germany. That same year, Madrid finally fell to Franco's forces.

View the Image
Hitler and Mussolini in Munich, 1940
at **www.myhistorylab.com**

By 1940 Hitler was sweeping through Europe, invading Denmark, Norway, Holland, Belgium, Luxembourg, and then France. In just six weeks, the Nazis had seized most of western Europe. Hitler then turned his forces on Great Britain. In the summer and fall of 1940, German raids on British air bases nearly destroyed the British Royal Air Force (RAF). Hitler ordered the bombing of London and other English cities, attacking civilians day and night in what came to be called the Battle of Britain.

In the Far East, events had taken an equally alarming turn. Nationalistic militarists gained control of the Japanese government in Tokyo and began a course of expansion. In 1931–1932, Japanese troops occupied the large Chinese province of Manchuria. Five years later, the Japanese launched a full-scale war against China. The United States extended aid to China and discontinued trade with Japan. In 1940 Japan joined Germany and Italy in the Axis alliance and invaded the French colony of Indochina.

The Great Debate over Intervention

In the mid-1930s, the overwhelming majority of Americans opposed intervention in foreign conflicts. Congress passed the Neutrality Acts of 1935, 1936, and 1937, outlawing arms sales or loans to nations at war and forbidding Americans from traveling on the ships of belligerent powers. When Japan invaded China in 1937, FDR refused to comply with the provisions of the latest Neutrality Act, on the technicality that neither combatant had officially declared war. By creatively interpreting the law, he was able to offer loans to the embattled Chinese. Roosevelt felt strongly that the United States should actively help to resist the Axis powers.

The largest organization to oppose Roosevelt's effort was the **America First Committee**. With 450 chapters, the group claimed several hundred thousand members, including famed aviator Charles Lindbergh. Centered largely in the Midwest, the America Firsters included some active Nazi supporters. Nevertheless, in 1940, the popular FDR became the first president elected to a third term.

Soon, public opinion began to shift. Many Americans were shocked when Hitler swiftly conquered much of Europe. News reports of the German occupation of France and the intense bombardment of England in the Battle of Britain bolstered FDR's efforts to take action. In his "Four Freedoms" speech to Congress in January 1941, FDR cited the freedoms he considered necessary for the postwar world and pledged his support for England against the Nazis. A few months later, Congress approved the Lend-Lease agreement to lend rather than sell munitions to the Allied countries.

When Hitler broke his promise to Stalin and attacked the Soviet Union in June 1941, FDR extended Lend-Lease to the Soviets. During the summer, FDR and British Prime Minister Winston Churchill met on a ship off the coast of Newfoundland to develop a joint declaration known as the Atlantic Charter. The two leaders announced that the United States and Britain sought no new territories, they recognized the right of all peoples to choose their own form of government, and they called for international **free trade** and navigation. Realizing the possible cost of losing colonies, Churchill retreated

TABLE 23-1			
The Election of 1940			
Candidate	**Political Party**	**Popular Vote (%)**	**Electoral Vote**
Franklin D. Roosevelt	Democratic	54.8	449
Wendell L. Willkie	Republican	44.8	82

Freedom of Speech   *Freedom of Worship*

Freedom from Want   *Freedom from Fear*

■ Norman Rockwell's depiction of the "Four Freedoms," which adorned the cover of the *Saturday Evening Post*, inspired the purchase of war bonds and came to symbolize the democratic values for which the nation was fighting. These four scenes by the popular artist evoked an American ideal of close families and harmonious communities.

from the global implications of the charter, while Roosevelt walked a fine line between contradicting Churchill and supporting the idea of empire. However, the charter emboldened anticolonial activists around the world.

The Attack on Pearl Harbor

For nearly a decade, tensions had been mounting between the United States and Japan as American leaders tried to contain Japan's expansion in Asia. Roosevelt assumed that a strong U.S. military presence in the Pacific would persuade Japan's premier, General Hideki Tojo, to avoid a confrontation with the United States. When Japan continued its aggression in Asia, FDR froze Japanese assets in the United States, putting trade with Japan under presidential control. This move, he hoped, would bring Japan to the bargaining table. Instead, on November 25, the Japanese dispatched aircraft carriers toward Hawaii.

Although U.S. intelligence sources had broken the codes with which the Japanese encrypted messages about their war plans, they did not realize that the Japanese intended to strike Hawaii. At 7:55 a.m. on December 7, Japanese planes swooped over Pearl Harbor and bombed the naval base. The assault caught the American forces completely off guard and destroyed most of the U.S. Pacific fleet. Only a few aircraft carriers that were out at sea survived. Two hours after the attack on Pearl Harbor, the Japanese also struck the main U.S. base at Clark Field in the Philippines, destroying half of the U.S. Air Force in the Far East.

When the smoke cleared, 2,323 American service personnel were dead. President Roosevelt somberly told millions of Americans gathered around their radios that the day of the attack would "live in infamy." Congress immediately declared war against Japan. Three days later, Germany and Italy declared war against the United States. Most former doubters now joined the war effort.

Japanese-American Relocation

The assault on Pearl Harbor sparked widespread rumors along the U.S. West Coast that Japanese and Japanese-Americans living there planned to sabotage the war effort. Although no charges of criminal activity or treason were ever brought against any Japanese Americans, powerful white farming interests eager to eradicate Japanese-American competition pushed for an evacuation.

Not everyone supported the internment idea. U.S. Attorney General Francis Biddle protested that there was "no reason" for a mass relocation. J. Edgar Hoover, director of the FBI, also opposed the plan, arguing that it reflected "hysteria and lack of judgment." Nevertheless, in February 1942, Roosevelt signed Executive Order 9066, which authorized the removal of 110,000 Japanese and Japanese Americans from the West Coast. Of those, 70,000 were *Nisei*, native-born American citizens. Families received at most a week's notice to evacuate their homes and move to prisonlike camps surrounded by barbed wire and guarded by armed soldiers. There were ten such camps in seven states, most of them located in arid, desolate spots in the West. At the camps, internees lived in makeshift wooden barracks, where entire families crowded into one room.

While the internment experience alienated some Japanese Americans, fully 33,000 joined the armed services—including 1,200 who enlisted from the internment camps—and proved their patriotism on the battlefield. In the Pacific, their knowledge of the Japanese language proved critical in translating intercepted Japanese military documents. The Japanese also served ably in Europe, suffering huge casualties. The Japanese Americans of the 442nd Regiment lost one-fourth of their soldiers in battles in North Africa and Italy. They suffered 800 casualties rescuing the Texan "Lost Battalion," 211 men surrounded by German troops in the Vosges Mountains of France. The U.S. government took its time acknowledging that

•••⊣ Read the Document

Executive Order 9066: Resulting in the Relocation of Japanese at **www.myhistorylab.com**

■ On December 7, 1941, the Japanese launched a surprise attack on the U.S. naval base at Pearl Harbor, Hawaii. The attack brought the United States immediately into World War II and was the only time that the war came to American soil.

the internment had been a grave injustice. The Supreme Court upheld the constitutionality of the policy, and Roosevelt would not rescind the evacuation order until after his reelection in 1944. The camps finally closed in 1945. All told, Japanese Americans lost property valued at $500 million. In 1988 Congress enacted legislation awarding restitution payments of $20,000 each to 60,000 surviving internees—a small gesture for Americans whose only "crime" was their Japanese ancestry.

Foreign Nationals in the United States

Although Japanese Americans were the only U.S. citizens interned solely because of their ancestry, German and Italian nationals living in the United States were also subject to new regulations, and in some cases relocation and incarceration. The Smith Act of 1940 required all foreign-born residents to be registered and fingerprinted, and broadened the grounds for deportation.

Six hundred thousand Italians and 314,000 Germans living in the United States were subject to these requirements. Several hundred were deemed potentially dangerous and interned for the duration of the war. Approximately 10,000 Italian nationals were forced to relocate from their homes on the West Coast. A few hundred German and Italian immigrants who were naturalized U.S. citizens were also relocated from designated coastal areas.

Wartime Migrations

Even before the United States officially entered World War II, the conflict had begun to change the face of the nation. The sleepy town of Richmond, California, perched near the north end

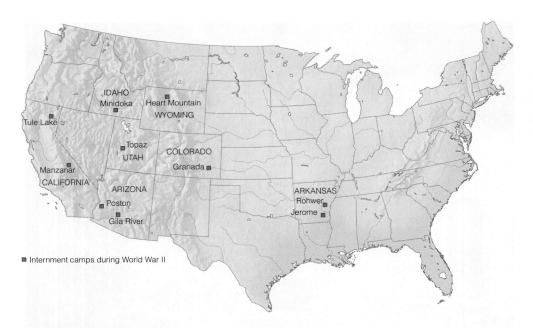

■ MAP 23.1
INTERNMENT OF JAPANESE AMERICANS DURING WORLD WAR II
After the Japanese attack on Pearl Harbor, President Franklin Delano Roosevelt signed an order authorizing the removal of people of Japanese descent from the West Coast. These Japanese Americans were relocated to internment camps built in arid and isolated areas in the West as well as in two locations in Arkansas.

of San Francisco Bay, underwent a profound transformation when the nation stepped up war production. The town's mostly white population of 23,000 ballooned to 120,000 after industrialist Henry Kaiser constructed four shipyards there. The yards employed over 150,000 workers, more than one-fourth of them African American.

Many cities, however, were ill equipped to handle the influx of migrants. An estimated 60,000 African Americans moved into Chicago, causing an enormous housing crisis. Many newcomers lacked even a modicum of privacy as they crowded into basements and rooms rented from total strangers. Huge numbers of whites also came north, many leaving hardscrabble farms and hoping to prosper in booming war industries.

Wartime also saw new migration from abroad and a reversal of earlier immigration policies. Because of the alliance with China in the war against Japan, in 1943 Congress repealed the Chinese Exclusion Act, and migrants from China became eligible for citizenship for the first time. An executive agreement between the United States and Mexico created the **bracero** program, under which 300,000 Mexican laborers, mostly agricultural workers, came to rural areas like California's San Joaquin Valley. By the mid-1960s, nearly 5 million Mexicans had migrated north under the program.

Total War

What were the major differences for the United States between the war in Europe and the war in the Pacific?

World War II consisted of two wars: one centered in Europe and the other in the Pacific. Combatants in both conflicts engaged in total war—the targeting of civilian as well as military targets. Of all the combatants, only the United States escaped physical destruction on its own national soil (with the exception of Pearl Harbor). Coming out of the war physically unscathed, economically sound, and politically strong, the United States became the most prosperous and powerful nation in the world.

The Holocaust

Hitler's war aims included conquering all of Europe and destroying European Jewry. Throughout the war, Nazi anti-Jewish policies escalated from persecution and officially sanctioned violence to imprisonment in concentration camps, slave labor, and ultimately Hitler's "Final Solution," genocide. Nazis developed increasingly efficient means of killing Jews. In the infamous Nazi death camps, guards herded prisoners into "shower rooms" that were actually gas chambers.

View the Image
Nazi Murder Mills at
www.myhistorylab.com

American officials knew of the Nazi persecution of the Jews but did little about it. Throughout the 1930s, American Jewish groups pressured the Roosevelt administration to ease immigration laws to allow Jewish refugees to enter the country. But the United States raised the legal quota of Jewish immigrants only slightly.

When the Nazis began their policy of extermination in 1941, they tried to keep it a secret. U.S. State Department officials heard reports of the Holocaust but decided to keep the information quiet. Despite official silence, Rabbi Stephen S. Wise, a prominent American Jewish leader, heard the news and held a press conference in November 1942. But the American press, preoccupied with military events and reluctant to publish stories of atrocities without official verification, gave the Holocaust little coverage. Meanwhile, despite reports of Nazi genocide, the U.S. government turned away boatloads of Jewish refugees, sending them back to Germany to their deaths.

> *The U.S. government turned away boatloads of Jewish refugees, sending them back to Germany to their deaths.*

Nazi persecution of the Jews raised American sensitivity to racism but did little to diminish antisemitism within the United States. In fact, American hostility toward Jews reached new heights during World War II and exceeded the level of prejudice against any other group. In 1944, when asked to identify the greatest "menace" to the nation, 24 percent of Americans polled listed Jews—more than those who listed Germans, Japanese, radicals, Negroes, and foreigners. In Europe, American military strategists knew of the existence and location of Nazi death camps, but they chose not to try to bomb them or the railroad lines leading to the camps.

The War in Europe

The leaders of the Allied powers, including the United States, Britain, and the Soviet Union, had to develop a strategy to defeat the Axis powers. But the Allies did not always agree on how to conduct the war, and relations between the United States and the Soviet Union remained strained. Unable to fully overcome the hostility and suspicion that had marked their earlier encounters, leaders of both countries fought the war with postwar power considerations in mind.

Like the United States at Pearl Harbor, the Soviet Union suffered a shocking blow when Germany launched a surprise invasion in June 1941 in violation of the nonaggression pact Hitler had signed with Stalin in 1938. With the full might of the Nazi forces now concentrated on the front lines against the Russians in eastern Europe, Soviet premier Joseph Stalin wanted the United States to open a second front in western Europe to divert the Nazis toward the west and relieve pressure on the Soviet Union. In May 1942, Roosevelt assured Stalin that the United States would support an Allied invasion across the English Channel into France. But the British prime minister, Winston Churchill, persuaded FDR to delay that dangerous maneuver and instead to launch an invasion of French north Africa, which was controlled by the Nazi occupation forces in Vichy, France.

While the Allies turned their attention to north Africa, the Soviets singlehandedly forced the German army into retreat at Stalingrad, where fierce fighting lasted from August 1942 to January 1943. The Battle of Stalingrad was a major turning point in the war. Axis soldiers in north Africa also surrendered in May 1943. The following summer, the Allied forces overran the island of Sicily and moved into southern Italy. Italians overthrew

Mussolini and opened communication with General Dwight D. Eisenhower, commander of the Allied forces in Europe. By 1944 the Allied forces reached Rome.

The long-awaited Allied invasion across the English Channel finally began on June 6, 1944, code named D-Day. At dawn, in the largest amphibious landing in history, more than 4,000 Allied ships descended on the French beaches at Normandy. As the troops splashed onto shore, they met a barrage of German fire. Many thousands died on the beach that day. Over the next ten days, more than 1 million soldiers landed at Normandy, along with 50,000 vehicles and more than 100,000 tons of supplies, opening the way for an advance into Nazi-occupied France.

In the months after D-Day, the western Allies liberated Paris and went on to defeat the Germans in Belgium at the Battle of the Bulge, sending the Nazis into full retreat. The Allied armies then crossed the Rhine River and headed for Berlin. Eisenhower stopped his

■ **MAP 23.2**
WORLD WAR II IN EUROPE
Along the eastern front of the war in Europe, Soviet troops did the bulk of the Allied fighting in Europe and sustained the highest casualties. The Battle of Stalingrad, in which Soviet troops finally drove back the Nazis after months of brutal fighting, was a major turning point in the war.

troops at the Elbe River to let Soviet troops take Berlin. Eisenhower hoped that giving the Soviets the final triumph would ease postwar relations with the Soviet Union—but he also wanted to save American lives. Huge numbers of Soviet troops died in the siege of Berlin, but the war in Europe was nearly over. With the Soviets approaching his bunker in April 1945, Hitler committed suicide. Germany surrendered on May 7, 1945—V-E (Victory in Europe) Day. FDR himself had died suddenly of a cerebral hemorrhage on April 12, 1945.

The War in the Pacific

As the conflict in Europe came to an end, the war in the Pacific continued to rage. Following the attack on Pearl Harbor, Japan continued its Pacific conquests. In April 1942, General Douglas MacArthur, driven from the Philippines to Australia, left 12,000 American and 64,000 Filipino soldiers to surrender on the Bataan peninsula and the island of Corregidor. On the infamous "Bataan Death March" to the prison at Camp O'Donnell, the Japanese beat, tortured, and shot the sick and starving troops. As many as 10,000 men died on the march.

■ A photograph taken on D-Day, June 6, 1944, as U.S. troops waded to shore from their landing craft and faced German artillery fire on Omaha Beach. This is a rare surviving photograph from the initial Normandy invasion because so many of the photographers, along with thousands of soldiers, died at the scene.

Now in control of Indochina, Thailand, the Philippines, and the chain of islands from Sumatra to Guadalcanal, Japan's military leaders planned to destroy what remained of the U.S. fleet. But MacArthur marshaled his forces and achieved a major victory in the Battle of the Coral Sea in May 1942. U.S. intelligence sources discovered that the Japanese were planning a massive assault on Midway Island, a naval base key to Hawaii's defense. Under the command of Admiral Chester Nimitz, the United States launched a surprise air strike on June 4, 1942, sinking four Japanese carriers, destroying 322 planes, and virtually eliminating Japanese offensive capabilities. Two months later, Nimitz's forces landed at Guadalcanal in the Solomon Islands, subduing the Japanese in five months of brutal fighting. Having seized the offensive, U.S. troops continued toward Japan. MacArthur's forces took New Guinea, and, by February 1944, Nimitz secured the Marshall Islands and the Marianas. Next came Saipan, Iwo Jima, and Okinawa in the spring of 1945.

Crucial to these victories were the sensitive radio communications of a special U.S. Marine unit of Navajo "code talkers." Keith Little was one of the young Navajo men who volunteered for military service. Little and 400 other Navajo became part of a special unit that developed an intricate code, based on the Navajo language, to transmit top-secret information without risk of decoding by the Japanese. Ironically, many of these men had been educated in government boarding schools that forbade them to speak their native language. Now that same government called upon them to use their language to help win the war. The Navajo language was particularly well suited to code because very few people besides Navajo knew it. In a process code named "Magic," the all-Navajo 382nd Platoon of the U.S. Marine Corps encoded and decoded sensitive military information almost instantly and flawlessly. In two days on the Pacific island of Iwo Jima, six code talkers transmitted more than 800 messages, working around the clock, without a single error. Signal Officer Major Howard Conner recalled, "Without the Navajos the Marines would never have taken Iwo Jima."

The war in the Pacific was particularly vicious. Racism on both sides fueled acts of extreme brutality. Japan's leaders believed that their racial superiority gave them a divine

■ MAP 23.3
WORLD WAR II IN THE PACIFIC
During World War II, the Japanese occupied vast territories in Asia and the Pacific. The Battle of Midway in 1942 was the first major victory for the United States in the Pacific and helped turn the tide of the war in favor of the Allies.

mission to conquer Asia. The Japanese tortured prisoners of war and civilians in their conquered lands. They tested biological weapons and conducted medical experiments on live subjects. Japanese troops forced Chinese and Korean women into sexual slavery, euphemistically calling them "comfort women."

Racial hostility also promoted American battlefield savagery. U.S. troops in the Pacific often killed the enemy instead of taking prisoners and desecrated the enemy dead with disrespect equal to that meted out by the Japanese on the bodies of their foes. War correspondent Ernie Pyle explained that "in Europe we felt that our enemies, horrible and deadly as they were, were still people. But . . . the Japanese were looked upon as something subhuman and repulsive, the way some people feel about cockroaches or mice."

■ The family pictured here was among thousands of loyal citizens of Japanese ancestry removed from their homes on the West Coast and relocated to internment camps. Here, the Hirano family, George, Hisa, and Yasbei (left to right), pose at the Colorado River Relocation Center in Poston, Arizona. Hisa holds a photo of her son, an American soldier, who is off fighting the war.

The Home Front

Wartime mobilization brought Americans from all regions and backgrounds together in shared service and sacrifice. Automobile manufacturers stopped making cars and instead turned out tanks, jeeps, and other military vehicles. Citizens made do with government-rationed basic staples, from food to gasoline. As able-bodied men left their jobs to fight the war, new work opportunities opened up for women as well as for disabled Americans. Cities and centers of war production brought together young women and men who found new opportunities for sexual experimentation, while gay men and lesbians discovered newly visible communities. The war raised expectations of women and minorities that they would achieve full inclusion in the American promise.

In what ways did World War II alter life for the Americans who remained at home?

Many Americans hoped that the liberal spirit of the New Deal would endure during the war; others were eager for an end to what they perceived as Depression-era class conflict and hostility to business interests. To some extent, both sides got their wish. Full employment, the increasing strength of unions, and high taxes on the wealthy pleased New Deal liberals. Profit guarantees, freedom from antitrust actions, no-strike pledges, and low-cost imported labor gratified probusiness conservatives. And Roosevelt was elected to an unprecedented fourth term in 1944.

TABLE 23-2			
The Election of 1944			
Candidate	**Political Party**	**Popular Vote (%)**	**Electoral Vote**
Franklin D. Roosevelt	Democratic	53.5	432
Thomas E. Dewey	Republican	46.0	99

Propaganda and Building Morale

The United States, like all other major powers involved in the conflict, mounted a propaganda drive to promote support for the war effort. The Office of War Information (OWI) coordinated morale-boosting and censorship initiatives. Working in partnership with the motion picture industry and other media outlets, the OWI sponsored movies, radio programs, publications, and posters. These productions portrayed the war as a crusade to preserve the "American way of life" and encouraged American women and men to work in war industries, enlist in the armed forces, and purchase war bonds. Eric Johnston, head of the Motion Picture Producers' Association and FDR's business adviser, insisted that Hollywood remove class conflict from its films: "We'll have no more *Grapes of Wrath*, we'll have no more *Tobacco Roads*, we'll have no more films that deal with the seamy side of American life. We'll have no more films that treat the banker as a villain."

Within the United States, government censors made sure that no photographs showing badly wounded soldiers or mutilated bodies reached the public. Rarely, if ever, did those on the home front see the true extent of the war's destructiveness and brutality.

Home Front Workers, Rosie the Riveter, and Victory Girls

Wartime opened up new possibilities for jobs, income, and labor organizing, for women as well as for men, and for new groups of workers. Disabled workers entered jobs previously considered beyond their abilities, fulfilling their tasks with skill and competence. Norma Krajczar, a visually impaired teenager from North Carolina, served as a volunteer aircraft warden where her sensitive hearing gave her an advantage over sighted wardens in listening for approaching enemy planes. Deaf people streamed into Akron, Ohio, to work in the tire factories that became defense plants, making more money than they ever made before.

■ Sailors relax in the Aircraft Repair Unit during their free time at Guadalcanal. The walls above their cots are decorated with "pinups" of young women in alluring poses, reminding the men of the pleasures that await them after the war.

■ Eight American presidents elected consecutively following World War II were veterans of that war. Pictured in wartime service, from top left, are: Dwight D. Eisenhower, John F. Kennedy, Lyndon Johnson, Richard Nixon, Gerald Ford, Jimmy Carter, Ronald Reagan, and George H. W. Bush.

Along with new employment opportunities, workers' earnings rose nearly 70 percent. Income doubled for farmers and then doubled again. Labor union membership grew 50 percent, reaching an all-time high by the end of the war. Women and minorities joined unions in unprecedented numbers. Energetic labor organizers like Luisa Moreno and Dorothy Ray Healy organized Mexican and Russian Jewish workers at the California Sanitary Canning Company into a powerful CIO cannery union that achieved wage increases and union recognition.

World War II ushered in dramatic changes for American women. Wartime scarcities led to increased domestic labor as homemakers made do with rationed goods, mended clothing, collected and saved scraps and metals, and planted "victory gardens" to help feed their families. Employment opportunities for women also increased. As a result of the combined incentives of patriotism and good wages, many women took "men's jobs" while the men went off to fight.

Rosie the Riveter became the heroic symbol of the woman war worker. Pictures of "Rosies" building planes or constructing ships graced magazine covers and posters. For the first time, married women joined the paid labor force in droves and public opinion supported them. During the Depression, 80 percent of Americans had objected to wives working outside the home; by 1942 only 13 percent still objected. However, mothers of young children found very little help. In 1943 the federal government finally responded to the needs of working mothers by funding some day-care centers. But meager to begin with and conceived as an emergency measure, government funding for child care would end after the war.

New opportunities for women also opened up in the armed services. Along with the 10 million men aged 21 to 35 drafted into the armed services and the 6 million who enlisted, 140,000 women volunteered for the Women's Army Corps (WACs) and 100,000 for the Navy WAVES (Women Accepted for Voluntary Emergency Service).

Most female enlistees and war workers enjoyed their work and wanted to continue after the war. The extra pay, independence, camaraderie, and satisfaction that their jobs provided had opened their eyes to new possibilities. Edith Speert, like many others, was never again content as a full-time housewife and mother. In a letter dated November 9, 1945, she wrote to her husband who was still overseas:

> *Sweetie, I want to make sure I make myself clear about how I've changed. I want you to know* now *that you are not married to a girl that's interested solely in a home—I shall definitely have to work all my life—I get emotional satisfaction out of working; and I don't doubt that many a night you will cook the supper while I'm at a meeting. Also, dearest—I shall never wash and iron—there are laundries for that! Do you think you'll be able to bear living with me? . . . I love you, Edith*

Wartime upheaval sent the sexual order topsy-turvy. For many young women, moving to a new city or taking a wartime job opened up new possibilities for independence, excitement, and sexual adventure. Some young women, known as "victory girls," believed that it was an act of patriotism to have a fling with a man in uniform before he went overseas. The independence of these women raised fears of female sexuality as a dangerous, ungoverned force. The worry extended beyond the traditional concern about prostitutes and "loose women" to include "good girls" whose sexual standards might relax during wartime. Public health campaigns warned enlisted men that "victory girls" would have their fun with a soldier and then leave him with a venereal disease, incapable of fighting for his country.

Wartime also intensified concerns about homosexuality. Urban centers and the military provided new opportunities for gay men and lesbians to form relationships and build communities. Although the military officially banned homosexuals from the forces, many served by keeping their orientation secret. If discovered, gay men faced severe punishment, including confinement in cages called "queer stockades" or in psychiatric wards. Lesbians faced similar sanctions, although the women's corps, in an effort to assure the civilian world of their recruits' femininity, often looked the other way.

Racial Tensions at Home and the "Double V" Campaign

The Holocaust, Nazi Germany's campaign to exterminate European Jews, demonstrated the horrors of racial hatred taken to its ultimate extreme. The U.S. government did little to help Jewish refugees or to stem the slaughter of Jews in Europe. Official indifference and widespread antisemitism prevailed throughout the war. Nevertheless, Nazi policies against the Jews discredited racial and ethnic prejudice, forcing Americans to confront the reality of racism in their own country. Anthropologist Ruth Benedict, in her 1943 book *The Races of Mankind*, urged the United States to "clean its own house" and "stand unashamed before Nazis and condemn, without confusion, their doctrines of a Master Race." As black leader W. E. B. Du Bois noted, World War II was a "War for Racial Equality" and a struggle for "democracy not only for white folks but for yellow, brown, and black."

Throughout the war years, racial tensions within the United States persisted. Black workers, who were excluded from the best-paying jobs in the defense industry, mobilized against workplace discrimination. Their most powerful advocate was African-American civil rights leader A. Philip Randolph, who had organized the overwhelmingly black Brotherhood of Sleeping Car Porters and won the union a contract with the railroads in 1937. In 1941, Randolph pressured FDR to ban discrimination in defense industries. He threatened to organize a massive march on Washington if Roosevelt did not respond. Roosevelt issued Executive Order 8802, which created the Fair Employment Practices Commission (FEPC) to ensure that blacks and women received the same pay as white men for doing the same job. The FEPC narrowed pay gaps somewhat, but it did not solve the problem.

Sometimes the presence of racial minorities in previously all-white work settings led to hostilities. In 1943 in Detroit, white workers at the Packard auto plant walked off the job when three black employees were promoted. With increasing numbers of white and black Southerners arriving to work in the city's war industries, overcrowding strained the boundaries of traditionally segregated neighborhoods. Clashes at a new housing complex escalated into several days of rioting, resulting in 34 deaths and 1,800 arrests.

In Los Angeles, the death of a Mexican-American youth, José Diaz, sparked sensational news coverage and whipped up anti-Mexican fervor. Although police never determined the cause of Diaz's injuries, they filed first-degree murder charges against 22 Mexican-American boys from the neighborhood. The jury found the young men guilty, but an appeals court overturned the convictions. Nevertheless, hostility continued to mount against Mexican-American youths, particularly *pachucos* who sported **zoot suits**, distinctive attire with flared pants, long coats, and wide-brimmed hats. Pachucos wore the zoot suit as an expression of ethnic pride and rebelliousness.

For eight days in June 1943, scores of soldiers hunted zoot-suiters in Los Angeles bars, theaters, dance halls, and even in their homes, pulling off their clothes and beating them. Soon the attacks expanded to all Mexican Americans, and then to African Americans as well, some of whom also wore the zoot-suit style. The Los Angeles police sided with the rioters. They stood by during the beatings and then arrested the naked and bleeding youths and charged them with disturbing the peace. The rioting raged until the War Department placed the entire city of Los Angeles off limits to military personnel.

In spite of discrimination at home, members of minority groups responded enthusiastically to the war effort. The numbers of blacks in the U.S. army soared from 5,000 in 1940 to 700,000 by 1944, with an additional 187,000 in the U.S. Navy, Coast Guard, and Marine Corps. Four thousand black women joined the WACs. Almost all soldiers fought in segregated units, despite protests by the NAACP that "a Jim Crow army cannot fight for a free world." African Americans fought for the "Double V"—victory over fascism abroad and racial discrimination at home.

American Indians all over the country declared their willingness to fight for the cause. Fully 25,000 Native Americans, including 800 women, served in the military during the war. By 1945 nearly one-third of all able-bodied Native-American men between 18 and 50 had served. Five percent of them were killed or wounded in action. Native Americans enlisted at a higher rate than the general population, prompting the *Saturday Evening Post* to editorialize, "We would not need the Selective Service if all volunteered like the Indians."

In addition to those who enlisted, half of all able-bodied Native-American men not in the service and one-fifth of women left reservations for war-industry jobs. At the beginning of the war, men on reservations earned a median annual income of $500, less than one-fourth the national average. One-third of all Native-American men living off reservations were unemployed. Worse, the average life expectancy for Native Americans in 1940 was just 35 years, compared with 64 years for the population at large. Like others who found new opportunities during the conflict, Native Americans hoped that their wartime economic progress would be permanent. But the boom would end for them when the war ended. Fewer than 10 percent of Native Americans who relocated to cities found long-term employment after the war.

⊙ Watch the Video

The Desegregation of the Military and Blacks in Combat at **www.myhistorylab.com**

INTERPRETING HISTORY

Zelda Webb Anderson became one of the first black women to enter military service during World War II. She served as an officer in the Women's Army Auxiliary Corps (WAAC), renamed the Women's Army Corps (WAC) in 1943. After the war she earned a doctorate in education at the University of California, Berkeley. Her 42-year career in education included a stint teaching at the University of East Africa in Dar-es-Salaam, Tanzania. She related her wartime experiences to the University of Nevada Oral History Program in 1995.

I reported for duty in January 1942. . . . This was so exciting to me. We had black officers, and our basic training was the same as for men. They would simply tell us, "You wanted to be in a man's army, so now you got to do what the men do." We learned military courtesy, history, how to shoot an M-1, go on bivouac, bathe in a teacup of water, eat hardtack rations. . . .

Every evening troops of male soldiers would march by our barracks en route to the mess hall. I told the commanding officer that we would like to have some shades at the windows. "Oh, no. You wanted to be in the man's army. Fine—you have to do what the men do." I told all the girls, "Listen, they won't give us any shades. So I want you to get right in front of the windows buck naked." The next day we had shades at all the windows. . . .

They pulled me out of basic training the third week and sent me to officer training in Des Moines. All of the instructors were white, but white and black officers were being trained in the same facility, in the same classes, and we slept in the same barracks. After OCS I was assigned to a laundry unit.

A black enlisted WAAC could either be in the laundry unit or she could be in the hospital unit. In the laundry unit, if she had a college degree, she could

Zelda Webb Anderson

work at the front counter. . . . If she had less than that, then she did the laundry—very demeaning. And in the hospital unit they let her wash walls, empty basins, wash windows—all that menial work. . . .

I was assigned to duty at Fort Breckenridge, Kentucky. The post commander's name was Colonel Throckmorton. In a pronounced southern accent he told me, "You're going over to that colored WAC company, and you're going to be the mess officer."

I said, "Sir, I have not had any mess training."

"All you nigras know how to cook."

I said, "You just met one who does not know how to cook; but if you send me to Fort Eustis, Virginia, for training I will come back and be the best mess officer you have on this post."

"I ain't sending you to no school, and you're going over there to be a mess

officer." When I about-faced, I kept on going. I didn't even salute him. . . .

[Much later, after developing a more cordial relationship with Colonel Throckmorton,] I told him that segregation has not allowed white people to know black people: "We know you very intimately, but you don't know how we think, how we react, and so you just try to push your stuff on us, not giving a damn about how we feel about this. And then when we rebel, or you meet somebody like me, who decides that you can't do this to me, then you think I'm cantankerous; you think I'm an agitator. I'm just trying to give you an education. . . ."

I lived out the rest of my days very happy in the Army. If I had succumbed to the treatment that they had given other blacks before, and not spoken up for myself, my morale would have been down. . . . In this life, you've got to speak up for yourself. You can't go around shuffling your feet with your head hung down acting apologetic. If you see something you want, you must go after it. One day somebody will recognize it, and it's a victory for you, especially when it's somebody who has denigrated you because of your race. . . .

Our country has not solved all of its problems. You have to live democracy before you can preach democracy. I've got four granddaughters, and I don't want them put in a position where they don't have equal opportunities, equal chances, and then they have to fight the same old battles that I fought again.

Questions

1. *Why do you think Anderson, as a woman and an African American, would choose to enlist in the U.S. Army during World War II?*
2. *According to Anderson, in what ways did the segregation of the armed forces distort white officers' views of blacks?*

The End of the War

Allied leaders met several times to plan for the postwar era. Roosevelt hoped to ensure American dominance and to limit Soviet power. At a conference in Teheran, Iran, in 1943, Roosevelt insisted that the eastern European states of Poland, Latvia, Lithuania, and Estonia should be independent after the war. As the war wound down, Churchill, Stalin, and Roosevelt met again at Yalta, in Ukraine, in February 1945. They agreed to demand Germany's unconditional surrender and to divide the conquered nation into four zones to be occupied by Britain, the Soviet Union, the United States, and France. It became obvious at Yalta that separate spheres of influence would prevail after the war. Poland was a source of contention. Although Stalin nominally agreed to allow free elections in eastern Europe, he intended to make sure that the countries bordering the Soviet Union would be under his control. He also pledged to enter the war against Japan and received assurances that the Soviet Union would regain the lands lost to Japan in the 1904–1905 Russo-Japanese War.

In July 1945, the newly sworn-in American president, Harry Truman, joined Stalin and Churchill (replaced by Clement Attlee after Churchill's election loss) at Potsdam, near Berlin. The three leaders issued a statement demanding "unconditional surrender" from Japan while privately agreeing to let Japan retain its emperor. The rest of the conference focused on postwar Europe.

As the war ended in Europe, Allied troops liberated the Nazi concentration camps. At that moment, the world finally learned the extent of Hitler's "Final Solution." Several Japanese Americans were among the first Allied soldiers to enter the camps. Ichiro Imamura described the sight at Dachau: "When the gates swung open, we got our first good look at the prisoners. . . . They were like skeletons—all skin and bones. . . . They were sick, starving and dying." Some of the survivors saw the Japanese-American soldiers and feared that they were Japanese allies of the Germans. A *Nisei* soldier reassured them, "I am an American soldier, and you are free."

The atomic bomb offered Truman a new means to end the war. In 1942 Roosevelt had authorized the Manhattan Project, the research program to develop nuclear weapons, at a top-secret laboratory in Los Alamos, New Mexico. Building the bomb required the work of 125,000 people and cost nearly $2 billion.

When Truman learned of the successful test on July 16, 1945, while at the Potsdam conference, he hoped to avoid an invasion of Japan that would have cost the lives of many American soldiers, and he wanted to send a message to the Soviet Union that the United States would be the dominant power in the postwar world. But some of the scientists who had developed the bomb urged a "demonstration" in a remote, unpopulated area that would impress the Japanese but would not cause loss of life. General George C. Marshall and other military leaders argued in favor of dropping the bomb on military or industrial targets, with ample warning ahead of time to enable civilians to leave target areas. But others agreed with Truman

What alternatives were available for ending the war in Europe and in the Pacific, and why did the United States choose the strategies it employed to end the war?

•••⌐Read the Document
Manhattan Project Notebook at **www.myhistorylab.com**

■ On V-J Day, August 14, 1945, New Yorkers of Italian descent celebrate Japan's surrender. Although the United States fought against the country of their ancestors, these Americans showed their spirited support for the Allied cause.

that dropping the bomb on a major city, without warning, would be the only way to persuade the Japanese to surrender unconditionally.

When the first bomb exploded over Hiroshima on August 6, 1945, and the second on Nagasaki two days later, the horrifying destructiveness of nuclear weapons became apparent. Even though Americans saw few images of the carnage on the ground, the huge mushroom cloud and the descriptions of cities leveled and people instantly incinerated shocked the nation and the world. In addition to the immediate devastation wreaked by the bomb, deadly radioactive fallout remained in the atmosphere, causing illness and death for months and even years after the attack. On August 14, 1945—V-J (Victory in Japan) Day—the Japanese agreed to surrender, and the official ceremony of surrender took place on September 2.

CONCLUSION

World War II left massive devastation in its wake all across the globe. Although 400,000 Americans died in the conflict, American casualties were far below those suffered by other countries. The wartime economy provided full employment and brought the nation out of the Great Depression.

The war changed life for Americans in profound ways. Although wartime forged a sense of unity as the nation came together to fight against fascism, it also highlighted fissures within American society. Members of minority groups fought in segregated units. Racial tensions and conflicts erupted at home, even as the country fought against a racist foe. Women joined the paid labor force and the armed services in unprecedented numbers, while at the same time being bombarded by official and cultural messages reminding them that their ultimate service to the nation was as wives and mothers.

While life at home changed dramatically, so did the place of the United States in the world. The war's conclusion did not usher in the era of peace Americans expected. European empires staggered on the brink of collapse. Only the United States and the Soviet Union remained as major military powers, shifting the international balance of power from a multipolar to a bipolar system. For the next half-century, the fallout from World War II, as well as the power struggle between the United States and the Soviet Union, would shape political relationships across the globe.

For Review

✓•⌐Study and Review at www.myhistorylab.com

1. What was the immediate impact of the Japanese attack on Pearl Harbor?

2. What is "total war" and how was it manifested in World War II?

3. What persuaded Truman to drop atomic bombs on Hiroshima and Nagasaki?

4. How did the relationship between the United States and the Soviet Union unfold and develop during the war?

Chronology: 1937–1945

1937   Japan invades China.

1939   Germany invades Poland, and Great Britain and France declare war.

1940   Germany invades Denmark, Norway, Holland, Belgium, Luxembourg, and France.

1941   A. Philip Randolph's March on Washington movement.
FDR's "Four Freedoms" speech.
Japan bombs Pearl Harbor.

1942   Executive Order 9066 (internment of Japanese and Japanese Americans).
Japan conquers the Philippines.

1943   Zoot-suit riots in Los Angeles. Attacks on blacks in Detroit.

1944   Normandy invasion on D-Day (June 6).

1945   Harry S. Truman becomes president upon death of Roosevelt.
First test of atomic bomb, Alamogordo, New Mexico.
Atomic bombs dropped on Hiroshima and Nagasaki.
V-E Day (May 7); V-J Day (September 2).

Key Terms

America First Committee A group that opposed Roosevelt's efforts to intervene in World War II against the Axis powers. p. 537

Axis Pact An alliance among Germany, Italy and Japan during World War II. p. 536

Bracero Mexican nationals working in the United States in low-wage jobs as part of a temporary work program between 1942 and 1964. (The *bracero* program was established by an executive agreement between the presidents of Mexico and the United States, providing Mexican agricultural labor in the Southwest and the Pacific Northwest.) p. 540

Fascism A form of right-wing dictatorship exalting nation and race above the individual. p. 536

Free trade International economic relations characterized by multinational investment and a reduction or elimination of tariffs. p. 537

Holocaust The name given to the Nazi genocide against the Jews during World War II. Six million Jews were murdered. p. 535

Pachuco Young Mexican American man who expressed attitudes of youthful rebellion in the 1940s. Many wore the Zoot Suit, also fashionable among urban African Americans. p. 549

Rosie the Riveter A heroic symbol of women workers on the homefront during World War II. p. 547

Zoot suits Distinctive clothing in the 1940s worn largely by Mexican American and African American men, characterized by flared pants, long coats, and wide-brimmed hats. p. 549

24

Cold War and Hot War, 1945–1953

At 11:30 a.m. on April 25, 1945, U.S. Army private Joseph Polowsky glimpsed what looked like the future. The young Chicago native was riding in the lead jeep of an American force along the Elbe River in central Germany when he spotted Russian soldiers on the far side, their medals glistening in the morning sun. Elated, he and five of his comrades found a small boat and paddled across to the eastern bank. Using Polowsky's knowledge of German to communicate, the American soldiers embraced their Soviet allies with laughs and tears. The Russians produced bottles of vodka, and toasts, pledges, singing, and dancing followed. After years of pressing Germany from east and west, the Allies had finally linked up in the heart of Hitler's empire. A reporter wrote of the scene, "You get the feeling of exuberance, a great new world opening up."

Despite his conservative Republican background, Polowsky spent much of the rest of his life advocating American-Russian friendship. He could not forget the transforming experience of that April day along the Elbe and the hopes it engendered for a peaceful future. However, what followed the Allied victory turned out to be not a "great new world" of international peace and brotherhood but the **Cold War** of U.S.-Soviet hostility that lasted for more than four decades. The opposing ideologies—**communism** and capitalist democracy—joined with conflicting national interests to produce this heavily armed standoff. The American effort to contain the expansion of communist influence entailed a radical reorientation of American involvement abroad in peacetime, including the nation's first peacetime military alliance, the North Atlantic Treaty Organization (NATO). At times the Cold War turned into a hot war of actual shooting, most importantly in the Korean War of 1950–1953 and the Vietnam War in the following decade.

In some ways, the Cold War encouraged efforts at social reform. America's new leading role in world affairs brought its domestic life into the spotlight of world attention. Racial discrimination and violence at home embarrassed American leaders as they spoke of leading the anticommunist "free world" abroad.

But in other ways, the Cold War constrained efforts to bring American life more fully into line with its democratic and egalitarian promise. Rising tensions with communist movements and governments overseas stimulated great anxieties about possible subversion within the nation's own borders. Anticommunist fervor put unions on the defensive and encouraged women to shun the workplace in favor of family life and parenting, particularly in the nation's growing suburbs. This second Red Scare—the first had followed World War I in 1919—reached flood tide by 1950 with the rise to prominence of Senator Joseph McCarthy, a Republican from Wisconsin. McCarthy made a career of blaming supposedly disloyal Americans at home for setbacks to U.S. goals abroad in places such as China and Korea. He left a bitter legacy that long outlasted his political demise in 1954.

The Uncertainties of Victory

Franklin Roosevelt's death in April 1945 stunned the nation and the world. Elected four times to the presidency, he had dominated American politics like no figure before or since. Just as the unprecedented destruction of World War II was finally ending, the leadership of the nation passed into the new and less tested hands of Harry Truman. Peace brought an array of uncertainties and immediate needs. The victors had to reconstruct a world that had been damaged, physically and psychologically, almost beyond recognition. Spared the destruction visited elsewhere, the United States faced the different challenge of demobilizing its military forces and reconverting to a peacetime economy. Intense conflicts along the color line and in the workplace revealed real differences among Americans about the shape of the democracy they had fought to defend.

How were the world and the United States different at the end of World War II than they had been at the beginning?

Global Destruction

World War II wrought death on a scale that defies comprehension. From England in the west to the islands of New Guinea in the east, from the Baltic Sea in the north to the Sahara Desert in the south, much of Europe and Asia was left in ruins. Soviet and American power had finally crushed the Axis, with Berlin now a "city of the dead" and Japan's urban landscape devastated by firebombing and nuclear attacks. Some of the victors were only marginally better off.

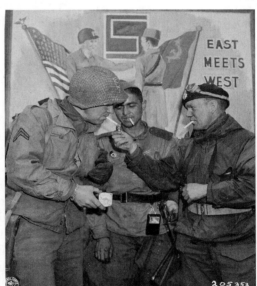

■ Soviet and American troops meet in central Germany in May 1945.

Only one of the major combatants emerged from the war in better shape than at the beginning. The American people, one official remarked in 1945, "are in the pleasant predicament of having to learn to live 50 percent better than they have ever lived before." Many Americans suffered terribly in the war, of course; 400,000 died, leaving behind desolate families, and millions of veterans returned with traumas that colored the remainder of their lives. But such casualties paled in comparison to those of other belligerent nations. With just 6 percent of the world's population and 50 percent of its wealth, the United States enjoyed a position of staggering economic advantage.

Americans' overriding fear was that the end of the fighting might return the country to the state it had faced when the war began: economic depression. The nation's awesome industrial productivity depended on government spending, which was now to be cut back sharply. International trade might pick up much of the slack, but the war had destroyed most of the purchasing power of U.S. trading partners in Europe and Asia. Rising tensions between the two primary victors—the United States and the Soviet Union—hampered the process of postwar reconstruction.

Vacuums of Power and a Turn to the Left

World War II altered the world's ideological and physical landscape. Japan and Germany, the centers of prewar power in Asia and continental Europe, were vacuums waiting to be filled and reshaped by their conquerors. In addition to defeating two nations, the Allies had also discredited the right-wing ideas on which those governments had been built: fascism and militarism. Fascism's murderous character tarred those who had collaborated with the Axis

■ Franklin D. Roosevelt's death at his vacation home in Warm Springs, Georgia, stunned a nation and a world that had not known another U.S. president for 13 years. Navy bandsman Graham Jackson was one of Roosevelt's favorite musicians. As the procession began to transport the president's body north for burial in Hyde Park, New York, Jackson captured the grief of millions of Americans as he played the sweet, slow strains of "Going Home."

during the war, primarily conservatives in countries such as France who preferred fascism to socialism.

Into many of the postwar vacuums of power flowed a newly prominent worldwide left. Socialists, communists, and other radicals espoused communal rather than individualistic values. The occupying Soviet forces installed communist governments in eastern Europe by force, and Socialist and Communist parties rose sharply in popularity in France, Italy, Belgium, and Scandinavia. Europeans across the continent established welfare states to provide a minimum standard of living for all their citizens.

This turn to the left encompassed most of the globe. Africans began organizing for eventual independence from European rule, and Asians launched the final phase of their anticolonial struggle for liberation. Indonesia fought its way free from the Dutch, and India gained its freedom from Britain. The Allies established the new United Nations (UN) in San Francisco in April 1945. Eventually housed in New York, its General Assembly gave all nations an equal voice and vote in deliberations, and its small Security Council—responsible for guiding any UN military actions—gave a permanent seat and veto power to five nations: the United States, the USSR, Britain, France, and China. The 1948 UN Human Rights Charter helped put practitioners of colonialism and racial discrimination on the defensive by declaring worldwide support for the principles of national self-determination and equal treatment for all peoples.

Postwar Transition to Peacetime Life

The fundamental task for Americans at home was to convert from a wartime society back to a peacetime one. They were especially eager to bring home the 12 million men in uniform serving abroad. Eager to resume civilian life, the veterans walked off ships' gangplanks into a country in transition. Wartime rationing was lifted on goods such as sugar and gasoline, and the 35-mph speed limit was withdrawn. But as orders for war materials dried up, taking jobs with them, wartime inflation persisted. Housing remained especially scarce. In the richest country in the world, one-third of the citizens still lived in poverty, with neither running water nor flush toilets.

To ease the transition home, Congress had passed the Servicemen's Readjustment Act of 1944 (the GI Bill) to extend crucial financial aid to veterans. It provided low-cost mortgages that helped create an explosion in home ownership. It created Veterans Administration hospitals to provide lifetime medical care. And it paid tuition and stipends for college and vocational training, making higher education broadly available for the first time. The 2 percent of veterans who were women also made use of these benefits. In the postwar era, when American politics generally became more conservative—shifting away from the New Deal reform spirit and toward an anticommunist emphasis—the GI Bill was the one area in which the United States expanded its own welfare state.

The postwar transition presented particular challenges to American women. Millions of them had gone to work outside the home during the war and found economic independence in doing so. Now they faced powerful pressures to leave the workforce and return to a domestic life of old and new families. Many women accepted this return to the domestic sphere, content to focus on marriage and family life. Others felt differently. "War jobs have uncovered unsuspected abilities in American women," one argued. "Why lose all these abilities?"

Challenging Racial Discrimination

African Americans faced a similar problem. After finding new opportunities in industrial employment during the war, they were laid off afterward in favor of returning white veterans. Like women, blacks were expected by others to retreat into deference. Black veterans spearheaded the resistance to this notion.

African-American efforts to overcome discrimination met fierce white resistance in 1946 and 1947. In the South, where most black Americans still lived, a wave of beatings and lynchings greeted black veterans in uniform and their attempts to register to vote. White Northerners also used violence to preserve the segregated character of neighborhoods in Chicago, Detroit, and other cities. They destroyed the property and threatened the lives of blacks who dared to move to previously all-white blocks, effectively confining African Americans to impoverished areas.

The retreat of European colonialism and American competition with the Soviet Union nonetheless encouraged many white Americans to acknowledge the contradiction between leading the "free world" and limiting the freedoms of Americans of color. A series of Supreme Court decisions validated the long-term strategy of the National Association for the Advancement of Colored People (NAACP) for contesting segregation in the courts. Court rulings outlawed segregation in voting primaries (*Smith v. Allwright*, 1944), interstate transportation (*Morgan v. Virginia*, 1946), contracts for house sales (*Shelley v. Kraemer*, 1948), and graduate schools (*Sweatt v. Painter* and *McLaurin v. Oklahoma*, 1950).

Popular culture moved in the same direction of breaking down racial barriers. *Billboard* magazine in 1949 changed the category of "race music" to "rhythm and blues" as white record producers and radio disc jockeys such as Alan Freed began to bring the early rock 'n' roll of African-American musicians to mainstream white audiences. By 1955 young white musicians such as Bill Haley and Elvis Presley joined black stars such as Chuck Berry and Little Richard in creating a wildly popular sound that transcended racial categories. Professional baseball erased its color line when Jackie Robinson, a former four-sport star at the University of California–Los Angeles and lieutenant in the U.S. Army, joined the Brooklyn Dodgers in 1947.

Native Americans and Mexican Americans faced similar discrimination in the Southwest and elsewhere. With war veterans in the fore, they also organized to contest unfair education and election practices. "If we are good enough to fight, why aren't we good enough to vote?" asked returning Navajo soldiers in New Mexico and Arizona, where the state constitutions

■ Japanese American women pack lima beans into boxes for freezing at Seabrook Farms, near Bridgeton, New Jersey, in 1947. Unlike the northern part of the state, which was closely tied to New York City, rural southern New Jersey was a rich fruit-and-vegetable-growing region. After their release from the internment camps of World War II, Americans of Japanese descent joined their fellow citizens in finding work where they could in a peacetime economy no longer shrouded by the Great Depression.

prohibited Indian residents from voting, until successfully challenged in 1948. The League of United Latin American Citizens (LULAC) followed a strategy similar to that of the NAACP regarding educational discrimination, leading to the Ninth Circuit Court's decision in *Mendez v. Westminster* (1947) outlawing segregated schools for Mexican Americans in California. In parallel fashion, indigenous Alaskans organized in the Alaska Native Brotherhood successfully lobbied the territorial legislature in Juneau to pass an antidiscrimination law in 1945.

Class Conflict between Workers and Owners

In many ways, 1946 seemed like 1919. A world war had just ended, in which corporations had made handsome profits. American workers had enjoyed nearly full employment and improving wages and had joined unions in large numbers. In 1946 one-third of the workforce held a union card, the largest portion ever. But the end of war-related orders led to job cuts and the loss of overtime wages, and by the spring of 1946, 1.8 million workers were out on strike.

Mirroring World War I, the conclusion of hostilities in 1945 revealed rising tensions between the United States and the Soviet Union. The spread of leftist revolutions abroad amplified fears of communist influence in American unions, especially because a few of the most effective Congress of Industrial Organizations (CIO) organizers were Communist party members or at least sympathetic to an emphasis on class conflict between owners and workers. As in 1919, a Red Scare began to develop, egged on by a business community that used the supposed threat of the tiny U.S. Communist party to weaken the much larger and less radical union movement. In contrast to the end of World War I, however, federal law guaranteed the right of workers to bargain collectively, and the strikes of 1946 resulted in some negotiated wage increases.

The tide turned against unions as anticommunism intensified. The Republican party claimed a sweeping victory in the 1946 congressional elections, taking control of both the House and the Senate in a stark rejection of Truman's leadership. Republicans and conservative Democrats then passed the Taft-Hartley Act in 1947 over the president's veto, weakening unions by prohibiting secondary boycotts (against the products of a company whose workers were on strike) and requiring union officials to swear anticommunist oaths. At the same time, the expanding U.S. economy after 1947 pulled many skilled workers up into the middle class and gave them a larger stake in the status quo.

The Quest for Security

How did the meaning of "security" change for the United States after 1945?

On February 21, 1947, a British official in Washington informed the U.S. government that Britain could no longer provide financial assistance to the anticommunist governments of Greece and Turkey. This information marked a watershed in modern world history. Long the greatest imperial power and the dominant outside force in the Middle East, Britain was beginning a slow retreat. Left in its wake were vacuums of power, particularly in the Middle East, South Asia, and Africa. President Truman and his advisers believed that either Soviet or American influence would flow into these regions. The Truman administration formulated a policy to contain communism in the eastern Mediterranean that it quickly expanded to encompass the entire noncommunist world. Powerful new nuclear weapons increased anxieties about the nation's security.

Redefining National Security

U.S. policymakers had ended World War II with one primary goal. They were determined to revive the global capitalist economy that had nearly dissolved in the Great Depression of the 1930s and had then been battered by the war. American prosperity and freedom, they believed, depended on a world system of free trade because Americans simply could not consume all the products of their efficient farms and factories. If they could not sell the surplus abroad, the United States would slide back into a depression.

"National security" was expanding to mean something very different from simply defending the nation's territory against invasion. For the disproportionately powerful United States, national security after 1945 came to be identified with the creation and preservation of a free-trading capitalist world order. American national security was seen to be at stake almost everywhere around the globe.

The primary threat to that security came from the Soviet Union. The danger lay in Soviet encouragement, by example and assistance, of revolutions that rejected market economies and individualist ethics. Demoralized by the war's destruction and by grim postwar economic conditions, western Europeans and others seemed to be considering the paths of socialism and communism. "Hopeless and hungry people," Secretary of State Dean Acheson warned, "often resort to desperate measures."

> *"Hopeless and hungry people," Secretary of State Dean Acheson warned, "often resort to desperate measures."*

Conflict with the Soviet Union

The antifascist alliance of the Soviet Union and the United States dissolved rapidly as their conflicting interests reemerged after the war. Long skeptical of the capitalist world it wanted to replace, the Soviet government viewed expansive U.S. interests as evidence of "striving for world supremacy." Yet Moscow was just as clearly expanding its own sphere of national security, with Soviet troops remaining in areas they had occupied during the war: Manchuria, northern Korea, Iran, and especially eastern and central Europe. Each side spoke of the other's goal as "world domination."

Contrasting experiences in World War II amplified historical and ideological differences. Whereas the war brought the United States out of the global capitalist depression (which the Soviets had avoided), it brought the USSR into a depression caused by the invading Germans' destruction of the western portion of the country. With a decimated population, a battered economy, and minimal air and naval forces, the postwar Soviet Union remained a regional power based on its army. The United States was the only truly global power, with a vast naval armada and air force projecting military might onto every continent, undergirded by the most productive economy in world history.

The two nations' visions of the postwar world order reflected these relative positions. Americans sought an open world for the free flow of goods and most ideas, and proved willing to tolerate and even embrace dictatorial governments as long as they were anticommunist and open to foreign trade and investment. Meanwhile, the Soviets called for a more traditional division into separate spheres of influence for the great powers.

Conflicts over specific areas liberated from the Nazis hastened the onset of the Cold War in the first 18 months after the end of World War II. Whereas the Soviets wanted reparations and a deindustrialized Germany that could never threaten it again, the United States considered a rebuilt industrial German state crucial for a healthy, integrated western European economy. Britain and France had gone to war in defense of an independent Poland, but for Stalin control of Poland was not negotiable because it had been "the corridor for attack on Russia." Moscow and Washington also clashed over Iran, where the Soviets briefly encouraged a leftist uprising in the northern part of the oil-rich country to counteract British and American influence in the capital city of Tehran. U.S. policymakers worried about Soviet requests to Turkey for greater control of the straits leading out of the Black Sea into the Mediterranean.

The Policy of Containment

Diplomat George Kennan best articulated the policy of **containment** in an influential telegram sent from his post at the U.S. embassy in Moscow in February 1946. Kennan explained

•••—Read the Document
Churchill's "Iron Curtain" Speech at
www.myhistorylab.com

Members of NATO (1949)
Members of Warsaw Pact (1955)
Nonaligned counties
Ⓢ **Participants in the Marshall Plan, 1947–1952**
🚗 **Year first atomic device was tested by that country**

ICELAND Ⓢ

NORWAY Ⓢ
Oslo
SWEDEN
Stockholm
FINLAND
Helsinki
U.S.S.R.
🚗 1949
Baltic Sea

U.S loan of $3.5 billion, 1946

IRELAND Ⓢ
Dublin
DENMARK
Copenhagen

GREAT BRITAIN 🚗 1952 Ⓢ
London

NETHERLANDS
Amsterdam
Brussels Ⓢ
BELGIUM
Bonn Ⓢ
WEST GERMANY
LUX.

Berlin blockade, 1948–1949
Berlin
EAST GERMANY
Warsaw
POLAND

ATLANTIC OCEAN

Paris

FRANCE 🚗 1960 Ⓢ

Withdrew forces from NATO, 1966

Joined NATO, 1955

SWITZ. Ⓢ
AUSTRIA Ⓢ
Vienna

Zones of occupation ended, 1955

Prague
CZECHOSLOVAKIA

Communist coup, 1948
U.S.S.R. invasion, 1968

Budapest
HUNGARY

Anti-communist revolution failed, 1956

ROMANIA
Bucharest

Black Sea

PORTUGAL Ⓢ
Lisbon
SPAIN
Madrid

Joined NATO, 1982

YUGOSLAVIA
Belgrade

Tito–Stalin Schism, 1948

BULGARIA
Sofia

Rome Ⓢ
ITALY

GREECE Ⓢ
Athens Ⓢ
ALBANIA

Withdrew from Warsaw Pact, 1968

TURKEY
Ankara Ⓢ

Truman Doctrine, 1947 joined NATO, 1952

■ **MAP 24.1**
EUROPE DIVIDED BY THE COLD WAR
For centuries Europe had controlled much of the rest of the world. After 1945, Russians occupied the eastern half of the continent and Americans wielded dominant influence in the western half. This division of Europe into communist and noncommunist blocs lasted until the end of the Cold War in 1989.

"The reins of world leadership are fast slipping from Britain's . . . hands. These reins will be picked up either by the United States or by Russia."

Soviet hostility as a function of traditional Russian insecurity overlaid with newer Marxist justifications. He called for "the adroit and vigilant application of counterforce" against all Soviet efforts at expanding their influence. One month later, on March 5, 1946, former British prime minister Winston Churchill warned that a Russian "iron curtain" had descended across Europe, imprisoning all those to the east of it. "The reins of world leadership are fast slipping from Britain's competent but now very weak hands," the State Department argued. "These reins will be picked up either by the United States or by Russia."

Picking up those reins meant a fundamental reorientation for the United States. No longer just the dominant force in the Western Hemisphere, it would have to maintain its wartime projection of military forces around the globe—permanently. In an address to Congress on March 12, 1947, asking for $400 million in aid for Greece and Turkey, Truman simplified the world system into two "ways of life," those of "free peoples" and those of "terror and oppression" under communist rule. All nations must choose between them, he declared, and the United States must support "free peoples who are resisting attempted subjugation by armed minorities or outside pressures."

The **Truman Doctrine**, as it became known, exaggerated a real problem in order to win public support for a new international role for the United States. It funded the governments of Turkey and Greece but it framed the new policy broadly, opening the path to supporting anticommunist regimes and opposing revolutions around the world for decades to come. The most important immediate step was the reconstruction of a vibrant, reintegrated western European economy. The United States provided $13 billion between 1948 and 1952 to fund the European Recovery Program, commonly known as the Marshall Plan for its chief architect, Secretary of State George Marshall (1947–1949).

Ensuring western European security against the Red Army also entailed the first U.S. military alliance in peacetime. The victors of World War II divided a defeated Germany into separate zones of occupation. The British, French, and American decision in March 1948 to create a unified state out of the western sectors of Germany led a few months later to a year-long Soviet blockade of western access to Berlin and fears of a general war. The creation of NATO in 1949 made the American military commitment to Europe permanent. The point of NATO for western Europe, its British first secretary general said, was to "keep the Americans in, the Russians out, and the Germans down."

The onset of the Cold War determined the fate of the defeated powers of World War II. Reconstructing Germany and Japan replaced initial concerns about rooting out Nazism and punishing war criminals, as at the Nuremberg trials of surviving Nazi leaders in 1945–1946. The American occupation under General Douglas MacArthur initially (1945–1947) emphasized democratization of Japanese society, including building labor unions, weakening corporate monopolies, ensuring women's political rights, and punishing war criminals. But rising U.S. tensions with the Soviets and the imminent victory of the Communist forces in China's civil war prompted American officials to shift course by 1948. Henceforth, they focused on rebuilding as quickly as possible Japan's industrial economy as the hub of capitalist Asia.

●●●┤Read the Document

The Marshall Plan at **www.myhistorylab.com**

Colonialism and the Cold War

Most of the world's nonwhite majority still lived under European colonial control, and for them the struggle for national independence and racial equality was the great issue of the late 1940s and 1950s. In this North-South conflict of **colonialism**, as opposed to the East-West conflict of the Cold War, the United States held an awkward position. Its primary NATO partners included the greatest colonial powers: Britain, France, Belgium, the Netherlands, and Portugal. Racial segregation in the United States further undercut American leadership of the "free world."

For the world's nonwhite majority, the struggle for national independence and racial equality was the great issue of the late 1940s and 1950s.

With European rule in Asia and Africa on the way out, the Truman administration sought a gradual transfer of colonial rule into the hands of local pro-West elites. The U.S. grant of official independence to the Philippines in 1946 was offered as a model, as was the British departure from India a year later. However, the importance of Europe for America meant supporting even those imperialists who did not leave peacefully, such as the French digging in against communist-led revolutionaries in Vietnam (part of French Indochina).

The British withdrawal from Palestine in 1948 created a peculiar dilemma for the United States. Jewish settlers—primarily from Europe and often survivors of the

◄●►─ Read the Document

Press Release Announcing U.S. Recognition of Israel at **www.myhistorylab.com**

Holocaust—proclaimed the new state of Israel against the wishes of the Arab majority. Secretary of State Marshall and others urged Truman not to recognize Israel in order to avoid imperiling U.S. relations with the Arab oil-producing states. The president sympathized with the Jewish desire for a homeland, however, and understood the importance of American Jews as constituents of the Democratic party in the 1940s. His decision to recognize Israel, which most Middle Easterners viewed as a new colonial state, set the United States on a course of enduring friendship with that nation and enduring conflict with Israel's Arab neighbors and the Palestinians.

The Impact of Nuclear Weapons

Scientists in the 1940s dramatically increased Americans' sense of personal safety by introducing the use of antibiotics. "Miracle drugs" such as penicillin cured common bacterial infections that had previously been debilitating or fatal. What science gave with one hand it threatened to take away with the other, however. The use of atomic weapons on Japan foreshadowed a future of utter insecurity in which instantaneous destruction of entire nations could occur without warning.

Even without being used again in war after 1945, nuclear weapons altered the American environment. Weapon tests released vast quantities of radiation into the atmosphere. Local cancer rates spiked upward for Bikini Islanders in the Pacific, where the first tests occurred, and then for farmers and ranchers in Utah and Nevada, when tests began 65 miles northwest of Las Vegas in 1953. Navajo Indians mining uranium in the Southwest paid dearly for

■ Soldiers watch as "Dog," a 21-kiloton nuclear device, is dropped from a bomber at the Nevada Test Site at Yucca Flat, northwest of Las Vegas, in November 1951. U.S. atomic specialists tested nuclear weapons first in the Marshall Islands of the western Pacific Ocean, especially the Bikini atoll, beginning in 1946, and then in Nevada beginning in January 1951. Residents downwind from the test sites suffered various adverse health effects from radiation exposure, including high cancer rates.

their intensive exposure to the poisonous material, as did thousands of workers involved in nuclear weapon production. Weapon assembly plants in Hanford, Washington, and Rocky Flats, Colorado, leaked radioactivity into the groundwater. In combination with the nuclear power industry, atomic weapon development resulted in an enormous supply of radioactive waste—deadly for 10,000 more years—that the U.S. government still does not know how to dispose of safely.

The government offered reassurances about the safety of the atom, and the Atomic Energy Commission covered up evidence of radioactivity's ill effects. But many Americans were deeply anxious about this destructive new power that loomed over their lives, especially as the Soviet-American arms race intensified. Science fiction movies painted frightening pictures of a future devastated by nuclear war and haunted by exposure to radiation. Concerns about a nuclear world escalated with the successful 1952 test of an American hydrogen bomb, a thousand times more powerful than the device that destroyed Hiroshima.

⚫Watch the Video
Duck and Cover at
www.myhistorylab.com

American Security and Asia

Japan did not conquer independent nations in its sweep southward at the start of World War II. Instead it defeated the forces of imperial powers: the French in Indochina, the Dutch in Indonesia, the British in Singapore and Malaya, and the Americans in the Philippines. In a single swoop, Japanese soldiers demonstrated the absurdity of white supremacy and cleared the way for the end of colonialism in Asia. Then Japan's retreat in 1945 left vacuums of power throughout the region. Into them flowed two contenders: the returning but gravely weakened European imperialists, and Asian nationalists such as Ho Chi Minh in Vietnam. Americans were not passive observers of this struggle, as they sought to establish a new free-trading order in the region. As communist forces won a civil war in China, the U.S. government bulked up its military and intelligence capacities and went to war in Korea.

Why was Asia particularly important to the United States during the early postwar period?

The Chinese Civil War

Americans had long felt a special connection to China. Half of the thousands of Christian missionaries sent out by American churches in the early twentieth century had been posted there. Entrepreneurs eyed the Chinese market, home to one-fifth of the world's potential consumers. During World War II, Chinese resistance to Japan's invasion occupied millions of Tokyo's soldiers who would otherwise have been shooting at American GIs. The close U.S. alliance with the government of Jiang Jieshi seemed to confirm American hopes that Asia's largest nation would follow a pro-American path.

But the partisans of the Chinese Communist Party (CCP) under Mao Zedong's leadership fought more effectively against the Japanese than Jiang's soldiers did. Japan's withdrawal from China in 1945 initiated four years of warfare between the Communists and Jiang's anticommunist Nationalists. The Truman administration provided $3 billion in aid to Jiang. Americans watched in frustration as the CCP defeated the Nationalists, who retreated to the island of Taiwan in 1949.

The People's Republic of China (PRC) was the first communist government created without the presence of Soviet troops. Profound suspicions on both sides prevented any Sino-American accommodation, and the U.S. government refused to recognize the People's Republic. Faced with U.S. hostility and sharing a common ideology with the Soviet Union, Mao papered over historic Chinese-Russian tensions and signed a mutual defense pact with Moscow in February 1950. For American policymakers, the so-called loss of China increased the importance of building capitalist societies in the rest of Asia, particularly Japan and—fatefully—South Korea and Vietnam. China's revolution also became a major issue in

■ Were all communists conspiring together against the United States and its interests? New Chinese leader Mao Zedong (left) helps Soviet ruler Josef Stalin celebrate his birthday on December 21, 1949. Two months later, the two men signed a mutual defense treaty. But, as their expressions suggest, they shared little personal warmth. Conflicting Chinese and Russian national interests soon strained— and eventually broke—their alliance.

American politics. "Who lost China?" Republicans demanded rhetorically and effectively, presuming that it had once been America's to lose.

The Creation of the National Security State

A week before Mao's announcement that China had become a communist country, President Truman shared some equally grim news with the American public: the Soviet Union had detonated its first nuclear device. The United States had lost the atomic monopoly that for four years assured Americans of their unique position of military strength. Truman asked his advisers for a full reevaluation of the nation's foreign policy.

The result was the top-secret National Security Council document 68 (**NSC-68**), which articulated the logic of what became the **national security state**: a government focused on the imperatives of military power, global involvement, and radically increased defense spending. NSC-68 argued that the United States had entered an era of permanent crisis because of the expansion of communism and the hostile intentions of the Soviet Union. America's worldwide interests meant that it must oppose revolutions or radical change anywhere on the globe. NSC-68 went beyond the containment policy of the Truman Doctrine to call instead for fostering "a fundamental change in the nature of the Soviet system." This armed struggle necessitated secrecy and centralization of power in the hands of the federal government.

The National Security Act of 1947 and its 1949 amendments created the institutions of the new national security state. The Central Intelligence Agency (CIA) organized spying and covert operations, the Department of Defense unified the separate branches of the military, and the National Security Council (NSC) coordinated foreign policy information for the president.

At War in Korea

Two months after NSC-68 arrived on the president's desk, troops from communist North Korea poured across the thirty-eighth parallel into South Korea on June 25, 1950. The alarmist

INTERPRETING HISTORY

NSC-68

Concerned about the trend of international events in the wake of the Communist revolution in China and the Soviet Union's acquisition of nuclear weapons, President Truman ordered his National Security Council on January 31, 1950, to conduct "a reexamination of our objectives in peace and war and of the effect of these objectives on our strategic plans." The resulting study, known as NSC-68, called for a military buildup to counter Soviet expansionism. Some specialists on the USSR, such as George Kennan, questioned NSC-68's accuracy regarding Soviet intentions and successes. But the subsequent North Korean invasion of South Korea seemed to confirm the idea of "international communism" on the march.

From NSC-68: U.S. Objectives and Programs for National Security (April 14, 1950)

The Soviet Union, unlike previous aspirants to hegemony, is animated by a new fanatic faith, antithetical to our own, and seeks to impose its absolute authority over the rest of the world. . . .

Any substantial further extension of the area under the domination of the Kremlin would raise the possibility that no coalition adequate to confront the Kremlin with greater strength could be assembled. It is in this context that this Republic and its citizens in the ascendancy of their strength stand in their deepest peril.

The issues that face us are momentous, involving the fulfillment or destruction not only of this Republic but of civilization itself. . . . The assault on free institutions is world-wide now, and in the context of the present polarization of power a defeat of free institutions anywhere is a defeat everywhere. . . .

Our policy and actions must be such as to foster a fundamental change in the nature of the Soviet system. . . . In

a shrinking world, which now faces the threat of atomic warfare, it is not an adequate objective merely to seek to check the Kremlin design, for the absence of order among nations is becoming less and less tolerable. . . .

The integrity of our system will not be jeopardized by any measures, covert or overt, violent or non-violent, which serve the purposes of frustrating the Kremlin design, nor does the necessity for conducting ourselves so as to affirm our values in actions as well as words forbid such measures. . . .

The total economic strength of the U.S.S.R. compares with that of the U.S. as roughly one to four. . . . The military budget of the United States represents 6 to 7 percent of its gross national product (as against 13.8 percent for the Soviet Union). . . . This difference in emphasis between the two economies means that the readiness of the free world to support a war effort is tending to decline relative to that of the Soviet Union.

It is true that the United States armed forces are now stronger than ever before in other times of apparent peace; it is also true that there exists a sharp disparity between our actual military strength and our commitments. . . . It is clear that our military strength is becoming dangerously inadequate. . . . In summary, we must . . . [engage in] a rapid and sustained build-up of the political, economic, and military strength of the free world.

Questions

1. What is the precise problem that the United States faces, according to NSC-68?
2. How does NSC-68's analysis of the Soviet threat in 1950 compare with American understandings today of the threat from Islamic terrorist organizations such as Al Qaeda?

Workers at the Douglas Aircraft Company's Santa Monica factory assemble Nike guided missiles for the U.S. Army in 1955. Large military contracts proliferated during the Cold War and stimulated the growth of Sunbelt states like California.

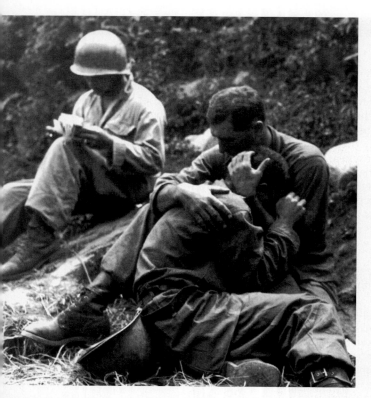

■ Near Haktong-ni, Korea, on August 28, 1950, an Army corpsman fills out casualty tags while one American soldier comforts another who has just seen a friend killed in action. Men who fought together on the front lines in Korea, as in other wars, experienced physical and psychological traumas unparalleled in civilian life. They often developed strong friendships with each other but sometimes had difficulty making the transition back to peacetime routines at home.

recommendations of NSC-68 now seemed fully justified to U.S. policymakers. But the origins of the conflict on the Korean peninsula were complicated.

Korea had been colonized by Japan since 1910. After Japan's defeat in 1945, Soviet and U.S. forces each occupied half of the peninsula. In the north, the Soviets installed a dictatorial Communist regime under Kim Il Sung, who had fought with the Chinese Communists in their common struggle against Japan. In the south, the Americans established an authoritarian capitalist regime led by Syngman Rhee, who had lived in the United States most of the previous four decades. The 38th parallel was an arbitrary dividing line for a nation that had been unified for 1,300 years, and both governments sought to reunite Korea under their control. Border skirmishes intensified after the Soviets and Americans withdrew in 1948, and leftist rebellions continued across much of the south. Some 100,000 Koreans lost their lives in the fighting between 1945 and 1950.

U.S. forces arrived in late June 1950, just in time to prevent the South Korean army from being driven off the peninsula, and then slowly pushed the North Koreans backward toward the 38th parallel in hard fighting. Truman received UN approval for this "police action," along with a small number of troops from several other nations.

Americans assumed the North Korean invasion had been orchestrated by Moscow as part of a plan of worldwide communist aggression. The Truman administration considered defense of South Korea crucial to demonstrate the credibility of U.S. power. The U.S. government took preemptive actions against possible aggression elsewhere. It sent the 7th Fleet to defend Taiwan, which it had previously assumed China would eventually conquer and reabsorb; it increased assistance to anticommunist forces in the Philippines and Vietnam; and it rearmed West Germany as part of NATO. The U.S. annual military budget increased from $13 billion in 1950 before the war to $50 billion in 1953, setting a pattern for vast military expenditures ever since.

General Douglas MacArthur's brilliantly executed landing of fresh U.S. troops at the port of Inchon behind North Korean lines on September 15, 1950, created a turning point in the war. South Korea was retaken; containment had succeeded. Should American commanders now shift to rolling back communism by proceeding north of the 38th parallel? The opportunity was irresistible, despite Truman's determination to keep this a limited war. MacArthur ignored signals that the Chinese would not allow U.S. soldiers to come all the way to their border at the Yalu River—the equivalent for Americans of having the Soviet Army arrive at the Rio Grande. On November 27, 200,000 Chinese soldiers struck hard, driving American soldiers south of the 38th parallel again in the longest retreat in U.S. history.

MacArthur wanted to take this "entirely new war" directly to the Chinese, using conventional or even nuclear bombing campaigns against the People's Republic. His growing insubordination forced Truman to fire the

TABLE 24-1			
The Election of 1948			
Candidate	Political Party	Popular Vote (%)	Electoral Vote
Harry S. Truman	Democratic	49.5	304
Thomas E. Dewey	Republican	45.1	189
J. Strom Thurmond	State-Rights Democratic	2.4	38
Henry A. Wallace	Progressive	2.4	—

■ MAP 24.2

THE KOREAN WAR, 1950–1953

The strategic location of the Korean peninsula enhanced the importance of what had originally been a civil conflict among Koreans. Korea's close proximity to China, the Soviet Union, and U.S.-occupied Japan made the outcome of that conflict very important to all of the great powers. The Americans and Chinese wound up doing the bulk of the fighting against each other in the full-scale war that unfolded in 1950.

popular general in April 1951 because the president had no desire to start a larger war that would draw in the USSR. The bloody fighting in Korea stalemated that spring close to the original dividing line, where the front remained as the two sides negotiated for two years before signing a ceasefire in July 1953. American deaths totaled 37,000, and China lost nearly a million soldiers. Three million Koreans on both sides died—10 percent of the population of the peninsula—and another 5 million became refugees. Containment succeeded at enormous cost, and the Korean peninsula is still divided and heavily armed today.

The Korean War shaped subsequent American politics and society in critical ways. The stalemate frustrated Americans, who agreed with MacArthur that there was "no substitute for victory." But the ominous threat of nuclear weapons meant that wars had to be limited. The fighting in Korea enabled McCarthy and the Red Scare to dominate political life in the United States. Republican presidential nominee General Dwight Eisenhower was perhaps the most popular American alive because of his leadership of the Allied victory in Europe in World War II, and he swept into the White House in 1952 over Democrat Adlai Stevenson, the governor of Illinois.

A Cold War Society

Which were the most important changes in Americans' lives in the early Cold War era?

Expanding economic opportunities and narrowing political freedoms characterized American society in the first decade of the Cold War. Anticommunist repression pushed dissident views to the margins of the nation's political life. Americans largely accepted this new conformity for two reasons: their desire to support their government during international crises, especially the Korean War, and a consumer cornucopia that surrounded them with attractive material goods. Americans moved to the suburbs, and to the South and West.

By 1947 the United States was launching into an era of extraordinary economic expansion that continued for 25 years. Since Ben Franklin's time, Americans had been known for thrift in their pursuit of wealth, but after 1945 the long-cherished principle of delaying gratification declined steeply. "Buy now, pay later," General Motors urged as it offered an installment plan to customers. Diner's Club introduced the first credit card in 1950. In a formulation breathtaking for its distance from Puritan and immigrant traditions of saving for the future, writer William Whyte observed that "thrift is now un-American."

> *Expanding economic opportunities and narrowing political freedoms characterized American society in the first decade of the Cold War.*

Family Lives

View the Image
Levittown at **www.myhistorylab.com**

Many white Americans embraced the opportunity to move to the suburbs after World War II. Seeking larger homes and yards and quieter neighborhoods, they flocked to new developments such as Levittown outside New York City on Long Island. Suburbs did not welcome all, however. Even as federal courts struck down segregation laws in some spheres of American life, agencies such as the Veterans Administration and the Federal Housing Administration were encouraging residential separation by race. Private banks did the same. Other government policies, including highway construction and tax benefits for homeowners, promoted the growth of suburbs at the cost of cities. A third epoch in American residential history began by 1970 when more Americans resided in suburbs than cities, parallel to the 1920 shift from a rural majority to an urban one.

Suburban life encouraged a sharpening of gender roles among the growing middle class. Men commuted to work while women were expected to find fulfillment in marriage and motherhood, including a nearly full-time job of unpaid housework. Despite this partial retreat from wartime employment, however, fully one-third of American women continued to work for pay outside the home. The economic circumstances of most black women offered them little choice, and most wound up doing double housework: their own and that of families employing them as domestics.

From 1946 to 1964, women giving birth at a younger age to more children created the demographic bulge known as the baby boom. Large families reinforced the domestic focus of most women, putting the work of child-rearing at the center of their lives. Fatherhood became increasingly a badge of masculinity.

Married mothers were celebrated, but unmarried ones were rebuked. Despite the greater freedom of the war years, the sexual double standard remained in place, with women's virtue linked directly to virginity in a way that men's was not. Birth control devices such as the diaphragm were legal only for married women and only in certain states. Women seeking to terminate unwanted pregnancies had to consider illegal abortions, the only kind available before 1970; millions did so, including one-fifth of all married women and a majority of single women who became pregnant. Two studies of American sexual behavior by Dr. Alfred Kinsey of Indiana University in 1948 and 1953 shocked the public with their revelation of widespread premarital and extramarital sexual intercourse as well as homosexual liaisons.

The Growth of the South and the West

Before World War II, American cultural, industrial, and financial power had always been centered in the urban North, but federal expenditures during the war began to change this. The U.S. Army built most of its training bases in the South, where land close to the coasts was thinly populated and inexpensive. Military bases and defense industries sprang up along the West Coast to project power into the Pacific against Japan. U.S. troops built the Alcan (Alaska–Canada) Highway, and millions of GIs passed through Hawaii en route to the Pacific battlefront. Fighting against the Japanese to defend Pearl Harbor and the Aleutian Islands brought the once-distant territories of Hawaii and Alaska more into Americans' consciousness, setting them on the path to statehood in 1959.

The **Sunbelt** of the South, the Southwest, and California grew rapidly after the war, whereas older Rustbelt cities of the Northeast and Midwest began to lose manufacturing jobs and population. Like the 440,000 people who moved to Los Angeles during the war, postwar migrants to California and Arizona appreciated the weather and the economic opportunities. Military spending underwrote half the jobs in California during the first decade of the Cold War. Migrants from south of the border, meanwhile, found work primarily in California's booming agricultural sector.

Two industries particularly stimulated the growth of the Sunbelt: cars and air conditioning. Automobiles helped shape the economies of western states, where new cities were built out of sprawling suburbs. New car sales shot up from 70,000 in 1945 to 7.9 million in 1955. Inexpensive gasoline, refined from the abundant crude oil of Texas and Oklahoma, powered

◉─ See the **Map**
Population Shifts, 1940–1950 at
www.myhistorylab.com

■ A new cloverleaf intersection on a freeway arches across the northern New Jersey suburbs in 1949. Multilane, limited-access highways became common after World War II. A new word, "smog" (from smoke and fog), appeared to describe the urban pollution caused by trucks and commuter vehicles.

this fleet. Automobile exhaust pipes replaced industrial smokestacks as the primary source of air pollution. Air conditioning also became widely available after World War II and contributed to the breakdown of the South's regional distinctiveness. From Miami and Atlanta to Houston and Washington, D.C., the new Sunbelt depended on the indoor comfort brought by controlling summertime heat and humidity.

Harry Truman and the Limits of Liberal Reform

On the political front, the onset of the Cold War narrowed the range of American political discourse. In seeking to consolidate the New Deal legacy, President Truman found himself boxed in by conservative Republican opponents. Allied governments in western Europe had embraced the idea that access to health care was a right of every citizen in a modern democratic state. But when Truman proposed a system of national health care, conservatives quashed his proposal in Congress.

Perhaps the most blatant omission of the New Deal had been protection against racial discrimination. Now, as the Cold War intensified, the fact that millions of Americans still lacked basic guarantees for their civil rights was an embarrassing contradiction to rhetoric about ensuring rights and liberties throughout the "free world." Truman campaigned for reelection in 1948 on a platform of support for civil rights that was unprecedented in the White House. That summer he ordered the desegregation of the armed forces and the federal civil service.

African-American voters in Chicago, Cleveland, and other northern cities played a key role in swing states; their solid support lifted Truman to a narrow and surprising victory over the heavily favored Republican candidate, New York governor Thomas Dewey. Truman's reelection was all the more impressive because of the fracturing of the Democratic party. Alienated by the civil rights plank, white Southerners walked out of the Democratic convention and ran South Carolina governor Strom Thurmond as an independent candidate. The "Dixiecrats" won four states in the Deep South, foreshadowing the abandonment by white Southerners of the party of their parents in the 1960s. Truman won as a man of the moderately liberal center, fierce against communism, usually supportive of the rights of organized labor, and opposed to discrimination.

Cold War Politics at Home

In a pattern that became known as **McCarthyism**, mostly Republican conservatives blamed liberal Democrats in the administration for communist successes abroad—especially in China and Korea—and accused them of sympathizing with and even spying for the Soviet Union. The hunt for domestic subversives to explain international setbacks was grounded in the reality of a handful of actual Soviet spies, most notably Julius Rosenberg (executed for treason in 1953 along with his apparently innocent wife, Ethel) and nuclear scientist Klaus Fuchs. But this second Red Scare expressed primarily the frustration of being unable to translate vast U.S. power into greater control of world events. And it served, above all, to cast suspicion on the patriotism of liberals at home.

Despite his general support for civil liberties, Truman helped set the tone for pursuing suspected traitors. In an unsuccessful effort to fortify his right flank against Republican attacks, he established a federal employee loyalty program in March 1947 as the domestic equivalent of the Truman Doctrine. Attorney General Tom Clark drew up a list of supposedly subversive organizations that the FBI and state committees on "un-American activities" then hounded. In a case with sobering implications for free speech, federal courts in 1949

TABLE 24-2

The Election of 1952

Candidate	Political Party	Popular Vote (%)	Electoral Vote
Dwight D. Eisenhower	Republican	55.1	442
Adlai E. Stevenson	Democratic	44.4	89

convicted the leaders of the U.S. Communist party of promoting the overthrow of the U.S. government. Words alone, the courts ruled, could be treasonable—the same logic as the wartime Sedition Act of 1918 (see Chapter 20).

Republicans reaped the benefits of the Red Scare. Most Americans who had sympathized in any way with the Soviet Union in the Depression years were by the late 1940s merely liberal Democrats, but the House Un-American Activities Committee (HUAC) zeroed in on their earlier records. Investigating Hollywood, the television industry, and universities as well as the executive branch of the U.S. government, HUAC destroyed the careers of prominent figures as well as average Americans.

The era found its name in the previously obscure junior senator from Wisconsin, Republican Joseph McCarthy. With a single speech in Wheeling, West Virginia, on February 9, 1950, this ambitious politician soared to prominence. "I have here in my hand a list of 205" Communist party members working in the State Department, he declared. Over the next four years, the numbers and names changed as McCarthy stayed one step ahead of the evidence while intimidating witnesses before his Senate subcommittee. He talked about communists, but his show was about Democrats. As the war in Korea raged, he mercilessly red-baited (attacked as "soft" on communism) the Truman administration. But after the Republican electoral victory in 1952, his excesses lost their partisan utility. With the end of the war in Korea and his ill-advised attacks on the U.S. Army as supposedly infiltrated by communists (the Army-McCarthy hearings), he was at last censured by his Senate colleagues in 1954 and died an early, alcohol-related death in 1957.

●●●—|Read the **Document**
McCarthy, Wheeling, WV Speech at
www.myhistorylab.com

> *McCarthy talked about communists, but his show was about Democrats. As the war in Korea raged, he mercilessly red-baited the Truman administration.*

Who Is a Loyal American?

The Cold War politics of inclusion and exclusion established a new profile for loyal Americans. Private familial and material concerns were expected to replace public interest in social reform. Anticommunists launched a withering assault on homosexuals as "perverts" and threats to the nation's security. Church membership climbed in tandem with condemnations of "godless Communism," and Congress added the words "under God" to the Pledge of Allegiance. Discrimination against Roman Catholics and Jews, though still evident, declined as Catholics such as McCarthy proved intensely anticommunist and as pictures and stories emerged to reveal the horrors of the Nazi Holocaust against the Jews. More inclusive references to the "Judeo-Christian tradition" became common.

American leadership of the global anticommunist cause strengthened the struggle for racial equality at home, within certain limits. The NAACP and most African Americans took an anticommunist position in accord with Truman, in return for his support of civil rights. They downplayed their concern for colonial independence in Africa and Asia to support NATO. The American GI Forum (Latino veterans) and the Japanese American Citizen League also worked within the confines of Cold War politics to end discrimination.

For impoverished Native Americans, the government seemed to give with one hand and take away with the other. In 1946 Truman established the Indian Claims Commission to consider payment for lands taken and treaties broken. But Dillon S. Myer, director of the Bureau of Indian Affairs, closed reservation schools, withdrew support for traditional cultural activities, and launched an urban relocation program, all intended to move Native Americans into the mainstream and get the government "out of the Indian business."

Immigrants, too, received mixed messages. The McCarran-Walter Act (1952) ended the long-standing ban on allowing people of Asian descent not born in the United States to become U.S. citizens. But it preserved the discriminatory 1924 system of "national origins" for allocating numbers of immigrants from different countries. The bill also strengthened the attorney general's authority to deport aliens who were suspected of subversive intentions.

■ From 1951 to 1953, Mexican American miners went on strike against the Empire Zinc Mining Company in Silver City, New Mexico. Women took on major roles in this labor action, which inspired a famous movie, *Salt of the Earth*. Defiant in the face of police and company shotguns and billy clubs, Elvira Molano (center) served as cochair of the union negotiating committee and became known as "the most arrested woman" during the strike.

CONCLUSION

McCarthyism at home and the war in Korea ensured a generation of hostility between the United States and China. It tied the People's Republic more closely to the USSR, strengthening the common belief that international communism was a unified movement. The United States committed itself to defending Taiwan from recapture by the Beijing government. The Korean War also jump-started the moribund Japanese economy as American dollars poured into Japan, where the U.S. war effort was based.

Frustrations with the course of war in Korea affirmed the inward focus of American society in the 1950s. Despite the organizing efforts of political activists such as civil rights workers, most citizens seemed to look increasingly to their personal and familial lives for satisfaction and meaning. From the powerful U.S. economy flowed an unprecedented river of consumer goods, including the new artificial materials—plastic, vinyl, nylon, polyester, Styrofoam—that have pervaded and polluted American life ever since. As peace came to Korea and U.S. soldiers returned from across the Pacific, Americans sought the good life at home.

For Review

✓●─Study and Review at www.myhistorylab.com

1. Which were the most important causes of the Cold War?

2. How were the Cold War and the struggle for decolonization related to each other?

3. In which ways did family life change for Americans in the late 1940s and early 1950s?

4. How were McCarthyism and the Korean War connected?

Chronology: 1945–1953

1945 Harry S. Truman becomes president upon death of Roosevelt.
Atomic bombs dropped on Hiroshima and Nagasaki.
V-E Day (May 8); V-J Day (August 14).
United Nations created.

1946 *Morgan v. West Virginia* outlaws segregation in interstate transportation.
Winston Churchill gives "Iron Curtain" speech, Fulton, Missouri.

1947 Jackie Robinson joins Brooklyn Dodgers.
Taft-Hartley Act limits labor union activities.
Truman Doctrine of containing communism announced.

1948 New Mexico and Arizona grant Indians right to vote.
Modern state of Israel founded.
U. S. armed services desegregated.

1949 Billy Graham launches his first evangelical crusade in Los Angeles.
Establishment of People's Republic of China.
USSR acquires nuclear weapons.

1950 Sen. Joseph McCarthy accuses State Department of harboring communists.
North Korean troops invade South Korea.

1951 Ethel and Julius Rosenberg convicted of treason.

1952 Dwight Eisenhower elected president.

1953 Korean War ends.

Key Terms

Cold War The conflict and competition between the United States and the Soviet Union (and their respective allies) that emerged after 1945 and lasted until 1989. p. 554

Colonialism The centuries-old system of mostly European nations controlling and governing peoples and lands outside of Europe. p. 561

Communism A totalitarian form of government, grounded in the theories of German philosopher Karl Marx and the practices of V. I. Lenin in Russia, that eliminated private ownership of property in supposed pursuit of complete human equality; the system of government also featured a centrally directed economy and the absolute rule of a small group of leaders. p. 554

Containment The U.S. policy during the Cold War of trying to halt the expansion of Soviet and communist influences. p. 559

McCarthyism The political campaign led by Senator Joseph McCarthy (R-Wisconsin) to blame liberals at home for setbacks to U.S. interests abroad, due to what he considered liberals' sympathies with communism. p. 570

National security state The reorientation of the U.S. government and its budget after 1945 toward a primary focus on military and intelligence capabilities. p. 564

NSC-68 The 1950 directive of the National Security Council that called for rolling back, rather than merely containing, Soviet and communist influences. p. 564

Sunbelt The band of states from the Southeast to the Southwest that experienced rapid economic and population growth during and after World War II. p. 569

Truman Doctrine President Truman's March 1947 speech articulating the new policy of containment. p. 561

PART NINE

The Cold War at Full Tide, 1953–1979

URING THE THIRD QUARTER OF THE TWENTIETH CENTURY, THE Cold War cast a long shadow over the United States and the rest of the world. Tensions mounted at home and abroad as the United States and the Soviet Union vied for power among the world's nations. In poor Third World countries, insurgents attempted to throw off the yoke of colonialism and play the two superpowers against each other. The United States used different strategies to counter Soviet influence in Latin America, Africa, the Middle East, and Southeast Asia, including military force in Korea and Vietnam, white-knuckle diplomacy in Cuba, extensive aid to nonaligned countries, and covert operations worldwide.

Soviet advances in science and technology spurred the U.S. government to sponsor bold new domestic initiatives in public education and space exploration. The Cold War even helped to shape a post–World War II domestic ideal: a nuclear family living in a suburban house, with a breadwinner father and a full-time homemaker mother. Many Americans believed that their prosperous, consumer-oriented economy, with its emphasis on individualism and personal choice, was a key weapon in the fight against communism.

In a feverish arms race, both the United States and the USSR rushed to stockpile weapons of mass destruction. Innovations in nuclear weapons technology (such as intercontinental ballistic missiles) made the bombers used in World War II obsolete. The hydrogen bomb, tested successfully for the first time in 1953, dwarfed the power of the atomic bomb that had leveled Hiroshima. Nevertheless, citizens who criticized the arms buildup risked being branded unpatriotic. More than ever before, domestic policy was intertwined with foreign policy.

The rise of multinational corporations meant that large, impersonal institutions, whether government or private, were shaping American life. Middle-level managers—men in "grey flannel suits"—represented the corporate ethos of loyalty to the company above all else. At the same time, many Americans sought to work within their local communities for social and political change. In the South, African-American men and women launched a dramatic assault on the system of legal segregation known as "Jim Crow." Working at the grassroots level, these activists boycotted buses, marched, engaged in sit-ins at lunch counters, and went to jail. Their efforts provoked the courts and Congress to act, culminating in the Civil Rights Acts of 1964 and 1965. For the first time in American history, the federal government assumed responsibility for eliminating discrimination in the workplace and guaranteeing all its citizens the right to vote.

Other groups also organized and entered the political arena. Indians, disabled Americans, California farm workers, and gay men and lesbians all formed organizations to counter discrimination and advance their civil rights. The women's movement affected all aspects of American society, enabling women to play a fuller role in the nation's political and economic life. A new environmental movement secured legislation protecting wilderness areas and endangered species and ensuring that Americans had clean air to breathe and clean water to drink.

Lyndon B. Johnson assumed the presidency after John F. Kennedy was assassinated in 1963. Johnson hoped to revitalize the New Deal legacy by expanding social welfare programs. His program, the Great Society, sought to address seemingly intractable problems such as poverty, lack of health care for the elderly, and the deterioration of inner-city neighborhoods. But Johnson also expanded the U.S. military presence in Vietnam, an effort that cost an increasing number of American lives. Even constant bombing proved futile to stem the civil war that pitted Americans and anticommunist Vietnamese against the National Liberation Front of South Vietnam and their comrades in the north. Johnson's successor, Richard M. Nixon, was also mired in a war that was increasingly unpopular among Americans.

Protests against the war in the late 1960s and early 1970s highlighted an emerging youth culture. The baby boom generation, born in the two decades after World War II, embraced sexual freedom and new forms of music (such as rock 'n' roll) in an apparent attempt to defy their parents and "the Establishment" in general. Many Americans felt betrayed by both Johnson and Nixon, believing that tens of thousands of American soldiers had died in vain in Vietnam. The Watergate break-in at Democratic headquarters, leading eventually to Nixon's resignation, contributed to a growing, widespread disenchantment with government authority.

By the late 1970s, developments abroad had greatly complicated Cold War politics. Middle Eastern oil-producing nations imposed an oil embargo on the United States, highlighting U.S. dependence on fossil fuels. Islamic fundamentalists were beginning to retaliate violently against the spread of American influence and culture in Muslim countries. And at home, a conservative backlash emerged to counter the expansion of the welfare state, the heightened visibility of the feminist movement, and widening civil rights protests.

1968 Martin Luther King Jr. assassinated
Robert Kennedy assassinated
My Lai massacre
Wild and Scenic Rivers Act
Tet offensive

1969 Huge antiwar protests in Washington, D.C.
Indians occupy Alcatraz, San Francisco Bay
Stonewall raid, New York City
Astronauts Neil Armstrong and Buzz Aldrin walk on the moon

1970 United States invades Cambodia
National Guardsmen kill four students, Kent State University

1971 Pentagon Papers published
Nixon administration creates "plumbers" for illegal activities

1972 Watergate break-in
Nixon visits China
Founding of *Ms.* magazine

1973 *Roe v. Wade* legalizes abortion
American Indian Movement members occupy Wounded Knee
Endangered Species Act
OPEC oil embargo
American troops withdrawn from Vietnam

1974 Nixon resigns; Gerald R. Ford becomes president

1975 *Mayaguez* incident
Vietnam reunified under communist rule
Congressional investigations of CIA covert operations

1976 Hyde Amendment prohibits use of Medicaid funds for abortions
Nation celebrates bicentennial

1977 President Jimmy Carter issues general amnesty for draft evaders
Trans-Alaska pipeline system completed
ABC airs miniseries *Roots*, based on book by Alex Haley

1978 *Bakke* Supreme Court decision
California Proposition 13

1979 Camp David peace accords
Partial meltdown of nuclear core at Three Mile Island nuclear plant
Iranian Revolution

25

Domestic Dreams and Atomic Nightmares, 1953–1963

CHAPTER OUTLINE

Cold War, Warm Hearth

The Civil Rights Movement

The Eisenhower Years

Outsiders and Opposition

The Kennedy Era

Conclusion

I
n 1959, Vice President Richard M. Nixon traveled to Moscow in the Soviet Union to visit the American National Exhibition, a showcase of American consumer goods and leisure equipment. The main attraction of the exhibition was a full-size, six-room, ranch-style house. In a heated debate with Soviet Premier Nikita Khrushchev at the opening of the exhibition, Nixon extolled the virtues of the American way of life while his opponent promoted the communist system. The two leaders did not discuss missiles, bombs, or government. Rather, they argued over the relative merits of American and Soviet washing machines, televisions, and electric ranges in what came to be known as the "Kitchen Debate," one of the most noted verbal sparring matches of the century.

The model home filled with consumer goods and appliances offered tangible proof, Nixon claimed, of the superiority of free enterprise over communism: "To us, diversity, the right to choose, . . . is the most important thing. We don't have one decision made at the top by one government official. . . . We have many different manufacturers and many different kinds of washing machines so that the housewives have a choice. . . . Would it not be better to compete in the relative merits of washing machines than in the strength of rockets?"

Nixon called attention to a built-in, panel-controlled washing machine. "In America," he said, "these [washing machines] are designed to make things easier for our women." Khrushchev countered Nixon's boast of comfortable American housewives by expressing pride in productive Soviet female workers. The Soviets, he claimed, did not share that "capitalist attitude toward women."

According to American journalists, Nixon's knockout punch in his verbal bout with the Soviet premier was his description of the American postwar domestic dream: successful breadwinners supporting attractive homemakers in well-appointed, comfortable homes. The American National Exhibition in Moscow seemed to demonstrate the superiority of the American way of life.

Scientific discoveries in the 1950s also inaugurated the modern era of exploration beyond Earth's atmosphere, fueled by the space race between the United States and the Soviet Union. The National Aeronautics and Space Administration (NASA), established in 1958, sent the first American into space in 1961. But science also brought pesticides, smog, and other pollutants. Americans at the time rarely considered the environmental consequences of consumer goods, cars, petrochemicals, or nuclear power.

The decade from 1953 to 1963, under the presidencies of Dwight Eisenhower and John Kennedy, was a time of expansive optimism

■ **Vice President Richard M. Nixon and Soviet Premier Nikita Khrushchev touring the 1959 American National Exhibition in Moscow.**

about the future. Hawaii and Alaska became states in 1959. The **baby boom** demonstrated widespread faith in the future for American children. It was also a decade of growth for U.S. influence abroad, the domestic economy, consumer culture, and television. Suburbs, highways, and shopping malls expanded to meet the needs of increasing numbers of families with young children. Some teenagers and others rebelled against what they saw as conformity in American life. But African Americans organized in the civil rights movement to gain full access to the freedoms and comforts of this increasingly middle-class society.

It was also a decade of anxiety. Americans worried about the perils of the atomic age as the nuclear arsenals of both superpowers continued to grow. Science fiction films about alien invaders reflected concerns about foreign dangers. The Soviet Union's 1957 launching of *Sputnik*, the first artificial satellite to orbit the Earth, alarmed Americans and forced the nation to confront the possibility of Soviet technological superiority. The United States appeared to be at the height of its strength and power, yet at the same time, more vulnerable than ever before.

Cold War, Warm Hearth

The postwar era was a time of deep divisions in American society, yet in certain ways Americans behaved with remarkable conformity. This is especially evident in the overwhelming embrace of the nuclear family. The GI Bill, with its provisions for home mortgage loans, enabled veterans of modest means to purchase homes. Although residential segregation prevailed throughout the postwar era, limiting most suburban developments to prosperous white middle- and

In what ways did the suburban family home promote Cold War ideology?

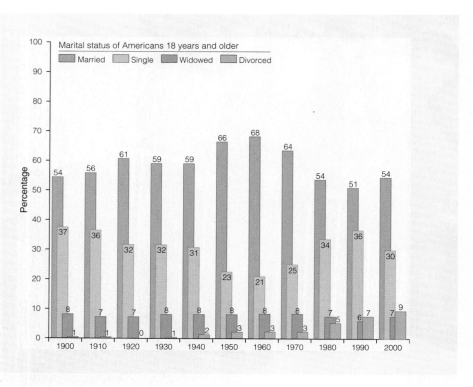

■ **FIGURE 25.1**
MARITAL STATUS OF THE U.S. ADULT POPULATION, 1900–2000
Following World War II, Americans married in record numbers. The high rate of marriage corresponded with a relatively low divorce rate. Beginning in the 1970s, the marriage rate plummeted and the divorce rate rose dramatically.

working-class families, many veterans of color were able to buy their first homes. Americans of all racial, ethnic, and religious groups, of all socioeconomic classes and educational levels, brought the marriage rate up and the divorce rate down. The "American way of life" embodied in the suburban nuclear family, as a cultural ideal if not a universal reality, motivated countless postwar Americans to strive for it, to live by its codes, and—for Americans of color—to demand it.

Consumer Spending and the Suburban Ideal

Between 1947 and 1961, national income increased more than 60 percent. Rather than putting this money aside for a rainy day, Americans were inclined to spend it. Investing in one's home, along with the trappings that would enhance family life, seemed the best way to plan for a secure future.

Between 1950 and 1970, the suburban population more than doubled, from 36 million to 74 million. Fully 20 percent of the population remained poor during this prosperous time. But most families of ample as well as modest means exhibited a great deal of conformity in their consumer behavior, reflecting widely shared beliefs about the good life. They poured their money into homes, domestic appliances, televisions, automobiles, and family vacations.

Nuclear families who settled in the suburbs provided the foundation for new types of community life and leisure pursuits, sometimes at the expense of older ones grounded in ethnic neighborhoods and kinship networks. Family-oriented amusement parks such as Disneyland in Anaheim, California, which opened in 1955, catered to middle-class tastes, in contrast to older venues such as Coney Island, known for thrill rides, class and ethnic mixing, and romantic environments. Religious affiliation rose to an all-time high as Americans built and joined suburban churches and synagogues, complete with youth programs and summer camps.

In 1949 fewer than 1 million American homes had a television. Within the next four years, the number soared to 20 million.

The Cold War made a profound contribution to suburban sprawl. Congress passed the Federal-Aid Highway Act of 1956, which provided $100 billion for building 41,000 miles of national highways. When President Dwight D. Eisenhower signed the bill into law, he stated one of the major reasons for the new highway system: "[In] case of atomic attack on our key cities, the road net must permit quick evacuation of target areas."

The worst-case scenario was communist takeover and the defeat of the United States in the Cold War. Pentagon strategists and foreign policy experts feared that the Soviet Union might gain the military might to allow its territorial expansion and, eventually, world domination. But observers also worried that the real dangers to America were internal: racial strife, emancipated women, class conflict, and family disruption. Most postwar Americans longed for security after years of economic depression and war, and they saw family stability as the best bulwark against the new dangers of the Cold War.

Race, Class, and Domesticity

After World War II, the nation faced a severe housing shortage. The federal government gave developers financial subsidies to build affordable single-family homes and offered Federal Housing Authority (FHA) loans and income tax deductions to homebuyers. These benefits enabled white working-class and middle-class families to purchase houses. Postwar prosperity, government subsidies, and the promise of assimilation made it possible for white-skinned Americans of immigrant background to blend into the suburbs.

■ Commuters, mostly men, left their suburban homes each morning to go to jobs in the cities, returning home at night. Suburbs served as "bedroom communities," inhabited mostly by women and children during the day.

Despite the expansion of the black and Latino middle class and the increase in home ownership among racial minorities, most suburban developments excluded nonwhites. The FHA and lending banks maintained policies known as **red lining**, which designated certain neighborhoods off limits to racial minorities. Although Americans of color remained concentrated in urban and rural areas, some did move to the suburbs, usually into segregated communities.

For Americans of color, suburban home ownership offered inclusion in the postwar American dream. In her powerful 1959 play *A Raisin in the Sun*, African-American playwright Lorraine Hansberry eloquently articulated the importance of a suburban home, not to assimilate into white America but to live as a black family with dignity and pride. Asian Americans also had good reason to celebrate home and family life. With the end of the exclusion of Chinese immigrants during World War II, wives and war brides began to enter the country, helping to build thriving family-oriented communities. After the disruptions and anguish of internment, Japanese Americans were eager to put their families and lives back together. Mexican Americans and Mexican immigrants, including *braceros*, established

■ **At a time when many corporations and professions excluded African Americans, many black entrepreneurs opened their own establishments to serve their own communities. This black-owned dress shop in Chicago catered to middle-class African American women.**

flourishing communities in the Southwest. Puerto Ricans migrated to New York and other eastern cities, where they could quadruple their wages on the island.

Racial segregation did not prevail everywhere. In Shaker Heights, Ohio, a suburb of Cleveland, white residents decided, as a community, to integrate their neighborhood. Drawing on postwar liberal ideals of civil rights and racial integration, they welcomed black homeowners. Their effort succeeded by emphasizing class similarity over racial difference. White residents encouraged other white families to move into Shaker Heights, pointing out that their prosperous black neighbors were "just like us."

As residents and businesses migrated to the suburbs, slum housing and vacant factories remained in the central cities. The Housing Acts of 1949 and 1954 granted funds to municipalities for urban renewal. However, few of those federal dollars provided low-income housing. Mayors, bankers, and real estate interests used the money to bulldoze slums and build gleaming office towers, civic centers, and apartment complexes for affluent citizens, leaving the poor to fend for themselves in the remaining dilapidated corners of the cities.

Although intended to revitalize cities, urban renewal actually accelerated the decay of inner cities and worsened conditions for the urban poor. Federally funded projects often disrupted and destroyed ethnic communities. In Los Angeles, the Dodgers' stadium built in Chavez Ravine offered baseball fans access to the national pastime, but it destroyed the historically rooted Mexican-American neighborhood in its path. The $5 million project displaced 7,500 people and demolished 900 homes.

Along with the urban poor, rural Americans reaped few benefits of postwar affluence. The 1950s marked the greatest out-migration from the South as the mechanization of farms—particularly the mechanical cotton picker—reduced the number of workers on the land. More than one-fourth of the population left Kentucky and West Virginia, where unemployment in some areas reached 80 percent.

Women: Back to the Future

The nuclear family ideal of the 1950s included a full-time wife and mother and a breadwinner husband. This vision of domesticity marked a giant step backward for many women, whose opportunities and experiences had expanded dramatically during World War II. The elevation of the housewife as a cultural icon contrasted sharply with the reality. The proportion of women who fit the mold of full-time homemaker was rapidly shrinking. Although most American women married, had children, and carried the lion's share of responsibility for housework and child-rearing, increasing numbers of married women also held jobs outside the home. The employment of married women began to rise during World War II and kept rising after the war, even though most of the well-paying and highly skilled jobs returned to men at the war's end.

Many women worked part-time while their children were at school, as they considered themselves homemakers not wage earners. With few other opportunities for creative work, women embraced their domestic roles and turned homemaking into a profession. Many fulfilled their role with pride and satisfaction and extended their energies and talents into their communities, where they made important contributions as volunteers in local parent-teacher associations (PTAs) and other civic organizations. Some expanded part-time employment into full-time occupations when their children left the nest. Others felt bored and frustrated and drowned their sorrow with alcohol or tranquilizers. In 1963 author Betty Friedan described the constraints facing women as the "problem that has no name" in her feminist manifesto *The Feminine Mystique.*

Education was one avenue available to women, as students as well as teachers. But higher education did not open its doors fully to women. Because few women gained access to graduate and professional schools and most well-paying jobs were reserved for men, college degrees for white women did not necessarily open up career opportunities or greatly improve their job and earning prospects. By 1956 one-fourth of white female students married while still in college. Many of these women dropped out of school to take jobs to support their husbands through college. But the situation was different for black women. Like their mothers and grandmothers, most black women had to work to help support their families. Job prospects for black women generally were limited to menial, low-paying occupations. Young black women knew that a college degree could mean the difference between working as a maid for a white family and working as a secretary, teacher, or nurse. Although few in number, more than 90 percent of black women who entered college completed their degrees.

Black women also aspired to the role of homemaker, but for very different reasons than white women. Although poverty still plagued large numbers of black citizens, the black middle class expanded during the 1950s. Postwar prosperity enabled some African Americans, for the first time, a family life in which the earnings of men were adequate to allow women to stay home with their own children rather than tending to the houses and children of white families. For black women, domesticity meant "freedom and independence in her own home." It is no wonder that in the early 1960s, women of color bristled when white feminists such as Betty Friedan called upon women to break free from the "chains" of domesticity.

The Civil Rights Movement

As the civil rights movement gained momentum in the South, African-American activists faced fierce opposition from local white authorities and contempt from national leaders. Persistent racial discrimination proved to be the nation's worst embarrassment throughout the Cold War. The Soviet Union pointed to American race relations as an indication of the hypocrisy and failure of the American promise of freedom for all. Yet national leaders paid only

What were the major goals of the civil rights movement in the 1950s?

lip service to racial justice and failed to provide the strong support necessary to defeat the system of racial segregation in the South known as "Jim Crow," a legal, or *de jure*, set of institutions that prevailed throughout the South. Although the nation's leaders acknowledged the need to address Southern segregation, they did nothing to address the unofficial, or *de facto*, segregation that prevailed throughout the country.

Nevertheless, at the grassroots level, racial minorities continued to work for equal rights. For example, Mexican Americans in the Southwest pressed for desegregation of schools, residential neighborhoods, and public facilities through organizations such as the middle-class League of United Latin American Citizens (LULAC) and the Asociacion Nacional México-Americana (ANMA), a civil rights organization that emerged out of the labor movement. It was not until 1963 that the power of the civil rights movement—and the violence of southern white opposition—finally compelled the federal government to take action.

■ **Children in segregated schools studied in wretched physical conditions but benefited from dedicated African American teachers. The Supreme Court struck down school segregation in the landmark 1954 case *Brown v. Board of Education*, arguing in its unanimous decision that separate facilites were inherently unequal.**

Watch the Video

How did the Civil Rights Movement change American Schools? at **www.myhistorylab.com**

Brown v. Board of Education

The first major success in the struggle to dismantle the Jim Crow system in the South came in the 1954 Supreme Court decision *Brown v. Board of Education*. Civil rights strategists decided to pursue their cause in the courts rather than through Congress. They knew that southern Democrats in Congress, who held disproportionate power there, would block any civil rights legislation that came before the House or Senate. They believed that they had a better chance of success through the courts.

NAACP lawyers filed suit against the Topeka, Kansas, Board of Education on behalf of Linda Brown, a black child in a segregated school. They were targeting the 1896 *Plessy v. Ferguson* decision, which justified Jim Crow laws on the grounds that they provided "separate but equal" facilities. The case reached the U.S. Supreme Court, where NAACP general counsel Thurgood Marshall argued that separate facilities, by definition, denied African Americans their equal rights as citizens.

Read the Document

Brown V. Board of Ed of Topeka, Kansas at **www.myhistorylab.com**

In 1953, during the three-year period that the Supreme Court had the *Brown* case before it, President Eisenhower appointed Earl Warren as chief justice. Warren had been state attorney general and then governor of California during World War II and had approved the internment of Japanese Americans—a decision he later deeply regretted. He now used his political and legal skills to strike a blow for justice. He knew that such a critical case needed a unanimous decision to win broad political support. One by one, he persuaded his Supreme Court colleagues of the importance of striking down segregation. On May 17, 1954, Warren delivered the historic unanimous ruling: "To separate [black children] from others of similar age and qualifications solely because of their race generates a feeling of inferiority as to their status in the community that may affect their hearts and minds in a way unlikely ever to be undone. . . . Separate educational facilities are inherently unequal."

White Resistance, Black Persistence

The *Brown* case was a great triumph, but it was only the first step. Desegregation would be meaningful only when it was enforced, and that was another matter entirely. At first, there seemed to be cause for optimism as many white officials in the South seemed resigned to accept the decision. However, few were willing to initiate action to implement desegregation. Even the Supreme Court delayed its decision on implementation for a full year and then simply called for the process to begin "with all deliberate speed" but specified no timetable. Political leaders did not begin to work on the task, leaving sympathetic educators and eager black Americans with no support. President Eisenhower was not enthusiastic about racial integration. He said, "I don't think you can change the hearts of men with laws or decisions."

In 1955, the year after the *Brown* decision, white Mississippians murdered 14-year-old Emmett Till for allegedly whistling at a white woman. Till was from Chicago but was visiting relatives in Mississippi. His mutilated body was found in the Tallahatchie River. Although Till's killers later confessed to the murder, an all-white jury found them not guilty. Eisenhower remained silent about Till's murder and the travesty of justice, even when E. Frederick Morrow, his one black adviser, beseeched him to condemn the lynching.

Eisenhower's hands-off policy emboldened southern segregationists to resist the Supreme Court's desegregation decision. When it became clear that the federal government would not enforce the ruling, white resistance spread across the South. State legislatures passed resolutions vowing to protect segregation, and most southern congressmen signed the 1956 "Southern Manifesto," promising to oppose federal desegregation efforts.

A crisis at Central High School in Little Rock, Arkansas, finally forced Eisenhower to act. Under a federal court's order to desegregate, school officials were prepared to comply and had carefully mobilized community support. But Arkansas Governor Orville Faubus, facing re-election, instructed National Guard troops to maintain "order" by blocking the entry of black students into the school. Eisenhower initially refused to intervene in the crisis. Hoping for a compromise, he met with Faubus, who agreed to allow the school to integrate peacefully. But Faubus broke his word, withdrew the National Guard troops, and left Little Rock, leaving the black students unprotected.

On September 23, 1957, as nine black students attempted to enter Central High, a huge angry crowd of whites surrounded them. With international news cameras broadcasting pictures of the shrieking and menacing mob, Eisenhower was forced to federalize the Arkansas National Guard and send 1,000 paratroopers to Little Rock. Eisenhower acted to maintain federal authority rather than to support integration.

●◦◦—Read the Document
Executive Order 10730: Desegregation of Central HS at
www.myhistorylab.com

Eisenhower acted to maintain federal authority rather than to support integration.

Boycotts and Sit-Ins

Under Jim Crow laws in the South, black passengers were required to sit in the back section of buses, leaving the front of the bus for whites. If the "white" section at the front of the bus filled up, black passengers were required to give up their seats for white passengers. On December 1, 1955, Rosa Parks and the black community of Montgomery, Alabama, were ready to take on the system. Parks, who worked as a seamstress, was a widely respected leader in Montgomery's black community, active in her church, and secretary of the local NAACP. On her way home from work, sitting in the first row of the "colored" section of the bus when the front of the bus filled with passengers, she refused to move when a white man demanded her seat. Parks was arrested, and black Montgomery sprang into action.

Literally overnight, the Montgomery bus boycott was born. For 381 days, more than 90 percent of Montgomery's black citizens sacrificed their comfort and convenience for the sake of their rights and dignity. As one elderly black woman replied when a white reporter offered her a ride as she walked to work, "No, my feets is tired but my soul is rested."

■ **MAP 25.1**

MAJOR EVENTS OF THE AFRICAN AMERICAN CIVIL RIGHTS MOVEMENT, 1953–1963
Most of the major events of the early stages of the black freedom struggle took place in the South.
Black southerners formed the backbone of the movement, but the grassroots protest movement drew
participants from all regions of the country, all racial and ethnic groups, cities and rural areas, churches
and universities, old and young, lawyers and sharecroppers.

Martin Luther King Jr., pastor of the Dexter Avenue Baptist Church, was a newcomer to
Montgomery when the bus boycott began. He embraced the opportunity to become the leader
of the boycott and, eventually, the most powerful spokesperson for the civil rights movement.
As he told the 5,000 listeners who gathered in his church on the first night of the boycott, "If
you will protest courageously and yet with dignity and Christian love, in the history books
that are written in future generations, historians will have to pause and say, 'there lived a great
people—a black people—who injected a new meaning and dignity into the veins of civilization.' This is our challenge and our overwhelming responsibility."

The bus boycott ended a year later when the Supreme Court ruled that Montgomery's buses
must integrate, but the momentum generated by the boycott galvanized the civil rights movement. King and other leaders formed the Southern Christian Leadership Conference (SCLC),
which united black ministers across the South in the cause of civil rights. The boycott tactic
spread to other southern cities. As boycotts continued, a new strategy emerged: the **sit-in**.

On February 1, 1960, four African-American students at North Carolina Agricultural and
Technical College in Greensboro, inspired by the bus boycott, entered the local Woolworth
store and sat down at the lunch counter. When they were told "We do not serve Negroes," they
refused to leave, forcing the staff at Woolworth's to physically remove the nonviolent protesters. Undaunted, they returned to the lunch counter the next day with 23 classmates. By the
end of the week, more than a thousand students joined the protest. By this time, white gangs
had gathered, waving Confederate flags and menacing the black undergraduates. But the
students responded by waving American flags.

In May 1961, members of the Congress of Racial Equality (CORE) organized the Freedom Rides, in which black and white civil rights workers attempted to ride two interstate
buses from Washington, D.C., to New Orleans in an effort to challenge segregation at facilities
used in interstate travel. Their journey began peacefully, but when they reached Rock Hill,
South Carolina, a group of whites beat John Lewis, one of the young black riders, for entering

a whites-only rest room. In Anniston, Alabama, a mob slashed the tires of one of the buses, threw a fire bomb through a window, and pummeled the riders with fists and pipes. After the brutal beatings, reinforcements from the Student Nonviolent Coordinating Committee (SNCC) arrived to continue the Freedom Rides. They persevered, facing beatings along the way until they reached Jackson, Mississippi, where they were immediately arrested and jailed. The spirit and strength of the civil rights workers inspired many others to join them in the movement.

The Eisenhower Years

Dwight D. Eisenhower's presidency was notable for moderation, with few major new initiatives and leadership that rested more on his personal stature than his actions. Ike, as he was known, presided during a time of great prosperity and his policies encouraged business expansion. However, the former general did try to stem the defense buildup. In his farewell address as president, Eisenhower warned the nation against the growing power of the **military-industrial complex**, the term he coined to describe the armed forces and the politically powerful defense industries that supplied arms and equipment to them.

TABLE 25-1			
The Election of 1956			
Candidate	Political Party	Popular Vote (%)	Electoral Vote
Dwight D. Eisenhower	Republican	57.6	457
Adlai E. Stevenson	Democratic	42.1	73

The Middle of the Road

As president, Eisenhower pursued a path down the middle of the road. His probusiness legislative agenda and appointments pleased conservatives, and he placated liberals by extending many of the policies of the welfare state enacted during the New Deal. He agreed to the expansion of Social Security and unemployment compensation and an increase in the minimum wage. He also made concerted efforts to reduce defense spending, believing that continued massive military expenditures would hinder the nation's economic growth. In December 1953, Eisenhower announced the New Look, a streamlined military that relied less on expensive conventional ground forces and more on air power and advanced nuclear capabilities.

Eisenhower's plans to reduce defense spending derailed in 1957 when the Soviet Union launched *Sputnik*, the first artificial Earth satellite. Although *Sputnik* could not be seen with the naked eye—it was only 22 inches in diameter—it emitted a beeping noise that was broadcast by commercial radio stations in the United States, making its presence very real and causing near hysteria among the public. The Soviet's launching of *Sputnik II* a month later confirmed widespread fears that the United States was behind in the space race and, more significantly, in the arms race. Eisenhower's popularity in the polls suddenly dropped 22 points.

Acquiescing to his critics, the president increased funds for military, scientific, and educational spending. NASA, which developed the program of space exploration, was one result. But Eisenhower believed that "the most critical problem of all" was the lack of American scientists and engineers. He led the federal government to subsidize additional science and math training for both teachers and students.

Eisenhower's secretary of defense, former head of General Motors Charles Wilson, commented that "what's good for General Motors business is good for America." But not everyone agreed. Eisenhower's probusiness policies often harmed the nation's environment. He promoted the Submerged Land Act, which removed from federal jurisdiction more than $40 billion worth of oil-rich offshore lands. Under the control of state governments, oil companies

••▶ Read the **Document**
National Defense Education Act at
www.myhistorylab.com

could—and did—gain access to them. The *New York Times* called the act "one of the greatest and surely the most unjustified give-away programs" in the nation's history. The administration's willingness to allow businesses to expand with little regulation, and with virtually no concern for the environment, contributed to increasing pollution of the air, water, and land during the 1950s and helped spark the environmental movement of the 1960s and 1970s.

Eisenhower also supported the Federal-Aid Highway Act of 1956. As the largest public works project the nation had ever mounted, this centrally planned transportation system contributed to the national pastime of family road vacations and tourism. Cheap gas fueled America's car culture. Cars gave Americans increased mobility and enabled suburban dwellers to drive to work in the cities. But reliance on the automobile doomed the nation's passenger train system and led to the decline of public transportation. Cars also contributed to suburban sprawl, air pollution, and traffic jams.

Eisenhower's Foreign Policy

The New Look, while containing military spending, shifted American military priorities from reliance on conventional weapons to nuclear deterrence and covert operations. During Eisenhower's presidency, the United States and the Soviet Union both solidified their separate alliances. The 12 original NATO nations agreed that an attack on any one of them would be considered an attack on all, and they maintained a force to defend the West against a possible Soviet invasion. NATO expanded in 1952 to include Greece and Turkey, and West Germany joined in 1955. The Soviet Union formed a similar alliance, the Warsaw Pact, with the countries of eastern Europe. Confrontations between the United States and the Soviet Union over the fate of Europe gave way to subtle maneuvers regarding the Third World—a term originally referring to nonaligned nations in the Middle East, Africa, Asia, and Latin America.

After Joseph Stalin died in 1953, Nikita Khrushchev became the new leader of the Soviet Union and called for peaceful coexistence with the United States. To limit military expenditures and improve relations, the superpowers arranged high-level summit meetings. In 1955 delegates from the United States, the Soviet Union, Britain, and France met in Geneva. Although the meeting achieved little of substance, it set a tone of cooperation. In 1959 Khrushchev came to the United States, met with Eisenhower, and toured the country. Despite the Soviet downing of an American U-2 spy plane in 1960, the superpowers began to discuss arms limitation. Both countries agreed to limit aboveground testing of nuclear weapons because of the health and environmental risks such tests posed. Soviet negotiations with the United States did not, however, mean greater liberty in eastern Europe, where Soviet forces crushed a 1956 uprising in Hungary.

The Eisenhower administration distrusted countries that maintained neutrality in the Cold War, fearing that those not aligned with the United States might turn to communism and become allies of the Soviet Union. Through covert operations including coups and assassinations, the Central Intelligence Agency (CIA) manipulated governments around the world. In 1953 the CIA helped to overthrow the elected government in Iran—which had seized control of Western-owned oil fields in the country—and to restore the dictatorship of Shah Reza Pahlavi, whose unpopular Western-leaning regime would be overthrown by Muslim funda-

Anticommunism became the guiding principle behind nearly all U.S. foreign policy, taking precedence over other American ideals.

mentalists in 1979. The CIA helped overthrow the elected government of Jacobo Arbenz in Guatemala in 1954. U.S. officials considered Arbenz a communist because he sought to redistribute large tracts of land, much of it owned by the Boston-based United Fruit Company. In 1959 revolutionary leader Fidel Castro established a regime in Cuba based on socialist principles. His government took control of foreign-owned companies, including many owned by Americans, alarming U.S. officials and investors in Cuba. Eisenhower's hostility encouraged Castro to forge an alliance with the Soviet Union. The CIA then launched a plot to overthrow Castro. In 1960–1961, the CIA also helped orchestrate the overthrow and assassination of the charismatic left-leaning Patrice Lumumba, the first minister of the Republic of the Congo in Africa, soon after its independence from Belgium.

The Middle East became a focus for U.S. foreign policy under Eisenhower. When Egyptian leader Gamal Abdul Nasser nationalized the British-controlled Suez Canal in 1956, arguing that canal tolls would provide funds for a dam, the British government, with the help of France and Israel, launched an attack against Egypt to regain control of the canal. Although he distrusted Nasser, Eisenhower criticized Britain for trying to retain its imperial position in the Middle East, a move applauded by leaders in Africa and Asia. The episode weakened U.S. relations with Nasser, who forged ties with the Soviet Union. Eisenhower now feared that "Nasserism" might spread throughout the Middle East.

In the spring of 1957, Congress approved the Eisenhower Doctrine, a pledge to defend Middle Eastern countries "against overt armed aggression from any nation controlled by international communism." However, U.S. policymakers rarely distinguished between nationalist movements and designs by "international communism," which they defined as Soviet aggression. Because American leaders believed that struggles for national self-determination in Third World countries were inspired and supported by the Soviet Union, they used the Eisenhower Doctrine to provide justification for U.S. military intervention to support pro-Western governments.

Cultural Diplomacy

In addition to political and military interventions, American foreign policy during the early Cold War era promoted cultural relationships. Initiatives to promote international friendship and a positive view of the United States, especially in the developing world, were part of American "cultural diplomacy."

One of the earliest and most successful diplomats for American culture was Dr. Tom Dooley, known as the "jungle doctor." Dooley joined the U.S. Navy medical corps during World War II and remained in the navy reserves until 1950. After earning his medical degree, he moved to Southeast Asia, where he set up clinics to provide medical care for impoverished villagers. He quickly became a major celebrity. In a 1960 Gallup poll, Dooley was among the ten most admired Americans.

Dooley personified the complex legacy of U.S. cultural diplomacy during the early years of the Cold War. A practicing Catholic, he rejected the role of the religious missionary—a role tied to racism and imperialism in the anticolonial post–World War II years. Rather, Dooley promoted modernization and development, embracing an internationalist vision grounded in respect and appreciation for the local culture and customs of the people with whom he lived. As a result, he was the nation's most effective ambassador.

Dooley's zeal to help the people of Southeast Asia went beyond medical care. A passionate anticommunist, in 1956 he assisted the CIA and the U.S. Navy in leading the exodus of 900,000 Catholic refugees from newly created communist North Vietnam to South Vietnam, where the United States backed a noncommunist dictatorship under Ngo Dinh Diem. The CIA supported Dooley's efforts and helped publicize his cultural diplomacy.

Dooley's work in Southeast Asia provided essential medical care to people in need and also served American interests in the early years of the Cold War. But his decision to live and work in the remote villages of Laos was not based simply on self-sacrifice. As a homosexual, Dooley would have had a difficult life within the United States in the 1950s. Anticommunist crusaders purged homosexuals from government employment, and gay men and lesbians faced harassment, ostracism, and often the loss of their jobs. Dooley escaped this intense homophobia by creating communal living situations with other men in remote areas of Laos, far from public view. There he could keep his sexual orientation private. If he had remained in the United States, the anticommunists whose political passions he shared would have purged him from their ranks.

■ **MAP 25.2**
COLD WAR SPHERES OF INFLUENCE, 1953–1963
During the early years of the Cold War, the United States and the Soviet Union developed formal military alliances, most importantly NATO and the Warsaw Pact. The American and Soviet informal spheres of influence also included trading and cultural ties to other countries. Many independent nations, especially those just emerging from colonialism, remained neutral in the Cold War.

Outsiders and Opposition

The 1950s often are remembered for political and cultural complacency among white Americans, with opposition to the nation's institutions emanating from people of color. But an increasing number of young whites, in the South as well as North, joined the struggle for civil rights. Others were drawn to the music and dance of black America, especially the fusion of rhythm-and-blues with country-and-western, a form of early rock 'n' roll. Distinct types of protest also emerged from the white middle class: the rebellion of the Beats who rejected staid conformity, the stirrings of discontent among women, and the antinuclear and environmental movements. The arts rejected mainstream values, as Jackson Pollock and other abstract expressionist painters challenged artistic conventions and shifted the center of the art world from Paris to New York. Even the sexual revolution of the 1960s had its roots in widespread defiance of the rigid sexual codes of the 1950s.

One clue that all was not tranquil was the widespread panic that the nation's young were out of control. Adults worried about an epidemic of juvenile delinquency, blaming everything from parents to comic books. New celebrities such as movie stars Marlon Brando and James Dean portrayed misunderstood youth in rebellion against a corrupt and uncaring adult world. In their films, and in J. D. Salinger's now-classic novel *Catcher in the Rye*, young women and men strain against the authority and expectations of their parents and the adult world, dreaming of freedom and personal fulfillment.

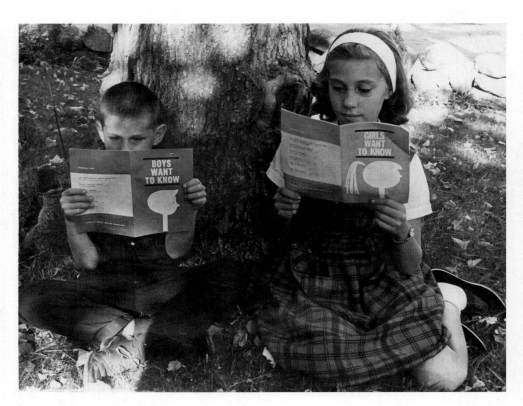

■ Since sex was rarely discussed in most middle-class families, many parents relied on schools to provide elementary sex education, and a generation of suburban children learned the facts of life from nervous teachers and a variety of simplified texts.

Sexual mores were rigid in the 1950s—and widely violated. Single young women who became pregnant faced disgrace and ostracism unless they married quickly, which many did. Abortion, which had been illegal since the late nineteenth century but tacitly accepted until after World War II, became increasingly difficult to obtain, with hospitals placing new restrictions on legal therapeutic abortions. A double standard encouraged men to pursue sexual conquest as a mark of manhood and virility but tarnished the reputation of women who engaged in sexual intercourse prior to marriage.

In many ways, the youth of the 1950s were already undermining the constraints that toppled in the next decade. Nowhere is this more obvious than in the explosion of rock 'n' roll, with its roots in African-American rhythm-and-blues, its raw sexuality, and its jubilant rebelliousness. Rock 'n' roll emerged from the fusion of musical traditions among artists from many ethnic backgrounds. Jewish songwriters Jerry Leiber and Mike Stoller wrote songs such as "Hound Dog" for black artists such as Willie Mae Thornton that were later recorded by white Southerner Elvis Presley. The first Mexican-American rock 'n' roll star, Ritchie Valens, sang ballads such as "Donna" along with jazzed-up versions of Mexican folk songs such as "La Bamba."

Rebellious Men

Men, too, were in revolt. According to widely read studies of the time, such as William Whyte's *The Organization Man* and David Reisman's *The Lonely Crowd*, middle-class men were forced into boring, routinized jobs, groomed to be "outer-directed" at the expense of their inner lives, and saddled with the overwhelming burden of providing for ever-growing families with insatiable consumer desires.

A few highly visible American men provided alternative visions. Hugh Hefner built his Playboy empire by offering men the trappings of the "good life" without its burdensome responsibilities. The Playboy ethic encouraged men to enjoy the sexual pleasures of attractive women without the chains of marriage and to pursue the rewards of consumerism in well-appointed "bachelor flats" rather than appliance-laden homes. *Playboy* magazine celebrated this lifestyle.

Beat poets, writers, and artists offered a different type of escape. In literary works such as Allen Ginsberg's poem *Howl* and Jack Kerouac's novel *On the Road*, and in their highly publicized lives, the Beats celebrated freedom from conformity, eccentric artistic expression, playful obscenity, experimentation with drugs, open homosexuality, and male bonding. While eschewing the luxurious consumerism Hefner extolled, the Beats shared with *Playboy* a vision of male rebellion against conformity and responsibility. The mainstream men who indulged in these fantasies were more likely to enjoy them vicariously than to bolt from the breadwinner role. The dads who were honored on the new consumer holiday of Father's Day far outnumbered the freewheeling Beats and bachelors.

The Kennedy Era

John Fitzgerald Kennedy was the first American president born in the twentieth century and the first Roman Catholic president. In his inaugural address, he claimed that "the torch has been passed to a new generation." It was a fitting metaphor for a young man who had been reared to compete and to win, whether the contest was athletic, intellectual, or political. But at the time of his election, it was not clear that a new generation had grabbed the torch. The young candidate was largely the creation of his father, Joseph, who rose to power and wealth as a financier, Hollywood executive, and ambassador to England. Ambitious and demanding, the elder Kennedy was known for his ruthlessness in business and politics and for his blatant philandering. He groomed his oldest son, Joseph P. Kennedy Jr., for greatness, specifically for the presidency. But when young Joe was killed in World War II, the father's ambitions settled on the next in line, John.

John (Jack) Kennedy became a hero during World War II, winning military honors for rescuing his crewmates on his patrol boat, PT-109, when it was rammed by a Japanese destroyer. The rescue left him with a painful back impairment and exacerbated the symptoms of Addison's disease, which plagued him all his life and necessitated daily cortisone injections. His father coached him to bear up under the pain, hide his infirmity, and project an image of health and vitality. "Vigor" was a word Kennedy used often and an aura he projected, inspiring a national craze for physical fitness that survives to this day. Young JFK also emulated his father's brash sexual promiscuity, even after his marriage to Jacqueline Bouvier in 1953.

In 1946 Kennedy won election to the House of Representatives, and in 1952 he defeated incumbent Republican Henry Cabot Lodge to become the Democratic senator from Massachusetts. JFK's father financed all of his political campaigns, and in 1960 the elderly Kennedy bankrolled and masterminded JFK's narrowly successful run for the White House. Kennedy selected as his running mate the powerful Senate majority leader, Lyndon B. Johnson of Texas, whom he had battled for the nomination.

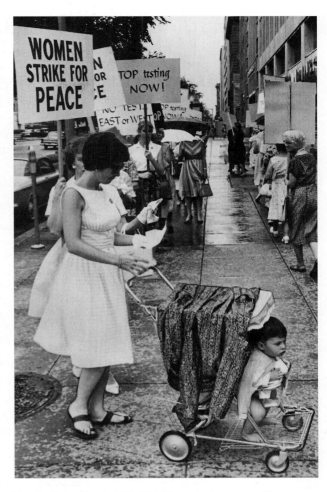

On November 1, 1961, 50,000 women in communities across the country took to the streets to protest nuclear testing. Under the sponsorship of Women Strike for Peace, these demonstrators used their authority as mothers, and brought along their children, to highlight their stake in the future. Participants lobbied government officials to "End the Arms Race—Not the Human Race." Within a year their numbers grew to several hundred thousand.

How did Kennedy's foreign and domestic policies differ from those of Eisenhower?

Watch the Video
Kennedy-Nixon Debate at
www.myhistorylab.com

TABLE 25-2

The Election of 1960

Candidate	Political Party	Popular Vote (%)	Electoral Vote
John F. Kennedy	Democratic	49.9	303
Richard M. Nixon	Republican	49.6	219

INTERPRETING HISTORY

Rachel Carson, *Silent Spring*

In 1962, Silent Spring, *Rachel Carson's eloquent exposé of the chemical industry's deadly impact on the health of the planet, landed on the best-seller list, where it stayed for months. The book, which eventually sold 1.5 million copies and remains in print today, galvanized the environmental movement of the 1960s and 1970s. Carson called the chemical industry "a child of the Second World War" and creator of "elixirs of death." She reported that annual pesticide production increased from 124 million pounds in 1947 to 637 million pounds by 1960. Twenty years later it had reached 2.4 billion pounds. "In the course of developing agents of chemical warfare," she noted, "some of the chemicals created in the laboratory were found to be lethal to insects. The discovery did not come by chance: insects were widely used to test chemicals as agents of death for man."*

It took hundreds of millions of years to produce the life that now inhabits the earth—eons of time in which that developing and evolving and diversifying life reached a state of adjustment and balance with its surroundings. The environment, rigorously shaping and directing the life it supported, contained elements that were hostile as well as supporting. Certain rocks gave out dangerous radiation; even within the light of the sun, from which all life draws its energy, there were short-wave radiations with power to injure. Given time—time not in years but in millennia—life adjusts, and a balance has been reached. For time is the essential ingredient; but in the modern world there is no time.

Environmentalist Rachel Carson, author of *Silent Spring*.

The rapidity of change and the speed with which new situations are created follow the impetuous and heedless pace of man rather than the deliberate pace of nature. Radiation is no longer merely the background radiation of rocks, the bombardment of cosmic rays, the ultraviolet of the sun that have existed before there was any life on earth; radiation is now the unnatural creation of man's tampering with the atom. The chemicals to which life is asked to make its adjustment are no longer merely the calcium and silica and copper and all the rest of the minerals washed out of the rocks and carried in rivers to the sea; they are the synthetic creations of man's inventive mind, brewed in his laboratories, and having no counterparts in nature.

To adjust to these chemicals would require time on the scale that is nature's; it would require not merely the years of a man's life but the life of generations. And even this, were it by some miracle possible, would be futile, for the new chemicals come from our laboratories in an endless stream; almost five hundred annually find their way into actual use in the United States alone. The figure is staggering and its implications are not easily grasped—500 new chemicals to which the bodies of men and animals are required some-how to adapt each year, chemicals totally outside the limits of biologic experience.

Among them are many that are used in man's war against nature. Since the mid-1940s over 200 basic chemicals have been created for use in killing insects, weeds, rodents, and other organisms described in the modern vernacular as "pests"; and they are sold under several thousand different brand names.

These sprays, dusts, and aerosols are now applied almost universally to farms, gardens, forests, and homes—nonselective chemicals that have the power to kill every insect, the "good" and the "bad," to still the song of the birds and the leaping of fish in the streams, to coat the leaves with a deadly film, and to linger on in the soil—all this though the intended target may be only a few weeds or insects. Can anyone believe it is possible to lay down such a barrage of poisons on the surface of the earth without making it unfit for all life? They should not be called "insecticides" but "biocides."

Questions

1. *What connection does Carson make between time and the environment?*
2. *Why does Carson believe insecticides should be called biocides?*

Kennedy's Domestic Policy

With a thin margin of victory, Kennedy lacked a popular mandate for change. But he quickly established himself as an eloquent leader. In his inaugural address, the new president inspired the nation with his memorable words, "My fellow Americans, ask not what your country can do for you; ask what you can do for your country." Focusing his address on foreign policy, he declared, "Let every nation know . . . that we shall pay any price, bear any burden, meet any hardship, support any friend, oppose any foe to assure the survival and the success of liberty." He initially sought to avoid division at home and to wage the Cold War forcefully abroad. He believed that prosperity was the best way to spread the fruits of affluence, rather than government programs that would redistribute wealth. Accordingly, he supported corporate tax cuts to stimulate the economy, which grew at a rate of 5 percent each year from 1961 to 1966.

Although Democrats held strong majorities in both houses, powerful southern conservatives often teamed up with Republicans in Congress to defeat reform legislation. Kennedy knew that it would be futile to champion the cause of civil rights in the face of that alliance. But he did support issues important to his working-class constituents and proposed a number of legislative initiatives, including increasing the minimum wage, health care for the aged, larger Social Security benefits, and the creation of the Department of Housing and Urban Development (HUD).

Kennedy's Foreign Policy

Kennedy was the first U.S. president to understand and recognize the legitimacy of movements for national self-determination in the Third World. He supported movements to end colonial rule while at the same time containing the spread of communism. His efforts earned him a great deal of good will among Africans and other non-Europeans. But if nationalist movements appeared friendly to the Soviet Union, Kennedy worked against them. He sharply increased military spending and nuclear arms buildup as a show of strength and preparedness against possible Soviet aggression.

One of Kennedy's most popular initiatives was the Peace Corps, a program that sent Americans, especially young people, to nations around the world to work on development projects. In 1961 Kennedy signed the Charter of Punta del Este with several Latin American countries, establishing the Alliance for Progress, a program designed to prevent the spread of anti-Americanism and communist insurgencies in Latin America. The alliance offered $20 billion in loans to Latin American countries for democratic development initiatives.

Kennedy continued the strategies of Truman and Eisenhower to fight communism in South Vietnam by supporting the corrupt regime of Ngo Dinh Diem. But the National Liberation Front (NLF), founded in 1960 and supported by Ho Chi Minh's communist regime in North Vietnam, gained the upper hand in its struggle against Diem. In response, Kennedy increased the number of military advisers there from 800 to 17,000. By 1963 it was obvious that Diem's brutal regime was about to fall to the NLF, and Kennedy allowed U.S. military advisers and diplomats to encourage Diem's dissenting generals to depose Diem.

Kennedy also faced a crisis in Cuba. Fidel Castro's revolution initially represented the sort of democratic insurgency that Kennedy wanted to support. But Castro's socialism turned the United States against him, and he established close ties with the Soviet Union. During the Eisenhower administration, the CIA began planning an invasion of Cuba with the help of Cuban exiles in Florida. Kennedy's national security advisers persuaded Kennedy to allow the invasion to proceed.

On April 17, 1961, U.S.-backed and -trained anticommunist forces, most of them Cuban exiles, landed at the Bahia de Cochinas (Bay of Pigs) on the southern coast of Cuba. Castro expected the invasion—his agents in Florida had infiltrated the Cuban exiles—so his well-prepared troops quickly surrounded and captured the invaders. No domestic uprising against Castro occurred to support the invasion. Kennedy pulled back in humiliating defeat but continued to support covert efforts that tried but failed to destabilize Cuba and assassinate Castro.

Another crisis soon erupted in Berlin. Located 200 miles deep in East Germany, with only two highways connecting it to West Germany, West Berlin was a showcase of western material superiority and an espionage center for the western powers. In June 1961, Khrushchev threatened to end the western presence in Berlin and unite the city with the rest of East Germany. In part, Khrushchev wanted to stop the steady stream of East Germans into West Berlin.

Kennedy refused to relinquish West Berlin. On August 13, 1961, the East German government constructed a wall to separate East and West Berlin. Two years later, Kennedy stood in front of the wall and pledged to defend the West Berliners.

The most serious foreign policy crisis of Kennedy's presidency came in 1962, when the Soviet Union, at Castro's invitation, began to install nuclear missiles in Cuba. Kennedy's advisers presented a series of possible responses. The most dramatic and dangerous would be a full-scale military invasion of the island, which would topple Castro but would surely have prompted military retaliation by the Soviet Union. Another option was a more limited military intervention, an air strike to destroy the missiles before they became operational. Others proposed a blockade of Cuban ports to prevent the missiles from entering. Another possibility was to negotiate secretly with Castro, Soviet leaders, or both. Kennedy decided against behind-the-scenes negotiations as well as the drastic move of military intervention and instead established a "quarantine" around the island to block Soviet ships from reaching Cuba, hoping that the Soviet Union would back down and withdraw the missiles. A quarantine, unlike a blockade, was not considered an act of war; nevertheless, Kennedy put the Strategic Air Command on full alert for possible nuclear war.

> *Kennedy put the Strategic Air Command on full alert for possible nuclear war.*

Watch the Video
The Cuban Missile Crisis at
www.myhistorylab.com

Read the Document
Test Ban Treaty at
www.myhistorylab.com

It was a risky move. On national television, Kennedy warned the Soviet Union to remove the missiles or face the military might of the United States. For the next five days tensions mounted, as Russian ships hovered in the water beyond the quarantine zone. Finally Khrushchev proposed an agreement, offering to remove the missiles if the United States would agree not to invade Cuba. Kennedy also privately promised to remove Jupiter missiles in Turkey as soon as the crisis was over. The two leaders managed to diffuse the crisis, but they were both sobered by the experience of having come to the brink of nuclear war. In 1963 they signed a nuclear test ban treaty.

1963: A Year of Turning Points

In 1963 the President's Commission on the Status of Women published a report that documented widespread discrimination against women in jobs, pay, education, and the professions. In response, Kennedy issued a presidential order requiring the civil service to hire people "without regard to sex," and he supported passage of the Equal Pay Act of 1963.

Also in 1963, in Birmingham, Alabama, Martin Luther King Jr. led a silent and peaceful march through the city. Chief of Police Bull Connor unleashed the police, who blasted the demonstrators with fire hoses and attacked them with vicious police dogs. Four black children were later killed when segregationists bombed an African-American church. The Kennedy administration responded by bringing the full force of its authority to bear on the officials in Birmingham. But the crisis intensified. Alabama's segregationist governor, George Wallace, refused to admit two black students to the University of Alabama, threatening to stand in the doorway to block their entrance.

View the Image
Civil Rights March on Washington at
www.myhistorylab.com

Finally, on June 10, 1963, Kennedy federalized the Alabama National Guard and for the first time went before the American people to declare himself forcefully on the side of the civil rights protesters and to propose a civil rights bill. A few months later, on August 28, more than 250,000 people gathered at the nation's capital in front of the Lincoln Memorial for the culmination of the March on Washington, a huge demonstration for jobs as well as freedom, where Martin Luther King Jr. delivered his inspiring "I Have a Dream" speech.

In the fall of 1963, a confident Kennedy began planning his reelection campaign for the next year. To mobilize support, he visited Texas. "Here we are in Dallas," he said on November 22, 1963, "and it looks like everything in Texas is going to be fine for us." Within an hour of uttering those optimistic words, the president lay dying of an assassin's bullet.

As shock and grief spread across the nation, a bizarre series of events confounded efforts to bring the assassin to justice. Police arrested Lee Harvey Oswald, who had previously lived in the Soviet Union and who had loose ties to organized crime and to political groups interested in Cuba. Oswald claimed he was innocent. But before he could be brought to trial, Oswald was murdered. Jack Ruby, a nightclub owner who also had links to organized crime, shot Oswald while he was in the custody of the Dallas police—an event witnessed by millions on live television. Ruby later died in prison. The newly sworn-in president, Lyndon B. Johnson, appointed a commission to investigate the assassination under the leadership of Supreme Court Chief Justice Earl Warren. The Warren Commission eventually concluded that Oswald and Ruby had both acted alone, although the report failed to end speculation about a possible conspiracy.

CONCLUSION

During the decade between the election of Dwight D. Eisenhower and the assassination of John F. Kennedy, the nation experienced unprecedented prosperity. Increasing numbers of Americans moved into middle-class suburbs and enjoyed the fruits of a rapidly expanding consumer economy. Men and women rushed into marriage and childbearing, creating the baby boom and a powerful domestic ideology resting on distinct gender roles for women and men. At the same time, fears of nuclear war, intense anticommunism, and pressures to conform to mainstream political and cultural values contributed to anxieties and discontent.

Beneath the apparently tranquil surface, some Americans began to resist the limitations and exclusions of the widely touted "American way of life." African Americans in the South demanded their rightful place as full citizens, challenging the Jim Crow system and accelerating the civil rights movement through nonviolent protests, boycotts, and sit-ins. Young people created a vibrant youth culture to the pulsating rhythms of rock 'n' roll. Beatniks, peace activists, and environmentalists expressed incipient political and cultural dissent. The rumblings of vast social change had already begun and would explode in the years ahead, pushed along by a divisive war in Vietnam.

For Review

✓●─Study and Review at www.myhistorylab.com

1. Who had access to the postwar suburban ideal? Who was excluded, and why?

2. What strategies did civil rights activists develop and use? How effective were they? What resistance did they encounter?

3. How did Eisenhower steer a path down the "middle of the road"?

4. What marked Kennedy as a new type of president?

Chronology: 1953–1963

1953   CIA engineers coup in Iran, restores shah to power.

1954   *Brown v. Board of Education* outlaws school segregation.

1955   Polio vaccine approved for use.
Disneyland opens in Anaheim, California.
Montgomery, Alabama, bus boycott begins.

1956   Interstate Highway Act.

1957   Central High School in Little Rock, Arkansas, integrated.
USSR launches satellite *Sputnik*.

1958   National Defense Education Act.

1959   Nixon–Khrushchev Kitchen Debate.
Cuban Revolution.

1960   Oral contraceptive pill comes on the market.
Beginning of lunch counter sit-ins (Greensboro, North Carolina).

1961   Bay of Pigs invasion of Cuba.
Berlin Wall constructed.

1962   Rachel Carson, *Silent Spring*.
Cuban missile crisis.

1963   Lyndon B. Johnson becomes president after assassination of John F. Kennedy.
Equal Pay Act of 1963.
Betty Friedan, *The Feminine Mystique*.

Key Terms

Baby boom The period of increased U.S. childbirths from roughly the early 1940s to the early 1960s. p. 577

Military-industrial complex The term given by President Dwight D. Eisenhower to describe the armed forces and the politically powerful defense industries that supplied arms and equipment to them. p. 585

Red lining Policies maintained by the Federal Housing Authority and lending banks which designated certain neighborhoods off limits to racial minorities. p. 579

Sit-in A form of civil disobedience in which activists sit down somewhere in violation of law or policy in order to challenge discriminatory practices or laws. The tactic originated during labor struggles in the 1930s and was used effectively in the civil rights movement in the 1960s. p. 584

The soft-spoken black man with the strange northern accent first showed up in small-town McComb, Mississippi, in the summer of 1961. Robert Parris Moses had come on a mission of democracy. An organizer for the new Student Nonviolent Coordinating Committee (SNCC), he was there to encourage impoverished African Americans to register to vote. Over the next four years in the Deep South, Bob Moses paid a price for his commitments. Local police imprisoned him, and white supremacists beat him severely and murdered dozens of his fellow activists in the black freedom movement. But Moses remained committed to nonviolence and racial integration. His quiet courage became legendary in the movement. One summer night in 1962, he returned to a deserted SNCC office in Greenwood, Mississippi, that had just been ransacked by a white mob. Three other SNCC workers had barely escaped with their lives. Moses simply looked around, made up a bed in the corner of the devastated main room, and went to sleep. He refused to be intimidated.

During the 1960s, an extraordinary number of idealistic young people became involved in public life in an effort to make real their nation's promises of freedom, justice, and equality. The civil rights movement inspired the social movements that followed: for ending the war, for preserving the environment, and for liberating women, Latinos, Indians, and gay men and lesbians. But organizing for change inevitably brought activists up against fierce resistance from what they called "the establishment." Disillusionment and radicalization often followed. Public life became deeply contentious by 1968 as young radicals challenged more conservative citizens on issues of race, war, and gender.

The escalating American war in Southeast Asia loomed over all. Lyndon Johnson brought the nation to its apex of liberal reform with his extensive Great Society legislation. However, the high-flying hopes of Democratic liberals crashed to earth with the destructive war that the Johnson administration waged against seasoned communist revolutionaries in far-off Vietnam. Out of the wreckage of 1968 emerged a Republican president, Richard Nixon, and a growing conservative backlash against the social changes advocated by people of color, the counterculture, the antiwar movement, and the rising tide of women's liberation.

26

The Nation Divides: The Vietnam War and Social Conflict, 1964–1971

CHAPTER OUTLINE

Lyndon Johnson and the Apex of Liberalism

Into War in Vietnam

"The Movement"

The Conservative Response

Conclusion

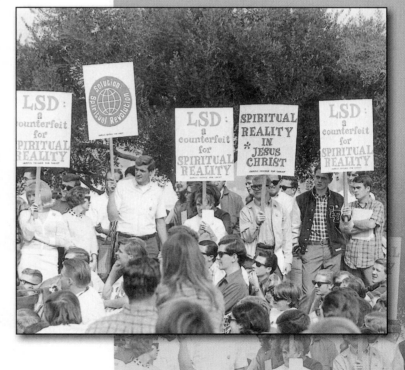

Lyndon Johnson and the Apex of Liberalism

Wealth provided the foundation on which the **Great Society** was built. American economic expansion after World War II had created history's richest nation by 1960. From 1961 to 1966, the economy accelerated at

A native of New York City, Bob Moses graduated from Hamilton College in upstate New York and did graduate work at Harvard University. He was inspired by the sit-in movement that began in 1960 in the American South and soon moved south to join SNCC.

What did Johnson hope to achieve with his Great Society programs?

an annual growth rate of more than 5 percent with very low inflation, stimulated by large tax cuts and extensive military spending. The 41 percent increase in per capita income during the 1960s was not evenly distributed, however. And the distribution of wealth (stocks and real estate) was far more skewed than that of income. The president and the Congress believed that economic expansion would continue indefinitely and the nation could therefore afford government policies to improve the welfare of less affluent Americans. The Supreme Court expanded individual liberties.

The New President

Lyndon Baines Johnson was one of the most remarkable American characters of the twentieth century, both a giant among political leaders and a bully with those who worked for him. Johnson entered Democratic politics early as an avid supporter of Franklin Roosevelt and the New Deal and rose like a rocket through Congress to become perhaps the most powerful Senate majority leader ever (1954–1960) and then vice president (1961–1963). Kennedy's assassination catapulted him into the Oval Office as the nation's first Texan president.

Johnson retained Kennedy's cabinet and advisers and used the memory of the fallen young president to rally support for his administration. Johnson turned out to be the more liberal of the two men, in part because his early years in Texas had given him a visceral understanding of poverty and discrimination that his predecessor lacked. Johnson's focus was different, too. He retained Kennedy's anticommunist commitments abroad, but his heart remained at home, where he wanted to perfect American society.

First he had to win reelection. Less than a year remained until voters went to the polls in 1964. The Republicans nominated right-wing Senator Barry Goldwater of Arizona, a sign of the party's sharp swing away from its moderate northeastern elements toward its fiercely conservative western and southern constituencies. Goldwater believed in unrestricted markets

Lyndon Johnson took the presidential oath of office on board *Air Force One*, returning to Washington from Dallas, where John Kennedy had just been assassinated on November 22, 1963. Johnson's wife, Lady Bird, is on his right, and Jacqueline Kennedy, still in blood-stained clothes, stands on his left. Johnson adroitly channeled the public outpouring of grief for the murdered young president into support for their shared legislative goals.

and a minimal role for the federal government in every aspect of American life except the military. He spoke casually about using nuclear weapons against communists abroad. Goldwater declared that "extremism in the defense of liberty is no vice," but Johnson zeroed in on that extremism and swept to the largest electoral majority of any president (61 percent).

TABLE 26-1			
The Election of 1964			
Candidate	Political Party	Popular Vote (%)	Electoral Vote
Lyndon B. Johnson	Democratic	61.1	486
Barry M. Goldwater	Republican	38.5	52

The Great Society: Fighting Poverty and Discrimination

In pursuit of what he called the Great Society, Johnson first declared a "War on Poverty." No citizen in the richest nation on earth should live in squalor, he believed. Yet more than one out of five Americans still lived below the conservatively estimated official poverty line.

The president and a large congressional majority passed several measures to alleviate poverty. They sharply increased the availability of money and food stamps through the Aid to Families with Dependent Children ("welfare") program, and they raised Social Security payments to older Americans. Several programs focused on improving educational opportunities as an avenue out of poverty: Head Start offered preschool education and meals for youngsters, the Elementary and Secondary Education Act sent federal funds to the least affluent school districts, and an expanded system of student loans facilitated access to college. The Job Corps provided employment training, and Volunteers in Service to America (VISTA) served as a domestic Peace Corps, funneling people with education and skills into poor communities to serve as teachers and providers of other social services.

No barrier to opportunity in the early 1960s was higher than the color bar. Both opportunist and idealist, Johnson as president shed his segregationist voting record (necessary for election in Texas before 1960) and became the most vocal proponent of racial equality ever to occupy the Oval Office. Two factors facilitated his change in position. One, blatant inequalities for American citizens weakened the United States in its competition with the Soviets and Chinese for the loyalty of the nonwhite Third World majority. Two, the African-American freedom struggle in the South had reached a boiling point. Black frustration was mounting over white brutality and the seeming indifference or even hostility of the national government.

The Civil Rights Act of 1964 fulfilled the implicit promise of the *Brown v. Board of Education* decision a decade earlier. The 1964 act made desegregation the law of the land as it outlawed discrimination in employment and in public facilities such as restaurants, theaters, and hotels. The Voting Rights Act of 1965 outlawed poll taxes and provided federal voting registrars in states that refused the ballot to African Americans. The single most important legislation of the twentieth century for bringing political democracy to the South, the Voting Rights Act increased the percentage of blacks voting in Mississippi from 7 percent to 60 percent in two years. Also in 1965, a new Immigration Act eliminated the discriminatory national-origins system, with most immigrants thereafter arriving from Asia and Latin America rather than Europe.

Read the Document

Johnson, "The War on Poverty" at www.myhistorylab.com

See the Map

Impact of the Voting Rights Act of 1965 at www.myhistorylab.com

The Great Society: Improving the Quality of Life

Johnson's vision of the Great Society extended to the broader quality of life in the United States. Health care was perhaps the most fundamental issue for citizens' sense of personal security. After 1965, the new Medicare system paid for the medical needs of Americans age 65 and older, and Medicaid underwrote health care services for the poor. In 1964, when more than half of adults smoked tobacco, the surgeon general issued the first government report linking smoking to cancer. Higher federal standards for automotive safety followed a year later. Public pressures also led to the establishment of new requirements for publishing the nutritional values of packaged food. The federally funded Public Broadcasting System

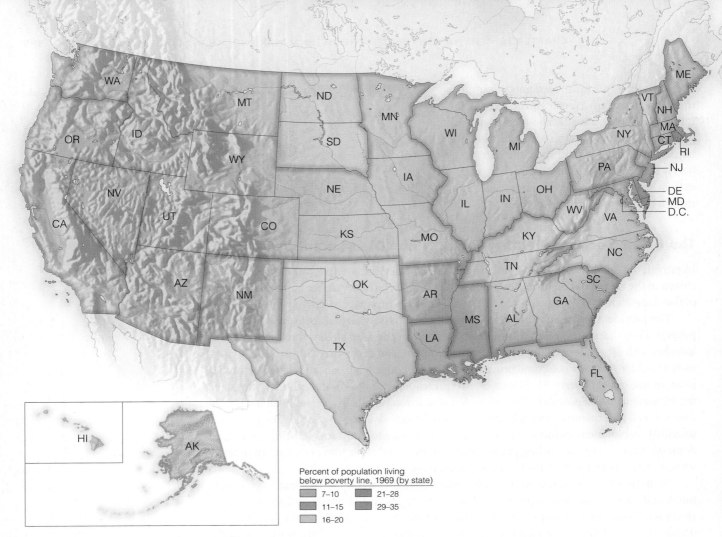

■ **MAP 26.1**

PERCENTAGE OF POPULATION LIVING BELOW THE POVERTY LINE, 1969 (BY STATE)
The United States in the 1960s was a nation of unprecedented wealth and comfort. Yet millions of Americans still lived in poverty. Prodded by other reformers, President Johnson sought to reduce the number of impoverished citizens through the Great Society programs. The southeastern and south-central states had the highest poverty rates, a legacy of slavery and limited industrialization.

(PBS) was established to provide television programs that were more educational than the fare tied to advertising on the three corporate networks (NBC, CBS, and ABC). In fact, most Great Society measures targeted all Americans rather than just the disadvantaged.

Nothing more directly threatened the quality of American life than the degradation of the natural environment. The costs of the unrestrained and much-heralded economic growth since World War II showed up in the pollution of the nation's air, water, and land. Growing public awareness prompted the Clean Air Act (1963) and the Clean Waters Act (1966), which set federal guidelines for reducing smog and preserving public drinking sources from bacterial pollution. Even the long dam-building tradition in the American West faced new questions, with the Wild and Scenic Rivers Act enacted in 1968. Meanwhile, Congress passed the Wilderness Act in 1964, setting aside 9 million acres of undeveloped public lands as a place "where man is a visitor who does not remain."

The Liberal Warren Court

The Supreme Court under the leadership of Earl Warren steadily expanded the constitutional definition of individual rights. This shift reached even those deemed to have lost many of their rights: prisoners. *Gideon v. Wainwright* (1963) established the right of indigent prisoners to legal counsel, and *Escobedo v. Illinois* (1964) confirmed the right to counsel during interrogation, a critical hindrance to the use of torture. After *Miranda v. Arizona* (1966), police were required to inform anyone they arrested of their rights to remain silent and to speak to a lawyer.

The Warren Court bolstered other rights of individuals against potentially coercive community pressures. Decisions in 1962 and 1963 strictly limited the practice of requiring prayers in public schools. In 1963 the Court narrowed standards for the definition of "obscenity," allowing freer expression in the arts but also in pornography. *Griswold v. Connecticut* (1965) established the use of contraceptive devices by married people as a matter of private choice protected by the Constitution. In 1967 the Court heard the case of Mildred Jeter, a black woman, and Richard Loving, a white man, Virginians who had evaded their state's ban on interracial marriage by traveling to Washington, D.C., for their wedding and then returning home to Virginia to live. In the aptly titled *Loving v. Virginia*, the Court declared marriage one of the "basic civil rights of men" and overturned the laws of the last 16 states restricting interracial unions.

The Supreme Court's interpreting of the Constitution to expand individual rights disturbed many conservative Americans. They saw the Court as another arm of an intrusive national government that was extending its control over matters previously left to local communities. For them, the goal of integration did not justify the busing of school children. Rising crime rates worried them more than police brutality. Many Roman Catholics were troubled by the legalization of contraceptives. Incensed by the ban on requiring school prayer, Protestant fundamentalists sought redress through political involvement, which they had previously shunned, initiating a grassroots religious conservative movement that helped bring Ronald Reagan to power in 1980.

Into War in Vietnam

The 1960s also marked the culmination of the U.S. government's efforts to control revolutionary political and social change abroad. Johnson's accomplishments at home were forever overshadowed by the war he sent Americans to fight in the quiet rice paddies and beautiful highland forests of Southeast Asia. An aggressive U.S. anticommunist policy abroad collided with leftist revolutionaries throughout the Third World, and it was ill fortune for the Vietnamese that this collision struck them hardest of all.

Why did the United States go to war in Vietnam, and why did it not win the war?

The Vietnamese Revolution and the United States

Vietnamese nationalists, varying in ideologies but led by Ho Chi Minh and the Indochinese Communist party, had sought since the 1930s to liberate their country from French colonial rule. Japanese advances during World War II put the Vietminh (Vietnamese nationalists) on the same side as the Americans, and Ho worked closely with the U.S. Office of Strategic Services (OSS), precursor to the Central Intelligence Agency (CIA).

After the defeat of Germany and Japan, the French wanted to regain control of their colonies in Africa and Asia, including Vietnam. The British provided troop transport ships for French soldiers, and the United States provided most of the funds to support France in its war against the Vietminh (1946–1954). Cold War priorities won out: a weakened France had to be bolstered as the linchpin of a reintegrated, anticommunist western Europe, while the Vietminh were led by Communist party members. But the Vietnamese defeated the much more heavily armed French at the battle of Dien Bien Phu in May 1954. Two months later, the Geneva Accords divided the country temporarily at the seventeenth parallel until national elections could be held within two years to reunify Vietnam. Ho's forces solidified their control of the north, the French pulled out entirely, and the Eisenhower administration made a fateful decision to intervene directly to preserve the southern part of Vietnam from communism. The United States created a new government led by the Roman Catholic, anticommunist Ngo Dinh Diem in a new country called "South Vietnam."

The Vietnamese Revolution was only half over, however. The French colonialists withdrew, but the Saigon regime did not hold elections. In North Vietnam, the sometimes brutal internal revolution for the creation of a socialist society proceeded with an extensive program of land redistribution. In South Vietnam, Diem ruled for eight years with increasing repression of communists and other dissenters. U.S. funding kept him in power. Southern members of the old Vietminh began a sabotage campaign against the Saigon government and formed the National Liberation Front (NLF) in 1960, with the support of North Vietnam. Diem and his American supporters called them Viet Cong or VC, roughly equivalent to the derogatory American term *Commies*. As the struggle to overthrow Diem intensified, several of his own generals assassinated him in November 1963 with the tacit support of U.S. officials in South Vietnam and Washington.

Johnson's War

Lyndon Johnson inherited his predecessors' commitment to preserving a noncommunist South Vietnam. Bolstered by Kennedy's hawkish advisers, he believed that American credibility was at stake. But Johnson faced a swiftly deteriorating military situation. The NLF, which the administration portrayed as merely a tool of North Vietnam, was winning the political war for the South, taking control of the countryside from the demoralized Army of the Republic of Vietnam (ARVN). Faced with the choice of escalating U.S. involvement to prevent an NLF victory or withdrawing entirely from the country, Johnson escalated.

How he did so was crucially important. There was neither a national debate nor a congressional vote to declare war. Johnson did not want to distract Congress from his Great Society agenda, nor did he want to provoke the Soviet Union or China. But he believed he had to preserve a noncommunist South Vietnam or else face a debilitating backlash from Republicans, who would skewer him as McCarthy had done to Truman over the "loss" of China 15 years earlier. So the president used deception, describing offensive American actions as defensive and opening up a credibility gap between a committed government and a skeptical public.

In August 1964, North Vietnamese ships in the Gulf of Tonkin fired on the U.S. destroyer *Maddox*, which was aiding South Vietnamese sabotage operations against the North. The president portrayed the incident as one of unprovoked communist aggression, and Congress expressed almost unanimous support through its Gulf of Tonkin Resolution. With this substitute for a declaration of war, Johnson ordered American planes to begin bombing North Vietnam, and the first American combat troops splashed ashore at Da Nang in South Vietnam on March 8, 1965. In July the administration made the key decision to add 100,000 more soldiers, with more to follow as necessary.

●●●—[Read the Document

Johnson, The Tonkin Gulf Resolution Message at **www.myhistorylab.com**

American strategy had two goals: to limit the war so as not to draw in neighboring China (to avoid a repeat of the Korean War) and to force the NLF and North Vietnam to give up their struggle to reunify the country under Hanoi's control. The problem was the political nature of the guerrilla war in the South: a contest for the loyalty of the population, in which NLF operatives mingled easily with the citizenry. This kind of war made the enemy difficult to find. The "strategic hamlet" program uprooted rural peasants and concentrated them in fortified towns, creating "free fire zones" in their wake where anything that moved was a target. The U.S. Air Force pounded the South as well as the North, dropping more bombs on this ancient land (smaller than either Germany or Japan) than had been used in all theaters on all sides in World War II. These tactics destabilized and traumatized society in South Vietnam as one-fourth of the population became refugees.

> *American strategy had two goals: to limit the war so as not to draw in neighboring China (to avoid a repeat of the Korean War) and to force the NLF and North Vietnam to give up their struggle to reunify the country under Hanoi's control.*

Americans in Southeast Asia

Who were the 3 million Americans who went to Vietnam? The initial forces contained experienced soldiers, but as the war escalated this professional army was diluted with hundreds of thousands of young draftees. Student deferments protected more comfortable Americans, so GIs were predominantly those who lacked money and education. Very few knew anything about Vietnamese history or culture, and almost none spoke the Vietnamese language. Although 70 percent were white men, black, Hispanic, and Native American enlistees shipped out in disproportionate numbers. In sharp contrast to the motives of the NLF and the North Vietnamese army, few of these young men (along with 10,000 women who volunteered as nurses) were in Vietnam to win the war regardless of the cost or duration. They had only to survive 12 months before returning home to the safety of a peacetime society.

President Johnson spoke of the conflict in Vietnam as a case of one sovereign nation—North Vietnam—invading another one—South Vietnam. However, few Vietnamese saw the war in those terms. The United States, dismissing the failure of the French before them, had intervened not so much in an international war as in an ongoing revolution that aimed to reunify the country. Few Vietnamese, whatever their opinions of communism, viewed the corrupt Saigon regime as legitimate or democratic. After all, it was kept in place by foreigners, whereas the North was ruled by people who had expelled the French foreigners.

Initial U.S. optimism reflected a grave underestimation of the NLF and the North Vietnamese. Ho Chi Minh was an extremely popular leader, and intervention from the other side of the world only strengthened his position. As the war expanded, NLF recruiting in the south snowballed, and the people of North Vietnam remained loyal to their authoritarian government. Communist forces proved willing to endure profound hardship and sacrifices to prevail. Their morale was much higher than that of the ARVN.

North Vietnamese regular army units came South to match the growing number of U.S. forces, and they occasionally engaged the Americans in large set battles, as at Ia Drang Valley in the fall of 1965. U.S. troops fought well in such firefights, making devastating use of their superior weapons and air power. However, the bulk of the fighting consisted of smaller engagements with deceptive enemies on their home turf who faded in and out of the civilian population with ease. Ambushes and unexpected death haunted Americans on patrol, and relentless heat and humidity wore them down.

American soldiers felt mounting frustration and rage over the nature of the war that they were ordered to fight. Lacking a clear battlefront and an understandable strategy for winning the war, they were commanded simply to kill the often mysterious enemy. Yet distinguishing civilians from combatants in a popular guerrilla war was not always easy, especially when so many civilians evidently supported the NLF and so few Americans spoke Vietnamese. Realizing that few of the people they were supposed to be defending actually wanted them there but under orders to produce enemy bodies, many U.S. troops on the ground began to slide toward a racial war against all Vietnamese.

Many GIs resisted this logic, sometimes showing real kindness to Vietnamese civilians. But atrocities on both sides inevitably followed from this kind of war. The worst came in the village

■ A North Vietnamese militia fighter named Kim Lai escorts an American pilot whom she captured after his plane crashed over the North. American GIs often were struck by the diminutive size of the average Vietnamese in comparison to the average American. Bigger, better equipped, and much more well-armed than their opponents, most U.S. soldiers and officers before 1968 went into the field in Vietnam certain that they would be victorious.

CHINA

NORTH VIETNAM

Red R.

U.S. air raids 1966–1968, 1972

Haiphong — *harbor mined 1972*

Hanoi

LAOS
(Communist Pathet Lao victory, 1975)

Mekong R.

Gulf of Tonkin

Hainan Island

Gulf of Tonkin incident Aug.4,1964

U.S. Seventh Fleet operations during the war

Vientiane

Demilitarized Zone (DMZ)

Invasion of Laos Feb. 6–Mar.,1971

Khe Sanh
Quang Tri
Hue: Tet offensive Jan. 30–Feb.,1968
Da Nang
Hoian

Lang Vei
A Chau
Kham Dua

THAILAND

Quang Ngai
Dak To

Kontum
Pleiku
Qui Niun

SOUTH VIETNAM

Tuy Hoi
Ban Me Thuoi

(Communist Khmer Rouge victory, 1975)

CAMBODIA

Nha Trang
Dalat

South China Sea

Cam Ranh Bay

Invasion of Cambodia Apr. 29–June 29,1970

Phnom Penh

Bien Hoa
Cholon
Saigon: Tet offensive Jan. 30–Feb.,1968

Chau Dua
Vinh Long

Saigon

My Tho

Gulf of Thailand

Ben Tre
Can Tho
Ca Mau

Vietnam | Capitals
Major battles or actions | U.S. and South Vietnamese troop movements
Major North Vietnamese supply routes into South Vietnam | "Boat People" refugees after 1975
NLF-North Vietnamese victory and U.S. withdrawal, April 30,1975

■ **MAP 26.2**

THE AMERICAN WAR IN VIETNAM

Before U.S. combat troops entered Vietnam in 1965, few Americans knew where this Southeast Asian country was. Vietnam's geography and place names quickly became familiar in the United States as hundreds of thousands of young Americans served there and some 58,000 died there. Vietnam's elongated shape, its borders with Cambodia and Laos, and its proximity to China all affected the course of the fighting between 1965 and 1973.

of My Lai on March 16, 1968, where 105 soldiers from Charlie Company—enraged by the recent deaths of several comrades in ambushes—slaughtered, often after torturing or raping, more than 400 Vietnamese women, children, and old men. The army covered up the massacre for a year and a half, and eventually found only Lieutenant William Calley, the leader of Charlie Company's First Platoon, guilty of murdering Vietnamese civilians.

1968: The Turning Point

In late 1967, the public face of the war effort remained upbeat. General William Westmoreland declared that he could now see "some light at the end of the tunnel." But hopes of an imminent victory were crushed by the startling Tet Offensive (named for the Vietnamese

New Year) that began on January 30, 1968. NLF insurgents and North Vietnamese troops attacked U.S. strongholds throughout South Vietnam. The blow to American public confidence in Johnson and his military commanders proved irreversible. Far from being on the verge of defeat, as the administration had been claiming, the communists had shown that they could mount simultaneous attacks around the country.

The Tet Offensive coincided with two other crises in early 1968 to convince American political and business elites that U.S. international commitments had become larger than the nation could afford. First, a week before Tet began, the North Korean navy seized the U.S. intelligence ship *Pueblo* in the Sea of Japan and temporarily imprisoned its crew. U.S. commanders were left scrambling to find enough forces to respond effectively without weakening American commitments in Europe and elsewhere. Second, a British financial collapse devalued the pound and caused the London government to announce its imminent withdrawal from its historic positions east of the Suez Canal, placing new military burdens on the United States in the Middle East. These events reduced international confidence in the U.S. economy, causing a currency crisis in March 1968 as holders of dollars traded them in for gold.

The political career of Lyndon Johnson was a final casualty of these events. His support on the left withered as the antiwar and **black power** movements expanded. Meanwhile, his more centrist supporters were joining the backlash against civil rights, urban violence, and antiwar protesters, peeling off to the Republican party. On March 12, antiwar challenger Senator Eugene McCarthy of Minnesota nearly defeated the incumbent president in the New Hampshire Democratic primary. Johnson's vulnerability was clear. Senator Robert Kennedy of New York joined the race two weeks later. In a televised speech on March 31 that caught the divided nation by surprise, Johnson announced an end to U.S. escalations in the war, the start of negotiations in Paris with North Vietnam, and an end to his own political career. He would not seek reelection.

"The Movement"

While national leaders were defending what they called the "frontiers of freedom" abroad, young Americans in the mid- and late 1960s organized to expand what they considered the frontiers of freedom at home. Television for the first time tied the country together in a common culture whose shared images were transmitted simultaneously around the nation. The expanding war in Vietnam radicalized people who had initially been optimistic about reforming American society. Black power, the New Left, the counterculture, women's liberation, and other liberation movements often had quite divergent goals. But participants overlapped extensively and activists spoke of "the Movement" as if it were a unified phenomenon. At the heart of the youth movements of the decade lay a common quest for authenticity—a rejection of hypocrisy and a distrust of traditional authorities—that fused cultural and political protest.

What did the protest movements of the 1960s have in common?

From Civil Rights to Black Power

By 1966 the civil rights movement fractured as it confronted the limits of its success. It had achieved the goals of ending legal discrimination and putting southern African Americans in the voting booth, but it had not brought about a colorblind society. Racial prejudice among white conservatives remained virulent, and white liberals, such as those in the Kennedy and Johnson administrations, revealed themselves as not always trustworthy allies.

The Justice Department and the Federal Bureau of Investigation (FBI) did little to restrain the violence of the Ku Klux Klan until white organizers Michael Schwerner and Andrew Goodman and black co-worker James Chaney were murdered in the summer of 1964. Two months later, at the national Democratic party convention in Atlantic City, New Jersey,

■ A leading spokesman for the Black Muslims, Malcolm X converted to orthodox Islam and softened his antiwhite rhetoric in the two years before his murder in 1965. Like SNCC's Bob Moses, Malcolm increasingly identified with the Third World. Here he is shown in Egypt on a 1964 pilgrimage to Mecca, Saudi Arabia.

Johnson crushed the effort of the biracial Mississippi Freedom Democratic party to replace the state's regular, all-white Democratic delegates. The president was determined to avoid further alienating white southern voters as he pursued a huge victory margin in the November elections.

For centuries, the black freedom struggle had woven together elements of racial separatism with elements of integration into the larger American culture. For many younger African Americans, the pendulum now swung toward a need for greater independence from the white majority. They took inspiration from Malcolm X, the fiery and eloquent minister of the Nation of Islam (Black Muslims), who until his murder in 1965 captivated listeners with denunciations of white perfidy and demands for black self-respect. In 1966, SNCC members began to speak of the need for "black power" rather than for the integrated "beloved community" they had initially sought in 1960.

The Black Panther party formed in Oakland, California, in response to police brutality. The heavily armed Panthers engaged in several shootouts with police and were eventually decimated by an FBI campaign against them. White Americans were shocked by the uprisings and riots that swept through black urban communities during the summers of 1964–1968. Triggered by the actions of white police, the riots expressed the fierce frustrations of impoverished people whose lives remained largely untouched by the achievements of the civil rights struggle. The most destructive outbreaks occurred in the Watts district of Los Angeles in 1965 and in Detroit and Newark in 1967.

Black power thrived primarily as a cultural movement that promoted pride in African-American and African history and life. The slogan "black is beautiful" captured this spirit: long degraded by their white compatriots as inferior, black Americans in the late 1960s and 1970s reversed this equation to celebrate their cultural heritage. This could be as basic as a hairstyle, the natural Afro replacing hair straightened to look like European-American hair. At universities, new departments of African-American studies fostered the exploration of black history. Unlearning habits of public deference to whites, most African Americans began referring to themselves as "black" rather than "Negro."

Cultural black power mixed with a different kind of political black power by the late 1960s: the election of black officials. Although militant black power advocates garnered the most media attention, most African Americans supported Lyndon Johnson and used the Voting Rights Act to pursue their goals in the realm of electoral politics. In 1966 Carl Stokes of Cleveland was elected the first black mayor of a major American city, and African Americans won local offices across the South.

The New Left and the Struggle Against the War

⊙ Watch the Video
"Protests Against the Vietnam War"
at **www.myhistorylab.com**

In 1962, a group of liberal college activists founded the Students for a Democratic Society (SDS). They called for a rejuvenation of American politics and society to replace the complacency that they saw pervading the country. Racial bigotry and poverty particularly troubled these optimistic young reformers, along with the overarching threat of nuclear destruction (highlighted anew by the missile crisis in Cuba). They hoped to become a kind of "white SNCC," promoting participatory democracy to redeem the promise of Cold War America.

SDS served as the central organization of the New Left. Communism was simply not important to these activists. Nor was conservatism, which was then at its lowest point. They focused instead on the behavior of the liberals who ran the U.S. government from 1961 to 1968. They developed a critique of "corporate liberalism" as promoting the interests of the wealthy and the business community far more than providing for the needs of the disadvantaged.

INTERPRETING HISTORY

Martin Luther King Jr. and the Vietnam War

Most Americans approved of the war in Vietnam until at least 1968. Appreciative of Lyndon Johnson's commitment to reduce poverty and end racial discrimination at home, African Americans generally supported the president's policies in Southeast Asia. However, younger, more radical civil rights workers were among those who opposed the first insertion of U.S. combat troops in 1965. Within two years, the nation's most prominent black leader, Martin Luther King Jr., decided that he could no longer keep quiet about his growing unease with the American war effort. A storm of criticism greeted his public denunciation of the war, most of it suggesting that he should limit himself to domestic civil rights work. But King no longer believed that events at home and abroad could be separated. The following excerpt is from his speech at Riverside Church, New York City, April 4, 1967.

A few years ago there was a shining moment in that struggle [against poverty and discrimination]. It seemed as if there was a real promise of hope for the poor—both black and white—through the Poverty Program. There were experiments, hopes, new beginnings. Then came the build-up in Vietnam and I watched the program broken and eviscerated as if it were some idle political plaything of a society gone mad on war. . . . I was increasingly compelled to see the war as an enemy of the poor and to attack it as such. . . .

We were taking the black young men who had been crippled by our society and sending them 8,000 miles away to guarantee liberties in Southeast Asia which they had not found in Southwest Georgia and East Harlem. So we have been repeatedly faced with the cruel irony of watching Negro and white boys on TV screens as they kill and die together for a nation that has been unable to seat them together in the same schools. . . .

As I have walked among the desperate, rejected and angry young men [in the ghettos of the North the last three summers] I have told them that Molotov cocktails and rifles would not solve their problems. I have tried to offer them my deepest compassion while maintaining my convictions that social change comes most meaningfully through non-violent action. But they asked—and rightly so—what about Vietnam? They asked if our own nation wasn't using massive doses of violence to solve its problems, to bring about the changes it wanted. Their questions hit home, and I knew that I would never again raise my voice against the violence of the oppressed in the ghettos without having first spoken clearly to the greatest purveyor of violence in the world today—my own government. . . .

[Our troops in Vietnam] must know after a short period there that none of the things we claim to be fighting for [such as freedom, justice, and peace] are really involved. Before long they must know that their government has sent them into a struggle among Vietnamese, and the more sophisticated surely realize that we are on the side of the wealthy and the secure while we create a hell for the poor.

His birthday now a national holiday, Martin Luther King Jr. has become widely accepted as a heroic figure in the American past. But in the last few years of his life, King's increasingly sharp criticisms of injustice in American society disturbed many fellow citizens.

Questions

1. How does King believe that the U.S. war in Vietnam is related to problems at home in American society?
2. What might have been the more negative and positive racial aspects of the Vietnam War?
3. What precisely does King believe to be wrong with the U.S. war in Vietnam?

Source: Martin Luther King, Jr., and the Vietnam War from Martin Luther King Jr., *Beyond Vietnam,* Reprinted by arrangement with the Heirs of the Estate of Martin Luther King Jr. and Writers House LLC. © 1967 Estate of Martin Luther King, Jr.

After 1965, SDS's initially broad reform agenda narrowed to stopping the Vietnam War. SDS members organized the first major antiwar protest outside the White House on April 17, 1965, bringing their organization into alliance with the small group of religious and secular pacifists already working against the war. Then mainstream Democrats began abandoning Johnson over the war as it grew. The president had alienated the powerful chair of the Senate Foreign Relations Committee, J. William Fulbright of Arkansas, by issuing misleading reports during the brief U.S. military intervention in the Dominican Republic in April 1965 to defeat a left-leaning but not communist coup attempt. Fulbright then held televised hearings on the American war in Southeast Asia in January 1966, raising grave doubts about its wisdom.

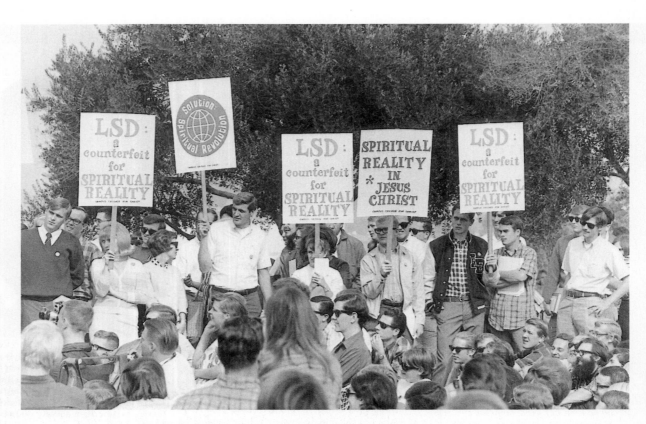

■ The search by many young people in the 1960s counterculture for greater consciousness led them to a spiritual path. These young evangelists held a Campus Crusade for Christ rally at the University of Texas at Austin in 1969. The emphasis of evangelical Christians on the person of Jesus rather than on a particular denominational tradition attracted many converts. The sandals, long hair, and gentleness associated with Jesus made a particularly good fit with the style and values of the "hippies," although most evangelicals appeared traditionally clean-cut and held conservative political views.

Draft resistance increased as young men moved to Canada, as did SNCC's Bob Moses, or went to jail, as did boxing champion Muhammad Ali.

Antiwar protesters followed the same trajectory of radicalization as black power advocates. Their dismay turned to rage as the Johnson administration continued to expand a war that was destroying much of Vietnam while killing tens of thousands of American soldiers and many more Vietnamese for no reason its opponents considered legitimate. In combination with or in support of black militants, white radicals took over buildings on university campuses in 1968–1969: Columbia, Cornell, Harvard, San Francisco State, and many others. SDS ultimately broke apart in the confusion and exhilaration of its growing demand for revolution against the larger systemic enemies, imperialism and capitalism, not just corporate liberalism. But radical rage could not be understood apart from the ongoing destruction of Vietnam by a government acting in the name of all Americans.

Cultural Rebellion and the Counterculture

While the New Left moved from wanting to reform American society to wanting to overthrow it, the counterculture sought to create an alternative society. Called "hippies" by those who disliked them, these young people were alienated by the materialism, competition, and conformity of American life in the Cold War. They tried to live out alternative values of gentleness, tolerance, and inclusivity. "Do your own thing" was a common slogan.

In reaction against the conformity of mainstream society, members of the counterculture explored the limitations of consciousness to expand their self-knowledge. They went beyond the nicotine and alcohol that were the common stimulants of their parents' culture to experiment with such mind-altering drugs as marijuana, peyote, hashish, LSD, and cocaine. Spirituality was an important path into consciousness for many in the counterculture. Religious traditions associated with Asia, particularly Buddhism, gained numerous adherents, as did spiritual customs and traditional practices of Native Americans. Others rediscovered the "authentic" Jesus obscured by the institutional structures of the formal Christian church (earning themselves the nickname "Jesus freaks"); Campus Crusade for Christ, InterVarsity, and other evangelical college groups spread across the country. Music served as the most common coin of the countercultural realm, from the political folk sound of Joan Baez and Bob Dylan to the broadly popular Beatles and the more distinctly countercultural rock 'n' roll of the Grateful Dead and Jefferson Airplane.

Older Americans experienced the counterculture largely as spectacle. The mainstream media emphasized the alternative aspects of the hippie lifestyle in its coverage. Viewers were varyingly disgusted by, attracted to, and titillated by the hair, clothing, nudity, and blurred gender distinctions. Meanwhile, entrepreneurs realized that they could market the antimaterialist counterculture profitably. Young Americans eagerly bought up records, clothing, jewelry, and natural foods, unintentionally revealing how consumer values pervaded American life.

One of the most visible changes of the 1960s was often called the sexual revolution. Changes in Americans' sexual behavior in the 1960s reflected in part the counterculture's goal of living an authentic, honest life in which words matched actions. The sexual revolution removed some of the penalties for the premarital and extramarital sex that had previously been fairly common but unacknowledged. The appearance of the birth control pill in 1960 underpinned the shift to more open sexual relationships by freeing women from the fear of pregnancy. Attitudes toward abortion also became more tolerant. New York passed the first state law legalizing some abortions in 1970, and three years later the Supreme Court established a woman's constitutional right to abortion in the landmark case of *Roe v. Wade*.

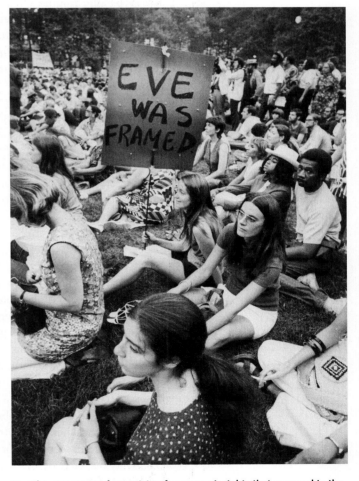

■ The new wave of organizing for women's rights that emerged in the late 1960s had many faces. Some protests against sex discrimination and disrespect for women were angry and others were gentle, as in this 1970 scene. "Raising consciousness" was a central strategy of the movement, as women and men became more aware of the gendered assumptions that had long governed—and channeled—their lives and their thoughts.

Women's Liberation

The movement for women's liberation built on developments earlier in the decade, including Betty Friedan's *The Feminine Mystique* (1963), a widely read book that captured the frustrations of many women who had accepted the role of suburban homemaker after World War II. Friedan and other liberal feminists founded the National Organization for Women (NOW) in 1966 to lobby against sexual discrimination in the public sphere in such areas as employment, wages, education, and jury duty. These challenges had radical implications for women's and men's earnings and thus for responsibilities within families, but NOW did not yet focus on issues inside the private sphere of the home.

The shift to the view that "the personal is political" came from younger women who had been active in the civil rights and antiwar struggles. Inspired by the courage and successes of the protest movements in which they figured prominently, these female activists had also learned that traditional gender roles restricted them even in organizations dedicated to participatory democracy. Ironically, radical men could be as patronizing and disrespectful of women's abilities as mainstream men. Younger feminists in 1967 and 1968 agreed with NOW's challenge to discrimination in the public sphere, but they focused even more on the personal politics of women's daily lives, on issues such as parenting, child care, housework, and abortion.

The new wave of feminism that washed through American culture at the end of the 1960s triggered fierce debates about the nature of gender. Was there a uniquely feminine way of knowing, seeing, and acting, or were women in essence the same as men, distinguishable ultimately by their individuality? Was womanhood biologically or only culturally constructed? Feminists disagreed sharply in their answers. But the women's movement that emerged out of the 1960s shared a common commitment to expanding women's possibilities that permanently transformed women's lives and gender relations in American society, in areas ranging from job and educational opportunities, sexual harassment, and gender-neutral language to family roles, sexual relations, reproductive rights, and athletic facilities.

●●●┤Read the Document

National Organization of Women, Statement of Purpose at **www.myhistorylab.com**

The Many Fronts of Liberation

Like the women's movement, the Chicano, pan-Indian, and gay liberation movements of the late 1960s were grounded in older organizing efforts within those communities. The struggles for "brown power," "red power," and "gay power" also reflected the newer influence of black power and its determination to take pride in what the dominant American society had denigrated for so long. Activists on college campuses successfully pressured administrations to establish interdisciplinary ethnic studies programs, such as the first Chicano studies program at California State University at Los Angeles in 1968. Ethnic cultural identity went hand in hand with the pursuit of political and economic integration into mainstream American life.

The most prominent push to organize Latinos was the effort led by Cesar Chávez and Dolores Huerta to build a farm workers' union in California and the Southwest. These primarily Mexican-American migrant workers harvested most of the hand-picked produce that Americans ate, but their hard work under severe conditions failed to lift them out of poverty. National consumer support for boycotts of table grapes and iceberg lettuce helped win recognition for the United Farm Workers (UFW) union and better pay by 1970.

●●●┤Read the Document

Cesar Chavez, From "He Showed Us the Way," April 1978 at **www.myhistorylab.com**

Puerto Ricans, the largest Spanish-speaking ethnic group located primarily on the East Coast, experienced a similar growth in militancy and nationalist sentiment during the late 1960s. By the 1960s, more than a million natives of the Caribbean island had moved to the East Coast, many to the New York City area. Despite being the only Latino immigrants already holding American citizenship when they arrived, Puerto Ricans experienced similar patterns of both discrimination and opportunity as Mexican Americans.

The most destitute of Americans, Indians also sought to reinvigorate their communities. On the Northwest Coast, they staged "fish-ins" in the mid-1960s to assert treaty rights. In 1968, urban activists in Minneapolis formed the American Indian Movement (AIM). On November 20, 1969, just days after the largest antiwar march in Washington, 78 Native Americans seized the island of Alcatraz in San Francisco Bay "in the name of all American Indians by right of discovery." For a year and a half, they used their occupation of the former federal prison site to publicize grievances about anti-Indian prejudice and to promote a new pan-Indian identity that reached across traditional tribal divisions. In 1973 armed members of AIM occupied buildings for two months at Wounded Knee, South Dakota, site of the infamous 1890 U.S. Army massacre of unarmed Sioux. Tribal governments sought "red power" in their own quieter way. They asserted greater tribal control of reservation schools across the country.

Although they lacked a unifying ethnic identity, gay men and lesbians also found opportunities to construct coalitions in the more open atmosphere of the late 1960s. Building on the earlier community organizing of older homosexuals in New York, San Francisco, and Los Angeles, more militant youth began to express openly their anger at the homophobic prejudice and violence prevalent in American society. The demand for tolerance and respect reached the headlines when gay patrons of the Stonewall Bar in New York fought back fiercely against a typically forceful police raid on June 27, 1969. Activists of the new Gay Liberation Front emphasized the importance of "coming out of the closet": proudly acknowledging one's sexual orientation as legitimate and decent.

The Conservative Response

What motivated the conservative revival of the late 1960s and early 1970s?

The majority of Americans had mixed feelings about the protests that roiled the nation. They were impressed by the courage of many who stood up against discrimination, and by 1968 they wanted to find a way out of the war in Southeast Asia. But they were alienated by the style and values of others who loudly demanded change in American society. Moderate and conservative citizens and generations of recent European immigrants resented what they saw as a lack of appreciation for the nation's virtues and successes. The political and social upheavals of 1968 opened the door to a Republican return to the White House, and Richard Nixon slipped through.

Backlashes

The backlash first developed in response to the increasing assertiveness of people of color. European Americans in every part of the United States had long been accustomed to deference from nonwhites and racial segregation, either by law in the South or by custom elsewhere. Like most white Americans, conservatives resented what they considered blacks' ingratitude at the civil rights measures enacted by the federal government, including black power's condemnation of whites as "crackers" and "honkies." Urban riots and escalating rates of violent crime, along with the Supreme Court's expansion of the rights of the accused, deepened their anger. They associated crime with urban African Americans, for although whites were still the majority of criminals, blacks (like any other population with less money) were disproportionately represented in prisons. Many European Americans were troubled by the militancy of Chicanos in the Southwest, Puerto Ricans in the Northeast, Indians on reservations and in cities, and African Americans almost everywhere.

Another backlash developed as a defense of traditional hierarchies against the cultural rebellions of the 1960s. Proud of their lives and values, conservatives rejected a whole array

Jules Fieffer

■ Cartoonist Jules Fieffer portrayed the generation gap that separated many younger Americans from many older ones by the early 1970s. Movements for black and Native American civil rights and against the U.S. war in Vietnam led to a profound shift in how many citizens, especially younger ones, understood their nation and its politics. A new generation of historians began to cast serious doubts on many long-accepted truisms about the American past.

of challenges to American society. Raised to believe in respecting one's elders, they resented the disrespect of many youth, who warned, "Don't trust anyone over 30." A generation that had fought and sacrificed in the "good war" against the Nazis found the absence of patriotism among many protesters unfathomable. The United States remained one of the most religious of industrialized societies, and conservative churchgoers emphasized obedience to authorities. They feared the effects of illegal drugs on their children.

The backlash against the social changes of the 1960s contained elements of class antagonism as well. Working-class whites resented the often affluent campus rebels and the black and Latino poor targeted by some Great Society programs. They believed that their values of hard work, restraint, and respectability were increasingly unappreciated and even mocked. Republican leaders from Goldwater to Nixon to Reagan gave voice to these resentments and drew votes away from Democratic blue-collar strongholds.

The Turmoil of 1968 at Home

The traumas of 1968 brought the conservative backlash to the critical stage. First came the Tet Offensive in Vietnam, creating fears that the war might become an interminable quagmire. Then, on April 4, a gunman named James Earl Ray assassinated Martin Luther King Jr. in Memphis, where he had gone to support a strike by sanitation workers. King had become more openly radical in his final years, opposing the war and working on class-based organizing of poor people. But he remained the nation's leading apostle of nonviolence, and his murder evoked despair among millions of citizens, especially African Americans. Police battled rioters and arsonists in black neighborhoods of 130 cities across the nation, with 46 people dying in the clashes.

Summer brought more shocking news. Charismatic senator Robert Kennedy's entry into the presidential campaign inspired renewed hopes among Democratic liberals. On the night of his victory in the June 5 California primary, Kennedy was killed by a deranged gunman. Vice President Hubert Humphrey seemed assured of the nomination at the Democratic convention in Chicago in August, despite his association with Johnson's war policies. Some 10,000 antiwar activists, including hundreds of FBI *agents provocateurs* (spies seeking to provoke violence), showed up to engage in protests outside the convention. Chicago's Democratic mayor Richard Daley unleashed thousands of police on protesters, bystanders, and photographers in an orgy of beatings that subsequent investigations called a police riot. Ninety million Americans watched on television as a deeply divided Democratic party appeared helpless before the violence.

Into the vacuum of public anger and alienation that accompanied the liberals' self-destruction in Chicago stepped two men. The spread of the conservative backlash from 1964 to 1968 gave Alabama governor George Wallace a wider constituency for his right-wing populist message of hostility to liberals, blacks, and federal officials. With the national Democratic party committed to racial integration, Wallace ran for president as an independent candidate and won 13.5 percent of the popular vote in November. Republican candidate Richard Nixon campaigned as the candidate of "law and order" and promised that he had a secret plan to end the war in Vietnam. Nixon won the popular vote by less than 1 percent.

TABLE 26-2

The Election of 1968

Candidate	Political Party	Popular Vote (%)	Electoral Vote
Richard M. Nixon	Republican	43.4	301
Hubert H. Humphrey	Democratic	42.7	191
George C. Wallace	American Independent	13.5	46

The Nixon Administration

A lonely, aloof man of great tenacity and ambition, Richard Nixon had worked hard to remake his public image for 1968. Widely viewed as a somewhat unscrupulous partisan since his early career in Congress, he had refashioned himself as a statesman with a broad vision for reducing international tensions between the great powers. He sounded like a conservative in the campaign against Humphrey, but once in the White House he governed as the most liberal Republican since Theodore Roosevelt, pressed by a Congress still controlled by Democrats.

Nowhere was this clearer than on issues related to natural resources. Much had happened to the environment since Republican Theodore Roosevelt's conservation efforts, none of it for the better. A powerful movement was building to protect natural resources and human health from the effects of air and water pollution. Biologist Paul Ehrlich's bestselling *The Population Bomb* (1968) warned of the dire consequences of the globe's runaway growth in human population. In 1969, the government banned the carcinogenic pesticide DDT. That same year a huge oil spill off Santa Barbara fouled 200 miles of pristine California beaches, and the Cuyahoga River in Cleveland, its surface coated with waste and oil, caught fire and burned for days. Environmentalists around the country proclaimed April 22, 1970, as "Earth Day."

Congress responded with legislation that mandated the careful management of the nation's natural resources. The Environmental Protection Agency was established in 1970. Amendments to the Clean Air (1970) and Clean Water (1972) acts tightened restrictions on harmful emissions from cars and factories. The Endangered Species Act (1973) created for the first time the legal right of nonhuman animals to survive, a major step toward viewing the quality of human life as inextricable from the earth's broader ecology.

What Nixon did care deeply about at home was politics, not policy. Antiwar demonstrations reached their height during Nixon's first two years in the White House (1969–1970). He and Vice President Spiro Agnew loathed the protesters, whom they saw as weakening the nation. The two men pursued what Agnew called "positive polarization": campaigning to further divide the respectable "silent majority," as the president labeled his supporters, from voluble liberal Democrats in Congress and radical activists on the streets, whom they associated with permissiveness and lawlessness. In this broad cultural battle for political supremacy, the president appealed to conservative white southern and northern ethnic Democrats.

Early in his administration, Nixon began wielding the power of the federal government to harass his political opponents. Johnson had used the FBI, the CIA, and military intelligence agencies to infiltrate and thin the ranks of antiwar demonstrators and nonwhite nationalists. Nixon continued these illegal operations. Nixon went beyond other presidents in assembling an "Enemies List" that included prominent elements of the political mainstream, especially liberals, the press, and his Democratic opponents. The president was particularly concerned about controlling secret information. The Pentagon Papers were a classified Defense Department history of U.S. actions in Vietnam revealing that the government had been deceiving the American public about the course of the war. When disillusioned former Pentagon official Daniel Ellsberg leaked the study to the *New York Times* for publication in 1971, Nixon was enraged. The White House created a team of covert operatives nicknamed "the plumbers" to "plug leaks" by whatever means necessary.

> *Antiwar demonstrations reached their height during Nixon's first two years in the White House (1969–1970).*

Escalating and De-escalating in Vietnam

Nixon and his national security adviser, Henry Kissinger, had ambitious plans for shifting the relationships of the great powers to America's advantage. To deal with China and the Soviet Union, they first had to reduce the vast U.S. engagement in the small country of Vietnam, which had grown wildly out of proportion to actual U.S. interests there. Under the Nixon Doctrine, the United States would provide military hardware rather than U.S. soldiers to allied governments, which would have to do their own fighting against leftist insurgencies.

In South Vietnam, this doctrine required "Vietnamization," or withdrawing American troops so ARVN could shoulder the bulk of the war.

The key to a successful withdrawal from Vietnam for Nixon was to preserve U.S. "credibility." The perception of power could be as important as its actual exercise, and the president wanted other nations, both friend and foe, to continue to respect and fear American military might. There was no immediate pullout but a gradual process that lasted for four years (1969–1973), during which almost half of the total U.S. casualties in Vietnam occurred. Nixon did his utmost to weaken the communist forces during the slow withdrawal. The president ordered the secret bombing and invasion of neighboring Cambodia and Laos, an intensified aerial assault on North Vietnam, and the mining of Haiphong Harbor near Hanoi. Enormous protests rocked the country after the announcement of the Cambodian invasion on April 30, 1970. National Guard troops killed four students at a demonstration at Kent State University in Ohio and two at Jackson State College in Mississippi, deepening the sense of national division.

A majority of Americans now opposed the nation's war effort, a level of dissent unprecedented in U.S. history. Most telling of all was the criticism of some veterans returning from Vietnam. The morale of American soldiers still in Vietnam plummeted as the steady withdrawal of their comrades made clear that they were no longer expected to win the war. Drug abuse and racial conflict increased sharply among GIs. Even "fragging" (killing one's own officers) escalated before the peace accords were signed in Paris and the United States evacuated its last combat troops in 1973.

View the *Image*
Kent State Demonstrations at **www.myhistorylab.com**

Read the *Document*
Richard Nixon, "Peace With Honor" (1973) at **www.myhistorylab.com**

CONCLUSION

Between 1964 and 1971, young, nonwhite, and female Americans laid claim to greater equality. The ratification of the Twenty-Sixth Amendment in 1971 reduced the voting age from 21 to 18, in acknowledgment of the sacrifices of young people sent to fight in Vietnam. In large numbers, women challenged and overcame traditional limits on their personal and work lives. Racial discrimination and segregation were outlawed.

These years also witnessed striking disjunctures. The nation accomplished humanity's age-old dream of walking on the surface of the moon when Neil Armstrong stepped out of the *Apollo 11* spacecraft on July 20, 1969, while at home the country sometimes appeared to be coming apart at the seams. Poverty rates dropped to their lowest point ever, yet violence seemed to pervade the land. The slaughter of 43 people (mostly African Americans) by white state police retaking the Attica prison in upstate New York after an inmate insurrection in 1971 was one of the single most deadly confrontations between Americans since the Civil War.

The deceptive manner in which Johnson and Nixon waged the war in Vietnam eroded Americans' faith in their public officials. American life also grew more informal as the egalitarian style of the various social movements of the 1960s spread into the broader culture. But the removal of some of the most blatant distinctions of race and gender did not extend to differences of class. In the watershed cases of *San Antonio Independent School District v. Rodriguez* (1973) and *Milliken v. Bradley* (1974), the Supreme Court ruled that wealthier districts did not have to share financing with poorer ones, nor did they have to share students by means of busing. The Court found that there was no constitutional right to an education of equal quality. The ladder of social mobility remained slippery in a nation whose neighborhoods were still stratified between the affluent and the poor.

For Review

✓●─[Study and **Review** at **www.myhistorylab.com**

1. What did Lyndon Johnson think was wrong with American society, and how did he try to fix it?

2. Why did the United States go to war in Vietnam, and why did it not win the war?

3. In which ways and how closely were the various protest movements of the 1960s related to each other?

4. How central were race relations to the conservative backlash that appeared in the late 1960s?

Chronology: 1964–1971

1964 Gulf of Tonkin Resolution (supporting Johnson on Vietnam).
Civil Rights Act of 1964 (employment and accommodations).
Wilderness Act.

1965 Voting Rights Act of 1965.
Griswold v. Connecticut legalizes birth control for married couples.
Watts (Los Angeles) uprising.

1966 Clean Water Act.
National Organization for Women (NOW) founded.

1967 Thurgood Marshall appointed first African American to U.S. Supreme Court.
Riots in Detroit, Michigan, and Newark, New Jersey.
Tet offensive (by Communist forces in Vietnam).

1968 My Lai massacre.
Martin Luther King Jr. assassinated.
Richard Nixon elected president.

1969 Huge antiwar protests in Washington, D.C.
Stonewall raid, New York City.
Astronauts Neil Armstrong and Buzz Aldrin walk on the moon.

1970 United States invades Cambodia (expanding war in Vietnam).
National Guard troops kill four students, Kent State University in Ohio.

1971 Pentagon Papers published.

Key Terms

Black power The slogan used by young black nationalists in the mid- and late 1960s. p. 605

Great Society In the 1960s, President Lyndon Johnson's programs for reducing poverty, discrimination, and pollution, and for improving health care, education, and consumer protection. p. 597

Reconsidering National Priorities, 1972–1979

ABC television news anchor Howard K. Smith began his coverage of a women's rights march in New York City in 1970 by quoting with approval the words of Vice President Spiro Agnew: "Three things have been difficult to tame. The ocean, fools, and women. We may soon be able to tame the ocean, but fools and women will take a little longer." Condescension toward women still pervaded American society, and few men even noticed it. The political upheavals of the 1960s had barely touched the relationships between most women and men by the start of the new decade. But all this changed as the 1970s unfolded.

The spread of ideas about women's liberation in the 1970s transformed the personal lives of almost every American, female and male alike. **Feminism** challenged the most basic and intimate assumptions about relationships, family, work, and power. It also sharply expanded women's opportunities. For example, Emily Howell Warner was born in 1939 and grew up in Colorado, wanting to be a flight attendant. Friends suggested she try flying lessons instead. On a regular commercial flight one day, a flight attendant took her up to see the cockpit. She was fascinated by "all those dials and switches" and knew she wanted to fly. After years of hard work and training, in 1973 Warner became the first woman hired as a pilot by a scheduled U.S. carrier, Frontier Airlines. Within three years, she was the first female promoted to captain, and in 1986 Warner commanded the first all-female flight crew on a commercial flight.

Feminism joined with other developments of the decade to force Americans to reexamine much that they had taken for granted. Elected on the promise to end the war in Southeast Asia "with honor," President Nixon escalated the fighting before eventually withdrawing U.S. forces from Vietnam. At the same time, he repaired relations with both China and the Soviet Union as those two communist powers drew apart. Americans thus suffered their first clear defeat in war while also seeing the Cold War splinter. Scandal in the White House then forced the first resignation of a U.S. president and deepened public distrust of political authorities. American economic growth—the foundation of the country's power—stumbled because of spending on the Vietnam War and oil shortages. High-paying manufacturing jobs declined as factories began to move overseas in pursuit of cheaper labor, and skilled blue-collar workers saw their status as middle-class Americans start to slip. Unemployment grew sharply. A growing environmental movement raised troubling questions about whether an expanding economy and exploitation of natural resources should continue to top the country's list of priorities.

Journalist Tom Wolfe dubbed the 1970s the "Me Decade." The label did have some merit: many Americans turned away from the public sphere after the exhilarating but divisive politics of the 1960s and pursued self-exploration and self-fulfillment instead. Crime, divorce, premarital and extramarital sex, and drug use all increased while the nation's economic health and international status declined. But the 1970s also witnessed a rethinking of long-standing assumptions: about how democracy should work at home, what role the nation should play in international affairs, how people ought to treat the environment, and how men and women should relate to each other.

■ Emily Howell Warner, the first woman hired as a pilot by a scheduled U.S. carrier.

Twin Shocks: Détente and Watergate

Richard Nixon had long been the nation's leading anticommunist. No one had more fiercely opposed leftists at home and communists in China and the Soviet Union. However, the president was more a savvy political opportunist than an ideologue. He and his national security adviser, Henry Kissinger, saw a chance to use mounting Chinese-Soviet tensions to the advantage of the United States as they withdrew American armed forces from Vietnam.

How did détente and the Watergate scandal affect U.S. foreign relations and American politics?

At the same time that Nixon manipulated the Cold War abroad, the Republican president initiated a campaign of illegal actions at home to weaken his political opponents in the Democratic party. This strategy backfired in the Watergate scandal, which drove him from office in 1974.

Triangular Diplomacy

Nixon and Kissinger prided themselves on their "realpolitik" approach to foreign policy: their pragmatic assessment of other powers' security needs, regardless of ideology, and their collaboration with those powers on issues of common concern. In 1969 China and the USSR gave Nixon and Kissinger an ideal opportunity to exercise their realpolitik skills. That year, tensions that had been building between the two communist states erupted in brief skirmishing between Chinese and Soviet troops on their shared border. Nixon envisioned a "triangular diplomacy" that he hoped would divide the communist world.

The president and Kissinger also shared a commitment to secrecy. Any fundamental revision of the nation's foreign policy, they believed, could happen only if they concentrated all decision-making in the White House. They set out to keep Congress, the press, and even their own State Department in the dark. Diplomatic innovation thus went hand in hand with an unprecedented extension of the secretive national security state.

Nixon's 1972 visit to China brought a host of benefits. Live television coverage showed Nixon toasting Mao Zedong, premier of the People's Republic of China, while a Chinese military band played "America the Beautiful" and "Home on the Range."

Americans' impression of the People's Republic as a grim, forbidding land began to give way to a renewed interest in China as an exotic but intriguing place. Cultural exchanges soon proliferated: first ping-pong teams, eventually legions of students. U.S. businesses also cast a covetous eye at the immense China market. Trade between the two nations rose dramatically over the next three decades.

Nixon and Kissinger now constructed the other leg of their diplomatic triangle. As they anticipated, the Soviets had taken alarm at the warming of relations between their two greatest rivals. Nixon flew to Moscow for a summit meeting with Soviet leader Leonid Brezhnev in May 1972 that initiated a policy of **détente** (relaxation of tensions). A trade pact quickly followed. The two superpowers also agreed to limit offensive nuclear weapons (the Strategic Arms Limitations Treaty, or SALT I) and to ban antiballistic missile defense systems (the ABM treaty).

Like the Soviet leaders, Nixon and Kissinger sought to preserve the existing international balance of power. Dealmaking with China and the USSR constituted one step in this process. In another, the two men sought to stifle socialist revolutions in Third World nations by bolstering pro-American allies there. For instance, the duo feared that the democratic election of socialist Salvador Allende in Chile in 1970 would lead to "another Cuba." A socialist leader might nationalize the investments of U.S. corporations in Chile and perhaps challenge Washington's capitalist hegemony in the Western Hemisphere. Determined to block these possibilities, the CIA secretly funded a right-wing military coup in Chile in September 1973. Allende died in the assault on the presidential palace, and the rebel forces murdered thousands of his supporters and established a brutal military dictatorship under General Augusto Pinochet. "I don't see why we need to stand by and watch a country go Communist because of the irresponsibility of its own people," Kissinger explained privately.

Scandal in the White House

Meanwhile, on the domestic front, Washington police caught agents of Nixon's reelection campaign breaking into the Democratic National Committee headquarters in the **Watergate** hotel and office complex on June 17, 1972. The burglars' goal was to put in place secret listening devices, or "bugs." Later, the White House tried to cover up its connections to the crime.

The Watergate break-in was only one part of the administration's broader campaign of illegal warfare against its political opponents. An insecure and unhappy loner, Nixon harbored an almost paranoid suspicion when he took office in early 1969. The president and his aides regularly discussed "how we can use the available federal machinery to screw our political enemies," in the words of White House counsel John Dean. They persuaded the FBI and the CIA to monitor and harass antiwar activists and pushed the Internal Revenue Service to investigate prominent Democrats. They extorted large contributions to the Republican party from corporate executives by making it clear that federal agencies would otherwise impede the pursuit of their business interests. The *New York Times*'s publication of the classified Pentagon Papers in 1971 stiffened the resolve of the Committee to Reelect the President (CREEP) to stop any further leaks. The committee assembled a group of undercover operatives (the "plumbers") to stop leaks and to engineer "dirty tricks" against the Democrats.

After the bungled Watergate break-in, the president directed the cover-up from the beginning, and then lied about it to the public. He also used the CIA to hinder the FBI's investigation into the matter. He approved payments of hush

TABLE 27-1			
The Election of 1972			
Candidate	Political Party	Popular Vote (%)	Electoral Vote
Richard M. Nixon	Republican	60.7	520
George S. McGovern	Democratic	31.5	17

money to the burglars to keep them quiet about their ties to the White House. Nixon's abuse of power escalated as he pressured his subordinates to perjure themselves in court. For most of a year, the cover-up held, and Nixon won reelection in 1972.

But the persistent investigations by *Washington Post* journalists Bob Woodward and Carl Bernstein kept the heat on. In early 1973, the administration began to crack due to a grand jury probe in the federal court of Judge John Sirica. The president's men lost confidence that the cover-up would hold and began looking for ways to save their own skins. Congress initiated its own televised investigations that mesmerized a national audience. The Senate Watergate committee, chaired by eloquent conservative North Carolina Democrat Sam Ervin, methodically exposed with growing bipartisan support the criminal actions in the White House. The key issue, as framed by Republican committee member Howard Baker of Tennessee, became, "What did the president know, and when did he know it?"

On July 16, 1973, White House aide Alexander Butterfield told the Senate committee that a built-in recorder taped all conversations in the Oval Office. Almost certainly, these tapes would provide answers to questions about the president's role. Both Congress and Justice Department special prosecutor Archibald Cox subpoenaed the White House tapes, but Nixon refused to hand them over. Instead, he fired Cox on October 20 in what became known as the Saturday Night Massacre. Outraged, Congress initiated impeachment proceedings against the president. In the spring of 1974, the House Judiciary Committee passed bills of impeachment for his specific abuses of power. Before the full House could vote to impeach him and the Senate decide on his guilt or innocence, the Supreme Court ruled that the White House had to turn over the subpoenaed tapes. The content of the tapes revealed the extent of the president's involvement in the cover-up and his personal crudeness, vindictiveness, and ethnic and racial prejudices. Facing a certain guilty verdict, Nixon resigned on August 9, 1974, less than halfway through his second term.

Watch the Video
Richard Nixon, "I am not a crook" at
www.myhistorylab.com

> *After the bungled Watergate break-in, the president directed the cover-up from the beginning, and then lied about it to the public.*

Read the Document
Committee's Conclusion on Impeachment at
www.myhistorylab.com

The Nation After Watergate

Never before had a U.S. president resigned from office. Many citizens celebrated the outcome of the Watergate investigations as evidence of democracy's resilience and power to uncover criminal activity in the White House and bring down a corrupt president. But the affair also discredited political institutions Americans had long respected. Indeed, the Nixon administration proved quite corrupt. A whole raft of senior officials, including the president's closest aides, H. R. Haldeman and John Ehrlichman, went to prison. Even Vice President Spiro Agnew had been forced to resign amid the Watergate investigations when a Maryland jury found him guilty of tax evasion dating back to his years as governor there. Congress swung strongly to the Democrats in the 1974 elections, slowing the Republicans' rise to the status of majority party.

The man who replaced Nixon in the White House faced a daunting situation. Gerald Ford, longtime Republican congressman and House minority leader from Grand Rapids, Michigan, had been tapped by Nixon to replace Agnew as vice president. Well liked by members of both parties, Ford seemed to embody the antidote to the extreme styles of both Nixon and Agnew. To restore decency and trust in the government, Ford saw his role as healing what he called "the wounds of the past." Within a month, he granted a "full, free, and absolute pardon" to Nixon for any crimes he may have committed as president, precluding any trial and punishment within a court of law. However, most Americans believed that Nixon should have faced justice for his actions, as had the people who carried out his orders. Ford's popularity plummeted overnight from 72 percent to 49 percent and never fully recovered.

■ Many South Vietnamese fled the communist victory in their country in 1975, including this woman and her children crossing the Mekong River. Most of the refugees undertook extremely perilous journeys by boat to other Southeast Asian nations, and hundreds of thousands eventually made their way to the United States.

If Ford inherited the fallout from Watergate at home, abroad he inherited the pending defeat in Vietnam. Military veterans returned to a nation determined to ignore or demean their sacrifices, and they quickly learned to keep their combat-induced traumas to themselves. When Saigon finally fell to the combined invasion of National Liberation Front and North Vietnamese fighters on April 30, 1975, Americans watched the televised images with both bitterness and relief. Two weeks later, Cambodian communist forces briefly seized the U.S. container ship *Mayaguez*, provoking Ford to demonstrate that the United States was still ready and willing to flex its military muscle. But 41 U.S. soldiers died in the rescue mission to save 39 sailors whom, it turned out, Cambodia had already released. Ford and Kissinger, continuing as the new president's secretary of state, pursued détente with the Soviets at summit meetings in Vladivostock (1974) and Helsinki (1975). At the same time, they supported anticommunist forces in various Third World conflicts, such as the civil war that erupted in Angola after that country achieved its independence in 1975.

Discovering the Limits of the U.S. Economy

How did the economic changes affect the way Americans felt about their country?

Defeat in Vietnam and corruption in the White House were soon joined by grim economic news. Generation after generation of Americans had watched their incomes rise. Since World War II had pulled the U.S. economy out of the Great Depression, median family income had doubled. But by 1973, the famous American standard of living began to decline. The three pillars of postwar prosperity—cheap energy, rising wages, and low inflation—simultaneously crumbled. The costs of the Vietnam War struck home at the same time that an oil embargo spawned by conflict in the Middle East gripped the country. Moreover, a widening environmental movement raised questions about the pursuit of endless economic growth on a planet that more and more people realized had limited natural resources.

The End of the Long Boom

During the 1970s, a terrible new economic scourge dubbed "stagflation" hit the United States. For the first time, employment and wages stagnated while prices climbed. What explained this phenomenon? Spending on the Vietnam War and on Great Society programs had pulled prices upward. The government had never raised enough taxes to cover the expense of the war, so it paid the bills by simply printing more dollars. In 1971 annual inflation stood at 4.3 percent, more than twice the pre-Vietnam rate; three years later it reached 11 percent, and by 1980 it topped out at 13.5 percent.

These figures devastated Americans' sense of economic security. Average real wages (income adjusted for inflation) dropped by an average of 2 percent a year from 1973 to the early 1990s. Unemployment rose to 9 percent in 1975. Only the continued flow of women into the workforce, seen by most families as an economic necessity, kept the majority of U.S. families afloat financially. The portion of citizens living in poverty, which had dropped sharply through the 1960s to 11 percent in 1973, rose again, hitting 15 percent by 1982. The gap between rich and poor began widening.

> *Only the continued flow of women into the workforce, seen by most families as an economic necessity, kept the majority of U.S. families afloat financially.*

This decline stemmed in part from competition from abroad, particularly West Germany and Japan. With U.S. assistance (and without the military expenditures that so burdened the United States), those countries had finally rebuilt their economies after World War II and boasted new, more efficient industrial facilities. The trade surplus that had long symbolized global U.S. economic superiority evaporated in 1971. That year, U.S. imports overtook exports for the first time in the twentieth century. Worried international investors traded in dollars for gold, forcing Nixon to end the 27-year-old Bretton Woods monetary system that had linked all other currencies to the dollar at fixed exchange rates. Freed from the fixed rate of $35 per ounce of gold, the value of the dollar dropped like a stone; by the end of the decade, it took $800 to buy an ounce of gold.

In this competitive environment, the *Wall Street Journal* reported, American companies "seek places where labor, land, electricity, and taxes are cheap." Corporations found those places in the American South and Southwest, regions characterized by few labor unions, low wage rates, minimal taxes, and negligible local government regulations. Many more such places were in neighboring Mexico, where U.S. companies established *maquiladoras*. These assembly plants, often just a few hundred yards across the Mexican-U.S. border, allowed corporations to hire primarily female workers at low wages and avoid strict U.S. environmental, labor, and safety laws. The long-term decline of the Rustbelt—the series of urban industrial centers strung across the American Northeast and Midwest—accelerated in the 1970s.

High unemployment and shrinking real wages contributed to rising anti-immigrant sentiment. Black Americans also faced an increasing backlash against hard-won civil rights gains. While court-ordered busing to integrate schools

■ White resistance to school busing in Boston sometimes turned violent in the mid-1970s. On April 5, 1976, white high school students from South Boston and Charlestown met with a city councilwoman who supported their boycott of classes. Outside City Hall, they chanced upon lawyer Theodore Landsmark and assaulted him. Photographer Stanley J. Forman won the Pulitzer Prize for this photo.

in segregated neighborhoods proceeded slowly but peacefully in the South, northern urban whites dug in their heels. In Boston, violence erupted in the school hallways and the streets from 1975 to 1978 as economically vulnerable working-class whites harassed African Americans attending schools in white ethnic neighborhoods of South Boston, and blacks defended themselves.

The Oil Embargo

Nothing revealed Americans' newfound economic vulnerability more than the 1973–1974 boycott initiated by the Oil Producing and Exporting Countries (OPEC). The largest producers of oil were the Arab countries around the Persian Gulf, especially Saudi Arabia. These nations had resented the creation of Israel in 1948 and the resulting displacement of the Palestinians. War broke out in 1967 and Israel seized control of the West Bank of the Jordan River and the Gaza Strip. Six years later, Egypt and Syria struck back, attacking and threatening to overrun Israel, but the United States gave the Israeli army a critical resupply of weapons that helped turn the tide of battle.

Henry Kissinger then shuttled between Tel Aviv and Cairo to negotiate a ceasefire. His diplomatic skills won him the Nobel peace prize and laid the groundwork for a warming of U.S. relations with Egypt (the most populous Arab nation though not an oil producer). However, the other Arab states expressed outrage at this demonstration of America's close links with the Israelis, and Arabs of all political persuasions were determined to voice their displeasure.

In October 1973, the OPEC nations initiated an embargo on selling oil to the United States and to western European nations that had supported Israel in the war. Oil supplies dwindled, and prices at gas pumps skyrocketed to four times their previous levels. Even when OPEC lifted the embargo after five months, it kept prices high by limiting production. Steeper energy costs powerfully accelerated inflation. Decades of easy access to cheap gasoline came to a sudden halt.

The Environmental Movement

The oil embargo encouraged many U.S. citizens to rethink the nation's cavalier use of natural resources. Environmental consciousness spread rapidly in the 1970s as evidence revealed the impact of industrial growth on the quality of life in the United States. Environmental

■ **FIGURE 27.1**
IMPORTED PETROLEUM AS SHARE OF U.S. PETROLEUM CONSUMPTION
Abundant natural resources, especially coal and oil, encouraged Americans' long-standing feeling of national strength and autonomy. After World War II, however, the United States switched from exporting oil to importing oil. Conservation measures in the 1970s temporarily reversed America's growing dependence on oil from abroad.

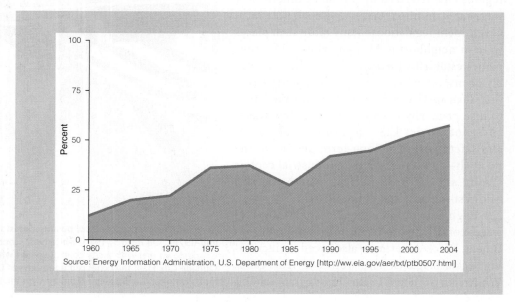

Source: Energy Information Administration, U.S. Department of Energy [http://ww.eia.gov/aer/txt/ptb0507.html]

organizations such as the Sierra Club, the National Wildlife Federation, and the Audubon Society saw their memberships soar. For the first time, the media began to examine the daunting range of environmental problems plaguing the United States and the rest of the world: acid rain, groundwater contamination, smog, rainforest destruction, oil spills, nuclear waste disposal, species extinction, ozone depletion, and global warming.

Environmentalists argued that the idea of unlimited consumption of natural resources was fundamentally irresponsible, both to future human generations and to other species. They urged Congress and the Environmental Protection Agency (EPA) to require fuel-efficient engines from carmakers and to promote renewable energy sources such as water, solar, and wind power. Citizen groups such as the Clamshell Alliance in New England and the Abalone Alliance in California protested the construction of new nuclear power plants. These operations, they pointed out, had no reliable method in place for disposing of nuclear waste.

Discovering the limits of the U.S. economy so soon after the Vietnam War and the Watergate scandal spawned a crisis of confidence.

A broad critique of the chemical industry's impact on public health also emerged in the 1970s. As it turned out, pesticides worked their way up the food chain into people's bodies. Some artificial sweeteners proved carcinogenic, and the lead that manufacturers had added to gasoline and house paint for generations caused brain damage. Long-standing industrial dumping of toxic chemicals made headlines.

The crisis at Love Canal in upstate New York helped bring the issue of toxic waste home to Americans. The Hooker Chemical Company had buried tons of poisonous waste in a dry canal in the town of Niagara Falls between 1947 and 1952 and then covered it over with dirt. The company gave the land to the town, which promptly built a school on it. A middle-class neighborhood soon grew up around the site. But the ground smelled odd and oozed mysterious substances. Sometimes it even caught on fire for no apparent reason. By the 1970s, local rates of cancer and other severe illnesses had soared. The chemical and industrial plant workers who lived in the neighborhood began to suspect that their

■ Thousands of runners surge up the Hayes Street hill in San Francisco in the annual 7-mile Bay-to-Breakers race across the city. In the 1970s, regular exercise began to become a common part of daily life for many Americans. At the same time, fast food and higher-fat diets contributed to a growing pattern of Americans being overweight and even obese.

quiet loyalty to their employers was no longer worth the risk to the health of their families. Persistent activism by community members finally overcame local, state, and company officials' efforts to keep the contents of the buried canal secret. In August 1978, New York governor Hugh Carey at last agreed to buy out the entire neighborhood, seal it off, and move residents elsewhere.

Discovering the limits of the U.S. economy so soon after the Vietnam War and the Watergate scandal spawned a crisis of confidence. Many Americans resented the idea of limits. But others began to embrace the idea of creating a healthier lifestyle that focused less on material consumption. Exercise, especially running, began to become an increasingly common activity for middle-class adults. The wildly successful Nike athletic shoe company was founded in 1972, and entrants in the New York City Marathon ballooned from 126 in 1970 to 10,000 by 1978. Interest in outdoor recreation—hiking, camping, and bicycling—grew exponentially. Recycling also started its climb from a fringe activity to common practice in a few parts of the country.

Reshuffling Politics

Which were the most significant political reforms of the 1970s?

The skepticism toward authority and tradition spawned by the counterculture, the Vietnam War, and the Watergate scandal spread through American culture in the 1970s. The use of illegal drugs, especially marijuana, was widespread. Casual sexual relationships proliferated in a decade when contraceptive pills had become widely available and the AIDS virus had not yet appeared. Popular and critically acclaimed films featured tales of malfeasance in high places. *All the President's Men* (1976) told the story of the Nixon administration's Watergate crimes. *Apocalypse Now* (1979) revealed the madness of the American war in Vietnam. *Three Days of the Condor* (1975) portrayed the CIA as a rogue agency beyond democratic control. *Blazing Saddles* (1974) hilariously spoofed the heroic Westerns that had long served as the staple of American moviegoers' diet. *One Flew over the Cuckoo's Nest* (1975) used novelist Ken Kesey's story of an insane asylum to suggest that those in charge were more dangerous than the inmates. In this atmosphere Congress began to reassert its authority against the "imperial presidency," and in 1976 voters put an obscure, devout Georgia peanut farmer and former one-term governor in the White House.

Congressional Power Reasserted

The double shock of defeat in Vietnam and the Watergate scandal reawakened a Congress that had grown accustomed to deferring to the White House in foreign affairs. Tellingly, Congress had never formally declared war on North Korea or North Vietnam, although such declaration is its constitutional duty. Angered by the illegalities and deception in both the Johnson and Nixon administrations, Congress passed the War Powers Act in 1973 to limit the president's capacity to wage undeclared wars. The bill required the chief executive to obtain explicit congressional approval for keeping U.S. troops in an overseas conflict longer than ninety days.

Defeat in Vietnam and the Watergate scandal reawakened a Congress that had grown accustomed to deferring to the White House in foreign affairs.

With encouragement from voters and journalists, Congress also uncovered its eyes and began to investigate the covert side of American foreign policy that had gathered momentum since 1945. After Watergate popped the cork on the bottled-up secret abuses of the executive branch, other troubling news spilled out about the nation's intelligence agencies, including CIA "dirty tricks" and the agency's Operation Chaos. The latter program of illegal domestic espionage against antiwar

INTERPRETING HISTORY

The Church Committee and CIA Covert Operations

In 1975–1976 the U.S. Senate Select Committee to Study Governmental Operations with Respect to Intelligence Activities engaged in the first comprehensive review by Congress of the actions of the Central Intelligence Agency. Under the leadership of Frank Church (D-Idaho), the committee investigated both intelligence gathering ("spying") and covert operations, the secret side of American foreign policy during the Cold War. One of the most controversial issues that the Church committee examined was evidence of the CIA's attempted use of assassination as a means of dealing with key figures in Cuba, the Congo, the Dominican Republic, South Vietnam, and Chile.

Alleged Assassination Plots Involving Foreign Leaders (Interim Report, November 20, 1975)

The Committee has received evidence that ranking Government officials discussed, and may have authorized, the establishment with the CIA of a generalized assassination capability. . . .

The evidence establishes that the United States was implicated in several assassination plots. . . . Our inquiry also reveals serious problems with respect to United States involvement in coups directed against foreign governments. . . .

Once methods of coercion and violence are chosen, the probability of loss of life is always present. There is, however, a significant difference between a coldblooded, targeted, intentional killing of an individual foreign leader and other forms of intervening in the affairs of foreign nations. . . .

A star baseball pitcher who once turned down an offer to sign with the New York Giants, Fidel Castro led a leftist, anti-American revolution in Cuba in 1959. U.S. hostility and Castro's evolving politics moved him to declare Cuba a communist state in 1961. The CIA tried unsuccessfully to arrange for Castro's assassination.

Non-attribution to the United States for covert operations was the original and principal purpose of the so-called doctrine of "plausible denial."

Evidence before the Committee clearly demonstrates that this concept, designed to protect the United States and its operatives from the consequences of disclosures, has been expanded to mask decisions of the President and his senior staff members. . . .

"Plausible denial" can also lead to the use of euphemism and circumlocution, which are designed to allow the President and other senior officials to deny knowledge of an operation should it be disclosed. . . .

It is possible that there was a failure of communication between policymakers and the agency personnel who were experienced in secret, and often violent, action. Although policymakers testified that assassination was not intended by such words as "get rid of Castro," some of their subordinates in the Agency

testified that they perceived that assassination was desired and that they should proceed without troubling their superiors. . . .

Running throughout the cases considered in this report was the expectation of American officials that they could control the actions of dissident groups which they were supporting in foreign countries. Events demonstrated that the United States had no such power. This point is graphically demonstrated by cables exchanged shortly before the coup in Vietnam. Ambassador Lodge cabled Washington on October 30, 1963, that he was unable to halt a coup; a cable from William Bundy in response stated that "we cannot accept conclusion that we have no power to delay or discourage a coup." The coup took place three days later. . . .

Officials of the CIA made use of persons associated with the criminal underworld in attempting to achieve the assassination of Fidel Castro. These underworld figures were relied upon because it was believed that they had expertise and contacts that were not available to law-abiding citizens. . . .

It may well be ourselves that we injure most if we adopt tactics "more ruthless than the enemy."

Questions

1. *What are the dangers to the United States of using assassination as a tool of U.S. foreign policy? Is the use of assassination compatible with the practice of democracy? How might it affect American society at home, as well as the way other nations perceive the United States?*

2. *Did the attacks of September 11, 2001, change the way Americans view the possible use by their government of assassination and other covert operations abroad? Should the attacks have altered Americans' attitudes about these issues?*

dissidents paralleled FBI abuses such as the Cointelpro campaigns to defame Martin Luther King Jr. and destroy the Black Panthers and the American Indian Movement. Congressional investigators documented CIA involvement in assassination attempts against foreign leaders such as Fidel Castro of Cuba and Patrice Lumumba of the Congo.

These revelations stirred fierce controversy among those who took an interest in national and international politics. Many citizens decried what their government had done in their names and without their knowledge. However, officials claimed that the extreme conditions of the Cold War and the duplicity of the Soviets necessitated secrecy. At the core of this controversy were two burning questions. How transparent could a democratic society and its government afford to be when they also had global interests to protect? And when democratic openness and imperial self-interest conflicted, which should win out?

Jimmy Carter: "I Will Never Lie to You"

In the backwash of Watergate, two presidential candidates—both outsiders to national politics—became advocates for opposing sides in the debate about power and openness in 1976. Former California governor Ronald Reagan made a strong run at the Republican nomination, falling just short at the Kansas City convention as incumbent Gerald Ford held on to head the GOP ticket. Reagan articulated conservative Americans' anger at seeing U.S. autonomy and power abroad hemmed in. He opposed détente with the Soviets, supported anticommunists everywhere, and warned against a treaty that would return control of the Panama Canal to the Panamanians. Ford found himself burdened by the faltering economy, weakened by Reagan's criticisms from the right, and hampered by widespread resentment of his pardon for Nixon.

TABLE 27-2			
The Election of 1976			
Candidate	**Political Party**	**Popular Vote (%)**	**Electoral Vote**
Jimmy Carter	Democratic	50.0	297
Gerald R. Ford	Republican	47.9	241

Jimmy Carter was the winner. The former Georgia governor based his candidacy on moral uplift. Contrasting himself to the Nixon administration, he told audiences, "I will never lie to you." Instead, Carter promised openness, accountability, and a government "as good and decent as the American people."

Carter was also a Naval Academy graduate, a former nuclear engineer, a successful peanut farmer and businessperson, and the first president from the Deep South in more than a century. A born-again Christian, he had supported civil rights during his governorship in Georgia. Carter kept his diminutive first name: Jimmy, not James nor even Jim. He wore denim, and he carried his own bags. At his inaugural parade, he and his wife Rosalynn chose to walk down Pennsylvania Avenue rather than ride in a limousine.

The new president entered the White House at a time of unusual resistance to executive authority. He encountered an assertive and suspicious Congress. He faced an economy still mired in stagflation as unemployment and prices kept rising and interest rates reached 21 percent.

Politics and ideology also hamstrung the new president, limiting his ability to lead his own party in governing the nation. The Georgian was the first Democratic president since the 1930s who did not fully subscribe to the New Deal principle of government regulation of the economy. As a social moderate but an economic conservative, Carter had a strong desire to balance the federal budget. This vision placed him closer to the Republicans than to many in his own party. Carter's tendency to take moralistic stands did not mesh well with the horse-trading style of compromise that characterized Congress. The president and his aides tried to govern as outsiders to the federal government. They viewed insiders as selfish and narrowminded. They failed to cultivate relationships with Democratic leaders in Congress such as powerful House Speaker Thomas ("Tip") O'Neill of Massachusetts. Meanwhile, seasoned legislators of both parties looked down on the new administration as inexperienced and naive.

Rise of a Peacemaker

Carter's idealism proved more effective, at least during his first two years, in refashioning U.S. foreign policy. The president started the national healing process with his first official act in office: he granted a "full, complete, and unconditional pardon" to those who had evaded the draft during the Vietnam War. He also tried to replace indiscriminate anticommunism with the promotion of human rights as the main theme in international affairs. "We are now free of that inordinate fear of Communism which once led us to embrace any dictator who joined us in that fear," he told an audience at Notre Dame University.

All presidents since 1945 had loudly supported human rights in the Soviet bloc. Carter defended dissidents in authoritarian countries friendly to the United States as well. His commitment to ending racial discrimination at home and his promotion of human rights abroad led to his administration's strong support for an end to white minority rule in southern Africa, including the establishment of Zimbabwe out of the old white-ruled Rhodesia in 1980.

Carter encouraged Americans to shift their attention from the East-West Cold War to the burgeoning problems between industrialized nations of the Northern Hemisphere and mostly poor countries of the Southern

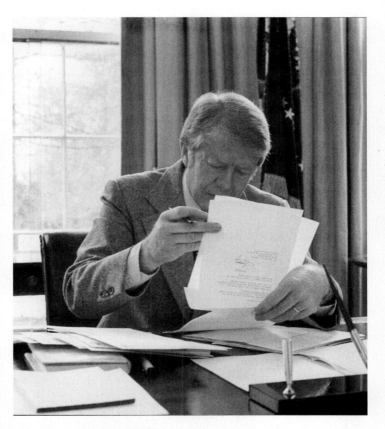

■ After his inauguration as president, Jimmy Carter got down to work in the Oval Office. Serious, conscientious, and extremely hard-working, Carter immersed himself in many of the details of his administration's policies. The image of him sequestered and industrious at his desk came to symbolize, for many, both the strengths and weaknesses of his presidency.

Hemisphere. The president made control over the Panama Canal a test case for this reorientation. The canal symbolized U.S. dominance of the hemisphere and served as a focus of resentment among many Latin Americans. Since 1903, the United States had ruled the 10-mile-wide Canal Zone as its own colony. Acknowledging this colonialist past, Carter signed treaties on September 7, 1977, to return sovereignty of the canal to Panama.

The Carter administration's other great diplomatic achievement came with the Camp David accords, an agreement between Egypt's president Anwar Sadat and Israel's prime minister Menachem Begin. The Arab-Israeli conflict had remained one of the most intractable problems in modern diplomacy. Sadat created an opening for diplomacy in 1977 by becoming the first Arab leader to visit Israel. Carter then invited Sadat and Begin to Camp David, the presidential retreat in rural western Maryland. There his persistence, plus promises of American aid to all parties, kept the marathon negotiations on track. In March 1979, the Egyptian and Israeli leaders signed two accords. Egypt became the first Arab state to grant official recognition to Israel. In turn, Israel agreed to withdraw its troops from the Sinai peninsula and apparently to stop building additional settlements on the Palestinian West Bank of the Jordan River. The framework for peace implied eventual autonomy for the Palestinians in the West Bank and Gaza.

Though promising, the Camp David accords failed to bring peace to the Middle East. Israeli settlements in the West Bank continued to proliferate, and anti-Israeli terrorism by Palestinians persisted. But Carter had persuaded two major players in the region to take a big step back from open hostility. The world rightly proclaimed him a peacemaker.

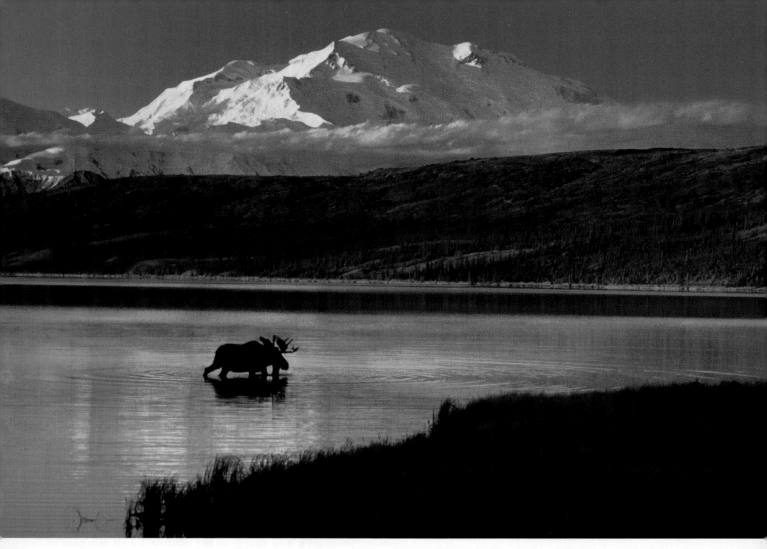

■ Mt. McKinley in Alaska's Denali National Park rises to 20,320 feet above sea level, the tallest peak in North America. Its scale and beauty inspired many supporters of the Alaska National Interest Lands Conservation Act of 1980, which dramatically expanded the nation's parklands and wilderness areas. The Alaska Lands Act and the new Trans-Alaska oil pipeline, completed three years earlier, helped residents of the lower 48 learn more about the nation's largest and most remote state.

The War on Waste

Within three months of taking office, Carter called for the "moral equivalent of war" to meet the deepening national energy crisis. He exhorted his fellow citizens to stop being "the most wasteful nation on Earth." Conserve energy, he implored them. Switch off lights and turn down thermostats.

The administration created the Department of Energy and granted tax incentives to promote development of alternative sources such as solar energy. The EPA required U.S. automakers to meet stricter fuel efficiency standards for their engines. High prices encouraged a renewed search for domestic sources of oil. In 1977 workers completed the 800-mile-long, 48-inch-wide Trans-Alaska Pipeline System. The system linked the state's northern oil fields at Prudhoe Bay on the Arctic Ocean with a tanker terminal in Valdez, on Alaska's southern coast on the Pacific Ocean. With new oil now flowing freely, Carter worked with Congress to pass the 1980 Alaska National Interest Lands Conservation Act. This legislation created the single largest addition ever to the nation's wilderness system, 47 million acres, and the new Wrangell–St. Elias National Park.

The most controversial power alternative came in the form of nuclear energy. Obtained by harnessing the force of splitting atoms, nuclear energy seemed to promise unlimited pollution-free power. But it entailed the use of a deadly radioactive fuel, uranium. In March 1979, the partial meltdown of the nuclear core of the Three Mile Island reactor near Harrisburg, Pennsylvania, leaked radiation and forced a major evacuation. Nevertheless, existing nuclear power plants continued to generate 11 percent of the nation's electricity in 1979, a figure that climbed to 22 percent by 1992 as other plants under construction came on line. However, because of negative public opinion and the high cost per unit of nuclear power, no new plants ordered by utility companies after 1974 were ever completed.

Diffusing the Women's Movement

"Good morning, boys and girls!" This standard classroom greeting suggests the central place of gender in how Americans identify people from a young age. Few people consider the phrase offensive, even though they probably would protest if a teacher addressed class members as "blacks and whites" or "tall people and short people." Should one's sex (a biological characteristic) or gender (the social assumptions associated with sex) constitute the fundamental dividing line among human beings? The spread of feminism through U.S. society from the 1970s onward raised this question.

How successful were feminists in their struggle for gender equality?

Pressing for Equality

In a decade marked by hard rethinking of major issues, feminists provided one of the most profound challenges of all. Few American households avoided at least some reconsideration of the roles of men and women. Just as the nation reimagined its foreign policy

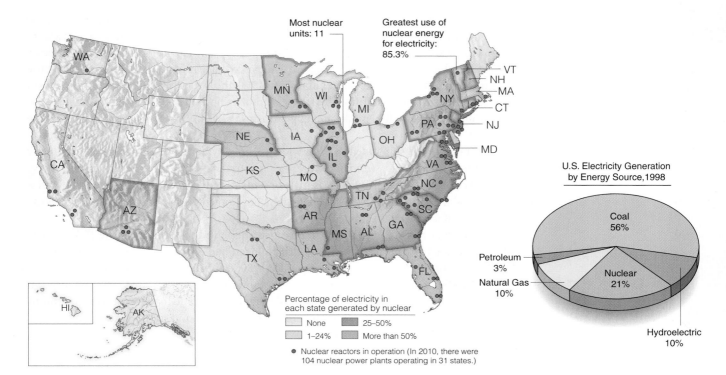

■ **MAP 27.1**
BUILDING NUCLEAR POWER PLANTS
Between 1969 and 1980, all of the nation's 104 commercial nuclear power reactors either came on line (56) or were in the process of being planned or built (48). The United States has roughly one-quarter of the 434 commercial nuclear power reactors in the world. Despite nuclear energy's important role in U.S. electricity production, there is still no system in place for the permanent disposal of radioactive waste.

in less assertive terms and with greater concern for human rights, feminists called for equality between the sexes while honoring their differences. The new title "Ms."—like Mr.—symbolized a desire not to have one's marital status revealed through the title of "Miss" or "Mrs." Thousands of consciousness-raising meetings also made women aware that their own experiences with discrimination were part of a broader pattern of injustice toward women.

The millions of American women who found their lives changing in the 1970s did not agree on all issues. African-American and Latino-American women balanced identities as women with identities as people of color, which aligned them closely with men of their communities. Working-class women of all colors often focused on issues common to all workers, including wages, workplace conditions, and union representation. Community organizers such as Lois Gibbs of Love Canal zeroed in on neighborhoods and families. The educated white women who formed the most visible part of the movement for equality differed among themselves on such issues as pornography: some found it inherently exploitive of women, while others considered it primarily a matter of free expression.

However, all women shared certain concerns. Even as many female Americans remained wary of the label *feminist*—fearing associations with anger, militancy, and dislike of men—they nonetheless tended to side with feminist positions on issues from equal pay for equal work to abortion rights and more egalitarian distribution of household chores within families. The women's movement also sought to unmask the violence constraining all women's lives: sexual harassment, domestic abuse, and rape.

New Opportunities in Education, the Workplace, and Family Life

In the 1970s, educated women gained access to a host of new opportunities in the workplace. Young women in college, unlike their mothers, expected to choose and develop a career after graduation even more than they anticipated getting married. The number of women entering graduate and professional schools soared. The percentage of female students in law school shot up from 5 percent to 40 percent between 1970 and 1980. In addition, most single-sex private colleges went coeducational. Many dormitories housed both men and women, allowing young people from the middle and upper classes to live in close physical proximity for the first time.

A similar process unfolded in the workplace. Employment in the United States, formerly divided into "men's" and "women's" work, saw a blurring of those lines. Help-wanted advertisements stopped categorizing jobs as male or female, and women joined the ranks of police officers and truck drivers. In 1980 more than half of women with children under six years old had paying jobs outside the home.

Not surprisingly, family life also changed shape in these years. In the 1950s, more than 70 percent of American families with children had a father who worked outside the home and a mother who stayed at home. By 1980, only 15 percent of families were configured that way. Yet society's growing acceptance of mothers in the workforce did not necessarily mean that these women enjoyed a lighter domestic load. Most working mothers still bore the brunt of the "second shift": child-rearing and housework in addition to a full-time paid job.

Changing roles brought new marital stresses, and divorce rates climbed in this decade. In 1970, one-third as many divorces as marriages occurred annually; in 1980, the figure was one-half. No-fault divorce laws, beginning with California's in 1970, eased the process and the stigma attached to divorce, although its emotional impact on adults and children remained difficult to measure. Men benefited financially when marriages split up. Their average living standard rose sharply, whereas that of women and their children plummeted.

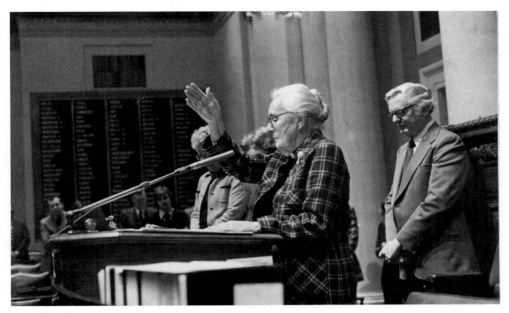

■ A scientist with a Ph.D. from the University of Minnesota, in 1934 Jeannette Piccard became the first woman to reach the stratosphere, piloting a balloon to a height of 57,000 feet. In a second career much later in life, Piccard joined the ministry of the Episcopal Church. In 1974, she and ten other women were ordained as Episcopal priests in Philadelphia, setting off a two-year controversy within the national church about the legitimacy of the ordinations in a previously all-male clergy. In 1976, the General Convention of the Episcopal Church voted to change church law and ordain both women and men. Here Piccard gives an invocation in the U.S. House of Representatives in Washington in 1977.

Equality Under the Law

Paralleling the logic of the black civil rights movement, the modern women's movement pressured lawmakers to eliminate the legal underpinnings of sex-based discrimination. Title IX of the Educational Amendments of 1972 required schools to spend comparable amounts on women's and men's sports programs. This critical step symbolized women's shift away from spectatorship and cheerleading to the female athleticism that helped define American popular culture by the end of the twentieth century.

After languishing for decades among failed proposals in Congress, the proposed Equal Rights Amendment to the Constitution finally rode to an overwhelming victory among senators and representatives in 1972. The legislature then sent it to the states for possible ratification by 1980. Simple in its language, the ERA declared: "Equality of rights under law shall not be denied or abridged by the United States or by any State on account of sex."

On January 22, 1973, in the landmark case of *Roe v. Wade*, the Supreme Court ruled (by a 7–2 vote) that constitutional privacy rights were "broad enough to encompass a woman's decision whether or not to terminate her pregnancy" in its first six months. This decision established women's constitutional right to determine the course of their own pregnancies.

●●●─Read the Document

Roe V. Wade at **www.myhistorylab.com**

Backlash

Even as the majority of Americans accepted the fundamental tenets of feminism, some fiercely defended existing gender roles. The mainstream media often painted women's rights activists as angry man-haters. Indeed, the media seized the opportunity to associate feminism with "bra-burning," a titillating way to blend women's rights with the sexual revolution and thus avoid the serious issues that women were raising. One Chicana worker involved in a strike against the Farah slacks company in Texas responded, "I don't believe in burning your bra, but I do believe in having our rights."

The women's movement posed a daunting challenge to traditional ideas about masculinity. Men wondered what equality for women really meant and how it might change their intimate and professional relationships with women. Should men still open doors for

> *Should men still open doors for women? Should they begin to do half (or more) of housework and parenting?*

women? Should they begin to do half (or more) of housework and parenting? Should they not comment on a female colleague's appearance? Women's growing economic independence and educational opportunities often altered the dynamics of power in male-female relationships. Many men from all classes and ethnicities, feeling defensive about assumptions and behaviors that were increasingly labeled sexist, resisted these changes. Some found the increasingly open acknowledgment of lesbianism threatening because it implied their potential irrelevance to women.

That men would have mixed feelings about women's liberation surprised no one. But some of the stiffest resistance came from women who had built their identities on motherhood and homemaking and now strongly defended that tradition. They sought to uphold an established family structure that they believed divorce, gay rights, abortion, and daycare would destroy. In their view, femininity meant service to one's family. "Feminists praise self-centeredness," antifeminist Phyllis Schlafly declared, "and call it liberation." In addition to defending their own choices, female antifeminists worried about the impact of dual-career families on children.

Opponents of women's liberation made two major legislative gains in the late 1970s. First, Congress passed the Hyde Amendment in 1976, which forbade the use of Medicaid funds for abortions. In practice, the amendment limited access to abortion to those women who could afford to pay for it themselves. Second, Schlafly's Stop-ERA campaign helped defeat the Equal Rights Amendment by limiting its ratification to only 35 of the required 38 states. Schlafly claimed that the amendment would "destroy the family, foster homosexuality, and hurt women." ERA opponents argued that it would also draw out the worst in men, letting husbands opt out of supporting their wives and freeing divorced men from paying alimony. Antifeminists resented the disrespect for motherhood that they felt from some feminists. Still, they agreed with feminists that tens of millions of American women were just one man removed from welfare. The two sides differed on the best way to protect women's interests: should women's economic independence be enhanced, or should men be tied more tightly to their families?

Though discouraging for some, the narrow defeat of the ERA could not mask feminism's growing influence throughout American culture. The "first woman" stories that began showing up in the media during the 1970s marked the entrance of women into previously all-male roles. Like physicians, lawyers, and other figures of cultural authority, religious leaders now increasingly consisted of women, including the first Lutheran pastor (1970), the first Jewish rabbi (1972), and the first Episcopal priest (1974). In 1981, Sandra Day O'Connor became the first female Supreme Court justice. And mainstream organizations such as churches and municipalities ran feminist-created community institutions, including rape crisis centers, women's health clinics, and battered women's shelters.

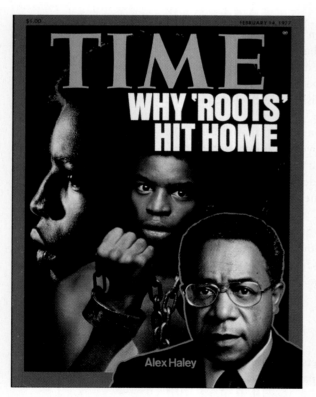

■ The 1977 miniseries version of Alex Haley's *Roots* captured the largest television audience ever to that time. The powerful drama about Haley's ancestors offered tens of millions of Americans an intimate and sympathetic understanding of the horrific story of black slavery and survival. *Roots* also represented the post-1960s emphasis on preserving and respecting group histories and identities rather than emphasizing only individual success and assimilation into the mainstream.

CONCLUSION

In 1978 a divided U.S. Supreme Court handed down a ruling on the contentious policy of **affirmative action**. The justices decided by a 5–4 vote in the *Bakke* case that strict racial quotas were unconstitutional, but that universities could consider race as one of several factors in determining a candidate's qualifications for admission. The Court, like the American public, was wrestling with the broader 1970s problem of how to reform American society in ways that would preserve its historic strengths while removing the ills that the previous decade's political activism had laid bare. One specific problem was the tension between the ideal of colorblind integration and new expressions of pride in distinctive racial and ethnic identities. Many white ethnic Americans in these years leavened their long-standing cultural assimilation with renewed attention to their own roots in particular European countries, especially Ireland and Italy.

Americans' self-confidence and pride as a nation had been deeply shaken by the combination of the Vietnam War, the Watergate scandal, and the economic downturn after 1973. Disillusioned by the corruptions of public life, many citizens turned inward and heeded the advice of Robert J. Ringer in his 1977 bestseller, *Looking Out for Number One*. But others found motivation in the decade's events—especially the revelation that presidents, corporate executives, and other authorities had lied to them. They learned what earlier Americans had discovered in the 1760s and 1770s about imperious British officials and the corrupting effects of managing a global empire. Like the revolutionaries of George Washington's generation, they sought to strengthen representative government.

For Review

✓●—[Study and **Review** at www.myhistorylab.com

1. How did détente and Watergate scandal affect U.S. foreign relations and American politics?

2. How did economic changes affect the way Americans felt about their country?

3. What were the most significant political reforms of the 1970s?

4. What did feminism mean, and what impact did it have in the United States?

Chronology: 1972–1979

1972   Watergate break-in.
Nixon visits China.
Founding of *Ms.* magazine.

1973   *Roe v. Wade* legalizes abortion.
American Indian Movement members occupy Wounded Knee.
Endangered Species Act.
OPEC oil embargo.
American troops withdraw from Vietnam.

1974   Nixon resigns; Gerald R. Ford becomes president.

1975   Vietnam reunified under communist rule.
Congressional investigations of CIA covert operations.

1976   Hyde Amendment prohibits use of Medicaid funds for abortions.

1977   Carter issues general amnesty for draft evaders.
Trans-Alaska Pipeline system completed.
ABC airs *Roots*, a miniseries based on a book by Alex Haley.

1978   Bakke Supreme Court decision.

1979   Camp David peace accords.
Partial meltdown of nuclear core at Three Mile Island nuclear plant.
Iranian revolution.

Key Terms

Affirmative action Policies designed to improve the educational and employment opportunities of historically underrepresented groups such as women and African Americans. p. 632

Détente The lessening of military or diplomatic tensions, as between the United States and the Soviet Union. p. 618

Feminism The belief that women and men are of equal value and that gender roles are, to a considerable degree, created by society rather than being simply natural. p. 616

Watergate The Washington, D.C. hotel-office complex where agents of President Nixon's reelection campaign broke into Democratic Party headquarters in 1972. Nixon helped cover up the break-in, and the subsequent political scandal was called "Watergate." p. 618

PART TEN

Global Connections at Home and Abroad, 1979–2006

AFTER THE UNCERTAINTIES AND REFORMS OF THE 1970s, many Americans sought reassurance about their country's direction. In the 1980s, President Ronald Reagan left his imprint on both domestic and foreign affairs. Reagan gave voice to conservatives, including those who favored a federal retreat from social welfare programs. Bolstered by the Moral Majority and other fundamentalist Christian groups, conservatives engaged in the so-called culture wars with liberals. Conservatives disapproved of feminists, black power advocates, gay rights activists, and environmentalists. Reagan and Congress implemented policies that shrank the federal government's commitment to social welfare programs. Reagan also reinvigorated Cold War rhetoric—he denounced the Soviet Union as an "evil empire"—and pushed military spending to unprecedented levels. Yet Reagan welcomed the initiatives of Soviet leader Mikhail Gorbachev, who sought to ease tensions with the West.

Unable to meet the basic needs of its own people and bogged down in an unwinnable war in Afghanistan, the Soviet Union disintegrated in 1991. Simultaneously, the United States embarked on a remarkable period of economic growth and expansion. President Bill Clinton favored free trade policies, such as the North American Free Trade Agreement (NAFTA), which he and others hoped would knit the world's nations together in pursuit of political and economic progress.

Nevertheless, domestic and foreign conflicts thwarted much of this hopeful vision. At home, the AIDS epidemic and drug addiction claimed many lives. Clashes among African Americans, Latinos, and Koreans in Los Angeles in 1992; the bombing of an Oklahoma City federal building by domestic antigovernment terrorists in 1995; attacks on abortion clinics; and a series of shootings by high school students revealed persistent faultlines in American society. Backed by the Supreme Court, a number of state and local governments passed anti-immigrant and anti-affirmative action laws. The culture wars were hot and, in some cases, deadly.

The most violent assault on the United States came from forces outside as well as within it. The Middle East had become a tinderbox of fears and resentments. In Iran, Islamic militants overthrew the U.S.-backed Shah in 1979. Throughout the region, many Islamic fundamentalists expressed their resentment over the military and political presence of the United States in Israel and Saudi Arabia. During the 1991 Persian Gulf War, the United States successfully reversed Iraq's seizure of oil fields in Kuwait. Yet U.S. attempts to protect its economic and political interests in the Middle East continued to outrage Islamic militants.

By the end of the 1990s, some Americans were able to focus inward and enjoy prosperity. The stock market was booming. Cheap gas prices encouraged affluent Americans to purchase huge sport utility vehicles with little regard for their environmental impact. However, ten years of high employment masked the hidden effects of a transformed economy, one characterized by a decline in labor union membership and the rise of an ill-paid service sector. A substantial proportion of Americans lived from paycheck to paycheck.

On September 11, 2001, Americans were forced to confront their own vulnerabilities. Anti-U.S. terrorists sponsored by Al Qaeda, a radical Islamist group, hijacked commercial airliners and flew them into the Twin Towers of the World Trade Center in New York City and into the Pentagon outside Washington, D.C. Some 3,000 people were killed. Within a month, anthrax-laced letters caused death and havoc in the offices where they were delivered and the postal centers that processed them, heightening pervasive fear and insecurity among Americans.

The events of September 11 highlighted a grim reality: certain foreign groups despised such cherished American values as democracy, liberalism, and consumerism. Moreover, U.S. foreign policies in the Middle East fanned the fires of anti-Western extremism. Terrorists were becoming more successful in enlisting people who were willing to die in attacks on the United States and more resourceful in using modern technology in those attacks. These terrorists were stateless, freed from the political tasks of protecting their own citizens, monitoring national borders, or dealing with internal dissidents.

In late 2001, these realities prompted the United States to invade Afghanistan and displace the ruling Taliban, hosts to Al Qaeda's training network. The following year the United States invaded Iraq in what the Bush administration called a preemptive attack on a dangerous, destabilizing regime—the dictatorship of Saddam Hussein. At home, issues related to war, terrorism, and civil liberties became increasingly divisive and bitter among Americans.

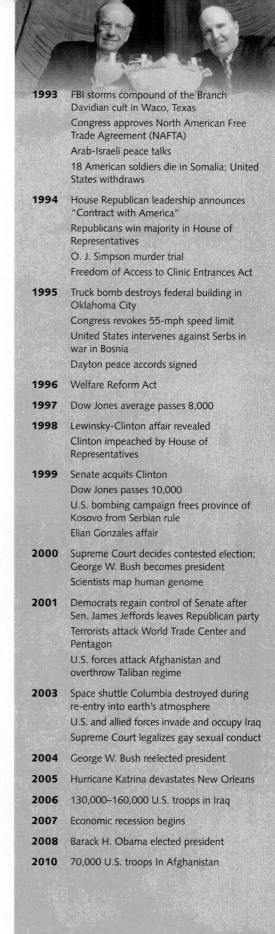

1993	FBI storms compound of the Branch Davidian cult in Waco, Texas
	Congress approves North American Free Trade Agreement (NAFTA)
	Arab-Israeli peace talks
	18 American soldiers die in Somalia; United States withdraws
1994	House Republican leadership announces "Contract with America"
	Republicans win majority in House of Representatives
	O. J. Simpson murder trial
	Freedom of Access to Clinic Entrances Act
1995	Truck bomb destroys federal building in Oklahoma City
	Congress revokes 55-mph speed limit
	United States intervenes against Serbs in war in Bosnia
	Dayton peace accords signed
1996	Welfare Reform Act
1997	Dow Jones average passes 8,000
1998	Lewinsky-Clinton affair revealed
	Clinton impeached by House of Representatives
1999	Senate acquits Clinton
	Dow Jones passes 10,000
	U.S. bombing campaign frees province of Kosovo from Serbian rule
	Elian Gonzales affair
2000	Supreme Court decides contested election; George W. Bush becomes president
	Scientists map human genome
2001	Democrats regain control of Senate after Sen. James Jeffords leaves Republican party
	Terrorists attack World Trade Center and Pentagon
	U.S. forces attack Afghanistan and overthrow Taliban regime
2003	Space shuttle Columbia destroyed during re-entry into earth's atmosphere
	U.S. and allied forces invade and occupy Iraq
	Supreme Court legalizes gay sexual conduct
2004	George W. Bush reelected president
2005	Hurricane Katrina devastates New Orleans
2006	130,000–160,000 U.S. troops in Iraq
2007	Economic recession begins
2008	Barack H. Obama elected president
2010	70,000 U.S. troops In Afghanistan

28

The Cold War Returns—and Ends, 1979–1991

CHAPTER OUTLINE

Anticommunism Revived

Republican Rule at Home

Cultural Conflict

The End of the Cold War

Conclusion

On July 16, 1979, just west of Albuquerque, New Mexico, a dam holding wastewater and residue from a uranium mine broke. Some 94 million gallons of radioactive water flooded into the Rio Puerco and on to the Rio Grande. Nearby, the Anaconda Copper Company operated the nation's largest uranium mine, producing the fuel for nuclear power. The mine closed in the early 1980s. At public hearings in 1986 concerning the future of the mine and its small mountain of poisonous tailings, Anaconda's scientists argued that the mine did not threaten human health in the area. Thus, they said, the tailing piles and the polluted ponds did not need to be cleaned up. Herman García, a Laguna Indian who lived in the adjoining village of Paguate, listened carefully but remained unconvinced. "We lost five people from cancer" last year in tiny Paguate alone, he explained. "I'm no expert," he concluded, but "I'd like for some of these experts to go out there and swim in those ponds. Then when I see them swim, then maybe I feel more secure."

The Native American West and the nuclear West have overlapped to a remarkable extent ever since participants in the Manhattan Project began building the first atomic bomb in 1942. Repeatedly, the U.S. government constructed major nuclear sites in the West on lands surrounded by Indian settlements. Some of this overlap resulted from geological coincidence: almost 90 percent of the nation's uranium lay on or adjacent to Indian lands. Some of it stemmed from politics. The sparse populations of Pueblo, Western Shoshone, and Yakima lacked the political clout to prevent their lands from becoming what the National Academy of Science called "national sacrifice areas."

In the 1980s, nuclear weapons and waste sparked controversy in the United States. President Ronald Reagan expanded the nation's nuclear arsenal, and his administration publicly discussed fighting and winning a nuclear war against the Soviet Union. A major accident in 1986 at the Chernobyl nuclear power plant outside the Soviet city of Kiev only heightened public concerns. Frightened by rising U.S.–Soviet tensions, citizens in western Europe and the United States organized an international movement to freeze further development of nuclear weapons.

In 1979, two international incidents raised questions about U.S. military effectiveness. A revolution in Iran led to the taking of American hostages and a dramatic rejection of American influence, and the Soviet Union sent troops into Afghanistan to prop up a Soviet-allied but weakening government.

Angered, Americans put tough-talking Republicans in the White House for 12 years. These leaders' emphasis on military might challenged the Soviet leadership, while changes in eastern Europe and the USSR brought an end to the Cold War and the breakup of the Soviet Union.

The Reagan administration also avidly promoted free markets. Its policies produced great wealth at the top of the socioeconomic ladder, increasing the distance between the daily experiences of the rich and the poor. These policies also catalyzed bitter struggles over natural resources, particularly those on western public lands.

Finally, the newly organized religious right clashed with liberal opponents over such issues as abortion and homosexuality. In these years, Christian fundamentalists and their allies sought to reverse cultural liberties that had emerged since the late 1960s.

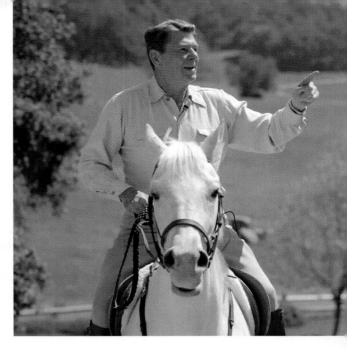

■ As President, Ronald Reagan loved spending time outdoors at his ranch near Santa Barbara, California.

Anticommunism Revived

"We're going down!" cried U.S. political officer Elizabeth Swift on the phone to the State Department. These were her last words as a crowd of young Iranians poured into the U.S. embassy in Tehran on the morning of November 4, 1979, and cut telephone lines. In a move that shocked Americans, Islamic militants seized 52 embassy personnel and held them hostage for over a year.

Why did Cold War tensions increase after 1979?

In the late 1970s, revolutionaries of a different political bent—socialist and leftist—took the offensive against authoritarian regimes in Central America. Indeed, the Third World seemed to be turning away from U.S. leadership in the wake of the American defeat in Vietnam. To make matters worse, the Soviet Union stepped up its support for leftists abroad. In December 1979, the Red Army invaded Afghanistan. Fed up with these humiliating events overseas and with relentless inflation at home, American voters elected Ronald Reagan as president—the most conservative chief executive since Calvin Coolidge. Reagan promised to resurrect the Cold War, and he delivered.

Iran and Afghanistan

In January 1979, the Iranian people overthrew the longtime authoritarian government of Shah Reza Pahlavi. Under the shah's rule, the nation's enormous oil wealth had flowed into the hands of a small elite. Meanwhile, the impoverished majority of devout Shi'a Muslims grew increasingly resentful of the shah's closeness with his American allies. His secret police had detained 50,000 political prisoners. The revolution found its leader in the austere religious figure Ruhollah Khomeini, who shouldered aside more moderate opposition groups. Returning from exile in Iraq and then Paris, Khomeini created a popular **theocracy** grounded in a strict interpretation of Islamic law.

Hunted by the rebels, the shah took his money and fled Iran. Several months later, the Carter administration let him fly to New York to seek treatment for cancer. Enraged that the United States harbored their nation's most wanted criminal, Iranians demanded the shah's extradition to Tehran to stand trial. Washington refused. Within a month, militants stormed the U.S. embassy—"that nest of spies," Khomeini called it, referring to the CIA's considerable presence in Iran.

■ Ruhollah Khomeini led the 1979 revolution in Iran that established the modern world's first Islamic theocratic state. The events in Iran encouraged Islamic revolutionaries across the Middle East, Asia, and North Africa. For Americans, the closest analogy was the Bolshevik revolution of 1917 in Russia, which provided a model for other communist revolutions abroad.

The hostages' captors paraded them before television cameras to force Washington to return the shah. Carter refused to give in. In April 1980, he finally approved a military rescue effort. But mechanical failures forced the mission to abort, and the collision of two helicopters during the attempt killed several U.S. soldiers. Not until after the shah's death in 1980 did the two governments finally negotiate the hostages' release in January 1981.

Khomeini and his followers despised the values they associated with modern U.S. culture: secularism, materialism, gender equality, alcohol consumption, and sexual titillation. They

> *Khomeini and his followers despised the values they associated with modern U.S. culture.*

sought to export the cleansing power of a puritanical Islamic faith throughout the Middle East and beyond. Indeed, the revolutionaries condemned the atheistic Soviets just as fiercely as they did the materialistic Americans.

Just seven weeks after the seizure of hostages in Tehran, the first of 110,000 Soviet troops rolled south across the USSR's border into neighboring Afghanistan. Their goal: to stabilize the pro-Soviet government there against anticommunist Islamic guerrilla fighters. Moscow had resolved to prevent the spread of **Islamist** revolution into the heavily Muslim southern regions of the USSR.

But few Americans saw this invasion as a defensive operation. Rather, they feared a push toward vulnerable Iran as Red Army troops marched beyond eastern Europe for the first time. The Carter administration halted most trade with the Soviets and withdrew the nuclear Strategic Arms Limitation Treaty (SALT II) from Senate consideration. In addition, the president organized a western boycott of the 1980 Olympics in Moscow and increased military spending. The "Carter Doctrine" proclaimed the U.S. commitment to preserve the status quo in the Persian Gulf region, even if it meant the use of military force. And the CIA began funding the Afghan guerrillas.

The Conservative Victory of 1980

By mid-1980, Carter's public approval rating had dropped to the lowest level of any preceding modern president. Inflation reached 13.5 percent. Even the president acknowledged a "crisis stage."

Onto this stage strode Ronald Reagan. Long considered too conservative to win the presidency, the former California governor projected the confidence and strength that many Americans wanted, even if they did not share all of his views. The 69-year-old one-time actor sailed through the Republican primaries. For his main tactic, he appealed to nostalgia, particularly among whites, for a rosier past—a time of rising wages and U.S. military might. While Carter spoke of learning to live within limits, Reagan insisted that "we are too great a nation to limit ourselves to small dreams."

The media loved Reagan. Indeed, his presidency fit with the new emphasis on constant entertainment, as cable television, VCRs (1976), ESPN (1979), MTV (1981), and CDs (1983) swept the culture. Daily newspaper readership plummeted from 73 percent to 50 percent during the 1980s. Equally telling, the average length of an uninterrupted "sound bite" on the evening news dropped from 42 seconds in 1968 to fewer than 10 seconds in 1988. Anything longer, the networks believed, would bore viewers. And no one projected simplicity with greater warmth or sincerity than Reagan.

Yet the 1980 election was about more than just Reagan's likable personality. It revealed the nation's renewed interest in conservative ideas. Republicans won control of the Senate for the first time since 1952. Several basic values united the party: an unhindered private sector and entrepreneurial initiative to create affluence, plus free markets and individual responsibility to solve the nation's social problems. Republicans, like most Democrats, also believed that the United States had a moral obligation to preserve world order and halt further expansion of communist influence. Reagan proclaimed that "government was the problem, not the solution."

■ MAP 28.1

TROUBLE SPOTS IN THE MIDDLE EAST, 1979–1993
Oil production around the Persian Gulf and the close American relationship with Israel made political instability in the Middle East a central concern of the U.S. government. American leaders particularly feared the spread of either Soviet influence or Islamic revolution, both of which opposed American cultural values and U.S. strategic interests.

Renewing the Cold War

"Sometimes in our administration," Reagan once joked, "the right hand doesn't know what the far-right hand is doing." But all hands in the White House agreed on the importance of restoring confidence in the nation's engagements abroad, particularly in the Third World. In the 1970s, leftist insurgencies in Asia, Africa, and Latin America had suggested the retreat of U.S. power.

TABLE 28-1			
The Election of 1980			
Candidate	**Political Party**	**Popular Vote (%)**	**Electoral Vote**
Ronald Reagan	Republican	50.7	489
Jimmy Carter	Democratic	41.0	49
John B. Anderson	Independent	6.6	

Reagan blamed the Soviet Union for "all the unrest that is going on." He rejected the 1970s policy of détente that had emerged during the Nixon administration and had taken further shape under Ford and Carter. Often, Reagan spoke as though the Chinese-Soviet split had never happened. His was "a kind of 1952 world," one aide recalled. "He sees the world in black and white terms." Pointing to the Soviet occupation of Afghanistan and its 1983 shootdown of a Korean Air Lines civilian jet that had strayed into Soviet airspace, the president denounced the USSR as "an evil empire."

•••–[Read the Document
Reagan, "Evil Empire" Speech at
www.myhistorylab.com

CENTRAL AMERICAN EYE CHART

P
OV
ERTY
HUNGER
INJUSTICE
CORRUPTION
REVOLUTION

DEMOCRATS

Sacramento Bee

'C - O - uh - M - M - uh - U - uh - N - uh - I - S - M!'

■ **Critics of Reagan's policies toward Central America believed that he ignored the indigenous problems encouraging revolutions there, blaming instead the USSR and Cuba. The cartoon suggests that the Democratic party took a different view than the president. Many Democrats in Congress did, and they were responsible for limiting Reagan's promotion of the Nicaraguan Contras. But many others went along with the popular president in defending the Contras and supporting right-wing regimes in the region.**

The Reagan administration backed up the president's words by launching the largest peacetime military buildup in American history. The Pentagon's budget increased 40 percent between 1980 and 1984. The new president also revived covert operations. He gave CIA director William Casey the green light to provide secret assistance to anticommunist governments and insurgencies throughout the Third World.

In Central America, extreme inequalities between landowning elites and vast peasant majorities had fueled insurgencies against the authoritarian governments of El Salvador, Guatemala, and Nicaragua. Moreover, some small assistance from Cuba and the Soviet Union had found its way to the rebels. Reagan passionately opposed these insurgents. He authorized the CIA to work hand in hand with the regimes, even though they used death squads to torture and murder dissidents and sometimes slaughtered whole villages and towns to wipe out possible resistance.

In Nicaragua, the Sandinista rebels managed to overthrow the pro-American dictatorship of Antonio Somoza in 1979. The Sandinistas set about building a more egalitarian and socialistic state while still preserving 60 percent of the nation's wealth in private hands. Carter had adopted a wait-and-see attitude. But after Reagan took office in 1981, the CIA created the counterrevolutionary "Contras," recruited primarily from Somoza's brutal former National Guard. The Contras waged an undeclared war on the new government in the Nicaraguan capital of Managua. By 1987, 40,000 Nicaraguans had died in the fighting, most of them civilians. Reagan called the Contras "freedom fighters" and declared them "the moral equal of our Founding Fathers."

Nevertheless, several European and Latin American allies considered the Contras an illegitimate force of terrorists. A large coalition of church and university groups in the United States agreed. Christian activists formed the "Sanctuary" movement to aid refugees from the right-wing dictatorships in Central America that sympathized with the Contras. The Pentagon, for its part, had no interest in sending troops to fight a popular government abroad. The opposition finally prevailed; Congress passed the Boland Amendments of 1982 and 1984 to restrict U.S. assistance to the Contras.

Republican Rule at Home

What did the Reagan administration want to change about American society?

While reasserting U.S. power abroad, Reagan also aimed to reorient domestic policies toward the free market. Lori was what the president called a "welfare cheat." Writer Barbara Ehrenreich told the story of a neighbor in New York City representative of welfare recipients: a single white mother with one child. Lori had been married for two years to a man who beat her and once chased her around the house with a gun. Welfare had made it possible for her to leave him, a move she described as like being born again, "as a human being this time." Lori sometimes earned close to $100 a week from cleaning houses and waiting tables—not enough to support herself and her daughter, but a useful supplement to the small government payments. She chose not to report this to the welfare office, spending it instead on little things deemed inessential by welfare regulations: deodorant, hand lotion, and an occasional commercial haircut.

Lori's story helps illuminate some of the major trends of the 1980s. Inflation finally eased and the stock market perked up. Congress and the White House slashed taxes. However, annual budget deficits and the national debt (the accumulation of previous deficits) soon soared as tax revenues declined and military spending increased. The administration shrank government programs for the poor and portrayed welfare recipients like Lori as lazy and irresponsible. Washington was unsympathetic to concerns over the environment and opened public lands in the West to new commercial uses. By the 1990s, the gap between rich and poor widened noticeably and the vaunted American middle class worried about its declining economic security.

"Reaganomics"

Taxes played a crucial role in the Reagan administration's efforts to reduce government involvement in the economy. In 1981 the president proposed a new tax law to lower federal income tax rates by 25 percent over three years. Congress passed the legislation, and the top individual rate—paid only by the wealthiest Americans— dropped from 70 percent to 28 percent. Congress also slashed taxes on corporations, capital gains, and inheritances, further benefiting the most affluent Americans.

Congress slashed taxes on corporations, capital gains, and inheritances, further benefiting the most affluent Americans.

While taxes shrank, federal spending on the military soared. The Pentagon bolstered its conventional and nuclear arsenals and gave service personnel a morale-boosting salary increase. After 1983, billions of dollars poured from the U.S. Treasury into the president's proposed Strategic Defense Initiative (SDI) for a missile defense system.

The funds for the weapons buildup could come from only one source: social programs at home. However, most domestic spending went to popular programs, such as Social Security and Medicare, which primarily benefited the middle class. Leaving those in place, Reagan instead reduced funding for welfare programs, including food stamps, school lunches, job training, and low-income housing.

The assault on welfare had links to racial issues as well. The Reagan administration opposed any form of affirmative action, calling instead for the "colorblind" application of law. The president and his supporters argued that prejudice no longer had any significant effect on the decisions that employers and others made. Ironically, Reagan's own Justice Department demonstrated the opposite: it sought unsuccessfully to win tax-free status for Bob Jones University in Greenville, South Carolina, and other schools and colleges that discriminated against people of color.

Reducing welfare spending did not close the budgetary gaps that lower taxes and higher military outlays had opened. To close these gaps, the government resorted to borrowing money. Formerly the world's largest creditor nation, the United States became its largest debtor nation. Between 1981 and 1989, the national debt ballooned to almost $3 trillion. Moreover, during the 12 years of Republican rule ending in 1993, annual budget deficits jumped from $59 billion to $300 billion.

Despite these problems, "Reaganomics" did help the national economy recover somewhat from the traumas of the 1970s. The tight money policies of the Federal Reserve Board after 1979 eventually tamed inflation, which dropped from 13.5 percent in 1980 to 3 percent in 1983. The Fed's high interest rates also choked off the nation's cash flow and provoked

TABLE 28-2			
The Election of 1984			
Candidate	**Political Party**	**Popular Vote (%)**	**Electoral Vote**
Ronald Reagan	Republican	59.0	525
Walter Mondale	Democratic	41.0	13

'SURELY,' SAYS I, 'NOT THE JAMES WATT, FOLK-HERO AND FAMOUS WILDERNESS RAPIST!' 'THAT'S ME.' SAYS HE. AND I SAYS, 'NOT THE RENOWNED DESPOILER OF OUR PRECIOUS NATIONAL HERITAGE!' 'RIGHT.' SAYS HE. SO I ATE HIM.'

■ **James Watt, Reagan's first secretary of the Interior Department, became one of the most polarizing figures in a polarized decade. He made clear that he considered environmentalists to be his opponents as he worked to promote the interests of mining and timbering companies as well as ranchers. The Interior Department manages the national parks, monuments, and wildlife refuges, as well as the Bureau of Land Management's extensive lands (national forests fall under the Department of Agriculture's jurisdiction).**

a severe recession in 1981–1982, with unemployment reaching above 10 percent. However, the economy revived again in 1983 and was growing at a robust annual rate of 6.8 percent by 1984. In that year, rising confidence in the economy helped Reagan soundly win reelection over his opponent, Carter's former vice president Walter Mondale.

The Environment Contested

The 1980 election marked the sharpest turn ever in American environmental policy. The new administration reversed two decades of growing bipartisan consensus on the need for greater protection of the environment. Reagan instead supported corporations' demands for fewer environmental regulations and easier access to natural resources on public lands. The president ridiculed the idea of preserving wilderness for its own sake. He even claimed that "trees cause more pollution than automobiles do."

The officials Reagan appointed to oversee these lands and assume responsibility for protecting them had little respect for the agencies they ran. Critics described the situation as "foxes guarding the chicken house." The officials openly disdained environmentalists, including those in the moderate wing of the Republican party, and explicitly rewrote regulations to favor private enterprise. They sold grazing, logging, and mining rights on public lands at prices far below market value, despite their stated commitment to market economics.

James Watt, the new Secretary of the Interior, declared that only two kinds of people lived in the United States: "liberals and Americans." Watt was also a Christian fundamentalist. In his Senate confirmation hearings, he suggested that the nation had little need for long-term public land management because Christ would soon be returning and the known world would pass away—an interpretation of stewardship that not even all fundamentalists shared, much less the broader American public. Watt's abrasive personal style eventually alienated even the White House, and he resigned in 1983.

The administration's reversal of federal environmental policies alarmed a wide range of citizens and stimulated a backlash. Membership in environmental organizations soared, in such traditional groups as the Sierra Club and the Audubon Society, as well as in more radical ones, such as Greenpeace. Most Americans wanted to breathe cleaner air, drink safe water, and make recreational use of national parks and national forests. In much of the rural West, jobs in the recreation industry outnumbered those in the logging, mining, and ranching businesses. In 1989 concerns intensified when the oil tanker *Exxon Valdez* ran aground in Prince William Sound in Alaska, coating 1,000 miles of pristine coastline with crude oil.

The Affluence Gap

As the Reagan administration eased corporate access to the nation's natural resources, the disparity between rich and poor expanded further. Whereas most Americans' real wages (wages after inflation is factored in) declined, the professional classes fared well, and the wealthiest citizens gained enormously. For example, the salary of an average corporate chief executive officer was 40 times greater than that of a typical factory worker in 1980; by 1989, it was 93 times greater. The top 1 percent of American families now possessed more assets than the bottom 90 percent—a ratio typical of Third World nations.

A series of corporate mergers and consolidations further enriched well-off Americans, as did financial speculation and manipulation on Wall Street. *Business Week* wrote of a "casino economy" in which insider trading and leveraged buyouts (business takeovers financed by debt) created paper wealth rather than actual products. This explosion of wealth at the top fueled an emerging culture of extravagance, reminiscent of similar trends in the late nineteenth century and in the 1920s. Newly identified "yuppies" (young urban professionals) embodied the drive for material acquisition, in contrast to the anticonsumerist inclinations of the late 1960s and early 1970s. Jerry Rubin, a member of the anarchist "yippies" in the 1960s, once dropped dollar bills onto the floor of the New York Stock Exchange—which traders scurried madly to grab—to dramatize the stock market's pursuit of profit. By the 1980s, however, Rubin was working as an investment banker. Ronald and Nancy Reagan were older but shared similar values. They relished lavish amenities like those made popular on the television shows *Dynasty*, *Dallas*, and *Lifestyles of the Rich and Famous*.

As the affluence gap widened, the broad middle class watched its job security slip. Early in the decade, the recession had prompted factory shutdowns and mass layoffs. More than a million industrial jobs disappeared in 1982 alone. Manufacturers' decisions to keep moving plants abroad for cheaper labor only worsened the situation. Although the 1980s saw the creation of 20 million new jobs, most of these were in the nonunionized service sector and offered low pay and few benefits.

The poorest Americans did not fare well in the 1980s. The bottom tenth saw their already meager incomes decline by another 10 percent. In 1986 a full-time worker at minimum wage earned $6,700 per year—almost $4,000 short of the poverty level for a family of four. Homelessness worsened in cities as the government cut funding for welfare and institutional care for the mentally ill while housing costs rose. More than 1 million people lived on the streets, one-fifth of them still employed. One out of eight children went hungry and 20 percent lived in poverty, including 50 percent of black children. These Americans received minimal sympathy from the nation's political leaders. By contrast, Congress and the White House provided large federal subsidies to "needy" businesses such as the Chrysler Corporation and the savings and loan industry.

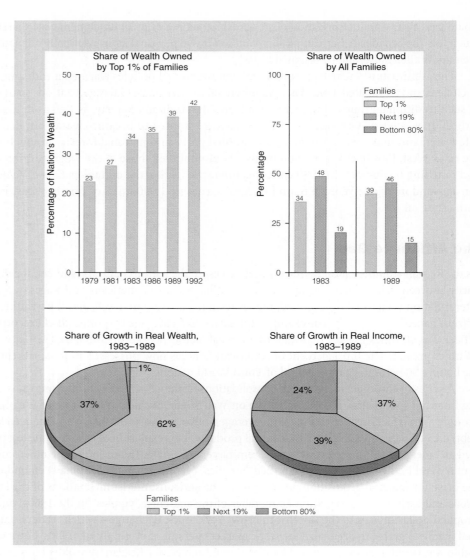

■ FIGURE 28.1

UNEQUAL DISTRIBUTION OF WEALTH AND INCOME

The 1980s were excellent years for wealthy Americans. The "trickle-down" effect touted by some Reagan administration officials—predicting that greater wealth accumulation among the rich would trickle down to the less affluent—had little impact.

Despite Reagan's record, 40 percent of union household members and 50 percent of all blue-collar workers cast their ballots for this staunch opponent of unions. Why? Part of the explanation lies in the decline of working-class voting during the 1970s. Disillusioned with a political process they saw as corrupt, numerous workers neglected to go to the polls on voting day. Many of those who did vote decided that the Democratic party had become increasingly co-opted by cultural liberalism and no longer spoke for the working class. Reagan's charisma and appeal to patriotism also attracted many citizens who might once have voted for their economic interests instead. Finally, white Americans increasingly defined their political loyalties on the basis of social and cultural issues—such as opposition to abortion, homosexuality, and affirmative action—rather than economic interests. Conservative Christians, in particular, strongly supported the Republican cause.

Cultural Conflict

One of the nation's foremost religious figures, Reverend Pat Robertson, controlled the Christian Broadcasting Network and ran unsuccessfully for the 1988 Republican presidential nomination. Like other social conservatives of this era, he promoted "family values" and traditional gender roles. Robertson went so far as to declare that feminism "encourages women to leave their husbands, kill their children [and] practice witchcraft." In contrast, author Susan Faludi wrote the 1991 best-seller *Backlash* about opposition to the women's movement. She became an important critic of gender roles in American society and how they limit people's life experiences and possibilities. In contrast to Robertson, Faludi concluded, "All women are feminists. It's just a matter of time and encouragement."

Which cultural issues did Americans most seem to disagree about?

Americans argued primarily about issues that had come to the fore during the social movements of the 1960s and 1970s.

As Robertson and Faludi demonstrate, Americans embroiled themselves throughout the 1980s in a contentious debate about values. Their society had changed in the previous generation in ways that some citizens disdained but others applauded. Americans argued primarily about issues that had come to the fore during the social movements of the 1960s and 1970s: sexuality, gender roles, the place of religion in public life, and multiculturalism. These often bitter "culture wars" dominated talk shows and newspaper editorial pages throughout much of the last two decades of the twentieth century.

The Rise of the Religious Right

Some of the Americans most troubled by the state of American society were conservative white Protestants, disproportionately from the South. Along with conservative Catholics, they criticized the post-1960s shift in mainstream values away from respect for traditional authorities—the church, political leaders, and the military—and toward freer sexual expression and general self-indulgence. What the nation needed, they believed, was a return to reverence for God. The growth of Christian fundamentalism paralleled rising religious fundamentalism around the globe, whether among Jews in Israel, Hindus in India, or Muslims in Iran and the Arab Middle East. For all their differences, religious people in these cultures shared a common quest: preserving spiritual purity and cultural traditions in an increasingly secular, integrated world.

Conservative Christians were not a fringe group. As many as 45 million Americans—20 percent of the population—indentified themselves as fundamentalist Christians in 1980. In combination with a similar number of Catholics, they represented a vast potential force in American politics. And their ranks were growing, while membership in the more liberal mainline Protestant denominations, such as the Presbyterians and Episcopalians, declined steadily after the 1960s.

Conservative Christians mobilized in the 1980 campaign to support Reagan's candidacy. Critics noted that Reagan himself attended church only occasionally and seemed an indifferent father. They contrasted the divorced candidate with his born-again, Sunday-school–teaching opponent, Jimmy Carter. But Reagan's conservative views on abortion and gay rights and his support for school prayer resonated with fundamentalists. They flocked to the Republican party and to new conservative religious organizations, such as the Moral Majority, founded in 1979 in Lynchburg, Virginia, by Reverend Jerry Falwell. More than 60 million people each week watched—and many sent money to—"televangelists," including Falwell, Robertson, and Jim Bakker.

Suffusing the GOP with a distinctly southern, grassroots flavor, the religious right also highlighted a major faultline in the modern Republican party: the tension between social conservatives, who emphasized community and tradition, and free marketeers, who promoted

INTERPRETING HISTORY

Religion and Politics in the 1980s

In 1979, Baptist minister Jerry Falwell founded the Moral Majority in Lynchburg, Virginia. The organization represented the growing engagement of conservative evangelical Christians in American politics, and Falwell emerged as the most prominent figure of the new religious right. However, not all Christians were conservative. Robert McAfee Brown, a Presbyterian minister and theologian, represented more liberal elements of the church that understood both the Bible and the problems of American society differently than Falwell.

Before he became involved in politics, Jerry Falwell had already made a name for himself in his hometown of Lynchburg, Virginia, as the senior minister of the large Thomas Road Baptist Church and the founder of Liberty University. His organization, the Moral Majority, became the most well-known conservative evangelical Christian organization of the 1980s.

The Goals of the Moral Majority (1980) by Jerry Falwell

We must reverse the trend America finds herself in today. Young people . . . have learned to disrespect the family as God established it. They have been educated in a public-school system that is permeated with secular humanism. They have been taught that the Bible is just another book of literature. They have been taught that there are no absolutes in our world today. . . . These same young people have been reared under

entrepreneurial capitalism. In its quest for profits, unrestrained capitalism had no inherent respect for tradition. Indeed, it could bring unwelcome changes, as Rustbelt industrial workers had discovered when their employers moved south and overseas. Marrying Jesus to the market proved difficult: should the state play a minimal role in the economy and society, as free-market libertarians believed, or should it monitor personal behavior, as social conservatives implied?

Gender and sexuality issues particularly aroused the ire of religious conservatives. They blamed feminism for weakening male authority in the family and for increasing divorce rates. A growing antiabortion movement gained national visibility by 1980, and religious conservatives opposed Americans' slowly increasing acceptance of gays and lesbians. Dismayed by the prevalence of casual sexual relationships in the 1970s, church conservatives urged abstinence on young Americans.

The heyday of the sexual revolution ended in the early 1980s, when researchers identified the human immunodeficiency virus (HIV), which causes acquired immunodeficiency syndrome (AIDS). The deadly epidemic spread swiftly through the gay male communities of San Francisco and New York as a result of unprotected sex. AIDS continued to spread during the 1990s and beyond, among gays and heterosexuals, both in the United States and the influence of a government that has taught them socialism and welfarism. . . .

I personally feel that the home and the family are still held in reverence by the vast majority of the American public. I believe there is still a vast number of Americans who love their country, are patriotic, and are willing to sacrifice for her. I remember that time when it was positive to be patriotic. . . . I remember as a boy . . . when the band struck up "The Stars and Stripes Forever," we stood and goose pimples would run all over me. . . .

It is now time to take a stand on certain moral issues. . . . We must stand against the Equal Rights Amendment, the feminist revolution, and the homosexual revolution. . . .

Americans have been silent much too long. We have stood by and watched as American power and influence have been systematically weakened in every sphere of the world. . . .

The hope of reversing the trends of decay in our republic now lies with the Christian public in America. We cannot expect help from the liberals. They certainly are not going to call our nation back to righteousness and neither are the pornographers, the smut peddlers, and those who are corrupting our youth.

The Politics of the Bible (1982)
by Robert McAfee Brown

In Christian terms, and I think in terms with which all Jews could also agree, my real complaint about the Moral Majority's intrusion of the Bible into American politics, is that they are not biblical enough. . . .

The Moral Majority's biblically inspired political agenda involves a very selective, very partial, and therefore very distorted use of the Bible. They have isolated a set of concerns that they say get to the heart of what is wrong with America—homosexuality, abortion, and pornography. . . .

Take the issue of homosexuality. If one turns to the scriptures as a whole, to try to come up with their central concerns, homosexuality is going to be very low on such a list even if indeed it makes the list at all. There are perhaps seven very ambiguous verses in the whole biblical canon that even allude to it. . . . [But there are] hundreds and hundreds of places where the scriptures are dealing over and over again with question of social justice, the tendency of the rich to exploit the poor, the need for all of us to have a commitment to the

hungry, . . . [and] the dangers of national idolatry, that is to say, making the nation into God, accepting uncritically whatever we have to do as a nation against other nations. . . .

When one looks over the agenda of the Moral Majority there is absolutely no mention of such things. . . . We seem to be living in two different worlds, reading two different books.

Questions

1. *Which specific issues in American society most trouble Jerry Falwell? What specifically about "liberals" seems to dismay him most?*

2. *What does Robert McAfee Brown find most unpersuasive about Jerry Falwell's use of the Bible to understand American society and its problems?*

3. *Which of these two interpretations do you find most persuasive, and why?*

Source: Irwin Unger and Robert R. Tomes, *American Issues*, 2nd ed. (Prentice-Hall, 1999), vol. 2, pp. 362–364, 375–377.

abroad—especially in such places as China, southern Africa, and Russia. New drugs slowed the onset of actual AIDS in many HIV-infected Americans while scientists continued the frustrating quest for a cure.

Yet another epidemic swept through the United States during the 1980s, striking impoverished urban neighborhoods especially hard. The culprit was crack cocaine. Powerfully addictive, it contributed to gang violence and record homicide rates in several cities. Drug-related convictions skyrocketed, stimulating a boom in prison building, a doubling of the nation's inmate population, and new police special weapons and tactics (SWAT) teams to deal with heavily armed drug operators.

Watch the Video
Evangelical Religion an Politics, Then and Now at **www.myhistorylab.com**

Dissenters Push Back

The liberal and radical reform energies that had percolated in the late 1960s and early 1970s did not evaporate entirely in the conservative 1980s. Nuclear threats engaged activists from both the peace and environmental movements. The accidents at Three Mile Island (1979) and Chernobyl (1986) intensified public anxieties about the dangers of nuclear energy. The sharp increases in both Soviet and U.S. nuclear arsenals alarmed residents in those countries and across Europe, where many of the missiles were located. The broad-based nuclear freeze movement that emerged in the United States and western Europe in the early 1980s encouraged arms control negotiations that would bear fruit a few years later.

Racial justice remained a primary concern for Americans of color and liberal and leftist activists, particularly in light of the Republican administration's opposition to affirmative action. Determined to honor the foremost leader of the civil rights movement, antiracists convinced Congress in 1983 to designate Martin Luther King Jr.'s birthday a national holiday. By 1985 a robust antiapartheid movement successfully campaigned to reduce U.S. investments in racially segregated South Africa. Perhaps the most prominent face of left-leaning politics in the decade was that of Reverend Jesse Jackson, a former aide to King. Jackson sought the Democratic nomination for president in 1984 and 1988, winning a handful of primaries in 1988 with his multiracial Rainbow Coalition. Jackson's candidacy encouraged several million African Americans to register to vote for the first time.

Gays and lesbians remained the only Americans against whom tens of millions of their fellow citizens openly believed it acceptable to discriminate.

Gay rights advocates also raised their voices in the 1980s. Faced with the twin scourge of AIDS and homophobic violence, homosexuals and their heterosexual supporters lobbied for the inclusion of sexual orientation as a category of discrimination in civil rights laws. Others took to the streets. In October 1987, nearly half a million Americans marched in Washington in support of gay rights. A few widely admired figures, such as tennis champion Martina Navratilova, publicly acknowledged their homosexuality, helping others to imagine this sexual orientation as acceptable rather than deviant. By the end of the 1980s, the record was mixed. Gays and lesbians remained the only Americans against whom tens of millions of their fellow citizens openly believed it acceptable to discriminate, but the rights of homosexuals, nonetheless, had much wider support than ever before.

The New Immigrants

For two decades after the restrictive immigration law of 1924, the flow of newcomers from abroad slowed to a trickle. The trickle became a stream again after World War II, and then legislation in 1965 opened the gates even wider. As a result, a wave of new immigrants, 3.3 million in the 1960s and 4.5 million in the 1970s, hit the United States. In the 1980s, 7.3 million people entered the country legally, along with a similar number without documentation.

These newcomers brought an unprecedented cultural and ethnic diversity. Only 10 percent of the most recent arrivals in the United States were Europeans. Forty percent came instead from Asia—particularly China, the Philippines, and South Korea—and 50 percent from Latin America and the Caribbean, particularly Mexico. From 1965 to 1995, 7 million Latinos and 5 million Asians moved to the United States.

The new immigrants came for the same reasons their predecessors had. Many were

■ While immigrants brought their own distinctive cultures to the United States, American popular culture spread abroad. The broadcast of National Basketball Association (NBA) games in dozens of other countries helped basketball climb to being the world's second most popular game (after soccer). Personable stars like Earvin "Magic" Johnson of the Los Angeles Lakers and particularly Michael Jordan of the Chicago Bulls became popular icons around the world.

fleeing political and religious persecution in their home countries, but most sought new economic opportunity. A small number, primarily from South Korea and Hong Kong, arrived with some assets that helped them get started in business. However, most came with few resources and took what work they could find in garment sweatshops, on farms, as domestic servants and janitors, and as gardeners. These immigrants willingly endured profound hardship to build better lives for their families. They also rekindled the nation's long-standing cultural diversity, especially in Sunbelt cities from Miami, Florida, to San Diego, California. In 1981, citizens of San Antonio elected Henry Cisneros as the first Mexican-American mayor of a major U.S. city. In Los Angeles, one-third of residents were foreign born by 1990.

Most Americans had foreign-born ancestors who had come to the United States with the same dreams that motivated the newest arrivals. Still, the non-European origins of the latest immigrants troubled some white citizens. Conservatives, in particular, worried about the growing diversity of American society and feared a decline of the Eurocentric culture they had grown up with. They were also anxious that poor immigrants might drain taxpayers' dollars by winding up on welfare. The Immigration and Naturalization Service (INS) stepped up patrols of the 2,000-mile U.S. border with Mexico to limit the rising number of undocumented Mexican workers heading north. By the early 1990s, the INS was apprehending and expelling 1.7 million undocumented workers every year.

⊙ See the **Map**
America's Move to the Sunbelt, 1970–1981 at **www.myhistorylab.com**

The End of the Cold War

For Americans, the greatest surprise of the 1980s was the warming of U.S.-Soviet relations after 1985. Few had imagined such a scenario during Reagan's first two years in office, when his administration became the first in four decades not to collaborate on nuclear arms control with the USSR. But in the Soviet Union, the rise to power of Communist party reformer Mikhail Gorbachev permanently changed the face of international politics. The American president finally agreed to work toward the common goal of reducing tensions between the two superpowers. Reagan eventually traveled to Moscow, embraced Gorbachev in front of Lenin's tomb, and announced that the Soviets had changed.

After 45 years, why did the Cold War end?

At the same time, the Reagan administration stumbled badly at home when a scandal involving Iran and the Nicaraguan counterrevolutionaries (Contras) came to light in 1986. The disaster revealed a secret foreign policy apparatus and a president out of touch with the daily governance process. Dramatic events in Europe then unfolded independent of the administrations of either Reagan or George H. W. Bush, his successor in the White House. In 1989 eastern Europeans tore down the Berlin Wall and ended Soviet rule in their countries. Two years later, the Soviet Union unraveled into its separate components, Russia being the largest. The end of the Cold War enabled Bush to focus on the Middle East, where an international force under his leadership drove Iraq out of occupied Kuwait and reestablished the status quo in that oil-rich region.

From Cold War to Détente

By the 1980s, the USSR's state-run economy was creaking to a halt. It simply could not provide the consumer products that Soviet citizens had learned about from the world outside their borders. Events further weakened the authority of the Soviet government. The USSR's occupation of Afghanistan became a quagmire resembling the United States' disastrous involvement in Vietnam, and the last Soviet troops finally withdrew in 1989. Initial government efforts to cover up the nuclear accident at Chernobyl only worsened matters, revealing the costs of corrupt communist rule. Nationalist movements for independence in the

Baltic states, the Caucasus region, and central Asia gathered momentum. In his six years in power (1985–1991), Gorbachev tried to preserve the Soviet system by reforming it through *glasnost* (greater political liberty) and *perestroika* (economic restructuring allowing some private enterprise). However, his government proved unable to control the forces for change that it had helped unleash.

Reagan's primary role in ending the Cold War was to support Gorbachev's quest for change within the Soviet Union. To that end, Reagan moved from confrontational rhetoric to pursuing a policy of détente. Gorbachev became head of the Soviet Communist party in 1985, at the start of Reagan's second term. The American president had already built up the U.S. military and was now thinking about his place in history. He wanted to leave office having earned a reputation as a peacemaker.

Beneath Reagan's strident rhetoric about national military strength ran a streak of radical idealism, including a desire to eliminate the threat of nuclear warfare. Once he felt convinced that Gorbachev was serious about internal reform and rapprochement with the United States, Reagan took action. In 1987 the two leaders signed the Intermediate Nuclear Force (INF) treaty. The agreement removed short-range and intermediate-range missiles from Europe and enabled each side to conduct on-site verification of the other side's compliance. The INF treaty marked the first actual reduction in the total number of nuclear weapons stored in the two nations' arsenals.

The Iran-Contra Scandal

Failures elsewhere offset Reagan's success with the Russians. His administration suffered its worst damage when it tried through illegal means to solve two foreign policy challenges with one stroke. Its main strategy consisted of linking a problem in the Middle East with one in Central America.

Revolutionary fervor intensified in the Middle East after the 1979 Iranian revolution, and hostage-taking and terrorism—the "poor man's nuclear bomb"—proliferated. In 1986, Americans bombed the Libyan capital of Tripoli in retaliation for apparent Libyan involvement in the killing of two U.S. soldiers in Germany. Things took an even nastier turn when an American warship in the Persian Gulf killed 290 civilians by shooting down an Iranian airliner, apparently by mistake. In revenge, pro-Iranian agents exploded a bomb on Pan Am Flight 109 over Lockerbie, Scotland, before the end of the year, killing 11 on the ground and 259 aboard the plane, including 35 students from Syracuse University.

Islamist revolutionaries also threatened moderate Arab leaders and assassinated Egyptian president Anwar Sadat in 1981. Lebanon became the center of a radical anti-Israeli campaign to seize Americans as hostages, especially after the United States' 1983 engagement against Muslim forces in the civil war there. Despite his 1980 campaign promise never to negotiate with terrorists, Reagan approved the illegal sale of U.S. arms to Iran in return for the freeing of a handful of hostages held by pro-Iranian radicals in Lebanon.

Events were heating up in Central America as well. The CIA-created Contras failed to overturn the new Sandinista government in Nicaragua. Even though the Contras lacked public support in Nicaragua and the United States, the president and his advisers were determined to keep them afloat. But they had a problem: how to fund the effort. Most Americans did not share Reagan's enthusiasm for the Contras and feared greater U.S. military involvement in Central America. Beginning in 1982, Congress passed the Boland Amendments, restricting aid to the Nicaraguan counterrevolutionaries. Faced with their chief's expressed desire to shore up the Contra cause, the president's men found an alternative solution.

The National Security Council (NSC) established a secret operation run by staff member Lieutenant Colonel Oliver North. Free from public or congressional oversight, North worked closely with CIA director William Casey. North and his colleagues solicited funds for the Contras from wealthy, conservative Americans and from sympathetic foreign governments, including Saudi Arabia and Taiwan. Then North hit on what he called the "neat idea" of "using the Ayatollah Khomeini's money to support the Nicaraguan freedom fighters." Iran desperately needed weapons for its war against neighboring Iraq (1980–1988), so North and his colleagues started diverting profits to the Contras from new sales of U.S. Army property to Tehran.

The NSC's action was illegal: it sold U.S. government property without authorization from the Pentagon, and it broke U.S. laws banning aid to the Contras. When news of the operation finally leaked out in November 1986, it shocked the nation. What did the president know, and when did he know it? The old Watergate question about Richard Nixon came to the fore again. Reagan called North a "national hero" but claimed ignorance of any illegal activities, including the diversion of funds from Iranian arms sales to the Nicaraguan rebels.

But in early 1987, 90 percent of Americans did not believe Reagan was telling all he knew. His job approval ratings dropped from 67 percent to 46 percent. The first round of memoirs by former aides also appeared in the final years of his administration, revealing an isolated president out of touch with the government he nominally headed. For example, the former actor breezily admitted that he was happiest when "each morning I get a piece of paper that tells me what I do all day long."

A Global Police Force?

Despite running a bruising presidential campaign in 1988, Reagan's vice president, George H. W. Bush, proved cautious once in office. Hemmed in by a Democratic-controlled Congress, he had what his chief of staff called a "limited agenda" at home. His most enduring domestic action came with his 1991 appointment of archconservative Clarence Thomas, an African-American lawyer from Georgia, to fill the seat of retiring Supreme Court justice Thurgood Marshall. Only 43 years old and with little experience as a judge, Thomas was chosen because of his conservative views and his race. The Senate narrowly confirmed him, 52–48, after contentious hearings in which a former aide, Anita Hill, accused Thomas of sexual harassment.

TABLE 28-3			
The Election of 1988			
Candidate	Political Party	Popular Vote (%)	Electoral Vote
George H. W. Bush	Republican	53.4	426
Michael S. Dukakis	Democratic	45.6	111

●●●Read the Document
George H.W. Bush, Inaugural Address (January 1989) at
www.myhistorylab.com

"I much prefer foreign affairs," the president once confided in his diary. Some of the most dramatic events of the twentieth century unfolded during his presidency. Poles, Czechs, and Hungarians—encouraged by Gorbachev's promise not to intervene militarily in other Warsaw Pact nations—peacefully overthrew their communist rulers in 1989. East Germans did the same. The Berlin Wall—the 28-year-old symbol of Cold War tensions—finally toppled on November 8. Three months later, anti-apartheid leader Nelson Mandela walked out of the South African prison where he had been held for 27 years. The white supremacist government there agreed to hold the first elections in which all South Africans could vote. The Baltic states of Lithuania, Latvia, and Estonia seceded from the USSR in 1990 and 1991. After a failed coup attempt by Communist hard-liners in August 1991, the Soviet Union broke into its 16 constituent states.

The Bush administration acted more boldly in its own hemisphere. In Panama, under the brutal leadership of Manuel Noriega, tensions grew between the Panamanian Defense Forces (PDF) and U.S. soldiers based in the Canal Zone. Noriega deepened his lucrative role as an intermediary in smuggling Colombian cocaine into the United States. Meanwhile, the crack cocaine epidemic tightened its grip in poor American neighborhoods. Rising popular concern about crack-related violence increased Americans' willingness to take action against Noriega. When the dictator overturned Panamanian election results that went against him and further confrontations erupted between American and Panamanian soldiers, Bush decided to step in.

In December 1989, 24,000 U.S. troops invaded the small Central American nation. They crushed the PDF, and thousands of civilians died in the crossfire. Noriega eventually surrendered and was brought to Miami, where he was convicted of drug trafficking and imprisoned.

Developments in the Middle East provoked the most important move of the George H. W. Bush administration: the initiation of the Persian Gulf War of 1991. In 1990 Iraq invaded tiny, neighboring, oil-rich Kuwait, annexing it as Iraq's "nineteenth province." With Americans and their Japanese and European allies dependent on Middle Eastern oil, Bush declared the invasion unacceptable. He rushed more than 200,000 troops to

■ **MAP 28.2**

THE SOVIET BLOC DISSOLVES

No change in world politics since World War II was greater than the collapse of the Soviet Union and its satellite states in eastern Europe. Eastern European countries soon sought membership in NATO and post-Communist Russia built closer relations with the United States and western Europe. The transition from socialist to capitalist economies was difficult, however, and many poorer citizens found daily life little easier than it had been before.

The Soviet Union and the Communist bloc in Eastern Europe dissolve

    Former Union of Soviet Socialist Republics (USSR), dissolved 1991

    Eastern European countries that overturned Communist rule, 1989–1990

Saudi Arabia in "Operation Desert Shield" to discourage further aggression by Iraqi leader Saddam Hussein. At the same time, the United Nations slapped economic sanctions on Iraq.

Within three months, Bush shifted his attention to liberating Kuwait. He doubled the number of U.S. troops in the region to 430,000. He also gained the support of the UN, which demanded Iraqi withdrawal by January 15, 1991. The U.S. Congress backed him as well, voting to support any actions necessary to drive Iraq out of Kuwait. Bush went on the offensive because he faced a shrinking window of opportunity. He had wide international support, including troops from several Arab nations, but growing clashes in Jerusalem between Israelis and Palestinians threatened to break up this alliance by rekindling Arab anger at Israel.

On January 16, 1991, U.S.-led coalition forces began five and a half weeks of bombing against Iraq. Then, on February 25, coalition forces poured across the border from Saudi Arabia in "Operation Desert Storm." The offensive freed Kuwait and sent Iraqi troops in headlong retreat toward Baghdad. The Iraqis burned oil wells as they fell back, blanketing the battlefield in smoke. Four days later, Bush halted the U.S. advance, having restored Kuwaiti sovereignty. Saddam Hussein remained in power and later crushed uprisings by Iraqi dissidents. The politics of coalition warfare helped prohibit further U.S. action, for no Arabs wanted Americans ruling Iraq.

The Gulf War's outcome seemed to validate two strategic lessons that U.S. commanders had learned during the Vietnam War. The first was the importance of preserving absolute control of the media. During the Persian Gulf conflict, the Pentagon kept journalists away from most of the action to control the images that Americans saw of the fighting. The public viewed endless videos of "smart" bombs hitting their targets in Baghdad but none of the tens of thousands of Iraqi soldiers being slaughtered during their retreat from Kuwait. The second lesson, advocated by General Colin Powell, the African-American chair of the Joint Chiefs of Staff who emerged from the war as a national hero, was to marshal overwhelmingly superior forces before going into battle, thus ensuring the success of the operation.

The Gulf War seemed to demonstrate a U.S. willingness to act as a global police force in the post–Cold War era. But the war also stimulated the further growth of anti-Americanism among Islamist revolutionaries, including Saudi-born Osama bin Laden; they considered it a sacrilege for non-Muslim American soldiers to operate bases in Saudi Arabia, home to Mecca, Islam's holiest site. Finally, the war foreshadowed Bush's defiant claim at a 1992 international environmental conference that, when it came to oil, "the American lifestyle is not negotiable."

Watch the Video
Bush's Early Response in the Persian Gulf War at **www.myhistorylab.com**

See the Map
The Middle East in the 1980s and 1990s at **www.myhistorylab.com**

CONCLUSION

The Republican era of Ronald Reagan and George H. W. Bush reshaped American relations with the rest of the world, as well as politics and economics in the United States. Both sets of changes hinged on the elevation of individualism and market forces above communal values and government planning. The collective dreams represented by the Soviet experiment evaporated into history in these years, leaving capitalism unchallenged as a system of economic organization across most of the globe. U.S. military power stepped into the vacuum left by the Soviet demise, most visibly in the 1991 Persian Gulf War. But that military revival came at the cost of vast deficit spending and a sharp recession in 1991–1992, which paved the way for Bill Clinton's victory over George H. W. Bush in the 1992 presidential campaign.

For Review

✓•⌐Study and Review at www.myhistorylab.com

1. Why did Cold War tensions increase after 1979?

2. Why did American voters elect Reagan twice to the presidency? Were they pleased with the results of his eight years in the White House?

3. Which cultural issues did Americans most seem to disagree about?

4. After 45 years, why did the Cold War end?

Chronology: 1979–1991

1979 Iranian revolution; militants take American hostages.
Soviet Union invades Afghanistan.

1980 Ronald Reagan elected president.

1981 Iran releases American hostages.
United States funds Contras to try to overthrow new leftist Nicaraguan government.

1983 HIV identified as virus that causes AIDS.
241 U.S. marines killed in bombing of Beirut barracks.

1984 Reagan reelected president.

1986 Chernobyl nuclear power plant disaster (Ukraine).
Iran-Contra scandal revealed.

1987 Intermediate Nuclear Force Treaty.
Stock market crash.

1988 Libyan terrorist bomb downs Pan Am Flight 103 over Lockerbie, Scotland.
George H. W. Bush elected president.

1989 Oil tanker *Exxon Valdez* runs aground off Alaska coast.
Berlin Wall falls.
United States invades Panama to seize Manuel Noriega.

1990 Iraq invades and occupies Kuwait.

1991 Persian Gulf War against Iraq.
Soviet Union dissolves into Russia and other component states.

Key Terms

Islamist Pertaining to an ideology promoting the creation of governments based on a fundamentalist interpretation of Islamic law. p. 638

Theocracy A government by officials who are regarded as divinely guided. p. 637

J ack Welch retired as chief executive officer of General Electric
in 2000. The previous year, his income had been $123 million,
mostly in stock and stock options. When he left the company, he
was granted the use of a Manhattan apartment for the rest of his life,
including food, wine, and laundry services. He was also given access
to corporate jets and other benefits worth more than $2 million per
year. Welch's enormous income and retirement package reflected the
upward redistribution of wealth that occurred throughout the 1990s.
A very small number of people, most of them corporate executives
like Jack Welch, became extremely wealthy while the majority
of Americans saw their real income decline.

As the gap between the wealthy and the poor grew, so did the
U.S. economy, which expanded throughout the 1990s. Increasing numbers of Americans invested in the soaring stock market, many for the
first time. The crime rate declined. Moreover, the strong economy also
emboldened consumers to buy and use products and resources, such
as huge gas-guzzling sport utility vehicles, with little concern for the
environmental impact. As the new millennium dawned, the economy
began to falter. The stock market fell, and there were signs of an impending recession.

The 2000 U.S. Census revealed a number of striking changes
in the nation's population during the 1990s. Among the most dramatic was the growth in the Latino population, from 22.4 million
to 35.3 million, making the number of Latinos—
most of them Mexican American—nearly equal to
that of African Americans. Immigrants from Asia
and Latin America also added increasing linguistic
diversity, fueling controversies over bilingual education and "English-only" political initiatives.

In national politics, the rifts between liberals
and conservatives that had opened up in the 1960s
persisted. Struggles over cultural issues such as
abortion and gay rights polarized the political
climate. In 1992 Democrats took back the White
House, but in 1994 Republicans swept into control
of Congress with a conservative agenda, hemming
in President Bill Clinton, a centrist Democrat who
presided over the final destruction of the Aid to
Families with Dependent Children (AFDC)
program, the central feature of the national welfare
system since the New Deal of the 1930s. In 2000 the
Supreme Court decided one of the closest and most
divisive elections in the nation's history, handing the
White House to the Republican candidate, George W.
Bush, son of the former president.

The post–Cold War era raised new questions about the role of the
United States in the world. Americans no longer looked to Russia as

29

Post–Cold War America, 1991–2000

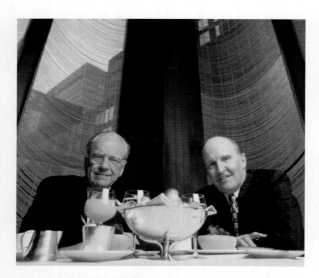

■ Jack Welch (right), former chief executive office of General Electric, dines with global media executive Rupert Murdoch.

a threat but to new international foes, especially terrorist networks operating outside the authority of particular countries. Within the nation, episodes of domestic terrorism, such as the bombing of a federal building in Oklahoma City and a series of school shootings by children, made Americans aware that dangers lurked within their previously safe havens.

The Economy: Global and Domestic

After the sharp recession of 1991–1992, by nearly all measures, the economy expanded in the 1990s. The stock market boomed, unemployment declined, and most Americans appeared to be better off financially at the end of the decade than at the beginning. But the overall growth of the economy did not benefit everyone, and many actually lost ground—especially those who lost jobs to automation, nonunionized workers who toiled for low wages under grim working conditions, and the nation's most vulnerable workers: poor single mothers, new immigrants, and unskilled people of color.

How did the expanding economy affect those at the top and bottom of the income ladder?

The Post–Cold War Economy

The end of the Cold War had a profound effect on the nation's economy. The demise of the Soviet Union finally ended the arms race against a superpower foe and made cutting the defense budget politically acceptable. But closing defense-related plants in southern California devastated the regional economy. By the mid-1990s, half the workers in the southern California aerospace industry had been laid off.

While defense industries shrank, the technology sector of the economy expanded, opening up new opportunities for young computer experts and entrepreneurs and generating fortunes for corporate executives. At the same time, mergers of giant multinational companies concentrated wealth and power in an ever-smaller number of ever-larger corporations. In the last three years of the decade, mergers totaled $5 trillion. Media giants America Online and Time-Warner merged in 2000. In 2001 Nestlé bought Ralston-Purina for $10 billion. Many of the largest mergers crossed national boundaries, such as German automobile maker Daimler-Benz and U.S. Chrysler.

Corporations expanded and consolidated, while some faced challenges to their power. Microsoft initially lost an antitrust suit that ordered the computer software giant to be split into two companies. Microsoft appealed the ruling in 2001, and ultimately the Justice Department settled the suit with minor sanctions against the company. In several states, civil suits against huge tobacco companies limited cigarette advertising and marketing and levied fines on tobacco companies totaling in the billions of dollars.

The nation's elite were not the only ones to capitalize on new entrepreneurial opportunities. The 1988 Indian Gaming Regulatory Act enabled Native Americans to build lucrative casinos on tribal lands, bringing new jobs and an estimated $4 billion a year to formerly impoverished communities. The Mashantucket Pequot east of Hartford, Connecticut, opened Foxwoods in 1992, and it quickly became the largest casino in the Western Hemisphere. The Oneida followed suit a few years later with the Turning Stone casino near Utica, New York. In Arizona casinos brought in $830 million a year. Some Indian casinos failed, however, and gambling took a largely hidden toll in the losses of already poor local residents.

Native Americans remained divided about the wisdom of trying to profit from America's growing inclination to take risks in hopes of winning big.

The Widening Gap Between Rich and Poor

In the last decade of the century, the bottom 60 percent of the population saw their real income decline, even as the economy boomed. Accumulated wealth—property and investments—was an even better measure of security and influence, and the top 1 percent of Americans owned more wealth than the bottom 90 percent combined. Microsoft chair Bill Gates alone was wealthier than the bottom 45 percent of all U.S. households together. A century earlier, famed capitalist J. P. Morgan said that no corporate chieftain should earn more than 20 times what his workers were paid, but by 1980 a typical chief executive of a large U.S. company took home forty times the earnings of an average factory worker; by 1990 the ratio had grown to 85 times, and by 2004 it reached 431 times.

■ Casino Sandia on the Sandia Pueblo in New Mexico. Many Native American communities across the country built gambling facilities on tribal lands. Although casinos brought needed income, they remained controversial.

Although one-third of the nation's African Americans were part of the middle class, black families had fewer assets and resources, making their hold on middle-class status more precarious than that of their white peers. The poorest African Americans were concentrated in low-paying jobs, lacking the quality health care and education that would make social and economic mobility possible. Full-time employment did not necessarily mean an escape from poverty. Among fully employed black heads of households without a high school education, 40 percent of the women and 25 percent of the men did not earn enough to achieve economic self-sufficiency. Almost 50 percent of all black children lived in households below the poverty line, compared to 16 percent of white children. The rate of unemployment was more than twice as high for blacks as for whites.

Recent immigrants from Asia, Africa, and Latin America joined African Americans in jobs at the bottom of the economy. Despite the controversy over illegal immigration, a quarter of a million undocumented workers toiled in the fields of agribusiness. At the same time, 2 percent of able-bodied citizens were in jail, nearly half of them black, because of the arrest and incarceration policies of the "war on drugs" that hit minority communities particularly hard. Prisoners were often required to work while incarcerated. Convicts entered data, packed golf balls, and filled a wide array of jobs for less than minimum wage, and most of their earnings went back to the government. These and other workers at the bottom of the labor force gained little or nothing from the economic boom of the 1990s.

Service Workers and Labor Unions

Low-wage workers in the service industries had one advantage over laborers working for multinational corporations: their jobs could not be exported. Some service workers organized successfully for better wages and working conditions. In 2000, for example, striking janitors of Service Employees International Union Local 1877 in Los Angeles achieved a wage increase of 26 percent, raising their hourly pay from less than $8 to more than $10. This was a tremendous triumph for a union whose membership was 98 percent immigrant: 80 percent Central Americans, more than half women, and all of them poor.

Other service workers also won improved contracts. Unionized hotel workers in San Francisco negotiated a five-year contract that increased pay for the lowest-paid workers, room

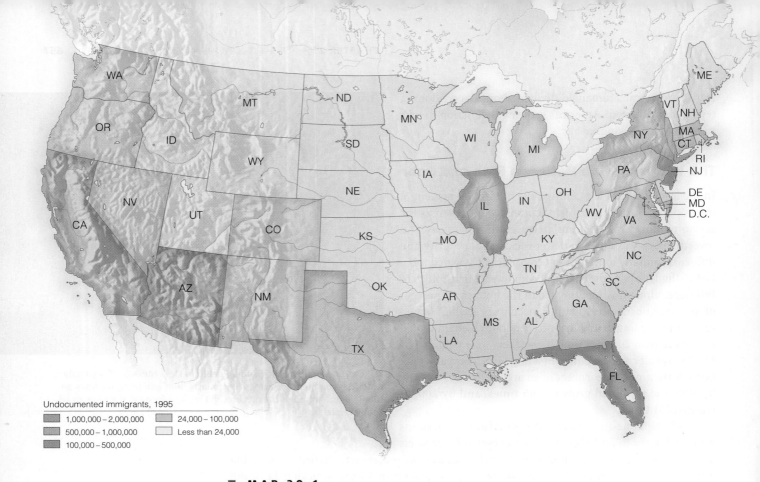

Undocumented immigrants, 1995

- 1,000,000 – 2,000,000
- 500,000 – 1,000,000
- 100,000 – 500,000
- 24,000 – 100,000
- Less than 24,000

■ **MAP 29.1**

STATES WITH LARGE NUMBERS OF UNDOCUMENTED IMMIGRANTS, 1995
Fully 77 percent of all undocumented immigrants entered the country legally, with visas in hand. During the 1990s, the total proportion of the foreign born in the United States, including those with and without legal status, increased from 9 to 11 percent, still less than the 15 percent in 1900. Immigrants paid $133 billion dollars annually in local, state, and federal taxes, and generated an annual contribution to the American economy in the range of $25 to $30 billion.

cleaners and dishwashers, by 25 percent, from $12 to $15 an hour. In Las Vegas, African-American hotel worker Hattie Canty helped organize 40,000 employees of large casino hotels. In the summer of 1997, 185,000 Teamsters went on strike against the United Parcel Service and won an improved contract with higher wages and benefits for part-time as well as full-time workers.

In spite of these successes, union membership declined. Moreover, strikes did little to benefit nonunionized workers, especially undocumented immigrants and sweatshop laborers both inside and outside the United States. There were some attempts to improve working conditions for those most exploited by the global economy. In April 1997, representatives from clothing manufacturers, human rights groups, and labor organizations drafted an agreement that tried to improve conditions for garment workers around the world. Companies that agreed to the voluntary pact would limit work weeks to 60 hours, with a maximum of 12 hours of overtime. The companies had to pay "at least the minimum wage required by local law or the prevailing industry wage, whichever is higher." The pact forbade children under 15 to work and contained policies protecting workers from harassment and unsafe working environments. But all of these efforts were voluntary and not legally enforceable.

Industry Versus the Environment

The global economy also affected the natural world. Environmental activists mobilized in response, with new forms of civil disobedience. Julia Butterfly Hill was one such activist. On a cold December night in 1997, the 23-year-old environmentalist climbed onto a small platform 180 feet above ground in a giant redwood tree in Humboldt County, California. She remained there for two years, trespassing on the property of the Pacific Lumber Company, which was threatening to cut down the 1,000-year-old tree as part of its logging operations.

Tree sitting was a strategy Earth First! activists developed to protest the destruction of the trees. Julia Hill took a forest name—Butterfly—and pledged that her "feet would not touch the ground" until the tree was safe from destruction. For two years, Hill endured rain and hail storms, ninety-mile-per-hour winds, bone-chilling cold, and harassment from the logging company. Finally, the president of Pacific Lumber, John Campbell, agreed never to cut down the tree or other trees in a 2.9-acre buffer zone, and Hill agreed to come down. For her civil disobedience, she paid a $50,000 fine, contributed by supporters, which the court designated to Humboldt State University for forestry research. Although her

■ Sweatshops like this one in the 1990s resemble those of a century earlier. Immigrant women labor in garment factories, working long hours in difficult conditions for meager wages.

success was modest in terms of saving endangered forests, her actions raised environmental awareness across the globe and called attention to the impact of economic expansion on the natural world.

Tolerance and Its Limits

Racial discrimination had eased over the course of the twentieth century, but persistent inequalities of power and economic opportunity continued to disadvantage Americans of color, who remained disproportionately poor, in prison, and on welfare. The economic downturn of the early 1990s widened the chasm between affluent white and poor nonwhite Americans. Highly publicized incidents of police brutality directed against Americans of color generated protests and, occasionally, violence. Nevertheless, there were signs that Americans were becoming more tolerant of one another and more willing to accept and even appreciate their diversity.

In what ways did Americans demonstrate increasing tolerance for those different from themselves?

The Los Angeles Riots: "We Can All Get Along"

On March 3, 1991, police pulled over Rodney King, an African-American motorist, after a high-speed chase on a Los Angeles freeway. The four officers dragged the unarmed black man from his car and kicked and beat him with their batons for fifteen minutes. A bystander recorded the beating on videotape, which was broadcast repeatedly on national television, sparking outrage among Americans of all races.

At the highly publicized trial in April 1992, defense lawyers for the police officers argued that King, who was clearly cowering on the videotape, was resisting arrest and that the police responded appropriately. The jury of ten whites, one Asian, and one Latino acquitted the officers. The acquittal ignited five days of rioting in the African-American community

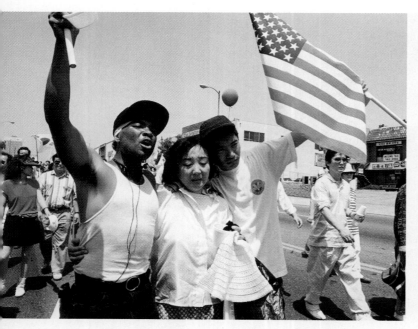

■ In the aftermath of the violent uprising that followed the acquittal of police officers in the beating of motorist Rodney King, Koreans and African Americans in Los Angeles express their solidarity, hoping to heal the wounds and divisions that had torn apart their city.

of South Central Los Angeles, leaving 58 people dead and $1 billion in property destroyed. Community leaders called for calm; even Rodney King implored the public: "We can all get along. We've just got to." Months later, a federal court in Los Angeles convicted two of the officers involved in the beating of violating King's civil rights—too late to avert the violence that erupted after the initial verdict.

Of the 58 people who died in the violence, 18 were Latino, 26 were black, ten were white, and two were Asian. Of the 4,000 businesses that were destroyed, most belonged to Latinos and Koreans. Perpetrators of the violence, as well as the victims, came from all racial groups. Antonia Hernandez, president of the Mexican American Legal Defense and Educational Fund, noted, "The hardest part is rebuilding the spirit of the city— what holds us together as Angelinos. It's the rebuilding of trust. . . . It's connecting communities that have never been connected." Several community groups came together in an effort to ease tensions, including the Japanese American Citizens League, Chinese for Affirmative Action, and the League of United Latin American Citizens.

Values in Conflict

Many citizens worried that the bonds holding Americans together might be fraying. In 1991 former University of Colorado football coach Bill McCartney formed the Promise Keepers, a fundamentalist Christian group dedicated to restoring the traditional privileges and responsibilities of husbands and fathers in the home. The Promise Keepers held evangelical revivals that drew tens of thousands of mostly working-class white and some black men to rallies across the country. They believed that men should be good providers for their families, strong role models for their children, and committed spouses.

Although white men continued to control nearly all the major economic and political institutions in the nation, a 1993 poll found that a majority of white men believed that their advantage in terms of jobs and income, along with their influence over American culture, was declining. African-American men also felt the need to bolster manhood and fatherhood. Efforts geared specifically toward African-American men included the 1995 Million Man March, organized by Nation of Islam Reverend Louis Farrakhan, which drew hundreds of thousands of black men to demonstrate their solidarity at a rally in Washington, D.C.

At the same time, gay men and lesbians mobilized to gain acceptance and legitimacy for the families that they formed. Although a 1994 poll showed that 52 percent of respondents "claimed to consider gay lifestyle acceptable," 64 percent were opposed to legalizing gay marriage or allowing gay couples to adopt children. In 2000, Vermont became the first state to grant legal status to civil unions between same-sex couples, although a fierce backlash threatened to overturn the legislation.

Values also collided around the rights and traditions of Native Americans as tribal communities came into conflict with non-Native environmentalists, sports enthusiasts, and scientists. In the upper Midwest, treaties with the government in 1837 and 1842 granted the Chippewa hunting, fishing, and gathering rights in the territories ceded to the United States. Federal courts consistently upheld these treaties, which include rights to take up to half of the fish and game allowed by state conservation requirements and to use methods such as spear fishing that are illegal for non-Indians. In the 1980s and 1990s, non-Indians challenged these policies and accosted Native Americans in fishing boats with rocks and insults. Native American cultural practices also clashed with environmentalist sensibilities over religious practices involving the gathering and sacrificing of golden eaglets.

Courtroom Dramas: Clarence Thomas and O. J. Simpson

Two of the most controversial legal clashes of the decade centered on accusations against successful black men and exposed deep chasms along class and gender as well as racial lines. The first of these episodes was the Senate hearing of October 1991 to confirm the appointment of conservative Judge Clarence Thomas to the U.S. Supreme Court. When University of Oklahoma law professor Anita Hill accused Thomas of sexual harassment when she had worked for him at the Equal Opportunity Employment Commission in the early 1980s, the question of Thomas's professional qualifications faded to the background and the hearings focused exclusively on Hill's accusations.

In live televised hearings, the African-American law professor testified that Thomas had made crude remarks to her as well as unwanted sexual overtures. Several of the all-white-male panel of senators questioned Hill's credibility, wondering why she continued to work for Thomas after the alleged harassment. Thomas drew on the long history of black men being falsely accused of sexual aggression to counter the charge of sexual harassment, accusing his Democratic opponents of conducting a "high-tech lynching." In the end, Thomas was confirmed. But Hill's testimony, and the insensitive behavior of the senators, brought the issue of sexual harassment to a high level of national consciousness. The hearings also highlighted the fact that Congress was overwhelmingly white and male, motivating female candidates and their supporters to alter that reality. After the 1992 elections, the number of female senators tripled from two to six, including the first black female senator, Carol Moseley Braun, Democrat from Illinois. The number of congresswomen rose from 28 to 47.

In 1994 television viewers were again riveted by a media spectacle, this time a sensational murder case in Los Angeles. The victims were the white ex-wife of black celebrity O. J. Simpson, former football star and film actor, and her male companion. Simpson's blood was found at the scene, hair and other forensic and DNA evidence linked him to the crime, he had no reliable alibi, and a motive was evident in his pattern of jealous rage and brutality against the murdered woman. No other suspects in the case were ever identified. But Simpson's team of lawyers unearthed evidence that, before the Simpson case, white police detective Mark Fuhrman had boasted of planting evidence and had made racist comments. The mostly black and female jury was sympathetic to the possibility that Fuhrman had framed Simpson. In Los Angeles, in the wake of the Rodney King beatings, African Americans had good reason to distrust the police. Simpson was acquitted, but he was later held responsible for the murders in a "wrongful death" civil suit.

In early October 1996, after a trial that lasted nearly a year, it took the jury only two hours to acquit Simpson of all charges. Pundits focused on the racial divide: blacks were more inclined to believe Simpson was innocent, and whites more likely to consider him guilty.

The Changing Face of Diversity

These highly charged events illuminated racial tensions, but there was also evidence that Americans were accepting the nation's diversity and adopting a more inclusive vision. The number of immigrants represented 10 percent of the population, the highest proportion of

INTERPRETING HISTORY

Vermont Civil Union Law

On April 26, 2000, Vermont became the first state to grant legal recognition to same-sex couples, affording them all the legal protections, privileges, and responsibilities of married couples. The law unleashed a storm of controversy and raised questions about the legal status in other states of civil unions contracted in Vermont. Nevertheless, in the first year after its enactment, 2,479 same-sex couples forged civil unions in Vermont, 478 of them among Vermonters, and the rest from other states. Two-thirds were lesbian unions. Several states began to consider similar bills, but others moved to prohibit such unions. Nebraska amended its state constitution to outlaw same-sex marriage and civil unions. On the national level, conservative lawmakers endeavored to introduce a constitutional amendment that would ban civil unions and restrict marriage to heterosexual couples. Among other provisions, the Vermont Civil Union Law stipulated that

Kathleen Peterson and Carolyn Conrad exchange vows in front of Justice of the Peace T. Hunter Wilson. The ceremony in Brattleboro, Vermont, on July 1, 2000, marked the first legal union under Vermont's Civil Union Law. Vermont was the first state to provide recognition and legal status to gay and lesbian couples.

(1) Civil marriage under Vermont's marriage statutes consists of a union between a man and a woman. . . .

(2) Vermont's history as an independent republic and as a state is one of equal treatment and respect for all Vermonters. . . .

(3) The state's interest in civil marriage is to encourage close and caring families, and to protect all family members from the economic and social consequences of abandonment and divorce, focusing on those who have been especially at risk.

(4) Legal recognition of civil marriage by the state is the primary and, in a number of instances, the exclusive source of numerous benefits, responsibilities and protections under the laws of the state for married persons and their children.

(5) Based on the state's tradition of equality under the law and strong families, for at least 25 years, Vermont Probate Courts have qualified gay and lesbian individuals as adoptive parents.

(6) Vermont was one of the first states to adopt comprehensive legislation prohibiting discrimination on the basis of sexual orientation. . . .

(7) The state has a strong interest in promoting stable and lasting families, including families based upon a same-sex couple.

(8) Without the legal protections, benefits and responsibilities associated with civil marriage, same-sex couples suffer numerous obstacles and hardships.

(9) Despite long-standing social and economic discrimination, many gay and lesbian Vermonters have formed lasting, committed, caring and faithful relationships with persons of their same sex. These couples live together, participate in their communities together, and some raise children and care for family members together, just as do couples who are married under Vermont law.

(10) While a system of civil unions does not bestow the status of civil marriage, it does satisfy the requirements of the Common Benefits Clause. Changes in the way significant legal relationships are established under the constitution should be approached carefully, combining respect for the community and cultural institutions most affected with a commitment to the constitutional rights involved. Granting benefits and protections to same-sex couples through a system of civil unions will provide due respect for tradition and long-standing social institutions, and will permit adjustment as unanticipated consequences or unmet needs arise.

(11) The constitutional principle of equality embodied in the Common Benefits Clause is compatible with the freedom of religious belief and worship guaranteed in Chapter I, Article 3rd of the state constitution. Extending the benefits and protections of marriage to same-sex couples through a system of civil unions preserves the fundamental constitutional right of each of the multitude of religious faiths in Vermont to choose freely and without state interference to whom to grant the religious status, sacrament or blessing of marriage under the rules, practices or traditions of such faith.

Questions

1. What political principles and values provided the foundation for Vermont's civil union law?

2. In what ways does the Vermont civil union law distinguish between civil marriages and civil unions?

foreign-born residents since the 1930s. The numbers of Asians and Pacific Islanders increased by 45.9 percent, with those of Chinese ancestry comprising the largest group, followed by those with origins in the Philippines. The Latino population grew by 39.7 percent. Among the nation's Latinos, nearly two-thirds were of Mexican ancestry.

Not everyone celebrated these developments. In California, with one-third of the nation's Latino population, voters responded with Proposition 187 to deny public education and most other public social services to undocumented immigrants, and Proposition 227 to end bilingual education. Large numbers of Latino voters opposed these measures. In subsequent elections, many young Latinos and new citizens marshaled their political power and voted for the first time. By 2000 whites no longer constituted a majority of California's multiethnic population, dropping from 57 percent in 1990 to 47 percent in 2000.

At the same time, politics and ideas based on distinct and rigid racial lines gave way to a growing recognition of intermixing. In the world of sports, young golfer Tiger Woods, son of a black Vietnam-veteran father and a Thai mother, became the reigning superstar of the sport most closely identified with the world of the white elite. Pop star Prince was one of many artists who crafted a persona that highlighted both racial and gender ambiguity. On job and college application forms, a growing number of mixed-race Americans refused to be identified as belonging to one particular racial group. Reflecting this development, the U.S. Census of 2000 allowed people to check more than one box to indicate their racial identity.

■ Hines Ward, son of a Korean mother and an African-American father, starred for the University of Georgia football team in the 1990s and became an All-Pro wide receiver for the NFL's Pittsburgh Steelers. He also became a respected advocate for biracial youths in South Korea.

The Clinton Years

What was the impact of the "Republican revolution" during Clinton's presidency?

🎬 **Watch** the **Video**
Clinton Presidential Campaign Ad (1992) at **www.myhistorylab.com**

William Jefferson Clinton was the first American president born after World War II. Raised in Arkansas in a working-class family, Clinton attended Georgetown University and studied at Oxford University in England as a Rhodes Scholar. Like many college students of his generation, he opposed the Vietnam War and avoided the draft. He attended Yale Law School, where he met Hillary Rodham from Illinois, whom he married in 1975. In 1978, at the young age of 33, he was elected governor of Arkansas. After one term, he was defeated in his bid for reelection. He made a comeback by defining himself as a New Democrat with centrist political inclinations and reclaimed his job as governor. When he ran for president in 1992, Clinton received the support of the Democratic Leadership Council, a group of **New Democrats** who shifted the national party to the right of its previous New Deal liberal position.

Clinton: The New Democrat

In 1992 the incumbent president, George H. W. Bush, faced an uphill battle. The recession of 1991–1992 hit white-collar as well as blue-collar workers as unemployment climbed above 8 percent. During 12 years of Republican presidents, the national debt had more than quadrupled to $4.4 trillion. Reflecting pressures from the right wing of the party, Republicans attacked permissiveness in American society, opposed abortion and gay rights, and called for a smaller government. The Democrats nominated the 46-year-old Clinton. A wildcard in the election was the Reform party candidacy of H. Ross Perot, a Texas billionaire who financed his own campaign and used the national media to tap into voter discontent with the two major parties.

Much of the campaign reflected the culture wars, pitting what many saw as the socially permissive legacy of the 1960s against conservative efforts to restore traditional "family values" to American public life. Many Americans worried that the prevalence of single-parent families, the high rate of divorce, and the pervasiveness of sex and violence in the popular culture all reflected a decline in moral standards and an erosion of American society.

Clinton won the election by a comfortable margin, but Perot garnered 19 percent of the popular vote, the largest showing for a third-party candidate since Theodore Roosevelt ran on the Progressive party ticket in 1912. Clinton began his term with a solidly Democratic House and Senate, which included a new infusion of women, along with the nation's first senator of American Indian descent, Ben Nighthorse Campbell of Colorado. Saying that he wanted his advisers to "look like America," Clinton appointed two Latinos, three blacks, and three women to the 14-member cabinet.

TABLE 29-1

The Election of 1992

Candidate	Political Party	Popular Vote (%)	Electoral Vote
William J. Clinton	Democratic	43.1	370
George H. W. Bush	Republican	37.4	168
H. Ross Perot	Independent	18.8	—

Clinton's Domestic Agenda and the "Republican Revolution"

Clinton ran into trouble early in his administration when he tried to fulfill his campaign promise to allow gays and lesbians to serve openly in the military, reversing a policy that dated back half a century. Top military officials, already unhappy with having a new commander in chief who had avoided military service during the Vietnam War, vehemently opposed lifting the ban against gays. Ultimately, Clinton compromised and established a new policy of **"don't ask, don't tell,"** which allowed homosexuals to serve as long as they did not make their sexual orientation known.

Clinton's effort to reform the health care system was equally unsuccessful. With rising health care costs and millions of uninsured citizens, efforts to provide national health insurance and reduce the cost of health care had wide public support but fierce opposition from the medical establishment and the pharmaceutical industry. Clinton appointed his wife, Hillary Rodham Clinton, an attorney and longtime advocate on behalf of children and families, to head a task force to develop a plan. But the task force, deliberating behind closed doors, failed to come up with a workable strategy acceptable to all sides. The Clintons abandoned the effort after a year of hearings and no action in Congress.

◄●◄ Read the Document
Clinton Healthcare Reform Proposals
at **www.myhistorylab.com**

Clinton succeeded in passing a budget that raised taxes on the wealthiest Americans, cut spending to reduce the deficit, and expanded tax credits for low-income families. In the next three years, the economy markedly improved. Other legislative successes included the Family and Medical Leave Act, which required employers to grant unpaid medical leave for up to twelve weeks. Clinton appointed two relatively liberal new Supreme Court Justices, Ruth Bader Ginsburg in 1993 and Stephen Breyer in 1994.

The 1994 congressional elections hurt Clinton's legislative agenda. In the midst of the campaign, about 300 Republican congressional candidates, under the leadership of Speaker of the House Newt Gingrich, endorsed a "Contract with America," calling for welfare reform, a balanced budget, more prisons and longer sentences, increased defense spending, an end to legal abortion, and other conservative measures. The Republicans declared a "Republican Revolution" as they took control of both the House and Senate for the first time in 40 years and pushed Congress to the right of center.

The new Congress passed a large tax cut and a tough anticrime bill, increased military spending, and reduced federal regulatory power over the environment. Clinton used his veto power to limit the Republican agenda, but he also took on some conservative issues as his own, such as free trade and welfare reform. In his 1996 State of the Union address, Clinton announced that the "era of big government is over," and he signed the Welfare Reform Act, abolishing the 60-year-old program Aid to Families with Dependent Children (AFDC). Clinton won reelection easily in 1996 while Republicans stayed in control of both houses of Congress.

TABLE 29-2

The Election of 1996

Candidate	Political Party	Popular Vote (%)	Electoral Vote
William J. Clinton	Democratic	49.24	379
Robert Dole	Republican	40.71	159
H. Ross Perot	Reform	8.4	—

The Impeachment Crisis

Clinton's personal behavior left him vulnerable to political enemies, who took full advantage of every opportunity to discredit him. Clinton's sexual behavior became an issue well before he entered the White House. During the 1992 campaign, Gennifer Flowers, a former nightclub singer, told a tabloid that she and Clinton had an affair when he was governor. Early in his presidency, Paula Jones, a former Arkansas state employee, filed a sexual harassment suit against Clinton, claiming that he had propositioned her when he was governor of Arkansas. The case was eventually dismissed, but it returned to haunt him. In 1998 Independent Council Kenneth Starr reported that he had evidence that Clinton had an extramarital affair with a young White House intern, Monica Lewinsky. Starr claimed that Clinton had broken the law in an effort to cover up the affair. Lewinsky and Clinton had both testified in the Paula Jones case, and both denied having had a sexual relationship. Starr claimed that Clinton had lied under oath and had instructed his close adviser and friend, Vernon Jordan, to find Lewinsky a job to keep her quiet. Starr charged Clinton with perjury, witness tampering, and obstruction of justice. Clinton vehemently denied the charges, but Lewinsky had saved a dress with a stain containing the president's DNA, providing the investigation with the "smoking gun" it needed.

As Starr and congressional Republicans pressed the investigation with relentless determination, the media saturated the nation and the world with sordid and graphic details of the president's sexual encounters with the young intern. Polls showed that Americans disapproved of Clinton's personal behavior, but they did not want him removed from office. With the economy booming, Clinton garnered high job performance ratings, rising to 79 percent at the height of the scandal. Negative sentiment against Kenneth Starr and congressional Republicans mounted as the investigation dragged on for four years at a cost to taxpayers of $40 million.

Public opinion notwithstanding, the House of Representatives impeached—that is, brought charges against—Clinton on December 19, 1998, accusing him of perjury and obstruction of justice. But the majority of senators determined that Clinton's misdeeds did not meet the standard for "high crimes and misdemeanors" required to remove a president from office, and acquitted him.

⊙ Read the Document

Articles of Impeachment Against Clinton (1999) at **www.myhistorylab.com**

Trade, Peacemaking, and Military Intervention

Stymied in Congress by Republican opposition, the president turned his attention to foreign policy. In 1993, with the president's strong encouragement, Congress approved the North American Free Trade Agreement (NAFTA), eliminating tariffs and trade barriers among the United States, Mexico, and Canada and thus creating the largest free trade zone in the world. In 1994, Congress approved the General Agreement on Tariffs and Trade (GATT), which reduced tariffs on thousands of goods and phased out import quotas imposed by the United States and other industrialized nations. Supporters argued that these measures would increase global competition and improve the U.S. economy. Businesses would benefit from the easing of trade barriers, and consumers would have access to lower-priced goods.

NAFTA and GATT barely passed Congress. Clinton faced strong opposition from liberal Democrats in industrial areas and from labor unions, who feared that these measures would result in jobs going abroad, declining American wages, and a relaxation of environmental controls over companies moving outside U.S. borders. In the first few years of NAFTA and GATT, these fears seemed justified. Some jobs went abroad, and threats of moving gave employers a negotiating edge over workers. In Mexico, the impact of NAFTA was even worse. The peso collapsed as money and goods flowed across the border, and the average wages for workers fell from $1.45 to $.78 per hour.

Equally controversial were Clinton's efforts to grant China **most-favored-nation** status, which would designate China as a full trading partner with the United States. Human rights activists argued that China's dismal record of violent suppression and imprisonment of political dissenters should preclude favorable trading terms. But with an eye to China's huge potential market for American goods and favorable site for U.S.-owned factories, Congress approved Clinton's proposal.

Cold War politics did not entirely disappear from foreign policy. The tiny communist nation of Cuba, suffering severe economic hardship since the collapse of its benefactor, the Soviet Union, remained off limits to U.S. trade and tourism. Cuban Americans in southern Florida, who had fled Cuba after Fidel Castro's successful revolution, blocked any efforts to ease relations between the two countries. Democrats as well as Republicans were reluctant to alienate these voters; their numbers and political clout in the nation's fourth largest state gave them considerable power.

Relations between the United States and Cuba were strained anew in November 1999 by an incident that began when a small boat carrying 14 Cubans trying to escape to Florida sank. The three survivors, who clung to inner tubes, included a six-year-old boy, Elian Gonzales. Elian's relatives in Miami argued that the boy should stay in the United States, where he could grow up in a democratic society—a goal his mother died trying to achieve. However, his father wanted him back in Cuba, and a court decided that the boy should be returned to his remaining parent. After months of intense media coverage in both countries and futile efforts at negotiation, U.S. government agents stormed the small house where Elian was staying and seized the boy, who eventually returned to Cuba with his father.

Most of Clinton's diplomatic efforts focused on peacekeeping and peacemaking. Clinton endeavored to ease hostilities in some of the world's most conflict-ridden areas. Northern Ireland had been fraught with violence for 30 years and the United States, with political and diplomatic connections to London as well as strong ties to the Irish, wanted to help resolve the crisis. Clinton made several trips to Ireland to promote peace between Irish Catholic nationalists who wanted to break ties with England and join the Republic of Ireland and Protestants loyal to Great Britain. Despite dissent and violence by extremists on both sides, by the time Clinton left office, an agreement had been reached that established a shared coalition government.

In the Middle East, Clinton brought Yasser Arafat, leader of the Palestine Liberation Organization (PLO), and Yitzak Rabin, Israeli prime minister, to Washington for talks that led to an historic 1993 handshake and pledges to pursue a peace agreement. Those efforts were hampered by violent extremists on both sides. Rabin was assassinated by a fanatical right-wing Israeli, leading to the election of a hawkish new prime minister, Benjamin Netanyahu. Large-scale violence between Palestinians and Israelis erupted again in the summer of 2000 and Clinton left office with no agreement in sight.

In the final weeks of Clinton's presidency in 2000, he made a historic visit to Vietnam—the first by an American president since the war. His administration was the first to reopen formal relations with the Vietnamese government. Although the United States lost the war, westernization had taken hold in Vietnam, with investment beginning to flow in from Europe, the United States, and Japan, as well as American popular culture and technology. Cheering crowds welcomed the president of the superpower that Vietnam had defeated 25 years earlier.

The legacy of the war in Vietnam and the end of the Cold War raised new questions about how and when to use American military force. Most of the overseas crises during Clinton's presidency stemmed from problems of national disintegration, ethnic conflict, and humanitarian disasters resulting from political chaos and civil wars.

■ Bill Clinton was the first American president to visit Vietnam since 1969. He is pictured here on November 17, 2000, walking with Vietnamese President Tran Duc Luong (left) as they passed Vietnamese soldiers during official welcome ceremonies.

■ **MAP 29.2**

THE BREAKUP OF THE FORMER YUGOSLAVIA

Created in 1919 as a multiethnic nation, Yugoslavia split apart in 1991–1992. After Slovenia and Croatia gained their independence swiftly, Bosnia deteriorated into fierce ethnic fighting dominated by Serb atrocities and encouraged by the Serbian government of Slobodan Milosevic. A brief U.S. bombing campaign in 1995 finally brought the Serbs to peace negotiations. Similar ethnic fighting in the province of Kosovo in 1999 led to another U.S. bombing campaign and Kosovo's current quasi-independence under NATO guidance. In 2006 Montenegro's citizens voted narowly to establish their full independence from Serbia.

In 1992, President Bush had sent U.S. marines to Somalia in east Africa as part of a UN effort to provide famine relief and to restore peace in the war-torn nation. After Clinton took office, Somali warlord Mohammed Farah Aidid killed 50 Pakistani UN peacekeepers. The U.S. forces then mobilized against Aidid, shifting the peacekeeping mission to military engagement. As part of the effort to hunt down Aidid, U.S. soldiers killed hundreds of Somali citizens, creating intense anti-American sentiment among the population. In September 1993, Aidid's forces killed 18 American soldiers in a firefight and dragged the body of one victim through the streets. The outraged American public viewed the grim spectacle on TV, and the experience left Clinton with no clear guidelines on humanitarian intervention abroad. Largely as a result of the disaster in Somalia, when ethnic conflict led to genocide in Rwanda in central Africa in 1994, the United States and other western nations refused to intervene.

Ethnic conflict was also the cause of trouble in the Balkans. From 1945 to 1980, Marshal Josip Broz Tito ruled over a unified communist Yugoslavia, maintaining stability by suppressing ethnic rivalries. But after Tito's death in 1980 and the end of the Cold

•◆•⊣ **Read** the **Document**

The Balkan Proximity Peace Talks Agreement at **www.myhistorylab.com**

War in 1989, ethnic nationalism pulled Yugoslavia apart, with Slovenia and Croatia breaking away in 1991–1992. The region erupted in bloody conflicts. After sustained Serbian attacks on Muslims in Bosnia between 1992 and 1995, Clinton reluctantly agreed to air strikes against the Serbs, leading to the 1995 Dayton Accords, which brought an end to the war. When Serbian president Slobodan Milosevic embarked on a murderous campaign to drive the majority Muslim ethnic Albanians out of Serbia's southern province of Kosovo, Clinton finally ordered air strikes that forced the Serbs to retreat. Milosevic was voted out of office in 2000. The following year, Serbian authorities arrested Milosevic and turned him over to the War Crimes Tribunal in The Hague, which had indicted Milosevic for crimes against humanity.

Terrorism and Danger at Home and Abroad

While the Clinton administration carved out a new role for the United States in the post–Cold War world, several international terrorist attacks against the United States killed hundreds of people in the 1990s and highlighted the strength of extremist groups whose members were deeply hostile to the United States and its interventions around the world.

International terrorism proved to be one of the most difficult issues to confront. In June 1996, a truck bomb killed 19 U.S. airmen in Dhahran, Saudi Arabia. Two years later, bombs exploded at two U.S. embassies in east Africa, killing 224 people in Nairobi, Kenya, and Dar es Salaam, Tanzania. Four men were convicted of conspiracy in the terrorist attacks. They were identified as followers of Islamist militant Osama bin Laden, a guerrilla who had been funded by the CIA in the 1980s to resist the Soviet invasion of Afghanistan. Bin Laden, originally from Saudi Arabia, was living in Afghanistan under the protection of the fundamentalist Taliban regime. He was known to be the leader of the Al Qaeda terrorist network operating in several countries throughout the Middle East. On October 12, 2000, a small boat carrying a bomb pulled up next to the destroyer USS Cole in Yemen's port of Aden and exploded, ripping a hole in the hull and killing 17 Americans and wounding 39 others. Two suicide bombers carried out the attack. U.S. officials believed that they, too, were associated with Osama bin Laden.

Islamist radicals also struck in New York City. On February 26, 1993, a bomb exploded in the parking garage underneath the World Trade Center, the skyscrapers dominating the New York skyline in Lower Manhattan. Six people were killed and more than a thousand were injured. Eight years later, the same twin towers were attacked again, with far more devastating consequences.

Not all terrorists came from abroad. On the morning of April 19, 1995, a two-ton home-made bomb exploded at the Alfred P. Murrah Federal Building in Oklahoma City. The huge building crumbled, killing 168 people, including 19 children. The attack was the worst act of terrorism in the nation's history to that date. Initial news reports speculated that the terrorists were Arabs, but it turned out that the attack was carried out by American citizens with a hatred for the government. Timothy McVeigh, a veteran of the 1991 Persian Gulf War, and his accomplice, Terry Nichols, were found guilty of the bombing.

Antigovernment individuals and groups had long operated within the United States, and during the 1990s their activities—as well as FBI efforts to curtail them—intensified. Investigations throughout the decade uncovered networks of antigovernment militias, tax resisters, and white supremacist groups, many of them heavily armed and isolated in remote rural areas. Some antigovernment extremists acted alone, like Theodore Kaczynski, known as the "Unabomber," who for two decades sent bombs through the mail, killing three people and injuring 29. His demand to have his antigovernment manifesto published in major national newspapers led to his identification and arrest.

•••—**Read** the **Document**

US of America v. Timothy James McVeigh—Sentencing (August 14, 1992) at **www.myhistorylab.com**

The FBI tried to prevent these extremists from causing harm, but some of their efforts went awry. In 1992, during a standoff in Idaho, an FBI agent shot and killed the wife and son of Randall Weaver, a former Green Beret and antigovernment militia supporter who had failed to appear for trial on weapons charges. The following year in Waco, Texas, the FBI stormed the heavily armed compound of an antigovernment religious sect known as the Branch Davidians. The leader of the group, David Koresh, had barricaded the compound. The FBI, acting on reports of abuse of members, particularly women and children, tried to force Koresh and his group out of the building. But a fire broke out, killing 80 men, women, and children inside. The FBI came under intense criticism for its aggressive tactics in these cases. For antigovernment extremists, these actions prompted revenge. The Oklahoma City bombing apparently was intended in part as retaliation for the FBI assault against the Branch Davidians precisely two years earlier. Timothy McVeigh was sentenced to death for the Oklahoma City bombing and was executed by lethal injection on June 11, 2001.

The McVeigh case revived a debate about the death penalty, particularly in light of recent evidence of many botched legal defenses in capital cases. Opponents pointed to the preponderance of convicts of color on death row, representation by incompetent attorneys, and the execution of mentally retarded offenders, to argue that the death penalty should be abolished. The governor of Illinois declared a moratorium on executions when a study revealed that many death row inmates were cleared of charges as a result of new DNA evidence. Public opinion began to shift, but the majority—including the U.S. presidents from both parties throughout the decade—continued to support the death penalty.

The Oklahoma City bombing was the worst but not the only example of domestic terrorist attacks. After the Supreme Court's 1973 decision in Roe v. Wade legalized abortion, antiabortion activists worked to have the decision reversed. Most antiabortion protesters were peaceful and law-abiding. But a small militant fringe of antiabortion crusaders switched their targets of protest from elected officials to abortion providers and turned to violence. In 1993, half of all abortion clinics reported hostile actions, including death threats, fires, bombs, invasions, blockades, and shootings. In 1993 and 1994, vigilantes shot and killed one abortion provider, tried to kill another, and shot employees at two clinics in Brookline, Massachusetts.

The violence spurred Congress to pass the Freedom of Access to Clinic Entrances Act in 1994, making it a federal crime to block access to clinics. But the intimidation and violence were effective. Although abortion remained legal, the procedure became increasing difficult to obtain. Few medical residency programs in obstetrics and gynecology routinely taught the procedure, and considering the dangers posed by antiabortion terrorists, few physicians were willing to perform abortions. By the end of the decade, there were no abortion providers in 86 percent of largely rural counties in the country. Abortions continued to be available in cities, mostly in specialized abortion clinics. Between 1990 and 1997,

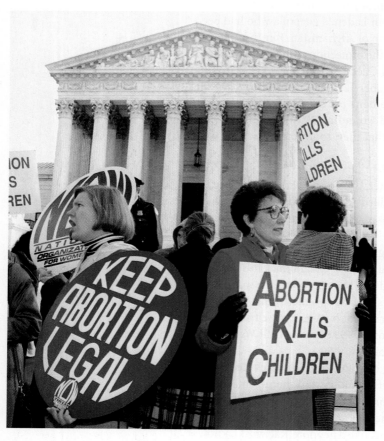

■ Abortion remained one of the most controversial political issues throughout the 1990s. Here abortion rights advocate Inga Coulter of Harrisburg, Pennsylvania, and antiabortion crusader Elizabeth McGee of Washington, D.C., take opposing sides in a demonstration outside the Supreme Court building on December 8, 1993.

the number of abortions declined by 17.4 percent. But the political battles continued. After years of controversy and debate, the abortion pill RU-486 received FDA approval for use in the United States, making it possible for individual doctors to prescribe the pill and for women to avoid surgery.

Weapons and Health

In spite of episodes of domestic terrorism, violent crime declined throughout the decade, especially crimes committed by youths. But a spate of school shootings in which children murdered other children sparked national soul searching and finger pointing as Americans wondered whom and what to blame. The murderers were mostly white middle-class boys who appeared to be "normal kids." The worst of these shootings occurred on April 20, 1999, at Columbine High School in a suburb of Denver, Colorado, where two boys opened fire and killed 12 of their schoolmates and a teacher before killing themselves.

The common factors in all of these killings were that the children used guns and that they got the weapons easily, often from their own homes. Gun control advocates noted that easy access to firearms in the United States was unique among Western industrial nations. In 1992, 367 people were killed by handguns in Great Britain, Sweden, Switzerland, Japan, Australia, and Canada combined. The total population of those countries equaled that of the United States, where in that same year, handguns killed 13,220 people. Public opinion polls showed that most Americans favored gun control, but the powerful gun lobby and the National Rifle Association argued that the Second Amendment to the Constitution guaranteed individuals the unlimited right to bear arms. Congress enacted the Brady Bill, a gun control measure named for James Brady, the White House press secretary who was gravely wounded in the 1981 assassination attempt on President Ronald W. Reagan. The bill required a waiting period for handgun purchases and banned assault rifles. Nevertheless, access to firearms remained easy.

Americans in the 1990s also harmed themselves in less violent ways. Despite the nation's near obsession with fitness, both the wealthy and the poor suffered from many afflictions. Eating disorders plagued millions of Americans. Among the affluent, anorexia nervosa (self-starvation) and bulimia (frequent binging and purging) affected an estimated 5 million Americans, especially young women, who were influenced in part by a fashion fad that glamorized emaciated bodies. Men also strove for a fashionable body, sometimes with the aid of drugs to enhance athletic performance or muscle buildup. In 2000, the Mayo Clinic reported a 30 percent annual increase in eating disorders, mostly among young women, but in a growing number of men as well. The opposite problem plagued the lower end of the economic ladder, where obesity increased dramatically, especially among children. With popular fast-food chains offering "supersized" high-fat meals, the proportion of overweight children jumped from 5 percent in 1964 to 20 percent in 2000.

Illegal drugs, including marijuana, cocaine, and heroin, remained popular in spite of official efforts to curb the trade.

■ **FIGURE 29.1**
CHILDHOOD OVERWEIGHT RATES FOR BOYS AND GIRLS AGE 6–17, 1960s AND 1990s
During the last half-century, obesity rates among children rose dramatically, especially in the 1990s. Childhood obesity is associated with a wide range of medical problems that can affect the health of overweight children throughout their lives. In the 1960s, boys and girls were equally likely to be more than 20% overweight. But by the 1990s, obesity had become more prevalent among boys.

However, illegal drugs represented only one dimension of Americans' desire to solve their problems through the use of chemical substances. Some mind-altering drugs, such as Prozac and other antidepressants, were legal and available by prescription. While these medications proved very effective in treating mental illness, some mental health experts worried that these drugs were being overprescribed, especially for children, as life's normal ups and downs were increasingly diagnosed as maladies such as depression and attention deficit disorder. Aging baby boomers also boosted the profits of pharmaceutical companies. Women turned to hormone replacement therapies to offset the effects of menopause. Skyrocketing sales of Viagra, a drug for treating male impotence, reflected middle-aged men's concerns about waning sexual potency.

Medical developments brought new cures and new worries. Antibiotics were so widely prescribed that forms of drug-resistant bacteria began to proliferate. Tuberculosis appeared in new deadly forms that did not respond to treatment with available antibiotics. In 1997, researchers in Scotland cloned a sheep, raising hopes that cloning could lead to new medical breakthroughs and fears that human cloning might be next. In 2000, scientists charted the entire human genome, or genetic code, offering the possibility of finding causes and cures for genetically linked diseases. As the century came to an end, scientific breakthroughs gave rise to new hopes as well as new questions.

The Contested Election of 2000

What flaws in the American electoral system did the 2000 election reveal?

The first presidential election of the new millennium was the most bitterly contested in more than a century. The Democratic candidate won the national popular vote, but with ballot counts disputed in Florida, a Supreme Court decision ultimately made the Republican candidate the victor. The election exposed defects in the election process, from faulty ballots and voting machines to the role of the media, and raised serious questions about the value of the electoral college. The election also revealed that flaws in the system disfranchised large numbers of poor and minority voters. But in the end, the transfer of power took place smoothly, and the nation accepted the outcome.

The Campaign, the Vote, and the Courts

The campaign pitted Vice President Al Gore, the Democratic party's candidate who hoped to benefit from Clinton's high approval rating and the healthy economy, against Republican George W. Bush, governor of Texas and son of the former president. Only half of the nation's eligible voters turned out to vote. As results were announced by the media, it became clear that whoever took Florida, where Bush's brother Jeb Bush was governor, would win the election. By the next day, Gore had won the national popular vote by half a million votes, but Bush was ahead in Florida. Bush's lead was so narrow that it triggered an automatic recount.

With all eyes on Florida, a number of serious irregularities surfaced. Some Florida voters were given confusing ballots while others were turned away at the polls because of inaccurate and incomplete voter registration lists. Most of the disfranchised voters were African American, who usually voted Democratic. For weeks after the election, the outcome was still unknown as Democrats and Republicans argued over how to recount ballots in contested

TABLE 29-3			
The Election of 2000			
Candidate	Political Party	Popular Vote (%)	Electoral Vote
George W. Bush	Republican	47.88	271
Al Gore	Democratic	48.39	266*
Ralph Nader	Green	2.72	—

*One District of Columbia Gore elector abstained.

counties. Florida's secretary of state, Katherine Harris, a Republican who headed Florida's campaign for George W. Bush, refused to extend the deadline to allow the recounts to take place and declared Bush the winner by 537 votes out of 6 million cast statewide.

Gore contested the results, and the Florida Supreme Court ordered that the recount proceed. Bush then appealed to the U.S. Supreme Court to reverse the decision of the Florida Supreme Court. After 36 days of partial vote counting and court battles, in a sharply divided 5–4 decision, the U.S. Supreme Court stopped any further vote counting, with the most conservative judges voting in support of the Bush request. The four dissenting judges issued a stinging rebuke of their five colleagues responsible for the decision. In his dissenting opinion, Justice Stephen Breyer wrote that the majority ruling "can only lend confidence to the most cynical appraisal of the work of judges throughout the land."

The Aftermath

What became clear in the months after the 2000 election were the widespread flaws in the election system in Florida and elsewhere. Across the country, outdated voting machines yielded inaccurate vote counts, and long lines at polling places prevented voters from casting ballots. Low-income and minority voters were more likely to be disfranchised because they lived in precincts with faulty voting machines or overcrowded polling places.

In addition to those whose votes did not count, many others were prevented from voting altogether. In Florida, "suspected felons" were removed from voter registration lists without being informed and without the opportunity to demonstrate that they were law-abiding citizens eligible to vote. According to the U.S. Civil Rights Commission, "Perhaps the most dramatic undercount in Florida's election was the nonexistent ballots of countless unknown eligible voters, who were turned away, or wrongfully purged from the voter registration rolls . . . and were prevented from exercising the franchise." As a result, hundreds of African-American citizens with no criminal record arrived at the polls only to discover that they had been disfranchised.

Policymakers and media moguls debated the role of the media in reporting election returns. Some argued for a blackout on early returns until all polls across the country were closed, to avoid the possibility that early results might influence voters who had not yet voted. Others proposed that only official results be announced, to avoid the problem of erroneous reporting that occurred on election night 2000. But media representatives countered that a free press should be able to report the news as it happens, although they agreed on the need to ensure accuracy.

Legacies of Election 2000

In addition to the unprecedented Supreme Court decision, the 2000 election was remarkable in other ways. For the first time, a First Lady was elected to public office: Hillary Rodham Clinton became a Democratic senator from New York. Third-party politics also critically influenced the outcome of the presidential election. Several third-party candidates achieved national visibility during the 1990s and won elections at the state and local levels, including professional wrestler Jesse Ventura, elected governor of Minnesota in 1998 on the Reform party ticket. In 2000 Green party candidate Ralph Nader gained fewer than 3 percent of the votes, but his candidacy drew off some of the left-leaning elements of the Democratic party—enough votes to cost Al Gore the election.

President George W. Bush immediately reversed several Clinton-era policies, including a number of environmental protections. His first major legislative success was the passage of a major tax cut. During his first year in office, the economy went from boom to bust and headed into a recession. Nevertheless, as the new millennium dawned, the

United States remained the wealthiest and most powerful nation in the world. Bush re-treated from international treaties on issues ranging from global warming to nuclear test ban agreements, and he revived the Reagan-era proposal for a nuclear missile shield. But the place of the nation in the global community was yet to be defined. Soon, monumental events shattered the nation's sense of security and forced Bush to engage in the world in unprecedented ways.

CONCLUSION

In the 1990s, the role of the nation in the world shifted and a half-century of political certain-ties evaporated. With the Cold War over, conflicts around the globe, many of them grounded in ancient ethnic hostilities, posed challenges for the world's most powerful nation. The United States focused on markets and trade, the nation's supply of oil, the need for political order to maintain international stability, and the danger of "rogue nations." President Clinton tried to be a peacemaker in hot spots around the world while attempting to respond to violent episodes of international terrorism.

At home, Americans demonstrated increasing tolerance for people who looked and acted differently from themselves. Polls showed declining levels of racial, ethnic, and religious hostility and greater acceptance of homosexuality, single parenthood, and family arrange-ments that deviated from the nuclear family model. But episodes of racial discrimination—by police, courts, and voting officials—continued. Politics remained an arena in which culture wars flared over abortion, gun control, and welfare reform. A Democratic president faced impeachment by his Republican foes in Congress while maintaining high approval ratings from the public.

At the dawn of the new century, several crises challenged Americans' sense of secu-rity. A deeply flawed presidential election revealed profound problems in the nation's vot-ing system. A sharp and sudden downturn in the economy shattered the optimism many middle-class people felt during the booming Clinton years and forced many of the working poor into desperate circumstances. Already reeling from these disturbing developments, the nation was soon shaken to its core by a terrorist attack that forced a new reckoning at home and abroad.

For Review

1. What contributed to the increasing gap between the rich and poor during the 1990s?

2. What were the effects of immigration and outsourcing on the American economy and workers?

✓●─ Study and Review at www.myhistorylab.com

3. What new fault lines appeared within American society during the 1990s, and what old ones seemed to ease?

4. How did Clinton respond to domestic and foreign challenges during his presidency?

Chronology: 1991–2000

1991 Los Angeles police beat and arrest Rodney King.

1992 South Central Los Angeles riots follow acquittal of police in Rodney King case.
FBI shootout at Ruby Ridge, Idaho.

1993 FBI storms compound of the Branch Davidian cult in Waco, Texas.
Congress approves North American Free Trade Agreement (NAFTA).
Arab–Israeli peace talks.
18 American soldiers die in Somalia; United States withdraws.

1994 House leadership announces "Contract with America."
O. J. Simpson murder trial.

1995 Truck bomb destroys federal building in Oklahoma City.
U.S. intervenes against Serbs in war in Bosnia.
Dayton peace accords signed.

1996 Welfare Reform Act.

1998 Lewinsky–Clinton affair revealed.
Clinton impeached by House of Representatives.

1999 Senate acquits Clinton.
Dow Jones passes 10,000.
U.S. bombing campaign frees province of Kosovo from Serbian rule.
Elian Gonzales affair.

2000 Supreme Court decides contested election; George W. Bush becomes president.

Key Terms

"Don't ask, don't tell" A policy established by the Clinton administration allowing gays and lesbians to serve in the military so long as they do not disclose their sexual orientation. p. 664

Most-favored-nation A designation allowing countries to export their products to the United States with tariffs no greater than those levied against most other nations. p. 666

New Democrat Member of the Democratic party, many of them organized in the Democratic Leadership Council, who espouse center to center-right policies. p. 664

30

A Global Nation in the New Millennium

At the beginning of the third millennium, the United States was more closely connected than ever to the rest of the world. The processes of globalization—increasing trade, communication, travel, and migration—linked the nation to the rest of a world that often seemed to be torn by ethnic and religious strife. That strife from abroad impinged on Americans in a shocking new way on September 11, 2001. On a sunny Tuesday morning, 19 hijackers—four of them trained as pilots—seized control simultaneously of four large commercial jets and turned them into suicidal missiles. At 8:48 a.m., one flew into the 110-story north tower of New York City's World Trade Center, igniting an enormous fireball. Fifteen minutes later, the second plane flew into the south tower. In less than two hours, both towers collapsed, killing the thousands of people still inside. Among the dead were hundreds of firefighters, police officers, and other rescue workers who had raced into the towers to evacuate the occupants. The third plane flew into the Pentagon. The fourth was also being directed toward Washington, apparently to destroy the White House or the Capitol Building, until it crashed in a field 75 miles southeast of Pittsburgh.

The carefully coordinated assaults killed almost 3,000 people, destroyed the two tallest buildings in the country's largest city, and left a gaping hole in the headquarters of the nation's military command. Who was responsible for the most horrific act of terrorism against civilians in U.S. history?

The 19 perpetrators were self-styled holy warriors of a secretive, extremist Islamist organization known as Al Qaeda, organized by wealthy, charismatic Saudi Arabian expatriate Osama bin Laden. Al Qaeda worked out of Afghanistan, hosted by the most repressive Islamic government on Earth, the Taliban, which rose to power in 1996 out of the chaos that followed the withdrawal of the Soviet army in 1989. The rage of bin Laden and other Islamist terrorists against the United States had been building throughout the 1990s, fueled by the presence of "infidel" American troops in Saudi Arabia since the 1991 Persian Gulf War, by American support for Israel, and by the rapid spread of secular American popular culture around the globe. At odds with moderate Islamic mainstream thought throughout the world, bin Laden announced in 1998: "To kill Americans and their allies is an individual duty of every Muslim who is able."

At the heart of American society remained a common assumption, that the United States is a democratic country. The events on United Airlines Flight 93, one of the four doomed planes on September 11, 2001, revealed the tenacity of the belief in majority rule. After the hijackers seized control and herded the passengers into the rear of the cabin, a dozen passengers and crew members were able to communicate by phone with people on the ground. They learned that two other planes had already crashed into the World Trade Center towers in New York City, and they realized that these hijackers—unlike previous ones who sought concrete gains and an escape—planned only destruction for them all. Face to face with imminent death and the certainty that many others would perish if they failed to act, the passengers discussed what to do. They made a plan to rush the hijackers, led by several large, athletic passengers, including Mark Bingham, a prominent gay businessperson and rugby player from San Francisco. Should they proceed? Quintessential Americans, they took a vote. GTE Airfone operator Lisa Jefferson heard the rest: "Are you guys ready?" asked Todd Beamer, a tall father of two from Cranbury, New Jersey. Screams and a sustained scuffle followed before the line went dead. The plane, headed for the heart of Washington, crashed in an unpopulated part of western Pennsylvania with no casualties on the ground.

■ **Smoke rises from the crash of United Airlines Flight 93 near Shanksville, Pennsylvania. For almost all Americans, the hijackings and destruction of September 11, 2001, came indeed out of a clear blue sky. Anti-American actions of the previous decade by Islamic terrorists had created little anxiety in a powerful nation that had imagined itself safe from major attack.**

The September 11 attacks both jolted the country's political course and highlighted anew certain continuing themes in American society and politics. President George W. Bush chose to invade Afghanistan and then Iraq as part of a global "war on terror." The September 11 attacks and their aftermath also underlined how intertwined were the U.S. economy and the global economy, and how access to key natural resources such as oil determined much of daily life and the country's foreign policy. The attacks and their aftermath demonstrated, too, how widely American popular culture had spread around the globe and how culturally diverse American society had become. The United States, still a nation of immigrants and their descendants, embodied the new global era.

> *The events on United Airlines Flight 93, one of the four doomed planes on September 11, 2001, revealed the tenacity of the belief in majority rule.*

Politics in the New Millennium

The attacks of September 11, 2001, constituted perhaps the most significant event in American life since Japan's surrender in 1945. The economy, already sliding into recession, accelerated its downward course. Just seven months in office, the administration of President George W. Bush responded by leading the nation into a "war on terrorism" abroad and at home. Within two years, U.S.-led efforts succeeded in overthrowing the governments of Afghanistan and Iraq. Complicated, long-term military occupations ensued, with U.S. forces continuing to engage in bloody battles against insurgents in both countries. In an effort to prevent further terrorist attacks at home, Congress passed the "USA Patriot Act," granting greater powers to the executive branch of the federal government. Authorities detained hundreds of immigrants, primarily young men of Middle Eastern descent. These policies then faced the test of public approval in the 2004 and 2006 elections.

What were the Bush administration's priorities, and how were they affected by the attacks on September 11, 2001?

The President and the War on Terrorism

George W. Bush did not have an auspicious record of achievement before his election as governor of Texas in 1994 and as president of the United States six years later. He grew up primarily in Midland, Texas, the grandson of a U.S. senator from Connecticut and the eldest son of a wealthy oilman, diplomat, and eventual U.S. president, George H. W. Bush. "W.," as he was sometimes called to distinguish him from his father, attended the elite Phillips Academy in Andover, Massachusetts, and he earned degrees from Yale and Harvard Business School, though his modest academic achievements hinted at the benefits of unofficial forms of affirmative action for the scions of wealthy and powerful families. His sociability and charisma earned him many friends. He avoided going to Vietnam when he was of draft age by serving in the Air National Guard, though he apparently failed to show up for much of a year of that service in 1972.

After a mixed career in business and a strong taste for the partying life, Bush gave up drinking at age 40 and became a devout, conservative Christian. This ambitious and now more serious man made his way up in Republican political circles, benefiting from family connections as well as a warm, "regular guy" personality that appealed to many working-class Americans. Before his presidency, Bush had traveled to few places other than Mexico. "I'm not going to play like a person who has spent hours involved with foreign policy," he admitted during the 2000 campaign. Once president, he took a unilateralist and almost isolationist stance, to the dismay of close U.S. allies. The United States rejected or withdrew from international agreements limiting global warming, weapons testing, and war crime prosecutions.

The events of September 11 stunned all Americans and gave the president a new focus. Finding and destroying Al Qaeda and its allies was now "the purpose of this administration," Bush told his cabinet. Four weeks after the attacks on New York and Washington, U.S. planes initiated the "war on terrorism" by bombing Taliban and Al Qaeda positions in Afghanistan. By October 19, U.S. special operations forces were working on the ground with anti-Taliban Afghan insurgents. Several European nations provided troops and other military assistance. By December, the Taliban had been driven from power throughout the country, and U.S. and allied forces had killed and captured hundreds of Taliban and Al Qaeda fighters. Many of the prisoners were transferred to the U.S. naval base at Guantanamo Bay, Cuba, to be held indefinitely and interrogated as enemy combatants. Despite continued pursuit and a reward of $25 million, the United States was not able to find Osama bin Laden, who was assumed to be hiding in the remote, snowy mountains of the Pakistan-Afghanistan border region.

•••⌐**Read** the **Document**

George W. Bush Address to Congress (September 20, 2001) at **www.myhistorylab.com**

Security and Politics at Home

•••⌐**Read** the **Document**

George W. Bush, From "National Security Strategy of the US (September 2002) at **www.myhistorylab.com**

The war on terrorism was not only a foreign affair. Just as the onset of the Cold War in the late 1940s had incorporated a hunt for domestic traitors, the war on terrorism in the early 2000s included a search for potential Al Qaeda sympathizers at home. Like the Cold War, the war on terrorism was framed as a long-term struggle against a maniacal, evil enemy who would not be easily defeated. Also as in the Cold War, American leaders announced that some civil liberties would have to be curtailed in order to protect the nation. The USA Patriot Act of October 2001 increased the U.S. Justice Department's range of options for spying on and detaining citizens and noncitizens suspected of pro-terrorist activities. Determined to prevent another major terrorist attack, Attorney General John Ashcroft oversaw the arrest of hundreds of illegal immigrants and their imprisonment in what the Justice Department later admitted were often unduly harsh conditions—not unlike Guantanamo, observers noted. Congress created the Department of Homeland Security (DHS) in an effort to better coordinate intelligence, police, and military authorities for defending the nation from future attacks.

Beyond terrorism, George W. Bush sought to move the nation in the direction of what he called "compassionate conservatism." One conservative activist noted that the new administration turned out to be "more Reaganite than the Reagan administration." In the economic realm, this meant promoting the private sector and reducing federal spending on social programs for the poor. It meant reducing the government's role in regulating health and safety issues in the workplace. And it meant pushing large tax cuts through Congress in 2001 and 2003 to the disproportionate benefit of the wealthiest 1 percent of Americans, including a doubling of the number of billionaires between 2003 and 2007. The budget surpluses of Bill Clinton's last years disappeared, as the Bush administration ran enormous annual deficits by retaining the tax cuts while sharply increasing military spending. Under Bush, the nation built the largest deficit in its history.

> *Like the Cold War, the war on terrorism was framed as a long-term struggle against a maniacal, evil enemy who would not be easily defeated.*

Bush's conservatism did not include conserving natural resources. Bush and Vice President Dick Cheney, both former oil executives, were strongly supported by corporate interests, particularly in the energy business, that sought easier access to public resources. The administration promoted oil drilling offshore and sought unsuccessfully to open Alaska's Arctic National Wildlife Refuge to oil production, encouraged mining and timber clear-cutting across western federal lands, and refused to regulate carbon dioxide emissions despite powerful evidence of global warming. The administration also loosened federal regulations on industrial air pollution, on water pollution by the coal industry, and on arsenic levels in drinking water.

Sexual issues remained flashpoints of political controversy. Explicit and suggestive sexuality pervaded popular culture, including two-thirds of television shows, causing particular concern among parents of young children. At the same time, Americans were increasingly accepting of homosexual couples. In *Lawrence v. Texas* (2003), the U.S. Supreme Court overturned state laws banning private homosexual behavior between consenting adults. A year later, Massachusetts legalized gay marriage, soon followed by Connecticut, Vermont, and Iowa. One-third of the nation's largest companies now offered employees in same-sex marriages or committed relationships the same benefits and supports, such as health care insurance, that they offered employees with traditional families. Marriage and family remained social institutions in transition, for better or worse: only 56 percent of adults were now married, compared with 75 percent 30 years earlier. And only 26 percent of American households consisted of a married couple with children.

Into War in Iraq

President Bush's most momentous decision was to invade and occupy Iraq in the spring of 2003. This was a very different proposition from the attack on Afghanistan. The effort to destroy Al Qaeda and its Taliban hosts in Afghanistan had widespread support in the United States and across much of the world. By contrast, invading a sovereign nation that had not attacked nor even threatened the United States divided Americans and alienated most of the rest of the world. The United Nations refused to support the invasion. America's western European allies were dismayed. Among America's major allies, only the British government of Prime Minister Tony Blair provided enthusiastic political support and a significant number of troops. Given this lack of support, why did the Bush administration invade Iraq?

Some observers pointed to personal reasons. Bush would be "finishing" the Persian Gulf War of 1991, when his father oversaw the liberation of Kuwait from Saddam Hussein's invading Iraqi forces but did not send troops to Baghdad to overthrow Saddam. Bush would also be avenging Saddam's effort to assassinate the elder Bush on a visit to Kuwait. Other

■ MAP 30.1

IRAQ AND AFGHANISTAN

The U.S. occupation of Iraq that began in 2003 placed more than 100,000 American soldiers in the center of the volatile Middle East. A multisided insurgency against those forces grew in strength, with Iraq increasingly divided ethnically into three parts, dominated respectively by Kurds in the north, Sunnis in the center, and Shi'a in the south. By 2007, civil war between Sunnis and Shi'a had convinced a majority of Americans that the United States should withdraw its troops from a situation growing only more perilous.

observers emphasized the centrality of Iraq's oil reserves, the fourth largest in the world. "If the Gulf produced kumquats, would we be doing this?" asked one administration official rhetorically. The president himself claimed two primary reasons for the invasion: that Saddam possessed "weapons of mass destruction"—chemical, biological, or nuclear—and could attack the United States or its allies "on any given day," and that Iraq had ties to Al Qaeda "and was equally as bad, equally as evil and equally as destructive." But after U.S. forces occupied Iraq, these two official reasons for the war evaporated. U.S. troops found no weapons of mass destruction (though Saddam had indeed used chemical weapons on dissident Iraqi civilians 15 years earlier), and Secretary of State Colin Powell admitted there was no "smoking gun" proof of a link between Al Qaeda's religious zealots and Saddam's fiercely secular dictatorship. The bipartisan reports of both the 9/11 Commission and the Senate Intelligence Committee in 2004 found that the primary reasons the president gave for invading Iraq were not true.

■ Nothing undercut the U.S. effort to extend its influence in the Middle East more than the photographs that emerged in the spring of 2004 of U.S. troops abusing Iraqi detainees at Abu Ghraib prison outside Baghdad. Here, two of these photographs are displayed on a street in neighboring Iran. The Abu Ghraib scandal dismayed America's allies, enraged Muslims everywhere, and almost certainly enhanced Al Qaeda recruiting. One Iraqi-American observed that the Bush administration had "done a good job of occupying the land of Iraq, but a horrible job of occupying the hearts of the Iraqi people."

A deeper reason for the U.S. invasion of Iraq appeared to be the administration's view of September 11 as an opportunity to preemptively reshape the Middle East into a region less hostile to the United States and Israel. A liberated Iraq, right in the center of the Middle East, might have a "demonstration effect" of pro-American capitalist democracy that would turn the rest of the region away from authoritarianism and Islamist revolution. Bush spoke of the overthrow of Saddam as "a watershed event in the global democratic revolution." This statement represented a highly optimistic view of how Americans might bring change to the Middle East, part of a new U.S. strategic doctrine emphasizing preemptive action against the nation's enemies. "We must take the battle to the enemy" in the war on terrorism, Bush declared in 2002, "and confront the worst threats before they emerge."

The U.S.-led offensive in Iraq that began on March 19, 2003, was a successful military action. Some 200,000 U.S. and British troops, with a few other allied forces, overran Saddam's defenses and occupied the nation of 25 million people within four weeks. Most Iraqis celebrated their liberation from Saddam's brutal regime, and many seemed to welcome the American soldiers. Seven months later, U.S. soldiers captured Saddam himself.

But military occupations rarely age well, especially without sufficient troops for the task. Widespread looting ravaged Baghdad, and essential services and personal security deteriorated in the aftermath of the old government's defeat. "Baghdad," one gasoline station owner observed, "is like the Wild West now." Saddam loyalists, Iraqi nationalists of various stripes, and arriving foreign Islamic revolutionaries initiated a multi-sided insurgency against the American occupiers. The number of U.S. and Iraqi deaths shot upward. The U.S. invasion of Iraq seemed to be increasing rather than reducing the threat of terrorism to Americans and others. Sunnis and Shi'a also faced off against each other in what began to look like civil war. The Bush administration turned over official sovereignty to a new Iraqi government on June 28, 2004, with 130,000 U.S. troops remaining in the country in an effort to provide security against insurgents. "We don't do empire," insisted Secretary of Defense Donald Rumsfeld. But two months earlier, photographs and eyewitness reports were made public of U.S. troops abusing, torturing, and sexually humiliating Iraqi detainees at the Abu Ghraib prison outside Baghdad—the same story as at Guantanamo. After a week's delay, the president finally apologized for Abu Ghraib. For most Middle Easterners and for Muslims around the world, however, this was compelling evidence that Bush's rhetoric about liberating Iraq was merely a cover for what they saw as fundamental American disdain for Muslims.

From Bush to Obama

President Bush entered his campaign for reelection in 2004 with solid support in his own party but mixed reviews from others. Most other nations considered the U.S. attack on Iraq unjustified and unwise. Western Europeans resented Bush's lack of interest in their concerns, making him probably the least-popular American president ever in Europe. The Democratic party hoped to exploit Bush's vulnerability by nominating Senator John Kerry of Massachusetts, a decorated Vietnam War hero with a moderately liberal legislative record. It did not quite work. The president prevailed in a narrow popular-vote victory. The Electoral College outcome hinged on Ohio, where a difference of 136,000 votes put Bush over the top. Christian conservatives were particularly important in getting Republican voters to the polls, and being at war made other voters wary of changing leadership.

TABLE 30-1			
The Election of 2004			
Candidate	Political Party	Popular Vote (%)	Electoral Vote
George W. Bush	Republican	50.7	286
John Kerry	Democratic	48.3	251
Ralph Nader	Independent	<1	—

The president's political fortunes declined swiftly after his reelection. At home, financial and sexual scandals brought down several prominent Republicans in Congress, including the once-powerful House majority leader, Tom DeLay of Texas. On August 29, 2005, Hurricane Katrina flooded New Orleans, causing hundreds of deaths and a massive evacuation of nearly the entire city. Republican Senator John McCain of Arizona joined a bipartisan and international chorus of voices that denounced the Bush administration's response to Katrina for "the terrible and disgraceful way that it was handled." In the November 2006 elections, the Republicans lost their majorities in both the House and the Senate.

Violence continued to ravage Iraq, rooted in deep ethnic and religious divisions that undermined American efforts to reconstruct a stable and orderly society. More than 4,000 U.S. military personnel had died in Iraq by the end of Bush's second term. In Afghanistan, a renewed Taliban insurgency increasingly challenged a deeply corrupt government backed by Washington. In June 2008 monthly U.S. and allied deaths in Afghanistan surpassed those in Iraq for the first time. Al Qaeda and Osama bin Laden, the original targets in the president's "war on terrorism," remained very much at large, their Islamist influence spreading dangerously across the border into an increasingly unstable and nuclear-armed Pakistan. Further details of the administration's abuse and torture of detainees continued to leak out, including what even conservative Republican Senator Lindsey Graham of South Carolina called "a pretty aggressive, bordering on bizarre, theory of inherent authority that had no boundaries."

Then the bottom dropped out of the economy. A largely unregulated bubble in the real estate market popped in 2007, revealing an entire array of irresponsible banking and investment practices that began to unravel in a major recession. The flow of credit in the United States slowed to a trickle. The stock market lost more than half its value from October 2007 to

March 2009, traumatizing investors and hollowing out citizens' retirement accounts. Consumers cut back dramatically on purchasing. Vulnerable industries such as automobiles teetered on the verge of bankruptcy. The global economy followed the U.S. economy into a downward spiral, with manufacturing and trade everywhere declining sharply and unemployment rising. By 2008, Bush's approval ratings reached a record presidential low, below even those of Richard Nixon on the eve of his resignation after the Watergate scandal. Bush's former speechwriter, David Frum, declared that the president "had led his party to the brink of disaster."

A young senator from Illinois, Barack Obama, emerged victorious from the Democratic presidential primary, having bested the much better known senator from New York and former First Lady, Hillary Clinton. The son of a Kenyan father and a white Kansas mother who divorced when he was young, Obama grew up in Hawaii and Indonesia with his anthropologist mother and her parents. He graduated from Columbia University and Harvard Law School, worked as a community organizer and law professor, and won seats in the Illinois state legislature and the U.S. Senate. Obama's opponent in the 2008 general election was Senator John McCain, who campaigned with the considerable burden of a Republican party associated with failure in governing abroad and at home, from diplomacy to the economy. Obama revealed himself to be a charismatic and inspiring campaigner, as well as a politician of unusually calm and deliberate demeanor. He inspired confidence in Democrats, independents, and even many Republicans, and he inspired hope around the globe. Obama defeated McCain soundly, 53 percent to 46 percent in the popular vote, and in January 2009 became the nation's first African-American president.

No president since Franklin Roosevelt had entered the White House facing such enormous challenges. *The Onion*, a satirical website, wryly announced: "Black man given nation's worst job." Obama set a new tone for a new administration, departing markedly from his predecessor: he opened previously closed government records, appointed distinguished scientists to deal with global warming, ordered the closing of the Guantanamo detention camp and of overseas CIA secret prisons, and warmed relations with traditional European allies of the United States. Obama declared that the United States "is not, and will never be, at war with Islam." He began reorienting U.S. foreign policy away from Iraq and toward Afghanistan. At home, Obama got a vast new stimulus bill passed by Congress in an effort to restart the ailing economy. Above all, the new president appeared pragmatic and levelheaded to most observers, including the more than 60 percent of the public approving his performance in the spring of 2009. Conservative columnist David Brooks called the president's personnel appointments "admired professionals" who were "not excessively partisan" and "not ideological." Conservative columnist Peggy Noonan noted Obama's "bearing and dignity" and the feeling he gave Americans that "now I know someone's in charge, finally someone's taken ownership of the mess" left in U.S. foreign policy and the American economy.

A year later, however, the challenges to the president and the nation remained stiff. First, stimulus spending under Bush and Obama helped stave off financial disaster, but unemployment rose to 10 percent and the federal budget deficit soared. Second, the Democrats' majorities in both houses of Congress were diverse in their interests and difficult to keep united, particularly in the face of solid opposition from Republicans to nearly all White House initiatives. The Democrats narrowly succeeded in their primary goal of reforming the U.S. health

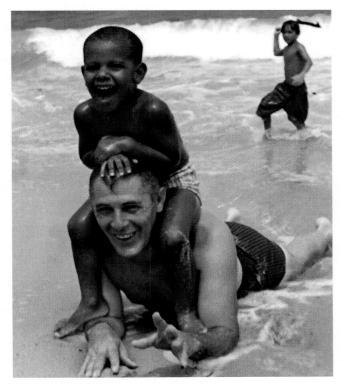

■ **Barack Obama plays on the beach with his maternal grandfather, World War II veteran Stanley Armour Dunham.**

care system—to provide insurance coverage for more Americans—in March 2010. Third, the wars in Iraq and Afghanistan had no clear end point in sight for Americans, continuing to pull in American lives and dollars. Americans who had hoped the 2008 election might bring greater bipartisanship and more effective governance in Washington were less optimistic in early 2010.

The American Place in a Global Economy

How did globalization affect Americans' lives?

While the new president navigated difficult political waters, average Americans struggled to find their place in a changing world economy. Mollie Brown James, for example, grew up in a small Virginia town west of Richmond. In 1950, at age 19, she moved to Paterson, New Jersey, joining the broad river of black Southerners who sought better economic opportunities and greater personal freedom in the North. She took a job in 1955 with the Universal Manufacturing Company in Paterson, with decent wages and benefits, unlike what had been available to her in Virginia. She stayed with Universal for 34 years. With union-negotiated wages, overtime work, and company-paid health insurance, she helped pull her family into the middle-class world of owning their own home and car and saving for retirement. But the peace of mind that came from a secure job vanished in 1989 when Universal closed the Paterson plant and moved its manufacturing operations to Matamoros, Mexico, just across the Rio Grande River from Brownsville, Texas.

James's job did not disappear. It moved and was inherited by 20-year-old Balbina Duque Granados. She, too, had grown up in a small town located in an agricultural area, in the Mexican province of San Luis Potosí, and she, too, had moved 400 miles north to find better-paying work in a booming manufacturing city. She was thrilled to land the difficult, repetitive job—her "answered prayer"—at a *maquiladora*, one of the foreign-owned assembly plants along Mexico's border with the United States that wed First World engineering with Third World working conditions. Her employer was also satisfied, paying her $.65 an hour to do what James had been paid $7.91 an hour for. But Granados's job was no more secure than James's had been. The beginnings of successful worker organizing in Matamoros encouraged the company to shift many of its operations 60 miles upriver to Reynosa, where the union movement was weaker. A journalist asked whether she would move there if her job did. "And what if they were to move again?" she replied. "Maybe to Juarez or Tijuana? What then? Do I have to chase my job all over the world?"

The Logic and Technology of Globalization

Like many other workers in the United States and abroad, Mollie James and Balbina Duque Granados learned firsthand the relentlessly international logic of the economic system known as capitalism. Those who have capital—extra money—invested it in corporations, whose purpose is to produce a profit for their shareholders. A corporation's profitability depends on keeping costs—labor and materials—down and expanding into new markets. Just as the telegraph and telephone had helped create a nation unified by rapid communication, the spread of personal computers and the Internet linked Americans even more closely to other nations.

At the start of the twenty-first century, engineering breakthroughs sped up the process of globalization. The integration of computers into every aspect of commerce and private life increased the efficiency with which businesses could operate. Computers boosted American productivity (the amount of work performed by a person in a given time period), which had declined between 1973 and 1996. Cable News Network (CNN) offered a standardized package of world news available 24 hours a day around the globe. CNN was so international in its aims that it banned the word *foreign* from its broadcasts.

Americans were also speeding up their daily routines in the new millennium. The desire for immediate gratification and efficiency that had nurtured fast food and microwave ovens encouraged the spread of cell phones, beepers, personal digital assistants, overnight package delivery, and constant news headlines scrolling across TV screens. Computers processed more information faster on ever-smaller silicon chips. Cell phones proliferated. Increased international air travel helped tourism compete with oil as the world's largest industry. The spread of the Internet—especially such popular sites as YouTube and Facebook—and the use of e-mail and instant-messaging epitomized the shift toward instant global communication.

Free Trade and the Global Assembly Line

The ideology of free trade underpinned the tighter meshing of Americans' lives with the world economy. Advocates of free trade argued that global markets unhindered by national tariffs benefited consumers everywhere by giving them access to the best goods at the lowest prices. America's NAFTA treaty with Canada and Mexico reflected this belief (see Chapter 29), as did the European Union with its newly unified currency, the euro. In the United States, by the start of the new millennium most leaders of both major political parties, corporate executives, bankers, and most other elites supported free trade.

"On the Internet, nobody knows you're a dog."

The Cartoon Bank

■ **The Internet provided both immediate connections with other people around the world and the safety of personal anonymity. Internet users could not be judged by their appearance or material possessions, only by the words they typed. Americans debated whether the popularity of the Internet represented a new kind of virtual community that would strengthen their connections to each other, or merely another way for citizens to remain isolated in their own homes rather than engaged with each other in civic organizations.**

But others objected to this internationalist economic ideology. Environmentalists warned of the pollution costs to the world's environment of U.S. factories relocating to poorer and less regulated nations, such as Mexico and China. Labor organizers decried the flight of American jobs as manufacturers sought less expensive and more compliant—often desperate—workers abroad. Human rights activists spotlighted the grim working conditions in many overseas plants, including the prevalence of child labor.

A "race to the bottom" for labor and environmental standards resulted from the development of a global assembly line. With capital able to move swiftly around the world and take its factories with it, nations and localities believed that they had little choice but to compete in offering multinational corporations the most advantageous terms possible. Such terms meant minimal government regulation, little protection for workers, nonexistent pollution standards, and local subsidies in place of corporate taxes. Corporate income taxes, which had been dropping since the 1950s, shrank by another third between 1986 and 2000. The *maquiladoras* on the Mexican border were part of a broader pattern of the corporate search for efficiency and profit, as companies, like Mollie James's Universal Manufacturing Company, took their production lines first to the American South and then abroad.

As a result, corporations and their products became less identifiable by nationality. Boeing Aircraft had long been the largest employer in the Seattle area, but was its new Boeing 777, manufactured piece by piece in 12 different countries, an "American" airplane? Japanese companies also moved many manufacturing plants overseas, including to the United States, to be closer to important markets. Was a Toyota made by American workers in Georgetown, Kentucky, a "foreign" car?

> *Was a Toyota made by American workers in Georgetown, Kentucky, a "foreign" car?*

Who Benefits from Globalization?

The increasing globalization of the U.S. economy at the end of the twentieth century created enormous wealth while sharpening class inequalities. The stock market skyrocketed. The Dow Jones average of the value of thirty top companies' stocks rose steadily from 500 in 1956, to 1,000 in 1972, to 3,000 in 1991. Then it more than quadrupled in value in just 16 years, surpassing 14,000 in 2007 before falling back sharply with the economic downturn that began later that year. Wealthy Americans who owned the bulk of corporate stock reaped the most gains, but middle- and even working-class Americans with retirement funds invested in the market also benefited handsomely. The process of globalization and the steady expansion of the U.S. economy after 1992 also encouraged a growing belief among Americans, especially affluent ones, that markets alone offered the best solution to social problems. But markets and their strict dependence on the profit motive proved unable to preserve the quality of the environment, to pull the 37 million officially poor Americans above the poverty line ($21,200 for a family of four in 2007), or to preserve the security of the vast middle class that had stabilized American politics since World War II.

American consumers enjoyed many of the fruits of the more integrated world economy. At least in industries not dominated by monopolies, the corporate quest for lower production costs, along with fierce international competition and technological innovation, reduced prices of many goods and services. Computers, airline travel, and gasoline were all significantly less expensive in real dollars (adjusted for inflation) than they had been a generation earlier. Competition abounded in the robust retail sector of the U.S. economy, including catalog and Internet shopping. Wal-Mart represented the epitome of how the globalized economy could benefit consumers. By 2000 the discount store surpassed General Motors as the largest American company, responsible for 6 percent of all U.S. retail sales. By 2007 Wal-Mart was also Latin America's largest retailer. Wal-Mart's success resulted from relentlessly cutting costs through sharp management, using cheaper imported goods and employing a nonunion workforce, and passing some of its savings along to customers in the form of lower prices.

The benefits that Americans experienced as consumers in the global economy were offset by their declining status as workers. As manufacturers moved to the Sunbelt and then overseas, high-wage, unionized jobs providing health insurance and pension benefits disappeared. Average real wages declined for more than two decades after 1973, and union membership shrank from one-third of the workforce in the early 1950s to one-tenth in 2000. Family incomes were maintained only by the addition of second and third wage earners, especially women. Americans spent more than they earned. The average household had 13 credit cards and carried $8,000 in debt on them, in addition to owing car and home mortgage payments. In 2005, the average personal savings rate dropped below zero.

Already wider in the United States than in any other industrialized nation, the distance between rich and poor continued to grow, whittling away at Americans' self-image as a middle-class society. The share of the national income going to the richest 1 percent nearly doubled in the last quarter of the twentieth century, while the share going

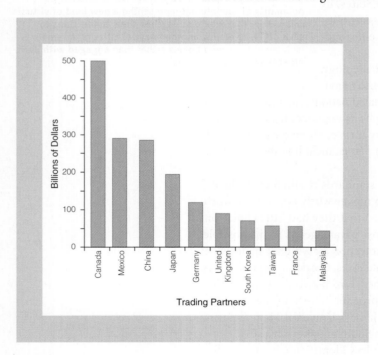

■ **FIGURE 30.1**
TOP TEN U.S. TRADING PARTNERS, 2005 (TOTAL VALUE OF IMPORTS AND EXPORTS IN BILLIONS OF DOLLARS)
Americans do the most business with Canada and Mexico, followed by east Asia and then western Europe. U.S. economic vitality has always depended to some extent on foreign trade, but that dependence grew steadily in the past generation.

to the bottom 80 percent shrank. Three million Americans lived in gated communities in extremely affluent suburbs, while one of five American children grew up in poverty, and 21 million citizens sought emergency food assistance each year.

The political system, which helps determine how wealth and opportunity are distributed in a society, seemed to offer little respite from the widening gap between haves and have-nots. The fraction of eligible citizens who made the effort to vote in presidential elections declined to just over half in 2004 and in off-year congressional elections to just over a third, with the likelihood of voting closely correlated to a person's affluence. The fierce partisanship, personal attacks, and culture of scandal that dominated American politics alienated many. Independents now outnumbered members of either major party. Citizens were also disillusioned by the blatant manner in which money came to dominate the political process. The average cost of a successful Senate campaign at $7.5 million and a House campaign approaching $1 million meant that few but the wealthy could campaign for Congress.

The Stewardship of Natural Resources

No issue in the early twenty-first century was more global or more significant than the environment. Winds and waters do not respect political boundaries, nor do the materials borne on them. The condition of the natural environment affects all living creatures, yet the prevailing calculus of the market and private ownership does not apportion responsibility for its care. The free market system has no mechanism for offsetting, or even measuring, the costs of depleted natural resources. A generation ago, biologist Garrett Hardin warned of "the tragedy of the commons": that individuals' incentives to preserve the quality of their own property do not carry over to resources held in common. Litter is an obvious example, and air, water, and ground pollution are the more serious cases. Global warming—or climate change—is the issue looming over all others.

American culture had long celebrated human domination of the natural world and the benefits it brought, especially the growth in productivity that permitted living standards to rise dramatically across decades and centuries. At the same time, the rise of environmentalism and ecological understanding since 1960 offered a different way of imagining people's place on the earth.

What are the most important ways in which the environment is changing, and how might these affect American society?

Ecological Transformation in the Twentieth Century

Ecosystems are always dynamic, and changes in weather and Native-American land use had reshaped the North American environment long before the followers of Christopher Columbus arrived on the continent. But European settlement and industrialization altered the face of the land in ways that would dumbfound a time traveler from the 1500s. Even a visitor from 1900 would be astonished by the intensity of human development of the land: vast cities with their sprawling suburbs and roads and highways everywhere. The key factor was population growth. Just as the number of people in the world quadrupled from 1.5 billion to 6 billion during the twentieth century, the population of the United States quadrupled from 75 million in 1900 to 300 million by 2006. Immigration and natural reproduction accounted for much of this, as did the much-longer average lifespan ushered in by antibiotics and antiviral vaccines.

The most dramatic changes in the land in the twentieth century resulted from the exploitation of wood, minerals, and water, particularly in the majority of the country lying west of the Mississippi River where the population grew 15 times larger. Commercial logging eliminated all but 3 percent of the old-growth forests of the 50 states. The clearcuts scarring the mountainsides and hillsides of the Pacific Northwest and Alaska told the tale, as did the erosion caused by the overgrazing by cattle of public lands managed by the Interior Department's Bureau of Land Management in Utah, New Mexico, and other western states. The Mining Act of 1872 still granted to private corporations the rights to such valuable minerals as gold and copper on public land for the remarkable nineteenth-century price of $2.50 per acre. Mining companies took full advantage of the opportunity, resulting in rock and chemical wastes piled in vast slagheaps and dumped in toxic holding ponds from Arizona to Montana. In the arid but increasingly populated western states, water was the most critical resource for population growth. Increasing diversions of the Rio Grande left that now misnamed river so dry that, by 2001, it failed to reach the Gulf of Mexico, trickling to a halt 50 feet short. Groundwater pumping for agricultural irrigation in the plains states and on the eastern slope of the Rocky Mountains was draining the vast underground Ogallala Aquifer at a rate that will empty it within a few more decades.

American prosperity came at a price. The prodigious growth of the U.S. economy in the twentieth century depended on the consumption of ever-increasing amounts of energy, most of it from coal, oil, and natural gas. Though making up less than 5 percent of the world's population, Americans accounted for a quarter of the globe's energy consumption. They depended on other countries to provide much of it for them: in the early 2000s, the United States imported 29 percent of its total energy needs and 58 percent of its oil, primarily from Canada, Mexico, Saudi Arabia, and Venezuela. Fossil fuels, such as coal and oil, could not be renewed; once burned, they were gone, and the world had a finite supply of such fuels. Americans were constructing a lifestyle that was unsustainable in the long run.

Pollution

The world's growing population was consuming five times as much fossil fuel in the early 2000s as in 1950, helping stimulate a steady rise in the earth's average temperatures. Americans caused 25 percent of carbon dioxide emissions, the largest contribution to the foremost environmental problem, global warming. In the summer of 2000, startled scientists found open water at the North Pole, a sight humans had never before seen. Greenhouse gases also contribute to a thinning of the ozone layer of the atmosphere, which enables more of the sun's ultraviolet rays to reach the earth's surface and causes skin cancer rates to soar.

The internal combustion engine had long since surpassed coal burning as the leading cause of pollution. The United States produced and used more cars and trucks than any other nation. With minimal public transportation outside a handful of major cities, Americans were deeply committed to a car-dependent lifestyle. The highway infrastructure strained under the pressure of a 60 percent rise in the number of licensed drivers from 1970 to 2000 but only a 6 percent growth in total miles of roads. Negotiating traffic jams became a standard part of the daily lives of the majority of Americans who lived in the suburbs created by urban sprawl, especially around such cities as Los Angeles and Atlanta. Smog increasingly obscured the once-spectacular vistas of Arizona's Grand Canyon.

No one knew yet how to dispose safely of millions of tons of materials impregnated with plutonium and other human-made radioactive elements.

Daily life in the United States came to depend in countless ways on the use of synthetic chemicals, production of which was hundreds of times greater than it had been before World War II. More than 50,000 known toxic waste dumps in the United States leached poisonous chemicals and heavy metals into the soil and water. No synthetic product was more pervasive in the United States than plastic, a post-1945 material made from petroleum. But the most deadly and durable pollutants remained the radioactive wastes created by six decades of nuclear development. No one knew yet how to dispose safely of millions of tons of materials impregnated with plutonium and other human-made radioactive elements. The U.S. nuclear weapon complex of some 3,000 sites put its often fatal touch on the lives of millions of Americans: uranium miners, military workers, soldiers used to observe test explosions at close range, and citizens living downwind from the Nevada Test Site in Nevada and Utah. The National Academy of Sciences concluded in 2000 that many of these sites would be permanent national sacrifice zones, toxic to humans for at least tens of thousands of years.

Environmentalism and Its Limitations

The ideas of most Americans about how to manage natural resources changed in the twentieth century. Environmental consciousness blossomed since the 1960s. Awareness of humans' connections with their broader ecological context led to significant reforms, such as the banning of carcinogenic pesticides and leaded gasoline, the cleaning up of polluted water in the Great Lakes, and the introduction of catalytic converters to reduce harmful emissions from automobile exhaust pipes and factory smoke-

■ The oil crises of the 1970s led automobile manufacturers to improve the efficiency of gas mileage in their cars. By the early 2000s, however, gasoline was once again inexpensive and growing numbers of Americans were buying large new sport utility vehicles (SUVs) such as the Chevrolet Suburban, despite their low gas mileage. A few environmentalists placed bumper stickers on other people's SUVs to highlight the key role of auto emissions in the accelerating process of global warming.

stacks. Recycling became common, and some dams were destroyed, freeing long-constricted rivers, such as the Penobscot in Maine. Yet issues of public land management and pollution control remained among the most controversial problems in American public life.

The relationship of Americans to their natural environment continued to be paradoxical. By large majorities in public opinion polls, Americans supported strong antipollution laws and the preservation of public lands from economic development. But in their daily lives, Americans consumed natural resources, especially gasoline, electricity, and water, at a rate unmatched by other societies. Measures that had reduced some of the nation's energy consumption since the 1970s were soon reversed: Congress revoked the national-55 mph speed limit in 1995, and ever larger cars, trucks, and especially sport utility vehicles steadily reduced the average gas mileage of passenger vehicles.

The Expansion of American Popular Culture Abroad

Just as the U.S. economy and American environmental problems could not be separated from the outside world, the nation's cultural life grew more closely tied to that of other nations at the dawn of the new millennium. By 2000, American popular culture rather than armed strength seemed to have emerged as the leading edge of U.S. influence around the world. American themes and products stood out in an increasingly global society, although they were resisted by some abroad who preferred more local identities and traditions, often rooted in ethnicity or religious conviction.

Why is American culture attractive to many peoples elsewhere?

A Culture of Diversity and Entertainment

Known for its informality and diversity, American culture proved powerfully attractive to peoples all over the world, partly because racial and ethnic diversity was more pronounced in the United States than in any other major nation. African Americans, Latino

> *The premium placed on acquiring material products seemed to many foreign observers the primary American value.*

Americans, and Asian Americans all figured prominently in the popular realms of sports, music, and films. Television was the leading medium for this culture of entertainment, beaming CNN, MTV, ESPN, and "reality" shows around the world. From jazz to rock 'n' roll to rap, American popular music spread across the globe, as did American jeans and sneakers, symbols of informality and comfort. Hollywood's movies dominated cinemas and DVD players everywhere, providing 85 percent of films screened in Europe.

Advertising grew in prominence as the central link between popular culture and the selling of products. Sports became steadily more commercialized. Postseason college football games began in 1985 to include the names of their corporate sponsors, creating such events as the Chick-fil-A Peach Bowl and the Weed Eater Independence Bowl. By the early 2000s, newspapers ranked bowl games—once hallowed for their own distinctive traditions—by the simple criterion of how much money sponsors paid to participating teams. In the 1990s and 2000s, "hoops" joined baseball as a popular U.S. export. National Basketball Association (NBA) games were telecast to more than 190 countries in 41 languages. Sports also brought foreigners to the United States as professional baseball and basketball teams began recruiting Latin American, European, African, and Asian athletes.

The Cartoon Bank

"Meritocracy worked for my grandfather, it worked for my father, and it's working for me."

■ An important tension in American history was the conflict between the ideal of equal opportunity for all and the reality of inherited wealth and privilege. The efforts of the George W. Bush administration to eliminate the federal estate tax, which affected the inheritances of less than 1 percent of U.S. citizens, represented the latest round in the debate about the relationship between political democracy and inherited economic inequality. In a pure meritocracy, all citizens would be rewarded for their personal achievements rather than those of their parents or ancestors.

U.S. Influence Abroad Since the Cold War

Cultural influences flowed both ways for Americans, with immigrants in particular bringing with them traditions and perspectives that refreshed the cultural mix of life in the United States. Japanese comics, Thai cuisine, Cuban salsa music, and soccer helped shape daily routines for many Americans. But increased trade and communication since the end of the Cold War above all enabled the further spread of American popular culture. American-accented English straddled the globe, the language of international commerce and of a large majority of postings on the World Wide Web. The informality and individualism of the Internet made it seem quintessentially American in style. The U.S. dollar remained one of the world's two primary trading currencies, along with the euro, and the dollar became the de facto and even the de jure currency of several other nations.

America's most popular eatery served 50 million customers a day at its 32,000 franchises across the globe. McDonald's Golden Arches appeared everywhere, from Japan and France to Russia and China. Even Mecca in Saudi Arabia, Islam's holiest site and the destination of millions of Muslim pilgrims, had a McDonald's. The company generated half of its revenues from non-U.S. operations.

America's cultural influence went beyond material interests. American religious missionaries worked in poor countries around the world, combining their spiritual mission with a commitment to improving daily life in concrete ways involving health care, education, and agriculture. Pentecostalists gained millions of converts in Latin America since the 1970s, and mainstream denominations, such as Lutherans, Episcopalians, and Roman Catholics, saw their numbers rise sharply in Africa. The most fully home-grown American religion was especially active in proselytizing abroad: the Church of Jesus Christ of Latter Day Saints (Mormons), headquartered in Salt Lake City. The Mormons claimed to have 5 million members in the United States and another 5 million worldwide.

Another channel for American influence abroad was the U.S. military. The United States retained its military superiority, with a defense budget larger than that of the next ten biggest military powers combined. When provoked, as by the September 11 attacks, American forces could wield extraordinary power and quickly reshape the histories of other nations, as demonstrated in Afghanistan and Iraq. But occupying other nations and charting the long-term future of other societies proved difficult. Instead, the expansion of American culture abroad seemed a safer and more effective way to influence other nations.

Resistance to American Popular Culture

Like Christian, Jewish, and Hindu fundamentalists, all of whom grew prominent in the final decades of the twentieth century, Muslim fundamentalists rejected the radical egalitarianism and the unbridled pursuit of pleasure so prevalent in American popular culture. The relative equality of women and the lack of respect for traditional social and religious hierarchies seemed to them emblems of American decadence, as the Islamic rulers of Afghanistan—the Taliban—demonstrated in the 1990s in their brutal repression of women's rights. Osama bin Laden and his followers resented U.S. policies of supporting Israel and certain oil-producing Arab nations, but they also fiercely condemned the secular, egalitarian character of American society, which they considered anti-Islamic. During the 1991 Persian Gulf War, Saudi Arabian officials tried to isolate U.S. troops from Saudi citizens, fearing the effects of contact with such diverse forces as female soldiers, bawdiness, Christianity, and American music and television.

The demise of communist regimes in Russia and eastern Europe opened the gates to a flood of western influences and brought the opportunities and inequalities of a suddenly privatized economy. State-provided safety nets disappeared, class differences widened, women's economic status declined, and the old Communist parties regained some popularity among voters frightened by the instabilities of American-style capitalism. Western Europeans also remained ambivalent about the spread of American values and lifestyles. Although many of them, especially among the young, found American culture attractive and learned English in record numbers, traditionalists who were proud of their own national culture took a dim view of such innovations as fast food.

Other nations sometimes found the U.S. government overbearing and resented its unparalleled military power. Rapidly modernizing China, the world's most populous country, seemed a growing rival to the United States in Asia, even as the two nations became major trading partners.

Two opposing trends characterized world affairs. One consisted of the unifying forces of economic internationalism and globalization, carrying with them a tide of American-dominated cultural styles. The other was made up of the resisting forces of political and ethnic nationalism. A world more tightly integrated in economic ways was at the same

INTERPRETING HISTORY

The Slow Food Movement

For many people in countries other than the United States, as for many Americans, McDonald's and other U.S.-based fast food restaurants offered an attractive dining experience. Customers everywhere appreciated the efficient and friendly service, clean surroundings, and the consistent quality of the food. Their enthusiasm explained the extraordinary international growth and profitability of such chains as Burger King and Kentucky Fried Chicken at the end of the twentieth century.

For other people, the rapid spread of fast food franchises around the globe threatened cherished values and lifestyles. The Slow Food Movement emerged in western Europe in the late 1980s as a loose-knit organization, headquartered in the northern Italian town of Bra. The movement sought to preserve and celebrate traditional cuisines and methods of food production in Europe and around the world. Slow Food's 60,000 members objected not only to the specific taste of fast food, but also to broader cultural changes symbolized by McDonald's and its competitors: the speeding up of daily life, including the loss of sociability around more leisurely meals; the gradual replacement of family farming and food production by corporate agriculture; and the erosion of distinctive local cooking and dining traditions.

The Slow Food Manifesto (November 9, 1989)

Our century, which began and has developed under the insignia of industrial civilization, first invented the machine and then took it as its life model.

We are enslaved by speed and have all succumbed to the same insidious virus: *Fast Life,* which disrupts our habits, pervades the privacy of our homes and forces us to eat *Fast Foods.*

To be worthy of the name, *Homo sapiens* should rid himself of speed before it reduces him to a species in danger of extinction.

A firm defense of quiet material pleasure is the only way to oppose the universal folly of *Fast Life.*

May suitable doses of guaranteed sensual pleasure and slow, long-lasting enjoyment preserve us from the contagion of the multitude who mistake frenzy for efficiency.

Our defense should begin at the table with *Slow Food.* Let us rediscover the flavors and savors of regional cooking and banish the degrading effects of *Fast Food.*

In the name of productivity, *Fast Life* has changed our way of being and threatens our environment and our landscapes. So *Slow Food* is now the only truly progressive answer.

That is what real culture is all about: developing taste rather than demeaning it. And what better way to set about this than an international exchange of experiences, knowledge, projects?

Slow Food guarantees a better future.

Slow Food is an idea that needs plenty of qualified supporters who can help turn this (slow) motion into an

time divided by ethnic conflicts. As people around the world felt themselves increasingly sucked into the vortex of a powerful global economy that they could not control, many responded by renewing their allegiances to older, more local traditions. Ethnic, religious, and national identities often offered more meaningful alternatives to a purely economic identity as consumers.

Identity in Contemporary America

What are the most important kinds of identity in the United States?

The 2000 U.S. Census revealed a society in the midst of change. Americans have long been known as a particularly restless and mobile people, and one out of five changed residences every year. The post-1965 wave of immigrants continued to rise (and foreign adoptions rose dramatically), bringing in millions of new Americans of Asian heritage. Latino Americans surpassed African Americans as the nation's largest minority. This latest surge in immigration boosted the number of Roman Catholics and Buddhists as American society remained the most openly religious—still primarily Protestant—of the industrialized nations. Geographically, Americans lived farther south and west than earlier generations, as none of the 20 fastest-growing states were in the Northeast or Midwest. And more than half of Americans lived in suburbs.

The spread of American fast food chains around the globe suggested that American culture may be a more powerful influence abroad than U.S. military might. The end of the Cold War led to McDonald's restaurants proliferating in downtown Moscow and Beijing, the capital cities of America's greatest opponents since World War II. The Golden Arches even invaded Mecca, Saudi Arabia, the holiest city of Islam.

international movement, with the little snail as its symbol.

Slow Food operates to protect the right to pleasure, the respect of the rhythms of life and a harmonious relationship with nature. It also seeks to explore, describe and improve the culture of food, to develop a proper education of taste and smell from childhood and to safeguard and defend the agroindustrial heritage while respecting the cuisines of each single country.

The Slow Food Manifesto was ratified in Paris at the Founding Congress of the International Slow Food Movement on December 9, 1989.

Source: http://www.slowfood.com

Questions

1. *What, precisely, do slow food advocates object to about fast food?*
2. *How important is fast food in the lives of people you know, and how does it affect their lives?*

Social Change and Abiding Discrimination

One of the most striking changes in American society over the past five decades has been the desegregation of public life. Latinos and Asians became much more numerous in the United States, and African Americans emerged from the enforced separation of Jim Crow into greater prominence. Roughly one-third of blacks were middle-class, and thousands won election to local, state, and national political offices. Black Americans became central in the nation's cultural life in music, literature, theater, and sports. By 2001 even a new president from the Republican party—known since 1964 for its lack of support from black voters—appointed two African Americans to direct the nation's foreign relations: Secretary of State Colin Powell and National Security Adviser (and later Secretary of State) Condoleezza Rice. In 2008, voters elected the first black President, Barack Obama. Workplaces were racially integrated to an extent that would have been hard to imagine in 1950, and interracial marriages became more common in the final decades of the twentieth century.

The lives of women in the United States also changed dramatically during the last half of the twentieth century. Most worked outside the home, from jobs in the service and manufacturing sectors to careers in the professions

TABLE 30-2

The Election of 2008

Candidate	Political Party	Popular Vote (%)	Electoral Vote
Barack Obama	Democratic	52.9	365
John McCain	Republican	45.7	173

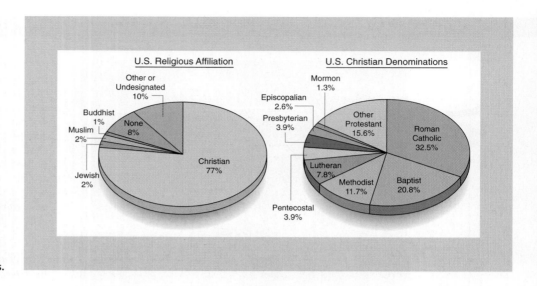

■ **FIGURE 30.2**
SELF-DESCRIBED RELIGIOUS AFFILIATION IN THE UNITED STATES, 2000
The most noticeable change of the last 30 years in American religious life has been the growth of evangelical and fundamentalist Protestant congregations (shown here as Pentecostals and "Other Protestants") and the shrinking of mainline Protestant denominations.

and politics. In 2000, women made up one-third of the students in the nation's medical schools and one-half in law schools. Their presence in leading political positions ranged from local officials to more than a dozen U.S. senators, two U.S. Supreme Court justices, a U.S. attorney general, and three U.S. secretaries of state. The passage of Title IX in 1972, prohibiting gender discrimination in school programs that received federal money, created a tidal wave of social change for American girls. In 1971, one in 27 girls played high school sports; by 1998 the ratio was one in three. Sports programs and teams for girls comparable to those for boys nourished a new generation of American women for whom athletic competition and achievement were the norm rather than the exception.

These improvements for the majority of Americans who were not heterosexual white men jostled against abiding forms of discrimination and inequality. Violence and the threat of violence against homosexuals, people of color, and particularly women (primarily domestic violence at the hands of husbands and lovers) remained very real, but most prejudices found more subtle avenues of expression. Working women continued to average about three-quarters the wages of working men. Many employers, police officers, store owners, bank loan officers, and others in positions of authority treated African Americans and Latinos with greater suspicion than they did other citizens, a practice that became known as racial profiling. Poverty and unemployment disproportionately affected black communities and families. Residential neighborhoods and public schools remained largely segregated by race, and the deeply symbolic Confederate flag still occupied a place of public honor in some southern states.

Native Americans shared this combination of improving status and continuing discrimination. Their numbers were reviving, from a mere 250,000 in 1900 to 2 million in 2000. A series of federal court decisions in the 1970s and 1980s strengthened Indians' "unique and limited" sovereignty over the tribal reservations, which constituted 2 percent of U.S. land. Starting with the Iroquois of upstate New York in 1970, several eastern Indian nations successfully sued state and federal governments for the return of parts of lands that had been illegally seized from them in the past, or for compensation. Beginning in the 1990s, casino revenues brought much-needed resources to a number of Indian nations. At the same time, the process of assimilation continued as a majority of Indians lived in urban areas and were married to non-Indians. Reservations suffered from severe unemployment rates and remained some of the poorest communities in the country, dependent on federal assistance for food and other basic necessities. Anti-Indian sentiments continued to surface in states as diverse as Montana, Wisconsin, Arizona, and New York.

Still an Immigrant Society

Economic opportunity and individual liberty still lured millions of people from other nations to the United States at the start of the new millennium. About a million now came legally each year, and another 300,000 entered without official papers. For the first time since the 1930s, one in nine Americans had been born abroad; in New York City the ratio was one in four. In 2004, 15 percent came from Europe, 33 percent from Asia, and 43 percent from Latin America and the Caribbean. Like Italy in 1900, Mexico in 2000 became the most important single source of new Americans. The demographic transition of California in 2000 from a white majority to a more diverse ethnic and racial mix like that of Hawaii symbolized the nation's turn to the South and West, even as the aspirations and work habits of the newcomers remained very much the same as those of their European predecessors. Only the hardiest and most motivated people made the difficult, emotionally wrenching, and often dangerous move to the United States.

> *Only the hardiest and most motivated people made the difficult, emotionally wrenching, and often dangerous move to the United States.*

Americans responded to the wave of newcomers with an ambivalence common in previous periods of high immigration. Many in the working class feared competition from highly motivated laborers accustomed to much lower wages. Many elites worried whether cultural diversity might weaken national unity. Conservative political leaders promoted new restrictions and stronger border patrols. Most Americans got used to having more immigrants around. Americans cheered for the one in four major league baseball players who were born in Latin America or had parents from there, and they became accustomed to the high number of Asian Americans in college classrooms. Many churches worked to help new arrivals adjust to life in the United States. Above all, American employers depended on immigrant workers to keep the nation's powerful economy afloat—to pick its fruits and vegetables, tend its young children, construct its new buildings, and work in its factories.

CONCLUSION

What held Americans together as they set off into the twenty-first century was a common loyalty to a set of ideas about economic opportunities and individual liberties. Unlike such nations as Germany and Israel, where citizenship was extended automatically only to people of a certain ethnicity, the United States awarded citizenship to all those who were born within its borders, regardless of ethnicity or race. Those born elsewhere became citizens on the basis not of their past lineage but of their future commitments—of their newly sworn loyalty to the U.S. Constitution, with its guarantees of freedom and its responsibilities of citizenship. In a vast society of multiple political and cultural beliefs, the scope of specific freedoms and the nature of individual responsibilities inevitably remained matters of ongoing tension and conflict. Nonetheless, the United States continued to address most of its problems through an orderly legal system, in contrast to the ethnic and religious strife marking so many of the world's nations.

Americans will face some basic challenges in the near future. Will the currently increasing inequality in American society—in terms of income, wealth, and power—weaken the bonds that hold the nation together? Policies regarding taxes, Social Security, health care, and welfare will help determine if most Americans will continue to see themselves as middle-class members of a mostly middle-class society. The process of globalization will not make this any easier. The tighter integration of the U.S. economy and the world economy has thus far helped create great wealth, but that wealth is distributed very unevenly among Americans. Who has how much wealth and influence will remain a crucial determinant of the nation's future.

Another challenge will be the use and distribution of natural resources, which will almost certainly become more contentious issues. As national and world populations continue to increase, so will the demand for oil, water, and timber. How will crowding and greater competition affect the quality of American life? How long can American society remain centered on the automobile and its emphasis on individual mobility? Behind all environmental issues looms the largest issue of all: global warming and how it may reshape societies around the globe.

The expansion of American influence abroad will continue to create problems as well as benefits for Americans. U.S. military, economic, political, and cultural leadership is clear. But the enormous reservoir of goodwill toward the United States that was evident around the world through much of the twentieth century has been draining rapidly in recent years. Ongoing U.S. military operations in Afghanistan and Iraq have convinced millions of peoples in those regions and elsewhere, rightly or wrongly, that the United States is an aggressive nation bent on dominating the world in general and humbling Islamic nations in particular. Whether the United States will gain more than it loses by its military engagements abroad remains an open question.

And finally, how well will Americans respond to the greater complexity of their society as their ranks come to include larger numbers of immigrants, non-Christians, people of color, open homosexuals, and people of other identities not previously considered mainstream? In comparison to most other cultures, American society has been unusually inclusive of people of diverse backgrounds and beliefs. Whether it will continue to be so will shape, as much as any other factor, the future of the United States.

For Review

✓●⌐Study and Review at www.myhistorylab.com

1. How successful was George W. Bush as president and in which ways?

2. How did globalization affect Americans' lives?

3. Why has the United States faced resistance and even hostility from many people and governments in the Middle East and elsewhere?

4. How do recent immigrants compare with previous immigrants in American history?

Chronology: 2001–Present

2001 Democrats gain control of Senate after James Jeffords leaves Republican party.
Al Qaeda terrorists attack World Trade Center and Pentagon.
U.S. forces attack Afghanistan and overthrow Taliban regime.

2002 Republicans regain control of Senate.

2003 Space shuttle *Columbia* disintegrates as it reenters Earth's atmosphere.
U.S. and allied forces invade and occupy Iraq.
U.S. forces capture Saddam Hussein.
Supreme Court legalizes gay sexual conduct in *Lawrence v. Texas*.

2004 George W. Bush reelected president.
Republicans increase their majority in Senate.

2005 Hurricane Katrina devastates New Orleans.
John Roberts becomes Chief Justice of Supreme Court and Samuel Alito becomes Associate Justice.

2006 Democrats gain majorities in both the House and Senate.
3000th U.S. military fatality in Iraq.

2007 130,000–160,000 U.S. troops still serving in Iraq.
Economic recession begins.

2008 Barack H. Obama elected president.

2010 70,000 U.S. troops still serving in Afghanistan.

APPENDIX

THE DECLARATION OF INDEPENDENCE

In Congress, July 4, 1776

The Unanimous Declaration of the Thirteen United States of America

When, in the course of human events, it becomes necessary for one people to dissolve the political bonds which have connected them with another, and to assume, among the powers of the earth, the separate and equal station to which the laws of nature and of nature's God entitle them, a decent respect to the opinions of mankind requires that they should declare the causes which impel them to the separation.

We hold these truths to be self-evident: That all men are created equal; that they are endowed by their Creator with certain unalienable rights; that among these are life, liberty, and the pursuit of happiness; that, to secure these rights, governments are instituted among men, deriving their just powers from the consent of the governed; that whenever any form of government becomes destructive of these ends, it is the right of the people to alter or to abolish it, and to institute new government, laying its foundation on such principles, and organizing its powers in such form, as to them shall seem most likely to effect their safety and happiness. Prudence, indeed, will dictate that governments long established should not be changed for light and transient causes; and accordingly all experience hath shown that mankind are more disposed to suffer, while evils are sufferable, than to right themselves by abolishing the forms to which they are accustomed. But when a long train of abuses and usurpations, pursuing invariably the same object, evinces a design to reduce them under absolute despotism, it is their right, it is their duty, to throw off such government, and to provide new guards for their future security. Such has been the patient sufferance of these colonies; and such is now the necessity which constrains them to alter their former systems of government. The history of the present King of Great Britain is a history of repeated injuries and usurpations, all having in direct object the establishment of an absolute tyranny over these states. To prove this, let facts be submitted to a candid world.

He has refused his assent to laws, the most wholesome and necessary for the public good.

He has forbidden his governors to pass laws of immediate and pressing importance, unless suspended in their operation till his assent should be obtained; and, when so suspended, he has utterly neglected to attend to them.

He has refused to pass other laws for the accommodation of large districts of people, unless those people would relinquish the right of representation in the legislature, a right inestimable to them, and formidable to tyrants only.

He has called together legislative bodies at places unusual, uncomfortable, and distant from the depository of their public records, for the sole purpose of fatiguing them into compliance with his measures.

He has dissolved representative houses repeatedly, for opposing, with manly firmness, his invasions on the rights of the people.

He has refused for a long time, after such dissolutions, to cause others to be elected; whereby the legislative powers, incapable of annihilation, have returned to the people at large for their exercise; the state remaining, in the mean time, exposed to all the dangers of invasions from without and convulsions within.

He has endeavored to prevent the population of these states; for that purpose obstructing the laws for naturalization of foreigners; refusing to pass others to encourage their migration hither, and raising the conditions of new appropriations of lands.

He has obstructed the administration of justice, by refusing his assent to laws for establishing judiciary powers.

He has made judges dependent on his will alone, for the tenure of their offices, and the amount and payment of their salaries.

He has erected a multitude of new offices, and sent hither swarms of officers to harass our people and eat out their substance.

He has kept among us, in times of peace, standing armies, without the consent of our legislatures.

He has affected to render the military independent of, and superior to, the civil power.

He has combined with others to subject us to a jurisdiction foreign to our constitution, and unacknowledged by our laws, giving his assent to their acts of pretended legislation:

For quartering large bodies of armed troops among us;

For protecting them, by a mock trial, from punishment for any murder which they should commit on the inhabitants of these states;

For cutting off our trade with all parts of the world;

For imposing taxes on us without our consent;

For depriving us, in many cases, of the benefits of trial by jury;

For transporting us beyond seas, to be tried for pretended offenses;

For abolishing the free system of English laws in a neighboring province, establishing therein an arbitrary government, and enlarging its boundaries, so as to render it at once an example and fit instrument for introducing the same absolute rule into these colonies;

For taking away our charters, abolishing our most valuable laws, and altering fundamentally the forms of our governments;

For suspending our own legislatures, and declaring themselves invested with power to legislate for us in all cases whatsoever.

He has abdicated government here, by declaring us out of his protection and waging war against us.

He has plundered our seas, ravaged our coasts, burned our towns, and destroyed the lives of our people.

He is at this time transporting large armies of foreign mercenaries to complete the works of death, desolation, and tyranny already begun with circumstances of cruelty and perfidy scarcely paralleled in the most barbarous ages, and totally unworthy the head of a civilized nation.

He has constrained our fellow-citizens, taken captive on the high seas, to bear arms against their country, to become the executioners of their friends and brethren, or to fall themselves by their hands.

He has excited domestic insurrection among us, and has endeavored to bring on the inhabitants of our frontiers the merciless Indian savages, whose known rule of warfare is an undistinguished destruction of all ages, sexes, and conditions.

In every stage of these oppressions we have petitioned for redress in the most humble terms; our repeated petitions have been answered only by repeated injury. A prince, whose character is thus marked by every act which may define a tyrant, is unfit to be the ruler of a free people.

Nor have we been wanting in our attentions to our British brethren. We have warned them, from time to time, of attempts by their legislature to extend an unwarrantable jurisdiction over us. We have reminded them of the circumstances of our emigration and settlement here. We have appealed to their native justice and magnanimity; and we have conjured them, by the ties of our common kindred, to disavow these usurpations, which would inevitably interrupt our connections and correspondence. They, too, have been deaf to the voice of justice and of consanguinity. We must, therefore, acquiesce in the necessity which denounces our separation, and hold them, as we hold the rest of mankind, enemies in war, in peace friends.

We, therefore, the representatives of the United States of America, in General Congress assembled, appealing to the Supreme Judge of the world for the rectitude of our intentions, do, in the name and by the authority of the good people of these colonies, solemnly publish and declare, that these United Colonies are, and of right ought to be, FREE AND INDEPENDENT STATES; that they are absolved from all allegiance to the British crown, and that all political connection between them and the state of Great Britain is, and ought to be, totally dissolved; and that, as free and independent states, they have full power to levy war, conclude peace, contract alliances, establish commerce, and do all other acts and things which independent states may of right do. And for the support of this declaration, with a firm reliance on the protection of Divine Providence, we mutually pledge to each other our lives, our fortunes, and our sacred honor.

JOHN HANCOCK

New Hampshire
Josiah Bartlett
William Whipple
Matthew Thornton

Massachusetts
John Adams
Samuel Adams
Robert Treat Paine
Elbridge Gerry

New York
William Floyd
Philip Livingston
Francis Lewis
Lewis Morris

Rhode Island
Stephen Hopkins
William Ellery

New Jersey
Richard Stockton
John Witherspoon
Francis Hopkinson
John Hart
Abraham Clark

Pennsylvania
Robert Morris
Benjamin Rush
Benjamin Franklin
John Morton
George Clymer
James Smith
George Taylor
James Wilson
George Ross

Delaware
Caeser Rodney
George Read
Thomas McKean

Maryland
Samuel Chase
William Paca
Thomas Stone
Charles Carroll of Carrollton

North Carolina
William Hooper
Joseph Hewes
John Penn

Virginia
George Wythe
Richard Henry Lee
Thomas Jefferson
Benjamin Harrison
Thomas Nelson Jr.
Francis Lightfoot Lee
Carter Braxton

South Carolina
Edward Rutledge
Thomas Heyward Jr.
Thomas Lynch Jr.
Arthur Middleton

Connecticut
Roger Sherman
Samuel Huntington
William Williams
Oliver Wolcott

Georgia
Button Gwinnett
Lyman Hall
George Walton

THE ARTICLES OF CONFEDERATION

Between the States of New Hampshire, Massachusetts Bay, Rhode Island and Providence Plantations, Connecticut, New York, New Jersey, Pennsylvania, Delaware, Maryland, Virginia, North Carolina, South Carolina, Georgia

Article 1

The stile of this confederacy shall be "The United States of America."

Article 2

Each State retains its sovereignty, freedom and independence, and every power, jurisdiction, and right, which is not by this confederation expressly delegated to the United States, in Congress assembled.

Article 3

The said states hereby severally enter into a firm league of friendship with each other for their common defence, the security of their liberties and their mutual and general welfare; binding themselves to assist each other against all force offered to, or attacks made upon them, or any of them, on account of religion, sovereignty, trade, or any other pretence whatever.

Article 4

The better to secure and perpetuate mutual friendship and intercourse among the people of the different states in this union, the free inhabitants of each of these states, paupers, vagabonds, and fugitives from justice excepted, shall be entitled to all privileges and immunities of free citizens in the several states; and the people of each State shall have free ingress and regress to and from any other State, and shall enjoy therein all the privileges of trade and commerce, subject to the same duties, impositions, and restrictions, as the inhabitants thereof respectively; provided, that such restrictions shall not extend so far as to prevent the removal of property, imported into any State, to any other State of which the owner is an inhabitant; provided also, that no imposition, duties, or restriction, shall be laid by any State on the property of the United States, or either of them.

If any person guilty of, or charged with treason, felony, or other high misdemeanor in any State, shall flee from justice and be found in any of the United States, he shall, upon demand of the governor or executive power of the State from which he fled, be delivered up and removed to the State having jurisdiction of his offence.

Full faith and credit shall be given in each of these states to the records, acts, and judicial proceedings of the courts and magistrates of every other State.

Article 5

For the more convenient management of the general interests of the United States, delegates shall be annually appointed, in such manner as the legislature of each State shall direct, to meet in Congress, on the 1st Monday in November in every year, with a power reserved to each State to recall its delegates, or any of them, at any time within the year, and to send others in their stead for the remainder of the year.

No State shall be represented in Congress by less than two, nor by more than seven members; and no person shall be capable of being a delegate for more than three years in any term of six years; nor shall any person, being a delegate, be capable of holding any office under the United States, for which he, or any other for his benefit, receives any salary, fees, or emolument of any kind.

Each State shall maintain its own delegates in a meeting of the states, and while they act as members of the committee of the states.

In determining questions in the United States, in Congress assembled, each State shall have one vote.

Freedom of speech and debate in Congress shall not be impeached or questioned in any court or place out of Congress: and the members of Congress shall be protected in their persons from arrests and imprisonments, during the time of their going to and from, and attendance on Congress, except for treason, felony, or breach of the peace.

Article 6

No State, without the consent of the United States, in Congress assembled, shall send any embassy to, or receive any embassy from, or enter into any conference, agreement, alliance, or treaty with any king, prince, or state; nor shall any person, holding any office of profit or trust under the United States, or any of them, accept of any present, emolument, office or title, of any kind whatever, from any king, prince, or foreign state; nor shall the United States, in Congress assembled, or any of them, grant any title of nobility.

No two or more states shall enter into any treaty, confederation, or alliance, whatever, between them, without the consent of the United States, in Congress assembled, specifying accurately the purposes for which the same is to be entered into, and how long it shall continue.

No State shall lay any imposts or duties which may interfere with any stipulations in treaties entered into by the United States, in Congress assembled, with any king, prince, or state, in pursuance of any treaties already proposed by Congress to the courts of France and Spain.

No vessels of war shall be kept up in time of peace by any State, except such number only as shall be deemed necessary by the United States, in Congress assembled, for the defence of such State or its trade; nor shall any body of forces be kept up by any State, in time of peace, except such number only as, in the judgment of the United States, in Congress assembled, shall be deemed requisite to garrison the forts necessary for the defence of such State; but every State shall always keep up a well regulated and disciplined militia, sufficiently armed and accoutred, and shall provide, and constantly have ready for use, in public stores, a due number of field pieces and tents, and a proper quantity of arms, ammunition and camp equipage.

No State shall engage in any war without the consent of the United States, in Congress assembled, unless such State be actually invaded by enemies, or shall have received certain advice of a resolution being formed by some nation of Indians to invade such State, and the danger is so imminent as not to admit of a delay till the United States, in Congress assembled, can be consulted; nor shall any State grant commissions to any ships or vessels of war, nor letters of marque or reprisal, except it be after a declaration of war by the United States, in Congress assembled, and then only against the kingdom or state, and the subjects thereof, against which war has been so declared, and under such regulations as shall be established by the United States, in Congress assembled, unless such States be infested by pirates, in which case vessels of war may be fitted out for that occasion, and kept so long as the danger shall continue, or until the United States, in Congress assembled, shall determine otherwise.

Article 7

When land forces are raised by any State for the common defence, all officers of or under the rank of colonel, shall be appointed by the legislature of each State respectively, by whom such forces shall be raised, or in such manner as such State shall direct; and all vacancies shall be filled up by the State which first made the appointment.

Article 8

All charges of war and all other expences, that shall be incurred for the common defence or general welfare, and allowed by the United States, in Congress assembled, shall be defrayed out of a common treasury, which shall be supplied by the several states, in proportion to the value of all land within each State, granted to or surveyed for any person, as such land and the buildings and improvements thereon shall be estimated according to such mode as the United States, in Congress assembled, shall, from time to time, direct and appoint.

The taxes for paying that proportion shall be laid and levied by the authority and direction of the legislatures of the several states, within the time agreed upon by the United States, in Congress assembled.

Article 9

The United States, in Congress assembled, shall have the sole and exclusive right and power of determining on peace and war, except in the cases mentioned in the 6th article; of sending and receiving ambassadors; entering into treaties and alliances, provided that no treaty of commerce shall be made, whereby the legislative power of the respective states shall be restrained from imposing such imposts and duties on foreigners as their own people are subjected to, or from prohibiting the exportation or importation of any species of goods or commodities whatsoever; of establishing rules for deciding, in all cases, what captures on land or water shall be legal, and in what manner prizes, taken by land or naval forces in the service of the United States, shall be divided or appropriated; of granting letters of marque and reprisal in times of peace; appointing courts for the trial of piracies and felonies committed on the high seas, and establishing courts

for receiving and determining, finally, appeals in all cases of captures; provided, that no member of Congress shall be appointed a judge of any of the said courts.

The United States, in Congress assembled, shall also be the last resort on appeal in all disputes and differences now subsisting, or that hereafter may arise between two or more states concerning boundary, jurisdiction or any other cause whatever; which authority shall always be exercised in the manner following: whenever the legislative or executive authority, or lawful agent of any State, in controversy with another, shall present a petition to Congress, stating the matter in question, and praying for a hearing, notice thereof shall be given, by order of Congress, to the legislative or executive authority of the other State in controversy, and a day assigned for the appearance of the parties by their lawful agents, who shall then be directed to appoint, by joint consent, commissioners or judges to constitute a court for hearing and determining the matter in question; but, if they cannot agree, Congress shall name three persons out of each of the United States, and from the list of such persons each party shall alternately strike out one, in the petitioners beginning, until the number shall be reduced to thirteen; and from that number not less than seven, nor more than nine names, as Congress shall direct, shall, in the presence of Congress, be drawn out by lot; and the persons whose names shall be drawn, or any five of them, shall be commissioners or judges to hear and finally determine the controversy, so always as a major part of the judges who shall hear the cause shall agree in the determination; and if either party shall neglect to attend at the day appointed, without shewing reasons which Congress shall judge sufficient, or, being present, shall refuse to strike, the Congress shall proceed to nominate three persons out of each State, and the secretary of Congress shall strike in behalf of such party absent or refusing; and the judgment and sentence of the court to be appointed, in the manner before prescribed, shall be final and conclusive; and if any of the parties shall refuse to submit to the authority of such court, or to appear or defend their claim or cause, the court shall nevertheless proceed to pronounce sentence or judgment, which shall, in like manner, be final and decisive, the judgment or sentence and other proceedings being, in either case, transmitted to Congress, and lodged among the acts of Congress for the security of the parties concerned: provided, that every commissioner, before he sits in judgment, shall take an oath, to be administered by one of the judges of the supreme or superior court of the State where the cause shall be tried, "well and truly to hear and determine the matter in question, according to the best of his judgment, without favour, affection, or hope of reward": provided, also, that no State shall be deprived of territory for the benefit of the United States.

All controversies concerning the private right of soil, claimed under different grants of two or more states, whose jurisdictions, as they may respect such lands and the states which passed such grants, are adjusted, the said grants, or either of them, being at the same time claimed to have originated antecedent to such settlement of jurisdiction, shall, on the petition of either party to the Congress of the United States, be finally determined, as near as may be, in the same manner as is before prescribed for deciding disputes respecting territorial jurisdiction between different states.

The United States, in Congress assembled, shall also have the sole and exclusive right and power of regulating the alloy and value of coin struck by their own authority, or by that of the respective states; fixing the standard of weights and measures throughout the United States; regulating the trade and managing all affairs with the Indians not members of any of the states; provided that the legislative right of any State within its own limits be not infringed or violated; establishing and regulating post offices from one State to another throughout all the United States, and exacting such postage on the papers passing through the same as may be requisite to defray the expences of the said office; appointing all officers of the land forces in the service of the United States, excepting regimental officers; appointing all the officers of the naval forces, and commissioning all officers whatever in the service of the United States; making rules for the government and regulation of the said land and naval forces, and directing their operations.

The United States, in Congress assembled, shall have authority to appoint a committee to sit in the recess of Congress, to be denominated "a Committee of the States," and to consist of one delegate from each State, and to appoint such other committees and civil officers as may be necessary for managing the general affairs of the United States, under their direction; to appoint one of their number to preside; provided that no person be allowed to serve in the office of president more than one year in any term of three years; to ascertain the necessary sums of money to be raised for the service of the United States, and to appropriate and apply the same for defraying the public expences; to borrow money or emit bills on the credit of the United States, transmitting, every half year, to the respective states, an account of the sums of money so borrowed or emitted; to build and equip a navy; to agree upon the number of land forces, and to make requisitions from each State for its quota, in proportion to the number of white inhabitants in such State; which requisitions shall be binding; and, thereupon, the legislature of each State shall appoint the regimental officers, raise the men, and cloathe, arm, and equip them in a soldier-like manner, at the expence of the United States; and the officers and men so cloathed, armed, and equipped, shall march to the place appointed and within the time agreed on by the United States, in Congress assembled; but if the United States, in Congress assembled, shall, on consideration of circumstances, judge proper that any State should not raise men, or should raise a smaller number than its quota, and that any other State should raise a greater number of men than the quota thereof, such extra number shall be raised, officered, cloathed, armed, and equipped in the same manner as the quota of such State, unless the legislature of such State shall judge that such extra number cannot be safely spared out of the same, in which case they shall raise, officer, cloathe, arm, and equip as many of such extra number as they judge can be safely spared. And the officers and men so cloathed, armed, and equipped, shall march to the place appointed and within the time agreed on by the United States, in Congress assembled.

The United States, in Congress assembled, shall never engage in a war, nor grant letters of marque and reprisal in time of peace, nor enter into any treaties or alliances, nor coin money, nor regulate the value thereof, nor ascertain the sums and expences necessary for the defence and welfare of the United States, or any of them: nor emit bills, nor borrow money on the credit of the United States, nor appropriate money, nor agree upon the number of vessels of war to be built or purchased, or

the number of land or sea forces to be raised, nor appoint a commander in chief of the army or navy, unless nine states assent to the same; nor shall a question on any other point, except for adjourning from day to day, be determined, unless by the votes of a majority of the United States, in Congress assembled.

The Congress of the United States shall have power to adjourn to any time within the year, and to any place within the United States, so that no period of adjournment be for a longer duration than the space of six months, and shall publish the journal of their proceedings monthly, except such parts thereof, relating to treaties, alliances or military operations, as, in their judgment, require secrecy; and the yeas and nays of the delegates of each State on any question shall be entered on the journal, when it is desired by any delegate; and the delegates of a State, or any of them, at his, or their request, shall be furnished with a transcript of the said journal, except such parts as are above excepted, to lay before the legislatures of the several states.

Article 10

The committee of the states, or any nine of them, shall be authorized to execute, in the recess of Congress, such of the powers of Congress as the United States, in Congress assembled, by the consent of nine states, shall, from time to time, think expedient to vest them with; provided, that no power be delegated to the said committee for the exercise of which, by the articles of confederation, the voice of nine states, in the Congress of the United States assembled, is requisite.

Article 11

Canada acceding to this confederation, and joining in the measures of the United States, shall be admitted into and entitled to all the advantages of this union; but no other colony shall be admitted into the same, unless such admission be agreed to by nine states.

Article 12

All bills of credit emitted, monies borrowed and debts contracted by, or under the authority of Congress before the assembling of the United States, in pursuance of the present confederation, shall be deemed and considered as a charge against the United States, for payment and satisfaction whereof the said United States and the public faith are hereby solemnly pledged.

Article 13

Every State shall abide by the determinations of the United States, in Congress assembled, on all questions which, by this confederation, are submitted to them. And the articles of this confederation shall be inviolably observed by every State, and the union shall be perpetual; nor shall any alteration at any time hereafter be made in any of them, unless such alteration be agreed to in a Congress of the United States, and be afterwards confirmed by the legislatures of every State.

These articles shall be proposed to the legislatures of all the United States, to be considered, and if approved of by them, they are advised to authorize their delegates to ratify the same in the Congress of the United States; which being done, the same shall become conclusive.

THE CONSTITUTION OF THE UNITED STATES OF AMERICA

Preamble

We the People of the United States, in Order to form a more perfect Union, establish Justice, insure domestic Tranquility, provide for the common defence, promote the general Welfare, and secure the Blessings of Liberty to ourselves and our Posterity, do ordain and establish this Constitution for the United States of America.

Article I

Section 1

All legislative Powers herein granted shall be vested in a Congress of the United States, which shall consist of a Senate and House of Representatives.

Section 2

The House of Representatives shall be composed of Members chosen every second Year by the People of the several States, and the Electors in each State shall have the Qualifications requisite for Electors of the most numerous Branch of the State Legislature.

No Person shall be a Representative who shall not have attained to the Age of twenty five Years, and been seven Years a Citizen of the United States, and who shall not, when elected, be an inhabitant of that State in which he shall be chosen.

Representatives and direct Taxes shall be apportioned among the several States which may be included within this Union, according to their respective Numbers, *which shall be determined by adding to the whole Number of free Persons, including those bound to Service for a Term of Years, and excluding Indians not taxed, three fifths of all other Persons.** The actual Enumeration shall be made within three Years after the first Meeting of the Congress of the United States, and within every subsequent Term of ten Years, in such Manner as they shall by Law direct. The Number of Representatives shall not exceed one for every thirty Thousand, but each State shall have at Least one Representative; *and until such enumeration shall be made, the State of New Hampshire shall be entitled to chuse three, Massachusetts eight, Rhode-Island and Providence Plantations one, Connecticut five, New York six, New Jersey four, Pennsylvania eight, Delaware one, Maryland six, Virginia ten, North Carolina five, South Carolina five, and Georgia three.*

When vacancies happen in the Representation from any State, the Executive Authority thereof shall issue Writs of Election to fill such Vacancies.

The House of Representatives shall chuse their Speaker and other Officers; and shall have the sole Power of Impeachment.

Section 3

The Senate of the United States shall be composed of two Senators from each State, *chosen by the Legislature thereof,* for six Years; and each Senator shall have one Vote.

Immediately after they shall be assembled in Consequence of the first Election, they shall be divided as equally as may be into three Classes. The Seats of the Senators of the first Class shall be vacated at the Expiration of the second Year, of the second Class at the Expiration of the fourth Year, and of the third Class at the Expiration of the sixth Year so that one third may be chosen every second Year; and if Vacancies happen by Resignation, or otherwise, during the Recess of the Legislature of any state, the Executive thereof may make temporary Appointments until the next Meeting of the Legislature, which shall then fill such Vacancies.

No Person shall be a Senator who shall not have attained to the Age of thirty Years, and been nine Years a Citizen of the United States, and who shall not, when elected, be an Inhabitant of that State for which he shall be chosen.

The Vice President of the United States shall be President of the Senate, but shall have no Vote, unless they be equally divided.

The Senate shall chuse their other Officers, and also a President *pro tempore,* in the Absence of the Vice President, or when he shall exercise the Office of President of the United States.

The Senate shall have the sole Power to try all Impeachments. When sitting for that Purpose, they shall be on Oath or Affirmation. When the President of the United States is tried the Chief Justice shall preside: And no Person shall be convicted without the Concurrence of two thirds of the Members present.

Judgment in Cases of Impeachment shall not extend further than to removal from Office, and disqualification to hold and enjoy any Office of honor, Trust or Profit under the United States: but the Party convicted shall nevertheless be liable and subject to Indictment, Trial, Judgment and Punishment, according to Law.

Section 4

The Times, Places and Manner of holding Elections for Senators and Representatives, shall be prescribed in each State by the Legislature thereof; but the Congress may at any time by Law make or alter such Regulations, except as to the Places of chusing Senators.

The Congress shall assemble at least once in every Year, *and such Meeting shall be on the first Monday in December, unless they shall by Law appoint a different Day.*

Section 5

Each House shall be the Judge of the Elections, Returns and Qualifications of its own Members, and a Majority of each shall constitute a Quorum to do Business; but a smaller Number may adjourn from day to day, and may be authorized to compel the Attendance of absent Members, in such Manner, and under such Penalties as each House may provide.

---

*Passages no longer in effect are printed in italic type.

Each House may determine the Rules of its Proceedings, punish its Members for disorderly Behaviour, and, with the Concurrence of two thirds, expel a Member.

Each House shall keep a Journal of its Proceedings, and from time to time publish the same, excepting such Parts as may in their Judgment require Secrecy; and the Yeas and Nays of the Members of either House on any question shall, at the Desire of one fifth of those Present, be entered on the Journal.

Neither House, during the Session of Congress, shall, without the Consent of the other, adjourn for more than three days, nor to any other Place than that in which the two Houses shall be sitting.

Section 6

The Senators and Representatives shall receive a Compensation for their Services, to be ascertained by Law, and paid out of the Treasury of the United States. They shall in all Cases, except Treason, Felony and Breach of the Peace, be privileged from Arrest during their Attendance at the Session of their respective Houses, and in going to and returning from the same; and for any Speech or Debate in either House, they shall not be questioned in any other Place.

No Senator or Representative shall, during the Time for which he was elected, be appointed to any civil Office under the Authority of the United States, which shall have been created, or the Emoluments whereof shall have been encreased during such time, and no Person holding any Office under the United States, shall be a Member of either House during his Continuance in Office.

Section 7

All Bills for raising Revenue shall originate in the House of Representatives; but the Senate may propose or concur with Amendments as on other Bills.

Every Bill which shall have passed the House of Representatives and the Senate, shall, before it become a Law, be presented to the President of the United States; If he approve he shall sign it, but if not he shall return it, with his Objections to the House in which it shall have originated, who shall enter the Objections at large on their Journal, and proceed to reconsider it. If after such Reconsideration two thirds of that House shall agree to pass the Bill, it shall be sent, together with the Objections, to the other House, by which it shall likewise be reconsidered, and if approved by two thirds of that House, it shall become a Law. But in all such Cases the Votes of both Houses shall be determined by yeas and Nays, and the Names of the Persons voting for and against the Bill shall be entered on the Journal of each House respectively. If any Bill shall not be returned by the President within ten Days (Sundays excepted) after it shall have been presented to him, the Same shall be a Law, in like Manner as if he had signed it, unless the Congress by their Adjournment prevent its Return, in which Case it shall not be a Law.

Every Order, Resolution, or Vote to which the Concurrence of the Senate and House of Representatives may be necessary (except on a question of Adjournment) shall be presented to the President of the United States; and before the Same shall take Effect, shall be approved by him, or being disapproved by him, shall be repassed by two thirds of the Senate and House of Representatives, according to the Rules and Limitations prescribed in the Case of a Bill.

Section 8

The Congress shall have Power To lay and collect Taxes, Duties, Imposts and Excises, to pay the Debts and provide for the common Defence and general Welfare of the United States; but all Duties, Imposts and Excises shall be uniform throughout the United States;

To borrow Money on the credit of the United States;

To regulate Commerce with foreign Nations, and among the several States, and with the Indian Tribes;

To establish an uniform Rule of Naturalization, and uniform Laws on the subject of Bankruptcies throughout the United States;

To coin Money, regulate the Value thereof, and of foreign Coin, and fix the Standard of Weights and Measures;

To provide for the Punishment of counterfeiting the Securities and current Coin of the United States;

To establish Post Offices and post Roads;

To promote the Progress of Science and useful Arts, by securing for limited Times to Authors and Inventors the exclusive Right to their respective Writings and Discoveries;

To constitute Tribunals inferior to the supreme Court;

To define and punish Piracies and Felonies committed on the high Seas, and Offences against the Law of Nations;

To declare War, grant Letters of Marque and Reprisal, and make Rules concerning Captures on Land and Water;

To raise and support Armies, but no Appropriation of Money to that Use shall be for a longer Term than two Years;

To provide and maintain a Navy;

To make Rules for the Government and Regulation of the land and naval Forces;

To provide for calling forth the Militia to execute the Laws of the Union, suppress Insurrections and repel Invasions;

To provide for organizing, arming, and disciplining, the Militia, and for governing such Part of them as may be employed in the Service of the United States, reserving to the States respectively, the Appointment of the Officers, and the Authority of training the Militia according to the discipline prescribed by Congress;

To exercise exclusive Legislation in all Cases whatsoever, over such District (not exceeding ten Miles square) as may, by Cession of particular States, and the Acceptance of Congress, become the Seat of the Government of the United States, and to exercise like Authority over all Places purchased by the Consent of the Legislature of the State in which the Same shall be, for the Erection of Forts, Magazines, Arsenals, dock-Yards, and other needful Buildings;—And

To make all Laws which shall be necessary and proper for carrying into Execution the foregoing Powers, and all other Powers vested by this Constitution in the Government of the United States, or in any Department of Officer thereof.

Section 9

The Migration or Importation of such Persons as any of the States now existing shall think proper to admit, shall not be prohibited by the Congress prior to the Year one thousand eight hundred and eight, but a Tax or duty may be imposed on such Importation, not exceeding ten dollars for each Person.

The Privilege of the Writ of Habeas Corpus shall not be suspended, unless when in Cases of Rebellion or Invasion the public Safety may require it.

No Bill of Attainder or ex post facto Law shall be passed.

No Capitation, or other direct, Tax shall be laid, unless in Proportion to the Census or Enumeration herein before directed to be taken.

No Tax or Duty shall be laid on Articles exported from any State.

No Preference shall be given by any Regulation of Commerce or Revenue to the Ports of one State over those of another: nor shall Vessels bound to, or from, one State, be obliged to enter, clear, or pay Duties in another.

No Money shall be drawn from the Treasury, but in Consequence of Appropriations made by Law; and a regular Statement and Account of the Receipts and Expenditures of all public Money shall be published from time to time.

No Title of Nobility shall be granted by the United States: And no Person holding any Office of Profit or Trust under them, shall, without the Consent of the Congress, accept of any present, Emolument, Office, or Title, of any kind whatever, from any King, Prince, or foreign State.

Section 10

No State shall enter into any Treaty, Alliance, or Confederation; grant Letters of Marque and Reprisal; coin Money; emit Bills of Credit; make any Thing but gold and silver Coin a Tender in Payment of Debts; pass any Bill of Attainder, ex post facto Law, or Law impairing the obligation of Contracts, or grant any Title of Nobility.

No State shall, without the Consent of the Congress, lay any Imposts or Duties on Imports or Exports, except what may be absolutely necessary for executing its inspection Laws: and the net Produce of all Duties and Imposts, laid by any State on Imports or Exports, shall be for the Use of the Treasury of the United States; and all such Laws shall be subject to the Revision and Controul of the Congress.

No State shall, without the Consent of Congress, lay any Duty of Tonnage, keep Troops, or Ships of War in time of Peace, enter into any Agreement or Compact with another State, or with a foreign Power, or engage in War, unless actually invaded, or in such imminent Danger as will not admit of delay.

Article II

Section 1

The executive Power shall be vested in a President of the United States of America. He shall hold his Office during the Term of four Years, and, together with the Vice President, chosen for the same Term, be elected, as follows:

Each State shall appoint, in such Manner as the Legislature thereof may direct, a Number of Electors, equal to the whole Number of Senators and Representatives to which the State may be entitled in the Congress: but no Senator or Representative, or Person holding an Office of Trust or Profit under the United States, shall be appointed an Elector.

The Electors shall meet in their respective States, and vote by Ballot for two Persons, of whom one at least shall not be an Inhabitant of the same State with themselves. And they shall make a List of all the Persons voted for, and of the Number of Votes for each; which List they shall sign and certify, and transmit sealed to the Seat of the Government of the United States, directed to the President of the Senate. The President of the Senate shall, in the Presence of the Senate and House of Representatives, open all the Certificates, and the Votes shall then be counted. The Person having the greatest Number of Votes shall be the President, if such Number be a Majority of the whole number of Electors appointed; and if there be more than one who have such Majority, and have an equal Number of Votes, then the House of Representatives shall immediately chuse by Ballot one of them for President; and if no Person have a Majority, then from the five highest on the List the said House shall in like Manner chuse the President. But in chusing the President, the Votes shall be taken by States, the Representation from each State having one Vote; A quorum for this Purpose shall consist of a Member or Members from two thirds of the States, and a Majority of all the States shall be necessary to a Choice. In every Case, after the Choice of the President, the Person having the greatest Number of Votes of the Electors shall be the Vice President. But if there should remain two or more who have equal Votes, the Senate shall chuse from them by Ballot the Vice President.

The Congress may determine the time of chusing the Electors, and the Day on which they shall give their Votes; which Day shall be the same throughout the United States.

No person except a natural born Citizen, *or a Citizen of the United States, at the time of the Adoption of this Constitution,* shall be eligible to the Office of President; neither shall any Person be eligible to that Office who shall not have attained to the Age of thirty five Years, and been fourteen Years a Resident within the United States.

In Case of the Removal of the President from Office, or of his Death, Resignation, or Inability to discharge the Powers and Duties of the said Office, the Same shall devolve on the Vice President, and the Congress may by Law provide for the Case of Removal, Death, Resignation or Inability, both of the President and Vice President, declaring what Officer shall then act as President, and such Officer shall act accordingly, until the Disability be removed, or a President shall be elected.

The President shall, at stated Times, receive for his Services, a Compensation, which shall neither be encreased nor diminished during the Period for which he shall have been elected, and he shall not receive within that period any other Emolument from the United States, or any of them.

Before he enter on the Execution of his Office, he shall take the following Oath or Affirmation:—"I do solemnly swear (or affirm) that I will faithfully execute the Office of President of the United States, and will to the best of my Ability, preserve, protect and defend the Constitution of the United States."

Section 2

The President shall be Commander in Chief of the Army and Navy of the United States, and of the Militia of the several States, when called into the actual Service of the United States; he may require the Opinion, in writing, of the principal Officer in each of the executive Departments, upon any Subject relating to the Duties of their respective Offices, and he shall have Power to grant Reprieves and Pardons for Offences against the United States, except in Cases of Impeachment.

He shall have Power, by and with the Advice and Consent of the Senate, to make Treaties, provided two thirds of the Senators present concur; and he shall nominate, and by and with the Advice and Consent of the Senate, shall appoint Ambassadors, other public Ministers and Consuls, Judges of the supreme Court, and all other Officers of the United States, whose Appointments are not herein otherwise provided for, and which shall be established by Law: but the Congress may by Law vest the Appointment of such inferior Officers, as they think proper in the President alone, in the Courts of Law, or in the Heads of Departments.

The President shall have Power to fill up all Vacancies that may happen during the Recess of the Senate, by granting Commissions which shall expire at the End of their next Session.

Section 3

He shall from time to time give to the Congress Information of the State of the Union, and recommend to their Consideration such Measures as he shall judge necessary and expedient; he may, on extraordinary Occasions, convene both Houses, or either of them, and in Case of disagreement between them, with Respect to the Time of Adjournment, he may adjourn them to such Time as he shall think proper; he shall receive Ambassadors and other public Ministers; he shall take Care that the Laws be faithfully executed, and shall Commission all the officers of the United States.

Section 4

The President, Vice President and all civil Officers of the United States, shall be removed from Office on Impeachment for, and Conviction of, Treason, Bribery or other high Crimes and Misdemeanors.

Article III

Section 1

The judicial Power of the United States, shall be vested in one supreme Court, and in such inferior Courts as the Congress may from time to time ordain and establish. The Judges, both of the supreme and inferior Courts, shall hold their offices during good Behaviour, and shall, at stated Times, receive for their Services, a Compensation, which shall not be diminished during their Continuance in Office.

Section 2

The judicial Power shall extend to all Cases, in Law and Equity, arising under this Constitution, the Laws of the United States, and Treaties made, or which shall be made, under their Authority;—to all Cases affecting Ambassadors, other public Ministers and Consuls;—to all Cases of admiralty and maritime Jurisdiction;—to Controversies to which the United States shall be a Party;—to Controversies between two or more States;— *between a State and Citizens of another State;*—between Citizens of different States;—between Citizens of the same State claiming Lands under Grants of different States, and between a State, or the Citizens thereof, and foreign States, Citizens or Subjects.

In all Cases affecting Ambassadors, other public Ministers and Consuls, and those in which a State shall be Party, the supreme Court shall have original Jurisdiction. In all the other Cases before mentioned, the supreme Court shall have appellate Jurisdiction, both as to Law and Fact, with such Exceptions, and under such Regulations as the Congress shall make.

The Trial of all Crimes, except in Cases of Impeachment, shall be by Jury; and such Trial shall be held in the State where the said Crimes shall have been committed, but when not committed within any State, the Trial shall be at such Place or Places as the Congress may by Law have directed.

Section 3

Treason against the United States, shall consist only in levying War against them, or in adhering to their Enemies, giving them Aid and Comfort. No person shall be convicted of Treason unless on the Testimony of two Witnesses to the same overt Act, or on Confession in open Court.

The Congress shall have Power to declare the Punishment of Treason, but no Attainder of Treason shall work Corruption of Blood, or Forfeiture except during the Life of the Person attainted.

Article IV

Section 1

Full Faith and Credit shall be given in each State to the public Acts, Records, and judicial Proceedings of every other State. And the Congress may by general Laws prescribe the Manner in which such Acts, Records and Proceedings shall be proved, and the Effect thereof.

Section 2

The Citizens of each State shall be entitled to all Privileges and Immunities of Citizens in the several States.

A Person charged in any State with Treason, Felony, or other Crime, who shall flee from Justice, and be found in another State, shall on Demand of the executive Authority of the State from which he fled, be delivered up, to be removed to the State having Jurisdiction of the Crime.

No Person held to Service or Labour in one State, under the Laws thereof, escaping into another, shall, in Consequence of any Law or Regulation therein, be discharged from such Service or Labour, but shall be delivered up on Claim of the Party to whom such Service or Labour may be due.

Section 3

New States may be admitted by the Congress into this Union; but no new State shall be formed or erected within the Jurisdiction of any other State; nor any State be formed by the Junction of two or more States, or Parts of States, without the Consent of the Legislatures of the States concerned as well as of the Congress.

The Congress shall have Power to dispose of and make all needful Rules and Regulations respecting the Territory or other Property belonging to the United States; and nothing in this Constitution shall be so construed as to Prejudice any Claims of the United States, or of any particular States.

Section 4

The United States shall guarantee to every State in this Union a Republican Form of Government, and shall protect each of them against Invasion; and on Application of the Legislature, or of the Executive (when the Legislature cannot be convened) against domestic violence.

Article V

The Congress, whenever two thirds of both Houses shall deem it necessary, shall propose Amendments to this Constitution, or, on the Application of the Legislatures of two thirds of the several States, shall call a Convention for proposing Amendments, which, in either Case, shall be valid to all Intents and Purposes, as Part of this Constitution, when ratified by the Legislatures of three fourths of the several States, or by Conventions in three fourths thereof, as the one or the other Mode of Ratification may be proposed by the Congress; Provided *that no Amendment which may be made prior to the Year One thousand eight hundred and eight shall in any Manner affect the first and fourth Clauses in the Ninth Section of the first Article;* and that no State, without its Consent, shall be deprived of its equal Suffrage in the Senate.

Article VI

All Debts contracted and Engagements entered into, before the Adoption of this Constitution, shall be as valid against the United States under this Constitution, as under the Confederation.

This Constitution, and Laws of the United States which shall be made in Pursuance thereof; and all Treaties made, or which shall be made, under the Authority of the United States, shall be the supreme Law of the Land; and the Judges in every State shall be bound thereby, any Thing in the Constitution or Laws of any State to the Contrary notwithstanding.

The Senators and Representatives before mentioned, and the Members of the several State Legislatures, and all executive and Judicial Officers, both of the United States and of the several States, shall be bound by Oath or Affirmation, to support this Constitution; but no religious Test shall ever be required as a Qualification to any Office of public Trust under the United States.

Article VII

The Ratification of the Conventions of nine States, shall be sufficient for the Establishment of this Constitution between the States so ratifying the Same.

Done in Convention by the Unanimous Consent of the States present the Seventeenth Day of September in the Year of our Lord one thousand seven hundred and Eighty seven and of the Independence of the United States of America the Twelfth* IN WITNESS whereof We have hereunto subscribed our Names,

GEORGE WASHINGTON
President and Deputy from Virginia

Delaware
George Read
Gunning Bedford Jr.
John Dickinson
Richard Bassett
Jacob Broom

Maryland
James McHenry
Daniel of St. Thomas Jenifer
Daniel Carroll

Virginia
John Blair
James Madison Jr.

North Carolina
William Blount
Richard Dobbs Spraight
Hugh Williamson

South Carolina
John Rutledge
Charles Cotesworth Pinckney
Charles Pinckney
Pierce Butler

Georgia
William Few
Abraham Baldwin

New Hampshire
John Langdon
Nicholas Gilman

Massachusetts
Nathaniel Gorham
Rufus King

Connecticut
William Samuel Johnson
Roger Sherman

New York
Alexander Hamilton

New Jersey
William Livingston
David Brearley
William Paterson
Jonathan Dayton

Pennsylvania
Benjamin Franklin
Thomas Mifflin
Robert Morris
George Clymer
Thomas FitzSimons
Jared Ingersoll
James Wilson
Gouverneur Morris

*The Constitution was submitted on September 17, 1787, by the Constitutional Convention, was ratified by conventions of the several states at various dates up to May 29, 1790, and became effective on March 4, 1789.

AMENDMENTS TO THE CONSTITUTION

Amendment I

Congress shall make no law respecting an establishment of religion, or prohibiting the free exercise thereof; or abridging the freedom of speech, or of the press; or the right of the people peaceably to assemble, and to petition the Government for a redress of grievances.

Amendment II

A well regulated Militia being necessary to the security of a free State, the right of the people to keep and bear Arms, shall not be infringed.

Amendment III

No Soldier shall, in time of peace be quartered in any house, without the consent of the Owner, nor in time of war, but in a manner to be prescribed by law.

Amendment IV

The right of the people to be secure in their persons, houses, papers, and effects, against unreasonable searches and seizures, shall not be violated, and no Warrants shall issue, but upon probable cause, supported by Oath or affirmation, and particularly describing the place to be searched, and the persons or things to be seized.

Amendment V

No person shall be held to answer for a capital, or otherwise infamous crime, unless on a presentment or indictment of a Grand Jury, except in cases arising in the land or naval forces, or in the Militia, when in actual service in time of War or public danger; nor shall any person be subject for the same offense to be twice put in jeopardy of life or limb; nor shall be compelled in any criminal case to be a witness against himself, nor be deprived of life, liberty, or property, without due process of law; nor shall private property be taken for public use, without just compensation.

Amendment VI

In all criminal prosecutions, the accused shall enjoy the right to a speedy and public trial, by an impartial jury of the State and district wherein the crime shall have been committed, which district shall have been previously ascertained by law, and to be informed of the nature and cause of the accusation; to be confronted with the witnesses against him; to have compulsory process for obtaining witnesses in his favor, and to have the Assistance of Counsel for his defence.

Amendment VII

In Suits at common law, where the value in controversy shall exceed twenty dollars, the right of trial by jury shall be preserved, and no fact tried by a jury, shall be otherwise re-examined in any Court of the United States, than according to the rules of the common law.

Amendment VIII

Excessive bail shall not be required, nor excessive fines imposed, nor cruel and unusual punishments inflicted.

Amendment IX

The enumeration in the Constitution, of certain rights, shall not be construed to deny or disparage others retained by the people.

Amendment X*

The powers not delegated to the United States by the Constitution, nor prohibited by it to the States, are reserved to the States respectively, or to the people.

Amendment XI
[Adopted 1798]

The Judicial power of the United States shall not be construed to extend to any suit in law or equity, commenced or prosecuted against one of the United States by Citizens of another State, or by Citizens or Subjects of any Foreign State.

Amendment XII
[Adopted 1804]

The Electors shall meet in their respective states, and vote by ballot for President and Vice President, one of whom, at least, shall not be an inhabitant of the same state with themselves; they shall name in their ballots the person voted for as President, and in distinct ballots the person voted for as Vice President, and they shall make distinct lists of all persons voted for as President, and of all persons voted for as Vice President, and of the number of votes for each, which lists they shall sign and certify, and transmit sealed to the seat of the government of the United States, directed to the President of the Senate;— President of the Senate shall, in the presence of the Senate and House of Representatives, open all the certificates and the votes shall then be counted;—The person having the greatest number of votes for President, shall be the President, if such number be a majority of the whole number of Electors appointed; and if no person have such majority, then from the persons having the highest numbers not exceeding three on the list of those voted for as President, the House of Representatives shall choose immediately, by ballot, the President. But in choosing the President, the votes shall be taken by states, the representation

---

*The first ten amendments (the Bill of Rights) were ratified and their adoption was certified on December 15, 1791.

from each state having one vote; a quorum for this purpose shall consist of a member or members from two-thirds of the states, and a majority of all the states shall be necessary to a choice. And if the House of Representatives shall not choose a President whenever the right of choice shall devolve upon them, before *the fourth day of March* next following, then the Vice President shall act as President, as in the case of the death or other constitutional disability of the President.—The person having the greatest number of votes as Vice President, shall be the Vice President, if such number be a majority of the whole number of Electors appointed, and if no person have a majority, then from the two highest numbers on the list, the Senate shall choose the Vice President; a quorum for the purpose shall consist of two-thirds of the whole number of Senators, and a majority of the whole number shall be necessary to a choice. But no person constitutionally ineligible to the office of President shall be eligible to that of Vice President of the United States.

Amendment XIII
[Adopted 1865]

Section 1

Neither slavery nor involuntary servitude, except as a punishment for crime whereof the party shall have been duly convicted, shall exist within the United States, or any place subject to their jurisdiction.

Section 2

Congress shall have power to enforce this article by appropriate legislation.

Amendment XIV
[Adopted 1868]

Section 1

All persons born or naturalized in the United States, and subject to the jurisdiction thereof, are citizens of the United States and of the State wherein they reside. No State shall make or enforce any law which shall abridge the privileges or immunities of citizens of the United States; nor shall any State deprive any person of life, liberty, or property, without due process of law; nor deny to any person within its jurisdiction the equal protection of the laws.

Section 2

Representatives shall be apportioned among the several States according to their respective numbers, counting the whole number of persons in each State, excluding Indians not taxed. But when the right to vote at any election for the choice of electors for President and Vice President of the United States, Representatives in Congress, the Executive and Judicial officers of a State, or the members of the Legislature thereof, is denied to any of the male inhabitants of such State, being twenty-one years of age, and citizens of the United States, or in any way abridged, except for participation in rebellion, or other crime, the basis of representation therein shall be reduced in the proportion which the number of such male citizens shall bear to the whole number of male citizens twenty-one years of age in such State.

Section 3

No person shall be a Senator or Representative in Congress, or elector of President and Vice President, or hold any office, civil or military, under the United States, or under any State, who, having previously taken an oath, as a member of Congress, or as an officer of the United States, or as a member of any State legislature, or as an executive or judicial officer of any State, to support the Constitution of the United States, shall have engaged in insurrection or rebellion against the same, or given aid or comfort to the enemies thereof. But Congress may by a vote of two-thirds of each House, remove such disability.

Section 4

The validity of the public debt of the United States, authorized by law, including debts incurred for payment of pensions and bounties for services in suppressing insurrection or rebellion, shall not be questioned. But neither the United States nor any State shall assume or pay any debt or obligation incurred in aid of insurrection or rebellion against the United States, or any claim for the loss or emancipation of any slave; but all such debts, obligations and claims shall be held illegal and void.

Section 5

The Congress shall have power to enforce, by appropriate legislation, the provisions of this article.

Amendment XV
[Adopted 1870]

Section 1

The right of citizens of the United States to vote shall not be denied or abridged by the United States or by any State on account of race, color, or previous condition of servitude.

Section 2

The Congress shall have power to enforce this article by appropriate legislation.

Amendment XVI
[Adopted 1913]

The Congress shall have power to lay and collect taxes on incomes, from whatever source derived, without apportionment among the several States, and without regard to any census or enumeration.

Amendment XVII
[Adopted 1913]

The Senate of the United States shall be composed of two Senators from each State, elected by the people thereof, for six years; and each Senator shall have one vote. The electors in each State shall have the qualifications requisite for electors of the most numerous branch of the State legislatures.

When vacancies happen in the representation of any State in the Senate, the executive authority of such State shall issue writs of election to fill such vacancies: *Provided*, That the legislature of any State may empower the executive thereof to make temporary appointments until the people fill the vacancies by election as the legislature may direct.

This amendment shall not be so construed as to affect the election or term of any Senator chosen before it becomes valid as part of the Constitution.

Amendment XVIII
[Adopted 1919, repealed 1933]

Section 1

After one year from the ratification of this article the manufacture, sale, or transportation of intoxicating liquors within, the importation thereof into, or the exportation thereof from the United States and all territory subject to the jurisdiction thereof for beverage purposes is hereby prohibited.

Section 2

The Congress and the several States shall have concurrent power to enforce this article by appropriate legislation.

Section 3

This article shall be inoperative unless it shall have been ratified as an amendment to the Constitution by the legislatures of the several States, as provided in the Constitution, within seven years from the date of the submission hereof to the States by the Congress.

Amendment XIX
[Adopted 1920]

The right of citizens of the United States to vote shall not be denied or abridged by the United States or by any State on account of sex.

Congress shall have power to enforce this article by appropriate legislation.

Amendment XX
[Adopted 1933]

Section 1

The terms of the President and Vice President shall end at noon on the 20th day of January, and the terms of Senators and Representatives at noon on the 3d day of January, of the years in which such terms would have ended if this article had not been ratified and the terms of their successors shall then begin.

Section 2

The Congress shall assemble at least once in every year, and such meeting shall begin at noon on the 3d day of January, unless they shall by law appoint a different day.

Section 3

If, at the time fixed for the beginning of the term of the President, the President elect shall have died, the Vice President elect shall become President. If a President shall not have been chosen before the time fixed for the beginning of his term, or if the President elect shall have failed to qualify, then the Vice President elect shall act as President until a President shall have qualified; and the Congress may by law provide for the case wherein neither a President elect nor a Vice President elect shall have qualified, declaring who shall then act as President, or the manner in which one who is to act shall be selected, and such person shall act accordingly until a President or Vice President shall have qualified.

Section 4

The Congress may by law provide for the case of the death of any of the persons from whom the House of Representatives may choose a President whenever the right of choice shall have devolved upon them, and for the case of the death of any of the persons from whom the Senate may choose a Vice President whenever the right of choice shall have devolved upon them.

Section 5

Sections 1 and 2 shall take effect on the 15th day of October following the ratification of this article.

Section 6

This article shall be inoperative unless it shall have been ratified as an amendment to the Constitution by the legislatures of three fourths of the several States within seven years from the date of its submission.

Amendment XXI
[Adopted 1933]

Section 1

The eighteenth article of amendment to the Constitution of the United States is hereby repealed.

Section 2

The transportation or importation into any State, Territory, or possession of the United States for delivery or use therein of intoxicating liquors in violation of the laws thereof, is hereby prohibited.

Section 3

This article shall be inoperative unless it shall have been ratified as an amendment to the Constitution by conventions in the several States, as provided in the Constitution, within seven years from the date of the submission hereof to the States by the Congress.

Amendment XXII
[Adopted 1951]

Section 1

No person shall be elected to the office of the President more than twice, and no person who has held the office of President, or acted as President, for more than two years of a term to which some other person was elected President shall be elected to the office of the President more than once. But this Article shall not apply to any person holding the office of President when this Article was proposed by the Congress, and shall not prevent any person who may be holding the office of President, or acting as President, during the term within which this

Article becomes operative from holding the office of President or acting as President during the remainder of such term.

Section 2

This article shall be inoperative unless it shall have been ratified as an amendment to the Constitution by the legislatures of three-fourths of the several States within seven years from the date of its submission to the States by the Congress.

Amendment XXIII
[Adopted 1961]

Section 1

The District constituting the seat of Government of the United States shall appoint in such manner as the Congress shall direct:

A number of electors of President and Vice President equal to the whole number of Senators and Representatives in Congress to which the District would be entitled if it were a State, but in no event more than the least populous State; they shall be in addition to those appointed by the States, but they shall be considered, for the purposes of the election of President and Vice President, to be electors appointed by a State; and they shall meet in the District and perform such duties as provided by the twelfth article of amendment.

Section 2

The Congress shall have power to enforce this article by appropriate legislation.

Amendment XXIV
[Adopted 1964]

Section 1

The right of citizens of the United States to vote in any primary or other election for President or Vice President, for electors for President or Vice President, or for Senator or Representative in Congress, shall not be denied or abridged by the United States or any state by reason of failure to pay any poll tax or other tax.

Section 2

The Congress shall have the power to enforce this article by appropriate legislation.

Amendment XXV
[Adopted 1967]

Section 1

In case of the removal of the President from office or his death or resignation, the Vice President shall become President.

Section 2

Whenever there is a vacancy in the office of the Vice President, the President shall nominate a Vice President who shall take the office upon confirmation by a majority vote of both houses of Congress.

Section 3

Whenever the President transmits to the President pro tempore of the Senate and the Speaker of the House of Representatives his written declaration that he is unable to discharge the powers and duties of his office, and until he transmits to them a written declaration to the contrary, such powers and duties shall be discharged by the Vice President as Acting President.

Section 4

Whenever the Vice President and a majority of either the principal officers of the executive departments or of such other body as Congress may by law provide, transmit to the President pro tempore of the Senate and the Speaker of the House of Representatives their written declaration that the President is unable to discharge the powers and duties of his office, the Vice President shall immediately assume the powers and duties of the office as Acting President.

Thereafter, when the President transmits to the President pro tempore of the Senate and the Speaker of the House of Representatives his written declaration that no inability exists, he shall resume the powers and duties of his office unless the Vice President and a majority of either the principal officers of the executive department or of such other body as Congress may by law provide, transmit within four days to the President pro tempore of the Senate and the Speaker of the House of Representatives their written declaration that the President is unable to discharge the powers and duties of his office. Thereupon Congress shall decide the issue, assembling within 48 hours for that purpose if not in session. If the Congress, within 21 days after receipt of the latter written declaration, or, if Congress is not in session, within 21 days after Congress is required to assemble, determines by two-thirds vote of both houses that the President is unable to discharge the powers and duties of his office, the Vice President shall continue to discharge the same as Acting President; otherwise, the President shall resume the powers and duties of his office.

Amendment XXVI
[Adopted 1971]

Section 1

The right of citizens of the United States, who are 18 years of age or older, to vote shall not be denied or abridged by the United States or any state on account of age.

Section 2

The Congress shall have the power to enforce this article by appropriate legislation.

Amendment XXVII
[Adopted 1992]

No law, varying the compensation for the services of the Senators and Representatives shall take effect, until an election of Representatives shall have intervened.

PRESIDENTIAL ELECTIONS

Year	Candidates	Parties	Popular Vote	Electoral Vote	Voter Participation
1789	**George Washington**		a	69	
	John Adams			34	
	Others			35	
1792	**George Washington**		a	132	
	John Adams			77	
	George Clinton			50	
	Others			5	
1796	**John Adams**	Federalist	a	71	
	Thomas Jefferson	Democratic-Republican		68	
	Thomas Pinckney	Federalist		59	
	Aaron Burr	Dem.-Rep.		30	
	Others			48	
1800	**Thomas Jefferson**	Dem.-Rep.	a	73	
	Aaron Burr	Dem.-Rep.		73	
	John Adams	Federalist		65	
	C. C. Pinckney	Federalist		64	
	John Jay	Federalist		1	
1804	**Thomas Jefferson**	Dem.-Rep.	a	162	
	C. C. Pinckney	Federalist		14	
1808	**James Madison**	Dem.-Rep.	a	122	
	C. C. Pinckney	Federalist		47	
	George Clinton	Dem.-Rep.		6	
1812	**James Madison**	Dem.-Rep.	a	128	
	De Witt Clinton	Federalist		89	
1816	**James Monroe**	Dem.-Rep.	a	183	
	Rufus King	Federalist		34	
1820	**James Monroe**	Dem.-Rep.	a	231	
	John Quincy Adams	Dem.-Rep.		1	
1824	**John Quincy Adams**	Dem.-Rep.	108,740 (30.5%)	84	26.9%
	Andrew Jackson	Dem.-Rep.	153,544 (43.1%)	99	
	William H. Crawford	Dem.-Rep.	46,618 (13.1%)	41	
	Henry Clay	Dem.-Rep.	47,136 (13.2%)	37	
1828	**Andrew Jackson**	Democratic	647,286 (56.0%)	178	57.6%
	John Quincy Adams	National Republican	508,064 (44.0%)	83	
1832	**Andrew Jackson**	Democratic	687,502 (55.0%)	219	55.4%
	Henry Clay	National Republican	530,189 (42.4%)	49	
	John Floyd	Independent		11	
	William Wirt	Anti-Mason	33,108 (2.6%)	7	
1836	**Martin Van Buren**	Democratic	765,483 (50.9%)	170	57.8%
	William Henry Harrison	Whig		73	
	Hugh L. White	Whig	739,795 (49.1%)	26	
	Daniel Webster	Whig		14	
	W. P. Magnum	Independent		11	
1840	**William Henry Harrison**	Whig	1,274,624 (53.1%)	234	80.2%
	Martin Van Buren	Democratic	1,127,781 (46.9%)	60	
	J. G. Birney	Liberty	7,069	—	

a Electors selected by state legislatures.

Year	Candidates	Parties	Popular Vote	Electoral Vote	Voter Participation
1844	**James K. Polk**	Democratic	1,338,464 (49.6%)	170	78.9%
	Henry Clay	Whig	1,300,097 (48.1%)	105	
	J. G. Birney	Liberty	62,300 (2.3%)	—	
1848	**Zachary Taylor**	Whig	1,360,967 (47.4%)	163	72.7%
	Lewis Cass	Democratic	1,222,342 (42.5%)	127	
	Martin Van Buren	Free-Soil	291,263 (10.1%)	—	
1852	**Franklin Pierce**	Democratic	1,601,117 (50.9%)	254	69.6%
	Winfield Scott	Whig	1,385,453 (44.1%)	42	
	John P. Hale	Free-Soil	155,825 (5.0%)	—	
1856	**James Buchanan**	Democratic	1,832,955 (45.3%)	174	78.9%
	John C. Frémont	Republican	1,339,932 (33.1%)	114	
	Millard Fillmore	American	871,731 (21.6%)	8	
1860	**Abraham Lincoln**	Republican	1,865,593 (39.8%)	180	81.2%
	Stephen A. Douglas	Democratic	1,382,713 (29.5%)	12	
	John C. Breckinridge	Democratic	848,356 (18.1%)	72	
	John Bell	Union	592,906 (12.6%)	39	
1864	**Abraham Lincoln**	Republican	2,213,655 (55.0%)	212[b]	73.8%
	George B. McClellan	Democratic	1,805,237 (45.0%)	21	
1868	**Ulysses S. Grant**	Republican	3,012,833 (52.7%)	214	78.1%
	Horatio Seymour	Democratic	2,703,249 (47.3%)	80	
1872	**Ulysses S. Grant**	Republican	3,597,132 (55.6%)	286	71.3%
	Horace Greeley	Dem.; Liberal Republican	2,834,125 (43.9%)	66[c]	
1876	**Rutherford B. Hayes**[d]	Republican	4,036,298 (48.0%)	185	81.8%
	Samuel J. Tilden	Democratic	4,300,590 (51.0%)	184	
1880	**James A. Garfield**	Republican	4,454,416 (48.5%)	214	79.4%
	Winfield S. Hancock	Democratic	4,444,952 (48.1%)	155	
1884	**Grover Cleveland**	Democratic	4,874,986 (48.5%)	219	77.5%
	James G. Blaine	Republican	4,851,981 (48.2%)	182	
1888	**Benjamin Harrison**	Republican	5,439,853 (47.9%)	233	79.3%
	Grover Cleveland	Democratic	5,540,309 (48.6%)	168	
1892	**Grover Cleveland**	Democratic	5,556,918 (46.1%)	277	74.7%
	Benjamin Harrison	Republican	5,176,108 (43.0%)	145	
	James B. Weaver	People's	1,041,028 (8.5%)	22	
1896	**William McKinley**	Republican	7,104,779 (51.1%)	271	79.3%
	William Jennings Bryan	Democratic People's	6,502,925 (47.7%)	176	
1900	**William McKinley**	Republican	7,207,923 (51.7%)	292	73.2%
	William Jennings Bryan	Dem.-Populist	6,358,133 (45.5%)	155	
1904	**Theodore Roosevelt**	Republican	7,623,486 (57.9%)	336	65.2%
	Alton B. Parker	Democratic	5,077,911 (37.6%)	140	
	Eugene V. Debs	Socialist	402,283 (3.0%)	—	
1908	**William H. Taft**	Republican	7,678,908 (51.6%)	321	65.4%
	William Jennings Bryan	Democratic	6,409,104 (43.1%)	162	
	Eugene V. Debs	Socialist	420,793 (2.8%)	—	
1912	**Woodrow Wilson**	Democratic	6,293,454 (41.9%)	435	58.8%
	Theodore Roosevelt	Progressive	4,119,538 (27.4%)	88	
	William H. Taft	Republican	3,484,980 (23.2%)	8	
	Eugene V. Debs	Socialist	900,672 (6.0%)	—	
1916	**Woodrow Wilson**	Democratic	9,129,606 (49.4%)	277	61.6%
	Charles E. Hughes	Republican	8,538,221 (46.2%)	254	
	A. L. Benson	Socialist	585,113 (3.2%)	—	
1920	**Warren G. Harding**	Republican	16,152,200 (60.4%)	404	49.2%
	James M. Cox	Democratic	9,147,353 (34.2%)	127	
	Eugene V. Debs	Socialist	919,799 (3.4%)	—	
1924	**Calvin Coolidge**	Republican	15,725,016 (54.0%)	382	48.9%
	John W. Davis	Democratic	8,386,503 (28.8%)	136	
	Robert M. La Follette	Progressive	4,822,856 (16.6%)	13	

[b]Eleven secessionist states did not participate.

[c]Greeley died before the electoral college met. His electoral votes were divided among the four minor candidates.

[d]Contested result settled by special election.

Year	Candidates	Parties	Popular Vote	Electoral Vote	Voter Participation
1928	**Herbert Hoover**	Republican	21,391,381 (58.2%)	444	56.9%
	Alfred E. Smith	Democratic	15,016,443 (40.9%)	87	
	Norman Thomas	Socialist	267,835 (0.7%)	—	
1932	**Franklin D. Roosevelt**	Democratic	22,821,857 (57.4%)	472	56.9%
	Herbert Hoover	Republican	15,761,841 (39.7%)	59	
	Norman Thomas	Socialist	881,951 (2.2%)	—	
1936	**Franklin D. Roosevelt**	Democratic	27,751,597 (60.8%)	523	61.0%
	Alfred M. Landon	Republican	16,679,583 (36.5%)	8	
	William Lemke	Union	882,479 (1.9%)	—	
1940	**Franklin D. Roosevelt**	Democratic	27,244,160 (54.8%)	449	62.5%
	Wendell L. Willkie	Republican	22,305,198 (44.8%)	82	
1944	**Franklin D. Roosevelt**	Democratic	25,602,504 (53.5%)	432	55.9%
	Thomas E. Dewey	Republican	22,006,285 (46.0%)	99	
1948	**Harry S. Truman**	Democratic	24,105,695 (49.5%)	304	53.0%
	Thomas E. Dewey	Republican	21,969,170 (45.1%)	189	
	J. Strom Thurmond	State-Rights Democratic	1,169,021 (2.4%)	38	
	Henry A. Wallace	Progressive	1,156,103 (2.4%)	—	
1952	**Dwight D. Eisenhower**	Republican	33,936,252 (55.1%)	442	63.3%
	Adlai E. Stevenson	Democratic	27,314,992 (44.4%)	89	
1956	**Dwight D. Eisenhower**	Republican	35,575,420 (57.6%)	457	60.6%
	Adlai E. Stevenson	Democratic	26,033,066 (42.1%)	73	
	Other	—		1	
1960	**John F. Kennedy**	Democratic	34,227,096 (49.9%)	303	62.8%
	Richard M. Nixon	Republican	34,108,546 (49.6%)	219	
	Other	—		15	
1964	**Lyndon B. Johnson**	Democratic	43,126,506 (61.1%)	486	61.7%
	Barry M. Goldwater	Republican	27,176,799 (38.5%)	52	
1968	**Richard M. Nixon**	Republican	31,770,237 (43.4%)	301	60.6%
	Hubert H. Humphrey	Democratic	31,270,533 (42.7%)	191	
	George Wallace	American Indep.	9,906,141 (13.5%)	46	
1972	**Richard M. Nixon**	Republican	47,169,911 (60.7%)	520	55.2%
	George S. McGovern	Democratic	29,170,383 (37.5%)	17	
	Other	—		1	
1976	**Jimmy Carter**	Democratic	40,828,587 (50.0%)	297	53.5%
	Gerald R. Ford	Republican	39,147,613 (47.9%)	241	
	Other	—	1,575,459 (2.1%)	—	
1980	**Ronald Reagan**	Republican	43,901,812 (50.7%)	489	52.6%
	Jimmy Carter	Democratic	35,483,820 (41.0%)	49	
	John B. Anderson	Independent	5,719,722 (6.6%)	—	
	Ed Clark	Libertarian	921,188 (1.1%)	—	
1984	**Ronald Reagan**	Republican	54,455,075 (59.0%)	525	53.3%
	Walter Mondale	Democratic	37,577,185 (41.0%)	13	
1988	**George H. W. Bush**	Republican	48,886,000 (53.4%)	426	57.4%
	Michael S. Dukakis	Democratic	41,809,000 (45.6%)	111	
1992	**William J. Clinton**	Democratic	43,728,375 (43.0%)	370	55.0%
	George H. W. Bush	Republican	38,167,416 (38.0%)	168	
	H. Ross Perot	Independent	19,237,247 (19.0%)	—	
1996	**William J. Clinton**	Democratic	47,401,185 (49.2%)	379	48.8%
	Robert Dole	Republican	39,197,469 (40.7%)	159	
	H. Ross Perot	Reform	8,085,294 (8.4%)	—	
	Ralph Nader	Green	684,871 (<1%)	—	
2000	**George W. Bush**	Republican	50,456,002 (47.9%)	271	51.2%
	Al Gore	Democratic	50,999,897 (48.4%)	266[e]	
	Ralph Nader	Green	2,882,955 (2.7%)	—	
	Other	—	834,774 (<1%)	—	
2004	**George W. Bush**	Republican	62,040,610 (50.7%)	286	55.3%
	John Kerry	Democratic	59,028,444 (48.3%)	251	
	Ralph Nader	Independent	465,650 (<1%)	—	
2008	**Barack Obama**	Democratic	69,456,897 (52.9%)	365	
	John McCain	Republican	59,934,814 (45.7%)	173	

[e]One District of Columbia Gore elector abstained.

GLOSSARY

Abolition Act of 1808   Also called the Slave Trade Act, prohibited the importation of foreign slaves into the U.S. p. 255

Affirmative action   Policies designed to improve the educational and employment opportunities of historically underrepresented groups such as women and African Americans. p. 632

Alien and Sedition Acts   Laws enacted by the Federalist-dominated Congress in 1798 to limit the speech of their critics and to make it more difficult for immigrants to become citizens. p. 223

Alien   Foreign-born resident of the United States who has not been naturalized as a U.S. citizen. p. 494

America First Committee   A group that opposed Roosevelt's efforts to intervene in World War II against the Axis powers. p. 537

Amphibious landing   A military assault that begins on the water and ends on land. p. 306

Anarchists   Persons who reject all forms of government as inherently oppressive and undesirable. p. 422

Annexation   Addition of territory that had belonged to one nation into another nation. p. 304

Anti-Federalists   A diverse and unsuccessful coalition that opposed ratification of the Constitution and feared the increased power of the proposed central government. The Anti-Federalists were named by their opponents, the Federalists. p. 210

Anti-semitism   Prejudice against Jews. p. 395

Archaic   The second long stage of North American habitation, covering about 7,000 years, from roughly 8,000 BCE to 1000 BCE (or from 10,000 to 3,000 years ago). During this period, inhabitants adapted to diverse local environments, gathering plants and hunting smaller animals than during the previous Paleo-Indian period. p. 6

Archipelago   A group of islands, such as the Hawaiian archipelago. p. 12

Asiento   A contract negotiated by the Spanish crown (between 1595 and 1789) with other European powers such as Portugal, France, England, and the Netherlands to provide a fixed number of slaves annually to Spain's American colonies for a set payment. p. 85

Assembly line   A form of industrial production popularized by the Ford Motor Company in which workers perform one task repeatedly as the products they are jointly assembling move along a conveyor. p. 464

Atlatl   A weighted, handheld device that enabled early Native Americans to throw spears with added power and velocity. p. 7

Axis Pact   An alliance among Germany, Italy and Japan during World War II. p. 536

Babel   A city described in the Old Testament where constructing a tower was made impossible by the confusion of varied languages. This term from the Book of Genesis is used to describe any scene of clamor and confusion. p. 111

Baby boom   The period of increased U.S. childbirths from roughly the early 1940s to the early 1960s. p. 577

Barracoon   An enclosure or barrack used for the confinement of slaves before their forced deportation from the African coast. p. 92

Bill of Rights   A set of amendments assuring basic rights, proposed by James Madison to help ensure acceptance of the newly drafted Constitution, and based on suggestions from the states. Ten of the twelve items passed by Congress were ratified by the states in 1791. Taken together, these first ten amendments to the Constitution became known as the Bill of Rights. p. 213

"Birds of passage"   A term applied to immigrants who came to the United States for a brief period of time, and then returned to their home countries. p. 457

Black Code   Southern state laws passed after the Civil War to limit the rights and actions of newly liberated African Americans. p. 364

Black power   The slogan used by young black nationalists in the mid- and late 1960s. p. 605

"Bloody shirt"   A partisan rallying cry used to stir up or revive sectional or party animosity after the American Civil War; for example, post–Civil War Republicans "waved the bloody shirt," associating some Democrats with a treasonous acceptance of secession during the war, while opponents had spilled their blood for the Union. p. 403

Bolsheviks   The Communist revolutionaries who overthrew the Russian czar in 1917 and established the Union of Soviet Socialist Republics (USSR). p. 485

Boston marriages   Unions of two women based on long-term emotional bonds in which the women live together as if married to each other. p. 466

Bracero   Mexican nationals working in the United States in low-wage jobs as part of a temporary work program between 1942 and 1964. (The *bracero* program was established by an executive agreement between the presidents of Mexico and the United States, providing Mexican agricultural labor in the Southwest and the Pacific Northwest.) p. 540

Bull Mooser   Supporter of Theodore Roosevelt in the 1912 presidential election when he broke from the Republican party and ran as a third-party candidate on the ticket of the Progressive (or Bull Moose) party. p. 456

Burgess   A representative elected to the popular branch of the colonial legislature in either Virginia or Maryland. p. 44

Cajuns   The Louisiana word for French-speaking people from Acadia (Nova Scotia) who were forced to move south in 1755 during the French and Indian War. Many of these refugees eventually moved to French Louisiana, where they have had a lasting impact on the culture. p. 118

Capitalism   The now almost worldwide economic system of private ownership of property and profit-seeking corporations. p. 514

Carpetbaggers   A negative term applied by Southerners to Northerners who moved to the South after the Civil War to pursue political or economic opportunities. p. 367

Checks and balances   The rules controlling interactions among the executive, legislative, and judicial branches of government, making up a novel system designed to prevent any single branch from overreaching its powers, as set forth in the Constitution in 1787. p. 207

Chinese Exclusion Act   Congressional legislation passed in 1882 to bar most Chinese workers from entering the United States. p. 395

Civil Rights Act of 1875   Congressional legislation that guaranteed black people access to public accommodations and transportation; the Supreme Court declared the measure unconstitutional in 1883. p. 383

Civil service reform   Measures designed to eliminate the spoils system in government hiring, in favor of maintaining professional standards in public service. p. 404

Coalition   An alliance of parties, factions, or nations. p. 279

Coffle   A procession or train of enslaved prisoners, bound together for travel (from the Arabic word for "caravan"). p. 92

Cold War   The conflict and competition between the United States and the Soviet Union (and their respective allies) that emerged after 1945 and lasted until 1989. p. 554

Colonialism   The centuries-old system of mostly European nations controlling and governing peoples and lands outside of Europe. p. 561

Columbian Exchange   The significant two-way interchange of plants, animals, microbes, and people that occurred once Christopher Columbus established regular contact by sea between the eastern and western hemispheres. For thousands of years before 1492, despite occasional encounters, these two separate and different "worlds" had remained isolated from each other. p. 17

Common school system   Tax-supported public education to provide elementary schooling free to young children. p. 298

Communism   A totalitarian form of government, grounded in the theories of German philosopher Karl Marx and the practices of V. I. Lenin in Russia, that eliminated private ownership of property in supposed pursuit of complete human equality; the system of government also featured a centrally directed economy and the absolute rule of a small group of leaders. p. 554

Compromise of 1850   Congressional legislation that provided that California would enter the Union as a free state that year, and that New Mexico and Utah would eventually submit the slavery question to their voters. As part of this compromise, the federal government abolished the slave trade in Washington, D.C. p. 312

Confederate States of America   The would-be new nation formed in February 1861 by seven southern states—South Carolina, Mississippi, Florida, Alabama, Georgia, Louisiana, and Texas—in a bid for independence from the United States of America. By late spring 1861, the Confederacy also included Virginia, Arkansas, Tennessee, and North Carolina. p. 338

Conservationist   Advocate of conserving and protecting the natural world through the use of renewable natural resources. p. 454

Conspicuous consumption   A term coined by the American social theorist Thorstein Veblen to describe the behavior of wealthy persons who flaunt their status through their purchase of fine clothes, large houses, fancy cars, and other highly visible material goods. p. 435

Consumer economy   An economic system in which most people work for wages, which they use to purchase manufactured goods and foodstuffs. p. 491

Containment   The U.S. policy during the Cold War of trying to halt the expansion of Soviet and communist influences. p. 559

Coverture   French term for the dependent and legal status of a woman during marriage. Under English law, the male family head received legal rights, and his wife lost independent status, becoming, in legal terms, a *femme covert*. p. 69

Czar   The title for a male ruler, or king, of Russia during the centuries before the Russian Revolution of 1917. p. 140

De facto   Latin phrase meaning "in reality," sometimes applied to a government that is exercising real power, though it has not been legally constituted. p. 157

Democratic-Republicans   The political party that emerged after the Revolution to oppose the Federalists' support for a strong central government; favored states' rights and the agrarian way of life. Thomas Jefferson, a leader of the Democratic-Republicans, was elected president in 1800. p. 218

Détente   The lessening of military or diplomatic tensions, as between the United States and the Soviet Union. p. 618

Diaspora   The dispersion of a population abroad, whether forced or voluntary. The term is often applied to Jewish settlement outside the eastern Mediterranean region, and to the spread of Africans across the Americas, due to the Atlantic slave trade. p. 107

Dispossession   Act of taking land or other property from a group of people. p. 313

"Dollar Diplomacy"   President William Howard Taft coined the term to refer to a policy that encouraged economic investment in foreign countries. p. 455

"Don't ask, don't tell"   A policy established by the Clinton administration allowing gays and lesbians to serve in the military so long as they do not disclose their sexual orientation. p. 664

Dred Scott v. Sandford   The 1857 case in which the Supreme Court held that residence on free soil did not render a slave a free person, for black people, enslaved and free, had (in the words of the court) "no rights which the white man was bound to respect." p. 330

Dust Bowl   The plains regions of Oklahoma, Texas, Colorado, and New Mexico and Kansas? affected by severe drought in the 1930s. p. 516

Edmunds Act   Congressional legislation passed in 1882 and aimed at Utah Mormons; it outlawed polygamy, stripped polygamists of the right to vote, and provided for a five-member commission to oversee Utah's elections. p. 404

Electoral college   An intricate system in which each state appoints electors, equal in number to its representation in Congress, to elect the president and vice president. The electoral college is a provision of the Constitution (Article II, Section 1) because the framers were unwilling to approve the direct election of president and vice president. This group, or "college," of electors still makes the selection, voting according to prior party commitments rather than individual choice. p. 208

Emancipation   National or state-sponsored program to free slaves. p. 311

Embargo Act of 1807   A law passed by Congress, at the urging of President Thomas Jefferson, to halt the shipment of U.S. goods to Europe in response to British military and naval aggression. p. 245

Encomienda   The Spanish encomienda system, imposed in Spain's American empire, requiring Indian communities to supply labor or pay tribute to a local colonial overlord (identified as an encomendero). p. 34

Entente   The alliance of Britain, France, and Russia, later joined by Italy and the United States, during World War I. p. 473

Equal Rights Amendment   (ERA) A proposed amendment to the United States Constitution that would have guaranteed equal rights for women. p. 493

Era of Good Feelings   A term used by historians to describe the presidency of James Monroe (1816–1820), when partisan tensions eased among voters and their political leaders. p. 251

Erie Canal   Waterway linking the New York cities of Troy and Albany, on the Hudson River, with Buffalo, on the eastern tip of Lake Erie; in the 1820s, the opening of the Erie Canal revolutionized trading between the Midwest and East Coast and established New York City as the most important financial center in the United States. p. 265

Evangelical Protestants   Christians who emphasize the importance of personal faith, as well as seeking new converts. p. 293

Fall line   The geographical division between the Piedmont and the Atlantic coastal plain where the land slopes sharply to the sea. p. 317

Family wage   A level of income sufficient for an individual worker, usually a man, to support a spouse and family through a single salary. p. 526

Fascism   A form of right-wing dictatorship exalting nation and race above the individual. p. 536

Federalists   A coalition of nationalist leaders who favored creating a stronger central government to replace the Articles of Confederation. They labeled their opponents as Anti-Federalists in the late 1780s. The strongest essays endorsing their proposed new Constitution were entitled *The Federalist*. p. 210

Federation   An alliance or compact between political units that agree to surrender certain powers to a central authority while still retaining other powers. p. 189

Feminism   The belief that women and men are of equal value and that gender roles are, to a considerable degree, created by society rather than being simply natural. p. 616

Fireside chats   The broadcasts by President Franklin Delano Roosevelt during which he spoke directly to American families, often gathered around a radio in their living room. p. 513

Flapper   Young woman in the 1910s and 1920s who rebelled against the gender conventions of the era with respect to fashion and behavior. p. 491

Flotilla   Any sizeable fleet of ships, or, more specifically, a naval term for a unit consisting of two or more squadrons of small warships. p. 134

Foundling home   A residence for orphaned children. p. 457

Freedmen's Bureau   Federal agency created by Congress in March 1865 and disbanded in 1869. Its purposes were to provide relief for Southerners who had remained loyal to the Union during the Civil War, to support black elementary schools, and to oversee annual labor contracts between landowners and field hands. p. 364

Freedmen's Bureau   Federal agency created by Congress in March 1865 and disbanded in 1869. Its purposes were to provide relief for Southerners who had remained loyal to the Union during the Civil War, to support black elementary schools, and to oversee annual labor contracts between landowners and field hands. p. 364

Free Labor Ideology   The ideas, represented most forcefully by the antebellum Republican party, that workers should profit from their own labor and that slavery is wrong. p. 317

Free trade   International economic relations characterized by multinational investment and a reduction or elimination of tariffs. p. 537

Fugitive Slave Law of 1850 Congressional legislation that required local and federal law enforcement agents to retrieve runaways no matter where they sought refuge in the United States. p. 324

Gadsden Purchase A total of 29,670 square miles of land (located in present-day southern Arizona and southwestern New Mexico) purchased by the United States from Mexico in 1853. p. 314

Globalization The process of integration—economic, but also cultural—of different parts of the world into a more unified system of trade and communication. p. 14

Grange An organization founded by Oliver H. Kelly in 1867 to represent the interests of farmers by pressing for agricultural cooperatives, an end to railroad freight discrimination against small farmers, and other initiatives. Its full name was National Grange of Patrons of Husbandry. p. 382

Great Awakening The title that was applied, in retrospect, to the interdenominational Christian revival that swept Britain's North American colonies between the 1730s and the 1750s, inspired at first by the preaching of Jonathan Edwards and George Whitefield (A religious revival in the early nineteenth century became known as the Second Great Awakening). p. 124

Great Migration The movement of African Americans out of the South to northern cities, particularly during World War I. p. 479

Great Society In the 1960s, President Lyndon Johnson's programs for reducing poverty, discrimination, and pollution, and for improving health care, education, and consumer protection. p. 597

Guerrilla war A conflict fought not on the basis of conventional warfare, but rather by mobilizing small groups of fighters who attack and harass superior forces. p. 289

Hayseeds A derogatory term applied to rural people deemed uneducated and naive (in contrast to self-proclaimed sophisticated city dwellers). p. 435

Headright Under the headright system, English colonial governments granted a fixed amount of land, usually 50 acres, to any head of household for every family member or hired hand that person brought into the colony. Sometimes fewer acres were granted for women and children on the grounds that they would clear and plant less land. p. 44

Hobos Migrant worker or poor and homeless vagrant who traveled on trains from location to location, usually in search of employment. p. 516

Holocaust The name given to the Nazi genocide against the Jews during World War II. Six million Jews were murdered. p. 535

Homestead Act Legislation passed in 1862 that granted 160 acres of land free to each settler who lived on and made improvements to government land for five years. p. 346

Hoovervilles Shantytowns, named for President Hoover and occupied largely by people who lost their homes and farms during the Great Depression. p. 506

Iberian Relating to Europe's Iberian Peninsula, the location of Spain and Portugal. p. 13

Imperialism The policy of extending a nation's authority by territorial acquistion (through negotiation or conquest) or by the establishment of political or economic control over other nations. p. 429

Impressment A policy that authorizes the seizure of persons or private property in the service of a government. p. 219

Indenture A document binding one person to work for another for a given period of time. Indentured servants received food, shelter, and clothing, plus "freedom dues" when their terms of service ended to help them get started independently. p. 88

Installment buying A system in which a consumer could make a down payment to purchase a product and then pay the remaining installments over time. p. 504

Iroquois League A Native American confederacy, located in central New York, originally composed of the Cayuga, Mohawk, Oneida, Onondaga, and Seneca Indians, and later including the Tuscarora as well. p. 37

Islamist Pertaining to an ideology promoting the creation of governments based on a fundamentalist interpretation of Islamic law. p. 638

Isthmus A narrow strip of land connecting two larger land areas (such as the isthmus of Panama). p. 18

Jim Crow The name given to the set of legal institutions that ensured the segregation of nonwhite people in the South. p. 414

Kachina An Indian religious system, inspired by Mexican traditions, and present in the American Southwest for more than 800 years. The kachina cult used masks for group performances associated with rain, curing, fertility, warfare, and the ancestors. Among many Pueblo and Hopi Indians, this tradition was epitomized by kachina (or katsina) dolls. p. 34

Kayak A highly maneuverable, decked-in canoe used by Native Alaskans for travel and hunting. The light frame is covered with skins, and the paddle has a blade at each end. Popular modern versions of this traditional boat are made with canvas or fiberglass. p. 140

Kentucky and Virginia Resolutions Resolutions issued by two state legislatures in 1798 in response to the Alien and Sedition Acts passed by Congress; proclaimed that individual states had the right to declare such measures "void and of no force." p. 223

Kickbacks Money paid illegally in return for favors (for example, to a politician by a person or business that has received government contracts). p. 373

Laissez-Faire a belief in little or no government interference in the economy. p. 403

Lecompton Constitution A Kansas state constitution drawn up by proslavery advocates in 1857; sought to nullify the doctrine of popular sovereignty in the state, decreeing that even if voters rejected slavery, any slaves already in the state would remain enslaved under the force of law. p. 330

Lewis and Clark expedition A "corps of discovery" commissioned by President Thomas Jefferson in 1804 to explore the newly acquired Louisiana Territory. Led by Meriwether Lewis and William Clark and lasting 28 months, the party reported on an array of subjects, including the cultural practices of western Indians and the natural features of the land, but failed to find a water route that would connect the Pacific Northwest to eastern markets. p. 242

Manifest Destiny The idea, first promoted in the 1840s, that the United States had a God-given right to expand its territory; used to justify territorial growth, expansion of economic markets, and conquest. p. 302

Manumission A formal emancipation from slavery; the act (by an individual owner or government authority) of granting freedom to an enslaved person or persons. p. 101

Marbury v. Madison An 1803 Supreme Court decision establishing the right of the judiciary to declare acts of both the executive and legislative branches unconstitutional. p. 237

Market Revolution The combined effects of transportation innovation, technological change, and economic growth, especially during the first half of the nineteenth century. p. 255

Mass consumption society The term refers to a shift in the early twentieth century from a society focused on frugality and production to one that embraced and celebrated consumer goods and leisure pursuits. p. 464

McCarthyism The political campaign led by Senator Joseph McCarthy (R-Wisconsin) to blame liberals at home for setbacks to U.S. interests abroad, due to what he considered liberals' sympathies with communism. p. 570

Mercantilism A commercial policy that sought to achieve economic self-suffiency and a favorable balance of trade (often by planting colonies) in order to promote a country's prosperity, strength, and independence. Rival European imperial powers favored the strategy of mercantilism in the seventeenth and eighteenth centuries. p. 58

Mesoamerica The transitional region between North and South America, composed of Mexico and Central America. p. 7

Mestizo A person of mixed European and American Indian ancestry. p. 65

Middle passage For European slave ships, the middle passage was the second of three legs in the triangular round-trip voyage from Europe to Africa to America and back to Europe. For enslaved Africans, the middle passage came to mean not only the transatlantic journey itself, but the entire process of removal from an African homeland and ultimate sale to an American master. p. 91

Military-industrial complex The term given by President Dwight D. Eisenhower to describe the armed forces and the politically powerful defense industries that supplied arms and equipment to them. p. 585

Monetary policy Government policies designed to affect the national economy through bank lending policies, interest rates, and control of the amount of money in circulation. p. 219

Monroe Doctrine Policy announced by President James Monroe in 1823 that the era of European colonization of the Americas had ceased; warned foreign powers, especially Russia, Spain, and Britain, that the United States would not allow them to intervene in the Western Hemisphere. p. 268

Morrill Act Legislation passed by Republican Congress in 1862 to create a system of agricultural (land-grant) public colleges. p. 346

Most-favored-nation A designation allowing countries to export their products to the United States with tariffs no greater than those levied against most other nations. p. 666

Muckrakers The name given to a group of investigative journalists in the early twentieth century whose exposés often challenged corporate and government power. p. 466

Mulattos A person of mixed European and African ancestry; the first-generation offspring of a Caucasian and a Negroid parent. p. 65

Muse In Greek mythology, one of the nine sister goddesses who preside over music, poetry, and the arts. p. 48

National Republicans A political party, led by John Adams in the 1820s, that favored a greater federal role in funding internal improvements and public education; forerunner of the Whigs, formed in opposition to President Andrew Jackson. p. 269

National security state The reorientation of the U.S. government and its budget after 1945 toward a primary focus on military and intelligence capabilities. p. 564

National Trades Union Organization formed in 1834 to help workers gain greater political influence. p. 293

Nativists American citizens born in the United States who oppose further immigration, especially from anywhere outside northwestern Europe. p. 296

New Democrat Member of the Democratic party, many of them organized in the Democratic Leadership Council, who espouse center to center-right policies. p. 664

New Nationalism Theodore Roosevelt's plan for a far-reaching expansion of the federal government to stabilize the economy and institute social reforms. p. 455

NSC-68 The 1950 directive of the National Security Council that called for rolling back, rather than merely containing, Soviet and communist influences. p. 564

Nullification The doctrine that a state has the right to ignore or nullify certain federal laws with which it disagrees. p. 272

Okie Migrant from Oklahoma who left the state during the Dust Bowl period in search of work. p. 517

Ordnance Cannons, artillery, and by extension general military supplies including weapons, ammunition, combat vehicles, and tools. p. 167

Pachuco Young Mexican American man who expressed attitudes of youthful rebellion in the 1940s. Many wore the Zoot Suit, also fashionable among urban African Americans. p. 549

Pacific Railroad Act   Legislation that granted to the Union Pacific and the Central Pacific railroads cash subsidies and a 400-foot right of way along the Platte River route of the Oregon Trail. p. 346

Paleo Indians   The earliest human inhabitants of North America, who first migrated to the continent from Siberia more than 15,000 years ago. Faced with a warming climate and the disappearance of many large game animals roughly 10,000 years ago (8,000 BCE), they learned to hunt smaller animals and adapted to varied local conditions during the Archaic Period (to c. 1000 BCE). p. 6

Panic of 1837   Economic crisis and depression caused by a combination of overspeculation—in bridges, canals, and turnpikes—and a large failure of grain crops in the West. p. 294

Pendleton Act   Congressional legislation passed in 1883; established a merit system for federal job applicants and created the Civil Service Commission, which administered competitive examinations to candidates in certain job classifications. p. 404

Pest house   In colonial times, a shelter to quarantine those possibly infected with contagious diseases (such as newcomers arriving in American ports from Africa or Europe) to prevent the spread of shipborne pestilence. p. 98

Planned obsolescence   A concept whereby producers intend for their products to eventually become obsolete or outdated and require replacement, thus perpetuating a cycle of production and consumption. p. 500

Plessy v. Ferguson   The 1896 case in which the Supreme Court decided that states could segregate public accommodations by race. p. 432

Pocket veto   An indirect veto of a legislative bill made when an executive (such as a president or governor) simply leaves the bill unsigned, so that it dies after the adjournment of the legislature. p. 364

Political machine   A group that effectively exercises control over a political party, usually at the local level and organized around precincts and patronage. p. 493

Popular sovereignty   The idea that residents of a state should be able to make decisions on crucial issues, such as whether or not to legalize slavery. p. 324

Populists   Agrarian reformers who formed the Populist, or People's party, a major (third) political party that emerged mostly in the Midwest and South in the late 1880s to address the needs of workers and farmers in opposition to government monetary policies and big business. The party faltered after its presidential candidate, William Jennings Bryan, lost in the 1896 election. p. 417

Privateers   Ships (and their crew members) licensed to harass enemy shipping in wartime. p. 78

Progressivism   A notion of political reform central to the "Progressive Era" (the first two decades of the twentieth century), when urban reformers with a faith in progress sought to address local and national social problems through political and civic means. p. 452

Race suicide   A fear articulated by Theodore Roosevelt and others that the low birthrate of Anglo-Saxon Americans, along with the high birthrate of immigrants from southern and eastern Europe and elsewhere, would result in a population in which "inferior" peoples would outnumber the "American racial stock." p. 463

Reconstruction era   The 12 years after the Civil War when the U.S. government took steps to integrate the 11 states of the Confederacy back into the Union. p. 363

Redemption system   An eighteenth-century arrangement in which potential migrants in Europe signed up with an agent who agreed to pay for their Atlantic passage. Reaching America, the newcomer signed a pact to work for several years for an employer. In exchange for much-needed labor, the employer agreed to pay back the shipper, "redeeming" the original loan that had been made to the immigrant "redemptioner." p. 117

Redress   A remedy for a wrong; a correction or reparation. As a verb, to redress means to correct, to set right, or to remove the cause of a grievance. p. 149

Red lining   Policies maintained by the Federal Housing Authority and lending banks which designated certain neighborhoods off limits to racial minorities. p. 579

Red Scare   Post–World War I repression of socialists, communists, and other left-wing radicals ("Reds"). p. 489

Republican mother   A wife and mother whose primary role is caring for and socializing future citizens (her children); an ideal favored by some elites after the American Revolution. p. 233

Republican party   Founded in 1854, this political party began as a coalition of Northerners who opposed the extension of slavery into the western territories. p. 327

Restitution   Giving back to the rightful owner something that has been lost or taken away. p. 307

Rosie the Riveter   A heroic symbol of women workers on the homefront during World War II. p. 547

Sachem   Algonquin Indian term for a Native American leader or chief. p. 72

Scalawag   A negative term applied by southern Democrats after the Civil War to any white Southerner who allied with the Republican party. p. 367

Second Great Awakening   A series of Protestant religious revivals that began in the 1790s and continued through the 1820s. Prominent revivalists such as Charles Grandison Finney sought to link the life of the spirit with political action and reform efforts. p. 279

Second New Deal   The agenda of policies and programs initiated by President Franklin Delano Roosevelt beginning in 1935 that was intended to strengthen the lot of American workers while simultaneously preserving the capitalist system. p. 521

Separation of powers   The novel idea that the powers of the three branches of government—legislative, executive, and judicial—should be kept separate from one another, so that each can check and balance the powers of the other two. p. 207

Sherman Anti-Trust Act   Congressional legislation passed in 1890 outlawing trusts and large business combinations. p. 405

Sit-down strike   A strategy employed by workers agitating for better wages and working conditions in which they stop working and simply sit down, thus ceasing production and preventing strikebreakers from entering a facility to assume their jobs. p. 530

Sit-in   A form of civil disobedience in which activists sit down somewhere in violation of law or policy in order to challenge discriminatory practices or laws. The tactic originated during labor struggles in the 1930s and was used effectively in the civil rights movement in the 1960s. p. 584

Social Darwinism   A late-nineteenth-century variation on the theories of British naturalist Charles Darwin, promoting the idea that only the "fittest" individuals will, or deserve to, survive (i.e., the idea that society operates on principles of evolutionary biology). p. 405

Social Gospel   A reform movement around the end of the twentieth century that stressed the responsibility of religious organizations to remedy a wide range of social ills related to urban life. p. 425

Social stratification   The schematic arrangement of a population into a ranking of horizontal of social layers (strata), or an identifiable hierarchy of classes within a society. p. 10

"Speakeasies"   Establishments where alcohol was illegally sold during the Prohibition era. p. 494

Substitute   During war, a man paid to serve in combat in another man's place. p. 344

Suffrage   The right to vote. p. 207

Sunbelt   The band of states from the Southeast to the Southwest that experienced rapid economic and population growth during and after World War II. p. 569

Tariff   A government tax on imported goods. p. 218

Tejanos   Spanish-speaking residents of the Mexican (and later, U.S.) state of Texas. p. 266

Temperance   A social movement embracing either total opposition to alcohol consumption or support for its moderate use. p. 296

Tenant farmer   A farmer who raises livestock and crops on land leased from wealthier owners. p. 316

Texians   The name used by U.S.-born citizens who lived in the Mexican state of Texas. p. 266

Theocracy   A government by officials who are regarded as divinely guided. p. 637

Three-fifths clause   A controversial clause of Article I, section 2, of the U.S. Constitution said that each slave would count as "three-fifths of all other Persons" when representatives and direct taxes were being apportioned to states according to population. Slaves had no rights of citizenship, but the clause gave southern slave states additional power in

Congress. Section 2 of the Fourteenth Amendment did away with the clause in 1868. p. 209

Tithe   A levy or donation (generally a tenth part) given to provide support, usually for a church. p. 23

Townsend Plan   A proposal by Dr. Francis Townsend in 1934 for a 2 percent national sales tax that would fund a guaranteed pension of $200 per month for Americans older than age 60. p. 525

Trail of Tears   The name Cherokee Indians gave to their forced removal from the Southeast to the West in 1838 and 1839 as part of the federal government's Indian removal policy. During the journey, U.S. troops destroyed the material basis of Cherokee culture and separated many families; over 4,000 Indians died. p. 290

Treaty of Ghent   Peace treaty signed by the United States and Great Britain in 1815, ending the War of 1812. p. 250

Truman Doctrine   President Truman's March 1947 speech articulating the new policy of containment. p. 561

Trust   A combination of firms or corporations created for the purpose of reducing competition and controlling prices throughout an industry. p. 393

Two-party system   A system of government characterized by two major political parties that compete against each other in "winner take all" elections. p. 218

Underground Railroad   A secret network of abolitionists developed during the antebellum period to help slaves escape and find refuge, many in the North or in Canada. p. 324

Unicameral   A legislative body that has only one chamber, or house. p. 70

Utopian   Relating to communities organized to strive for ideal social and political conditions. p. 300

Vigilantes   People who seek to take the law into their own hands and punish or intimidate alleged criminals or persons who resist a certain social order (for example, white supremacy). p. 302

Wage slavery   The idea that wage earners are exploited by employers as harshly as slaves are exploited by their owners. p. 318

War hawks   Politicians who favor specific forms of military action as a tool of U.S. foreign policy. p. 246

War of 1812   A military and naval conflict that pitted U.S. forces against the British and their Indian allies. The end of the war eliminated the post-Revolutionary British threat to U.S. sovereignty. p. 247

Watergate   The Washington, D.C. hotel-office complex where agents of President Nixon's reelection campaign broke into Democratic Party headquarters in 1972. Nixon helped cover up the break-in, and the subsequent political scandal was called "Watergate." p. 618

Welfare state   A nation in which the government provides a "safety net" of entitlements and benefits for citizens unable to economically provide for themselves. p. 514

Whigs   A national political party formed in 1834 in opposition to the presidency of Andrew Jackson and his policy of expanding the power of the president. The Whigs favored congressional funding for internal improvements and other forms of federal support for economic development. p. 273

Whiskey Rebellion   Protest in 1794 by western Pennsylvania farmers and grain distillers who objected to a high federal tax on the whiskey they produced. p. 220

Wildcat banks   Small banks that make loans unsupervised by the state or other financial institutions. p. 267

Wobblies   Members of the Industrial Workers of the World (IWW), a radical labor union formed in 1905. p. 469

Yellow journalism   Newspaper articles, images, and editorials that exploit, distort, or exaggerate the news in order to inflame public opinion. p. 444

Yeoman   A farmer who owns a modest amount of land (but no slaves). p. 316

Zoot suits   Distinctive clothing in the 1940s worn largely by Mexican American and African American men, characterized by flared pants, long coats, and wide-brimmed hats. p. 549

CREDITS

Part One Opener
Page 2, 3: Collection of the New-York Historical Society, (Neg #1049)

Chapter 1
Page 4: Richard A. Cooke / CORBIS; **5:** Illustration by Andy Buttram courtesy of the Illinois State Museum; **6:** Kenneth Garrett/National Geographic Image Collection; **12:** Richard A. Cooke/CORBIS; **14:** Courtesy, Algarve Tourism Board; **15:** Courtesy, Bancroft Library, University of California, Berkeley (SF309 G7 M25 1769 pl.20); **19:** The Pierpont Morgan Library/Art Resource, NY; **20:** Bibliothèque Nationale, Paris; **20:** Excerpt from *These Gods that we worship* . . . in Kenneth Mills and William B. Taylor, *Colonial Spanish America: A Documentary History*. Wilmington: Scholarly Resources, 1998. **22:** Huntington Library, Art Collections, and Botanical Gardens, San Marino, California/SuperStock; **25:** New York Public Library; **28:** British Museum

Chapter 2
Page 30: Jerry Jacka Photography. All Rights Reserved; **31:** Leonard Harris/Stock, Boston, LLC; **34:** Kevin Fleming/CORBIS; **35:** Jerry Jacka Photography. All Rights Reserved; **36:** Florida Division of Historical Resources; **40:** Collection of the New-York Historical Society, (Neg #1049); **43:** National Geographic Society. © 1998. Photo by Steve Rawls; **47:** Worcester Art Museum, Worcester, MA. Gift of Mr. and Mrs. Albert W. Rice; **48:** Courtesy of the Harvard University Archives; **48:** Anne Bradstreet, *Verses Upon the Burning of Our House, July 18, 1666*, 1666.

Chapter 3
Page 56: Harald Sund/Getty Images; **57:** Courtesy, Peter Wood; **58:** Réunion des Musées Nationaux/Art Resource, NY; **60:** Granger Collection, New York; **62:** Smithsonian American Art Museum, Washington DC/Art Resource, NY; **65:** Harald Sund/Getty Images; **68:** Pepys Library, Magdalene College, Cambridge; **73:** Benjamin Henry Latrobe, *View of Greenspring House*, 1796. Maryland Historical Society, Baltimore, MD (II-33); **74:** Jan Wyck, *William III Landing at Torbay*, 1688. National Maritime Museum Picture Library; **78:** New York Public Library

Part Two Opener
Page 82, 83: George Morland, *Traite Des Negres*, 1790–91. Colonial Williamsburg Foundation

Chapter 4
Page 84: Werner Forman Archive/Art Resource, NY; **85:** *Voyage Pittoresque dans le Bresil*, Rugendas plate 10, 2nd part. The Newberry Library, Chicago; **87:** Anonymous, *Vue du Cap Français et du nvr La Marie Seraphique de Nantes*, 1772–1773. *Le Jour de l'Ouverture de sa Vente, Troisieme Voyage d'Angole*. Musée du Château des Ducs de Bretagne (950.4.3); **89:** Alice Ravenel Huger Smith, *The Threshing Floor with a Winnowing-House* (The Carolina Rice Plantation Series). Gibbes Museum of Art/CAA, 37.09.22; **94:** Public Domain; **95:** Werner Forman Archive/Art Resource, NY; **100:** Courtesy, Florida Museum of Natural History. Photo by James Quine; **105:** George Morland, *Traite Des Negres*, 1790–91. Colonial Williamsburg Foundation; **105:** Thomas N. Ingersoll, *'Releese Us out of This Cruell Bondegg': An Appeal from Virginia in 1723*. *William and Mary Quarterly*, Third Series, 51 (October 1994): 776–782; **106:** William Hogarth, *The Gaols Committee of the House of Commons*, c. 1729, National Portrait Gallery, London; **107:** I. N. Phelps Stokes Collection of American Historical Prints. Prints Division, New York Public Library

Chapter 5
Page 110: John Moale, engraving, 1752. I. N. Phelps Stokes Collection, New York Public Library; **111:** Theodore Gentilz, *San Francisco del Espada en 1844*. Yanaguana Society Collection. Daughters of the Republic of Texas Library; **112:** Harrison Begay, *Night Chant Ceremonial Hunt*, 1947. Museum purchase, The Philbrook Museum of Art, Tulsa Oklahoma (1947.40); **116 (Figure):** Excerpted from *Mapping America's Past: A Book* by Mark C. Carnes and John A Garraty with Patrick Williams. © 1996 by Arcadia Editions Limited. Reprinted by permission of Henry Holt and Company, LLC. **118:** John Wollaston, *Mary Spratt Provoost Alexander*, undated. Museum of the City of New York, Gift of William Hamilton Russell (50.215.4); **119:** John Moale, engraving, 1752. I. N. Phelps Stokes Collection, New York Public Library; **126:** Paul Rocheleau Photography; **127:** Courtesy, Winterthur Museum (63.639); **129:** http://research.amnh.org/paleontology/collections/fossil-mammals/history-fossil-mammal-collection; **129:** Edmund Berkeley and Dorothy Smith Berkeley, eds., The Correspondence of John Bartram, 1743–1777 (Gainesville: University Press of Florida, 1992), 568–569. Text condensed and modernized for clarity. **130–131:** CENTRE DES ARCHIVES D'OUTRE-MER; **134:** Thomas Johnson, engraving, 1759. I. N. Phelps Stokes Collection of American Historical Prints, Prints Division, New York Public Library

Chapter 6
Page 137: Photo courtesy of Tryon Palace Historic Sites & Gardens; **138:** Edward Savage, *John Hancock and his Wife*, n.d., (48.8). In the Corcoran Gallery of Art, Washington, D.C. Bequest of Woodbury Blair; **139:** John Webber, *A View of Kealakekua Bay*, c. 1781–1783. Dixson Library, State Library of New South Wales, Sydney; **140:** University of Alaska Anchorage; **144:** Library of Congress; **151:** Photo courtesy of Tryon Palace Historic Sites & Gardens; **151:** William S. Powell, James K. Huhta, and Thomas J. Farnham, eds., The Regulators of North Carolina: A Documentary History, 1759–1776 (Raleigh: State Department of Archives and History, 1971), pp. 187–189; **153:** Library of Congress; **155:** *The Bostonians Paying the Excise-Man, or Tarring and Feathering* (1774). Library of Congress; **159:** Amos Doolittle, *The Battle of Lexington, Plate I*, 1775. The Connecticut Historical Society, Hartford, Connecticut (Acc. #1844.10.1)

Part Three Opener
Page 162, 163: William Ranney, *Veterans of 1776 Returning from the War*, c. 1848. Dallas Museum of Art, Museum League Fund, Special Contributors and General Acquisitions Fund

Chapter 7
Page 164: © 1992 Angel Art Ltd.; **165:** North Carolina Museum of Art, Raleigh, Purchased with funds from the State of North Carolina (52.9.25); **166:** Charles Willson Peale, *George Washington in the Uniform of a British Colonial Colonel*, c. 1772. Washington-Custis-Lee Collection, Washington and Lee University, Lexington, VA; **170:** Courtesy, American Antiquarian Society; **171:** William Mercer, *Battle of Princeton*, date unknown. Courtesy of the Historical Society of Pennsylvania Collection, Atwater Kent Museum of Philadelphia; **172:** Eric Foner, ed., Thomas Paine: Collected Writings

(New York: Library of America, 1995), pp. 100–115; **172:** Independence National Historical Park; **180:** Pennsylvania Capitol Preservation Committee; **183:** © 1992 Angel Art Ltd.; **186:** Louis Nicolas Van Blarenberghe, *The Storming of Yorktown in 1781*, 1784. Reunion des Musées Nationaux/Art Resource, NY; **187:** Benjamin West, *Signing of the Peace Treaty*. Courtesy, Winterthur Museum

Chapter 8
Page 189: George Davidson, *Attacked at Juan de Fuca Straits*, c. 1792; **190:** CORBIS; **192:** William Ranney, Veterans of 1776 Returning from the War, c. 1848. Dallas Museum of Art, Museum League Fund, Special Contributors and General Acquisitions Fund; **192:** James Kirby Martin, ed., *Ordinary Courage: The Revolutionary War Adventures of Joseph Plumb Martin*, 2nd ed. (New York: Brandywine Press, 1999), pp. 159–164; **195:** Natural History Museum, London; **198:** University of Michigan, William L. Clements Library, Map Division; **200:** Courtesy, Monroe County Historical Commission, Monroe, MI; **203:** Public Domain; **207:** Florida Stage; **209:** Susan Anne Livingston Ridley Sedgwick, *Elizabeth 'Mumbet' Freeman*, 1811. Watercolor on ivory. Courtesy of the Massachusetts Historical Society (MHS image number 28); **211 (Both):** Courtesy, American Antiquarian Society; **212:** Collection of the New-York Historical Society, (#1176)

Chapter 9
Page 216: James Peale, *The Artist and His Family*, 1795. Pennsylvania Academy of the Fine Arts, Philadelphia (1922.1.1). Gift of John Frederick Lewis; **220:** Ralph Earl, *Elijah Boardman*. Metropolitan Museum of Art. Bequest of Susan W. Tyler, 1979. (1979.395); **221:** Courtesy, American Canal and Transportation Center; **222:** Frederick Kemmelmeyer, *General George Washington Reviewing the Western Army at Fort Cumberland the 18th of October*, c. 1794. Winterthur Museum (58.2780); **224:** New Bedford Whaling Museum (#803); **225:** *The Old Plantation*, c. 1790–1800. Abby Aldrich Rockefeller Folk Art Museum. Colonial Williamsburg Foundation, Williamsburg, VA; **229:** Courtesy, Museo de America, Madrid. Photo by Iris Engstrand; **231:** Shaker Village of Pleasant Hill, Harrodsburg, KY; **233:** C. William Manning, *The Key of Liberty* (1798), in Major Problems in American History, Vol. 1: To 1877, Elizabeth Cobbs Hoffman and Jon Gjerde (Houghton Mifflin, 2002), 170–171; **234:** James Peale, *The Artist and His Family*, 1795. Pennsylvania Academy of the Fine Arts, Philadelphia (1922.1.1). Gift of John Frederick Lewis

Part Four Opener
Page 240, 241: Unknown Artist, *La Amistad*, c. 1840. New Haven Colony Historical Society, New Haven, CT (#1972.1)

Chapter 10
Page 242: John Antrobus, *Plantation Burial*, c. 1860. Historic New Orleans Collection, accession no. 1960.46; **243:** Library of Congress; **244:** William Clark, *Eulachon (T. Pacificus)*, 1806, Voorhis Journal #2. William Clark Papers, Missouri Historical Society Archives; **246:** Library of Congress; **247:** Courtesy, Dartmouth College Library; **249:** Library of Congress; **252:** Peter Turnley/CORBIS; **252:** Cherokee Women to Cherokee Council, May 2, 1817, series 1, Andrew Jackson Presidential Papers. **253:** Unidentified Artist, *Benjamin Hawkins and the Creek Indians*, c. 1805. Greenville County Museum of Art, Greenville, SC, Gift of The Museum Association, Inc., with funds donated by Corporate Partners: Ernst and Young; Fluor Daniel; Director's Circle Members: Mr. and Mrs. Alester G. Furman III; Mr. and Mrs. M. Dexter Hagy; Thomas P. Hartness; Mr. and Mrs. E. Erwin Maddrey II; Mary M. Pearce; Mr. and Mrs. John Pellett, Jr.; Mr. W. Thomas Smith; Mr. and Mrs. Edward H. Stall; Eleanor and Irvine Welling; Museum Antiques Show, 1989, 1990, 1991, Eliot, Davis, and Company, CPAs, sponsor; Collector's Group 1990, 1991; **257:** John Antrobus, *Plantation Burial*, c. 1860. Historic New Orleans

Collection, accession no. 1960.46; **258:** Chicago Historical Society, ICHi-22005

Chapter 11
Page 261: Richard T. Nowitz/CORBIS; **262:** John Gadsby Chapman, *Davy Crockett*, date unknown. Harry Ransom Humanities Research Center, The University of Texas at Austin (neg. #65.349); **265:** William Henry Brown, *Hauling the Whole Weeks Picking*, 1842. Historic New Orleans Collection (1975.93.1 & 1975.93.2); **269:** Library of Congress; **274 (Top):** Richard T. Nowitz/CORBIS; **274 (Bottom):** Newberry Library, Chicago; **277:** David Muench/ CORBIS; **277:** Eileen Boris and Nelson Lichtenstein, eds., Major Problems in the History of American Workers, 2nd ed. (New York: Houghton Mifflin, 2002), 93–95; **281:** Henry F. Darby, *The Reverend John Atwood and His Family*, 1845. Gift of Maxim Karolik for the M. and M. Karolik Collection of American Paintings, 1815–1865, 62.269. Museum of Fine Arts, Boston. Reproduced with permission. Copyright 2003 Museum of Fine Arts, Boston. All Rights Reserved

Chapter 12
Page 284: Joseph Vollmering, *The U.S. Naval Expedition Under Comore. M.C. Perry, Ascending the Tuxpan River*, 1848. Amon Carter Museum, Fort Worth, TX (1976.33.2); **285:** Minnesota Historical Society; **291:** Scotts Bluff National Monument, Nebraska. United States Department of the Interior, National Park Service; **294:** Samuel J. Miller, *Frederick Douglass*, 1847/52. Cased half-plate daguerreotype, plate: 14 × 10.6 cm; plate in closed case: 15.2 × 12 × 1.4 cm; plate in open case: 15.2 × 24 × 2 cm. Major Acquisitions Centennial Endowment, 1996.433. Reproduction, The Art Institute of Chicago. Photography © The Art Institute of Chicago; **295:** Library Company of Philadelphia (1835-7/P.8658); **297 (Top):** Unknown Artist, *La Amistad*, c. 1840. New Haven Colony Historical Society, New Haven, CT (#1972.1); **297 (Bottom):** Library Company of Philadelphia (59541.D); **300:** Fenimore Art Museum; **304:** CENTRE DES ARCHIVES D'OUTRE-MER; **307:** Joseph Vollmering, *The U.S. Naval Expedition Under Comore. M.C. Perry, Ascending the Tuxpan River*, 1848. Amon Carter Museum, Fort Worth, TX (1976.33.2); **305:** Clyde A. Milner, ed., Major Problems in the History of the American West: Documents and Essays (1989), pp. 219–221.

Part Five Opener
Page 310, 311: State Historical Society of Wisconsin, WHi (D32) 821

Chapter 13
Page 312: George Caleb Bingham, *Raftsmen Playing Cards*, 1847. Saint Louis Art Museum, Ezra H. Linley Fund; **313:** Courtesy of the California History Room, California State Library, Sacramento, California. Mines & Mining: Gold: Scenes from Dag. #3 *Head of Auburn Ravine*, 1852 (Neg. #912); **317:** American Textile History Museum, Lowell, Massachusetts; **319:** George Caleb Bingham, *Raftsmen Playing Cards*, 1847. Saint Louis Art Museum, Ezra H. Linley Fund; **321:** Courtesy of the Georgia Historical Society, Savannah, Georgia. D.M. Wright Papers, #1277, Box 36, Folder 286; **321:** George Howe, The Endowments, Position and Education of Woman. An Address Delivered Before the Hemans and Sigourney Societies of the Female High School at Limestone Springs, July 23, 1850 (Columbia, SC: I. C. Morgan, 1850), pp. 5, 9, 10–11; **322:** Bettmann/CORBIS; **332 (Both):** Library of Congress; **333:** Ohio Historical Society

Chapter 14
Page 336: Carl G. von Iwonski, *Block House, New Braunfels*. Yanaguana Society Collection. Daughters of the Republic Texas Library, CT96.8; **337:** Chicago History Museum, ICHi-22172; **341:** Library of Congress; **341:** Ira Berlin, Barbara J. Fields, Thavolia Glymph, Joseph P. Reidy, and Leslie S. Rowland, eds., Freedom: A Documentary History of Emancipation, 1861–1867, Series 1, Vol. 1, The Destruction of Slavery (1985), pp. 782–83;

343: Carl G. von Iwonski, *Block House, New Braunfels.* Yanaguana Society Collection. Daughters of the Republic Texas Library, CT96.8; **344:** Western History Collections, University of Oklahoma Library; **346 (Both):** Library of Congress; **347 (Left):** Library of Congress; **347 (Right):** National Archives; **348:** Library of Congress; **349:** The Museum of the Confederacy, Richmond Virginia; 347; **351:** Library of Congress; **356:** Colorado Historical Society (WPA-834; 10025492)

Chapter 15

Page 361: *Harper's Weekly*, September 16, 1871; **362:** Courtesy of the Georgia Historical Society, William Wilson Collection; **365:** CORBIS; **366:** Library of Congress; **366:** M. C. Fulton to Brig Gen. Davis Tillson, 17 April 1866, Unregistered Letters; **368:** H.P. Moore/ Collection of the New-York Historical Society, Neg. #37497; **372:** Library of Congress; **375:** Robert Benecke, photographer. DeGolyer Library, Southern Methodist University, Dallas, Texas, Ag1982.86.80; **376:** Union Pacific Historical Collection; **378 (Table):** Michael Williams, *Americans and Their Forests (1989), 352. Cambridge University Press.* **381:** State Historical Society of Wisconsin, WHi (D32) 821; **383:** *Harper's Weekly*, September 16, 1871

Part Six Opener

Page 386, 387: The Granger Collection

Chapter 16

Page 388: Library of Congress; **389 (Top):** Getty Images Inc. - Hulton Archive Photos; **389 (Bottom):** Carnegie Library of Pittsburgh; **392:** Detroit Public Library; **394:** Oregon Historical Society; **398:** CORBIS- NY; **401:** The Denver Public Library; **402:** New Mexico State University; **406:** Library of Congress; **406:** Andrew Carnegie, "Wealth," *North American Review* (1889)

Chapter 17

Page 409: Nebraska State Historical Society; **410:** Museum of New Mexico; **411:** California State Library Foundation; **413:** San Diego Historical Society; **414:** William Lawrence Katz; **418:** Nebraska State Historical Society; **419:** The Beinecke Rare Book and Manuscript Library; **421:** Library of Congress; **421:** *New York Herald,* August 30, 1886; **423:** Museum of the City of New York; **424:** Hampton University Museum; **426:** Library of Congress

Chapter 18

Page 428: UCR/California Museum of Photography; **429:** The Huntington Library, Art Collections, and Botanical Gardens; **430:** National Archives and Records Administration; **433:** National Anthropological Archives; **439:** Bridgeman Art Library/Virginia Historical Society; **440:** California Historical Society; **442:** American Museum of Natural History; **443:** The Granger Collection; **447:** UCR/California Museum of Photography; **447:** Proceedings of the Congressional Committee on the Philippines, in Harvey Graff, ed., *American Imperialism and the Philippine Insurrection* (Boston, 1969), pp. 64–79

Part Seven Opener

Page 450, 451: Art Resource/Jewish Museum

Chapter 19

Page 452: International Museum of Photography; **454:** The Granger Collection; **455:** Library of Congress; **457:** Art Resource/Jewish Museum; **460:** California Historical Society; **461:** International Museum of Photography; **463:** Minnesota Historical Society; **465:** Minnesota Historical Society; **467:** International Museum of Photography; **468:** Brown Brothers

Chapter 20

Page 472: Hagley Museum and Library; **473:** The Granger Collection; **476:** Library of Congress; **477:** The Denver Public Library; **479:** Getty Images Inc. - Hulton Archive Photos; **480:** Stock

Montage, Inc./Historical Pictures Collection; **483:** Hagley Museum and Library; **484:** National Archives and Records Administration; **484:** Addie W. Hunton and Kathryn M. Johnson, *Two Colored Women with American Expeditionary Forces* (New York: Brooklyn Eagle Press, 1920), pp. 28–30, 182–183, 186; **486:** Public Domain; **489:** Museum of History and Industry

Chapter 21

Page 491: Photofest; **492:** Columbia University in the City of New York; **493:** CORBIS- NY; **494:** CORBIS- NY; **498:** From The Collected Poems of Langston Hughes, published by Knopf and Vintage Books. Copyright © 1994 by the Estate of Langston Hughes. All rights reserved. Used by permission of Harold Ober Associates Incorporated; **499:** Photofest; **500:** Art Resource/ Schomburg Center for Research in Black Culture; **503:** Cartoonbank.com; **504:** The Advertising Archives; **507:** Princeton University Library; **507:** © 1925 by Scribner and Sons; renewed by Frances Scott Fitzgerald Lanahan

Part Eight Opener

Page 510, 511: Franklin D. Roosevelt Library

Chapter 22

Page 512: Library of Congress; **513:** Library of Congress; **514:** Getty Images, Inc – Liaison; **518:** Library of Congress; **519:** Franklin D. Roosevelt Library; **520:** CORBIS- NY; **520:** Florence Reece/ Stormking Music, 1947; **521:** Woody Guthrie, TRO-© Copyright 1961. Ludlow Music, Inc., New York, NY; **521:** Woody Guthrie, TRO-© Copyright 1963. Folkways Music Publishers, Inc., New York, NY; **522:** Library of Congress; **524:** AP Wide World Photos; **529:** Don Beatty; **530:** National Archives and Records Administration; **531:** National Air and Space Museum Smithsonian Institution

Chapter 23

Page 534: National Archives and Records Administration; **535:** Elaine Tyler May; **537:** Norman Rockwell Family Agency, Inc.; **539:** AP Wide World Photos; **543:** National Archives and Records Administration; **545:** National Archives and Records Administration; **546:** National Archives and Records Administration; **547 (Top Left):** Dwight D. Eisenhower Presidential Library-Museum; **547 (Top Center Left):** John F. Kennedy Library and Museum, Boston; **547 (Top Center Right):** LBJ Library Photo; **547 (Top Right):** The Richard Nixon Library & Birthplace Foundation, Album 43:6; **547 (Bottom Left):** Courtesy Gerald R. Ford Presidential Library; **547 (Bottom Center Left):** Jimmy Carter Library; **547 (Bottom Center Right):** Courtesy Ronald Regan Library; **547 (Bottom Right):** George Bush Presidential Library; **550:** University of Nevada; **550:** University of Nevada Oral History Program, 1995; **551:** National Archives and Records Administration

Chapter 24

Page 554: ChinaStock; **555:** National Archives and Records Administration; **556:** Getty Images/Time Life Pictures; **557:** National Life Insurance Company; **562:** CORBIS- NY; **564:** ChinaStock; **565:** CORBIS- NY; **566:** US Department of Defense; **569:** CORBIS- NY; **572:** Arizona State University Libraries

Part Nine Opener

Page: 574, 575: Dan Weiner

Chapter 25

Page 576: Library of Congress; **577:** AP Wide World Photos; **579:** Dan Weiner; **580:** Library of Congress; **582:** Getty Images/Time Life Pictures; **590:** University of Minnesota Libraries; **591:** Getty Images/Washington Post Writers Group; **592:** Getty Images/Time Life Pictures; **592:** Rachel Carson, *Silent Spring*, Boston: Houghton

Mifflin, 1962; **592:** Excerpt from "The Obligation to Endure," from *Silent Spring* by Rachel Carson. Copyright ©1962 by Rachel L. Carson, renewed 1990 by Roger Christie. Reprinted by permission of Houghton Mifflin Harcourt Publishing Company. All rights reserved

Chapter 26

Page 597: Campus Crusade for Christ; **598 (Top):** Take Stock-Images of Change; **598 (Bottom):** Lyndon Baines Johnson Library Collection; **603:** University of Maine; **606:** StockPhotos, Inc./Globe Photos, Inc.; **607:** Getty Images/Time Life Pictures; **608:** Campus Crusade for Christ; **609:** CORBIS- NY; **611:** Universal Uclick

Chapter 27

Page 616: Jimmy Carter Library; **617:** Hill Aerospace Museum; **620:** CORBIS- NY; **621:** Stanley Forman; **623:** Stock Boston; **625:** CORBIS- NY; **625:** Martin Luther King, Jr., and the Vietnam War from Martin Luther King Jr., "Beyond Vietnam," Reprinted by arrangement with the Heirs of the Estate of Martin Luther King Jr. and Writers House LLC. ©1967 Estate of Martin Luther King, Jr.; **627:** Jimmy Carter Library; **628:** CORBIS- NY; **631:** Minnesota Historical Society; **632:** Getty Images/Time Life Pictures

Part Ten Opener

Page 634, 635: CORBIS- NY

Chapter 28

Page 636: AP Wide World Photos; **637 (Top):** Ronald Reagan Presidential Library; **637 (Bottom):** CORBIS- NY; **640:** The Sacramento Bee; **642:** Universal Uclick; **646:** New York Times - Maps and Graphics; **646:** Irwin Unger and Robert R. Torres, *American Issues,* 2nd ed. (Prentice Hall, 1999), vol. 2, pp. 362–364, 375–377; **647:** Irwin Unger and Robert R. Torres, *American Issues,* 2nd ed. (Prentice Hall, 1999), vol. 2, pp. 362–364, 375–377; **648:** AP Wide World Photos

Chapter 29

Page 655: AP Wide World Photos; **656:** CORBIS- NY; **657:** CORBIS- NY; **659:** SIPA Press; **660:** SIPA Press; **662:** Getty Images, Inc – Liaison; **663:** AP Wide World Photos; **667:** AP Wide World Photos; **670:** AP Wide World Photos

Chapter 30

Page 676: Newscom; **677:** Val MacClatchey; **681:** Getty Images, Inc – Liaison; **683:** Newscom; **685:** Cartoonbank.com; **689:** AP Wide World Photos; **690:** Cartoonbank.com; **693:** AP Wide World Photos; **693:** http://www.slowfood.com

INDEX

Entries followed by *f, t, m,* and *i* refer to figures, tables, maps, and illustrations, respectively

A

Abalone Alliance, 623
Abenaki people, 79
Abolition
  18th century
    early efforts, 102–105
    manumission and, 101–102, 195
    post-Revolution advocacy, 217, 236
  19th century
    Abolition Act (1808), 255–256
    abolitionist literature, 294, 295*i*, 329
    Amistad case, 296, 297*i*
    Emancipation Proclamation, 349, 352
    Free-Soil Party stance on, 326–327, 330
    Harpers Ferry raid, 310, 331–332, 338
    support for movement, 294
    suppression of movement, 294–296, 295*i*
    Underground Railroad, 324, 328–329, 328–329*m*
    women and, 294, 301, 322–323
Abortion
  antiabortion movement, 634, 646, 670–671, 670*i*
  legalization of, 609, 631, 670
  post-World War II access to, 568
  restrictions on, 590, 632
  violence over, 634, 670
Abu Ghraib prison, 681*i*, 682
Acadia National Park, 479
Acadians, 118
Acoma (Sky City), 32, 34*i*
Adams, John
  on American liberty, 195
  on Boston Massacre, 154
  as Constitutional Convention participant, 207
  as Federalist, 218, 221–222, 222*t*, 235, 236*t*, 237
  legislative model of, 177–178
  as president, 218, 222–223, 237
  as Second Continental Congress participant, 168
  on Stamp Act resistance, 149
  as Treaty of Versailles diplomat, 186–187, 187*i*
Adams, John Quincy
  as *Amistad* case lawyer, 296
  as Democratic-Republican, 268–269, 268*t*, 269*t*
  as president, 268–269
  as Secretary of State, 268
  on southern view of slavery, 264–265
  as War of 1812 treaty negotiator, 250

Adams, Samuel, 152, 153, 157–158
Adams, Will, 31
Addams, Jane, 425, 469
Administration of Justice Act (1774), 156
Advertising
  consumer culture and mass advertising, 386, 389, 401, 402, 504–505, 504*i*
  mail-order catalogs, 402
  radio, 500
  sports events and, 690
Affirmative action, 632, 641
Affluence gap
  19th century, 403, 405
  20th century, 515, 621, 637, 641, 643–644, 644*f*, 655, 657, 686–687
  21st century, 687
Afghanistan
  20th century
    CIA involvement in, 638, 669
    Soviet presence in, 634, 636, 637, 638, 649
  21st century
    Al Qaeda in, 635, 669, 676, 678, 679
    U.S. invasion of, 635, 677–678, 679, 680*m*, 682
Africa. *See also specific countries by name*
  15th century slave trade, 14, 18, 19*i*, 85
  16th century slave trade, 27, 85
  17th century
    slave trade, 41, 43, 69, 85–86, 91–92
    trade with, 69, 92, 92*i*
  18th century slave trade, 82–83, 91–96, 93*m*, 94*i*, 96–97*m*, 202
  19th century
    African American repatriation to, 275, 333*i*
    Barbary war, 237
    slave trade, 255–256, 288, 296
  20th century
    African American affiliation with, 495, 606*i*
    independence movements in, 556
    missionaries in, 691
    terrorist attacks in, 669
    U.S. involvement in, 587, 593, 626, 627, 668
    World War II and, 536, 541
African Americans. *See also* Civil rights movement; Segregation; *slave-related entries*
  17th century free blacks, 85, 88, 91, 101
  18th century
    American Revolution participation, 165, 166–167, 179–180
    free blacks, 100, 101–102, 104, 163, 167, 179, 216–217, 224–227, 235
    liberty revolts by, 144*i*, 146
    music, 225–226, 225*i*
    post-Revolution status, 216–217, 223–227

    sailing/whaling occupation of, 224*i*
    women, 235
  19th century
    Black Codes, 364–365, 367
    black elite rise, 413
    buffalo soldiers, 414–415, 414*i*
    citizenship/voting rights for, 275, 364–365, 367, 371–373, 431
    Civil War role of, 336–337, 337*i*, 340–341, 341*i*, 344, 346, 351–352, 351*i*, 355
    culture of, 256, 257*i*, 258–259
    discrimination based on group identity, 318–323
    discrimination protests, 410–411, 412–415
    education of, 299, 361, 370–371, 433–434
    first in Congress, 372*i*, 373
    free blacks, 229, 240, 274–276, 288, 317, 318
    free communities of, 370–371
    Freedmen's Bureau aiding, 361, 364, 365*i*, 366–367, 368–369
    group identity of, 322
    Ku Klux Klan violence against, 367, 371, 373
    labor issues, 288, 294*i*, 318, 352, 363–364, 368–369*i*, 368–370, 397
    legal rights of, 310
    migration of, 288
    music, 258
    population of, 439
    post-Civil war challenges/tensions, 361–373, 362*i*, 365*i*, 366*i*, 368–369*i*
    repatriation to Africa, 275, 333*i*
    sailing/whaling as occupation, 244, 247*i*
    white supremacist/Ku Klux Klan violence against, 367, 371, 373, 431–432
    women, 322, 322*i*, 346, 440
  20th century
    Black Power, 605–606, 606*i*
    business ownership by, 580*i*
    culture, 465, 491, 498–499, 606
    discrimination against, 474, 479–480, 515–516, 557–558, 579–580
    education of, 473*i*
    first black mayor, 606
    Great Depression impacting, 515–516, 527
    home ownership, 578, 579–580
    judicial proceedings involving, 661
    labor issues, 450, 474, 479, 548–549, 581
    middle class status, 579, 581, 657
    migration of, 479–480, 480*i*, 540
    music, 465, 491, 499
    political involvement of, 525, 570, 606

PRESENT DAY WORLD

ARCTIC
OCEAN

*Beaufort
Sea*

GREENLAND

*Baffin
Bay*

ICELAN

ALASKA
(U.S.)

*Bering
Sea*

*Gulf of
Alaska*

*Hudson
Bay*

*Labrador
Sea*

C A N A D A

*Great
Lakes*

ATLANTIC
OCEAN

U N I T E D   S T A T E S

MEXICO

*Gulf
of
Mexico*

MOR

WESTERN
SAHARA

*PACIFIC
OCEAN*

Hawaiian Is. (U.S.)

BELIZE

GUATEMALA

EL SALVADOR

Galapagos Is. (EQ.)

MAURITAN

CAPE
VERDE

THE GAMBIA

SENEGA

GUIN

SURINAME

FRENCH
GUIANA
(FR.)

GUINEA
BISSAU

SIERR
LEON

LIBERI

CÔTE
D'IVOIRE

GHANA

SÃO TO
PRÍN

Kiribati

Tokelau

Samoa

Am.
Samoa

Cook
Is.

French
Polynesia

ECUADOR

Tonga

PERU

BRAZIL

BOLIVIA

PARAGUAY

CHILE

URUGUAY

ARGENTINA

Falkland Is. (U.K.)

South Georgia (U.K.)

UNITED
STATES

0   200   400   600 mi

0   200   400   600 km

ATLANTIC
OCEAN

BAHAMAS

Turks and
Caicos Is. (U.K.)

CUBA

DOMINICAN
REPUBLIC

Cayman Is. (U.K.)

U.S. Virgin Is.

JAMAICA

HAITI

PUERTO
RICO

Antigua and
Barbuda

HONDURAS

*Caribbean
Sea*

Guadaloupe

Dominica

Martinique

St. Lucia

Barbados

NICARAGUA

St. Vincent and
the Grenadines

Curaco

Grenada

COSTA
RICA

*Weddell
Sea*

Trinidad
and Tobago

VENEZUELA

GUYANA

A N T A R C T I C A

PANAMA   COLOMBIA

Svalbard Is. (NOR.)   Novaya
                      Zemlya
                                        *Kara
                                         Sea*   *Laptev
                                                                      Sea*   New Siberian Is.   *ARCTIC
                                                                                                     OCEAN*   *East
*Barents   Siberian
  Sea*   Sea*

                              RUSSIA

                                                                                              *Sea
                                                                                               of
                                                                                              Okhotsk*
                                                              *Lake
                                                              Baikal*   Sakhalin

        KAZAKHSTAN   MONGOLIA
*Aral   *Lake
 Sea*   Balkhash*   N. KOREA
                                                                                        JAPAN
                                            PEOPLE'S   S. KOREA
            AFGHAN.   REPUBLIC   *East   *PACIFIC
ISRAEL   IRAQ   PAKISTAN   OF CHINA   BHUTAN   China*   OCEAN*
   JORDAN   IRAN   Sea
EGYPT   BAHRAIN   NEPAL   TAIWAN
        QATAR   BANG.   BURMA   MACAO
        SAUDI   U.A.E.   INDIA   (MYANMAR)   LAOS   Northern
CHAD   ARABIA   OMAN   VIETNAM   Mariana
                          *Arabian   *Bay of   *Philippine   Is.
ERITREA YEMEN   Sea*   Bengal*   Sea*   Marshall
SUDAN   THAILAND   PHILIPPINES   Is.
        DJIBOUTI   CAMBODIA   *South
CENT.   SOMALIA   SRI   China*
RICAN REP.   ETHIOPIA   LANKA   Sea
ROON   MALAYSIA BRUNEI
EQUA. UGANDA   SINGAPORE   PAPUA   Nauru
GUINEA   KENYA   NEW GUINEA
DEM. REP.   RWANDA   INDONESIA   Solomon Is.
OF   BURUNDI   Tuvalu
CONGO   TANZANIA   *INDIAN
NGOLA   MALAWI   OCEAN*   *Coral
     ZAMBIA   Sea*   Vanuatu   Fiji
BIA ZIMB.   MADAGASCAR   New Caledonia (FR.)
BOTSWANA   MAURITIUS
        MOZAMBIQUE   AUSTRALIA   *Tasman
SOUTH   SWAZILAND   Sea*
AFRICA LESOTHO
                                                                              NEW
                                                                              ZEALAND